AMERICAN HISTORY

Grateful acknowledgment is made to the scholars and teachers who reviewed *American History* in manuscript or in classroom tests.

REVIEWERS

Félix D. Almaráz, Jr.
University of Texas at San Antonio

Willard Bill
University of Washington

Ray A. Billington
Late of the Huntington Library

John Morton Blum
Yale University

Robert Divine
University of Texas

Robert Ferrell
Indiana University

William Harbaugh
University of Virginia

Ari Hoogenboom
Brooklyn University

Michael Holt
University of Virginia

Arthur S. Link
Princeton University

Robert Middlekauff
University of California, Berkeley

Edmund Morgan
Yale University

Robert V. Remini
University of Illinois

Joyce Stevos
Providence Public Schools,
Rhode Island

READERS

Sylvester Brown
Glenn Hills Junior/Senior High School
Augusta, Georgia

Mary H. Clarke
Eliot Junior High School
Washington, D.C.

Anthony DiNardo
Liverpool Middle School
Baldwinsville, New York

LeRoy William Halter II
Parkview Middle School
Jeffersonville, Indiana

Lela Kerford
Martin Luther King, Jr., Junior High
Kansas City, Missouri

Barbara Lebda
Lindblom High School
Chicago, Illinois

Victor Megenity
Scribner Junior High School
New Albany, Indiana

Carl Metoxen
Centennial Junior High School
Friedley, Minnesota

Betty Jane Miller
Andrew Jackson Academy
Ehrhardt, South Carolina

Chris Miller
R. E. Byrd Junior High School
Van Nuys, California

Joseph A. Morrison, Jr.
William Annin Junior High School
Basking Ridge, New Jersey

Joseph Pasternak
Kosciuszko Junior High School
Thompsonville, Connecticut

Gail A. McNeil
Rotterdam-Mohonasen Central
Schenectady, New York

Elizabeth Peden
Beck Middle School
Greensville, South Carolina

William H. Wappas
Sweetwater Union High School
Chula Vista, California

CLASSROOM TESTING

Gerald Cavanaugh
East Junior High School
East Weymouth, Massachusetts

Margaret Ferguson
West Milbrook Junior High School
Raleigh, North Carolina

Bernard Fleming
Dedham Junior High School
Dedham, Massachusetts

David Gnong
East Junior High School
East Weymouth, Massachusetts

Linda Gresham
Lintom M. Adamson Junior High School
Rex, Georgia

Mary Jackman
Martin Junior High School
Raleigh, North Carolina

Woodie Persons
Riverwood High School
Atlanta, Georgia

Lou Rubidoux
South Junior High School
Arlington Heights, Illinois

Don Schaede
Larson Junior High School
Elgin, Illinois

Joe Schafer
South Junior High School
Arlington Heights, Illinois

Chris Schowengerdt
South Junior High School
Arlington Heights, Illinois

Lucelia Selden
Daniels Junior High School
Raleigh, North Carolina

AMERICAN HISTORY

REVISED EDITION

JOHN A. GARRATY

Aaron Singer

Michael J. Gallagher

 Harcourt Brace Jovanovich, Publishers

Orlando   San Diego   Chicago   Dallas

JOHN A. GARRATY is a distinguished historian and writer and Professor of History at Columbia University. His books include the widely adopted college textbook *The American Nation* and biographies of Henry Cabot Lodge and Woodrow Wilson. He has held Guggenheim, Ford, and Social Science Research Council Fellowships. Professor Garraty is a former president of the Society of American Historians, editor of the *Dictionary of American Biography,* a coeditor of the *Encyclopedia of American Biography,* and a member of the advisory board of *American Heritage* magazine.

AARON SINGER, who assisted John A. Garraty in the writing of *American History,* is a coauthor of *The Development of American Economic Life* with Robert L. Heilbroner and a member of the history faculty of Manhattan College in New York.

MICHAEL GALLAGHER, who prepared the teaching strategies for *American History,* is a teacher and chairman of the department of social studies at Dwight D. Eisenhower Junior High School in Schaumburg, Illinois.

The Cover: Johns, Jasper, *Flag.* 1954–55. Encaustic, oil, and collage on fabric mounted on plywood, $42\frac{1}{4}'' \times 60\frac{5}{8}''$ (107.3 × 153.8 cm). Collection, The Museum of Modern Art, New York. Gift of Philip Johnson in honor of Alfred H. Barr, Jr.

Design: Kirchoff/Wohlberg, Inc.

Photo Research: Harcourt Brace Jovanovich, Inc.

Cartography Editor: Valerie Wulf Krejcie

Cartography: H. Shaw Borst

Time Line Credits

Pp. xvi–1, Civico Museo, Como; BBC-Hulton; National Maritime Museum, Greenwich; Metropolitan Museum of Art; New York State Historical Assn., Cooperstown; Fogg Art Museum; Massachusetts Historical Society; 120–21, Granger Collection; Yale University Art Gallery; Granger Collection; Winterthur Museum; Granger Collection; 236–37, Thomas Gilcrease Institute, Tulsa; White House Historical Assn.; New York Historical Society; Smithsonian Institution; New York Historical Society; St. Louis Art Museum; 316–17, Missouri Historical Society; Ladies Hermitage Assn.; Texas Memorial Museum; National Portrait Gallery; Chicago Historical Society; Library of Congress; Brown Brothers; Gemini-Smith; 418–19, Brooklyn Museum; Museum of the Confederacy; Michigan State Library; Library of Congress; Historical Society of Pennsylvania; Appomattox Court House; Granger Collection; 520–21, Museum of the City of New York; Thomas Gilcrease Institute; Museum of the City of New York; A T & T; Culver; 610–11, Chicago Historical Society; Granger Collection; National Portrait Gallery; Johnson Publishing Co.; 674–75; Culver; National Gallery; Brown Brothers; National Portrait Gallery; United Press International; 772–73, Culver; Wide World; United Press International; Frank James-Taurus; Eisenhower Library; 838–39, Fred Ward, Black Star; Francis Kelley, LIFE Magazine, © Time, Inc.; United Press International; NASA; Robert Ellison, Black Star; FPG; William Karel, Sygma; Wide World.

CONTENTS

Unit Two
THE AMERICAN NATION

Unit Six
A CHANGING AMERICA

Maps

READING PRACTICE IN SOCIAL STUDIES

The Parts of a Book

As you begin to read *American History*, learn to use the various parts of this book. Begin by turning back to Contents on page v. A quick skimming of the *table of contents* shows you how a book is organized and gives you an idea of what to expect from your reading.

This book is divided into ten units covering American history from the arrival of the first Americans to the economic policies of President Ronald Reagan. The units are divided into 30 chapters, each covering approximately equal periods of our history. And the chapters are divided into sections, all listed in the table of contents. A sample is shown below.

This table of contents also highlights some special features of *American History*. The titles of bonus readings are shown in italic type and printed in blue ink. These brief looks at sidelights to our history are found throughout the book.

Also shown in italic type are the titles of two kinds of special lessons that appear often in the book. On tan pages you will find Building Skills in Social Studies. These lessons help you to read maps, charts, and graphs, and to use primary and secondary sources. A sample page is printed at the top of the next column. This lesson also includes a sample of the time lines found in the book. These two-page illustrated time lines open each unit and give a year-by-year picture

of America's history. Each one-page skill lesson gives you an opportunity to show that you have mastered new skills.

On green pages you will find Reading Practice in Social Studies. These one-page lessons help you practice reading skills and develop confidence. Like Building Skills, the Reading Practice lessons draw all their material from this book itself.

The table of contents also shows, at the end of each chapter, a one-page Review and a one-page Test. Further, at the end of each unit is a one-page Unit Test. These pages are printed in blue. A sample appears on the facing page. Each Review is organized in the same way. There are 20 persons, terms, or events to identify. Next are ten questions for you to show your understanding of American history. There then appear five activities for you to use your various talents in classroom projects based upon *American History*.

The tests may be easily scored for 100 points and are included in the book to help you review what you have learned. They include matching, chronological order, classifying, multiple

CHAPTER 16 REVIEW

Identification
Tell briefly why each of the following persons, terms, or events is important.
1. Abraham Lincoln
2. Jefferson Davis
3. Robert E. Lee
4. Thomas J. "Stonewall" Jackson
5. George B. McClellan
6. Ulysses S. Grant
7. William Tecumseh Sherman
8. Fort Sumter
9. Army of the Potomac
10. Army of Northern Virginia
11. Copperheads
12. Blockade runners
13. Antietam
14. Emancipation Proclamation
15. Draft riots
16. Battle of Chancellorsville
17. Battle of Gettysburg
18. Siege of Vicksburg
19. Sherman's March to the Sea
20. Appomattox Court House

Understanding American History
1. Compare and contrast Abraham Lincoln and Jefferson Davis as leaders. What were the strengths and weaknesses of each?
2. What were the advantages and disadvantages of the North and South at the start of the Civil War?
3. Describe the life of a typical soldier in the Civil War.
4. In what sense was the Civil War good for the northern economy?
5. How did the Civil War affect the South's economy?
6. What did the draft riots show about northern attitudes toward blacks?
7. Why was the Battle of Vicksburg a turning point of the war?
8. Compare and contrast Grant and Lee.
9. What were the two parts of General Grant's plan to end the war?

10. Why did General Sherman use total war in his March to the Sea?

Activities
1. Prepare a bulletin board to show the major battles of the Civil War. Southerners named battles after nearby towns, northerners after bodies of water. Give both names when there are two. Arrange the battles in the order in which they were fought. Include as much information as you need to show how the war progressed. Choose appropriate symbols for North and South, northern and southern victories, fighting on land and water, troop movements in the South and West.
2. There have been an enormous number of books published to describe and illustrate the Civil War. Check the card catalog of your school or public library. Choose one aspect of the war — food shortages, prison life, conscription, blockade running, newspaper coverage — for a short report to the class. If possible, illustrate your report by using an overhead projector or charts and drawings you can make yourself.
3. Use your historical imagination to write a letter home as a soldier or nurse in either the Confederate or Union army. Include a description of a general you might have glimpsed in camp, or describe conditions in a hospital for the war wounded.
4. With your classmates use your historical imagination to present a newscast just after the Battle of Gettysburg. Include interviews with the commanding generals as well as with typical soldiers for both armies. As a follow-up, return to the site to interview spectators who have just heard Lincoln deliver his Gettysburg Address.
5. Make a diorama or model of one of the Civil War battlefields. Consult reference books to be sure that your details are accurate. Describe the battle in class, perhaps by using toy soldiers to show troop movements.

489

choice, and always a short essay topic. The answers to all of the questions may be found by careful reading of each chapter and unit.

At the back of the book are a number of helpful study aids. A portion of the *glossary* is reproduced below. It shows key words and new terms which are printed in boldface type in the book. For each entry a page reference is given so you may use the term in context. Pronunciations are also provided for difficult words. A key to pronunciation is at the beginning of the Glossary on page 911.

Conestoga (kon′is-tō′gə) **wagon.** A sturdy covered wagon used by pioneers who moved westward. **322**

Confederate States of America. A federation of 11 independent southern states formed after their secession from the Union in 1860–61. **452**

Conquistadors (kon-kēs′tə-dôrs). Spanish soldiers who conquered Mexico and Peru. **28**

Conscience Whigs. Northern members of the Whig party who were against slavery (see **Cotton Whigs**). **430**

Also in the back of the book is a special feature titled Our Living Heritage. It begins on page 924 and tells you how you and your family may visit historical sites in your state.

A valuable reading tool is the *index*. The Index to *American History* begins on page 929. A sample is reproduced below.

Each name in the book is shown in alphabetical order in the index. For topics such as "Economy," a number of subentries are made. The term *See also* tells you where additional information appears elsewhere in the index.

Practice your reading skills by skimming the various parts of this book. Then use the table of contents, glossary, and index to find specific items named by your teacher.

UNIT ONE

1480 · **1490** · **1500** · **1510** · **1520** · **1530** · **1540**

Columbus sails
to America,
1492
•
Cabot explores
Newfoundland,
1497

Balboa sights
Pacific Ocean,
1513
•
Cortés invades
Aztecs, 1519

Magellan's crew
sails around
world, 1519-21
•
Verrazano sails
Atlantic Coast,
1524

Pizarro
marches on
Incas, 1531
•
Mendoza
founds
Buenos Aires,
1536

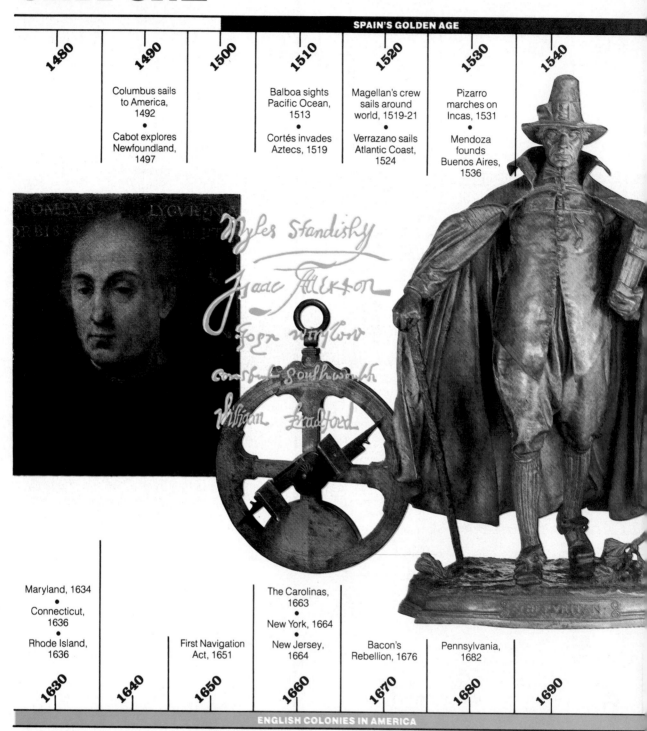

Maryland, 1634
•
Connecticut,
1636
•
Rhode Island,
1636

First Navigation
Act, 1651

The Carolinas,
1663
•
New York, 1664
•
New Jersey,
1664

Bacon's
Rebellion, 1676

Pennsylvania,
1682

1630 · **1640** · **1650** · **1660** · **1670** · **1680** · **1690**

THE AMERICAN COLONIES

1550 — 1560 — 1570 — 1580 — 1590 — 1600 — 1610 — 1620

1580
Colonies at Roanoke, 1580, 1587
•
British navy defeats Spanish Armada, 1588

1600
Virginia, 1607
•
Quebec, 1608

1610
Starving time in Virginia, 1609-11
•
First African slaves in America, 1619

1620
Massachusetts Bay, 1620
•
Thanksgiving, 1621
•
New Hampshire, 1623

Poor Richard, 1733.
AN
Almanack

by RICHARD SAUNDERS, Philom.
PHILADELPHIA:
Printed and sold by B. FRANKLIN, at the New Printing-Office near the Market

Delaware, 1704

Georgia, 1733

The Great Awakening, 1739-41

Albany Plan of Union, 1754
•
French and Indian War, 1755-63

Sugar Act, 1764
•
Stamp Act, 1765
•
Townshend Acts, 1767

Boston Massacre, 1770

1700 — 1710 — 1720 — 1730 — 1740 — 1750 — 1760 — 1770

1

CHAPTER 1
Three Discoveries
of America

America was discovered three times, each time by accident. The first time was about 30,000 years ago, when people from northern Asia touched foot on American soil in what is now Alaska. The exact year, decade, or century will never be known, for no historian recorded the adventures of these pioneers. Their graves are unmarked. The ashes of their campfires have been scattered by the winds of the ages. These were accidental discoverers, hunters following wild game or herders driving their flocks to find greener pastures over the next hill.

THE ICE AGE

Today Asia is separated from Alaska by the Bering Strait, a body of water more than 50 miles (80 kilometers) wide. When the first humans made the crossing, that stretch was dry land. The earth was then passing through a great **Ice Age,** a period when the weather was much colder than at present. What in warmer times would have fallen as rain and drained back into the oceans fell as snow instead. Gradually, enormous amounts of this snow piled up in the northern and southern regions of the earth, far more than could melt during the short summers. Vast ice fields called glaciers formed. So much water was trapped in these thick glaciers that the water level of the oceans dropped sharply, exposing a land bridge between Asia and North America.

Animals and plants crossed over this bridge. The bones of ancient Asian elephants, called mammoths, and of saber-toothed tigers have been found in dozens of places in the United States. Then came people, the first Americans.

The first American immigrants came in waves, for there were warmer periods when some of the ice melted and the water level rose. The last crossed about 10,000 years ago. At about that time the great glaciers began to melt, and the Bering land bridge was flooded over by the rising ocean.

■ How did the Ice Age lead Asian people to the first discovery of America?

■ Why did the first American immigrants come in waves? Why did the last cross some 10,000 years ago?

The identity of the early Americans who made these stone implements and spear points has been lost to history. These artifacts tell of hunts for bison and other game perhaps 8,000 years ago during the Stone Age. Why is so little known about the first Americans?

THE GREAT MIGRATION

What did it feel like to be among the first humans to reach this great, empty land? We know what the first astronauts experienced when they set foot on the moon. They were aware that they were doing something no one had ever done before. We do not know exactly what the first Americans experienced. They did not know that they were exploring a new continent. Understanding the difference calls for an act of **historical imagination.** Having a good historical imagination means being able to look at past events from the outside, keeping in mind what the people of the day knew, but at the same time remembering what they did not know.

Once in North America, the wanderers moved slowly southward and to the east, following the life-giving game and grasses. The distances they covered were enormous. It is 15,000 miles (24,000 kilometers) from their homeland in Asia to the southern tip of South America and 6,000 miles (9,600 kilometers) to what is now New

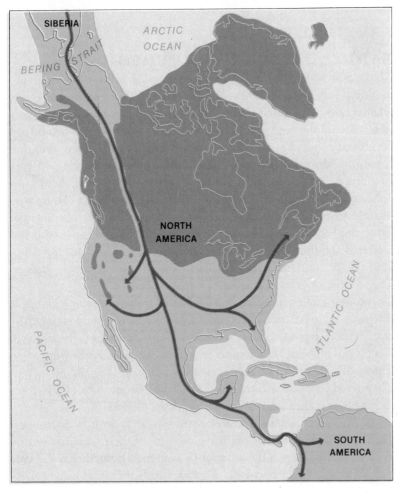

MIGRATION TO AMERICA

- Places covered by glaciers
- Land areas
- → Migration routes

England. Many thousand years passed before they had spread over all of North and South America.

As they advanced and multiplied, the first Americans gradually changed their ways of life. Some made their homes in fertile valleys, others in tropical jungles. Some settled in mountainous regions or in deserts. Each group had different problems, and each learned to see the world in different ways. As a result each **society** created its own **culture**. A *society* is a group of families who live and work together and who have common values and patterns of behavior. The *culture* of a society consists of the special characteristics of the people who make it up: the language they speak, their government, how they make a living, their family relationships, how they educate their children.

Some sense of how many different cultures these first Americans and their descendants created comes from the fact that the peoples of North and South America spoke between 1,000 and 2,000 languages.

- What are some of the reasons why the first Americans gradually changed their ways of life?
- What is a *society*? What is a *culture*?

EARLY AMERICAN CULTURES

About 500 years ago there were more than 25 million people living in North and South America. Only about 1 million of these inhabited what is now the United States and Canada. Partly because they were so few in number and spread over such a huge area, these people had developed a number of distinct cultures. But they had many things in common. Most did not rely entirely on hunting and living off berries, fruits, and other wild plants. Many were farmers. Seed corn 4,000 years old has been found in caves in the Southwest. Those who planted seeds and cultivated the land instead of merely hunting and gathering food were more secure and comfortable. People who had mastered farming, or agriculture, could settle in one place instead of roaming in constant search of food. They built permanent houses. Their societies grew to include more members.

None of the groups made much progress in developing simple machines or substituting mechanical or even animal power for their own muscle power. They had no wagons or other vehicles with wheels and no horses or oxen to help plow the land. Aside from a few copper objects and some gold and silver jewelry, they had no metals. They lived in what anthropologists call the **Stone Age.** Their tools and weapons were made of wood or stone or bone.

Most leaders, or chiefs, were chosen in a fairly democratic manner. That is, most chiefs ruled with the consent of their societies, not by force or written law. Life was mostly governed by tradition and custom. People tended to work in groups rather than alone. Usually

Both of these stone artifacts were found by archeologists at a site in Ohio. Perhaps the head was carved to represent an ancestor, and the little toad is a pipe that might have been used in the ceremonies of the ancient Hopewell people, who are named for the site where these art works were discovered. What might such artifacts show us about the culture of the first Americans who carved them?

they did not own their land as individuals. Their "hunting ground" or homeland was the general region in which the group lived. It was not, like a modern state or nation, an area with specific boundaries. This was true even of the farmers, who could not go far from the crops they tended.

These agricultural people were mostly peaceful, though they could fight fiercely to protect their fields. The hunters and wanderers, on the other hand, were quite warlike because their need to move about brought them frequently into conflict with other groups.

Some early American cultures were **matrilinear,** which means that family relationships were controlled by the female side. When a man and woman married in such a society, the man became a member of his wife's social group, or **clan.** A typical household might consist of an older woman, her daughters, and her granddaughters. Of course, the woman's husband, her sons-in-law, and her grandsons would also live in the household group. But only the female members were truly permanent members of the clan.

This water jar was one of the fine pieces of clay pottery made by the Zuni in the desert of the Southwest. Water was scarce and precious to these early Americans. Look closely at the decorations on the jar. What generalizations might you make about the Zuni from this artifact?

All of these statements are **generalizations.** They are true of most of the groups we are discussing. Yet every one of these communities was somewhat different from all the others. No generalization about them can be completely accurate. History is full of such "mostly but not entirely true" statements. This is unfortunate, but we must learn to live with this weakness. Remember, as you read, to add words like "usually" or "nearly always" when they are not on the page.

- How did the agricultural peoples differ from the hunters and wanderers in early America?
- What is a generalization? What words should the reader of history add?

5

This site in Mesa Verde, Colorado, was once a *pueblo*, or town, of 300 dwellings built upon the edge of a cliff. The circular ruin standing in the left foreground was once the entrance to a *kiva*, an underground chamber used for ceremonies by the cliff dwellers who built their pueblo between the 11th and 14th centuries. What building material was used by these people of the pueblos?

EARLY AMERICAN SOCIETIES

Land and climate strongly influenced the way the first Americans lived. They adjusted to nature—their **environment**—far more than they tried to change it. A brief look at some of the early American societies gives us an idea of the variety of American Indian cultures that evolved over hundreds of years.

The Southwest. As much as 1,000 years ago in the Southwest, the Hopi and Zuni were building with **adobe**—sun-baked brick plastered with mud. Their homes looked remarkably like modern apartment houses. Some were four stories high and contained quarters for perhaps a thousand people, along with storerooms for grain and other goods. These buildings were usually put up against cliffs, both to make construction easier and for defense against enemies. They were really villages in themselves, as later Spanish explorers must have realized since they called them **pueblos.** *Pueblo* is Spanish for town.

The people of the pueblos were peaceful and gentle. They raised what are called **the three sisters**—corn, beans, and squash. They made excellent pottery and wove marvelous baskets, some so fine that they could hold water. The Southwest has always been a dry country, with water scarce. The Hopi and Zuni brought water from streams to their fields and gardens through irrigation ditches. Water was so important that it played a major role in their religion. They developed elaborate ceremonies and religious rituals to bring rain.

The Great Basin. The way of life of less-settled groups was simpler and more strongly influenced by nature. Small tribes such as the Shoshone and Ute wandered the dry and mountainous lands between the Rocky Mountains and the Pacific Ocean. They gathered seeds and hunted small animals such as rabbits and snakes. In the Far

BUILDING SKILLS IN SOCIAL STUDIES

The Parts of a Map

You can learn to read a map with confidence when you look first at its parts. All of the maps in this book—and most maps in any book you look at—begin with a *title* and a *scale*.

The *title* tells you what the purpose of the map is. Always read the title carefully in order to know which areas of the map to look at most closely. The title of the map below, for example, has two parts. It shows both the location of American Indian tribes and also their larger culture regions. How are the various tribes and cultures identified on the map?

The *scale* shows distance in miles (*mi.*) or kilometers (*km.*)—or both, as in this book. Use a ruler with the scale to calculate approximate distances on a map.

Use the map below to answer these questions:
1. Choose one American Indian culture region and name all of the tribes found within it.
2. Which were the largest culture regions?
3. Which tribe lived closest to the Creeks?
4. Which is the greater distance—600 miles or 600 kilometers? What is the approximate distance across the Great Plains culture region?
5. Which of these two tribes would have been more likely to encounter the Huron—the Shoshone or the Seneca? Tell why.

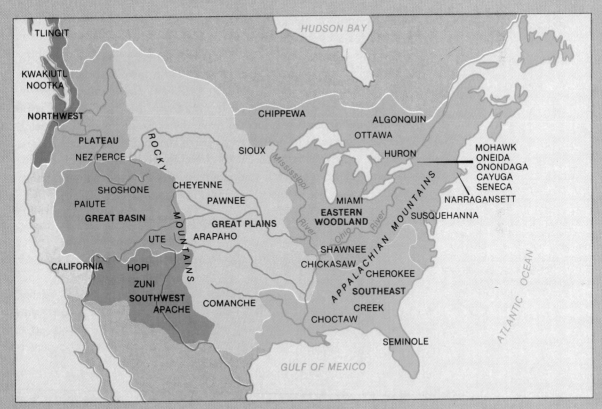

AMERICAN INDIAN TRIBES AND CULTURE REGIONS

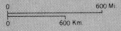

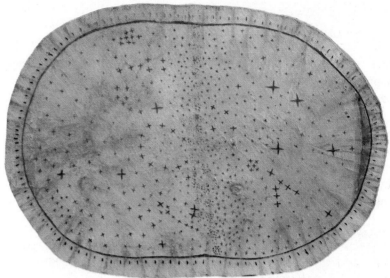

An early astronomer of the Pawnee painted this star chart on buckskin to show the stars and planets of the night sky. It was used to foretell the future. A reverence for the heavens was a part of the Pawnee tradition. What are some other uses Plains Indians made of animal hides?

North the ancestors of today's Eskimo hunted seals, walruses, and the great whales. They lived right on the frozen seas in shelters called igloos built of blocks of packed snow. When summer came, they fished for salmon and hunted the lordly caribou.

The Great Plains. The Cheyenne, Pawnee, and Sioux tribes, known as the Plains Indians, lived on the grasslands between the Rocky Mountains and the Mississippi River. They hunted the bison, commonly called the buffalo. Its meat was the chief food of these tribes, and its hide was used to make their clothing and the covering of their tents and teepees. Every part of the animal was used, even its waste, which when dried served as fuel for cook fires in that treeless region. Little wonder that the buffalo was an important symbol in the religious life of the Plains Indians.

This Kwakiutl ceremonial mask was carved from wood and later painted. Perhaps its three heads look to past, present, and future. Early Americans of the Northwest carved masks and totem poles to represent their ancestors. Why are artifacts of the Northwest Indians generally made of wood?

The Northwest. Fishing was the mainstay of the Kwakiutl, Nootka, and Tlingit tribes. These people lived mostly on salmon and other fish caught in the northwestern coastal waters. The magnificent forests of redwood, pine, and cedar that grew right down to the ocean supplied them with lumber to build their homes and canoes and to carve their ancestral totem poles.

The Southeast. The Ohio Valley was once the home of the ancestors of such important tribes as the Choctaw and the Creek. They were called the **Mound Builders** because they buried their dead in elaborate earthen mounds built in the shape of birds or snakes, or in human form. These were very large, as high as an eight-story building, and one has been found that covers an area as large as 50 modern

city blocks. We know that the people of the mounds traded with tribes as far away as the Rocky Mountains and the Gulf of Mexico because objects made of stone and ornaments made of the teeth of sharks and alligators have been found in their settlements. Tribes such as the Cherokee, Natchez, and Chickasaw gradually moved southeast from the Ohio Valley.

The Eastern Woodlands. The Mohawk, Oneida, Onondaga, Cayuga, and Seneca were a group of tribes that were later called the **Five Nations** or League of the Iroquois. They lived in the densely wooded central region of what is now New York State. The Iroquois group, or **confederation,** was very powerful because it could assemble many warriors. The Iroquois men were hunters, the women farmers. The Iroquois women also participated in tribal decision making, choosing new chiefs, for example.

An air view reveals this mound in the Ohio Valley in a way that the Hopewell artists who made it could not have seen. It is in the shape of a snake or serpent. In what way is this mound both a work of art and a religious site?

For thousands of years these tribal societies knew nothing of the rest of the world. They were as isolated from their original homeland in Asia and from Europe and Africa as if they were on the moon.

■ What are some examples of how environment shaped customs of the various North American tribal societies?

Uncovering the Past

Georg Gerster, Photo Researchers

The La Brea tar pit in Los Angeles yielded up this skull of a saber-toothed tiger, shown here in final restoration by an archeologist.

Since the first Americans did not record their history in books, we must reconstruct it from those objects they created that have survived the centuries. These include campsites and buildings, engraved stones, clay pots, tools and weapons, jewelry—what are known as **artifacts.** Putting together these fragments is like solving an enormous jigsaw puzzle with many missing pieces. It is a difficult but fascinating task.

Scientists who search for and study artifacts are called **archeologists.** In America archeologists have located and carefully dug up ancient camps, burial grounds, and entire cities. They have found hundreds of thousands of artifacts from arrowheads to huge stone statues.

We can estimate the age of these artifacts by using the technique called **carbon-14 dating.** Carbon is present in all living things, and some of this carbon takes a form called carbon-14. When a living thing dies, its carbon-14 begins to break down at a very slow but steady rate. Thus, by measuring what remains of the carbon-14 in, say, a human bone or even a piece of charcoal from a campfire, an expert can tell about how long ago the person was alive or the fire put out. Carbon-14 dates are accurate only to within a few hundred years. They are not of much use for studying recent events. But for the history of the peoples who first settled America, the method is most useful.

In addition to what archeologists can tell us about the first Americans, we can also learn by studying their living descendants. The scientists who do this research are called **anthropologists.** Some anthropologists live with and observe the descendants of the first Americans. They ask how these peoples explain their relation to one another. What are their religious ideas and other values? Do they tell stories called **folk tales** that have been handed down from generation to generation? What are their habits and traditions? The answers to these questions throw light on how early Americans lived and thought. In such ways historians have been able to learn a great deal about these first settlers of America.

THE VIKING SAGAS

The second discovery of America was much less important than the first. It occurred about the year 1000, less than a thousand years ago, but we know little for certain about the event or the European people who took part in it. The discoverers were Norwegian sailors who are called **Norsemen** or **Vikings.**

In 982 a red-headed Viking, aptly named Eric the Red, sailed from Iceland and founded a settlement near the southern tip of the island of Greenland in the North Atlantic. The story of Eric and his family and their adventures was passed down from generation to generation in **sagas,** a traditional Scandinavian story form. These sagas were told and retold. They were not written down until 200 years after the events they describe.

The two major sagas about their adventures, *Eric the Red's Saga* and the *Greenlanders' Saga*, contradict each other at many points. They are obviously a mixture of fact and fancy. Nevertheless, there is little doubt that either Eric's son Leif or some other Viking sailor was the first European to set foot on the North American continent.

Archeologists have discovered the remains of only one Viking camp in North America. It is at a place called **L'Anse aux Meadows** (the Creek of the Meadows) in Newfoundland. But the sagas speak of a land called **Vinland** (Wine Land) which must have been farther south since grapes do not grow as far north as Newfoundland. According to the *Greenlanders' Saga*, Leif sailed to Helluland (Baffin Island today) and Markland (Labrador). He then passed around a large island (Newfoundland) and reached a country "so choice, it seemed to them that none of the cattle would require fodder for the winter."

A Norse ship such as the Vikings might have sailed to America is depicted on this seal of the city of Bergen, Norway. It was carved in about 1300. How many centuries earlier was the Viking discovery of America?

THE VIKING EXPEDITIONS

There he found the grapevines. Leif and his crew loaded their boat with grapes and vines and timber and sailed back to Greenland.

Next, the saga tells us, Leif Ericson's brother Thorvald sailed to Vinland. While exploring, he and his party encountered nine men in kayaks, which are a kind of canoe. They killed eight of them but the ninth escaped, soon to return with a larger force. The Vikings drove them off. But Thorvald was killed in the battle.

According to the sagas, other expeditions followed, one led by Eric's daughter Freydis. The Vikings gathered grapes, traded for furs with the natives, whom they called *Skraelings*, and fought with them repeatedly. Sometime around the year 1010 the Vikings stopped visiting Vinland, perhaps because of these troubles with the Skraelings. Outside Norway and Iceland no one knew of their adventures. Five hundred more years passed before the original Americans were again disturbed by outsiders.

■ What is our source of information about the Vikings? What problems are there with this information?

EUROPE IN THE YEAR 1000

If the Vikings could make their way to North America, why did no other Europeans attempt to explore the western seas for such a long time? There were several reasons for the delay. Life in Europe was slow paced. Little changed from one year to the next. The people were mostly poor and uneducated. Curiosity about the rest of the world was at a low point. Each village, or **manor,** was a tiny world in itself, ruled by a lord. The lord's fields were cultivated by peasants called **serfs.** Serfdom was a condition halfway between freedom and slavery. Serfs could not leave their village. They were said to be bound to the soil. They labored to feed themselves and their families, but a large part of what they produced went to the lord of the manor. In exchange the lord protected his serfs against enemies and acted as lawgiver and judge for the community.

Nations as we know them did not yet exist. True, there were kings of places called England and France, but these rulers had relatively little power. The lesser nobles, the lords of the manor, owed their power to a great duke or count, he in turn to a king. Under what was called the **feudal system** each lord owed certain payments or services to a higher authority. In return for these "feudal dues" the higher noble protected him. But the lords of the manors controlled the land and the people, which meant that more often than not they were practically independent.

There was little trade between one manor and the next. Nearly everything that was eaten, worn, or used was made right in the community. Such a life had advantages. There were few surprises. Every-

This detail from a mural painted on a castle wall in Trent, Italy, is titled "Month of August." The 15th-century artist represented the feudal system with some ladies of the manor in the foreground, poor villagers going to market in the midground, and serfs harvesting grain in the background. Why was the lord of a manor quite independent?

one knew what to expect of everyone else. Misunderstandings were rare. But it was a narrow existence in a small world. People lacked not only the wealth and free time to explore but even the urge to do so.

- What kind of life did Europeans lead in the year 1000?
- How did the feudal system work?

THE CRUSADES

Outside pressures eventually ended Europe's sleepy period. One was a series of religious wars, the **Crusades,** organized by the Roman Catholic popes in order to get control of the city of Jerusalem and the rest of the **Holy Land** of Palestine, what is now Israel. This region had been overrun by the followers of the Arab prophet Mohammed, founder of **Islam,** a new religion. *Islam* means "submission to God." Believers in Islam are called **Moslems.** Eventually the Moslems created a huge empire extending from India in the East through the Holy Land and across North Africa to the Atlantic Ocean. They also conquered most of Spain.

Knights who may have done battle in the Crusades are shown in this splendid page from an illuminated manuscript decorated by monks in about 1400. This scene comes from "The Books of the Grand Khan" by a Venetian traveler to the Far East named Marco Polo. The fighting is led by Genghis Khan, whose vast empire at one time spread as far westward as the Holy Land. What holy city did the Crusaders seek to set free?

The Bodleian Library, Oxford

About the time that the Vikings were exploring the lands west of Greenland, the Moslem ruler of Palestine, the Caliph Hakam, began to persecute Christians in his domain. It became impossible for Europeans to visit the Holy Land.

Therefore, in 1095 Pope Urban II summoned Catholics to take up the cross (*crusade* means "marked with a cross") and drive the Moslems out of Palestine. All over Europe lords and serfs responded. Thousands sewed crosses to their garments and marched off, first to Constantinople, which is today the city of Istanbul in northwestern Turkey, and then on to Palestine. In 1099 the crusaders captured Jerusalem and founded the Christian Kingdom of Jerusalem.

The Moslems did not meekly submit to Christian control of a region that was equally holy to their faith. For the next 200 years war raged almost continuously. The sultan Saladin recaptured Jerusalem in 1187. Gradually the Moslems pushed the Christians back. Crusade after crusade was organized in Europe to help the Christian Kingdom and regain the lost territory. Finally, in 1291, the last Christian stronghold, the city of Acre, was forced to surrender.

- Who were the Moslems? How large was their empire?
- What was the purpose of the Crusades? Were the Crusades successful?

THE COMMERCIAL REVOLUTION

The Crusades caused great changes in the ways that Europeans thought and acted. The tens of thousands who traveled by land and sea to the Holy Land saw another world and heard new ideas. In the markets they tasted new foods such as dates and rice and oranges. They discovered pepper and cinnamon, ginger, nutmeg, cloves, and other spices to flavor and preserve foods they already knew. They bought garments made of silk and cotton, finer and more comfortable than the wool they were accustomed to. Jewels, rugs, and countless other beautiful objects excited them. Almost all of these products came to the Holy Land by old trade routes from India, China, and the islands off the east coast of Asia. Europeans called India the **East,** China the **Orient,** and the Asian islands the **Indies.**

When they returned to their homelands, the crusaders brought samples of Eastern products for others to see. The desire for more quickly spread. European society began to pass through what we call the **Commercial Revolution.**

To pay for goods from Asia, Europeans had to produce more goods of their own. They manufactured more woolen cloth, trapped more fur-bearing animals, cut more lumber. The isolated life of the self-sufficient manor ended. People left the manors. Cities grew larger. Since townspeople produce no food, the remaining farmers in-

Crusaders might have brought home fine pottery like this bowl made by a 15th-century Moorish artisan in Spain. Few travelers would have seen a graceful ship like this one, however, for goods were moved by land. Where did the trade routes begin?

The Bodleian Library, Oxford

creased their production to feed them. Lords of the manor cleared more land. To get their serfs to do more work, the lords had to grant them more privileges.

Life became more exciting—and more uncertain and dangerous, too. Trade between East and West made merchants and bankers more important. They needed strong rulers who would build roads, protect trade routes against robbers, and keep the peace. They willingly lent money to these rulers. The rulers used the loans to raise armies to protect their lands against foreign enemies and also against robbers and highwaymen who preyed on traveling merchants and their goods. Thus, merchants and kings helped one another. The kings became more powerful, the merchants richer. The European economy expanded.

In another illuminated page from "The Books of the Grand Khan," Marco Polo sails from Venice on his travels to the East. Much of this scene from the year 1400 may be seen today, including the bronze horses of St. Mark's, far left; the Doges's Palace left of the canal; and the statues of the winged lion of St. Mark next to St. Theodore stepping on a crocodile. Why were many treasures of the East sought by Europeans?

■ What was the connection between the Crusades and the Commercial Revolution?
■ How did Europe change during the Commercial Revolution?

BUILDING SKILLS IN SOCIAL STUDIES

Reading a Time Line

Historians tell events in the order in which they happened. Another way of putting this is to say that "the skeleton of history is chronology." The dictionary defines *chronology* as "the science that deals with measuring time by regular divisions and that assigns to events their proper dates." Historians arrange the events they write about in *chronological order*.

One of the best ways to show chronological order is by a *time line.* Time lines appear at the beginning of each unit in this book. They show events happening in order, one after the other. Time lines also show the length of time between events.

Time lines are divided into equal periods of time. Those in this book are divided by years, except in this first unit, which is divided by ten-year periods (decades). Each year is marked on the time line, even when no event is listed. Sometimes the length of time between events is as important as the events themselves. A color bar shows long-term events.

A time line is drawn to *scale.* The space between each date—the *interval*—is always the same. In this book the scale is approximately 1 inch (about 2.5 centimeters) for each year.

The time line shown oh this page is a much simpler version than the illustrated time lines at the beginning of each unit. Also, this time line covers a much greater period of time. The interval is by hundred years (centuries). Because so many early dates are uncertain, the symbol c. appears before many dates. This stands for *circa*, which means approximately.

Use the time line on this page to answer these questions:
1. When did the Vikings sail to America?
2. How long was the time of the Crusades?
3. When did the population of the Americas reach 25 million people?
4. How long after the invention of the compass did the Portuguese sail to Africa?
5. What happened to Spain in 1588?

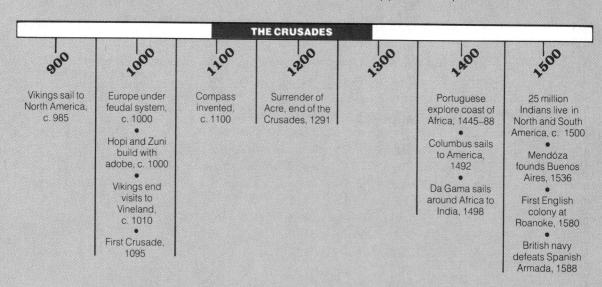

| 900 | 1000 | 1100 | 1200 | 1300 | 1400 | 1500 |

THE CRUSADES

| Vikings sail to North America, c. 985 | Europe under feudal system, c. 1000 • Hopi and Zuni build with adobe, c. 1000 • Vikings end visits to Vineland, c. 1010 • First Crusade, 1095 | Compass invented, c. 1100 | Surrender of Acre, end of the Crusades, 1291 | | Portuguese explore coast of Africa, 1445–88 • Columbus sails to America, 1492 • Da Gama sails around Africa to India, 1498 | 25 million Indians live in North and South America, c. 1500 • Mendóza founds Buenos Aires, 1536 • First English colony at Roanoke, 1580 • British navy defeats Spanish Armada, 1588 |

EUROPE STIRS TO NEW IDEAS

Both, National Maritime Museum, Greenwich

The religious ideals that had inspired the Crusades were not forgotten. But Europeans became more concerned about this world, less about the hereafter. More people were buying and selling, enjoying luxuries, appreciating art, gaining scientific knowledge. Advances in **printing** made by Johann Gutenberg of Germany in the 1450s did still more to break down barriers. With Gutenberg's press a printer could make any number of copies of a book simply by setting the type once. It was no longer necessary to copy books and manuscripts one at a time by hand. Books became much cheaper. As a result ordinary people as well as rich learned to read. They improved their minds with the powerful new knowledge found in books.

Great improvements were soon made in designing and sailing ships. The Vikings had crossed the Atlantic without navigation instruments. They steered by watching the stars and the sun, hoping for the best. By about 1100 the **compass** had been invented. Its magnetized needle always pointed north, which enabled sailors to know their direction even when sun and stars were hidden by clouds. By the 1400s sailors were also using the **astrolabe,** an instrument that measured a ship's latitude—that is, its distance north or south of the equator. These instruments made navigation more accurate.

When it was possible to travel farther, larger ships were designed and built. The stage was set for the third and final discovery of America and for the exploration and invasion of many other parts of the world by Europeans.

- How did Gutenberg's printing press help Europeans discover new ideas?
- Which inventions made longer sea voyages possible?

THE AGE OF DISCOVERY

As we said at the start, all of the discoveries of America were made by accident. The third one was made by explorers who were looking for a better way to get to China.

The compass of ivory and inlay at the top and the astrolabe of brass below it are both from the 15th century. How did sailors use each for navigation?

Trade between Europe and the East was dominated by Italian merchants whose ships sailed from Venice, Naples, and other ports. Their ships carried cloth, furs, metals, and other European products to Constantinople and brought back the silks, spices, jewels, and other Oriental goods that Europeans craved. These goods were very costly.

The merchants of Constantinople justified their high prices by pointing out how dangerous and expensive it was to bring goods to Constantinople from places half the world away. Their caravans had to cross high mountain passes infested with bandits and burning deserts where roving bands might strike at any time. Goods passed

17

This colored engraving shows the seaport of Lisbon in Portugal as it appeared in 1564. The armed ships stand at anchor with sails furled. Why had the Portuguese sought a sea route to the East?

Giraudon

Prince Henry of Portugal kneels at prayer in this oil painted on wood in about 1566, a century after his death. At his side is the youthful king of Portugal, Alfonso V, whom Henry helped protect until he came of age to rule. Why was Henry later known as the Navigator?

through many **middlemen.** Each of these earned a profit, adding to the final cost. Local lords taxed the travelers and their goods. There were tolls to be paid at bridges and ferries. Little wonder that the people of western Europe were eager to find easier and less expensive routes to the East.

The obvious path east was by no means the shortest. It was the all-sea route around Africa to India, the East Indies, and China. This longer route had many advantages. Ships sail day and night, while land travelers and the horses, donkeys, and camels that haul their belongings must stop each night to rest. The sea route would save time and labor. Once packed in a vessel's hold, goods would not have to be unloaded and reloaded until a home port was reached. Still more important, only one shipper would profit from the sea voyage, and no tolls or taxes need be paid along the way.

No one had ever sailed from Europe all the way to the Orient. There were no maps or charts, little knowledge of winds and currents. Indeed, no European had even seen the west coast of Africa below the Sahara Desert. Prince Henry of Portugal, who became known as Prince Henry the Navigator, took the lead in opening the African route.

Henry created a kind of research center for the study of geography and **navigation,** the science of sailing ships. Experts from many lands came to work there. Their information about tides and the position of the stars in different regions was of great value to Henry's captains. Armed with this information and financed by Henry, these brave sailors gradually explored the African coast. In 1445 one of Henry's ships reached the site of present-day Dakar, in Senegal, where the great western bulge of Africa turns to the south and east.

By the 1470s, after Henry's death, Portuguese ships had reached the equator. In 1488 another expedition managed to sail around the southern tip of the continent, only to turn back when the crew panicked, afraid to venture into the unknown seas ahead. Finally, in 1498, Vasco da Gama sailed around Africa and on to India.

- What made Europeans search for a new route to the Indies?
- What contributions did Henry the Navigator make to the Age of Discovery?

CHRISTOPHER COLUMBUS

Meanwhile, another explorer traveled in a different direction. His name was Christopher Columbus. Instead of sailing far to the south around Africa, he headed for Asia by sailing directly west. This possibility had attracted little attention. Educated people no longer believed that the world was flat. They did not think a ship sailing too far to the west would reach the edge and "fall off." But they believed that there was no land on the "other side" of the globe. Since it was at least 10,000 miles (16,000 kilometers) from western Europe to Asia, no ship could carry enough food and water to make the journey. The trip was out of the question.

Or was it? Columbus did not think so, and few captains knew the Atlantic Ocean as well as he. Columbus was a sturdily built man of above average height, red-haired, and with a ruddy complexion. He was born in Genoa, in northern Italy, in 1451. He went to sea at an early age. While still a young man, he had sailed south to the Guinea coast of Africa and north to the waters around the British Isles. He may even have visited Iceland.

In 1476 Columbus was shipwrecked off Portugal. He settled in Lisbon and along with his brother Bartholomew became a chart maker. Columbus studied every map and book of geography he could get his hands on. A doctor who knew him wrote that Columbus had a "noble and grand desire to go to the places where the spices grow." He was particularly fascinated by the famous tales of Marco Polo, a citizen of Venice who had traveled in the Far East in the late 1200s. If Columbus could get to China and the Indies by sailing west, fame and fortune would be his.

There were islands in the Atlantic—the Madeiras 350 miles (560 kilometers) from southern Portugal, the Azores 600 miles (960 kilometers) farther west. Columbus heard stories about an island called Antila, only 1,000 miles (1,600 kilometers) from Japan. He persuaded himself, moreover, that China was only 4,500 miles (7,200 kilometers) west of Spain and Portugal, Japan nearer still.

When he decided to sail westward, Columbus first sought the backing of the king of Portugal, John II. John believed, quite cor-

This oil portrait is believed to be an accurate likeness of Christopher Columbus although it was painted some years after his death. His face seems proud and strong-willed. Why was Columbus more apt than most sailors to find a new route to the Far East?

This is the queenly gaze Isabella of Spain might have given Columbus when he sought ships. The portrait in oil was made in the 15th century by the artist Bermejo. What did the Spanish monarchs promise to give Columbus?

rectly, that Columbus was greatly underestimating the distance to be covered. He refused to invest in such a foolhardy expedition. Columbus, he said, was a "big talker and boastful . . . and full of fancy and imagination." The Columbus brothers then attempted to interest Henry VII of England, Charles VIII of France, and the Spanish monarchs, Ferdinand and Isabella. All rejected their proposals.

But Columbus persisted. Finally, early in 1492, Queen Isabella agreed to outfit three tiny ships. The *Santa María*, which Columbus personally commanded, was about 85 feet (about 26 meters) long and had a crew of 39. The *Pinta* and the *Niña* were about half the size of the *Santa María*. The entire expedition consisted of 87 men.

On Friday, August 3, 1492, the little fleet set sail from Palos, Spain. After a stopover in the Canary Islands off northwestern Africa, the ships headed into the unknown. For over a month they sailed on, always toward the west, always alone, never another sail in sight. Columbus was a magnificent sailor. The *Santa María*'s compass guided him westward, but to judge his position he had only a sand-glass that had to be turned each half hour to measure time and only his years of experience at sea to estimate his speed. Yet he reckoned the distance traveled each day with amazing accuracy.

As day followed day into mid-October, Columbus's men grew tense. They had sailed far beyond where land was supposed to be, and before them lay only the endless ocean. They demanded that Columbus turn back. He would not. Be of good hope, he urged them. Finally he promised to abandon the search if land were not sighted by October 12.

The breeze freshened and the three ships picked up speed. Now broken branches, land birds, and other hopeful signs began to appear. At last, by moonlight at two o'clock in the morning of October 12, the lookout Rodrigo de Triana spotted the foam of waves breaking on a distant shore. *"Tierra! Tierra!"* he shouted. Land! Land!

- What was Columbus's goal? In what ways was he well qualified for his undertaking?
- Why did the king of Portugal refuse to support Columbus?

COLUMBUS IN AMERICA

When day broke, Columbus approached the land, which was a small island. He was absolutely certain that he had reached the East Indies. Now he had earned the title given him by Ferdinand and Isabella— Admiral of the Ocean Sea. He named the island **San Salvador,** or Holy Saviour, out of gratitude for having reached it safely. He found no spices there, no silks or rugs. Except for tiny bits that some of the inhabitants wore in their noses, he found no gold.

The natives of the island of Guanahaní, for that was its name in their language, were astonished and awed by the Europeans. Columbus, certain in his belief that he was in the Indies, called them Indians. All native Americans would thereafter be thus mistakenly described. They came forth shyly, bearing gifts. "They invite you to share everything they possess," Columbus recorded. He in turn gave them small presents—beads, bits of cloth, and tiny brass bells that particularly delighted them. When Luis de Torres, a member of the crew who knew Arabic, tried to speak to these "Indians," not a one understood him. This seemed odd, for Arabic was a common language in the Indies.

By signs the Indians told Columbus that many other islands lay to the west and south. So he pushed on, taking a few Indians along as interpreters. Everywhere he found the same charming, generous people. But he found no spices and no gold.

Soon the explorers reached Cuba. Perhaps this was China! At every harbor along this large landmass, Columbus expected to find a fleet of Chinese junks. Some of the local people told him that gold could be found at *Cubanacan*, by which they meant "in the middle of Cuba." Columbus thought they were saying *El Gran Can*—in Spanish, "the Great Khan"—and sent a delegation headed by de Torres to present his respects to the Emperor of China! Of course, the delegation found only tropical jungle.

Finally, in December 1492, Columbus reached the island of Haiti, which he named **Hispaniola,** the Spanish Isle. There the inhabitants had substantial amounts of gold; one chief gave him a belt with a solid gold buckle. The Spaniards could not find the source of the

Here is how the artist John Vanderlyn pictured the landing of Columbus and his crew in the Americas. This large painting is one of eight that hang in the Rotunda of the Capitol building in Washington, D.C. Columbus holds up the royal banner of Spain. Why did he call the native Americans Indians?

gold, but there was enough of it to convince them that there must be mines nearby. When the *Santa María* ran aground and had to be abandoned, Columbus decided to leave some of his crew on the island to look for the gold. He then sailed home in the *Niña*, still sure that he had reached the Far East.

- What kind of welcome did Columbus receive from the island people?
- What puzzles were there for Columbus as he sailed from island to island in America?

COLUMBUS RETURNS TO SPAIN

Columbus landed a hero at Palos, Spain, on March 15, 1493. Everywhere, crowds lined his route, gazing in wonder at the Indians he was bringing to show the king and queen. When he reached Barcelona, Ferdinand and Isabella showered honors upon him. They made him their personal representative, or viceroy, in the Indies and governor of the new territories.

No one yet had a very clear picture of where these new territories were. Columbus had made the Spanish claim, but Portugal, which already owned the Azores islands, claimed rights to lands farther into the Atlantic. The two Catholic countries turned to Pope Alexander VI to decide the issue. In May 1493 the Pope divided the ocean about 300 miles (480 kilometers) beyond the Azores. The dividing line was called the **Line of Demarcation.** New lands to the west of the line were to belong to Spain, those to the east to Portugal. The next year

COLUMBUS'S VOYAGES TO THE AMERICAS

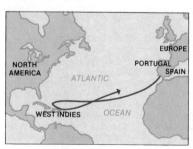

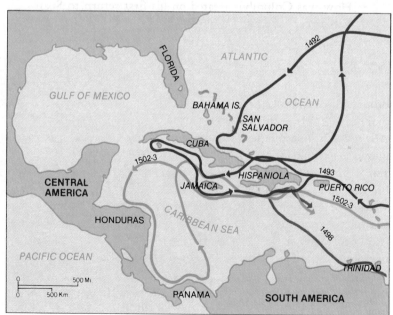

Spain and Portugal signed a treaty which moved the line somewhat farther west.

When Brazil, which extends well east of the line, was discovered in 1500, it became Portuguese. This explains why today Brazilians speak Portuguese while most other South American people speak Spanish.

Meanwhile, in September 1493 Columbus sailed again westward, this time with a fleet of 17 ships and 2,000 colonists. When he reached Hispaniola, he discovered that the crew members he had left there had been killed by the Indians. Columbus built a new settlement, named Isabela, then sailed off on a further futile search for China. When he returned to Isabela, he found the town in very bad condition. Many colonists were sick, others were squabbling with one another. More fighting had broken out with the Indians. Little gold had been collected. Much discouraged, Columbus sailed back to Spain.

Columbus was a great sailor and a brave and determined man. But he was not good at politics or business. He made two more trips across the Atlantic. On one he discovered the island of Trinidad off the north coast of South America. On the other he explored the coast of Central America from Honduras to Panama and spent more than a year on the island of Jamaica. He never obtained the wealth he had hoped for. The king took away most of his power. The great discoverer even spent a short time in jail. He died, almost forgotten, in 1506. He never accepted the fact that he had not reached the East Indies.

■ How was Columbus treated on his first return to Spain?
■ What were some of Columbus's strengths and weaknesses?

AMERICA: A NEW WORLD

News of Columbus's voyage and the wonderful things he had brought back with him spread rapidly through Europe. Gradually more new lands were discovered as explorers ventured across the Atlantic. On one of these voyages an Italian named Amerigo Vespucci visited the northern coast of South America. Later he traveled along the coast of Brazil. The voyages were not in themselves path breaking, and Vespucci was more a tourist than an explorer. But he wrote a description of his adventures that attracted much attention. Europeans were beginning to realize that an entire new continent existed out there in the Atlantic Ocean. Amerigo Vespucci did not mention "the Indies." He wrote about a **New World.**

In 1507 a German geographer who had read Amerigo's account suggested that the "New World" should be called America in his honor. The idea caught on, and by the 1530s people in every Euro-

Amerigo Vespucci is shown in this detail from a 1507 map that was made by Martin Waldseemüller of Germany. The map was the first to show the full size of the New World, which Waldseemüller chose to call *America*. How readily was the new name accepted?

23

pean country except Portugal and Spain were calling the new regions **America.** But 300 years after Columbus, Spain still called the chief governing body for its colonies the Ministry of the Indies.

▓ What was the significance of Vespucci's voyages to the "New World"?

Ferdinand Magellan is depicted in this oil painted in 1582, then half a century after his voyage to find a water passage to the ocean west of the Americas. Which ruler agreed to finance his expedition?

BALBOA AND MAGELLAN

Vespucci showed that America was very large. Two Spanish explorers soon proved that it was nowhere near Asia.

The first was Vasco Núñez de Balboa. Balboa was the governor of a Spanish settlement in what is now the Republic of Panama, in Central America. In 1513 he set out with about 200 Spanish soldiers and several hundred Indians to explore the area. The party made its way through a thick jungle that was infested with insects and poisonous snakes. They crossed tangled swamps and climbed up rugged mountains. In three weeks they covered only about 60 miles (96 kilometers). Finally, when they neared the top of the mountains, Balboa ordered his men to stop. He climbed to the summit alone. There before him, glittering in the sun as far as the eye could see, stretched an endless ocean.

After giving thanks to God, Balboa and his men pushed onward until they reached the shore. Where breakers came roaring in over the sand flats, he waded in, sword in hand, and took possession of the new ocean for Spain.

Balboa had crossed the **Isthmus of Panama,** where the Panama Canal would be dug 400 years later. His discovery that another great body of water lay beyond America proved that it was a long way to the Indies. To get there by sailing west, one would have to find a passage through or around the land barrier.

Since Balboa had shown that only a narrow neck of land separated the oceans at Panama, surely somewhere there must be a water passage, or **strait,** through to Balboa's ocean. In 1518 a Portuguese captain named Ferdinand Magellan presented King Charles V of Spain with a plan to find such a route. Magellan was a short, stocky man, dark, bearded, and very, very tough. He was a veteran of several wars in the East and knew the area well. He approached Charles after his own king, Manuel I of Portugal, had refused to back his expedition.

Charles V agreed to finance Magellan's voyage. On September 20, 1519, the explorer set sail from Sanlúcar, Spain, with five ships and a crew of 237 men. Their first stop was in the Canary Islands. From there they sailed to Brazil, then southward along the coast of South America. Magellan and his sailors searched always for a way through to the west.

Off what is now Argentina they ran into a terrible storm. One of the ships sank. This disaster frightened the sailors, and they urged Magellan to turn back. When he refused, some of them mutinied. Magellan crushed this rebellion before it could spread and put the leaders to death. Then he sailed on.

Finally the voyagers reached the southern tip of South America. As the fleet entered the narrow passage between the land and the island of **Tierra del Fuego** (Land of Fire), fierce storms and huge waves tossed the ships about wildly. The sailors on one ship, shaken and discouraged, turned tail before the tempest and fled homeward. Sadly, this vessel contained a large part of the expedition's supplies.

The three remaining ships battled head winds and powerful currents for 38 days. At last they made their way through the passage, which we now call the **Strait of Magellan,** into a broad and tranquil sea. Because it seemed so calm and safe after the long struggle with the turbulent strait, Magellan named it the **Pacific Ocean.** (*Pacific* means "peaceful.")

Magellan now happily pointed his fleet toward the west. But the greatest ordeal lay ahead. For 98 days the three ships sailed onward. They sighted only two uninhabited islands. When their food ran out, the hungry sailors ate the rats in the ships' holds, then leather from the rigging, then sawdust. Many died. Those who remained grew steadily weaker and weaker.

Finally, early in 1521, they reached the island we call Guam. Magellan was now directly south of Japan. After seizing food and water from the peaceful inhabitants, he pushed on to the Philippine Islands. There, in a battle against local warriors, Magellan was killed. Following Magellan's death, Juan del Cano assumed command.

The fleet wandered about in the East Indies for many months. Two more ships were lost. The one that remained, the *Victoria*, managed to sail across the Indian Ocean, around the tip of Africa, and home to Sanlúcar, Spain. On September 6, 1522, almost three years after they had set out, del Cano and the other 17 who were still alive set foot again on Spanish soil. They were the first to **circumnavigate,** or sail around, the entire globe.

This was one of the greatest sea voyages of all time, which is reason enough for remembering it. But it brought few benefits to Spain. By proving that Asia was so far west of Europe, the expedition demonstrated that sailing there in that direction was much more dangerous and expensive than anyone had imagined. So ended Columbus's dream of capturing the rich trade of Asia by sailing west.

- What was Balboa's discovery?
- What was the significance of the voyage of Magellan and del Cano? What did the voyage demonstrate?

BUILDING SKILLS
IN SOCIAL STUDIES

Finding Latitude and Longitude

In order to show locations on the earth, maps are often drawn with lines which are called *latitude* and *longitude*. It is possible to plot exact locations by using these lines. They can help in finding the location of a city, a ship at sea, or a crashed airplane in a jungle.

Maps are always drawn with the direction north at the top. The lines that run east and west are called *parallels of latitude*. 0° latitude is also called the *equator*. Other parallels of latitude are numbered up to 90° north and 90° south of the equator. Thus, latitude tells you how far north or south a point is from the equator.

The lines that run north and south on a map are called *meridians of longitude*. 0° longitude runs through Greenwich, England, and is called the *prime meridian*. Other meridians of longitude are numbered up to 180° east and 180° west of the prime meridian. Thus, longitude tells you how far east or west a point is from the prime meridian.

By combining latitude and longitude, you can quickly find exact locations on earth. Columbus and other explorers of his time knew only how to find latitude. Can you explain why they would have had an easier time if they had been able to calculate both their latitude and longitude?

Use the map below of the voyages of Balboa and Magellan and del Cano to answer these questions:
1. On this map how many degrees are between each parallel of latitude and each meridian of longitude?
2. Since north is at the top of the map, in which direction did Magellan sail from the prime meridian?
3. Which continent lies approximately between 40° west longitude and 80° west longitude?
4. What spot visited by Juan del Cano lies at 120° east longitude above the equator?
5. What was the farthest latitude south reached by Magellan in his voyage?

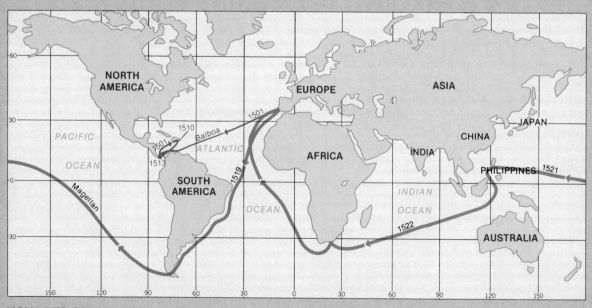

**VOYAGES OF BALBOA
AND MAGELLAN**

CORTÉS AND MONTEZUMA

While Magellan and del Cano were making their great voyage, the Spaniards were extending their control in America. Colonies were founded in all the larger islands of the Caribbean Sea. By 1519 most of the coastline around the Caribbean had been explored, and some knowledge of the peoples of the interior had been gathered.

The most powerful interior nation was the **Aztec** empire of central Mexico. In 1519 the governor of the Spanish colony of Cuba sent Hernán Cortés and about 450 soldiers to make contact with the Aztecs. The Aztec society and culture was mighty and wealthy. The Aztecs had built great stone temples. The capital city, Tenochtitlán, located on an artificial island in a shallow lake, housed 200,000 people. They had a written language, and they had mastered mathematics and astronomy.

The Aztecs were also warlike. They had conquered most of the other people of Mexico. According to their religion, human sacrifices had to be offered to the god of war to insure victory in battle. Each year thousands of people were slaughtered for this purpose. The victims were chosen from among the captives taken in earlier wars. The Aztecs also forced those they had conquered to pay heavy taxes.

As Cortés and his handful of Spanish soldiers marched inland from the coast, many local people eagerly joined forces with him. By the time he reached Tenochtitlán, he had an army of many thousands. With this army Cortés defeated the Aztecs.

The Aztec emperor, Montezuma, was a thin, fair-skinned man of about 40, delicate and refined in manner. His people treated him as a god. Members of the nobility had to bow low three times before approaching him. They addressed him as "Lord, my lord, great lord," and spoke with eyes lowered, not daring to look at his face.

Here we must use historical imagination. Montezuma probably believed that Cortés, with his steel armor, powerful weapons, and large war horses, was also a god. Perhaps Cortés was Quetzalcoatl, the chief rival of the Aztec war god. In any case the Aztecs did not resist the Spaniards. Montezuma gave them rich gifts of gold and precious stones, and he allowed them to take control of his empire.

For a time Cortés permitted Montezuma to remain as emperor while the Spaniards looted the Aztec treasures. But in 1520 the Aztec people suddenly revolted. They drove the Spaniards out of the city. Montezuma, however, was killed in the fight. The Spaniards quickly regrouped and, aided by their native allies, surrounded Tenochtitlán. In August 1521 they recaptured it. By 1540, when he returned to Spain, Cortés ruled over an empire that included all of modern Mexico and more.

▩ What kind of empire had the Aztecs built?

These drawings come from an early Aztec manuscript. The one at the top shows Montezuma's meeting with Cortés. Montezuma is seated at left with members of his court. Cortés is seated at the right with an interpreter. In contrast to this peaceful greeting, the second scene shows the fighting between the Spaniards and Aztecs. What might have caused the Aztecs to revolt in 1520?

THE CONQUISTADORS

Cortés was the most important of the Spanish **conquistadors,** or conquerors. There was no excuse for the invasion of Montezuma's empire. The conquistadors were greedy and ruthless. Yet Cortés and his men had mixed motives. Adventure for its own sake was one of these, and who can blame them? Uncovering the secrets of two vast, unknown continents was the greatest adventure in human history. Especially after gold and the other rich resources of America were discovered, most Spaniards believed that America was a paradise, a kind of Garden of Eden where they could live splendidly while also doing good. They developed a sense of special purpose, or **mission**—a belief that God had appointed them to do His work in this entirely new world. Here were people to be converted to Christianity, even if the task was a bloody one.

One of Cortés's soldiers summed up the motives of the conquistadors in a sentence: "We came here to serve God and the King, and also to get rich." The conquistadors were not only brave and ambitious but absolutely sure of the rightness of their beliefs. This gave

This splendid illustration might be the earliest actual depiction of the conquistadors in the Americas. It was made in about 1534 for the book called the Köhler Codex of Nuremberg. How did the Spanish conquerors view America?

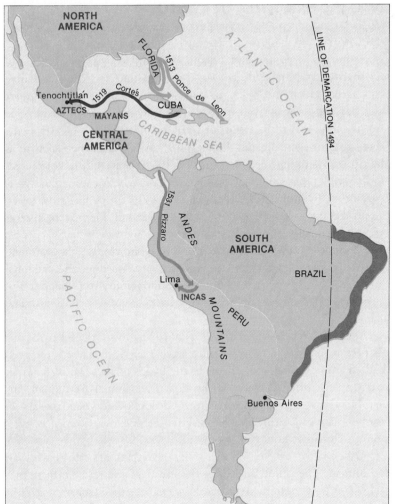

SPAIN'S GOLDEN AGE IN 16TH CENTURY AMERICA

Spanish lands in 1600

Portuguese lands

them the energy to accomplish great deeds—and also to do great harm. By the 1530s they had created an empire.

Already, in 1513, Ponce de León had made the first Spanish landing on the mainland of North America. De León was searching for the Fountain of Youth, a magical spring that was said to prevent anyone who bathed in it from growing old. Of course, he did not find such a magic fountain, but he did claim **Florida** for Spain.

In 1531 Francisco Pizarro marched into the snow-capped Andes Mountains of South America. There he found and overwhelmed the **Incas,** a people with a culture as rich and complex as the Aztecs'. Pizarro and his men seized a huge treasure of silver. Then they forced the defeated Incas to work their silver mines for Spain's benefit.

▧ What was the "sense of mission" that the conquistadors developed when they came to America?

THE EUROPEAN INVASION

When Columbus stepped ashore on Guanahaní island in October 1492, he planted the Spanish flag in the sand and claimed the land as a possession of Ferdinand and Isabella. He did so despite the obvious fact that the island already belonged to someone else—the "Indians" who gathered on the beach to gaze with wonder at the strangers who had suddenly arrived in three great, white-winged canoes. He gave no thought to the rights of the local inhabitants. Nearly every later explorer—French, English, Dutch, and all the others as well as the Spanish—thoughtlessly dismissed the people they encountered. What we like to think of as the discovery of America was actually the invasion and conquest of America.

In these new lands Europeans felt ten feet tall. Here were discoveries to be made, fame and fortune to be won. The native people would offer little or no resistance. Of what use were spears and arrows against men clad in steel and armed with guns and cannons? Surely the natives at first thought the Europeans were superior in every way. Had they not gently greeted the adventurers with gifts and affection?

With historical imagination it is not hard to see the Spanish conquerors as the first Americans must have seen them. Here were gods come from heaven to rule them. In the hands of these gods, flaming, roaring "fire-sticks" could strike down an animal or human, invisibly, across great distances. These gods looked down at frail canoes from enormous floating fortresses. How strong they seemed in their shining clothing, how rich in color.

Quickly the native Americans learned that these gods were all too human. Then they turned on the invaders and resisted them bitterly. But first came their peaceful acceptance, their innocent delight in the mysterious strangers and their gifts. Here a pattern was established that shaped the dealings between native Americans and Europeans for hundreds of years.

There was another reason why Europeans were able to seize so much of America so swiftly. This was disease. When Cortés invaded the land of the Aztecs in 1519, there were perhaps as many as 25 million people in Mexico. A hundred years later, there were barely 1 million. Smallpox, measles, and typhoid fever—not Spanish guns—accounted for so many deaths.

The germs that caused these diseases were brought to America from Europe, where people had suffered from them for countless generations. But while many Europeans died each year from diseases like smallpox, most people had developed considerable resistance to them, called **immunity.** The inhabitants of America lacked immunity. Measles was a "childhood disease" in Europe. Adults seldom caught it. But it struck down Americans by the thousands. No one can blame the Europeans for this terrible destruction. Indeed, the causes of the plagues were not then known. Nevertheless, this terrible loss of life was another tragic result of the third discovery of America.

- How did the Europeans treat the native Americans they encountered?
- How did the native Americans view the Europeans when they first met them? How did their view change?
- Why was disease able to "conquer" the native Americans?

THE END OF SPAIN'S GOLDEN AGE

By 1536, when Pedro de Mendoza founded the city of Buenos Aires in Argentina, Spain had control of the mightiest empire in the world. The inhabitants of lands 20 times the size of Spain recognized the Spanish king as overlord. The red and gold Spanish flag flew on staffs all over the Caribbean islands and from Buenos Aires to the land of the Zuni. This empire made Spain enormously rich. Gold and silver poured into the royal treasury. With this wealth and with the arms the wealth could buy, Spain seemed indestructible.

But there were cracks in the Spanish armor. Spain's own ability to produce goods—its economy—was weak and inefficient. In the 1500s about 95 per cent of the Spanish people were peasant farmers. Even so, because of poor soil and bad farming methods, they could not raise enough food to support the rest of the population. Spain had to import wheat from other parts of Europe. Manufactured articles had to be imported too, because Spain had almost no industry. Instead of using the gold and silver of America to improve farmland and finance manufacturing, the Spanish government bought what it needed abroad, paying for its imports with the treasure of America. While the flow of gold and silver continued, all was well. When the flow slowed to a trickle in the early 1600s, the Golden Age ended.

- What made Spain's empire so rich? What problem did Spain have at home that drained away its riches?
- What brought Spain's Golden Age to an end?

CHAPTER 1 REVIEW

Identification

Tell briefly why each of the following persons, terms, or events is important.

1. Leif Ericson
2. Johann Gutenberg
3. Henry the Navigator
4. Christopher Columbus
5. Amerigo Vespucci
6. Vasco Núñez de Balboa
7. Ferdinand Magellan
8. Hernán Cortés
9. Montezuma
10. Ponce de León
11. Francisco Pizarro
12. Ice Age
13. Feudal system
14. Crusades
15. Commercial Revolution
16. Line of Demarcation
17. Aztec empire
18. Conquistadors
19. Spain's Golden Age
20. Historical imagination

Understanding American History

1. Why did the first Americans develop so many cultures? Give three examples to support your answer.
2. How do archeologists and anthropologists help historians learn about the past?
3. How did environment influence the culture of the Indians of the Southwest? The Northwest? The Great Plains?
4. What is meant by historical imagination? Why is it important to use historical imagination when studying the past?
5. Which of the three discoveries of America do you think was the *least* important? Why?
6. How did the Crusades help bring about the Commercial Revolution?
7. How did the Commercial Revolution lead to the discovery of America by Columbus?
8. What were some of the hardships faced by Magellan and his crew?
9. How did the conquistadors treat the American Indians? What was their "sense of mission"?
10. Why was the discovery of America by the Europeans actually an invasion?

Activities

1. Using the maps in this chapter as a guide, trace the voyages of Leif Ericson, Columbus, Balboa, Magellan and del Cano, and de León on a large map of the world.
2. Using the time line at the beginning of Unit One as a guide, prepare your own illustrated time line of Spain's Golden Age. Decide which dates to include and copy or trace pictures to illustrate major events. This may be a class project for the bulletin board.
3. Choose one of the American Indian tribes named in this chapter for a research project. You might prepare a booklet on the tribe or build a model of a typical village. Perhaps a visit to a local museum may be arranged.
4. Find out if there is an archeological site in your area. You might begin by inquiring at a nearby museum, college, or university. Try to find out how the site was discovered and report on some of the finds. It may even be possible to visit a site. Information on archeological sites in the United States may be obtained from the National Science Foundation, the Smithsonian Institution, and the National Geographic Society, all in Washington, D.C.
5. Use your historical imagination to prepare a series of interviews to present in class as a TV news show. One show could feature Cortés and Montezuma, another Columbus and his crew meeting the natives of Guanahaní. Yet another could feature Juan del Cano and other survivors of Magellan's voyage.

CHAPTER 1 TEST

Matching (30 points)
Number your paper 1–10 and match the description in the first column with the term in the second column.

1. Scientists who study artifacts to learn about the past
2. Helps scientists determine the age of artifacts
3. Scientists who study living descendants to learn how groups lived in the past
4. A vast ice field that formed during the Ice Age
5. The measure of distance north or south of the equator
6. A person's surroundings
7. The way of life of a society, including language, government, and family relationships
8. Joined Asia and North America together, allowing people to make the first discovery of America
9. Helped sailors know what direction they were sailing
10. The science of sailing ships

a. Glacier
b. Culture
c. Environment
d. Navigation
e. Anthropologist
f. Archeologist
g. Compass
h. Latitude
i. Bering land bridge
j. Carbon-14 dating

Matching (20 points)
Number your paper 11–15 and match the description in the first column with the person in the second column.

11. Established an important research center for the study of geography and navigation
12. Made advances in printing leading to less expensive books so that more people could learn how to read
13. Ruler treated like a god
14. Conquered the Aztecs and claimed their gold for Spain
15. Agreed to outfit three ships for Columbus's voyage to search for a new Indies route

a. Hernán Cortés
b. Montezuma
c. Henry of Portugal
d. Isabella of Spain
e. Johann Gutenberg

Chronological Order (20 points)
Number your paper 16–20 and place the following events in order by numbering 1 for the first, 2 for the second, and so on.
16. Crusades
17. Age of Discovery
18. Ice Age
19. Commercial Revolution
20. Vikings sail to America

Essay (30 points)
Which of the three discoveries of America do you think was the *most* important? Write at least one full paragraph, taking care to spell and punctuate correctly.

CHAPTER 2
English Colonies in America

This oil painting seems to have its own light playing upon the sails of John Cabot's ship. He receives a final blessing before setting forth on his voyage to North America in 1497. Titled "The Departure of the Cabots," it was painted in 1906 by Ernest Board. It clearly shows the elaborate trappings of 15th-century England. What lands were claimed by the British following this voyage of exploration?

ENGLAND CHALLENGES SPAIN

The wealth and splendor of Spain's American empire attracted other Europeans the way flowers in springtime attract honeybees. The English in particular were envious of Spain. They longed to build an empire in the Americas. They hoped for a share of the gold and silver that almost everyone believed was so plentiful in the new land, and they wanted American products such as sugar and rice, which could not be grown in their cold northern climate.

In 1497, not very long after the news of Columbus's discovery reached England, King Henry VII sent John Cabot on a voyage of exploration. Cabot sailed along the coast of Newfoundland, giving England a claim to the northern regions of America. At that time

City of Bristol Museum and Art Gallery

Spain seemed too powerful to challenge. Only in the 1550s, after Queen Elizabeth I inherited the throne, did English interest in America become serious.

Elizabeth, ruling England alone in a world dominated by men, was a person of the strongest will and ambition. She was a shrewd ruler and a clever diplomat who paid little attention to right and wrong. Elizabeth never married, perhaps because no man could be her equal. She had a temper to match her fiery red hair and a tongue to match her sharp features. She was well aware of England's limited strength compared to Spain's. She proceeded cautiously.

One way to weaken Spain without openly going to war was to attack Spanish merchant ships on the high seas. In those days a ship out of sight of land was at the mercy of any more powerful vessel. There was no way to call for help or even to send an alert. A fast, powerfully armed ship could overtake a clumsy Spanish galleon loaded with treasure. The crew would be easily overcome, the cargo taken off, and the ship sent to the bottom. No one could prove that the ship had not run on a rocky reef in a fog and been dashed to pieces, or gone down in a storm, as in fact frequently happened.

The Spanish considered such attackers pirates, and rightly so. Nevertheless, Elizabeth encouraged English captains to roam the trade routes between Spain and its colonies in America in search of such prey.

The most famous of what the English affectionately called their **sea dogs** was Francis Drake. In 1577 Drake began the most famous of his many escapades. From England he sailed his ship, the *Golden Hind*, across the Atlantic and through the Strait of Magellan. In the Pacific he captured the *Cacafuego*, a Spanish galleon carrying a fortune in silver from Peru. Then he sailed north to California, which he claimed for England.

From California Drake crossed the Pacific and Indian Oceans, rounded Africa, and returned home. When he reached England in 1580, Drake presented Queen Elizabeth with treasure worth about twice her normal annual income. Little wonder that Elizabeth made him Sir Francis Drake, a knight of the kingdom, right there on the deck of the *Golden Hind*.

Drake sailed again into Spanish waters in 1585. This time he terrorized Spanish towns in the Caribbean islands. "Drake the Dragon," the Spanish called him. Furious, the king of Spain, Philip II, collected the largest fleet the world had ever seen—130 ships carrying 30,000 men and armed with 2,400 cannons. In 1588 this mighty **Spanish Armada** sailed from Spain to invade England.

Not one Spanish sailor or soldier set foot on English soil, except as a captive. Elizabeth's ships were fewer but easier to maneuver and more powerful. They sank many of the attackers. Storms finished off

The exquisite oil painting of Queen Elizabeth I, *above,* shows her fiery red hair and the elaborate jeweled costumes of her time. *Below* is Sir Francis Drake, the English sea dog. Why did Elizabeth make "Drake the Dragon" a knight of her kingdom?

still more. Only about half the Armada limped back to Spanish ports. With Spain's navy shattered and shaken, the stage was set for England to carve a place for itself in America.

- Why did England decide it would challenge Spain's power in America?
- How did Queen Elizabeth try to weaken Spain?
- What was the significance of the defeat of the Spanish Armada?

FALSE STARTS IN AMERICA

Even before the defeat of the Armada, English sailors were visiting North American waters in increasing numbers. By the 1570s about 50 vessels were catching fish on the Grand Banks off the coast of Newfoundland. Some of the fishermen established temporary camps ashore. In 1578 Queen Elizabeth issued a document called a **charter** to Sir Humphrey Gilbert. This charter gave Gilbert the right to establish and control a colony in America. Operating under the charter, Gilbert landed on Newfoundland with a party of 200. He officially claimed the island for England. This group did not stay, and Gilbert was drowned when his ship went down in a storm while returning home.

When Humphrey Gilbert was eight, his father had died. Later his mother married a man named Raleigh. They had a son, Walter, Humphrey's half-brother. He grew up to be the handsome and charming Sir Walter Raleigh, a close adviser of Queen Elizabeth. Two years after Humphrey Gilbert's death, Raleigh sent seven ships carrying over a hundred men to America. They were to establish a colony and look for gold.

Raleigh did not accompany the group. Some said Queen Elizabeth was in love with him at this time and would not let him leave her court. His colonists passed the winter on an island called **Roanoke** off the coast of what is now North Carolina. One of them, an artist and mapmaker named John White, painted many fascinating watercolors of the Indians of the region and of the plants and animals there. These pictures tell us a great deal about the life and culture of the American Indians of the Atlantic Coast.

No gold was found at Roanoke. The colonists fought with the local Indians. Life was hard. When Sir Francis Drake arrived at Roanoke in June 1586 on his way back from his raid in the Caribbean, the colonists eagerly accepted his offer of passage back to England.

Ever hopeful, in 1587 Raleigh dispatched another hundred-odd colonists to Carolina, headed by John White. For the first time women were sent out, among them White's married daughter, Ellinor Dare. These colonists landed at Roanoke in July, and on

Here stand the swashbuckling Sir Walter Raleigh and his son Wat, proud Englishmen in Queen Elizabeth's court. The artist who painted this lifelike oil in 1602 is unknown. What American colony did Raleigh sponsor?

36

August 18 Ellinor Dare gave birth to a daughter, Virginia, the first English child born in America.

A few days later John White sailed back to England for more supplies. He intended to return promptly, but he could not because of the national crisis caused by the attack of the Spanish Armada. Other delays followed and White did not get back to Roanoke until 1591. The island was deserted. No one has ever discovered what happened to the inhabitants of this **Lost Colony** of Roanoke.

- Why did the first settlers on Roanoke Island want to return to England?

MOTIVES OF THE COLONIZERS

Despite the setbacks, many important people in England remained very interested in America. For the queen and other political leaders, a major attraction was the hope of finding gold and silver to increase the wealth and power of England. Another was to reduce the power of Spain, which already controlled so much of the Americas. For upper-class gentlemen like Raleigh and Gilbert, the chief goals were adventure, honor, and fame.

There were more practical, down-to-earth reasons. Many people were out of work in England. Because of a rising demand for woolen cloth, many landowners had stopped farming and begun raising sheep. They fenced in, or enclosed, their fields and planted them in grass for the sheep. This was known as the **enclosure movement.** Raising sheep took much less labor than growing grain, so many serfs and tenants who had farmed the land now had to look for work elsewhere. Some found jobs in the towns. Others wandered about the countryside, often stealing and disturbing the peace. These people, put out of work and home by the enclosure movement, drained strength from England. Perhaps they could be resettled and made useful workers again in American colonies. People who thought this way saw America as a safety valve to get rid of troublemakers and keep English jails from overflowing.

The expanding cloth industry in England gave a boost to foreign trade and made many merchants rich. These merchants were eager to invest their profits in colonial ventures. For them America was a new business opportunity. Finally, there was still the hope for a practical westward route to the Indies. Although the trip around South America was too long to be profitable, maybe a **northwest passage** around or through North America could be discovered.

- Why were each of the following interested in colonizing America: the queen and other political leaders? gentlemen? landowners? merchants? explorers?

John White of Roanoke made these lovely watercolors of an American flamingo and an alligator in about 1585. Why are White's drawings valuable in the study of history?

37

READING PRACTICE IN SOCIAL STUDIES

Roots, Prefixes, and Suffixes

Many words that may seem difficult to you at first are often words whose *roots* are familiar. Their meanings, however, may have been changed by the addition of a *prefix* or a *suffix*. When you learn to break words down into their roots, prefixes, and suffixes, you can find their meanings without looking them up in a dictionary.

A *root* is a basic word from which many other words can be formed. Many English words come from Latin and Greek roots. For example, the word *migrate* comes from the Latin *migrare,* which means "to move from one place to another."

A *prefix* is a syllable added to the beginning of a root word. Prefixes usually change or add to the meaning of the root word. For example, if we add the prefix *e-* to migrate, we have the word *emigrate.* Migrate, remember, means to move from one place to another. The prefix *e-* means "out" or "out of." So emigrate means "to move out of a place."

If we add the prefix *im-* to migrate, we have the word *immigrate.* The prefix *im-* means "into." So immigrate means "to move into a place."

A *suffix* is a syllable added to the end of a word. A suffix may change a word's meaning, but usually it only changes the way the word is used—its part of speech. For example, migrate can be used as a verb. However, if we substitute the suffix *-ant* to form the word *migrant,* we now have a word that can be an adjective (as in "He is a migrant farm worker"). If we add the suffix *-tion,* we have the word *migration,* which is a noun (as in "The migration of the first Americans was across the Bering Strait.").

You can improve your reading skill by learning the following prefixes and suffixes.

Prefixes	Suffixes & Part of Speech	
ab- = from	*-al*	usually adjective
ad- = to, toward	*-ate*	usually verb
ante- = before	*-ic*	adjective
anti- = against	*-ful*	adjective
circum = around	*-fully*	adverb

Prefixes	Suffixes & Part of Speech	
ex-, e- = out, out of	*-ish*	adjective or verb
	-ism	noun
in-, im- = in, into	*-y*	noun or adjective
	-ity	noun
inter- = between, among	*-ant, -ent*	adjective
intra- = within	*-ance, -ence*	noun
post- = after		
pre- = before	*-able*	adjective
pro- = favoring	*-bly*	adverb
trans- = across	*-ive*	adjective
un- = not	*-ion*	noun
	-ous	adjective
	-ial	adjective

Number your paper 1–5 and write the common root word for each of the following groups.
1. governor, government, governing
2. manuscript, manufacture, emancipate
3. portable, import, transport
4. depend, pendulum, suspension
5. conscription, manuscript, inscription

Number your paper 6–10 and choose a prefix to form the best word for each blank.
Example: The first *im*migrants came from Asia.
6. Gold shipped to Spain was one of America's first ___ports.
7. Crusaders believed the people they called infidels were ___holy.
8. Juan del Cano ___navigated the earth.
9. Artifacts show that the mound builders had ___continental trade.
10. The Ice Age occurred in ___historic times.

Number your paper 11–15 and copy each of the underlined words. Circle the suffix and tell what part of speech it is.
11. The Shoshone were a <u>nomadic</u> people.
12. The <u>exploration</u> of America took centuries.
13. The <u>mighty</u> Spanish Armada was defeated
14. Columbus <u>hopefully</u> set sail for the Indies.
15. Tenochtitlán was a <u>marvelous</u> city.

MERCHANT ADVENTURERS

The experiences of men like Gilbert and Raleigh proved that founding a colony was expensive and risky. Most English merchants and manufacturers were shrewd and cautious in business, not daring adventurers or high-born court favorites. Instead of outfitting expeditions as individuals, they organized what they called **joint-stock companies.** These companies were ancestors of our corporations. They were owned by many stockholders who shared in the profits and losses of the enterprise.

The London merchant Sir Thomas Smythe was typical of these **merchant adventurers.** Smythe backed the first English attempt to sail around Africa. In 1600 he helped found the East India Company, which received exclusive rights from the English government to trade with the Indies. He also invested money in a number of expedi-

SCALA/EPA

This happy country scene hides the dark passions caused by the rustic fence. It separates the wheat field from the sheep who are yielding up their wool to the shearers. When the enclosure movement made work scarce, some Englishmen looked to America. A monk hand-colored this page from a breviary, a book used for daily prayers, and titled his work "Month of August." What caused the landowners to enclose their fields and graze sheep?

tions into Arctic waters in search of the northwest passage. Smythe was the treasurer of the Virginia Company of London and its guiding spirit.

The joint-stock Virginia Company was given charters by James I, who became king of England after his cousin Queen Elizabeth died in 1603. In 1606 James gave the **London Company** the right to develop a huge area of North America. The region was named **Virginia** in honor of Queen Elizabeth, who because she never married was known as the Virgin Queen.

Virginia extended along the Atlantic Coast from about the latitude of New York City to what is now South Carolina, and west "from sea to sea"—that is, all the way to the Pacific Ocean! Obviously neither King James nor the merchants nor anyone else in England had the slightest idea of how enormous this grant was. The country had never been explored. The charter shows what big ideas the colonizers had, as well as their disregard for the rights of the native inhabitants of America. Because a few of his explorers had nosed their way along the Atlantic beaches, King James claimed the right to dispose of the whole continent.

- Why were joint-stock companies organized?
- What boundaries were established by the Virginia Company charter?

JAMESTOWN: THE FIRST COLONY

A few days before Christmas 1606, the London Company sent off three ships, the *Discovery*, the *Susan Constant*, and the *Godspeed*, bearing 104 settlers. Their destination was Virginia, their purpose to build a town and search for gold, silver, and copper.

The three little ships reached Virginia on April 26, 1607. They sailed up a river, which they named after the king. A few days later they chose a place to build a fort on a peninsula jutting out into the river. They called this settlement **Jamestown.**

From the start life in Jamestown was an endless series of troubles. The site was easy to defend but swampy and infested with fever-bearing mosquitoes. By the end of summer half the colonists had died, and many of those who remained were down with malaria. Because the planting season had ended before the colonists had finished building houses and walling the town, they were unable to get a crop in the ground. Soon they were desperately short of food. When the first ship from England arrived the next spring, only 38 colonists were alive to greet it.

The colony also suffered from poor leadership. King James named a council to rule it. He appointed mostly stockholders in the London Company. They did not go to Jamestown and knew almost nothing

about the difficulties the settlers faced. For example, there was no sign of gold in the area around Jamestown. Yet the London authorities insisted that the colonists spend much of their energy searching for the precious metal. The Londoners did create a local council in Virginia, supposedly to handle day-to-day problems, but they gave the councilors no real authority.

Still worse, the Virginia councilors quarreled among themselves and allowed the colonists to neglect the basic tasks of planting crops and making the settlement safe.

The Jamestown settlers were poorly prepared for the great challenge of living in the new country. The 36 so-called gentlemen among them had none of the skills needed by pioneers, such as carpentry and farming. They were unaccustomed to hard labor of any kind. As for the others, there were goldsmiths, perfumers, and jewelers, who were certainly skilled—but in the wrong trades. Not one of them had ever been a real farmer. Too many settlers apparently believed that in America wealth grew on trees. They did not realize that it was necessary to work hard if they wished to stay alive.

Fortunately, one man among these colonists had the courage to take command. He was John Smith. Smith was a swashbuckler, a **soldier of fortune,** who was prepared to sell his sword to whoever would pay for it. He was a short, bearded fellow of 27, a man of action. He had seen far more of the world than any of the other settlers. He had fought in a number of wars in eastern Europe against the

The Jamestown settlers clear land and put up houses while living in tents in this engraving from the 19th century. Others bring stores from one of the ships at anchor in the James River of Virginia. How were the actual experiences of the first colonists different from the peaceful scene shown here?

41

John Smith was 27 years old when he took command of the Jamestown settlement. This engraving portrays Smith at the age of 33. Why was he known as a soldier of fortune?

Turks. In one war he was captured, taken to Constantinople, and sold into slavery. However, he managed to kill his master and escape. After many other remarkable adventures Smith found himself in Virginia.

In 1608 Smith was elected president of the Virginia council. Once in charge, he bargained with the Indians for food. He stopped the foolish searching for gold. Instead he put people to work building shelters and planting food crops. Hard work and strict discipline became the order of the day.

- Why did so many of the first settlers in Jamestown die?
- Why did the colonists have such a hard time obtaining food?
- What changes did John Smith make when he became president of the Virginia council?

REFORMS FOR VIRGINIA

Virginia's difficulties finally convinced the merchant adventurers in England that the London Company needed to be reorganized. In 1609 Sir Edmund Sandys, a councilor who was also a member of Parliament, England's legislative body, obtained a new charter from King James. This charter called for the appointment of a powerful governor who would rule the colony from Jamestown rather than from London.

The London Company then raised a good deal more money and outfitted a fleet of nine ships to carry about 600 new settlers across the Atlantic. Those who paid their own fare received one share of stock in the company. Those who could not pay agreed to work as servants of the company for seven years in return for their passage. Until 1616 everything the colonists produced was to be put into a common storehouse or fund. On that date the servants would have worked off their debt to the company. Then the profits of the enterprise were to be divided among the shareholders—both the investors back in England and the settlers. Every shareholder would also receive a grant of Virginia land.

These were fine plans but hard to put into effect. Conditions in Virginia got worse and worse. The first governor, Lord De La Warr, put off coming to Jamestown. The years from 1609 to 1611 were a **starving time.** Settlers ate dogs and mice. They ate the remains of an Indian killed in battle. According to John Smith, one hungry colonist butchered his own wife for food. For this crime, Smith explained, "he was executed, as he well deserved." At one point the colonists almost decided to abandon the settlement and return to England.

Then things began to improve in 1611 when the council appointed Thomas Dale, a soldier with a reputation for sternness, as governor. Dale arrived with fresh supplies and a new group of set-

A Colony Built Upon Smoke

In the long run what made Virginia prosper was tobacco. When the colonists realized that there was no gold and silver to be found, they looked for other sources of wealth. They tried to raise silkworms, to make glass, to grow wine grapes —all without success. Tobacco was a different story. The plant was native to America. The Indians prized it highly, using it for personal enjoyment and in their ceremonies. Sir Francis Drake brought tobacco to England from the West Indies after his raid, and Sir Walter Raleigh made smoking fashionable in high society. The habit spread quickly in England.

It is interesting that from the very start many people argued that smoking was unhealthy. King James himself opposed the use of tobacco. Although he considered it beneath his dignity to engage in public debate, he published anonymously an essay on the subject. This "Counterblast to Tobacco" described smoking as a "vile and stinking" habit that would injure the lungs and the brain. Thousands of King James's subjects ignored his warning. Demand for tobacco soared in England.

The Indians of Virginia grew and smoked tobacco, but this local plant had a harsh and bitter taste. A colonist named John Rolfe, who came to Jamestown about 1610, solved the problem by bringing in tobacco seeds from the Spanish colonies. This variety of tobacco flourished in Virginia and produced a much milder smoke. In 1616 Virginia farmers exported about 2,200 pounds (1,000 kilograms) of tobacco to England. Two years later they exported more than 20 times that amount.

The Virginians now had a cash crop they could sell in England. They were able to purchase the manufactured items they could not yet produce themselves: cloth, tools, furniture, guns. Little wonder that King Charles I, who succeeded James I in 1625, joked that Virginia was "built upon smoke."

Ingham Foster Collection, courtesy Jamestown Foundation

tlers in March. He promptly resumed the tough course set by John Smith. He soon became very unpopular because of his harsh rule. A man convicted of stealing some oatmeal was chained to a tree and allowed to starve to death. The colonists charged that Dale was a tyrant. Nevertheless, they began to plant corn, repair the fort, and work to make sure that the colony would survive.

- How severe was the "starving time" of 1609 to 1611?
- What helped conditions in Jamestown begin to improve?

HEADRIGHTS AND INDENTURES

In 1618 the London Company launched a campaign to attract more investors and settlers to Virginia. Colonists who paid their own way or that of others would receive 50 acres (20 hectares) of land for each "head" transported. This was called a **headright.** The company relaxed the rigorous discipline that Thomas Dale had imposed as governor of the colony. It guaranteed all settlers the same legal rights that English subjects had at home. It also gave settlers a voice in the local government of the colony. They would be allowed to elect representatives to an assembly known as the **House of Burgesses.** This was the first elected government body in America. Along with the governor's council, the House was given the power to make laws for the colony. It first met at Jamestown in 1619.

The London Company made an all-out effort to develop many kinds of products in the colony. But tobacco remained Virginia's most important commodity by far. As the price of tobacco rose, everyone rushed to plant more of it. The broad, green leaves of tobacco plants could be seen growing in the streets of Jamestown.

Growing tobacco required a great deal of labor. In Jamestown hands to work the land were in short supply. Those settlers who had money had a tremendous advantage in obtaining workers because of the headright system. Poor people who wanted to come to Virginia signed contracts called **indentures.** They agreed to work for seven years to pay off the cost of getting to America. These contracts of indenture could be bought and sold. The newcomer, who was called an **indentured servant,** had to work without wages for the person who owned the indenture. That same person also received the headright issued by the colonial government for bringing the newcomer to Virginia. He could therefore claim 50 acres (20 hectares) of land. In other words, the person who paid the passage of the immigrant received both land and the labor needed to farm the land for one price.

The great tobacco boom did the London Company little good. By the time the boom began, the original colonists had already served their seven years and were no longer working for the company.

 ▨ How did the London Company try to attract new settlers?
 ▨ How did the indenture system bring some a double benefit?

BLOODSHED IN JAMESTOWN

The colonists treated their Indian neighbors far worse than they treated their indentured servants. In the early days Jamestown could not have survived without the Indians. They gave the starving colonists food. They taught them how to live in the wilderness. The land around Jamestown was a dense forest. Corn, a native American plant grown by the Indians, would not grow for the colonists in forest shade. It would take years to cut down the huge trees and root out their stumps. The Indians showed the colonists how to kill the trees by cutting a ring around the trunks. Sunlight could then shine through the dead and leafless branches, and corn planted by the colonists sprouted between the trunks.

The colonists accepted the Indians' help and advice and then tried to take control of their homelands! The local Indians of course resisted. In a sudden attack in 1622 they killed about 350 colonists, almost one third of Virginia's European population. The bloodshed convinced King James that the colony, which was already being mismanaged, should be taken away from the London Company. In 1624 he canceled the charter and put Virginia under direct royal control. The Company was bankrupt. The stockholders lost their investment.

■ How did the Indians help the Jamestown colonists?
■ Why did the local Indians attack the colonists?

THE PILGRIMS

In 1617 Sir Edwin Sandys was trying to put Virginia's affairs in order. A community of people who were living in Holland asked him for permission to settle in America somewhere within the London Company's grant. These **Pilgrims,** as we now call them, had left England in 1608 to escape religious persecution. Pilgrims were people who had "separated" themselves from the Anglican Church, the Church of England. They were **Separatists.** The Dutch had not inter-

From this harbor in Plymouth the Pilgrims sailed from England to Holland in 1608. Charles Shimmin painted this oil in 1918, taking care to show the simple Pilgrim dress. Why did the Pilgrims leave their homes in England?

Woolaroc Museum

fered with their religious practice, but the Pilgrims were not happy in their new home. They could not get good jobs. Their children were beginning to speak Dutch instead of English.

Sandys admired the Pilgrims, but other company officials considered them dangerous **radicals.** (Radicals are people who favor sudden and widespread changes.) There were long delays, but finally in 1619 the London Company and the King granted them permission to migrate. Because the Pilgrims were poor people without money to pay for their voyage, they accepted a proposal by a group of English merchant adventurers. The merchants would put up the money to found a new settlement. The Pilgrims would do the work. In September 1620 a party of 35 Pilgrims and 66 other colonists sailed from Plymouth, England, on the *Mayflower* bound for Virginia. They were the first English settlers who came to America for religious reasons.

- Who were the Separatists?
- Why did the Pilgrims leave Holland for America?

PLYMOUTH PLANTATION

The little party on the *Mayflower* never reached Virginia. On November 9 they sighted land on Cape Cod Bay, north of the London Company's territory. With winter so near, they decided not to test their ship any longer in the stormy waters of the Atlantic and to settle where they were.

Because Cape Cod was outside the region controlled by the London Company, there was no existing government. Therefore, the Pilgrims decided to draw up a document which would provide a legal basis for governing the area and themselves. This document is called the **Mayflower Compact.** Its signers first acknowledged the authority of King James. They were not seeking to create a new nation. They then pledged "submission and obedience" to the officers they would themselves elect and to the laws they might pass "for the general Good of the Colony."

The Mayflower Compact is a short and simple document. To us it might seem a rather obvious and necessary statement, made by decent and honest people about to settle in a new land. Yet the Compact tells us a great deal about life in America, then and later. So far as any record shows, this was the first time in human history that a group of people consciously created a government where none had existed before.

The Pilgrims decided to settle at a place they called **Plymouth.** The rock on which they are thought to have landed is now a national monument. They came ashore with almost nothing, no "butter or oil, not a sole to mend a shoe." They were true pilgrims, these wanderers, uncertain of what lay over the next hill.

46

The Pilgrim Society

In some respects the Pilgrims were like the first immigrants from Asia, people who owned little more than what they had on their backs, isolated in an unknown land. They were totally dependent on one another, but this was their strength. They recognized their common purpose and the need for unity. Above all they trusted in "the good providence to God." They were ready to give up the familiar world for the uncertain wilderness.

Their early experiences were similar to those of the Jamestown settlers. Disease swept through the exhausted party. The survivors might well have starved to death if an Indian named Squanto had not befriended them. Squanto taught the Pilgrims how to grow corn. He showed them the best streams for fishing.

Things changed for the better in the spring. Unlike the first Virginians, the Pilgrims worked hard, planted their crops, and in the autumn gathered in a bountiful harvest. For this, in November 1621, the settlers came together to give thanks to God. Thus was established the American tradition of **Thanksgiving Day.**

Mysterious in the moonlight, the *Mayflower* lies at anchor on Cape Cod Bay, Massachusetts, in 1620. This oil was painted in 1882 by W. F. Halsall. What was the Pilgrims' original destination?

47

However, Plymouth remained a very small colony. Life there was hard. The courage, determination, dignity, and piety of the Pilgrims—not wealth or power—has assured them a permanent place in our nation's history.

The Pilgrims came to America for very different reasons than the settlers of Virginia. Even at this early date it was clear that America attracted ordinary people in many ways. For nearly all, however, there was hope of finding a better life in the land of opportunity.

- How were the experiences of the Pilgrims similar to those of the first Jamestown settlers?
- How did the Pilgrims differ from the Jamestown settlers?

THE FRENCH IN AMERICA

In 1524, not long after John Cabot's voyage in the service of Henry VII of England, the French king, François I, sent an Italian explorer, Giovanni da Verrazano, along the Atlantic Coast from North Carolina to Nova Scotia in search of a northwest passage. Ten years later Jacques Cartier sailed up the St. Lawrence River as far inland as the present site of Montreal. In 1608, while the English settlers were struggling at Jamestown, Samuel de Champlain founded the first permanent French settlement in America at **Quebec.**

In 1673 Father Jacques Marquette and Louis Joliet explored the upper Mississippi River. Soon after, in 1679, Robert La Salle set sail aboard the first vessel on the Great Lakes. By 1700 French explorers

Joslyn Art Museum

"Europeans Encountering Indians" is the title given to this oil painted as long ago as 1700. Perhaps it shows the early Americans as they appeared to the French explorers who sailed down the Mississippi. In which centuries did the French make their North American claims?

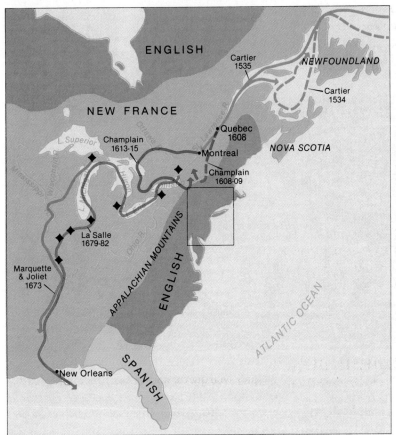

DUTCH AND SWEDISH COLONIES IN AMERICA

had sailed through the Great Lakes, down the Mississippi River to the Gulf of Mexico, and up the Missouri River to the Rocky Mountains. In addition to what is now Canada, France claimed the entire Mississippi valley, lands also covered by grants of the English king to Virginia. Many wars with England would be fought for control of these overlapping territories.

■ What French claims were made in America at the time of the British claims?

DUTCH AND SWEDISH CHALLENGES

In 1620 the English had founded only two tiny settlements in America—Jamestown and Plymouth. Nevertheless, they claimed all the territory from Newfoundland to Florida. The claim, however, was impossible to enforce. The first to challenge it were the Dutch people of Holland, also called The Netherlands. The Dutch were excellent sailors and master shipbuilders. Like the English they were dependent for their prosperity on foreign trade. The English rightly considered them their greatest rival on the high seas.

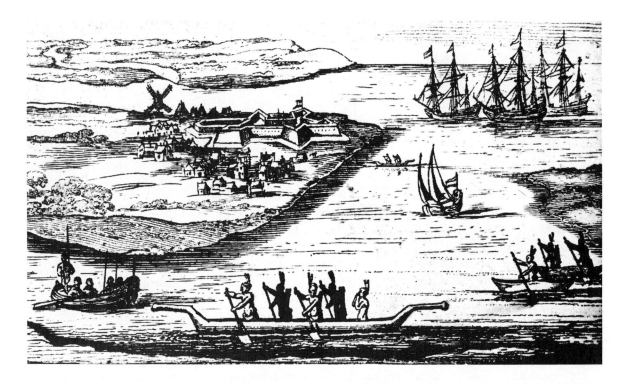

Here is the earliest view of what is today New York City. The engraving shows the Dutch Fort Amsterdam at the tip of Manhattan Island. Indians in canoes are entering the Hudson River while tall ships lay at anchor at the mouth of the East River. This part of the island is today the site of the World Trade Center. Why did the Dutch claim Manhattan Island?

Holland claimed the region drained by the Hudson River, basing their right to it on the discovery of the river by Henry Hudson in 1609. They called it **New Netherland.** In 1624 Dutch fur traders opened a post at Fort Orange, the site of present-day Albany. Two years later they founded New Amsterdam, on Manhattan Island at the mouth of the Hudson. Peter Minuit, the governor of the colony, bought Manhattan from its Indian inhabitants for some knives, beads, and trinkets. Eventually the island became the center of what is New York City, one of the most valuable pieces of property in the world. It has become fashionable to call Minuit's purchase the greatest real estate bargain of all time.

In 1629 Kiliaen Van Rensselaer, a jeweler from Amsterdam who owned stock in the Dutch West India Company, persuaded the company to issue a "Charter of Privileges of Patroons" to encourage American settlement. A **patroon** was a landholder with powers like those of a feudal lord of the manor. Anyone who brought 50 new settlers to New Netherland was to receive a great estate in the Hudson River valley and the powers to rule it. Rensselaer was the only patroon to set up an estate under the charter. Not many people came to New Netherland. The Dutch West India Company ruled it with an iron hand. The colonists had no voice at all in running the colony.

Two directors of the Dutch West India Company, Peter Minuit and Samuel Blommaert, were also involved in a Swedish West India Company that founded **New Sweden** on the Delaware River near

50

what is now the city of Wilmington. The Swedes built the first log cabins in America. These homes, so easy to build in a land covered with forests, were much copied.

The Swedes traded for furs with the Indians, but they did not prosper. When a Dutch force captured their settlement, Fort Christina, in 1655, New Sweden ceased to exist. The colonists, only about a hundred in all, were allowed to remain, and the region became a part of New Netherland.

The history of New Netherland was brief. The English saw the Dutch as intruders on English soil. Worse, Dutch merchants based in New Amsterdam were buying Virginia tobacco and selling it in Holland, much to the annoyance of English tobacco merchants. And the Dutch colony's excellent harbor at the mouth of the Hudson River was a tempting target.

In 1664 King Charles II sent four British warships carrying 400 soldiers to capture New Amsterdam. The town had only 1,500 inhabitants. The Dutch authorities had been too heavy-handed. The people had no will to fight. When their governor, Peter Stuyvesant, tried to organize a defense, they pushed him aside and turned the town over to the English without firing a shot.

- ▧ How did the Dutch West India Company try to attract settlers to America?
- ▧ What was the success of the early Dutch and Swedish settlements in America?

Queen Christina of Sweden, *above*, made American grants. In 1655 the Dutch in America captured Fort Christina, and New Sweden's brief history was ended. The oil portrait of the queen by Sébastian Bourdon was painted from life in the 17th century. What trade did the Swedes engage in? *Below,* Governor Peter Stuyvesant, the conqueror of New Sweden, is himself conquered by English invaders when the New Netherland colonists surrender. He lost his leg during a battle in the West Indies. This oil by J. L. G. Ferris was done in the 19th century. Why did the Dutch refuse to fight?

The Puritans of Massachusetts are represented by this sculpture in bronze by Augustus Saint-Gaudens, whose work was done in the 19th century. What did Puritans intend their "city upon a hill" to be?

Metropolitan Museum of Art

THE PURITANS

While the London Company was making plans to settle Virginia, another joint-stock company, the Virginia Company of Plymouth, tried to establish a settlement far to the north near the mouth of the Kennebec River in what is now Maine. The settlers arrived in 1607 but remained only one winter. However, fishermen and traders continued to set up temporary camps in the area. In 1614 the Plymouth Company sent John Smith to explore the region further. It was Smith who first called the area **New England.**

In the early 1620s the Plymouth Company, now called the Council of New England, gave away several tracts of land in the northern regions, including much of what are now **Maine** and **New Hampshire.** The council's most significant grant was made to a

52

group of religious reformers. Like the Pilgrims, these people were critical of the Church of England. But they were not Separatists. They had not given up hope of reforming the Church from within. They sought to purify it. Hence they were known as **Puritans.**

The efforts of the Puritans to reform the Church of England met strong resistance. Puritan ministers were even denied the right to preach. When they were persecuted, many Puritans began to think of moving to America. Perhaps there they could create a perfect church and community. As one of their leaders explained, they sought to build "a city upon a hill," a community other people could look up to and admire and eventually copy.

Before taking advantage of the council's grant, the Puritans obtained a new charter from the king and organized the **Massachusetts Bay Company.** Under the charter their colony was to be practically self-governing. They planned their venture carefully. Their first group was large—about a thousand people—and adequately supplied. In 1630 their 11-ship convoy reached Massachusetts.

The governor of Massachusetts Bay, John Winthrop, was well aware of the difficulties involved in founding a settlement in a wilderness. He was a practical person who preferred compromise and persuasion to force. The charter put all political power in the hands of the stockholders. But Winthrop feared that unless ordinary colonists had some share in governing the settlement, there would be trouble. Therefore he and the other stockholders decided to make about a hundred additional settlers **freemen,** which meant that they could vote for the governor of the colony and for members of its legislature, which was called the General Court. Some of the new freemen were not even members of the Puritan church. However, after this increase of the voting population, only church members were admitted to freemanship.

The Puritans were not democratic in the modern sense of the term. They did, however, try earnestly to create a **commonwealth,** a society devoted to the common welfare for the good of all.

Within a year of their arrival the Puritans had "planted," as they called it, several communities centered around their chief town, Boston. During the next ten years, about 15 or 20 thousand people came, far more than to any earlier colony. Soon some groups, or congregations, were pushing out on their own. In 1636 the Reverend Thomas Hooker led his congregation from Massachusetts to the fertile valley of the Connecticut River. There in **Connecticut** they established the town of Hartford. Other "river towns" sprang up in the valley. These towns formed a common government and drafted a written constitution, the **Fundamental Orders.** The system outlined in the Fundamental Orders was not very different from the government of Massachusetts Bay. Its main distinction was that it allowed male resi-

John Winthrop, first governor of Massachusetts Bay, was painted from life in the 17th century. Why did Winthrop give ordinary people a share in governing the colony?

This is Madame Penobscot, known by the name of her tribe in Maine. She was one of several American Indians taken to England in 1605, where she was an early promoter for the English colonizers. Who were among Maine's first settlers?

Religious conflicts drove both of
these Puritans from Massachusetts.
Roger Williams, *above,* became the
founder of Rhode Island. And Anne
Hutchinson, *below,* shown on trial in
a 19th-century engraving, became
a founder of Portsmouth in Rhode
Island. How did both Williams and
Hutchinson obtain their new lands?

dents who were not church members to become freemen. The document is very important historically because it was the first written frame of government in America, a kind of ancestor of all the state constitutions and of the Constitution of the United States.

■ Who were the Puritans? How did the Puritans differ from the Separatists? Why did they leave England?
■ What is the significance of the Fundamental Orders?

RELIGIOUS CONFLICTS

Because religion was so important to the Puritans, they would not tolerate anyone whose religious beliefs differed from their own. They believed theirs was the true faith and thought all others must be the work of the devil. Our concept of freedom of religion would have made little sense to them at all. Thomas Hooker left Massachusetts because of religious disagreements that now seem quite trivial. These differences were certainly unimportant compared with those of another minister, Roger Williams.

Williams was charming, the kind of person nearly everyone liked on first sight. But he was impulsive and easily excited. He was very stubborn about anything he considered a matter of principle, and he was a man of many principles. He was out of place in Massachusetts because he questioned many Puritan beliefs. He did not believe the government should have any power over religious questions, whereas the Puritans thought it should enforce all the Ten Commandments as well as civil law. He even insisted that, despite their charter, the colonists had no right to the land of Massachusetts until either they or the king purchased it from the Indians who lived there.

By 1635 the members of the General Court had heard enough of Williams's criticisms. They ordered him to leave the Commonwealth. He went off with a few followers and the next year founded the town of Providence, on Narragansett Bay. There he put his theories about religious freedom and fair treatment of the Indians into practice. In 1644 he obtained a charter for the colony of **Rhode Island and Providence Plantations.**

No sooner were the Puritans rid of Williams than they had to face another attack on their religious beliefs. This one came from Anne Hutchinson. Mrs. Hutchinson was one of the most remarkable of all the early colonists. She was both learned and deeply emotional. She and her husband William arrived in 1634, and soon she became known for her many acts of kindness and for her thorough knowledge of the Bible. She was very strong willed and, if possible, even more strict about matters of principle than Roger Williams. When she disagreed with some of the sermons delivered by her minister, she said so openly. She also began to hold meetings in her home to discuss religious questions. She told the people who attended these meetings that formal religion, church attendance, and prayer were less important than leading a holy life. One could go to Heaven without them.

These ideas horrified the Puritans. In 1638 Anne Hutchinson was brought to trial. Although she was able to defend her ideas brilliantly, she was found by the court to be "a woman not fit for our society." She too was banished, or expelled, from Massachusetts. Later, she and other exiles bought an island from the Narragansett Indians and founded Portsmouth, Rhode Island.

■ Why did the Puritans expel Roger Williams?
■ Why did the Puritans banish Anne Hutchinson?

MARYLAND

By this time another English colony had been founded in the region immediately to the north of Virginia. It had a different origin than any of the others, being essentially the property of a single person. The English rulers claimed America as their private possession to do with as they wished. For this reason few people objected when Charles I gave 10 million acres (4 million hectares) of land around Chesapeake Bay to an important English nobleman, George Calvert, Lord Baltimore. The grant gave Calvert enormous power. He could found manors such as had existed in feudal times and hold the residents as serfs. He could act as the prosecutor and judge of anyone accused of breaking the law. He was known as the proprietor, or owner, of the area, and his colony was thus a **proprietary** colony.

Calvert died before the king's seal was attached to the charter making the grant. His son Cecilius Calvert became the first proprietor of the colony, which was called **Maryland** in honor of Queen Henrietta Maria, the wife of Charles I. The Calverts were Catholics and hoped to make Maryland a Catholic colony.

The first settlers landed in 1634 and founded the town of St. Mary's. Life was relatively easy for them because Virginia, now prosperous, was nearby. They could get food and other supplies without waiting for ships from distant England. They also wasted little time hunting for gold. Instead they turned promptly to growing tobacco.

Despite the charter Cecilius Calvert soon realized that he could not rule Maryland like a feudal lord. In order to attract settlers, he had to allow people to own land and to have some say in the government. Although he encouraged Catholics to settle in Maryland, a majority of the people who came there were Protestants. The Catholics received large land grants and held most of the important positions in the colony. The Protestants resented this favoritism. To have made the Catholic church the official church of Maryland might have caused a revolution.

Cecilius Calvert, the second Lord Baltimore, founded the colony of Maryland in 1634. He is shown in this 17th-century oil attended by a grandson and his young servant. Why did Charles I grant so much land to the first Lord Baltimore?

BUILDING SKILLS
IN SOCIAL STUDIES

Comparing and Contrasting Maps

The pair of maps below may be *compared* because they have the same *base*. Their base is the land area of North America along the Atlantic Coast. Although there is a difference of 100 years between the two maps, the base does not change. That is because the base of a map generally shows *physical features* such as land areas, oceans, lakes, and rivers.

The pair of maps may be *contrasted* (their differences noted) because each also shows *political features* such as boundaries of the colonies and cities and towns. The political features of America changed greatly between 1650 and 1750, but the physical features did not

change at all. Both maps show colonial claims of Britain, France, and Spain. The right-hand map also shows the thirteen colonies.

1. Name four physical features that both maps have in common.
2. Name two political features that change from the first map to the second.
3. Which nations held American claims in 1650 but not in 1750?
4. What are two physical features of areas settled by 1650?
5. What physical feature did the spread of settled area follow by 1750?

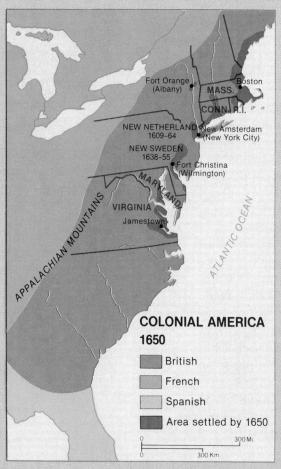

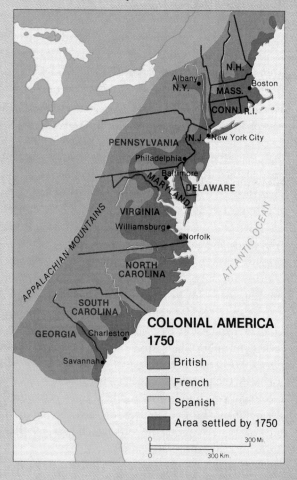

Calvert dealt with this problem shrewdly. He encouraged the local legislature to pass the Toleration Act of 1649, which guaranteed freedom of religion to all Christians. On the surface the Catholics were "tolerating" the Protestants. In fact, the Catholic minority was protecting itself.

■ What kind of powers did the king's grant give Lord Baltimore? Why were these powers never used?

Colonial Williamsburg

THE CAROLINAS

In 1663 Charles II gave the land between Virginia and Spanish Florida to eight noblemen, among them Sir George Carteret, who was probably the richest person in England, and Sir Anthony Ashley Cooper. The grateful proprietors named the region **Carolina** in honor of Charles I, whose name in Latin was *Carolus*. The Carolina proprietors hoped to attract settlers from the older colonies in order to avoid the expense of financing expeditions from England.

A number of Virginians did drift into the northernmost part of the grant, but settlement there was scattered and isolated. There were few roads and practically no villages, churches, or schools. Most of the colonizers became small farmers who grew food crops and a little tobacco.

When it became clear that settlers from the older colonies were not moving to the Carolinas in any number, Sir Anthony Ashley Cooper brought in people from the island of Barbados in the West Indies. In 1670 Charleston (originally Charles Town) was founded. Charleston soon became a busy trading center, as well as the social and political center of Carolina.

The proprietors of Carolina had broad political authority—on paper. They dreamed of creating a land of great estates where lords with feudal titles reigned over lowly tenants. Two fifths of the land was to be owned by the noble class.

The harbor and town of Charleston, South Carolina, are pictured in this watercolor. This earliest known view of Charleston is believed to be the work of Bishop Roberts, who painted there from 1735 to 1739. Why was Charles Town, as it was known, important to the new colony of Carolina?

57

The system was "almost unbelievably ill-suited to the American scene," as a modern historian has written. Most of the intended tenants quickly obtained land of their own. In 1719 the settlers rebelled against the proprietary government and asked the king to take over the colony. Ten years later this was done. The area was officially separated into **North Carolina** and **South Carolina,** each under a royal governor.

- Where did the proprietors of Carolina hope to find settlers?
- How did the proprietors intend to run Carolina? Why did their plan fail in the American colony?

NEW YORK AND NEW JERSEY

When New Netherland was taken over by the English in 1664, the name of the colony was changed to **New York** in honor of the Duke of York, its new proprietor. The duke had control of the entire region between Connecticut and Maryland. He immediately began to hand out generous chunks of it to his friends. The largest prize was **New Jersey,** which included everything between the Hudson and Delaware Rivers. He gave this region to Sir George Carteret and another of the Carolina proprietors, Lord John Berkeley.

To attract colonists, Carteret and Berkeley offered land on easy terms. They also promised settlers religious freedom and the right to elect a legislature. In 1674 Berkeley sold his half interest to two Quakers. Quakers were one of the Separatist groups. They were religious radicals—that is, they favored rapid and widespread religious change. They believed that everyone could communicate directly with God. For this reason they did not depend upon ministers, church services, or even the Bible. They stressed religious tolerance, "brotherly love," and simplicity. They were opposed to warfare and any use of force.

Another group of Quakers bought the rest of New Jersey in 1680 from the heirs of George Carteret. In 1702 the two sections were reunited as one colony.

- Who were the Quakers?

PENNSYLVANIA AND DELAWARE

Another large colonial grant was awarded to a very unlikely candidate, William Penn. Penn was a person of great wealth and high social status, the son of a much-decorated English admiral. While at Oxford University, he became a Quaker.

Because of their radical, anti-establishment beliefs, Quakers, both at home and in America, were often imprisoned, tortured, or even hanged. Penn himself spent some time in jail. To protect other Quak-

Shelburne Museum, Shelburne, Vermont

ers from such persecution, Penn hoped to create a refuge in America. Charles II was agreeable. He owed a large sum of money to Penn's father, who had died in 1670. To cancel this debt, in 1681 he gave William the region between New York and Maryland, suggesting that it be called **Pennsylvania** in honor of Penn's father.

William Penn was strongly religious and held to high ideals. He also had a solid understanding of the value of money and how to make it. Pennsylvania was to be "a holy experiment" in Christian living and self-government. Penn personally came to Pennsylvania to oversee the laying-out of Philadelphia, his city of "brotherly love." Like Roger Williams, he insisted that the Delaware Indians be paid for their land and treated fairly by the settlers. He was shrewd in business. To attract settlers he wrote glowing accounts of Pennsylvania's soil and climate and circulated them throughout Europe. These, along with his promises of a voice in the government and religious liberty, lured settlers from many lands. Among these were large numbers of Germans, who were popularly known as the Pennsylvania Dutch. "Dutch" was the way English settlers pronounced the word *Deutsch*, which means German.

Pennsylvania prospered from the start. Farmers produced large crops of wheat and other foodstuffs. To obtain a port to export their surplus, Penn in 1682 obtained a grant of land on Delaware Bay. This region, known as **Delaware,** became a separate colony in 1704.

The spirit of brotherly love seems to lay at the heart of Edward Hicks's "Penn's Treaty with the Indians," an oil painted toward the close of the 18th century. Penn is at the center of the Quakers who offer gifts to the Delaware chief. How did Penn treat the Delaware Indians?

- Why did William Penn found a colony in America?
- Why did many Europeans come to Pennsylvania?

GEORGIA

The last of the English colonies in America, **Georgia,** was not settled until 1733. It was founded by a group of well-to-do, charitable Englishmen who hoped to provide a new start for English people who had been imprisoned for debt. Their leader was James Oglethorpe, a man deeply committed to helping victims of political, economic, and religious oppression.

Armed with a charter granting him and his associates the authority to manage Georgia as **trustees** for 21 years, Oglethorpe came to America in 1733 with about a hundred settlers. They founded the town of Savannah. Each settler was given 50 acres (20 hectares) of land, tools to work it with, and enough supplies for the first year. Oglethorpe was stubborn and very straitlaced. He tried to make the settlers grow things like olive trees and silkworms that would not flourish in Georgia. He demanded that no lawyers be allowed in the colony, insisting that all lawyers were born troublemakers. He attempted to ban liquor.

Georgia was an out-of-the-way colony. A hostile Spanish settlement in Florida on its southern border kept it from growing very fast. Few people lived there. The people who did come there resented the strict rules. They made it impossible to keep out liquor, or even lawyers. In 1752, a year before their charter was due to run out, the discouraged trustees turned the colony over to the king.

- Why was Georgia founded?
- Why did Georgia fail to flourish?

Georgia's fields stretch farther than the eye can see in this interesting engraving. It is an idealized view of the founding of Georgia in 1733. When the colonists finish felling the tall tree in the foreground, they will seem to have cleared land all the way northwest to the foothills of the Blue Ridge Mountains. What did each of the first settlers receive?

CHAPTER 2 REVIEW

Identification
Tell briefly why each of the following persons, terms, or events is important.

1. Elizabeth I
2. Sir Francis Drake
3. Sir Walter Raleigh
4. Squanto
5. Peter Minuit
6. John Winthrop
7. Roger Williams
8. Anne Hutchinson
9. William Penn
10. James Oglethorpe
11. Roanoke
12. Enclosure movement
13. Northwest Passage
14. Joint-stock companies
15. Jamestown
16. Pilgrims
17. Puritans
18. Indentured servants
19. House of Burgesses
20. Mayflower Compact

Understanding American History
1. What were the various reasons why the English wanted to establish colonies in America?
2. How did forming joint-stock companies help the English to explore and colonize in America?
3. What was a headright? What were the terms of an indentured servant? How did wealthy settlers profit from the headright system?
4. How did the Jamestown settlers treat the local Indians?
5. Explain why the Mayflower Compact and the Fundamental Orders are important documents in American history.
6. How alike and how different were the Pilgrims and the first Jamestown settlers?
7. How did religious disagreements in Massachusetts help bring about the founding of new colonies in America?
8. How did Roger Williams and William Penn differ from earlier colonists in their dealings with American Indians?
9. By 1700 what French claims were made in America? What Dutch claims? What Swedish claims?
10. How were colonists attracted to New Jersey? To Pennsylvania? To Georgia?

Activities
1. Prepare a bulletin board to show the colonies and settlements in America described in Chapters 1 and 2. You might list each colony and the date of its founding on one side. Make a large map of North America for the other side and show the Spanish, English, Dutch, and Swedish colonies and the French settlements, each in its own color.
2. Read about the Lost Colony of Roanoke in an encyclopedia or another American history book. Then use your historical imagination to create a diary that one of the settlers might have kept hidden in a tree.
3. The first Jamestown settlers had the wrong trades and skills needed for survival. Some were goldsmiths and jewelers. Use historical imagination to make a list of five important occupations that would have made the Jamestown settlers stronger. Explain the reasons for each choice. Make a similar list for a group today going to an unexplored area of South America. Are your lists similar? Why or why not?
4. Use an encyclopedia and American history books to prepare a short report on one of the following women in history:

    Elizabeth I   Ellinor White Dare
    Christina of Sweden   Anne Hutchinson
5. Prepare with your classmates a large outline map of North America. Fill in the 13 states that grew from the original colonies. Show the state capitals and major cities. As the year progresses, add the remaining 37 states as each is admitted to the Union. The maps in this book will guide you.

CHAPTER 2 TEST

Completion (30 points)
Number your paper 1–10 and write the names or places to fill in the blanks after each number.

1. The most famous of the English sea dogs was _____.
2. A courageous soldier of fortune, _____ took command at Jamestown.
3. Many Pilgrims might have starved to death if _____ had not shown them how to grow corn and where to catch the best fish.
4. Peter Minuit bought _____ from its Indian inhabitants for knives, beads, and trinkets.
5. The governor of Massachusetts Bay, _____, preferred persuasion to force.
6. After being driven from Massachusetts for his religious beliefs, _____ founded Rhode Island and Providence Plantations.
7. At a trial in 1638 _____ was found to be "a woman not fit for our society" by the Puritans of Massachusetts.
8. The city of _____, named for the king of England, became the social and political center of Carolina.
9. In order to create a refuge for his fellow Quakers, _____ founded Pennsylvania.
10. The last English colony in America, _____, was settled in 1733.

Matching (20 points)
Number your paper 11–15 and match the description in the first column with the term in the second column.

11. Grant made to each colonist who paid the passage of settlers to America
12. A document that gave a person or a group the right to establish and control a colony
13. An organization in which the owners shared in both the profits and losses of outfitting expeditions
14. A land grant that gave a person or group as much power as a lord of the manor in feudal times
15. A contract a person signed agreeing to work for seven years in return for passage to America

a. Joint-stock company
b. Charter
c. Headright
d. Proprietary colony
e. Indenture

Matching (20 points)
Number your paper 16–20 and match the colony in the first column with its founder in the second column.

16. Connecticut
17. Rhode Island and Providence Plantations
18. Maryland
19. Delaware
20. Georgia

a. Roger Williams
b. James Oglethorpe
c. Thomas Hooker
d. Lord Baltimore
e. William Penn

Essay (30 points)
Tell what it is in our history that makes religious freedom so important to all Americans. Use specific examples from colonial times to make your point. Write at least one full paragraph, taking care to spell and punctuate correctly.

CHAPTER 3
Life in Colonial America

The English colonies in North America were separate communities scattered along the Atlantic coast from New England to Georgia. Few people in the Carolinas ever saw or spoke with a person from Massachusetts or New York or Pennsylvania. People did not often use the word "American" to describe themselves or their country. Most thought of themselves as English or Dutch or French—whatever their homeland. Yet they and their children soon became more American than European, for they were changed by the land.

LAND AND PEOPLE

In the beginning America was a very large country with a very small population. There was much work to be done and few people to do it. This situation had enormous effects on the colonists. For one thing it tended to make them more flexible. To succeed, one needed to be

An artist traveling in about 1735 painted this view of the New York farm of Martin van Bergen. The oil was put directly on the paneling above the van Bergen's fireplace. The owners stand in front of their Dutch-style farmhouse watching a milk cart pass. The Catskills rise in the background. Why did rural colonists need to be open-minded and flexible?

New York State Historical Association, Cooperstown

This oil painting shows "Abigail Gerrish and Her Grandmother" in about 1750. It was painted by John Greenwood, who with a handful of other New England painters, broke from English traditions to create art that was truly American. One of his fellow artists was Winthrop Chandler, who painted the portrait shown on page 80 of Mrs. Samuel Chandler. How were most children treated in colonial America?

open-minded. Historical imagination can help us to see why this attitude was important. Everything was so different in America. Those who were willing to experiment, to try new ways of doing things, usually did better than those who insisted on following traditional paths. For the same reason, Americans had to be jacks-of-all-trades. Farming in the wilderness meant being one's own carpenter, tailor, butcher, even one's own doctor.

With so much land to farm and with the woods and streams full of game and fish, there was always plenty to eat. Children grew big and strong. Sons and daughters were usually taller than their parents. The grandchildren grew taller still. Because there was so much work to be done, another child was an asset, not merely another mouth to feed. A six-year-old could tend the chickens, a ten-year-old weed vegetables or milk cows. Large families were the rule. There was plenty of land. When they were grown, the children could have farms of their own.

Children were well treated and given much love by most American parents. Europeans claimed that American children were spoiled. Compared to how children were treated in Europe, this may have been so, but by modern standards it was far from true. American youngsters worked hard, and family discipline was quite strict.

▨ How did the great amount of land in America influence the size of the family?

RIVERS SHAPE LIFE

In a country without roads the first colonists relied on rivers to get themselves and their goods from place to place. In Virginia, rivers like the James and the Potomac were broad, deep, and slow moving. Ocean-going vessels could sail up them for many miles. The ships brought the products of Europe to inland tobacco farmers and took away their barrels of cured tobacco for sale in England. For this reason the population of Virginia was scattered thinly over the land. Farms spread along the riverbanks. Land between the rivers lay untouched for many years. There were few towns because buying and selling could take place at each farmer's riverside dock.

In New England the rivers were shallow and full of rapids. Ships could not sail up them. Seaports were essential from the beginning. Boston, New Haven, Newport, and other coastal towns became quite large early in their histories. Inland transportation had to be by road.

Building roads was an expensive business. Settlers remained close together so that few had to be built. The New England village made its appearance. Around a small, parklike town square—the **town common**—the villagers built their church, meeting house, and

school. Each family received a small plot of land for a house and a garden around this town common. Outside the village lay the fields where crops were grown. Workers went out each morning, tilled their individual strips, and returned at day's end to their snug village homes.

Thus, people in New England were community minded. In Virginia and other southern colonies people were more family centered. There were more schools in New England, not only because Puritans believed that education was very important, but also because enough families lived within walking distance of the schools to support them. Southerners were more apt to educate their children at home. Perhaps because their lives were more isolated, southerners tended to welcome strangers with a special warmth. This was one origin of **southern hospitality.**

- How did rivers shape life in the South?
- Why were seaports essential in the North?

This engraving is the earliest view of Baltimore and surrounding farms in Maryland. It was made in 1752. Notice how close both farmland and homes are to the water. Why were southern farmers able to buy and sell goods at their own docks?

65

The Road to America

Gemini-Smith

John White painted this fanciful watercolor in a corner of a map of the Atlantic Coast, probably in the 1580s. He was the head of the expedition that became the Lost Colony of Roanoke.

For all American colonists there was first of all the Atlantic Ocean. If the Atlantic was the road the colonists traveled to America, it was the great barrier to travel and communication too. Few people who crossed the Atlantic as settlers ever returned to Europe. We can use historical imagination to picture the voyage to America. The trip took many weeks, sometimes months. It was dangerous, especially in winter when ferocious storms tossed tiny ships about like corks. At other times, when there was no wind, the ships were prisoners of the seas. A Congregationalist minister named Richard Mather wrote in 1635 of the hardships endured on a ship becalmed at sea:

> A great calm, and very hot all that forenoon. Our people and cattle were much afflicted with faintness, sweating, and heat; but (lo, the goodness of our God) about noon the wind blew at north and by east, which called us from our heat and helped us forward in our way.

Another writer, an English woman writing in 1609, chose these words to describe the end of her Atlantic crossing:

> After three and one-half months of living on this ship, I long to plant my feet on firm earth. How I long for home, but yet the New Land, America, offers us so much more.

Colonists who crossed the Atlantic could not depend on their home country, as the settlers at Roanoke had learned to their sorrow. Home was more than 3,000 miles (4,800 kilometers) away. Small wonder that the Americans would come to be known as a self-reliant people.

WOMEN IN COLONIAL AMERICA

Most of the first settlers were young men. Once a colony was established, however, it was important to these men and to the merchant adventurers or colonial proprietors that more women be recruited. The London Company shipped whole boatloads of unmarried women to Virginia. When they married, their husbands would pay the cost of their passage. Women often came to America as indentured servants and frequently ended up marrying their masters. Colonists tended to take a practical rather than a romantic view of marriage.

Yet people familiar with European attitudes almost always noticed that American men were more respectful of women and more considerate of their wives than European men were. Women were needed more as workers and as mothers—and as companions too.

Compared to their status today, women had few rights in colonial times. They were kept by law and custom under the thumb of

66

men. Married women could not own property. If they earned any money, it belonged legally to their husbands. Almost none had the right to vote. Divorce was next to impossible. Needless to say, wives also worked very hard. In addition to keeping house, rearing children, and performing hundreds of farm chores, the typical colonial woman had to devote much time to teaching her children, to making clothing for the whole family, to caring for anyone who was sick. If men were jacks-of-all-trades, women were surely jills-of-all-trades. The advantages of having many children in America were not weighed against the health of the mothers of these children. Constant child-bearing caused many women to die at an early age.

Yet, when all these things have been said, it remains true that America offered women more opportunities than was common in Europe. Women learned to handle guns and to defend themselves against attack. Some women ran large farms and plantations because "the man of the house" was away or had died. Martha Dandridge Custis, still in her twenties when her husband died, became one of the wealthiest women in America. A few are known to have run newspapers, served as lawyers in colonial courts, and done other things that would have been almost impossible for women in Europe.

- What was the attitude toward women in colonial America?
- What hardships did women face in colonial America?

Colonial Williamsburg

Martha Dandridge Custis was one of the richest women in America. This oil portrait was painted by John Wollaston before the death in 1757 of Daniel Custis. At 26 Martha Custis had become the owner of the Custis lands in Virginia. What were some of the tasks of a young colonial woman?

A young couple harvest their fields in this beautiful needlepoint made by Mary Woodhull in the late 1700s. They use scythes to cut the grain while doves circle overhead. Why were American women respected more than women in Europe?

"Burning Fallen Trees in a Girdled Clearing, Western Scene" is the title of this fine engraving by W. J. Bennett. The girdle is the band cut in the tree in the foreground. It was a way of killing trees learned from the Indians by the first settlers of Jamestown. What name was given settlers who cleared wild land and planted crops on it?

LAND AND LABOR

In Europe landowners were the kingpins of society. Membership in the nobility meant control of large territories and the people who lived in them. For lesser people, owning land brought prestige as well as whatever profit could be made from it. Except for highly skilled artisans, people who lived by their labor in Europe tended to be poor.

In America there was so much unused land that without labor land was worth almost nothing. With labor it could be used productively. This meant that working people earned more than European workers and were better treated by their employers.

High wages and cheap land meant that most Americans owned land. In Massachusetts and the other New England colonies the legislatures gave large tracts of land to groups of settlers who wanted to found new towns. The people then cleared as much of this land as they could farm and divided it up among the families. The rest, called the **commons,** remained town property. As the town grew, newcomers were given some of the common land so that they could have farms of their own.

In other colonies people got land in many ways. Those with headrights received it for nothing. Others bought land or got large grants from the king or from colonial authorities. Indentured servants could get money to buy land by working for wages after their terms of service were completed. Still others, impatient and willing to live under crude and dangerous conditions, moved west to the edge of the settled area. This region, vaguely defined and shifting always westward, was called the **frontier.** On the frontier a person could clear a tract of wild land, build a cabin, and plant a crop. Such people were called **squatters.** By the time settlement had expanded to their region, most squatters had made enough money to buy their property. If not, they usually sold their "improvements" to a newcomer and moved farther west to repeat the process.

■ What were some of the ways colonial Americans got land?

LAND AND THE RIGHT TO VOTE

The fact that most Americans owned land affected how the colonies were governed, in unexpected ways. Today we believe that all adult citizens should have the right to vote. One does not have to be rich or own property to participate in elections. This principle is known as **political equality,** a basic element of what we call **democracy.**

During the colonial era people did not believe in democracy as we now know it. For example, women were not allowed to vote. In addition, only white men who owned a certain amount of land or had some other substantial wealth were considered qualified to vote.

There was almost no difference between the attitudes of the English and the Americans on this point. Most colonists believed that the people who *owned* a country should have a say in running it, not those who merely *lived* in a country. Yet, since a majority of the colonists owned land, having to meet a "property qualification" to vote did not disqualify many.

Thus, while the colonists did not believe in the idea of democracy, in practice their governments were quite democratic. In most of the colonies about as large a percentage of the adult white men voted in elections as does today. With time, people became accustomed to voting. Since the property requirement had so little practical effect, it ceased to seem important. Gradually, the *idea* of democracy began to catch up with what was actually happening.

In the early days settlers could remember England, where a handful of great landowners completely dominated elections. These settlers considered voting a privilege that they had gained by coming to America. Their grandsons, who grew up in a society where nearly every white man voted, began to see voting as a natural right, not a privilege. This was one of the most important results of the ease of obtaining land in America.

- Which colonists were considered qualified to vote?
- In what way were colonial governments democratic?
- How did the ease of owning land in America change ideas about voting?

THE ORIGINS OF SLAVERY

Indentured servants got land and eventually political power in America because the need for their labor was so great. Other laborers in America were cruelly used. These were the black slaves brought from Africa. It takes a strong historical imagination to think as the European colonizers did about slavery. Most had certain deep-seated prejudices about people and their rights. Most believed that some people were better than others. Most assumed that the values and customs of their society were better than any others. Being Christians, they felt certain that Christianity was the only true religion. Non-Christians were "heathens." They were thought to be sinful and evil by nature.

We have seen how this point of view affected the way other Europeans dealt with the Indians. In the English colonies, however, the newcomers were not often able to make the Indians work for them. The land was large, the Indian population small. In most cases the Indians—those that were not wiped out by warfare or disease—eventually gave up their lands and moved west. A few Indians were enslaved. A few took on European ways. Most simply melted into

69

DESCRIPTION OF A SLAVE SHIP.

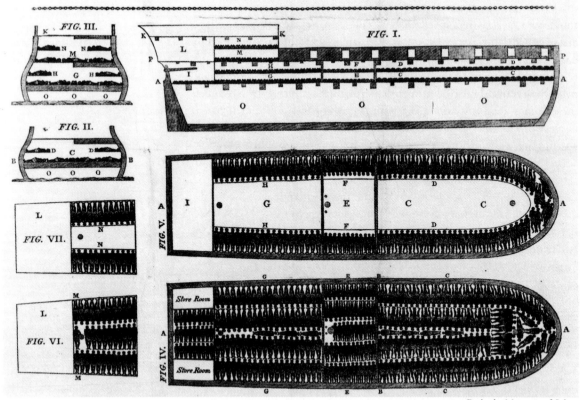

Peabody Museum of Salem

Seven views of a slave ship show the cold calculations made to get the greatest number of captured black Africans aboard. Everywhere the ship carries human cargo. The "Description of a Slave Ship" was published in 1789. When were the first African slaves brought to the English colonies?

the forest rather than submit to white control. There was nothing the colonists could do to stop them from leaving.

Another source of labor then became available—that of black Africans. The story of how these innocent people were brought to America and compelled to work as slaves is the most tragic and shameful chapter in our history. It is even more shameful than the ill use of the Indians, who at least had the means of fighting back, however hopeless the odds.

The Spaniards brought black slaves from Africa to America before the founding of Jamestown. It may be that the English colonists got the idea of enslaving blacks from the Spanish example. The word *negro* is Spanish for "black." The English must have borrowed it. Yet the English did not begin to use it to describe black people until after the Spanish had begun to enslave Africans. In any case the first Africans were brought to the English colonies by Dutch traders, who sold them to the Jamestown colonists in 1619.

At first few blacks were imported. Tobacco farmers and others in need of laborers much preferred indentured servants to Africans. The Africans could not speak English. Many lacked the skills needed by farmers. And it cost much more to buy a slave than to purchase the labor of a white servant for a limited period of time.

For a long time there were plenty of indentured servants. When they completed their service, most of them became independent farmers. They then competed with their former masters. The more servants a tobacco planter hired, the more small farmers would be planting tobacco for themselves seven years later. The price of tobacco and other crops tended to fall as production increased. Under slavery this kind of competition did not occur.

- Why were the English not able to make the Indians work for them?
- Why did the colonists originally prefer indentured servants to African slaves? What caused a change in attitude?

SLAVE LIFE

By 1690 there were slaves in all the English colonies. The **peculiar institution,** as some slaveholders called it, was firmly fixed in American society. It was to last for another 175 years.

It is hard for persons in a free society to conceive of what it was like to be a slave. We must use historical imagination carefully. The idea that slaves were constantly beaten or worked to death like prisoners in a concentration camp is incorrect. Slaves were too valuable to be treated like that—unless they refused to work or rose up against their owners. They were usually given adequate food, clothing, and

This detail comes from "Mulberry Plantation," an early oil painted by Thomas Coram. The slave quarters stand in orderly rows behind the owner's mansion. What did some slaveholders call slavery?

Carolina Art Association/Gibbes Art Gallery

shelter, again because it made sense to take good care of expensive property. But slaves had absolutely *no rights.* It was not simply that they could not vote or own property. Their owners had complete control over their lives. An owner could separate a husband and wife, or sell a child and keep the child's parents. Slaves were considered a form of living property, like cattle or horses. They worked for the exclusive benefit of their owners. Slavery was almost literally inhuman. But those who were enslaved were human beings.

Still using historical imagination, it must have been far worse to become a slave than to be born one. Most who became slaves were prisoners taken in wars in Africa or unsuspecting villagers captured by African slave hunters. These people made a business of preying upon others. They marched their captives in chains to prison pens on the coast, then sold them to white traders.

Next came the dreadful **Middle Passage,** the voyage across the Atlantic. The blacks were crowded below deck as closely as the captain thought possible without causing all to smother. How many died on the crossing was usually a matter of luck. If the winds were strong and favorable, the trip would be reasonably short. Most would survive. If the ship was delayed by bad weather, or if smallpox or some other contagious disease broke out, the death toll would be enormous.

Once in America, the slaves were put on public display and sold to the highest bidder. They were prodded and poked at by prospective buyers the way traders examine the teeth of an old horse.

One can imagine how confused and depressed most new slaves were after these experiences. Separated from home and family, unable to communicate, drained of strength and hope, there was little likelihood that they would try to resist or run away. Where could they run to? Surely children born into slavery bore its weight with less pain, having never known freedom.

It is one of the many strange aspects of slavery that those who were born into slavery and particularly those who had the easiest places in the system, such as those skilled at crafts like carpenters, were the ones who most frequently ran away or tried to organize slave revolts. Another puzzle is that by teaching slaves specific skills, their owners increased their usefulness but made them less willing to accept being slaves. Slaves who could read and write and practice a trade were far less willing to accept their condition than illiterate "field hands."

New Haven Historical Society

This handsome African slave was the proud son of a Mendi chief. He crossed the Middle Passage in chains. Later he was painted by Nathaniel Jocelyn. How were most slaves captured?

- How were African slaves usually treated by their owners in America?
- Why was the Middle Passage so dreaded?
- Who was more likely to rise up against an owner—a slave who had been taught a craft or a field hand?

72

John Carter Brown Library

SOUTHERN AGRICULTURE

What the colonists needed most were European manufactured goods. The money to buy these goods could be earned if the colonists raised crops that Europeans wanted but could not grow themselves. These were called **cash crops** because they brought the growers money to buy farm tools, furniture, clothing, guns and ammunition, pots and pans, books, glassware—the list seems endless. The southern colonists had an advantage in the search for cash crops because of their warm climate. The island settlements in the West Indies, for example, raised sugar, a tropical plant that Europeans wanted badly but could not grow. By selling their sugar to their home countries, Spanish, English, French, and Dutch colonists in the South could get the money they needed to buy European manufactured goods.

Tobacco provided a cash crop for the colonists of Maryland, Virginia, and the Carolinas. The seeds of tobacco are so small that a tablespoon will hold about 30,000 of them. The colonists planted these tiny seeds in beds of finely powdered soil. When the seeds sprouted, the little plants were moved to the fields. The best tobacco was made from the largest leaves. As the plants matured, the side shoots of each plant were cut off. At a certain point the top bud was

In the West Indies slaves refine sugar by boiling sugar cane under the watchful eyes of overseers, who inspect the sugar drying in bins. An English artist made this colored lithograph in the 19th century. Why was sugar a popular crop in the South?

73

clipped to stop growth. This pruning concentrated the plant's energies in the big leaves. In the fall these leaves were removed and carefully cured, or dried, in airy sheds. Then the tobacco was packed in barrels for shipping.

When tobacco first became popular in England, the price of American tobacco was very high. Anyone with even a small plot of land could make a good living growing it. More and more tobacco was planted as the tobacco colonies expanded. Gradually the price fell. The large planters could still live well enough earning a small profit on each barrel of tobacco. But many small farmers were forced to sell out and move west. When the news of this change reached Europe, poor people were less eager to come to America as indentured servants. With fewer Europeans coming to the tobacco colonies, African slaves became the chief source of labor on the tobacco plantations.

In parts of South Carolina and later in Georgia too, **rice** became the chief cash crop. Rice needs a warm climate and much water. It grew well in swamps and low-lying lands along the Atlantic coast. The fields were flooded by building dikes and canals and trapping river water that was backed up by the incoming ocean tides. Coastal areas of the South were called the **tidewater** because their rivers were affected in this way by the ocean tides.

Slaves are harvesting indigo in this 19th-century color engraving. The delicate tropical plants are carried in bundles to be soaked in the vats at the center and then dried on the racks at the right. Indigo was much in demand for its blue dye. Who first grew indigo in America?

Malaria and other tropical fevers struck down many of the people who had to work in the rice fields. For this reason slave labor was used almost exclusively. The whites claimed that blacks were immune to these diseases because of their African origin. It may have been that they suffered less because of natural immunity, but large numbers of blacks caught malaria and many died. Working knee-deep in mud with the temperature in the nineties and humidity high, the air swarming with mosquitoes, was not good for anyone.

South Carolina farmers also grew **indigo,** a plant that produced a blue dye used by the English cloth manufacturers. Indigo was first grown in America by Eliza Lucas, who while still in her teens was running three large South Carolina plantations owned by her father, a colonial official in the British West Indies. An inventive person, Lucas also produced silk and experimented with other products, although without much success.

The great pine forests of the South yielded tall, straight logs that became the masts of ships in the Royal Navy. The sap, or resin, of pine trees was made into tar and pitch that were used to preserve rope and make the hulls of ships watertight. These products were called **naval stores.**

- Why were cash crops important to the South? What are some examples of southern cash crops?
- Why did African slaves become the chief labor source in raising southern cash crops? What excuse was made for using the slaves?
- What are some examples of naval stores?

NORTHERN PRODUCTS

The northern colonies also produced naval stores, but the climate from Pennsylvania to Massachusetts Bay and New Hampshire was too cold to grow most of the southern cash crops. Put differently, the climate in these colonies was similar to the climate in England. England already produced all it needed of the crops that grew best in the North—crops such as wheat, barley, and oats.

One American product, more northern than southern, highly valued in Europe was fur. Fur-bearing animals were scarce in Europe but abundant in the forest wildernesses of America. Americans hunted and trapped beaver, deer, and other animals and sent the skins to Europe, where they were made into coats and wraps or converted into felt for hats. The colonists also traded for furs with the Indians. The **fur trade** was essentially a frontier activity. As the colonies grew larger, fur traders and hunters had to go farther and farther west.

Some northerners did a great deal of **fishing,** especially in the waters off Newfoundland. The English worked that area too, so there

BUILDING SKILLS IN SOCIAL STUDIES

Reading a Resource Map

Maps can carry a great amount of information because *symbols* are used when there are many similar items. A simple use of symbols is the **x** that represents a battle in the War for American Independence, as shown in the maps on pages 146 and 152. The part of the map that explains what the symbols stand for is the *key*. The key to the map on this page appears just below the title. Sometimes the key is found in a separate box.

The map "Colonial Products 1775" is a *resource map*. It uses many symbols—11 in all—to represent various products of the northern and southern colonies. These include natural resources such as trees and fish, crops such as tobacco and indigo, and manufactured goods such as sugar and paper. A simple symbol represents each category of products. The map would be too complicated if a product's name had to be printed in each colony where it was found.

Study the resource map carefully. Notice that major cities are identified but that the names of the colonies are not given. If you are unsure of the location of any of the thirteen colonies, review the map on page 56. Then answer the following questions.

1. Name three colonies in which tobacco was grown.
2. Name four colonies where ships were built.
3. Name three colonies where paper was made.
4. Name a southern colony and a northern colony where timber was harvested.
5. In which region of colonial America were the resources mostly agricultural? In which region were the resources mostly manufactured products?

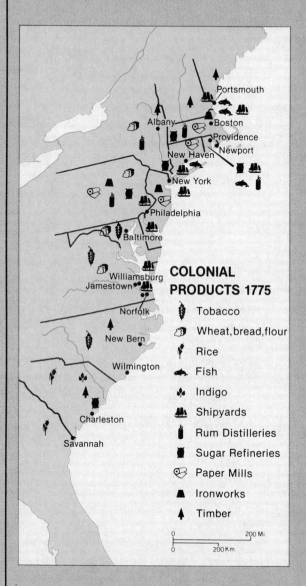

COLONIAL PRODUCTS 1775

	Tobacco
	Wheat, bread, flour
	Rice
	Fish
	Indigo
	Shipyards
	Rum Distilleries
	Sugar Refineries
	Paper Mills
	Ironworks
	Timber

0   200 Mi.
0   200 Km.

These colonial fur traders inspect a pelt held by a Northern Indian while they smoke their pipes. The engraving is a detail from a map of Canada made in 1777 by William Faden. Why were furs so valued in Europe?

was no market in England for the American catch. The Americans instead exported large quantities of dried and salted fish to southern Europe.

Yet, not many northerners trapped fur-bearing animals or fished. Most had to find other means of paying for the European manufactured goods they craved. The problem turned out to be a great advantage, for it encouraged northerners to try different things. It stimulated their imagination, or what has come to be called **Yankee ingenuity**—a knack for solving difficult problems in clever ways.

Since most people were farmers, the northern colonists produced much more food than they could eat. Where could they sell this surplus? The answer they came up with was the sugar-producing islands of the West Indies. These islands were all small. Every acre of fertile soil was devoted to raising sugar cane. Moreover, producing sugar requires a great deal of labor. The islands were densely populated, mostly by black slaves. The sugar planters worked their slaves very hard. They realized that the slaves had to have plenty to eat if they were to work well.

American merchants and sailors soon discovered that they could make excellent profits shipping grain and fish to the sugar islands, and also horses for plowing and hauling and barrels to pack sugar in. They could invest the profits of this trade in sugar and carry the sugar to England. When the sugar was sold, they could buy English manufactured goods and sell these at another fat profit when they returned to their home port.

■ What were some of the major northern crops? Why did these crops produce a surplus?

■ Why did the West Indies become so important in trade with the northern colonies?

THE TRIANGULAR TRADE

The trade between the northern colonies, the sugar islands, and England was called the **triangular trade** because three separate voyages were involved. There were many variations, some quite complex. American merchants frequently bought molasses in the sugar islands instead of sugar. Molasses is what is left over after the crystallized sugar has been boiled out of the sugar cane. It was almost a waste product in the islands, and very cheap. The Americans took it back to the mainland, most frequently to Rhode Island, where it was distilled into rum, a powerful alcoholic drink. The rum was then shipped to West Africa, where it was traded for slaves. The slaves, in turn, were taken to the West Indies, or perhaps to the colonies in America. Then the cycle might be repeated: slaves for molasses, molasses into rum, rum for slaves. If the African slaves were sold in Virginia, the captain of the vessel might buy tobacco and take that to England. He might then purchase manufactured goods for sale back home.

The triangular trade was extremely profitable. The Americans bought things where they were plentiful and cheap and sold them where they were in great demand. Each leg of the voyage added to the gain. The more complicated the route, the more money could be made. Sometimes a ship was away from its home port for years. When it finally returned, the owners were rich indeed.

TRIANGULAR TRADE ROUTES 1700s

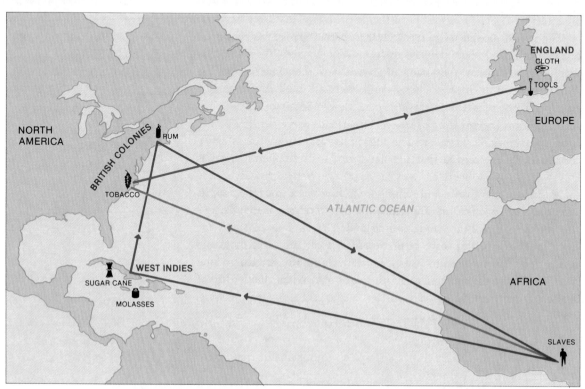

The St. Louis Art Museum

Thus what looked like a disadvantage—the fact that England did not need what northern colonists could produce—became an advantage, especially for the merchants and shipowners. A typical example was Thomas Amory, Irish born, who settled in Boston in 1720. Amory's ships traded with the West Indies, the Azores, England, and several European nations. He manufactured rum and naval stores and also built ships. He was so wealthy that when he married the daughter of a Boston tavern keeper, he could speak of his wife's fortune as *only* £1,500, although that was quite a large sum at the time. Another Boston merchant, James Bowdoin, son of a French Protestant who came to America to escape religious persecution, acquired a fortune of over £182,000.

Trade was the key to prosperity in the northern colonies, just as cash crops were the key to prosperity farther south. For this reason merchants were the most admired people in the North, the leaders of society, and often the political leaders too. The southern planter, owner of large estates and many slaves, played a similar role in the South.

■ How was the triangular trade conducted?
■ What were some variations of the triangular trade?

Sea captains relax in port on a leg of their triangular trade. This oil was painted on bed ticking by John Greenwood in the late 18th century. Called "Sea Captains Carousing in Surinam," it shows that the artist disapproved of such carryings on. For how long might sea captains be away from their home ports?

79

RURAL LIFE IN AMERICA

The northern colonies were almost as rural as the southern. In 1690 Boston was the largest town in North America, but it had a population of only about 7,000. A very large proportion, probably 90 per cent, of all the people north of Maryland were farmers.

Despite the importance of trade and the foreign manufactured goods that trade made possible, most farm families made many of the things they needed right in their own homes. They spun wool sheared from their own sheep into thread. They wove the thread into cloth from which they made their coats and dresses and shirts and trousers. They used the skins of deer for "buckskin" leggings and moccasins. They carved buttons out of bone and made plates and spoons of wood. They built most of their own furniture, oftentimes using homemade tools. Instead of nails, they fastened things together with wooden pegs. All this was especially true of families on the frontier and those living in districts far removed from rivers and roads. These people had to be almost entirely self-sufficient.

▓ In what ways were rural people self-sufficient?

VILLAGE AND TOWN LIFE

The towns were centers of activity, really the hearts and minds of the colonies. In even the smallest villages there were group activities like discussion clubs and sewing circles that people enjoyed.

The largest towns, in addition to Boston, were New York, Philadelphia, Charleston, Newport, and New Haven. All were **seaports,** their economy based upon sea trade and shipbuilding. Though small by modern standards, all were bustling, vital communities. Their harbors were forests of ships' masts and spars. Their docks were piled high with barrels, boxes, crates, chests, and bales of every sort. On the dockside streets one could hear many languages spoken. "We are a people thrown together from various quarters of the world," one proud citizen of Philadelphia explained.

In the shops and warehouses of the towns could be found fine English cloth and chinaware, tea from India, wine from Portugal and the Madeira islands, molasses from the sugar islands, as well as products from all the mainland colonies. Their taverns were crowded with sailors and dockworkers and artisans of all sorts. Every colonial town of any size had a weekly newspaper. Some had theaters too. The wealthy merchants built fine houses in the towns and filled them with good furnishings, some made by colonial cabinetmakers, silversmiths, and other artisans.

▓ What geographical feature did all the large towns have in common?

Mrs. Samuel Chandler, shown in a remarkable oil painted by Winthrop Chandler c. 1780, was married to a wealthy merchant. She has fine clothing that probably came from her husband's trade abroad. What kinds of homes did the merchants build in colonial towns?

READING PRACTICE IN SOCIAL STUDIES

Reading with a Purpose

An active reader is one who gets the most from reading assignments in the best possible time. Active readers go after information. One way to make yourself an active reader is to *set a purpose* for your reading. For reading without a purpose is like taking a trip without knowing where you are going. You may ramble along without knowing what to look for, and when your trip is over, you may wonder where you have been and what you have done. Not so when you read with a purpose.

One way to make your reading more purposeful is to use a strategy sometimes called *5WH,* which stands for "the five w's and how." When you read, you ask *who? what? when? where? why?* and *how?*

You might take the title of a section in this book. Before reading further, turn the title into a series of questions. For example, look at the section on page 78 titled "The Triangular Trade." You might ask questions such as these:

What was the triangular trade?
Why was it called the triangular trade?
Who took part in the triangular trade?
When was the triangular trade carried on?
Where was the triangular trade carried out?
How was the triangular trade conducted?

These questions give you a purpose for reading the section because you read to find answers. When you have the answers to your 5WH questions, you will find that you know a great deal about the triangular trade. You can quickly form new 5WH questions and move on to the next section.

You can also use the 5WH questions with the illustration program in this book. Illustrations include paintings, drawings, maps, diagrams, graphs, time lines, and the like.

When you are assigned a number of pages to read in this book, thumb quickly through the pages and look at the illustrations. They have been selected to show in pictures what the author says in words. The illustrations *support* the story. A quick look at the illustrations will give you a general idea of what a section is about.

Look quickly at the illustrations in this chapter and form a general idea about its content. Then use the illustrations to make up your 5WH questions. You might ask the following:

Who are the people pictured in this chapter?
What story do the pictures of black slaves illustrate?
When were the pictures in this chapter made? Hint: *Why* are there no photographs?
Where are the farms and plantations shown in the pictures located?
How did the black slaves come to America?

As you read the chapter, you will find that you can readily answer these questions.

The 5WH questions may also be asked to help you read a map. Look at the map of the triangular trade on page 78. Ask 5W questions like these:

What is the purpose of this map? (The title will tell you.)
Who engaged in the triangular trade? *Where* did they go, and *when?*
Why was the triangular trade carried on, and *how* did it work?

Not all of these questions can be answered from the map alone, but careful study of both the map and the section "The Triangular Trade" will give you the answers you seek.

With your classmates form a series of 5WH questions for each of the following:
1. The section at the beginning of Chapter 3 on page 64 titled "Rivers Shape Life."
2. The part of the section titled "Slave Life" on pages 71–72 about the Middle Passage.
3. The illustration on page 82 next to the section titled "The Great Awakening."
4. The special section on page 83 titled "Self-Taught Americans."
5. The section on pages 88–89 titled "Bacon's Rebellion."

George Whitefield, whose fervent preaching brought about the Great Awakening, is the subject of this mezzotint made in 1769 by John Greenwood. What were the feelings most colonists held about religion?

THE GREAT AWAKENING

American colonists were deeply religious and made great efforts to maintain their churches. Particularly on the frontier where the population was spread over great distances, people would travel for miles to attend services. Frontier ministers also rode from place to place on horseback, preaching and holding church meetings wherever a group could be brought together.

Just how deeply most colonists felt about religion was revealed by what is called the **Great Awakening** of the 1740s. In November 1739 a young English preacher named George Whitefield arrived in Philadelphia. He was on his way to Savannah, Georgia, where the trustees had appointed him minister and where he intended to found an orphanage.

Whitefield was a small, fair-skinned man with sparkling, deep-blue eyes. While preaching, he radiated energy and enthusiasm, bounding about, waving his arms to emphasize his points. He would undoubtedly have made a brilliant actor had he chosen the stage as a career. In Philadelphia, and then while traveling south to Savannah, he spoke wherever he could find a church. Sometimes he held services in the open air. Later he returned to the northern colonies, again preaching almost daily. Everywhere he went, he stirred intense religious emotions in his listeners. Thousands of colonists came forward to confess their sins and resolve to lead blameless lives in the future.

Dozens of other preachers followed in Whitefield's steps. The colonies from Georgia to New Hampshire were swept by repeated waves of religious excitement. Whitefield and most of the others played down the differences of doctrine that separated many of the Protestant sects. What mattered, they said, was to have sincere religious feelings. Philosophy and logic would get no one into Heaven.

The Great Awakening was a force for religious toleration because of its come-one-come-all spirit. Many people were carried away by the excitement in the crowd when they heard a dynamic speaker like Whitefield preach. They announced that they were converted. They swore to lead saintly lives in the future. They were perfectly sincere, but most of them could not change their old habits. In rural areas some of the people who gathered to listen were attracted more by the festival atmosphere that surrounded the meetings than by the desire to save their souls. Although the Awakening petered out after 1741, it had permanently changed American religious attitudes.

- What was the Great Awakening?
- In what way was the Great Awakening a force for religious toleration?

82

Colonial America had only a few colleges—Harvard in Massachusetts, William and Mary in Virginia, Yale in Connecticut, and the College of New Jersey, now called Princeton. But many colonists were caught up by the spirit of the Enlightenment in the 1770s and taught themselves.

David Rittenhouse was a clockmaker who made valuable contributions to the construction of telescopes and other instruments. He also built an orrery, a mechanical model of the sun and the planets which copied their movements exactly.

John Bartram was a farm boy who had little formal education but a passionate interest in all growing things. He traveled far and wide in America, collecting strange plants for his garden outside Philadelphia. He sent carefully packed samples of his discoveries to the leading European naturalists and received from them their own unusual finds. Distinguished visitors from Europe made detours to see his collection, and prominent Americans like George Washington and Benjamin Franklin came frequently to his garden.

Self-Taught Americans

Princeton University Observatory

Rittenhouse's orrery.

THE SEARCH FOR KNOWLEDGE

During the 1770s many people in the colonies were caught up by the spirit of what is known as the **Enlightenment.** The name describes a belief that in an orderly universe human reason will prevail. This time is sometimes called the Age of Reason because "enlightened" people believed that they could improve themselves and the world around them by careful study and hard thought.

Two great scientific advances set the stage for the Enlightenment. One was the invention of the telescope by the Italian scientist Galileo in 1609. Through his telescope Galileo was able to arrive at a much better understanding of the size of the universe and makeup of our own solar system than was earlier possible. The other advance was Sir Isaac Newton's discovery of the laws of gravity, which explained why the stars and planets behaved as they did.

The work of Galileo and Newton and other scientists changed the way educated people thought and the value they gave to thinking. The orderliness of the movements of the planets seemed to suggest that the universe was like a gigantic watch, complicated but operating according to fixed laws. If laws or rules governed the universe, surely no mystery of nature was beyond human solution. Surely humans, once they had solved the mysteries of nature, were destined to march steadily forward to greater and greater achievements.

These ideas found a welcome home in the colonies. It was easy to believe in progress in America because the colonies were so obviously making progress. The dense forest was being pushed back. The people

83

were growing richer and more numerous. It was easier still to believe that thought and study would push back the frontiers of knowledge. Explorers and scientists were constantly finding new rivers and mountains, new plants and animals. Americans continued to produce clever new ideas and ingenious ways of doing things.

▓ What was the Enlightenment? Why was its spirit welcome in the colonies?

BENJAMIN FRANKLIN

The greatest American of the Enlightenment was Benjamin Franklin. The story of his life begins in Boston, where he was born in 1706. His father was a soap and candle maker. Benjamin was the youngest of 17 children. He had only two years of schooling. At ten he became an apprentice in his father's shop, but after two years he shifted to the printer's trade, working for one of his nine older brothers.

In this earliest known portrait of Benjamin Franklin, he is shown in about 1746, just before he gave up his printing business to pursue his inventions. Robert Feke is the artist of this oil. *Right,* a page taken from the 1733 edition of *Poor Richard's Almanack.* What had Franklin done in his Boston days to learn a trade?

Poor Richard, 1733.

A N

Almanack

For the Year of Christ

I 7 3 3,

Being the First after LEAP YEAR.

And makes since the Creation Years
By the Account of the Eastern *Greeks* 7241
By the Latin Church, when ☉ ent. ♈ 6932
By the Computation of *W.W.* 5742
By the *Roman* Chronology 5682
By the *Jewish* Rabbies. 5494

Wherein is contained

The Lunations, Eclipses, Judgment of the Weather, Spring Tides, Planets Motions & mutual Aspects, Sun and Moon's Rising and Setting, Length of Days, Time of High Water, Fairs, Courts, and observable Days.

Fitted to the Latitude of Forty Degrees, and a Meridian of Five Hours West from *London,* but may without sensible Error, serve all the adjacent Places, even from *Newfoundland* to *South Carolina.*

By *RICHARD SAUNDERS,* Philom.

PHILADELPHIA:
Printed and sold by *B. FRANKLIN,* at the New Printing Office near the Market

Fogg Art Museum
Harvard University Portrait Collection

When he was 17, Benjamin left Boston to seek his fortune in Philadelphia. Soon he owned his own printing shop, then also a newspaper, the *Pennsylvania Gazette.* He published books and wrote the annual *Poor Richard's Almanack,* each volume full of practical advice, weather predictions, odd bits of information, and what he called "scraps from the table of wisdom." One of the best-known examples

84

of these "scraps" was the slogan "Early to bed, and early to rise, makes a man healthy, wealthy, and wise." Other typical examples are "God helps them that help themselves," "One today is worth two tomorrows," and "When the well is dry, they know the worth of water." He was so successful that by the time he was 42 he had enough money to live comfortably for the rest of his life.

At this point Franklin retired from the printing business so that he could pursue his other interests. These were almost endless. He invented a cast-iron fireplace (the Franklin stove) which radiated most of its heat into the room instead of allowing it to escape up the chimney. He invented bifocal eyeglasses so that people who were both nearsighted and farsighted need have only one pair. His famous experiment with a kite in a thunderstorm proved his theory that lightning was a form of electricity. This alone made his reputation among the leading European scientists of the time.

In addition to his scientific discoveries, Franklin was an outstanding citizen and public servant. He helped found the first library in Philadelphia, and the first fire department, and the first hospital, and a school—the Academy for the Education of Youth, which became the University of Pennsylvania. He was the town postmaster and later, by appointment of the king, postmaster for all the colonies.

In 1754 Franklin drafted the first scheme for uniting the colonies —the **Albany Plan of Union.** At this time he had no idea that the colonies might break away from England. Under his proposal England would still have had the final say about American affairs. But long before most other colonists understood the need, Franklin realized that the common interests of the different colonies were making it necessary for them to have some sort of common government. To make the point he drew a sketch of a snake divided into many pieces representing the different colonies. He attached to this drawing the title **Join, or Die.**

In 1754 Franklin was already world famous. But, as we shall see, the most important and exciting part of his life still lay ahead of him.

■ For what reasons was Benjamin Franklin the greatest American of the Enlightenment?

J O I N, or D I E.

EAST-WEST DISPUTES

America was indeed a land of opportunity. In England the cities and highways were crowded with ragged beggars and tramps. Few white people in America were that poor and hopeless. Some colonists were rich by any standard, but none was nearly as rich as the great English noble families or the merchant princes of London. Most Americans had what was called "middling" wealth. They lived comfortably, not lavishly. And they worked hard. Even the rich were rarely idle rich.

Edward Hicks's "The Peaceable Kingdom" was painted in oil in the early 19th century. In a detail above, a lion is as tame as a lamb, and children are as free as angels. William Penn's peaceful meeting with the Delaware Indians can be glimpsed in the background. For another view by Hicks of Penn's treaty, look again at page 59. How did colonial society differ from the world Hicks portrayed?

Yet colonial society was not really the "peaceable kingdom" that the Quaker artist Edward Hicks liked to portray. Sharp conflicts frequently occurred. Some even led to bloodshed.

By about 1750 settlement in most colonies had reached the eastern slopes and valleys of the Appalachian Mountains—that long range that runs from Georgia to New York and New England. In those days this was "the West" to the English colonists. It was only 100 miles (160 kilometers) or so from the seacoast where settlement had begun. But travel was slow and difficult. Most people rarely saw anyone from far outside their own communities.

Most colonists did not like Franklin's Albany Plan of Union. They were afraid of losing some of their independence to what seemed to them a "foreign" institution. The average person was loyal to only one colony and to only one village or county in particular. If the colonists had any common loyalty beyond that, it was to England or to the British Empire of which they were a part.

Colonial governments sometimes engaged in bitter disputes over territory. Boundaries were vague, mostly because the original land grants were made before the territories involved had been explored. The boundary between Maryland and Pennsylvania caused endless disputes and court battles. It was finally settled in the 1760s when Charles Mason and Jeremiah Dixon surveyed what came to be called the **Mason-Dixon line.** David Rittenhouse designed some of the instruments used by Mason and Dixon to survey this boundary. Disagreements of this type occurred so frequently that during his career Rittenhouse served on boundary commissions for more than half the English colonies.

Different interest groups in a single colony often came into conflict with one another. In already-settled areas people tended to think that defense against attack was a local matter. They argued, usually correctly, that frontier settlers were responsible for their own troubles. Therefore they should have to face the consequences without outside help.

The Quakers of Philadelphia, who opposed war as a matter of principle, were particularly smug about blaming the "hot-headed" Scotch-Irish settlers in the frontier sections of Pennsylvania for their conflicts with the local Indians. Whether the Quakers were correct or not, pioneers whose fields were burned or whose neighbors slain in surprise attacks were furious at the attitudes of these easterners, who were safe from such attacks.

People in the frontier sections of most colonies favored policies that made it easy for them to get land cheaply. Eastern landowners usually objected to such policies. If land was cheap in the West, the value of their own property would go down. A seaport merchant in the fur trade might be willing to sell guns to the Indians because guns made them better hunters. Westerners opposed such sales because they were afraid the Indians might use them to shoot settlers rather than deer or bear.

There were many such honest differences between the West and the East. The problem was that easterners made the policies because they controlled the colonial governments. The Quakers were so smug because they had a large majority in the Pennsylvania colonial legislature. They and similar groups in most colonies had more representatives than their numbers should have entitled them to.

The American system was and still is to elect legislators by geographical districts. Today, under the principle **one person, one vote,** all election districts must have approximately the same number of residents. A city district may be very small in area, one in farm country quite large. But their populations must be about equal.

When the first assemblies were formed in any colony, the election districts were fairly even in population. As the colony grew, people moved westward beyond the boundaries of the original districts. Soon these western settlers were demanding the right to elect representatives. They asked the assemblies to create new election districts.

Because of the East-West disagreements, the colonial assemblies were often reluctant to create new election districts, except in New England, where all the townships were the same size. A western

David Rittenhouse was one of the self-taught Americans who caught the spirit of the Enlightenment. He designed many tools for surveyors, telescopes, and other instruments. What part did he have in settling the boundary between Maryland and Pennsylvania?

87

legislator would have to represent several times as many voters as the eastern legislators did. In this way the East continued to control the colonial government long after the western population greatly exceeded the eastern.

Because they were under-represented, westerners deeply resented laws regulating land, road construction, and other matters that conflicted with their interests. Sometimes they even resorted to force to correct the injustice.

- Why did colonial governments have disputes so often over territory?
- Why did people in the frontier sections of most colonies resent the eastern sections?

BACON'S REBELLION

A good example of an East-West conflict occurred in Virginia in 1676. The trouble began along the Maryland-Virginia border when Indians killed a shepherd. White settlers responded by killing 24 Indians, including several of the Susquehanna tribe. Since the Susquehannas had not been involved in the murder of the shepherd, they were furious. Sweeping south out of Maryland, they killed at least 36 frontier settlers.

Howard Pyle illustrated Bacon's Rebellion with this late 19th-century black and white wash. Bacon, in the center, leads his followers in the burning of Jamestown. What made Bacon turn on Virginia's governor?

One of the men killed in this raid worked for a tobacco planter named Nathaniel Bacon. Not much is known about Bacon except that he was a thin, dark, rather sad-faced man who had come to Virginia from England only two years earlier. He had considerable money and was related to the wife of the governor of Virginia, Sir William Berkeley. Bacon promptly took charge of a large force of volunteers and marched them off to punish the Indians.

Governor Berkeley, however, tried to stop the violence. When Bacon refused to heed his order to lay down his arms, the governor proclaimed him a rebel. Bacon's force, in the meantime, had wiped out the Occaneechi, an Indian community that had nothing to do with the troubles. Indians, Bacon insisted, were "all alike." Then Bacon turned on the government. He drove the governor out of Jamestown and burned the town to the ground. Next he resumed his assaults on the Indians. In October 1676 Bacon died. The rebellion then collapsed.

Nathaniel Bacon was not a pure villain, despite his slaughter of innocent people and his refusal to obey the governor's orders. Most of the western planters considered him a hero. Many people felt that the legislature—the House of Burgesses—was not responsive to their needs and desires. There had not been an election in Virginia in 15 years.

Governor Berkeley had a long and distinguished career, but he had grown bad tempered in his old age. His wish to protect the Indians may not have been based entirely on his sense of fairness and justice. He seems to have had a considerable investment in the fur trade. If so, this would help explain why he did not want to see the Indians, on whom this profitable trade depended, killed or driven off.

After **Bacon's Rebellion** there were new elections in Virginia. The local Indians, most of whom had abandoned their lands when faced by Bacon's bloodthirsty army, were allowed to return after they agreed that they held the land under the authority of "the Great King of England." Some of their descendants still live on these lands. The entire conflict might have been avoided and many lives saved if the House of Burgesses had represented the interests of all the people concerned.

Fortunately, incidents like Bacon's Rebellion were rare in the colonial period. Displacing the Indians, slavery, unfair representation, and other sources of conflict seemed to be balanced by the opportunities that a new country made possible. America was not paradise. Life was hard and often dangerous. But to nearly every white colonist, the future seemed promising.

- What was Bacon's Rebellion?
- Why did many Virginians consider Bacon a hero?

CHAPTER 3 REVIEW

Identification

Tell briefly why each of the following persons, terms, or events is important.

1. Eliza Lucas
2. George Whitefield
3. David Rittenhouse
4. Benjamin Franklin
5. Nathaniel Bacon
6. Southern hospitality
7. Frontier
8. Squatters
9. Democracy
10. Peculiar institution
11. Middle Passage
12. Cash crops
13. Tidewater
14. Naval stores
15. Yankee ingenuity
16. Triangular trade
17. Great Awakening
18. Enlightenment
19. Albany Plan of Union
20. Mason-Dixon line

Understanding American History

1. Why did the colonists have to be self-reliant? Give at least two examples of ways the colonists were self-reliant.
2. Explain why river transportation was not as important in New England as it was in Virginia.
3. Why were large families important to the colonists?
4. Why did women have more opportunities in the colonies than in England? Give examples of some of these opportunities.
5. Why did working people in the colonies earn more and get better treatment than workers in England?
6. How did the availability of land help make colonial America more democratic than England?
7. Why did wealthy colonists prefer to buy slaves rather than purchase the labor of indentured servants?
8. How did northerners use Yankee ingenuity to find a means of paying for the European goods they craved?
9. What was the Enlightenment? Why is Benjamin Franklin a good person to represent the spirit of the Enlightenment?
10. What larger conflict lay beneath the conflict between Nathaniel Bacon and Sir William Berkeley?

Activities

1. Make your own map of the layout of a typical New England town or a Virginia farm. Begin by rereading the descriptions in this book and by reading the colonial sections of other American history books.
2. An important point in this chapter is that the great amount of land affected the lives of the colonists. Write a brief essay explaining how the abundance of land affected one of the following: women, indentured servants, slaves, American Indians.
3. Some colonial business leaders advertised in England to persuade more settlers to come to America. Imagine that you have been hired to conduct the advertising campaign for a group of these business leaders. Draw an eye-catching poster with an attention-getting slogan or prepare with your classmates a multimedia presentation to attract new settlers to America.
4. On page 85 there are examples of slogans or wise sayings from *Poor Richard's Almanack*. With your classmates make a list of your own slogans. Consider such subjects as good health, friendship, and good study habits. Put your slogans on the chalkboard. What do you conclude makes a good slogan?
5. Use your historical imagination to pretend that you are among the first group of settlers in a new colony in America. Write a letter to a friend back in England and describe your experiences. Describe one exciting moment, one happy time, and one sad time.

CHAPTER 3 TEST

Matching (20 points)
Number your paper 1–5 and match each term in the first column
with its description in the second column.

1. Frontier
2. Tidewater
3. Peculiar institution
4. Join, or Die
5. Democracy

a. Franklin's slogan to urge colonists to unite
b. The edge of settled area
c. Term used by some to describe slavery
d. Government based on political equality
e. The coastal areas of the South

Classifying (20 points)
Number your paper 6–15. For each of the following statements write
NE if it was characteristic of New England and *S* if it was character-
istic of the South.

6. Slaves were especially important.
7. People tended to live closer together.
8. Cash crops brought money to buy goods.
9. Rivers were broad and deep.
10. Inland transportation was by road.
11. Salted fish was sent to southern Europe.
12. Villages were built around a town common.
13. Children were usually educated at home.
14. Grain was shipped to the sugar islands.
15. Tobacco was an important crop.

Completion (30 points)
Number your paper 16–25 and next to each
number write the words from the list below that
best complete each sentence.

Bacon's Rebellion   squatters
self reliance   Eliza Lucas
Yankee ingenuity   Middle Passage
naval stores   Benjamin Franklin
Great Awakening   Enlightenment

16. The colonists needed ____ because they
could not depend upon others to help them.
17. ____ were people who farmed land they
cleared themselves on the frontier.
18. The voyage across the Atlantic on slave
ships was called the ____.
19. The period of great religious excitement
during colonial times was called the ____.
20. The pine forests of the South yielded the
products known as ____.
21. *Poor Richard's Almanack* and the Albany
Plan of Union were both written by ____.
22. The knack of northern colonists for solving
difficult problems is sometimes called
____.
23. A time when many people believed they
could improve themselves and their world
by careful study was known as the ____.
24. The first to grow indigo in America, ____
operated three large southern plantations.
25. The uprising known as ____ was the most
serious incident in the East-West conflict.

Essay (30 points)
Describe the triangular trade and explain why the northern colonists developed this system. Write at least one full paragraph, taking care to spell and punctuate correctly.

CHAPTER 4
Governing the American Colonies

As their colonies in America developed, the English worked out a system to govern and control them. The system applied to all the English colonies, not just those that eventually became the United States. Jamaica and Barbados in the West Indies, Bermuda, English possessions everywhere in the world, including its colonies in North America—all were part of one whole, the **British Empire.** The people of Massachusetts Bay may have felt a little closer to the people of Virginia than to the sugar planters of Jamaica, but the difference must have been small. All were English, and all were colonists. All recognized the same king, all flew the same flag.

ROYAL GRANTS AND CHARTERS
In theory the colonies belonged to the king himself, not to the English government. At one time the king owned all the land. He could dispose of it in whatever way he wished. Over the years, as we have seen, the kings established colonies in America in various ways. James I granted Virginia to the London Company in a kind of business deal. James gave the Company the right to look for gold and silver, and in return the Company was supposed to pay James one fifth of the gold and silver it found.

Charles II gave captured New Netherland to his brother, the Duke of York, as a present. He used Pennsylvania to pay off his debt to William Penn's father.

Each royal grant or charter was different from the others. But in every case the king remained the ruler, and his government supervised colonial affairs. The colonies remained English. They were not independent nations. England was an ocean away, but decisions made by the king and British lawmakers affected every colonist.

Of course, the kings did not personally manage the everyday affairs of the colonies. It is important to keep in mind that the colonies were much less important to the kings and to the English government than dozens of local matters. Colonial policy was set by the king's principal advisers, who made up what was called the **Privy Council.** *Privy* originally meant "private." A subcommittee of the council, the **Lords of Trade,** made the major decisions and handled particular colonial problems as they arose. At the same time the law-making

The Franklin Institute, Boston (photo Gabor Demjen)

body of England, **Parliament,** could and did pass laws that applied specifically to the colonies.

- Why could the king dispose of the American colonies in any way he wished?
- Which groups made policies that governed England's colonies in America?
- Which body passed laws to govern the colonies?

ENGLISH COLONIAL GOVERNMENT

There were also governments in each colony. These carried out the policies and enforced the laws of England and attended to all sorts of local matters that were of no direct concern to England. The colonial governments were modeled after the government of England. At the head of each colony was a **governor.** The governor was the chief executive. He represented the king. He was supposed to oversee the colonial government and make sure that the laws were executed, or enforced. Some governors were American born but most were English. Governors received orders and policy statements from London and put them into effect. When local problems arose, they decided what was to be done. For example, when Nathaniel Bacon raised a force to attack the Indians in Virginia, Governor Berkeley, on his own authority, ordered him to put down his arms.

Governors were assisted by **councils,** which had roughly the same powers and duties that the king's Privy Council had in England.

Benjamin Franklin stands at the bar of the English House of Commons in 1766 in this oil painting. Members of Parliament have assembled for Franklin's report from the American colonies. His red-robed questioner is Prime Minister George Grenville. The members of Parliament include Edmund Burke and William Pitt, both speakers for better treatment of the American colonies. What great whole was made up of all English colonies?

93

In most of the colonies members of the council were appointed, not elected by the voters. Councilors tended to be picked from among the wealthiest and most socially prominent people in each colony. This was true also of colonial judges.

Local laws were made by elected bodies. These **assemblies,** or legislatures, were modeled on the House of Commons in England. On paper their powers were strictly limited. Both the colonial governor and the government in England could disallow, or cancel, any law passed by an assembly. In practice the assemblies had a great deal of power because they controlled the raising of money by taxes and the spending of that money too. Governors could call the assemblies into session and dismiss them at their pleasure. They could order new elections, thus ending the terms of the legislatures. A governor could not, however, make the legislators pass any law they did not want to pass.

Because the assemblies had control over money, they could control the governor. They would refuse to spend money on projects the governor wanted unless he agreed to approve laws they wanted to enact. In extreme cases they could attach a sentence providing money for the governor's salary to a bill he had threatened to disallow. Then, if the governor disallowed the law, he got no pay!

■ Which groups assisted the governors of the English colonies?
■ How could assemblies control colonial governors?

LOCAL GOVERNMENT

Each town or community also had a governor of its own. In New England **townships** ran their affairs through what were called **town meetings.** Almost all citizens were entitled to take part in these gatherings. At the meetings they set the rate of town taxes, approved applications of new settlers for admission to the community, set aside land for the newcomers, hired teachers and ministers, and settled all kinds of local issues.

In the southern colonies local government was in the hands of **county courts.** These courts decided when and where to build roads, license taverns, raise taxes, try criminals, settle lawsuits. In general they oversaw all local matters. The chief officials of the county courts were **justices of the peace.** They were appointed by the governor.

The colonial system of government was quite well suited to the needs and wishes of all involved. The king and his advisers in London made the big decisions and appointed the people who put these decisions into effect. The colonists, however, were able to influence the decision makers in many ways. Purely local questions were left in the hands of the community. It was a complicated system, and often those who ran it were not efficient. But for about 150 years it

BUILDING SKILLS
IN SOCIAL STUDIES

Reading a Picture Graph

You may have heard the expression, "A picture is worth a thousand words." In this lesson you will find that a *picture graph* may also be worth a thousand words.

A graph is a visual way of arranging numbers, or *statistics*, to show what the numbers tell. In this graph small figures 👤 are used to make a simple comparison of the population of the American colonies in 1730. Each symbol stands for 10,000 persons. A partial 👤 figure represents a fraction of 10,000. For example, the population of Delaware in 1730 was 9,170 persons, so it is represented by part 👤 of a figure.

Use the graph on this page to answer the following questions:

1. What does this picture graph show?
2. Why doesn't the symbol 👤 represent one person?
3. Which two colonies had the largest populations in 1730? About how many people lived in each?
4. Which of the colonies had the smallest population in 1730? About how many people lived there?
5. Which colony was not founded in 1730?
6. Compute the total population of the northern colonies as closely as you can.
7. Compute the total population of the southern colonies as closely as you can.
8. Thinking back to your reading, why was the northern population larger than the southern population?
9. About how many colonists were there in 1730?
10. Explain how a colony's founding date may relate to its population.

POPULATION OF THE AMERICAN COLONIES 1730

NORTH		SOUTH	
New Hampshire	👤⌃	Maryland	👤👤👤👤👤👤👤👤⌃
Massachusetts	👤👤👤👤👤👤👤👤👤👤⚲	Virginia	👤👤👤👤👤👤👤👤👤👤👤⚲
Connecticut	👤👤👤👤👤👤⚲	North Carolina	👤👤👤
Rhode Island	👤👤	South Carolina	👤👤👤
New York	👤👤👤👤	Georgia	not founded
New Jersey	👤👤👤		
Pennsylvania	👤👤👤👤⌃		
Delaware	👤		

👤 = 10,000 persons   👤 = 6,000 persons

👤 = 8,000 persons   ⚲ = 4,000 persons

                 ⌃ = 2,000 persons

The town meeting depicted in this 18th-century engraving has gotten highly heated. No one knows what question brought out such strong emotions, but certainly these New Englanders valued their freedom to meet openly. What were some of the matters settled at these town meetings?

worked reasonably well. The raw materials of America flowed to England in exchange for manufactured goods. The colonies grew and prospered.

- Who handled local government in New England?
- Who handled local government in the southern colonies?

THE DOMINION OF NEW ENGLAND

Most colonists liked the fact that the British Empire was divided into so many separate units. It allowed each colony a great deal of control over its own affairs. English leaders felt differently. If they could combine the colonies into a few regional groups, it would be easier to manage them.

The most serious attempt to unify a group of colonies occurred after the death of Charles II in 1685. Since Charles had no children, his brother James, the Duke of York, became king. James was already proprietor of the colony of New York. In 1686 he created the **Dominion of New England.** As finally organized, the Dominion included New York, New Jersey, Connecticut, Rhode Island, Massachusetts, and New Hampshire. Sir Edmund Andros, a soldier who had formerly been governor of New York, was appointed governor of the Dominion.

All the colonies in the Dominion resented the loss of their independence. Moreover, the new governor was given enormous power. He could make laws on his own, including tax laws. Indeed, he ruled like a dictator, deciding by himself all questions of importance. The colonial assemblies ceased to meet.

Fortunately for the citizens of the Dominion, Andros's rule did not last very long. James II proved to be extremely unpopular in England. He ignored laws that Parliament had passed and adopted a strongly pro-Catholic policy that alarmed the many powerful Protestant groups in the nation. When his second wife, Queen Mary of Modena, gave birth to a son who would be raised a Catholic, the leaders of Parliament staged what was soon known as the **Glorious Revolution.** They invited James's daughter Mary, who was a Protestant, and her Dutch husband, William of Orange, to become joint rulers of England. James was so unpopular that he could not raise an army to put down the revolution. It was won without a shot being fired. William and Mary crossed over from the Netherlands in November 1688 to take the throne.

Sir Edmund Andros is the subject of this 17th-century oil portrait. He was governor of New York and later governor of the Dominion of New England. How much power did this governor have in the colonies?

Both, National Portrait Gallery, London

William and Mary ruled Britain after the Glorious Revolution of 1688. The oil painting of William III is dated 1677, and that of Mary II is undated but probably was painted at the time she became queen. Childless, these monarchs left no heirs to the throne of England. How did Parliament bring about the Glorious Revolution?

When news of the Glorious Revolution reached Boston the next April—the delay provides a good example of the slowness of communication between England and America—an angry crowd gathered. Andros and other Dominion officials were arrested. A council of leading citizens took over the government. The other colonies in the Dominion also revolted. Within a few weeks the Dominion had fallen apart.

Thereafter the English authorities gave up trying to unify the colonies. The new king, William III, had little interest in America.

He relied on the Lords of Trade to manage the colonies, but that committee was made up of weak and inefficient men. Local self-government once again flourished in America.

- ▨ Why did the English government want to combine the colonies into a few regional groups?
- ▨ What effect on the Dominion of New England did the Glorious Revolution have?

ENGLISH COLONIAL POLICY

The English did not give up the idea of regulating their American colonies. Colonies were supposed to be profitable. The English expected to add to their national wealth by developing and using American raw materials. They passed laws designed to control what the colonists produced and where they sold it. The object was to have the colonists concentrate on goods that England needed and to make sure that these goods were sold in England rather than in another country.

Another way of explaining English policy is to point out that all the European nations were trying to obtain as much gold and silver as possible. Gold and silver seemed at that time to be the true source of national power and wealth. Since neither England nor its colonies had gold or silver mines, England had to trade for these metals. Foreigners would pay gold and silver for English and colonial goods. The more the colonies could produce, the more there was to sell. Moreover, it was important to have what was called a **favorable balance of trade.** That is, England must sell more than it bought because every English purchase of foreign goods reduced the amount of gold and silver that could be held in the country.

In other words, trading goods for gold and silver was the key to prosperity. Trade, said Daniel Defoe, the author of *Robinson Crusoe,* was "the Wealth of the World." Colonies were helpful in making trade grow. That is why the Lords of Trade had been put in charge of them.

- ▨ How were the colonies supposed to be profitable for England?
- ▨ What was meant by a "favorable balance of trade"?

THE NAVIGATION ACTS

To make sure that the colonies raised the right products and sold them in the right places, Parliament passed many laws regulating colonial commerce. These laws were known as the **Acts of Trade and Navigation.** The first Navigation Act was passed in 1651. The last important one was not enacted until 1733. We need not consider each law separately because they were all part of one system, known as the **Old Colonial System.**

The Navigation Acts provided that all goods passing between England and the colonies must be carried in ships that had been built either in England or in its colonies. The owners of these vessels must be English or American. The captain and most of the crew must be English or American too. For example, a Boston merchant could own a ship made in London or Philadelphia and carry goods from Virginia to New York or to any port in England. But the merchant could not use a French-made ship for these voyages or hire a Dutch or Portuguese captain.

European goods could be brought into the American colonies *only* after being taken to England. American colonists could import French wine, for instance, but only after it had been brought to England. Once in England, of course, the wine could only be carried to the colonies in an English or colonial ship because of the first rule.

Colonial producers could sell certain products only within the British Empire. The names of these products were listed, or enumerated, in various ways. They were known as **enumerated articles.** Only goods that England needed but could not produce at home were enumerated. Sugar, tobacco, furs, naval stores, cotton, and the dye indigo were the most important enumerated articles. Many very important colonial products, such as fish and wheat, were not enumerated because England already had adequate supplies. Colonists could sell these products anywhere they could find a buyer.

Many British ships sailed out from Bristol, shown in this painting, on their voyages to explore and later colonize America during the 16th and 17th centuries. At the broad quay ships took on provisions or unloaded cargo from the colonies. What were some of the enumerated articles brought from America?

City of Bristol, Museum and Art Gallery

In addition, the English could buy enumerated products only from their own colonies. English sugar planters in the West Indies and tobacco planters in Virginia and Maryland could not sell their crops in France or Spain or Holland. In return English consumers could not buy sugar or tobacco raised in colonies controlled by the French, Spanish, or Dutch.

Parliament put restrictions on a few colonial manufactured products that competed with English goods. Exporting woolen cloth and fur hats was prohibited, although not their manufacture for local use. Late in the colonial period the construction of any new forges, or shops to make iron products, was outlawed. The English believed that these laws were perfectly fair to the colonists. They were trying to make their empire self-sufficient. If the colonies concentrated on producing raw materials that England needed, and if England concentrated on manufacturing, each would benefit. No precious gold or silver would have to be spent for foreign goods. The favorable balance of trade could be maintained.

The Navigation Act system worked quite well for more than a hundred years. The complicated triangular trade described in Chapter 3 did not conflict with it. The laws followed the natural trends of trade. The colonies were not well enough developed at this time to produce large amounts of manufactured goods. England, on the other hand, was by far the most efficient producer of manufactured goods in the world.

Moreover, the Navigation Acts were not enforced very strictly. Smuggling was common. America was far from England. It had a long coastline with many isolated harbors and tiny coves where small ships could slip in under cover of night and easily unload their cargoes of contraband goods.

For many years the English government did not try very hard to prevent smuggling. Most Americans obeyed the laws. England was getting all the colonial products it needed. It hardly seemed worth the effort and expense to stop shippers who tried to sneak past the British navy with a cargo of tobacco bound for Amsterdam, or with French wine or silk that had not been taken first to England.

Although American smugglers considered the Royal Navy their natural enemy, most colonists believed that the British army and navy were vital to their safety and well-being. Like children, the colonists were under the control of a mother country, and they needed its protection.

- What was the overall purpose of the Navigation Acts?
- What were enumerated articles?
- Why did the Navigation Act system work well for more than a hundred years?

READING PRACTICE IN SOCIAL STUDIES

Using Vocabulary Clues

Readers will sometimes come across terms that are new or unfamiliar. Very often these terms, whether a new word or a familiar word used in a new way, are found in a sentence that has its own *vocabulary clues*. These clues help you to understand the meaning of the new term.

For example, the term *Parliament* used by itself might not be familiar. However, this is how it appears at the beginning of Chapter 4: "At the same time the law-making body of England, **Parliament**, could and did pass laws that applied specifically to the colonies." Here the term is defined *in context* — that is, its meaning is made clear by its use in the sentence. Boldface type is used because Parliament is a new term in the book. It is set off by commas to show that Parliament is another way of saying "the law-making body of England."

Look closely at some of the ways the author of this book uses vocabulary clues. Oftentimes these clues come after a signal such as a mark of punctuation or a specific word. For example, the word *or* often signals a vocabulary clue. Early in the chapter you read, "The names of these products were listed, *or* enumerated, in various ways." Here *or* is a signal that enumerated is another way of saying "listed."

Boldface type in this book indicates a new and important term usually defined in the Glossary. Generally, new terms are also defined in context. For example, you read, "A subcommittee of the council, the **Lords of Trade**, made the major decisions and handled particular colonial problems as they arose." Using context clues alone and without looking in the Glossary at the back of the book, you know that the Lords of Trade were responsible for handling colonial problems.

Commas often signal vocabulary clues. You will read on page 109, "These import taxes, called **duties**, were not particularly high." Thus, duties are taxes on goods brought into a country. The word *duties* is in boldface type in the sentence, but it could also appear in italics, *duties,* or in quotation marks, "duties," or it could be signaled by commas only: Import taxes, duties, were collected under the Sugar Act of 1764.

Some new words are explained without being defined. In this chapter Sir Edmund Andros is described in this way: "Indeed, he ruled like a dictator, deciding by himself all questions of importance." Even if *dictator* is an unfamiliar word, you know that it means "a ruler who makes all important decisions by himself."

You will still want to use the Glossary and your dictionary to find the meanings of new words. But vocabulary clues can help you to find the meanings of words that may be right under your nose.

Each of the following sentences from Chapter 4 has a difficult new term italicized. Number your paper 1–5 and write the meaning of each term, using whatever vocabulary clues you find.

1. The British minister in charge of colonial affairs, Lord Hillsborough, ordered Massachusetts to *rescind,* or cancel, the Circular Letter.
2. Colonial policy was set by the king's principal advisers, who made up what was called the *Privy Council*. Privy originally meant "private."
3. In 1767 Charles Townshend, the *Chancellor of the Exchequer,* or finance minister, made another attempt to tax the colonists.
4. He was supposed to oversee the colonial government and make sure that the laws were *executed,* or enforced.
5. Moreover, it was important to have what was called a *favorable balance of trade.* That is, England must sell more than it bought because every English purchase of foreign goods reduced the amount of gold and silver that could be held in the country.

FRENCH AND ENGLISH WARS

From the time of the Glorious Revolution until the 1760s, England was almost constantly at war in Europe, always against France. Americans were involved in these wars because the French had also become a colonial power in North America.

The French, who had begun their explorations of America in 1524, did not build many permanent settlements in America. While the English were clearing land and planting crops along the Atlantic Coast, the French were ranging deep into the continent, hunting, trapping, and setting up trading posts where they bought furs from the American Indians.

Whenever war broke out in Europe between England and France, French and English colonists fought in America. It was difficult for them to get at each other because their posts and settlements in America lay far apart in the wilderness. Most of the battles consisted of sneak attacks and raids on frontier outposts. Relatively few colonists actually took up arms. Much of the fighting was done by Indians allied with one side or the other.

The first colonial conflict was known as King William's War. It went on with interruptions from 1689 to 1697. The French, with Indian support, attacked **Schenectady** in New York and a few villages in New England. American colonists responded by marching against Port Royal in Nova Scotia, which they captured and then lost. An attempted invasion of Canada failed miserably. When the war ended, the treaty of peace returned all captured territories to their colonial owners.

Both sides followed a similar strategy in Queen Anne's War, which began in 1702 and ended in 1713. France's Indian allies attacked several New England settlements and destroyed **Deerfield,** Massachusetts. The English colonists responded by making raids on Nova Scotian villages. Once again they captured Port Royal. Far to the south a force of Carolinians struck a blow at France's ally, Spain, by burning **St. Augustine,** Florida. The outcome of this war was decided in Europe, where England won a series of decisive victories. The Treaty of Utrecht in 1713 gave England control of Nova Scotia, Newfoundland, and Hudson Bay.

The third English-French clash in America, King George's War, lasted from 1744 to 1748. Once again Indians friendly to France crossed the St. Lawrence and attacked settlements in New England. New Englanders sailed north and captured **Louisbourg,** a fort on Cape Breton island that guarded the mouth of the St. Lawrence River. England fared badly in the European phases of this war. To the New Englanders' disgust Fort Louisbourg was given back to France at the peace conference ending the war.

The French and English wars involved few of the colonists. Still,

France's Indian allies are shown attacking Deerfield, Massachusetts, in this watercolor. It was painted as a diorama for a museum. In this raid Deerfield was destroyed. How did English colonists respond?

they increased tensions between settlers of both nations, who blamed each other for their troubles on the frontier.

- How were French colonies in America different from English colonies?
- What kinds of battles did the American colonists fight during the French and English wars?

THE FRENCH MENACE

Though considerable blood had been spilled between 1689 and 1748, neither England nor France had gained much from the other in America. In 1752 the French governor of Canada, the Marquis Duquesne de Menneville, ordered the construction of a new chain of forts running from Lake Erie south to the Ohio River, in what is now western Pennsylvania. These forts, Duquesne believed, would keep English fur traders and settlers from crossing the Appalachian Mountains into territory claimed by France.

Duquesne's action alarmed many people in the English colonies, none more so than Lieutenant Governor Robert Dinwiddie of Virginia. Dinwiddie, a Scot, had served in Barbados, Bermuda, and other colonies before being assigned to Virginia. He was very interested in buying land beyond the frontier, which could later be sold to settlers at a big profit.

When Dinwiddie learned what the French were doing, he sent a young planter and land surveyor named George Washington to warn them that they were trespassing on Virginia property. Washington was only 21 years old, but as a surveyor he knew the western land well. In November 1753 he set out with a party of six to find the French commander. After weeks of tramping through the icy western forests, Washington delivered Dinwiddie's message. But Duquesne rejected it with contempt.

In the spring of 1754, Dinwiddie sent another group of Virginians to build a fort where the Monongahela and Allegheny join to form the Ohio River. He also appointed Washington as lieutenant colonel of the Virginia militia and ordered him to lead a force of 150 soldiers to protect the new post against a possible French attack.

Before Washington could reach the Ohio, the French drove off the construction party and completed the post on their own, naming it **Fort Duquesne.** They occupied it with a force of about 600 men.

Washington should have turned back at this point or at least called for reinforcements. But he was young, ambitious, and headstrong. He marched straight toward Fort Duquesne. On the way he surprised a small French scouting party, killing their leader. The main French force then advanced against him. He set up a defensive post, Fort Necessity, but the French easily surrounded it. After an all-day attack Washington had to surrender. The French commander then allowed him and his men to go free. They returned to Virginia, leaving the disputed territory to the French.

- Why did the French order construction of a chain of forts from Lake Erie west through the Ohio Valley?
- Why was Washington not able to take Fort Duquesne from the French?

THE FRENCH AND INDIAN WAR

With Washington's retreat the war began in earnest. In all North America there were no more than 90,000 French settlers. The population of the English colonies was about 1.5 million. Thousands of British soldiers took part in the struggle. Yet for about two years the outnumbered French won all the battles. They were experts at forest warfare. Most of the Indians sided with them, for unlike the English the French colonists were mostly interested in the fur trade. They did not try to force the Indians to give up their lands or abandon their ways of life.

The British were not easily discouraged. The tide began to turn after a brilliant English politician, William Pitt, took over management of the war effort. In 1758 English troops finally captured Fort

"Britain's Glory, or the Reduction of Cape Breton" is the title given this engraving circulated in 1758. After King George's War, Louisbourg had been returned to France. Now the British fleet will avenge the loss. Cannonballs fly through the air as the British ships in the foreground advance toward the burning French warship at the front of the fort. What turned the tide of the French and Indian War?

Courtesy, New Brunswick Museum, Canada

The war that settled the future of North America began with a headstrong young colonel named George Washington holed up in a place called Fort Necessity.

Early in 1755 Major General Edward Braddock arrived in Virginia with two regiments of red-coated British soldiers. His orders were to drive the French out of Fort Duquesne. Braddock was a veteran with over 40 years in the British army. But his long military experience proved a disadvantage in America. Instead of moving swiftly along forest trails, guided by Indian scouts, he carved a road through the wilderness so that he could haul heavy cannon for the attack on the French.

Under such conditions surprise was impossible. As the troops approached Fort Duquesne, the French were ready for them. When Braddock's force of 1,400 men was passing through a narrow gulch about 8 miles (13 kilometers) from the fort, the woods suddenly exploded with gunfire. Redcoats fell by the hundreds. Panic spread among the survivors. Braddock fought bravely but finally went down, a bullet through his lungs.

Colonel Washington, who was serving under Braddock, miraculously escaped injury. A big man, well over six feet, he must have presented a tempting target as he tried to rally and organize the British soldiers. Two horses were shot out from under him. After he had finally led the 500 survivors back to safety, he discovered four bullet holes in his coat.

Washington's Escape

Washington/Custis/Lee Collection, Washington and Lee University

Duquesne. They changed its name to **Fort Pitt,** which is why the modern city on the site is named Pittsburgh.

Gradually other key French posts were taken. The most decisive battle occurred at the city of Quebec in 1759. Quebec is located on a cliff overlooking the St. Lawrence River. The British attack force, led by General James Wolfe, could not at first find a way to get up the cliff without being exposed to murderous fire.

Then one day Wolfe noticed some women washing clothes on the bank of the St. Lawrence. The next day he saw the same clothes hung out to dry on the cliff above. There must be a hidden path up the cliff! Wolfe investigated, found the path, and in the dead of night moved his army up to the city. There on a field called the **Plains of Abraham** the battle took place. Both Wolfe and the French commander, General Louis Joseph de Montcalm, were killed in the fight, which ended with the surrender of the city to the English.

By this time the conflict had spread throughout the world, including Europe, where it has been called the **Seven Years' War.**

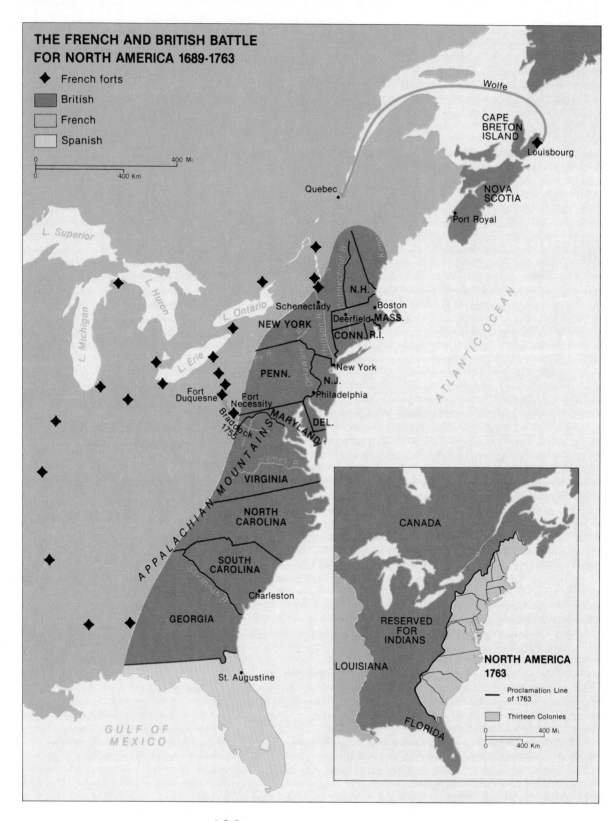

THE FRENCH AND BRITISH BATTLE
FOR NORTH AMERICA 1689-1763

◆ French forts
█ British
▢ French
░ Spanish

400 Mi.
400 Km.

Wolfe

CAPE
BRETON
ISLAND
◆ Louisbourg

NOVA
SCOTIA

Port Royal

Quebec

L. Superior

L. Michigan

L. Huron

L. Ontario

L. Erie

Schenectady

N.H.

Boston
MASS.

NEW YORK

Deerfield

CONN. R.I.

New York

PENN.

N.J.

Fort
Duquesne

Fort
Necessity

Philadelphia

MARYLAND

DEL.

Braddock
1755

APPALACHIAN MOUNTAINS

James R.

VIRGINIA

NORTH
CAROLINA

SOUTH
CAROLINA

Savannah R.

Charleston

GEORGIA

St. Augustine

GULF OF
MEXICO

ATLANTIC OCEAN

CANADA

RESERVED
FOR
INDIANS

LOUISIANA

FLORIDA

NORTH AMERICA
1763

—— Proclamation Line
of 1763

▢ Thirteen Colonies

400 Mi.
400 Km.

Everywhere the British were victorious. French outposts in Asia and Africa were captured. Spain entered the conflict on the side of France in 1761, only to see its colonies in Cuba and the Philippine Islands overwhelmed by the British.

When the war ended in 1763, the British were able to redraw the map of the world. Outside North America they were remarkably generous. They returned most of the lands they had conquered. France had to surrender Canada and all claims to the Ohio and Mississippi Valleys. Spain turned over Florida and the Gulf Coast as far west as the Mississippi River.

Nearly everyone in the English colonies in America was delighted with the outcome of the war. The French threat had been removed. Spain had been pushed back from the southern frontier. The way to the West lay open.

Although some of the colonies had contributed men and money to the conflict, British soldiers and sailors had done most of the fighting. The Royal Treasury paid most of the bills. Never did Americans feel more loyal to the king or more grateful to England than in 1763.

■ Why did France win most of the early battles in America?
■ What were the results of the French and Indian War?

Benjamin West painted "Death of General Wolfe" in 1770. The oil shows the general's last breath on the Plains of Abraham, where he was the victor in 1759. The French commander Montcalm died in the same battle. Which city in Canada was surrendered to the British after this battle?

National Gallery of Canada, Ottawa

107

POSTWAR PROBLEMS

As often happens after wars, peace brought new problems and caused new conflicts. The British government had borrowed huge sums during the war to pay its heavy costs. The new, larger empire would also be more expensive to maintain and defend. Where was the money to come from?

And how was the new, larger empire in America to be governed? The old system of thirteen separate colonies each controlled from London worked well enough when the colonies were separated from one another by thick forests. Now the wilderness was shrinking. Four colonies—Virginia, Pennsylvania, Connecticut, and Massachusetts—each claimed parts of the Ohio Valley just won from France. Each based its case on a royal charter drafted before anyone knew much about American geography. Who would untangle these conflicting claims?

There were also the Indians in the Ohio Valley. Everyone expected them to stop fighting when the French surrendered. Instead they organized behind Pontiac, a chief of the Ottawa, and tried to drive the whites back across the Appalachians. How could an area claimed by so many different colonies be defended? Who would pay the cost if British troops were used?

These last questions were the most pressing in 1763. The answers were that the British put down **Pontiac's Rebellion** and paid the cost of doing so. To keep the peace the British stationed 6,000 soldiers in the land won from the French and closed the entire region beyond the Appalachian Mountains to white settlers. This decision was announced in the **Proclamation of 1763.** Only licensed fur traders might enter the Ohio region. No one could purchase Indian lands.

Most American colonists did not like the Proclamation of 1763. It seemed to put the great West as far out of reach as it had been when the forts built by Governor Duquesne had first barred the way ten years earlier.

■ What was the purpose of the Proclamation of 1763? How did most American colonists react to it?

THE SUGAR ACT

The Proclamation of 1763 made sense as a temporary policy designed to make peace with the Indians and to buy time to untangle the complicated colonial claims in the Ohio Valley. The problem of governing the empire as a whole and paying the costs involved proved much more difficult.

In 1763 the British prime minister was George Grenville. Grenville had the mind of a bookkeeper: he saw the colonies in terms of money taken in, money spent. Running the colonies was expensive.

New York Public Library Rare Books Room

Most of the tax money collected in the colonies was also spent in the colonies. They were no longer so profitable for the mother country. In England taxes were high. In America taxes were low. To Grenville the conclusion was obvious: Parliament should raise the money to run the colonies by taxing the colonists.

The first of Grenville's tax measures was the **Sugar Act** of 1764. Under this law sugar, coffee, and a number of other products the colonists imported were to be taxed upon entry into any colonial port. These import taxes, called **duties,** were not particularly high. One of the most controversial, the duty on foreign molasses, actually reduced the existing molasses tax from sixpence a gallon to threepence.

The Sugar Act resembled many of the earlier laws regulating colonial trade. Actually it marked a drastic change in British policy. The old sixpenny tax on foreign molasses, put into effect by the Molasses Act of 1733, was not designed to raise money. It was passed to protect planters in the English sugar islands from foreign competition by making foreign molasses so expensive that no American would buy it. In other words, the tax was not supposed to be collected. The Molasses Act of 1733 was one of the Navigation Acts, part of the effort to make the Empire self-sufficient and hold down the importing of foreign products. However, a tax of only threepence a gallon would not be high enough to keep French molasses out of America.

Americans did not want to pay any new taxes. They were particularly alarmed by Grenville's determination to crack down on smugglers so that the new taxes could be collected. Remember that the Navigation Acts had never been strictly enforced. A merchant

At a French West Indian plantation sugar is being refined in a 1667 engraving by Jean Baptiste Duerte. Black slaves carry the sugar cane stems to the press, at upper right, where juice is squeezed out to be piped to the hut in the center. There the liquid is boiled until the sugar forms. The leftover liquid becomes molasses. How did the Molasses Act of 1733 protect planters in the English sugar islands?

who wanted to import French molasses could slip into a remote cove at night and bring his kegs ashore in small boats. If caught and brought to trial, a local jury would probably set him free. Or, more likely, he could pay bribes of about a penny a gallon to the customs officials and in perfect safety unload at his own wharf in broad daylight.

The Sugar Act contained regulations requiring shippers to file papers describing their cargoes in detail. Persons accused of smuggling could be tried in **admiralty courts,** where there were no juries and where the judges were stern British officials. If convicted, offenders lost both the cargo involved and the ship that carried it.

Americans disliked the Sugar Act, both for selfish reasons and because an important principle was involved. That they did not want to pay new taxes was understandable but hard to justify. The money raised was to be spent in the colonies and for the defense and development of the colonies. That the colonists should bear part of the expense of maintaining the Empire was certainly reasonable.

The moral principle behind their objection, however, was very important. Did Parliament have the right to tax people who had no say in the election of its members? *No,* most Americans answered. It was **taxation without representation.** People should be taxed only by legislative bodies they had themselves elected. The Sugar Act violated the laws of God and nature. Taxing people without their consent was little different from outright robbery. A Boston lawyer named James Otis put the issue clearly in his essay *The Rights of the British Colonies Asserted and Proved.* Colonists, being subjects of the king, had the same rights as his subjects in England. "No part of His Majesty's dominions can be taxed without their consent."

- How did Prime Minister Grenville propose to pay the high costs of administering the American colonies?
- For what two reasons did colonists dislike the Sugar Act?
- What is meant by taxation without representation?

THE STAMP ACT

Most colonists did no more than complain about the Sugar Act. Prime Minister Grenville moved ahead with his plans to raise money in America. In March 1765 Parliament passed another tax measure, the **Stamp Act.** This law taxed the use of all sorts of printed matter—deeds to land, marriage licenses, advertisements and handbills, newspapers, diplomas, customs documents, even packets of playing cards. Actual stamps or special stamped paper had to be purchased and used before any of these items could be sold.

Seldom has a political leader been so wrong about what the public would accept. When the terms of the law became known in

America, nearly all the colonists spoke out in opposition. The colonial assemblies wrote petitions urging that the law be done away with. They drafted stern resolutions denying Parliament's power to tax the colonies. A **Stamp Act Congress** attended by representatives of nine colonies met in New York and passed 14 polite but firm resolutions. Laws such as the Stamp Act, one resolution stated, "subvert the rights and liberties of the colonists."

The first open resistance to British authority now occurred. Groups calling themselves **Sons of Liberty** began to organize. These "Liberty Boys" believed in action rather than talk. Grenville had appointed a stamp master who was to receive the stamps and sell them to the public. In Boston the Liberty Boys stormed the house of stamp master Andrew Oliver even before he had received any stamps to sell. They broke his windows and made off with many of his valuables. Similar **Stamp Act Riots** erupted in other colonies. Many of the stamp masters found their very lives in danger. No one could safely distribute the hated stamps.

Essex Institute, Salem

This English teapot was probably made in 1766 at Derby to be sold in the colonies or to British who supported the American cause. How did the Liberty Boys protest the Stamp Act in Boston?

Metropolitan Museum of Art

These New Hampshire colonists are protesting the Stamp Act by throwing stones at the effigy of a stamp master. The mob taunts and jeers. At the left a mock funeral procession is formed. This wood engraving was done in 1829 by J. W. Barber. How were the stamp masters chosen?

Colonists also began to refuse to buy anything English until the law was repealed. A thousand merchants signed agreements not to import British goods. This **boycott** was effective because it hurt the business of exporters in England. They were soon urging Parliament to back down. Finally, since the law was not bringing a single penny into the treasury, Parliament repealed it.

■ How did the colonists react to the Stamp Act?
■ Why did Parliament repeal the Stamp Act?

THE DECLARATORY ACT

The issue was far from settled. The British were puzzled by the colonial argument against taxation without representation. Many older laws of Parliament applying to the colonies, such as the Molasses Act of 1733, had been tax laws. If representation was so important, what was the difference between the Stamp Act and any of the English laws that colonists had been obeying without argument for the past 150 years?

Furthermore, English leaders claimed, Parliament *did* represent the colonies. Every member of Parliament was said to represent every person in the Empire. The fact that no colonist sat in Parliament or voted for members seemed unimportant. Many thousands of people living in England could not vote for members of Parliament. Many parts of England, including some entire cities, were not represented in Parliament.

The members of Parliament did not think the colonists' objections were sincere. Nor did they want the repeal of the Stamp Act to seem like a surrender. They therefore passed the **Declaratory Act** at the same time that they repealed the Stamp Act. The act was only a statement of power, not an exercise of power. It had no specific effects. The colonies, it said, were "subordinate"—that is, under the control of Parliament. Parliament could pass *any* law regarding the colonies that it desired.

The colonists were so happy to learn that the Stamp Act had been repealed that they ignored the threat contained in the Declaratory Act. Still, they did not accept the principle that Parliament was supreme. When the colonies were tiny and isolated settlements struggling to survive, they had submitted to Parliament in return for aid and protection. By the 1760s the colonies were strong and solidly established. Like children, they were now growing up. The mother country no longer commanded their unquestioning obedience. If trouble was to be avoided, England would have to recognize that time had changed its relationship with its American offspring.

The Declaratory Act was not merely ill-advised. It was both untrue and unwise—untrue because the colonies were in fact no longer completely "subordinate," and unwise because by claiming that the colonies were subordinate, it was sure to encourage them to prove that they were not.

- How did Parliament answer the charge of taxation without representation?
- What did Parliament state in the Declaratory Act? Why was it passed?

THE TOWNSHEND ACTS

The Declaratory Act did nothing about Great Britain's need for money. In 1767 Charles Townshend, the Chancellor of the Exchequer, or finance minister, made yet another attempt to tax the colonists. Townshend was an attractive, witty person, the kind of man often described as clever. But he was short of common sense. Like many upper-class English of that time, he had a low opinion of colonists, whom he thought crude and rather dull.

If the colonists considered direct taxes like the stamp duties beyond Parliament's authority, Townshend reasoned, then let them pay **indirect taxes.** Taxes on imports collected from shippers and paid by consumers in the form of higher prices were indirect taxes. The Sugar Act taxes were an example. The colonists had not liked that law, but they had not done much about it but grumble.

British troops landed in Boston in 1768 to restore order. A sailor by the name of Christian Remick made this watercolor of the blockade of Boston Harbor. What was the spirit of the colonists at this time?

Massachusetts Historical Society

Townshend therefore proposed a number of additional tariffs on colonial imports. The **Townshend Acts** of 1767 taxed glass, lead, paper, paint, and tea—all things in everyday use that were not produced by the Americans. Like Grenville before him, Townshend also tried hard to collect the taxes. He appointed a Board of Customs Commissioners with headquarters in Boston to make it easier to enforce the law. The commissioners turned out to be greedy racketeers.

Under the law the customs officials received a third of the value of all ships and cargoes seized for violations. But these commissioners were not satisfied with what they could collect by enforcing the regulations strictly. They trapped merchants by allowing minor technical violations to go unpunished for a time and then cracking down when the merchants had grown used to doing business this way. They brought false charges of smuggling against shippers and paid witnesses to swear falsely to obtain convictions. When their thievery caused local citizens to riot against them, they demanded that the British government send troops to Boston to protect them against "the mob."

The colonists responded to the Townshend Acts and the greed of the customs commissioners by organizing another boycott. After all, no one could collect the taxes if no tea or glass or paint was imported. The Massachusetts legislature also sent a **Circular Letter** to the other colonial assemblies. No more taxation without representation, it said. Let us take action together.

The British minister in charge of colonial affairs, Lord Hillsborough, ordered Massachusetts to rescind, or cancel, the Circular Letter. When the legislature refused, he ordered it dissolved by the governor. He also transferred two regiments of British soldiers from the frontier to Boston.

▓ What is an indirect tax?
▓ How did the colonists respond to the Townshend Acts?

THE BOSTON MASSACRE

Before the French and Indian War, English troops had never been stationed in the colonies. Now, during peacetime, several thousand Redcoats were suddenly quartered in Boston. Tensions mounted. Most people in Boston did not hesitate to show their dislike for the soldiers, but they avoided violence. On March 5, 1770, serious trouble erupted. A squad of soldiers guarding the hated customs house was being taunted by a crowd of sailors, loafers, and small boys. Snowballs filled the air, harmless to the soldiers but infuriating. Suddenly the Redcoats began to fire into the crowd. When order was restored, three Americans lay dead on the ground. Two others died later of their wounds.

Museum of Fine Arts, Boston (Gift of Joseph W., William B., and Edward H. R. Revere)

Silversmith, engraver, firebrand, later hero of the Midnight Ride, Paul Revere was painted in oil by John Singleton Copley in 1765-70. He is shown musing over a piece of his handsome silver. Examples of Revere's work are displayed in many American museums. How is Revere best remembered?

The captain of the guards, Thomas Preston, and five of his men were arrested and accused of murder. A few Boston radicals, led by Sam Adams, now began to hint that the colonies should declare their independence. Adams was a founder of the local Sons of Liberty and one of the authors of the Massachusetts Circular Letter. Another radical, the silversmith Paul Revere, made and distributed an engraving of this **Boston Massacre** that portrayed Captain Preston commanding his sneering soldiers to fire at innocent, unarmed American civilians.

■ What British move led to the tensions that touched off the Boston Massacre?

Metropolitan Museum of Art

Unhappy Boston! begins the poem that is printed beneath this widely circulated engraving made by Paul Revere of "The Bloody Massacre." Captain Preston is shown at lower right, commanding his soldiers to fire. In fact the Redcoats were not in an orderly line, but this was fine propaganda for Boston radicals to circulate. The customs house is at the rear center. What prompted the British to fire?

THE CALM BEFORE THE STORM

Cooler heads prevailed. Sam Adams's cousin John Adams, a respectable lawyer, was a prominent Boston critic of British policy. Nevertheless, he came forward to defend the accused soldiers to make sure they had a fair trial. He eventually obtained their freedom.

Frustrated once again in its effort to raise money in America, Parliament repealed all the Townshend duties except the tax on tea. That

Boston radical Sam Adams is the subject of this fine 1771 oil by the great John Singleton Copley, who also painted Paul Revere, shown on page 114. Adams is pointing to the charter of Massachusetts. How was he a leader in the movement to declare America's independence?

tax was kept, not for the money it might bring, but to demonstrate that Parliament still claimed the right to tax the colonies.

The crisis seemed to have ended. Lord Hillsborough announced that the government would not try to raise any more money in America. Normal trade relations between the colonies and England resumed. Business was good. Colonial merchants even imported a good deal of tea, in most cases quietly paying the threepenny duty.

This period of calm hid a basic change in attitude in both Great Britain and in the colonies. Until the late 1760s few colonists had considered England unfair to them. Most were proud to be known as English. They might complain about this or that action of the government in London, but only in the way that citizens today may complain about their political leaders in Washington. Hardly anyone had thoughts of breaking away from England.

Still, the conflicts resulting from the Sugar, Stamp, and Townshend Acts did draw colonists together. Many began to fear that the English might try to take away their rights or destroy their liberty. This fear led them to cooperate more with people in other colonies. They recognized that they had common interests. During the calm following the repeal of the Townshend duties, the colonists were less fearful. Yet they remembered the heavy hand of the British. When new threats appeared, the colonists would readily join together to protect themselves.

The English leaders had failed to make Americans pay reasonable taxes for their own defense and administration. This struck a terrible blow to English pride. Unfortunately, the English could do nothing about it at the moment. Their frustration made them boil inside. They too would react differently—and forcefully—when a new crisis developed.

In the early 1770s most people who had lived through the turmoil of the previous ten years thought that the threat to the peace and stability of the British Empire had ended. Nearly all were genuinely relieved. Nearly all were convinced that no serious trouble would ever again disturb this happy state of affairs. Of course they were wrong. On both sides of the Atlantic people were ready in their minds for separation, whether they knew it or not. More and more they were thinking of those on the other side of the ocean as "them" rather than "us." John Adams had this in mind many long years later when he wrote, "The revolution was complete in the minds of the people, and the Union of the colonies, before the war commenced."

- What action did Parliament take to achieve calm after the Boston Massacre?
- How did the conflicts over the Sugar, Stamp, and Townshend Acts draw colonists together?

116

CHAPTER 4 REVIEW

Identification
Tell briefly why each of the following persons, terms, or events is important.
1. Sir Edmund Andros
2. Robert Dinwiddie
3. George Washington
4. William Pitt
5. James Wolfe
6. Pontiac
7. George Grenville
8. Charles Townshend
9. Samuel Adams
10. John Adams
11. Lords of Trade
12. Acts of Trade and Navigation
13. Fort Pitt
14. Proclamation of 1763
15. Sugar Act of 1764
16. Stamp Act
17. Stamp Act Congress
18. Sons of Liberty
19. Townshend Acts
20. Boston Massacre

Understanding American History
1. Explain how the colonies were governed from England.
2. What was the purpose of the Navigation Acts?
3. Why did most Indian tribes side with the French rather than the English?
4. What were three outcomes of the French and Indian War?
5. What actions did the British take in ending Pontiac's Rebellion and in the Proclamation of 1763?
6. Why did the colonists think the Sugar Act of 1764 and other British tax laws unfair?
7. What was the Declaratory Act? Why did Parliament pass this law?
8. How did the colonists respond to the Townshend Acts of 1767?
9. How did the conflicts that resulted from the Sugar, Stamp, and Townshend Acts help to unite the colonists?
10. Explain what John Adams meant when he wrote, "The revolution was complete in the minds of the people . . . before the war commenced."

Activities
1. With your classmates prepare a diagram to show how the American colonies were governed from Britain. On another diagram show colonial governments in America. On a third diagram show local government in New England and in the South.
2. Prepare a chart with a column headed *Cause* and a column headed *Effect* to show the consequences of British actions from the Proclamation of 1763 to the Boston Massacre of 1770. Include the following example in your chart:

Cause	Effect
Townshend Acts ⟶	Greedy customs officials cause local riots
	Colonists organize a boycott
	Massachusetts legislature sends Circular Letter

3. Use your historical imagination to pretend that you were one of the British soldiers accused of the Boston Massacre. Write a letter to your family in England to give your eyewitness account and to present your side of the story.
4. Use your historical imagination to pretend that you and your classmates are members of Parliament in 1763. Hold a spirited discussion on the question, "How should the American colonies be governed?"
5. With several classmates prepare a skit in which you attend a meeting of the Sons of Liberty. What actions of the British upset you? What actions of your own might you take? Have at least one member argue for proceeding with caution.

CHAPTER 4 TEST

Matching (20 points)
Number your paper 1–10 and match the person or group in the second column with the place or event in the first column.

1. Ohio Valley rebellion
2. Fort Necessity
3. Glorious Revolution
4. Boston Massacre
5. French forts
6. Sugar Act
7. Plains of Abraham
8. Dominion of New England
9. Boston Massacre engraving
10. Stamp Act riots

a. Captain Thomas Preston
b. Prime Minister George Grenville
c. Governor Edmund Andros
d. General James Wolfe
e. Colonel George Washington
f. Sons of Liberty
g. William and Mary
h. Pontiac
i. Marquis Duquesne
j. Paul Revere

Cause and Effect (20 points)
Number your paper 11–15 and match the cause in the first column with the effect in the second column.

11. Navigation Acts
12. French and Indian War
13. Boston Massacre
14. Stamp Act
15. Proclamation of 1763

a. Caused the British to raise taxes in the colonies
b. Angered colonists who wanted to move West
c. Increased hatred toward British soldiers
d. Angered merchants, who could not trade freely
e. Led to a boycott of British goods

Completion (30 points)
Number your paper 16–25 and next to each number write the words from the list below that best complete each sentence.

Parliament
justice of the peace
Navigation Acts
Sugar Act
king

enumerated articles
townships
governor
duties
county courts

All colonies in the British Empire belonged in theory to the __16__. Within each colony there was a __17__ who was the chief representative of the crown. He was supposed to make sure that the laws passed by __18__ were followed.

In New England local governments were organized by __19__, while in the southern colonies local governments were called __20__. The chief official in the South was the __21__.

Parliament controlled the shipping of goods from the colonies by the __22__. Further, colonial producers could sell only __23__ within the British Empire. Import taxes, called __24__, were levied on such products as sugar, coffee, and molasses. Most Americans resented this __25__ of 1764.

Essay (30 points)
Write at least one paragraph giving the British reasons for taxing their American colonies and write at least one paragraph giving the American argument against taxation. Take care to spell and punctuate correctly.

UNIT ONE TEST

Multiple Choice (20 points)
Number your paper 1–5 and write the letter of the phrase that best completes each sentence.

1. The cultures of the first Americans changed as they spread across the land because of
   a. reaction to Europeans.
   b. religion.
   c. environment.
   d. language.
2. The first English colonies in America were
   a. along the Atlantic Coast.
   b. in Canada.
   c. in Mexico.
   d. near the Mississippi River.
3. Working people in the colonies were treated better than in England because
   a. colonial employers were kinder persons.
   b. workers in England were lazy.
   c. colonial workers were more skilled.
   d. workers were scarce in the colonies.
4. The triangular trade was important to northerners because
   a. they wanted to trade farm products.
   b. they wanted to buy English manufactured goods.
   c. they didn't have enough slaves.
   d. the king ordered them to trade more.
5. The main quarrel between the British and the colonists was over
   a. slavery.
   b. the colonists' treatment of the Indians.
   c. Britain's right to tax the colonists.
   d. the colonists' friendship with France.

Chronological Order (25 points)
Number your paper 6–10 and place the following events in order by numbering 1 for the first, 2 for the second, and so on.
6. France loses its colonies in North America.
7. Jamestown settlers face a starving time.
8. Spain establishes colonies in the Americas.
9. Pilgrims come to America for religious freedom.
10. Bloodshed occurs in the Boston Massacre.

Matching (25 points)
Number your paper 11–15 and match the person in the second column with his or her description in the first column.
11. Expelled from Massachusetts for religious beliefs
12. A radical who founded a Boston chapter of the Sons of Liberty
13. British leader who tried to increase taxes in the American colonies
14. Conqueror of the Aztecs
15. A strong leader of the Jamestown colonists

a. John Smith
b. Hernán Cortés
c. George Grenville
d. Anne Hutchinson
e. Sam Adams

Essay (30 points)
Look as far back as you can in the history covered in Unit One to determine for yourself the events that brought the colonies to the eve of war in the 1770s. Describe a number of these events in a short essay, taking care to spell and punctuate correctly.

UNIT TWO

1770   1771   1772   1773   1774   1775   1776

COMMON SENSE;

1773 — Boston Tea Party

1774 — First Continental Congress

1775
- Lexington and Concord
- Second Continental Congress
- Washington takes command

1776
- *Common Sense*
- Declaration of Independence
- Mission Dolores (San Francisco) founded

Northwest Ordinance
-
Constitutional Convention

Constitution ratified

Washington elected President

Bill of Rights adopted

1785   1786   1787   1788   1789   1790   1791

THE AMERICAN NATION

1777 **1778** **1779** **1780** **1781** **1782** **1783** **1784**

Winter at
Valley Forge

Treaty of
Alliance with
France

Cornwallis
surrenders at
Yorktown
•
Los Angeles
founded

Peace of Paris

1792 **1793** **1794** **1795** **1796** **1797** **1798** **1799**

Neutrality
Proclamation

Adams elected
President

XYZ Affair

Alien and
Sedition Acts

CHAPTER 5
The War for American Independence

THE TEA ACT

The calm before the storm of the revolution ended in 1773. In May of that year Parliament passed a law known as the **Tea Act.** This law was designed to help the British East India Company, which was in very bad shape. After its founding in 1690, the **East India Company** had prospered, bringing riches to its stockholders and employees by its trade with India. But by 1773 the Company had fallen upon hard times. King George III and Parliament felt that something must be done to revive the Company's fortunes.

One of the chief products of the East India Company was tea. In 1773 it had about 17 million pounds (7.65 million kilograms) of unsold tea stored in English warehouses. Normally the Company sold its tea at auction in London to wholesale merchants. The merchants then sold the tea to English storekeepers or to American wholesalers, who in turn sold it to retail merchants in the colonies. These merchants sold the tea to the colonists. The tea was taxed first in England and then again—the threepenny Townshend duty—in the colonies.

The Tea Act authorized the East India Company to sell tea directly to American retailers. This would eliminate the handling charges and profits of both British and American wholesalers. In addition, the act repealed the English tax on tea so that only the Townshend tax remained.

Frederick, Lord North, who had become prime minister of England in 1770, assumed that the colonists would not object to the Tea Act. The cost of tea would be greatly reduced for Americans, and opposition to paying the Townshend duty had been gradually dying out. Now, with the price much lower because of the elimination of the middlemen's profits and the English tax, surely the colonists would not mind paying the threepenny charge. East India tea, even with the tax, would be as cheap as tea from the Dutch East Indies, which smugglers were selling in America. Many people thought the prime minister's reasoning made sense.

The East India Company promptly shipped 1,700 chests containing about 500,000 pounds (225,000 kilograms) of tea to its agents in Boston, New York, Philadelphia, and Charleston.

Contrary to Lord North's hopes, news of the Tea Act caused great resentment in the colonies. What bothered most people was not only the tea tax but the fact that Parliament had given an English company what amounted to a monopoly of the tea trade in America. American importers of English tea would be cut out of the business. Even smugglers of foreign tea could not beat the Company's price. Both groups were furious.

Other merchants were nearly as angry. If Parliament could give the East India Company a monopoly of the tea business, could it not give other monopolies to the Company or to any other favored group? If that happened, one excited Philadelphian warned, "every Tradesman will groan under dire Oppression."

The American merchants were very influential people. No doubt their dislike of the Tea Act affected how other citizens responded to it. Ordinary people rarely protest when the cost of living goes down. Yet in this case they did. The strength of the public reaction showed how mistrustful the Americans were of the British by 1773.

The Tea Act seemed part of a devilish plot to make the colonies totally subordinate to England. Had not Parliament itself revealed that intention in the Declaratory Act back in 1766? Only recently, in 1772, the British government had begun to pay the salaries of colonial governors. Now the governors were no longer dependent upon the colonial assemblies, which had been able to threaten not to pay governors who disregarded colonial opinion. For years English leaders had been complaining about the high cost of governing the colonies. Why were they now taking on an additional expense? Many Americans believed that Lord North and his associates intended to crush local self-government in America.

■ What was the purpose of the Tea Act? Why did the British think the colonists would be pleased with the Act? Why did the colonists resent it?

THE BOSTON TEA PARTY

When the ships carrying the East India Company's tea began to arrive in American ports, public protest rose to new heights. The ship *London* arrived in Charleston, South Carolina, on December 2. An angry crowd gathered and persuaded the Company agent who was to receive the tea to resign. The tea was brought ashore and stored in a warehouse, but it could not be sold. In Philadelphia and New York public feeling was so strong that the captains of the tea ships did not dare unload. Instead they sailed back to England.

In Boston, however, an explosive situation developed when the tea ship *Dartmouth* tied up in the harbor on November 27. The governor of Massachusetts, Thomas Hutchinson, was determined to en-

The Granger Collection

Townspeople dressed as Mohawks dump chests of East Indies tea from one of the ships in Boston Harbor. In this early, hand-colored wood engraving some citizens of Boston watch from the pier on the right. What caused this famous protest?

force the law. Hutchinson was American born. He had opposed all the British efforts to tax the colonies after the French and Indian War. But he believed that Parliament had the *right* to tax the colonies and to pass laws like the Tea Act.

Over the years Hutchinson had become the chief target of the Boston Sons of Liberty and of Sam Adams in particular. His house had been looted by rioters during the Stamp Act crisis. It was he who had announced, with obvious pleasure, the alarming news that the English had decided to pay the salaries of colonial governors.

Now Hutchinson stood firm. With his support the East India agents in Boston refused to resign. Customs officers denied the captains of tea ships permission to leave the port. For more than two weeks tension mounted in the town. Crowds milled in the streets. Sam Adams and other radicals stirred public feeling at mass meetings.

Finally, on the night of December 16, Adams gave the signal to a group of townspeople disguised as Mohawks. They boarded three tea ships and dumped the tea chests into the harbor. Tea worth about £15,000, a considerable fortune, was destroyed while a huge crowd watched silently from the shore.

- What were Thomas Hutchinson's views on England's policies toward the colonists?
- How did members of the "tea party" disguise themselves?

THE COERCIVE ACTS

The **Boston Tea Party** was, as the name suggests, a kind of celebration in the eyes of those who participated in it. In British eyes (and, it must be admitted, to any unprejudiced observer) it was a serious crime. Obviously it had been carefully planned. The "Mohawks" had gathered at the home of Benjamin Edes, editor of the Boston *Gazette*, to put on their costumes and await Sam Adams's signal.

When the news reached England, government leaders were furious. Parliament promptly passed a series of laws to force Massachusetts to pay for the tea.

The first of these laws, known as the **Coercive Acts,** was the Boston Port Act. It provided that no ship could enter or leave Boston harbor until the town had paid for the tea. The second, the Administration of Justice Act, gave the governor power to transfer the trials of soldiers and royal officials accused of serious crimes to courts outside of Massachusetts. This would be done when the governor felt that a fair trial could not be had in the colony.

The third law, the Massachusetts Government Act, further increased the governor's power by giving him control over town meetings, and it replaced the elected colonial council with a council appointed by the king. Another law, not directly related to the Tea Party but equally disliked by the colonists, ordered citizens to house British soldiers in their homes. A general, Thomas Gage, commander of British troops in America, replaced Thomas Hutchinson as governor of Massachusetts. Hutchinson promptly set sail for England to report to the king. He never returned to America.

Many Americans who had been critical of British policies spoke out against the Tea Party as an unnecessary act of violence. But the Coercive Acts angered and frightened everyone. To punish the entire community because some tea had been destroyed by extremists was the act of tyrants. Benjamin Franklin wrote that if the English government wanted to make up for the East India Company's loss, it ought to pay the money itself. It could subtract the sum from the far larger amount it had "extorted" from the colonies by its many illegal policies.

The Americans called the Coercive Acts the **Intolerable Acts.** The two names reflect the two views of the crisis. To the British the time had come to *coerce*, or force, the colonists into obedience. To the colonists the use of such force was *intolerable*—more than they could be expected to put up with.

   How did Great Britain react to the Boston Tea Party?

THE FIRST CONTINENTAL CONGRESS

Lord North hoped to accomplish two things by punishing Massachusetts so severely. One was to frighten the other colonies into accepting more British control over their affairs. The other was to tempt the other colonists to take advantage of Massachusetts's suffering. Ships that could not unload at Boston could unload at New York or Philadelphia or Baltimore to the benefit of those towns.

Lord North was assuming that the colonies were still separate societies. He was quite mistaken. Even before the Tea Act, radicals in

Boston had formed a **Committee of Correspondence** to keep in touch with radicals elsewhere in Massachusetts and in the other colonies. A network of such committees existed by the time news of the Coercive Acts reached America. Almost without intending to, these committees were becoming an informal central government, a kind of United States waiting to be born.

The leaders of the other colonies did not even consider taking advantage of Massachusetts's misfortune. When the Massachusetts committee sent out a message in June 1774 calling for a meeting of colonial leaders, all but Georgia sent delegates. In September these delegates gathered in Philadelphia for what we now call the **First Continental Congress.**

The Congress took a firm but moderate position. It condemned the Intolerable Acts, and it urged full support for the citizens of Boston. It passed resolutions demanding the repeal of all the British laws aimed at raising money in the colonies. Only the colonial assemblies, it declared, had the right to tax Americans. The delegates denounced the British practice of maintaining an army in the colonies in peacetime. The Congress also set up a **Continental Association** to enforce a ban on importing British products of all kinds.

No one spoke openly about independence. Indeed, the delegates sent off a "loyal address" to George III, asking him politely to help them in their struggle for the rights of English subjects. Yet the Congress concluded its session in October with this stern warning: "We have *for the present* only resolved to pursue . . . peaceable measures." Then they adjourned, agreeing to meet again the following May if their demands had not been met.

- What did Lord North hope to accomplish by punishing Massachusetts so severely?
- How did Lord North misjudge the other colonies?
- What actions did the First Continental Congress take?

LEXINGTON AND CONCORD

Meanwhile, in Massachusetts hatred of the Intolerable Acts had turned the colony into an armed camp. General Gage ruled in Boston, supported by his regiments of Redcoats. Outside the city no British law could be enforced. With the colonial legislature no longer functioning, local groups calling themselves **Patriots** took over. In the towns and villages citizens began to form militia companies. These civilian-soldiers could soon be seen drilling on town commons all over the colony. They were called **Minute Men** because they were supposed to be ready for action on a moment's notice.

Parliament now declared Massachusetts to be in a state of rebellion. The government decided to send more Redcoats to General

These American soldiers were drawn for a 1770s *broadside*, a printed handout. Broadsides were sometimes given out as recruiting posters. What name was given to local civilian-soldiers?

Gage in Boston and ordered him to "arrest and imprison" the radical leaders. On the night of April 18, 1775, Gage sent a force of 700 men commanded by Lieutenant Colonel Francis Smith to seize a supply of weapons that the Patriots had gathered at **Concord,** a town about 15 miles (24 kilometers) west of Boston. On the way the troops could also arrest Sam Adams and the merchant John Hancock, another Patriot leader, who were at **Lexington.**

When the British troops set out, Paul Revere, who had made the engraving of the Boston Massacre, and another Patriot, William Dawes, rode ahead to rouse the countryside. Revere reached Lexington at midnight and warned Adams and Hancock to flee. Dawes reached the town about half an hour later. They then rode on toward Concord, accompanied by Dr. Samuel Prescott, a young man from Concord who had been visiting a lady in Lexington. Revere and Dawes were captured by a British patrol. Prescott escaped by jumping his horse over a stone wall, and he got to Concord in time to warn the people of the coming attack.

The British advance guard under Major John Pitcairn reached Lexington at dawn. Before them, lined up on the common, were some 70 Minute Men. The group included a number of men in their sixties as well as youngsters in their teens. Such a tiny force could not hope to stop the Redcoats.

The Minute Men at Lexington fall before the Redcoats led by Major John Pitcairn on April 19, 1775. This is the first of a series of hand-colored engravings by Amos Doolittle. How many Minute Men faced the 700 Redcoats?

Major John Pitcairn (with spyglass) and Lieutenant Colonel Francis Smith are in the foreground of this hand-colored engraving by Amos Doolittle. Behind them the Redcoats march into Concord. What fate awaited these Redcoats on their march back to Boston?

Major Pitcairn rode forward and with a sneer ordered the Minute Men to move off. They were about to do so when someone fired a shot. British accounts say it was an American, American accounts blame a British soldier. More shots followed, and suddenly the Redcoats, "so wild," as one witness put it, "they could hear no orders," fired a volley directly into the American line.

When the smoke cleared, eight Minute Men lay dead. Ten other Americans and one Redcoat were wounded. The Britishers then marched on to Concord. They managed to occupy the town and destroy whatever supplies the Americans had not carried off or hidden.

It was now mid-morning. The Redcoats had been on the march since midnight. Outside Concord, Minute Men from every nearby town were rapidly gathering. One group drove back three British infantry companies guarding Concord's **North Bridge.** Two more Americans were killed in this skirmish, but three Redcoats also fell. Colonel Smith decided to head back to Boston.

The march back was like a trip through the corridors of Hell. All along the route American snipers peppered the weary Redcoats with bullets. Hundreds and hundreds of local citizens picked up their muskets and followed the sound of gunfire to join in the fight. By the time the British were safely back in Boston, they had suffered 273 casualties. American losses came to just under 100.

■ Why did Parliament declare Massachusetts to be in a state of rebellion?

■ Why were British troops sent to Concord?

Albany Institute of History and Art

BREED'S HILL

The **War for American Independence** had begun. Within 48 hours nearly 20,000 angry American militiamen had gathered in and around Cambridge, across the Charles River from Boston. The new **Massachusetts Provincial Assembly** appointed Artemas Ward, a veteran of the French and Indian War, to command this large force. Ward, however, was not a good organizer. Militiamen from other New England colonies had their own commanders. Everywhere there was confusion.

Fortunately the one important British force in America was penned up in Boston. In May militiamen from Connecticut and Massachusetts took **Fort Ticonderoga** on Lake Champlain, capturing some valuable heavy cannon. Then, on June 16, the Americans occupied **Bunker Hill** and **Breed's Hill,** two high points in Charles Town, a peninsula across the harbor from Boston. Working all night, they built an earthen *redoubt,* or fort, on Breed's Hill.

From this strong point cannon would be able to pound Boston and the British warships in the harbor. The British realized at once that they must clear the Americans from this position or abandon the city.

Three weeks earlier, three leading English generals had arrived in Boston to advise Gage. One of them, Major General William Howe, a veteran of King George's War and the French and Indian War, was assigned the task of driving the Americans back. Howe was a brave man and a skillful soldier. It was he who had led General Wolfe's advance guard during the surprise attack at Quebec in 1759.

American snipers in the foreground fire upon a retreating brigade of Redcoats led by Lieutenant Colonel Francis Smith. This is another in Amos Doolittle's series of hand-colored engravings. The burning houses are in Lexington. What were the British and American losses in these battles?

129

CHARLES TOWN

BOSTON

Smoke fills the skies over Breed's Hill and Bunker Hill under British attack. This oil painting is called "Attack on Bunker Hill with the Burning of Charles Town." However, the real battle is being fought on Breed's Hill, which the Redcoats are attempting to scale. What use did the British make of the barges in the bay?

On the morning of June 17, Howe ferried 1,500 Redcoats across the bay on barges. He himself led one force around the base of Breed's Hill, hoping to cut off the Americans' retreat and attack their position from the rear. The rest of the Redcoats, commanded by Brigadier General Robert Pigot, marched straight up Breed's Hill. They advanced in three broad lines, pushing through tall grass and climbing over fences as they went.

It was a dramatic sight. Across the bay hundreds of Bostonians watched the brewing battle from their windows and rooftops. The Americans on Breed's Hill were tired and hungry after their night's labor with spades and shovels. Fresh troops were supposed to relieve them, but none arrived. The inexperienced civilian soldiers now faced hardened professional troops—skilled British bayonet fighters eager to avenge the bloody retreat from Concord.

The Americans knew how to shoot, and their commander, Colonel William Prescott, knew how to maintain discipline. Legend

130

has it that the men were told not to fire until they could see the whites of the enemy's eyes. The British came on, firing with no effect against the earthen wall of the redoubt. They were prepared to take losses until they could scale the wall and end the battle with their bayonets. When the British were almost to the wall, Prescott gave the signal. A wall of flames erupted as the Americans fired. The heavy musket balls tore through the British lines. A second volley sent the Redcoats back down the hill in confusion. The field before the redoubt was littered with dead and dying men.

Meanwhile, General Howe's force had met a similar fate in front of an American defense line along the shore. Both British generals then regrouped and sent their brave soldiers forward once more against the American defenses. Once more they were thrown back.

Instead of landing behind the two hills as he could easily have done, Howe had probably attacked the Americans directly to shock them. He thought the untrained colonials would turn and run when faced by his disciplined veterans. Once the Redcoats had taken the hill by direct assault, the weakness and cowardice of the defenders would be exposed. The rest of the rebel army would melt away and the war would be over. After all, American militiamen had proved very poor soldiers in earlier wars. Howe's former commander, General Wolfe, had described the American soldiers attached to his command during the French and Indian War as "the dirtiest, most contemptible cowardly dogs you can conceive."

After two charges Howe knew that he had made a terrible mistake. Now he *had* to take the hill or face a defeat that would shatter morale. Reinforced by fresh troops, the Redcoats advanced up the hill for the third time. Inside the redoubt the Americans were almost out of ammunition. Those who had no more bullets loaded their muskets with nails and pieces of glass. Their last volley tore fresh holes in the British line. Then the Redcoats were over the wall.

Now American blood flowed freely as the veteran Redcoats proved their skill in hand-to-hand fighting. Among those killed was Dr. Joseph Warren, leader of the Massachusetts Patriot government.

The battle ended with the British in control of the vital high ground. For some reason it has been remembered as the **Battle of Bunker Hill** rather than Breed's Hill. Over a thousand English soldiers were dead or wounded, more than four out of every ten in the battle. About a hundred Americans were killed. Three hundred more were wounded or taken prisoner. Most of the American casualties came after the men had used up their ammunition.

- Why did the Americans occupy Bunker Hill and Breed's Hill?
- What were the strengths and weaknesses of both sides at Breed's Hill?

THE SECOND CONTINENTAL CONGRESS

Lexington, Concord, and Bunker Hill had been fought by Massachusetts with some help from neighboring New England colonies. The rest of the colonies were now to enter the conflict. In May the **Second Continental Congress** met in Philadelphia. Some of the most important men in America had been elected delegates. Others not yet well known would soon become important. The Massachusetts radicals Sam Adams, John Adams, and John Hancock were there. So was Benjamin Franklin of Pennsylvania. Virginia sent its fiery orator Patrick Henry, who had just urged the arming of the Virginia militia in a speech ending with the sentence, "I know not what course others may take; but as for me, give me liberty or give me death!" Virginia was also represented by George Washington, well known for his role in the French and Indian War, and by a young lawyer named Thomas Jefferson. Jefferson had recently attracted attention by writing a pamphlet, *A Summary View of the Rights of British America*, in which he argued that kings should be "the servants of the people," not their masters.

Not all the delegates took such extreme positions. The Congress proceeded cautiously. It sent an **Olive Branch Petition** asking the king to protect them against Parliament. (An olive branch is a symbol

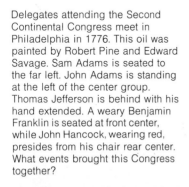

Delegates attending the Second Continental Congress meet in Philadelphia in 1776. This oil was painted by Robert Pine and Edward Savage. Sam Adams is seated to the far left. John Adams is standing at the left of the center group. Thomas Jefferson is behind with his hand extended. A weary Benjamin Franklin is seated at front center, while John Hancock, wearing red, presides from his chair rear center. What events brought this Congress together?

Historical Society of Pennsylvania

Courtesy, The Henry Francis du Pont Winterthur Museum

George Washington in 1782 with his white horse. John Trumbull painted this oil in 1790. In which earlier war was Washington a fighter?

of peaceful intentions.) The next day it issued a "Declaration of the Causes and Necessity of Taking Up Arms." Earlier, on June 15, two days before the Battle of Bunker Hill, Congress had created an official American army and appointed George Washington as its commander in chief.

Washington looked like a general. He was over six feet tall, strong, a fine athlete, yet dignified and reserved. His bravery in battle had been demonstrated in the western wilderness on the day the French ambushed General Braddock. Yet Washington was also known for his sound judgment and his sense of responsibility. He was the kind of person people trusted and respected from the first meeting.

Actually, Washington had much to learn about warfare and running an army. The other possible commanders, however, knew still less. The fact that Washington was from Virginia, the most powerful of the southern colonies, was another reason why he was chosen. The appointment symbolized the union of the colonies that was rapidly taking place.

133

Martha Dandridge Custis married
George Washington in 1759. "Dear
Patsy" he called her. He carried
this miniature with him while he
fought the Revolutionary War. It
was painted by Charles Wilson
Peale in about 1776. Peale made
the fine portrait of Washington
on page 105. Why did marriage
make it possible for Washington
to refuse a salary as commander
in chief?

Washington accepted the assignment eagerly and set out at once
for Massachusetts. It was typical of the man that he refused to take a
salary. Of course, he could afford not to be paid. He was married to
Martha Custis Washington, one of the richest women in America.

- What was the mood of the Second Continental Congress?
- What were Washington's major assets as a general?

THE AMERICAN ARMY

When Washington arrived outside Boston on July 2, 1775, he found
himself in charge of an army of about 14,000 men. Some were living
in dormitories on the campus of Harvard College. Others were in
private homes. A few units had set up tents. Nearly all the men wore
their ordinary outdoor clothing. There were no American uniforms.
The soldiers even had to supply their own guns. Most of them were
armed with muskets, a weapon that fired a round bullet with murderous effect at close range. Beyond 50 yards (about 46 meters) it
was wildly inaccurate. Some soldiers had only spears or axes. Gunpowder and cannon were very scarce.

There was very little discipline. Men commanded by leaders like
Colonel Prescott, the hero of Breed's Hill, made good soldiers. Those
with lazy or cowardly officers seldom performed well. Most units
had elected their own officers and made a point of treating them as
equals rather than as their superiors. This was not a force for military
efficiency.

Washington was very unhappy with the army he found. As a
southern planter and slave owner he was accustomed to ordering men
about and being obeyed. He set out at once to turn what he called
"this mixed multitude" into his own idea of an army. He made the
men build barracks and taught them to march in step. He weeded out
officers who could not maintain discipline. Any soldier found drunk
was given a good whipping.

Then Washington sought to persuade the men to sign up for a
year's service in the new Continental Army. Only about 10,000 did
so. Many had families to support at home. Moreover, Washington's
stern discipline was not popular with many units. Officers in this
army were appointed, not elected. Washington chose mostly men like
himself from the upper classes of society. He believed that ordinary
soldiers would obey their "betters" more readily than people of their
own level. There were 28 regiments, each with 8 companies of about
90 men. Units from the more distant colonies arrived, and gradually
a national army emerged.

- What was the condition of the American army when Washington took command? What changes did he make?

Rifle companies from the southern colonies were particularly impressive in Washington's army. Their guns, called "Pennsylvania rifles," had grooved barrels which set a bullet spinning when fired. In the hands of sharpshooters, these rifles were accurate at 150 yards (135 meters) or more. They were greatly feared by the British, especially when snipers began to pick off sentries at what seemed to be incredible distances. The British sent one captured rifleman back to England to demonstrate his weapon. His aim proved so deadly that the exhibition was said to have discouraged many English civilians from enlisting.

Pennsylvania rifles still had to be loaded and fired in the same slow and cumbersome way that muskets were. Gunpowder was poured down the barrel. Then the bullet and some kind of wadding were packed in with a ramrod. Next a small amount of powder was sprinkled on the firing pan. When the marksman pulled the trigger, a sparking arrangement similar to that of a cigarette lighter ignited the powder in the pan. That flame entered a small hole in the barrel and exploded the main charge, firing the bullet. Occasionally the powder in the pan "flashed" without causing the gun to fire. This is the origin of the expression "a flash in the pan."

Obviously it was difficult and dangerous for a soldier to reload either a rifle or a musket while moving and under fire.

Pennsylvania Rifles

Anne S. K. Brown Military Collection

THE BRITISH ARMY

In July 1775 the British had fewer than 4,000 soldiers in Boston. It was a force much different from the army Washington commanded. The generals were members of the aristocracy. Often they were prominent in politics too. William Howe and two other generals then in Boston, John Burgoyne and George Clinton, were members of Parliament. Such men paid little heed to instructions from London that did not please them.

Officers of lower rank normally obtained their commissions by buying them. Prices were high. A colonel's post might go for £5,000, a substantial fortune in the 1700s. This meant that only wealthy men could hope to be officers. The gap between officer and enlisted man could not be bridged.

Ordinary soldiers were mostly drawn from the very bottom of society. Criminals were often allowed to enlist to avoid jail or execution. Vagrants and idle persons of all sorts were frequently "pressed" into service. Discipline was brutal, in part because it seemed the only way to control such types. A marine in the Boston garrison who was

135

British infantrymen march forth into battle in three regular columns. This oil painting by the famous illustrator Howard Pyle is titled "The Battle of Bunker Hill." It was painted in 1898, then more than 100 years after the famous battle. How is this painting a closeup of the same battle shown on page 130?

convicted of punching an infantry officer was sentenced to receive 800 lashes with a cat-o'-nine-tails.

The principal weapon of the British infantry was a musket similar to that used by colonial troops but heavier and equipped with a bayonet. Soldiers "leveled" their muskets before firing, but they did not really try to aim. The guns did not even have rear sights. If a whole line fired at once in the general direction of the enemy, some damage would be done. The smoke alone caused by the exploding gunpowder could screen the soldiers as they plodded methodically ahead. The object was to get close enough to the foe to go for him with cold steel. Their bright red uniforms made British soldiers easy targets for marksmen, but against the inaccurate muskets of the day what the men wore made little difference. The attack on Breed's Hill is an excellent example of the strengths and weaknesses of British tactics.

Despite the harsh treatment of enlisted men, the British army was an excellent fighting machine. Both officers and men were brave, enduring, effective. The system reflected English society just as the American system reflected American society. Conditions that today might seem cruel and mindless were accepted as normal and necessary by most of those on the bottom as well as by their leaders. Perhaps the typical soldier took a kind of pride in his ability to stand up to the punishing life he had to lead. All ranks could take pride in being English, members of the most powerful nation in their world.

- How did British officers of lower rank obtain their commissions in the army? *by buying it*
- Why was discipline of ordinary British soldiers so harsh? *because most were criminals or of low society*

WASHINGTON'S FIRST VICTORY

For long months after the Battle of Bunker Hill, the British army sat pinned down in Boston. The American forces ringing the city greatly outnumbered them. Washington was eager to attack, but he was persuaded not to assault the city directly. In January 1776 Colonel Henry Knox, a very stout but energetic and talented young artillery officer, reached camp with the heavy brass and iron cannon that had been captured at Fort Ticonderoga. Using sleds and teams of oxen, Knox and his men had dragged the cannon nearly 300 miles (480 kilometers), a tremendous achievement. In March Washington had these guns pulled up **Dorchester Heights,** south of Boston. He built strong defenses to protect them. From this position the cannon could have methodically blown the British positions in the city below to bits.

The Joseph Dixon Crucible Company Collection

Colonel Henry Knox and his men use sleds and oxen to drag the captured cannon and guns of Fort Ticonderoga through the winter snow of 1776. Tom Lovell painted this oil, titled "The Noble Train of Artillery." One of the huge mortars was nicknamed "Old Sow." Where did Washington have these guns and cannon placed?

General Howe realized at once that he must either capture Dorchester Heights, a task far more difficult than the capture of Breed's Hill, or abandon Boston. He had neither the men nor the desire to attack. He let the Americans know that if they did not allow him to leave peacefully, he would destroy the city. Washington wisely agreed to let Howe move his troops. On March 17, 1776, the British departed for their naval base at Halifax, Nova Scotia, there to await reinforcements and supplies from home. With the fleet went more than 1,500 Americans. These people preferred exile to rebellion against a king and country they considered their own. They and others like them, perhaps a fifth of the American population, were called **Loyalists, or Tories.**

For the moment the thirteen colonies were entirely clear of British troops. But the struggle was just beginning. By July 1776 General Howe was back on American soil with a powerful army. By then the colonies had given up trying to persuade England to treat them more fairly. Instead they had declared their independence and become the **United States of America.**

■ Why did Washington allow Howe to leave Boston?

So Howe wouldn't destroy the city

THE MOVEMENT FOR INDEPENDENCE

The conflict was bound to turn into a war for independence once large numbers of Americans had been killed by British soldiers. Bayonets had been used on the brave defenders of Breed's Hill after their ammunition had run out. Any peaceful solution seemed most unlikely.

For many months the colonists had tried to believe that King George was their friend. He was being misled by evil advisers, the argument ran. Of course, this was not true, and eventually the colonists realized that it was not.

The person most responsible for opening the colonists' eyes was an Englishman who had just recently emigrated to America. His name was Thomas Paine. In January 1776 Paine published a pamphlet, **Common Sense.** In it he attacked not only George III, whom he called a "Royal Brute," but the whole *idea* of monarchy. *Any* king was a bad thing, Paine insisted. People have "a natural right" to rule themselves. Therefore, the colonies should throw off all connection with Great Britain and create a republic of their own.

Common Sense was an immediate best seller. Nearly everyone in the colonies read it or heard it discussed. Once the idea of independence was freely talked about, more and more people accepted it.

By June 1776 nearly all the members of the Second Continental Congress were ready to act. Richard Henry Lee of Virginia introduced a resolution for independence on June 7. The "United Col-

COMMON SENSE;

ADDRESSED TO THE

INHABITANTS

OF

A M E R I C A,

On the following interesting

S U B J E C T S.

I. Of the Origin and Design of Government in general, with concise Remarks on the English Constitution.

II. Of Monarchy and Hereditary Succession.

III. Thoughts on the present State of American Affairs.

IV. Of the present Ability of America, with some miscellaneous Reflections.

Man knows no Master save creating Heaven,
Or those whom choice and common good ordain.
THOMSON.

PHILADELPHIA;

Printed, and Sold, by R. BELL, in Third-Street.

MDCCLXXVI.

Thomas Paine's *Common Sense* stirred the colonists when it was published in January 1776. This is the cover of the original pamphlet. What institution did Paine attack in this publication?

onies" were "free and independent States," Lee's resolution said. "All allegiance to the British Crown" should be broken.

Before passing this resolution, Congress appointed a committee to prepare a statement explaining why independence was necessary. The members of this committee were Benjamin Franklin of Pennsylvania, John Adams of Massachusetts, Roger Sherman of Connecticut, Robert Livingston of New York, and the youngest delegate, 33-year-old Thomas Jefferson of Virginia. The document they drafted, the **Declaration of Independence,** was written mainly by Jefferson. On July 2, voting by states, the delegates resolved to declare their independence. Then, on the **Fourth of July,** they officially approved the Declaration.

- What was the significance of Thomas Paine's *Common Sense?*
- Why did Congress appoint a committee to prepare the Declaration of Independence?

THE DECLARATION OF INDEPENDENCE

Jefferson's Declaration of Independence is one of the best-known and most influential political documents ever written. No one has expressed so well the right of people to overthrow a government they do not like and make a new one they do like. The argument is easy to follow. It is shown by the notes at the margins of the Declaration, reprinted, with reading aids, on pages 140-43 of this chapter.

Jefferson originally wrote that the truths set forth in the Declaration were "sacred and undeniable." In polishing the Declaration, Franklin changed the phrase to read "self-evident"—that is, obvious. They make up only a small part of the document. Nevertheless, they are the part that makes the Declaration so important. For the first time in history, a group of revolutionaries were carefully explaining to the world why they had the right to use force to change their government.

The Declaration of Independence is a superb statement of the principles on which **democratic government** is based. (Political power in a **democracy** comes from the people and is for the benefit of all.) Using historical imagination reminds us that the Declaration was also wartime propaganda. As a description of the causes of the Revolution, the Declaration is very one-sided. Many of the charges made against George III were strongly exaggerated. Some were untrue. The king had many faults. But he was not a tyrant, and he had no desire to become one.

Those who put their names on the Declaration of Independence were burning their bridges behind them. In English eyes they were now traitors. If they lost the war, they could expect the treatment commonly given traitors—death.

139

THE DECLARATION OF INDEPENDENCE
In Congress, July 4, 1776

The unanimous Declaration of the thirteen united States of America,

When in the Course of human events, it becomes necessary for one people to dissolve the political bands which have connected them with another, and to assume among the powers of the earth, the separate and equal station to which the Laws of Nature and of Nature's God entitle them, a decent respect to the opinions of mankind requires that they should declare the causes which impel them to the separation.—

We hold these truths to be self-evident, that all men are created equal, that they are endowed by their Creator with certain unalienable Rights, that among these are Life, Liberty, and the pursuit of Happiness.—

That to secure these rights, Governments are instituted among Men, deriving their just powers from the consent of the governed,—

That whenever any Form of Government becomes destructive of these ends, it is the Right of the People to alter or to abolish it, and to institute new Government, laying its foundation on such principles and organizing its powers in such form, as to them shall seem most likely to effect their Safety and Happiness. Prudence, indeed, will dictate that Governments long established should not be changed for light and transient causes; and accordingly all experience hath shown, that mankind are more disposed to suffer, while evils are sufferable, than to right themselves by abolishing the forms to which they are accustomed. But when a long train of abuses and usurpations, pursuing invariably the same Object evinces a design to reduce them under absolute Despotism, it is their right, it is their duty, to throw off such Government, and to provide new Guards for their future security.—

Such has been the patient sufferance of these Colonies; and such is now the necessity which constrains them to alter their former Systems of Government. The history of the present King of Great Britain is a history of repeated injuries and usurpations, all having in direct object the establishment of an absolute Tyranny over these States. To prove this, let Facts be submitted to a candid world.—

He has refused his Assent to Laws, the most wholesome and necessary for the public good.—

He has forbidden his Governors to pass Laws of immediate and pressing importance, unless suspended in their operation till his Assent should be obtained; and when so suspended, he has utterly neglected to attend to them.—

He has refused to pass other Laws for the accommodation of large districts of people, unless those people would relinquish the right of

---

impel: force.

endowed: provided.

All people have God-given or "natural" basic rights.

People create governments to insure that their natural rights are protected. Governments are the servants of the people who establish them.

If a government does not serve its purpose, the people have a right to abolish it. Then the people have the right and duty to create a new government that will safeguard their security.

Despotism: unlimited power.

This document will explain to the world why Americans had the right to use force to change their government.

usurpations: unjust uses of power.

Tyranny: absolute power.

candid: impartial; fair.

Assent: approval.

Twenty-six paragraphs list the supposed crimes of George III.

relinquish: give up.

140

Representation in the Legislature, a right inestimable to them and formidable to tyrants only.—

He has called together legislative bodies at places unusual, uncomfortable, and distant from the depository of their public Records, for the sole purpose of fatiguing them into compliance with his measures.—

He has dissolved Representative Houses repeatedly, for opposing with manly firmness his invasions on the rights of the people.—

He has refused for a long time, after such dissolutions, to cause others to be elected; whereby the Legislative powers, incapable of Annihilation, have returned to the People at large for their exercise; the State remaining in the meantime exposed to all the dangers of invasion from without, and convulsions within.—

He has endeavored to prevent the population of these States; for that purpose obstructing the Laws for Naturalization of Foreigners; refusing to pass others to encourage their migrations hither, and raising the conditions of new Appropriations of Lands.—

He has obstructed the Administration of Justice, by refusing his Assent to Laws for establishing Judiciary powers.—

He has made Judges dependent on his Will alone, for the tenure of their offices, and the amount and payment of their salaries.—

He has erected a multitude of New Offices, and sent hither swarms of Officers to harass our people, and eat out their substance.—

He has kept among us, in times of peace, Standing Armies without the Consent of our legislatures.—

He has affected to render the Military independent of and superior to the Civil power.—

He has combined with others to subject us to a jurisdiction foreign to our constitution, and unacknowledged by our laws; giving his Assent to their Acts of pretended Legislation:—

For quartering large bodies of armed troops among us:—

For protecting them, by a mock Trial, from punishment for any Murders which they should commit on the Inhabitants of these States:—

For cutting off our Trade with all parts of the world:—

For imposing Taxes on us without our Consent:—

For depriving us in many cases, of the benefits of Trial by Jury:—

For transporting us beyond Seas to be tried for pretended offences:—

For abolishing the free System of English Laws in a neighboring Province, establishing therein an Arbitrary government, and enlarging its Boundaries so as to render it at once an example and fit instrument for introducing the same absolute rule into these Colonies:—

For taking away our Charters, abolishing our most valuable

---

inestimable: priceless.
formidable: causing dread.

Annihilation: destruction.

convulsions: violent disturbances.

Naturalization of Foreigners: the process by which foreign-born persons become citizens.
Appropriations of Lands: setting aside land for settlement.

tenure: term.

a multitude of: many.

quartering: lodging.

Arbitrary: not based on law.
render: make.

abdicated: given up.

Laws, and altering fundamentally the Forms of our Governments:—

For suspending our own Legislatures, and declaring themselves invested with power to legislate for us in all cases whatsoever.—

He has abdicated Government here, by declaring us out of his Protection and waging War against us.—

He has plundered our seas, ravaged our Coasts, burnt our towns, and destroyed the Lives of our people.—

foreign Mercenaries: soldiers hired to fight for a country not their own.

perfidy: violation of trust.

He is at this time transporting large Armies of foreign Mercenaries to complete the works of death, desolation and tyranny, already begun with circumstances of Cruelty & perfidy scarcely paralleled in the most barbarous ages, and totally unworthy the Head of a civilized nation.—

He has constrained our fellow Citizens taken Captive on the high Seas to bear Arms against their Country, to become the executioners of their friends and Brethren, or to fall themselves by their Hands.—

insurrections: rebellions.

He has excited domestic insurrections amongst us, and has endeavored to bring on the inhabitants of our frontiers, the merciless Indian Savages, whose known rule of warfare, is an undistinguished destruction of all ages, sexes and conditions.

Petitioned: asked in a formal manner.
Redress: correction of wrongs.

In every stage of these Oppressions We have Petitioned for Redress in the most humble terms: Our repeated Petitions have been answered only by repeated injury. A Prince, whose character is thus marked by every act which may define a Tyrant, is unfit to be the ruler of a free people.

unwarrantable jurisdiction: unjustified authority.

magnanimity: generous spirit.
conjured: called upon.

Nor have We been wanting in attentions to our British brethren. We have warned them from time to time of attempts by their legislature to extend an unwarrantable jurisdiction over us. We have reminded them of the circumstances of our emigration and settlement here. We have appealed to their native justice and magnanimity, and we have conjured them by the ties of our common kindred to disavow these usurpations, which would inevitably interrupt our connections and correspondence. They too have been deaf to the voice of justice and of consanguinity. We must, therefore, acquiesce in the necessity, which denounces our Separation, and hold them, as we hold the rest of mankind, Enemies in War, in Peace Friends.—

consanguinity: common ancestors.
acquiesce in: consent to.

rectitude: rightness.

We, therefore, the Representatives of the united States of America, in General Congress, Assembled, appealing to the Supreme Judge of the world for the rectitude of our intentions, do, in the Name, and by Authority of the good People of these Colonies, solemnly publish and declare, That these United Colonies are, and of Right ought to be Free and Independent States; that they are Absolved from all Allegiance to the British Crown, and that all political connection between them and the State of Great Britain, is and ought to be totally dissolved; and that as Free and Independent States, they have full Power to levy War, conclude Peace, contract Alliances, es-

Here is the actual declaration of independence.

tablish Commerce, and to do all other Acts and Things which Independent States may of right do.—

And for the support of this Declaration, with a firm reliance on the protection of divine Providence, we mutually pledge to each other our Lives, our Fortunes and our sacred Honor.

John Hancock	Benjamin Harrison	Lewis Morris
Button Gwinnett	Thomas Nelson, Jr.	Richard Stockton
Lyman Hall	Francis Lightfoot Lee	John Witherspoon
George Walton	Carter Braxton	Francis Hopkinson
William Hooper	Robert Morris	John Hart
Joseph Hewes	Benjamin Rush	Abraham Clark
John Penn	Benjamin Franklin	Josiah Bartlett
Edward Rutledge	John Morton	William Whipple
Thomas Heyward, Jr.	George Clymer	Samuel Adams
Thomas Lynch, Jr.	James Smith	John Adams
Arthur Middleton	George Taylor	Robert Treat Paine
Samuel Chase	James Wilson	Elbridge Gerry
William Paca	George Ross	Stephen Hopkins
Thomas Stone	Caesar Rodney	William Ellery
Charles Carroll	George Read	Roger Sherman
of Carrollton	Thomas McKean	Samuel Huntington
George Wythe	William Floyd	William Williams
Richard Henry Lee	Philip Livingston	Oliver Wolcott
Thomas Jefferson	Francis Lewis	Matthew Thornton

What did the Declaration of Independence tell the world?

Yale University Art Gallery

This detail from John Trumbull's "Declaration of Independence" shows the five-member drafting committee for the Declaration. From left, John Adams, Roger Sherman, Robert Livingston, Thomas Jefferson, and Benjamin Franklin. They are arranged in the painting according to their contributions, so Jefferson is the strongest figure.

READING PRACTICE IN SOCIAL STUDIES

Using Historical Imagination

When we read history, we tend to form opinions about events in the past. Sometimes these opinions can keep us from fully understanding history. To judge the people and events of 200 years ago using only today's standards can lead to a false picture of history. We need instead to read with *historical imagination*. We need to put ourselves in the place of those who lived in the past to see why they thought and acted as they did. One opportunity to read with historical imagination comes with the Declaration of Independence.

Over the years people have argued heatedly about what Jefferson meant by the first of his "self-evident" truths—"that all men are created equal." First of all, Jefferson surely meant by *men* "people," just as, when he spoke of "the opinions of mankind," he meant the opinions of all people, women and men alike.

This is not to suggest that Jefferson or any other signer of the Declaration of Independence believed in equal rights for women as the term is used today. The delegates who signed the Declaration believed that women were entitled to life, liberty, and the pursuit of happiness so long as they behaved as men thought they should behave.

During the Revolution women held many jobs performed by men in peacetime. Many women ran farms and shops while their husbands, fathers, and brothers were at war. Abigail Adams called herself a "farmeress" and really did manage the Adams farm. Some women served as nurses with the army. A few actually fired guns in defense of liberty. But women remained legally subordinate to men. No movement to improve the position of women grew from the Revolution.

On the other hand, Jefferson certainly meant that only *free* men were created equal. How else could he, a slaveholder, claim that liberty was a God-given right of "all men"?

During the Revolutionary War about 5,000 blacks served in the American armed forces. Most were given dirty, non-combat jobs. Yet a black man, Prince Estabrook, was among the militiamen on the Lexington common when the first shots were fired. Another black, Salem Poor, was among the defenders of Breed's Hill. Indeed, blacks fought in every major battle. Still, most white Americans accepted slavery.

Nearly every white person in America of the 1770s was in some ways prejudiced against blacks by today's standards. Further, most men, black as well as white, were "male chauvinists" by today's standards. We must use our historical imagination if we want to understand these men and their time. To condemn George Washington for owning slaves and taking control of his rich wife's property would only show that we did *not* understand Washington or the Revolutionary Era. We would be equally wrong if we took the Declaration of Independence so literally as to believe that the signers were perfect democrats.

As you read history, remember to use historical imagination. You will make your own judgments, but try to understand why people of another time thought and acted as they did.

1. What is historical imagination?
2. How does historical imagination help us to understand the past?
3. What did Jefferson mean by "all men are created equal"?
4. What was the status of women like Abigail Adams during the Revolution? Of men like Salem Poor?
5. Using historical imagination, why might Washington have felt it was proper for him to keep slaves or control his wife's property?

AMERICA'S DARK HOUR

The British were now determined to crush the American rebellion. General Howe had left Boston in March 1776 with 4,000 soldiers. He returned to New York City in July 1776 with 32,000. This army was supported by a huge fleet of over 400 warships and transports under the command of General Howe's brother, Richard, Lord Howe.

By capturing New York and patrolling the Hudson River with their warships, the British could split New England from the rest of what they still called "the colonies." General Howe first established a base on Staten Island. Then, late in August, he landed 20,000 soldiers on Long Island. Instead of attacking directly, he brilliantly outmaneuvered Washington's army. Then he struck from two directions. The **Battle of Long Island** revealed that Washington was inexperienced at managing a complicated operation. He barely managed to withdraw his battered troops across the East River to New York City.

The victory greatly heartened the British. Howe became a national hero. King George knighted him. Sir William, as he was thereafter called, again proceeded slowly and carefully. Apparently the losses he had suffered in the Battle of Bunker Hill had made him overly cautious.

After delaying several weeks Howe finally moved his army across the East River. Once more the British troops routed Washington's force. The Americans fled to the northern end of Manhattan Island, leaving Howe in control of New York City. New York was not like Boston. A large proportion of the citizens were Loyalists. They welcomed the British with open arms.

This was one of the low points of the war for the Americans. If Howe had been more aggressive, he could probably have destroyed Washington's army completely.

Finally, after more fighting, Washington crossed the Hudson to New Jersey, where Howe could not use the British fleet to maneuver around him. Half of Washington's army had been captured by now, nearly 3,000 at Fort Washington at the northern end of Manhattan Island. Washington had left this garrison behind when he moved his main force to New Jersey. Through late November and into December, the disheartened army retreated in the direction of Philadelphia, followed by Howe. The Continental Congress, thoroughly alarmed, shifted its sessions from Philadelphia to Baltimore. In mid-December the American army retreated across the Delaware River into Pennsylvania.

In this dark hour Washington devised a daring and brilliant plan. Winter was closing in. The enlistments of most of his men were about to expire. Something had to be done to revive their spirits and

BUILDING SKILLS
IN SOCIAL STUDIES

Tracing Movements on a Map

Oftentimes a map must show movement. Maps in Chapter 1, for example, show the migration of the first Americans (page 3) and the voyages of discovery of Columbus (page 22) and Balboa, Magellan and del Cano (page 25).

Many maps in this book show the movement of troops in wartime. "The Turning Point of the War" shows the movements of British and American troops in 1776–77 on land and sea. Separate colors are used to represent each army, and arrows indicate the direction of troop movements.

By studying troop movements closely, you gain a sense of the sweep of an army from battle to battle—the victors in pursuit, the defeated in retreat. You can see where armies gathered strength and where desperate fighters played out their final hours.

Like all good maps, the one on this page tells a story. But the story may be fully appreciated only by carefully reading the descriptions in your book on pages 145–49. Then turn to the map to see Generals Howe and Burgoyne moving their British armies across the Atlantic and down from Canada (and into the jaws of defeat by the Americans).

Study the map carefully before answering the following questions.

1. Where was General Howe's first landing? Where did he next move his troops by water?
2. Where did the Americans move after leaving Long Island? Which battles did they win at the end of their march?
3. What are three bodies of water crossed by the British army?
4. Where did General Burgoyne begin his march? Where did he win? Where did he lose?
5. From your reading, why did Washington retreat across the Hudson River?

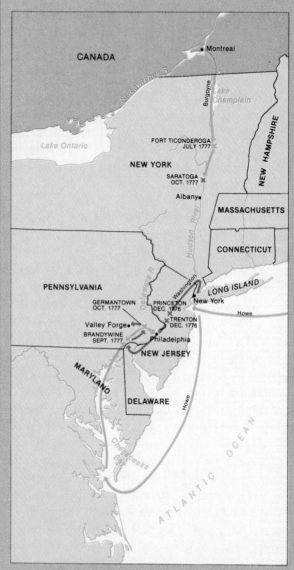

THE TURNING POINT
OF THE WAR 1776-77

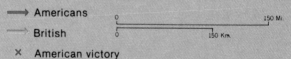

⟶ Americans

⟶ British

× American victory

× British victory

raise the hopes of the people. As Thomas Paine wrote in another of his powerful pamphlets, too many Americans were **sunshine patriots,** enthusiastic for independence when things were going well, cowards and shirkers when the future looked grim.

Across the Delaware in Trenton, New Jersey, 1,400 of General Howe's soldiers were encamped. These men were not English but Hessians—German troops from the principality of Hesse-Cassel. Americans hated and feared the Hessians, partly because they were tough soldiers known to be fond of looting and mistreating civilians, partly because they were **mercenaries,** hired soldiers, killing for money. Actually, the Hessians were not really mercenaries. The real mercenary was their ruler, Prince Frederick II of Hesse-Cassel. It was the prince who had ordered his soldiers to America, and it was he who pocketed the money paid by the British.

Washington decided to attack the Hessian camp. On Christmas night, amidst a snowstorm, he led his men back across the Delaware River, 9 miles (about 15 kilometers) above Trenton. The soldiers marched swiftly on the town. At dawn they overwhelmed their astonished foe. More than 900 Hessians were taken prisoner. So complete was the surprise that only 30 Hessians were killed before the brief **Battle of Trenton** was over. Not a single American lost his life and only 3 were wounded.

Washington quickly struck the British again, this time at Princeton, where he drove two British regiments from the town, with heavy losses. Then he made camp for the winter at Morristown, New Jersey, only about 30 miles (48 kilometers) west of New York.

■ Why did the British want to capture New York?
■ Why did Howe fail to destroy Washington's army?
■ What was the significance of Washington's victories in New Jersey?

1777: THE YEAR OF DECISION

When the snows melted, the war resumed. The British developed a complicated strategy for 1777. General Henry Clinton would hold New York with a small force while General Howe took the bulk of his troops by sea to Chesapeake Bay in order to attack Philadelphia from the south. At the same time another British army led by General John "Gentleman Johnny" Burgoyne would march down from Canada toward New York.

Howe carried out his part of the plan. He moved slowly, as usual, but effectively. He landed his men in Maryland on the Chesapeake in August. Washington hurried southward as soon as he learned where Howe was. The two armies clashed at Brandywine Creek, southwest of Philadelphia, on September 11.

The **Battle of Brandywine** resembled the Battle of Long Island both in the tactics used and the result. Howe cleverly outmaneuvered Washington. He sent part of his force around the American right side and then struck from two directions. The Americans were badly defeated. On September 26 Howe marched into Philadelphia.

In October Washington staged a surprise counterattack. At the **Battle of Germantown** he gave a better account of himself than at Brandywine, but his battle plan was too complicated. A heavy fog led to much confusion. Once more the British held the field when the shooting stopped.

These losses were very discouraging. Nevertheless, at year's end Washington still held his army together. Its will to fight had not been broken. Howe won the battles, but he failed to smash the American army. With the approach of winter, Washington and his men retreated into camp at Valley Forge, northwest of Philadelphia.

- What strategy for 1777 was developed by the British generals Clinton, Howe, and Burgoyne?
- In what way was General Washington a victor in 1777, even though he lost the Battles of Brandywine and Germantown?

THE BATTLE OF SARATOGA

The British were able to occupy and hold seaport towns and the surrounding countryside because of their powerful navy. However, it was gradually becoming clear that fighting in the interior was much more difficult for them. The fate of General Burgoyne illustrates this point effectively.

Burgoyne was a typical upper-class Englishman of his day—rich, pleasure loving, accustomed to having his own way. He was, however, more talented than most. He wrote a number of plays that were good enough to be performed in London. He had fought with distinction in Europe during the Seven Years' War. Ordinary soldiers loved him because he treated them as human beings, not as the scum of the earth.

Yet like General Braddock in the 1750s, Burgoyne did not adapt well to American conditions. He set out from Montreal in June 1777 with 6,000 regulars (half of them German mercenaries), a small force of Loyalists, and about 500 Indians. He also brought with him 138 pieces of artillery and an enormous amount of baggage of every sort. Burgoyne's personal baggage alone filled 30 carts.

A large crowd of peddlers and other civilians tagged along behind the army. Some of the officers brought their wives. Baron von Riedesel, commander of the German troops, and Frederika von Riedesel even brought their three small children, the youngest only a year old.

148

Both, The Granger Collection

The wealthy upper-class English general John Burgoyne had been a brave fighter in Europe. But in America he surrendered his army at Saratoga in October 1777. The splendid portrait in oil is by the distinguished English painter Joshua Reynolds. The bronze medal was ordered struck by Congress to commemorate the surrender at Saratoga. Burgoyne, left, hands his sword to General Horatio Gates. Why did General Burgoyne's soldiers love him?

This cumbersome army sailed smoothly enough down Lake Champlain and recaptured Fort Ticonderoga on July 5. But thereafter, moving overland, the advance slowed to a crawl. The retreating Americans chopped down huge trees to block the forest paths. It took the army 24 days to reach Fort Edward, 23 miles (about 37 kilometers) south of Ticonderoga.

With every passing day more and more American militia gathered. Like the Minute Men at Concord, these were local farmers who picked up their rifles or muskets and gathered to defend their own districts. "Wherever the King's forces point," Burgoyne noted with dismay, "three or four thousand [militiamen] assemble in twenty-four hours."

The commander of the regular troops facing Burgoyne was General Horatio Gates. Gates was very cautious. He avoided a major battle as long as possible. On September 19 the two armies finally clashed in the battle of **Freeman's Farm.** American units led by Colonel Daniel Morgan and Major General Benedict Arnold, who was as daring as Gates was cautious, dealt Burgoyne's army a smashing blow. The British advance was stopped. On October 7 Burgoyne was defeated again, suffering heavy losses.

By this time Burgoyne's army was surrounded. Supplies were running low. On October 17 he surrendered at Saratoga. The Americans took 5,700 prisoners.

- Why was it more difficult for the British to defeat the Americans in the interior?
- What difficulties did General Burgoyne have in moving his army down from Montreal?

149

THE ALLIANCE WITH FRANCE

The **Battle of Saratoga** was probably the great victory that won the United States its independence. It increased the Americans' confidence. It discouraged the British so much that they offered to promise never again to try to tax the colonists if they would lay down their arms. This offer was refused.

But the most important result of the Battle of Saratoga occurred in France. When the news of the victory reached Paris, the French officially recognized the government of the United States. In February 1778 Benjamin Franklin and two other American diplomats negotiated a **treaty of alliance.** France promised to fight to protect the independence of the United States. France then declared war on Great Britain.

The French were eager to see the Americans win their independence because that would weaken their enemy, Great Britain. They had been helping the Americans with loans and war supplies from the start of the revolution. Many French officers had already come to America to fight. The best-known of these was the youthful Marquis de Lafayette, who was only 19 when he joined the American army. Now the French army and navy joined in the conflict directly. By the summer of 1778, a French fleet was operating in American waters. In 1780 an army of 6,000 men under Count Rochambeau landed in Rhode Island. Spain also entered the war against England in 1779, and Holland in 1780.

■ What was the most important result of the Battle of Saratoga?
■ What did the French promise in the 1778 treaty?

WINTER AT VALLEY FORGE

We can see now that victory was almost certain after the Battle of Saratoga. This happy future was much less clear to Washington and the weary soldiers wintering at **Valley Forge.** Supplies of food and especially of clothing were scarce. According to Washington himself, in December 1777 2,898 of his men were barefoot. Many were ill.

The problem was bad organization and the lack of enough horses and wagons to bring supplies to Valley Forge. Not far away, civilians had plenty to eat and adequate clothing. Knowing this made Washington boil with rage and discouraged many of his men. Thousands of the troops deserted.

The soldiers who did not leave were strengthened by their suffering. They also benefited from the training they got from a German volunteer, General Friedrich von Steuben. Von Steuben was something of a faker. He claimed to be a baron and a former lieutenant general in the army of King Frederick of Prussia. Actually, he had no noble title, and he had been only a captain in the Prussian army. He

was perfectly sincere, however, in his wish to help the American cause. And he was an excellent soldier.

Von Steuben taught Washington's veterans how to maneuver in the field and how to use bayonets properly. He was a stern taskmaster who made the soldiers drill for hours. He lost his temper frequently, and since he knew very little English, he tended to shout at the Americans in a mixture of German and French, substituting curses for clear instructions. Nevertheless, the Americans came to love him. He worked himself as hard as the men he was drilling. His devotion to them was obvious. Despite his foreign background, he knew how to manage the Americans. In Prussia, he said, when an officer says, "Do this," the soldiers do it without argument. In America, "I am obliged to say, 'This is the reason why you ought to do that.'"

■ Why were the conditions at Valley Forge so bad?

Astride his white horse, General Washington reviews his troops at Valley Forge during the winter of 1777-78. John Trego painted this 1883 oil. What made Washington so angry at Valley Forge?

THE WAR IN THE SOUTH AND WEST

In May 1778 General Howe resigned his command. General Henry Clinton replaced him. Clinton marched the British army in Philadelphia back to New York. The Americans then put General Benedict

151

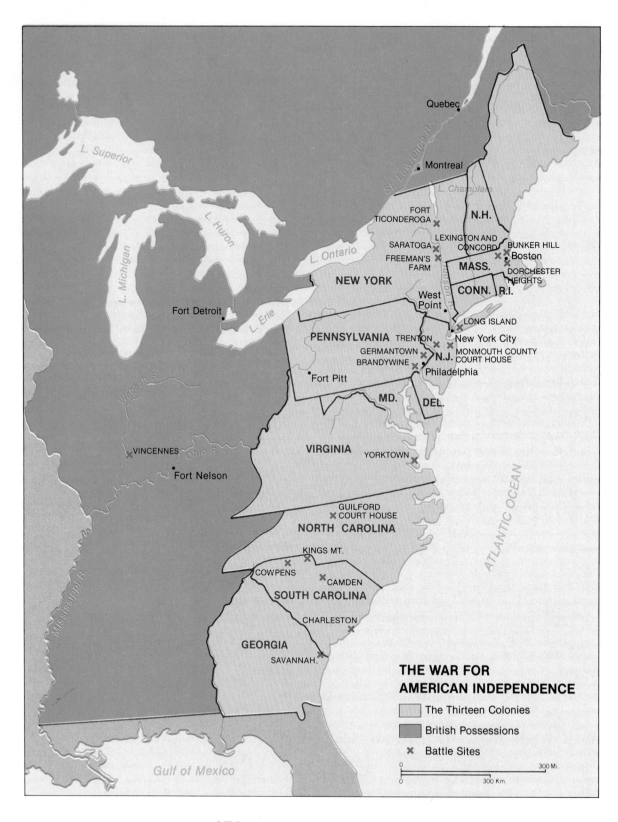

Quebec

Montreal

L. Superior

L. Huron

L. Michigan

L. Ontario

Fort Detroit

L. Erie

St. Lawrence R.

L. Champlain

FORT TICONDEROGA ✕

N.H.

SARATOGA ✕

LEXINGTON AND CONCORD ✕

BUNKER HILL ✕

Boston

FREEMAN'S FARM

MASS.

DORCHESTER HEIGHTS ✕

NEW YORK

West Point

CONN.

R.I.

LONG ISLAND ✕

New York City

Wabash R.

PENNSYLVANIA

TRENTON ✕

GERMANTOWN ✕

BRANDYWINE ✕

N.J.

MONMOUTH COUNTY COURT HOUSE ✕

Fort Pitt

Philadelphia

MD.

DEL.

Ohio R.

VINCENNES ✕

Fort Nelson

VIRGINIA

YORKTOWN ✕

Mississippi R.

GUILFORD COURT HOUSE ✕

NORTH CAROLINA

KINGS MT. ✕

COWPENS ✕

CAMDEN ✕

SOUTH CAROLINA

CHARLESTON ✕

GEORGIA

SAVANNAH ✕

ATLANTIC OCEAN

Gulf of Mexico

THE WAR FOR AMERICAN INDEPENDENCE

The Thirteen Colonies

British Possessions

✕ Battle Sites

0   300 Mi.

0   300 Km.

Arnold, one of the heroes of the Battle of Saratoga, in charge of the American troops in reoccupied Philadelphia. While Clinton's troops were marching across New Jersey, Washington attacked. His victory at the **Battle of Monmouth Court House** was a small one, but it gave a valuable boost to American morale.

Thereafter the British concentrated their efforts in the South, where they hoped to find many Loyalists. Using the navy effectively, the British captured **Savannah,** Georgia, in 1778. In 1780 another naval expedition led by Clinton captured **Charleston,** South Carolina. Clinton took as many Americans prisoner in Charleston as the British had lost at Saratoga. He then returned to his base at New York, leaving General Charles Cornwallis in charge of the southern campaign. Later in 1780 Cornwallis routed an American army under the command of General Horatio Gates at **Camden,** South Carolina.

The British in the South counted on local support, but they soon found guerrilla bands picking away at them. These irregular soldiers, led by men like Francis Marion, the "Swamp Fox," and Thomas Sumter, continued to resist the Redcoats. Soon Cornwallis was in serious trouble in the South.

After Gates's defeat at Camden, Nathanael Greene was put in charge of the American forces in the South. General Greene used hit-and-run tactics against Cornwallis with brilliant results. A band of militiamen had already trapped a Tory force at **King's Mountain** in South Carolina. Now Greene divided his forces and staged a series of scattered raids. At the **Battle of Cowpens** in South Carolina one flank soundly defeated the British. They then rejoined Greene and attacked Cornwallis's army at **Guilford Court House,** forcing the British to retreat to the coast. There Cornwallis would be supported and supplied by the Royal Navy. But soon most of Georgia and the Carolinas were back in American hands.

The Americans' fortunes also improved in the West, while fighting in the North was at a standstill. George Rogers Clark, financed by Virginia's governor, Patrick Henry, swept into Illinois country. There he won several battles against the British and their Indian allies, including **Vincennes,** on the Wabash River, which he took in 1778 and recaptured in February 1779. Clark built **Fort Nelson,** now Louisville, Kentucky, and planned a campaign to march upon **Fort Detroit.** But he was unable to proceed when adequate supplies did not arrive from Virginia.

In the North there was treason. Benedict Arnold had persuaded Washington to make him commander of the key American fort at **West Point,** on the Hudson River north of New York City. He had secretly agreed to turn over the fort to the British for a large sum of money and a commission in their army.

Francis Marion, the "Swamp Fox," *above,* and George Rogers Clark, conqueror of the Northwest, *below,* were both painted in watercolor by James Barton Longacre in the early 19th century. How did each help America win its war?

Fortunately for the United States, a British officer, Major John André, was captured while returning from West Point with papers confirming Arnold's treachery. André was hanged as a spy, but Arnold escaped to New York and later became a British general.

In May 1781 Cornwallis marched north into Virginia, hoping for a decisive victory. Again local militiamen and regular army units began to pick away at his army. Again he retreated to the sea. This time he fortified himself at **Yorktown,** a small tobacco port located where the York River flows into Chesapeake Bay. An American force under General Lafayette took up positions outside the town to keep the British under observation.

■ Why were the British unable to hold the South?
■ How did George Rogers Clark carry the war to the West?

SURRENDER AT YORKTOWN

Now came the final act of the long struggle. Washington had originally intended to assault New York City with the support of the French army that Count Rochambeau had brought to Rhode Island. Rochambeau urged a joint attack on Yorktown instead. Washington finally agreed. Leaving a small force to trick General Clinton into thinking the Americans intended to attack New York, the combined American and French armies marched swiftly south.

At the same time two French fleets, one from the West Indies, the other from Newport, Rhode Island, came together off Yorktown. The squadron from the West Indies landed 3,300 more French soldiers outside the Yorktown defenses. After Washington and Rochambeau arrived in early September 1781, there were 16,000 allied soldiers and 36 warships in position. Cornwallis had only 8,000 men under his command, and many of them were ill. When a British fleet sought to relieve him, it was driven off by the French. Cornwallis's army was doomed.

On October 6 Washington began to batter Cornwallis's fortifications with heavy artillery. The assault was under the able direction of French gunners and of the same Henry Knox, now a general, who had brought the guns of Fort Ticonderoga to Boston to make possible Washington's first victory back in 1776. Cornwallis sent off a last message to General Clinton: "If you cannot relieve me very soon, you must be prepared to hear the Worst." No relief arrived.

Cornwallis had to surrender on October 19. His men marched out, their flags furled, while the band played "The World Turned Upside Down." The French troops, in beautiful white uniforms, were lined up on the right. On the left were the Americans. Only the front ranks wore the buff and blue uniform of the Continental Army. The rest were, in the words of General von Steuben, "a ragged set of

fellows." As the British soldiers threw down their arms angrily in formal surrender, Lafayette told the band to strike up "Yankee Doodle." This dramatic scene took place on a field no more than 10 miles (16 kilometers) from Jamestown, where the first English settlers had landed 174 years before.

The last battle was over. The British still had control of New York City, Charleston, Savannah, and some frontier posts, but they no longer had the will to fight. In March Parliament voted to give up "further prosecution of offensive war on the Continent of North America." A few days later Lord North resigned as prime minister. Although a peace treaty was still to be signed, the War for American Independence had been won.

For Cornwallis's British troops this is "The World Turned Upside Down" as they surrender to the Americans at Yorktown in October 1781. Center is General Benjamin Lincoln leading the Redcoats past the Americans, in buff and blue, on the right, General Washington slightly in front. On the left are French allies, in white, with Polish and Prussian fighters behind. John Trumbull painted this oil. How did regular American soldiers look by the time of this last battle?

■ Why was Washington able to defeat the British at Yorktown?

CHAPTER 5 REVIEW

Identification
Tell briefly why each of the following persons, terms, or events is important.

1. Sam Adams
2. General William Howe
3. George III
4. General John Burgoyne
5. General Friedrich von Steuben
6. Benedict Arnold
7. Count Rochambeau
8. Tea Act
9. Sons of Liberty
10. Fort Ticonderoga
11. Intolerable Acts
12. First Continental Congress
13. Committees of Correspondence
14. Lexington and Concord
15. Breed's Hill
16. Second Continental Congress
17. Loyalists
18. General Henry Knox
19. Valley Forge
20. Battle of Yorktown

Understanding American History
1. Explain why the Coercive Acts eventually led to fighting at Lexington and Concord.
2. Explain how the war changed from a struggle to protect colonists' rights into the War for American Independence.
3. Why might Washington have been considered a poor general in the first years of the war? Name three battles that support your answer.
4. Explain why the Battle of Saratoga was so important to the American cause.
5. What was the last major battle of the war? Explain the role of the French in this battle.
6. Why were the Committees of Correspondence important in helping the colonies against Britain?
7. Why did the British usually have more success fighting near the coast than inland?
8. Use your historical imagination to explain what "all men are created equal" meant to the leaders of the American Revolution.
9. Compare and contrast the American and British armies.
10. How did the publication of *Common Sense* cause more colonists to favor the idea of independence?

Activities
1. Make your own time line of major events discussed in Chapter 5. Label political events on one side of the time line and military events on the other side. You may wish to use the time line in this book as a model.
2. Make a recruiting poster for Washington's army. Make up a slogan for your poster. A slogan is a short phrase that catches people's attention and advertises a group's purpose. Display your posters.
3. Write your own eyewitness account of the Boston Tea Party, first as a member of the Sons of Liberty and then as a captain of one of the tea ships.
4. Use your historical imagination to write a newspaper report of the Battle of Lexington. Try to give as fair an account as you can of the events on April 19, 1775. You may wish to include one or two eyewitness descriptions and perhaps interviews with fighters from both sides.
5. Prepare with your classmates a map of the major battles of the War for American Independence. Make your map large enough to display in the classroom. Decide whether or not you will show troop movements and how you will distinguish on your map between American forces and British forces.

CHAPTER 5 TEST

Matching (40 points)
Number your paper 1–10 and match the description in the second
column with the person or place in the first column.

1. Paul Revere
2. Thomas Paine
3. Boston
4. Charles Cornwallis
5. Lexington
6. Saratoga
7. Thomas Jefferson
8. Valley Forge
9. George Washington
10. Trenton

a. He was chief author of the Declaration of Independence.
b. The American victory here was the turning point in the war.
c. He was commander of the American army.
d. The first shots of the Revolution were fired here.
e. He was the general who surrendered to the Americans and the French at Yorktown.
f. The Sons of Liberty dumped tea into the harbor here.
g. He was the patriot who warned the citizens of Lexington that the British were coming.
h. Washington's army suffered many hardships here during the winter of 1777–78.
i. He was the author of *Common Sense*, which said the Americans should establish their own nation.
j. The American victory here was important to keep up morale.

Completion (30 points)
Number your paper 11–20 and write the words to fill in the blanks after each number.

11. The American civilian-soldiers who drilled on town commons in Massachusetts called themselves _____.
12. Thomas Hutchinson was paid by the British government when he held the office of_____ of Massachusetts.
13. The fort on Lake Champlain that supplied much heavy artillery after the Americans captured it was _____.
14. The fiery orator who said "give me liberty or give me death" was _____ of Virginia.

15. Washington's soldiers were drilled at Valley Forge under the supervision of _____ of Prussia.
16. The principal weapon of both British and American soldiers was a _____.
17. Another name for the Tories was the _____.
18. In *Common Sense* Thomas Paine called _____ a "Royal Brute."
19. The Second Continental Congress met in _____.
20. A government in which political power comes from the people and is for the benefit of all is a _____.

Essay (30 points)
From your reading of Chapter 5, what do you think was the major cause of the War for American Independence? Support your answer by being as specific as possible. Write at least one full paragraph, taking care to spell and punctuate correctly.

CHAPTER 6
Creating the United States

THE REVOLUTION CONTINUES

Yorktown was the last battle of the War for American Independence. Great Britain gave up its thirteen American colonies, and the fighting ended. But the Battle of Yorktown did not end the American Revolution that had begun in the early 1770s. Ending the Revolution was something only the Americans could do. The British had tried to stop the Revolution by force. When they failed, the Revolution went forward.

In other words, there was more to the Revolution than the War for American Independence. Breaking free from British control did not answer this question: What kind of government shall America have instead? Nor did it answer these questions: What kind of society should the people of America create? What kind of economic system?

The Americans began to look for answers to these questions during the war. They continued to search and to experiment for many years after General Cornwallis surrendered.

The John Carter Brown Library

Vendors display their wares on the corner of Third and Market Streets in Philadelphia. This scene is one of a number of fine hand-colored engravings made by William Birch in 1799. Street scenes such as this greeted delegates to the Second Continental Congress. What task lay before this Congress?

Creating a new system of government was the most obvious task. It had two parts. One was to change the governments of the individual colonies into governments that were independent of England. The other was to find a substitute for the British colonial system—that is, to establish a new central government that could deal with common problems and advance the common interests of the new independent governments.

The first part meant creating the states. The second meant creating the United States. The first part was more important in those days because the state governments affected the lives of the people much more than the central government. The second part was more difficult because it meant deciding what power the United States should have over the separate states that made it up.

- How was the American Revolution different from the War for American Independence?
- What two tasks lay before the Americans who were creating a new system of government during the Revolution?

STATE GOVERNMENTS

Changing a colony into a state meant getting rid of all British controls on local government and then deciding what, if any, new controls should be substituted. The original colonial charters had been grants of power by the king. In place of these royal charters, the people of the states substituted **constitutions.** These constitutions were written descriptions of the system of government the people wanted and of the powers that each part of the government was to have.

The constitutions were all more or less alike, although each state made its own. They divided government into three parts: an elected **legislature,** where proposed laws were to be debated and either passed or rejected; an **executive,** who was to carry out the laws and manage the day-to-day operations of the government; and a system of **courts,** where the laws could be enforced.

The state legislatures replaced the colonial assemblies. The assemblies had always been the part of the colonial governments most influenced by public opinion. They had become centers of popular opposition to British control. Naturally the new constitutions gave the legislatures a great deal of power.

On the other hand, state governors were given very little power by the constitutions. They lost the right to dismiss the legislatures and the power to keep a particular legislature in office for years without its members having to stand for reelection. The powers to declare war, to conduct foreign relations, and to appoint government officials were generally assigned to the legislatures, not to the governors. Governors, in other words, were intended to be mere administrators, not rulers or even policy makers. This change was a natural result of the widespread resentment of the way colonial governors had tried to dominate the assemblies.

One state, Pennsylvania, decided not to have a governor at all. The work usually done by a governor was to be done by a Supreme Executive Council of 12 persons elected by the people. Another state, Virginia, dealt with the problem of controlling the governor by having the legislature elect him. Even with this control the Virginia constitution went on to order that the governor's salary be "adequate *but moderate.*"

The powers of state judges were also limited by the constitutions. Even the legislatures were subject to strict checks. They were increased in size so that individual representatives would have less power. Terms of office were usually only one year, kept short so that voters could quickly get rid of representatives whose actions they disapproved of. Most of the constitutions also contained **Bills of Rights,** lists of what the state governments could *not* do and liberties that the people could not be deprived of. The troubles that led to the Revolution had made Americans suspicious of *all* government.

Some of the constitutions were more conservative than others. Some made greater changes in the colonial patterns. Qualifications for voting varied. The Pennsylvania constitution gave the right to vote to all adult free men who paid taxes. In South Carolina property qualifications for voting were kept high, and a person running for office needed a considerable fortune.

What was common to all constitutions and what made them all fundamentally democratic was that the people were establishing the rules by which political life was to be organized and run. The constitutions were contracts, written legal agreements. They demonstrated that governments existed to do what the people wanted them to do, but no more. They made government officials **public servants,** not the public's masters.

The creation of these constitutions also proved that people could change their government peacefully. The American states were created in an orderly, legal manner. Making constitutions caused hot debates and sharp arguments, but there was no rioting and bloodshed, no use of any kind of force. It was particularly remarkable that governments could be changed in this peaceful and orderly way even while the people were fighting a war for survival. The creation of the state constitutions was the most significant event of the Revolution.

- Why did the state constitutions give so much power to the legislatures?
- Why was the creation of the state constitutions the most significant event of the Revolution?

REPRESENTING THE PEOPLE

The new governments did not try to make radical changes. Many people worried about the government being controlled by a few "aristocrats." By aristocrats they meant the rich and socially prominent people of their communities. Other groups feared control by "the mob," meaning the artisans and manual laborers of the towns and other relatively poor people who owned little or no property. Since the great majority of the people were neither "aristocrats" nor members of "the mob," most of the constitutions tried to protect the owners of property and at the same time to prevent these well-to-do citizens from using their wealth and influence to take advantage of the poor. The result was usually to keep things more or less as they had been in colonial times.

In some cases the constitutions were drafted by special assemblies called **conventions** elected by the voters specifically for that purpose. This method made sure that the ideas and intentions of those who prepared the constitutions were known and approved of in advance. The convention system was one of the most original political ideas to come out of the Revolution.

Most of the new governments finally gave their western districts fairer representation in the state legislatures. Many did away with state support for one particular region. The constitutions did not attempt, however, to do away with slavery.

The high ideals of the times had led many owners to free their slaves, but they did so as individuals, not in response to state law. However, in the northern states the legislatures gradually passed laws to free the children of slaves born after a certain date. These laws did not deprive any owner of any existing human property. No such laws were passed in the South, where most of the slaves were. The movement to free slaves was probably caused more by economic changes than by a belief in freedom for all inspired by the Declaration of Independence. In Virginia, for example, the price of tobacco was very low in the 1770s and 1780s, so owning slaves was not very profitable. When conditions changed, the attitudes of southern slave owners changed also, as we shall see later.

■ What were conventions? What was their importance in the American political system?

FORMING A CENTRAL GOVERNMENT

Forming a central government for all the colony-states was much more complicated. In a sense it began with the Plan of Union drafted by Benjamin Franklin at the Albany Congress in 1754. The Stamp Act Congress was another step. So were the colonial committees of correspondence and the informal organizations designed to enforce bans on importing British goods. The First Continental Congress followed. All these attempts at union were responses to the same pressures that led Benjamin Franklin to say, "we must all hang together or we shall hang separately."

The Second Continental Congress was the first central government, the first true United States. It had a continuing existence, and it ran the country on a day-to-day basis. In the beginning this government had no constitution or specific duties. Then the new state constitutions provided for the regular election of representatives to the Congress, and it was firmly and legally established.

From the start the Congress assumed a great deal of power. It appointed Washington commander in chief of the army and selected other generals. It drafted the Declaration of Independence. It operated a postal service. It sent representatives to foreign countries to obtain support. The diplomats who negotiated the crucial treaty with France after the Battle of Saratoga were assigned by the Continental Congress. The Congress also figured out how much money would be needed each year to carry on the war and perform other government functions. It decided how much each state should contribute to this total. It then sent bills for these amounts, called **requisitions,** to the states. These were often ignored by the states and rarely paid in full. Congress had to borrow large sums of money to make up the difference. It even printed paper money.

The Congress was a kind of American parliament. But there was no American equivalent to the English king or the prime minister. Instead committees of Congress carried out the functions of the head of state and executive leader of the country.

> In what ways was the Second Continental Congress the first central government of the United States?

THE ARTICLES OF CONFEDERATION

By November 1777 a committee of Congress had drafted a written constitution, the **Articles of Confederation.** This charter made no important change in the way what it called "The United States of America" was already operating. It put in writing the powers that the Continental Congress was already exercising. It stressed the independence of the separate states. The United States was to be only a "league of friendship"—that is, a kind of alliance. The Articles of Confederation provided that each state should have but one vote in Congress. All laws passed by Congress had to be approved by 9 of the 13 states. The Articles themselves could not be amended unless all the states agreed.

Limits were set on the power of the United States, even while the nation was fighting a war for its very survival. This reveals how sus-

picious people were of a central government. In particular they feared being taxed by the central government. This was obviously a result of their resentment of the Stamp Act and the other taxes that Parliament had tried to make them pay. Thus Section 8 of the Articles of Confederation said Congress should decide how much money had to be raised, but actual tax laws would have to be passed by the state legislatures.

Many states were reluctant to give Congress the authority that the Articles proposed, even though it was severely limited. However, after a little more than a year had passed, all the states except Maryland had **ratified,** or approved, the document. Maryland's objections had nothing to do with the fear of a central government. In fact, it was demanding an increase in the power of Congress.

At issue was the old question of who should control the western lands. Maryland's colonial charter did not include a "sea-to-sea" land grant such as that of Virginia, Massachusetts, and other colonies. Maryland insisted, therefore, that all state claims to lands beyond the

Philadelphians line up at their new theater. This gentle hand-colored engraving is another in the popular series done by William Birch. The theater is to the right of Chestnut Street, the back of Congress Hall to the left. What document did the Congress draft in 1777?

163

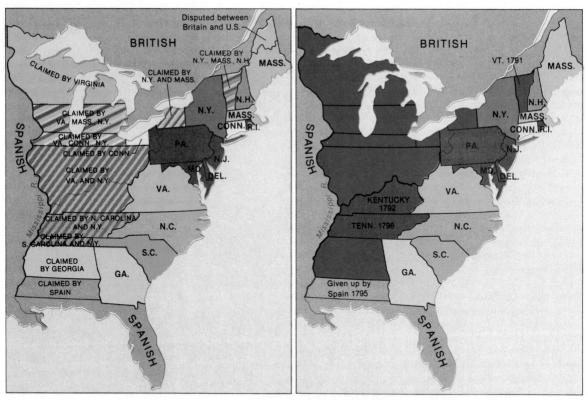

COLONIAL CLAIMS TO WESTERN LANDS 1776

THE STATES CEDE THEIR CLAIMS TO THE UNITED STATES 1781-1800

■ Territory ceded by the States

■ New States

Appalachian Mountains be turned over to the United States. Some of the states agreed, but Virginia, which had enormous western claims, refused to do so. Maryland was equally stubborn. Therefore the Articles of Confederation could not go into effect. Finally, in January 1781, Virginia gave up its western claims, and Maryland ratified the Articles.

No one could have known this at the time, but the decision to put all western lands under the control of the central government was one of the most important in the entire history of the United States. The incident is an example of how the give-and-take of political compromise in a democratic system can have unintended results. In this case the results were all good.

Maryland had held out for national control of the western lands for selfish reasons. People in the state seeking to make a fast profit buying and selling land, including the governor himself, hoped to get huge tracts of Indian land in the Ohio Valley. Virginia gave up its claims for equally selfish reasons. Benedict Arnold's raiders had invaded the state in December 1780. Cornwallis was preparing to march his powerful army north from the Carolinas. Virginia was obviously going to need the help of the other states. Giving up its western claims was a kind of goodwill gesture.

■ How did the Articles of Confederation stress the independence of the separate states?
■ Why did the question of who should control the western lands become so important?

THE TREATY OF PARIS

The importance of settling the western claims became fully clear only after a peace treaty was signed with Great Britain officially ending the War for American Independence. Negotiating the treaty was complicated because the struggle had become another world war. Spain and France were deeply involved, and their interests were not always the same as America's. Spain, for example, wanted to extend its control in America into what are now Mississippi and Alabama. France was not eager to see the United States become too large and powerful either. Both these nations wished to settle many issues with the British. In the complicated negotiations they might sacrifice American goals to advance their own.

Another problem was that the British leaders resented having lost a war to colonists. Their pride was hurt. To have to negotiate with "rebels" was a bitter pill for them to swallow. They might prefer to give more to the French and Spanish to avoid giving in to the Americans.

The peace negotiations took place in Paris in 1782 and 1783. Congress appointed an extremely distinguished delegation consisting of Benjamin Franklin, Thomas Jefferson, John Adams, Henry Laurens, and John Jay. Franklin, Jefferson, and Adams were probably the best-known and most respected Americans of their generation. Henry Laurens had made a fortune as a merchant and planter in South Carolina. He had served as president of the Continental Congress. During the war he had been captured by the British while sailing to Holland on a diplomatic assignment. He had spent more than a year locked up in the Tower of London. Finally he was released in exchange for General Cornwallis, who had surrendered after the Battle of Yorktown.

John Jay, a New York lawyer and drafter of the first New York state constitution, had also been a president of the Continental Congress. Jay came to Paris directly from service as United States minister to Spain. He was a humorless person but extremely intelligent and a shrewd diplomat. Franklin tended to accept the

American delegates in Paris for the peace talks with Great Britain in 1782-83. This detail is from an oil painted by Benjamin West in about 1783. British delegates refused to pose, so the painting is unfinished. The Americans, from left, are John Jay, John Adams, Bejamin Franklin, Henry Laurens, and Franklin's grandson, who was secretary to the delegation. Why were Americans eager for a treaty?

suggestions of the French foreign minister, Count Vergennes. Jay did not trust Vergennes, and he was right not to.

Fortunately for the United States, Jay did the most important negotiating with the chief British delegate, Richard Oswald. He persuaded Oswald that a strong United States in North America would be less of a threat to England than a strong France or Spain.

In the end Oswald accepted Jay's argument. In November 1782 he signed an agreement that gave the United States just about everything it could have hoped for. Besides official recognition of the

166

United States, the British accepted the Great Lakes as the northern boundary of the new nation and the Mississippi River as the western boundary. The southern boundary was set at 31° north latitude. Florida and the southern parts of present-day Alabama, Mississippi, and Louisiana remained under Spanish control.

The British also agreed to remove their armies from American soil "with all convenient speed." In return the Americans promised not to seize any more property from American Loyalists. They would urge the state governments to give back property that had already been taken. Finally, they agreed not to try to prevent British subjects from recovering debts owed them from before the Revolution by Americans. This agreement, the **Peace of Paris,** was officially accepted by both sides in September 1783.

■ What were the major points of the Treaty of Paris?

HEROES OF THE REVOLUTION

In the flush of victory Americans celebrated their first national heroes. Benjamin Franklin had been widely known for his experiments with electricity and for *Poor Richard's Almanack.* Now he was admired everywhere for his staunch support of the Revolution.

Thomas Jefferson had also become a national hero by the 1780s. American pride in the Declaration of Independence swelled when the Revolution succeeded and the courage of the document's signers could be fully appreciated.

The greatest hero of all was Washington. "The Father of His Country" was, by all accounts, a stern man who stood alone and said little. Yet all Americans admired his personal sacrifice and his careful use of power. One admirer called him "no harum Starum ranting Swearing fellow but Sober, steady, and calm."

A Scot, John Paul Jones, was revered as the founder of the strong United States naval tradition. In his little ship *Bon Homme Richard* ("Poor Richard," named in admiration of Franklin), Jones came upon a British convoy led by the powerful *Serapis.* He lashed his ship to the *Serapis* and fought from sunset into moonlight until both ships were seriously damaged. Still Jones refused to surrender. "I have not yet begun to fight," he proclaimed. Finally the British vessel surrendered and was boarded by Jones as the *Bon Homme Richard* sank in a storm of fire.

All men and women who had been brave enough to take up arms against the British were now heroes. One, Andrew Jackson, was only a boy of nine when war broke out. For refusing to black the boots of a British officer, he was struck sharply in the face with the flat of a sword. He carried the scar to his grave.

■ What qualities of George Washington were widely admired?

John Paul Jones, the Scottish founder of the strong American naval tradition, is portrayed in this heroic bust. It was cast in bronze from a plaster sculpture by a French artist, John-Antoine Houdon, c. 1780. How did Jones and his sailors defeat the British *Serapis?*

167

THE LAND ORDINANCES

With peace and with the United States recognized as a member of the family of nations, Congress turned to other problems. One of the most important was the organization of the territory beyond the Appalachian Mountains. As early as 1780 Congress had decided that western territories under its control should be "formed into distinct republican States which shall become members of the Federal Union." After the war was won, Congress put the policy into effect by passing two laws called **Land Ordinances.**

The first, the **Land Ordinance of 1785,** established a method of selling the land. This method combined the New England idea of carving up the wilderness into large townships and the southern practice of giving land in smaller units to individuals. Unsettled regions were to be surveyed into squares 6 miles (about 10 kilometers) on a side. Half of these **townships** would then be subdivided into 36 sections, each 1 square mile (640 acres, or 256 hectares) in area. The townships and sections were to be sold at public auction. The money would go into the treasury of the United States, but the money from the sale of one section in each township would be given to the local community for the support of its schools.

The **Land Ordinance of 1787,** also known as the **Northwest Ordinance,** provided a way to govern the lands bounded by the Ohio and Mississippi Rivers and the Great Lakes while they were growing from territory to statehood. The new regions could have been carved up into colonies the way the English had done with their American possessions. But the American people had just fought a war to get rid of colonialism. The Ordinance provided that the Northwest be divided into units called **territories.** Each territory was to be ruled by a governor and three judges appointed by Congress. When 5,000 men of voting age had settled a territory, they could elect a local legislature to deal with their own affairs and a nonvoting delegate to represent their interests in Congress.

Cincinnati, on the Ohio River, lay in the new Northwest Territory. A. J. Swing painted this oil of Cincinnati as it appeared in 1800, 13 years after the Northwest Ordinance was passed. Fort Washington is in the background at the right. How did a territory such as this one in Ohio become a state?

Courtesy, Cincinnati Historical Society

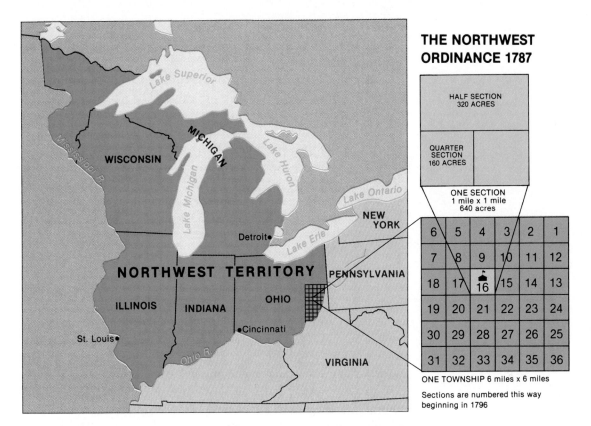

THE NORTHWEST ORDINANCE 1787

HALF SECTION
320 ACRES

QUARTER SECTION
160 ACRES

ONE SECTION
1 mile x 1 mile
640 acres

6	5	4	3	2	1
7	8	9	10	11	12
18	17	16	15	14	13
19	20	21	22	23	24
30	29	28	27	26	25
31	32	33	34	35	36

ONE TOWNSHIP 6 miles x 6 miles

Sections are numbered this way
beginning in 1796

When the population of the territory reached 60,000, the voters were to draft a state constitution. After Congress approved this document, the territory would become a state, equal to all the other states. The only limitations placed by Congress were that the state government must be **republican**—that is, its power must lie in representatives elected by the people—and that slavery must be prohibited.

Under the Northwest Ordinance, the states of Ohio, Indiana, Illinois, Michigan, and Wisconsin were eventually formed. As the nation expanded westward, the same method was used again and again. Thus the original 13 states became the present 50. This development was not always smooth. Many controversies marked the history of westward expansion. Slavery, for example, was not ruled out in all new territories. Bitter conflicts erupted over this issue, as we shall see.

Without the Land Ordinance system there would surely have been far more bitter conflicts. If Congress had tried to give the West less power than the original states, the United States would almost certainly have become a number of separate nations.

- How would new states come into being under the Land Ordinance system?
- What two limitations did Congress place on states that were formed from territories?

PEACETIME TROUBLES

The end of the War for American Independence was a great blessing. The bloodshed stopped. Normal life could resume. American ships could sail the seas without fear of attack. Merchants could buy and sell in markets such as China that formerly had been closed to them.

However, peace brought out the weaknesses of a government that was only a "league of friendship." When the need to "hang together" to save their necks ended, the states tended to go off in different directions. The great Land Ordinances could never have been passed if Virginia had not given up its western claims. And the Virginians would never have given them up if they had not felt threatened by the coastal invasions of Benedict Arnold and General Cornwallis.

Once the war was over, rivalries between the various states became more troublesome. As every American sports fan knows, members of leagues, however friendly, can compete with one another fiercely! There was a brief economic downturn, or **depression.** Farmers and merchants experienced hard times. This depression lasted from 1784 to 1786. During the hard times the states were stingier than ever about supplying the money that the United States needed to run its affairs. Each state would pay only for direct benefits and ignore national needs. States like North Carolina and Georgia had frontier districts where there could be fighting with the Indians or possible invasion by Spanish forces. These states were willing to contribute to national defense. South Carolina, protected from danger by Georgia and North Carolina, was unwilling to pay its share of national defense.

■ What were some of the peacetime troubles for the "league of friendship"?

THE TRADE PROBLEM

Many Americans were hurt by British regulations of trade with the United States after the war. To the British the United States had become a foreign country. They therefore applied the Navigation Acts to American commerce. They barred American dried and salted fish from the sugar islands in the British West Indies. This hurt New England fishermen. They required that other American products be carried to the West Indies in British ships. This hurt American merchants and shipbuilders.

British manufacturers had not been able to sell their products in America during the war. Local manufacturing had begun to spring up to supply the needs of the people. With peace restored the British began to sell goods in America at extremely low prices in order to win back the customers they had lost.

The New York Historical Society

This practice, called **dumping,** could have been checked by taxing British imports. High **tariffs,** or taxes on imports, might also have persuaded the British to remove the restrictions on American trade with the West Indies. But the United States government did not have the power under the Articles of Confederation to put tariffs on foreign goods.

One need only recall how Americans felt about the Townshend duty on tea to understand why the states had been unwilling to allow the central government to tax imports. Yet if one or another individual state taxed British goods, British merchants would simply ship their products to a port in a state that had not passed tariff laws.

Soon many Americans began to suggest that Congress be given the power to tax foreign goods. This could be done only if all the states agreed to change the Articles of Confederation. Despite many attempts this unanimous consent could not be obtained.

American manufacturing expanded during the war. Pewter dishes were widely used. The members of the American Society of Pewterers of New York City carried this silk banner when they marched in July 1788. The banner proclaims that "art shall flourish in Columbia's land." What happened to the price of British imports when the war ended?

- How did British restrictions on trade hurt Americans after the war had ended?
- How might a tariff on British goods have helped Americans?

171

States could issue their own paper money in the early 1780s. This five-dollar bill was issued by Rhode Island. It is hand numbered in the upper left. Why did the citizens of Rhode Island want "cheap" paper money after the war?

THE MONEY PROBLEM

Another power denied the United States under the Articles of Confederation was the power to tax. The system of asking the states for money never worked well, even during the war. To pay its bills Congress printed more and more paper money, called **Continental dollars.** This money fell in value because people had no confidence in it. They preferred **hard money**—gold and silver coins that simply as metal were worth the value stamped on them. The lower the real value of the Continental dollar, the more dollars the government had to print. A vicious circle developed. Soon people were using the expression "not worth a Continental" to mean "worthless."

The state governments did have the power to tax their citizens. They could issue paper money too, and all did so. This paper money caused **inflation.** That is, prices rose because the amount of dollars in people's pockets increased without an increase in the amount of goods available for sale. People lost confidence in state money for the same reason that they distrusted Continentals.

Some states therefore cut down on their paper issues. To pay their expenses they increased taxes. Money paid in taxes was money that otherwise might have been spent on goods, so the demand for goods declined. Sellers then had to lower their prices.

Not everyone benefited from lower prices, not even all the people who could buy things more cheaply. People who had borrowed money in the past preferred inflation, which made it easier for them to pay their debts. A farmer who borrowed $10 when wheat was selling for 25 cents a bushel would have to raise 40 bushels to pay his debt. If the price of wheat went up to 50 cents a bushel, he would only have to produce 20 bushels to pay it.

Popular pressure for "cheap" paper money was particularly strong in Rhode Island. That state had been hard hit by the postwar depression. Taxes were a heavy burden on the farm population. Farmers also resented the prosperity of the merchants of Providence and other towns.

In 1786 the Rhode Island legislature passed a bill allowing property owners to borrow fixed amounts of money from the government at a very low interest rate for 14 years. The state would simply print the money and hand it over to any Rhode Island landowner who applied. When lenders refused to accept this paper money in payment of debts, the legislature passed a law allowing the debtors to deposit the money with local judges, who would declare the loan repaid. When storekeepers refused to accept the paper at face value, the legislature passed a law to heavily fine them.

These laws caused business in Rhode Island to come to a standstill. Storekeepers closed their shops rather than sell goods for money they believed worthless. People who were owed money went

172

into hiding. Some fled the state. One jokester suggested that instead of paper the state issue money made of rope. Then people who refused to accept it could be whipped with the rope, and if they continue to refuse, hanged with it.

One tough-minded butcher, John Weeden of Newport, Rhode Island, refused to accept paper money from a customer, John Trevett. When he was fined for refusing, Weeden went to court. In the case of *Trevett v. Weeden*, the Rhode Island Supreme Court refused to make Weeden pay the fine on the grounds, never before used by an American court, that the law was **unconstitutional.** It violated the state constitution. The constitution had not given the legislature the power to pass the law. After the Court's decision it became impossible to make people accept Rhode Island paper money. It fell rapidly in value.

- Why did Congress begin to print paper money?
- Why did Americans prefer "hard" money to paper money?
- What was the fate of paper money in Rhode Island?

SHAYS'S REBELLION

Conservative people in all the states had been greatly concerned by the actions of the Rhode Island legislature. Events in Massachusetts soon alarmed these conservatives even more. There the reverse of the Rhode Island situation existed. The Massachusetts legislators were determined to pay off the large state debt by raising taxes.

Daniel Shays brought his protest against taxes to the steps of the state supreme court in Springfield, Massachusetts, in 1786. Howard Pyle made this engraving more than 100 years later. What action prompted Shays's Rebellion?

These taxes hit people in the western part of the state very hard. Poor farmers who did not have the money to pay them had their farms seized and sold. Resentment mounted. Crowds gathered to prevent local courts from meeting to condemn the property of debtors so that it could be sold to pay the taxes. In September 1786 a mob marched on Springfield, Massachusetts, to prevent the state supreme court from meeting.

The leader of the protesters was Daniel Shays, a veteran of the War for American Independence. Shays had fought at Lexington, Bunker Hill, and Saratoga. Although he was uneducated, he had risen to the rank of captain. He was a poor man, much troubled by the determination of the state to prevent inflation and pay off the debt.

After breaking up the meeting of the supreme court, Shays tried to attack the Springfield arsenal in order to get more weapons. However, his force of 1,200 men was routed by militia units. A second battle with the militia in January 1787 had the same result. **Shays's Rebellion** collapsed and Shays fled to Vermont.

- Why did the farmers in western Massachusetts rise up against their government?
- What were the events of Shays's Rebellion?

THE CONSTITUTIONAL CONVENTION

The Rhode Island and Massachusetts disturbances raised questions in the minds of many conservatives about the future of republican government. Was this what happened when the people were allowed to govern themselves? Would the poor always use their votes to cheat the rich when they had the votes to do it, as in Rhode Island, or resort to force when they did not, as in Massachusetts?

One result of such questions was to make people want to increase the power of the United States government at the expense of the states. Then it would be more difficult for a minority to frighten the majority or for one group to get control of the machinery of government.

A stronger central government could maintain order better. It could develop a unified policy for the whole country. Those who favored giving the national government control over foreign trade expected prosperity to result. These objectives—**unity, order,** and **prosperity**—made a powerful combination. The time had come to revise the Articles of Confederation.

In September 1786 delegates from five states met at Annapolis, Maryland, to discuss the foreign trade problem. They could do nothing about it unless all the states participated. Reform was impossible. One of the men present was Alexander Hamilton of New York, a young lawyer who had served on General Washington's staff

174

during the war. He suggested that the group call another meeting. Delegates to this meeting should consider a plan for revising the entire Articles of Confederation.

Congress voted to recommend this proposal to the states. All the legislatures except Rhode Island's sent delegates to the meeting. The sessions began at the Pennsylvania State House in Philadelphia on May 25, 1787.

The delegates' first decision was to elect George Washington president, or chairman, of the conference. The presence of Washington, who was 55, and of Benjamin Franklin, who was over 80, added prestige to the group. But most of the work was done by much younger people like James Madison of Virginia, who was 36.

The next major step was the decision to try to draft a new constitution. The delegates had been authorized by the state legislatures only to try to patch up the Articles of Confederation. Instead they wiped the slate clean. The meeting then became the **Constitutional Convention.** This was technically illegal. The delegates justified their

The Constitutional Convention assembles in Philadelphia. This engraving is the earliest known of the meeting. George Washington, quill in hand, stands before the delegates. For what purpose did the delegates assemble?

action by pointing out that they were only recommending changes. The states could always reject their proposals.

■ What were some of the arguments made for having a stronger central government?
■ What surprising result came from the meeting of the delegates to consider revising the Articles of Confederation?

THE SUPREME LAW OF THE LAND

On May 30, only five days after beginning their first discussion, the delegates agreed in principle to the most fundamental change. The Articles of Confederation had created a "league of friendship." A league is a kind of treaty signed by basically independent nations. The delegates at Philadelphia proposed **a national government** instead. Gouverneur Morris of Pennsylvania, one of the best speakers at the convention, explained the difference between the two. The "league of friendship" was "a mere compact resting on the good faith of the parties." A national government was "a complete and compulsive" authority, able to enforce its laws directly on the people.

This principle was spelled out in the famous first sentence of the **Constitution,** the Preamble. It reads: "We the *People* of the United States . . . do ordain and establish this Constitution," not "We the states . . ." In Article VI the Constitution further states that it is to be "the supreme Law of the Land." Judges in the states are to be bound by it without regard for anything in the state constitutions. Even the members of the state legislatures were to be required to take an oath to support the United States Constitution.

Such a drastic change was agreed upon so quickly because the delegates were determined to create a more effective central government. Of course, some Americans disapproved of the change. When Sam Adams, who was not a delegate, saw that the Preamble to the Constitution began "We the People" rather than "We the states," he remarked, "As I enter the Building I stumble at the Threshold." Nevertheless, the Philadelphia delegates had been appointed by *state* legislatures. The legislatures would not have selected them if they were not prepared to see the United States made stronger.

Historical imagination helps us to understand another reason why people were ready for a more powerful government. The War for American Independence had stirred **nationalism,** a feeling of national pride. It had given people their first heroes and their first flags. Thousands of soldiers had traveled far from home and seen other parts of the country. They had fought alongside soldiers from other states. Their horizons had been broadened. Afterwards, they were less likely to think of themselves as Virginians or Pennsylvanians or New Yorkers. They had become first of all Americans.

176

No one wanted the central government to swallow up the states. The state governments should remain strong and active and independent. However, to the powers already possessed by the United States, the delegates now added several. The most important were the power to tax and the power to regulate trade between the states and between all the states and foreign countries. The Constitution also took away from the separate states the right to coin money and print paper money and the right to tax imports and exports.

Now the United States could raise money to pay its expenses without depending on the state legislatures. Therefore it could pay its bills and avoid printing too much money. The dollar would be worth a dollar, whether in the form of silver or gold coins or in the form of a dollar bill.

Now the United States could place tariffs on imported goods, either to raise money or to regulate foreign trade. These were powers Parliament had tried to exercise before the Revolution. Now Congress was to exercise them.

Moreover, reducing the power of the states to "make" money meant that incidents like Rhode Island's paper money problems could no longer occur. Any future Daniel Shays could be checked by the power of the whole nation if necessary.

The states, however, would still have enough power to manage their local affairs. They could not print money, but they could obtain money by taxing their citizens. The states and the local communities within them could continue to have their own police, and state governors could call up militia units in emergencies.

The Preamble of the Constitution neatly summarizes what these changes were meant to accomplish. "We the People" were creating "a more perfect Union" where "Justice" would be assured and order maintained (the founders used the term "domestic Tranquility"). The new system would "provide for the common defense" against foreign enemies too. It would "promote the general Welfare" and secure for Americans and their descendants "the Blessings of Liberty." In other words, the Constitution would supply the nation with the *unity, order,* and *prosperity* that had been lacking under the Articles of Confederation.

The complete text of the Constitution, with aids for reading, follows on pages 178-197 of this chapter.

- What is the difference between a "league of friendship" and a national government?
- Why did the delegates agree so quickly to have a new Constitution?
- What are some of the powers the Constitution gave to the United States government?

THE CONSTITUTION
OF THE UNITED STATES OF AMERICA

Preamble

We the People of the United States, in Order to form a more perfect Union, establish Justice, insure domestic Tranquility, provide for the common defense, promote the general Welfare, and secure the Blessings of Liberty to ourselves and our Posterity, do ordain and establish this Constitution for the United States of America.

Article I

Section 1. All legislative Powers herein granted shall be vested in a Congress of the United States, which shall consist of a Senate and House of Representatives.

Section 2. The House of Representatives shall be composed of Members chosen every second Year by the People of the several States, and the Electors in each State shall have the Qualifications requisite for Electors of the most numerous Branch of the State Legislature.

No Person shall be a Representative who shall not have attained to the Age of twenty-five Years, and been seven Years a Citizen of the United States, and who shall not, when elected, be an Inhabitant of that State in which he shall be chosen.

Representatives and direct Taxes shall be apportioned among the several States which may be included within this Union, according to their respective Numbers, which shall be determined by adding to the whole Number of free Persons, including those bound to Service for a Term of Years, and excluding Indians not taxed, three fifths of all other Persons. The actual Enumeration shall be made within three Years after the first Meeting of the Congress of the United States, and within every subsequent Term of ten Years, in such Manner as they shall by Law direct. The Number of Representatives shall not exceed one for every thirty Thousand, but each State shall have at Least one Representative; and until such enumeration shall be made, the State of New Hampshire shall be entitled to choose three; Massachusetts eight; Rhode Island and Providence Plantations one; Con-

---

The people establish the Constitution and thus the government. See pages 176-77.

domestic Tranquility: establishment of order within the country.

Posterity: future generations.
ordain: order; decree.

Article I describes the legislative, or law-making, branch of government.

vested: held or established.

States may decide who is qualified to vote, but now they also must abide by the Fifteenth, Nineteenth, Twenty-fourth, and Twenty-sixth Amendments. Representatives are to be elected every two years.

Electors: voters.

requisite: required.

attained: reached.

By custom a representative is also expected to reside in the district he or she represents.

apportioned: divided up.

Material lined through has been deleted from the Constitution by time limits or by amendments.

This is the "Three-Fifths Compromise." See pages 198-99.

Enumeration: the counting; census.

By law the number of representatives has now been set at 435.

necticut five; New York six; New Jersey four; Pennsylvania eight; Delaware one; Maryland six; Virginia ten; North Carolina five; South Carolina five; and Georgia three.

When vacancies happen in the Representation from any State, the Executive Authority thereof shall issue Writs of Election to fill such Vacancies.

The House of Representatives shall choose their Speaker and other Officers; and shall have the sole Power of Impeachment.

Section 3. The Senate of the United States shall be composed of two Senators from each State, chosen by the Legislature thereof, for six Years; and each Senator shall have one Vote.

Immediately after they shall be assembled in Consequence of the first Election, they shall be divided as equally as may be into three Classes. The Seats of the Senators of the first Class shall be vacated at the Expiration of the second Year, of the second Class at the Expiration of the fourth Year, and of the third Class at the Expiration of the sixth Year, so that one third may be chosen every second Year; and if Vacancies happen by Resignation, or otherwise, during the Recess of the Legislature of any State, the Executive thereof may make temporary Appointments until the next Meeting of the Legislature, which shall then fill such Vacancies.

No Person shall be a Senator who shall not have attained to the Age of thirty Years, and been nine Years a Citizen of the United States, and who shall not, when elected, be an Inhabitant of that State for which he shall be chosen.

The Vice President of the United States shall be President of the Senate, but shall have no Vote, unless they be equally divided.

The Senate shall choose their other Officers, and also a President pro tempore, in the Absence of the Vice President, or when he shall exercise the Office of President of the United States.

The Senate shall have the sole Power to try all Impeachments. When sitting for that Purpose, they shall be on Oath or Affirmation. When the President of the United States is tried, the Chief Justice shall preside: And no Person shall be convicted without the Concurrence of two thirds of the Members present.

Judgment in Cases of Impeachment shall not extend further than to removal from Office, and disqualification to hold and enjoy any Office of honor, Trust or Profit under the United States: but the Party convicted shall nevertheless be liable and subject to Indictment, Trial, Judgment and Punishment, according to Law.

Section 4. The Times, Places and Manner of holding Elections for Senators and Representatives, shall be prescribed in each State by the Legislature thereof; but the Congress may at any time by Law make or alter such Regulations, except as to the Places of choosing Senators.

The Congress shall assemble at least once in every Year, and such Meeting shall be on the first Monday in December, unless they shall by Law appoint a different Day.

Section 5. Each House shall be the Judge of the Elections, Returns and Qualifications of its own Members, and a Majority of each shall constitute a Quorum to do Business; but a smaller Number may adjourn from day to day, and may be authorized to compel the Attendance of absent Members, in such Manner, and under such Penalties as each House may provide.

constitute: form; make up.
Quorum: the number of persons needed to be present to conduct business.
In practice each house of Congress conducts business without a quorum unless a member objects and calls for a quorum.

Each House may determine the Rules of its Proceedings, punish its Members for disorderly Behavior, and, with the Concurrence of two thirds, expel a Member.

Concurrence of two thirds: each house can expel a member with a two-thirds vote.

Each House shall keep a Journal of its Proceedings, and from time to time publish the same, excepting such Parts as may in their Judgment require Secrecy; and the Yeas and Nays of the Members of either House on any question shall, at the Desire of one fifth of those Present, be entered on the Journal.

Yeas and Nays: votes for and against.

One fifth of the members of either house can call for a roll-call vote.

Neither House, during the Session of Congress, shall, without the Consent of the other, adjourn for more than three days, nor to any other Place than that in which the two Houses shall be sitting.

Section 6. The Senators and Representatives shall receive a Compensation for their Services, to be ascertained by Law, and paid out of the Treasury of the United States. They shall in all Cases, except Treason, Felony and Breach of the Peace, be privileged from Arrest during their Attendance at the Session of their respective Houses, and in going to and returning from the same; and for any Speech or Debate in either House, they shall not be questioned in any other Place.

Compensation: salary. It was $57,500 a year in 1981.
ascertained: determined.

Treason: betrayal of one's country. See Article II, Section 3.
Felony: a serious crime.
Breach of the Peace: illegal violence.

No Senator or Representative shall, during the Time for which he was elected, be appointed to any civil Office under the Authority of the United States, which shall have been created, or the Emoluments whereof shall have been increased during such time; and no Person holding any Office under the United States, shall be a Member of either House during his Continuance in Office.

A senator or representative may not also be an employee of government.

Emoluments: payments; salary.

Section 7. All Bills for raising Revenue shall originate in the House of Representatives; but the Senate may propose or concur with Amendments as on other Bills.

Bill: a proposed law.
Revenue: money; income.
originate: start; begin.

The Senate may propose changes in revenue bills.

This section describes how a bill becomes law. See page 201.

Every Bill which shall have passed the House of Representatives and the Senate, shall, before it become a Law, be presented to the President of the United States; If he approve he shall sign it, but if not he shall return it, with his Objections to that House in which it shall have originated, who shall enter the Objections at large on their Journal, and proceed to reconsider it. If after such Reconsideration two thirds of that House shall agree to pass the Bill, it shall be sent, together with the Objections, to the other House, by which it shall

180

likewise be reconsidered, and if approved by two thirds of that House, it shall become a Law. But in all such Cases the Votes of both Houses shall be determined by Yeas and Nays, and the Names of the Persons voting for and against the Bill shall be entered on the Journal of each House respectively. If any Bill shall not be returned by the President within ten Days (Sundays excepted) after it shall have been presented to him, the Same shall be a Law, in like Manner as if he had signed it, unless the Congress by their Adjournment prevent its Return, in which Case it shall not be a Law.

Every Order, Resolution, or Vote to which the Concurrence of the Senate and House of Representatives may be necessary (except on a question of Adjournment) shall be presented to the President of the United States; and before the Same shall take Effect, shall be approved by him, or being disapproved by him, shall be repassed by two thirds of the Senate and House of Representatives, according to the Rules and Limitations prescribed in the Case of a Bill.

Section 8. The Congress shall have Power To lay and collect Taxes, Duties, Imposts and Excises, to pay the Debts and provide for the common Defense and general Welfare of the United States; but all Duties, Imposts and Excises shall be uniform throughout the United States;

To borrow Money on the credit of the United States;

To regulate Commerce with foreign Nations, and among the several States, and with the Indian Tribes;

To establish an uniform Rule of Naturalization, and uniform Laws on the subject of Bankruptcies throughout the United States;

To coin Money, regulate the Value thereof, and of foreign Coin, and fix the Standard of Weights and Measures;

To provide for the Punishment of counterfeiting the Securities and current Coin of the United States;

To establish Post Offices and post Roads;

To promote the Progress of Science and useful Arts, by securing for limited Times to Authors and Inventors the exclusive Right to their respective Writings and Discoveries;

To constitute Tribunals inferior to the supreme Court;

To define and punish Piracies and Felonies committed on the high Seas, and Offences against the Law of Nations;

To declare War, grant Letters of Marque and Reprisal, and make Rules concerning Captures on Land and Water;

To raise and support Armies, but no Appropriation of Money to that Use shall be for a longer Term than two Years;

To provide and maintain a Navy;

To make Rules for the Government and Regulation of the land and naval Forces;

To provide for calling forth the Militia to execute the Laws of

This section describes the powers of Congress.
Duties: taxes on imported or exported goods.
Imposts: taxes on imported goods.
Excises: taxes on products manufactured within the country.

Rule of Naturalization: the steps by which foreign-born persons can become United States citizens.
Bankruptcies: persons or businesses unable to pay their debts.

Securities: money and government bonds

post Roads: improved roads on which the mail was carried.

Right to . . . Writings and Discoveries: copyright and patent laws to protect the rights of authors and inventors.
Tribunals inferior to the supreme Court: the system of lower courts, district courts, and appeals courts.

Letters of Marque and Reprisal: licenses once used to allow privately owned ships to capture enemy ships.
Appropriation: an amount of money set aside for a special purpose.

Militia: citizen-soldiers who are not in the regular army. Today it refers to the National Guard units of the states.
execute the Laws: carry out the laws.

181

the Union, suppress Insurrections and repel Invasions;

To provide for organizing, arming, and disciplining, the Militia, and for governing such Part of them as may be employed in the Service of the United States, reserving to the States respectively, the Appointment of the Officers, and the Authority of training the Militia according to the discipline prescribed by Congress.

Congress is to have authority over the seat of government, established as the District of Columbia, and over facilities and buildings owned and operated by the federal government in the various states. This is known as "the elastic clause." See page 218.

To exercise exclusive Legislation in all Cases whatsoever, over such District (not exceeding ten Miles square) as may, by Cession of particular States, and the Acceptance of Congress, become the Seat of the Government of the United States, and to exercise like Authority over all Places purchased by the Consent of the Legislature of the State in which the Same shall be, for the Erection of Forts, Magazines, Arsenals, dock-Yards, and other needful Buildings;—And

To make all Laws which shall be necessary and proper for carrying into Execution the foregoing Powers, and all other Powers vested by this Constitution in the Government of the United States, or in any Department or Officer thereof.

This section puts limits on the powers of Congress to ban slavery before 1808. See pages 198–199.

Section 9. ~~The Migration or Importation of such Persons as any of the States now existing shall think proper to admit, shall not be prohibited by the Congress prior to the Year one thousand eight hundred and eight, but a Tax or duty may be imposed on such Importation, not exceeding ten dollars for each Person.~~

Writ of Habeas Corpus: a court order that protects a person from being held in jail when there is not enough evidence to charge him or her with a crime.

The Privilege of the Writ of Habeas Corpus shall not be suspended, unless when in Cases of Rebellion or Invasion the public Safety may require it.

Bill of Attainder: a legislative measure that condemns and punishes a person without benefit of jury trial.

ex post facto Law: a law that punishes a person for doing something before the law making it illegal was passed. *Modified by the Sixteenth Amendment.*

No Bill of Attainder or ex post facto Law shall be passed.

~~No Capitation, or other direct, Tax shall be laid, unless in Proportion to the Census or Enumeration herein before directed to be taken.~~

No Tax or Duty shall be laid on Articles exported from any State.

No Preference shall be given by any Regulation of Commerce or Revenue to the Ports of one State over those of another: nor shall Vessels bound to, or from, one State, be obliged to enter, clear, or pay Duties in another.

Only money approved by Congress may be spent.

No Money shall be drawn from the Treasury, but in Consequence of Appropriations made by Law; and a regular Statement and Account of the Receipts and Expenditures of all public Money shall be published from time to time.

Title of Nobility: titles of rank that can be inherited, like "princess," "baron," "king."

No Title of Nobility shall be granted by the United States: And no Person holding any Office of Profit or Trust under them, shall, without the Consent of the Congress, accept of any present, Emolument, Office, or Title, of any kind whatever, from any King, Prince, or foreign State.

This section limits the powers of the states.

Section 10. No State shall enter into any Treaty, Alliance, or

Confederation; grant Letters of Marque and Reprisal; coin Money; emit Bills of Credit; make any Thing but gold and silver Coin a Tender in Payment of Debts; pass any Bill of Attainder, ex post facto Law, or Law impairing the Obligation of Contracts, or grant any Title of Nobility.

No State shall, without the Consent of the Congress, lay any Imposts or Duties on Imports or Exports, except what may be absolutely necessary for executing its inspection Laws: and the net Produce of all Duties and Imposts, laid by any Senate on Imports or Exports, shall be for the Use of the Treasury of the United States; and all such Laws shall be subject to the Revision and Control of the Congress.

No State shall, without the Consent of Congress, lay any Duty of Tonnage, keep Troops, or Ships of War in time of Peace, enter into any Agreement or Compact with another State, or with a foreign Power, or engage in War, unless actually invaded, or in such imminent Danger as will not admit of delay.

emit Bills of Credit: issue letters or bonds to be used as money.
Tender: money offered in payment of a debt.

net Produce: income from duties and imposts after expenses have been paid.

Duty of Tonnage: duty collected at a given amount per ton of cargo.

imminent: threatening to happen soon.

Article II

Section 1. The executive Power shall be vested in a President of the United States of America. He shall hold his Office during the Term of four Years, and, together with the Vice President, chosen for the same Term, be elected, as follows.

Each State shall appoint, in such Manner as the Legislature thereof may direct, a Number of Electors, equal to the whole Number of Senators and Representatives to which the State may be entitled in the Congress: but no Senator or Representative, or Person holding an Office of Trust or Profit under the United States, shall be appointed an Elector.

The Electors shall meet in their respective States, and vote by Ballot for two Persons, of whom one at least shall not be an Inhabitant of the same State with themselves. And they shall make a List of all the Persons voted for, and of the Number of Votes for each; which List they shall sign and certify, and transmit sealed to the Seat of the Government of the United States, directed to the President of the Senate. The President of the Senate shall, in the Presence of the Senate and House of Representatives, open all the Certificates, and the Votes shall then be counted. The Person having the greatest Number of Votes shall be the President, if such Number be a Majority of the whole Number of Electors appointed; and if there be more than one who have such majority, and have an equal Number of Votes, then the House of Representatives shall immediately choose by Ballot one of them for President; and if no Person have a Majority, then from the five highest on the List the said House shall in like Manner choose

Article II describes the executive department, which is headed by the President. See pages 199-200. Electors are chosen today by conventions or committees of the political parties in each state. On election day the people vote for electors, who then in turn choose the President. See page 200.
Presidential elections are held the first Tuesday after the first Monday in November. Electoral votes are cast on the first Monday after the second Wednesday in December.

Modified by the Twenty-fifth Amendment.

the President. But in choosing the President, the Votes shall be taken by States, the Representation from each State having one Vote; A quorum for this Purpose shall consist of a Member or Members from two thirds of the States, and a Majority of all the States shall be necessary to a Choice. In every Case, after the Choice of the President, the Person having the greatest Number of Votes of the Electors shall be the Vice President. But if there should remain two or more who have equal Votes, the Senate shall choose from them by Ballot the Vice President.

The Congress may determine the Time of choosing the Electors, and the Day on which they shall give their Votes; which Day shall be the same throughout the United States.

No Person except a natural born Citizen, or a Citizen of the United States, at the time of the Adoption of this Constitution, shall be eligible to the Office of President; neither shall any Person be eligible to that Office who shall not have attained to the Age of thirty-five Years, and been fourteen Years a Resident within the United States.

In Case of the Removal of the President from Office, or of his Death, Resignation, or Inability to discharge the Powers and Duties of the said Office, the Same shall devolve on the Vice President, and the Congress may by Law provide for the Case of Removal, Death, Resignation or Inability, both of the President and Vice President, declaring what Officer shall then act as President, and such Officer shall act accordingly, until the Disability be removed, or a President shall be elected.

Compensation: salary. The President's salary in 1981 was $200,000.

The President shall, at stated Times, receive for his Services, a Compensation, which shall neither be increased nor diminished during the Period for which he shall have been elected, and he shall not receive within that Period any other Emolument from the United States, or any of them.

By tradition the oath is administered by the Chief Justice of the Supreme Court.

Before he enter on the Execution of his Office, he shall take the following Oath or Affirmation:—"I do solemnly swear (or affirm) that I will faithfully execute the Office of President of the United States, and will to the best of my Ability, preserve, protect and defend the Constitution of the United States."

Sections 2 and 3 describe the powers and responsibilities of the President. As Commander in Chief the President exerts civilian control over military power.

Section 2. The President shall be Commander in Chief of the Army and Navy of the United States, and of the Militia of the several States, when called into the actual Service of the United States; he may require the Opinion, in writing, of the principal Officer in each of the executive Departments, upon any Subject relating to the Duties of their respective Offices, and he shall have Power to grant

Reprieve: the temporary suspension of a sentence.

Reprieves and Pardons for Offenses against the United States, except in Cases of Impeachment.

He shall have Power, by and with the Advice and Consent of the Senate, to make Treaties, provided two thirds of the Senators present concur; and he shall nominate, and by and with the Advice and Consent of the Senate, shall appoint Ambassadors, other public Ministers and Consuls, Judges of the supreme Court, and all other Officers of the United States, whose Appointments are not herein otherwise provided for, and which shall be established by Law: but the Congress may by Law vest the Appointment of such inferior Officers, as they think proper, in the President alone, in the Courts of Law, or in the Heads of Departments.

The President shall have Power to fill up all Vacancies that may happen during the Recess of the Senate, by granting Commissions which shall expire at the End of their next Session.

Section 3. He shall from time to time give to the Congress Information of the State of the Union, and recommend to their Consideration such Measures as he shall judge necessary and expedient; he may, on extraordinary Occasions, convene both Houses, or either of them, and in Case of Disagreement between them, with Respect to the Time of Adjournment, he may adjourn them to such Time as he shall think proper; he shall receive Ambassadors and other public Ministers; he shall take Care that the Laws be faithfully executed, and shall Commission all the Officers of the United States.

Section 4. The President, Vice President and all civil Officers of the United States, shall be removed from Office on Impeachment for, and Conviction of, Treason, Bribery, or other high Crimes and Misdemeanors.

Article III

Section 1. The judicial Power of the United States, shall be vested in one supreme Court, and in such inferior Courts as the Congress may from time to time ordain and establish. The Judges, both of the supreme and inferior Courts, shall hold their Offices during good Behavior, and shall, at stated Times, receive for their Services, a Compensation, which shall not be diminished during their Continuance in Office.

Section 2. The judicial Power shall extend to all Cases, in Law and Equity, arising under this Constitution, the Laws of the United States, and Treaties made, or which shall be made, under their Authority;—to all Cases affecting Ambassadors, other public Ministers and Consuls;—to all Cases of admiralty and maritime Jurisdiction;—to Controversies to which the United States shall be a Party; —to Controversies between two or more States;—between a State and Citizens of another state;—between Citizens of different States; —between Citizens of the same State claiming Lands under Grants of different States, and between a State, or the Citizens thereof, and foreign States, Citizens or Subjects.

The Senate must give its Advice and Consent to major appointments of the President and to treaties.

Inferior Officers: government employees who do not hold major appointments. The majority of federal government positions are now held by those who have passed examinations given by the Civil Service Commission, established by Congress in 1883. See pages 588–90.

expedient: suitable; advisable.

convene: call together.

If the Houses of Congress disagree on when to adjourn, the President may decide for them.

Article III describes the third major branch of the government, the judiciary. See page 202.

Equity: fairness.
The Constitution and laws under it are the basis of all judicial decisions.
Ambassadors . . . public Ministers and Consuls: representatives of other governments.
Jurisdiction: lawful right to exercise authority. Cases involving representatives of other nations go directly to the Supreme Court. Other cases go to the Supreme Court on appeal and after they have been tried in lower courts.

In all Cases affecting Ambassadors, other public Ministers and Consuls, and those in which a State shall be Party, the supreme Court shall have original Jurisdiction. In all the other Cases before mentioned, the supreme Court shall have appellate Jurisdiction, both as to Law and Fact, with such Exceptions, and under such Regulations as the Congress shall make.

The Trial of all Crimes, except in Cases of Impeachment, shall be by Jury; and such Trial shall be held in the State where the said Crimes shall have been committed; but when not committed within any State, the Trial shall be at such Place or Places as the Congress may by Law have directed.

Section 3. Treason against the United States, shall consist only in levying War against them, or in adhering to their Enemies, giving them Aid and Comfort. No Person shall be convicted of Treason unless on the Testimony of two Witnesses to the same overt Act, or on Confession in open Court.

The Congress shall have Power to declare the Punishment of Treason, but no Attainder of Treason shall work Corruption of Blood, or Forfeiture except during the Life of the Person attainted.

Article IV

Section 1. Full Faith and Credit shall be given in each State to the public Acts, Records, and judicial Proceedings of every other State. And the Congress may by general Laws prescribe the Manner in which such Acts, Records and Proceedings shall be proved, and the Effect thereof.

Section 2. The Citizens of each State shall be entitled to all Privileges and Immunities of Citizens in the several States.

A Person charged in any State with Treason, Felony, or other Crime, who shall flee from Justice, and be found in another State, shall on Demand of the executive Authority of the State from which he fled, be delivered up, to be removed to the State having Jurisdiction of the Crime.

No Person held to Service of Labor in one State, under the Laws thereof, escaping into another, shall, in Consequence of any Law or Regulation therein, be discharged from such Service or Labor, but shall be delivered up on Claim of the Party to whom such Service or Labor may be due.

Section 3. New States may be admitted by the Congress into this Union; but no new State shall be formed or erected within the Jurisdiction of any other State; nor any State be formed by the Junction of two or more States, or Parts of States, without the Consent of the Legislatures of the States concerned as well as of the Congress.

The Congress shall have Power to dispose of and make all needful Rules and Regulations respecting the Territory or other Property

---

levying War: calling for war.
adhering to: supporting.

overt: open to view; observable.

The punishment for treason is death or a fine of $10,000 and imprisonment for not less than five years.

no Attainder of Treason shall work Corruption of Blood, or Forfeiture: the punishment for treason does not extend to the children of a traitor. They cannot be deprived of their rights or property, as had been done in England.

Article IV describes relations among the states.

Immunities: protections.
The process of returning a criminal to the state in which the crime was committed is called "extradition."

Deleted by the Thirteenth Amendment.

Junction: joining together.

belonging to the United States; and nothing in this Constitution shall be so construed as to Prejudice any Claims of the United States, or of any particular State.

Section 4. The United States shall guarantee to every State in this Union a Republican Form of Government, and shall protect each of them against Invasion; and on Application of the Legislature, or of the Executive (when the Legislature cannot be convened) against domestic Violence.

Republican Form of Government: a government formed of representatives elected by the people.

Article V

The Congress, whenever two thirds of both Houses shall deem it necessary, shall propose Amendments to this Constitution, or, on the Application of the Legislatures of two thirds of the several States, shall call a Convention for proposing Amendments, which, in either Case, shall be valid to all Intents and Purposes, as Part of this Constitution, when ratified by the Legislatures of three fourths of the several States, or by Conventions in three fourths thereof, as the one or the other Mode of Ratification may be proposed by the Congress; Provided that no Amendment which may be made prior to the Year One thousand eight hundred and eight shall in any Manner affect the first and fourth Clauses in the Ninth Section of the first Article; and that no State, without its Consent, shall be deprived of its equal Suffrage in the Senate.

Article V describes the process for amending the Constitution. Congress could not prohibit the importation of slaves before 1808, according to this Article. After 1808 Congress did prohibit bringing slaves into the United States.

Suffrage: right of voting.

Article VI

All Debts contracted and Engagements entered into, before the Adoption of this Constitution, shall be as valid against the United States under this Constitution, as under the Confederation.

valid: legally binding.

Confederation: the government formed under the Articles of Confederation. See pages 162-65.

This Constitution, and the Laws of the United States which shall be made in Pursuance thereof; and all Treaties made, or which shall be made, under the Authority of the United States, shall be the supreme Law of the Land; and the Judges in every State shall be bound thereby, any Thing in the Constitution or Laws of any State to the Contrary notwithstanding.

The Constitution is to form the basis of all laws. Legislators and judges shall take oaths to support it.

The Senators and Representatives before mentioned, and the Members of the several State Legislatures, and all executive and judicial Officers, both of the United States and of the several States, shall be bound by Oath or Affirmation, to support this Constitution; but no religious Test shall ever be required as a Qualification to any Office or public Trust under the United States.

Oath or Affirmation: a formal pledge or promise.

Article VII

The Ratification of the Conventions of nine States, shall be sufficient for the Establishment of this Constitution between the States so ratifying the Same.

Ratification: approval. See pages 204-06 for a description of the ratification of the Constitution.

DONE in Convention by the Unanimous Consent of the States present the Seventeenth Day of September in the Year of our Lord one thousand seven hundred and Eighty seven and of the Independence of the United States of America the Twelfth. IN WITNESS whereof We have hereunto subscribed our Names.

George Washington—
President and deputy from Virginia

New Hampshire
John Langdon
Nicholas Gilman

Massachusetts
Nathaniel Gorham
Rufus King

Connecticut
William Samuel Johnson
Roger Sherman

New York
Alexander Hamilton

New Jersey
William Livingston
David Brearley
William Paterson
Jonathan Dayton

Pennsylvania
Benjamin Franklin
Thomas Mifflin
Robert Morris
George Clymer
Thomas FitzSimons
Jared Ingersoll
James Wilson
Gouverneur Morris

Delaware
George Read
Gunning Bedford, Jr.
John Dickinson
Richard Bassett
Jacob Broom

Maryland
James McHenry
Daniel of St. Thomas Jenifer
Daniel Carroll

Virginia
John Blair
James Madison, Jr.

North Carolina
William Blount
Richard Dobbs Spaight
Hugh Williamson

South Carolina
John Rutledge
Charles Cotesworth Pinckney
Charles Pinckney
Pierce Butler

Georgia
William Few
Abraham Baldwin

Attest: *William Jackson*, Secretary

THE AMENDMENTS

ARTICLES in addition to, and Amendment of the Constitution of the United States of America, proposed by Congress, and ratified by the Legislatures of the several States, pursuant to the fifth Article of the original Constitution.

First Amendment

[The First through Tenth Amendments, now known as the Bill of Rights, were proposed on September 25, 1789, and declared in force on December 15, 1791.]

Congress shall make no law respecting an establishment of religion, or prohibiting the free exercise thereof; or abridging the freedom of speech, or of the press; or the right of the people peaceably to assemble, and to petition the Government for a redress of grievances.

The first ten amendments are called "The Bill of Rights." See pages 212-14.

abridging: limiting.
petition: a formal request. Today the word usually means a written request to which persons sign their names.
redress of grievances: a correction of injustices.

Second Amendment

A well regulated Militia, being necessary to the security of a free State, the right of the people to keep and bear Arms, shall not be infringed.

infringed: limited; curtailed.

Third Amendment

No Soldier shall, in time of peace, be quartered in any house, without the consent of the Owner, nor in time of war, but in a manner to be prescribed by law.

quartered: lodged; housed

Fourth Amendment

The right of the people to be secure in their persons, houses, papers, and effects, against unreasonable searches and seizures, shall not be violated, and no Warrants shall issue, but upon probable cause, supported by Oath or affirmation, and particularly describing the place to be searched, and the persons or things to be seized.

Warrants: judicial orders authorizing arrest, search, or seizure.

Fifth Amendment

No person shall be held to answer for a capital, or otherwise infamous crime, unless on a presentment or indictment of a Grand Jury, except in cases arising in the land or naval forces, or in the Militia, when in actual service in time of War or public danger; nor shall any person be subject for the same offence to be twice put in jeopardy of life or limb; nor shall be compelled in any criminal case to be a witness against himself, nor be deprived of life, liberty, or property, without due process of law; nor shall private property be taken for public use, without just compensation.

capital . . . crime: a crime punishable by the death penalty.
presentment or indictment: formal accusations.

jeopardy: danger or loss; the peril a defendant faces when put on trial for a crime.

Sixth Amendment

In all criminal prosecutions, the accused shall enjoy the right to a speedy and public trial, by an impartial jury of the State and district wherein the crime shall have been committed, which district shall have been previously ascertained by law, and to be informed of the nature and cause of the accusation; to be confronted with the witnesses against him; to have compulsory process for obtaining witnesses in his favor, and to have the Assistance of Counsel for his defense.

Seventh Amendment

In Suits at common law, where the value in controversy shall exceed twenty dollars, the right of trial by jury shall be preserved, and no fact tried by a jury shall be otherwise reexamined in any Court of the United States, than according to the rules of the common law.

Eighth Amendment

Excessive bail shall not be required, nor excessive fines imposed, nor cruel and unusual punishments inflicted.

Ninth Amendment

The enumeration in the Constitution, of certain rights, shall not be construed to deny or disparage others retained by the people.

Tenth Amendment

The powers not delegated to the United States by the Constitution, nor prohibited by it to the States, are reserved to the States respectively, or to the people.

Eleventh Amendment
[*Proposed March 4, 1794; declared ratified January 8, 1798*]

The Judicial power of the United States shall not be construed to extend to any suit in law or equity, commenced or prosecuted against one of the United States by Citizens of another State, or by Citizens or Subjects of any Foreign State.

Twelfth Amendment
[*Proposed December 9, 1803; declared ratified September 25, 1804*]

The Electors shall meet in their respective states and vote by ballot for President and Vice President, one of whom, at least, shall not be an inhabitant of the same state with themselves; they shall name in their ballots the person voted for as President, and in distinct ballots the person voted for as Vice President, and they shall make distinct lists of all persons voted for as President, and of all persons

---

impartial: not favoring one side or another.

ascertained: determined.

compulsory process: the authority to force witnesses to appear in court.
Counsel for . . . defense: a lawyer who defends an accused person in court.

Twenty dollars does not represent the wealth it once did. Suits involving money are generally not tried in federal courts unless they involve much larger sums.

bail: money posted with the court that allows a person accused of a crime to be released from jail and acts as a guarantee that the person will appear in court for trial.

enumeration: listing.
construed: interpreted.
disparage: discredit.

A person cannot sue a state in federal court. The only way in which an individual can sue a state is to introduce the case in the courts of the state being sued.

Article II, Section 1, Clause 3 of the Constitution specified that the President would be the one receiving the largest number of votes and the Vice President would be the one receiving the next largest number of votes. This resulted in confusion in the elections of 1796 and 1800. See pages 228–29 and 241–43. This amendment requires that there be two separate ballots: one for President and one for Vice President.

voted for as Vice President, and of the number of votes for each, which lists they shall sign and certify, and transmit sealed to the seat of the government of the United States, directed to the President of the Senate;—The President of the Senate shall, in the presence of the Senate and House of Representatives, open all the certificates and the votes shall then be counted;—The person having the greatest number of votes for President, shall be the President, if such number be a majority of the whole number of Electors appointed; and if no person have such majority, then from the persons having the highest numbers not exceeding three on the list of those voted for as President, the House of Representatives shall choose immediately, by ballot, the President. But in choosing the President, the votes shall be taken by states, the representation from each state having one vote; a quorum for this purpose shall consist of a member or members from two thirds of the states, and a majority of all the states shall be necessary to a choice. And if the House of Representatives shall not choose a President whenever the right of choice shall devolve upon them, before the fourth day of March next following, then the Vice President shall act as President, as in the case of the death or other constitutional disability of the President;—The person having the greatest number of votes as Vice President, shall be the Vice President, if such number be a majority of the whole number of Electors appointed, and if no person have a majority, then from the two highest numbers on the list, the Senate shall choose the Vice President; a quorum for the purpose shall consist of two thirds of the whole number of Senators, and a majority of the whole number shall be necessary to a choice. But no person constitutionally ineligible to the office of President shall be eligible to that of Vice President of the United States.

Deleted by the Twentieth Amendment.

Thirteenth Amendment
[*Proposed January 31, 1865; declared ratified December 18, 1865*]
Section 1. Neither slavery nor involuntary servitude, except as a punishment for crime whereof the party shall have been duly convicted, shall exist within the United States, or any place subject to their jurisdiction.

Section 2. Congress shall have power to enforce this article by appropriate legislation.

Slavery is made illegal. See page 494.

This amendment extended civil rights to former slaves and is the basis on which subsequent civil rights legislation was passed. See pages 497–98.

Fourteenth Amendment
[*Proposed June 13, 1866; declared ratified July 28, 1868*]
Section 1. All persons born or naturalized in the United States, and subject to the jurisdiction thereof, are citizens of the United States and of the State wherein they reside. No State shall make or enforce any law which shall abridge the privileges or immunities of citizens of the United States; nor shall any State deprive any person of life, liberty, or property, without due process of law; nor deny to any

abridge the privileges or immunities: take away rights or freedoms to which citizens are entitled.
due process of law: fair and legal proceedings.

person within its jurisdiction the equal protection of the laws.

Section 2. Representatives shall be apportioned among the several States according to their respective numbers, counting the whole number of persons in each State, excluding Indians not taxed. But when the right to vote at any election for the choice of electors for President and Vice President of the United States, Representatives in Congress, the Executive and Judicial officers of a State, or the members of the Legislature thereof, is denied to any of the male inhabitants of such State, being twenty-one years of age, and citizens of the United States, or in any way abridged, except for participation in rebellion, or other crime, the basis of representation therein shall be reduced in the proportion which the number of such male citizens shall bear to the whole number of male citizens twenty-one years of age in such State.

This section was never carried out. States that denied males over 21 the right to vote did not, in fact, lose representation in Congress. American Indians gained citizenship rights in 1924.

Section 3. No person shall be a Senator or Representative in Congress, or elector of President and Vice President, or hold any office, civil or military, under the United States, or under any State, who, having previously taken an oath, as a member of Congress, or as an officer of the United States, or as a member of any State legislature, or as an executive or judicial officer of any State, to support the Constitution of the United States, shall have engaged in insurrection or rebellion against the same, or given aid or comfort to the enemies thereof. But Congress may by a vote of two thirds of each House, remove such disability.

Leaders of the Confederacy could not hold office, either at the federal or at the state level.

Section 4. The validity of the public debt of the United States, authorized by law, including debts incurred for payment of pensions and bounties for services in suppressing insurrection or rebellion, shall not be questioned. But neither the United States nor any State shall assume or pay any debt or obligation incurred in aid of insurrection or rebellion against the United States, or any claim for the loss of emancipation of any slave; but all such debts, obligations and claims shall be held illegal and void.

Validity: legality.

incurred for: made necessary by.

bounties: payments made to men in the armed forces.

The federal government refused to honor any debts of the Confederacy.

Section 5. The Congress shall have power to enforce, by appropriate legislation, the provisions of this article.

Fifteenth Amendment
[*Proposed February 26, 1869; declared ratified March 30, 1870*]

Section 1. The right of citizens of the United States to vote shall not be denied or abridged by the United States or by any State on account of race, color, or previous condition of servitude.

Section 2. The Congress shall have power to enforce this article by appropriate legislation.

Sixteenth Amendment
[*Proposed July 12, 1909; declared ratified February 25, 1913*]

The Congress shall have power to lay and collect taxes on incomes, from whatever source derived, without apportionment among the several States, and without regard to any census or enumeration.

The income tax is today the major source of the government's revenues. See page 666.

Seventeenth Amendment
[*Proposed May 13, 1912; declared ratified May 31, 1913*]
The Senate of the United States shall be composed of two Senators from each State, elected by the people thereof, for six years; and each Senator shall have one vote. The electors in each State shall have the qualifications requisite for electors of the most numerous branch of the State legislatures.

This amendment provides for senators to be elected directly by the people rather than by the state legislatures. See page 652.

requisite: required.

When vacancies happen in the representation of any State in the Senate, the executive authority of such State shall issue writs of election to fill such vacancies: *Provided,* That the legislature of any State may empower the executive thereof to make temporary appointments until the people fill the vacancies by election as the legislature may direct.

This amendment shall not be so construed as to affect the election or term of any Senator chosen before it becomes valid as part of the Constitution.

Eighteenth Amendment
[*Proposed December 18, 1917; declared ratified January 29, 1919; repealed by the Twenty-first Amendment December 5, 1933*]
Section 1. After one year from the ratification of this article the manufacture, sale, or transportation of intoxicating liquors within, the importation thereof into, or the exportation thereof from the United States and all territory subject to the jurisdiction thereof for beverage purposes is hereby prohibited.

The "Prohibition Amendment" placed certain restrictions on intoxicating liquor. See page 667.

Section 2. The Congress and the several States shall have concurrent power to enforce this article by appropriate legislation.

Section 3. This article shall be inoperative unless it shall have been ratified as an amendment to the Constitution by the legislatures of the several States, as provided in the Constitution, within seven years from the date of the submission hereof to the States by the Congress.

Nineteenth Amendment
[*Proposed June 4, 1919; declared ratified August 26, 1920*]
The right of citizens of the United States to vote shall not be denied or abridged by the United States or by any State on account of sex.

Women have the right to vote. See page 710.

Congress shall have power to enforce this article by appropriate legislation.

Twentieth Amendment

[Proposed March 2, 1932; declared ratified February 6, 1933]

Section 1. The terms of the President and Vice President shall end at noon on the 20th day of January, and the terms of Senators and Representatives at noon on the 3rd day of January, of the years in which such terms would have ended if this article had not been ratified; and the terms of their successors shall then begin.

Section 2. The Congress shall assemble at least once in every year, and such meeting shall begin at noon on the 3rd day of January, unless they shall by law appoint a different day.

Section 3. If, at the time fixed for the beginning of the term of the President, the President elect shall have died, the Vice President elect shall become President. If a President shall not have been chosen before the time fixed for the beginning of his term, or if the President elect shall have failed to qualify, then the Vice President elect shall act as President until a President shall have qualified; and the Congress may by law provide for the case wherein neither a President elect nor a Vice President elect shall have qualified, declaring who shall then act as President, or the manner in which one who is to act shall be selected, and such persons shall act accordingly until a President or Vice President shall have qualified.

Section 4. The Congress may by law provide for the case of the death of any of the persons from whom the House of Representatives may choose a President whenever the right of choice shall have devolved upon them, and for the case of the death of any of the persons from whom the Senate may choose a Vice President whenever the right of choice shall have devolved upon them.

Section 5. Sections 1 and 2 shall take effect on the 15th day of October following the ratification of this article.

Section 6. This article shall be inoperative unless it shall have been ratified as an amendment to the Constitution by the legislatures of three fourths of the several States within seven years from the date of its submission.

Twenty-first Amendment

[Proposed February 20, 1933; declared ratified December 5, 1933]

Section 1. The eighteenth article of amendment to the Constitution of the United States is hereby repealed.

Section 2. The transportation or importation into any State, Territory, or possession of the United States for delivery or use therein of intoxicating liquors, in violation of the laws thereof, is hereby prohibited.

Section 3. This article shall be inoperative unless it shall have been ratified as an amendment to the Constitution by conventions in the several States, as provided in the Constitution, within seven years

Before this amendment was passed, those elected in November did not take office until March 4. The long delay was necessary when the Constitution was written because both communication and transportation were slow. By having the new Congress convene on January 3, the amendment limits the power and influence of members of Congress who were not reelected in November (called "lame ducks").

President elect: the person who has been elected President but who has not yet taken office.

This amendment repeals the Prohibition Amendment but retains to the government the right to enact laws controlling the transportation and possession of intoxicating liquors. See page 667.

from the date of the submission hereof to the States by the Congress.

Twenty-second Amendment
[Proposed March 24, 1947; delcared ratified March 1, 1951]

Section 1. No person shall be elected to the office of the President more than twice, and no person who has held the office of President, or acted as President, for more than two years of a term to which some other person was elected President shall be elected to the office of the President more than once. But this Article shall not apply to any person holding the office of President when this Article was proposed by the Congress, and shall not prevent any person who may be holding the office of President, or acting as President, during the term within which this Article becomes operative from holding the office of President or acting as President during the remainder of such term.

Section 2. This article shall be inoperative unless it shall have been ratified as an amendment to the Constitution by the legislatures of three fourths of the several States within seven years from the date of its submission to the States by the Congress.

Although the original Constitution did not set a limit on the number of terms a President could serve, George Washington set a precedent (an example) of serving only two terms. Franklin Roosevelt broke the precedent by being elected to a third and fourth term. The amendment makes it law that no person may be elected President more than twice nor serve more than ten years. See page 811.

Twenty-third Amendment
[Proposed June 16, 1960; declared ratified April 3, 1961]

Section 1. The District constituting the seat of Government of the United States shall appoint in such manner as the Congress may direct:

A number of electors of President and Vice President equal to the whole number of Senators and Representatives in Congress to which the District would be entitled if it were a State, but in no event more than the least populous state; they shall be in addition to those appointed by the States, but they shall be considered, for the purposes of the election of President and Vice President, to be electors appointed by a State; and they shall meet in the District and perform such duties as provided by the twelfth article of amendment.

Section 2. The Congress shall have power to enforce this article by appropriate legislation.

This amendment gives residents of the District of Columbia the right to vote for President and Vice President.

Twenty-fourth Amendment
[Proposed August 27, 1962; declared ratified February 4, 1964]

Section 1. The right of citizens of the United States to vote in any primary or other election for President or Vice President, for electors for President or Vice President, or for Senator or Representative in Congress, shall not be denied or abridged by the United States or any State by reason of failure to pay any poll tax or other tax.

Section 2. The Congress shall have power to enforce this article by appropriate legislation.

In 1964 five states used a poll tax, which is a tax a person had to pay in order to vote. This amendment forbade the poll tax in federal elections; in 1966 the Supreme Court declared that poll taxes were illegal as requirements to vote in state and local elections.

This amendment defines procedures to be followed in the case of the death, disability, or resignation of a President or Vice President. The Vice President can become Acting President in two ways: if the President declares in writing that he cannot do his duties or if the Vice President and a majority of the Cabinet officers declare that the President is unfit to carry out his powers and duties. See page 878.

Twenty-fifth Amendment
[Proposed July 6, 1965; declared ratified February 23, 1967]

Section 1. In case of removal of the President from office or of his death or resignation, the Vice President shall become President.

Section 2. Whenever there is a vacancy in the office of the Vice President, the President shall nominate a Vice President who shall take office upon confirmation by a majority vote of both Houses of Congress.

Section 3. Whenever the President transmits to the President pro tempore of the Senate and the Speaker of the House of Representatives his written declaration that he is unable to discharge the powers and duties of his office, and until he transmits to them a written declaration to the contrary, such powers and duties shall be discharged by the Vice President as Acting President.

Section 4. Whenever the Vice President and a majority of either the principal officers of the executive departments or of such other body as Congress may by law provide, transmit to the President pro tempore of the Senate and the Speaker of the House of Representatives their written declaration that the President is unable to discharge the powers and duties of his office, the Vice President shall immediately assume the powers and duties of the office as Acting President.

Thereafter, when the President transmits to the President pro tempore of the Senate and the Speaker of the House of Representatives his written declaration that no inability exists, he shall resume the powers and duties of his office unless the Vice President and a majority of either the principal officers of the executive department or of such other body as Congress may by law provide, transmit within four days to the President pro tempore of the Senate and the Speaker of the House of Representatives their written declaration that the President is unable to discharge the powers and duties of his office. Thereupon Congress shall decide the issue, assembling within forty-eight hours for that purpose if not in session. If the Congress, within twenty-one days after receipt of the latter written declaration, or, if Congress is not in session, within twenty-one days after Congress is required to assemble, determines by two-thirds vote of both Houses that the President is unable to discharge the powers and duties of his office, the Vice President shall continue to discharge the same as Acting President; otherwise, the President shall resume the powers and duties of his office.

Twenty-sixth Amendment
[Proposed March 23, 1971; declared ratified July 5, 1971]

Section 1. The right of citizens of the United States, who are eighteen years of age or older, to vote shall not be denied or abridged by the United States or by any State on account of age.

Section 2. The Congress shall have power to enforce this article by appropriate legislation.

Proposed Equal Rights Amendment
[*Proposed March 22, 1972*]

Section 1. Equality of rights under the law shall not be denied or abridged by the United States or by any State on account of sex.

Section 2. The Congress shall have the power to enforce, by appropriate legislation, the provisions of this article.

Section 3. This amendment shall take effect two years after the date of ratification.

This proposed amendment failed to win ratification by three fourths of the state legislatures. See pages 884-886.

Proposed Twenty-seventh Amendment
[*Proposed August 22, 1978*]

Section 1. For purposes of representation in the Congress, election of the President and Vice President, and Article V of this Constitution, the District constituting the seat of government of the United States shall be treated as though it were a state.

Section 2. The exercise of the rights and powers conferred under this article shall be by the people of the District constituting the seat of government, and as provided by the Congress.

Section 3. The twenty-third article of amendment to the Constitution is hereby repealed.

This proposed amendment would give the District of Columbia full voting representation in Congress by election of senators and representatives. Its deadline for ratification is August 22, 1985.

- According to the Preamble to the Constitution, what are some reasons for preparing this document? State each in your own words.
- What is to be the source of all legislative power granted by the Constitution, according to Article I?
- What are qualifications for election to the House of Representatives, as stated in Article I, Section 2?
- What are the qualifications for election to the Senate, as stated in Article I, Section 3?
- In Article I, Section 8, what are some powers granted to Congress?
- In Article II, Section 2, what are some powers granted to the President? In Section 3 what are some duties of the President?
- What kinds of courts are described in Article III?
- What rights are guaranteed by Article IV?
- How are amendments made to the Constitution, according to Article V?
- What are the first ten amendments to the Constitution usually called?

EXECUTIVE

President
Vice President
Cabinet

LEGISLATIVE

Senate   House of
                Representatives

JUDICIAL

Supreme Court
Appellate Courts
District Courts

THE "MORE PERFECT UNION"

Giving new power to the United States was relatively simple. Deciding who should control and use the power was more difficult. The problem was complicated. Should the authority of the United States government remain concentrated in Congress? Or should it be separated into executive, legislative, and judicial branches as in most state constitutions? Further, should each state have an equal weight in electing representatives to the United States as was true under the Articles of Confederation? Or should representation depend upon population? That would give the larger states more representatives and thus more influence than the smaller ones.

Early during the Convention, Governor Edmund Randolph of Virginia, a member of that state's delegation, presented the **Virginia Plan.** It provided for a government with three separate branches and for representation by population. William Paterson then offered the **New Jersey Plan,** which would have left all power in Congress and continued the one-state, one-vote system.

The delegates adopted the basics of the Virginia Plan with little debate. There was to be an executive branch headed by a **President of the United States;** a legislative branch, the **Congress,** with two chambers, a **Senate** and a **House of Representatives;** and a system of courts, the **national judiciary,** including the **Supreme Court.**

The delegates from the smaller states, however, dug in their heels on the question of representation by population. The debate went on for weeks. Both camps realized they must find some way to agree or the entire Constitution would be defeated. Finally they worked out the so-called **Great Compromise.** Members of the House of Representatives would be elected on the basis of population. (In the first House, Virginia, the largest state, elected 11 representatives, New Hampshire chose 3, Pennsylvania 8, and so on.) But each state was to have two seats in the Senate. Further, to protect the influence of the state governments, the Constitution provided that senators were to be elected by the state legislatures, not by the people.

■ What was the Virginia Plan? What was the New Jersey Plan?
■ What was the Great Compromise?

SLAVERY IN THE CONSTITUTION

When the delegates spoke of "the People," they were not talking about black people. The delegates decided to allow each state to determine who could vote and who could not. The only limit they imposed was a clause saying that the same rules must apply to the elections to Congress as to the "most numerous" branch of the state's own legislature. This meant that almost no blacks could vote, not even those who were free.

Northern and southern delegates did clash over whether slaves should be counted in determining the number of representatives a state should have in Congress. The issue was decided by what is called the **Three-Fifths Compromise**—three fifths of the slaves were counted in the population of a state.

Actually, the delegates were very squeamish about slavery. They did not even mention the word in the final document. The Three-Fifths Compromise provided for counting "the whole Number of free Persons" and "three fifths of all other Persons." In another so-called compromise Congress was denied the power to outlaw bringing slaves from abroad until 1808. The ban was worded this way: "The Importation of such Persons as any of the States . . . shall think proper to admit, shall not be prohibited" before 1808. Still another clause required the free states to return any slave who managed to escape into a free state. It referred to slaves as persons "held to Service or Labor."

Historical imagination helps us here. Some of the delegates surely had guilty consciences about allowing slavery to exist in a nation where "all men" were supposed to be equal and where the government was committed to providing "the people" with "Blessings of Liberty." But their feelings of guilt did not prevent them from protecting the interests of slave owners in the ways just mentioned. They believed that if they did not, the southern colonies would not stay in the Union.

- What was the Three-Fifths Compromise?
- How did the Constitution protect the interests of slave owners?

William Paterson offered the New Jersey Plan at the Constitutional Convention in 1787. This fine portrait in oil was painted by Mrs. B. S. Church. What did Paterson propose?

THE PRESIDENCY

The most drastic change put into effect by the Constitutional Convention was the creation of a powerful Presidency. As we have seen, under the Articles of Confederation there was no chief executive. In discussing the new office, the delegates were torn in two directions. They wanted a national leader. But they did not want to make the chief executive too powerful. Neither did they want a mere figurehead.

Some delegates wanted to give the executive power to a group. Others preferred a President sharing authority with an elected council. Some suggested that the state legislatures choose the President.

The delegates settled for one President—and a President with a great deal of power. Besides being responsible for administering the laws passed by Congress, the President was to be commander in chief of the army and navy. He alone was in charge of foreign relations. He was to appoint judges and other important government officials. And

FIRST in WAR,
FIRST in PEACE
&
FIRST in the Hearts
of his
COUNTRYMEN

Liberty places a crown of laurel leaves on a bust of Washington. This scene was painted in oil on a tavern window shade in about 1800. The artist used many symbols such as the British crown crushed under Liberty's feet. The pine tree and the cap of liberty on a pole above the pine tree are often symbols of freedom. How does this painting make George Washington heroic?

the President was also given the power to veto laws passed by Congress.

Everyone assumed that the first President would be George Washington. This was one reason why the office was given so much power. Washington was so admired and trusted that the delegates made the Presidency worthy of his talents. For example, who but Washington could serve as commander in chief of the army?

Of course, Washington would not be President forever. Looking ahead, the delegates worked out a complicated system for choosing his successors. Each state was to select in whatever manner its legislature wished as many **electors** as it had senators and representatives in Congress. The electors in each state would then meet to vote for President. Each elector would vote for two people, only one of whom could be a resident of that state. The votes would then be counted and the results forwarded under seal to the national capital. On an appointed day the ballots from the different states would be opened and counted in the presence of the Senate and the House of Representatives. The person with the largest number of votes would become President, the second largest, Vice President.

However, if the leading candidate did not receive a majority, the House of Representatives would choose a President from among the five persons with the largest number of votes. In this voting each state delegation in the House would have only one vote.

There were good reasons why the delegates created such a complicated system of election. The country was large. Communication was slow and limited. It seemed unlikely that any person less famous than a Washington could be well-known all over the country. Yet it was important that the President be a person of outstanding character as well as ability. If candidates were selected in each region by persons who knew them well, the high standard needed could probably be met. Then the people's representatives in Congress could discuss the merits of the best of these and make a final selection. The rule that the House of Representatives vote by states was another concession to the smaller states.

- Why did the delegates to the Constitutional Convention give so much power to the President?
- What was the reasoning behind the complicated system of Presidential electors?

THE CONGRESS

Some of the reasons for a **two-branch Congress** have already been discussed. The lower branch, the House of Representatives, was to be popularly elected to represent the ordinary people of the United States. It alone could introduce bills to raise money.

BUILDING SKILLS IN SOCIAL STUDIES

Reading a Flow Chart

Each year approximately 10,000 bills are introduced in Congress. Only about 1,000 become laws. Passing a bill into law is a complicated process that may be better explained by a *flow chart* than by a written description. A flow chart shows a step-by-step procedure. The flow chart on this page shows the path taken by a bill until it becomes law or is killed.

Study the flow chart carefully and then answer the following questions.

1. In which house of Congress are bills to raise money introduced?
2. Does a bill usually move through the House and Senate in the same way?
3. Must bills pass both houses of Congress in the same form in order to be sent to the President?
4. May a bill that was originally passed by the Senate later be killed by a committee in the House?
5. When the House and Senate pass a bill in different forms, where are the two versions of the bill sent?
6. If the House and Senate pass a bill in the same form, does it automatically become law?
7. If the President vetoes a bill, is it automatically dead?
8. What is a pocket veto?
9. How quickly must the President act on a bill?
10. What happens to a bill when no compromise can be reached by the members of the joint committee?

How a Bill Becomes Law

House of Representatives
(any bill may start here)

1. Bill introduced
2. Bill sent to committee where it may be
   a. killed
   b. passed
   c. amended and passed
   d. amended and defeated
3. Bill sent back to House where it may be
   a. defeated
   b. passed
   c. amended and passed
   d. amended and defeated

Senate
(any bill *except* those to raise money may start here)

1. Bill introduced
2. Bill sent to committee where it may be
   a. killed
   b. passed
   c. amended and passed
   d. amended and defeated
3. Bill sent back to Senate where it may be
   a. defeated
   b. passed
   c. amended and passed
   d. amended and defeated

If bill passes one house, it must be sent to other house for consideration

Bill passed in different form by House and Senate

Bill passed in identical form by House and Senate

4. Bill sent to joint committee of House and Senate
   a. With compromise wording, bill is sent back to Step 3 in House and Senate
   b. Without compromise, bill is killed

5. Bill sent to President, who must within ten days
   a. Sign bill into law
   b. Veto, sending bill and objections back to Step 3 where a two-thirds majority of each house may pass bill into law (a veto override)
   c. Take no action

If Congress is still in session, bill automatically becomes law

If Congress adjourns before ten days, bill is dead (called a pocket veto)

PRESIDENT

Commands the armed services
Administers the law
Supervises domestic affairs
Conducts foreign policy
Appoints high officials
Recommends legislation
May veto legislation

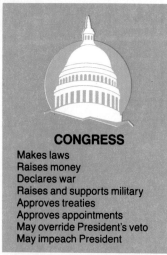

CONGRESS

Makes laws
Raises money
Declares war
Raises and supports military
Approves treaties
Approves appointments
May override President's veto
May impeach President

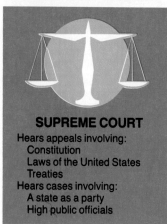

SUPREME COURT

Hears appeals involving:
  Constitution
  Laws of the United States
  Treaties
Hears cases involving:
  A state as a party
  High public officials

The Senate, which originally had 26 members, was seen as the upper house, a kind of advisory council. It was the Senate that must give its **advice and consent** to major appointments of the President or to treaties made by the President. Members of the Senate were also expected to represent the interests of what Alexander Hamilton called "the rich and the well-born," just as members of the House were expected to represent "the great mass of the people." But senators were not expected to be snobs. Their main task was to try to look after the interests of their separate states as well as the well-being of the United States.

The Congress, not surprisingly, is the first of the three branches of government described in the Constitution. After all, the members of the Constitutional Convention were themselves a Congress. More important was the fear of being dominated by a king or prime minister. The Americans who drew up the Constitution remembered vividly what had happened to the colonies under English rule.

■ Which branch of the Congress was supposed to represent the ordinary people of the United States? Which branch was supposed to look beyond the interests of the separate states?

THE JUDICIARY

The Constitution also provided for a system of United States courts, separate from the courts of the individual states. It only mentioned specifically a Supreme Court. It left it to Congress to decide how many judges to have on the Supreme Court and how many lower courts to set up under the Supreme Court. (There are now nine **Supreme Court Justices** and two kinds of lower federal courts—the **district courts** and the **appellate courts**, or appeals courts.)

Under the Constitution all United States judges serve "during good Behavior." This means that they cannot be removed once appointed unless they commit a crime or are unable to perform their duties for some reason, such as insanity. The Constitution gives the federal courts the responsibility of hearing all cases involving the laws and treaties of the United States and also cases involving foreigners, two or more states, and the citizens of different states.

■ What is the only court mentioned specifically in the Constitution? What are its judges called?
■ What are the two kinds of lower federal courts?

CHECKS AND BALANCES

Although they were creating a more powerful government, the delegates at Philadelphia were very concerned about the possible misuse of power. They tried to prevent misuse by dividing power among

Franklin's Advice

The Granger Collection

many people and institutions and by a clever system of **checks and balances.** Here are a few samples of how the President's powers are checked. The other branches are subject to similar restraints.

The President can **veto,** or reject, bills passed by Congress. This is a check on the power of Congress, but Congress can **override** a veto. If both houses again pass the bill by two-thirds majorities, it becomes law.

The President is commander in chief of the army and navy. But Congress controls the raising of money to maintain the armed forces, and Congress alone has the power to declare war.

The President or representatives of the President can negotiate treaties with foreign countries. But such treaties become law only when approved by two thirds of the Senate.

The President has the power to appoint judges, ambassadors, and other important officials. But the Senate can vote to reject any of these appointments.

Finally, if the President commits a serious crime, he can be brought to trial by a process called **impeachment.** In such cases the House of Representatives brings the charges against the President, and the Senate acts as judge and jury. A two-thirds vote is necessary for **conviction** and removal from office.

■ How does the Constitution guard against misuse of power?

203

RATIFYING THE CONSTITUTION

The Constitution was to go into effect when nine states (two thirds) had approved it. In each state interest in the document was high. Everywhere citizens read and discussed the new form of government. Then they elected representatives to **ratifying conventions** where the decision to approve or disapprove was to be made. Since it was complicated and involved many important changes, the Constitution did not win everyone's approval. Sharp divisions of opinion were common.

Supporters of the Constitution called themselves **Federalists.** Those who opposed it are known as **Antifederalists.** The second name is confusing because a *federal* form of government is one that involves a combination of independent states. We speak of the United States today as the federal government. The so-called Antifederalists actually were federalists in this sense.

Both groups, in other words, wanted a federal form of government. They differed about how strong the federation known as the United States should be. Almost no one wanted to center all power in the federal government, and very few were satisfied with the old "league of friendship" the Constitution proposed to replace.

Since there was no nationwide vote on the Constitution nor public opinion polls to sample popular attitudes, it is impossible to know whether or not a majority of the people favored the new system. In some states there was little organized opposition. In others opinion was sharply divided. Those who disapproved of the Constitution did so mostly because they were afraid the new central government would be so powerful that it would soon destroy the independence of the states. The Constitution, one excited Antifederalist said, was "a beast, dreadful and terrible," which "devours, breaks into pieces, and stamps [the states] with his feet." Supporters of the Constitution did their best to persuade Antifederalists that the state governments would remain powerful and free to manage local affairs as they wished.

The first state to hold its ratifying convention was Delaware. On December 7, 1787, the delegates voted unanimously to accept the Constitution. By the middle of January four more states had ratified by large margins—Pennsylvania, New Jersey, Georgia, and Connecticut.

Sentiment in a number of other states was also running strong for ratification. Nine states would be enough to put the Constitution into effect, but how effective could the government of the United States be if Massachusetts, New York, and Virginia refused to join the Union? The Antifederalists in these important states were numerous and well organized.

The Massachusetts convention met in early January 1788 and

debated the question for nearly a month. At first the Antifederalists seemed to have a majority. The memory of Shays's Rebellion was on everyone's mind. Representatives from the troubled districts were strongly against ratification. The men Paul Revere had gone to Lexington to warn in April 1775, Sam Adams and John Hancock, were delegates. They were believed to oppose the Constitution.

The Federalists, however, proved to be shrewd politicians. They organized a mass meeting in Boston in favor of ratification. This show of support in his home district persuaded Sam Adams to vote for the Constitution in spite of his doubts. The Federalist leaders promised Hancock, who was very ambitious, that they would not oppose him for governor in the next election if he would vote for the Constitution. They even hinted that he might be a good candidate for Vice President of the United States if the new government was accepted.

Hancock then came out for the Constitution. He also made an important practical suggestion that helped persuade others in Massachusetts and other states to go along. Once the Constitution was accepted, amendments should be submitted dealing with the objections that had been raised against it. The convention then voted 187 to 168 to ratify.

The contest was also close in Virginia, but again the Federalists won out. By the end of June ten states had ratified. Only Rhode Island, North Carolina, and New York had yet to act.

New York was crucial. Because of its geographical location the nation would be split almost in two if New York did not join. And 46 of the 65 delegates at the New York convention were Antifederalists. Defeat seemed certain.

The leader of the Federalists at the convention was young Alexander Hamilton. Although he did not have a very high opinion of the Constitution—he thought it too weak rather than too strong—he was determined to see it ratified. He, John Jay, and James Madison had already written a series of newspaper articles explaining and defending the Constitution, the now-famous **Federalist Papers.** At the ratifying convention he advanced all the arguments developed in those essays and invented some new ones on the spot.

Although Hamilton probably did not change many minds, the Antifederalists were in a difficult position. If the United States needed New York, so did New York need the United States. Moreover, opinion in New York City was strong for the Constitution. Hamilton and other city leaders threatened to break away from the state and join the Union on their own if the Constitution was rejected. For practical reasons rather than because their minds had been changed, enough Antifederalists voted on July 26, 1788, to ratify the Constitution, 30 to 27.

George Washington took the oath of office as President at Federal Hall in New York City. This fine statue in bronze by J. Q. A. Ward marks the site. It was sculpted in 1883. What was the source of Washington's oath of office?

- How was the Constitution to be ratified?
- What did the Federalists and the Antifederalists have in common? Where did they disagree?
- How did the Federalists win support for the Constitution in Massachusetts?
- Why did New York decide to ratify the Constitution?

THE UNITED STATES OF AMERICA

Now the new system would have its chance. The first Congress was elected early in 1789. The state legislatures chose their Presidential electors. On April 6, on order of the last Continental Congress, the new Congress gathered for the formal counting of the electoral votes in New York City, the temporary national capital. No one was surprised when John Langdon of New Hampshire, the President of the Senate, announced that George Washington was the unanimous choice of the 69 electors. John Adams, who received 34 votes, was declared elected Vice President.

On April 30 Washington stood on the balcony of Federal Hall, at the corner of Broad and Wall Streets in New York City, and took the oath of office as President. A fine statue of Washington marks the site today. The oath he recited has been repeated by every President, for it is part of the Constitution:

> I do solemnly swear that I will faithfully execute the Office of President of the United States, and will, to the best of my ability, preserve, protect, and defend the Constitution of the United States.

Thus ended the Revolution. Thirteen English colonies in America had become one independent nation. What would the Americans make of their independence and their new union?

Washington tips his hat to cheering sailors in New York Harbor. This imaginary scene was painted in oil in the 19th century by L. M. Cooke. Washington is on his way to take the oath of office as President on April 30, 1789. Why did he take the oath of office in New York City?

CHAPTER 6 REVIEW

Identification
Tell briefly why each of the following persons, terms, or events is important.
1. Benjamin Franklin
2. George Washington
3. Alexander Hamilton
4. James Madison
5. John Jay
6. Treaty of Paris
7. Articles of Confederation
8. Shays's Rebellion
9. Northwest Ordinance
10. *Trevett v. Weeden*
11. Constitutional Convention
12. Great Compromise
13. Three-Fifths Compromise
14. Federalist Papers
15. Legislative branch
16. Executive branch
17. Judicial branch
18. Nationalism
19. Ratifying conventions
20. Checks and balances

Understanding American History
1. Why did the new state constitutions give much more power to the legislatures than to governors?
2. What did Benjamin Franklin mean when he said, "We must all hang together or we shall hang separately"?
3. What were some of the powers the Second Continental Congress gave to itself?
4. In what ways did the Articles of Confederation show that Americans were suspicious of a central government?
5. What were the major provisions of the Treaty of Paris?
6. Explain the difference between a "league of friendship" and a national government.
7. Why did Americans eventually come to support a strong central government when they had opposed a strong government under British rule?
8. How did the Virginia Plan and the New Jersey Plan differ? How did the Great Compromise resolve the differences?
9. What are some of the major duties of each of the three branches of the federal government under the Constitution?
10. Explain the difference between the American Revolution and the War for American Independence.

Activities
1. Prepare with your classmates a large map of North America as it appeared in 1783. Use one color to show the 13 United States and separate colors to show the territories claimed by European nations. Indicate major bodies of water.
2. Find other history texts or reference books to read further about the Constitutional Convention and the ratifying conventions. Prepare a report for the class.
3. Make charts for the bulletin board showing the duties of each of the three branches of the federal government—legislative, executive, and judicial.
4. Clip articles from current newspapers and magazines that deal with activities of the three branches of the federal government. Group the articles that deal with each branch and add them to bulletin board charts. See how many different kinds of activities you can find for each branch of the government.
5. Who are your United States senators and representatives? Write to one of these members of Congress for information on a timely topic such as national health care, energy conservation, defense spending, or balancing the federal budget.

CHAPTER 6 TEST

Matching (40 points)
Number your paper 1–10 and match each item in the first column
with its description in the second column.

1. Articles of Confederation
2. Treaty of Paris
3. Northwest Ordinance
4. *Trevett v. Weeden*
5. Great Compromise
6. Three-Fifths Compromise
7. Electors
8. Checks and balances
9. Federalist Papers
10. Bills of Rights

a. These told what the state governments could not do and named liberties that people could not be deprived of.
b. The Rhode Island Supreme Court declared a law unconstitutional because the state legislature did not have the power to pass it.
c. This officially ended the War for American Independence.
d. They directly elect the President.
e. This was the first written constitution of the United States.
f. This determined the number of representatives and senators each state is allowed.
g. These articles were written to explain and defend the new Constitution.
h. This determined how slaves would be counted as part of a state's population.
i. This established a way of governing the lands bounded by the Ohio and Mississippi Rivers and the Great Lakes while they were growing from territory to statehood.
j. This system in the Constitution is meant to keep the power of all three branches of government equal.

Matching (30 points)
Number your paper 11–20 and match the power in the first column
with the branch of government in the second column.

11. Passes bills
12. Signs bills into law
13. Vetoes bills
14. Impeaches
15. Approves treaties
16. Decides if laws are legal
17. Hears cases concerning two or more states
18. Has charge of foreign relations
19. Appoints judges
20. Has charge of the military

a. Legislative
b. Executive
c. Judicial

Essay (30 points)
Explain why many Americans were ready to accept a strong central government at the time the Constitution was written and approved by the states. Write at least one full paragraph, taking care to spell and punctuate correctly.

CHAPTER 7
Setting Up the Government

ESTABLISHING PRECEDENTS

Like all later Presidents, Washington's first task was to appoint officials to run the government departments. He also had to decide what jobs needed to be done and how the work should be organized and supervised. The task was complicated by the need to cooperate with the Congress. Of course, the Senate had to approve the major appointments. In addition, laws had to be passed to create the positions and provide money to pay salaries. Washington's government seems simple when compared to the enormous federal government of today. It was not so simple to design and staff it back in 1789.

Washington was extremely conscientious. He knew that as the first President he was establishing a **precedent,** a guide for later action, every time he made a decision. The Constitution had given him a great deal of power. He was a strong and determined person. He wanted to use his power to the full. Yet he knew that many citizens were worried about the misuse of Presidential power, not so much by Washington as by unknown later Presidents.

Washington sincerely believed in the separation of powers. In particular he was careful not to tread on the toes of Congress. It was the job of Congress to make the laws. His job was to execute, or carry out, the laws.

Congress created three main departments: the **Department of State,** the **Treasury,** and a **War Department.** Each of these was headed by a secretary appointed by the President. Today the Secretary of State has charge of the relations of the government with foreign countries. In 1789 the Secretary also had to manage all domestic affairs except those handled by the War and Treasury heads. Yet Thomas Jefferson, the first Secretary of State, had a staff of only five persons.

The War Department, headed by General Henry Knox, was just as small. Only the Treasury Department, under Alexander Hamilton, had a fairly large staff. By 1790 70 persons were working for the Treasury. Washington made Edmund Randolph, presenter of the Virginia Plan at the Constitutional Convention, **Attorney General.** Randolph was only a part-time employee, a kind of legal adviser to the President.

The New York Public Library

Washington's Cabinet did not meet as a group. This engraving, based on a painting by Alonzo Chappel, shows, left to right, Henry Knox, Secretary of the War Department; Thomas Jefferson, Secretary of State; Alexander Hamilton, Secretary of the Treasury; and President Washington. Which of these men became Washington's most influential adviser?

Washington called upon the secretaries for advice on many issues, but he did not meet with them as a group. What we call the **Cabinet,** a group of department heads meeting more or less regularly with the President to discuss current issues, did not exist in Washington's day.

General Knox, who worshiped Washington, his former commander, ran the War Department efficiently. He was mostly a follower who merely agreed with whatever decision Washington made. Jefferson was just the opposite. He disliked routine office details and sometimes neglected his duties as head of the State Department. He often disagreed with Washington about important matters. Hamilton was a bundle of energy and wide ranging in his interests. He was eager to increase his own power. Gradually he became Washington's most influential adviser.

- What is a *precedent*? Why was Washington especially careful about the precedents he established?
- What was Washington's view on the use of Presidential power?
- What were the first three departments of the government?

WASHINGTON AS PRESIDENT

Washington would have preferred to serve without salary, as he had during the War for American Independence, but Congress voted him a salary of $25,000. That was a very large sum for the time. Congress did not give him an expense account, however, so the salary was not as generous as it seemed. Washington actually spent about $5,000 a year of his own money on official business.

Congress did rent a fine three-story mansion near the Federal Building for the President. The house was, according to the first lady, Martha Custis Washington, "handsomely furnished, all new." Washington supplied his own servants. He brought seven of his slaves up from Mount Vernon, his Virginia plantation. He hired another 14 white servants locally. He served the best food and wines at official dinners. He drove about in a fine carriage drawn by six horses. At receptions he appeared in rich formal clothes and wore his dress sword in a splendid white leather scabbard.

On the other hand, the small size of the government made for simplicity. New York City was still a small town. Its population was about 30,000 in 1789. On Tuesday afternoons from three to five o'clock, President Washington received guests. Every Friday evening Martha Washington gave a tea party. No invitations were necessary for these affairs. Anyone who was properly dressed could simply walk in. Washington particularly hated the afternoon affairs, which were for men only. The visitors tended to stand and stare in awe at the Great Man, or else they ignored him and spent their time gobbling up the refreshments.

Martha Washington received guests at tea parties on Friday evenings in the Presidential mansion in New York City. This oil painted by Daniel Huntington in 1861 turns the tea party into "The Republican Court." All eyes are on the first lady at left center. On her right stand John Jay, in red, John Adams, and Alexander Hamilton. Standing in the corner is Thomas Jefferson, under the portrait of the lady. President Washington is near the center. In front center are Abigail Adams and Sarah Jay. Why did President Washington not enjoy receptions?

The Brooklyn Museum

Abigail Smith Adams managed the Adams farm while John Adams took part in the politics of the American Revolution. She called herself a "farmeress." This portrait is done in watercolor. When John Adams participated in the Constitutional Convention, Abigail Adams wrote him many wise and warm letters of advice. How did Abigail Adams describe President Washington?

The tea parties were different. Washington enjoyed chatting with the women at these affairs very much. The President was a tall, powerfully built man. Women often found him charming. According to Abigail Adams, the wife of the Vice President, Washington was much more dignified and well mannered than King George III of England. Of course, Abigail Adams was an ardent patriot. She may have been prejudiced!

To many people of the time Washington seemed more like a statue on a pedestal than a human being. That is still the case. He seemed almost too formal and dignified to be a real person. This was because he was so aware of his responsibilities. He could hardly ever relax. Americans considered him the greatest hero of their Revolution. He felt that he had to live up to the almost godlike image the people had made of him.

This must have made life difficult for Washington at times. He frequently complained of the burdens of his office. He looked forward to the day when he could retire to his plantation at Mount Vernon. Yet he never neglected his duties. Although he only looked like a perfect man, he was as close to a perfect first President as the young nation could have hoped for.

■ What kind of manner did Washington think appropriate for the President of the United States?

THE BILL OF RIGHTS

One of the first tasks that Congress took up was preparing the **amendments** to the Constitution that the Federalists had promised the Antifederalists. The purpose was to reassure people who were afraid that the new government had too much power. About 80 proposed amendments had been suggested by one or another state. After debating through the summer of 1789, the Congress passed 12. Ten of these were ratified by the states.

These first ten amendments are known as the **Bill of Rights.** They did not give rights to the people or to the states. The rights already existed. The amendments stated simply and clearly that the government had no authority to take them away. The First Amendment begins, "Congress shall make no law . . ." That was the basic principle.

The rights so protected include freedom of religion, freedom of speech, freedom of the press, and the right of people to gather together in groups peacefully—that is, the right of assembly. The right of privacy is protected too—no "unreasonable searches and seizures" are permitted. Several amendments deal with the rights of persons accused of committing crimes. Trial by jury is guaranteed. People may not be forced to testify against themselves. All accused persons are en-

READING PRACTICE
IN SOCIAL STUDIES

Scanning and Skimming

Setting a purpose for reading is important. When you read with a purpose, you determine how you should read the material at hand. One purpose for reading might be to find a specific piece of information. Another might be to look quickly at some part of a book to get a general idea of its contents.

Since you read for different purposes, you need to develop different reading styles. Two important reading styles are *scanning* and *skimming.* Both can help you to read quickly and to save time. It is important to know how and when to use each of these reading skills.

Scanning is reading for specific details. You glance quickly at a reading assignment, looking only for specific information which you decide upon before you begin reading. You ignore all other information. In order to use scanning successfully you must be sure of your purpose in reading and have a general idea of where to find the information you seek.

Suppose you want to know who General Henry Knox was. You need not scan this entire book, beginning with page 1. What you should do is scan the Index to find the name *Knox.* On what page of the text does he first appear? Turn to that page and quickly scan for his name. Once you find Henry Knox, read the entire sentence in which the name appears. You might also read a sentence or two before or after. By scanning you readily find what you need. You save valuable reading time.

Skimming is reading quickly to get a general impression about printed matter. When you skim, you are not concerned with facts and details. You are reading only to get a sense of the material.

Skimming is very useful when you begin to read new material. Suppose you are assigned a chapter of a new book to read. You should first skim the chapter to get a general overview. Skim by looking at chapter and section titles. Look next at illustrations. What information do the pic-tures, charts, graphs, and maps give you? Quickly read the first sentence of each paragraph. After you have skimmed, you should have a good idea of what the chapter is about. Skimming will make your close reading of the chapter go faster. You will understand the chapter better because you have a general idea about its purpose and direction.

Scanning and skimming will be useful to you many times in your reading. Simply remember to first set your purpose for reading. If scanning or skimming will help you, use these reading skills to save time and to become a better reader.

Number your paper 1–5 and write *Scan* if you would use scanning, *Skim* if you would use skimming.
1. You want to find which words in a chapter are introducted in boldface type.
2. You want to find the specific date of a historical event.
3. You want to get a general idea of what a chapter is about by reading its section headings.
4. You want to find the pages on which a particular historical event is discussed by using the index.
5. You want to get an overview of a unit by looking at the timeline which appears at the beginning of it.

Scan pages 209–212 in this chapter and answer the following questions.
1. What is a precedent?
2. Who was the first Secretary of State?
3. What is the President's Cabinet?
4. What was President Washington's salary?
5. What was the population of New York City in 1789?

Skim pages 209–212 in this chapter and list five of the main ideas you find.

titled to be told in advance what crime they are accused of. All have the right to be helped by a lawyer.

The Tenth Amendment states that all powers not given to the United States government by the Constitution or denied by the Constitution to the states are "reserved" to the states or to the people as individuals.

Two points about the Bill of Rights are particularly important. One is that most of the amendments did not protect people's rights against violation by the state governments. The First Amendment says that *Congress* may not interfere with freedom of religion, speech, or the press. It did not prevent Massachusetts or South Carolina or any other state from doing so. Some states permitted and protected slavery, the most complete denial of human rights imaginable.

The second point is that the rights protected were what the people of that day called **natural rights.** People also have **legal rights,** those given them by laws. For example, our present old-age pension law gives persons over a particular age fixed amounts of money each month. The people have a right to these payments. But the law can be and many times has been changed by Congress. If for some reason Congress voted to repeal the old-age pension law, that right would disappear. The right of free speech, however, is one of our natural rights, or as we would now say, **human rights.** Under the Constitution the government cannot take that right away.

■ What is the purpose of the Bill of Rights?
■ What is the difference between legal rights and human rights?

HAMILTON AND THE NATIONAL DEBT

One of the main reasons for strengthening the national government was the poor condition of the finances of the United States. Congress therefore acted quickly to use its new power to tax. In 1789 it placed a tariff, or tax, of 5 per cent on all foreign goods entering the country. This law was quite similar to the measures Parliament had employed in the 1760s to raise money in America. Those laws had caused a revolution. The **Tariff Act of 1789** was accepted by everyone. The vital difference was that the new taxes were agreed to by the people's own representatives. These taxes were not imposed by an outside power.

These taxes raised enough money to meet the day-to-day expenses of the government. They did not deal with the problem of paying off the large debts that the government had accumulated during and after the War for American Independence. This debt included money lent by foreign governments during the Revolution and bonds sold to private citizens by the government to raise money during the Revolution. It included bonuses and other payments prom-

Alexander Hamilton was a genius of finance. John Trumbull painted this oil portrait of Hamilton. What was the financial condition of the United States when Hamilton was named Secretary of the Treasury?

214

BUILDING SKILLS IN SOCIAL STUDIES

Reading a Bar Graph

The graph on this page is called a *bar graph* because it shows statistics (numerical facts) as colored bars. Bar graphs are especially useful for comparing sets of statistics. This bar graph compares income and expenditures of the federal government for its first 70 years.

To read a bar graph, look first at its title to see what is being compared. This bar graph not only compares income and expenditures but also permits comparisons to be made between each 10-year period.

A bar graph has a *horizontal axis* and a *vertical axis*. The horizontal axis is the line at the bottom of the graph that runs across the page. The vertical axis is at the left side of the graph and runs up and down.

Most bar graphs use separate colors or shades of color to make comparisons. Find the color key that explains what the different color bars represent. Now you should be able to read the graph and explain what these statistics tell

us about the growth of federal government from Washington's first term, beginning in 1789, to 1860, 70 years later.

Use the bar graph to answer these questions:
1. What information is shown on the horizontal axis? On the vertical axis?
2. What was the federal income for the three years 1789–91? For 1840? For 1860?
3. What was the federal expenditure for the three years 1789–91? For 1840? For 1860?

When the government has more income than expenditures, it has a *budget surplus*. When expenditures are greater than income, there is a *budget deficit.*
4. Did the federal government have a surplus or a deficit in the three-year period 1789–91? In 1830? In 1840?
5. Use the bar graph to make a general statement about the income and expenditures of the federal government from 1789 to 1860.

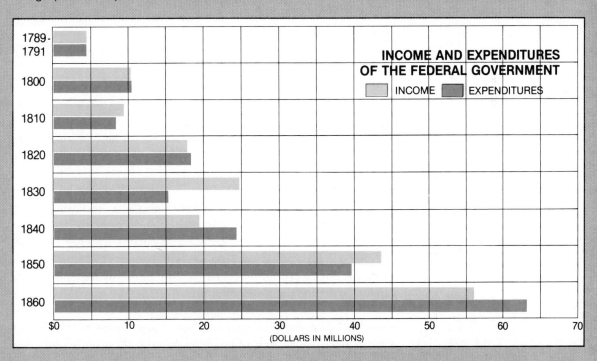

INCOME AND EXPENDITURES OF THE FEDERAL GOVERNMENT

INCOME   EXPENDITURES

(DOLLARS IN MILLIONS)

ised to soldiers. The government also owed money to merchants and manufacturers who had supplied it with various goods.

Because of the large national debt, investors were unwilling to lend the government more money. They considered the United States a poor credit risk. The **bonds of the United States,** certificates representing the money the nation had borrowed, had fallen far below their face value. A person who owned a $1,000 bond might not be able to sell it for even $500.

It was the responsibility of the Secretary of the Treasury, Alexander Hamilton, to find a way to pay off the debt and restore the credit of the government. Many people admired Hamilton extravagantly during his lifetime. Others considered him a villain. This division of opinion remains today.

Everyone recognizes that Hamilton was a genius of finance. But his ideas about government and about human nature remain controversial. Hamilton had a low opinion of the average person's honesty and judgment. He believed that most people were selfish and easily led astray by crafty, power-hungry leaders.

Hamilton did not trust the rich any more than he did what he called "the great mass of the people." If "aristocrats" had power, they would oppress the rest of society. If the poor controlled the government, they would use their power to seize the property of the rich. A good government, he thought, was one that balanced rival interests. This attitude was not unusual, as we have seen. However, Hamilton went beyond most political thinkers of his day. He thought that the selfish desires of the rich could be used to strengthen the government and thus the whole nation.

Many of the people who had bought government bonds had sold them at a loss. Others had been forced to accept the government's promises to repay them when the money owed them became available. They had sold these paper promises to investors for less than their face value. These investors were what we call **speculators.** They were gambling that some day the government would be able to pay off its bonds and other debts at full value. Speculators were obviously wealthy or well-to-do people who had spare cash.

Hamilton proposed gradually raising enough money by taxes to pay off all the national government's debts. He also wanted the United States to assume, or take over, the debts of the states. He wanted to pay all at their face value. A speculator who had bought a $1,000 bond for $500 would receive $1,000. Hamilton reasoned that by doing this he would make the wealthy bond owners enthusiastic supporters of the national government. With such powerful people behind it, the government would be strong.

Some Americans felt that this policy was unfair to the former soldiers and other owners of bonds or government promises who had sold them cheaply. They wanted the original owners of these securities to receive at least some of their increased value. Hamilton refused. The speculators had paid what the bonds were worth when they bought them, he pointed out. They had taken the risks. Now they were entitled to the profits. After some hesitation Congress passed the necessary laws.

- Why did Hamilton want to pay off the national debt?
- How did speculators profit when the government paid its debts?

The John Carter Brown Library

On Philadelphia's Third Street this Bank of the United States stood in 1799. It was engraved by William Birch, who hand colored this view. The building was among the finest examples of architecture known as Greek Revival. Notice its graceful columns and marble front. In what way was this bank established?

THE BANK OF THE UNITED STATES

Hamilton next asked Congress to pass a bill establishing a **Bank of the United States.** There were almost no banks of any kind in the country in 1790. Hamilton argued that the bank would provide a safe place to store the money the government took in taxes. The bank would also be able to lend money to merchants and manufacturers, thus speeding the growth of business. For example, a manufacturer of shoes might ask the bank for a loan to buy leather. The leather and the shoes made from it would be **security** for the loan. If the shoemaker did not repay it, the bank would seize the goods. The bank would print new paper money, called **bank notes,** and lend them to the manufacturer. Thus he would be able to produce more shoes, earn more money, and repay the loan. Without such a bank the shoe manufacturer and all sorts of other people in business would have to operate on a much smaller scale. Once again Hamilton's scheme would greatly benefit the nation, especially the rich.

Congress passed a bank bill, but President Washington hesitated to sign it. He could not find anything in the Constitution giving Congress the power to create a bank. He therefore asked Hamilton and also Secretary of State Jefferson if they thought the bill was constitutional.

Hamilton, naturally enough, said the bill was constitutional. Jefferson, however, insisted that it was not. What is most interesting about their arguments is that they relied on the *same* clause in the Constitution, yet reached opposite conclusions.

Besides spelling out the powers of Congress, such as the power to tax and the power to borrow money, the Constitution says that Congress can "make all laws that are necessary and proper" to put its powers into effect. This clause means, for instance, that since Congress has the power to coin money, it may also build and operate a mint. But the **necessary and proper clause** is vague. Hamilton concluded that the bank had "a natural relation" to the power to collect taxes and regulate trade. A bank was a *proper* way to make use of that power.

The First Bank of the United States issued this 10-dollar bank note in 1796. The X marks probably show that it was redeemed, or turned in for payment in gold or silver coin. The name of the holder of the bank note and the date were written in by hand. Which branch of government had the power to coin money and issue bank notes?

On the other hand, Jefferson claimed that Congress could only pass laws that were *necessary,* "not those which are merely '*convenient.*'" Since the government could function without a bank, a bank was "not *necessary* and consequently not authorized," Jefferson said.

Washington accepted Hamilton's argument. He signed the bank bill. In most cases since, government leaders have done the same. The necessary and proper clause is often called the **elastic clause** because it has been used so often to stretch the powers of Congress. Yet the clause can be read two ways. If only the Constitution had said "necessary *or* proper," many later arguments would have been avoided.

Critics of Hamilton's financial policies objected more to his desires to help already powerful interests than to the policies themselves. The policies were so effective that almost everyone approved of them. The credit of the United States was soon as good as that of any nation in the world. The Bank of the United States proved a most valuable institution, both to the government and to business.

- Why did Hamilton want a Bank of the United States?
- Why did Jefferson oppose the bank bill?
- What is meant by the "elastic clause" of the Constitution?

THE FRENCH REVOLUTION

The first serious political conflicts in the United States were not caused by Hamilton's schemes but by events that occurred on the other side of the Atlantic Ocean. The American Revolution had been very popular in France. Of course, it had weakened France's chief European rival, Great Britain, but the Revolution also seemed a great step forward to the liberal-minded French people. Washington and Jefferson were almost national heroes to them.

Thus the American Revolution was one of the causes of the **French Revolution,** which began in 1789. That revolution, in turn, was greeted with enormous enthusiasm in America. Did it not prove that American republican ideas were spreading?

This enthusiasm slackened, however, when the French Revolution took a more radical turn. By 1793 extremists were in control of France. King Louis XVI and many members of the nobility were executed. Radical social changes were being put into effect. Then, in 1793, war broke out between France and Great Britain.

The United States had signed a treaty of alliance with France in 1778. French help had made it possible for America to win its independence. The treaty was still in effect. Furthermore, the United States had not yet managed to get the British to live up to all the terms of the treaty that had ended the War for American Independence. Was the United States not duty bound to side with France?

- How did Americans greet news of the French Revolution in 1789?
- What reasons were there for America to side with France in the war?

THE NEUTRALITY PROCLAMATION

Should the United States come to the aid of France by declaring war on Great Britain? Many Americans thought that was the honorable course the country should follow. But Washington felt otherwise. He issued a **neutrality proclamation** warning American citizens not to aid either side. The government would try to be "friendly and impartial" to both.

The revolutionary government in France paid little attention to this proclamation. It sent a special diplomatic representative, Edmond Charles Genet, to rouse support for France in the United States.

Giraudon

The French Revolution erupted in 1789. This detail is from a large oil painting by Hubert Robert. It shows the "Fall of the Bastille," the fortress which the revolutionaries stormed to set free political prisoners. How did America's Revolution inspire the French?

219

Edmond Genet preferred to call himself simply "Citizen" Genet. This oil portrait on wood shows Genet in his older days. It was done by Ezra Ames, a traveling portrait painter from Albany, New York. What sort of man was Genet?

Genet was a charming, red-haired man of 30, an enthusiastic supporter of his country's cause. He spoke English fluently. Although the son of an important French diplomat, he called himself simply "Citizen" Genet. He arrived at Charleston, South Carolina, in April 1793. While making his way northward to present himself to President Washington, he persuaded a number of Americans who owned merchant ships to mount guns on their vessels and sail off to attack unarmed British ships on the high seas. These ships and the men who sailed them were called **privateers.** They flew the French flag and carried papers issued by the French government making them part of the French navy.

Privateering was a common practice at the time. Americans had often engaged in it under the British flag in earlier wars. It was possible during the days of wooden sailing ships because the differences between a warship and a merchant vessel were slight. A small privateer was designed for speed and easy maneuvering. Armed with a few cannon, it could capture or destroy an unarmed cargo vessel. It could also escape large pursuing warships. Since Genet's privateers were entitled to keep two thirds of the value of the cargo and ships they captured, the business could be very profitable.

A privateer was certainly not acting in a neutral manner. When Washington learned what Genet was up to, he was furious. When Genet reached the capital, which had been moved to Philadelphia, Washington ordered him to stop these activities at once. Genet ignored the orders. Privately he called Washington *le vieillard,* which is French for "the old man." He continued to recruit and arm privateers. He tried to persuade several Americans to organize private armies to attack Spanish Florida and Louisiana, since Spain was also at war with France at this time. He even tried to raise an army to invade Canada. Washington finally demanded that the French replace him.

The removal of Genet did not stop the efforts being made to involve the United States in this latest European war. Washington and his advisers believed that neutrality was the proper policy for America. Maintaining neutrality was not easy. Both France and Great Britain wanted to trade with the United States. Since they were at war with each other, each also wanted to prevent the other from getting American products. The navies of both began to seize unarmed American merchant ships on the Atlantic. In a single year several hundred American vessels loaded with valuable goods were captured. The British attacks were much more damaging than the French because Great Britain had a much larger navy than France.

■ What was Washington's response to the war between Great Britain and France?

■ What actions of "Citizen" Genet made Washington's neutrality policy harder to maintain?

THE INDIAN CONFEDERACY

Americans were also troubled by the refusal of the British to remove their troops from forts on American soil in the Great Lakes area. These outposts were not important in themselves, but American frontier settlers claimed that the British were supplying the Indians of the area with guns to use against them.

The War for American Independence had not won the Indians of the country their independence. During the conflict Indians fought on both sides. When the war ended, the British coldly betrayed those Indians who had helped them. They did so by signing the peace treaty granting all the land between the Appalachian Mountains and the Mississippi River to the United States. The Indians properly claimed that they, not the British, owned this land.

The tribes of the region north of the Ohio River resisted the invasion of American settlers who pressed into the area after 1783. They joined together in a **confederacy** and pledged not to sell any territory to the whites. Unlike the tribes who lived by hunting, many of these Indians had taken up farming. For them, moving would mean more than having to find another hunting ground.

By the late 1780s 10,000 white settlers were pouring into the Ohio Valley each year. They disregarded the fact that the land had always been owned by the Indians. The white settlers demanded that the government protect them. Finally in 1790 an army of 1,400 led by General Joseph Harmar advanced against the Indian confederacy.

The leader of the Indian confederacy was Michikinikua, or Little Turtle, chief of the Miamis. Despite his mild name, Little Turtle was a brave and skillful fighter. He defeated Harmar's force badly. The next year Little Turtle and his warriors defeated an even larger army commanded by Major General Arthur St. Clair. They killed over 600 of St. Clair's 2,000 men and wounded 250 others. These battles were among the fiercest and bloodiest in the entire history of warfare between whites and Indians.

General Arthur St. Clair, *above,* fought Michikinikua, or Little Turtle, *below,* in the Ohio Valley. The oil portrait of St. Clair is by Charles Willson Peale. The drawing of Little Turtle is based on an earlier painting and is probably true to life. What was the outcome of the battle of these two leaders?

In 1792 Washington placed General "Mad Anthony" Wayne in command of the army. Wayne was "mad" only in the sense that he was a tough professional soldier. He loved a good fight, but he was certainly not crazy.

Wayne had more than 3,600 regulars under his command. He spent months training and drilling them. In October 1793 he headed north from a base on the Ohio River near Fort Washington (present-day Cincinnati). As he advanced he built a series of forts to protect his rear. Scouts ranged ahead and on each side to protect the army against surprise. He passed the winter at Fort Greenville, about halfway between Fort Washington and Lake Erie.

Observing Wayne's careful preparations, Little Turtle decided that it would be hopeless to resist. "The Americans are now led by a

chief who never sleeps," he warned his fellows. But hotter heads prevailed. Led now by Blue Jacket, a chief of the Shawnees, in June 1794 the Indians attacked part of Wayne's force near the place where St. Clair had been routed. They won a minor victory. Still, Wayne continued his slow, steady advance. The showdown battle occurred in August near Fort Miami, one of the British posts a few miles southwest of Lake Erie.

This **Battle of Fallen Timbers** was a great victory for Wayne. He had more men and he "outgeneraled" Blue Jacket. The Indians fled in disorder. When they sought safety in Fort Miami, the British commander refused to let them in. Wayne then set fire to the Indians' cornfields and homes. Their defeat was total, their spirits were broken.

- What was the cause of the tension between Indians and whites in the 1780s?
- What was the fate of the Indian confederacy in the Ohio Valley?

JAY'S TREATY

Earlier in 1794 Washington had sent John Jay, Chief Justice of the United States, to England to try to work out a solution to all the conflicts that had developed between the two nations. Jay had done well in the negotiations leading to the treaty of 1783 ending the War for American Independence. This time he was far less successful.

Jay got the British to agree to withdraw their troops from the western forts. They also agreed to let American ships trade with their colonies in Asia. And they promised to pay damages to the shipowners whose vessels they had illegally seized in the West Indies. But that was all.

The British refused to stop attacking American merchant ships elsewhere in the world. They would not allow American ships to trade with the British sugar islands in the West Indies. They rejected the American view of the trading rights of neutral nations during wartime. They would not pay for the slaves who had fled to their lines during the War for American Independence.

Jay's Treaty was disliked by most Americans. Many leading politicians urged Washington to reject it. Washington, however, decided to accept it, and he managed to persuade the Senate to ratify it. He considered it unfair and in some respects insulting. Americans had proper claims that the British had flatly refused to recognize. Nevertheless, he realized that the United States had some gains from the treaty. More important, the treaty made it possible to avoid going to war again. Washington knew that time was on the nation's side. Each year the United States was becoming larger, richer, and stronger. A war with Great Britain, or any other European nation, would cost much and could gain little.

The removal of the British troops and the defeat of the Indians at the Battle of Fallen Timbers opened the northwest to peaceful settlement. In August 1795 General Wayne and 92 leading chiefs signed the **Treaty of Greenville.** The Indians agreed to turn over the entire southern half of what is now Ohio to the whites.

America obtained an additional and unexpected benefit from Jay's Treaty. Relations between the United States and Spain were not good. The Spanish government had refused to recognize the boundary between Florida and the southern United States that had been fixed by the peace treaty ending the War for American Independence. The Spanish also controlled the west bank of the Mississippi River and both sides of the mouth of the river, including the city of **New Orleans.**

The Spanish refused to allow Americans to load and unload cargo freely at New Orleans. This hurt the western farmers. They needed what they called **the right of deposit** at New Orleans in order to transfer their farm products from river craft to ocean-going ships.

General "Mad Anthony" Wayne makes peace with leaders of the Indian confederacy in the Ohio Valley. This oil shows the 1795 Treaty of Greenville. What land was exchanged by this treaty?

The Chicago Historical Society

The Whiskey Rebellion

Imagine the President of the United States, on horseback, leading an army westward across the United States, with the Secretary of the Treasury as second in command. In 1794 this surprising turn of events came about when western farmers rioted to protest a tax placed on the manufacture of whiskey. This was the so-called Whiskey Rebellion.

Congress had placed a tax of about 25 per cent on the value of any whiskey distilled, or manufactured, in the United States. The tax was one of the measures designed by Hamilton to pay off the debts of the United States and the states. This very heavy tax angered frontier farmers, who usually distilled a large part of their corn and other grain into whiskey. They did so because land transportation was so difficult and expensive. There were few roads, and they were rough and impassable in bad weather. It was much cheaper to ship whiskey the long distances to market over these bad roads than bulky farm products.

In 1794 farmers in western Pennsylvania had rioted to protest the tax. They bullied tax collectors, prevented courts from meeting, and threatened to march on Pittsburgh. Washington promptly called up 12,900 militiamen to duty and marched westward. Alexander Hamilton was his second in command. When the soldiers reached the troubled area, not a single "rebel" could be found. No one dared to stand up before this huge force, which was actually larger than any army Washington had commanded during the war! The "rebellion" ended, or perhaps it would be more accurate to say it disappeared.

Some historians feel that Washington overreacted to the Whiskey Rebellion. Perhaps he did. Still, the contrast was sharp between his swift and painless enforcement of the law and the bloodshed of Daniel Shays's rebellion only eight years earlier. This time there was a strong central government backed by the new Constitution.

When the Spanish read the Jay Treaty, they were greatly alarmed. They suspected that the published version was incomplete. Perhaps there was a secret clause outlining a joint British-American attack on Spain's possessions in North America. They decided to try to make friends with the United States. In 1795 they signed a treaty accepting the America view of the Florida boundary line and granting Americans the right to ship goods freely down the Mississippi. This agreement is known as **Pinckney's Treaty** because it was negotiated

for the United States by Thomas Pinckney, a son of Eliza Lucas Pinckney, the remarkable woman who introduced the cultivation of indigo in America.

■ Why did Washington sign Jay's Treaty?
■ What did Americans gain from Pinckney's Treaty?

President Washington, on his white horse, reviews the Western Army of Cumberland, Maryland, in 1794. This oil painting is probably by James Peale, a son of Charles Willson Peale, whose portrait of the younger Washington appears earlier in this book. Why did the President lead the army westward in 1794?

WASHINGTON'S FAREWELL ADDRESS

By 1796 Washington could justly feel that he had set the United States well on its way as an independent nation. The Jay and Pinckney Treaties had assured the United States the boundaries first laid out in the treaty of 1783. The bloody fighting between whites and Indians had been ended, at least for the moment. Settlers were pushing west across the Appalachian Mountains. Kentucky had enough people to become a state by 1792. Tennessee entered the Union in 1796. Ohio would soon follow.

Besides his sense of having completed his main tasks, Washington was tired after serving two terms as President. Political bickering was beginning to affect his reputation as a national hero. Although he could surely have been elected to a third term had he wished one, Washington decided to retire.

His **Farewell Address** of September 1796 announced his decision. It also contained his final advice to the American people. That advice can be boiled down to two ideas—unity at home, neutrality abroad.

First, **unity.** Washington disliked political squabbling, but his argument mostly concerned conflicts between special interest groups in different sections of the country. Too often northerners, southerners, and westerners thought only of what was best for their own region and tried to gain their objectives no matter what the effect on other sections. Washington called these rivalries "the jealousies and heartburnings" of "geographical discriminations." Such attitudes were shortsighted. Northern manufacturers needed southern raw materials. Southern farmers sold their crops in northern markets. East and West had similar common interests. All sections of the country profited from the increase in trade that resulted. To understand why Washington put so much emphasis on so obvious a point, one must remember how new the United States was. Local pride remained strong. Washington stressed the argument that national unity was "the main pillar . . . of real independence."

As for **neutrality,** Washington urged a policy of avoiding "passionate attachments" to any foreign country. The United States was fortunate. Its "detached and distant" location meant that it did not have to become involved in European conflicts. The "great rule of conduct" for America ought to be to encourage trade with the rest of the world but to "steer clear of permanent alliances."

Washington did not mean by this last statement that the United States should isolate itself from the rest of the world. The Jay and Pinckney Treaties are proof that he did not want the country to retreat into a shell and avoid all diplomatic agreements with Europe. He was against *permanent* ties with any particular nation but not against evenhanded dealings with all foreign countries.

■ What arguments did Washington make for unity in his Farewell Address? For neutrality?

THE FIRST POLITICAL PARTIES

The election of a President to succeed Washington was the first in which political parties played a role. Today we think of political parties as the machinery by which office seekers work out programs and present issues to the voters. The **two-party system**—Democratic and Republican—makes it possible for this large country to have an effective national government. If every candidate or local group set up a different organization, no one would ever have a majority. No satisfactory decisions could be made.

The framers of the Constitution, however, disliked and distrusted political parties. They made no provision for them. They called parties **factions.** The word suggests fringe groups conspiring to dominate the rest of society. The framers believed that individuals representing small districts could arrive at agreements based on the national interest. In their eyes parties meant corruption. Leaders, they thought, should take personal responsibility for their decisions.

Yet very soon after the Constitution was ratified, political parties began to form. They did so because the Constitution created a strong national government. Because it was powerful, the government made important decisions. National politics therefore *mattered*. People joined together in parties to attempt to control the decisions of the government.

The first parties were more influenced by personalities than by issues. The principal figures were Secretary of the Treasury Hamilton and Secretary of State Jefferson. Members of Congress who favored Hamilton's financial policies took the name **Federalists.** They began to vote as a group on most issues, even those not related to Hamilton's programs.

Those who opposed Hamilton and his ideas began to call themselves **Democratic-Republicans.** James Madison, now a Congressman from Virginia, was the chief organizer and manager of the Democratic-Republican party. Jefferson was its best-known leader. He was the person most responsible for the ideas it stood for.

- Why did the framers of the Constitution dislike and distrust political parties?
- Why were political parties formed so soon after the Constitution was ratified?

JEFFERSON AND HAMILTON

Thomas Jefferson considered Alexander Hamilton to be a dangerous **reactionary.** A reactionary is one opposed to political or social change. Jefferson thought that Hamilton wished to undo the gains of the Revolution and go back to a less democratic form of government. He even thought that Hamilton wanted to make the United States into a monarchy, perhaps with George Washington as king.

Yet Jefferson himself was not a democrat in the modern sense. He distrusted human nature almost as much as Hamilton did. Since governments consisted of people, Jefferson therefore distrusted *all* government. He wanted to keep the government as small as possible. Hamilton, on the other hand, wanted to use the government to control the weak and selfish elements in human nature.

In Jefferson's opinion the best way to keep government small was to keep society simple. The United States was a free country, he believed, because it was a nation of farmers. The population was spread out. Most families owned their own land. They managed their own affairs. Countries with crowded seaports and industrial towns needed more government controls to preserve order. City workers seldom owned land. They had less interest in protecting property and

Thomas Jefferson wanted to keep government as small as possible. This fine miniature oil portrait is by John Trumbull. Later Jefferson stopped wearing powdered wigs. Why did Jefferson dislike cities?

in having orderly government. "When we get piled upon one another in large cities," Jefferson said, "we shall become corrupt." Hamilton disagreed with all these ideas. He wanted the United States to have a strong and varied economy. He urged the government to do everything it could to encourage the growth of industry.

When Hamilton proposed paying off the national debt, Jefferson did not oppose him. Jefferson also went along with the plan to take over the state debts. In exchange Hamilton agreed that the permanent capital of the United States (the **District of Columbia**) should be located in the South, on land donated by Maryland and Virginia.

Jefferson *did* object to Hamilton's Bank of the United States and to the Whiskey Tax. Those measures favored eastern merchants and other city interests. Southern and western farmers had little to gain from a national bank, and they were the ones who had to pay the Whiskey Tax.

- Why did Jefferson distrust Hamilton?
- Why did Jefferson distrust all government?

THE ELECTION OF 1796

The growth of political parties ruined the complicated system for choosing the President established by the Constitution. Instead of voting for local electors whose judgment they trusted, voters in 1796 were presented with lists of names. The party leaders drew up these lists. They picked persons who had promised to vote for the party's choice for President. Ballots containing the names of the party's electors were sometimes printed and handed out to voters in advance.

John Adams, who had been Washington's Vice President, was the logical choice of the Federalists for President. Jefferson was the Democratic-Republican favorite. For Vice President the Federalist party leaders decided to run Thomas Pinckney of South Carolina, who had negotiated the popular treaty with Spain. The Democratic-Republican candidate for Vice President was Senator Aaron Burr of New York.

Hamilton, who was very influential in the Federalist party, disliked Adams. However, he dared not openly oppose him for President. Instead he worked out a clever, but very shady, scheme. The Federalists seemed likely to win a majority of the electors. If all these electors voted for Adams and Pinckney, both would have the same number of electoral votes. Since Adams was known to be the Presidential candidate, he would be chosen President and Pinckney Vice President. To prevent this from happening, Hamilton persuaded a few Federalist electors in South Carolina not to vote for Adams. If Pinckney got even one more vote than Adams, according to the rules he would be President and Adams Vice President.

John Adams was elected President in 1796. This detail is from an oil portrait by John Singleton Copley. Why was Adams the logical choice for President?

Unfortunately for Hamilton, news of his plan leaked out. A large number of Federalist electors who were friendly to Adams reacted by not voting for Pinckney. When the electoral votes were counted in the Senate, Adams had 71, Pinckney only 59. Jefferson, who had the united support of the Democratic-Republican electors, received 68 votes. He, not Pinckney, now became the new Vice President!

■ What was Hamilton's strategy to block the election of Adams in the election of 1796? What was the surprising consequence when his plan backfired?

THE XYZ AFFAIR

From the beginning of his Presidency, John Adams had to deal with a serious problem with the French. France was still at war with Great Britain. French leaders were angry at the United States for agreeing to the Jay Treaty. French warships and also numerous French privateers called **picaroons** were stopping American merchant ships on the high seas and seizing their cargoes. In 1795 alone they captured 316 vessels. When President Washington sent Charles C. Pinckney, Thomas Pinckney's brother, to France to try to settle these problems, the government refused to receive him. The French even ordered him out of the country.

When he became President, Adams decided to make another effort. He sent three special commissioners to France: Charles Pinckney; John Marshall, a Federalist from Virginia; and Elbridge Gerry of Massachusetts, a personal friend of his who happened to belong to the Democratic Republican party.

In those days diplomats had much greater responsibilities than they do today. It took Marshall almost seven weeks to get from Philadelphia to Paris. Without radios or cables diplomats could not send back home for new instructions. They had to make many important decisions on their own. This explains why the negotiations between the French and the three American commissioners developed as they did.

The French foreign minister, Talleyrand, was brilliant, but he could not be trusted. He was of noble birth and had been a bishop of the Catholic church before the French Revolution. During the Revolution he became a leading diplomat of the new republican government. When the Revolution became more radical, however, Talleyrand had to flee the country to save his life. He spent about two years in the United States. In 1796 he returned to France after a more conservative government, known as the Directory, took office. Soon thereafter he was named foreign minister.

The three Americans expected Talleyrand to be friendly because the United States had given him refuge. They were completely

Independence National Historical Park

The Granger Collection

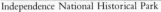
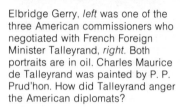
Elbridge Gerry, *left* was one of the three American commissioners who negotiated with French Foreign Minister Talleyrand, *right*. Both portraits are in oil. Charles Maurice de Talleyrand was painted by P. P. Prud'hon. How did Talleyrand anger the American diplomats?

wrong. He had disliked America. "If I have to stay here another year," he had written to a French friend, "I shall die." Moreover, Talleyrand loved money. He would not discuss the issues unless he received a large bribe.

The Americans did not know what to do. For weeks they had a series of meetings and exchanged letters with three secret agents of Talleyrand—one a Swiss banker, another a German merchant, the third a French diplomat. Besides the outright bribe, Talleyrand expected the United States to make a large loan to France that would be practically a gift. The United States must also apologize to France for certain harsh remarks about the French nation that President Adams had made in a speech to Congress.

Bribing officials was not as frowned upon then as it later became. Yet Talleyrand wanted $250,000, a huge sum. (At today's prices it would have amounted to several million dollars.) He would not stop the attacks on American ships or even begin to negotiate until the money was promised. "It is money," the Swiss banker reminded the Americans. "It is expected that you will offer money." Pinckney, the only American commissioner who could speak French properly, burst out angrily, "No, no. Not a sixpence!" Finally the commissioners gave up. Pinckney and Marshall returned home very much discouraged by Talleyrand's greed.

Gerry remained in Paris because he feared that France would declare war on the United States if the negotiations were broken off. President Adams was very upset by the attempt to bribe his representatives. He ordered Gerry to return to America. He published the letters of the commissioners, substituting the letters *X, Y,* and *Z* for the names of Talleyrand's secret agents.

The publication of the **XYZ correspondence** caused a sensation. Congress ordered 10,000 additional copies distributed free in rural areas where there were few newspapers. When John Marshall reached Philadelphia, Federalist members of Congress gave a huge banquet in his honor. "Millions for defense, but not one cent for tribute"—that is, for bribes—became a Federalist slogan. Congress created a new **Department of the Navy** and appropriated money for 40 new warships. It increased the size of the tiny United States army from 3,500 to about 10,000 men. It officially suspended the treaty of alliance with France.

War seemed unavoidable. Public feeling against France was bitter. Children in the streets played games of French against Americans. Washington came out of retirement to command the army. Suddenly Adams, who had been elected President by such a narrow margin, became a national hero.

■ Why did President Adams send commissioners to France?
■ What was the American response to the publication of the XYZ correspondence?
■ How did the XYZ Affair affect President Adams?

The XYZ Affair is the subject of this American political cartoon of 1798. It is entitled "Cinque-Têtes, or the Paris Monster." The five-headed monster stands for the Directory, the French government. The three American commissioners, Pinckney, Marshall, and Gerry, are on the left. The symbolic monster of the French Revolution sits top right in front of a guillotined citizen. The interesting "Civic Feast" on the right-hand side seems to consist of live frogs. Why does the five-headed monster say, "Money, money, money"?

The Granger Collection

THE ALIEN AND SEDITION ACTS

War with France would certainly have been popular in 1798. President Adams, however, wished to avoid it. He was right to do so. France had the most powerful army in the world. Its commander, Napoleon Bonaparte, was a military genius. The French navy completely outclassed the American. Although three powerful new warships called **frigates** were being built, the largest American warships ready for action were tiny coast guard patrol boats with crews of only six men. French privateers waited outside American harbors and picked off merchant ships almost at will.

Nevertheless, many Federalist leaders, including Hamilton, hoped for war. War would give them an excuse to destroy what they called their "internal enemies." Jefferson's Democratic-Republicans had long been supporters of France and some of the radical ideas of the French Revolution. Would they not side with France if war broke out? It was time to crack down on "Democrats and 'all other kinds of rats,'" these Federalists claimed.

Taking advantage of the war scare and the public anger over the XYZ Affair, the Federalists pushed several laws through Congress in the summer of 1798. These laws are known as the **Alien and Sedition Acts** because they were aimed at foreigners in the United States and at people who were supposed to be trying to undermine the government in order to help France.

One of these laws increased from 5 to 14 years the length of time foreigners had to live in the United States before they could become citizens. Another gave the President the power to jail or order out of the country foreigners whom he thought were "dangerous to the peace and safety of the United States."

Still more severe was the Sedition Act, which outlawed conspiracies against the government and attempts to start riots or uprisings. There were reasonable arguments for this part of the act. But the act also made it a crime for anyone to "write, print, utter, or publish" even merely "scandalous" statements critical of the government, of either house of Congress, or of the President.

The Sedition Act was an attempt to frighten the Democratic-Republicans into silence. In practice it made criticism of the Federalists a crime but not criticism of the Democratic-Republicans. It was against the law to "defame" the President but not the Vice President.

Such an attack on freedom of speech and of the press was a threat to everything the American Revolution had sought to protect. In 1798 the great American experiment in republican government was little more than 20 years old. Was it about to end in a new tyranny?

- Why did President Adams resist going to war against France?
- At which political party was the Sedition Act aimed?

CHAPTER 7 REVIEW

Identification
Tell briefly why each of the following persons, terms, or events is important.
1. George Washington
2. Thomas Jefferson
3. Alexander Hamilton
4. Citizen Genet
5. Anthony Wayne
6. James Madison
7. John Adams
8. Cabinet
9. Bill of Rights
10. Bank of the United States
11. Elastic clause
12. Neutrality Proclamation
13. Jay's Treaty
14. Pinckney's Treaty
15. Whiskey Rebellion
16. Washington's Farewell Address
17. Federalist party
18. Democratic-Republican party
19. XYZ Affair
20. Alien and Sedition Acts

Understanding American History
1. What is a precedent? Why were Washington and other Americans concerned about the precedents the first President established?
2. Explain the difference between natural rights and legal rights. Which of these are protected by the Bill of Rights?
3. Why did Hamilton want the national government to assume state debts and pay state and national debts at face value?
4. Contrast the views of Hamilton and Jefferson as they applied the "necessary and proper clause" to the bank bill.
5. Why did Washington want to avoid going to war against Great Britain or aiding the French?
6. Name some of Washington's accomplishments as President.
7. Explain the two main ideas expressed in Washington's Farewell Address.
8. Contrast the views of Jefferson and Hamilton on the uses of government.
9. What actions did Congress take after the XYZ correspondence was published? How did ordinary Americans respond?
10. Why did political parties begin to form so soon after the Constitution was ratified?

Activities
1. Interview a police officer from your community. Ask what things he or she must do to protect the rights of a suspect. Your teacher may arrange for a representative of the police department to speak to the class. Prepare questions to ask after the talk.
2. Do research in your library to prepare a short report on the life of one of the following persons:

   Thomas Jefferson   James Madison
   Alexander Hamilton   Aaron Burr
   Anthony Wayne   John Adams
   John Jay   Thomas Pinckney
3. Prepare a bulletin board on the President's Cabinet as it exists today. Show each department, the name of its leader, and its major responsibilities.
4. Assemble a collage, using pictures and headlines from newspapers and magazines, to illustrate the freedoms protected by the Bill of Rights.
5. Research with your classmates the Battle of Fallen Timbers. Then use your historical imagination to prepare interviews with members of both armies—the Indian confederacy and the United States. Questions and answers should explain why each side fought, describe the battle itself, and explain the results and consequences of the battle.

CHAPTER 7 TEST

Completion (30 points)

Number your paper 1–10 and next to each number write the words that best complete each of the following statements.

1. The _____ was added to the Constitution in order to protect peoples' natural rights.
2. The group of government department heads that meets regularly with the President to review current issues is the _____.
3. Washington issued the _____ to warn that the United States would aid neither side in the war between Britain and France.
4. Investors who bought government bonds at less than their face value in the hope that the government would later pay off the bonds at full value were called _____.
5. In his _____ Washington urged unity at home and neutrality abroad.
6. The attempt by French secret agents to get bribes from United States diplomats was known as the _____.
7. Private ships with guns that were hired by one country to attack the ships of another country were called _____.
8. The section of the Constitution that stretches the power of Congress by allowing it to pass laws on subjects not specifically mentioned is known as the _____.
9. The _____ were pushed through Congress by the Federalists in an attempt to silence the Democratic-Republicans.
10. The framers of the Constitution called political parties _____ and made no provision for them.

Matching (20 points)

Number your paper 11–15 and match the person in the second column with the description in the first column.

11. His victory over Blue Jacket in the Battle of Fallen Timbers opened the Northwest to peaceful settlement.
12. He was President during the XYZ Affair.
13. He was the financial genius who wanted the United States to pay off all state and national debts in order to establish good credit.
14. He was the best-known leader of the Democratic-Republicans.
15. He knew that his decisions were especially important in establishing precedents for future Presidents to follow.

a. George Washington
b. Thomas Jefferson
c. Alexander Hamilton
d. Anthony Wayne
e. John Adams

Classifying (20 points)

Number your paper 16–20. For each of the following statements write *J* if it was an idea of Thomas Jefferson, *H* if it was an idea of Alexander Hamilton.

16. He was a strong supporter of France and the French Revolution.
17. He wanted the United States government to establish a bank in order to loan money to help businesses grow.
18. He argued to stretch the elastic clause.
19. He hoped the nation would be made up of small independent farmers.
20. He wanted the national government to be strong enough to balance rival interests.

Essay (30 points)

How did George Washington's personal qualities and his far-reaching vision make his Presidency so successful? Write at least one full paragraph, taking care to spell and punctuate correctly.

UNIT TWO TEST

Multiple Choice (20 points)
Number your paper 1-5 and write the letter of the phrase that best completes each sentence.

1. The British fought better near the coast than inland because
   a. they were experienced coast fighters.
   b. most American cities were inland.
   c. their strong navy supported them.
   d. their Indian allies fought near water.
2. The Declaration of Independence
   a. gave equal rights to all Americans.
   b. divided government into three branches.
   c. forced Britain to give up the war.
   d. told the world why Americans revolted.
3. A weakness of the Articles of Confederation was that
   a. Congress could not tax the states.
   b. the President could not veto bills.
   c. only Congress could print money.
   d. the Supreme Court was too strong.
4. The Bill of Rights protects
   a. the authority of the Supreme Court.
   b. individual citizens.
   c. the powers of the President.
   d. the lawmaking power of Congress.
5. The first political parties were formed because
   a. the central government was weak.
   b. the Constitution established them.
   c. the national government was powerful.
   d. Washington had such great popularity.

Chronological Order (25 points)
Number your paper 6–10 and place the following events in order by numbering 1 for the first, 2 for the second, and so on.

6. The Constitution is ratified.
7. The War for American Independence ends.
8. The Declaration of Independence is written.
9. The Boston Tea Party takes place.
10. Washington presents his Farewell Address.

Matching (25 points)
Number your paper 11–15 and match the description in the first column with the American leader in the second column.

11. The diplomat who negotiated a treaty with Britain
12. A strong promoter of a national bank
13. The chief author of the Declaration of Independence
14. The Federalist President during the XYZ Affair
15. The chief organizer of the Democratic-Republican party

a. Thomas Jefferson
b. James Madison
c. Alexander Hamilton
d. John Jay
e. John Adams

Essay (30 points)
Explain what "all men are created equal" meant to most American leaders at the time the Declaration of Independence was written. Write at least one full paragraph, taking care to spell and punctuate correctly.

UNIT THREE

1800
Jefferson elected President

1801
Jefferson's inaugural in new Capitol
•
Whitney makes muskets with interchangeable parts

1802

1803
Louisiana Purchase

1804
Burr kills Hamilton in duel
•
Lewis and Clark Expedition departs
•
Jefferson reelected

1810
Macon's Bill Number Two

1811
Battle of Tippecanoe

1812
Congress declares war on Great Britain
•
Madison reelected

1813
Battle of Put-In-Bay
•
Battle of the Thames
•
Creek War

1814
Battle of Horseshoe Bend
•
Burning of Washington
•
Peace of Ghent

WAR OF 1812

A GROWING AMERICA

1805

1806
Lewis and Clark
return

1807
Embargo Act
•
Clermont
powered by
steam

1808
Madison
elected
President

1809
Non-Intercourse
Act
•
Tecumseh and
the Prophet
found Red Stick
Confederacy

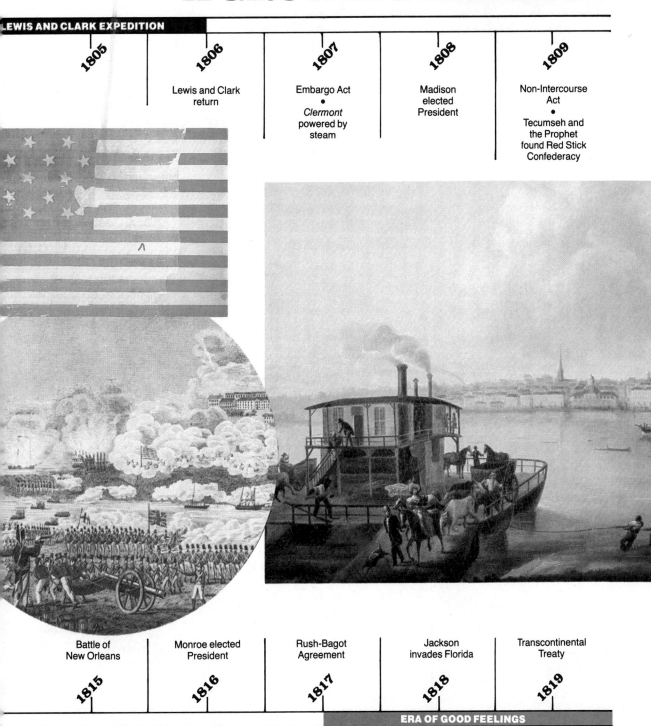

Battle of
New Orleans

1815

Monroe elected
President

1816

Rush-Bagot
Agreement

1817

Jackson
invades Florida

1818

Transcontinental
Treaty

1819

ERA OF GOOD FEELINGS

CHAPTER 8
The Age of Jefferson

A Federalist editor strikes phrases from America's great documents in this 1799 political cartoon. 'Peter Porcupine' says, "I hate this country & will sow the seeds of discord in it." Liberty weeps over Ben Franklin. At right the devil whispers, "Let us destroy this Idol liberty," while the British lion purrs, "Go on, dear Peter my friend, and I will reward you." What act inspired this cartoon?

ATTACKS ON THE SEDITION ACT

The Sedition Act was an attempt to frighten critics of the Federalist government into silence. Although it had been passed because of the war scare abroad with France, its real motives had to do with politics at home. Remember that the Sedition Act made it a crime to criticize the President, who was a Federalist, but not a crime to criticize the Vice President, who was a Democratic-Republican. In that sense the act was purely political.

The Granger Collection

Only about ten people were convicted of violating the Sedition Act. Not one of these was accused of plotting against the government. All the convictions were for *criticizing* the government or some important Federalist leader. Charles Holt, a newspaper editor, published an article calling the United States army "a band of disorganized . . . ruffians, a burden, a pest, and a terror to the citizens." For this and similar statements he was sentenced to six months in jail and fined $200. James Callender, another editor, claimed that President Adams was "repulsive," a "fool," and "the blasted tyrant of America." His punishment was nine months in jail and a $200 fine.

Such statements were untrue and in very bad taste. Still, the right to make them was protected by the **First Amendment** of the Constitution, which guarantees freedom of speech and of the press. Moreover, equally unfair criticisms of Jeffersonian leaders were made by Federalist editors. These were ignored by the government.

Vice President Jefferson reacted swiftly to the obvious political bias of the Sedition Act against his party. Above all, he believed that Congress did not have the power under the Constitution to pass any of the Alien and Sedition Acts. They were **unconstitutional,** in his opinion. He wrote out a series of statements called *resolutions* which explained his reasoning. A friend of his introduced these resolutions at a session of the legislature of the new state of Kentucky, where the Jeffersonians had a large majority. The legislature voted to approve them in November 1798.

At the time the public did not know that Jefferson had written the resolutions. They were called the *Kentucky Resolutions*. About a month later a similar set of resolutions was passed by the Virginia legislature. These were written by James Madison.

The **Kentucky and Virginia Resolutions** did not claim that the rights of free speech and the free press had no limits. The issue was whether the federal government had the power to limit them. Jefferson and Madison argued that because of the First Amendment, it could not. Only the state legislatures could restrict these rights.

When Congress goes beyond its legal powers, what can be done? Jefferson had a simple answer. The Constitution, he wrote, was a contract. It was an agreement made by separate states. It gave certain powers to the federal government created by the states. What if Congress broke the contract by passing a law that the Constitution did not give it the power to pass? Jefferson argued that any state could **nullify,** or cancel, the law. The law would no longer exist within that state. Each state, said Jefferson, "had an equal right to judge for itself" whether or not a law of Congress is constitutional.

If put into practice, this **doctrine of nullification** would have meant the end of the United States as one nation. If any state could refuse to obey a law of Congress, the national government would

James Madison was author of the Virginia Resolutions. He sat for this likeness in oil by Gilbert Stuart, the most celebrated portrait painter of the early 1800s. (A Stuart portrait of Washington is engraved on the one-dollar bill.) How did Madison protest the Sedition Act?

soon collapse. Even the friendly Kentucky legislature found the idea of nullification too radical. It changed that resolution. Instead it urged Congress to repeal, or cancel, the unconstitutional law. The Virginia Resolutions took the same position.

The Kentucky and Virginia Resolutions had no practical effects. The other states did not respond favorably to them. Congress did not repeal the Alien and Sedition Acts. The resolutions are important, however, because they put forth an argument about **states' rights** that was to reappear many times in American history.

- What was the political purpose of the Sedition Act?
- How did Jefferson react to the Sedition Act?
- What is the historical importance of the Kentucky and Virginia Resolutions?

THE HEROISM OF JOHN ADAMS

The Federalists, of course, did not think that the Alien and Sedition Acts were unconstitutional. President John Adams had special reason for believing them both legal and desirable. The coarse personal attacks of Democratic-Republican editors like James Callender made him very angry. He was understandably delighted to see such people punished.

Adams also wanted to be reelected President in 1800. He knew that his strong stand against France at the time of the XYZ Affair had made him very popular. The people saw him as the defender of the nation's honor and security during a national crisis. The danger of war with France was a political advantage for him. If war actually broke out, he would almost certainly be reelected.

John Adams, however, was too honest and too patriotic to put personal gain ahead of duty. He learned that the French foreign minister, Talleyrand, was eager to repair the damage caused by the XYZ Affair. Adams decided to try again to solve the nation's difficulties with France by negotiation. Late in 1799 he sent three new commissioners to Paris.

This made Hamilton and his Federalist supporters furious. They wanted the conflict between America and France to continue. But they could not prevent Adams from acting.

The American commissioners were greeted "with a friendly dignity." After months of discussion the diplomats signed a treaty known as the **Convention of 1800.** Peace was restored between the two nations. France agreed to release the United States from its obligations under the treaty of alliance of 1778. Little else was gained, for the French would not agree to pay for the damages their warships and privateers had done to American vessels and their cargoes.

On October 4, 1800, Napoleon Bonaparte, who was now dictator of France, gave an enormous party for the American commissioners. It took place at his brother's estate outside Paris. There were 180 guests, including all the high officials of the French government. A magnificent meal was eaten. Champagne toasts were drunk to "perpetual peace," to "freedom of the seas," and to President John Adams. Later there were fireworks and a concert.

■ Why was John Adams heroic in reestablishing negotiations with the French?

THE ELECTION OF 1800

President Adams had stopped the threat of war with France. He was quite rightly proud of what he had done. Many years later he said that the treaty was his greatest achievement. "The most splendid diamond in my crown," was the way he put it. Peace ended the crisis that had led to passage of the Alien and Sedition Acts. Equally important, it ended the threat to democracy these laws posed. It also lessened the fear of many Americans that the Jeffersonians preferred France to their own country. This helped Jefferson in his campaign for the Presidency in 1800.

This detail of a portrait of Napoleon Bonaparte, emperor of the French, is from an oil by Jacques-Louis David, First Painter to the emperor. We see Napoleon in 1798 at the age of 29. In 1804 he proclaimed himself emperor. How did Napoleon receive the Americans who came to make peace in 1800?

Thomas Jefferson, at left, and Aaron Burr, at right, were the Democratic-Republican party's candidates for President and Vice President in 1800. Jefferson's oil portrait is by Rembrandt Peale, c. 1800, and Burr was painted in oil on wood by John Vanderlyn in 1809. Who were the Federalist candidates?

The Democratic-Republican party again nominated Jefferson for President and Aaron Burr for Vice President. The Federalists ran Adams for President and Charles C. Pinckney of XYZ fame for Vice President. In the campaign the Jeffersonians were united, the Federalists badly divided. Hamilton disliked Adams so much that he published a pamphlet on "The Public Conduct and Character of John Adams" in which he described Adams as jealous, vain, and stubborn. According to Hamilton, Adams was totally unfit to be President.

The Capital City

Jefferson was the first President to be inaugurated in the new capital city, which was named after George Washington, who had died in 1799. The land where **Washington** was built, which is called the **District of Columbia,** had been chosen by President Washington himself. He selected a site a few miles down the Potomac River from his plantation, Mount Vernon.

Washington also selected the designer of the capital, Pierre Charles L'Enfant, a French-born engineer who had come to America to serve in the Revolutionary Army. L'Enfant had remodeled Federal Hall, the first home of Congress, in New York City. Washington liked his work and asked him to design the permanent capital. It was a remarkable opportunity, and L'Enfant did a brilliant job.

L'Enfant's plan provided for broad avenues reaching out like spokes in a wheel from two main centers where the President and Congress would be located. The plan left generous room for parks as well. It has been widely regarded as one of the finest examples of city planning in the world.

In 1801, however, Washington was a tiny village. Only one wing of the Capitol building had been erected. The Treasury Department building and the still-unfinished President's mansion were the only other solidly constructed buildings. There were a few clusters of houses and shops. The streets were unpaved, dusty in dry weather, ankle deep in mud after every rain. Living was uncomfortable. Members of Congress slept and ate in rough hotels called boarding houses. A room and three meals a day in one of these places cost about $15 a week. There was little to do after sessions of Congress. Most senators and representatives hurried back to their home districts as soon as Congress adjourned. In summer the village was almost deserted. President Jefferson flatly refused to stay there in July and August because of the heat and humidity.

Once again Hamilton tried to manage the votes of the Federalist electors in order to make the Federalist candidate for Vice President get more votes than Adams. Again this trick failed. The Democratic-Republican party won the election. Jefferson received 73 electoral votes, Adams only 65.

Because the Democratic-Republicans were united and well organized, all their electors had voted for Burr as well as Jefferson. He, too, had 73 electoral votes! The electors intended, of course, that Burr be Vice President. Nevertheless, the tie meant that the House of

Representatives would have to choose between them. Under the Constitution each state, no matter how many representatives it had, would have one vote.

Since there were 16 states, 9 were needed for a majority. The Democratic-Republicans controlled 8 states. The Federalists had 6, and 2 were divided evenly. The Federalists voted for Burr, partly just to make trouble for the opposition, partly because they thought Burr less radical than Jefferson. Thus, on the first ballot Jefferson got 8 votes and Burr 6. The votes of the equally divided states did not count. For an entire week all the delegates held firm. They voted 35 times without anyone changing his vote. Finally, Federalist James A. Bayard of Delaware, that small state's only representative, changed from Burr to Jefferson. That gave Jefferson the Presidency, 9 states to 6. Burr became Vice President.

Everyone now realized that with the development of well-organized political parties, tie votes between members of the same party would become common. The **Twelfth Amendment** was added to the Constitution. Thereafter the electors voted separately for President and Vice President.

- Why did the election of 1800 and the growth of political parties lead to the Twelfth Amendment to the Constitution?

This engraving shows Georgetown, the Potomac River, and dimly in the distance the Federal City planned by a veteran of the Revolutionary War, Pierre Charles L'Enfant. Washington, D.C. was but a tiny village when this view was made in 1801. Who chose the site on which the new capital city was built?

243

BUILDING SKILLS IN SOCIAL STUDIES

Using Primary Sources

First-hand information is always best. That is why so many original works of art are included in this book. The original materials that historians study are called *primary sources.* These include documents and letters, maps and drawings, paintings and photographs—anything that will throw light on the past.

Three primary sources appear on this page. The first is Pierre Charles L'Enfant's plan for the new capital city of Washington, D.C. Notice how the broad avenues radiate from the centers of power. The plan is widely praised.

The drawing of the President's House was made in 1792 by its Irish architect, James Hoban. His was the prize-winning plan in a national competition, defeating an anonymous entry by Thomas Jefferson, among others.

The first architect of the Capitol was the Quaker doctor William Thornton. His drawing was presented to President Washington in 1793.

Library of Congress

United States Capitol

The Granger Collection

Maryland Historical Society

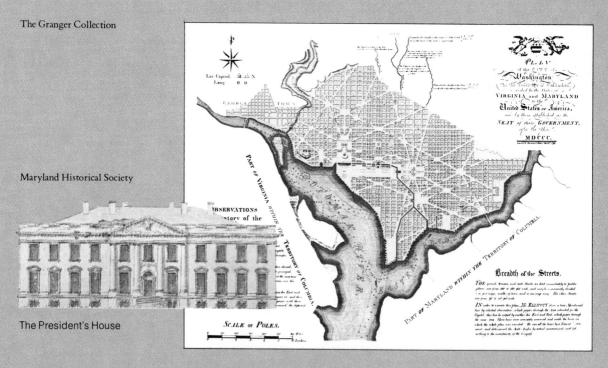

The President's House

JEFFERSON'S INAUGURAL ADDRESS

Jefferson's inaugural address, delivered in the Senate chamber of the Capitol on March 4, 1801, was a fitting beginning for the new city and his administration. Jefferson believed that his election was a kind of second American Revolution that had checked the Federalists' attempt to make the United States into a monarchy. The speech, however, showed that he intended to make few changes. The tone was similar to that of Washington's Farewell Address. Like that speech, its main themes were unity at home and neutrality abroad.

Majority rule was the first principle of democracy, Jefferson reminded his audience. But minorities also have rights and "to violate [them] would be oppression." His main point was that political differences could be smoothed over by discussion and compromise. "Every difference of opinion is not a difference of principle," he said. "We are all Republicans, we are all Federalists." With this clever reference to the political parties, he was reminding the people that everyone wanted America to be a *republic* rather than a monarchy, and also that everyone believed in a *federal* system, with power divided between the central government and the states.

As for the rest of the world, Jefferson tried to show that he did not intend to make the United States dependent on France, as the Federalists had claimed during the election campaign. His policy would be "honest friendship for all nations, entangling alliances with none."

He also spoke with deep feeling about American democratic ideals. The United States, he said, was "the world's best hope." It had "the strongest government on earth," because the people felt that they were part of the government. They were therefore eager to protect and defend it.

Jefferson's speech promised a moderate and reasonable program. The Alien and Sedition Acts were either repealed or allowed to expire. By 1802 all were gone. Jefferson got Congress to repeal the Whiskey Tax too. And he canceled the Federalists' program for expanding the army and navy. On the other hand, he continued Hamilton's policy of paying off the national debt and made no effort to do away with the Bank of the United States.

The author of the Declaration of Independence had no taste for pomp and ceremony in the White House. Plain citizens and foreign diplomats were each seen in their turn, for Jefferson told them, "Nobody shall be above you, nor you above anybody."

- What were the main themes of Jefferson's inaugural address?
- What did Jefferson mean by "We are all Republicans, we are all Federalists"?
- What did Jefferson say his foreign policy would be?

THE LOUISIANA PURCHASE

Jefferson's most important accomplishment was adding a huge new western region to the nation. This came about in a most unexpected manner. The settlers who crossed over the mountains into Kentucky, Tennessee, and the lands north of the Ohio River cleared the land and planted crops. As the country developed, traffic down the Mississippi River increased rapidly. Frontier farmers floated their wheat, lumber, tobacco, and other produce down the river on log rafts. These goods had to be stored in warehouses and on docks in New Orleans while waiting to be reshipped to East Coast ports or to Europe on ocean-going vessels. As we have seen, Pinckney's Treaty of 1795 with Spain guaranteed Americans what was called the **right of deposit** at New Orleans. Without the right of deposit, western settlers could not get their produce to market.

All went well until 1802, when Spain, under pressure from the powerful Napoleon Bonaparte, agreed to give New Orleans and the rest of the land called Louisiana back to France. For more than a year Spain continued to govern New Orleans. But France was obviously preparing to take over the city as part of a general expansion of its overseas empire. Napoleon planned to use Louisiana as a breadbasket to feed the French West Indian sugar islands. France's most important island colony, **Santo Domingo,** had broken away during the French Revolution. Slaves led by Toussaint L'Ouverture, the "Black Napoleon," took control of the island. In 1801 Napoleon had sent 20,000 soldiers to put down the rebellion.

Jefferson had long been an admirer of France and of French civilization. He disliked the English. Yet the mere thought of France controlling New Orleans made him willing to consider an alliance with Great Britain against France. If France canceled the right of deposit, he wrote to his diplomatic representative in Paris, Robert R. Livingston, we must "marry ourselves to the British fleet."

Spain was a weak nation. It could not seriously threaten American interests. If Spain closed New Orleans to Americans, the city could probably be captured by a force of arms. With a great military power in control, the result might be very different. To solve the problem, Jefferson instructed Livingston to offer to buy the city of New Orleans from France.

Livingston spent the greater part of 1802 trying to arrange a deal. Talleyrand, who was still in charge of French foreign relations, looked down his nose at him. He would not even tell Livingston whether or not Spain had also given Florida to France. Napoleon seemed to be the only person able to make decisions, and he was hard to reach. "He seldom asks advice," Livingston complained in a letter to James Madison, who was Jefferson's Secretary of State. "His ministers are mere clerks."

The Granger Collection

Toussaint L'Ouverture is shown in this early engraving in his military dress. He led a fight for liberty on the island of Santo Domingo. Who was the French leader who fought L'Ouverture?

Louisiana State Museum

"Raising the Flag at New Orleans" is the title of this oil painted by an artist named DeThulstrup. The Stars and Stripes replaces the French tricolor in a ceremony on December 20, 1803, after the Louisiana Purchase. This scene is set in the French quarter of the city, the Vieux Carré (old square). The flag flies over the Place d'Armes (now Jackson Square) at the front of the government building on the left— the Cabildo, built in 1795—and St. Louis Cathedral, on the right, built in 1794. Both buildings may be visited today. Which country claimed New Orleans before the French?

In October 1802 Spain canceled the American right of deposit at New Orleans. The situation was at once critical. Much alarmed, Jefferson sent a trusted adviser, James Monroe, to join Livingston in France. He authorized Monroe to offer Napoleon $10 million for New Orleans. Meanwhile, the French expedition to Santo Domingo had been wasted by yellow fever and jungle warfare.

Now Napoleon needed money. Soon he planned to resume his long war with England. The French possessions in America would then be easy targets for Britain's powerful navy. Early in 1803 he ordered Talleyrand to offer to sell New Orleans and all the rest of Louisiana to the United States. The Americans quickly took the offer.

▨ Why did Jefferson want to buy New Orleans from France?
▨ Why did Napoleon suddenly decide to sell New Orleans and all of Louisiana to the United States?

READING PRACTICE IN SOCIAL STUDIES

Using Reference Books

Oftentimes you need to find information quickly. You may search for the meaning of a word or the location of a country. Perhaps you need statistics (numerical facts) for a report, or you seek general information about the life of a famous person. All of this information may be found in *reference books*.

The word *reference* comes partly from a Latin word that means "to bring back." Reference books help you to bring back the facts you need for a class report or a research project. They help you to go beyond your history book.

Four of the most useful reference books are the *dictionary, encyclopedia, atlas,* and *almanac.* Knowing how to use each will help you to bring back information.

You already know that a *dictionary* can help you spell and define words. But a dictionary gives other information too. Dictionaries divide words into syllables and give their correct pronunciations. They also give the part of speech and etymology (the source) of words. Many of our English words come from Latin, Greek, or other languages, and the etymology explains where the English word originated.

Most important, dictionaries give the meanings of words. Many words have more than one meaning. The first meaning given is the most commonly used. However, the meaning you seek may not be the most common one, so be sure to read through all the meanings and see which makes most sense.

To find a word quickly in its alphabetical order in the dictionary, use the *guide words* at the top or bottom of each page. Guide words, printed in **bold type,** show the first and last words defined on the page. Thumb quickly past the guide words to find the page on which the word you seek appears.

An *encyclopedia* is usually a set of several volumes that contains brief articles about many topics, arranged in alphabetical order. For some topics you will find *see* or *see also*. The word *see* tells you to look on another page for the topic you seek. The words *see also* tell you to look on another page for additional information.

An *atlas* is a book of maps. Many atlases are organized by regions of the world. Some contain current maps of cities, states, countries, and continents. Historical atlases show maps of various regions as they existed in the past. The type of atlas you use will depend on the information you seek.

An *almanac* is a book of facts. It gives statistics and other kinds of factual information on a wide variety of topics—politics, religion, sports, population, and so forth. Almanacs are issued yearly and include facts about the past year as well as facts for several previous years.

Knowing which of these reference books to use and how to use it will save you time and make your search for information in social studies more productive.

The following questions may be answered by using standard reference books in your school.
1. Write the word *adventurer* in syllables.
2. What meanings does your dictionary give for the word *revolution?*
3. What is the etymology of the word *explore?*
4. Arrange the following words in alphabetical order: govern, gouge, governor, gourd, government.

Tell which reference book would be the *best* source to find each of the following. Then report on the information you find.
5. What is the current population of the United States?
6. Name the countries that border Iran.
7. Give an account of Thomas Jefferson's early years.
8. What is the meaning of *agriculture?*
9. What is the true course of the Mississippi River?
10. Give an account of the Milan Decree of 1807.

When Napoleon offered to sell Louisiana, he did not simply mean what is now the state of Louisiana. Rather he meant all the land between the Mississippi River and the Rocky Mountains! When Talleyrand, the French foreign minister, passed this news on to Robert Livingston, the American negotiator was dumbfounded. But he recovered swiftly. He offered $5 million for the territory. Not enough, said Talleyrand. He urged Livingston to think the matter over.

The very next day James Monroe arrived in Paris to represent President Jefferson. After considerable discussion he and Livingston decided to offer $15 million. If Jefferson thought $10 million a fair price for New Orleans, surely $15 million was not too much to pay for that city and the entire western half of the Mississippi Valley. Talleyrand accepted the offer.

This Louisiana Purchase was one of the greatest real estate bargains in history. When the Americans asked Talleyrand about the exact boundaries of Louisiana, he could not tell them. No one knew. "You have made a noble bargain for yourselves," Talleyrand said. "I suppose you will make the most of it."

A Noble Bargain

Missouri Historical Society

This bronze plaque by Karl Bitter honors the signing of the Louisiana Purchase. Shown from left to right are James Monroe, Robert Livingston, and Charles Maurice de Talleyrand.

HAMILTON AND BURR

Adding all this new territory to the United States alarmed many of the leaders of the Federalist party. Jefferson was popular with farmers and with western settlers in general. Federalist strength was greatest in New England and among merchants and other city residents. When people began to settle Louisiana, and new states were formed beyond the Mississippi, the power and influence of the Federalists in Congress seemed sure to decline.

A group of angry Federalists in the New England states, led by former Secretary of State Timothy Pickering, began to scheme to withdraw their states from the Union. Such a withdrawal, the technical name for which is **secession,** would be more likely to succeed if New York joined the movement. Then a strong northeastern confederacy could be formed. Pickering and his friends therefore tried to persuade Vice President Aaron Burr of New York to join with them.

Burr did not enjoy being Vice President. He had decided to seek election as governor of New York. When he was approached by the Federalists, he did not agree to join the plot. He did not reject the idea either. However, he was defeated in the New York election, which took place in April 1804. Without the support of New York, the secession scheme had to be abandoned.

With steady aim Aaron Burr has just fired the fatal shot in his duel with Alexander Hamilton, who clutches his forehead. The bullet tore through his torso. Hamilton lay dead in the morning. In this early engraving the seconds for the duel watch. Why did Burr and Hamilton quarrel?

During his campaign for governor, Burr had become very angry with Alexander Hamilton, who had criticized him in a most insulting manner. Hamilton had strongly opposed the idea of secession. He disliked Burr even more than he disliked Jefferson. After Burr had lost the election, Hamilton continued to make insulting remarks about him. Finally Burr challenged Hamilton to a duel.

Dueling was against the law in New York and in many other states. Hamilton had performed bravely during the War for American Independence. Therefore no one could accuse him of cowardice. Like many Americans of his day, Hamilton believed that a challenge to duel could not honorably be refused. He accepted. On July 11, 1804, the two men met secretly in New Jersey, across the Hudson River from New York City. At the signal to fire, Hamilton discharged his pistol into the air. Burr aimed his gun carefully. Hamilton fell. The bullet had passed through his liver and come to rest against his backbone. Nothing could be done. The next morning he died.

In a way, this senseless tragedy marked the decline of the Federalist party that Hamilton had created. The Louisiana Purchase was popular nearly everywhere. Jefferson was easily reelected President in 1804. Four years later his friend and adviser, James Madison, became President. Madison served two terms, and then another of Jefferson's friends, James Monroe, was President for eight more years.

■ What was the plan of the bitter New England Federalists? Why was Vice President Burr important to their plan?

250

THE LEWIS AND CLARK EXPEDITION

This famous watercolor portrait is of Captain Meriwether Lewis, who was painted in 1806 by a French artist, Charles Saint-Mémin. We see Lewis after his return from the expedition to explore the Louisiana Territory. Why did Jefferson choose Lewis to lead the Corps of Discovery?

Long before the shooting of Hamilton, President Jefferson had begun to plan for the development of the Louisiana Territory. In fact, he had first asked Congress for money to explore the region even before Spain had returned it to France. Congress supplied him with $2,500. He then appointed his private secretary, a young ex-soldier named Meriwether Lewis, to head the expedition. According to Jefferson, Lewis was brave, careful, and "habituated to the woods."

Lewis persuaded another soldier, William Clark, to become co-leader of the expedition. The two had met while both were fighting under General Anthony Wayne against the Indian confederacy in the Ohio Valley. These two experienced outdoorsmen made an excellent team.

Jefferson gave the explorers very detailed instructions. These instructions reflected his own interests, which were as varied as Benjamin Franklin's. Besides describing and mapping the country, Lewis and Clark were to keep careful records of its climate—the temperature, the number of rainy days, wind directions, and so on. They were to locate and map the course of all rivers in order to find "the most direct . . . water connection across this continent." In addition, Jefferson ordered them to take note of soil conditions and to look for traces of valuable minerals. They were to collect plant and animal specimens and even to bring back the bones of any "rare or extinct" animals they could find.

Jefferson was particularly interested in the many American Indian cultures. As a young man he had been one of the first persons to find and excavate a settlement of the ancient civilization of the Mound Builders. He instructed Lewis and Clark to gather all sorts of information about the western Indians. He wanted to know about their languages, their clothing, what they ate, how they lived, their diseases. He gave Lewis and Clark a list of basic English words and told them to take note of the corresponding words in the languages of the Indians they met.

Lewis and Clark prepared for their journey carefully. They consulted with leading scientists. They gathered the necessary equipment, such as guns, warm clothing, gifts for Indians, and medicines. They even secured navigational instruments so that they could map the country accurately.

They chose with equal care the members of what they called their **Corps of Discovery.** They employed a half-French, half-Indian interpreter who was skilled in the sign language used by Indians of different tribes to communicate with one another. One member was an expert at repairing guns, another a carpenter. Twenty-one members of the Corps were army men. The Secretary of War had authorized Lewis to "detach" any volunteers he wanted from their mili-

BUILDING SKILLS
IN SOCIAL STUDIES

Using Scale on a Map

The map on this page shows the Lewis and Clark Expedition to explore the Louisiana Purchase. Look at the map carefully. With a ruler practice using the scale. Let inches stand for miles, centimeters for kilometers. Then answer the following questions.

1. Which color is used to show the United States? Which shows the Northwest Territory? Which the Louisiana Purchase?
2. Which countries claimed Oregon Country?
3. What river did the explorers travel on in 1804?
4. How far was Fort Mandan from St. Louis?

5. What mountains did Lewis and Clark have to cross in 1805?
6. What is the approximate distance between Fort Mandan and Fort Clatsop?
7. Where did Lewis and Clark separate on their return? Where did they rejoin?
8. On his return, what direction did Lewis take after crossing the Continental Divide?
9. Why do you suppose Lewis and Clark so often followed rivers?
10. How many months did it take Lewis and Clark to travel from St. Louis to the Pacific? How many months did it take for the Expedition to return?

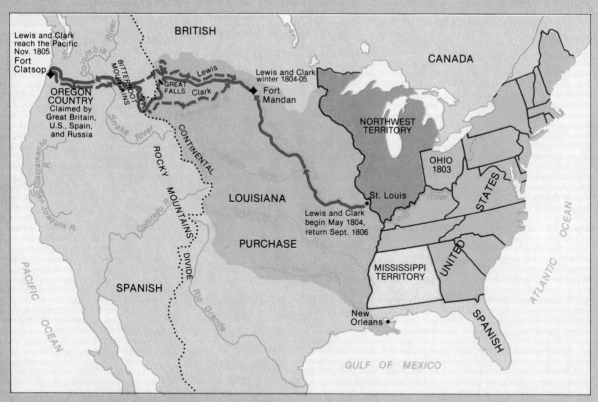

**LEWIS AND CLARK EXPLORE
THE LOUISIANA PURCHASE 1804-06**

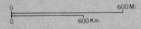

tary duties. Only strong men used to living in the woods were chosen, for as Lewis said, hard work was "a very essential part of the services required of the party." The group finally chosen consisted of 45 persons. One of these, an enormously strong man named York, became the first black person to cross the continent. He was a slave owned by William Clark.

Charles Marion Russell is a famous painter of the American West. Once a trapper and cowboy, Russell lived for some time with Indians whose ancestors greeted Lewis and Clark. He painted many scenes of Lewis and Clark's expedition to explore the Louisiana Purchase. In this oil Lewis and Clark are seen in the right background with the Flathead Indians of the Northwest. How did the explorers talk to the Indians?

- What action did Jefferson take to plan for the development of the Louisiana Territory?
- What kinds of tasks were Lewis and Clark given?

WESTWARD TO THE PACIFIC

On May 14, 1804, the explorers set out from their base at the junction of the Mississippi and Missouri Rivers. Up the Missouri they went. They traveled in three boats, the largest a 55-foot (about 17-meter) keelboat manned by 22 oarsmen. Their first objective was the "mountains of rock that rise up in the West."

By August they had reached what is now **Council Bluffs,** Iowa. There they had their first meeting with Indians belonging to the tribes of the Great Plains. Lewis and Clark put up the United States flag, which at the time had 17 stars. Through an interpreter Lewis told the Plains Indians that "the great Chief of the seventeen nations of America" wanted to live in peace and was eager to trade with them for their furs. He then gave out gifts and left an American flag with them. What use the Plains Indians made of the flag is not recorded, but Jefferson's hopes for peace were doomed to disappointment.

By October the explorers were deep in the northern plains. Cold weather was fast approaching. They built **Fort Mandan,** and in this snug, easily defended post they passed a long, bitterly cold winter.

When spring came, Lewis and Clark shipped the many boxes of plants, Indian craft objects, and animal bones and skins that they had collected back to St. Louis in the keelboat. Everything was carefully labeled. Then they pushed on. A Canadian white man, Toussaint Charbonneau, accompanied them as an interpreter, as did Sacagawea (Bird Woman), a Shoshone married to Charbonneau, and their newborn son.

Sacagawea became a very important member of the party. High in the Rockies, near the present-day border of Montana and Idaho, they met up with the Shoshone. Lewis had pushed ahead with Charbonneau and the guide who knew Indian sign language. Most Indians of the region were very wary and difficult to find, but the explorers came upon three Shoshone women. After giving them gifts, they persuaded these Shoshone to lead them to their camp. There they found 60 warriors on horseback. The Shoshone people greeted the explorers in friendly fashion, giving them food and smoking a ceremonial pipe of peace. When Sacagawea and the rest of the party reached the Shoshone camp, she discovered to everyone's delight that the chief was her brother!

The Shoshone sold Lewis and Clark 29 horses for the trip across the **Continental Divide,** the ridge of the Rocky Mountains that separates the streams that flow east into the Mississippi Valley from those that flow west to the Pacific Ocean. Equally important, one of the warriors, whom the explorers called Toby, guided them through the Bitterroot Mountains. Without Toby's help they might easily have become hopelessly lost in the rugged High Plateau country.

In this fine Charles Russell painting Sacagawea is shown in 1805 in the embrace of her Shoshone relatives, who lived in the mountain country. Captain Lewis stands alertly in the foreground. The grand vista is near the present-day border of Montana and Idaho. The leader of the Indian scouting party signs a question to Toussaint Charbonneau, interpreter for the party. Although this scene is tense, what were usual relations with the Indians whose homeland was the Louisiana Territory?

The Thomas Gilcrease Institute, Tulsa

Amon Carter Museum

In this Charles Russell water scene, painted in 1905, leaders of the Corps of Discovery encounter Indians of the lower Columbia River. In the boat are Lewis, Clark, York, and Sacagawea, who signs their greeting. The canoes were carved from the thick trunks of ponderosa pine trees. These may be the Clatsop Indians, after whom the winter fort of 1805–06 was named. What was the diet for these travelers during the rainy winter months?

Lewis and Clark were the first outsiders to describe the Shoshone people and many of the other Indians of the mountain area. They obtained more horses from a tribe called the Flatheads. Eventually they reached the great Columbia River. In November 1805, having floated down the Columbia in dugout canoes carved from the trunks of the great ponderosa pine trees, they reached the Pacific.

They settled for the winter near the mouth of the Columbia River. There they built **Fort Clatsop,** named after the local Indians. The fort was 50 feet (15 meters) square. It consisted of two rows of huts made of pine logs facing each other across a courtyard. During the rainy winter months when food was scarce, the men ate a good deal of dog meat and whale fat, called blubber. According to Captain Lewis, the men became "extremely fond" of dog meat. "For my own part," Lewis added, "I think it is an agreeable food and would prefer it vastly to lean venison or elk."

After a long, rainy winter the explorers began the trip back. They reached St. Louis late in September 1806. Their exciting but difficult adventure had been remarkable for its harmony. There had been no serious clashes with the many Indians they met along the way. The explorers had managed to get along with one another too, even when cooped up far from home with little to do during two winters.

Captain Lewis deserves much of the credit for this harmony. He was a firm but considerate leader. He treated all members of the party fairly. He was careful not to exclude the slave York or Sacagawea, as when he called for a vote on where to build Fort Clatsop.

- What was Sacagawea's surprise discovery when the Lewis and Clark Expedition met the Shoshone?
- How did Captain Lewis maintain harmony?

255

The pen and ink drawings are from notes made in the field by Captain Clark during his exploration of the Louisiana Territory. These sketches show new species of flora and fauna. In what way was Lewis and Clark's Expedition a voyage of discovery?

LEWIS AND CLARK'S ACHIEVEMENT

Besides giving the United States a claim to territory in the Northwest, this remarkable expedition produced an amazing amount of new information about the Great West. Lewis and Clark discovered the true course of the Missouri River. They proved that the continent was much wider than most persons had thought. They found and mapped a number of passes through the Rockies. In later years their maps would help settlers make their way through the mountains and on to the Pacific. Hundreds of hunters, trappers, scientists, and ordinary settlers profited from Lewis and Clark's maps and reports.

Lewis and Clark also discovered and brought back many new plants. They were the first whites to see many animals as well. They sent back large numbers of skins of animals for scientific study, as well as many live animals of the region.

Lewis and Clark's accounts of the Indian tribes they met provided much fresh information. In some cases the very existence of large tribes was unknown until the reports of Lewis and Clark were published. All in all, their expedition was one of the great voyages of discovery of modern times.

■ What were some achievements of Lewis and Clark?

JEFFERSON AND THE NAVY

Only a few weeks after selling Louisiana to the United States, France was again at war with England. Once again the struggle between these two European nations had powerful effects upon the United States.

The country's prosperity depended to a large extent on foreign trade. America still needed foreign manufactured goods, and farmers sold a great deal of their produce abroad. French and British warships and privateers hurt this trade by capturing American merchant ships bound for each other's ports.

During 1806 the British seized 120 American ships carrying cargoes to and from the French West Indies. The British also claimed the right to seize American ships headed for European countries that Napoleon had conquered, such as Holland and Belgium. Napoleon, in turn, issued orders to his captains to capture any neutral vessel that had allowed itself to be inspected on the high seas by a British warship. Such vessels "have become English property," Napoleon announced in his **Milan Decree** of 1807.

Jefferson had said in his inaugural address that he favored "honest friendship" with all nations. How could the United States be friendly with countries that attacked its ships in this manner? What could be done to prevent these attacks?

One obvious way to protect American shipping would be to build a navy powerful enough to escort convoys of merchant ships and drive off or sink privateers. When John Adams was President, a naval building program had been undertaken. The frigates *Constitution, Constellation,* and *United States* had performed well against French armed vessels in the late 1790s. They were without doubt the most powerful warships of that type afloat at the time. But frigates cost several hundred thousand dollars each and were expensive to maintain. Once peace with France had been reached, Jefferson saw no need to expand the navy further. He preferred to rely on small gunboats, which cost only about $10,000 apiece to build. These tiny gunboats were useless on the high seas or in combat with a large warship.

Mariners Museum, Newport News

The most famous ship ever to have flown the American flag, the U.S.S. *Constitution* is the subject of this 1893 watercolor by Nicolas. A 44-gun frigate launched in 1794, "Old Ironsides" sailed the high seas on and off for nearly 100 years. It now is on display in Boston Navy Yard. Why did Jefferson prefer gunboats to frigates such as this one?

Jefferson's trouble was that he was very upset when foreign powers threatened the rights of American citizens, but he was unwilling to spend large sums of public money to defend those rights. In a way, the whole country suffered from the same confusion. War in Europe caused attacks on American ships. These attacks were a blow to American pride. Yet the war greatly increased the demand for American goods in Europe. Sales doubled between 1803 and 1805. The same situation that was causing the trouble was also producing prosperity.

■ How did the war between France and England hurt the United States on the high seas?
■ Why was war in Europe both good and bad for America?

TROUBLE ON THE HIGH SEAS

Merchants could protect themselves against the loss of ships and their cargoes by insuring them. Insurance rates were high in wartime, but the prices merchants could get for their goods were high in wartime too. More irritating was the loss of men.

For hundreds of years the Royal Navy had claimed the right to *impress* any British civilian into the navy in a national emergency. **Impressment** was a hit-or-miss way of drafting men for military service. As the system developed in the 1700s, a ship's captain in need of sailors would send what he called a *press gang* ashore. Perhaps some of his crew had been killed in a battle at sea. More likely, some may have deserted when the vessel reached port.

New York Public Library Picture Collection

This 19th-century engraving shows an unfortunate sailor who has been impressed. The motley fellows at his sides are the press gang who carried him off to their ship. Now they bring him before their British officers, who inspect the unwilling recruit. Other sorrowful victims stand behind him. How did these press gangs capture their victims?

The press gang, composed of members of the warship's crew, would go ashore armed. They would roam the waterfront area searching for men who looked as though they were experienced sailors. The press gang seized anyone they wanted and carried them away to their ship. Sometimes they found it easiest just to drag off drunks from shoreside bars. The unfortunate men who were impressed received one shilling, called press money, to "compensate" them for having been forced to serve in His Majesty's navy.

Press gangs were not supposed to take anyone who was not a British subject. But sometimes they made mistakes. Particularly in

British ports in the West Indies, American sailors on shore leave were often taken. These men naturally protested loudly that they were Americans. But Englishmen who wanted to avoid being impressed frequently claimed that *they* were Americans. Because they spoke the same language, it was not always easy to tell the difference. Real Americans often did not have any way of proving they were citizens when arrested by a press gang. English sailors sometimes carried false papers, pretending that they were Americans. The gangs seldom troubled to check carefully in any case. They took any man they wanted. When the captains of British warships sent press gangs ashore, they were not accustomed to having them come back empty-handed. By the time an American was reported missing, he would be far at sea, beyond reach of rescuers.

The United States government did not deny the right of the British to impress British sailors from American merchant ships. But most Americans considered the practice shameful, even if no sailors were taken. British naval officers were often arrogant and domineering. Sometimes they treated the Americans rudely and with contempt. "On board our good old ship *Leander,*" one British officer later admitted, "we had not enough consideration for the feelings of the people we were dealing with."

- For what purpose was impressment originally intended?
- How were Americans victims of impressment?

THE EMBARGO ACT

In December 1807 Congress passed the **Embargo Act.** This law prohibited all exports from the United States. Jefferson reasoned that if merchant ships could not carry goods abroad, no American sailor could be forced into a foreign navy. This was, of course, a drastic way of dealing with the problem, not unlike trying to kill a fly on a window by throwing a brick at it.

Stopping exports caused unemployment among sailors and among workers who had been making goods that were usually exported. The busy shipbuilding industry came almost to a standstill. Still more workers were then unemployed. Even more serious, foreign shipowners would not carry goods to America if they had to return to their home ports empty. The value of all the goods imported in 1808 was less than half that of 1807. The embargo policy was an economic disaster.

People in the New England states and in other areas where foreign trade was important deeply resented the Embargo Act. Many broke the law because they considered it unwise and unfair. There were many ways of doing so. Trade by sea between one American port and another was allowed. A captain could sail from Boston to

Thomas Jefferson Memorial Foundation (Photo: Ed Roseberry)

"You shall be King hereafter," says the emperor Napoleon, standing just behind President Jefferson in this English political cartoon. Its satire is directed at the Embargo Act and its effects on American merchants. The only profits go to the French. "My warehouses are full," says one man. Says another, "My family is starving." Yet Jefferson talks only theory. He tells his audience, "This is a Grand Philosophical Idea. If we continue the Experiment for about fifteen or twenty years, we may begin then to feel the good Effects." This is all too much for the man at the back. He remembers "Great Washington." Even the little dog is upset. Why was the Embargo Act of 1807 passed?

New York or from Philadelphia to Charleston or to any other American port. Many announced that they were sailing on such a voyage and went instead to Europe or the West Indies. If caught, they claimed that a storm had driven them off course.

The captain of the merchant ship *Commerce,* supposedly headed for New Orleans, sailed to Havana, Cuba. The excuse he gave was that he had run out of water for his crew. At the same time that he filled his water barrels, he sold his cargo and bought a shipload of sugar.

Besides tricks such as these, many Americans resorted to direct smuggling in order to sell their goods abroad. Large amounts of American products were carried illegally from the northern states to Canada. That long and still almost unsettled border was very difficult to patrol. When smugglers were caught and brought to trial, juries made up of their fellow citizens usually found them not guilty. It was as hard to convict a merchant charged with violating the Embargo Act as it had been in the 1770s to convict someone of violating the Townshend Act by importing Dutch tea to avoid the tea tax.

■ How was the Embargo Act supposed to protect Americans? How did it hurt Americans?

AMERICA ON THE EVE OF WAR

In the fall of 1808, Secretary of State James Madison, Jefferson's longtime friend, was elected to succeed him as President. After the election Jefferson gave up the struggle to enforce the Embargo Act. Early in 1809 Congress repealed it. Congress then passed a law to prohibit importing British and French goods into the United States. Under this **Non-Intercourse Act** no English or French ship could enter an American harbor. The law also gave the President the power to end the boycott against either nation whenever it "shall cease to violate the neutral commerce of the United States."

The Non-Intercourse Act was even harder to enforce than the Embargo Act. A ship's captain could set out officially for Spain or Holland or any other nation and then land his cargo wherever he liked. English and French attacks on American ships continued.

In desperation Congressman Nathaniel Macon of North Carolina proposed a bill allowing American ships to trade with England and France but prohibiting English and French ships from trading with the United States. How this would reduce attacks on American ships and sailors was hard to see. Congress did not pass Macon's bill. But in 1810 it did pass **Macon's Bill Number Two.**

This law removed all restrictions on trade with England and France. It also provided that if either nation stopped attacking American merchant ships, the President could cut off all trade with its rival nation unless it also stopped its attacks. For example, if the English would leave American ships alone, the Americans would boycott England's rival—France.

Macon's Bill Number Two seemed to treat England and France in exactly the same way. In fact, trade with England quickly became as great as it had been before the Embargo Act. But there was little trade with France because by 1810 the British navy dominated the Atlantic Ocean. Few neutral merchant ships dared try to get to French-controlled ports. And the British practice of impressing American sailors continued. The policies of Jefferson and Madison had failed. To more and more people it seemed that the only way to protect the right to trade freely was to go to war.

▪ After the Non-Intercourse Act and Macon's Bill Number Two, why did America still have troubles on the high seas?

CHAPTER 8 REVIEW

Identification

Tell briefly why each of the following persons, terms, or events is important.

1. Thomas Jefferson
2. John Adams
3. Pierre Charles L'Enfant
4. Robert R. Livingston
5. James Monroe
6. Napoleon Bonaparte
7. Hamilton-Burr duel
8. Toussaint L'Ouverture
9. Lewis and Clark Expedition
10. Sacagawea
11. Kentucky and Virginia Resolutions
12. Doctrine of nullification
13. Louisiana Purchase
14. Continental Divide
15. Fort Clatsop
16. Right of deposit
17. Impressment
18. Embargo Act
19. Non-Intercourse Act
20. Macon's Bill Number Two

Understanding American History

1. What was Jefferson's doctrine of nullification? Why could this idea have meant the end of the United States as one nation?
2. Why was the Twelfth Amendment added to the Constitution after the election of 1800?
3. What was the importance of Jefferson's statement, "We are all Republicans, we are all Federalists"?
4. Why did Jefferson want to buy Louisiana? Why did Napoleon want to sell it?
5. Explain why the Louisiana Purchase and the death of Hamilton weakened the Federalist party.
6. Why was Sacagawea important to the success of the Lewis and Clark Expedition?
7. What were some accomplishments of the Lewis and Clark Expedition?
8. What was impressment? Why did it anger many Americans?
9. Why did many Americans break the Embargo Act of 1807?
10. What conditions on the Atlantic Ocean by 1810 put America on the eve of war with Great Britain?

Activities

1. Using the map in this chapter as a guide, trace the routes followed by the Corps of Discovery on a large map. Show where the expedition began in 1804 and identify the major sites of exploration until the Corps returned in 1806. Prepare a bulletin board to illustrate the highlights of the Lewis and Clark Expedition.
2. Read further about the Lewis and Clark Expedition in an encyclopedia or other reference book. Then use historical imagination to prepare diary entries that you might have written as a member of the expedition. Try to describe one ordinary day and one very exciting day.
3. Drawings and plans of Fort Mandan and Fort Clatsop may be found in many history books. Prepare a scale model of one of the forts, or prepare a scale model of Lewis and Clark's keelboat.
4. Find out what you can about the life of Aaron Burr. Some people consider the former Vice President a near traitor, while others think that history has treated him unfairly. Report on your findings to your classmates. See if others in class form a different picture of Burr than you do.
5. Use your historical imagination to hold a public meeting in your classroom. The year is 1807. The British have seized 120 American ships. Now the French emperor has issued orders to capture any American ship that allows itself to be searched on the high seas by the British. First, why must American ships sail the Atlantic? Second, what are some ways to protect America's shipping? Listen to several points of view.

CHAPTER 8 TEST

Completion (30 points)
Number your paper 1–10 and write the names or places to fill in the numbered blanks.

___1___ and ___2___ led the Corps of Discovery in exploration of the ___3___. This land had been bought from the country of ___4___ while ___5___ was President. ___6___ was the Shoshone woman who helped the expedition succeed.

The purchase of this new territory alarmed the ___7___ party. With the death of the party's leader, ___8___, the party began its decline.

Meanwhile, the United States was alarmed by the ___9___ of Americans who were forced to sail on British ships. This problem continued when ___10___ succeeded Jefferson as President.

Matching (20 points)
Number your paper 11–20 and match the description in the first column with the name or term in the second column.

11. A group of sailors sent ashore to capture men to serve as crewmen on ocean-going ships
12. The idea that a state does not have to obey federal laws it does not agree with
13. Emperor who sold Louisiana to the United States
14. Vice Presidential candidate in the election of 1800 who almost became President due to a tie vote
15. Leader who put the nation above politics by trying to settle the problems the United States had with France.
16. The withdrawal of a state or territory from the government of the United States
17. Prohibited importing British and French goods into the United States
18. Farmers who shipped their goods down the Mississippi needed this guarantee
19. Architect who planned Washington, D.C.
20. American diplomat to whom the offer to sell Louisiana was made by Talleyrand

a. Nullification
b. Napoleon Bonaparte
c. Non-Intercourse Act
d. John Adams
e. Pierre Charles L'Enfant
f. Robert R. Livingston
g. Aaron Burr
h. Right of deposit
i. Secession
j. Press gang

Classifying (20 points)
Number your paper 21–25. For each of the following statements write which country was involved, *France* or *England*.

21. Made peace with the United States in 1800
22. Impressed civilians into its navy
23. Sold Louisiana to the United States
24. Dominated the Atlantic Ocean
25. Obtained New Orleans from Spain

Essay (30 points)
By 1810 the young United States was threatened by both Britain and France. Tell which country seemed the greater threat. Use specific actions of the British and French to support your answer. Take care to spell and punctuate correctly.

CHAPTER 9
War and Peace, 1812–1823

When America declared war on Great Britain in 1812, the people of the Northeast were bitterly opposed. Strangely enough, they were also the people most injured by British attacks on American ships and their crews. Those who favored the war were westerners and southerners, called **War Hawks,** many of whom had never even seen the Atlantic Ocean. If war broke out, these "hawks" hoped to gobble up British-owned Canada. They also expected to take Florida from Spain, because Spain had now taken the side of England in the long war the British were fighting against Napoleon.

This is an early oil portrait of William Henry Harrison, governor of Indiana Territory. It was painted by Ralph Earl. What tactics did Harrison use to take land from the Indians?

TROUBLES ON THE FRONTIER

The War Hawks and other frontier settlers also blamed England for the troubles between Indians and whites in the Northwest Territory. They felt that the British in Canada kept the Indians riled up to make trouble. They correctly believed that if war broke out, the Indians in the Great Lakes region would side with the British.

The huge area of land in southern Ohio that was turned over to the white settlers by the Indians in the Treaty of Greenville in 1795 was not enough to satisfy the land-hungry pioneers for long. Their most cold-blooded leader was General William Henry Harrison. Harrison was governor of Indiana Territory, the region directly west of the new state of Ohio. He considered the Indians "wretched savages" blocking the forward march of what he called "civilization." By "civilization" Harrison meant his own way of life.

Harrison used trickery, bribery, and military force to push Indians off more and more land. Other government leaders who seemed milder and more tolerant than Harrison did the Indians almost as much harm. They tried to get Indians to settle down on farms and become "good Americans." They wanted Indians to give up their customs and religions and copy the culture of the whites. They did not care that this would destroy the Indians as a distinct group of people. They believed that the change would be the best thing that could happen both to the Indians and to their white neighbors on the frontier.

As President Jefferson put it, if the Indians settled down and gave up hunting, more land would be available for the white settlers. By

The Thomas Gilcrease Institute, Tulsa

becoming farmers, the Indians would increase what Jefferson called their "domestic comforts"—that is, their standard of living.

Many Indians found some parts of the white way of life attractive. Guns, for example, made them more efficient hunters and warriors. Knives and metal tools, bright-colored cloth, whiskey, cheap jewelry, and other trinkets appealed to them powerfully. White traders took great advantage of the Indians' desire for these things, swapping nearly worthless goods or whiskey for their valuable furs.

- Why did the whites on the frontier borders resent the Indians?
- How did some government leaders want to change the Indian way of life?

"Indian Village" was painted in oil by Jules Tavernier. Tepees stretch as far as the eye can see, for this village is a large one. We see here a way of life that is peaceful and serene. Yet land-hungry settlers soon took away the Indian way of life for what whites called "civilization." Why did Thomas Jefferson want Indians to settle down and give up hunting?

TECUMSEH AND THE PROPHET

By about 1809-10 a brilliant leader was rising among the Indians of the Ohio Valley. He was Tecumseh, a Shawnee chief. Tecumseh had fought under Chief Little Turtle against United States troops in the 1790s. He took part in the Battle of Fallen Timbers, where one of his brothers was killed.

Tecumseh was against all grants or sales of land to the whites. He believed that God, "the Great Spirit," had created the land for all Indians to *use,* not to own. Indians had no right to sell the land, even to one another, he said. If one could sell land, "why not sell the air, the clouds, and the great sea?" Tecumseh asked. "White people," he said, "are never satisfied. . . . They have driven us from the great salt water, forced us over the mountains. . . . We are determined to go no farther." Tecumseh was also against torture and other forms of cruelty in warfare.

In September 1809 General Harrison signed a treaty with the chiefs of a number of tribes. The Indians gave up 3 million acres (1.2 million hectares) in return for about $10,000. That was not even half a cent an acre. The United States government was selling similar land for $2 an acre. Clearly, the Indians were being cheated.

Tecumseh was furious. No Shawnees signed the treaty. He went to see General Harrison. He warned the General not to try to take over the lands just purchased. The local "village chiefs" who had signed the treaty had no right to do so. "We are prepared to punish those chiefs who . . . sell their land," Tecumseh said. And he added sternly, "If you continue to purchase . . . it will produce war."

Tecumseh realized that war was likely to break out between the United States and Great Britain. He intended to organize the many Indian tribes south of the Great Lakes. Then he would threaten to side with the British forces in Canada. Perhaps that would persuade the **Big Knives,** as he called the whites, to allow the Indians to hold their land in peace.

Tecumseh made this promise to Harrison: If the United States would give up its claims to the Indian lands purchased by the 1809 treaty, the Indians would become loyal allies and help the United States in any war against the British in Canada.

Harrison told Tecumseh frankly that the President would never agree to this. Tecumseh then said that he hoped the Great Spirit would put some sense in the President's head. Otherwise, "he may sit still in his town and drink his wine," but "you and I will have to fight it out."

Tecumseh then set out to organize all the Indian tribes east of the Mississippi to resist white expansion. The alliance he formed was called the **Red Stick Confederacy,** possibly because the members painted their war clubs red.

Tecumseh was an inspiring leader. He was a tall, handsome man with a long, thin face. He wore simple deerskin clothing with few decorations. Usually he had a single eagle's feather in his hair. He was a marvelous speaker and very intelligent. Even General Harrison admitted that Tecumseh was "one of those . . . geniuses which spring up occasionally to produce revolutions."

All along the southern and western frontiers Tecumseh preached Indian unity and resistance to white expansion. Resistance meant more than fighting with gun and tomahawk. Indians must cast off every sign of white culture. Tecumseh was aided in his crusade by his brother Tenskwatawa, known as the Prophet. Tenskwatawa had

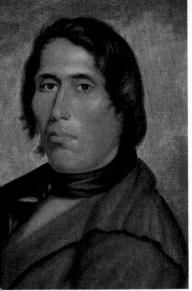

Field Museum of Natural History

National Museum of American Art

These handsome Shawnee brothers led Indians east of the Mississippi in a Red Stick Confederacy. Tecumseh, *left,* and Tenskwatawa, known as the Prophet, *right,* held out hope for their people when whites pushed farther onto Indian land. The portrait in oil of Tecumseh is not signed. The one of Tenskwatawa is by George Catlin. It was painted 1830–39 by the great 19th-century painter of American Indians. According to William Henry Harrison, what kind of leader was Tecumseh?

been a heavy drinker and troublesome as a young man. He was sometimes called Laulewasikaw, which in Shawnee means Loud Mouth. In 1805 he experienced a religious vision. He dropped all his bad habits and began to preach against drinking and against copying white ways. He claimed to have magical powers and to be able to see the future.

The Prophet attracted many Indians to the Red Sticks, but he was a poor leader. General Harrison marched against his headquarters at the village called Prophetstown in the fall of 1811. The Prophet ordered a night attack. The battle took place near Tippecanoe Creek in Indiana on November 7. The fighting was fierce and extremely bloody. Harrison drove the Indians off and destroyed their town, but almost a fifth of his own force of about a thousand men were killed or wounded.

The chief result of this **Battle of Tippecanoe** was to make Harrison a popular hero. Tecumseh had been away from Prophetstown recruiting more men for the Red Stick Confederacy. He was annoyed with his brother, who should not have started the fighting. But he did not think that the battle was very important. He referred to it as a "scuffle with the Big Knives."

No one could doubt, however, that the Red Sticks were preparing to fight these Big Knives. The British in Canada would probably help the Indians in such a contest. Because white westerners blamed the British for the Indians' warlike behavior, sentiment for declaring war on England was strong on the frontier by 1812.

- Why was Tecumseh so opposed to the Indian land sale in 1809? What else did he oppose?
- Why did Tecumseh organize the Red Stick Confederacy?
- Why was sentiment for declaring war on England strong on the frontier by 1812?

BUILDING SKILLS IN SOCIAL STUDIES

Reading a Line Graph

A *line graph* is useful for making comparisons. The line graph on this page shows the value of United States exports to Great Britain and France from 1790 to 1815. You can see at a glance the value of exports to each country. You can also see quite clearly that exports to Great Britain were nearly always greater than those to France.

Like other graphs, a line graph has a *horizontal axis* and a *vertical axis*. On this graph the years from 1790 to 1815 are shown on the horizontal axis. Dollars in millions are given on the vertical axis. To find the value of exports for each country for a given year, find the point where a line from the horizontal axis *intersects*, or cuts across, a line from the vertical axis.

Study the line graph carefully before answering the following questions.

1. Which axis shows years on this graph?
2. Which color line stands for exports to Great Britain? Which for France?
3. In which year was the value of exports to Great Britain highest? Approximately what was that value in millions of dollars?
4. In which years was the value of exports to France highest? What was that value?
5. In which years was the value of exports to France greater than those to Britain?
6. How many millions of dollars of goods went to France in the period 1805–09?
7. The Embargo Act was in effect by 1808. What was its effect on U.S. exports?
8. Why did exports drop off in 1813–14?
9. What was the value of exports to Britain in 1815?
10. From your reading of history, why were exports to Britain usually higher?

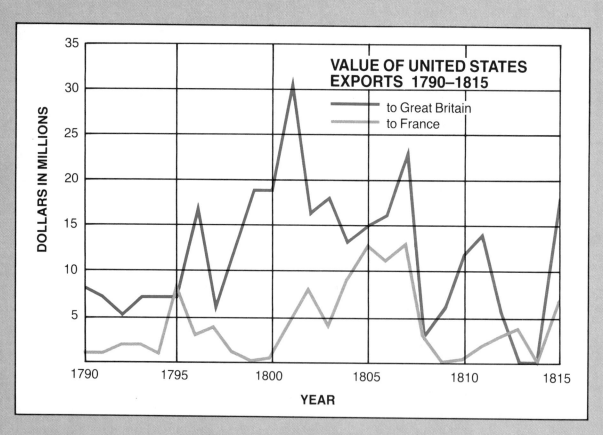

VALUE OF UNITED STATES EXPORTS 1790–1815

— to Great Britain
— to France

THE WAR OF 1812 BEGINS

In June 1812 Congress declared war on Great Britain. The vote was fairly close in both the Senate and the House of Representatives. Nearly all the members of Congress who voted against the war came from the northeastern states where shipping and foreign trade were important. Although these people were angered by the impressment of sailors and by British attacks on American ships, they realized that war with England would seriously injure their trade. They would rather suffer the insults and losses and wait for the war in Europe to come to an end.

Probably they were correct in thinking that this **War of 1812** was a mistake. The British were engaged in a life-and-death struggle with Napoleon, now emperor of France. Napoleon was seeking to conquer and control all Europe. French attacks on American commerce were fewer in number than British attacks only because France had a much smaller navy.

The British had no real quarrel with the United States. Nor could the United States gain anything by fighting Britain that it would not get anyway once the war between Great Britain and France was over. By forcing Britain to fight in America, the United States was obviously making it more difficult for the British to bring the war in Europe to an end.

- Why did northeastern members of Congress vote against war with Britain?
- What problem did Britain have in Europe?

THE WAR AT SEA

The first battles of the War of 1812 occurred at sea. They resulted in some spectacular American victories. The most powerful ships in the American navy were its seven **frigates.** These three-masted, square-rigged ships varied in length from about 140 to 175 feet (about 42 to 53 meters). The *Chesapeake* was one of the vessels in this class. Others bore such names as *Constitution, United States,* and *President.* The frigates were all quite new. They had been built as a result of the war scare following the XYZ Affair of 1797. They were beautifully designed—fast, easy to maneuver, and armed with from 40 to 50 or more cannon. Their officers were young but highly skilled and experienced. Morale in the navy was very high.

The British fleet in the Atlantic was many times larger than the American. To begin with, there were seven **ships of the line.** Ships of the line were armed with from 60 or 70 or more cannon. Then there were 34 frigates. These were somewhat smaller and less heavily armed than the American type. Dozens of smaller ships and transports completed the British force.

The *Constitution*, America's prized frigate, commenced firing on the British *Guerrière* on August 12, 1812. Under the deadly hail of its cannon the *Guerrière* was smashed out of the sea. This oil painting is thought to be by Thomas Birch. It shows the maneuver known as "crossing the T," in which the *Constitution*, flying flags of the United States, fires broadside at the listing *Guerrière*. What were British and American casualties?

The British had excellent officers and sailors. Their one mistake was in not reckoning how able the American navy had become.

In August 1812 the *Constitution* met with the British frigate *Guerrière* off the coast of Maine. The *Guerrière*, a French-built ship, had been captured by the British in 1806. Captain Isaac Hull of the *Constitution* held his fire until the two ships were side by side. Then he said to his gun crews, "Now, boys, pour it into them."

The *Constitution*'s first volley broke the *Guerrière*'s mizzenmast. With sails and rigging trailing over its stern, the *Guerrière* could not be managed. Captain Hull then crossed in front of the crippled ship. This maneuver, called **crossing the T,** enabled him to fire broadsides while the British ship's guns could not be aimed at the *Constitution*.

270

The Americans' cannon fired again and again, splintering the Britisher's hull and smashing down masts, sails, and rigging. From above, perched high in the *Constitution*'s rigging, American riflemen picked off sailors on the *Guerrière*'s deck. After half an hour the British captain surrendered. His ship was a total wreck. Of its crew of over 270, 79 were killed or wounded. There were only 14 American casualties.

The *Constitution* later defeated the frigate *Java* in another famous battle. **Old Ironsides,** as it is now called, is the most famous ship ever to have flown the American flag. It has been preserved as a museum and monument at the Boston Navy Yard.

In October 1812 the American frigate *United States* sighted H.M.S. *Macedonian* near the Azores. Captain Stephen Decatur of the *United States* was already famous for his exploits while fighting North African pirates when Jefferson was President. Now he outmaneuvered the captain of the *Macedonian* brilliantly. Taking advantage of the fact that he had more powerful, long-range guns, he pounded the *Macedonian* from a distance. When the *Macedonian* finally surrendered, 100 cannon holes were counted in her hull. Decatur put an American crew aboard the captured ship and sailed it to New York. There the vessel was sold for $200,000, the money going, according to the custom of the time, to the crew of the *United States*.

These and other victories at sea were won because the American frigates were better fighting machines than the British ships. The American sailors proved to be superior fighters too. The fire of their guns was extremely accurate, and the tactics of the American captains were often brilliant.

After early losses the British high command ordered captains to avoid single-ship battles with American frigates. Instead the huge British navy was used to bottle up most American warships in their home ports. By early 1813 the British fleet in American waters had been increased to 17 ships of the line, 27 frigates, and about 50 other warships.

The frigates *Essex* and *President* both got to sea, the latter to be defeated by a squadron of four British ships.

Dozens of American privateers roamed the oceans during the war. These privateers were fast, light, and beautifully designed. They could easily outsail the best frigates of the Royal Navy. One privateer, the *True-Blooded Yankee,* captured 27 British merchant ships off the coast of Ireland and Scotland in a little more than one month. By the end of the war, privateers were capturing an average of nearly two ships a day. All told, they took about 1,300 vessels during the conflict.

- What were some strengths of the young United States navy?
- Why were so many victories at sea won by the United States?

Victories at Sea

Captain David Porter was one of the American naval captains whose tactics were particularly brilliant. One time, while captain of the frigate *Essex*, Porter saw a British ship approaching. He turned the *Essex* away and set more sails to make the enemy captain think he was trying to escape. At the same time he ordered weights dragged from the stern so that in fact the ship was moving more slowly.

The commander of the British ship, the 22-gun *Alert*, fell for this trick and sped after the *Essex*. Then, when the *Alert* was in range, Porter turned and let loose with his 46 cannon. Within eight minutes the battle was over, the *Alert* a wreck. In two months on the high seas, Captain Porter captured seven British ships.

The *Essex* later managed to slip past the British in the Atlantic and sail around South America into the Pacific Ocean. There it destroyed or captured many English ships that were hunting whales. The *Essex*, one historian writes, "was like a wolf in a pasture of unguarded sheep." Eventually, British "guardians" arrived. Then the *Essex* was trapped off the coast of Chile by three British warships and forced to surrender.

THE FIGHT FOR CANADA

The land-fighting during the War of 1812 was a seesaw struggle. It seemed at the start that Canada would be an easy target. The population was small, and many Canadians sympathized with the United States. Yet when a force commanded by General William Hull, an uncle of Captain Isaac Hull of the *Constitution,* crossed the border from Detroit, it quickly ran into trouble. Indians under Tecumseh ambushed one militia unit. Confused, Hull retreated to Detroit without making a real fight. Far worse, he surrendered the fort to a small Canadian force commanded by General Isaac Brock. Brock then announced that Michigan had been annexed to the British Empire! And for the moment it had. Indeed, by the end of 1812, most of what is now Indiana and Illinois was also controlled by Canadian troops.

In 1813 the Indian-hater William Henry Harrison, who was nevertheless a competent general, was put in charge of the war on the border. Before he could invade Canada, however, a British naval squadron had to be cleared from Lake Erie. The officer who accomplished this task was Oliver Hazard Perry.

Perry came from a navy family. His father, his four brothers, and two of his brothers-in-law were naval officers. To win control of Lake Erie he built a fleet, including two 20-gun ships, right on the

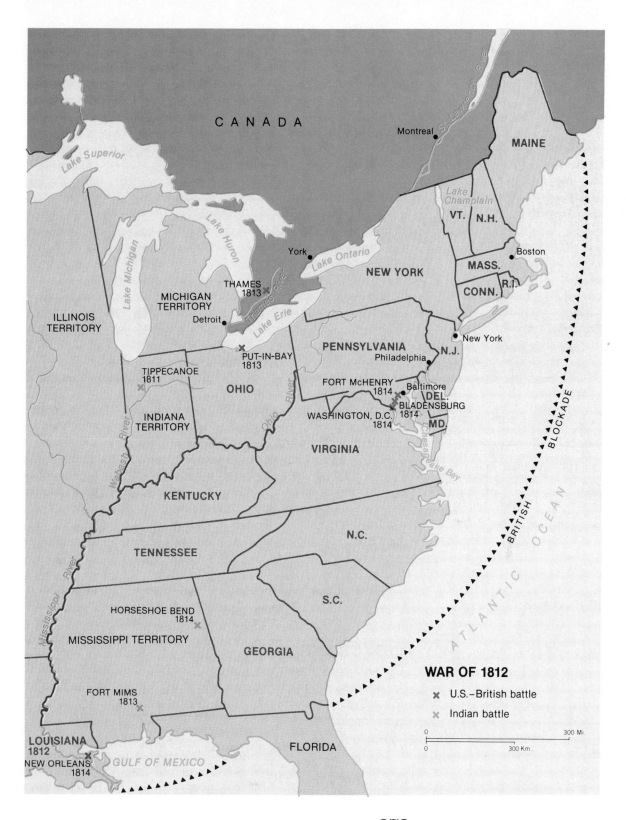

C A N A D A

Montreal

St. Lawrence River

MAINE

Lake Superior

Lake Huron

Lake Michigan

York

Lake Ontario

Lake Champlain

VT.

N.H.

MASS.

Boston

CONN.

R.I.

NEW YORK

THAMES
1813

Thames River

Lake Erie

MICHIGAN
TERRITORY

Detroit

ILLINOIS
TERRITORY

PUT-IN-BAY
1813

TIPPECANOE
1811

OHIO

Ohio River

PENNSYLVANIA

Philadelphia

New York

N.J.

FORT McHENRY
1814

Baltimore

DEL.

BLADENSBURG
1814

WASHINGTON, D.C.
1814

MD.

Chesapeake Bay

INDIANA
TERRITORY

Wabash River

VIRGINIA

KENTUCKY

N.C.

TENNESSEE

Mississippi River

S.C.

HORSESHOE BEND
1814

MISSISSIPPI TERRITORY

GEORGIA

BRITISH BLOCKADE

ATLANTIC OCEAN

FORT MIMS
1813

WAR OF 1812

✕ U.S.–British battle

✕ Indian battle

LOUISIANA
1812

NEW ORLEANS
1814

GULF OF MEXICO

FLORIDA

0   300 Mi.

0   300 Km.

273

Oliver Hazard Perry stands beneath a tattered Stars and Stripes. Both are survivors of the Battle of Put-in-Bay, where Americans won control of Lake Erie. This watercolor was painted by J. L. G. Ferris in the late 19th century. A national monument at Put-in-Bay commemorates this battle fought in September 1813, when Perry became a national hero. What message did he send to General Harrison?

scene. Finally, in September 1813, in the bloody **Battle of Put-in-Bay** he defeated the British squadron. "We have met the enemy and they are ours," he informed General Harrison.

Harrison was then able to capture Detroit and advance into Canada. At the Thames River, which flows through southern Canada to Lake Erie, he defeated Canadian troops and their Indian allies in the **Battle of the Thames.** The victory won back the Great Lakes region for the United States. But the most significant result of the battle was the death of Tecumseh. Without the great chief it was easier for whites to get full control of the northwestern region.

■ What was the significance of the Battle of Put-in-Bay?
■ What was the significance of the Battle of the Thames?

THE CREEK WAR

The southern Indians were also soon crushed. Tecumseh, it will be remembered, had traveled extensively in the South persuading the Indian tribes there to join his Red Stick Confederacy. He had won many supporters among the younger Creek warriors in Alabama and Georgia.

These Indians, with some support from both British and Spanish agents, began to attack southern frontier outposts. The most serious of their assaults during this **Creek War** occurred in August 1813

274

when Red Eagle, leader of the warring Creeks, surprised and overwhelmed the defenders of **Fort Mims** in western Alabama. Red Eagle's warriors killed between 400 and 500 persons, many of them women and children.

General Andrew Jackson, commanding a force of Tennessee militiamen, then marched into Creek country. Jackson had fought in the War for American Independence while still a boy. After the Revolution he had moved to Tennessee, where he prospered as a lawyer and plantation owner. He served for a time in both houses of Congress, and he was a judge of the Tennessee Supreme Court.

Jackson was at heart a fighting man, a natural leader of soldiers. Most frontier militia units were hard to discipline. Being used to living on their own, frontiersmen disliked taking orders and being controlled in any way. Jackson's soldiers, however, accepted his orders without question. This was because they both feared and respected him. He had a reputation for being very tough. The men called him "Old Hickory" because the wood of the hickory tree is extremely hard. But he was also known for his loyalty to his men and for his concern for their welfare.

In a series of battles Jackson's army smashed the Creek forces. The climax came in March 1814 at the **Battle of Horseshoe Bend,** on the Tallapoosa River in Alabama. There 1,200 of Red Eagle's Red Sticks had dug in, protected, they thought, by the curve of the river and a wall of earth. Jackson's soldiers swept over the wall and killed 700 of the Indians, losing only 26 of their own men. Jackson thereafter forced the Creeks to surrender 20 million acres (8 million hectares) to the whites. The Indians in the South could resist no longer.

■ What was the significance of the Battle of Horseshoe Bend?

THE BURNING OF WASHINGTON

The British had thus far depended mostly upon Canadian militia units and Indian allies to fight the United States. But by the spring of 1814 Napoleon had been defeated in Europe. The British then sent 14,000 soldiers to fight in America.

The British set out to destroy Washington. The capital city was supposed to be protected by a fleet of 26 gunboats on Chesapeake Bay. When a British squadron led by a 74-gun ship of the line entered the bay, the gunboats' commander hastily pulled his tiny ships back into a shallow stream. There they were out of range of the British cannon but useless for the defense of Washington.

In August an army of 4,500 Redcoats came ashore south of Washington. It was commanded by General Robert Ross, who had fought against Napoleon under the great British general, the Duke of Wellington. At the village of **Bladensburg,** Ross's troops attacked a

This panorama shows the capture of Washington by the British on August 24, 1814. Across the Potomac the public buildings are aflame, even as flags fly over the Capitol and White House (hidden by smoke). Where was President Madison at the time the British took the capital city?

Dolley Payne Todd Madison grew up as a Quaker. Her first husband died in a yellow fever epidemic in 1793. The next year the 26-year-old widow was married to Congressman James Madison of Virginia. Dolley Madison had grace, charm, wit, and tact. She was official White House hostess for the widowed Thomas Jefferson, as well as for the eight years of the Madison Presidency. How was she brave in 1814?

large but poorly organized force of American militiamen. The Americans fled in panic. On the night of August 24 the British marched straight into Washington and set fire to all the public buildings. Even the President's mansion, the White House, was set afire.

President James Madison had been at the battlefield at Bladensburg. He escaped by fleeing up the Potomac River into Virginia. Dolley Madison, the First Lady, protected by a slave named Jennings, got away from the White House only minutes before the British entered. All she could save was some silverware and an oil painting of George Washington.

■ Why were the British able to burn Washington so easily in 1814?

THE DEFENSE OF BALTIMORE

The British had no intention of remaining in Washington. Their next objective was Baltimore, Maryland, at the head of Chesapeake Bay. Transport ships of their fleet put General Ross's army ashore on September 12 about 14 miles (about 23 kilometers) south of the city. Then the ships advanced toward **Fort McHenry,** which guarded the entrance to Baltimore Harbor.

Unlike the assault on Washington, the attack on Baltimore was a failure. General Ross's troops ran into stiff resistance about 7 miles (about 11 kilometers) from the city. When the general himself rode forward to investigate, he was killed by a sharpshooter. The Americans retreated a few miles, but their line held.

Meanwhile, the fleet could not get within cannon range of Fort McHenry. The water was too shallow for most of the warships. Five special ships armed with rockets and bombs did get to within 3 miles (almost 5 kilometers) of the fort. At dawn on September 13 Admiral Sir Alexander Cochrane ordered these vessels to open fire.

After a day and night of firing on Fort McHenry, the British fleet withdrew. Baltimore was safe. Now the tide of the war was turning. The shame of having the nation's capital destroyed roused people to fight harder. The defense of Baltimore showed their new determination. Thousands of young men came forward to enlist in the army.

■ Why was the defense of Fort McHenry so important?

The bombardment of Fort McHenry, which began at dawn, went on all that day and the following night. It had little effect. The distance was too great for accurate fire. Many of the bombs burst harmlessly in the air. Only four soldiers in the fort were killed. Its walls remained unbroken.

While the firing was in progress, Francis Scott Key, a Washington lawyer, was aboard one of the larger British vessels. He had been sent to try to obtain the release of an American doctor who had been arrested by the British after the Battle of Bladensburg. Admiral Cochrane had agreed to let the doctor go free, but he would not allow the Americans to go ashore until the battle was over.

Key watched the attack on Fort McHenry. Until darkness fell, he could see the fort's flag, an enormous banner 36 feet long and 29 feet wide (about 11 × 8 meters). During the night the continuing glare of the British rockets and the bursting bombs gave proof that the Americans were holding out. Then, when dawn came, Key could again see the flag, waving proudly over Fort McHenry. He was so inspired by the sight that he wrote "The Star-Spangled Banner." This poem, when set to the music of an English song, became our national anthem. The great flag, the original "star-spangled banner," now hangs in the Smithsonian Institution in Washington.

The Star-Spangled Banner

Smithsonian Institution

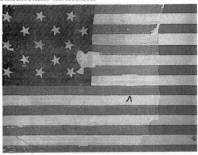

This is the actual flag whose broad stripes and bright stars flew over Fort McHenry. It was the second U.S. flag, with 15 stars and 15 stripes.

THE BATTLE OF NEW ORLEANS

Now the British were planning a still greater attack. This one came in the South, near the city of New Orleans. During the fall of 1814 they gathered an army of 11,000 veterans of the war against Napoleon at a base on the island of Jamaica in the Caribbean Sea. A fleet of 60 ships carried this force to the Louisiana coast.

The Redcoats landed east of the mouth of the Mississippi River and marched through the swampy country without being discovered. They were only 7 miles (about 11 kilometers) from New Orleans when muddied messengers burst in with the news upon the American

An imposing Andrew Jackson is the subject of this flattering portrait in oil by Ralph Earl. The artist, who lived from 1751 to 1801, claimed to have been an eyewitness to the Battle of Lexington in 1775. *Below*, "Defeat of the British Army" in the Battle of New Orleans. This aquatint was made in 1815 from a drawing done directly on the field of battle by Hyacinthe Laclotte, an army engineer. Along Rodriguez Canal ranks of British and American soldiers draw sabers to fight hand-to-hand. Jackson's regular troops and militia units line the middle of the broad field. Who were among Jackson's militiamen?

general who was in charge of defending the city. The date was December 23, 1814.

The American general was Andrew Jackson, who had been put in command of southern defenses after his victories over the Creeks. Although surprised by the British advance, Jackson reacted at once. "Gentlemen," he announced, "the British are below. We must fight them tonight." Quickly he ordered every available unit forward. A force of cavalry advanced on the left. Down the Mississippi went a warship to bombard the enemy from the right. In the center went Jackson's regular troops with hastily organized militia units. Among the militiamen were a company of free black citizens of New Orleans. Even a group of pirates had come forward "patriotically" to defend the city in exchange for Jackson's promise not to arrest them.

The battle began at 7:30 that very evening. It lasted for two hours and ended in a draw. Jackson then retreated and began to build an earth-wall defense line behind a canal only 5 miles (8 kilometers) from New Orleans.

The sudden American attack made the British delay their advance. They should have abandoned it altogether. Jackson had brought up many cannon and had his men properly positioned to defend the wall. When the British commander, General Sir Edward Pakenham, finally attacked on January 8, 1815, his men were mowed down by a hail of iron and lead. They suffered over 2,000 casualties in about an hour. General Pakenham and both his second and third in command were killed. When the smoke cleared, even the toughest

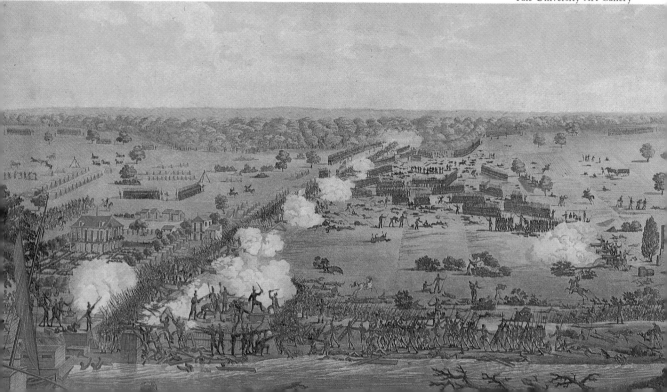

American veterans were stunned by the sight of the battlefield. "You could have walked a quarter of a mile . . . on the bodies," one of them reported. Only 71 Americans were killed, wounded, or missing in action in this **Battle of New Orleans.**

■ Why were the British defeated at the Battle of New Orleans?

THE PEACE OF GHENT

The loss of life at New Orleans was particularly tragic because the battle should never have been fought. Although the soldiers did not know it, the war was officially over!

Since August 1814 five American commissioners had been trying to negotiate a peace treaty with British diplomats at the city of Ghent in Belgium. The British demanded that the United States return most of the Northwest Territory to the Indians. The Americans wanted the British to give up the right to impress sailors from American ships. Neither side would compromise.

The discussions dragged on for months. Finally everyone realized that the reasons for fighting had simply disappeared. With Napoleon defeated, the British did not need to stop American ships from carrying goods to Europe. There was no longer any need to seize sailors and force them into the Royal Navy.

On December 24, 1814, the day after Jackson had rushed his men out from New Orleans to stop the British advance, the delegates signed the **Peace of Ghent.** The terms of this treaty were simple. Peace was restored. No territory changed hands. No promises were made. The United States did not get what it had set out for in 1812. As one witty historian has said, "It surrendered nothing except the right to shoot Englishmen." That was a right no one any longer wished to exercise.

Nowadays, of course, the whole world would have known about the treaty within hours after the signing. But in 1814 it took weeks for the news to reach Washington and more weeks for word to be sent to the troops around New Orleans. Thus, the brave men who fell before Jackson's defense wall died in vain.

The Battle of New Orleans did serve some purpose. It restored American military morale, which had been damaged by the ill-organized battles along the Canadian border and by the burning of Washington. It also made a popular hero of Andrew Jackson.

The peace treaty itself was equally popular. In New England, where most people had been opposed to fighting Great Britain, some Federalist leaders had revived talk of seceding from the Union. Late in 1814 they held a meeting, the **Hartford Convention,** to consider this step. Fortunately, moderates at the convention managed to prevent such an extreme act. When the war ended without serious loss to the United States, the Federalist party suddenly seemed out of date and almost unpatriotic. Trade with Europe also picked up rapidly after the war. In the 1816 Presidential election, Rufus King, the Federalist candidate, got only 34 votes in the electoral college to James Monroe's 183.

- What were the terms of the Peace of Ghent?
- Why was the Battle of New Orleans particularly tragic?

SOLVING PROBLEMS WITH ENGLAND

Still another result of the War of 1812 was that it convinced Europe that the United States was here to stay. The British no longer dreamed of regaining their former colonies. This did not mean that England and the United States suddenly became allies or even particularly friendly. The new attitude was one of respect rather than friendship.

Many sore spots remained between the United States and Great Britain. After 1815, however, these conflicts were solved by diplomats, not by soldiers and sailors.

The first step was to negotiate a treaty in 1815 removing many restrictions on trade between the two nations. Then, in 1817 they signed the **Rush-Bagot Agreement,** which provided that neither would maintain a fleet of warships on the Great Lakes. Each was to have four small vessels on the lakes to act as a kind of police force, but the border between the United States and Canada—one of the longest in the world—was to remain forever unfortified.

A difficult problem was deciding the exact boundary between Canada and the United States. Special commissions made up of American and English experts worked on this. In 1818 one of these commissions fixed the northern boundary of the Lousiana Purchase at 49° north latitude. At this time the two nations also agreed to joint control of the area west of the Louisiana territory, known as the Oregon Country.

- What did the Rush-Bagot Agreement provide?

JACKSON'S INVASION OF FLORIDA

Many westerners had hoped that the war of 1812 would pry Florida from Spanish control. They were disappointed. But soon after the war the United States got possession of both Florida and a huge chunk of Spanish territory west of Louisiana.

According to settlers who lived along the southern frontier, Seminoles from Florida were raiding white settlements. The Seminoles had been reinforced by many Creek warriors after their terrible defeat by Andrew Jackson at the Battle of Horseshoe Bend.

280

READING PRACTICE
IN SOCIAL STUDIES

Finding Main Ideas in Paragraphs

Facts and details are important in reading history. But they are only important because they illustrate *main ideas*. Good readers pay attention to facts and details, but they are always on the lookout for main ideas. To understand and remember what you read, you first need to determine what is the main idea of each paragraph.

A paragraph is a group of related sentences that develop or explain a main idea. It is the main idea which holds the paragraph together and gives meaning to its details.

When you find the main idea of a paragraph, you can see how it is supported by details. You understand how one detail makes another more meaningful. You recognize which details are the most important.

There are two steps to finding the main idea of a paragraph. First you need to find the person, place, or thing that the paragraph is about. This is called the *topic.* Topics can be simply stated in a word or a phrase. For example, read the second paragraph on page 279 under the heading "The Peace of Ghent." What is the topic?

The topic of the paragraph may be stated in a phrase: *negotiating a peace treaty.*

Once you find the topic, your second task is to ask, "What is the most important thing the writer is saying about this topic?" Your answer to this question will give you the main idea of the paragraph. Main ideas should be stated in complete sentences.

In the paragraph you read on the topic *negotiating a peace treaty,* the main idea is stated in the first sentence, which says, "Since August 1814 five American commissioners had been trying to negotiate a peace treaty with British diplomats at the city of Ghent in Belgium." Notice how the rest of the details in the paragraph develop the main idea. They tell what the British demanded, what the Americans wanted, and that neither side would compromise.

Often the main idea is given in the first sentence of a paragraph, but this is not always the case. Good writers put variety into their work by arranging paragraphs in as many ways as possible. So the main idea can occur anywhere in the paragraph. Look, for example, at the third paragraph on page 279, still under the heading "The Peace of Ghent." The main idea is found in the second sentence: "Finally everyone realized that the reasons for fighting had simply disappeared." The first sentence of the paragraph is called a *transition*—that is, a bridge between the thoughts of the previous paragraph and this one. The last two sentences of the paragraph give details to support the main idea.

There are times when the main idea is not stated in a single sentence but may be found by putting two sentences together. There are also paragraphs that have an *unstated main idea.* In these cases read the entire paragraph carefully and decide for yourself what main idea its details point to. Finally, a few paragraphs may not state a main idea at all. They may contain additional details to support the main idea of the paragraph that comes just before, or they may introduce the paragraph that follows.

The important thing to remember is to look for the main idea by first finding the topic and then by asking yourself what is the most important thing the writer is saying about the topic. Knowing how to recognize main ideas will help you to read with confidence.

Look at the section titled "Solving Problems with England" on page 280. There are four paragraphs. In the first three paragraphs the main idea of each is stated in a single sentence. The main idea of the fourth paragraph is unstated. Number your paper 1–4. For each paragraph write the topic and the main idea. Then turn to other sections in this chapter and determine for yourself what main idea may be found in each paragraph.

The white settlers also complained that many of their slaves were escaping into Florida. About 250 of these runaways controlled what was known as the **Negro Fort** on the Apalachicola River, about 60 miles (96 kilometers) south of the American border. Knowing there was a black-controlled fort encouraged other slaves in the United States to run away. In 1816 an American force marched into Florida and blew up the fort, killing most of the blacks.

Early in 1818 General Jackson was sent to crush the Seminoles. Again ignoring the boundary line, he boldly pursued them into Florida at the head of an army of 3,000 soldiers and 2,000 Indian allies. The Seminoles fell back, avoiding a battle.

Jackson was furious. When two Indian chiefs were captured by trickery, he had them hanged. At the town of St. Marks on the Gulf of Mexico he seized Alexander Arbuthnot, a harmless, 70-year-old British trader. Arbuthnot's crime had been to warn the Seminoles that the army was coming. Shortly thereafter Jackson captured another British civilian, Robert Ambrister, a former British marine who was indeed working with the Seminoles.

Jackson believed that all the conflicts with the Indians were caused by foreign agents. He decided to put Arbuthnot and Ambrister on trial. It was obviously illegal to try English civilians before an American military court on territory belonging to Spain. Jackson nevertheless did just that. The two men were found guilty and sentenced to death. Arbuthnot was hanged. Because of his military background, Ambrister was executed by a firing squad.

Since he was unable to find any Indians to attack, Jackson next marched into West Florida and captured the capital, **Pensacola.** He dashed off a letter to President Monroe, explaining what he had done. Then he went home to Tennessee.

■ Why did General Jackson march into Florida?
■ How did General Jackson go beyond the law?

Seminoles attack an American fort in Florida in this 1837 lithograph. The Seminole raids soon brought Andrew Jackson in bold pursuit. Who owned Florida when Jackson invaded its borders in 1818?

THE TRANSCONTINENTAL TREATY

Jackson's invasion proved that Spain could no longer control Florida. In Washington the Spanish minister to the United States, Luis de Onis, bitterly protested the seizure of Pensacola. It was "an outrage," he said. Jackson must be punished.

President Monroe was embarrassed. He did not want to approve of what Jackson had done. But he did not want to give up the territory Jackson had taken. He dared not criticize the popular general publicly. So he told Onis that he agreed that Jackson had gone beyond his orders. But he had done so because of military necessity.

Onis knew then that the United States was not going to give back West Florida. The rest of Florida was surely lost as well.

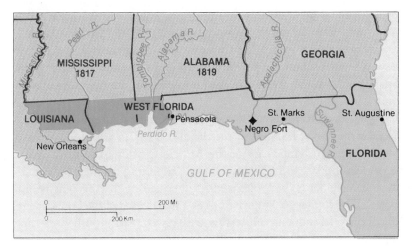

Occupied by U.S. 1810-13

Ceded by Spain 1819

UNITED STATES

Museum of Fine Arts, Boston

Onis was already negotiating with Secretary of State John Quincy Adams about the boundary between the Louisiana Purchase and Spanish Mexico. Perhaps he could get better terms in this discussion by agreeing to give up Florida.

John Quincy Adams, the son of ex-President John Adams, had been in public service since he was teenaged. Like his father he was very intelligent, hard-working, stubborn, and shrewd as a Yankee trader. He suggested to Onis that Spain should give up Florida. The United States would then be willing to postpone settling the Louisiana boundary. As Adams well knew, this was exactly the opposite of what Onis wanted.

Onis was afraid that a delay would only increase American demands in the West. Already Adams was claiming that the Mexican province of Texas was part of the Louisiana Purchase. So Onis insisted that a "safe and permanent" line be agreed to quickly.

Adams pressed Onis to accept the Rio Grande as the line. Since this would have given Texas to the United States, Onis practically spat out his refusal. After further dickering Adams suggested a compromise. A western boundary would be drawn that left Texas in Spanish hands. But he added the idea that from a point north of Texas the boundary line should extend west *"straight to the Pacific Ocean."*

This would give the United States a boundary all the way across North America. Onis tried to get Adams to give up this claim. He failed. Finally he wrote his superiors in Spain: "If His Majesty . . . hasn't sufficient forces to make war on this country, then I think it would be best not to delay making the best settlement possible."

In October 1818 the Spanish government gave in. It agreed in principle to Adams's demand. In a few months the details were ironed out by Adams and Onis. Spain sold Florida to the United States for $5 million. The line between Mexico and the United States followed

The young John Quincy Adams sat for this oil portrait by John Singleton Copley at about the time of the War for American Independence: Those who knew both his subjects and his work claimed that Copley mirrored his time with great faithfulness and accuracy. What government rank did Adams hold when he negotiated the Transcontinental Treaty?

roughly the present eastern and northern boundaries of Texas, then went north to 42° north latitude, then west to the Pacific Ocean.

Adams drove such a hard bargain that he forced Onis to agree that where the boundary followed rivers, it would run along the Spanish side of the river, not the middle of the stream as most such boundaries do.

The **Transcontinental Treaty** was a great triumph for Adams and for the United States. Great Britain's Proclamation of 1763 had set the western boundaries of the American colonies at the Appalachian Mountains. In 1783 the peace treaty ending the War for American Independence had extended that boundary to the Mississippi River. The Louisiana Purchase of 1803 had extended the boundary to the Rocky Mountains. Now this treaty with Spain pushed the line on to the Pacific Ocean. In little more than 50 years the nation had grown from a string of settlements along the Atlantic Coast to a powerful country a continent wide. John Quincy Adams was not exaggerating when he said that the day he and Onis signed the treaty was "the most important day of my life."

- Why did Onis agree to negotiate the Florida question with Adams?
- What were the terms of the Transcontinental Treaty?

THE WHOLE CONTINENT ONE NATION

When Adams first suggested extending the boundary line between Mexico and the United States west to the Pacific, Onis argued that there was no need for such a boundary. He insisted that the entire Pacific coast belonged to Spain. He denied that the United States had a right to any territory west of the Louisiana Purchase.

Adams declared that Onis's argument was "nonsense." He reminded the Spaniard that Great Britain claimed the Oregon Country and was willing to share control of it with the United States. Russia also had a number of trading posts along the northern Pacific Coast.

Adams, of course, won the argument. But his success was more a sign of Spain's weakness than of the correctness of his argument. Aside from the explorations of Lewis and Clark, the United States had little on which to base its claims in the region beyond the Rocky Mountains. Jefferson had *purchased* Louisiana from France. Was this not proof that the nation had not owned that land before 1803? How could it claim a right to land still farther west?

The answer to this question was very simple. The people were pushing steadily westward. They assumed that the land beyond the mountains was eventually to be a part of the United States. John Quincy Adams, for example, was convinced that God intended the

The Shelburne Museum

United States to control all of North America. "The whole continent," he wrote in 1811, "appears to be destined . . . to be peopled by one nation."

No European country was strong enough or determined enough to resist United States claims very vigorously. Of course, the native Americans of the Northwest were another matter. They fought hard to protect their own claims. But that came much later. When Adams and Onis divided the land by drawing a line on a map, the actual invasion of the region by white settlers still lay far in the future.

■ What claims did the United States make for the territory west of the Louisiana Purchase?

REVOLUTION IN LATIN AMERICA

Spain sold Florida to the United States and signed the Transcontinental Treaty because it was no longer strong enough to protect its vast holdings in the Americas. The great empire that Columbus and Cortés and the other *conquistadors* had created was falling apart. Indeed, by 1822 all of Spain's colonies in South and Central America had revolted and declared their independence.

These Latin American revolutions delighted most people in the United States. The new nations seemed to be copying the example of their North American neighbor. As free countries they would be

People and goods moved westward in Conestoga wagons much like this one in an oil painted by Thomas Birch in 1816. The scene is set on a Pennsylvania turnpike. What destiny did John Quincy Adams see for the North American continent?

A great hero of revolutionary South America, Simon Bolivar is known as the Liberator. In this color engraving he is shown in 1819 at the age of 36. Against which country did the South Americans revolt?

open to ships and goods from the United States. This had not been so under Spanish rule. President Monroe promptly established diplomatic relations with the new republics.

Great Britain also profited from Spain's declining influence. But it did not intend to recognize the new republics officially, as the United States had done. The British found themselves in a difficult position. On the one hand, they did not want to encourage revolutions or the formations of republics anywhere. British leaders feared that revolutionary ideas might spread and "infect" their own colonies. On the other hand, they did not want to see the South American republics destroyed. They were worried about other European powers that did not trade heavily with South America. Might they not help Spain regain control of its former colonies? Already there was talk of a large French army being sent to South America for this very purpose.

In 1823 George Canning, the British foreign minister, proposed that the United States and Great Britain issue a joint statement warning other nations not to try to restore Spanish control in America. The two countries themselves should promise not to try to take over these former colonies, Canning added.

This was most flattering for the United States—this opportunity to join with Great Britain in a joint statement of international policy. But this particular statement was not really one that the United States wished to make. Secretary of State Adams had two reasons for rejecting Canning's suggestion. The island of Cuba was still a Spanish colony. Someday, Adams hoped, the United States might be able to take it over. Canning's plan would rule out this possibility. And why should the United States help the British increase trade with the new republics?

Why trail along like a rowboat in the wake of a warship? It would be better, Adams advised President Monroe, for the United States to issue a statement of its own. The statement, he added, should deal with the whole question of relations between the United States, the other countries of the Western Hemisphere, and the nations of Europe. After much discussion the President agreed.

On December 2, 1823, the members of Congress gathered to hear the President's annual State of the Union message. The message, like most such speeches, dealt with many subjects. What Monroe said about foreign relations made up a relatively small part of it. He did not stress the subject in any special way.

- Why did the revolutions in Latin America delight most people in the United States?
- What joint statement did Great Britain want to issue with the United States? Why did the United States refuse?

READING PRACTICE IN SOCIAL STUDIES

Finding Main Ideas in Sections

Finding the main idea of a paragraph is an important reading skill. In this book, as in many, several paragraphs make up a section. Just as an individual paragraph has a main idea, so does each section have at least one main idea. The main ideas of the paragraphs in a section develop the main idea of the section as a whole.

Remember that there are two steps in finding the main idea of a paragraph. First find the topic—the person, place, or thing that the paragraph is about. Then ask yourself, "What is the most important thing the writer is saying about the topic?"

To find the main idea of a section, you will do well to follow the same two steps. Often the topic of a section is stated in its heading. Using the heading as a guide, look for the topic and main idea of each paragraph. Then see how all the paragraphs together develop the topic and main idea of the section.

This will soon become an automatic process for you. You will see how writers build ideas paragraph by paragraph, section by section.

Turn to page 296 and read through the seven paragraphs of the section titled "Mass Production." Then answer the following questions.

1. What is the topic of the first paragraph?
   a. Natural resources
   b. Forests
   c. Iron
   d. Waterpower
2. The main idea of the first paragraph is stated in the
   a. First sentence
   b. Second sentence
   c. Third sentence
   d. Fourth sentence
3. What is the topic of the second paragraph?
   a. Obstacles to production
   b. Mass production
   c. Tools and machines
   d. Shoemakers and clockmakers
4. The topic of the third paragraph is
   a. Eli Whitney
   b. Technology
   c. Muskets
   d. The new government arsenal
5. The main idea of the fourth paragraph is stated in the
   a. First sentence
   b. Second sentence
   c. Third sentence
   d. Fourth sentence
   e. Fifth sentence
6. The main idea of the fifth paragraph is
   a. Unstated
   b. Given in the first sentence
   c. Given in the second sentence
   d. There is no main idea in this paragraph
7. The main idea of the sixth paragraph is
   a. Wolcott was Secretary of the Treasury.
   b. Whitney's offer to make muskets was accepted by the government.
   c. Whitney received a $5,000 advance.
   d. The government needed guns.
8. The main idea of the seventh paragraph is
   a. Whitney was a clever man.
   b. Whitney became rich.
   c. Whitney successfully demonstrated muskets made by mass production and received a new government contract.
   d. Whitney produced 500 muskets by 1801.
9. The topic of this section is
   a. Mass production
   b. Eli Whitney
   c. Making muskets
   d. Interchangeable parts
10. The main idea of this section is
    a. Eli Whitney was an American genius.
    b. Eli Whitney showed that mass production would succeed with interchangeable parts.
    c. The government purchased muskets.
    d. American manufacturers had a treasure store of natural resources.

A Protective Tariff

Danbury Scott-Fanton Museum and Historical Society

A protective tariff works this way: Suppose a hat manufacturer in Danbury, Connecticut, could make a hat for $3. After adding a profit the hat might be sold for $4. But an English hat manufacturer, having lower labor costs, might be able to make a similar hat for $2.50. Even after adding a dollar for profit, the English manufacturer could undersell the American. As a result the American manufacturer would be driven out of business.

The Tariff of 1816, therefore, put a tax of 30 per cent on imported hats. Since 30 per cent of $3.50 is $1.05, the English hat would now cost $4.55. The American manufacturer's business would be safe. Even if the English hatmaker sold hats at cost, the duty—30 per cent of $2.50—would raise the price to $3.25, still leaving the American with a small advantage.

Of course, American consumers had to pay higher prices because of the new tariff. But the theory was that the whole country would benefit. Business activity would increase because of the protection given to manufacturers. More people, for example, would be employed in making hats. And these hatmakers would spend their earnings, thus helping other businesses to grow.

MASS PRODUCTION

American manufacturers had a treasure store of natural resources to draw on. Abundant forests provided lumber for buildings and machines and also logs for fuel. There was iron for making tools and nails. Swift-running streams supplied waterpower to run machinery.

Still, American manufacturers had to overcome many obstacles. It was difficult to turn out goods in large quantities. The shoemakers of Lynn, Massachusetts, made boots one pair at a time for particular customers. The clockmakers of Philadelphia made timepieces only after individuals placed their orders. Americans did not yet have the manufacturing know-how to **mass produce** articles. Their **industrial technology**—that is, the tools, machines, and other things used to produce goods—was very inefficient.

One of the first Americans to improve the nation's industrial technology was Eli Whitney. When war threatened between the United States and France in the 1790s, Congress decided to purchase 7,000 muskets. Muskets were still in short supply in America. The new government arsenal at Springfield, Massachusetts, had turned out only about 1,000 muskets in three years.

Muskets were made by hand. A gunsmith shaped each barrel and fitted it with its own trigger and other parts. If a part broke, a new one had to be made and fitted to that particular gun. The barrel or trigger of one musket could not be substituted for another. It would not fit.

Whitney decided that he could manufacture muskets by the thousands if he could make them from **interchangeable parts.** If all triggers and barrels for a certain model of gun were exactly the same, the parts from any musket could be used with those of any other.

Yale University Art Gallery

Eli Whitney's muskets made with interchangeable parts led to a gun factory at Whitneyville, Connecticut. The oil painting is by William Giles Munson. Later, Samuel Colt carried on the manufacture. An illustration of Colt's first patent for firearms is shown below. Note the many parts that could be mass produced. How did Whitney demonstrate his new muskets in Washington?

Museum of Connecticut History

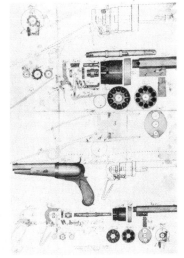

In 1798 Whitney wrote to Oliver Wolcott, the Secretary of the Treasury. He offered to turn out 10,000 muskets. His offer must have astonished Wolcott, but the government needed the guns badly. Whitney got the contract and an advance payment of $5,000 to get his business started.

It took Whitney two years to produce the grinders and borers and lathes that would enable him to produce identical parts. By September 1801 his shop in New Haven, Connecticut, had produced 500 muskets. He took ten of these to Washington. There he appeared before an amazed but delighted group of officials, which included President John Adams and Vice President Thomas Jefferson. Whitney took the muskets apart. He mixed the parts so that it was no longer possible to know which trigger went with which barrel, and so on. Then, choosing pieces at random, he reassembled the parts into ten muskets. Whitney's demonstration led to a revised contract. The new contract gave him an advance of $30,000.

- What assets did American manufacturers have? What obstacles did they have to overcome?
- How did Eli Whitney set out to improve the nation's industrial technology?

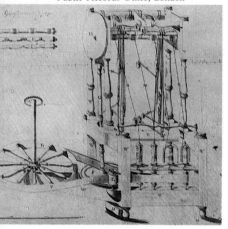

Above is the 1769 patent drawing for the spinning machine invented by Richard Arkwright. Cotton fibers were twisted between its rollers to produce strong thread. Below it is James Hargreaves's spinning jenny, first built in 1765. The one shown is an improved model. At it a spinner could operate all the spindles at once by cranking the wheel. When the cotton fibers were stretched, the fine thread was made. Where were these machines invented?

THE INDUSTRIAL REVOLUTION

While Whitney was developing his method of producing interchangeable parts, English manufacturers were shifting their work from hand tools to power-driven machinery. This is what is meant by the **Industrial Revolution.**

The process began in the 1700s. In those days almost every home had a spinning wheel for making thread and a loom for weaving cloth. Families made a good deal of their own clothing, working in their spare time. But it took about six times as long to make thread as it took to weave the same thread into cloth. This meant that one weaver used all the thread that six spinners could produce.

In 1765 an English weaver and carpenter named James Hargreaves built a machine called the **spinning jenny.** (Some say the machine was named after his wife. Others say the name came from "gin," a short form of the word "engine.") The spinning jenny was a mechanical spinning wheel. It was small, cheap, and easy to build. It could be operated by hand. Soon Hargreaves's invention found its way into thousands of English homes.

The spinning jenny increased output, but it did not reduce the price of cotton cloth very much. Because cotton fibers are not very strong, cotton could only be used for the short threads running across the cloth. Linen had to be used for the thousands of threads running lengthwise. And linen, which was made from the flax plant, was much more expensive than cotton.

In 1768 Richard Arkwright, a barber, solved this problem. He invented a spinning machine that produced much stronger cotton thread. Now cloth could be made entirely of cotton. The price fell.

Arkwright's machine was much bigger and heavier than Hargreaves's jenny. It could not be kept in a home or operated by hand. It required a mechanical force, such as waterpower, to run it. Thus

it was called the **water-frame.** In 1771 Arkwright formed a partnership and constructed what the English called a "mill." Americans sometimes called mills **factories.**

- What is meant by the Industrial Revolution?
- What was the importance of Hargreaves's spinning jenny? Of Arkwright's waterframe?

THE FACTORY COMES TO AMERICA

Arkwright's water-frames proved so successful that by the late 1780s over 100 cotton mills in England were using them. Cotton cloth production increased greatly. Soon English cloth was being exported to every part of the world.

The British government had no intention of sharing the secrets of its Industrial Revolution with other countries. It would not allow the export of textile-making machinery. Nor would it allow workers who were familiar with the machines to leave the country. But a number of these skilled workers, called **mechanics,** still made their way to America. The most important was Samuel Slater, who at one time had worked for Arkwright. When Slater decided to go to America, he memorized the designs for the new cotton-spinning machinery.

Slater landed in New York in 1789, the year the new Constitution went into effect. He soon met up with Moses Brown of Providence, Rhode Island. Brown was a member of a family that had been engaged in commerce and small-scale manufacturing in Rhode Island for generations. Slater agreed to build cotton-spinning machines for Brown in Pawtucket, Rhode Island, on the Blackstone River. By 1791 the work was done. Slater's machines spun cotton thread, using waterwheels turned by the current of the Blackstone for power. This

This engraving of Samuel Slater was made by W. G. Jackson. Slater came to America in 1789 with memorized plans for cotton-spinning machinery. What were skilled workers such as Slater called in England?

A gentle watercolor shows the noisy Blackstone River, which produced the power to turn Samuel Slater's machines at Pawtucket Falls, Rhode Island. This factory was erected in 1790 by Moses Brown. Why had he and Slater become partners?

This craggy, disheveled fellow is one of America's early benefactors of education. Moses Brown put up the money for the factory to house Samuel Slater's spinning machines. He prospered and later gave large sums of money to the Quakers and to Brown University, named for his brother. How did Brown dispose of the thread made by his factory?

thread was both better and cheaper than homespun cotton. The day of the factory had arrived in America.

Slater's machines made only thread. Brown sold some of this thread in his Providence store. The rest he supplied to workers who wove it into cloth on looms in their own homes. This was known as *putting out* the thread. The weavers returned the cloth to Brown, who paid them so much a yard for their work. He then sold the cloth in his store.

The **putting-out system** was widely used in America. It persisted long after factories became common. Hats, shoes, stockings—many products—were made in this manner, as well as cloth. The system made one workshop out of many homes. Brown's weavers worked for wages, but they did so at home. They were less dependent upon Brown than the workers in Slater's factory. They owned their own tools and had control over when and how hard they worked.

- How did the British government try to protect the secrets of its Industrial Revolution?
- How did the putting-out system work?

RECRUITING A LABOR FORCE

The Rhode Island System. Who wanted to work in factories? In England most factory jobs were filled by former tenant farmers who had been thrown out of work when owners fenced the land and planted grass in order to raise sheep. But there had been no enclosure movement in the United States. Most white American farmers worked their own land for themselves. They were **self-employed.** So were most artisans, such as carpenters and shoemakers. Few people in America worked for wages. Still fewer were willing to work in factories.

American manufacturers tried to solve this problem in two ways. The **Rhode Island system** made much use of children. Slater's first spinning machines were operated by seven boys and two girls ranging in age from 7 to 12. Slater could use these young children because his machinery was relatively easy to operate. He could pay them much less than adults. Children in the Slater mills received between 33 and 67 cents a week, while adult workers in Rhode Island were earning between $2 and $3 a week. As late as 1820 more than half of the workers in the Rhode Island mills were children.

Child labor seemed perfectly reasonable to most people. Farm children had always worked. In those days children were not required by law to go to school. Poor families were delighted to have any money their children could earn. Often entire families, parents and children together, worked in the early factories, answering advertisements like the one on page 301 from a Providence newspaper.

300

The Lowell System. The second method of getting workers for the factories was invented by Francis Cabot Lowell, a prominent Boston merchant. In 1810 Lowell visited spinning and weaving mills in England. He was deeply impressed by their efficiency. Like Slater, he carefully memorized the layout of the mills. He hoped to be able to reproduce them in New England.

Lowell's opportunity to test his memory came sooner than he had expected. When he returned to America, the War of 1812 was under way. Foreign trade had come to a standstill. No English goods were available. Lowell therefore organized a group of investors called the Boston Associates and hired a brilliant young engineer named Paul Moody.

Lowell and Moody spent a year constructing power looms copied from English designs. Meanwhile, the Associates built a factory at **Waltham,** Massachusetts, where they could use the water-power of the Charles River. By the end of 1813 the factory and machinery were ready to operate. This plant both spun cotton and thread *and* wove it into cloth by machine.

Lowell did not copy British labor practices. He and other manufacturers were disturbed by the poverty that the Industrial Revolution had brought to English workers. Lowell was as much concerned with the well-being of his workers as with his own profits. He was determined not to use children and poor families, as was being done in England and Rhode Island.

Instead, the **Lowell system** employed young unmarried women from neighboring farms. Many of these young women were willing to work before settling down. They could save part of their wages, and the idea of life in the factory community seemed interesting and even exciting to them. Their lives, however, were hard.

- What was the Rhode Island system for recruiting a labor force?
- What was the Lowell system for recruiting a labor force?

HANNAH BINDING SHOES

Poor lone Hannah,
Sitting at the window, binding shoes:
    Faded, wrinkled,
Sitting, stitching, in a mournful muse.
    Bright-eyed beauty once was she,
    When the bloom was on the tree:
        Spring and winter,
Hannah's at the window, binding shoes.

Lucy Larcom, a poet and millworker in Lowell, Massachusetts, is shown above in an engraved likeness. The women workers at Lowell submitted poetry to a magazine they published themselves. Although life was hard and the days long, the women tried to improve their lives by taking part in cultural activities sponsored by the factory owners. For a few hours they could shut out the humdrum of the damp, noisy factory. There they labored before blackened windows that could not be opened for fear the thread would dry and snap. What is the message of the poem?

IMMIGRATION FROM EUROPE

Many women walked out of the factories to protest wage reductions in 1834 and 1836. They were replaced by men and women recently come from Europe. These people were very poor and willing to take any job they could find. The number of people coming to America was increasing yearly. Only about 250,000 immigrants entered the United States between the end of the Revolutionary War and 1820. During the next 20 years more than 700,000 crossed the Atlantic.

The majority of these immigrants came from England, Ireland, and Germany. Most came as families. Nearly all came to the United States because they were poor and hoped to earn a better living in what Europeans considered "the land of opportunity."

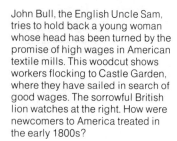

John Bull, the English Uncle Sam, tries to hold back a young woman whose head has been turned by the promise of high wages in American textile mills. This woodcut shows workers flocking to Castle Garden, where they have sailed in search of good wages. The sorrowful British lion watches at the right. How were newcomers to America treated in the early 1800s?

Museum of the City of New York

No one rolled out the red carpet for these newcomers. Some Americans opposed unlimited immigration. They wanted to keep the country for "native Americans." These **nativists** believed that too much immigration would destroy American institutions. They conveniently forgot that the only real native Americans were the Indians!

The nativists were members of various Protestant churches. They were particularly hostile to Irish Catholics, who were entering the country in large numbers. In 1834 a nativist mob burned a Catholic convent near Boston. Similar shameful incidents occurred in other parts of the country.

- Where did most immigrants come from after 1820?
- Who were nativists and whom did they oppose?

302

CITY LIFE IN AMERICA

Most of the immigrants who came to America between 1820 and 1840 settled in the cities of the Northeast. These were still communities where a person could easily walk from one end to the other in half an hour—a place where church steeples stood out on the skyline and the masts and spars of ships at the wharves towered over the roofs of the houses, shops, and warehouses. There were no skyscrapers or great factories. The largest manufacturer in New York City in the 1830s employed only about 200 people.

New York Historical Society

These eastern cities were mainly shipping centers. Manufacturing was not very important. Most industries which did exist, such as shipbuilding and barrel making, were linked to trade and commerce.

The cities to the west were also mainly commercial centers. We think of cities as developing in already settled areas, but these western cities developed on the edge of settlement. They made up what may be called an **urban frontier.** They were founded even before most of the surrounding forests were cleared by farmers. Indeed, they acted as outposts and depots from which settlers spread out. Many people went west not to farm but to live in these communities and supply the needs of farmers.

All American cities underwent similar growing pains in this period. Since few city streets were paved, there was always mud in rainy weather. This gave rise to a famous joke: A passing citizen

The hustle and bustle of New York City is seen in this large oil painting by Francis Guy. The time is 1799. At the left is the Tontine Coffee House, built at the corner of Water and Wall streets in 1792. The Stock Exchange and insurance companies had offices there. Down the street is a forest of masts and spars from the wharves on the East River. Where did most immigrants settle?

303

offers help to a man who has sunk up to his neck in a huge mud puddle. "No need to worry," replies the man. "I have a horse under me."

Garbage littered city streets. In all parts of the country goats and hogs were allowed to roam about rooting through the waste. Charleston, South Carolina, passed a law against shooting turkey buzzards because these scavengers ate the dead cats and dogs and rotting food left lying about the town.

The lack of sanitation and polluted water often led to epidemics of contagious diseases. The most dreaded was cholera. This terrible disease is caused by bacteria spread in polluted water, but no one knew this at the time. During cholera epidemics people living in dirty, crowded slums died by the hundreds. Many people, therefore, thought the disease was a punishment for poverty.

Many American cities had neither police nor fire departments. Even the largest cities had no more than a dozen police, and these were only part-time employees. They refused to wear uniforms, arguing that uniforms were for servants.

Fires were put out by volunteer fire companies. There was often much competition between these associations. When fires broke out, fire companies sometimes fought each other rather than the blaze. More than glory was at stake. Cash prizes were frequently awarded to the companies that responded most quickly to alarms.

In 1790 there were only 24 towns in the United States with a population of 2,500 or more. By 1840 there were 131. Many people moved into the cities, but many left them too. There was, in other words, a great deal of turnover among the urban population. Between 1830 and 1840, for example, 35,775 families either came into or left the city of Boston.

Rapid city growth caused crowded slums to develop. Most cities simply could not absorb people as fast as the newcomers arrived. The poor crowded into the attics and basements of houses. Large apartments were broken up into many small ones. Buildings with many families crowded together were called **tenements.** Rents were low. But because there were so many apartments in each, the profits made by owners of tenements could be very large. Little, if any, of the profit went to keep the tenement buildings in repair. They were unsanitary and unsafe.

Despite all of these problems, the cities remained the cultural centers of American life. Cities, with their theaters, cafes, taverns, and libraries, attracted people in large numbers—artists, writers, ordinary people searching for excitement and adventure.

- In what sense were western cities an urban frontier?
- What caused slums to develop in cities?

BUILDING SKILLS IN SOCIAL STUDIES

Mapping Population Change

The growth of the United States, from a nation of 4 million people in 1790 to 17 million in 1840, may readily be seen on a map showing population change. By using the skills of *comparison and contrast* (page 56), you can quickly see not only how much population increased but also where the changes were the greatest.

Maps that show population are sometimes called *population density maps* or *census maps.* Density means the amount of something per unit—in this case the number of people by area. The census is the official count of the population. The census is taken every ten years in the United States, the last being in 1980.

Color is particularly useful to show population density, although some maps use dots. Such a map, of present-day population density, is on pages 900–901. In the map below five colors represent the various numbers of people, varying from less than 100,000 to more than 1 million.

1. By 1840 which areas, by state, had the greatest population density?
2. In which area was there greatest population growth between 1790 and 1840?
3. How are cities of over 20,000 people represented? Which cities reached 20,000 by 1790?
4. Which cities reached 20,000 people *after* 1790?
5. From your reading on page 303, which cities on the 1840 map might be part of the urban frontier?

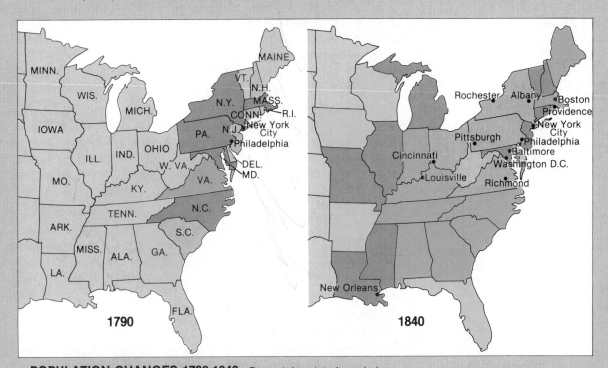

POPULATION CHANGES 1790-1840 Present-day state boundaries

- More than 1 million people
- 500,000 to 1 million people
- 250,000 to 499,999 people
- 100,000 to 249,999 people
- Less than 100,000 people
- • Cities with over 20,000 people

305

With the crack of a whip the driver of this stagecoach urges his team to pull westward. The fine watercolor is by George Tattersall. The wheels of the stagecoach sink into the muddy road, which is marked by stumps of the trees felled to make the bridge at right. Whenever the horses galloped around a curve such as this, there was always the chance that overland travelers would "be stumped." Who were the builders of most American roads in the early 1800s?

NEW ROADS AND TURNPIKES

As the cities expanded, it was no longer easy to walk from one end to the other. A new means of transportation was necessary. In 1827 Abraham Brower began running a **stagecoach** up and down Broadway in New York City. By 1833 there were about 80 stagecoaches in New York. The coaches were drawn by two horses and seated 12 passengers. In the winter some drivers replaced their wheels with runners, turning them into sleighs. Stagecoaches could soon be found in every city, and service between many cities was also available.

Travel overland could be effective only if there were good roads. America's roads were poor indeed. Most were unpaved. They turned into seas of mud after every heavy rain. In dry weather they were bumpy and rutted, and every passing wagon sent up clouds of dust. An inexpensive way to build weatherproof roads had not yet been found. Most roads were built by private companies that hoped to earn profits. The roads these companies built marched straight up and down hill and dale rather than around a more level but longer and more expensive way.

Builders collected tolls from people who traveled over their roads. The tollgate was usually a pole, or pike, blocking the road. When the traveler paid the toll, the pike was raised or turned aside to let the traveler pass. Hence these toll roads were called **turnpikes.**

Travel overland was both expensive and time-consuming. In the early 1800s it cost more to haul a ton of goods only 9 miles inland (about 14 kilometers) than to bring the same ton all the way across

306

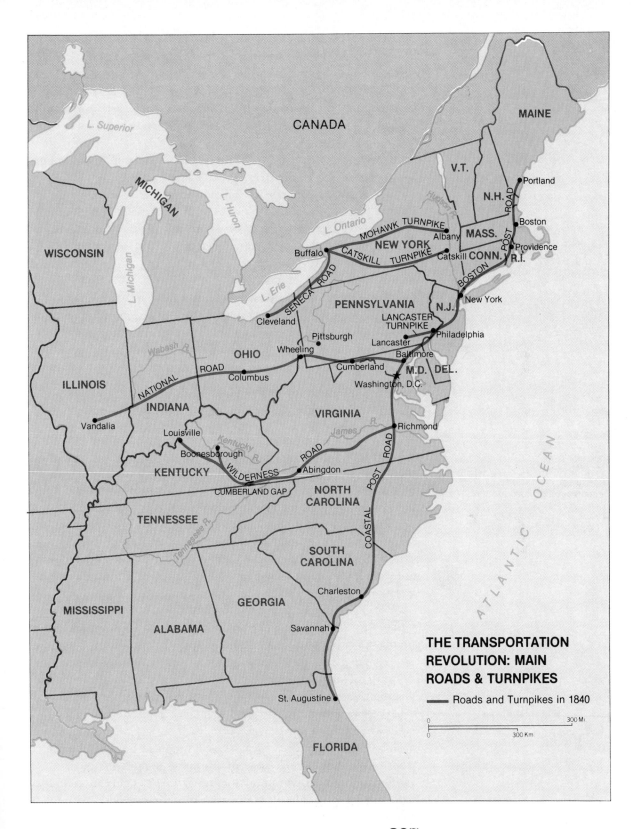

THE TRANSPORTATION
REVOLUTION: MAIN
ROADS & TURNPIKES

—— Roads and Turnpikes in 1840

CANADA

MAINE

V.T.

N.H.

MASS.

CONN. R.I.

N.J.

MICHIGAN

WISCONSIN

NEW YORK

PENNSYLVANIA

OHIO

ILLINOIS

INDIANA

VIRGINIA

KENTUCKY

M.D. DEL.

NORTH
CAROLINA

TENNESSEE

SOUTH
CAROLINA

MISSISSIPPI

ALABAMA

GEORGIA

FLORIDA

ATLANTIC OCEAN

L. Superior

L. Huron

L. Michigan

L. Ontario

L. Erie

Hudson R.

Wabash R.

Kentucky R.

James R.

Tennessee R.

Portland

Boston

Providence

Albany

Catskill

Buffalo

New York

Philadelphia

Lancaster

Cleveland

Pittsburgh

Wheeling

Baltimore

Columbus

Cumberland

Washington, D.C.

Vandalia

Louisville

Boonesborough

Abingdon

CUMBERLAND GAP

Richmond

Charleston

Savannah

St. Augustine

MOHAWK TURNPIKE

CATSKILL TURNPIKE

LANCASTER TURNPIKE

SENECA ROAD

NATIONAL ROAD

WILDERNESS ROAD

COASTAL POST ROAD

BOSTON POST ROAD

0   300 Mi.
0   300 Km

307

the Atlantic Ocean. Little wonder that in the 1790s the rebellious farmers of Pennsylvania had turned their corn into whiskey. In bulk form corn was far too expensive to ship to eastern markets.

During the War of 1812, a wagon drawn by four horses took 75 days to go from Worcester, Massachusetts, to Charleston, South Carolina. It would have been quicker to sail to Europe, stay a week or two, and return to America—and cheaper too. Any profits that might have been earned would have been "eaten up" by the four horses during the 75-day trip.

The roads of this period did not unite the country. In 1806 Thomas Jefferson took the first steps to link the eastern regions with the western. He authorized the building of the **Cumberland, or National Road.** Construction began in 1811 at Cumberland, Maryland. The route crossed over the mountains in southern Pennsylvania and ended at the site of present-day Wheeling, West Virginia. Later it was extended as far west as Vandalia, Illinois.

The National Road was a remarkable engineering achievement. It was built on a solid stone foundation with a gravel topping. Over it rolled an almost endless caravan of coaches, carts, and wagons. Its sturdy stone bridges still carry traffic today.

- In what ways were America's roads poor in the 1800s?
- Why was the Cumberland, or National Road, built?

CANALS

The easiest means of moving goods and people was by water. But, like America's roads, its rivers and lakes were not connected. Fortunately many of them could be joined by digging **canals.**

Goods were carried through canals on barges towed by horses or mules. The animals plodded patiently along what were called towpaths on the bank of the canal. A mule could pull a load of 50 times or more heavier on water than it could over any road. Thus, canal transportation was much cheaper than transportation by road.

Canals were very expensive to build. They could not be dug without government support. In 1816 De Witt Clinton, the canal commissioner of New York, persuaded the state legislature to build a canal running from the Hudson River across the state all the way to Lake Erie. This route offered the most attractive passage from the Atlantic Coast to the Great Lakes. It passed through the Mohawk Valley, a gap in the Appalachian Mountains. Thus the land was relatively level. The water did not have to be raised and lowered too much by **canal locks.** In 1817 work on Clinton's "Big Ditch" began. Much of the digging was done by European immigrants.

The first section was opened to traffic in 1819, and in 1825 the **Erie Canal** was completed. It was an engineering wonder: 363 miles

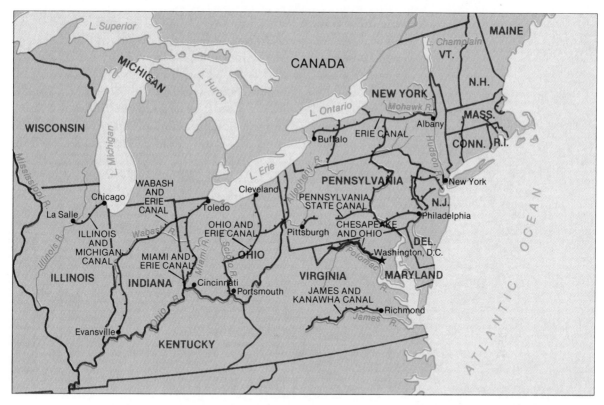

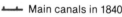 Main canals in 1840

long, 40 feet wide, and 4 feet deep (about 580 kilometers long, 12 meters wide, and 1 meter deep). It cost the state $7 million, an enormous sum for those days, but it attracted so much traffic that the tolls collected soon paid its cost. Because of this high volume, the rates charged for using the canal were very low. The cost of shipping a ton of goods fell from 19 cents a mile before the canal was built to 1 cent. The canal became the busiest route for goods and people moving between the Atlantic Coast and the western cities and farms.

When they saw how profitable the Erie Canal was, other states hastened to build canals of their own. Soon a wave of canal building was under way. In 1816 there were only about 100 miles (160 kilometers) of canals in the entire nation. By 1840 there were more than 3,300 miles (5,280 kilometers). This meant that the combined length of the canals of the United States was greater than the distance in North America between the Atlantic and Pacific Oceans.

The canals created a network that united the different sections of the country and stimulated their economies. Bulky farm products could now be shipped cheaply to distant markets. Eastern manufactured products no longer had to be lugged over the Appalachians.

- What problem was there in moving people and goods inland?
- Why were rates charged for canals very low?

STEAMBOATS

Travel by canal was slow. It still depended on animal power. Mules would only walk about 3 miles an hour (about 5 kilometers) pulling a barge. What was needed was a new source of power. Once again, British technology supplied the answer. In the 1760s a Scot named James Watt had invented a practical **steam engine.** Watt's invention used the energy of burning wood and coal to replace the energy of beasts and human beings. When the steam engine was used to run machines in factories, it replaced waterpower. This meant that factories did not have to be located near dams or swiftly moving rivers. They could be built anywhere.

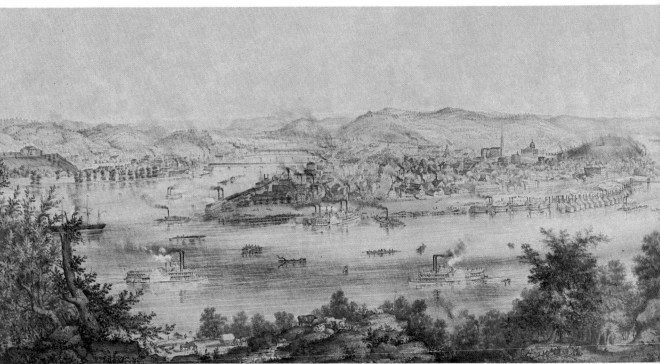

New York Public Library Print Room

In 1849, when this lithograph was made, Pittsburgh was often called the "Gateway to the West." From its crowded docks steamboats set out to carry settlers on the Ohio River as they began their journeys westward. In the years after Fulton sailed his *Clermont,* steamboats had become huge floating palaces, gliding from city to city. What problems did the designers of early steamboats have to solve?

If steam can move machines, can it not be used to move boats? One of the first Americans to ask this question was John Fitch, a silversmith and clockmaker. In 1787 Fitch launched a **steamboat** propelled by 12 paddles on the Delaware River. Among the many spectators who witnessed the launching of Fitch's smoke-belching monster were several of the delegates from the Constitutional Convention in nearby Philadelphia. Shortly afterwards, Fitch built another boat which carried passengers between Philadelphia and Burlington, New Jersey. But this enterprise was a commercial failure. Fitch's boat was so small and uncomfortable that people preferred to use other means of transportation.

310

For another 20 years steamboats were neither efficient nor reliable. Then, in 1807, Robert Fulton, an artist turned inventor, began building a steamboat on the East River in New York City. Fulton called it the *Clermont,* but those who had watched it being built called it **Fulton's Folly.** In August the boat made its first voyage up the Hudson River from New York City to Albany. The 300-mile trip (480 kilometers) took 62 hours, but the *Clermont* soon proved that a steam vessel could earn a profit.

The construction of new and improved steamboats went quickly ahead. In 1811 Nicholas Roosevelt, an associate of Fulton and a distant relative of two future Presidents, built the *New Orleans* at Pittsburgh. In the winter of 1811-12 this boat made the 1,950-mile trip (3,120 kilometers) from Pittsburgh to New Orleans in only 14 days. Previously the journey had taken four to six weeks.

An even more dramatic breakthrough occurred in 1815 when the *Enterprise* was piloted up the Mississippi from New Orleans to Pittsburgh against the current. Before that time a trip upstream by sail or keelboat from New Orleans to Pittsburgh took more than four months. Soon dozens of steamboats were sailing up and down the western rivers. In 1817 there were only 17. By 1840 there were 536.

    ■ What are some advantages of steam power?
    ■ What did Robert Fulton's steamboat *Clermont* prove?
    ■ What breakthrough did the *Enterprise* achieve?

Robert Fulton's oil portrait is the work of Benjamin West, who also painted America's delegation to the Peace of Paris on page 166. Fulton had been a Philadelphia portrait painter before he turned his mechanical apptitude to canal engineering and steamboats. What popular nickname was given to the *Clermont* while Fulton built it on New York City's East River?

RAILROADS

Soon after the canals and steamboats, there came a still more significant technological advance—the **railroad.** The first steam-driven locomotive, the **Tom Thumb,** was built by Peter Cooper for the Baltimore & Ohio Railroad in 1830. The track on which the *Tom Thumb* made its first run had previously been used by horse-drawn coaches. To demonstrate the engine, Cooper raced *Tom Thumb* against a horse-drawn coach. The locomotive swept ahead from the start. But it broke down before the finish line. The horse won the race.

Railroads had many advantages over canals and steamboats. They could go practically anywhere. They were much faster. They could pull greater loads. And they could operate all year round in the northern states, where the canals and many rivers were frozen solid in the winter months.

In the beginning many Americans considered railroads dangerous. The sparks from their engines set fields afire and frightened farm animals. The engines often jumped their tracks. But the advantages of railroads could not be resisted. In 1830 the Baltimore & Ohio, the nation's only railroad, had 13 miles (about 21 kilometers) of track.

The Chessie System, B&O Railroad Museum Archives (Photo: Robert Sherbow/UNIPHOTO)

"The Race of the Tom Thumb" is an oil painting by Herbert D. Stitt. It was completed in 1927 as part of a series for the Fair of the Iron Horse in celebration of 100 years for the Baltimore & Ohio Railroad. Which won the race—the horse or train?

By 1840 there were dozens of lines operating more than 3,300 miles (5,280 kilometers) of track, most of it in the Northeast.

The railroads gave the economy a great boost. Besides reducing travel time and cost, they caused many other businesses to expand. The demand for iron for engines and rails greatly increased the mining and smelting of iron. Remote areas boomed once the trains reached them. Farmers expanded output. Land prices rose.

The railroads completed the web of transportation which began with the turnpikes. This **Transportation Revolution** brought about dramatic changes. It tied westerners to easterners. It made it easier for people in one region to know and do business with people in other regions. It made nearly everyone more prosperous. In a way, the Transportation Revolution had almost as much to do with creating the *United States* as the American Revolution itself.

- What were some advantages of railroads over canals and steamboats?
- How did the railroads give the economy a boost?

CHAPTER 10 REVIEW

Identification
Tell briefly why each of the following persons, terms, or events is important.
1. Eli Whitney
2. Samuel Slater
3. Francis Cabot Lowell
4. De Witt Clinton
5. Robert Fulton
6. Nature's nation
7. Diversified economy
8. Protective tariff
9. Mass production
10. Industrial technology
11. Industrial Revolution
12. Putting-out system
13. Rhode Island system
14. Lowell system
15. Nativists
16. Urban frontier
17. Tenements
18. National Road
19. Erie Canal
20. Transportation Revolution

Understanding American History
1. In the early 1800s why were most Americans opposed to the growth of industry?
2. After the War of 1812 why did many Americans become convinced that manufacturing must become an important part of their economy?
3. Explain how a protective tariff works. Use an example to illustrate your answer.
4. What advantages did American manufacturers have in the early 1800s? What obstacles did they have?
5. Explain the contribution Eli Whitney made to American technology.
6. Describe some of the changes that occurred during the Industrial Revolution.
7. What advantages did workers in the putting-out system have over the factory system?
8. Compare and contrast the Rhode Island and Lowell systems for recruiting labor.
9. What were some of the problems of American cities in the period 1790–1840?
10. What were some effects of the Transportation Revolution on American life?

Activities
1. Use your historical imagination to present a skit showing a visit to your country cousin in the early 1800s. What will you tell your cousin about the city where you live? Discuss with your cousin the merits of city life and country life. Two other classmates may turn the situation around so that the country cousin visits relatives in the city.
2. Prepare a bulletin board showing some of the problems faced by cities in 1790–1840. Add newspaper and magazine articles to illustrate problems which continue to this day. Other students may report on the solutions found to some city problems of 1790–1840 and of today.
3. In 1801 Eli Whitney showed his muskets made from interchangeable parts to officials in Washington, including President Adams and Vice President Jefferson. Use your historical imagination to join the onlookers at Whitney's demonstration. What questions will you ask Whitney as he takes apart and reassembles the ten muskets?
4. Young women in the factories of Lowell worked 12 hours a day, six days a week. They shared a bedroom with seven other women. Workers came from all over New England, for wages in Lowell were higher than women could earn in any other occupation. Still, factories were hot, damp, and stuffy, and the work was usually boring. Use historical imagination to write a letter home to your family on the farm. Tell what you like and dislike about Lowell.
5. Prepare a bulletin board or multimedia display to show the scope of the Transportation Revolution in the United States. Show major rivers, canals, roads, and railroads that made up the American network by 1840.

CHAPTER 10 TEST

Matching (30 points)
Number your paper 1–10 and match the description in the first column with the name or term in the second column.

1. Manufacturing existing side by side with agriculture
2. Developed the idea of using interchangeable parts
3. Persuaded the State of New York to build the Erie Canal
4. The shift from hand tools to power-driven machinery
5. Skilled workers who operated machines
6. Improved trade and travel between East and West
7. Built the new cotton-spinning machines in America
8. The ability to turn out goods quickly in large quantities
9. City housing where many families lived in crowded conditions
10. Made a workshop out of many homes

a. Eli Whitney
b. Tenements
c. Diversified economy
d. National Road
e. Samuel Slater
f. Mass production
g. Industrial Revolution
h. De Witt Clinton
i. Putting-out system
j. Mechanics

Matching (20 points)
Number your paper 11–15 and match the invention in the first column with the person in the second column.

11. Reliable steamboat
12. Steam-driven locomotive
13. Spinning jenny
14. Practical steam engine
15. Water-frame

a. James Watt
b. James Hargreaves
c. Robert Fulton
d. Richard Arkwright
e. Peter Cooper

Completion (20 points)
Number your paper 16–25 and next to each number write the words that best complete each sentence.

16. The cost of foreign-made goods was kept higher than American-made goods by _____.
17. Fulton's steamboat, the _____, showed that a steam vessel could earn a profit.
18. The _____ wanted to keep the country for "native Americans."
19. The National Road was sometimes known as the _____.
20. What the English called mills, Americans sometimes called_____.
21. _____ were dug so that lakes and rivers could be better used to transport goods.
22. Eli Whitney used _____ to mass produce his muskets.
23. Western cities on the edge of settlement made up the area called the _____.
24. The early 1800s saw a_____ with the building of roads, canals, and railroads.
25. The first travel other than on foot in New York City was by Abraham Brower's _____.

Essay (30 points)
Explain how the Industrial Revolution caused each of the following: increased immigration to America, urbanization, and the Transportation Revolution. Plan your essay to show clearly how the *cause* led to each *effect*. Write at least three paragraphs and proofread your paper carefully.

UNIT THREE TEST

Multiple Choice (20 points)

Number your paper 1–5 and write the letter of the phrase that best completes each sentence.

1. The British practice of impressment
   a. violated the rights of American citizens.
   b. was meant to weaken the United States.
   c. persuaded Americans to enlist in its navy.
   d. increased Britain's trade with America.
2. The Louisiana Purchase was important to western farmers because
   a. they could then trade with Mexico.
   b. it gave U.S. control of the Mississippi River.
   c. gold was discovered in California.
   d. they could sell supplies to the Indians.
3. Most westerners favored war with Britain in 1812 because they wanted
   a. protection of their sea trade routes.
   b. control of Canada.
   c. more factories in the Northeast.
   d. better treatment for American Indians.
4. The Treaty of Ghent ending the War of 1812
   a. gave Britain large amounts of territory.
   b. gave New Orleans to the United States.
   c. brought a promise to end impressment.
   d. brought only a pledge to stop fighting.
5. Many Latin American nations won their independence from Spain in the early 1800s because
   a. Spain had become very weak.
   b. the United States aided the new nations.
   c. Britain had soundly defeated the Spanish.
   d. Spain lost interest in its colonies.

Chronological Order (25 points)

Number your paper 6–10 and place the following events in order by numbering 1 for the first, 2 for the second, and so on.

6. The United States and Britain sign the Treaty of Ghent.
7. The United States and Spain sign the Transcontinental Treaty.
8. Lewis and Clark explore the Louisiana Purchase.
9. American troops defeat the British at New Orleans.
10. Dolley Madison is forced to flee the White House.

Matching (25 points)

Number your paper 11–15 and match the person in the second column with the description in the first column.

11. Persuaded Congress to pass the Embargo Act
12. Guided Lewis and Clark on part of their expedition
13. American Indian fighter and victor in the Battle of New Orleans
14. Made muskets with interchangeable parts
15. Organizer of the Red Stick Confederacy

a. Andrew Jackson
b. Tecumseh
c. Thomas Jefferson
d. Eli Whitney
e. Sacagawea

Essay (30 points)

Write a few well-planned paragraphs on *one* of the following: Identify and explain two of the reasons why the United States went to war with Great Britain in 1812, *or* Explain how the Industrial Revolution in the United States led to the growth of cities and increased immigration.

UNIT FOUR

1820
Monroe reelected
•
Missouri Compromise

1821
Austin leads settlers to Texas
•
Lundy publishes antislavery paper

1822

1823

1824
Adams elected President

1825

1826

Texans revolt against Mexico
1835

Fall of the Alamo
•
Republic of Texas
•
Van Buren elected President
1836

Panic of 1837
1837

Cherokee Trail of Tears
1838

Sutter settles in California
1839

Log Cabin Campaign
•
Harrison elected President
1840

Tyler succeeds to Presidency
1841

A WESTERING AMERICA

1827	1828	1829	1830	1831	1832	1833	1834
	Tariff of Abominations • Jackson elected President		Indian Removal Act • Treaty of Dancing Rabbit Creek	Garrison founds *The Liberator* • Nat Turner's uprising	Nullification Crisis • Bank Veto • Jackson reelected		National Trades' Union

1842	1843	1844	1845	1846	1847	1848	1849
	Whitman leads settlers on Oregon Trail	Polk elected President	Texas annexed	Wilmot Proviso • Oregon boundary settled by Treaty of 1846 • Congress declares war on Mexico	Battle of Buena Vista • Republic of California • Mormons found Salt Lake City	Treaty of Guadalupe Hidalgo • Taylor elected President • Seneca Falls Declaration	Gold Rush to California

317

CHAPTER 11
The Age
of Jackson

President James Monroe was one of the luckiest persons ever to hold high office in the United States. He got on easily with most people, but he was really quite an ordinary fellow. He was little brighter than the next person. He seldom had an original idea. Nevertheless, in his long and happy life he advanced from one success to another. He achieved nearly every goal he set out after.

THE ERA OF GOOD FEELINGS

Because the Federalists were so unpopular after the War of 1812, Monroe was elected President in 1816 without serious opposition.

In 1817 he made a goodwill tour of New England. That part of the country had been a Federalist stronghold. Yet everywhere the President went, enthusiastic crowds gathered. Local officials—Federalists and Republicans alike—greeted him warmly. As one Boston newspaper wrote, "an **Era of Good Feelings**" had begun. When Monroe ran for reelection in 1820, no one ran against him. Only one Presidential elector refused to vote for him.

A crowd assembles on the streets of Philadelphia on election day, 1815. A German-born artist, John Lewis Krimmel, made this watercolor and ink drawing of American democracy in action. What name was given to this time after the War of 1812?

Historical Society of Pennsylvania

The country was at peace with all nations. It was prosperous and growing rapidly. There were 15 stars in the flag that Francis Scott Key saw waving over Fort McHenry in 1814 when he wrote "The Star-Spangled Banner." By 1821 the flag that flew over the fort had 23 stars. Indiana, Illinois, Alabama, Mississippi, Missouri, and Maine had been admitted to the Union as states during that seven-year period.

As the United States grew larger and richer, people noticed more differences between one region and another. These differences were in many ways for the good. People in one section produced one thing, those in another section something else. A large percentage of the nation's shoes were made in or near Lynn, Massachusetts. Fairfield County, Connecticut, especially the town of Danbury, was a center of hat manufacturing. Such **specialization** meant that there was a great deal of trading, not only of goods but also of ideas.

These regional differences came to cause conflicts and arguments over government policies. New leaders came forward who tended to represent their own sections of the country rather than the country as a whole. The Era of Good Feelings ended, to be replaced by an era of **sectional conflicts.** The nation seemed divided into three geographic regions: the Northeast, the South, and the West.

- Why were the years after 1817 known as the Era of Good Feelings?
- What caused sectional conflicts to replace the Era of Good Feelings? Into which sections did the nation seem divided?

THE NORTHEAST

The northeastern section, consisting of the New England states, New York, New Jersey, and Pennsylvania, became the major manufacturing area of the United States. Most of the important seaports were also located in this section.

These seaports and other towns were growing rapidly. New York City had 200,000 people by 1830. Europeans began coming to the United States in increasing numbers about 1830, and many settled in New York City and other eastern cities. The hustle and bustle of city life was exciting. Theaters and concert halls were built, book and magazine publishing flourished. But overcrowding turned older neighborhoods into slums. The rich seemed to get richer while the poor grew poorer.

Because city life had such variety, it is not possible to describe a typical city resident, particularly the poor because so little note was taken of their lives. Far more is known about a well-to-do urban family like that of John Ellerton Lodge and Anna Cabot Lodge of Boston.

John Ellerton Lodge is the subject of this engraved portrait by John A. J. Wilcox. We see Lodge here as a young man. How did Lodge make his fortune?

The Lodges of Boston. The Lodges lived in a big, square stone house in a quiet residential neighborhood. Their home was surrounded by a beautiful garden. Off to one side were the stables where the Lodge horses and carriage were kept. The house was full of fine English and early American furniture.

John Ellerton Lodge was a merchant whose ships were mostly engaged in trading with China. His business was located on Commercial Wharf. From his office overlooking the harbor, he could see the masts and spars of his many ships, which bore such varied names as *Magnet, Kremlin,* and *Sarah H. Snow.* These vessels brought in equally varied Chinese goods—tea, silk, chinaware, ginger, and other spices, even fireworks.

John Ellerton Lodge was an extremely hard worker who was also active in charitable affairs. Private charity was especially important in those days, for there were few government welfare programs. Lodge was interested in the cultural life of Boston too. He was president of the board of directors of the Boston Theater, the local opera house.

Despite the growth of cities in the Northeast, agriculture remained the occupation of a large majority of the people. Farmers grew wheat, corn, and other grains and raised cattle, sheep, and hogs. Farms tended to be small, run by a single family with perhaps one or two "hired hands." Since most people had large families, many sons and daughters of farmers moved to the towns and cities when they grew up. Others headed west to seek their fortunes.

■ What were two major occupations of the Northeast?

THE SOUTH

By the South we mean the states south of Pennsylvania and east of the Mississippi River. These were the states where slavery was still legal. As in colonial times, tobacco was the most important crop in Maryland, Virginia, and North Carolina. By 1815 and after, cotton was the main crop of South Carolina, Georgia, and, as the country grew, of Alabama, Tennessee, and Mississippi too. Southern farmers also grew grain and other food crops and raised hogs and cattle.

Tobacco and cotton were especially important to the South. There was a great demand for these crops in Europe and in the northern states. Southerners did not develop much manufacturing. They could buy the clothing, tools, and other manufactured goods they needed with the money earned by exporting cotton and tobacco.

Cotton was grown on small family farms of a few dozen acres and on large plantations worked by a hundred or more slaves. There were far more small farms than plantations, but the great cotton plantation was the ideal of southern society. The planters were the most influential leaders of the region.

320

National Portrait Gallery

The Calhouns of South Carolina. A good example of an important planter was John C. Calhoun, master of Fort Hill plantation in South Carolina. Fort Hill is in the northern part of the state, in hilly country within sight of the Blue Ridge Mountains. John and Floride Calhoun built their place in 1825, after he had been elected Vice President of the United States.

Despite their wealth, their many slaves, and his importance as Vice President, the Calhouns' life was not that of the idle rich. Floride was responsible for managing the entire household. Besides raising her nine children, she had to make sure that any slave who was ill or injured was properly cared for. She made some of the women slaves' clothing. She rarely had a free moment between sunrise and nightfall.

When not in Washington, the Vice President worked at dozens of farm chores. He was up at dawn and in the fields by 7:30. He checked with his plantation manager, the **overseer.** He experimented with new varieties of crops. He had to keep his eye on every detail of a very large operation.

John C. and Floride Calhoun built Fort Hill, *upper left,* on their 550-acre (220 hectares) plantation. The mansion is now part of the Clemson College campus. The oil painting of John C. Calhoun is probably by Charles Bird King c. 1818–25. The engraving of Floride Calhoun was not signed but pictures her as the young mistress of Fort Hill. What office did Calhoun hold?

■ What were the two major crops of the South?

■ Why was so little manufacturing developed in the South?

THE WEST

In the early 1800s so many families were moving west that an Englishman on the way to Ohio in 1817 wrote, "Old America seems to be breaking up and moving westward. We are seldom out of sight as we travel . . . of family groups, behind and before us."

People of every sort were on the move. In the South well-to-do planter families accompanied by a dozen or more slaves shared the roads with poverty-stricken farmers who had nothing more than the clothes on their backs and a few tools. Along the National Road, which crossed the mountains, individuals on horseback passed weary couples pulling handcarts. Many poor people actually walked all the way from the eastern states to Ohio and Indiana.

Sometimes several families banded together for the trip. One traveler described a group that included 42 children crowded into three wagons.

The **Conestoga wagon** was developed to handle the heavy loads of the pioneers. It was built with strong, wide wheels to withstand the ruts and mud and bumps of unpaved roads. A canvas cover protected the travelers from rain and snow and sheltered them at night. Conestoga wagons were not known for speed or comfort. But they were tough, roomy, and not very expensive. A good one cost about as much as the horse that pulled it.

Their Conestoga wagon loaded, this family bids a tearful goodbye to the older folks they will leave behind as they join the movement westward. "Leaving the Old Homestead" is the title James Wilkins gave to this oil painted in the 19th century. What were some virtues of the Conestoga wagon?

Missouri Historical Society

Of course, after the opening of the Erie Canal across New York in 1825, traveling west became far less difficult. But the trip was never easy.

Throughout the West nearly everyone began as a farmer. For the settlers of Indiana or Alabama the work of clearing land and building a house was little different from what it had been 200 years earlier for the settlers of Massachusetts and Virginia. Huge trees had to be chopped down, or at least killed by stripping their bark, so that sunlight could shine on the pioneers' first crops. Their first houses were usually made of logs. No one could spare the time or energy to saw logs into boards. The kitchen was often an open shed or lean-to on the side of the cabin.

READING PRACTICE
IN SOCIAL STUDIES

Details

Readers of history sometimes feel lost in a sea of names and dates. These *details* often stand out on the printed page. But names and dates have no historical significance unless they are part of the writer's larger story.

Compare the following two accounts of the building of a southern plantation:

John and Floride Calhoun built their plantation, Fort Hill, in 1825.

A good example of an important planter was John C. Calhoun, master of Fort Hill plantation in South Carolina. Fort Hill is in the northern part of the state, in hilly country within sight of the Blue Ridge Mountains. John and Floride Calhoun built their place in 1825, after he had been elected Vice President of the United States.

The second account is clearly more interesting because of the details added to the bare bones of historical fact. Details tell us something about the builder of Fort Hill. They give a picture of its location and point out its significance in the larger sweep of history — it is one of the great southern plantations that represented the ideal of its society.

Writers use details to support main ideas. You may already have practiced finding main ideas in paragraphs (page 281) and in sections (page 295). Details help you to remember the main idea. They may describe, explain, or give examples of the main idea.

Look closely at the following paragraph:

The **Conestoga wagon** was developed to handle the heavy loads of the pioneers. It was built with strong, wide wheels to withstand the ruts and mud and bumps of unpaved roads. A canvas cover protected the travelers from rain and snow and sheltered them at night. Conestoga wagons were not known for speed or comfort. But they were tough, roomy, and not very expensive. A good one cost about as much as the horse that pulled it.

The paragraph comes from the section "The West" on pages 321–22.

The main idea of this paragraph is found in its first sentence. The other five sentences are filled with details that give a description of the Conestoga wagon and the needs of the pioneers who depended upon it. The details make the main idea easy to understand because they are specific.

Other kinds of details help you to remember a main idea because they give a large amount of factual information in an interesting way. For example, on page 318 you read that "an Era of Good Feelings" began in 1817. Then you read the following details:

The country was at peace with all nations. It was prosperous and growing rapidly. There were 15 stars in the flag that Francis Scott Key saw waving over Fort McHenry in 1814 when he wrote "The Star-Spangled Banner." By 1821 the flag that flew over the fort had 23 stars. Indiana Illinois, Alabama, Mississippi, Missouri, and Maine had been admitted to the Union as states during that seven-year period.

The details — a list of state names, two dates, and a handful of proper names — all support the main idea. At the same time they continue the story of American history in an imaginative way.

Read the section titled "The Election of 1824" on page 326 and answer the following questions.
1. Which are the details that explain why John Quincy Adams seemed a logical choice for President in 1824?
2. List the details that describe William H. Crawford as a candidate for President.
3. List the details that describe Henry Clay as a candidate for President.
4. Which details explain what was meant by internal improvements?
5. Which details explain Henry Clay's plan called the American System?

"Settlers Cabin in Indiana" is the work of Karl Bodmer, a Swiss artist. This detail is from the unfinished watercolor showing a rustic cabin, a spring house in front for storing food, and split-rail fences. Lincoln the Rail-Splitter would have been at home here. What hardships did the western frontier offer?

The Lincolns of Indiana. A famous example of the hardships faced by these pioneers is the story of Thomas and Nancy Lincoln, who settled with their two children in Indiana in the winter of 1816. The land was covered with dense forest. Thomas Lincoln, a carpenter as well as a farmer, began by building a "half-faced camp." This was a crude, three-sided shelter of logs and branches, entirely open on the south. It was December when Thomas Lincoln built his camp. The family survived only by keeping a roaring fire going day and night in front of the camp. Thomas hastened to build a more permanent log cabin, complete with a stone fireplace and chimney.

That winter the family lived on deer, turkey, and other forest animals shot by Thomas Lincoln. The Lincolns' young son, Abraham, who was only seven when they arrived, had to fetch their water from a spring some distance from the cabin. Once the cabin was finished, Abraham helped his father clear land for their first crop. He soon became expert with an axe. (Later, when Abraham Lincoln became a politician, he was known as "the Rail-Splitter" because of his skill at splitting long logs into fence rails.)

The Lincolns suffered many hardships of the frontier. Nancy Lincoln died of a mysterious disease called "the milk sickness." Abraham had almost no formal schooling. He loved to read, but there were few books to be bought or borrowed. After ten years of backbreaking labor, Thomas sold the farm for only $125.

Abraham Lincoln was an exceptional person who would surely have made his mark in any situation. He rose easily in the rough-and-tumble frontier world. He was able to become a lawyer and make an excellent living, despite his humble origins and lack of education. Westerners respected ability and paid little mind to a person's origins.

Corn was the first crop usually planted in the West. It was easy to grow and could feed both the pioneers and their farm animals. After the work of clearing and fencing the land was finished, wheat, tobacco, and cotton would be grown in one place or another. And although the West remained mostly agricultural, small-scale manufacturing of all kinds soon sprang up everywhere. Transportation was so expensive that westerners made all kinds of goods for themselves. Everything from nails and pots and stoves to paper and barrels and clocks was made in dozens of western communities.

- At what occupation did nearly everyone in the West begin?
- Why did small-scale manufacturing spread throughout the West?

By 1820 there were almost as many people west of the Appalachian Mountains as there had been in the original 13 states at the time of the American Revolution. Settlers thought of this area between the Appalachians and the Mississippi River as the West. It was indeed the western frontier of the United States.

By 1850 the land called the Northwest Territory lay in the eastern half of the Middle West. Its location, like other areas of the growing nation, was redefined by the rush west. In this way the meaning of the term "the West" kept changing as the United States grew westward.

The first Americans had lived in western America for perhaps 30,000 years or more. By the 1770s there were many Spanish and Russian settlements, mostly trading posts and missions, in the Far West along the Pacific coastline. These western peoples either had separate societies or were colonists of Spain, Russia, or Great Britain. Some would later come to refer to themselves as Americans. But they did so only after the United States had grown to include them at the western edge of the continent. Then the West came to mean the land between the Rockies and the Pacific Ocean.

Even the present-day use of the terms "West" or "Far West" is not particularly accurate when talking about the nation. What of those most western of all the United States—Alaska and Hawaii?

America Grows Westward

California Historical Society

This detail from a lithograph by V. Adam, c. 1822, shows the fort in San Francisco known as the Presidio.

THE ELECTION OF 1824

By 1824 the three sections of the United States had produced strong leaders, each of whom was favored by a particular section. No one had opposed Monroe for President in 1820. Four candidates, each strong in his section of the country, competed for the office when Monroe retired four years later.

One candidate was John Quincy Adams. He seemed the logical choice in 1824 because he was Monroe's Secretary of State. Monroe had been Madison's Secretary of State before becoming President, and Madison had been Jefferson's. Adams had also been very successful as Secretary. The Adams name and his long career of public service were other advantages. But he had few supporters outside New England and the other northeastern states.

The favorite in the southern states was William H. Crawford of Georgia. Crawford was Monroe's Secretary of the Treasury. Like Adams he had been a diplomat in the past. He had served in the Georgia legislature and in the United States Senate.

Crawford was a tall, attractive man who got on easily with all sorts of people. He was a politician's politician, a master of all the ins and outs of that craft. Although his support was mainly southern, some important northern leaders backed him for President. He seemed likely to be elected, until he suffered a stroke that left him partly paralyzed.

The other two candidates were westerners. One was General Andrew Jackson. He was one of the few nationally popular persons of the time. He was not much of a politician, and he had relatively little interest in sectional issues like roads and tariffs. The second western candidate was Henry Clay of Kentucky. Like Crawford, Clay was handsome and charming. He loved the give-and-take of political debate and the behind-the-scenes negotiations that were necessary to get important bills through Congress.

Clay had been a prominent War Hawk in 1812, but he was best known for his superb ability to solve sectional conflicts by working out clever compromises. He was the father of a plan for sectional cooperation that he called the **American System.** Easterners wanted the government to place **high tariffs** on foreign manufactured goods that competed with their own products. Westerners wanted the government to help pay for what were called **internal improvements**—the roads and canals needed to get western goods to market cheaply.

Clay proposed that western members of Congress vote for high tariffs in exchange for eastern votes for internal improvements. By helping each other, he explained, both sections would profit. In 1824 Clay was well known throughout the country because he was Speaker, or presiding officer, of the House of Representatives. But his support in the election was only in the West.

Chicago Historical Society

Three times Henry Clay saved the Union when sectional conflict led to crisis. For his efforts he was known as the Great Compromiser. This oil portrait was painted by Matthew Jouett in 1824. What was Clay's American System?

When the electoral votes were counted, Jackson had 99, Adams 84, Crawford 41, and Clay 37. Since no one had a majority, under the Constitution the House of Representatives had to choose the President from among the three candidates with the most votes. This meant that Henry Clay was eliminated. But although he could not hold the office himself, Clay decided who would be President. He urged his supporters to vote for Adams, who was then elected.

- How did sectional issues cause the election of 1824 to differ from the reelection of President Monroe in 1820?
- How was the outcome of the election of 1824 determined?

THE SECOND PRESIDENT ADAMS

John Quincy Adams, like his father President John Adams, was intelligent, strong willed, energetic, and totally dedicated to serving his country. Naturally he had been brought up a Federalist. But in the early 1800s he realized that Federalist ideas were out of date. He switched to the Jeffersonian Republican party.

Adams believed firmly, like Alexander Hamilton, that the federal government should encourage the development of manufacturing and stimulate all kinds of economic activity. He considered Clay's American System an excellent idea. He also hoped to establish a national university in Washington, and he urged Congress to spend large sums on scientific research and exploration.

Adams favored big government that would look after national interests, but the country was still sharply divided. People were mostly caught up in their own sectional interests. Even as brilliant a politician as Clay or Crawford would have found it difficult to bring the people together. And Adams was a very poor politician. His administration was a disaster.

Like his Presidential father, John Quincy Adams put service to country ahead of personal gain. However, he lacked the common touch, and critics found him hard and stern. In this oil portrait painted in 1815 by Pieter Van Huffel, his appearance is formal but friendly. How did he make others in the government uncomfortable?

Adams was extremely hardworking. Every morning he got up at five o'clock. In the dead of winter he would throw open his window and take a sponge bath with ice-cold water to prepare for his day's work. He assumed that everyone in government was as devoted to duty and as energetic as he was. When his associates did not live up to his expectations, he managed, without intending to, to make them feel guilty.

An example of Adams's clumsiness as a politician was his appointment of Henry Clay as Secretary of State. Clay was certainly able, and he had some diplomatic experience. But naming him looked like a political payoff. It had been Clay's friends in the House of Representatives who had cast the votes that made Adams President. Furthermore, the last four Secretaries of State had moved up from that office to the Presidency. The supporters of Andrew Jackson were outraged. They charged Adams with having made a "corrupt bargain" with Clay by promising to try to make Clay his successor in return for votes in the election.

Once in office, Adams quickly showed that he did not know how to use the power of the Presidency to get his program adopted. He would not replace government officials who resisted his policies with people who supported them. When he was sure he was right, he was rigid and stubborn. And he was nearly always sure that he was right.

His plan for a national university had no chance of being accepted by Congress. "Let us not recommend anything so unpopular," the practical-minded Henry Clay suggested. But Adams made the recommendation anyway. "I feel it is my indispensable duty," he explained to Clay.

- What kind of government did the second President Adams believe in?
- Why was Adams's appointment of Henry Clay as Secretary of State clumsy politics?

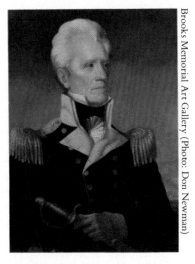

Ladies' Hermitage Association

Brooks Memorial Art Gallery (Photo: Don Newman)

Andrew Jackson wore military dress for his 1833 oil portrait by Ralph W. Earl. He always wore the miniature, *right,* of Rachel Donelson Jackson, his beloved wife. She was buried on Christmas Eve, 1828, in the white dress she had planned to wear for Jackson's inauguration. Her likeness is by Louisa Catherine Strobel. What present-day political party formally began with Andrew Jackson?

THE ELECTION OF ANDREW JACKSON

By 1828 Adams was discouraged and depressed. None of his policies had succeeded, but he was determined to seek reelection. This time he faced only one opponent, Andrew Jackson. The Jacksonians were now calling themselves simply **Democrats** instead of Democratic-Republicans. This was the formal beginning of the Democratic party.

In those days candidates for President did not campaign in their own behalf. To do so was considered undignified. Their supporters were not so restrained. The campaign of 1828 was bitterly fought and very dirty.

The Jacksonians said little about issues like the tariff and internal improvements. They again accused Adams of having made a "corrupt bargain" to win the Presidency in 1824. When they discovered that he had bought a chess set and a billiard table for the White House, they charged him with wasting public money on gambling devices. One Democratic newspaper claimed that Adams was so pro-British that he intended to move to England when he retired and buy a noble title.

The President's supporters replied with lies of their own. Jackson was a reckless gambler and a murderer, they said. They told shady stories about his mother and then about his wife Rachel. Understandably, by the end of the campaign Jackson and Adams were furious with each other.

These lies and wild charges probably had little effect on the election, nor did any of the real issues. Jackson won chiefly because he was so popular while Adams was so ramrod straight and remote from ordinary voters.

■ Why did Jackson win the election of 1828?

In the Era of the Common Man the White House was open to all. Robert Cruikshank engraved this caricature titled "The President's Levee, or all Creation going to the White House" in 1829. What was the role of women in the Era of the Common Man?

JACKSONIAN DEMOCRACY

Jackson's victory marked a turning point in American history. Although he was neither poor nor ordinary in any sense, he presented himself as being in tune with the **common man.** (Women were not counted in politics at that time because they could not vote.) Jackson's position was shrewd politics, and there was some truth to it. He was not an ignorant man, but he was poorly educated. He wrote with a terrible scrawl. His spelling was even worse. He had the manners of a gentleman, but he was capable of behaving like a rowdy. He was utterly unlike any earlier President.

329

After Jackson delivered his inaugural address on March 4, 1829, he held open house at the White House. Anyone could come. The mansion became so crowded that Jackson was almost crushed to death. Furniture was broken, mud tracked over expensive carpets. Huge amounts of food and drink were consumed. Jackson finally had to escape out a side door and spend the night in a hotel.

This was a new kind of democracy, quite different from that of Thomas Jefferson. Jefferson had tried to teach people that public officials were their servants. No person had *rights* superior to those of anyone else. The Jeffersonians believed that the people should have the right to choose their leaders. Yet they assumed that the people would choose exceptional persons to lead them.

The Jacksonians claimed that any ordinary person could be a leader. The common sense of the "common man" was all that was required to handle public office or a government job.

This faith in ordinary people led to a number of democratic reforms. State property qualifications for voting and holding office were dropped. More and more, Presidential electors were chosen by popular vote, not by the state legislatures.

Soon national meetings of party leaders began to be held. These **nominating conventions** were attended by large numbers of delegates from all over the nation. The delegates chose the party's Presidential and Vice Presidential candidates. Then, at the Presidential election, voters cast ballots for the electors in their states who were pledged to vote for the candidates selected at the party conventions. Both the Democrats and their opponents adopted the convention method of choosing candidates.

Not all results of this new faith in the good sense of the "common man" were for the good. Politicians soon learned to attract voters by slogans and flattery rather than by discussing the issues. Probably this was bound to come with the spread of democratic ideas and the pressures of closely fought elections.

In Jackson's case there was no way to avoid making personality more important than issues. No party had been led by as popular and colorful a figure as "Old Hickory" Jackson, ex-Indian fighter and Hero of New Orleans. Since then, personality has been important for many candidates.

Election campaigns were becoming a spectator sport with voters watching from the sidelines while office seekers and speechmakers competed for what became known as the **spoils of office.** The Jacksonian Democrats went further. They made politics a team sport which a great many ordinary citizens could play. When they won a local, state, or national election, they used their power as elected officers to appoint as many of their followers as possible to government jobs as postmasters and clerks.

Philadelphia Museum of Art

Everywhere, Andrew Jackson was a celebrated hero of common citizens. This pine writing desk has the Hero of New Orleans painted on a drawer. It was made c. 1825 by Pennsylvania Dutch craftsmen. Why was Jackson's personality a campaign issue?

The Jacksonians then added the idea known as **rotation in office.** After a certain length of time, usually four years, most jobholders were replaced by other members of the team. The purpose was to get as many people as possible involved in party politics by holding out to all loyal party workers the possibility of a government job.

■ How did Jacksonians differ from Jeffersonians in their idea of democracy?

■ What was the system known as the spoils of office?

THE IDEA OF NULLIFICATION

Jackson was popular in all parts of the country, but sectional disagreements did not end when he was elected President. The **tariff question** was particularly troublesome. Many members of Congress represented districts whose products had to compete with foreign-made goods, such as cotton and woolen cloth. These districts, mostly in the northeastern states, favored high protective tariffs. The southern states produced few such products. They opposed tariffs that would raise the prices of goods they had to buy.

A few months before the Presidential election, Congress had passed a tariff law with very high duties. People who opposed it disliked it so much that they called it the **Tariff of Abominations.** They considered it abominable, or disgusting. Most southerners were among this group.

What made the tariff argument so serious was the belief of some experts that protective tariffs were **unconstitutional.** They argued that the Constitution gave Congress the power to tax imports only in order to raise money. To tax imports to keep foreign goods out of the country was an abuse of power and therefore illegal.

One person who considered the Tariff of Abominations unconstitutional was Vice President John C. Calhoun, whose South Carolina cotton plantation we have described. In 1828 Calhoun wrote an essay insisting that a state had the right to prevent an unconstitutional law from being enforced within its territory.

Jefferson and Madison had made a similar argument in the Kentucky and Virginia Resolutions protesting the Alien and Sedition Acts of 1798. But Calhoun went further. He described an orderly, legal way for a state to be free of a law it found unconstitutional. When a state legislature considered a law of Congress unconstitutional, he wrote, it could order a special election to choose delegates to decide the question. If the delegates elected by the voters agreed, they could pass an act called an **ordinance of nullification.** The law would then be *nullified*—that is, cease to exist—in the state.

Neither South Carolina nor any other state tried to nullify the Tariff of Abominations. Calhoun believed that Jackson agreed with

This caricature of John C. Calhoun is from a lithograph made early in the 19th century. The U.S. Capitol is in the background. In a larger version of this cartoon, Calhoun is portrayed commanding the sun to stand still, like the Biblical Joshua, so "that the nation of Carolina may continue to hold Negroes & plant Cotton till the day of Judgment!" What position of Calhoun's is this cartoonist attacking?

Prints Division, New York Public Library

him about tariffs. He supported Jackson for President in 1828 and was himself elected to a second term as Vice President, running this time with Jackson on the Democratic ticket. He assumed that after the election Congress would pass a new law lowering the tariff.

But the influence of manufacturers in Congress was growing steadily. When a new tariff was finally passed in 1832, it lowered the duties only slightly. Most southerners were disappointed and very angry.

■ Why did some people argue that protective tariffs were unconstitutional?

■ What way did Vice President Calhoun propose for a state to be free of a law it thought unconstitutional?

THE NULLIFICATION CRISIS

The South Carolina legislature decided to put Calhoun's theory of nullification into practice. It ordered a special election. The delegates chosen by the voters met in November 1832 and passed an **ordinance,** or act, nullifying the tariff laws. After February 1, 1833, the collection of tariffs would be prohibited in South Carolina. (The delay was decided upon in hopes that Congress would avoid a showdown by lowering the tariff before the deadline.) When the ordinance was passed, Calhoun resigned as Vice President and returned to South Carolina. The legislature then elected him United States Senator.

President Jackson was not particularly interested in tariffs. Unlike Calhoun, he was not brilliant at political theory. But he knew the United States would fall apart if a state could refuse to obey any federal law it did not like. As President he had sworn to protect and defend the Constitution. He therefore acted as decisively as he had acted in 1815 when he learned that General Pakenham's Redcoats were approaching New Orleans.

First Jackson issued a *Proclamation to the People of South Carolina.* This warned them that he would use the army if necessary to enforce tariff laws if nullification was actually tried. Then he announced that he would march personally into South Carolina at the head of his troops and hang the leading nullifiers. "Union men, fear not," he said. *"The Union will be preserved."*

If other southern states had supported South Carolina by nullifying the tariff, civil war would probably have resulted.

But most southerners were not ready to break up the Union over such an issue. Northerners were also eager to avoid a fight. In Congress, Calhoun and Henry Clay worked out a compromise tariff bill that provided for a gradual lowering of duties. When it passed and was signed by Jackson, the South Carolina legislature **repealed,** or did away with, the Ordinance of Nullification.

The crisis was over. But the question remained unanswered. Did a state have the right to refuse to obey a federal law that it considered unconstitutional?

- Why did Jackson oppose the South Carolina Ordinance of Nullification?
- What actions did Jackson take after South Carolina passed the Ordinance of Nullification?

THE BANK OF THE UNITED STATES

The **Nullification Crisis** showed Andrew Jackson at his best. He was determined, coolheaded, and confident. He stood firm for the great principle of saving the Union. Yet he was willing to compromise on the particular issue of the tariff. The same cannot be said for his handling of another controversy of his Presidency. This was the question of whether or not to renew the charter of the **Second Bank of the United States.**

After the Second Bank of the United States was founded in 1816, many state-chartered banks lost business to it. Several states therefore passed laws placing heavy taxes on branches of the Bank within their borders. The Bank refused to pay these taxes. In the case of *McCulloch v. Maryland* (1819), the Supreme Court declared that the Bank was

BUILDING SKILLS IN SOCIAL STUDIES

Reading a Diagram

A *diagram* is a graphic design that explains how its different parts are related. Diagrams are particularly useful for showing a series of activities that depend one upon the others. Such is the case in the diagram on this page. It shows that banks today hold a position in our economy as important as in the time of Andrew Jackson.

Study the diagram carefully. Notice the four points at which branches of the business cycle begin and end. Trace the flow of each branch. When you feel that you understand the purpose of the diagram and the reason for its design, answer the following questions.

1. What four major categories are shown?
2. Which two categories are sources of taxes?
3. Which two categories make deposits?
4. What are two ways growing businesses help the general economy?
5. According to this diagram, what are three things workers do with their money?
6. Where do banks get the money they lend to businesses?
7. When business is bad and many workers are unemployed, what happens to the amount of money banks are able to lend? Explain.
8. When business is bad, what happens to the amount of money collected in taxes?
9. How does money deposited by the government eventually come back to workers?
10. Explain in your own words why banks are important to our economy.

A HEALTHY BUSINESS CYCLE

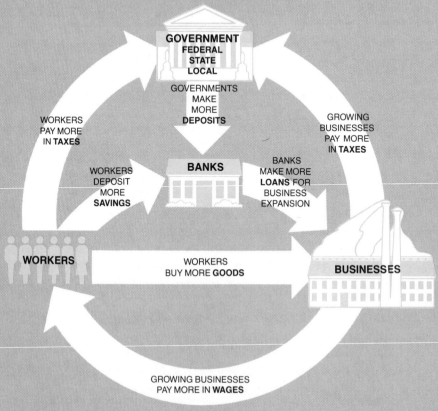

GOVERNMENT
FEDERAL
STATE
LOCAL

GOVERNMENTS MAKE MORE **DEPOSITS**

WORKERS PAY MORE IN **TAXES**

GROWING BUSINESSES PAY MORE IN **TAXES**

WORKERS DEPOSIT MORE **SAVINGS**

BANKS

BANKS MAKE MORE **LOANS** FOR BUSINESS EXPANSION

WORKERS

WORKERS BUY MORE **GOODS**

BUSINESSES

GROWING BUSINESSES PAY MORE IN **WAGES**

constitutional and therefore that no state could tax it. That appeared to answer the constitutional question first raised by George Washington when Alexander Hamilton proposed the first Bank of the United States in 1790. After 1819 the new Bank prospered.

The president of the Bank, Nicholas Biddle, was an excellent financier. He used the resources of the powerful Bank to stimulate the economy of the nation by lending money to businesses to expand their operations. At the same time he tried to prevent state banks from lending money too recklessly.

Banks made loans by issuing paper money to borrowers who put up some sort of security, such as a deed to land, to guarantee that the loan would be repaid. Each bank created its own paper money, with its name printed on the bills. This paper money, called **bank notes,** was supposed to represent gold or silver coins in the bank's safe. These bank notes passed from hand to hand, as money does today. Anyone who received any bank's note had the right to go to that bank and exchange the note for coins, called **hard money.**

So long as people were sure a bank would exchange hard money for bank notes, few would trouble to make the exchange. For this reason banks issued far more notes than they had gold and silver in their vaults. Up to a point this was reasonable and safe.

But some banks were tempted to issue very large amounts of notes. The more notes issued, the more loans there were earning interest for the bank. This was dangerous, for if people suddenly began turning in these notes, the bank would not have enough gold and silver. It would then be **bankrupt,** and people who owned its paper money or who had deposited their savings in it would be hurt.

However, Nicholas Biddle had a way to force state banks to be conservative about making loans. He could threaten to turn in all of the state bank notes that the Bank of the United States received in the course of its far-flung activities and demand payment in gold or silver in return.

Many state bankers objected to Biddle's policies. They wanted the government to let the Bank go out of business when its 20-year charter ran out in 1836. Then they would be able to make loans more freely and thus earn larger profits.

Andrew Jackson also wanted to do away with the Bank of the United States. His reasoning, however, was far different from that of the state bankers. Jackson was what was called a hard money man. His reasoning went this way: Bank notes were supposed to represent gold and silver coins. A bank that issued any more notes than it had gold and silver in its vaults was committing a fraud. Since *all* banks did so, including the Bank of the United States, Jackson considered them all dangerous. "I do not dislike your Bank any more than all banks," the President told Biddle. And he added that he was "afraid

Nicholas Biddle is the subject of this watercolor portrait by James Barton Longacre. How did Biddle attempt to stimulate the national economy?

of banks." For this tough old frontier fighter to admit that he was afraid of anything was most unusual. The Bank of the United States was in deep trouble.

Jackson also had more logical reasons for disliking the Bank. He believed that its conservative policies had caused a depression in 1819. And he was convinced that a private corporation ought not to have so much power over the nation's economy. The fact that Biddle had used the Bank to influence political events angered him further. Biddle had employed Senator Daniel Webster and other opponents of Jackson, and he made loans to newspaper editors who supported anti-Jackson candidates.

- Why did state-chartered banks dislike the Bank of the United States?
- For what reasons did President Jackson dislike the Bank of the United States?

THE BANK VETO

Biddle and supporters of the Bank in Congress knew that Jackson hoped to destroy it. They decided to introduce a bill in Congress to recharter the Bank in 1832, four years before its charter would ex-

In this political cartoon President Jackson attacks the many-headed Bank of the United States. Center is Nicholas Biddle in his top hat. The heads of the 24 bank directors spring up from the "nasty varmint." Jackson cuts with his 'veto stick,' aided by Vice President Van Buren, who is choking Massachusetts and Delaware. Why did Jackson veto the bank bill?

pire. This would extend the charter before campaigning began for the Presidential election of 1832.

Jackson could sign the bill if he believed the Bank was popular, or he could veto it. If he signed it, the Bank would be safe. If he vetoed it, his decision could be used against him in the election. Perhaps he would be defeated. Then Congress could pass another recharter bill which the new President would sign.

Jackson vetoed the bill. He gave many reasons: The Bank was unconstitutional. It was a dangerous financial monopoly. It allowed a few wealthy investors to make profits from "the earnings of the American people." Many of its stockholders were foreigners.

Some of these arguments made little sense. But most ordinary people were impressed by Jackson's attack on monopoly and uncontrolled wealth. The veto was very popular. The Bank was still in business, but its charter was running out. In the election Jackson defeated his opponent, Henry Clay, by 219 electoral votes to 49.

■ Why was Jackson's bank veto so popular?

BOOM AND BUST

Jackson then set out to close down the Bank of the United States. He began to withdraw the government money that was already in the Bank to pay bills. At the same time he stopped depositing government money in the Bank. Instead he ordered that the income from taxes and land sales be deposited in various state banks. Jackson's opponents charged that the government was showing favoritism in this matter. They called banks that received these deposits "Jackson's pets" or "pet banks." This was somewhat unfair because the money was soon spread out among nearly 100 different state banks.

Biddle tried to fight back by forcing state banks to convert their paper money to gold. This was done to limit the number of business loans they could make. His policies only turned more people against the Bank. Many of the banks began to lend money recklessly. More and more bank notes were put into circulation.

With so much paper money available, prices began to rise rapidly. Many people borrowed money in order to buy land. The price of city lots soared. As the price of land rose, more people hastened to buy land. The federal government sold undeveloped western lands in enormous amounts. In 1832 government land sales came to $2.6 million. Four years later the total was nearly $25 million.

Jackson's battle with the Bank outlasted his time in office. In 1837 there was an **inflationary spiral**—that is, a continuous rise in prices when the higher cost of one product or service causes the prices of other goods and services to go up too. This inflationary spiral, called a **boom,** ended as most booms do in a sudden collapse of prices

Library of Congress

"I have no money, and cannot get any work," says the worried father. The Panic of 1837 brings hard times for the hungry children and mother. She asks, "Cannot you contrive to get some food for the children?" A son suggests "specie claws," which is worthless paper money. Eviction notice in hand, the landlord waits at the door. What was the fate of banks after the Panic of 1837?

and business activity. This collapse, the **Panic of 1837,** was followed by a period when economic activity generally slowed down. This is called a **depression.** Worried depositors all over the country suddenly began rushing to the banks to change their bank notes into gold or silver. Banks swiftly ran out of coin and had to close their doors.

■ How did Jackson try to close the Bank of the United States?
■ What was the result of reckless lending and putting more and more bank notes into circulation?

THE SOUTHERN INDIANS

The third great issue of Jackson's Presidency was the "removal" of the southern Indians to undeveloped territory west of the Mississippi River. In 1830 about 120,000 Indians still occupied parts of Florida, Georgia, Alabama, and Mississippi.

These southern Indian tribes would not agree to blend into white society. They insisted on keeping their tribal governments, so there were what amounted to governments within governments in these states. The Indians' attitude was understandable. The southern states treated Indians almost as harshly as they did black slaves. They did not allow Indians to vote or testify in court. Yet they wished to tax them and make them serve in the state militia. They refused to recognize the existence of tribal governments.

Jackson backed up the states in these matters. In the opinion of Chief Justice John Marshall in the case of *Worcester v. Georgia* (1832), Georgia law did not extend to the **Cherokee Nation,** which was located entirely within that state. Jackson refused to enforce the Court's decree. "John Marshall has made his decision," the President is supposed to have said. "Now let him enforce it."

Although he had been a fierce Indian fighter, Jackson did not hate Indians. He respected their courage and fighting ability. But since they were unwilling to give up their ancient customs and way of life, he believed they should move to open territory west of the Mississippi River.

This seemed a reasonable proposal to the President. After all, he explained, every year thousands of white Americans left family and friends "to seek new homes in distant regions."

But since it would be unfair and maybe dangerous to try to force the Indians to move, Jackson set out to persuade them to go. He offered to pay for their present lands, to transport them west at government expense, and to give them new land beyond the frontier. The place chosen was west of Arkansas in what is now Oklahoma.

- In what sense did the southern Indians have governments within governments?
- How did Jackson attempt to persuade the southern Indians to move west?

INDIAN REMOVAL

In 1830 Congress passed a **Removal Act** providing money to carry out Jackson's policy of Indian removal. The first Indians approached were the **Choctaws,** who lived in central Mississippi. In September 1830 government agents organized a great conference at Dancing Rabbit Creek in Mississippi. Between 5,000 and 6,000 Choctaws attended. The agents supplied food for this huge gathering. They distributed cloth, soap, razors, and other gifts. They promised the Choctaws land in the West, free transportation, expense money for a year while they were settling in their new home, and annual grants to support the tribal government. Any Choctaw who wished to remain in Mississippi as an individual farmer would be given a plot of land. Failure to move, agents warned, could mean destruction of their society by Mississippi whites. The federal government could offer them no protection.

In the **Treaty of Dancing Rabbit Creek** the Choctaws accepted these terms. Jackson was eager to carry out the removal smoothly. As one government agent put it, if the removal could be handled well, it would "break the ice and pave the way for future removals." A full year was devoted to preparations. Still, the move was badly managed.

The first group of Indians set out during the winter of 1831–32. That winter turned out to be bitterly cold, even in Mississippi and Arkansas. Many died of exposure and starvation. Later groups in 1832 and 1833 fared better. All in all, about 15,000 Choctaws settled be-

Did travelers on the Trail of Tears have this much dignity, such warm blankets and sturdy ponies? Or has the artist Robert Lindneux painted an ideal picture of Indian removal? This oil depicts the trek westward in 1831–32. In the well-organized party even the dog at the far left helps carry. What may be a truer picture is "Choctaw Removal," from which the detail on the opposite page is taken. Thinly clad walkers fight wintry winds and snow. This 20th-century painting is by Valjean Hessing, an American Indian. Why were the Choctaws removed?

yond the Mississippi. The federal government had cut costs of the relocation wherever possible. Sometimes the Indians were supplied with spoiled meat and other bad food. Even so, the move still cost much more than had been expected. Nevertheless, Jackson went ahead with the Indian removal policy. More than 45,000 southern Indians were resettled.

By the 1840s scarcely an Indian remained in the southern states. The tribes that were removed had suffered heavy losses. For the moment the survivors were free to go their own way, but not for long.

- What was the outcome of the Treaty of Dancing Rabbit Creek?
- How did the federal government handle the removal of the Choctaws?

The most tragic story of Indian removal was that of the Cherokees of Georgia. Of all the American Indians, the Cherokees made the greatest effort to accept white customs. They developed a written language and published their own newspaper. They drafted a written constitution for the Cherokee Nation. Many took up farming. Some built houses similar to those of the whites. They even copied their white neighbors by buying a considerable number of black slaves!

The Cherokees would not surrender their independence. They fought against removal in the federal courts. When the Supreme Court upheld their claims, President Jackson ignored the Court's decision. In 1835 a small group of Cherokees agreed to go west, but the vast majority still refused.

In 1838 Martin Van Buren, Jackson's successor as President, sent General Winfield Scott to Georgia with orders to round up the Cherokees and force them to leave the area. Seven thousand soldiers swiftly herded together 15,000 Cherokees and marched them off. They were forced to leave nearly all their possessions behind. About 4,000 of them died on the long Trail of Tears to Oklahoma. It was, one white soldier later recorded, "the cruelest work I ever knew."

The Trail of Tears

Philbrook Art Center

THE LOG CABIN CAMPAIGN OF 1840

Martin Van Buren had been Secretary of State during Jackson's first term and Vice President during his second. Van Buren came from New York. He was a small, red-haired man, one of the shrewdest politicians of his day. He was so clever at political dealing that he was frequently called "the Little Magician" or "the Red Fox."

In 1836, with Jackson's approval, the new Democratic party nominated Van Buren for President. When the opposition, now calling itself the **Whig** party, put up three different Presidential candidates, Van Buren won the election easily. He got 170 electoral votes, while his closest opponent, General William Henry Harrison, received only 73.

As President, Van Buren was hurt by the economic depression that followed the Panic of 1837. Many state banks closed. Others had shaky finances. The federal government had no safe place to store tax payments and other income. At Van Buren's urging, Congress established an **Independent Treasury System.** Thereafter, all money due the government was to be paid in gold or silver. This money was simply stored in government vaults until needed.

In 1840 Van Buren sought reelection. This time the Whigs united behind General Harrison. They correctly guessed that this old

341

BUILDING SKILLS IN SOCIAL STUDIES

Photographs as Primary Sources

On this page are the likenesses of the first three Presidents of the United States to sit before the camera. It is with a start that we peer this far into the past. The camera makes it possible for us to see the actual images of all but 5 of the 40 Presidents. Because the camera is so honest, a photograph is an ideal *primary source*.

John Quincy Adams, *upper right*, appears in a daguerreotype taken by Philip Haas in 1843. This image was made by an early version of today's camera.

Andrew Jackson, *below*, managed to sit for this picture in 1845. By that time he was fatally ill but still of sound mind.

Martin Van Buren, *lower right*, posed for Matthew Brady in about 1856. Brady later became famous as a Civil War photographer.

Portraits or photographs of each of the 40 Presidents await your study in this book.

Metropolitan Museum of Art

George Eastman House

National Portrait Gallery

Indian fighter would have an appeal to voters similar to that of Andrew Jackson. Their strategy was the **Log Cabin Campaign.**

In 1828 the Democrats had ignored most issues and concentrated on describing the virtues of that friend of the common man and savior of his country, Andrew Jackson. Now the Whigs sang the praises of "Old Tippecanoe," the conqueror of Tecumseh. Harrison was a simple man of the people, the Whigs claimed. He lived in a log cabin

Western Reserve Historical Society/Smithsonian Institution

This 1840 campaign banner is of William Henry Harrison astride a white horse, approaching his log cabin. The former frontier fighter, 68 years old when he took office, sits ramrod straight. Harrison was in real life a Virginia aristocrat. What charges did the Whigs make against President Van Buren?

and always had a warm welcome for strangers. He drank that wonderful beverage of the people, homemade hard cider, right out of the jug. On the other hand, the Whigs insisted, Van Buren was an aristocrat who dined off gold plates in the White House and misused the people's money on expensive French wines. When Van Buren tried to discuss issues such as the tariff and banking policy, they shouted, "Van, Van, is a used-up man." Then they launched into speeches describing the Battle of Tippecanoe. At every Whig gathering cider flowed freely.

These tactics worked perfectly. The campaign was mindless but very exciting. Voters by the thousands were fascinated. In the election of 1836, 1.5 million citizens had gone to the polls. In 1840 the total soared to 2.4 million. Harrison won by a big margin, 234 electoral votes to 60. The ideas set in motion by the Jacksonians in 1828 had proved unbeatable. American politics would never be the same.

How did the Whigs win the election of 1840?

CHAPTER 11 REVIEW

Identification
Tell briefly why each of the following persons, terms, or events is important.

1. James Monroe
2. John Quincy Adams
3. Andrew Jackson
4. Henry Clay
5. John C. Calhoun
6. Nicholas Biddle
7. Martin Van Buren
8. William Henry Harrison
9. Era of Good Feelings
10. American System
11. Internal improvements
12. Spoils of office
13. Tariff of Abominations
14. Nullification Crisis
15. Pet banks
16. Panic of 1837
17. Treaty of Dancing Rabbit Creek
18. Cherokee Nation
19. Trail of Tears
20. Log Cabin Campaign

Understanding American History

1. What is meant by the "Era of Good Feelings"? Why did it end?
2. How was Henry Clay's American System to help both westerners and easterners?
3. Describe the major economic differences among the Northeast, the South, and the West after the Era of Good Feelings.
4. What was the "corrupt bargain" President Adams was accused of making? How did it affect the election of 1828?
5. What was Jacksonian democracy? What two reforms in elections did it lead to?
6. Explain Calhoun's idea of nullification. Why was nullification a threat to the future of the United States?
7. How did the Tariff of Abominations lead to the Nullification Crisis?
8. Why did Jackson veto the rechartering of the Second Bank of the United States?
9. Describe Jackson's removal of the southern Indians to western lands.
10. Who was "Old Tippecanoe"? Describe his campaign in the election of 1840.

Activities

1. Working in teams, prepare multimedia presentations to give in class on one section of the country—Northeast, South, or West—in the early 1830s. Give an accurate picture of life in one region. Describe work and home, reporting on as many details as you can find by library research.
2. Make a model or a large-scale drawing of a southern plantation. Explain its importance in the economy of the South. Then, based on your outside reading and research, describe a day on a typical plantation. Have other classmates do the same for the Conestoga wagon in the West and the merchant ships of the Northeast.
3. Prepare and deliver in class a brief campaign speech to endorse one of these four candidates for the Presidency in 1824: John Quincy Adams, William H. Crawford, Andrew Jackson, or Henry Clay. Learn about your candidate by reading and research. Then try to persuade others to vote for your candidate in a class mock election.
4. A Cherokee named Sequoyah invented what is called a syllabary—a system that permitted writing the sounds of spoken Cherokee in 85 different characters. By 1828 a weekly newspaper was published in the Cherokee language. Use your historical imagination to prepare reports for the Cherokee newspaper about events leading to Indian removal in the 1830s and the Trail of Tears.
5. Political slogans were chanted throughout the 1840 Log Cabin Campaign. Report on slogans used to elect Ronald Reagan in 1980, or research a Presidential election of the 1960s or 1970s for your report.

CHAPTER 11 TEST

Matching (30 points)
Number your paper 1–10 and match the description in the first column with the name in the second column.

1. President of the Second Bank of the United States
2. Vice President and later senator from South Carolina
3. Popular Secretary of the Treasury from Georgia
4. President during the Era of Good Feelings
5. Chief Justice of the Supreme Court
6. Proposed the American System to bind East and West
7. "Little Magician" who later became President
8. Accused of a "corrupt bargain" to win the Presidency
9. "Old Tippecanoe" who became President in 1840.
10. The President of the "common man"

a. James Monroe
b. John Quincy Adams
c. Andrew Jackson
d. Henry Clay
e. John C. Calhoun
f. William Crawford
g. William Henry Harrison
h. Martin Van Buren
i. Nicholas Biddle
j. John Marshall

Classifying (20 points)
Number your paper 11–20. Classify the following statements by writing *NE* if it is a characteristic of the Northeast, *S* for the South, or *W* for the West.

11. Tobacco and cotton were major crops.
12. This was the major manufacturing area of the nation.
13. Most people here favored building roads and canals.
14. This region had the most important seaports.
15. Slaves worked on large plantations.
16. Most people here were against high tariffs.
17. The largest cities were in this region.
18. The United States grew mainly in this direction.
19. Most people here favored high tariffs.
20. The idea of nullification had appeal here.

Completion (20 points)
Number your paper 21–25 and next to each number write the words that best complete each sentence.

21. At national meetings called _____, candidates for President and Vice President are chosen by party leaders.
22. The idea that winners of elections should reward supporters with jobs is called the _____.
23. The Tariff of Abominations was a high tax on _____.
24. A _____ is a time when economic activity is very slow.
25. Harrison's plan to win the Presidency in 1840 was the _____.

Essay (30 points)
Write a brief essay explaining President Jackson's position on *two* of the following issues and what action he took: a) nullification, b) the Second Bank of the United States, c) Indian removal.

CHAPTER 12

Manifest Destiny

William Henry Harrison took the oath of office as President on March 4, 1841. He was 68 years old, then the oldest man elected President. Exactly one month later, on April 4, he died of pneumonia. His successor, Vice President John Tyler of Virginia, was 50, the youngest President up to that time.

"Tippecanoe and Tyler too" was the Whig campaign slogan in 1840. But Harrison died one month after his swearing in, and John Tyler became President. This is his Presidential portrait by George Peter Alexander Healy, painted in oil in 1859. Why had the Whigs nominated Tyler?

"HIS ACCIDENCY" THE PRESIDENT

John Tyler was the first Vice President to become President because of the death of his running mate. He was not a success as President. The Whig party had nominated him only because he was a former Democrat who had opposed the policies of Andrew Jackson. They had not taken the trouble to study his own position on important issues.

When Henry Clay and other Whigs in Congress attempted to push through a bill creating a new Bank of the United States, they discovered that Tyler considered a federal bank unconstitutional. He vetoed the bill.

The Whig politicians were furious. They referred to Tyler as "His Accidency" instead of "His Excellency." Unfortunately, neither they nor later political leaders learned from this experience. Even today much less attention is paid to the qualifications of Vice Presidential candidates than Presidential ones. Yet eight Vice Presidents have become President because of the death of their running mates.

■ Why did Whigs call John Tyler "His Accidency"?

THE TEXAS QUESTION

Since they disliked him so much, the Whigs did not nominate Tyler for a second term in 1844. Instead they chose Henry Clay, even though he had been defeated for that office twice before, in 1824 and 1832. The Democrats were expected to nominate former President Martin Van Buren.

But a new issue had developed by 1844 that caught even experienced politicians like Clay and Van Buren by surprise. This issue caused Van Buren to lose the Democratic nomination to James K.

346

Polk, a former governor of Tennessee. Polk was what is called a **dark horse** candidate. A dark horse is one who seems to have no chance at the start of a convention but wins the nomination when the favored candidate or candidates cannot obtain the required majority of the convention delegates.

The new issue was whether or not the Republic of Texas should be **annexed,** or added to the Union as a state. As we have seen, Texas lay on the Spanish side of the boundary negotiated by John Quincy Adams in the Transcontinental Treaty of 1819. Two years later, Texas became part of independent Mexico when that nation revolted against Spain.

At that time hardly anyone lived in Texas, but pioneers were beginning to trickle in. One of the first was Stephen F. Austin, a judge from Arkansas Territory. In 1821 Austin obtained permission from the Mexican government to bring in 300 families, each of whom was given a large grant of land. Most of these settlers grew cotton on their land. They prospered. More immigrants from the United States followed. By 1830 there were about 22,000 of them in Texas, 20,000 whites and 2,000 black slaves.

Stephen Austin became a citizen of Mexico and for several years was governor of the province of Texas. Most of the United States immigrants felt no loyalty to Mexico. There were so few native Mexicans in Texas that the United States immigrants began to feel that Texas was their country and that they were the real Texans. Few troubled to learn Spanish. When the Mexican government abolished slavery in the nation, the Texans found tricky legal ways to keep control of their slaves.

- What new issue surprised politicians in the Presidential election of 1844?
- Why did the United States immigrants to Texas come to feel it was their country?

TEXAS WINS ITS INDEPENDENCE

Government leaders in Mexico City naturally disliked the Texans' attitude. They tried to stop further immigration to Texas. When Austin came to Mexico City to explain the feelings of the Texans, he was thrown in jail and held for a year without trial. Finally, in 1835, the Texans revolted.

The President of Mexico, Antonio López de Santa Anna, marched northward at the head of his army to put down the rebellion. In February 1836 he captured the town of San Antonio. But 155 Texans in the town retreated into the **Alamo,** the stronghold built by the Spanish missionaries. They refused to surrender. Another 32 men later joined them under siege.

James K. Polk, the first dark horse, was a strong President, a promoter of westward growth. He worked so hard that he died a few months after leaving office. This portrait in oil is by Max Westfield (after one made by G. P. A. Healy), painted in 1882. Who was the nominee of the Whigs in the election of 1844?

Stephen F. Austin is often called the 'Father of Texas.' He is seen as a young man in this oil painted in the 1830s. How did Austin lead the pioneer settlement of Texas?

Antonio López de Santa Anna was the general who called himself the Napoleon of the West. But he lost a leg fighting the French at Veracruz in 1838. In 1836 his Mexican army began their siege of the Alamo, in San Antonio, against 187 Texans. Below, Davy Crockett swings his rifle Betsy. By nightfall on March 6 these fighters lay dead—Crockett, Bowie, Travis, all 187. The Texan who painted this scene is Robert Ondermonk. Who built the Alamo?

Santa Anna's army attacked the Alamo again and again. Repeatedly his men were driven back with heavy losses. But after ten days of fighting, they broke into the Alamo. Then every one of the defenders, even the wounded, were killed on the spot. Among the dead were Davy Crockett, a colorful frontier character who had represented Tennessee in Congress, and James Bowie, who is thought to have designed the Bowie knife.

Enraged Texans now declared themselves independent. They appointed Sam Houston commander of the Texas army. For a time Houston retreated eastward. Then, at **San Jacinto,** he turned and attacked the Mexicans. It was a small battle. Houston had only 783 soldiers, Santa Anna about 1,300. Yet this battle determined who would win the war. On the afternoon of April 21, Houston surprised the Mexican soldiers. The Texans broke through Santa Anna's defenses, making effective use of two cannon, which they nicknamed "the Twin Sisters." "Forward!" Houston shouted. "Charge! *Remember the Alamo!*"

The Texans rushed into the Mexican camp, this slogan on their lips. The Mexicans fought bravely but were soon defeated. Many died. The others fell back in disorder, calling out fearfully "*Me no Alamo,*" although in fact these were the very men who had slaughtered the defenders of the mission.

The victory was total. "The fierce vengeance of the Texans could not be resisted," Houston later explained. Santa Anna was captured. But instead of killing him, Houston wisely gave him his freedom in

exchange for his promise to take his army out of Texas. The **Republic of Texas** then elected Houston its first president.

The people of the republic, however, were eager to see Texas become one of the United States. Andrew Jackson, who was still President at the time, was unwilling to accept Texas. He was worried about the political problem that might result if another slave state were admitted to the Union. The next President, Van Buren, took the same position.

President Tyler, being a southerner, favored admitting Texas. He had his Secretary of State negotiate a treaty of annexation in 1844. The Senate refused to ratify this agreement. That is why the Democrats rejected Van Buren as their 1844 Presidential candidate and nominated Polk, who favored both slavery and the annexation of Texas. To balance this pro-southern policy, Polk proposed ending the agreement for joint control of the Oregon country with Great Britain. The United States should take over all that area, which extended far beyond the present northern boundary of the nation.

■ Why did Sam Houston tell his men to "remember the Alamo" when they went into battle?
■ Why did President Jackson oppose statehood for Texas?

Sam Houston, an adopted son of the Cherokee, commanded Texas's army. He sits astride his horse in this oil painted by Steven Seymour Thomas. In his later years, while Houston was governor of Texas, he refused to be part of the stampede to secede from the Union and was removed from his office. Why did Houston grant Santa Anna his freedom in 1836?

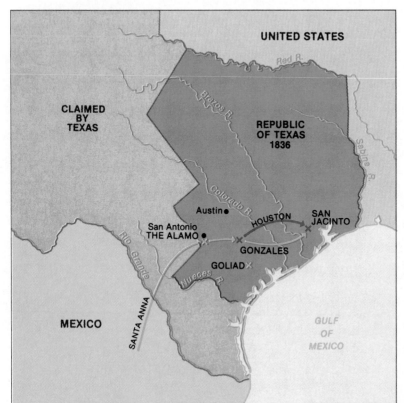

TEXAS WINS ITS INDEPENDENCE FROM MEXICO 1835-36

⟶ Texans
✕ Texan victory
⟶ Mexicans
✕ Mexican victory

0   300 Mi.
0   300 Km.

BUILDING SKILLS IN SOCIAL STUDIES

Using Art as a Primary Source

A painting such as Asher Durands's "Progress," below, may be studied as a *primary source*. It gives first-hand information—one artist's view of America during that time in its history known as *manifest destiny*. Even if the term "manifest destiny" is a new one, a first glance at the picture suggests that it had something to do with Nature and the vast reaches of America.

Manifest destiny was a belief in the 1840s that the United States was meant to overspread the continent "from sea to shining sea." Durand shared this belief when he exhibited "Progress" in 1853. Another title for it is "The Advance of Civilization." The painting is full of clues that Durand had an optimistic view of American progress—from the seemingly endless hills rolling westward to the new cities springing up along the riverbanks.

Study the painting carefully. See how many of these symbols of "civilization" you can find.

1. Noble American Indians gazing down from their rocky perch upon a growing America.
2. A peaceful, productive farm, the basis of American economy in the 19th century.
3. Canal barges, linking East to West, an early sign of technological progress.
4. A mill on the water, drawing from a plentiful source of energy.
5. A church, symbol of American faith.
6. A sprawling city where industry already sends smoke into the clear skies.
7. Telegraph poles spanning the continent.

Use the same step-by-step technique to discuss the painting on page 351 as a primary source. Its caption will help you study its parts.

Warner Collection, Gulf States Paper Corp., Tuscaloosa, Ala.

Museum of the City of New York

MANIFEST DESTINY

Now westward expansion became a hot political issue. In the 1840s the speed of westward expansion was picking up. For 200 years moving west had seemed like climbing up a steep incline—slow and difficult work. It was as though North America were an enormous plank balanced just west of the Mississippi River like a seesaw. Once the midpoint was passed, the balance tilted. The road ahead now seemed downhill, therefore easy.

People rushed westward eagerly. Suddenly it appeared possible that the entire continent might be theirs! This new attitude was given a name by a writer named John L. O'Sullivan. It was, O'Sullivan announced, the **manifest destiny**—that is, the obvious future role of the people of the United States—"to overspread the continent."

The way west only seemed easy. Wild animals and mighty forests lay in the path of eastern travelers. John Adams had written of "conquering" the West "from the trees and rocks and wild beasts." The pioneers of the 1840s had to cross rugged and dangerous country to reach the Pacific Coast. But neither the Rocky Mountains nor the great western desert could stop them. One enthusiastic speaker referred to the Rockies as "mere molehills."

The movement west began in the 1830s when a few Christian

This picture, "Westward the Course of Empire Takes Its Way," is in more American histories than any other by Currier & Ives. No other engraving seems to show as well how hopefully people looked westward in the 1830s. Symbols of progress are everywhere: the puffing railroad locomotive on its endless tracks, the hardworking men and women who cleared the land to build their school and church in the foreground, and the covered wagons departing this settlement for farther frontiers. The engraving was made by Fanny Palmer and James M. Ives in 1868. Ives and Nathaniel Currier were America's most popular makers of hand-colored prints. How is the main title of this engraving, "Across the Continent," another way to say manifest destiny?

351

THE UNITED STATES

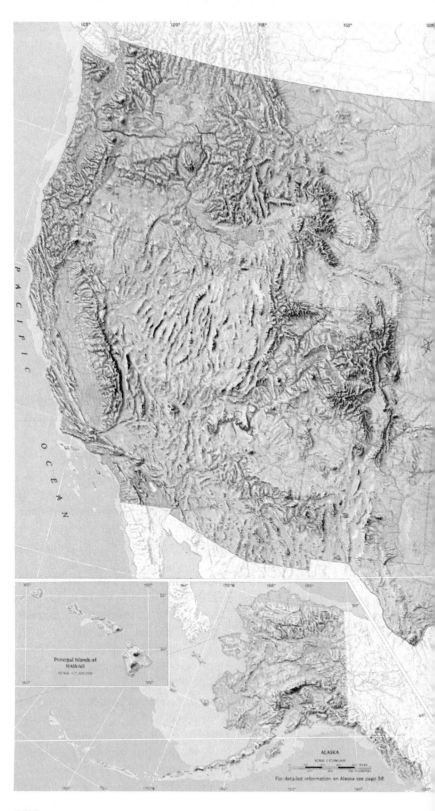

The map on these pages shows the United States in *physical relief.* By studying the color key at right, you can see which are the lowest and highest areas, or *elevation.* Notice especially the rugged lands of the western third of the nation that had to be crossed by the pioneers who were fired with the idea of manifest destiny.

LAKE SUPERIOR

LAKE MICHIGAN

LAKE HURON

LAKE ONTARIO

LAKE ERIE

ATLANTIC OCEAN

ELEVATION TINTS

SHADED RELIEF

Richard Edes Harrison, 1969

Albers Equal Area Projection

SCALE 1:7,500,000

353

missionaries settled in the **Willamette Valley** in Oregon. They had little success in persuading the local Indians to become Christians. But their descriptions of the country gradually attracted more easterners. By 1840 about 120 families were living there.

Others were making their way to the Mexican province of California. John A. Sutter was one of the first from the United States to do so. Sutter had immigrated to New York City from Switzerland in 1834. From New York he had made his way to Oregon. Then he sailed to the Hawaiian Islands. In Hawaii he purchased a ship and transported a cargo of local produce to San Francisco.

Somehow Sutter persuaded the Mexican governor of California to grant him a large tract of land in the Sacramento River valley. He settled on the American River, a branch of the Sacramento, in 1839. Gradually he built a fortified town, which he called **Sutter's Fort.** The entire place was surrounded by a thick wall 18 feet high (about 6 meters) topped with cannon for protection against unfriendly Indians. Sutter's Fort attracted weary, westward-moving pioneers the way a magnet attracts iron.

- What was meant by manifest destiny?
- How did the settlers of Willamette Valley persuade others to settle in Oregon?
- What was the importance of Sutter's Fort?

This engraving shows Sutter's Fort on the American River. John Sutter called his original settlement New Helvetia, after a poetic name for Switzerland. Sacramento, the state capital of California, stands today on the site, where the remains of Sutter's Fort may be visited. How had Sutter obtained his land?

Scottsbluff National Monument

THE OREGON TRAIL

From small beginnings there came a mass movement westward in 1843. All over the eastern states people caught what they called "Oregon fever" and prepared to move west. They gathered in groups in western Missouri to make the 2,000-mile voyage (3,200 kilometers) over the **Oregon Trail.** This trail followed the Platte River to Fort Laramie in Wyoming and then crossed the Rockies by way of South Pass before descending to Oregon along the Snake and Columbia Rivers.

One such group set out on May 21, 1843. One of its guides was the Reverend Marcus Whitman, an early missionary settler in Oregon who had returned east on church business. Almost a thousand people were involved. They rode in 120 canvas-covered wagons pulled by oxen. About 5,000 cattle and a small army of dogs accompanied them.

Such a large group was really a community on wheels. It had to be governed and, when whites pushed into Indian country, ruled like

"Barlow Cut-Off" is the title given by William H. Jackson to this 1930 oil painting. It shows a caravan of covered wagons as they cross the continent on the Oregon Trail. How far did they travel?

an army. An elected council of ten settled disputes. A guide or pilot planned the route and decided where and when to stop for food and rest. Each wagon had its special place in the caravan. A bugler summoned everyone to rise at dawn and signaled the time to settle down for the night. Each night the wagons were formed in a great circle as protection against possible Indian attack.

The group traveled 15 or 20 miles (24 to 32 kilometers) on an average day. Getting the entire company across a river could take as long as five days, for there were no ferries or bridges along the way. Nevertheless, progress was steady. On October 27, 1843, the caravan reached the Willamette Valley safely.

The next year five groups made the trip overland to Oregon and California. Although California belonged to Mexico and control of Oregon was in dispute with the British, these pioneers gave no thought to the fact that they were going to foreign countries. In this respect they were like the people who were settling Texas. Here is a song people sung on the Oregon Trail:

The hip-hurrah for the prairie life!
Hip-hurrah for the mountain strife!
And if rifles must crack, if swords we must draw,
Our country forever, hurrah, hurrah!

▓ In what sense were the wagons moving westward "a community on wheels"?

TAKING TEXAS AND OREGON

The mood of the country was aggressive and confident. In such an atmosphere the Presidential election was held. James K. Polk emerged the winner.

Polk had promised to bring both Texas and Oregon into the Union. He was soon able to do so.

Congress voted to annex Texas a few months after the election. In December 1845 Texas became a state. At the same time Polk began diplomatic negotiations with the British about Oregon. He made it clear that if England did not agree to a satisfactory settlement, he was ready to take the territory by force. The British had no stomach for a fight over Oregon. But they were unwilling to surrender all of the area. In 1846, after considerable discussion, the negotiators reached a compromise. The territory was divided by extending the already existing boundary between the United States and Canada to the West Coast.

▓ How did Texas become a state?
▓ How was the dispute with the British over the Oregon territory settled?

Texas Memorial Museum, Austin

The Lone Star flag was adopted as the national banner of Texas while the Alamo was under siege. It is today the state flag.

WAR WITH MEXICO

Annexing Texas led to war. Although Mexico had not been able to prevent Texas from becoming independent, the Mexicans did not accept the Texans' claim that the new republic extended all the way to the Rio Grande, the "Great River." They insisted that the Nueces, a river farther to the east, was the boundary between Mexico and Texas.

National Portrait Gallery

General Zachary Taylor, kerchief at his neck, is seen with his aides at Walnut Springs in 1847. Earlier these soldiers fought the battles of the Mexican War. One of them, Braxton Bragg is sixth from right. He became a general himself for the Confederacy later in the Civil War. William Carl Brown, Jr. is the painter of this oil. Why had President Polk ordered Taylor to march to the Rio Grande?

After Texas was annexed, President Polk sent troops commanded by General Zachary Taylor across the Nueces River. Then he sent a diplomatic representative, John Slidell, to Mexico City. The Mexican leaders were unwilling even to discuss the boundary question. National pride was involved. The Mexicans once again stated their claim for all of Texas. Polk then ordered General Taylor to march straight to the Rio Grande. When he did so, a Mexican force promptly crossed the river and attacked one of his patrols. When word of this skirmish reached Washington, Congress declared war on Mexico on May 13, 1846.

Mexico was a large country and far from the supply depots of the United States. Yet the United States forces quickly defeated the Mexican armies. General Taylor was not a brilliant commander, but his troops were devoted to him and also very well trained. By the end of the summer of 1846 they had won three major battles. Then, in February 1847, in the **Battle of Buena Vista** they soundly defeated the last important Mexican force in northern Mexico.

The famous Bear Flag of California first flew over Sonoma, north of San Francisco, in 1848.

Mexico City fell to the U.S. Army in September 1847. General Scott and his troops are shown riding in triumph into the great plaza at the heart of the city. How had Scott moved his troops to Mexico City?

In California other United States units, including a naval squadron and a militia force raised by residents of the area around Sutter's Fort, defeated the small Mexican forces based in the Southwest. The victors announced the founding of the **Republic of California.** They designed a simple flag, a grizzly bear on a plain background. By February 1847 the important California towns of San Francisco, Los Angeles, and San Diego had been won from Mexico.

- Why did the United States go to war with Mexico?
- What was the outcome of fighting between settlers and the Mexican forces in California?

THE CAPTURE OF MEXICO CITY

These early victories posed a political problem for President Polk. General Taylor had become a national hero. He was a plain, unassuming soldier made in the mold of William Henry Harrison and Andrew Jackson. His troops affectionately called him "Old Rough and Ready." Taylor belonged to the Whig party. Polk was afraid that Taylor might decide to run for President in 1848. The President had no intention of seeking a second term himself, but as a loyal

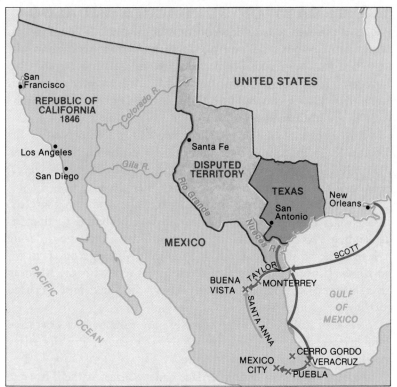

THE MEXICAN WAR 1846-47

→ Mexican forces

→ United States forces

× United States victory

Democrat he did not want Taylor to be *too* successful on the battle-field. He therefore put a different general, Winfield Scott, in command of the army which had the task of capturing Mexico City.

General Scott, a powerful man nearly six feet, six inches tall, was also a Whig. He lacked Taylor's easy-going style. He was stuffy and rather vain. Behind his back his troops called him "Old Fuss and Feathers." Scott therefore seemed less of a threat to the Democrats than Taylor. Fortunately for the nation, Scott was an excellent general, actually far more competent than Taylor.

Scott approached Mexico City from the sea. In March 1847 his fleet of 200 ships put 10,000 men ashore near the city of **Veracruz,** on Mexico's east coast. The United States army captured Veracruz easily and then marched inland. They won an important battle at **Cerro Gordo** and another at **Puebla.** By September they were at the outskirts of **Mexico City.**

There the showdown clash occurred. It was hard fought with 1,000 United States soldiers and 4,000 Mexican soldiers killed or wounded. But again Scott's troops were victorious. The capital city was occupied, the Mexicans forced to surrender.

■ Why did President Polk put General Winfield Scott in command of the army that was to capture Mexico City?

359

THE TREATY OF GUADALUPE HIDALGO

Polk had attached a state department official, Nicholas P. Trist, to Scott's army. Trist's task was to negotiate a peace treaty once the Mexicans had been defeated. In addition to insisting on the Rio Grande boundary of Texas, he was told by Polk to offer as much as $30 million if Mexico would sell California and the rest of the Southwest to the United States.

Trist proved to be an excellent negotiator. He persuaded the defeated Mexicans to turn over all that territory for a little more than $18 million. The negotiations took a great deal of time, however, because of the confusion in Mexico City after the battle.

President Polk became impatient and also somewhat greedy. Mexico had been so thoroughly beaten that he began to think of demanding even more territory. He sent Trist a message ordering him to break off the discussions and return to Washington. Trist ignored the order. He completed the negotiations with the Mexican government and sent the resulting **Treaty of Guadalupe Hidalgo** back to the United States.

President Polk was furious. Out of pure spite he had Trist fired from his state department job. He would not even pay Trist his salary for the time he had spent in Mexico.

Nevertheless, Polk found that he had to agree to the Treaty of Guadalupe Hidalgo. The terms, after all, were better than he had originally hoped for. The war had become extremely unpopular in some parts of the country. Particularly in the North, many people felt there had been no reason for seizing so much of Mexico over what was really a minor boundary dispute. Adding more territory where slavery might be established was another concern in the North. Polk therefore swallowed his anger and submitted the treaty to the Senate, which ratified it easily.

- Why did President Polk tell Nicholas Trist to break off negotiations with Mexico?
- Why did the President go along with the Treaty of Guadalupe Hidalgo?

CALIFORNIA AND THE RANCHEROS

The great prize that the United States won in the Mexican War was the province of California. In the 1840s most of the region beyond the Rocky Mountains was untouched by any other than its native Indians. But, as we have seen, the Spanish had been living in California and New Mexico since the late 1700s. By the 1830s there were 21 mission settlements in a kind of broken string from San Diego to Sonoma, north of San Francisco. The landholdings of the missions were enormous.

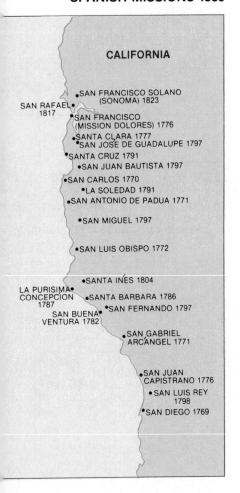

SPANISH MISSIONS 1830

CALIFORNIA

SAN FRANCISCO SOLANO (SONOMA) 1823
SAN RAFAEL 1817
SAN FRANCISCO (MISSION DOLORES) 1776
SANTA CLARA 1777
SAN JOSÉ DE GUADALUPE 1797
SANTA CRUZ 1791
SAN JUAN BAUTISTA 1797
SAN CARLOS 1770
LA SOLEDAD 1791
SAN ANTONIO DE PADUA 1771
SAN MIGUEL 1797
SAN LUIS OBISPO 1772
SANTA INÉS 1804
LA PURISIMA CONCEPCION 1787
SANTA BARBARA 1786
SAN FERNANDO 1797
SAN BUENA VENTURA 1782
SAN GABRIEL ARCANGEL 1771
SAN JUAN CAPISTRANO 1776
SAN LUIS REY 1798
SAN DIEGO 1769

Around the missions founded by the Spanish were clustered large Indian villages, for Father Junípero Serra and other priests had converted thousands of Indians to Christianity. These Indians were practically slaves. They did all the work that supported the missions. They tended large herds of cattle and grew corn, grapes, and other crops. They also made cloth, leather goods, wine, soap, and many other manufactured products.

The missions were so prosperous that other Mexicans demanded that the government open mission lands to settlers. In the early 1830s it did so. Thereafter any Mexican citizen with cattle could obtain a huge **rancho** free. These landholders were called **rancheros.** Within a few years 700 *ranchos* were established in California, most of them about 50,000 acres (20,000 hectares) in area. Each *ranchero* had an enormous amount of land.

Thomas Gilcrease Institute, Tulsa

The pride of the Spanish *rancheros* is evident in this color lithograph, titled "Hacendado y Su Mayordomo," "The Landowner and His Foreman." This drawing is by Julio Michaud, a Mexican artist. How were *ranchos* obtained from the government?

Life on one of these great ranches was rich but simple. People ate enormous quantities of meat at every meal. Horses were so plentiful that travelers merely lassoed a new one when their own mounts became tired. Most of the hard work of caring for the herds and raising crops was still done by the Indians, who were even worse off than when they had lived outside the missions.

Yet in spite of their wealth, the ranchers had few comforts and conveniences. Their homes were unheated and poorly furnished. Window glass was scarce. Most homes had dirt floors. People lived so far apart that they had few visitors. There were no newspapers. The days stretched out one after another.

- What was life like in the mission settlements of California?
- What was life like on one of the *ranchos* in California?

361

BUILDING SKILLS IN SOCIAL STUDIES

Finding Boundaries on a Map

During the 1840s the United States overspread the continent. At this time of manifest destiny the boundaries of new territories followed both *physical* and *political* divisions.

Physical boundaries are natural boundaries such as landforms or bodies of water that separate one area from another. Physical boundaries twist and turn on a map like the rivers that form boundaries between many of the states.

Political boundaries are likely to follow the straight lines of surveyors. U.S. state boundaries running east and west tend to be political. But boundaries running north and south are often both physical and political.

Study the map on this page carefully before you answer the following questions.
1. Which was the largest land area acquired?
2. Which three territories came from Mexico?
3. How did the U.S. acquire Texas?
4. How did the U.S. acquire Florida?

Tell whether each of the following is defined by a physical or political boundary, or both.
5. The border of Texas and Mexico?
6. The border of California and Oregon Country?
7. The borders of present-day Utah?
8. The borders of present-day Arizona?
9. Where is the longest political boundary?
10. In what direction did the U.S. grow?

MANIFEST DESTINY 1853

—— Territorial boundary line

····· Natural boundary line

—— Present-day state boundaries

THE MORMONS OF UTAH

The signing of the Treaty of Guadalupe Hidalgo increased interest in westward expansion. During the Mexican War one of the most remarkable migrations of American history had taken place into what is now Utah. This was the settlement that spread out next to the Great Salt Lake. It consisted of members of a uniquely American religious sect, the **Mormons.**

The Mormon religion was begun in the 1820s by Joseph Smith, a young farmer in western New York. According to Smith, an angel named Moroni gave him golden tablets on which was written the *Book of Mormon.* Smith's English version of the book was published in 1830. It became the basis of the Mormon Church.

Smith attracted many followers, and in 1831 he founded a new community in Ohio. In 1837 the Mormons moved to Missouri. In 1839 they moved again to a town they called **Nauvoo,** in Illinois. The close-knit, cooperative society that the hard-working Mormons developed enabled them to prosper. Nauvoo grew rapidly. By 1844 it was the largest city in Illinois, with a population of 15,000.

The Mormons adopted religious practices that tended to set them apart. One was polygamy, which permitted a man more than one wife at the same time. Smith also became quite domineering as the church grew. He organized a private army, the Nauvoo Legion. He refused to allow critics of his group to publish a newspaper in Nauvoo. By 1844 opposition to the Mormons in Illinois led to Smith's arrest. Then a mob formed. He was dragged from jail and lynched.

After the murder of Smith the Mormons decided that to practice their religion they would have to find a place far removed from other people. Brigham Young became their new leader. Young was

"Exodus from Nauvoo" recalls the Biblical Exodus of the Jews from Egypt. Here, Mormons in covered wagons leave their Illinois homes to resettle in the Great Salt Lake Valley. This scene is one of the 22 remarkable oil paintings made by C. C. A. Christensen, an artist from Denmark, who became a devout Mormon. He pulled his belongings West in a handcart. Years later he rolled up his paintings in order to travel in his wagon throughout all Utah to keep alive the memory of the Mormon Exodus. What kind of society had the Mormons founded at Nauvoo?

Brigham Young University

TRAILS TO THE WEST

present-day state boundaries

0 ———————— 600 Mi.

0 ———————— 600 Km.

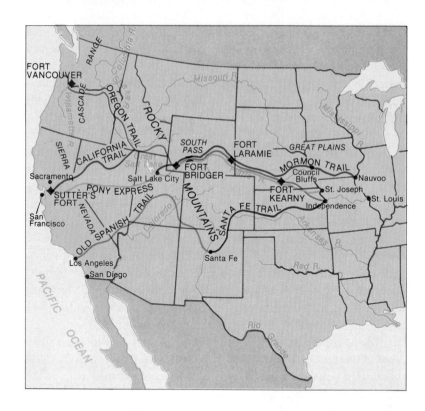

This fine daguerreotype of Brigham Young shows the Mormon leader in the later years of his life. Under his leadership Salt Lake City grew to a prosperous community and the territory of Utah was established. Why was Young so successful as a leader?

devoutly religious, handsome, and tremendously strong. He was also an excellent organizer. He realized that moving 15,000 people across the country would require very careful planning.

First he divided the Mormons into small groups. He himself led the first group west in 1846. The party proceeded slowly across Iowa, stopping to build camps and to plant crops at several points so that those who followed would have food and shelter. In western Iowa they built a large camp on the Missouri River. It contained nearly a thousand cabins.

Then, in April 1847, Young led a small advance party west. Now they moved swiftly. In July they reached a dry, sun-baked valley near Great Salt Lake. There they established **Salt Lake City,** their permanent home. Their route, followed by many later pioneers, came to be known as the **Mormon Trail.**

The Mormons' success was possible because Brigham Young had almost total control over the community. He headed both the church and the regular government. Most Mormons believed that Young was inspired by God. They considered him all-wise and devoted to their happiness. They accepted his leadership without questions.

- Why did the Mormons move westward?
- What are some of the reasons why the Mormons were able to successfully move so many people across the country?

364

The valley near Great Salt Lake was almost a desert. It was here upon the salt flats under the strong sun that the Mormons made their home. The streams running down from the mountains were ordered dammed up by Brigham Young. Irrigation ditches were dug so that fields could be watered and crops planted.

As more groups of Mormons arrived, the place became a beehive of activity. Indeed, a beehive is one of the symbols of the Mormon religion. Everything was organized to serve the common good.

Salt Lake City was a planned community. By 1849 it had broad streets lined with neat houses that were set off by well-tended gardens. The surrounding fields were rich with wheat, corn, and potatoes. There were large herds of cattle, horses, and sheep.

Passing travelers marveled at the Mormons' prosperity and at the speed with which they had turned their desert into a garden.

A Desert in Bloom

B. McKechnie—Shostal Associates

GOLD IN CALIFORNIA

John H. Gerard—DPI

By 1848 the Oregon travelers, the Mormons, and other westward-moving pioneers had made crossing the continent a fairly common experience. The trip was still long and tiring. Sometimes it could be dangerous. But the routes were well marked, and there were a number of forts and settlements along the way where travelers could rest and obtain fresh supplies.

After the Mexican War California attracted more easterners. Many of them settled in and around John A. Sutter's well-known fort on the American River. As the area developed, Sutter, with an eye to new business, expanded his activities. To supply lumber for new settlers, he decided to build a sawmill about 40 miles (64 kilometers) up the river from Sutter's Fort.

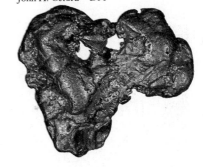

First the river bed next to the mill had to be dug out so that a large water wheel could be installed to produce power to run the saws. James W. Marshall was in charge of building the mill. During the digging he noticed bits of shiny yellow metal shimmering in the water. He collected some of them and had them tested. They were pure gold.

This discovery took place in January 1848. Other people then began to **prospect,** or search for, gold. When they found gold, they told friends about their good luck. More people became prospectors. By May the town of San Francisco was buzzing with the news. "Gold! Gold! *Gold* from the American River!"

This watercolor shows "William D. Peck, Rough and Ready, California." It was painted by Henry Walton in 1856. Perhaps Peck posed for this portrait to send to the folks back home. He holds a miner's scale. On the floor is a pan used to search for gold. What name was given to searchers for gold?

The Oakland Museum History Department

By the end of the year the whole country was talking about the discoveries. Then, in December 1848, President Polk himself announced that the gold was "more extensive and valuable" than had been thought.

◾ How was gold discovered in California in 1848?

THE FORTY-NINERS

After the President's announcement the **Gold Rush** was on. In 1848 at least 80,000 people came to California to look for gold. The historian Samuel Eliot Morison has described "the gold-fever of '49" in these words: "Farmers mortgaged their farms, workmen downed their tools, clerks left counting-rooms, and even ministers abandoned their pulpits."

Most of these **Forty-Niners** followed the overland trails across the Rocky Mountains. Some, however, took longer but more comfortable water routes. Some sailed from the East to Panama, crossed the isthmus on foot, and then sailed north to San Francisco. Others took the all-water route around South America.

Sometimes it took half a year to make the long ocean voyage. But for those who could afford the fare (about $1,000), **clipper ships** made the trip around in much less time. The sleek, three-masted clippers were incredibly fast. Several are known to have sailed over 400 miles (640 kilometers) in 24 hours. The best modern racing yachts have never approached their records.

The clipper ships were 200 to 300 feet (60-90 meters) or more in length. Their towering masts supported clouds of sails. Their sharp, graceful bows knifed through the seas smoothly. The most famous clipper ship was *Flying Cloud* designed by Donald McKay. In 1851 *Flying Cloud* sailed from Boston to San Francisco in 89 days, less than three months. Remember that it had taken Magellan 38 days just to sail through the Straits of Magellan!

> What were some of the means of travel used by the Forty-Niners to get from the East to California?

MINING CAMPS

Gold was worth $16 an ounce in 1849. About 10 million ounces (28 million grams) were mined in California that year. Production increased in 1850 and 1851. By 1852 100,000 prospectors were mining in California. They found 81 million ounces (2.3 billion grams) during that one year. Some miners became millionaires. Others made smaller fortunes. But most made very little.

When a miner found gold, he **staked a claim** to the spot. Then no one else could legally work that place. Soon dozens of other prospectors would flock to the surrounding area to stake out claims. Disputes about boundaries and other rights frequently broke out.

Villages called **mining camps** sprang up wherever gold was found. These camps were given colorful names such as Whiskey Flat, Hangtown, Roaring Camp, and Volcano. Life in the camps was uncomfortable, expensive, and sometimes very dangerous. A person could be flat broke one day and worth thousands of dollars the next.

Flying Cloud, the beautiful clipper ship, cuts the waves in this 20th-century oil painting by Frances Vining Smith. Below is an *allegory,* "Sunday Morning at the Mines," to show the struggle of evil on the left, good on the right. Charles Christian Nahl painted the scene in the 1870s. The bad miners break the Sabbath by rough riding to the gambling tent. But the good miners hear the Bible read aloud, while two wash clothes. How many miners had come to California by 1852?

Such an up-and-down life, combined with the hardships the miners faced, encouraged a devil-may-care attitude. Many miners were heavy drinkers and reckless gamblers. This situation attracted all sorts of thieves and tricksters, as well as shrewd business dealers, saloonkeepers, and merchants who sold the miners everything from pickaxes and tents to fancy clothes and fine horses at extremely high prices. As a group these types made far more money than the miners. Fighting in the mining camps—with fists, knives, and guns—was common.

People from all over the United States, from Mexico and South America, from Europe, and from as far away as China and Australia flocked to the gold regions. With so many people crowding into the camps, disputes of all kinds occurred. Mexican Californians were badly treated and often prevented from prospecting. The Chinese were also mistreated, although none of the gold seekers were more hard working. The local Indians were driven off by brute force, although as always they were the original settlers of the land. Blacks who made their way to the gold country also faced discrimination.

Nevertheless, some from these various groups found gold, and a few became rich. Two black miners, forced by white prospectors to dig in a most unpromising spot, hit a deposit so rich that the site was named Negro Hill. These two men found gold worth $80,000 in four months. By 1852 there were 2,000 blacks in California, half of them working in the mining area.

Despite the problems of camp life the majority of the prospectors and storekeepers in the mining country were decent people eager to found schools and churches and live at peace with one another. The difficulty was that most of the camps sprang up too quickly to establish orderly governments. They tended to be abandoned when the gold ran out. Then the prospectors rushed off to other strikes in other regions. The old camps became **ghost towns,** inhabited only by a stray cat or two or a few hermits or vagabonds.

■ What was life like in the gold-mining camps of California?

SLAVERY IN THE SOUTHWEST

Adding California to the Union caused new problems. In the past the movement of white settlers into new lands had forced most of the native Indian population to retreat westward. But the California Indians had their backs to the ocean. As a result those who had not been forced to labor on the great California ranches were practically wiped out by the invading white settlers.

In earlier times most new territories had been added to the United States before many settlers had entered them. But California already had a well-established Spanish population. Then the gold

California State Library

Perhaps 1,000 black prospectors came to California. The miner in this 1852 photograph is working a Long Tom, a device to wash gold out of gravel. How were nonwhite miners generally treated?

rush, as we have just seen, greatly increased the population. Everyone realized that California did not need to go through the territorial stage of development. Like Texas, it would enter the Union directly as a state. But should California be a free state or a slave state?

Always in the past, northern territory had become free, southern slave. The Northwest Ordinance of 1787 had declared that the land north of the Ohio River and east of the Mississippi should be free. Kentucky and the territory south of the Ohio became slave states.

In 1820 a sharp conflict had developed over the admission of Missouri as a state. Missouri, which was part of the Louisiana Purchase, extended far north of any of the slave states. But its white citizens wanted slavery. The **Missouri Compromise** of 1820 allowed Missouri to become a slave state. Congress balanced this decision by creating a free state, **Maine,** which had been part of Massachusetts.

The Missouri Compromise also divided the rest of the Louisiana Purchase into free and slave territory. The land south of Missouri's southern border—latitude 36° 30'—was opened to slavery. The land west and north of Missouri was to be free.

After the Treaty of Guadalupe Hidalgo some people favored extending this line dividing free territory from slave all the way to the Pacific. That would have split California in two. The people who were living in California did not want any of it to become a slave state. The Spanish in California had no wish to hold slaves. The gold miners were opposed to slavery because they were afraid that big mining companies would bring in large numbers of blacks to compete with individual prospectors.

If California became a free state, the eastern slave states would expect something in return. What about slavery in the rest of the territory obtained from Mexico? The problem led to a great debate in Congress and throughout the country.

- What had the Missouri Compromise decided about free and slave states?
- What problem was caused by the question of adding California to the Union?

THE ELECTION OF 1848

The debate over free and slave territories began even before the discovery of gold. It played an important part in the Presidential election of 1848. Since President Polk did not seek a second term, the Democrats nominated Senator Lewis Cass of Michigan. Cass had been Secretary of War in Andrew Jackson's Cabinet. He favored a system known as **popular sovereignty.** This system would let settlers in new territories make their own decision about whether or not they would have slavery.

Zachary Taylor, twelfth President, was the popular 'Rough and Ready' of the Mexican War. Sixteen months after he took office, Taylor spoke at Fourth of July ceremonies held at the base of the new Washington Monument. The day was scorching. Five days later he was dead. This lithograph is by Francis D'Avignon, made while Taylor was President. Which qualities did the Whig party stress during Taylor's campaign?

Many northern Democrats were unhappy about the nomination of Cass. They considered popular sovereignty a victory for slavery because it would allow southerners to bring their slaves into new land. These Democrats founded a new organization, the **Free-Soil** party. Their candidate was former President Martin Van Buren.

The Whig party chose General Zachary Taylor as its candidate. President Polk's worst fears had come true. "Old Rough and Ready" had no political experience, but he was very popular. He refused to express an opinion on any of the controversial issues of the day. During the campaign the Whigs stressed his victories in the war, his courage, and his personal honesty. As had been the case with General Harrison in 1840, this tactic worked perfectly. In the election Taylor got 163 electoral votes to Cass's 27. Van Buren received about 10 per cent of the popular vote but no electoral votes because he did not get a majority in any state.

- What was popular sovereignty?
- Why did northern Democrats leave their party in 1848 and form the Free-Soil party?

THE COMPROMISE OF 1850

After the election the debate continued. Besides the future of California and the other new territory, every aspect of the slavery issue was discussed. There were lengthy arguments on the question of the slave trade in Washington, D.C., and on the question of how to force northern officials to return slaves who had escaped into their states.

On each issue there was a northern and a southern position. Many northerners hoped to keep slavery out of all the new territory. In August 1846, long before the end of the Mexican War, Congressman David Wilmot of Pennsylvania introduced the **Wilmot Proviso** in the House of Representatives. The proviso called for prohibiting slavery "in any territory [taken] from the Republic of Mexico."

Southerners, of course, wanted to be able to take their slaves into all such territory. They controlled enough votes in Congress to defeat the Wilmot Proviso. But for both groups slavery was becoming a moral question—that is, a question of right and wrong.

As we shall see in the next chapter, many northern people believed strongly that it was sinful for one person to own another. Few of these northerners believed that it was legally possible to abolish slavery in states where it already existed. But large numbers were determined that it should not spread into new lands. Since Congress had always had the power to decide whether or not to allow slavery in new territories, people who felt this way were urging their representatives and senators to support measures like the Wilmot Proviso that would ban slavery in the entire Southwest.

Congress also controlled the city of Washington because the District of Columbia was not part of any state. Those who disliked slavery urged Congress to abolish the institution there. At the very least they wanted Congress to prohibit the buying and selling of slaves in the capital.

The more extreme southerners wanted a law guaranteeing the right of owners to bring their slaves into all the new territories. Even moderate southerners would not agree to the abolition of slavery in Washington. Some were not opposed to a law which would prohibit buying and selling of slaves there. In return they demanded that Congress pass a stricter fugitive slave law. They argued, with considerable truth, that many northern police officials and northern judges were refusing to help in the capture and return of slaves who had escaped into the free states.

"Slaves Escaping Through the Swamp" was painted in 1863 by Thomas Moran. Bloodhounds scramble down the river bank as they track these fugitives, their pursuers barely visible behind the dense underbrush. How does this oil painting reflect a popular northern view of slavery in the 1850s?

Philbrook Art Center

National Portrait Gallery

Henry Clay, 72 years old and ailing, pleads with the Senate to reach the Compromise of 1850. Seated at left, his ear cupped, is Daniel Webster. He soon will rise in strong support of Clay's plan. But attacks will be made by John C. Calhoun, standing third from the right, and William H. Seward, seated in the left front. Vice President Millard Fillmore is presiding. This engraving was done in 1855 by Robert Whitechurch. For what reason was this debate held?

All the important members of Congress took part in the debate over these issues. Old Henry Clay, three times an unsuccessful candidate for President and now Senator from Kentucky, worked out the compromise that was eventually accepted.

Congress should admit California as a free state, Clay urged. The rest of the land obtained from Mexico should be organized as New Mexico Territory. Slavery should neither be prohibited nor specifically authorized there. In other words, Clay supported Lewis Cass's popular sovereignty plan for this territory.

To please antislavery northerners, Clay suggested that the buying and selling of slaves in the District of Columbia be prohibited. To please southerners, he proposed a very harsh fugitive slave bill. Another of Clay's bills provided that some lands claimed by Texas were to be transferred to New Mexico Territory. In exchange the debts that Texas had built up while it was an independent republic were to be paid by the United States.

Daniel Webster of Massachusetts, another important senator, delivered a powerful speech in support of Clay's compromise proposals. On the other side Senator William H. Seward of New York spoke against making any concessions to the slave interests. Clay's fugitive slave bill must not pass, Seward said. Although the Constitution of the United States required the return of fugitives, a "higher law," the law of God, would keep decent people from helping to capture an escaped slave.

The bitterest attack on Clay's ideas came from John C. Calhoun, the father of nullification. Calhoun was also old and so ill that his speech had to be delivered by another senator. Slaves were a form of property, Calhoun said. All citizens had the right to take their property into all the territories of the United States. Unless Congress allowed owners to bring their slaves into the territories, the southern states would **secede,** or leave the Union. There was nothing evil or immoral about slavery, Calhoun argued. Northerners must accept the fact that it existed. If they wanted to live at peace with the South, they must stop criticizing slavery.

In the midst of the debate on Clay's bills, President Taylor fell ill and died. Vice President Millard Fillmore of New York succeeded him. Fillmore favored Clay's compromise. Nevertheless, the arguments dragged on into the summer months.

Finally the various proposals came to a vote. California was admitted to the Union as a free state. The rest of the former Mexican lands were organized into two large territories, Utah and New Mexico, without mention of slavery. Texas was given $10 million to pay its debts. The slave trade in the District of Columbia was abolished. A new Fugitive Slave Act was passed.

Few Americans, North or South, approved of all these laws. But nearly everyone was pleased with the result as a whole. The **Compromise of 1850** appeared to put an end once and for all to the conflict between the free and slave states. All the territory owned by the United States had now been organized. Never again would Congress have to decide the future of slavery on American soil. As Senator Stephen A. Douglas of Illinois put it, a "final settlement" had been reached. At least that was how it seemed in 1850.

- What did the Wilmot Proviso call for?
- In the great debate over the slavery issue, what was the position of Henry Clay? Of John Calhoun?
- What did the Compromise of 1850 seem to accomplish?

Daniel Webster of Massachusetts sat for this oil painting in 1828. It is the work of Chester Harding, who taught himself to paint. A detail is shown. How did Webster support Clay's Compromise of 1850?

Millard Fillmore completed Zachary Taylor's term as President. He later became the nominee of the American party (or Know-Nothing party) rather than the Republican party, a choice which ended his political career. This daguerreotype was taken about 1850, when Fillmore succeeded to the Presidency. What stand did he take on the Compromise of 1850?

CHAPTER 12 REVIEW

Identification

Tell briefly why each of the following persons, terms, or events is important.

1. Henry Clay
2. James K. Polk
3. Stephen F. Austin
4. Antonio López de Santa Anna
5. Sam Houston
6. John A. Sutter
7. Zachary Taylor
8. Winfield Scott
9. Brigham Young
10. Manifest destiny
11. Oregon Trail
12. Treaty of Guadalupe Hidalgo
13. *Ranchero* system
14. Mormon Trail
15. Forty-Niners
16. Missouri Compromise
17. Popular sovereignty
18. Free-Soil party
19. Wilmot Proviso
20. Compromise of 1850

Understanding American History

1. Describe the events that led Texans to declare their independence from Mexico.
2. What was the "Texas question"? How did it affect the election of 1844?
3. What was manifest destiny? What effect did this idea have on westward expansion?
4. What was the chief cause of the war with Mexico? In what sense was the idea of manifest destiny a cause of the war?
5. What were some of the outcomes of the war with Mexico?
6. Describe the events that led the Mormons to move from Nauvoo to Utah.
7. Describe life in a typical Forty-Niner mining camp.
8. Why was the Democratic party split in the election of 1848?
9. What were the provisions of the Compromise of 1850?

10. Why did North and South quarrel whenever the United States added territory?

Activities

1. Make a large map for the bulletin board to show the expansion of the United States from 1790 to 1853. Use different colors to show the expansion into the Southwest and West. Be sure to label each new territory separately and indicate who first held it.
2. With your classmates make a plaster of paris or papier-mâché model of the Alamo. Show the model in class and tell the history of the Alamo from the time of its founding to the battle of 1836. Others might give brief biographical sketches of fighters at the Alamo, including Davy Crockett, James Bowie, and Antonio López de Santa Anna.
3. Do research in your school or public library on the *ranchero* system. Prepare an oral or written report on life on one of the *ranchos* in the 1830s. You might illustrate your report with pictures and drawings to show *ranchero* life. Some of your classmates might prepare a plan or model of a typical *rancho* to display.
4. Tell the story of the Mormon trek westward in stories and pictures. Working in small groups, let each group tell one part of the story. Begin with Joseph Smith in New York. Describe the moves to Ohio, Missouri, and Illinois. Then give a picture of life in Nauvoo. Explain the preparations made for the move west under Brigham Young. Describe the winter camps. Tell about the establishment of Salt Lake City and report on the Mormons' achievements.
5. Use your historical imagination to write diary entries describing daily life either as a member of a wagon train moving west or as a resident of a mining camp. Try to give a sense of everyday activity, but also tell about any happenings that are out of the ordinary.

CHAPTER 12 TEST

Completion (30 points)

Number your paper 1–10 and next to each number write the word from the list below that best completes each sentence.

manifest destiny   Missouri Compromise
"Oregon fever"   Free-Soil party
Forty-Niners   Compromise of 1850
popular sovereignty   secede
dark horse   Great Salt Lake

1. California was admitted to the United States as a free state by the _____.
2. The permanent home of the Mormons, near _____, is on land that was once a near desert.
3. The southern states threatened to _____ if slave owners were not allowed to bring their slaves into the territories.
4. Gold miners known as _____ rushed to stake claims in California.
5. In 1848 a group of Democrats who were against the spread of slavery into the territories formed the _____.
6. _____ was the belief that the future of the nation was to overspread the continent.
7. Under the _____ the number of free and slave states remained equal.
8. In the 1830s some easterners caught _____ and moved westward.
9. A candidate who seems to have no chance at a convention and yet wins the nomination is called a _____.
10. The idea that settlers of a territory should make their own decision about whether or not to allow slavery is called _____.

Matching (30 points)

Number your paper 11–20 and match the person in the second column with the description in the first column.

11. President of Mexico when Texas revolted
12. Chief author of the Compromise of 1850
13. Died fighting for Texan independence
14. President when the United States acquired Oregon and California
15. Gold was discovered on his land in California
16. Leader of the Mormon trek westward
17. Commander of the Texan army when Texas won its independence from Mexico
18. Obtained Mexico's permission to bring American settlers into Texas
19. "Old Rough and Ready," he commanded United States forces early in the Mexican War
20. "Old Fuss and Feathers," he was an excellent general who eventually captured Mexico City

a. Henry Clay
b. James K. Polk
c. Antonio López de Santa Anna
d. Sam Houston
e. John A. Sutter
f. Winfield Scott
g. Stephen F. Austin
h. Davy Crockett
i. Zachary Taylor
j. Brigham Young

Essay (40 points)

Explain point-by-point the provisions of the Compromise of 1850 and tell why most people felt this was the final settlement of the slavery question. Plan your brief essay carefully. If time permits, begin with a draft copy. Be sure to proofread your paper, taking care to spell and punctuate correctly. After making any changes you feel necessary, write out your final copy.

CHAPTER 13
Slavery
and Abolitionism

200 YEARS OF SLAVERY

Right after the American Revolution slavery seemed to be dying out. The northern states passed laws gradually doing away with it. Many southerners freed their slaves voluntarily. In 1808 Congress prohibited bringing any more slaves into the country. Yet in 1850 slavery persisted in America, where it had existed some 200 years.

"Slave Market in Richmond, Virginia" was painted in oil by Eyre Crowe in 1852. While slaves await on benches, the white gentlemen make their bids to the auctioneer, his arm stretched out. Yet surely this is a "prettified" picture—the freshly starched aprons, the smiling mother, the boy wearing his Sunday best. Who knows if these children will still sit in Mother's lap when the auctioneer raps down his gavel? When did Congress prohibit bringing more slaves into America?

Collection of Honorable and Mrs. John Heinz III, Washington, D.C. (Gemini-Smith)

Some people who thought that slavery was bad for the country proposed freeing the black slaves and sending them back to Africa. In 1817 they founded the **American Colonization Society.** They purchased land in Africa for former slaves to settle on. Most free American blacks were not interested in living in Africa. However, the American Colonization Society did persuade several thousands to make the move to what became the nation of Liberia, on the west coast of Africa.

Few white **colonizationists** genuinely wanted to help blacks. The colonization movement was mostly aimed at getting rid of the former slaves. Nevertheless, the movement was another sign that many white southerners were unhappy with slavery.

▨ What was the purpose of the American Colonization Society?

THE IMPORTANCE OF COTTON

Southern attitudes about slavery changed after the discovery of a new crop that greatly increased the need for slave labor. This crop was cotton. In the 1790s cotton was in great demand in many parts of the world because of the new spinning machinery that had been invented in England. It was just at this time that Samuel Slater was building the first spinning machines in America. These machines could produce thread so rapidly that they were soon using up cotton faster than the world was producing it.

Most cotton came from Egypt. Egyptian cotton was of very high quality. It had long, soft fibers that grew around and protected the seeds of the plant. When the plant ripened, the **cotton boll** burst open. Then the fluffy white fibers could easily be separated from the shiny black seeds.

A little of this cotton was grown in America on the Sea Islands along the coast of Georgia and South Carolina. The winters there were very mild. But **Sea Island cotton** would not grow on the mainland. The plants were so tender that they were killed by the slightest spring frost.

Another variety of cotton, called **upland cotton,** could withstand colder temperatures. It was hardy enough to be grown almost anywhere in the southern states. Unfortunately, the fibers of this plant were short and tightly woven about the seeds. It took a whole day for a skilled person to remove the seeds by hand from a single pound of this cotton.

If only someone would invent a machine for removing the seeds from upland cotton! Many farmers in South Carolina and Georgia were expressing this hope in one way or another in the 1790s. Rice cultivation could not be increased much in those states. Rice needed a great deal of water. It could only be grown where the fields could be flooded. Indigo, the plant introduced in the 1740s by Eliza Lucas, was not worth growing after the Revolution because the British government no longer paid a bounty for producing it.

- Why did the demand for cotton suddenly increase in the 1790s?
- What was the advantage of growing upland cotton? What problem did it give farmers?

ELI WHITNEY AND THE COTTON GIN

In 1793 Eli Whitney was visiting a friend on a plantation near Savannah, Georgia. Whitney had just graduated from Yale College. He had learned about metalworking from his father, a nail maker. He had not yet turned his inventive mind to thinking about making guns from interchangeable parts.

Samuel F. B. Morse completed this oil portrait of Eli Whitney in 1827, two years after the inventor's death. Morse no doubt admired the genius who devised the cotton gin, shown at right, and manufactured muskets with interchangeable parts as well. Morse was himself an inventor. His telegraph took him some 12 years to perfect. What led Whitney to the invention of the cotton gin?

The Granger Collection

During his visit he talked with a number of Georgia farmers. They mentioned their interest in growing cotton and showed him how difficult it was to remove the seeds from upland cotton bolls. Young Whitney had never seen a cotton plant before. Perhaps that was an advantage. He studied the plant carefully. "If a machine could be invented that would clean the Cotton," he explained in a letter to his father back in Connecticut, "it would be a great thing both to the Country and to the inventor."

After a few days of thinking, he designed a machine that he called a **cotton gin.** It consisted of a box that opened at the top and had rows of narrow slits down one side. The box was stuffed with cotton, seeds and all. Against the side of the box Whitney set a roller or cylinder. The cylinder had rows of wire teeth around it. These rows of teeth were arranged so that when someone turned the cylinder, the teeth passed into the box through the slits. The cotton in the box caught on the teeth as they turned. As the teeth came out of the box, they pulled the cotton fibers with them.

But the seeds, which were wider than the slits in the box, could not pass through with the fibers. The fibers therefore pulled free of the seeds. A second cylinder, turning in the other direction, brushed the fibers from the teeth. As the first cylinder continued to turn, the teeth reentered the box to catch up more of the cotton.

One person turning the handle of a cotton gin could remove the seeds of not one pound of cotton in a day but of fifty! A gin was easy to make and cheap. Even a small farmer could afford one. The owners of large plantations soon were building large gins powered by horses or mules. Quickly it became profitable to grow cotton.

▨ How did Eli Whitney's cotton gin make it profitable to grow cotton?

EFFECTS OF THE COTTON GIN

All over the South farmers began to plant the new crop. In 1793 they grew about 10,000 bales, each containing 500 pounds (225 kilograms) of cotton. In 1801 American production reached 100,000 bales. By 1835 it had passed a million bales. Cotton was worth about 25 cents a pound in the 1790s. The price remained in the 15- to 20-cent range even after output had increased enormously. Cotton planters therefore prospered.

Most of the people who flocked westward into Alabama, Mississippi, Arkansas, Louisiana, and on into Texas became cotton planters. Of course they also raised large quantities of corn, wheat, cattle, and other food products. But cotton was their most important crop. Indeed, it became the key to prosperity for the South and almost as important for the rest of the country.

The Granger Collection

Cotton cultivation made possible the rapid growth of the northern cotton cloth industry. Citizens everywhere benefited from cheap cotton clothing, which was cool in summer and much easier to keep clean than woolen garments. Exports of cotton to England and other European countries paid for badly needed foreign imports of all kinds.

The great cotton boom increased the need for workers to cultivate the fields and to pick and gin the fluffy white fibers when the crop was ripe. Cotton growing seemed especially well suited for the institution of slavery because it kept the slaves busy the year

This beautiful 1884 lithograph was one of the popular Currier & Ives American scenes. "Cotton Plantation on the Mississippi" portrays slaves picking cotton while their overseer in the field watches from his mule. A wagon pulls a load of baled cotton in the left foreground. It is typical of Currier & Ives that the institution of slavery appears to be as peaceful as a Sunday afternoon outing. Cotton seeds were machine separated after Whitney invented the gin, but how did cotton have to be picked?

round. (Slave owners always feared that if their workers had too little to do, they would get into trouble!)

The year began with spring planting, whether on a small farm worked by a single white family and one or two black slaves or on a large plantation with a hundred slaves. First, corn and other food crops were planted in March. When these were in the ground, the cotton seeds were sown. Once sprouted, the corn needed little care, but the small, tender cotton plants required much labor. The young shoots had to be thinned out. As the plants grew, the soil had to be hoed and cultivated frequently to keep down weeds. Insect pests had to be watched for and killed before they could do serious damage to the crop. This work kept all hands busy during the long southern summers.

By September it was time to harvest the corn. The cornstalks were gathered and stored away to make winter food for cows and pigs. Picking the cotton took up the rest of the fall because the cotton bolls did not all ripen at the same time. Unless the white fluff was gathered as soon as the bolls burst open, rain and dust would dirty it and thus reduce its value. The slaves had to go through the fields almost daily.

Cotton is packed into bales under pressure from the screw-down top of this cotton press. A mule can turn the heavy screw by patiently plodding its circular path. This wood engraving was made in 1871. Where is the baled cotton likely to be sent?

Picking took skill and patience but not a great deal of stength. Women and children worked the fields side by side with the men. A skilled picker could gather 200 pounds (90 kilograms) in a day.

After picking, the cotton had to be put through the gin to remove the seeds. Then it was packed in bales. This was done in a **cotton press,** a box-like affair with a heavy screw-down top. The bales were bound in burlap and tied with wire or twine.

Harvesting was usually over by Christmas time. Then, for about a week, all work stopped. During this brief period the harsh and cruel side of slavery was put aside, if not forgotten. There were feasts, singing and dancing, a Christmas tree bright with candles. One South Carolina slave described a tree he remembered as "a picture of beautifulness." There were also small presents for everyone. Some masters even dressed up as Santa Claus and distributed gifts to the black children.

After this brief holiday it was time to clear new land. Fences had to be repaired, tools sharpened. Thus the winter passed. Soon it was time for the next spring planting.

Although cotton increased the demand for slave labor, there could be no sudden increase in the supply of slaves. Congress had forbidden bringing any more slaves into the country. Farmers therefore competed with one another for American blacks. The natural increase of the population could not satisfy the demand. The price of slaves rose rapidly. By 1850 slaves were selling for three or four times as much as they had cost before the invention of the cotton gin.

- Why did cotton increase the demand for slave labor?
- Why could there be no increase in the supply of slaves?

HOW COTTON AFFECTED SLAVES

In some respects the fact that slaves were becoming more valuable meant that their owners treated them better. Prosperous owners could afford to feed, clothe, and house slaves adequately. Probably most did so, if only because it made sense to take good care of such useful property.

The slaves ate simple food. It consisted mainly of corn, pork fat, and molasses. This did not make a balanced diet, for no one at that time understood the importance of vitamins and minerals for good health. Fortunately, most slaves were allowed to have small vegetable gardens of their own. They could fish in the streams and hunt and trap small forest animals such as opossums and raccoons. They got enough to eat, even if their food was plain and simple.

The slaves wore clothing that was also simple but sufficient—overalls, cotton and woolen shirts, a pair of heavy work shoes, a hat for protection against rain and summer heat.

This 19th-century engraving shows a typical slave cabin of the South. Many others like it would make up a separate village on a plantation. The girl outside the door is using a washboard and a cake of lye soap to clean the family's few clothes. How much room would this family have in a slave cabin?

State Department of Archives and History, Raleigh, North Carolina

Slave cabins were small and poorly furnished. Most families lived in a single room. The cabins had fireplaces for cooking and to provide heat in winter. Some had board floors, but many were built directly on the earth. Windows rarely had panes of glass. These living conditions were primitive by modern standards. They were not, however, unhealthy. They tended to improve as time passed. Poor white farm people, in the North as well as in the South, were not much better off in these respects.

However, the cotton gin also made life much more difficult for most black people. When slaves were worth more, owners changed their attitude toward slavery. The number of blacks who were freed by their owners declined after 1800. Most southern state governments even passed laws making it difficult for owners who wanted to release their slaves to do so. Owners also tended to try to make their slaves work harder. The high price of cotton encouraged them to increase production by any possible means.

The westward expansion of cotton cultivation was extremely hard on thousands of slaves. Blacks and whites moved west together from Virginia and the Carolinas to Alabama, Mississippi, and Texas. But they made the move under very different circumstances.

White pioneers endured the dangers and hardships of the frontier willingly. They hoped to obtain a better way of life. They were prepared to take risks and suffer inconveniences to do so. The blacks whom they brought with them faced the same dangers and hardships. But they had no hope of benefiting as a result.

■ How did the cotton gin make life more difficult for most black people?

BUILDING SKILLS IN SOCIAL STUDIES

Comparing Statistics

Statistics are numerical facts. In order to compare statistics, visual aids are especially helpful. On this page a pair of *bar graphs* and a map show the relationship of slavery and the amount of cotton grown in the United States from 1820 to 1860.

The bar graphs show the steady growth of the slave population of the United States and the increase in bales of cotton produced. The map shows the area in the South where cotton was grown in 1839 and the area where cotton was grown in 1859.

Look at each of the bar graphs. Both show the years from 1820 to 1850 on the horizontal axis. What does each show on its vertical axis? Now answer the questions in the next column.

1. In which southern states was most cotton grown in 1839? In 1859?
2. Compare the cotton-growing area of 1859 to the cotton-growing area of 1839. Describe the growth by states.
3. What numbers does the top graph show on its vertical axis? The bottom graph?
4. About how many slaves were held in 1830?
5. About how many slaves were held in 1850?
6. About how much cotton was produced in 1840?
7. About how much cotton was produced in 1860?
8. Between which years did the amount of cotton production increase the most?
9. A *trend* is the general course of events. What trend is shown by the top graph? By the bottom graph? By the map?
10. What general statement can you make about the increase of slavery and cotton growing?

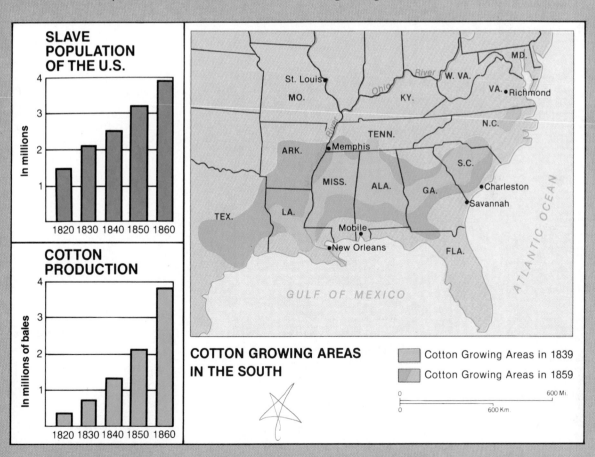

SLAVE POPULATION OF THE U.S.

In millions

1820 1830 1840 1850 1860

COTTON PRODUCTION

In millions of bales

1820 1830 1840 1850 1860

COTTON GROWING AREAS IN THE SOUTH

Cotton Growing Areas in 1839
Cotton Growing Areas in 1859

600 Mi.
600 Km.

Sold Down the River

"Slave Auction at Richmond" is an oil painting by Eyre Crowe. With the rap of the auctioneer's hammer a young slave on the platform will become the property of the highest bidder in this close, narrow hall.

White pioneers often left loved ones behind. Young men and women setting out for the West had to bid farewell to parents and friends knowing they would probably never see them again. It was very sad. For slaves these separations were cruel rather than sad. They had no choice in the matter. Since few could read or write, they did not even have the possibility of writing letters to those they had to leave behind forever.

It was bad enough for slaves whose owners took their human property west along with the farm tools, furniture, and other goods. Much worse was the fate of those who were sold to professional slave traders. These traders made a business of buying slaves wherever they could find them. They herded the poor captives together, chained them, and carted them off to regions where their labor was in great demand. Busy markets developed in cities like New Orleans, where slaves from the Upper South were collected.

At these markets the black slaves were sold at auction, one by one, to the highest bidder. Mothers were often separated from their children, wives from their husbands—all by the fall of the auctioneer's hammer. To be sold down the river in this way was a terrible fate.

THE PECULIAR INSTITUTION

By the 1830s most white southerners were convinced that slavery—"the peculiar institution"—was absolutely necessary to their well being. They thought their whole way of life depended upon their ownership of the black population. They even persuaded themselves that slavery was good for the slaves as well as for the owners. They wrongly argued that blacks were childlike by nature and of lower intelligence than whites. The whites reasoned that under slavery they could protect and guide these "inferior" people. Compare the life of the slave with that of the northern free worker, they urged. Did slaves ever have to worry about where their next meal was coming from? Did anyone ever see a black beggar in the South? Sick slaves were cared for by their masters. Old slaves were certain of support as long as they lived and a decent burial when death finally came.

Southerners especially liked to compare the living conditions of plantation workers with those of poor immigrants and low-paid factory workers in northern cities. They insisted that the workers who planted and picked cotton were better fed, better housed, and better clothed than the workers in the northern textile factories who spun the cotton into thread and wove it into cloth.

■ What arguments did some southerners put forth to justify slavery?

PRIDE AND PREJUDICE

Slaveholders also took pride in the importance of American cotton to the whole world. **"Cotton is King"** was a southern slogan. Southern whites meant by this slogan that their cotton was essential to the prosperity of the United States and to most of Europe as well. Since cotton depended on slavery, criticism of slavery seemed to them unpatriotic and downright dangerous.

Of course, cotton was *not* king in the sense that southerners imagined. It was the nation's most valuable export, but the national economy would not have collapsed if no cotton were grown. Still, southerners were hardly alone in boasting about the importance of their system. Like Americans in all sections, they were proud of their country and their way of life.

That pride was understandable. The United States was a rich and growing country. The American experiment in republican government was proving a success. Most ordinary people in other nations greatly admired America. European reformers studied the Declaration of Independence and the Constitution. They looked forward to a time when they might create similar governments in their own lands. Each year more and more foreigners were crossing the Atlantic Ocean hoping to find wealth and happiness in the United States.

Gentlemen of the cotton trade cast practiced eyes on samples in this detail from an oil painted by Edgar Degas, one of the greatest French artists. The setting is the cotton exchange at New Orleans. How did "the peculiar institution" support the profitable cotton trade?

Noticing these things, Americans tended to sing the praises of their country and of themselves. Frontier settlers in particular liked to brag about their own abilities. "I am a real ring-tailed roarer . . . from the thunder and lightning country," one western character explained. "I make my breakfast on stewed Yankee and pork steak and rinse them down with spike nails. I can lick my weight in wildcats or raccoons. . . . I can out-eat, out-drink, out-work, out-grin, out-snort, out-run, out-lift, out-sneeze, out-lie any thing in the shape of man or beast from Maine to Louisiana." It was this kind of thinking that explains the foolish confidence of the western War Hawks who had expected to conquer Canada so easily when war broke out with Great Britain in 1812.

Collection of the Boatmen's National Bank of St. Louis

"Stump Speaking" shows a politician campaigning in rural Missouri. His speech, which may have lasted hours, seems to interest most listeners in an era when people paid particular attention to the spoken word. George Caleb Bingham, who painted this oil in 1854, was a politician himself as well as a fine American painter. Why did Americans have strong national pride during the 1830s?

Most easterners and southerners were more restrained than western types like the War Hawks and the "ring-tailed roarer." But Americans in every section felt deep national pride. Each **Fourth of July** people gathered in towns and villages to celebrate the anniversary of the signing of the Declaration of Independence. There were fireworks, parades, brass bands, and many stirring speeches by politicians, ministers, and war veterans. The words of the Declaration were sometimes read aloud, reminding listeners that "all men are created equal." On the outskirts of plantation lawns and city parks black slaves heard these words as they tended the horses and waited for their owners.

Americans of the day were quite pleased with their achievements. This was often harmless enough. But among the slaveholders this pride had very serious effects. They could not accept even the mildest criticism of "the peculiar institution."

- What did southerners mean when they boasted that "Cotton is King"?
- Why did southerners believe that criticism of slavery was unpatriotic and dangerous?

THE MOVEMENT TO ABOLISH SLAVERY

Gradually, a small number of white Americans, mostly but not entirely people from the free states, began to argue that slavery was wrong and ought to be abolished. These **abolitionists,** as they were called, were influenced by the same typically American pride and self-confidence that led so many southerners to insist that slavery was the best possible social system. The abolitionists believed in the ideal of freedom. They insisted that America was the land of liberty. They were impatient with any imperfection in their society. It was sinful, they said, to stand by idly while a flaw like slavery existed.

Abolitionists quoted the Declaration of Independence to show that slavery was contrary to American principles. They also put forth religious arguments stressing that all human beings are equal in the eyes of God. It was hard to disagree with these arguments. Nevertheless, most people, even non-slaveholders, considered the abolitionists to be dangerous radicals.

This was so because there seemed no legal way to do away with slavery in the United States. Under the Constitution each state could decide whether or not to allow slavery to exist within its borders. The northern states had abolished it after the Revolution. But nearly all white citizens in the southern states favored the slave system. There was no chance that the voters of Virginia or Georgia or Mississippi would ever voluntarily agree to free their slaves.

Slavery could, of course, be abolished by amending the Constitution. But an amendment would require the approval of three fourths of the states. In 1850 half of the 30 states in the Union permitted slavery. No antislavery movement could possibly be ratified. To campaign for abolition under these circumstances seemed like urging revolution and civil war.

Nevertheless, some important foes of slavery demanded action. One of the prominent early ones was Benjamin Lundy, a saddle maker from New Jersey. Lundy probably became interested in abolition because he was a Quaker. Even during the colonial period many Quakers had spoken out against slavery. In 1821 Lundy began to publish an antislavery paper, *The Genius of Universal Emancipation.*

Benjamin Lundy was an early leader in the movement to abolish slavery. He edited several publications that called for abolition. What were the legal steps needed to end slavery?

Lundy's paper never had more than 700 subscribers. His influence, however, was quite large. He worked tirelessly for the cause. He demanded that free blacks in the North be treated fairly. He urged Congress to abolish slavery in the District of Columbia and to prohibit its spread into the western territories. He bitterly attacked the plan to annex slaveholding Texas.

At first Lundy favored granting freedom to the slaves gradually. Perhaps if the children of all slaves born after a certain date were set free, the South could accept abolition. When this idea of **gradual emancipation,** or freedom, attracted no southern support, Lundy became more radical. He began to demand **immediate emancipation.**

- What arguments did the abolitionists make against slavery?
- Why did most people consider the abolitionists to be dangerous radicals?

RADICAL AND MODERATE VOICES

In 1829 Benjamin Lundy appointed a young man from Massachusetts, William Lloyd Garrison, as assistant editor of *The Genius of Universal Emancipation.* Garrison turned out to be much more radical than Lundy. Lundy had always hoped to persuade owners to free their slaves. He tried, for example, to show them that slavery was neither efficient nor economical. Garrison simply insisted that it was criminal and sinful to own a human being. He denounced not only slaveholders but all Americans who were willing to put up with the institution.

Garrison soon disagreed with Lundy. He left his job as editor and in 1831 began publishing a paper of his own, *The Liberator.* "I will not excuse," he announced in the first issue, "I will not retreat a single inch—and *I will be heard.*"

Garrison's position was so radical that even most northerners who disliked slavery turned against him. He blamed *everyone* who tolerated slavery for the existence of the institution. He urged the northern states to secede from the United States. "No Union with Slaveholders," was one of his slogans. Garrison publicly set fire to a copy of the Constitution. The Constitution, he said, was a "compromise with tyranny" and an "agreement with Hell."

In 1833 Garrison and other abolitionists founded the American Anti-Slavery Society. But Garrison's radical position caused conflict in the organization. The first president of the Society was Arthur Tappan, a well-to-do New York merchant. He helped to finance the abolitionist movement, but eventually he broke with Garrison. So did Tappan's brother Benjamin, and so did two important southern abolitionists, the sisters Sarah and Angelina Grimké.

In 1836 Angelina Grimké published a pamphlet, *Appeal to Christian Women of the South.* The *Appeal* urged southern women to "over-

William Lloyd Garrison, publisher of *The Liberator,* is shown in this engraved portrait by H. W. Smith. In an editorial for *The Liberator* Garrison proclaimed, *"I will be heard."* Whom did he blame for the institution of slavery?

READING PRACTICE IN SOCIAL STUDIES

SQ3R—A Helpful Study Plan

SQ3R is a study plan that can make you a more efficient reader. With practice it will save you time.

SQ3R stands for Survey, Question, Read, Recite, and Review. The method is easy to learn and to use.

When you begin a reading assignment in this book, first *survey* the sections. Use the skills of skimming and scanning taught in the Reading Practice on page 213. Skim over the section titles, boldface type, study questions, illustrations and their captions, and maps. Scan for unfamiliar vocabulary and for words that appear in italics.

Surveying the assignment gives you a general idea of what lies ahead in your reading. You become aware of new words and new terms before you actually read the material.

When your survey is completed, set a purpose for your reading. (The Reading Practice on page 81, "Reading with a Purpose", can help you here.) Use the information from your survey to *question* what lies ahead. Turn section heads into questions. Ask who? what? when? where? why? and how? For example, the section title "The Importance of Cotton" becomes the question "Why was cotton important?" Or the illustration of the cotton plantation on page 379 leads to the question "Why were cotton plantations so important in the South?"

Write down your questions as a study guide for yourself. Then *read* to answer the questions. You needn't try to remember everything you read in the sections. Usually the answers to the questions you form will give you the main ideas and the most important details.

Next, *recite*. Write down answers to your questions in your own words. This gives you an immediate check on your reading and helps you not to forget what you read. Using your own words makes you think carefully about the material and ensures that you understand it.

Finally, you *review*. There are two times for useful review—immediate and later. When you finish writing down answers to all your questions, immediately answer the questions a second time without looking at your written answers. Reread any parts of the chapter that give rise to questions you still find difficult to answer.

A few days later, perhaps while preparing for a test, review again by answering your set of questions without looking back to your written answers. Again reread if necessary.

SQ3R may seem to take a great amount of time and effort. But as you learn to use SQ3R, you will soon see that it actually saves both reading and study time.

The guidelines below will help you to complete this Reading Practice. Study the guidelines carefully. Then use SQ3R to read the rest of Chapter 13.

SQ3R Guidelines

1. *Survey*
   Read headings and study questions.
   Scan for specific details.
   Skim for unfamiliar words.
   Look at illustrations and their captions.
2. *Question*
   Make up a set of questions from your survey.
   Turn titles into questions.
   Ask who? what? when? where? why? how?
3. *Read*
   Read to find answers to your questions.
4. *Recite*
   Write down the answers to your questions in your own words.
5. *Review*
   Immediately answer your questions without looking at your earlier answers. Reread if necessary.
   Later, while studying for a test, answer your questions again. Reread if necessary.

The Granger Collection

Angelina Grimké Weld, shown in a 19th-century engraving, and Sarah Grimké appealed to women of the South to reject slavery. Why did they urge its overthrow?

throw this horrible system of oppression and cruelty." Next she made speeches attacking slavery before small groups of women in private homes. As her reputation grew, she began to lecture in public to larger groups. Sarah Grimké also spoke and wrote for the cause of abolition.

In 1838 Angelina Grimké married Theodore Dwight Weld, a clergyman who was a leader of the more moderate opponents of slavery. When Garrison demanded "immediate emancipation" of the slaves, he meant exactly that—right now and entirely free. Weld spoke in favor of what he called "immediate abolition gradually achieved." By this he meant that his *goal* was complete freedom for all slaves but that it would take time to change the minds of slaveholders and to persuade northerners to take a stand.

To attract recruits, Weld and his group collected and published stories showing how slaves were being mistreated. They organized support for members of Congress who sympathized with their views. They ran candidates of their own in many elections.

■ How did the following work for abolition: William Lloyd Garrison? Angelina and Sarah Grimké? Theodore Dwight Weld?

BLACK ATTACKS ON SLAVERY

It is surely correct to assume that every slave was at least a silent abolitionist. A few were so outraged by slavery that they rose in rebellion against it. The chances of success were slight. Slaveholders feared slave uprisings so much that they reacted to them with terrible brutality. When captured, rebellious slaves were always killed.

One rebel slave was Denmark Vesey of Charleston, South Carolina. Vesey had purchased his freedom after winning some money in a lottery. Yet he was not satisfied with escaping from bondage himself. For years he planned his uprising, gradually gathering a group of blacks ready to take up arms. In 1822 he was ready to act. At the last moment one of his men lost his nerve and betrayed the plot. Although the rebellion never took place, Vesey and 26 others were hanged.

The bloodiest slave uprising was that organized by Nat Turner, a slave in Southampton County, Virginia. To whites who knew him, Turner had seemed the last person who might be expected to resort to violence. He was mild mannered and deeply religious. Yet in 1831 he and his followers murdered 57 people before they were captured. Historians still argue about whether or not Turner was insane. The point is that nearly every slave hated bondage. Nearly all were eager to see something done to destroy the system.

■ How did some slaves protest bondage?

390

The Granger Collection

BLACK ABOLITIONISTS

Only free blacks in the free states could speak openly against slavery. Many did so well before abolitionism became an important movement among white Americans. There were a large number of antislavery societies organized by black Americans long before the creation of the American Anti-Slavery Society.

Black abolitionists varied in their specific ideas just as white abolitionists did. One of the first whom we know much about was Paul Cuffe. Cuffe was born free in Massachusetts Bay in 1759. As a youth he went to sea. Gradually he saved enough to buy a ship. He prospered. Eventually he owned a fleet of six merchant vessels. By 1800 he was probably the richest black in the United States.

Cuffe favored the return of blacks to Africa. Most white colonizationists wanted to send former slaves to Africa in order to get rid of them. Cuffe saw colonization as a way for black people to free themselves from prejudice and mistreatment by the white majority. He transported 38 black volunteers to West Africa in 1815 at his own expense. He intended to bring a new group each year, but he died before he could carry out his plan.

Henry Highland Garnet was more bitterly antislavery than Paul Cuffe. Garnet was born a slave in 1815 but escaped to the North with his parents when he was a small boy. His father became a shoemaker in New York City. Garnet managed to get a high school education. He went to sea and lost a leg as a result of an accident.

The Granger Collection

Abolitionist Henry Highland Garnet is shown in this 1881 engraving. He urged slaves to strike for freedom. What did other black abolitionists believe was the best way to do away with slavery?

Harriet Ross Tubman, *above,* sat for H. B. Lindsley's photographic study. Below is a detail from an 1867 oil by Theodor Kaufmann, "On to Liberty." The escaping slaves surge forward as they realize that they may be free at last. How did Tubman aid runaway slaves such as these?

Garnet was a man of fierce determination. He had an eye, a friend said, "that looks through you." During the 1830s and 1840s he preached abolition to black and white audiences alike. Here is an example of his radical argument:

> Brethren arise, arise! Strike for your lives and liberties. Now is the day and the hour. Let every slave throughout the land do this and the days of slavery are numbered . . . . *Rather die freemen than live to be slaves.*

A number of black women joined the attack on slavery. Harriet Ross Tubman, for example, escaped from Maryland into Pennsylvania when faced with the threat of being "sold down the river" after the death of her owner. She got a job as a cook in Philadelphia. But she was not satisfied merely to be free or even to make speeches urging the abolition of slavery. She became a specialist at the highly dangerous task of helping slaves to escape into the northern states. She helped between 200 and 300 escaped slaves make their way to freedom.

- How did Paul Cuffe fight slavery?
- How did Henry Garnet fight slavery?
- How did Harriet Ross Tubman fight slavery?

Gemini-Smith

FREDERICK DOUGLASS

The most famous black abolitionist was Frederick Douglass. Douglass had been a slave in Baltimore. In 1836 he ran away but was captured before he could get to a free state. Two years later he tried again, this time succeeding. He settled in Massachusetts.

One day in 1841 Douglass attended a meeting of the Massachusetts Anti-Slavery Society. Garrison himself was present. Without preparation Douglass stood up and delivered a powerful speech. The members of the society were so impressed that they urged him to become an agent of the society and work full time for abolition.

White abolitionists found that black speakers, particularly former slaves like Frederick Douglass, were the best possible advertisements for their cause. Former slaves understood the horrors of slavery as no white person could.

Frederick Douglass proved to be the most moving and persuasive of all the black abolitionists. He was a big, handsome man with what would today be called a magnetic personality. He was an excellent speaker. At first he followed the lead of Garrison, demanding instant abolition and refusing to make the slightest compromise. Eventually he decided that the only way to change the system was to work within it. He then began to engage in political activity. He also published his own abolitionist paper, *The North Star*.

■ How did Frederick Douglass fight for abolition?

A photograph of Frederick Douglass taken in the 1880s shows his power. Douglass was a much-admired orator. How did he change in his methods of seeking abolition of slavery?

THE INFLUENCE OF THE ABOLITIONISTS

In the 1840s and 1850s American abolitionists were a small minority in every part of the country. The followers of William Lloyd Garrison were a small minority of this minority. Nevertheless, the abolitionists had a large influence on public opinion, and Garrison and his followers had a large influence on other abolitionists.

Even people who considered abolitionists dreamers who threatened the peace of the Union were affected by their arguments against slavery. Such people were unwilling to act. But their dislike of slavery grew. Their consciences bothered them. Moderate abolitionists found themselves listening more closely to Garrison. Their own efforts to persuade others to support gradual change had come to nothing.

Many abolitionists became discouraged by their apparent lack of success in getting rid of slavery. But in one important sense they were succeeding better than they knew. They were convincing the people of the North that slavery was a bad institution. They had yet to convince northerners that it was possible to free the nation of slavery.

■ How did the abolitionists influence opinion in the North?

CHAPTER 13 REVIEW

Identification

Tell briefly why each of the following persons, terms, or events is important.

1. Eli Whitney
2. Benjamin Lundy
3. William Lloyd Garrison
4. Angelina Grimké
5. Theodore Dwight Weld
6. Denmark Vesey
7. Nat Turner
8. Paul Cuffe
9. Henry Highland Garnet
10. Harriet Ross Tubman
11. Frederick Douglass
12. American Colonization Society
13. Upland cotton
14. Cotton gin
15. Cotton press
16. "Cotton is King"
17. "The peculiar institution"
18. Abolitionists
19. Emancipation
20. American Anti-Slavery Society

Understanding American History

1. How did the cotton gin help make cotton the most important crop in the South?
2. How did the cotton gin affect southerners' desire for new land and more slaves?
3. How did increased cotton production affect both the North and the South?
4. Describe the yearly cycle of life on a cotton plantation.
5. How did the lives of the slaves change as cotton production increased?
6. What arguments did some southerners use to defend "the peculiar institution"?
7. Why were Americans in all sections proud of their country and their way of life in the 1830s?
8. What were some of the arguments used by abolitionists to attack slavery?
9. How did most white northerners feel about the abolitionists? Explain.
10. Why did William Lloyd Garrison split with many other abolitionists?

Activities

1. Make a large diagram of a cotton gin to explain how it works to the class. Use large sheets of cardboard that can be seen easily by all students, or prepare your diagram for an overhead projector. Then plan a short talk to explain the importance of Eli Whitney's invention.
2. Working in small groups, plan skits to show how North and South viewed each other in the 1830s. Use your historical imagination. Suppose that you have just returned to your southern plantation home from a visit to relatives in a northeastern city. While there, you were taken to an abolitionist meeting. Tell your southern family and friends what opinions and attitudes you found in the North. Another group can reverse the situation. While visiting in the South, you were taken to the cabin of an elderly slave who was in the care of family members and the slaveowner. Explain your impressions to your family in the North.
3. Prepare a short Fourth of July address to deliver in class. Use historical imagination to make the time the 1830s and the place a bandstand in a city park. Tell which achievements of your section of the country and of the nation as a whole fill you with pride. Be sure that all sections of the country are represented—Northeast, South, and West.
4. Prepare a short biographical sketch of one of these early abolitionists:

    Benjamin Lundy   Henry Highland Garnet
    Angelina Grimké   Frederick Douglass
    William Lloyd Garrison   Paul Cuffe
5. Do library research into the remarkable life of Harriet Ross Tubman. Then write a short paper describing her achievements or prepare a short dramatic scene based on one episode in her life.

CHAPTER 13 TEST

Matching (30 points)
Number your paper 1–10 and match the person in the second column with the description in the first column.

1. A moderate who believed in "immediate abolition gradually achieved"
2. Former slave who helped many slaves escape to the North
3. Inventor of the cotton gin
4. A radical who wanted immediate abolition of all slaves
5. Famous black abolitionist who became a great speaker and writer against slavery
6. Free black who became wealthy and wanted to return all blacks to Africa
7. A Quaker and early abolitionist who at first favored gradual emancipation but later favored immediate emancipation
8. Slave whose rebellion never started because he was betrayed
9. Moderate abolitionist who wrote *Appeal to the Christian Women of the South*
10. Executed leader of the bloodiest slave uprising in the South

a. Eli Whitney
b. Benjamin Lundy
c. William Lloyd Garrison
d. Angelina Grimké
e. Theodore Dwight Weld
f. Denmark Vesey
g. Nat Turner
h. Paul Cuffe
i. Harriet Ross Tubman
j. Frederick Douglass

Completion (30 points)
Number your paper 11–20 and next to each number write the words from the list below that best complete each sentence.

North   emancipation
South   cotton press
"the peculiar institution"   abolitionists
cotton gin   "King Cotton"
upland cotton   slaves

Tobacco was the major crop of the __11__ before the invention of the __12__. But once it became easier to separate the fibers, __13__ could be grown in most climates. It was shipped north and abroad after being packed in bales by an invention called the __14__. Growing cotton increased the demand for __15__ to work in the fields. Southerners came to believe in the power of the export they called __16__. Some argued that slavery, or __17__, was necessary for their way of life. Still, slavery was increasingly criticized by persons called __18__, who demanded its end. These people were divided between radicals who demanded immediate __19__ and moderates who favored a more gradual course. Slowly many people in the __20__ came to the belief that slavery was an evil institution.

Essay (40 points)
In a short paper explain three reasons that southerners used to defend slavery *and* give three arguments abolitionists used to attack slavery. If time permits, write a first draft for your teacher to review before you make a clean copy.

CHAPTER 14

The Age of Reform

Phelps-Stokes Collection, The New York Public Library

At the dawn of the Age of Reform Broadway was abustle with wagons, carriages, and horse-drawn trolleys. This New York City street scene is an aquatint created by John Hill and Thomas Horner in about 1835. Behind this broad street and these sturdy storefronts lie the crowded sweatshops and narrow tenements that reformers sought to improve. Why were Americans optimistic in the time from 1830 to 1850?

From the 1830s through the 1850s the effort to get rid of slavery was only one of many reform movements. This was truly an **Age of Reform.** The rapid growth of the country was causing changes of all sorts. These changes were mostly good for the average person. But sometimes they had undesirable side effects. Using machines for mass production reduced the price of goods. But the introduction of machinery often caused skilled workers to lose their jobs. The growth of cities opened up all sorts of opportunities for thousands of people. But it also led to crowded, unhealthy living conditions.

Since Americans were so proud of their society, they found any flaw or weakness in it frustrating and annoying. Because they were so self-confident, they took these imperfections as a challenge. At every hand they could see signs of growth and progress. This made them optimistic about the future. Something *could* be done. Therefore something *must* be done. That was the dominant attitude of the reformers.

396

WOMEN IN JACKSONIAN AMERICA

One of the strangest things about the movement to free slaves was that many of its most active supporters were themselves not entirely free. When women came forward to speak out against slavery, they were attacked by people who believed that it was "unfeminine" for a woman to speak in public to a mixed audience. Even many male abolitionists took this position. At an international antislavery convention held in London in 1840, the men in charge refused to allow women delegates to participate. Two American delegates, Lucretia Mott and Elizabeth Cady Stanton, had to watch the proceedings from the balcony.

Nowhere were women placed in more lofty positions than in America. Nowhere were they more respected. But they were still treated as second-class citizens. They could not vote, hold public office, or sit on juries. Married women had no control over their own property. In the eyes of the law they were in the same position as children. They were subject to control by their husbands. Single women fared slightly better. At least they could manage their own property.

Women also had few opportunities to get a good education or have an interesting career. They could not get into most high schools and colleges. People of the time believed that women's brains and nervous systems could not stand the strain of studying difficult subjects such as chemistry and mathematics!

What was woman's role in Jacksonian America? To serve man, according to this 19th-century painting. Only the very old or very young are seated at the 'pic nick' table. This is a detail from an oil by Jerome B. Thompson of an outdoor banquet in Camden, Maine. The women either serve the meal or stand aside—shy, silly, sorrowful— plaiting garlands to amuse a violin player, staring pensively away when a suitor proposes marriage. What was the status of women at this time?

M. and M. Karolik Collection, Museum of Fine Arts.

This daguerreotype shows women students of Emerson School in about 1850. It was taken by Southworth and Hawes. The instructor who sits comfortably on a raised platform is of course a man. What opportunities did women have to take classes such as this one in 1830–50?

Metropolitan Museum of Art

Even most women who tried to improve women's education believed this to be true. Emma Hunt Willard's *Plan for Improving Female Education,* published in 1819, called for teaching young girls religion, housekeeping, literature, and music. The goal was to prepare them for marriage and motherhood, not for a "masculine" career. When Catherine and Mary Beecher decided to teach chemistry at their Female Seminary in Connecticut, they assured parents and prospective students that knowledge of chemistry would make their graduates better cooks.

- What were some of the things women could not do in America of the early 1830s and 1840s?
- What purpose was given for women's education?

WOMEN IN THE PROFESSIONS

The ideal woman was expected to be religious, mild mannered, obedient, and totally domestic—nothing more. Practically all careers but marriage and teaching school were considered unfeminine. To be married and "live happily ever after" was supposed to be the goal for every young girl.

Nevertheless, a few women made their careers in male-dominated fields. Elizabeth Blackwell, a teacher, was determined to be a doctor. She read medical books at night. A sympathetic doctor gave her private lessons so that she could qualify for the Geneva Medical College in New York. She graduated first in her class in 1849 and became the first woman licensed to practice medicine in the United States.

Elizabeth Blackwell went on to establish her own hospital, the New York Infirmary for Women and Children, and a medical college for women. Her sister-in-law, Antoinette Brown Blackwell, became

398

Schlesinger Library, Radcliffe College

Early achievements by women were made by Elizabeth Blackwell, *left*, a medical doctor, and Sarah J. Hale, *right*, the editor of *Godey's Lady's Book*, from which comes the fashion plate shown below. This watercolor appeared in November 1842. Which careers were considered 'feminine' at this time?

the first woman to be ordained a minister. Antoinette Blackwell was also active in many reform movements. Yet she found time to raise six children and to write no less than ten books.

Another such professional, Sara Josepha Hale, became the editor of the leading women's magazine of the day, *Godey's Lady's Book*. Hale worked to improve the education of women. She also wrote poetry for children, including "Mary Had a Little Lamb."

The overwhelming majority of professional women of the period were elementary school teachers. By the 1850s Philadelphia had 699 women and 82 men teaching in its school system. Brooklyn, New York, had 103 women and only 17 men. Yet nearly all the school principals were men, and male teachers were paid higher salaries.

The Granger Collection

- What was Elizabeth Blackwell's achievement?
- In what field were the overwhelming majority of professional women?

WOMAN AS GUARDIAN OF THE HOME

Elementary school teaching fit in neatly with women's role as mother. Child-rearing had always been their responsibility. In the 1830s and 1840s it seemed more important than ever. People were beginning to leave the farms for the cities. Instead of the whole family working on one plot of land, the father became the "breadwinner," the mother guardian of the home.

Factory work kept fathers away from home from early morning to late evening, six days a week. The mother had almost complete charge of rearing the children. Men no longer shared in most house-hold chores. That was "woman's work."

- Why did the role of woman as guardian of the home become more important in the 1830s and 1840s?

THE WOMEN'S RIGHTS MOVEMENT

City life and increasing prosperity meant more leisure time for middle- and upper-class women. These women had household servants to help them with their domestic chores. Therefore they could develop new interests and activities. Many became involved in the reform movements of the day. In particular, many became abolitionists.

Women who protested against slavery soon became aware of their own lowly position in society. One argument against slavery was the statement in the Declaration of Independence that all men were created equal. If slaves were entitled to equality, surely "free" women were too. Yet when women tried to speak out against slavery, they were often prevented from doing so. Even most male abolitionists did not believe in true equality for females.

Both Sarah and Angelina Grimké experienced so much resistance when they made public speeches attacking slavery that they became militant feminists. In *Letters on the Equality of the Sexes and the Condition of Women* (1838), Sarah Grimké wrote that "history teems with women's wrongs" and "is wet with women's tears."

For women abolitionists this was what would today be called a "consciousness-raising" experience. They began to believe that besides trying to free the slaves, they must try to free themselves and their sisters from forms of bondage based on sex. Elizabeth Cady Stanton, one of the women who had not been allowed to participate in the London antislavery conference of 1840, wrote: "I now fully understood the practical difficulties most women had to contend with. . . . The wearied, anxious look of the majority of women impressed me with the strong feeling that some measures should be taken."

Brown Brothers

National Portrait Gallery

Organizers of the Women's Rights Convention in 1848 were Elizabeth Cady Stanton, *left,* and Lucretia Coffin Mott, *right.* Mott is shown in an 1842 oil portrait by Joseph Kyle. Which conference would not allow these women participation?

The Granger Collection

In 1848 Stanton, with Lucretia Mott, organized a **Women's Rights Convention** at Seneca Falls, New York. The delegates to the convention issued a *Declaration of Sentiments* modeled on the Declaration of Independence. "All men *and women* are created equal," it said. The history of mankind, it went on, "is a history of repeated injuries . . . on the part of man toward woman." These injuries included denials of the right to vote, the right to equal educational opportunities, and the right to own property. The **Seneca Falls Declaration** closed with the demand that women be given "all the rights and privileges which belong to them as citizens of the United States."

Similar meetings were soon being held throughout the nation. In the 1850s several national feminist conventions took place. Women were on the move. Their cause won many new supporters. The most important of these was Susan B. Anthony of New York.

In the 1850s Anthony organized campaigns on behalf of equal pay for women teachers and for equal property rights. Her efforts encouraged other feminists to continue the struggle. Soon Massachusetts and Indiana passed more liberal divorce laws. In 1860 New York gave women the right to sue in court and to control their earnings and property. But nowhere were women able to win the right to vote. They made some progress during the Age of Reform, but the vote was not yet theirs.

- How did the fight against slavery lead to the women's rights movement in the 1840s?
- What did women demand in the Seneca Falls Declaration?
- For what did Susan B. Anthony campaign?

A newspaper cartoonist showed the Women's Rights Convention held at Seneca Falls with this caricature. In the balcony men yawn, stretch, and jeer, while the ladies hold up their heads and scowl at the interruption of their speaker. The title given this cartoon reveals its attitude toward 1840s women: "The Orator of the Day Denouncing the Lords of Creation." What important right was denied to women during the Age of Reform?

READING PRACTICE
IN SOCIAL STUDIES

How Paragraphs Form Sections

Paragraphs are made up of details, one added to another. Details can develop a main idea, suggest an unstated main idea, add interesting information, or clarify other details. Just as paragraphs are made from details, so are sections in this book made up of paragraphs.

Paragraphs have several different functions in a section. Four of the basic functions are to *introduce,* to *develop* a topic, to *make transitions* from one idea to another, and to *summarize or conclude* a section. By looking closely at one section from this book, you can readily see how paragraphs form sections.

The section titled "The Women's Rights Movement" on page 400 consists of seven paragraphs. Three of these have specific functions while the others serve to develop the topic.

The first paragraph introduces the topic by describing the conditions which made some women seek equal rights. It reads:

> City life and increasing prosperity meant more leisure time for middle- and upper-class women. These women had household servants to help them with their domestic chores. Therefore they could develop new interests and activities. Many became involved in the reform movements of the day. In particular, many became abolitionists.

The topic is *Women becoming involved in reform movements*.

The next two paragraphs develop the topic by giving particulars such as the following:

> Both Sarah and Angelina Grimké experienced so much resistance when they made public speeches attacking slavery that they became militant feminists. In *Letters on the Equality of the Sexes and the Condition of Women* (1838), Sarah Grimké wrote that "history teems with women's wrongs" and "is wet with women's tears."

The fourth paragraph is transitional — it acts as a bridge from the ideas of the first paragraphs to those which follow. Not all transitional paragraphs state a main idea. Some simply are intended to help the writing flow smoothly from one idea to another. However, there is a main idea in the following transitional paragraph:

> For women abolitionists this was what would today be called a "consciousness-raising" experience. They began to believe that besides trying to free the slaves, they must free themselves and their sisters from forms of bondage based on sex.

After the topic is developed further by two more paragraphs, there is the following concluding paragraph:

> In the 1850s Anthony organized campaigns on behalf of equal pay for women teachers and for equal property rights. Her efforts encouraged other feminists to continue the struggle. Soon Massachusetts and Indiana passed more liberal divorce laws. In 1860 New York gave women the right to sue in court and to control their earnings and property. But nowhere were women able to win the right to vote. They made some progress during the Age of Reform, but the vote was not yet theirs.

Most sections in this book are formed like the model examined in this Reading Practice. However, there are always exceptions since it is variety that makes writing interesting.

Read the section titled "Horace Mann" on page 403 and then answer the following questions.
1. What is the topic of the section?
2. What idea, in your own words, does the first paragraph introduce?
3. Which details in the third paragraph develop the topic of the section?
4. Give some reasons why the fourth and fifth paragraphs are transitional.
5. Which sentences in the final paragraph are intended to conclude the section?

Addison Gallery of American Art, Phillips Academy, Andover, Massachusetts

FREE PUBLIC SCHOOLS

Unlike the women's rights movement, the fight for public education made a great deal of progress during the Age of Reform. Before the 1820s only a handful of communities maintained free schools. By the 1850s villages, towns, and cities all over the nation had established such schools. Education had become a public responsibility.

Educational reformers argued that a democracy could not exist unless all people could read and write. Schools would train students to be patriotic, hardworking, law-abiding citizens. In addition, ordinary working men and women supported public education because they hoped that schools would enable their children to rise in the world. The growth of public education for all had far-reaching effects. By 1860 90 per cent of all adult whites in America could read and write.

▓ Why did Americans support public education?

HORACE MANN

The effort to improve public education was particularly strong in Massachusetts. The early Puritans had established elementary and secondary schools in all but the smallest of their towns. Now, in the Age of Reform, the state built on this Puritan foundation.

Much of the credit belongs to Horace Mann, a lawyer and state legislator. When Massachusetts established a state board of education

"New England Country School" was painted in oil in about 1878 by the fine American artist Winslow Homer. The movement for free public schools offered education to this handful of pupils who recited their lessons in one room that housed all grades. At this time teaching was one of a few occupations permitted women. Why did reformers believe in teaching all people to read and write?

National Portrait Gallery

Horace Mann led efforts to improve public schools. This lithograph was made c. 1859 by Francis D'Avignon. On what foundation did Mann build?

Winslow Homer was best known for watercolors. "Homework" offers this portrait of a young pupil reading his lessons while the sun is still strong. What would his school have been like in the 1830s-1850s?

in 1837, Mann became its secretary. He worked for laws that required school attendance. He called for special schools to train teachers. He favored higher salaries for teachers and better equipment for schools.

In 1839 Mann founded the first teacher training institute in the United States. Similar schools were soon established throughout the country. These institutes were called **normal schools,** the word coming from *norm,* meaning a "model" or "standard."

Before 1839 teachers had rarely received any direct training. There were no established qualifications a teacher had to meet. One man being interviewed for a job in a mining town was asked only, "Do you retain a clear recollection of the twenty-six letters of the alphabet?" Apparently that was all he was expected to know to "educate" the local children.

Mann was also interested in building new schools. He was exaggerating only a little when he said that "there is more physical suffering endured by our children" in badly constructed schoolhouses "than by prisoners in our jails."

Down through the 1840s wood-frame, one-room "little red schoolhouses" were the rule. In these small buildings 60 or more children of all ages were crowded into one classroom. A single teacher had to deal with first graders and teenagers at the same time. It was difficult to learn with so many distractions. But in the Boston of Horace Mann's day there were few schoolhouses of any kind. Most classes were held in stores and cellars.

By modern standards the best schools of the 1830s and 1840s were very uncomfortable. They had no washrooms. Students sat on narrow, backless benches. Yet, thanks to Horace Mann, by 1848 Massachusetts had built 50 well-equipped and comfortable public schools. Other states soon followed Massachusetts's lead.

■ For what reforms in education did Horace Mann work?

THE SCHOOL CURRICULUM

The main subjects students of the early 1800s learned were known as **"the three R's"**—reading, writing, and 'rithmetic. They were taught quite differently than they are today. Before the 1840s most American schools used a teaching method developed in England by Joseph Lancaster. Lancaster used a **monitor system** in which teachers instructed older students who, in turn, taught younger pupils their lessons.

The **Lancasterian system** appealed to American educators and politicians because it provided instruction at the lowest possible cost. It did nothing, however, to encourage individual growth or to open the imagination.

404

In the 1840s and 1850s some educators began to question the Lancasterian system. Reformers like Horace Mann wanted to make education more exciting. Students should be encouraged to give free play to their imaginations. But like all educators, the reformers agreed that the schools' main purpose should be to build character and train children to become good citizens.

- What main subjects were students taught in the early 1800s?
- Why did educators and politicians like the Lancasterian system of education? How did reformers like Horace Mann want to change education?

IDEAL COMMUNITIES

Relying on education to improve society was likely to be a slow process. Few educational leaders were calling for drastic change. Yet many reformers were dreaming of totally reorganizing society. Some thought it wrong that a few people were much richer than all the others. They hoped to create a world where wealth would be shared equally.

Others thought that family life drew people into a small, closed circle and shut others out. They believed that people should live in community houses and that children should be raised and trained in common, not by their individual parents.

Most Americans considered such schemes foolish and unworkable, if not downright dangerous. The reformers tended therefore to establish small communities in thinly settled parts of the country. The huge tracts of cheap, undeveloped land still to be found in the United States made it relatively easy to do so. Between 1820 and 1850 at least 58 such **ideal communities** were founded.

Many of these were very short-lived. Some lasted many years. A few evolved into institutions that still survive. The Mormons went west to Utah for much the same reason that the Puritans had come to Massachusetts Bay. Both groups wished to practice their religion without interference from people in their country who considered them dangerous and wrongheaded. The settlement on the Great Salt Lake was the Mormons' ideal community, organized according to their distinct beliefs.

Many other ideal communities were created by religious sects. One of the first to do so was the **Shakers.** This sect was founded by an Englishwoman, "Mother Ann" Lee. Mother Ann believed that she was God. She predicted that the world would soon come to an end. There was no point, therefore, in anyone having children.

Life in Shaker communities, which were called "families," was strictly regulated by a group of elders, half of them men, half women. Members wore simple black clothes. The two sexes lived separately.

Metropolitan Museum of Art

Shaker furniture is widely admired for its simple and functional design. This chair of wood and cane would hang on the wall when not in use. Who founded the Shakers?

405

Everyone was expected to work very hard. All profits belonged to the group. Contacts with the outside world were few.

Despite these strict rules the Shakers seemed to enjoy life. Singing, listening to sermons, work itself were all seen as serious religious activities and profoundly satisfying group experiences. New recruits entered the sect. When time passed without the world coming to an end, the Shakers began to adopt orphans in order to renew the membership. By the 1840s there were 20 Shaker communities in America.

Members of the Oneida community have assembled for their dinner in this 19th-century engraving. They share in this communal meal just as they share the work of the ideal community. How did the members support themselves?

The **Amana community,** founded by a German immigrant, Christian Metz, and the **Oneida community,** founded by John Humphrey Noyes, were two other important communities of this type. Metz founded his settlement in western New York and later moved it to Iowa. The Noyes group began in Vermont and eventually settled in Oneida, New York. Both prospered. They owned much rich farmland and also developed manufacturing.

People who joined these communities made large personal sacrifices. Obviously most of them were deeply committed to the goals of the group. They were hardworking and skillful. Shaker furniture, simple and graceful, is still highly prized. The handiwork of both Oneida and Amana has evolved into modern manufacturing companies, Oneida making silverware, Amana electrical appliances.

- How did most Americans view ideal communities?
- What was life like in a Shaker community?

HELPING THE DISADVANTAGED

Many people were unwilling to live in isolated communities and abandon all the customs and patterns of ordinary life. They were nonetheless sincerely interested in improving society. Some devoted their energies to helping people in need. Samuel Gridley Howe, a Boston doctor, specialized in the education of the blind. In the 1830s he founded a school, the **Perkins Institution.** He developed a method for printing books with raised type so that blind people could learn to "read" with their fingertips. Howe's greatest achievement was teaching Laura Bridgman, a child who was both blind and deaf, to read in this way and to communicate with others through signs called a manual alphabet. Another of his pupils, Anne Sullivan, learned the manual alphabet to communicate with Laura. She later became the teacher of Helen Keller, a remarkable woman who lost her sight and hearing as an infant.

Another Massachusetts reformer, Dorothea Dix, practically revolutionized the treatment of the mentally ill. Dix was a schoolteacher. One day in 1841 she was asked to teach a Sunday school class in a jail in Cambridge, Massachusetts. When she went to the jail, she discovered to her horror that insane and feeble-minded people were being kept there and treated like ordinary criminals.

Compassion for the disadvantaged led Samuel Gridley Howe, *above*, to found Perkins Institution. Anne Sullivan, a graduate of the school, became the teacher of Helen Keller, who could not see, hear, or speak. The famous teacher and her pupil are pictured below. How did Anne Sullivan communicate with pupils?

Brown Brothers

Granger Collection

Dorothea Lynde Dix is the subject of this daguerreotype taken about 1848. What reform did she lead?

Thereafter, Dix devoted her life to improving the care of the insane. She visited prisons all over the country and wrote reports describing conditions and exposing their faults. Dix insisted that insanity should be treated as a disease and that it could be cured. Through her efforts many states set up asylums for the care of the mentally ill.

■ How did Samuel Gridley Howe help blind people?
■ How did Dorothea Dix work to help the insane?

CHILD CARE

The social problem of **juvenile delinquency** was also attacked by reformers. As cities grew larger, an increasing number of children and teenagers began to get into trouble with the law. When a boy or girl was caught stealing, for example, the "criminal" was handled the same way that adult thieves were. If convicted, these young people were thrown into the same jails that older convicts were kept in.

Many other children who had not committed crimes wandered homeless about the cities. They were orphans or runaways or youngsters who had been abandoned by their parents. When found, these children were often put into the local poorhouse, called an **almshouse.** Again they were kept along with adults, many of them tramps, drunkards, and similar types.

Reformers realized that this system only increased the chances

"Buffalo Newsboy" was painted in oil by Thomas Le Clear in 1853. At this time boys and girls in trouble with the law were jailed with adults. Homeless children wandered city streets. Reformers opened houses of refuge to care for children. What was the daily routine in a house of refuge?

View of the Berks — County — Almshouse. 1880.
DIRECTORS: MAHLON FOGLEMAN, FRANCIS ROLAND, JOHN H. BOWER.
STEWARD: BENJ. ANDERSON. UNDER STEWARD: G. E. WISNER.
INSANE HOSPITAL STEWARD: JAMES W. SALLADE. CLERK: J. B. KNORR.

Metropolitan Museum of Art

that young delinquents and wanderers would become dangerous criminals when they grew up. As one put it, the jails turned "little Devils" into "great ones." Instead, the delinquent children should be reformed and the homeless ones protected and taught a trade so that they would be able to earn their livings.

To accomplish these goals, **houses of refuge** were founded as early as the 1820s in New York, Boston, and Philadelphia. Life in these houses was hard, discipline strict. The children rose at dawn, dressed, and were marched off to the washroom. After passing inspection to make sure that they were neat and clean, they had an hour or so of lessons. Only then was there a recess for breakfast.

The rest of the day, except for the noon break, was spent working in shops. The boys made such things as cane chair seats, nails, and candles. The girls spent the time sewing. Work ended at about five o'clock. Then, after a light supper, the children marched back to school. The evening classes went on until bedtime.

This system was very harsh by modern standards. Children who violated the rules were often beaten, even put in solitary confinement. But it was a true reform. These houses of refuge represented the first attempt to treat delinquent children differently from adult criminals.

Gold paint on zinc is used to show the poorhouse in this 1880 oil made by John Rasmussen. It shows the Berks County Almshouse, which is actually several stout structures. Who were the inhabitants of such a place?

409

Charles Loring Brace is the subject of this 19th-century engraving. The New York social reformer removed homeless children from slums. How were these children more victims than criminals?

Gradually some of the people who studied juvenile delinquency began to realize that in many cases the children were more victims than criminals. The terrible poverty of the slums made it difficult for them to lead decent, normal lives.

One such person was Charles Loring Brace, one of the first American social workers. Brace founded the **Children's Aid Society** of New York in 1853. The society opened lodging houses where homeless boys and girls could live without actually being confined as they were in a house of refuge. It also established schools to teach children trades.

Brace persuaded manufacturers to give some of the children jobs. But his main goal was to be able to relocate homeless children with farm families. He believed that the terrible conditions of slum life in the cities was the main reason why delinquent children were getting into trouble. "The best of all Asylums for the outcast child," he said, is a "farmer's home."

- Why did reformers want children taken out of almshouses?
- Where did Charles Loring Brace believe homeless children could have the best lives?

THE ATTACK ON "DEMON RUM"

Some reformers worked to improve the training of the deaf. Others worked for world peace. Still others tried to get citizens to give up what the reformers considered bad habits, such as drinking or playing games on Sundays. (Many critics considered these people not reformers but busybodies.)

The campaign against alcohol was the most important attempt made to control the personal behavior of citizens. The effort to restrict drinking began as a call for **temperance.** It was a fight against drunkenness, not against drinking in moderation. But it soon became a campaign for **total abstinence** and the **prohibition** by law of the manufacture and sale of all alcoholic beverages. Those who favored prohibition called drinkers sinners and potential criminals.

The members of the **American Temperance Union,** which was founded in 1826, went about the land lecturing and distributing pamphlets. Despite the name they were outright prohibitionists. They urged drinkers to "sign the pledge"—that is, to promise in writing that they would give up alcohol completely.

The campaign reached a high point in 1851 when the state of Maine outlawed the manufacture and sale of alcoholic drinks. The person most responsible for the passage of this law, Neal Dow, was a manufacturer who became alarmed because many of the men who worked for him were ruining their lives with drink.

- What was the high point of the temperance campaign?

A popular series of engravings made in the 19th century showed a family destroyed by alcohol. Timothy Shay Arthur offered these scenes entitled "The Bottle and the Pledge." In the pleasant family scene we watch as the head of the household persuades his wary wife to join him in a friendly drink. The bottle takes its toll. While the children huddle together, their father dozes drunkenly. Meanwhile the mother trades household effects to buy more liquor. Now the table is bare, the cupboard empty, the cat scrawny, and the fireplace cold. What was "the pledge" members of the Temperance Society signed?

ECONOMIC REFORM

There were also reformers who wished to change the American economic system. Most people in the nation were better off by far than the average European. But some were not. Many who worked hard had not been able to rise above poverty. Furthermore, as the economy expanded, some people were growing very rich. The gap between wealthy merchants and manufacturers and people of ordinary income seemed to be widening.

Reformers found these trends to be alarming. "Does a man become wiser, stronger, or more virtuous and patriotic because he has a fine house?" asked William Leggett, a New York newspaper editor. "Does he love his country the better because he has a French cook and a box at the opera?"

Leggett blamed the growing gap between rich and poor on what

BUILDING SKILLS IN SOCIAL STUDIES

Following a Time Sequence

The social progress in the United States during the Age of Reform from the 1830s through the 1850s is clearly seen on the *time line* below. It is arranged in five-year intervals and is a part of the time line that opens the unit on pages 316-17.

Because the discussion of social reforms in this chapter is arranged by *categories* — women, education, the disadvantaged — the time line is helpful to show *time sequence*. It shows the order of events by listing *landmarks* — dates that are high points.

Use the time line to answer these questions.
1. How many years are covered by this time line? How do you find each entry's date?
2. Which three landmarks are shown in the struggle by women to gain equal rights?
3. Which two landmarks are shown in the efforts to control the sale of alcoholic drinks?
4. How many years passed between Sarah Grimké's *Letters on the Equality of the Sexes* and the Women's Rights Convention?
5. What is a landmark in improved treatment of the disabled? Of homeless children?

AGE OF REFORM

1820 — 1825 — 1830 — 1835 — 1840 — 1845 — 1850

American Temperance Union, 1826

Howe founds Perkins Institution, 1832
• National Trades' Union, 1834

Massachusetts Board of Education, 1837
• Grimké writes *Letters on the Equality of the Sexes*, 1838
• Mann founds teacher training institute, 1839

Dix begins to improve care of the insane, 1841

Women's Rights Convention, 1848
• Blackwell licensed to practice medicine, 1849

Maine bans sale of alcoholic drinks, 1851
• Brace founds Children's Aid Society, 1853

he somewhat vaguely called "concentrated money power." He supported Andrew Jackson's attack on the Second Bank of the United States. And he favored reducing tariffs because high tariffs increased the profits of the manufacturers and caused prices to rise.

Leggett's policies were less drastic than those put forth by some other economic reformers. Thomas Skidmore, for example, proposed that rich people not be allowed to leave their wealth to their children. He even proposed that all the personal property of all the people in the country be taken over by the government. It would then be spread among the people in equal shares.

George Henry Evans, publisher of a newspaper called *The Working Man's Advocate,* had a more practical suggestion. Evans's slogan was "Vote Yourself a Farm." He wanted the government to limit the amount of land that any one person could own. He urged Congress to stop the sale of unoccupied land in the West. Publicly owned lands should be divided up into farm plots and given to citizens who were willing to cultivate them. "Are you an American citizen?" one land-reform statement ran. "Then you are a joint owner of public lands. Why not take enough of your property to provide yourself a home? Why not vote yourself a farm?"

William Leggett, shown as a young man in this engraving, was one who struggled to close the gap between rich and poor in Jacksonian America. What did he fear as the economy expanded?

■ What did economic reformers mean by "Vote Yourself a Farm"?

EFFORTS TO HELP WORKERS

One of William Leggett's favorite proposals was that workers should organize into unions. Although there were some labor organizations during the colonial period, unions had always been considered illegal. They were thought to be conspiracies, plots organized by workers to "control" wages at the expense of employers and the public. Yet by the 1830s many skilled workers were founding unions. In 1834 several trade groups even managed to create a national organization, the **National Trades' Union.** Finally, in 1842, a Massachusetts judge, Lemuel Shaw, ruled in the case of *Commonwealth v. Hunt* that labor unions were not conspiracies unless the members engaged in specific criminal activity. "For men to agree together to exercise their . . . rights," is no crime, Judge Shaw declared. Thereafter, the courts of other states accepted this argument.

Few factory workers organized unions during these years. But the hard conditions and long hours of factory work caused a number of reformers to try to improve the lives of these workers.

Seth Luther, a carpenter and cotton textile worker, was one of the most radical critics of the factory system. Most of the reformers came from farms or from well-to-do city families. They had no actual experience as laborers. Unlike these types, Luther knew what life in

413

the factories was like. He criticized the system vigorously. In particular he denounced the employment of children in factories. Instead of laboring all day over a loom, every child in the nation, he said, should receive a good education at public expense. He called for shorter work hours for all laborers and for better working conditions. He compared the New England textile mills to prisons, the workers to slaves. The employers he said, "wish to control their men in all things; to enslave their bodies and souls, make them think, act, vote, preach, pray, and worship, as it may suit 'We the Owners.'"

Many less radical reformers supported the movement to reduce the working day from the usual dawn-to-darkness routine to ten hours. Unfortunately, the ten-hour movement made little progress. But in 1840 the federal government set a ten-hour limit on the workday of its own employees.

- How did the general public view labor unions?
- What reforms did Seth Luther seek for factory workers?

THE END OF THE AGE OF REFORM

The Age of Reform was a time of high hopes. Today some of the reformers' suggestions seem either undesirable or totally impractical. Others seem quite moderate. At the time the volume and variety of the proposals gave a special excitement to life. But the hectic urge to improve everything at once could not go on forever. What ended it was the conflict between North and South over the future of slavery.

CHAPTER 14 REVIEW

Identification
Tell briefly why each of the following persons, terms, or events is important.
1. Lucretia Mott
2. Elizabeth Cady Stanton
3. Emma Hunt Willard
4. Elizabeth Blackwell
5. Antoinette Brown Blackwell
6. Sara Josepha Hale
7. Susan B. Anthony
8. Horace Mann
9. Samuel Gridley Howe
10. Dorothea Dix
11. Charles Loring Brace
12. William Leggett
13. Seneca Falls Declaration
14. Lancasterian system
15. Normal schools
16. Ideal communities
17. Shakers
18. Houses of refuge
19. American Temperance Union
20. National Trades' Union

Understanding American History
1. Why was the period from 1830 through the 1850s known as the Age of Reform?
2. How were women treated as second-class citizens in Jacksonian America?
3. How did many women make use of increased leisure time?
4. What did most people of the 1830s and 1840s think was the proper role for women?
5. Why did most Americans support the idea of free public schools?
6. What were some of the reforms Horace Mann sought for public education?
7. For what reasons did people try to establish ideal communities between 1820 and 1850?
8. Describe the reforms Dorothea Dix brought to the treatment of the mentally ill.
9. What were some reforms in the treatment of juveniles from 1820 through the 1850s?
10. Explain the difference between temperance and prohibition. What arguments were made for and against prohibition?

Activities
1. The Seneca Falls Declaration declared that "all men *and women* are created equal." Yet it is clear at this point in your study of American history that men are better remembered. In an ongoing class project you can begin to make up for this historical injustice. Set aside a bulletin board or other display space in the classroom. Feature a Woman of the Week whose role in American history, important though it may be, has largely gone unnoticed. You may choose a woman to research from this book, or you may find a strong candidate by reading in other histories or the encyclopedia for the period covered by each chapter. Plan your display so that it will make the life of each Woman of the Week memorable for her achievements. By taking turns, all members of the class can participate in this activity. Place highlights from each display in a scrapbook titled "Women of America."
2. In the Lancasterian system of education older students, called monitors, taught younger pupils. Working in small groups, have several students be monitors and teach history lessons from this chapter. Then discuss the advantages and disadvantages of this method of education.
3. In the Age of Reform some people realized that they could improve society by helping the disadvantaged. What efforts are made by the government or volunteers in your community to help disadvantaged people? Is it possible for you to observe some of these efforts without disturbing others?
4. Research the work of Samuel Gridley Howe for a report on the Perkins Institution.
5. Discuss with your classmates an ideal community you would like to found. How will you ensure fair treatment of all people?

CHAPTER 14 TEST

Matching (30 points)
Number your paper 1–10 and match the description in the first column with the name in the second column.

1. Founder of the Children's Aid Society and one of the first American social workers
2. First woman licensed to practice medicine in the United States
3. Organized campaigns for equal pay and property rights for women
4. Developed the monitor system of education used in America until the 1840s
5. Wrote *Plan for Improving Female Education,* which encouraged the goal of marriage and motherhood
6. An organizer of the Women's Rights Convention
7. Favored economic reform aimed at closing the gap between rich and poor
8. Editor of *Godey's Lady's Book* who worked to improve the education of women
9. Revolutionized the treatment of the mentally ill
10. Educational reformer who worked for better teacher training and more equipment for schools

a. Lucretia Mott
b. Emma Hunt Willard
c. Elizabeth Blackwell
d. Sara Josepha Hale
e. Susan B. Anthony
f. Horace Mann
g. Joseph Lancaster
h. Dorothea Dix
i. Charles Loring Brace
j. William Leggett

Completion (30 points)
Number your paper 11–20 and next to each number write the words from the list below that best complete each sentence.

Perkins Institution
Women's Rights Convention
normal schools
ideal communities
Seneca Falls Declaration

monitor system
Shakers
"the three R's"
Age of Reform
temperance

The period from 1830 through the 1850s in America is called the __11__. In 1848 Lucretia Mott and Elizabeth Cady Stanton organized the __12__, which said in the __13__ that "all men *and women* are created equal."

Meanwhile, the reformer Horace Mann tried to change the __14__ of education favored by Joseph Lancaster. Students learned mainly what were called __15__. Mann established __16__ to train teachers.

Members of religious sects such as the __17__ lived in what were called __18__, where they withdrew from society.

Samuel Gridley Howe founded the __19__ to educate the blind. Other reformers urged the practice of __20__ to restrict drinking.

Essay (40 points)
List at least four rights denied to women in the early 1800s. Tell why you think each of these rights was denied. Use your historical imagination to be sure you judge the situation fairly.

UNIT FOUR TEST

Multiple Choice (20 points)
Number your paper 1–5 and write the letter of the phrase that best completes each sentence.

1. The Era of Good Feelings was followed by
   a. efforts to unite the nation.
   b. the rise of sectionalism.
   c. the War of 1812.
   d. the closing of the frontier.
2. The Missouri Compromise and the Compromise of 1850 were both attempts to
   a. end slavery.
   b. keep the Democrats in office.
   c. gain new territory from Mexico.
   d. avoid conflict over the slave question.
3. Nullification was dangerous to the future of the United States because it would have
   a. given equal rights to women.
   b. raised tariffs.
   c. encouraged the British to invade.
   d. allowed states to disobey federal laws.
4. The invention of the cotton gin
   a. increased the demand for slaves.
   b. lowered the demand for slaves.
   c. had no effect on the demand for slaves.
   d. encouraged the growth of southern cities.
5. Many southerners strongly defended slavery because
   a. they hated abolitionists.
   b. more immigrants were coming from Europe.
   c. their way of life depended on slaves.
   d. slaves were needed to settle the West.

Chronological Order (25 points)
Number your paper 6–10 and place the following events in order by numbering 1 for the first, 2 for the second, and so on.
6. Gold is discovered in California.
7. Jackson orders the southern Indians removed to the West.
8. The Era of Good Feelings comes to an end.
9. William Henry Harrison conducts the Log Cabin Campaign.
10. The United States and Mexico go to war.

Matching (25 points)
Number your paper 11–15 and match the person in the second column with his or her description in the first column.
11. Led the Mormons west to Utah
12. Radical abolitionist who called for slavery's immediate end
13. Author of many compromises and Adams's Secretary of State
14. Aided many slaves in their escape to the North
15. An organizer of the convention at Seneca Falls

a. Henry Clay
b. Elizabeth Cady Stanton
c. William Lloyd Garrison
d. Brigham Young
e. Harriet Ross Tubman

Essay (30 points)
Write a brief essay on *one* of the following topics. What were the provisions of the Missouri Compromise and the Compromise of 1850? What was the main purpose of the compromises? *or* Explain the effects of the invention of the cotton gin on the economy and society of the South.

UNIT FIVE

1850	1851	1852	1853	1854	1855	1856
Compromise of 1850		*Uncle Tom's Cabin*	Gadsden Purchase	Kansas-Nebraska Bill		Pottawatomie Massacre • "Bleeding Kansas" • Buchanan elected President

Lee surrenders to Grant at Appomattox
•
Lincoln assassinated
•
Johnson succeeds to Presidency
•
Black Codes

Civil Rights Act

Reconstruction Act

Johnson impeached and acquitted
•
Grant elected President

1865	1866	1867	1868	1869	1870	1871

RECONSTRUCTION

A DIVIDED AMERICA

CIVIL WAR

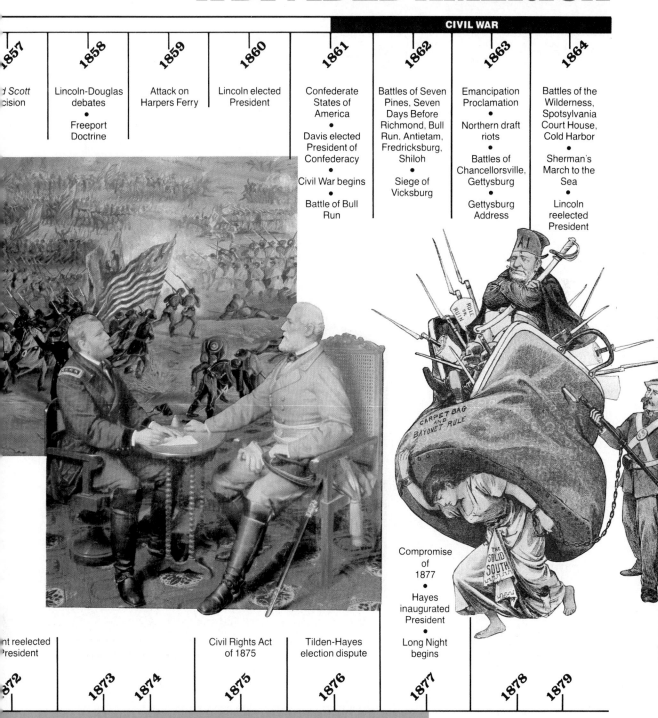

1857	1858	1859	1860	1861	1862	1863	1864
d Scott cision	Lincoln-Douglas debates • Freeport Doctrine	Attack on Harpers Ferry	Lincoln elected President	Confederate States of America • Davis elected President of Confederacy • Civil War begins • Battle of Bull Run	Battles of Seven Pines, Seven Days Before Richmond, Bull Run, Antietam, Fredricksburg, Shiloh • Siege of Vicksburg	Emancipation Proclamation • Northern draft riots • Battles of Chancellorsville, Gettysburg • Gettysburg Address	Battles of the Wilderness, Spotsylvania Court House, Cold Harbor • Sherman's March to the Sea • Lincoln reelected President

nt reelected *President*			Civil Rights Act of 1875	Tilden-Hayes election dispute	Compromise of 1877 • Hayes inaugurated President • Long Night begins		
872	1873	1874	1875	1876	1877	1878	1879

419

CHAPTER 15
Causes of the Civil War

Most Americans had expected the Compromise of 1850 to put an end to the slavery controversy. Events quickly proved that it had not done so.

SLAVE CATCHING

As soon as the new **Fugitive Slave Act** went into effect, southerners began to try to reclaim slaves who had escaped into the free states. Blacks who had escaped to the North found themselves in grave danger of recapture. Blacks accused of being runaways could not testify in their own defense. Many in the North who had not run away also felt threatened.

COLORED PEOPLE
OF BOSTON, ONE & ALL,
You are hereby respectfully CAUTIONED and
advised, to avoid conversing with the
Watchmen and Police Officers
of Boston,
For since the recent ORDER OF THE MAYOR &
ALDERMEN, they are empowered to act as
KIDNAPPERS
AND
Slave Catchers,
And they have already been actually employed in
KIDNAPPING, CATCHING, AND KEEPING
SLAVES. Therefore, if you value your LIBERTY,
and the Welfare of the Fugitives among you, Shun
them in every possible manner, as so many HOUNDS
on the track of the most unfortunate of your race.
Keep a Sharp Look Out for
KIDNAPPERS, and have
TOP EYE open.
APRIL 24, 1851.

The Brooklyn Museum

Eastman Johnson painted this oil, "A Ride for Freedom — The Fugitive Slaves," c. 1862. Johnson is well known as a *genre* painter — that is, his frequent subject was everyday life. But this is no everyday event for the family riding fearfully north toward freedom. Will they heed the poster warning that slave catchers lie waiting in the North? Why were northern blacks also fearful?

Thousands pulled up stakes and moved to Canada. Among the blacks who left the country were many of the more outspoken black leaders. "We have lost some of our strong men," Frederick Douglass mourned. He himself did not flee. "The only way to make the Fugitive Slave Law a dead letter," he wrote, "is to make half a dozen or more dead kidnappers." By kidnappers Douglass meant the men who sought to reclaim runaway blacks under the Fugitive Slave Law.

During the next few years about 200 blacks were captured and sent back into slavery under the new law. This was a small percentage of the number that had escaped. Even these cases, however, had a powerful effect on northern public opinion.

Most white northerners were prejudiced against blacks. Only five states, all in New England where very few blacks lived, permitted blacks to vote freely. Some states prohibited blacks from settling within their borders. Nowhere were blacks allowed to mix with whites on trains or in restaurants, theaters, or hotels. Except in Massachusetts, this **segregation** extended to public schools.

The segregation of public schools was practiced both North and South. In this engraving the black pupils are told to turn back by the school master. In what other places were blacks and whites not permitted to mix together?

Yet in spite of their prejudices, many northerners were sympathetic to the plight of runaway slaves. Runaways had risked their lives to win freedom. It was hard not to be impressed by them, especially when they had gone on to raise families, learn trades, and become hard-working, law-abiding citizens.

When northerners saw such people seized and dragged off without being given a chance to defend themselves in court, thousands were outraged. In Indiana, for example, a black man named Mitchum was arrested and turned over to a southerner who claimed that Mitchum had run away 19 years earlier. Whether or not Mitchum had really run away, it seemed cruel and unjust to separate him from his wife and children after so many years.

A Philadelphia woman, Euphemia Williams, escaped a somewhat different fate. She was arrested, but a judge released her at the last moment. Had he not, her six children, all born in Pennsylvania, would have been enslaved with her. Under southern law the status of black children depended on the mother, not the father.

Even northerners who were unmoved by the way the new fugitive slave law affected black people objected to it. It required citizens of the northern states to help capture runaways when ordered to do so by a law enforcement officer. Thousands considered this a violation of their rights. Yet it was the abolitionists, black and white, who led the attack on the law.

In Boston a group headed by the respectable clergyman Theodore Parker rescued a runaway couple, William and Ellen Craft. The group so threatened the man who had arrested the Crafts that he fled the city in fear for his life. In Syracuse, New York, a fugitive named Jerry McHenry was freed when a crowd of 2,000 people broke into the jail where he was being held. In Pennsylvania some blacks actually killed a slave catcher.

Not many of the runaways who were arrested were freed by force. In most cases they were brought to trial as the law provided. Some were released. Others were sent back into slavery without the public taking much notice. The law was disliked throughout the North, even though a majority of whites did nothing to stop it from being enforced. More and more northerners were becoming "uncomfortable" about the existence of slavery in the country.

 ▧ Why did many northerners support runaway slaves?
 ▧ Why did many northerners object to the Fugitive Slave Law?

A NOVEL ABOUT SLAVERY

Discomfort in the North increased when people began to read **Uncle Tom's Cabin,** a novel about slavery published in 1852. The author, Harriet Beecher Stowe, was not an active abolitionist. In her book she tried to make the point that the slave system was at fault, not the whites who owned the slaves and profited from their labor. She made the villain of her story, Simon Legree, a northerner.

The plot of *Uncle Tom's Cabin* is as hard to believe as that of a modern soap opera. The main character is the slave Uncle Tom, who accepts slavery with "patient weariness." He speaks to whites in a soft voice and has "a habitually respectful manner." He is content to remain a slave as long as his master is kind. Indeed, most of the blacks in the book quietly accept slavery and all its injustices.

Tom is first owned by a kindly Kentucky planter named Shelby. Next he becomes the property of a noble gentleman from New Orleans named St. Clare. All goes well. Then St. Clare dies. Tom is sold to the Yankee-born Simon Legree, who owns a cotton plantation in Louisiana.

Simon Legree is one of the arch villains of American literature. He enters and exits twirling his moustaches, his lips curled in a sneer. Legree cares only for money. He drives his slaves unmercifully, whipping them repeatedly to make them work harder. He controls them by fierce bulldogs who would "jest as soon chaw one of ye up

Harriet Beecher Stowe sat for this oil portrait in 1853, one year after publication of *Uncle Tom's Cabin*. The artist is Alanson Fisher. What was the subject of this novel?

as eat their dinner," and by Sambo and Quimbo, evil black overseers whom "Legree had . . . trained in savageness and brutality as systematically as he had his bulldogs." At one point the saintly Tom refuses to whip a slave woman who is too tired to pick as much cotton as Legree wishes. Legree has Tom brutally beaten by Sambo and Quimbo. One lashing follows another. Finally Tom dies of his injuries.

The Granger Collection

Uncle Tom's Cabin was applauded widely in the North, both the novel and a traveling melodrama based on it. Many people saw no spectacle to rival the pursuit of Eliza Harris by snarling bulldogs on the icy Ohio River. Thus this scene advertises the play in the poster, *left.* Below is a poster praising "the greatest book of the age." Did Stowe write accurately about slavery?

Stowe's description of slavery was not very realistic. She had grown up in Connecticut and Ohio. She had seen slaves only once, during a visit to a plantation in Kentucky. But while the characters in *Uncle Tom's Cabin* are all either saints or the worst of sinners, the black characters are shown as human beings with deep feelings. This was something new in American fiction. Stowe's tale of the sufferings of blacks made her readers weep.

The book was an immediate popular success. Within a year of publication 300,000 copies were sold. It was made into a play and presented before packed houses in theaters all over the northern states. We cannot know how many of the millions of people who read the book or saw the play became abolitionists as a result. But the historian David Potter was unquestionably correct when he wrote, "The northern attitude toward slavery was never quite the same after *Uncle Tom's Cabin.*"

Culver Pictures

- What point did Harriet Beecher Stowe try to make in *Uncle Tom's Cabin?*
- In what way was *Uncle Tom's Cabin* something new in American fiction?

423

THE KANSAS-NEBRASKA ACT

The concern of northerners about slavery increased dramatically in 1854. In 1853 Senator Stephen A. Douglas of Illinois had introduced a bill setting up a territorial government for the frontier west of Missouri and Iowa. On the surface it was a routine measure. As settlers pushed the frontier westward, Congress always organized the districts they were entering by setting up governments for them. This had been done repeatedly, beginning with the Northwest Ordinance of 1787.

Douglas's bill, however, ran into trouble. Once California entered the Union, plans for building a railroad to the West Coast sprang up everywhere. Being from Illinois, Douglas favored a route running west from Chicago. No such line could be built until the land beyond Missouri and Iowa had a territorial government.

Museum of the City of New York

Wars, fires, American heroes, and trains were ever-popular subjects for Currier & Ives. This engraving shows the American Express train, its locomotive billowing the smoke that excited 19th-century America. What event sparked plans to build a railroad to the West Coast?

Southern interests wanted the railroad to run west from New Orleans or some other southern city. All the lands such a route would cross had already been organized. In 1853 the United States had bought from Mexico a tract on the border known as the **Gadsden Purchase.** This land contained a pass through the mountains. A railroad could be constructed over this pass and on to the Pacific Ocean. Southerners in Congress did not want to encourage the building of a northern rail line. They refused to vote for the Douglas bill.

Stephen A. Douglas was extemely ambitious. In 1852, when he was only 39, he announced himself a candidate for the Democratic Presidential nomination. Other party leaders considered him much

424

too young for that office. They nominated Franklin Pierce of New Hampshire. Pierce went on to defeat the Whig candidate, General Winfield Scott, in the 1852 election.

Douglas did not let this failure discourage him. All his life he had gotten what he wanted. He had made a fortune as a lawyer and real estate operator. He had been a state legislator, a judge, and a member of the House of Representatives before being elected to the Senate. Although he was very short, people spoke of him with awe as the "Little Giant." He seemed to give off energy and determination.

Douglas was a shrewd politician. When he realized that southern congressmen were opposed to his bill, he looked for a way to change their minds. He came up with a scheme. Why not open the new territory to slavery? To prevent an uproar in the North, however, no new slave territory would be specifically created. Instead, settlers of the area would themselves decide whether or not to permit slavery.

This was the principle of **popular sovereignty** that had already been applied to New Mexico and Utah territories by the Compromise of 1850. As a further compromise the area would be split into two territories—Kansas, west of the slave state of Missouri, and Nebraska, west of the free state of Iowa.

Douglas knew that many northerners would dislike this **Kansas-Nebraska Bill.** But he thought most of them would merely grumble. The possibility of slavery actually being established in the new territories was small. The climate was unsuitable for growing cotton or any other plantation crop. Douglas himself considered slavery a terrible institution. But he did not think the development of the West should be held up over the principle of whether or not to permit it. On January 4, 1854, he introduced the bill in the Senate.

Franklin Pierce was elected to the Presidency in 1852. He served one unhappy term, the Pierces grieving at the loss of their only son, who was killed in a train wreck before the inauguration. This oil portrait is by G. P. A. Healy, done in 1853. Whom did Pierce defeat to win the Democratic nomination in 1852?

- For what two reasons had Senator Douglas introduced a bill to establish the new territories of Kansas and Nebraska?
- How did Senator Douglas hope to persuade southerners to support his Kansas-Nebraska Bill? How did he hope to avoid a northern uproar?

THE STRUGGLE FOR KANSAS

Antislavery northerners responded to the Kansas-Nebraska Bill with roars of protest. Although it did not do so specifically, Douglas's bill repealed the ban on slavery in that region which had been imposed by the Missouri Compromise. It was a "criminal betrayal" of the interests of free laborers eager to settle in the new land. It was "an atrocious plot" to make the territory "a dreary region . . . inhabited by masters and slaves."

For months the Kansas-Nebraska Bill was debated in Congress. Finally, with the votes of southerners who approved of the slavery

BUILDING SKILLS
IN SOCIAL STUDIES

Combining Reading and Map Skills

The question of extending slavery into the western territories was hotly debated for more than half a century. Three times Congress acted to settle the matter. But it was not resolved by the Compromise of 1820 nor by the Compromise of 1850. Four short years later Congress once again struggled with the problem before passing the Kansas-Nebraska Act of 1854.

Such a complicated matter as the slavery issue may be better understood by combining reading and map skills. First, review the accounts of the political attempts at solving the difficult question. Reread the sections that describe the three measures passed by Congress. They are as follows:

"Slavery in the Southwest," pages 368–69
"The Compromise of 1850," pages 370–73
"The Kansas-Nebraska Act," pages 424–25

Use your reading skills to find the main idea in each section. Then study the maps on this page. They show clearly which states and territories were free and which were slave as a result of each law. Use your map skills to first read the key and then to read each map.

When you combine reading and map skills, each makes the other easier to understand. Reading the sections explains political considerations and gives reasons why each act was passed. Reading the maps shows at a glance the results of each Congressional decision.

Combine your reading and map skills to answer the following questions.
1. In the Compromise of 1820 how did Congress "balance" admitting Missouri as a slave state?
2. Which new state was admitted with the Compromise of 1850? Which new territories?
3. Which free territories existed in 1854?
4. Which two territories were created in 1854?
5. Which area on the 1854 map shows the idea of popular sovereignty?

COMPROMISE OF 1820

OREGON COUNTRY

MAINE

MISSOURI COMPROMISE LINE 36°30′

MISSOURI

COMPROMISE OF 1850

OREGON COUNTRY

UTAH TERRITORY

CALIFORNIA

NEW MEXICO TERRITORY

KANSAS-NEBRASKA ACT 1854

WASHINGTON TERRITORY

OREGON TERRITORY

NEBRASKA TERRITORY

MINNESOTA TERRITORY

UTAH TERRITORY

KANSAS TERRITORY

NEW MEXICO TERRITORY

THE SLAVERY ISSUE
1820-1854

Free territory	Slave state
Free state	Decision of the people in the territory
Slave territory	

provision, it passed both houses and was promptly signed by President Pierce.

Douglas had hoped that northerners who opposed his bill would quiet down once the issue was settled. Instead they grew more bitter. Antislavery critics were determined to prevent slavery from gaining a foothold in Kansas. "Gentlemen of the Slave States," said Senator William H. Seward of New York, "we will engage in competition for the virgin soil of Kansas, and God give the victory to the side which is . . . right." Eli Thayer, a member of the Massachusetts legislature, organized the **Massachusetts Emigrant Aid Company** to help pay the moving expenses of antislavery families willing to settle in Kansas.

Hundreds of **free soilers** might now rush to Kansas and use popular sovereignty to keep slaves out. Alarmed proslavery groups in Missouri therefore hastened across the state line to Kansas. When the first territorial governor took a census of Kansas late in 1854, he found fewer than 3,000 adult males in the territory. But when a territorial legislature was elected in March 1855, more than 6,300 votes

Kansas State Historical Society

"Free-Soil Battery" is the title of this 1856 daguerreotype. The early photograph shows a gun crew with cannon protecting Topeka, capital of the free soilers. At whom would they have directed their fire?

were cast! About 5,000 Missourians had crossed over into Kansas to vote. Their ballots were illegal since they were not residents of the territory. Still their votes were counted. As a result a large majority of the men elected to the territorial legislature were proslavery.

The new legislature moved quickly to pass laws authorizing slavery in Kansas territory. It even passed one that provided the death penalty for anyone giving help to runaway slaves. "Free Soil" Kansans were furious. They refused to recognize the right of this legislature to govern them. Instead they set up their own government at the town of **Topeka.**

The engraving at the right shows a group of antislavery men who have gathered in 1855 in Topeka, Kansas. Most are armed, perhaps with the rifles sent by the Reverend Henry Ward Beecher from New York. His photograph, *below,* was taken by Napoleon Sarony c. 1880. Why did Kansans need the rifles known as "Beecher's Bibles"?

National Portrait Gallery

With two governments claiming to rule the same territory, it is not surprising that fighting broke out. Abolitionists in the East began to send guns to the antislavery forces. One was the Reverend Henry Ward Beecher of Brooklyn, New York, a brother of Harriet Beecher Stowe. He was so active in collecting money for guns that people began to speak of the weapons as **Beecher's Bibles.**

Fighting was common in most rough-and-ready frontier communities. In Kansas tension between northern and southern settlers made the situation explosive. In November 1855 a free soil settler was killed by a proslavery man in an argument over a land claim. His friends then burned down the killer's cabin. A proslavery sheriff, Samuel Jones, arrested one of these men. *His* friends promptly attacked the sheriff and forced him to release his prisoner. Sheriff Jones, backed by a force of 3,000 Missourians, then set out to track down the rescuers. Luckily the territorial governor put a stop to this activity before more blood could be spilled.

- How did antislavery northerners hope to prevent slavery in Kansas?
- How did proslavery groups influence the Kansas territorial election in 1855?

"BLEEDING KANSAS"

Trouble broke out again in Kansas the following spring. The town of **Lawrence** had become the headquarters of the antislavery settlers. Bands of armed men marched about the town much the way the Minute Men had paraded about the towns of Massachusetts in 1775. A United States marshal tried to arrest some of the leaders, but they fled before he could do so.

Then, on May 21, Sheriff Jones, again at the head of an army of Missourians, marched into Lawrence. In broad daylight they threw the printing presses of two newspapers into a river. They burned down the Free State Hotel and other buildings. Antislavery Kansans seethed with rage.

Yale University Art Gallery

A few days later a man named John Brown set out to avenge the attack on Lawrence. During his 56 years Brown had moved restlessly from place to place. He tried many businesses but failed time after time. His behavior had often been on the borders of the law, if not outside it. Yet he was sincerely opposed to slavery and devoted to the cause of racial equality. He had come to Kansas in October 1855.

When Brown learned of the attack, he led a party of seven men, four of them his own sons, to a settlement near Pottawatomie Creek, south of Lawrence. In the dead of night they entered the cabins of

These travelers from Missouri have crossed the Kansas border to make trouble for antislavery settlers. If their faces leave any doubt about the artist's sympathies, the title does not, for F. O. C. Darley called this wash drawing "Border Ruffians Invading Kansas." What kinds of damage did proslavery forces do in Lawrence, Kansas?

three unsuspecting families. For no apparent reason they murdered five people. They split open their skulls with heavy, razor-sharp swords. They even cut off the hand of one of their victims.

The **Pottawatomie Massacre** brought Kansas to the verge of civil war. Free soilers and proslavery men squared off to fight as irregular soldiers, or *guerrillas*. Brown was one of many of these. Very few people were killed. But politicians played up the unrest to win popular support. Soon horror-stricken citizens in the Northeast were reading exaggerated newspaper reports about **"Bleeding Kansas."**

- How did proslavery and antislavery forces square off in Kansas?
- What was the consequence of the Pottawatomie Massacre?
- How did northern newspapers report the events in Kansas?

POLITICAL BREAKUPS

The controversy over slavery in the western territories once again became a major political issue. It brought about major shifts in the nation's political parties. The Kansas-Nebraska Act had been a Democratic party measure. Its passage caused that party to lose thousands of supporters in the North. The Whig party, however, was shattered completely. Southern **Cotton Whigs** and Northern **Conscience Whigs** could not remain in the same organization. Most of the southerners supported the Kansas-Nebraska Act.

The northern Whigs went in two directions. The huge increase of immigration in the 1840s and 1850s hurt the Whig party greatly. For various reasons about 90 per cent of the new Irish citizens became Democrats. The tendency of German immigrants to vote Democratic was almost as strong. Most of these immigrants were Catholic, while most Whigs belonged to one or another of the Protestant churches. So the Whigs disagreed in both politics and religion with the new Democrats. As a result many Whigs became **nativists.** They favored strict controls on the admission of foreigners into the country. They joined a new political organization, the **Native American party.** Many former Democrats also joined this new party. Native Americans were often called **Know-Nothings** because when asked about the organization, they replied, "I know nothing."

Perhaps without realizing it, the nativists were trying to make the slavery issue go away by ignoring it. They were also bucking a tide that could not be stemmed without ruining the country. A steady flow of immigrants was essential if the United States was to expand. The very people who joined the Native American party benefited from the work the new immigrants did. By spending their wages, the immigrants stimulated the whole economy. Fortunately most American-born citizens realized this. The Know-Nothings won

some important local elections in the 1850s, but they never replaced either of the two major political parties.

The other new organization that northern Whigs and Democrats joined was the **Republican** party. It sprang up in many northern states immediately after passage of the Kansas-Nebraska Act. The exact birthplace of the party is still in dispute.

The Republican platform was simple: Keep slavery out of the western territories. Dislike of slavery was not the only reason the party took this stand. Indeed, many Republicans shared the common prejudice of northern whites against blacks. They feared that white farmers could not compete with slave owners who could bring their blacks into the territories. This reason probably appealed to the average Republican voter more than concern for the freedom of blacks.

When the ranks of voters swelled with newcomers from Ireland, nearly all the Irish-born citizens joined the Democratic party. They were poor and unskilled, so they competed with free northern blacks for jobs. These Irish interpreted Republican talk about free soil and free men as being pro-black. While not in favor of slavery, the Irish found Democratic politics more to their liking.

Blood flows in the streets of the City of Brotherly Love. This engraving of an anti-Catholic riot in Philadelphia in 1844 shows a mob attacking new immigrants to America. But how did Nativists benefit from this flow of immigrants?

■ How did the Democratic party suffer from passage of the Kansas-Nebraska Act? Why was the Whig party shattered?

■ What did the Native American party favor?

■ What was the platform of the Republican party?

THE ELECTION OF 1856

The political situation in 1856 was most unsettled. Neither President Pierce nor Senator Douglas could get the Democratic nomination for the Presidency. Their support of the Kansas-Nebraska Act convinced party leaders that they could not win in the northern states. Instead the Democrats chose James Buchanan of Pennsylvania.

Buchanan seemed well qualified for the Presidency. He had been a congressman and also a senator. He was an experienced diplomat, having been minister to both Russia and Great Britain. He had been President Polk's Secretary of State. But the chief reason the Democrats picked him was that his service as minister to Britain had kept him out of the country during the bitter fight over the Kansas-Nebraska Act.

National Portrait Gallery

U.S. Naval Academy Museum

James Buchanan, *left,* and John C. Frémont, *right,* were the candidates for President in 1856. Buchanan was painted in oil by G. P. A. Healy in 1859. Frémont is shown in a detail from N. C. Wyeth's "Frémont and the Pathfinder Flag." Frémont had his own flag, but Buchanan won the election. Wyeth was an especially popular illustrator of children's adventure books. Why was Frémont a popular American hero?

The Republicans nominated John C. Frémont, "the Pathfinder." Unlike Buchanan, who was 64, Frémont was a relatively young man in his early forties and something of a national hero. As his nickname indicates, he was an explorer. He had also played an important role in taking California during the Mexican War. A strong, silent type, Frémont had almost no political experience. With voters so divided, that too was a political advantage. Former President Millard Fillmore was also a candidate in 1856. He received the nomination of the Native American party and also of the rapidly declining Whig party.

The Republicans did not even attempt to campaign in the South. Fillmore got many northern votes that might otherwise have gone to Frémont, but he did not even come close to winning a single free state. So the contest was between Buchanan and Frémont in the North and between Buchanan and Fillmore in the South. Buchanan's strength in both sections gave him a great advantage among undecided voters and people who put sectional peace ahead of any particular issue.

Buchanan proved to be much more popular than Fillmore in the South. He lost only Maryland. Frémont was the stronger of the two in the North. But Buchanan won narrow victories in Illinois, Indiana, New Jersey, and his home state, Pennsylvania. These gave him a majority of the electoral vote, 174 to Frémont's 117 and Fillmore's 8.

Again the danger of the Union breaking up over slavery seemed to have been avoided. Buchanan's conservatism and his long political experience encouraged people to believe that he would proceed cautiously and with good judgment.

■ What were Buchanan's qualifications for the Presidency? Why did the Democrats nominate him?

THE DRED SCOTT CASE

Before Buchanan had a chance to demonstrate his abilities, a new crisis erupted. This one was produced by the Supreme Court. It involved the case of a slave named **Dred Scott.**

We know very little about Dred Scott, the man. He was short and had a dark skin. He could neither read nor write. He must have been a very determined person because he carried on a long struggle for his freedom.

In 1833 Scott had been purchased by John Emerson, an army doctor in St. Louis, Missouri, who used him as a servant. When the army assigned Doctor Emerson to duty at Fort Armstrong in Illinois, he took Scott with him. Then, in 1836, Emerson was transferred to Fort Snelling, a post in the western part of Wisconsin Territory, now Minnesota. Again Scott accompanied him. While there, Scott met and married a slave named Harriet Robinson.

After further moves Emerson was transferred to Florida. He sent the Scotts to St. Louis with his wife. When Emerson died in December 1843, his wife inherited them. Exactly what happened next is not clear. But in 1846, with the help of the white family that had originally sold Scott to Emerson, the Scotts sued for their freedom in a Missouri court. Their cases were separate but identical. In effect, what happened to Dred determined what happened to Harriet and their two children.

Scott argued that since slavery had been banned in Illinois by state law, he had become free when Emerson brought him to that state. Furthermore, slavery was also illegal in Wisconsin Territory because Wisconsin was in the northern part of the Louisiana Pur-

Although little is known about Dred Scott, we do have this portrait done by Louis Schultze in 1858. The oil portrait was made after a photograph and was painted in St. Louis in the year Scott died. Why did Dred Scott become famous?

chase. Slavery had been banned there by Congress in the Missouri Compromise of 1820. In other words, Scott claimed that when he returned to the state of Missouri, he was no longer a slave. Since he had not been reenslaved, he was still free.

This complicated case shuttled from one Missouri court to another for many years. In 1852 the Missouri Supreme Court ruled against Scott. The matter did not end there, however. In 1851 Mrs. Emerson had moved to Massachusetts and remarried. She either sold or gave the Scotts to her brother, John Sanford.

Sanford lived in New York. This offered fresh hope for Scott. Again with the support of white friends, he started a new suit for his freedom, this one in the federal courts.

▨ Why did Dred Scott argue that he should be free?

THE COURT AND THE CONSTITUTION

The case of *Dred Scott v. Sanford* began in 1854. Eventually it came to the Supreme Court for final settlement. On March 6, 1857, only two days after the start of James Buchanan's term as President, the Court announced its decision.

The decision turned out to be more complicated than the case itself. Chief Justice Roger B. Taney ruled against Scott. Blacks, he said, were "a subordinate and inferior class of beings." They had "none of the rights and privileges" of citizens of the United States. Since Scott was black, he was not a citizen. Therefore he had no right to bring a suit in a federal court even if he had been free! This amazing statement was enough to keep Scott a slave.

Taney had more to say. Living in Illinois and Wisconsin Territory had not made Scott free. By returning to Missouri he came again under Missouri law, and Missouri was a slave state. And, Taney went on, going to Wisconsin Territory could not have made Scott free in any case because Congress did not have the right to keep slaves out of a federal territory.

Taney's argument ran as follows: Slaves were property. Any law which prevented owners from bringing their slaves into a territory would deprive them of property. Since the Fifth Amendment to the Constitution states that "no person shall be . . . deprived of life, liberty, or property without due process of law," the Missouri Compromise was in violation of that amendment. It was **unconstitutional** and therefore **void**—the law could no longer be in force.

Congress had already repealed, or canceled, the Missouri Compromise by passing the Kansas-Nebraska Act. Taney's argument was therefore against a law that no longer existed. It was particularly annoying to people who were opposed to opening western territories to slavery. The Court was using part of the Bill of Rights to keep

Granger Collection

National Portrait Gallery

people in chains. Furious abolitionists were joined in their outcry by thousands of other people who considered slavery wrong.

Only once before the Dred Scott case had the Supreme Court declared a law passed by Congress to be unconstitutional. That had occurred over 50 years earlier, in the case known as **Marbury v. Madison** (1803).

The Constitution does not specifically say that the Supreme Court can declare federal laws unconstitutional. *Marbury v. Madison* was significant because it established the power of the Court to do so.

The particular question at issue in the Marbury case was not very important. It involved the appointment of a justice of the peace in the District of Columbia. Chief Justice John Marshall had ruled on a law creating certain federal courts. He held that a clause in the law violated the Constitution. This established the **precedent** for declaring an act of Congress unconstitutional. Without this precedent to look back to, the justices who decided the Dred Scott case might not have dared declare that an important law passed by Congress was unconstitutional.

The Dred Scott decision was greeted with a storm of criticism, and with good reason. Whether or not free blacks were citizens of the Unites States, many states treated such blacks as citizens. Everyone agreed that a citizen of one state could sue a citizen of another in the federal courts. Still worse, why was the Supreme Court declaring the Missouri Compromise unconstitutional? That law no longer existed.

The Dred Scott ruling was handed down by Roger B. Taney, *left*, Chief Justice of the Supreme Court. This photograph is by Matthew Brady. At right is Chief Justice John Marshall. His portrait in oil was made c. 1831 by James Reid Lambdin. What was the ruling in the case of *Marbury v. Madison?*

435

The Republicans simply had to come out against this part of the decision. It made their reason for existence—keeping slavery out of the territories—illegal.

The justices had acted as they did in hopes of settling the question of slavery in the territories once and for all. Instead they only made the controversy more heated.

- What did the Supreme Court rule in *Dred Scott v. Sanford*?
- What argument did Chief Justice Roger Taney make?
- How was precedent important to the Court's decision?
- Why was the Court's decision strongly criticized?

SENATOR DOUGLAS'S DILEMMA

Conditions in Kansas Territory grew still worse. Meeting at the town of Lecompton, the proslavery convention in Kansas had drawn up a proposed state constitution authorizing slavery. The delegates represented only a minority of the people of the territory. But since they were Democrats, President Buchanan supported them. He urged Congress to accept this **Lecompton Constitution** and admit Kansas as a state. Of course, antislavery forces in Kansas and throughout the nation objected strongly.

These developments put Senator Stephen A. Douglas in a difficult position. He was a Democrat. The President had made the matter a party issue. On the other hand, Douglas sincerely believed in popular sovereignty. And it was obvious that a majority of the people in Kansas were opposed to the Lecompton Constitution and to the opening of the territory to slavery.

To complicate his problem, Douglas had to stand for reelection to the Senate in 1858. If he went against the Democratic party, he would suffer. If he supported the Lecompton Constitution, he might lose his Senate seat, for thousands of Illinois Democrats objected bitterly to that document.

Douglas did not hesitate for long. He announced that he opposed the Lecompton Constitution. When President Buchanan tried to put pressure on him to change his mind, he flatly refused.

When a vote was finally taken on the Lecompton Constitution, the people of Kansas rejected it by a huge majority, 11,300 to 1,788. Southern Democrats and President Buchanan were furious. They blamed Douglas for this defeat.

In Illinois the Democratic party split into factions, one group pro-Buchanan, the other pro-Douglas. Illinois Republicans were of course delighted. It gave them a chance to defeat Douglas and win his seat in the United States Senate.

In those days senators were still chosen by the state legislatures, not by popular vote. Ordinary citizens often had no idea who would

National Portrait Gallery

Here stands the "Little Giant" from Illinois, Stephen A. Douglas. One of two remarkable politicians then from Illinois, Douglas posed for this photograph in about 1859. Why did Douglas oppose Buchanan on the Lecompton Constitution?

be chosen senator when they cast their ballots for their representatives to the state legislature. The 1858 Illinois election did not follow this pattern. Douglas was too important and his quarrel with the President too public. Illinois voters were very much aware that the state representatives they chose would reelect or defeat Douglas. Douglas campaigned hard for his seat. Technically, he and his Republican opponent were speaking in behalf of local candidates for the legislature. But everyone knew that their votes—Democratic or Republican—would decide who Illinois would send to the Senate.

- Why did Senator Douglas speak out against the Lecompton Constitution?
- How did the Illinois election of 1858 become a "popular" election for the Senate seat held by Douglas?

THE LINCOLN-DOUGLAS DEBATES

The Republican candidate for the Senate was Abraham Lincoln, a lawyer and former member of the state legislature. He had served a term in Congress in the 1840s. Lincoln had moved to Illinois in 1830 when he was 21 years old. He had little formal education. As a youth he had attended school only during the few winter weeks when he was not needed to work on his father's farm. But he had read widely on his own. He was a hard worker and intensely ambitious.

Lincoln also had a reputation for honesty. Early in life people began to call him "Honest Abe." He had an excellent sense of humor. Once he saw a woman, who was wearing an enormous feathered hat, slip and fall in a mud puddle. "Reminds me of a duck," he said to a friend he was with. "What do you mean?" asked the friend. "Feathers on her head and down on her behind," Lincoln replied. These qualities helped him in politics. In 1834 he was elected to the Illinois legislature.

Although Lincoln had prospered as a lawyer, his political career had been only modestly successful. After his term in Congress ended in 1849, he had held no further public office. He had always been a loyal member of the Whig party, but people in Illinois thought of him as a rather ordinary local politician.

All this changed when the Kansas-Nebraska Act revived the question of slavery in the territories. "If slavery is not wrong," Lincoln said, "nothing is wrong." Still, he was not an abolitionist. Slavery was like a cancer, he said, but cutting it out might cause the patient—the United States—to "bleed to death." However, there must be no further extension of slavery in the West. By 1856 Lincoln had joined the new Republican party.

Lincoln expressed his ideas well. He had a remarkable gift for words. What called him to the attention of Republican leaders, how-

Lincoln the "Rail Splitter" was the other remarkable politician from the state of Illinois. In this photograph the young Lincoln is beardless. It was made at the time he opposed Senator Douglas in the election of 1858. Which qualities of Lincoln's helped him in politics?

437

A huge crowd has assembled in the summer of 1858 to hear Lincoln and Douglas debate. This oil painting shows Lincoln speaking, Douglas seated to his right. This debate is being held in Charleston, Illinois. How was each candidate a strong debater?

ever, was his conservatism and good judgment. Although he hated slavery, he did not hate slave owners. He did not blame them for the existence of the institution. He admitted that he did not know how to do away with slavery in states where it already existed.

These views appealed to moderates in the North. The Republicans had to attack the Dred Scott decision to survive as a party. Their problem was that they did not want to appear to be abolitionists or to favor racial equality. Lincoln seemed the kind of candidate who could manage this difficult task. His good mind and clever tongue were also important because Stephen A. Douglas was a brilliant orator and a master of every detail of the issues of the day.

Lincoln challenged Douglas to debate the issues with him in different sections of Illinois. Douglas agreed. Their meetings attracted large crowds, for each debate was a great local occasion. Because of the importance of the election, newspapers all over the country reported on the debates in detail.

Douglas tried to persuade the voters that Lincoln and the Republicans were dangerous radicals. He accused them of being abolitionists and of favoring equality. Lincoln "thinks the Negro is his brother," the Little Giant sneered. As for the western territories,

Stephen A. Douglas put on a great show for his debates with Abraham Lincoln. He arrived in a private railroad car. Attached to the train was a flatcar with a brass cannon mounted on it. As the train approached the town, a campaign worker fired off blank charges to alert Douglas's local supporters. Lincoln stressed a "man of the people" approach. He traveled in an ordinary coach on the trains.

Local party leaders met the candidates at the station. A parade formed and marched through town to the field or square where the speeches were delivered. There were flags, banners, brass bands, flowers, and floats carrying pretty girls. Like most political meetings of that era, the event took on a carnival atmosphere like a county fair. Crowds of 15,000 and more were common as farmers flocked to town from surrounding areas.

Even without his tall "stovepipe" hat, the six-feet, six-inch Lincoln towered over the Little Giant. He wore a formal black suit, usually rumpled and always too short for his long arms and legs. Douglas was what we would call a flashy dresser. He wore shirts with ruffles, fancy embroidered vests, a broad felt hat. He had a rapid-fire way of speaking that contrasted with Lincoln's slow, deliberate style. (We know this partly because, while the two men spoke for equal lengths of time, Douglas got out far more words. A copy of his remarks at one of the debates takes 22 pages to Lincoln's 18 pages in one published version.)

Lincoln's voice was high pitched, Douglas's deep. Both had to have powerful lungs to make themselves heard over street noises and the bustle of the crowds. They had no public address systems to help them.

Douglas claimed that all were destined by climate and soil conditions to become free. *Allowing* slave owners to settle in Kansas would not in fact mean that they would do so.

It was obvious that most Illinois voters shared the Little Giant's low opinion of blacks. Lincoln's own feelings were less extreme but not essentially different. He stated firmly that he was against permitting blacks to vote or sit on juries. Marriage between blacks and whites should remain illegal. Blacks should not be allowed to become citizens of Illinois. But, Lincoln insisted, blacks did have the "natural rights" described in the Declaration of Independence: the right to life, liberty, and the pursuit of happiness. He made much of the right of every black to "the bread . . . which his own hand earns."

Neither Douglas nor most others in Illinois would have disagreed with this statement. About the best that can be said for Lincoln's treatment of the race question during the campaign is that he overreacted in trying to prove that he was not an abolitionist.

- Why did the Republican party promote Abraham Lincoln's candidacy for the Senate?
- What position did Senator Douglas take in his debates with Lincoln? What position did Lincoln take?

THE FREEPORT DOCTRINE

On the question of slavery in the territories Lincoln took a firm stand. He put Douglas in a difficult political position by asking him if the people of a territory could exclude slavery *before* the territory became a state. After all, did not the Dred Scott decision mean that slavery could not be banned in any territory?

Lincoln asked Douglas these questions during their debate at Freeport, Illinois. Douglas's answer is now known as the **Freeport Doctrine.** "It matters not what way the Supreme Court may . . . decide" about slavery, he said. "The people have the lawful means to introduce or exclude it as they please, for the reason that slavery cannot exist . . . unless it is supported by local police regulations."

Obviously, Douglas was correct. If local authorities did not back up the owners, all the slaves could simply walk off and do as they pleased. This being the case, the people of a territory could effectively prevent slaves from being brought into their regions merely by doing nothing.

This argument helped Douglas in Illinois, where many voters were eager to believe that popular sovereignty could work in the territories despite the Dred Scott decision. It hurt him in the slave states, however. Thus it reduced his chances of winning the Democratic Presidential nomination in 1860.

On election day in November the voters gave the Democrats a small majority in the state legislature. Douglas was therefore reelected to the Senate. But Lincoln was helped by the campaign too. The publicity and his effective speeches attracted much national attention. His own account of his feelings are worth recording. "It gave me a hearing," he said. "I believe I have made some marks." But he also said, "I feel like the boy who stumped his toe. I am too big to cry and too badly hurt to laugh."

- What was Douglas's argument in the Freeport Doctrine? How did it help him in Illinois but hurt him nationally?
- How was Lincoln helped by his campaign for the Senate, even though he was not elected?

READING PRACTICE
IN SOCIAL STUDIES

Reading a Time Sequence

One way that writers organize information is by *time sequence.* This arrangement is particularly useful for writers of history, who set down events in *chronological order* — that is, in the order in which they occurred.

Recognizing time sequence is an important reading skill. When you know that a section is organized by time sequence, you are better able to see the relationship of one event to another.

Many time clues may be found in your reading. Dates are the most obvious. Specific dates such as 1492 or July 4, 1776, stand out clearly when you skim a page. So do more general dates such as "the 1840s and 1850s."

Approximate dates such as "thousands of years ago" or "half a century later" are also time clues.

A number of specific words may be time clues when they indicate the passage of time. Among these are *first, second, then, next, finally, yesterday, today, tomorrow,* and *soon.*

Finally, phrases may also show passage of time: *a month before, at that moment, shortly after.*

When reading for time sequence, you are apt to find that not all writers proceed in chronological order. Some writers go back and forth in time, particularly when explaining larger movements or cause and effect. Time clues then become very important, for they help you to give order to what you read and remember.

As you look for time clues, here is an important point to keep in mind: Time sequence is used for more than listing a series of events that occurred over a period of time. It is also used to show how a series of events is related to some larger event or idea. For example, look at the section "The Attack on Harpers Ferry" on page 442. The events of John Brown's raid and its aftermath are listed in time sequence to tell the story of the attack. But these events are only part of the much larger story of the abolitionist movement and of reactions to John Brown's raid in both the North and the South.

Read "The Attack on Harpers Ferry" on page 442 before completing the following exercises. Number your paper 1–5 and list the time clues in each of the following sentences.

1. On the evening of October 16, 1859, Brown and his commandos crossed the Potomac.
2. Brown then sent some of his men off to capture two local slaveholders as hostages.
3. When workers began to arrive in the morning, Brown also took some of them prisoner.
4. In a matter of hours Brown's force was under siege, pinned down in the armory.
5. After a fair but swift trial he was convicted and sentenced to be hanged.

Number your paper 6–11 and place the following events in chronological order.

a. Brown's men are killed or captured.
b. Brown is tried and sentenced to death.
c. Brown's men take two hostages.
d. Brown's men capture the armory at Harpers Ferry.
e. Brown becomes a hero to many northerners.
f. Brown makes plans to raid Harpers Ferry.

Number your paper 12–15 and answer these questions about "The Attack on Harpers Ferry."

12. The topic of the section is a) John Brown, b) the attack on Harpers Ferry, c) slavery.
13. The purpose of the first three paragraphs is to a) explain who John Brown was, b) give the background of the attack on Harpers Ferry, c) review "Bleeding Kansas."
14. The purpose of paragraphs 4–6 is to a) explain the raid in time sequence, b) explain why the raid took place, c) give examples of abolitionism.
15. The most important idea in this section is that a) Brown was insane, b) the attack further split North and South, c) John Brown was a hero.

Harpers Ferry lies peacefully in the Shenandoah Valley. Here the U.S. arsenal was located in 1796. This tranquil scene was disturbed by the commando raid of John Brown's tiny army in October 1859. This view is a lithograph by Edward Beyer, made in 1857 and "taken from Nature," in the words of the artist. Today this region is a national park. What was the outcome of Brown's raid?

THE ATTACK ON HARPERS FERRY

At this point John Brown again appeared on the national scene. Brown was never punished for his part in the Pottawatomie massacre. He believed that God had commanded him to free the slaves by force. Kansas had seemed the best place to wage this battle. But violence was no longer necessary to keep slavery out of Kansas, and its settlers had little interest in fighting to get rid of it anywhere else.

Brown had to develop a new scheme. He decided to organize a small band of armed followers, march into the South, and seize land in some remote area. What would happen next he never made clear. Apparently he expected slaves from all over the region to run away and join him. With their help he would launch raids throughout the South aimed at rescuing more blacks from slavery.

Brown managed to persuade six important Massachusetts abolitionists to give him enough money to organize and supply his attack force. The goal of his miniature 18-man army was a United States government armory in the town of **Harpers Ferry,** Virginia, on the Potomac River northwest of Washington.

On the evening of October 16, 1859, Brown and his commandos crossed the Potomac. They overpowered a watchman and occupied the armory and a government rifle factory. Brown then sent some of his men off to capture two local slaveholders as hostages. One of these was Lewis Washington, a great-grandnephew of George Washington. When workers began to arrive in the morning, Brown also took some of them prisoner. Then he sat back to wait for local slaves to rise up and join his rebellion.

Not one slave did so. But the local authorities reacted promptly. In a matter of hours Brown's force was under siege, pinned down in the armory. A detachment of marines commanded by Lieutenant-Colonel Robert E. Lee arrived from Washington. Brown refused to surrender. On October 18 Lee sent the marines forward with fixed bayonets. They quickly overwhelmed the rebels.

Ten of Brown's men were killed, but he was taken alive. He was charged with murder, conspiracy, and treason. After a fair but swift trial he was convicted and sentenced to be hanged.

John Brown was almost certainly insane. He was so disorganized that he did not even attempt to let the slaves know that he had come to free them. The affair might have been dismissed as the act of a lunatic if Brown had acted like a disturbed person after his capture, but he did not do so. Indeed, he behaved with remarkable dignity and self discipline.

Even Brown's judge and jailors admired his calm courage. When he was condemned to death, he said that he had acted in the name of God. "To have interfered as I have done . . . in behalf of His despised

The Metropolitan Museum of Art

"The Last Moments of John Brown" is the way the North imagined his execution. Horace Greeley wrote for his newspaper a description of the black woman waiting with her little child: "He stopped a moment, and stooping, kissed the child." But Greeley was not present, and in fact only soldiers met Brown. Thomas Hovenden painted the oil. How did Brown behave after being sentenced to death?

poor, is not wrong, but right. Now, if it is . . . necessary that I should forfeit my life for the furtherance of the ends of justice . . . I say, let it be done." And he added calmly, "I feel no consciousness of guilt."

Brown became a hero to the abolitionists and to many other northerners. They considered him a noble freedom fighter. His bloody murders in Kansas and his wreckless assault at Harpers Ferry were conveniently forgotten. When northerners made Brown a near saint, white people in the slave states became even more concerned. They began to think that northerners intended to destroy slavery, not merely limit its expansion. Once again, northerners and southerners looked at each other with suspicion, fear, and even hatred.

- Why did John Brown and his small army raid Harpers Ferry?
- Why did some northerners consider Brown a hero?
- How did feelings about John Brown's raid further divide North and South?

THE ELECTION OF 1860

As the 1860 Presidential election drew near, the Democrats became even more sharply divided. The northern faction supported Senator Douglas. The southern wing was led by President Buchanan, although he was not a candidate for a second term. The party's nominating convention was held in April 1860 at Charleston, South Carolina. Douglas controlled a small majority of the delegates, but the rules of the convention required a two-thirds majority for nomination. This he could not get. The convention then adjourned.

The delegates gathered again in June in Baltimore. Once more they failed to agree. This time the party broke formally in two. The northerners then nominated Douglas for President. The southerners selected Buchanan's Vice President, John C. Breckinridge of Kentucky.

In the meantime the Republican Presidential convention had taken place in Chicago. To broaden their appeal, party leaders drafted a program of economic reforms to go along with their demand that slavery be kept out of the territories. They called for a **Homestead Act** giving 160 acres (64 hectares), enough land for a family farm, to anyone who would settle on it. They urged government support for a railroad to the Pacific and higher tariffs on manufactured goods in order to protect producers from foreign competition. They rejected the idea of nativist support. They promised not to restrict immigration into the country.

Before the convention Senator William H. Seward of New York seemed the person most likely to get the Republican Presidential nomination. However, to win the election, the Republicans would have to carry Pennsylvania, Indiana, and Illinois—the northern states

William H. Seward of New York is the subject of this photograph made by Alexander Gardner. Were it not for his strong antislavery views, he might have been the Republican's candidate for President in 1860. Who was the Republican nominee?

444

Reynolda House, Inc.

that Buchanan had carried in 1856. Seward was thought to be too antislavery to persuade doubtful voters in those states. After much political "horse-trading" the delegates nominated Abraham Lincoln.

Many proslavery radicals had threatened that the southern states would secede from the Union and set up an independent country of their own if a Republican was elected President. This possibility was particularly alarming to many people in the Upper South, the so-called **border states** of Maryland, Virginia, Kentucky, and Missouri. Should civil war break out, it would surely be fought on their soil.

These people formed still a fourth party, the **Constitutional Unionist** party, in 1860. The Constitutional Unionist's platform was simple: They stood for "the Constitution and the Union." In other words, they tried to ignore the controversial issues that were dividing the country. If the party had lived long enough to develop a symbol like the Democratic donkey and the Republican elephant, the symbol should have been an ostrich with its head buried in the sand.

The Constitutional Unionists nominated John Bell, for many years a congressman and senator from Tennessee. Bell was a stiff, rather colorless person. He was chosen because of his long, conservative record and the fact that although he was a slave owner, he had voted against the Kansas-Nebraska Act.

With four candidates running, no one could hope to get a majority of the popular vote. Lincoln received 1,866,000, nearly all in the northern states. Douglas got 1,383,000, also mostly in the North.

Thomas Cole's "Pioneer Home in the Woods" is from about 1845. Family farms sprang up everywhere on the western frontier after the Homestead Act made land available to anyone who would settle it. Which political party called for the Homestead Act in its 1860 platform?

445

Breckinridge received 848,000 and Bell 593,000. But Lincoln won a solid majority of the electoral votes, 180 of the 303 cast.

What had happened was this: In the free states the election was between Lincoln and Douglas. It was a fairly close contest, but Lincoln won in every state. Despite his large popular vote, Douglas got only 12 electoral votes, Missouri's 9 and 3 from New Jersey.

A POLITICAL RACE

Price 10 cents.

Prints Room, New York Public Library

A political cartoonist saw the race for President in 1860 this way. A long-legged Lincoln outdistances Douglas, Breckinridge, and Bell as he strides to the White House. Why was this a four-way race?

In the slave states Breckinridge and Bell divided the votes. Breckinridge had a majority in all the states of the Deep South. Bell carried the border states of Tennessee, Kentucky, and Virginia.

- How did the Republican party try to broaden its appeal in the election of 1860?
- How did the four-way race for President help Abraham Lincoln get elected?

THE SECESSION CRISIS

Although he got much less than half the popular vote, Lincoln had been legally elected President. Even the southerners recognized that this was so. The more radical of them therefore prepared to take their states out of the Union.

For several years there had been much talk of the South seceding if a "black Republican" was ever elected President. Lincoln and other northerners had convinced themselves that this talk was merely bluff. Stephen A. Douglas recognized how serious the threat was. As the campaign progressed, he sensed the trend of popular opinion. A month before the election he realized that Lincoln was almost certainly going to win. "Mr. Lincoln is the next President," he told his secretary. "We must try to save the Union. I will go South." During the remaining weeks he campaigned in Tennessee, Georgia, and Alabama. Everywhere he spoke not for himself but for preserving the Union.

His noble effort failed. Within days of the news of Lincoln's election, the legislature of South Carolina summoned a special convention to consider the question of secession. Before the end of the year the delegates to that convention voted to take the state out of the Union. Other southern states followed quickly. Only the states of the Upper South held back, and leaders in these states were seriously considering leaving the Union.

The reasons why the South seceded have puzzled historians for more than a hundred years. Probably no completely satisfactory explanation is possible. But this much can be said: The slave system was at the root of the difficulties between the sections. White southerners felt that the security of their peculiar institution was being threatened. By leaving the United States and setting up a country of their own, they hoped to protect not only slavery but what they considered their whole way of life.

The southern states based their right to leave the Union on the fact that the original 13 states had existed separately before they joined together to form the United States. The states drafted and then approved the United States Constitution. Surely each had the right to cancel its allegiance if its citizens so desired. This was the doctrine of **states' rights,** first argued by Jefferson in the 1790s. It was given its most complete expression by John C. Calhoun in the 1820s and 1830s when he argued that a state could nullify a federal law it did not consider constitutional.

Belief in states' rights was the legal justification of secession, but it was not the reason why the southern states seceded. That was more a matter of **southern nationalism**—loyalty to the region and to the slave system. The national controversy over slavery had weakened the southerners' loyalty to the entire United States. For a person like Lincoln to say, "If slavery is not wrong, nothing is wrong," was a slap in the face to most white southerners. No matter that Lincoln and other moderates had no intention of trying to destroy slavery where it already existed. Southern defenders of slavery could not accept the idea that the system was "wrong." When Lincoln's point of view triumphed and Lincoln became President of the United States, southerners no longer wished to be part of the Union.

- What event prompted the Deep South to secede from the Union?
- What was the southerners' legal argument for their secession?
- What was another reason for the South's secession?

447

CHAPTER 15 REVIEW

Identification

Tell briefly why each of the following persons, terms, or events is important.
1. Harriet Beecher Stowe
2. Stephen A. Douglas
3. John Brown
4. James Buchanan
5. Millard Fillmore
6. Roger B. Taney
7. Abraham Lincoln
8. John C. Breckinridge
9. William H. Seward
10. John Bell
11. Segregation
12. Kansas-Nebraska Act
13. Popular sovereignty
14. Pottawatomie Massacre
15. Republican party
16. Dred Scott case
17. Lincoln-Douglas debates
18. Freeport Doctrine
19. Harpers Ferry
20. States' rights

Understanding American History

1. For what reasons did northerners object to the Fugitive Slave Act?
2. What was the impact of *Uncle Tom's Cabin* on northern readers?
3. Why did Stephen A. Douglas want Kansas and Nebraska organized into territories? How did he secure southern votes for his Kansas-Nebraska Bill?
4. What was meant by "Bleeding Kansas"?
5. What was the platform of the new Republican party? In what section of the country were most of its members?
6. What did the Supreme Court decide in the case of *Dred Scott v. Sanford?* Why was the decision strongly criticized?
7. How did Senator Douglas risk his political career by his opposition of the Lecompton Constitution?

8. What effect did the raid on Harpers Ferry have on northerners and southerners?
9. Who were the four candidates for President in 1860, and which was the party of each?
10. Explain states' rights and southern nationalism as reasons why the South seceded.

Activities

1. The play made from *Uncle Tom's Cabin* was enormously successful, partly because it is a melodrama. George and Eliza Harris are its hero and heroine, Simon Legree its snarling villain. The classic melodrama usually has a sweet young heroine saved from a dastardly landlord by a handsome hero who appears just in the nick of time. Obtain a copy of a melodrama from your school or public library and prepare a scene to present with your classmates. If possible, find a copy of the play made from *Uncle Tom's Cabin* and present a scene from it.
2. Many books, plays, and songs were written about John Brown. Use the card catalog in your library to find information for a report on John Brown. Also check other American history books and the encyclopedia. You might sing "John Brown's Body Lies a Moulderin' in the Grave" for the class and explain what its lyrics mean.
3. Prepare a bulletin board to show the new political parties that came into being in the 1850s. Include information about the party platforms, candidates, and region of strongest support.
4. Use your historical imagination to present a television news special on the Lincoln-Douglas debates. Give your viewers background information, highlights of the debates, and a sampling of crowd opinion.
5. Present a short campaign speech to endorse one of the four candidates for President in the election of 1860: John Bell, John C. Breckinridge, Stephen A. Douglas, or Abraham Lincoln.

CHAPTER 15 TEST

Completion (30 points)
Number your paper 1–10 and next to each number write the words from the list below that best complete each sentence.

free soilers

popular sovereignty

Lecompton Constitution

Fugitive Slave Act

Native American party

Missouri Compromise

states' rights

Freeport Doctrine

border states

Harpers Ferry

1. The Supreme Court ruled that the _____ was unconstitutional because Congress could not outlaw slavery in the territories.
2. Senator Douglas said in the _____ that slavery cannot exist without local support.
3. People who were against the spread of slavery into the territories were called _____.
4. John Brown raided _____ in an attempt to start a slave rebellion in the South.
5. The doctrine of _____ was used by southerners to defend seceding from the Union.
6. The Kansas-Nebraska Act called for citizens of the territories to use _____ to determine whether or not to permit slavery.
7. Proslavery forces in Kansas drew up the _____ to authorize slavery in the state.
8. Southerners were angered when northerners did not enforce the _____ and return runaway slaves.
9. Residents of the _____ feared that if war broke out, it would be fought on their soil.
10. The Know-Nothings were members of the _____.

Matching (20 points)
Number your paper 11–15 and match the person in the second column with the description in the first column.
11. Chief Justice of the Supreme Court who held that blacks were not citizens and therefore could not sue in courts
12. Proposed the Kansas-Nebraska Act
13. Author of *Uncle Tom's Cabin*
14. Slave who sued for freedom but lost
15. Republican nominee for President in 1860

a. Abraham Lincoln
b. Stephen A. Douglas
c. Harriet Beecher Stowe
d. Roger B. Taney
e. Dred Scott

Matching (20 points)
Number your paper 16–20 and match the political party in the second column with its description in the first column.
16. Favored strict controls on the admission of foreigners into the United States
17. Nominated Stephen A. Douglas for President
18. Opposed the spread of slavery
19. Ignored the issue of slavery completely
20. Shattered by the Kansas-Nebraska Act

a. Republican party
b. Whig party
c. Native American party
d. Constitutional Union party
e. Northern Democratic party

Essay (30 points)
Choose *three* of the following and explain how they divided North from South: Fugitive Slave Act, *Uncle Tom's Cabin,* Dred Scott case, Kansas-Nebraska Act, Harpers Ferry. Plan your essay carefully, perhaps by making a simple outline before you begin to write.

CHAPTER 16

The Civil War

BETWEEN PEACE AND WAR

The states of the Deep South left the Union during a time when the United States government was particularly weak. President-elect Lincoln would not take office until March 4, 1861. Furthermore, he showed no interest in dealing with the problem of secession or taking responsibility of any kind before that date. The retiring President, James Buchanan, seemed paralyzed by the crisis. He announced that secession was illegal. Then he added that it would also be illegal for the federal government to try to prevent a state from seceding!

The American eagle guards its nest of states in this 1861 cartoon. But while the eagle warns "Annihilation to Traitors," the southern states in the foreground hatch rebellion. The war propaganda cartoon is a color lithograph done by E. B. and E. C. Kellogg of Hartford, Connecticut. The subtitle gives their position: "The Union! It Must and Shall Be Preserved." Which states seceded from the Union?

THE EAGLE'S NEST.
"THE UNION! IT MUST AND SHALL BE PRESERVED."

Connecticut Historical Society

Matters drifted throughout the winter. Several members of Congress tried to work out compromises that would satisfy the fears of southerners without stirring up northern foes of slavery. None succeeded. More southern states withdrew from the Union. Each seceding state tried to take over federal property within its borders—post offices, army forts, court houses.

Buchanan did not try to hold on to government property in the states that left the Union. But there were three forts in Charleston,

Harper's Weekly

This 1861 illustration comes from a popular magazine, *Harper's Weekly*. It shows the heavy guns and crew that occupied Fort Johnson. These South Carolinians stand ready to fire their cannon upon Fort Sumter. Why had national attention focused on Forts Johnson and Sumter?

South Carolina, that did not fall into local hands. One of these, **Fort Sumter,** was on an island in Charleston harbor. The others were on the mainland. They were held by about 100 soldiers commanded by Major Robert Anderson.

Gradually, national attention focused on these forts. Would South Carolina use force to seize them? If so, would Buchanan try to defend the forts? Major Anderson was a southerner. But he was a patriotic soldier who had taken an oath to protect the flag of the United States. Major Anderson realized that he could not protect all the forts with his tiny force. One night in December 1860 he moved his men to the more easily protected Fort Sumter.

South Carolina troops then occupied the abandoned forts on the mainland. When Buchanan sent an unarmed ship with men and supplies to Fort Sumter, the South Carolinians drove it off with cannon fire from the shore. For the first time shots were fired in anger. Yet no one was injured. Major Anderson remained in control of Fort Sumter.

■ Why was there no strong Presidential reaction in the winter of 1861 to the secession of the Deep South?

THE CONFEDERATE STATES OF AMERICA

On February 4, 1861, 37 delegates representing six southern republics met at **Montgomery,** Alabama, to create a central government. Southern leaders knew that the seceding states had to design a strong union if they were to stay independent. They had to work fast. They wanted to have the new government in operation before Abraham Lincoln became President of the United States on March 4.

The delegates began work on February 5 and adopted a constitution only three days later. This was possible because the document was almost a copy of the United States Constitution. The differences were small but significant. The new nation was to be a **confederacy** of independent states, not a union. Hence the delegates called it the **Confederate States of America.** The constitution also specifically mentioned slavery and guaranteed the rights of citizens to own slaves. Congress was forbidden to pass any law "denying . . . the right of property in negro slaves."

Despite a stress on the rights of the separate states, the Confederate constitution, like the United States Constitution, was to be the "supreme law of the land." The President was to hold office for six years instead of four. But he could not be reelected. Congress could not spend money unless two thirds of the representatives approved. The constitution could be amended if two thirds of the states approved, not three fourths as under the United States Constitution.

▦ What were the major differences between the constitutions of the Confederate States and the United States?

JEFFERSON DAVIS

The day after finishing the constitution, the delegates unanimously elected Jefferson Davis of Mississippi to be President of the Confederate States of America. They chose Alexander Stephens of Georgia as Vice President.

Davis was in the rose garden at his plantation, Brierfield, overlooking the Mississippi, when a telegram announcing his election was delivered. The President was a tall, slender man with high cheekbones, fair hair, and blue-gray eyes. He was 52 years old, the tenth child of a pioneer family in Todd County, Kentucky. He attended Transylvania University in Lexington, Kentucky, and was graduated from the United States Military Academy in 1828. He resigned his commission in 1835 to become a cotton planter in Mississippi.

Davis had long and varied experience in public life before becoming President of the Confederacy. He was elected to the House of Representatives in 1845. The next year the Mexican War broke out. He gave up his seat in Congress to serve as a colonel in the army. He was wounded in the foot at the Battle of Buena Vista. The wound was quite serious because the bullet drove pieces of his brass spur into his foot. He came back to Mississippi on crutches but recovered fully. In 1847 he was elected to the United States Senate. When Franklin Pierce became President in 1853, he named Davis Secretary of War.

In his inaugural address President Davis insisted that he desired to maintain peaceful relations with the United States. His speech was not very inspiring. Davis was an extremely hard worker, but he did

Jefferson Davis, elected President of the Confederacy in 1861, is the subject of this 1863 oil portrait by Robertson. How long was his term of office under the newly adopted constitution of the Confederacy?

not get on well with people. He often quarreled with members of his Cabinet and with other government officials. He could be very stubborn. His feelings were easily hurt by criticism. He wasted far too much of his time handling unimportant details. Once he spent a whole day dictating one 4,000-word letter.

■ What were Jefferson Davis's strengths when he became President of the Confederacy? What were his weaknesses?

LINCOLN BECOMES PRESIDENT

In 1861 Jefferson Davis's strengths were much more obvious than his weaknesses. Indeed, when Abraham Lincoln was inaugurated as President of the United States on March 4, many people thought him a far less inspiring leader than the President of the new Confederacy.

Smithsonian Institution

The Republican ticket is the focus of this 1860 campaign poster. Most prominent are Abraham Lincoln and his running mate, Hannibal Hamlin. The 15 previous Presidents appear in the borders. How many can you identify from their portraits, which appear elsewhere in this book?

453

Mary Todd married Abraham Lincoln in 1842. She was from Kentucky and met Lincoln in Springfield, Illinois, where she had come to live near her relatives. This is a daguerreotype. Mary Todd Lincoln made a tasteful and comfortable home for the family in Springfield which is now open to the public. What kind of people were the Lincolns thought to be at the time they came to Washington?

Lincoln had chosen a Cabinet that reflected a wide variety of attitudes and regions. This was understandable at a time of national crisis. Yet would this backwoods lawyer be able to control such a group? Or would he become a figurehead, a kind of homespun master of ceremonies? He had appointed the best-known Republican in the United States, William H. Seward, as Secretary of State. Seward did not resent Lincoln's having defeated him for the Republican Presidential nomination. But he did not think Lincoln competent to be President. He was ready, he told his wife, "to save freedom and my country" by making the major government decisions himself.

Lincoln, however, did not intend to be dominated by Seward or anyone else. People like Seward misunderstood him. They took his slow, deliberate, rather uncertain manner to mean confusion and lack of intelligence. Nothing could have been further from the truth.

Lincoln first revealed his depth and determination in his inaugural address. He assured the South that he would not send troops into the region to prevent secession. He promised again not to interfere with slavery in the states. Nevertheless, secession was illegal, even "revolutionary," he said. "No state upon its own mere motion can lawfully get out of the Union." In any case, secession would not end any of the existing disagreements between North and South. Conflicts of interest would remain. The only sensible solution was to negotiate as friends. "We are not enemies but friends," Lincoln said in closing. Angry disagreements "must not break the bonds of our affection."

- How did the national crisis influence Lincoln's choice of his Cabinet?
- What was Lincoln's message to the Confederacy in his inaugural address?

THE WAR BEGINS

The immediate problem Lincoln faced was what to do about Fort Sumter. Major Anderson and his men could not hold out forever without fresh supplies. After considering the question for about a month, Lincoln decided to send food to the besieged garrison but no troop reinforcements or ammunition. He informed the governor of South Carolina of his intention.

The Confederates would not accept even this small "invasion" of what they considered their territory. On April 12, acting on orders from President Davis, they began to bombard Fort Sumter. By the next day the fort was in ruins. When his ammunition was almost exhausted, Major Anderson surrendered.

The **Civil War** had begun. Southerners felt that they were fighting for what we would call the right of self-determination. They believed that the people of a state ought to be able to decide what

454

Museum of the Confederacy

kind of government they wanted for themselves. They had no intention of injuring the states that remained in the Union. What right had the United States to prevent them from going their own way?

Lincoln's answer to this argument was simple: A nation has the right to protect itself against destruction. If one part could separate itself from the rest whenever it disapproved of the result of an election, the nation would swiftly break up into many tiny fragments.

Lincoln's reasoning made it possible to go to war for patriotic reasons. Slavery was obviously the major cause of the war. But the war was not fought to abolish slavery. White people in the northern states did not suddenly become abolitionists when Confederate cannon began to pound Fort Sumter. They fought "to save the Union," not "to free the slaves."

▨ What reason did President Lincoln give for going to war?

The Stars and Bars, new flag of the Confederacy, flies over Fort Sumter after its capture by South Carolina forces in 1861. A lone sentry gazes at the departing Union relief ships, which came no closer because of the heavy Confederate cannon. The oil was painted c. 1863 by Conrad Wise Chapman. Why did the South bombard Fort Sumter?

455

RAISING THE ARMIES

After the attack on Fort Sumter, Lincoln called for 75,000 volunteer soldiers to put down the rebellion. Recruits came forward enthusiastically all over the North. But news that Lincoln intended to use force against the Confederacy caused Virginia, North Carolina, Tennessee, and Arkansas to secede and join the other Confederate states. When Virginia joined the Confederacy, the government shifted its capital from Montgomery, Alabama, to **Richmond,** Virginia.

Richmond, Virginia, the Capital of the Confederacy, stately stands in this view from Belle Isle. With two flags flying overhead, its capitol is in the background, to the right. E. Crehen made this lithograph in the late 1850s. Which city was the first Confederate capital?

In both North and South, recruiting was left to the states. Young men enlisted with high hopes for an exciting adventure that would take them far from farm or factory. A passion for "Zouave" units swept both sides. Prospective soldiers joined these Zouave companies to wear their broad sashes and baggy red breeches.

Since northern and southern soldiers were so much alike, any differences had to come from their generals. Lincoln's first choice for commander of the Union army had been Colonel Robert E. Lee, the officer who captured John Brown. Although Lee was a Virginian and the owner of 200 slaves, he was known to have opposed secession. His great hero was George Washington, and he was married to the first President's step-granddaughter.

Lee had been the top student in his class at the United States Military Academy. He had higher grades than any other cadet in the academy's history. As a young officer in the Mexican War, he had

456

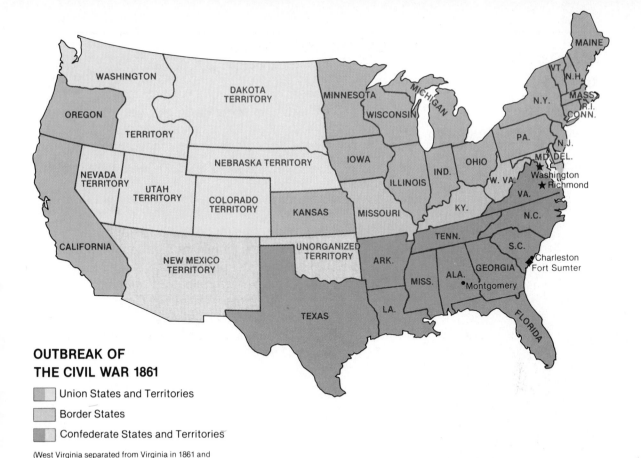

OUTBREAK OF
THE CIVIL WAR 1861

Union States and Territories

Border States

Confederate States and Territories

(West Virginia separated from Virginia in 1861 and
joined the Union in 1863).

Virginia Historical Society

Robert E. Lee on his horse Traveller
was photographed during the Civil
War by Michael Miley. Lee was a
hero both South and North for his
strong personal character. Traveller
was nearly as celebrated. Visitors
after the war pulled the hairs from
his tail for souvenirs. Lee's home
is today part of Arlington National
Cemetery. Who was Lee's hero?

Soldiering in the Civil War

Cooper-Hewitt Museum,
Smithsonian Institution

The typical soldier in the newly formed armies of the North and South had no previous military experience. Most knew how to handle guns, but the rest of soldiering was a mystery to nearly all. To teach recruits how to march, drill sergeants sometimes tied a piece of hay to each man's left foot and a piece of straw to the right. Then, lining the men up on the drill field, the sergeant would chant, "Hay-foot, straw-foot, hay-foot, straw-foot," until the troops caught on.

Most ordinary soldiers joined the armies with no idea of what actual warfare was like. Some were looking for personal glory. Others joined in hopes of visiting distant places and getting to know Americans from other parts of the country. North and South, love of country was the main motive. The names of volunteer companies reflected this patriotism and sought to inspire fear in the enemy ranks. Confederate regiments had names like the Southern Avengers, Rejectors of Old Abe, and Barton Yankee Killers. Northern regiments took names like Detroit Invincibles and Union Clinchers.

Most regiments were made up of men from one town or county. Since the soldiers elected their own officers, popularity rather than ability often determined who would be leaders. One Confederate regiment picked as colonel the fellow who gave the men two jugs of whiskey.

This system did not make for strict discipline. In one Union regiment drilling on a hot parade ground, a private was heard saying to the company commander, "Tom, let's quit this foolin' around . . . and get a drink."

performed brilliantly. If he had accepted Lincoln's offer, the Civil War might not have lasted as long as it did.

Unfortunately for the United States, Lee decided that he could not fight against his own state. He resigned from the army and joined the Confederates. Lincoln then turned to General Irvin McDowell, who was an efficient officer but without battle experience.

By July 1861 30,000 Union soldiers were training in camps outside Washington. Twenty miles (32 kilometers) to the south other thousands of Confederate soldiers were gathered at **Manassas** railroad junction, on a small stream called **Bull Run.** The Southern troops at Manassas were commanded by General Pierre Beauregard of Louisiana. Beauregard had also seen action in the Mexican War. In the attack on Mexico City he was twice wounded.

■ Why did Lincoln wish Lee to command his army?

READING PRACTICE IN SOCIAL STUDIES

Comparison and Contrast

One of the ways writers organize information is by *comparison and contrast.* Comparison is used to show how things are both similar and different, while contrast is used to show only the differences.

Comparison and contrast is often used to organize information in history. It readily gives the larger picture of events that led to debate and compromise. It helps readers understand why one side prevailed over another. It shows how sectional or political divisions came about

Comparison and contrast also helps us to understand how the central players in our history stood out from more ordinary people.

The author of this book uses comparison and contrast in the preceding chapter to describe the Lincoln-Douglas debates:

Even without his tall "stovepipe" hat, the six-foot, six-inch Lincoln towered over the Little Giant. He wore a formal black suit, usually rumpled and always too short for his long arms and legs. Douglas was what we would call a flashy dresser. He wore shirts with ruffles, fancy embroidered vests, a broad felt hat. He had a rapid-fire way of speaking that contrasted with Lincoln's slow, deliberate style.

Oftentimes word and phrase clues signal the use of comparison and contrast Examples include *similar, both, same, whereas, while, also, almost, than, exactly like, different from.*

Comparison and contrast may be either *direct* or *implied.* When it is direct, key words such as those below in italics act as signals. Look at this paragraph from page 453:

In 1861 Jefferson Davis's strengths were much *more* obvious *than* his weaknesses. Indeed, when Abraham Lincoln was inaugurated as President of the United States on March 4, many people thought him a far *less* inspiring leader *than* the President of the new Confederacy.

When comparison and contrast is implied, it is suggested or understood without signal words. The reader must decide what is being likened or contrasted in this passage from page 454:

Lincoln had chosen a Cabinet that reflected a wide variety of attitudes and regions. This was understandable at a time of national crisis Yet would this backwoods lawyer be able to control such a group? Or would he become a figurehead, a kind of homespun master of ceremonies?

Here a comparison is implied between Lincoln the man and Lincoln the President.

A useful way to take notes on a section organized by comparison and contrast is to divide each category into columns on a chart. A typical entry would begin like this:

Northern generals	Southern generals

Then take details from the section to fill in the columns of your chart. Look for both direct and implied comparisons and contrasts.

Read the section titled "North Versus South" on page 461 and then answer the questions that follow. If you wish to review *topic* and *main idea,* look back to page 281.

1. What is the topic of this section?
2. Copy the following chart. Use comparison and contrast to fill in the chart with details from "North Versus South."

Advantages of the North	Advantages of the South

3. How do the details on your chart support the topic of this section?
4. Keeping your chart in mind, write a general statement that gives the main idea of the section.
5. Tell whether your chart compares, contrasts, or does both, and explain why.

Johnny Reb and Billy Yank

During the Civil War most soldiers still used clumsy, muzzle-loading rifles. The most skillful rifleman could get off no more than two shots a minute. This gun had a range of nearly a mile and was deadly accurate up to 250 yards (225 meters). To advance in mass formation against troops armed with such rifles was to invite wholesale slaughter.

Army food ranged from fair to awful. It consisted mostly of salt or pickled beef or pork and bread—cornbread for the Confederate troops and hardtack for the Union. Hardtack was a solid cracker made from wheat. It came in thick, square chunks. The men generally soaked it in their coffee and ate it with a spoon. Coffee was therefore especially important to Union soldiers. They ground the coffee beans by pounding them with a stone or musket butt.

In camp Confederate "Johnny Reb" and Union "Billy Yank" passed the time playing cards, organizing horse races, and taking care of their equipment. Baseball was popular. When bats and balls were not available, the men made do with a board or a section of some farmer's fence rail for a bat. A walnut or stone wrapped with yarn made a usable ball.

Music was a popular pastime in both armies. Soldiers gathered around campfires in the evening to sing songs like "Home, Sweet Home" and "John Brown's Body," the favorite on the Union side. "I don't believe we can have an army without music," said Robert E. Lee.

At left is the Palmetto Battery near Charleston, South Carolina. This Confederate group of artillerymen was photographed in 1863. At right, a typical Union infantry company.

Library of Congress

National Archives

NORTH VERSUS SOUTH

In numbers the Confederacy seemed no match for the United States. The North had about 22 million people, the South only 9 million. Nearly 4 million of the southerners were slaves. Since white southerners were unwilling to put guns in the hands of blacks, the Confederate army could draw upon only 1,280,000 white men between the ages of 15 and 50 to fill its ranks.

In 1860 over 90 per cent of the nation's factories were in the northern states. New York, Pennsylvania, and Massachusetts each manufactured more goods than the entire Confederacy. There were only two gunpowder factories in the South, both small. There was not one factory capable of handling orders for uniforms and shoes.

The North also had more than twice as many miles of railroad tracks as the South and twice as many horses, donkeys, and mules. The government had little trouble moving its troops and supplies from the farms and the cities to its armies in the field. Since the United States was already in existence, it had an army, navy, and ways of raising money. The South had to create these institutions from scratch.

Just to begin operations, Confederate officials were forced to borrow from the state of Alabama and from bankers in New Orleans. The Confederate treasury was originally located in the back room of a bank in Montgomery. The secretary of the treasury and his one assistant had to furnish the office with their own money.

On the other hand, the Confederacy had certain advantages over the Union. Like the colonists during the War for American Independence, the southerners were defending their homeland. The invading northern armies had to maintain longer and longer lines of communication as they advanced. The southerners' homes and their whole way of life were at stake. This added to their determination and helped make up for the shortage of men and supplies.

> What advantages did the North have at the beginning of the Civil War? What advantages did the South have?

FROM BULL RUN TO RICHMOND

It took time to raise and train an army. The northern people were impatient. "On to Richmond" was the popular cry in Washington. In July 1861, long before the troops were ready, General McDowell ordered them forward.

On July 21 at **Bull Run** this poorly trained force of 30,000 met the Confederate army, which was not much better prepared. At first the Confederates fell back. But troops under Thomas J. Jackson stopped the Union advance cold, winning for General Jackson the nickname "Stonewall." Then the southerners counterattacked. The

"The Army of the Potomac" is an oil painting by James Hope, 1865. The panorama shows the Union camp at Cumberland Landing, which is on the Pamunkey River. McClellan rides ahead of his staff in the foreground. Why did Lincoln name McClellan as his commander of the army?

Union army was thrown into confusion and then panic. Hundreds of soldiers threw down their guns and fled northward toward Washington. If the Confederate soldiers had not been so green, they might have captured the capital before the northern army could regroup.

After this disgraceful defeat President Lincoln put General George B. McClellan in command of the army. McClellan was an excellent organizer. He was also popular with rank-and-file soldiers. He soon whipped the **Army of the Potomac** into excellent shape.

Yet McClellan had a number of serious weaknesses as a leader. He was very vain and had too high an opinion of his own abilities. He thought President Lincoln stupid and incompetent. He even had vague visions of taking over control of the government in order to save the Union single-handedly.

These flaws would have been bad enough. But McClellan was also overly cautious when it came to fighting. Despite his dashing appearance and bold talk, he never seemed ready to march against the enemy. When he was first appointed, caution was the right policy. The army had to be trained and disciplined. Yet when this task had been accomplished, McClellan still delayed. Finally, in March 1862, he prepared to attack.

McClellan's plan for capturing Richmond was complicated but sensible. Instead of marching directly south, he moved his army by boat down the Potomac River and through Chesapeake Bay to the mouths of the York and James Rivers, southeast of the Confederate capital. He then advanced up these streams. By the middle of May he had over 110,000 men, a huge force, within 25 miles (40 kilometers) of Richmond.

Instead of striking at the Confederate capital swiftly, McClellan delayed. On May 31 he was moving his army across the Chickahominy River, a branch of the James. While his troops were divided by the river, the Confederate commander, General Joseph E. Johnston, launched a fierce attack. The loss of life in the **Battle of Seven Pines** was heavy on both sides. Yet neither side gained an advantage.

General Johnston was wounded in this battle and had to give up his command. The new leader of the **Army of Northern Virginia** was Robert E. Lee.

The North quickly learned how much it had lost when Lee decided to fight for the Confederates. Although outnumbered, Lee realized how cautious McClellan was. He therefore reduced his force by sending General Stonewall Jackson and his men into the Shenandoah Valley north and west of Richmond to attack small Union forces stationed there.

Jackson specialized in the swift movement of troops. Soon his force was closer to Washington than to Richmond. This caused alarm in Washington. President Lincoln ordered large numbers of Union troops to the Shenandoah region. These units were in the wrong place to help McClellan. This was exactly what Lee had hoped for. While the Union soldiers were marching westward, Jackson was hurrying back toward Richmond!

The moment Jackson's regiment had rejoined his own, Lee ordered an all-out attack. What followed is known as the **Seven Days Before Richmond.** The Union army fell back to Harrison's Landing, a base on the James River. Over 15,000 Union soldiers were killed or wounded. The Confederates lost nearly 20,000 men. Neither side could be said to have won the battle.

- What did the Battle of Bull Run reveal about both North and South?
- What were some of General McClellan's weaknesses, and how did they endanger his Union troops?
- What strategy against McClellan did Robert E. Lee use?
- How did both the Confederacy and the Union suffer in the Seven Days Before Richmond?

BEHIND THE NORTHERN LINES

By the summer of 1862 northern leaders realized that the Civil War would not be won quickly. It was sure to cost many more thousands of lives and great sums of money. It would affect everyone in the nation, women and men, civilians and soldiers.

The early months of the war brought a business depression and much confusion to many parts of the North and West. The loss of southern trade injured many businesses. Hundreds of millions of dollars owed by southern borrowers could not be collected. Many banks in the North collapsed. About 6,000 companies went bankrupt.

The demands of the army and navy for uniforms, guns, and other supplies soon caused business to pick up again. Union soldiers wore out about 1.5 million uniforms and about 3 million pairs of shoes a year. The clothing and shoe industries boomed. Between 1860 and 1865 the consumption of wool more than tripled.

The Union forces also needed enormous amounts of everything from coal and nails to soap and writing paper. The demand for horses, ambulances, and wagons rose steadily. An army ambulance cost the fair sum of $170. By October 1862 the army had purchased 3,500 of them.

International Harvester Corp./HBJ Photo

Ripe wheat bows to the McCormick reaper in this 20th century painting. The traditional scythe and cradle were replaced by its sharp "straight reciprocating blade." What was the result of the North's wartime boom?

An army marches on its stomach. But food had to be raised by fewer people because so many young farmers were in uniform. Fortunately, the **mechanical reaper** came into general use at just this time. One reaper could harvest as much wheat as five field hands using scythes and cradles. Cyrus Hall McCormick, the inventor of the reaper, sold about 165,000 of these machines during the war.

The wartime boom caused prices to rise rapidly. The wages of the men and women of the North who produced war supplies and other goods did not keep pace with the rising cost of living. However, work was plentiful. Nearly all people were able to take care of themselves.

- What effects did the Civil War have on northern business?
- Why was Cyrus Hall McCormick's mechanical reaper so important during the war?

NORTHERN OPPONENTS OF THE WAR

Many people in the North and West were not willing to fight a war to prevent the southern states from seceding. Some believed that the United States would be better off without the South. Others had no objection to slavery. Still others felt that the southern states had a right to secede.

People who opposed the war came to be popularly known as **Copperheads.** Most of the Copperheads supported the Democratic party. They were sympathetic to the South and argued that it was not worth the cost to force the Confederacy to surrender.

465

Radical Copperheads organized secret societies with such names as Knights of the Golden Circle and Sons of Liberty. They tried to persuade Union soldiers to desert, and they helped Confederate prisoners to escape. Some Copperheads even smuggled guns and ammunition into the South.

The most important Copperhead leader was Clement L. Vallandigham, a congressman from Ohio. Vallandigham charged that Lincoln intended to abolish slavery if the United States won the war. He demanded that the government try to negotiate a reunion with the South. In 1863 he was thrown in prison by the military authorities. President Lincoln, however, ordered him released and deported to the Confederacy. Vallandigham went from the South to Canada, and in 1864 he came back to Ohio. Although he resumed his criticisms of the government, Lincoln decided it would be better not to silence him.

Liberty with her Union shield draws back from the Copperheads in this 1863 cartoon. These are snakes who strike without warning. Their stern faces portray Clement Vallandigham, the Copperhead leader. Why was he upset with President Lincoln?

Harper's Weekly

Lincoln did not let all critics off so easily. In 1861 he suspended the right of people to *habeas corpus* (from the Latin for "you shall have the body"). This is the legal process for ensuring that an accused person is not imprisoned unlawfully. It is a right guaranteed by the Constitution. But during the war over 13,000 Americans were held in jail without formal charges made against them.

Lincoln insisted that his first duty was to protect the Union. He exercised more power than any earlier President. But Lincoln did not try to be a dictator. The government did not censor newspapers or prevent citizens from voting as they wished in elections. When Union soldiers were sentenced to death for running away during a battle, Lincoln tended to pardon them. He called them "leg cases" rather than cowards, adding, "It would frighten the poor fellows too terribly to kill them." In a more serious mood, while pardoning one deserter, he said, "This boy can do us more good above ground than below ground."

- Who were the Copperheads?
- How did Lincoln treat critics of the war?

SHORTAGES IN THE SOUTH

Unlike the North, the Confederate economy was injured by the war. Paying for the war was the South's most difficult task. It could not raise enough by borrowing or taxing to meet all its bills. So the government had to print money that it could not back with gold or silver. It issued over $1 billion in bank notes during the war.

The South promised to pay off these notes in gold or silver after the war ended. When the South began to lose the war, people doubted that it would be able to pay its debts. Confederate paper money then fell rapidly in value. By early 1865 50 Confederate paper dollars were worth less than one gold dollar. Prices of goods in the South skyrocketed. In 1864 eggs cost six Confederate dollars a dozen. In the North eggs cost about 25 cents a dozen.

Almost every kind of manufactured product was scarce in the South because the region had been almost entirely agricultural. Shortages of clothing sent people rummaging in their attics in search of spinning wheels and hand looms that their grandparents had used. Soldiers marched in ragged uniforms. Sometimes they had no shoes. For civilians thorns took the place of pins. The blank side of wallpaper served as a substitute for writing paper.

- How did the Civil War affect the economy of the South?

Harper's Weekly

Far too long and lean already, these southern citizens stare with sunken eyes at the poster, which proclaims further hunger for the South. In this political cartoon a horned Jefferson Davis watches from the left. What happened to Confederate money?

THE BLOCKADE

The navy remained loyal to the Union. After the fall of Fort Sumter President Lincoln ordered it to blockade all southern harbors. This naval blockade gradually choked off the South's foreign trade. About 6,000 ships had entered and left southern ports in 1860. The next year only 800 managed to slip past northern warships. Thereafter almost none escaped.

Many southern captains tried to break through the blockade. Their ships, like the privateers of earlier wars, were small and fast. These **blockade runners** operated out of Charleston or Savannah or out of Mobile, Alabama, on the Gulf of Mexico.

The British island of Bermuda, only 400 miles (640 kilometers) off the North Carolina coast, was the blockade runners' favorite destination. There they exchanged cotton or other farm products for guns, medicines, blankets, and coffee, as well as for fancy silks and

BLOCKADE OF THE SOUTH
1861

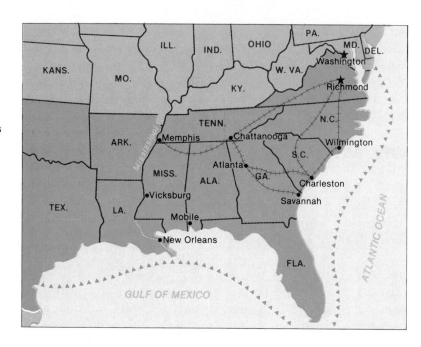

Union States

Confederate States

▲ ▲ ▲ Union Blockade

++++ Important Southern Railroads

0   600 Mi.

0   600 Km.

The C.S.S. *Nashville* is running the blockade in this 1862 watercolor by the Earl of Dunmore. Which were the key ports for the blockade runners?

Mariners Museum

other luxuries. The blockade runners brought in whatever they thought would sell for the best price. Since they were private citizens, the government could not control their activities or order them to import only war supplies.

■ How successful was the naval blockade of the South?
■ What goods were exchanged by the blockade runners?

COTTON DIPLOMACY

At the start of the war southern leaders thought that the economies of England and France would collapse without southern cotton. Those nations imported immense amounts of cotton for their textile factories. If their mills were forced to shut down, thousands of workers would lose their jobs. The southerners believed that England and France would enter the war on the side of the Confederacy to prevent this from happening.

Southerners who believed that **cotton diplomacy** would work tried to increase the pressure on England and France by preventing the export of cotton. "We have only to shut off your supply of cotton for a few weeks," one boasted to an English journalist, "and we can create a revolution in Great Britain."

These southerners were wrong. When the war broke out, English warehouses were bulging with cotton. By the time the supply had been used up, the British had discovered that they needed northern wheat more than southern cotton. Most British and French government leaders wanted the Confederacy to win the war. But they were unwilling to enter the war themselves.

Cotton was of little use to the South itself during the war. Planters shifted to growing corn and wheat and to raising pigs and cattle.

■ What did southerners believe cotton diplomacy would bring?

THE DRAFT IN THE SOUTH

Another difficulty faced by the Confederacy was raising a large enough army to defend its borders. Thousands of men enlisted. But because the white population was small, it became necessary in 1862 to **conscript,** or draft, men to serve as soldiers by law.

This draft law was very unpopular. It favored the rich, because a man who was conscripted could hire a substitute. Anyone who owned 20 or more slaves was exempted. The government believed that these large slave owners were needed at home to control the blacks. Many southerners complained that the draft law made the conflict "a rich man's war and a poor man's fight."

■ Why did southerners dislike the draft?

Urging their oxen onward, fugitive slaves ford the Rappahannock River in this 1862 photograph, which was taken by Timothy O'Sullivan. They are following the retreat of General Pope's army as it makes its way to Washington after the Second Battle of Bull Run. What name was given to the slaves who crossed over the Union lines?

SLAVES IN THE WAR

By 1865 the Southern government decided to use slaves as soldiers. Slaves had been used by the Confederate army throughout the war as laborers, bakers, blacksmiths, shoemakers, and nurses. Slaves also worked in factories. Half of the 2,400 employees of the Tredegar Iron Works in Richmond, the largest factory in the South, were slaves.

Many persons thought that the blacks would riot or run off by the thousands during the war. Few did. But whenever northern armies invaded a district, some slaves slipped away and crossed the Union lines. Often northern officers put them to work building fortifications. These blacks became known as **contrabands.**

How did the Confederate army use slaves during the war?

THE SECOND BATTLE OF BULL RUN

In the summer of 1862, under orders from Lincoln, McClellan began to withdraw the Union army from its positions near Richmond. The plan was to combine his veterans with a new army being organized south of Washington by General John Pope. As soon as the northerners pulled back, Lee moved northward. He was determined to destroy General Pope's army before McClellan could join with it. He knew that it was not enough simply to defend Richmond. To end the war, he had to deliver such a stinging defeat that the people of the North would lose the will to fight.

In a daring maneuver Lee sent 25,000 men commanded by Stonewall Jackson to hit Pope's army from the rear. Once again Jackson marched swiftly, then struck silently. He cut off the railroad

470

running from Washington to the Union front and set fire to most of Pope's supplies.

In desperation, on August 29 Pope attacked Lee. This **Second Battle of Bull Run** was fought on almost the same ground as the first. The Army of Northern Virginia halted the Union assault and then drove Pope's troops back toward Washington. Dismayed by Pope's failure, Lincoln dismissed him and again gave McClellan command of the Army of the Potomac. Ben Wade, a congressman from Ohio, objected strongly to McClellan's appointment. Lincoln asked him whom he should appoint instead. "Anybody," Wade answered impatiently. "Wade," said Lincoln calmly, "anybody will do for you, but I must have somebody."

■ What did General Lee believe he must do to end the war?

ANTIETAM

Lee now marched around the defenses of Washington. On September 5 he crossed the Potomac River to Maryland. McClellan was unsure of Lee's exact position. So he too crossed the river. On September 9 one of McClellan's soldiers found a copy of Lee's battle plans wrapped around some cigars in an abandoned Confederate camp. With this information McClellan was able to track down Lee's army. The armies met in battle on September 17 at **Sharpsburg,** a town on a branch of the Potomac called Antietam Creek. Lee had fewer than 50,000 men, McClellan about twice that number.

Missouri Historical Society

This is ever the price of war. Here lie Confederate soldiers who have fallen in front of Dunker Church at Antietam in September 1862. How did Lee's plans for this campaign become known?

It was a foggy, gray morning when this **Battle of Antietam** began. When the bloody struggle ended at twilight, the Confederates had lost 13,000 men, the Union forces 12,000. For yet another time in this bloody war neither side had won much of an advantage.

All next day the exhausted armies faced each other silently. Then, that night, the Confederates retreated back across the Potomac. The North had finally won a battle.

■ What was the significance of the Battle of Antietam?

THE EMANCIPATION PROCLAMATION

The cost of the war in blood and money was changing the way ordinary people in the North felt about slavery. Anger at white southerners more than sympathy for the blacks caused this change. The first result of it came in April 1862 when Congress abolished slavery in the District of Columbia.

Gradually Lincoln came to the conclusion that the United States should try to free all the slaves. He would have preferred to have the states buy the blacks from their owners and then **emancipate** or free them. This idea was known as **compensated emancipation.**

The Emancipation Proclamation was reprinted in this elaborate poster in 1888. One corner has been damaged. How would Lincoln have preferred to emancipate the slaves?

But Lincoln was a clever politician. He knew that many citizens would oppose paying anything to rebels and slave owners. Others still objected to freeing the slaves for the sake of doing away with an evil institution. Lincoln therefore decided to act under his war powers. He would free slaves not because slavery was wrong but as a means of weakening the rebel government.

Lincoln hesitated until after the Union victory at the Battle of Antietam. Then he issued the **Emancipation Proclamation.** This proclamation stated that after January 1, 1863, "all persons held as slaves within any States . . . in rebellion against the United States shall be . . . forever free."

Notice that the Proclamation did not liberate a single slave that the government had any control over. It applied only to areas ruled by the Confederates. Slaves in Maryland, Kentucky, Missouri, and even in those parts of the Confederacy that had been captured by Union armies, remained in bondage.

Chicago Historical Society

National Portrait Gallery

Yet when the armies of the United States advanced into new territory after January 1, 1863, the slaves there were freed. At last the war was being fought for freedom, not only to save the Union. Lincoln also ordered that blacks should be encouraged to enlist in the army. All told, about 180,000 black soldiers fought for the United States during the Civil War. More than 38,000 lost their lives in the struggle.

"Come and Join Us Brothers" is the title of the recruiting poster at left, published in Philadelphia after the Union army actively sought black regiments. At right is Major Martin R. Delany, c. 1865. He became the first black field officer. This hand-colored lithograph commemorates his promotion on the battlefield for bravery. How many black soldiers fought in the Civil War?

▩ What were the conditions of the Emancipation Proclamation?
▩ What was necessary to actually free slaves?

THE DRAFT RIOTS

The benefits of the Emancipation Proclamation were slow in coming. Its disadvantages appeared at once. Probably it made white southerners more determined than ever to maintain their independence. Many northern whites resented it because they feared that slaves liberated under the Proclamation would flock into the North to compete with them for jobs. The Democratic party made large gains in the 1862 Congressional elections.

A few months after the Proclamation went into effect, Congress passed a conscription law. Like the Confederate draft, this measure allowed men who were drafted to hire substitutes. They could even avoid military service by paying the government $300.

RALLY ROUND
THE FLAG, BOYS!
100 MEN WANTED!!
For the 23d Mich. Infantry.

Enlist before April 1st, secure the Government Bounty of $300 00,
AND "KEEP OUT OF THE DRAFT!"

Government Bounty, $300; State Bounty, $100; Town Bounty, $100.
Apply to WM. SICKELS. St. Johns, or
O. L. SPAULDING,
Lieut. Col., 23d Mich. Infantry. Corunna.
March , 1864.   "REPUBLICAN" PRINT, ST. JOHNS.

"Rally Round the Flag, Boys!" says this 1864 Michigan recruiting poster. And "Keep Out of the Draft!" which passed the month the poster went to press. The unpopular draft brought about New York City's draft riots, shown in the engraving at right. It was published in 1864 in *Leslie's*, a popular magazine. What warning did these riots give both North and South?

Poor men could not possibly raise $300, which was as much as a laborer could earn in a year. Many made a connection between the draft law and emancipation. They resented having to risk their lives in order to free blacks who could then compete with them for work.

Draft riots broke out in many parts of the country in the spring and summer of 1863. The worst occurred in New York City, where Irish-born workers ran wild for four days in July. The rioters burned buildings, looted shops, and terrorized innocent local blacks. Over a hundred black New Yorkers were murdered. These riots and other signs of anti-black feeling in the North should have been a warning. The war might free the slaves, but it was not likely to produce racial harmony, neither in the North nor South.

▨ What feelings led to the draft riots in 1863?

474

FREDERICKSBURG

Meanwhile the Emancipation Proclamation had not much effect on the battlefields. When McClellan failed to attack the Confederates as they retreated after the Battle of Antietam, Lincoln again removed him from command of the Army of the Potomac. He chose General Ambrose E. Burnside to succeed him. Unlike McClellan, Burnside was a bold, even reckless officer. He decided to push directly toward Richmond. In December 1862 he crossed the Rappahannock River over pontoon bridges and occupied the town of Fredericksburg, about 50 miles (80 kilometers) north of Richmond.

The Confederate army was entrenched on a ridge behind Fredericksburg called **Marye's Heights.** It was an extremely strong position. Looking across the field that lay before the Confederate lines,

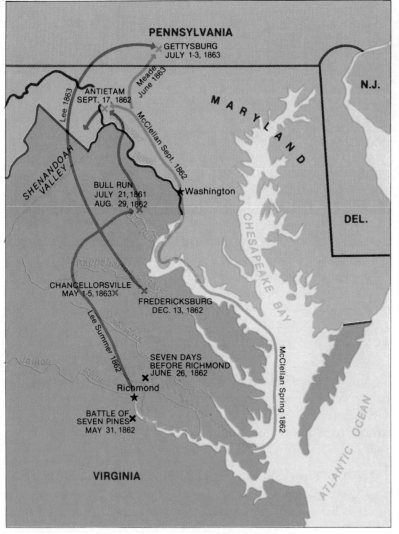

THE WAR IN THE EAST 1861-63

× Union Victory

→ Union Forces

× Confederate Victory

➤ Confederate Forces

× No Victor

Only the bayonet would do, firing was useless—these the instructions to raw recruits from Pennsylvania in the 1862 assault on Marye's Heights. This detail is from an oil painted by Union Lieutenant Frederick Cavada. Why did the Confederates have such a strong position during this Battle of Fredericksburg?

General E. P. Alexander, Lee's chief of artillery, remarked, "A chicken could not live in that field when we open on it."

Burnside nevertheless attacked. He had 120,000 men to Lee's 75,000. The **Battle of Fredericksburg** was fought on December 13. It began in heavy fog. About eleven o'clock in the morning the fog lifted. The Confederates could see the Union soldiers coming across the frozen plain. They commenced firing.

Burnside sent his blue-coated soldiers charging at Lee's position six separate times. Each time they were driven back by musket and cannon fire, leaving the field littered with their dead. At the end of the day they had suffered 12,000 casualties. Utterly defeated, Burnside crossed back across the Rappahannock. Shortly afterwards, at his own request, Burnside was relieved of command.

- Why was Lee able to soundly defeat Burnside in the Battle of Fredericksburg?
- What decision did General Burnside reach after crossing back over the Rappahannock?

CHANCELLORSVILLE

Lincoln next turned the Army of the Potomac over to General "Fighting Joe" Hooker. General Hooker concentrated his units at Chancellorsville, a village in the densely wooded area of Virginia known as the **Wilderness.** While he was preparing to advance, Lee attacked him. This **Battle of Chancellorsville** on May 1-5, 1863, showed Lee at his best. Although he had only 60,000 soldiers to Hooker's 125,000, he divided his army again. Stonewall Jackson's troops slipped quietly around the right side of the Union army. Then Jackson and Lee attacked at the same time. After days of bloody fighting, Hooker retreated. Lee had won another brilliant victory.

The victory was a costly one. General Jackson was wounded by stray bullets from his own lines. Three bullets hit him, one in the right hand and two in the left arm. Nowadays such wounds would not be fatal. But the bone in his arm was badly broken. The arm had to be amputated. Stonewall died from shock and loss of blood.

A photograph of Stonewall Jackson made shortly before he died in the Battle of Chancellorsville shows a face that is at once disciplined and compassionate. What accident led to Jackson's death?

- How did Lee achieve his victory in the five days of fighting at Chancellorsville?
- Why did Lee's victory turn out to be a costly one for the southern army?

GETTYSBURG

A month after the battle of Chancellorsville, Lee again invaded the North. He still hoped that a decisive victory on northern soil would cause the United States to give up the struggle.

As gray-clad Confederates marched through Maryland and into Pennsylvania, Union forces raced across country to intercept them. General George G. Meade was now in command, the fifth officer to hold this post in less than a year.

On July 1, 1863, one of Meade's units made contact with a Confederate detachment at the town of Gettysburg, in southern Pennsylvania. Lee's army was spread out, traveling in three separate columns. Now he quickly concentrated his forces. Meade placed his Union troops outside the town on a ridge that curved like a fishhook. A hill called **Cemetery Ridge** was the center of their position. Lee's Confederate forces occupied another ridge half a mile away. The center of the Confederate line was on **Seminary Ridge.**

For two days the battle raged back and forth. On July 3, while Confederate artillery pounded Cemetery Ridge, General George E. Pickett led a charge of 15,000 infantrymen at the Union position. For a brief moment these Confederates reached the Union trenches on Cemetery Ridge. But Union reserves counterattacked swiftly. Pickett's surviving infantrymen were driven off. This was the last Confederate charge. The battle was over. Again Lee retreated into

"Battle of Gettysburg" was painted in oil by James Walker. Its design came from Col. John Bachelder in about 1870. In this detail southern soldiers charge in the background while Yankee reinforcements rush forward. General Meade is visible with field glasses at right center. In the foreground soldiers aid the dying Confederate General Lewis Armistead. How might this battle have ended the Civil War?

Virginia. Had Meade pursued the Confederates quickly, he might have destroyed them and ended the war. Instead he delayed, and the war dragged on for nearly two more years.

Some months after the **Battle of Gettysburg,** President Lincoln dedicated a cemetery there where thousands of Union soldiers were buried. He delivered a short speech. Lincoln's <u>Gettysburg Address</u> attracted little attention at the time. It is now recognized as his noblest expression of the purpose of the Civil War and of the ideals of American democracy. The speech concluded with these words:

> From these honored dead we take increased devotion to that cause for which they gave their last full measure of devotion—that we here highly resolve that these dead shall not have died in vain— that this nation, under God, shall have a new birth of freedom— and that government of the people, by the people, for the people, shall not perish from the earth.

- What advantage did General Pickett briefly gain at Gettysburg? Why was he unable to hold Cemetery Ridge?
- Why is the Battle of Gettysburg so well remembered?

478

Medical treatment in the Civil War was terribly crude by modern standards. Thousands of soldiers died of blood poisoning. Operations were performed without anesthetics. Still worse, about twice as many soldiers died of disease as of wounds.

Typhoid fever took countless lives. No one knew its cause or how to cure it. Army doctors treated pneumonia by blood-letting, a procedure which surely increased the chances that the sick soldier would die.

The best military hospital in the South was run by Sally L. Tompkins in Richmond. President Jefferson Davis made Tompkins a captain. She was the only woman officer of the Confederate army. Like her many counterparts North and South, she saw thousands of amputations performed to halt deadly gangrene.

On the Union side heroic work was performed by the nurse Clara Barton. She cared for sick and wounded soldiers at Antietam and Fredericksburg. By wagon caravan she carried supplies from one Union hospital to another, calming the frightened horses when cannon shells exploded in their pathway. In 1864 she was appointed superintendent of nurses for the Union army. Later Barton founded the American Red Cross Society. She served as president of the Red Cross from 1882 to 1904.

Binding Up the Wounds of War

The Granger Collection

Above, Clara Barton at the time she ministered to the war wounded. The photograph below shows a ward of the Carver General Hospital in 1864. Many of the men have lost limbs to save their lives.

Library of Congress

BUILDING SKILLS
IN SOCIAL STUDIES

Eyewitnesses to War

The Civil War was recorded for history by both the camera and the sketchbook when artists were dispatched to the battlefield by newspapers and magazines. Examples of these eyewitnesses to war are below and throughout this book.

At right is the wagon headquarters of the *New York Herald* at Culpeper Court House. This was probably taken by Matthew Brady, the most famous Civil War photographer. Below is a pencil sketch by Alfred R. Waud for *Harper's Weekly* of Confederates leaving Mechanicsville, Virginia, in 1862. At the bottom is a Timothy Sullivan photograph of Sharpsburg Bridge at Antietam.

june 26 1862

THE WAR IN THE WEST

In the West the Union objective was to control the Mississippi River. Then it would be impossible for the Confederates to bring men and supplies to the eastern front from Arkansas, Louisiana, and Texas. The South would be cut in two.

The struggle for the river began in 1862. It was long and bitter. Out of it came the great general that Lincoln had been searching for since the beginning of the war. His name was Ulysses S. Grant.

Unlike Robert E. Lee, Grant had done poorly at West Point. He served well enough in the Mexican War. But he found army life boring in peacetime. He began to drink too much. In 1854 he resigned his commission in the army. He tried a number of businesses but succeeded in none. He seemed a totally undistinguished person.

When the Civil War broke out, Grant was working in a leather shop in Galena, Illinois. He joined an Illinois regiment. Since experienced officers were scarce, he was made a brigadier general.

Grant was a shy, slight man. He did not look like a soldier, much less a general. He was constantly chewing a cigar. He rarely stood up straight. His uniforms were rumpled and ill fitting. Often Grant did not wear his officer's insignia. Yet he was brave and determined, and he turned out to be an excellent military strategist.

National Portrait Gallery

Riders for the Union are assembled in this 1865 portrait of its generals by Ole Peter Hansen Balling. *Left to right:* Devin, Custer, Kilpatrick, Emory, Sheridan, McPherson, Crook, Merritt, Thomas, Warren, Meade, Parke, Sherman, Logan, Grant, Burnside, Hooker, Hancock, Rawlins, Ord, Blair, Terry, Slocum, Davis, Howard, Schofield, and Mower. In what ways did Grant turn out to be an able leader?

In February 1862 Grant organized a successful land-and-river attack on **Fort Henry,** a Confederate strong point on the Tennessee River. After the Confederates surrendered the fort, he laid siege to **Fort Donelson,** on the Cumberland River. When the Confederate commander asked Grant what terms he would offer for the surrender of the fort, Grant replied, "immediate and unconditional surrender." With this brief remark U. S. Grant won the nickname "*Uncondi- tional Surrender*" Grant.

▨ How did General Grant receive his nickname?

SHILOH

Grant next marched his men up the Tennessee River. He intended to destroy railroad lines near Corinth, Mississippi. On April 6, 1862, about 30 miles (48 kilometers) from Corinth, his army was surprised by Confederates under General Albert Sidney Johnston. The result- ing **Battle of Shiloh** caught Grant completely off guard. During the first day's fighting, his army was forced back to the river.

Fortunately, 25,000 fresh Union troops arrived during the night. The next day they drove the Confederates back. But Shiloh was an extremely costly victory. In two days about 13,000 Union soldiers were killed or wounded. Grant was so shaken by the surprise atttack that he allowed the Confederates to escape. He was relieved of his command. His reputation seemed ruined.

▨ What happened to General Grant at Shiloh?

THE WAR IN THE WEST 1862-64

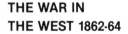 Union States
 Confederate States
→ Union Forces
✕ Union Victory

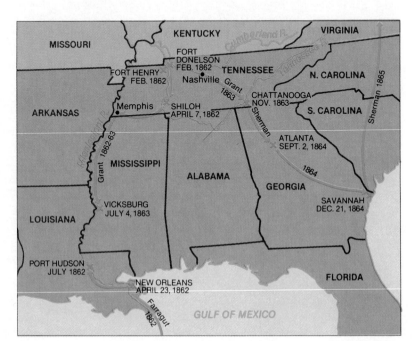

THE SIEGE OF VICKSBURG

Gradually, other Union forces gained control of the Mississippi River. On April 23, 1862, a naval task force commanded by Captain David Farragut sailed up from the Gulf of Mexico and captured New Orleans. By autumn only a 250-mile stretch (400 kilometers) of the river between Vicksburg, Mississippi, and Port Hudson, Louisiana, was still in Confederate hands.

At this point Lincoln put Grant back in command of a powerful army. Grant decided to attack Vicksburg. The town was located high on cliffs overlooking a bend in the Mississippi. It was defended by the southern army commanded by General John C. Pemberton.

Grant approached Vicksburg from the north in November 1862. His artillery pounded Vicksburg's fortifications. But marshy land around the city blocked a possible infantry attack. Grant therefore moved his entire army to the other side of the Mississippi. Then he marched past the Vicksburg fortifications at night and recrossed the river south of the city.

After driving off a Confederate army east of Vicksburg, Grant began the **Siege of Vicksburg,** pinning down Pemberton and his army. The siege began in mid-May. For weeks the Confederates held out. Eventually they ran short of food and ammunition. On July 4, 1863, Pemberton surrendered. Shortly afterwards, the remaining southern stronghold on the river, **Port Hudson,** was also captured. The Confederacy had been snipped in two.

■ What tactics did Grant use to lay siege to Vicksburg?

Captain Farragut's flagship *Hartford* leads his naval task force past the guns of Port Hudson in this detail from an 1864 oil painting by Edward Arnold. What major city had already been captured by Farragut?

483

U. S. Grant, *above,* faced the Armies of the Confederacy. Its officers are shown below in a painting entitled "Summer" by Charles Hoffbauer. It shows the generals in 1863. *Left to right:* Hood (standing), Hampton (on horseback), Ewell (foot on stump), Gordon (arms folded), Jackson (on horseback), F. Lee (pointing), Hill (with sword), R. E. Lee on Traveller, Longstreet (holding field glasses), Johnston (horseback), Beauregard (holding map), and Stuart (beside his horse). How many soldiers had Grant and Lee each in May 1864?

LINCOLN FINDS HIS GENERAL

Lincoln now put Grant in command of all Union troops west of the Appalachian Mountains. In November 1863 a series of battles was fought around **Chattanooga,** Tennessee, an important railway center. There Grant defeated a Confederate army under General Braxton Bragg. Bragg retreated into northern Georgia. A few months later, in March 1864, Lincoln called Grant to Washington. He was promoted to lieutenant general and named general-in-chief of all the armies of the United States.

Grant decided to try to end the war by mounting two great offensives. He himself would lead the Army of the Potomac against Lee, seeking a showdown battle in northern Virginia. A western army commanded by General William Tecumseh Sherman would march from Chattanooga into northern Georgia. Its immediate objective was to capture Atlanta.

Grant had given command of the western army to General Sherman because he was a tough soldier who had served under Grant at the bloody battle of Shiloh and in the fighting around Chattanooga. Sherman's father, an Ohio lawyer and judge, had named his son after the Shawnee leader Tecumseh, whom he admired greatly.

■ What was General Grant's strategy to end the war?

GRANT VERSUS LEE

In May 1864 Grant crossed the Rappahannock and Rapidan Rivers and marched into the tangled forest of the Wilderness, where Lee had defeated Hooker one year earlier. This time Lee was reluctant to fight. He had only 60,000 men. Grant had more than 100,000.

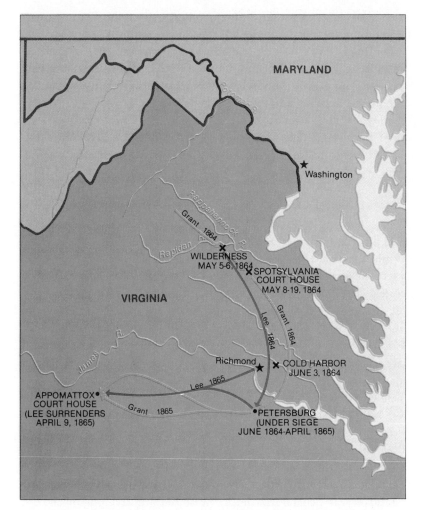

THE FINAL BATTLES
OF THE WAR 1864-65

→ Union Forces
➡ Confederate Forces
✕ Battle

0   75 Mi.

0   75 Km.

MARYLAND

★ Washington

Grant 1864

WILDERNESS
MAY 5-6, 1864

✕ SPOTSYLVANIA
COURT HOUSE
MAY 8-19, 1864

VIRGINIA

Lee 1864   Grant 1864

Richmond ★ ✕ COLD HARBOR
JUNE 3, 1864

Lee 1865

APPOMATTOX ●
COURT HOUSE
(LEE SURRENDERS
APRIL 9, 1865)

Grant 1865

● PETERSBURG
(UNDER SIEGE
JUNE 1864-APRIL 1865)

Grant made Lee fight. For two days Union and Confederate forces hammered away at each other in the **Battle of the Wilderness.** The Army of the Potomac suffered 18,000 casualties, far more than their Confederate enemy.

Scarcely had this battle ended when Grant pressed stubbornly on. He was trying to march around Lee's smaller army and get between it and Richmond. At **Spotsylvania Court House** the two armies clashed again. This time 12,000 Union soldiers fell in a single day.

Again Grant advanced. In another bloody clash at Cold Harbor 7,000 Union soldiers died in less than an hour. In one month of fighting Grant had lost 55,000 men, Lee 31,000.

Despite the tremendous human cost, Grant was gaining his objective. Lee was running short of equipment. Union factories were turning out almost unlimited amounts of supplies. The larger population of the North was beginning to tip the scales toward the Union. Lee could not replace all his casualties. But bolstered by a steady

485

stream of volunteers and draftees, the Army of the Potomac was larger after the **Battle of Cold Harbor** than at the start.

In June 1864 Grant crossed the James River in order to strike at **Petersburg,** a town a few miles south of Richmond. Petersburg was an important railroad junction. If Grant could capture it, supplies to Richmond and Lee's army would be cut off.

Lee's weary veterans managed to stop the Union army outside Petersburg. Grant had to place the city under siege. Both sides dug in. The trenches stretched for miles around the city. For nine months the Confederate defenses held.

■ What was Grant's objective in pressing Lee battle to battle?

SHERMAN'S MARCH TO THE SEA

While Grant was stalled outside Petersburg, General Sherman advanced toward **Atlanta** at the head of a force of 100,000. The Confederate general resisting him, Joseph E. Johnston, had only 60,000 men. He tried to avoid a showdown battle. President Jefferson Davis did not approve of this. He replaced Johnston with General John B. Hood. An aggressive officer, Hood twice attacked Sherman's much larger army. Both attacks failed. On September 2 the Union army marched triumphantly into Atlanta. Hood retreated northward into Tennessee.

News of Sherman's victory reached Washington just before the Presidential election of 1864. Lincoln had been renominated by Republicans and pro-war Democrats on a National Union ticket. The Vice Presidential candidate was Andrew Johnson, a Tennessee Democrat who had remained loyal to the Union. The Democratic candidate was General McClellan. With the war dragging on and on, Lincoln had expected to lose the election. Now, Sherman's victory helped him and his party immensely. Lincoln was reelected in a landslide, 212 electoral votes to 21.

After capturing Atlanta, Sherman burned the city to the ground. The next day, November 15, his army set out eastward toward the city of **Savannah** on the Atlantic Coast.

As Sherman's army went "marching through Georgia," as the song goes, "from Atlanta to the sea," it left a path of destruction behind it 60 miles wide (96 kilometers). On Sherman's order his troops destroyed or consumed everything in their path.

The Union soldiers slaughtered chickens and cattle. They burned barns and houses. When the men crossed a railroad line, they tore up the rails, piled up and set fire to the ties, and placed the rails on the roaring fire. When the rails were red hot, they bent and twisted them so that they were useless. Sometimes they wound the rails around tree trunks. These were known as "Sherman's neckties."

General William Tecumseh Sherman was photographed by Matthew Brady in 1865. He is wearing a mourning sash on his left arm for Abraham Lincoln. How wide was the wake of destruction left by Sherman and his army?

486

Sherman was carrying out what is now called **total war.** He sought to destroy the resources of the civilian population as well as the opposing army. He was trying to break the southerners' will to resist. When his harsh policy was questioned, Sherman simply said, "War is cruelty."

On December 21 the Union army entered Savannah. That city, too, went up in flames. Next Sherman marched north, destroying large sections of South Carolina and North Carolina with the same cold-blooded efficiency.

The entire South was savaged by the war. Two thirds of its railroad mileage was destroyed. The Confederate capital at Richmond met the same fate as the cities in Sherman's path. On April 3, 1865, fires raged through its shattered streets.

- How did Sherman's capture of Atlanta help Abraham Lincoln be reelected President?
- Why did Sherman engage in total war?

The Confederacy evacuated from its capital of Richmond, Virginia, on April 3, 1865. Flames roared through its streets and buildings where once flowered the Capital of the Confederacy (page 456). Today Richmond remembers the Confederate dead at Hollywood Cemetery, burial place of three Presidents and 18,000 southern soldiers. Why were major cities of the South destroyed?

Library of Congress

SURRENDER AT APPOMATTOX

In April 1865 Grant finally cut the railroad line to Petersburg. Lee abandoned Petersburg and Richmond and retreated westward. His army was now thinned to 30,000 men. His last hope was to escape into North Carolina and join with the army that Sherman was driving before him. But Grant's pursuing troops sealed off this escape route. On April 8 Lee made the painful decision to surrender.

Lee and Grant met at the home of Wilmer McLean in the village of **Appomattox Court House** on Sunday, April 9. Lee wore his best dress uniform. He carried a jewel-studded sword at his side. Grant had on a muddy officer's coat and an ordinary private's shirt, unbuttoned at the neck.

It was a moving scene. Lee was dignified in defeat, Grant gracious in victory. "I met you once before, General Lee, while we were serving in Mexico," Grant said after they had shaken hands. "I think I should have recognized you anywhere."

At Appomattox Court House, in the quiet of a parlor, the Civil War is ended. "Surrender of General Lee to General Grant" was painted in oil by Louis Guillaume. How did each general react to this moving scene?

Appomattox Court House National Historical Park

The two great generals talked briefly about that war of long ago when they had been comrades. Then Grant sat down at a little table and wrote out the terms of surrender. The terms were generous. The Confederates must merely surrender their weapons and depart in peace. When Lee hinted that his men would benefit greatly if allowed to keep their horses for the spring planting, Grant said, "Let all the men who claim to own a horse or mule take the animals home with them to work their little farms." Both men then signed the surrender paper. The war was over.

■ What were the terms of surrender at Appomattox?

CHAPTER 16 REVIEW

Identification

Tell briefly why each of the following persons, terms, or events is important.

1. Abraham Lincoln
2. Jefferson Davis
3. Robert E. Lee
4. Thomas J. "Stonewall" Jackson
5. George B. McClellan
6. Ulysses S. Grant
7. William Tecumseh Sherman
8. Fort Sumter
9. Army of the Potomac
10. Army of Northern Virginia
11. Copperheads
12. Blockade runners
13. Antietam
14. Emancipation Proclamation
15. Draft riots
16. Battle of Chancellorsville
17. Battle of Gettysburg
18. Siege of Vicksburg
19. Sherman's March to the Sea
20. Appomattox Court House

Understanding American History

1. Compare and contrast Abraham Lincoln and Jefferson Davis as leaders. What were the strengths and weaknesses of each?
2. What were the advantages and disadvantages of the North and South at the start of the Civil War?
3. Describe the life of a typical soldier in the Civil War.
4. In what sense was the Civil War good for the northern economy?
5. How did the Civil War affect the South's economy?
6. What did the draft riots show about northern attitudes toward blacks?
7. Why was the Battle of Vicksburg a turning point of the war?
8. Compare and contrast Grant and Lee.
9. What were the two parts of General Grant's plan to end the war?
10. Why did General Sherman use total war in his March to the Sea?

Activities

1. Prepare a bulletin board to show the major battles of the Civil War. Southerners named battles after nearby towns, northerners after bodies of water. Give both names when there are two. Arrange the battles in the order in which they were fought. Include as much information as you need to show how the war progressed. Choose appropriate symbols for North and South, northern and southern victories, fighting on land and water, troop movements in the South and West.

2. There have been an enormous number of books published to describe and illustrate the Civil War. Check the card catalog of your school or public library. Choose one aspect of the war — food shortages, prison life, conscription, blockade running, newspaper coverage — for a short report to the class. If possible, illustrate your report by using an overhead projector or charts and drawings you can make yourself.

3. Use your historical imagination to write a letter home as a soldier or nurse in either the Confederate or Union army. Include a description of a general you might have glimpsed in camp, or describe conditions in a hospital for the war wounded.

4. With your classmates use your historical imagination to present a newscast just after the Battle of Gettysburg. Include interviews with the commanding generals as well as with typical soldiers for both armies. As a follow-up, return to the site to interview spectators who have just heard Lincoln deliver his Gettysburg Address.

5. Make a diorama or model of one of the Civil War battlefields. Consult reference books to be sure that your details are accurate. Describe the battle in class, perhaps by using toy soldiers to show troop movements.

CHAPTER 16 TEST

Matching (30 points)
Number your paper 1–10 and match the person in the second column with the description in the first column.

1. Led the March to the Sea
2. Issued the Emancipation Proclamation
3. Commander of the Army of Northern Virginia
4. Led a gallant charge for the South at Gettysburg
5. Invented the mechanical reaper
6. President of the Confederacy
7. A leading Copperhead who criticized the Union for fighting the South
8. Important southern general whose firm stand earned him the nickname "Stonewall"
9. Union general whose strategy finally forced the Confederacy to surrender
10. Union general who was a good organizer but overly cautious

a. Abraham Lincoln
b. Jefferson Davis
c. Robert E. Lee
d. Ulysses S. Grant
e. George B. McClellan
f. William T. Sherman
g. Thomas J. Jackson
h. Cyrus Hall McCormick
i. George E. Pickett
j. Clement Vallandigham

Chronology (20 points)
Number your paper 11–15 and place the following events in order by numbering 1 for the first, 2 for the second, and so on.

11. Lincoln issues the Emancipation Proclamation
12. Creation of the Confederate States of America
13. Lincoln is sworn in as President
14. Grant leads the Army of the Potomac
15. Lee leads the Army of Northern Virginia

Classifying (20 points)
Number your paper 16–20. For each of the following statements write *N* if it was a strength of the North, *S* if it was a strength of the South.

16. Most factories were here.
17. Its soldiers fought to defend their homeland.
18. Far more people lived here.
19. Shorter lines of communication were necessary here.
20. This army began with more able military leaders.

Essay (30 points)
How did the Civil War affect the economies of both North and South? Give as many specifics as you can to support your answer. Plan your short essay with an opening statement that sets forth your position and choose details which support your conclusion.

CHAPTER 17

Reconstruction

On the evening of April 9, 1865, President Lincoln received a telegram from General Grant: "GENERAL LEE SURRENDERED THE ARMY OF NORTHERN VIRGINIA THIS MORNING." Next day the whole country had the news. Bells rang out, bands played, flags and banners flew everywhere. A crowd gathered outside the White House. "Tad" Lincoln, the President's 12-year-old son, appeared at the window happily waving a captured Confederate flag. Everyone cheered.

Library of Congress

Shortly before an assassin took his life, President Lincoln sat for this photograph with his son Tad. It was taken by Brady Studio. How many days after the end of the Civil War was Lincoln assassinated?

Unfortunately, this happy national mood did not last. On the evening of April 14 Abraham and Mary Todd Lincoln were attending a play at Ford's Theater in Washington. Suddenly a shot rang out. John Wilkes Booth, a little known actor who sympathized with the South, had slipped into the President's box and fired a bullet into his head. The next day the President died.

"The South is avenged!" shouted John Wilkes Booth as he leapt from the Presidential box after firing the shot that killed Lincoln. What was Booth's fate?

Booth escaped from the theater in the confusion and fled to Virginia. He was hunted down and trapped in a barn. The barn was set on fire, but Booth was killed by a bullet. Whether he was shot or killed himself is not clear. The people of the North were grief-stricken. The Confederacy had surrendered, but the nation was still badly divided.

PRESIDENT ANDREW JOHNSON

Much now depended on Andrew Johnson, who became President after the **assassination** of President Lincoln. Before the Civil War Johnson had served in both houses of Congress and as governor of Tennessee. The Republicans had picked him to run for Vice President in 1864, even though he was a Democrat. He was one of the few pro-Union politicians who came from a slave state. His home state of Tennessee was not even a member of the Union when he became President!

All through his career Johnson had been a champion of the small farmer. He favored laws to improve public education and provide free farms, or **homesteads,** for families who would settle on the public lands. He was always critical of great wealth. This helps explain his hatred of the southern planters, whom he called "traitorous aristocrats."

Most Republican politicians expected Johnson to make a fine President. Moderate Republicans believed he would be lenient toward the South. They hoped, as Lincoln had put it in his moving speech at his second inauguration, "to bind up the nation's wounds" quickly.

Johnson pleased the **Moderates** by issuing an **amnesty,** or pardon, to most former Confederates. Those who would take an oath of loyalty to the United States would regain full citizenship. The states of the former Confederacy could hold elections and send representatives and senators to Congress.

On the other hand, less-forgiving Republicans, called **Radicals,** expected Johnson to act on his well-known dislike of the southern planter class and punish them severely. Congressman Thaddeus Stevens of Pennsylvania was one of the Radical leaders. He demanded that the United States seize the property of the large slaveholders and give it to the ex-slaves. There would be plenty of "rebel land," he said, to give a 40-acre farm (16 hectares) to every adult male ex-slave in the South.

- What did the Moderate Republicans think should be done to the South after the Civil War?
- What did the Radical Republicans propose to do to the South after the Civil War?

BUILDING SKILLS IN SOCIAL STUDIES

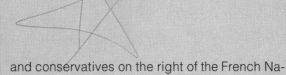

The Language of Politics

In this chapter the terms *radical, moderate,* and *conservative* have been used to describe different political groups during the time of Reconstruction. These are but a few of the terms used in this book to describe political positions. Similar terms are *liberal* and *reactionary.*

Nowadays people are more apt to describe themselves as being a *Republican,* a *Democrat,* or an *Independent.* Nearly twice as many voters are registered with the Democratic party as with the Republican party. Yet the Republican candidate for President in 1980 won all but 6 of the 50 states. Part of the reason for Ronald Reagan's victory was the strong support he received from the close to 30 per cent of the voters who described themselves as Independents. Their politics are often said to be "middle-of-the-road."

Political positions are frequently described as being *left, right,* and *center.* This comes from the days of the French Revolution in 1789 when radicals sat on the left, moderates in the center, and conservatives on the right of the French National Assembly.

Most Americans consider themselves to be middle-of-the-road, either moderately liberal or moderately conservative. Sixty-nine per cent are in the political center. A way to illustrate this is by drawing *bell curves,* as the diagram below shows.

Use the diagram to answer these questions.
1. Which political positions make up the political center?
2. Are Republicans more likely to take a liberal position or a conservative one?
3. How would most Independents describe themselves politically?
4. A member of which political party would be more likely to take a radical position? Which a reactionary position?
5. Why is it difficult to describe someone as being "a Democrat" or "conservative"?

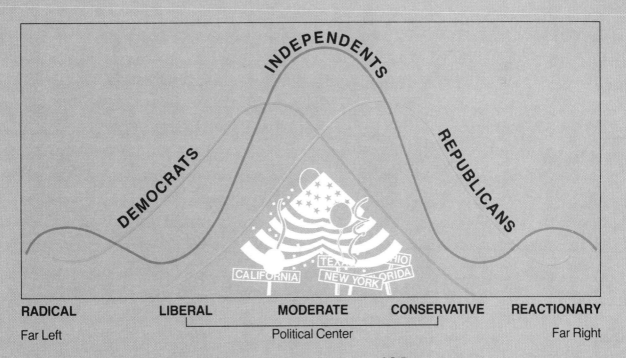

| RADICAL | LIBERAL | MODERATE | CONSERVATIVE | REACTIONARY |

Far Left — Political Center — Far Right

THE BLACK CODES

The Radicals were also concerned about the way former slaves, called **freedmen,** were being treated in the South. By the end of 1865 all the southern state governments set up under Johnson's amnesty plan had ratified the new **Thirteenth Amendment** to the Constitution, which officially abolished slavery. But the whites were a majority in most parts of the South. They were powerful and well organized. Southern blacks could not protect their new rights without northern help. The new southern governments did not allow blacks to vote. Their legislatures swiftly passed regulations called **Black Codes** designed to keep blacks in a kind of semi-slave condition.

These codes barred blacks from any kind of work except farming and household service. Some states forced blacks to sign labor contracts with landowners at the beginning of each year. If they left their work, they received no pay. If they refused to sign, they were arrested and charged with being tramps. The "sentence" was to work for one of the landowners for the year.

These Black Codes alarmed most northerners. The results of the new southern elections alarmed them even more. Southern voters, all of them white, chose as leaders many of the same people who had led them during the rebellion. Several Confederate generals were elected to Congress. The Georgia legislature picked Alexander H. Stephens, Vice President of the Confederacy, to represent the state in the United States Senate. Stephens had recently been paroled from prison after being charged with treason for his role in the Confederacy.

Many blacks were kept in a kind of semi-slave condition after the Civil War. Such is the plight of these farmers in Virginia c. 1900. What work were they allowed to do?

The Granger Collection

While northerners argued over President Johnson's plan for Reconstruction, southerners took stock of their ruined land. Where Sherman's troops had marched, cities were burned, crops pulled up, rails tied in knots. There was little seed to plant new crops. As Generals Grant and Lee had recognized at Appomattox, a horse or mule was a precious thing. There was an uneasy truce between the defeated whites and newly freed slaves. Many blacks stayed on at the plantations, but their former owners could not afford to feed or clothe them.

Mary Boykin Chesnut (right) of Mulberry plantation in South Carolina made these diary entries in 1865:

A Nation in Mourning

National Portrait Gallery

February 29
Trying to brave it out. [The Yankees] have plenty, yet let our men freeze and starve in their prisons. Would you be willing to be as wicked as they are? A thousand times, no!

April 19
We are to stay here. Running is useless now; so we mean to bide a Yankee raid, which they say is imminent. Why fly? They are everywhere, these Yankees, like red ants, like the locusts and frogs which were the plagues of Egypt.

May 2
Nothing but tall blackened chimneys to show that any man has ever trod this road before. This is Sherman's track. It is hard not to curse him. I wept incessantly at first. The roses of the gardens are already hiding the ruins. My husband said Nature is a wonderful renovator. He tried to say something else and then I shut my eyes and made a vow that if we were a crushed people, crushed by weight, I would never be a . . . slave.

August 2
Dr. Boykin and John Witherspoon were talking of a nation in mourning, of blood poured out like rain on the battlefields—for what? Never let me hear that the blood of the brave has been shed in vain! No; it sends a cry down through all time.

The newly elected representatives were members of the Democratic party. Admitting them to Congress might give the Democrats a majority. This was too much even for Moderate Republicans to accept. Both houses of Congress voted not to admit the new southern representatives. Johnson's plan for the **Reconstruction** of the South was rejected.

- What did the Thirteenth Amendment do?
- What was the purpose of the Black Codes?
- Why did Congress refuse to admit the newly elected southern representatives?

JOHNSON AND THE REPUBLICANS

The Republicans in Congress then began to reconstruct the South according to their own ideas. Before the end of the war Congress had created a **Freedman's Bureau** run by the army to care for refugees. Early in 1866 a new bill was passed increasing the power of the Bureau to protect southern blacks.

Liberated blacks line up for aid at the Freedmen's Bureau in Memphis, Tennessee. This engraving is from about 1866. Which agency ran the original Freedmen's Bureau?

President Johnson decided to **veto** this Freedmen's Bureau Bill. He claimed that he approved of the purpose of the bill. He was eager, he said, "to secure for the freedmen . . . their freedom and property and their entire independence." But he argued that it was unconstitutional to apply military law to civilians in peacetime.

Congress therefore attacked the Black Codes by passing a **Civil Rights Act.** This law made blacks citizens of the United States. It was necessary to state this specifically because the Dred Scott decision had declared that even free blacks were not American citizens. The bill also forbade the southern states from restricting the rights of freedmen by special laws like the Black Codes.

President Johnson vetoed this bill too. It was a mistake to make blacks citizens, he now insisted. They needed to go through a period of "probation" before receiving this "prize." It was unconstitutional to give blacks "safeguards which go infinitely beyond any that the . . . Government has ever provided for the white race," he said.

As this veto made clear, Johnson's dislike of southern planters did not keep him from being very prejudiced against blacks. Great wealth in the hands of a few plantation owners was what he really hated, not slavery. Before the war he once said that he wished every white family in America could have one slave "to take the drudgery" out of life!

In April 1866 both houses of Congress again passed the Civil Rights Act. They obtained the two-thirds majority necessary to **override** the President's veto. This was the first veto ever to be overridden. Thus the Civil Rights Act became law a year after the war ended.

- What was the purpose of the Freedmen's Bureau law? Why did President Johnson veto it?
- Why was it necessary for Congress to pass the Civil Rights Act? Why did President Johnson veto this bill too? How did Congress respond to this second Presidential veto?

THE RECONSTRUCTION ACTS

Next, Congress passed and sent to the states for ratification what became the **Fourteenth Amendment** to the Constitution. In many ways this measure was even more important than the Thirteenth Amendment. The Republicans in Congress drafted it in order to put the terms of the Civil Rights Act directly into the Constitution.

"All persons born or naturalized in the United States," the amendment said, "are citizens of the United States *and of the State wherein they reside.*" This made blacks citizens no matter where in the nation they lived. Then the amendment struck down the Black Codes. "No State shall . . . abridge the privileges and immunities of citizens of the United States; nor shall any State deprive any person of life, liberty, or property, without due process of law."

The Fourteenth Amendment did not make racial segregation illegal. It did not even tell states to allow blacks to vote. Nevertheless, most white southerners objected to it strongly. Since the southern states refused to ratify the amendment, it was impossible to

New York Public Library Picture Collection

Under the watchful eyes of a U.S. soldier, Richmond, Virginia, holds its first municipal election after the Civil War. Blacks and whites alike stand in line to cast their ballots. When blacks were made citizens, why could some still not vote?

get the approval of three fourths of the states necessary to make it part of the Constitution.

President Johnson made his conflict with the Republicans an issue in the Congressional elections of November 1866. He campaigned up and down the country, arguing for his own approach. He failed to change many minds. Indeed, most historians believe that Johnson's angry charges probably lost more votes for his policies than they gained. The Republicans easily maintained their large majorities in both houses of Congress.

As a result Congress passed the **Reconstruction Act** of March 1867. This stern measure divided what it called "the rebel states" into five military districts. "Sufficient military force" to "protect all persons in their rights" was stationed in each district. To get rid of army rule, each former state would have to draw up a new constitution that guaranteed blacks the right to vote. The state would also have to ratify the Fourteenth Amendment.

In other words, Congress ordered a military occupation of the South. Lincoln's hope that the nation could bind up its wounds in harmony had come to nothing.

White southerners hated military rule. They hated the idea of racial equality even more. They still refused to ratify the Fourteenth Amendment. A second, and a third, and finally a fourth Reconstruction Act were passed by Congress. Each put more pressure on "the rebel states." At last, in June 1868, southern governments in which blacks participated began to be formed. These governments ratified the amendment. The final state to complete the process was Georgia, in July 1870, more than five years after the end of the Civil War.

- What did the Fourteenth Amendment do?
- How did Republicans use the Reconstruction Act to force southerners to give blacks the right to vote?

PRESIDENT JOHNSON IS IMPEACHED

Radical Republicans blamed President Johnson for much of the stubborn resistance of white southerners to the Reconstruction Acts. He had urged the states not to accept the Fourteenth Amendment. He had vetoed each of the Reconstruction bills, even though their repassage by large majorities was certain. In February 1868 angry Congressional leaders decided to try to remove the President from office by impeaching him.

The Constitution provides that the House of Representatives, by majority vote, can bring charges against a President. This is called **impeachment.** The charges are judged by the Senate, with the Chief Justice of the Supreme Court presiding over the trial. A two-thirds majority vote is required for **conviction.**

There is an arrogance in the face of Andrew Johnson in this Presidential portrait by Eliphalet F. Andrews. But his conflicts with the Congress were not sufficient grounds for his impeachment. For what did Radical Republicans blame Johnson?

New York Historical Society

The Radicals brought 11 charges against the President. Most of them were totally without merit. The most serious accusation was that he had violated the **Tenure of Office Act** of 1867 by dismissing Secretary of War Edwin M. Stanton. This law prohibited the President from *discharging* appointed officials without the consent of Congress.

Johnson believed that the Tenure of Office Act was unconstitutional. The Constitution states only that Senate approval is necessary for the *appointment* of high officials. In the past no one had challenged the right of a President to remove an appointee without consulting the Senate.

Johnson dismissed Stanton deliberately to bring the issue before the Supreme Court, where it could properly be decided. Impeaching the President was clearly not justified by the facts. Indeed, his term was almost over. But many members of Congress believed that Reconstruction would never be successful unless Johnson were removed from office.

The President was spared conviction by a single vote. On each charge the Senate failed to obtain a two-thirds majority by only one vote.

The Senate sits as a court to judge whether or not Andrew Johnson will be convicted in his impeachment of 1868. This engraving appeared in *Harper's Weekly* on April 11. Below is a ticket to the proceedings. By how narrow a margin did President Johnson escape conviction?

Granger Collection

Andrew Johnson remained in office until March 1869. He was a poor President. All his life he had been a valuable public servant when he was battling for reform, a lone "outsider" stubbornly attacking "the Establishment." When fate made him the head of that Establishment, he proved unable to adjust. He could not work well with other people. He made a dreadful mess of his time in the White House.

Yet Johnson was not an evil man. His Reconstruction policies seem wrong to us today, but he did not deserve to be accused of committing crimes against the nation.

- Why did the Republican leaders of Congress want to remove the President from office?
- What is the difference between *impeachment* and *conviction*?

THE ELECTION OF 1868

A majority of the white people of his generation shared Andrew Johnson's low opinion of the character and intelligence of blacks. As we have seen, some northern states did not allow blacks to vote. However, the results of the Presidential election of 1868 led to a dramatic change in this situation.

Blacks in the southern states *had* voted in that election. Federal troops stationed there under the Reconstruction Act prevented whites from keeping blacks from the polls. When the blacks voted, they naturally cast their ballots overwhelmingly for the Republican party.

The Republican Presidential candidate, General Grant, won an easy victory in the electoral college, 214 votes to 80 for the Democratic candidate, Horatio Seymour. But in many northern states the popular vote was extremely close.

When Republican politicians studied the election statistics, they realized that if northern blacks had been able to vote, Grant would have won in a landslide. They reasoned that blacks could never get much power in the North. Blacks made up less than 10 per cent of the population in that section. Why not allow them to vote? With blacks voting solidly Republican, the hated Democrats could be kept out of power forever.

Early in 1869 Congress drafted still another Constitutional amendment: "The right of citizens of the United States to vote shall not be denied . . . on account of race, color, or previous condition of servitude." Within about a year this **Fifteenth Amendment** was ratified by the states. With the Thirteenth and Fourteenth Amendments, it is one of the **Civil War Amendments.**

- How would northern blacks have influenced the election of 1868 if they had been allowed to vote?

Ulysses S. Grant is the subject of this formal portrait by Thomas Le Clear, made c. 1880. After leaving the White House, Grant wrote his *Personal Memoirs*, which became a national best seller. What did the Fifteenth Amendment, passed when Grant took office, provide?

Corcoran Gallery of Art

THE USES OF FREEDOM

The Civil War Amendments did bring certain freedoms to black Americans. Freedom meant first of all the right to decide what to do with one's own time, from minute to minute and day to day. It meant lifting a terrible weight off the *minds* of nearly 4 million former slaves. It meant freedom to move about.

With leisure time most blacks had to work less hard. Now they could put down their hoes and stretch their tired muscles for a few minutes without fear of a blow or a harsh word. Parents did not send the youngest children into the fields as their former owners would have done. Old people labored less and rested more. Mothers devoted more time to their homes and children, less to planting, hoeing, and harvesting.

Another use that blacks made of freedom was to seek education. Very few slaves could read and write. There had been no schools for slave children, and indeed it was against the law in most southern states even to teach a slave to read.

The Freedmen's Bureau established schools in the South as soon as the war ended. Private groups from the North also contributed time, money, and teachers.

The preacher comes to call, making the children watchful and shy. "A Pastoral Visit" was painted in oil by Richard N. Brooke in 1881. The aged preacher and the adults he sits with at table are all former slaves. How many slaves were freed by the war?

501

Blacks responded eagerly to this opportunity for schooling. In South Carolina, for example, a school for blacks was set up in Charleston as soon as the Union army captured the city. By 1867 there were about 20,000 blacks attending school in that state. All over the South elderly ex-slaves could be seen learning their ABC's alongside their grandchildren.

At first most white southerners sneered at the very idea of educating the freedmen. But many came to admit that blacks could learn as well as whites. Most blacks who were educated became good and useful citizens. Thus all but the most prejudiced whites changed their minds. These whites continued, however, to oppose teaching black and white children in the same schools.

■ What were some uses blacks made of their new freedom?

Both adults and children recite their lessons in this Freedmen's Bureau school. The engraving was probably published in *Harper's Weekly*. How did the success of these schools change the view many whites held about blacks?

BLACKS IN GOVERNMENT

While the United States army occupied the South, blacks voted and held office in all the states of the former Confederacy. Nothing made white southerners more bitter and resentful than to be "ruled" by the very people they had totally dominated for so long.

"Rule" is not, however, the proper word to describe the role of blacks in southern politics during Reconstruction. Only a handful ever served in Congress or in high state office during the period. Blacks held many local offices, but they seldom controlled any branch of a local government. The only state legislature that ever had a black majority was South Carolina's between 1868 and 1877.

Most of the members of the **"Black Republican"** governments were whites. Those who came from the northern states were called

Chicago Historical Society

Robert B. Elliott of South Carolina addresses Congress on civil rights on January 6, 1874. Elliott served two terms in Congress. He studied at Eton College in England. When did blacks hold a majority in the South Carolina state legislature?

Carpetbaggers because travelers of the period usually carried their belongings in soft-sided bags made of carpeting. Southern white Republicans were referred to scornfully by their Democratic neighbors as **Scalawags.**

Carpetbaggers and Scalawags came from all walks of life. Some genuinely wanted to help blacks achieve political influence. Others

Granger Collection

The Solid South staggers under the weight of the carpetbag carrying General Grant in this cartoon from the humor magazine *Puck*, 1880. The South is chained to two Union soldiers whose bayonets support the unusual Presidential chariot. In the left background is a Hall of Justice surrounded with cannon. At right is a sunken riverboat and the shell of a southern plantation. To which party did Carpetbaggers and Scalawags belong?

intended to win power for themselves by controlling black votes. Some were plain thieves. Black politicians in the South also varied widely in ability and devotion to duty.

During the 1870s white people who objected to blacks holding office emphasized the numerous examples of black corruption and incompetence that came to light. A northern observer, James S. Pike, reported that the 1873 session of the South Carolina legislature was marked by total confusion. "No one is allowed to talk five minutes without interruption," Pike complained. There was "endless chatter" and much "gush and babble." Pike said of one speaker, "He did not know what he was going to say when he got up . . . and he did not know what he had said when he sat down."

A black politician in Arkansas collected $9,000 for repairing a bridge that had cost the state only $500 to build in the first place. The black-controlled South Carolina legislature spent $16,000 a year on paper and other supplies. The average spent on these materials before the war was $400. The black South Carolina senators had a kind of private club in the capitol building where fine food and wines and the most expensive cigars were always available. Many black legislators routinely accepted money in exhange for their votes on important issues.

Such things did indeed happen. What white critics failed to mention was that many white politicians were just as corrupt and inefficient. One commentator watched the disorderly behavior of members of the United States House of Representatives at about this time. He said that trying to make a speech in the House was like trying to speak to a crowd in a passing trolley while standing on the curb of a busy city street.

As for corruption, the main difference between white and black thieves was that the white ones made off with most of the money. After studying the actions of black and white officials during Reconstruction, the historian Joel Williamson concludes that "the most gigantic steals" were engineered by white politicians like "Honest John" Patterson, a Carpetbagger who systematically bribed South Carolina legislators to vote for a bill worth nearly $2 million to a railroad Patterson controlled.

Furthermore, the southern state governments accomplished a great deal of good during these years. They raised taxes in order to improve public education, which had been badly neglected before 1860. They also spent large sums on roads, bridges, railroads, and public buildings damaged during the war.

- Who were Carpetbaggers and Scalawags? What were some reasons these politicians sought public office?
- How did corrupt white and black politicians differ?

504

Sharecroppers are baling cotton in the 1870s photograph at left. Below is an engraving made at the time of the Civil War, showing a slave with his sack of cotton. How were these sharecroppers paid?

SHARECROPPING

Nearly all the slaves had been farm workers and nearly all continued to work on the land after they became free. The efforts of Radicals like Thaddeus Stevens to carve up the large plantations and give each black family **forty acres and a mule** never attracted much support among northern whites. In theory, a freedman could get a 160-acre farm (64 hectares) under the Homestead Act of 1862. Only a handful of blacks were able to do so. They lacked the tools, seed money, and the means of getting to the distant frontier. The price of land was only a small part of the cost of starting a farm.

Most of the former slaves therefore continued to cultivate land owned by whites. At first they worked for cash wages. But the South was poor after the war. Most landowners were very short of cash. So a new system was worked out called **sharecropping.**

Sharecropping means sharing the crop. Under this system the landowner provided the laborers with houses, tools, seeds, and other supplies. The **sharecroppers** provided the skill and muscle needed to grow the crops. When the harvest was gathered, it was shared, half to two thirds for the landowner, the rest for the sharecropper.

This system allowed black workers to be free of the close daily control they had endured under slavery. Each black family had its own cabin and tilled its own land as a separate unit. Sharecroppers could at least hope that by working hard and saving they might some day have enough money to buy a farm of their own. Then they would be truly free. For this reason most blacks much preferred sharecropping to working for wages.

A long time passed before many sharecroppers owned their own farms. Partly this was because most whites tried to keep blacks from obtaining land of their own. The landowners wanted to make sure they had enough workers for their own farms. And they wanted to keep all the blacks dependent upon them.

Some landowners cheated the sharecroppers when the harvest was divided. Local storekeepers sometimes also cheated them. Share-croppers had to buy supplies on credit. They ran up bills at the general store during the growing season. When the crop was sold in the autumn, they used the money to pay off this debt. Frequently the merchant added items to the bill that the farmers had never purchased. Blacks who objected were threatened with the loss of credit in the future, or with violence. The local courts were not likely to give justice to blacks who sued any white person.

Even when dealing with honest landowners and merchants, it was hard to make much more than a bare living as a sharecropper. Prices were high in the stores because the storekeepers also had to borrow to get the goods they sold. They paid high interest rates because money was so scarce in the South. They had to charge high prices to cover that expense. So it was lack of money more than cheating by whites or racial prejudice that kept black sharecroppers from getting farms of their own. White sharecroppers hardly fared better. Yet the cheating was common and the prejudice almost universal.

- Why was it difficult for freedmen to begin farming under the Homestead Act of 1862?
- Why was it so difficult to make much more than a bare living as a sharecropper, especially for blacks?

THE CROP-LIEN SYSTEM

The shortage of money made everyone dependent on bankers and other people with funds to invest. These investors wanted to be sure that the loans they made in the spring were repaid in the fall after the crops had been harvested. They demanded that the landowners pledge the future crop as security for the loan. This meant that they had a claim on the crop, called a **lien,** before it was even planted. If the borrower failed to pay when the loan fell due, the lender could take possession of the crop.

This **crop-lien system** was fair enough on the surface. However, it had an unfortunate side effect. The lenders insisted that the borrowers grow one of the South's major cash crops, such as cotton or tobacco. These were products for which there was a **world market.** They could be converted into cash anywhere and at any time. If the price was low, they could be safely stored until market conditions improved.

The Granger Collection

Under the crop-lien system these former slaves cultivate tobacco in this engraving. Ever so slowly their standard of living improved, but the South became a slave to the crop-lien system and stayed poor. What progress was made by blacks at this time?

The landowners and sharecroppers of the South would have been better off if they could have grown many different things—vegetables and fruits as well as cotton and the other cash crops. By concentrating on one crop, they exhausted the fertility of the soil more rapidly. If they had a larger-than-normal harvest, the price of the cash crop fell steeply because supply was greater than demand.

Everyone was caught up in the system. The bankers put pressure on the landowners and storekeepers. They, in turn, forced the sharecroppers to plant what the bankers wanted. The tendency is to blame the bankers. The charge is that they were greedy and short sighted. But the bankers really had little choice. It would have been extremely risky, for example, to lend a farmer money to grow tomatoes, for they had to be sold locally when they were ripe or they would rot and become worthless within a few days.

So most southern black people stayed poor. The South itself stayed poor. It took about 20 years for the region to get production back to where it had been when the Civil War broke out. As we shall see, during those years the rest of the country was increasing its output at a rapid rate.

Yet for black southerners the Reconstruction era was a time of genuine progress. Any change from slavery had to be an improvement. Gradually the standard of living of blacks improved. They had more to eat, better clothes, and more comfortable houses. When they supplied these things for themselves by their own labor, they were better off than when they got only what their owners chose to give them.

■ How did the crop-lien system work? What were its unfortunate side effects?

507

RESISTANCE TO RECONSTRUCTION

It is safe to say that the great majority of white southerners strongly resisted the changes forced upon them during Reconstruction, sometimes openly, sometimes in the dead of night. The Black Codes were one attempt to keep blacks in a lowly state. In 1866 the whites also began to form secret organizations to hold blacks down by terror.

Blacks attempting to vote are halted by White Leaguers in this engraving by J. H. Wares. The man at the door holds a "Republican ticket," but it will not gain him admission past the hatchet-faced election judge whose gun is at the ready beside the ballot box. Why were these secret white groups determined to keep blacks from voting?

New York Public Library Picture Collection

The most important of these organizations was the **Ku Klux Klan.** Klan members were determined to keep blacks from voting and thus influencing political events. Klansmen tried to frighten blacks by galloping through the night dressed in white robes, hoods, and masks. They claimed to be the ghosts of Confederate soldiers. They burned crosses on the hillsides, a hint of the terrible tortures that awaited blacks who tried to vote. When blacks refused to be frightened, the Klan often carried out its threats. Hundreds of black southerners were beaten, other hundreds actually murdered by the Klan.

The federal government managed to check the Klan by about 1871. It sent troops to areas where violence had broken out. Many Klan leaders were arrested. Gradually, more white southerners joined in efforts to keep blacks from voting. In 1874 groups in Mississippi calling themselves **Red Shirts** formed military companies. These Red Shirts marched about in broad daylight. They gave merciless beatings to those they called "uppity" or rebellious blacks. Many blacks fought back against this kind of violence. In some areas small-scale but bloody battles broke out between armed bands of whites and blacks.

■ Why did some southern whites organize the Ku Klux Klan?

THE ELECTION OF 1876

Since blacks were in the minority in the South and had fewer weapons than whites, they lost most battles when they clashed. Northern whites, meanwhile, began to lose interest in controlling the South by means of the army. They became satisfied that southern whites did not actually intend to reenslave blacks. They began to put the South's problems out of their minds. Gradually the number of troops stationed in the southern states was reduced. Many blacks then chose not to risk voting and exercising their other rights.

In state after state during the 1870s **Conservative** parties, made up entirely of whites, took over the government from the Republicans. The Republican party was further hurt by the failure of President Grant to live up to expectations as President. The military hero was honest and a true democrat, but he was a poor Chief Executive. He became the innocent victim of scandals and corruption in his administration. Although he was reelected in 1872 by 800,000 votes more than the Democratic party nominee, Horace Greeley, his party grew weaker. By 1876 the Republicans controlled only three southern states—Louisiana, Florida, and South Carolina.

The Presidential election of 1876 pitted Governor Samuel J. Tilden of New York, the Democrat, against Governor Rutherford B. Hayes of Ohio, the Republican. Tilden won in his home state, New York, in neighboring New Jersey and Connecticut, in Indiana, and in all the southern states. This gave him a substantial majority of the electoral vote, 203 to 165. In the popular vote he won by 250,000 votes—4.28 million to 4.03 million.

But when Republican leaders added up the votes on election night, they discovered that switching the electoral votes of the three southern states they still controlled would give the majority to Hayes, 185 to 184! Republican officials in these three states swiftly threw out enough Democratic ballots to change the result. Then they

Switching votes by three southern states kept American history from remembering President Samuel J. Tilden. Instead it was Rutherford B. Hayes who became President after the disputed election of 1876. The photograph of Hayes, *above,* was taken c. 1875. Tilden, *below,* was painted by Thomas Hicks c. 1870. To which party did each of the candidates belong?

forwarded to Washington "official" results showing Hayes the winner.

Of course the Democrats protested loudly. They filed another set of "official" results that showed Tilden the winner in the three disputed states.

For weeks no one knew who the next President would be. Congress appointed a special commission to settle the issue. It was made up of ten members of Congress, five Democrats and five Republicans, and five members of the Supreme Court. The Supreme Court justices were supposed to be nonpolitical, but three were Republicans, the other two Democrats.

The commission held an investigation and heard evidence from both sides. It soon became clear that both parties had behaved in a completely corrupt manner in the three states in dispute. More Democrats had almost certainly voted than Republicans. But large numbers of blacks who would surely have voted Republican had been kept away from the polls by force and threats.

   ■ Why was the outcome of the 1876 Presidential election in doubt? How did Congress attempt to determine whether the President would be Tilden or Hayes?

THE COMPROMISE OF 1877

When the commissioners finally voted, they split 8 to 7 on each of the disputed states. Every Republican voted for Hayes, every Democrat for Tilden. Obviously they had not paid much attention to the evidence. The Democrats felt cheated. Many were ready to fight to make Tilden President. For a time another Civil War seemed about to break out.

In this crisis the leaders of the two parties worked out what is known as the **Compromise of 1877.** Hayes agreed to recall all the remaining federal troops stationed in the South. He promised to appoint a conservative southerner to his Cabinet. He said also that he sympathized with a proposal sponsored by southerners to build a railroad from Texas to southern California.

In exchange the Democrats promised not to use their power in the southern states to prevent blacks from voting and to guarantee blacks their own rights. After all these details had been settled in a series of informal, behind-the-scenes discussions, the Democrats agreed to go along with the electoral commission's decision. On March 4, 1877, Hayes was inaugurated as President in an orderly, entirely peaceful ceremony.

   ■ What danger was there for the nation in 1877?
   ■ What were the results of the Compromise of 1877?

READING PRACTICE
IN SOCIAL STUDIES

Reading Items in a List

Writers who wish to show a process that has several steps often organize their thoughts in the form of a list. This is called organization by *enumeration*. Enumeration means "the orderly listing of items that relate to the same topic." *Enumerated items* are subtopics.

This type of organization is quite easy to recognize. An author generally signals enumeration in the introduction to a section. For example, on page 168 of this book the author writes:

> With peace and the United States recognized as a member of the family of nations, Congress turned to *other* problems. *One* of the most important was the organization of the territory beyond the Appalachian Mountains. . . . After the war was won, Congress put the policy into effect by passing *two* laws called **Land Ordinances.**
>
> The *first,* the **Land Ordinance of 1785**, established a method of selling the land.

Among the clues that signal enumeration are specific words like *first, second, third* and general words and phrases like *several, few, a number of.* Usually a number introduces each subtopic—*in the first place, second, thirdly*—although general words such as *next, then,* or *also* may signal enumeration.

When you skim a section before reading it closely, look for clues that show enumeration. These clues serve as pointers to the topic and its subtopics. The topic and subtopics taken together will give you the main idea. For instance, in the passage from page 168 above, the topic might be stated *as Congress organizing the territories*. The main idea may be stated as "Congress organized the western territories by passing the Land Ordinances."

Outlining is an excellent way to arrange notes on sections that contain items in a list. If you take notes on the material in this chapter, which treats civil rights for blacks during Reconstruction, your outline might look like this:

Gains and Losses for Blacks
I. Black Codes hold down former slaves.
II. Civil Rights Act makes blacks citizens.
III. Civil War Amendments guarantee rights.
IV. Blacks lose rights as Long Night begins.
V. Segregation outlawed by Civil Rights Act of 1875.
VI. Court strikes down Civil Rights Cases.
VII. Atlanta Compromise urges blacks to accept accommodation.

Practice reading items in a list by looking at the section "The Long Night Begins" on page 512. Then do the following exercises.

1. What best describes this section's topic?
   a. The Long Night
   b. Poll taxes
   c. Blacks deprived of right to vote
2. What phrase in the first paragraph is a clue that "The Long Night Begins" is organized by enumeration?
3. What phrase in the second paragraph is a clue to enumeration? What is the topic of this paragraph?
4. What phrase in the third paragraph is a clue to enumeration? What is its topic?
5. What main idea is expressed by the fourth paragraph?
6. How do the details in the fourth paragraph develop its main idea?
7. What clue in the fifth paragraph shows enumeration? What is this paragraph's topic?
8. What sentence in the last paragraph gives the conclusion to this entire section?
9. The three items enumerated in this section are subtopics of what topic? What is the main idea of the section?
10. Based on your answers to these questions, what do you think is meant by the term "the Long Night"?

THE LONG NIGHT BEGINS

After the Compromise of 1877 the white citizens of the North turned their backs on the black citizens of the South. Gradually the southern states broke their promise to treat blacks fairly. Step by step they deprived them of the right to vote and reduced them to the status of second-class citizens.

The first step was to pass **poll tax** laws. A poll tax is a charge made for voting. It can be avoided simply by not going to the polls. For poor people, paying a poll tax was a great sacrifice. Many preferred to spend what little money they had in other ways. In most southern states the tax *accumulated* when not paid. That is, a person who skipped one election would have to pay double if he wished to vote at the next. A person who voted only in Presidential elections would pay four times the regular tax.

Another technique for keeping blacks from the polls was to require a **literacy test** for voting. People who could not read could not vote. And those blacks who could read were usually asked to read a difficult, technical legal passage of some kind. Poll taxes and literacy tests did not violate the Fifteenth Amendment because they were not directly based on "race, color, or previous condition of servitude."

These measures prevented many poor white people from voting too. But when they wanted to, the authorities could find ways of allowing whites to vote anyway. One method was to permit people who could not read to vote if they could "understand" and explain a passage that an election official read to them. A white person might be asked to explain a clause in the state constitution that said: "The term of the governor shall be four years." A black person who sought to qualify would then be asked to explain a more complicated passage. And whatever the black said, he would be told his explanation was incorrect and that he had not "understood."

Another technique was the so-called **grandfather clause.** Grandfather clauses provided that literacy tests and poll taxes did not apply to persons who had been able to vote before 1867, nor to their children and later descendants. Of course most whites came under this heading, but no blacks did at all. By about 1900 only a handful of black citizens were voting in the southern states.

 ▓ What were three methods used in the South to keep blacks from voting?

THE COURT AND SEGREGATION

When blacks ceased to have an influence on elections, elected officials stopped paying much attention to their needs and desires. The separation of blacks and whites in public places—**segregation**—became widespread.

There had always been a good deal of segregation in the North and South alike. In part it had been based on economics. Poor people could not afford to eat in the same restaurants as rich people, for example, and most blacks were poor. On the other hand, in the decades before the Civil War blacks and whites had often met together informally. This happened perhaps even more in the South than in the North.

After the destruction of the Confederacy, Congress had ruled out segregation in the South. The **Civil Rights Act of 1875** provided specifically that "citizens of every race and color" were entitled to "the full and equal enjoyment" of restaurants, hotels, trains, and all "places of public amusement."

But after 1877 whites began to ignore this law. In part they were more eager now for segregation because blacks were now unquestionably free. Separation had seemed less important to whites when blacks were clearly in lowly positions and under white "command." The typical southern white did not object to sitting next to a black on a streetcar if the black was a nursemaid caring for a white child. The same woman entering the car alone would cause the white to bristle if she tried to occupy the next seat.

When blacks began to be turned away from public places like theaters in cities all over the country, some went to court to seek their constitutional rights. In one case, W. H. R. Agee protested against being denied a room in a hotel in Jefferson City, Missouri. In another, Sallie J. Robinson sued because she was forced to ride in a second-class car while traveling from Tennessee to Virginia, even though she had a first-class ticket.

These and other suits, known as the **Civil Rights Cases,** were decided by the Supreme Court in 1883. The majority of the justices ruled that the Civil Rights Act was unconstitutional. It was therefore not illegal for private businesses to practice racial segregation. The guarantees of the Fourteenth Amendment were protections against actions by state governments, not private persons.

After this, segregation became more and more the rule, especially in the South. Then, in 1896, the Supreme Court ruled further in the case of **Plessy v. Ferguson** that even in public schools segregation was legal, provided that schools for black children were as good as those for whites.

One justice, John Marshall Harlan, born in Kentucky, a slave state, objected to this **separate-but-equal** argument. Harlan's family had owned slaves. But the experiences of Reconstruction had caused him to change his mind about race questions. "Our Constitution is color blind," he said. It "neither knows nor tolerates classes among citizens." But in 1896 Harlan's was the minority view of the Court and among white citizens in all parts of the country.

Justice John Marshall Harlan, shown in the photograph above, came from a family that had once owned slaves in Kentucky. But Harlan believed that segregation was in violation of the Constitution. How did Harlan describe the Constitution?

New York State Historical Association, Cooperstown

"Kept In." In this 1888 oil painting by Edward L. Henry the voices of schoolchildren at recess can nearly be heard through the open window. One sorrowful little girl remains in the classroom. Her loneliness is a reminder of the physical barriers of segregation. In what other places was segregation practiced?

Efforts to prevent segregation practically ended as a result of these court decisions. Blacks could not stay at hotels used by white travelers. Theaters herded them into separate sections, usually high in the balcony. Blacks had to ride in the rear sections of streetcars. They could not enter "white" parks or swim at "white" public beaches. Even cemeteries were segregated.

The schools, parks, and other facilities open to blacks were almost never as good as those open to whites. The separate-but-equal rule was ignored everywhere. In 1876 South Carolina spent the same amount on the education of each child, black or white. By 1895, when school segregation was complete in South Carolina, the state was spending three times more on each white child.

- What was the result of the Civil Rights Cases decided by the Supreme Court in 1883?
- What was the importance of the Court's decision in *Plessy v. Ferguson?* Why did Justice Harlan object to the separate-but-equal argument?

514

THE ATLANTA COMPROMISE

It is easy to imagine how depressed and angry American blacks must have been in the 1890s. Segregation was only the visible surface of the way they were mistreated. In almost any conflict between a black person and a white, the white had every advantage. Blacks were punished more severely when they were convicted of crimes. Many kinds of jobs were entirely closed to blacks. When they did the same work as whites, they received lower pay. If they refused to act humbly and politely to whites, they were insulted or even beaten. If they wanted to adjust to white ideas of how they ought to act, they had to behave like children or clowns.

Some blacks protested violently against all this injustice. Those who did were dealt with still more violently by the white majority. **Lynchings,** the killing without trial of supposed criminals by mobs, became evermore frequent, especially in the southern states.

(Both) Library of Congress

The school band plays an outdoor concert at Tuskegee Institute In 1902 this photograph was taken by Francis Benjamin Johnson, one of the first women to be assigned by the U.S government to document the rural South. At right is Booker T. Washington, who established Tuskegee. Why did he found this famous school?

Faced with these handicaps, many black Americans adopted the strategy proposed by Booker T. Washington, the founder of a trade school for blacks in Alabama, **Tuskegee Institute.** Washington had been born a slave. He obtained an education by working as a janitor at the school he attended. His experiences convinced him that a person of lowly origins could rise in the world by a combination of hard work and a willingness to go along with the wishes and prejudices of powerful people. He had seen first hand what happened to black people, especially in the South, who openly fought the prejudices of whites.

Washington was expert at obtaining the support of well-to-do whites who wanted to help blacks without actually treating them as equals. His school prospered. He was already well known when, in a speech at Atlanta, Georgia, in 1895, he proposed what became known as the **Atlanta Compromise.**

Blacks should accept the separate-but-equal principle, Washington said. They should learn skilled trades so that they could earn more money and thus improve their lives. And there was nothing shameful about working with one's hands. "There is as much dignity in tilling a field," he said, "as in writing a poem." Furthermore, it would be "the extremest folly" for blacks to demand truly equal treatment from whites. The way to rise in the world was to accept the system and try to get ahead with it.

Washington asked whites only to be fair. Help blacks who went along with segregation, he argued, by making sure that what was separate was really equal.

Most important white southern leaders claimed to be delighted with the Atlanta Compromise. In fact they made very little effort to change the attitude and behavior of average white citizens.

Today Washington seems to have buckled under with the Atlanta Compromise. Yet the failure of Reconstruction had awakened old fears and suspicions about blacks. Once again they had to move with caution. Historical imagination helps us see the Atlanta Compromise as a desperate effort to hold on to the few gains blacks had made. For black people who had to live through those years, **accommodation,** going along, was not cowardice but survival.

- What happened to blacks in the 1890s who protested against injustice?
- Why did Booker T. Washington propose the Atlanta Compromise?

CHAPTER 17 REVIEW

Identification
Tell briefly why each of the following persons, terms, or events is important.

1. Andrew Johnson
2. John Marshall Harlan
3. Booker T. Washington
4. Radical Republicans
5. Black Codes
6. Freedmen's Bureau
7. Civil Rights Act
8. Reconstruction Act
9. Impeachment
10. Civil War Amendments
11. Carpetbaggers
12. Scalawags
13. Sharecropping
14. Crop-lien system
15. Ku Klux Klan
16. Compromise of 1877
17. Segregation
18. Civil Rights Cases
19. *Plessy v. Ferguson*
20. Atlanta Compromise

Understanding American History

1. Compare and contrast the plans of the Moderate and Radical Republicans for Reconstruction of the South.
2. How did the three Civil War Amendments attack the Black Codes?
3. What were the provisions of the Reconstruction Act of 1867?
4. How did the election of 1868 show Republicans the importance of the black vote?
5. What were some of the motives of Carpetbaggers and Scalawags in the "Black Republican" governments of the South?
6. Explain the crop-lien system. How did it work to keep the South poor?
7. What situation was resolved by the Compromise of 1877? What were its terms?
8. What were some ways blacks were deprived of the right to vote in the South during the Long Night that began after 1877?
9. What did the Supreme Court rule when it reviewed the Civil Rights Cases in 1883? What was meant by the "separate-but-equal" argument in *Plessy v. Ferguson?*
10. What did Booker T. Washington propose in the Atlanta Compromise?

Activities

1. The assassination of President Lincoln caused great national mourning. Report on the aftermath of the tragedy by doing research in your school or public library. Topics might include the following:
    Newspaper Accounts of the Assassination
    Booth and the Assassination Conspiracy
    Trials of the Conspirators
    Ford's Theater—Then and Now
    Mary Todd Lincoln's Ordeal
    The Capital Mourns Its Slain President
    The Lincoln Funeral Train
    Walt Whitman Mourns President Lincoln
2. Working with your classmates, research the impeachment trial of Andrew Johnson. Then use your historical imagination to act out scenes from the trial, presenting fairly the case for and against the President. Since Johnson did not appear at his trial, you may wish to place certain scenes in the White House. Members of the class, acting as the Senate, should then decide the case.
3. Prepare a flow chart to show the crop-lien system. Include bankers, landowners, storekeepers, and sharecroppers.
4. Use your historical imagination to write diary entries describing Reconstruction. The entries on page 495 provide a model.
5. Prepare a chart to show the seesaw struggle to guarantee rights for blacks during and just after Reconstruction. Include the Black Codes, the Civil Rights Act, the Civil War Amendments, the Long Night, the Civil Rights Act of 1875, the Supreme Court rulings on the Civil Rights Cases and *Plessy v. Ferguson,* and the Atlanta Compromise.

CHAPTER 17 TEST

Completion (30 points)
Number your paper 1–10 and next to each number write the word from the list below that best completes each sentence.

Black Codes
Ku Klux Klan
Chief Justice
Long Night
Radical Republicans

impeachment
Moderate Republicans
Reconstruction
freedmen
Senate

President Johnson's main task was the ___1___ of the South after the Civil War. His plans pleased ___2___ but angered ___3___, who wished to treat the South like a conquered country. The President's enemies wanted to remove him by ___4___. He was tried by the ___5___ with the ___6___ presiding.

Former slaves, called ___7___, faced prejudice in both North and South. Southerners passed laws called ___8___ to keep blacks in a lowly position. Secret organizations such as the ___9___ terrorized blacks. Now began the time called the ___10___ when civil rights were denied blacks.

Matching (30 points)
Number your paper 11–20 and match the term in the second column with the description in the first column.

11. Made blacks citizens of the United States and outlawed the Black Codes
12. The idea that blacks should accept the separate-but-equal principle and work within the system to get ahead
13. Northerners who came South to take part in "Black Republican" governments
14. The separation of blacks and whites in public places
15. Organization to help former slaves adjust to their new lives
16. Freed all slaves, made them citizens, and gave male blacks the right to vote
17. A pardon Moderate Republicans wanted to give most former Confederates
18. The pledge of a future crop as security for a loan
19. Settled when the Supreme Court ruled that the separation of blacks and whites by private businesses was not illegal
20. System by which laborers worked for part of the crop they grew rather than for cash wages

a. Freedmen's Bureau
b. Civil War Amendments
c. Civil Rights Act
d. Carpetbaggers
e. Amnesty
f. Atlanta Compromise
g. Segregation
h. Civil Rights Cases
i. Crop-lien system
j. Sharecropping

Essay (40 points)
State simply and clearly the goals of Reconstruction, beginning with Lincoln's hope "to bind up the nation's wounds." Then tell what, in your opinion, were the chief reasons why Reconstruction went so badly for the South and for the nation as a whole.

UNIT FIVE TEST

Multiple Choice (20 points)
Number your paper 1- 5 and write the letter of the phrase that best completes each sentence.

1. The Fugitive Slave Law and *Uncle Tom's Cabin* tended to
   a. make Lincoln more popular.
   b. help pass the Kansas-Nebraska Act.
   c. further divide North and South.
   d. bring an end to Reconstruction.
2. States' rights was the argument to defend
   a. the right of the South to secede.
   b. the use of troops during Reconstruction.
   c. the Dred Scott decision.
   d. Sherman's March to the Sea.
3. Which of the following was the *immediate* cause of the Civil War?
   a. The Kansas-Nebraska Act
   b. *Uncle Tom's Cabin*
   c. The attack on Fort Sumter
   d. The raid on Harpers Ferry

4. Sherman's March to the Sea showed
   a. the importance of the navy.
   b. careless planning.
   c. habeas corpus.
   d. total war.
5. The economy of the North
   a. improved during the Civil War.
   b. was not affected by the Civil War.
   c. fell sharply during the Civil War.
   d. was destroyed by the Civil War.

Matching (25 points)
Number your paper 6–10 and match the person in the second column with the description in the first column.

6. President who was impeached but not convicted
7. Brilliant southern general in the Civil War
8. Author of *Uncle Tom's Cabin*
9. Favored acceptance of the separate-but-equal principal
10. Author of the Emancipation Proclamation

a. Robert E. Lee
b. Booker T. Washington
c. Andrew Johnson
d. Abraham Lincoln
e. Harriet Beecher Stowe

Chronological Order (25 points)
Number your paper 11–15 and place the following events in order by numbering 1 for the first, 2 for the second, and so on.
11. The Emancipation Proclamation is issued.
12. *Plessy v Ferguson* upholds separate-but-equal segregation.
13. Reconstruction of the South begins.
14. Confederates fire on Fort Sumter.
15. The Kansas-Nebraska Act is passed.

Essay (30 points)
Write a brief essay on *one* of the following topics. Compare and contrast the strengths and weaknesses of the North and South at the start of the Civil War and tell which side had the advantage, *or* List and explain at least four of the major causes of the Civil War.

UNIT SIX

Vanderbilt's railway network
•
Rockefeller founds Standard Oil

Cable cars in San Francisco
•
Crime of 1873

9 million buffalo slaughtered in two years

Battle of Little Bighorn
•
Bell demonstrates telephone

Chief Joseph surrender
•
Edison invents phonogra

Haymarket bombing
•
Statue of Liberty
•
American Federation of Labor

Blizzards end open range
•
Interstate Commerce Act
•
Electric street railways in Richmond

Harrison elected President

Pan-American Conference
•
Jane Addams founds Hull House

Sherman Antitrust Act
•
Sherman Silver Purchase Act

Cleveland returned to Presidency
•
Homestead strike
•
Populist par

1885	1886	1887	1888	1889	1890	1891	1892

A CHANGING AMERICA

THE CLOSING OF THE FRONTIER

1878
Bland-Allison Act

1879
Edison's electric light

1880
Garfield elected President

1881
A Century of Dishonor
•
Garfield assassinated
•
Arthur succeeds to Presidency

1882

1883
Civil service reform, Pendleton Act

1884
Cleveland elected President

1893
Depression of 1893

1894
Pullman strike
•
Coxey's Army

1895

1896
Bryan's "Cross of Gold" speech
•
McKinley elected President

1897

1898
Spanish-American War

1899

CHAPTER 18

The Last Frontier

THE GREAT AMERICAN DESERT

The vast region we call the **Great Plains** extends from western Texas north to the Dakotas and on into Canada. Endless acres of grassland roll westward, gradually rising until they reach the towering ranges of the Rocky Mountains. Explorers and white hunters once described this region and the mountains beyond as the **Great American Desert.** Before the 1850s the Spanish-Americans in the Southwest and the Mormons in Utah were the only whites who had made permanent settlements in this huge and lonely area.

The land of the Great Plains is mostly level. There are few trees. In winter, blizzards roar unchecked out of the Arctic. Temperatures fall far below freezing. Yet in summer the thermometer can soar halfway to the boiling point when hot winds sweep north from Mexico.

Until well after the Civil War, farming on the plains seemed impossible. There was too little rain and no wood to build houses or

The Great Plains is strewn with skulls in Albert Bierstadt's 1889 oil painting, "The Last of the Buffalo." Buffalo and deer wait by the water while this hunt sweeps on. But Plains Indians would never have been such wasteful killers as these. They took only enough for food, clothing, and shelter. This work is one of the most popular paintings by Bierstadt, who traveled widely in the American West in 1859. How like the description of the Great Plains on this page is Bierstadt's painting?

Corcoran Gallery of Art

fences. Most people thought the desert was home only for the donkey-eared jackrabbit, the prairie dog, the antelope, the wolflike coyote, and the great, shaggy buffalo. The buffalo in particular seemed the lords of the Great Plains. About 12 million of them were grazing there at the time the Civil War ended.

■ Why did farming on the Great Plains seem impossible?

THE PLAINS INDIANS

Long before the white settlement of America, many people lived on the Great Plains. They knew it was not really a desert. These were the Plains Indians. They had survived and prospered there for thousands of years.

There were 31 Plains tribes. The **Apache** and **Comanche** lived in Texas and eastern New Mexico. The **Pawnee** occupied western Nebraska, the **Sioux** the Dakotas. The **Cheyenne** and **Arapaho** were the principal tribes of the central plains. In 1850 these tribes contained about 175,000 people. Although they spoke many different languages, all could communicate with one another. They had developed a complex and efficient sign language.

The Plains Indians differed from tribe to tribe. Some were divided into several groups, or **bands,** of about 500 people each. The Cheyenne, for example, consisted of ten bands with names like the Aorta Band, the Hairy Band, the Scabby Band, and the Dogmen Band. Although each band was a separate community, bands joined together for religious ceremonies and to fight other tribes or the white invaders. Their chiefs and councils of elders acted mostly as judges. Their decisions were enforced by small groups of warriors called **soldier bands.** The soldier bands settled disputes between band members, punished those who broke tribal laws, and protected the group against surprise attacks.

Within the circle of their band, warriors tried to prove their courage and daring on the battlefield. To touch an enemy or capture his weapon was proof of highest bravery.

The Plains Indians, as we have seen, had always depended heavily on the buffalo. After the European invasion of America they also captured and tamed wild horses. Spanish explorers had brought the first horses with them to America. Some of these animals escaped and ran wild. Eventually, large herds roamed the West.

The Indians quickly became expert riders. On horseback they were better hunters and fighters. They could cover large distances swiftly and run down buffalo and other game. Horses became so important to the Plains Indians that many tribes went to war against their neighbors for them. Many counted their wealth in horses. Some paid their debts with horses. Some men swapped horses for wives.

Maria Longworth Nichols established Rookwood Pottery in 1880. From its kilns in Cincinnati this unique group of artisans produced beautiful pottery such as this vase decorated by Grace Young in 1901. This is a portrait of a Sioux warrior, Hollow Horn Bear. In which part of the Great Plains did the Sioux make their camps?

523

Amon Carter Museum

In the moonlight White Quiver leads a string of ponies he has stolen from the Crow. Charles Marion Russell painted "The Horse Thieves" in 1901. In raids on neighboring tribes, Indians showed their skill and bravery. White Quiver once stole 50 Crow ponies and restole them twice afterwards, including the chief's favorite buffalo horse. One of these ponies became Monte, Russell's own horse for 25 years. In what other ways did Indians show their bravery?

Indians wore many kinds of clothing. In some tribes the men wore breechcloths and long leggings which went from hip to ankle. During the winter they wore buffalo robes. Women might wear sleeveless dresses made of deerskin. In desert regions Indians wore moccasins with double leather soles for protection against the hard ground.

The typical Plains warrior carried a bow about three feet long (nearly one meter). It was usually made of bone or ash wood. His arrows had points made of bone, flint, or metal. Some warriors were armed with long, stone-tipped lances and carried round shields made of buffalo hide. These buffalo-hide shields were smoked and hardened with glue made from buffalo hooves. They were so tough that bullets striking them at an angle would not go through.

In battle an Indian warrior could fire off half a dozen arrows from his stubby, powerful bow while a white soldier was cramming a single bullet into his muzzle-loading rifle. Galloping on horseback at full speed, a warrior could shoot arrows so fast that the next would be in the air before the first found its target. These arrows struck with great force. At short range an Indian could sink the entire shaft of an arrow into the body of a buffalo.

- How were many Plains Indian tribes organized?
- What were some of the ways in which Plains Indian life was changed by the horses brought by the Spanish explorers?

REMOVING THE PLAINS INDIANS

The Plains Indians rarely came into conflict with whites before the 1850s. They usually traded in peace with white hunters. The pioneers who crossed the plains on their way to Oregon generally avoided the Indians.

In the early 1850s white settlers began moving into Kansas and Nebraska. After the Mexican War, promoters planned to build railroads to the Pacific through the newly won territory. They demanded that the government remove the Plains Indians from this territory.

In 1851 agents of the United States called a meeting of the principal Plains tribes at Fort Laramie, in what is now Wyoming. The agents persuaded the Indians to stay within limited areas. In exchange the government would give them food, money, and presents.

Beinecke Library, Yale University

This new system was called **concentration.** It was a way of dividing the Indians so that they could be conquered separately. **Divide and conquer** is a very old military strategy. Once a tribe had agreed to live in a particular region, it could be forced to give up its holdings without arousing the others.

As soon as Senator Stephen A. Douglas pushed the Kansas-Nebraska Act through Congress, settlers and storekeepers came pouring into lands that had been reserved for the Indians. The Indians were pushed into even smaller areas. By 1860 there were very few native Americans left in Kansas and Nebraska.

Fort Laramie, shown in this watercolor sketch by Alfred Jacob Miller, was a fur trading post built in 1834. In 1849 the army bought it to protect travelers on the Oregon Trail. When Indians met at the fort in 1851, what agreement did they reach with government agencies?

■ What was the purpose of the system called concentration?

RAILROADS IN THE WEST

In 1862 Congress passed the **Pacific Railway Act.** This law granted a charter to the Union Pacific Railroad Company to build a line westward from Nebraska. Another company, the Central Pacific Railway of California, was authorized to build a connecting line eastward from the Pacific.

The government granted each company the **right of way**—the thin strip of land on which the tracks were actually laid. In addition it gave them large amounts of land for every mile of track built. This land could be sold and the money used for construction. Or it could be held in reserve and sold later when the land became more valuable. The government also lent the companies large amounts of money at a low rate of interest to help them with the work.

While Chinese railroad workers watch, this Central Pacific train enters a snow shed in the Sierra Nevada Mountains. This oil was painted by Joseph Becker. Snow sheds kept tracks clear and gave some protection to the wooden cars in the event of an avalanche. Why was building the transcontinental railroad extremely difficult?

Thomas Gilcrease Institute, Tulsa

The Central Pacific employed thousands of Chinese immigrants to lay its tracks. Most of the Union Pacific workers were immigrants from Ireland. Construction got under way in 1865.

Building the railroad was tremendously difficult. The Central Pacific had to cross the snow-capped Sierra Nevada range. **Omaha,** Nebraska, where the Union Pacific began, had not yet been connected to eastern railroads. Thousands of tons of rails, crossties, and other supplies had to be shipped up the Missouri River by boat or hauled across Iowa by wagon.

The two companies competed with each other in order to get the lion's share of the land and money authorized by the Pacific Railway Act. Charles Crocker, manager of the Central Pacific's construction crews, drove his men mercilessly. During one winter they dug tunnels through 40-foot snowdrifts (12 meters) high in the Sierras in order to lay tracks on the frozen ground.

Yale University Library

This famous photograph shows "East and West Shaking Hands" in the 1869 meeting of the Union Pacific and the Central Pacific at Promontory, Utah. How was this event celebrated?

The two lines met on May 10, 1869, at **Promontory,** Utah. The Union Pacific had built 1,086 miles of track (1,738 kilometers), the Central Pacific 689 miles (1,102 kilometers). There was a great celebration. Leland Stanford of the Central Pacific was given the honor of hammering home the last spike connecting the two rails. The spike was made of gold, the hammer of silver.

RAILROADS IN THE WEST

(present-day state boundaries)

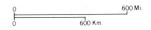

600 Mi.

600 Km.

Soon other **transcontinental railroads** were built. These included the Atchison, Topeka & Santa Fe and the Southern Pacific in the Southwest and the Northern Pacific, which ran south of the Canadian border. The transcontinentals connected with the eastern railroads at Chicago, St. Louis, and New Orleans. Once they were completed, a traveler could go from the Atlantic Coast to San Francisco and other Pacific Coast cities in a week's time. The swiftest clipper ship had taken three months to make the journey from New York to San Francisco.

- What were some ways Congress used to encourage the building of a transcontinental railroad?
- How did transcontinental railroads change travel time from coast to coast?

INDIAN WARS

The transcontinental railroads brought many more whites into the West. Wherever they went, fighting with the Indians followed. Even before the Civil War there was trouble in the **Pikes Peak** area of Colorado, where gold was discovered. By 1859 a seemingly endless stream of wagons was rolling across the plains. Many had the slogan "Pikes Peak or Bust!" lettered on their canvas covers.

About 100,000 of these **Fifty-Niners** elbowed their way onto Cheyenne and Arapaho land. The Indians fiercely resisted this invasion. Between 1861 and 1864 they rode several times into battle against army units. Then, in November 1864, Colonel John M. Chivington attacked a peaceful Cheyenne encampment at Sand Creek

Washita is the sorrowful spot where the Cheyenne and Arapaho lay down their weapons in 1868. There George Armstrong Custer's Seventh Cavalry destroyed Black Kettle's village and the Indian way of life. The painting is by Charles Schreyvogel. Why had Indians and whites begun fighting in the early 1860s?

Thomas Gilcrease Institute, Tulsa

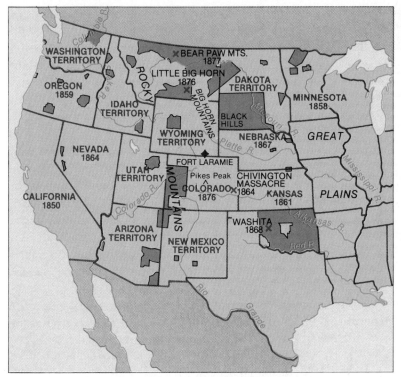

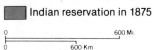
without warning. The Cheyenne, under Chief Black Kettle, tried to surrender by first raising an American flag and then a white flag of truce.

Chivington ignored these flags. "Kill and scalp all, big and little," he ordered. His soldiers scalped the men, ripped open the bodies of the women, and clubbed the little childen to death with their gun butts.

During this **Chivington Massacre** about 450 Cheyenne were killed. The Cheyenne answered with equally bloody attacks on undefended white settlements. In 1868 the Cheyenne and Arapaho were defeated at **Washita,** in present-day Oklahoma. They were forced to settle on reservations, one in the Black Hills of Dakota, the other in Oklahoma.

Meanwhile, the Pikes Peak boom had become a bust. Little gold was found. About half the miners returned to their homes. This time the signs on their wagons read "Busted, By Gosh!"

Yet if Colorado had proved a bust, many prospectors still believed that gold could be found elsewhere. New prospectors crossed the Great Plains and spread through the mountains in the 1860s. Many followed a route pioneered by John M. Bozeman, a prospector from Georgia. This **Bozeman Trail** ran from Fort Laramie in Wyoming north to Montana. It cut through the rolling

Above, Red Cloud, the Oglala Sioux chief, and his great-granddaughter Burning Heart. They were painted by Henry Cross. Below is a remarkable photograph of a Sioux camp, taken in 1891 near Pine Ridge, South Dakota, after some 150 Hunkpapa Sioux were massacred by the Seventh Cavalry. What was Red Cloud's victory?

foothills of the Big Horn Mountains, the hunting grounds of the western Sioux.

The Sioux pitched their teepees beneath the sheltering mountains. There they hunted the plentiful game—deer, buffalo, elk, antelope, and bear. The Sioux chief, Red Cloud, protested strongly when whites began to use the new Bozeman Trail. He warned that the Sioux would fight to save their hunting grounds.

In 1865 Red Cloud's warriors made repeated attacks on white parties. The United States army responded by building forts along the trail. In December 1866 an army supply caravan approaching one of the forts was attacked. When a small troop of soldiers commanded by Captain W. J. Fetterman appeared, Red Cloud's warriors quickly dashed off into the wilderness. Captain Fetterman foolishly followed them. He blundered into a trap, or **ambush.** Fetterman and all 82 of his soldiers were killed. A few months later John Bozeman himself was killed crossing the Yellowstone River on the trail he had marked.

At this point prospectors stopped crossing the Sioux country. A new treaty was signed in 1868. The Sioux agreed to live on a reservation in Dakota Territory west of the Missouri River.

- What was the Chivington Massacre?
- Why did the Sioux try to stop white prospectors from using the Bozeman Trail?

CUSTER'S LAST STAND

Still the fighting went on. Between 1869 and 1875 over 200 clashes between Indians and army units took place. In 1876 the territory of the Sioux was again invaded, this time by the construction crews of the Northern Pacific Railroad and by prospectors looking for gold in the **Black Hills.** War broke out.

At this time General George Armstrong Custer made his famous last stand in the **Battle of the Little Bighorn** in southern Montana. George Custer looked more like an actor than a soldier. He had long, flowing yellow hair. He wore buckskin trousers, red-topped boots,

Thomas Gilcrease Institute, Tulsa

National Portrait Gallery

In the Battle of the Little Bighorn the Sioux chief Sitting Bull, *left,* defeated General George Armstrong Custer, *right,* and his Seventh Cavalry. The portrait of Sitting Bull is by Henry Cross, and Custer's photograph was taken by Matthew Brady. What were the personal qualities of each of these leaders?

and a broad-brimmed hat. He was a good soldier, a graduate of the United States Military Academy at West Point. During the Civil War he fought at Bull Run and Gettysburg, and he accepted the final Confederate surrender on the battlefield near Appomattox. But he sometimes deliberately led his men into dangerous situations in hopes of winning what he called "glory."

On June 25, 1876, Custer led a cavalry troop of 264 men toward what he believed to be a small Sioux camp. Instead, at the Little Bighorn River, his tiny force stumbled upon between 2,500 and 4,000 Sioux, commanded by chiefs Sitting Bull, Crazy Horse, and Rain-in-the-Face.

Sitting Bull led the attack. He had become chief of his band nine years earlier. He was a solid, muscular man, 42 years old in 1876. He had a slightly hooked nose and piercing black eyes. Deep lines marked his weather-beaten brow. His dark hair hung in two heavy braids in front of his shoulders.

Sitting Bull was a fiercely proud and independent man. He resisted all efforts to get his people to give up their ancient customs. He would never sign a treaty with the whites, no matter how favor-

531

Custer's Last Stand is the subject of this lithograph by Kurtz and Allison. Custer stands at the center. How is this artist's view similar to the real battle as described on this page?

able the terms might seem. More than most Indians, he believed that no compromise with the whites was possible.

Now Sitting Bull faced Custer. Swiftly the Sioux warriors surrounded Custer's little force. Racing round and round on their ponies, they poured a deadly fire upon the troops. Desperately the soldiers dismounted and tried to use their horses as shields. Their situation was hopeless. A hail of bullets and arrows poured upon them from every direction. One bullet struck Custer in the temple, another in the chest. Within half an hour the entire company was wiped out.

This great victory at the Little Bighorn only delayed the final defeat of Sitting Bull and the rest of the Sioux. The chief held out until 1881. Then, his people near starvation, he surrendered to army units. In 1883 he was placed on the Standing Rock reservation in the Dakotas.

▓ What victory did the Sioux win at Little Bighorn? How were they finally the losers?

CHIEF JOSEPH

The search for gold also drew miners to Indian lands in the mountains of western Idaho. The whites called the Indians of this region the **Nez Perce,** or "pierced nose," because they wore nose ornaments made of shell. They were a peace-loving people. They claimed that no member of their tribe had ever killed a white. When Lewis and Clark traveled through Nez Perce lands on their expedition to the Pacific Coast, the explorers had been treated as honored guests.

The Nez Perce chief was a man the whites called Joseph. His real name was Hinmaton-Yalaktit, which means "Thunder coming out of the water and over the land." Like Tecumseh, the great Shawnee leader, Joseph believed that Indians had no right to sell the land they lived on. When his father was dying, he had told Joseph: "This land holds your father's body. Never sell the bones of your father and mother."

Now the government insisted that Joseph make way for the whites and move his band to the Lapwai Reservation in Oregon. Joseph had only 55 men of fighting age. He decided to yield. He selected land on the reservation in May 1877. Then the government gave him only one month to move his people and their possessions to the reservation.

While on the march to Oregon, a few angry Nez Perce killed some white settlers. Troops were sent to capture them. Chief Joseph decided that he must take his people to Canada instead of Oregon. For months the band slipped away from thousands of pursuing troops in the rugged country along the border between Oregon and Montana. In September 1877 they reached the **Bear Paw Mountains,** only 30 miles (48 kilometers) from Canada.

Joseph thought they were safe at last. He stopped to rest, for many of his people were sick. Then army cavalry units suddenly attacked. Joseph and his warriors held out for four days. Finally they surrendered.

"I am tired of fighting," Joseph told his captors. "It is cold and we have no bullets. The little children are freezing to death. My people . . . have no blankets, no food. . . . I will fight no more forever."

The Nez Perce were settled on a barren reservation in Oklahoma. Far from the mountains of Idaho, this land was "the malarial bottom of the Indian Territory." Joseph, however, was sent to a reservation in Washington state. There he lived in exile, separated from his people and removed from the land he loved. When he died in 1904, the official cause of his death was listed as a broken heart.

- What did Chief Joseph believe about selling land?
- What caused the peace-loving Nez Perce to flee?
- Why did Chief Joseph surrender in 1877?

The likeness of Chief Joseph, the well-spoken Nez Perce leader, is one of many photographic records that document the disappearance of the first Americans. What claim did the Nez Perce make to prove they were a peace-loving people?

The Buffalo Vanishes

What finally put an end to Indian independence was the killing off of the buffalo. Thousands had been slaughtered to feed the gangs of laborers who built the western railroads. In one 18-month period the scout William Cody (shown at left) shot some 4,000 buffalo for the Kansas Pacific Railroad construction camps. This won him the nickname Buffalo Bill.

Once the railroads were built, shooting buffalo became a popular sport for tourists and hunters from the East. Bored passengers on the trains sometimes opened their windows to blast away at the grazing buffalo.

In 1871 a Pennsylvania tanner discovered that buffalo hides could be made into useful leather. Hides that were once worthless now brought $1 to $3 each. Buffalo hunting then became a profitable business. Between 1872 and 1874, 9 million buffalo were killed. By 1900 there were fewer than 50 buffalo left in the entire United States! The buffalo had been nearly sacred to many Indian tribes. It gave them food, clothing, and shelter. Without it, the Indians were powerless to resist the advance of the whites.

Library of Congress

Head held in his hand, Hunkpapa Sioux chief Sitting Bull stares at the camera in an 1882 photograph. Here at Standing Rock reservation on the Dakota Territory the chief has come back from exile in Canada after the massacre of Custer and his cavalry. Sitting Bull performed for a time in Buffalo Bill's Wild West Show. The woman at his right is his ninth wife. On his left is Catherine Weldon, a Boston widow and admirer. Sitting Bull offered to make her his wife but she declined. Below is Helen Hunt Jackson, whose novel *Ramona* told the plight of the Indian people when the frontier closed. How did many Americans react to the government's treatment of the Indians?

THE END OF INDIAN INDEPENDENCE

All of the wars between the Indians and the army were hard fought. Yet many of the white soldiers sympathized with their enemies. They understood why the Indians were fighting. Even Colonel John Gibbon, who discovered the bodies of Custer's men after the Battle of the Little Bighorn, blamed the wars on the whites. Another officer said, "If I had been a red man . . . I should have fought as bitterly."

The way the government treated Indians shocked many Americans. They were particularly upset when the government broke treaties it had made with the tribes. In *A Century of Dishonor,* published in 1881, Helen Hunt Jackson showed how the government broke promises to Indians. In her novel *Ramona* she tried to do for the Indians what Harriet Beecher Stowe's *Uncle Tom's Cabin* had done for the black slaves.

Another fighter for Indian rights was Sarah Winnemucca, the daughter of a Paiute chief. Winnemucca wrote a book and gave lectures describing how unjustly the Indians had been treated. She demanded that the United States return much of the land it had taken from her people.

Congress finally responded by passing the **Dawes Severalty Act** of 1887. This law broke up reservation lands into individual family units. Each family got 160 acres (64 hectares). To protect the owners against speculators, they were not allowed to sell the property for 25 years. Only then did they have full rights to the land. And only then were they allowed to become citizens of the United States.

The Dawes Act was supposed to protect and help the Indians. However, it was written entirely from a white point of view. It ignored the Indians' culture and traditions. Its aim was to turn them into farmers and destroy their tribal organizations. It was well meant, but it simply showed once again that most white Americans had little sympathy for the plight of the Indians. In this sense it was typical of most of the laws that Congress passed affecting the lives of the original Americans.

- How did Helen Hunt Jackson fight for Indian rights?
- How did Sarah Winnemucca fight for her people?
- What was the purpose of the Dawes Act? Why was it not a good law from the Indian point of view?

"Old Pancake" and "Old Virginia" held shares in the famous Comstock Lode. "Old Pancake" is shown in a photograph above. His true identity was Henry Tompkins Paige Comstock. Where was the Comstock Lode?

THE COMSTOCK LODE

The Dawes Act spoke of encouraging the Indians to adopt "the habits of civilized life." The lawmakers apparently wanted them to copy the life-styles of their white neighbors. How "civilized" those life-styles were is another question!

The miners of the West offered one model. They carried their "civilization" into the mountains of Colorado, Nevada, Arizona, Idaho, Montana, and Wyoming. In each case they struck the region like a tornado.

The first important strikes after the California discovery of gold in 1848 came in Nevada in 1859. The center of this activity was Gold Canyon, a sagebrush-covered ravine on the southern slope of Mt. Davidson. At first the miners panned for gold in the gravel beds of streams. When their yields began to decline, the prospectors moved farther up the mountainside. Among these miners was Henry Comstock, known to his friends as "Old Pancake." His partner, James Fennimore, was called "Old Virginia." They began digging at the head of Gold Canyon on a small rise called Gold Hill. Another pair, Peter O'Riley and Patrick McLaughlin, started digging at Six Mile Canyon, a ravine on the northern slope of Mt. Davidson.

O'Riley and McLaughlin soon came upon a dark, heavy soil sprinkled with gold. Just as they were shouting news of their discovery, Henry Comstock came riding by. Jumping from his horse, he made a quick examination of the find. "You have struck it, boys!" he announced.

Then the old prospector bluffed his way into a partnership. "Look here," he said, "this spring was Old Man Caldwell's. You know that. . . . Well, Manny Penrod and I bought this claim last winter, and we sold a tenth interest to Old Virginia the other day. You two fellows must let us in on equal shares."

At first O'Riley and McLaughlin said no. Then they were afraid they might lose everything, so they said yes.

The partners went to work at once. They found very little gold. Instead they struck large deposits of heavy, bluish sand and blue-gray quartz. Not knowing what that "blasted blue stuff" was, they simply piled it beside the mine. Another miner, however, gathered up a sack of the blue quartz and had it tested, or **assayed.** The assayers' reports went beyond anyone's wildest dreams. The "blue stuff" was rich in silver and gold. The partners had hit upon what was known as a **bonanza**—a large find of extremely rich ore.

News of the discovery caused 15,000 people to swarm into the region in the next few months. Henry Comstock gained everlasting fame by giving the find his name. The enormous **Comstock Lode** ran along the eastern face of Mt. Davidson. It crossed the heads of Gold and Six Mile Canyons and dipped underneath the crowded mining camps.

Most of the gold and silver the prospectors sought was buried deep in veins of hard quartz rock. Heavy machinery was needed to dig it out. Tunneling operations called for experienced mining engi-

Frederic Remington, like Charles M. Russell, brought his love of the Old West to his paintings. This copy of "The Gold Bug" shows a prospector with his mules and dog. The tools of the prospector's trade are easily at hand — pick and shovel, pan, and a canteen, gun, and coffeepot. Which states attracted miners in the 1850s?

The Anaconda

In Montana and Arizona the mining riches were in copper, not gold and silver. In the late 1870s Marcus Daly bought a small silver mine in Butte, Montana, for $30,000. For some reason this mine was named **Anaconda**. An anaconda is a large snake like a python or a boa constrictor. Perhaps the silver ore ran in a curved, snakelike vein.

To develop the Anaconda, Daly turned to George Hearst, a millionaire California developer who had already invested in many western mines. Daly began operations in 1880.

The silver of Anaconda soon gave out. Beneath it, however, Daly found a rich vein of copper. Hearst supplied the huge sums needed to mine and smelt this copper. By the late 1880s the Anaconda Copper Corporation had become the greatest producer of copper in the world. Eventually, Daly and his associates took over $2 billion worth of copper out of the "richest hill in the world."

Montana Historical Society

Marcus Daly is said to have planned the town of Anaconda, Montana, seen here in 1887, by pointing to a grazing cow and pronouncing, "Main Street will run north and south in a direct line through that cow."

neers. Prospectors like Comstock, O'Riley, and McLaughlin did not have the skill and money such operations required. Comstock eventually sold his share of the mine for a mere $10,000.

The real "bonanza kings" were John W. Mackay, James G. Fair, James C. Flood, and William S. O'Brien. All were of Irish ancestry. All had been born poor. All had come to California during the Gold Rush. In 1868-69 these four men formed a partnership. They used the profits of one strike to buy up other mines. Eventually they took precious metals worth over $150 million from the rich Nevada lode.

▣ What was the Comstock Lode?

MINING CAMP LIFE

Whenever a strike was made, **mining camps** seemed to sprout out of the surrounding hillsides like flowers after a desert rain. The camps were ramshackle towns of tents and noisy saloons. The most famous was **Virginia City,** Nevada. It was given its name by Henry Comstock's partner, "Old Virginia." While on a spree, "Old Virginia" tripped and fell, smashing his bottle of whiskey. Rising to his knees he shouted drunkenly, "I baptize this town Virginia Town."

Thomas Gilcrease Institute, Tulsa

Virginia City was a typical **boom town,** so crowded that a horse and wagon could take half an hour to cross the main street. In these mining towns it was difficult to keep the peace. Smooth-talking gamblers, gunslingers, and other outlaws sidled alongside **claim jumpers,** shifty types who specialized in seizing ore deposits that had been staked out by others. Some camps were taken over by these outlaws, who ruled the terror-filled citizens at gunpoint.

When conditions in a mining camp got too bad, the respectable residents took action. They formed **vigilance committees** to watch over their towns. Sometimes they even drew up formal constitutions, pledging their members, who were called **vigilantes,** to cooperate until order was restored.

As soon as enough vigilantes had been signed up, the worst troublemakers were hunted down. These villains were given speedy trials before judges and juries made up of the same vigilantes who had run them down. The trials, of course, were not legal. The usual punishment for the guilty was death by hanging. In one six-week period Montana vigilantes hanged 22 outlaws.

Under the star-lit sky, in front of the Long Horn, a westerner falls from his horse in this Charles Russell painting. What kind of trouble there was at the Long Horn is left to the viewer's imagination. What were the conditions of a typical boom town?

539

Once a town was properly governed, more and more settlers moved in. Some opened stores. Others turned to farming. Lawyers, ministers, teachers, and doctors gradually appeared. The people built schools and churches. They started newspapers and opened hospitals. They built roads to connect with other communities. They put down solid roots.

■ Who were the vigilantes? How did vigilante law work?

THE CATTLE KINGDOM

While the miners were searching the mountains for gold and silver, other pioneers were seeking their own fortunes on the grasslands of the High Plains. The land that formed the **cattle kingdom** stretched from Texas into Canada and from the Rockies to eastern Kansas. This area made up nearly one quarter of the entire United States.

Spanish explorers had brought the first European cattle into Mexico in the early 1500s. Over the years their cattle had grown to enormous herds. Many ran wild. New breeds developed. These great herds spread northward as far as Texas.

By 1860 about 5 million wild cattle were grazing in Texas. These were the famous **Texas longhorns,** so named because their horns had a spread of as much as seven feet (over two meters). After the Civil War, cattle that were worth from $3 to $5 a head in Texas

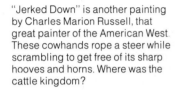

"Jerked Down" is another painting by Charles Marion Russell, that great painter of the American West. These cowhands rope a steer while scrambling to get free of its sharp hooves and horns. Where was the cattle kingdom?

Thomas Gilcrease Institute, Tulsa

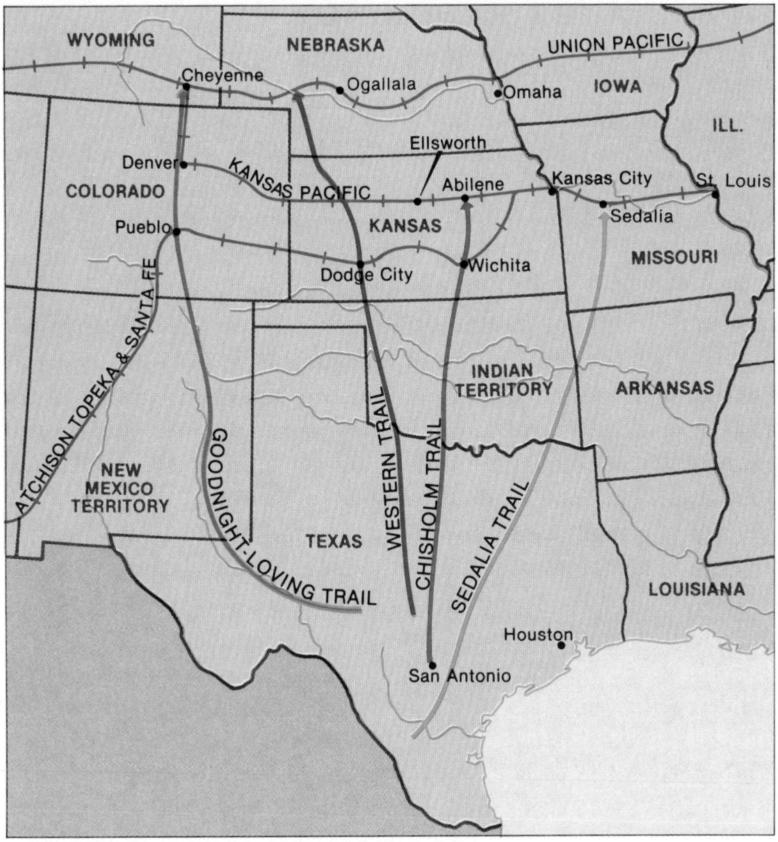

Map labels:

WYOMING

NEBRASKA

UNION PACIFIC

Cheyenne

Ogallala

Omaha

IOWA

ILL.

Ellsworth

Denver

KANSAS PACIFIC

Abilene

Kansas City

St. Louis

COLORADO

Pueblo

KANSAS

Sedalia

Dodge City

Wichita

MISSOURI

ATCHISON TOPEKA & SANTA FE

INDIAN TERRITORY

ARKANSAS

GOODNIGHT-LOVING TRAIL

WESTERN TRAIL

CHISHOLM TRAIL

SEDALIA TRAIL

NEW MEXICO TERRITORY

TEXAS

LOUISIANA

Houston

San Antonio

0 — 300 Mi.

0 — 300 Km.

could be sold for $30 to $50 a head in the cities of the eastern United States. The problem was how to get them there. Joseph G. McCoy, an Illinois meat dealer, thought he knew the answer. He could make a fortune, he believed, if he could establish a convenient meeting place for eastern buyers and Texas cattle ranchers.

McCoy chose **Abilene,** Kansas, as this meeting place. There he put up a hotel for the cowhands and dealers and built barns, pens, and loading chutes for the cattle. He persuaded officials of the Kansas Pacific Railroad to ship cattle to **Chicago,** the meat packing center of the United States, at special low rates.

To get Texas longhorns to Abilene and other **cattle towns** meant herding them slowly northward over the empty plains. This **long drive** was a two-month journey. On the first drive Texans herded 35,000 longhorns over the **Chisholm Trail** to Abilene. During the next 20 years about 6 million head of cattle were driven north over the grasslands.

- What was the origin of wild cattle?
- How did Joseph G. McCoy solve the problem of getting Texas longhorns to eastern cities?

OPEN-RANGE RANCHING

The key to the success of the long drive was the grass and water along the trail northward from Texas. Cattle ranchers discovered that prairie grass made an excellent food for their cattle. Then they discovered that the tough, rangy longhorns got along very well in the harsh winters of the northern plains. Soon millions of cattle were grazing on land belonging to the government. Ranchers could fatten their herds on this **open range** of lush grass without paying a cent for it. The cattle roamed freely across the unfenced plains.

Of course the cattle also needed water. It was a very dry region, almost a desert. Water rights, or **range rights,** along a stream meant control of all the land around it. Ranchers quickly bought up all the land around their water supply. By owning a few acres along a small river, a rancher could control thousands of acres of surrounding grasslands without actually owning it.

One Colorado **cattle baron,** John F. Iliff, had the use of an area the size of Connecticut and Rhode Island. Yet he owned only about 15,500 acres (6,200 hectares). His land consisted of 105 small parcels on which there was running water.

To secure adequate range rights, a number of ranchers would band together into an association. They would buy up all the land along the banks of a stream or claim it under the Homestead Act. Only their cattle would be allowed on this private property. Only their cattle could drink from the stream. Although the rest of the range was public property, no other rancher for miles around could graze cattle without water.

"Stampede" is the thundering tramp of this herd of longhorns spooked by a cloudburst. The easily frightened steers would stampede at a snapped twig or the hiss of a rattlesnake. It was the cowhand's risky work to halt this senseless rush. Henry Jackson painted this stunning scene, which hangs in the Buffalo Bill Historical Center in Cody, Wyoming. Why did the longhorns roam the plains?

Buffalo Bill Historical Center, Cody, Wyoming

Under this system the cattle belonging to the ranchers who owned the banks of the stream became thoroughly mixed. Each spring and fall, cowhands would **round up** all the animals to a central place. The cowhands would fan out across the range, each riding up a canyon or hill. Each would return driving all the cattle in the area before him.

Next the cowhands sorted each rancher's cattle from the rest by checking every animal's marking, called a **brand.** The brank mark was a scar made by pressing a red-hot branding iron onto the animal's hide. Each rancher's brand had a distinct shape, so it was easy to determine who owned which cattle. Those that were ready for market were penned up and shipped off by rail. The rest were turned loose, free to roam the range again until the next roundup.

Of course, newborn calves had not been branded. But calves always trailed close beside their mothers, so it was easy to tell whose property they were. They were branded and sent bawling back to their mothers.

- Why was the open range so important to cattle ranchers?
- Why was it necessary to have cattle roundups?

THE COWHAND

That colorful figure, the cowhand or cowboy, was the master of the long drive and the roundup. Mexican-Americans were the first cowhands. These **vaqueros** invented almost all the tools of the cowhand's trade, from his broad-brimmed felt hat, his cotton bandana, and his rope lariat to his special western saddle. The word *rodeo* is the Spanish word for "roundup."

A cowhand's life was a hard one. The men worked sunup to sundown and received lower wages than most factory workers. Their legs became bowed from long days in the saddle. They developed permanent squints from peering into the glaring sunlight of the treeless plains. Their faces were lined and leathery, their hands calloused from constantly handling coarse ropes.

Not all cowhands were the strong, silent types portrayed in the movies by white actors. Many came from poor families or from groups outside the mainstream. About one third of the men who worked cattle on the open range were either Mexican-Americans or blacks.

Every item of the cowhand's clothes and equipment served a necessary function. The wide brim of his "ten-gallon hat" could be turned down to shade his eyes or drain off rainfall. His bandana could be tied over his nose and mouth to keep out the dust raised by the pounding hooves of countless cattle. The bandana also served as a towel, a napkin, a bandage, and a handkerchief. Cowhands sometimes

The cowhand and the *vaquero* show the tools of their trade in Frederic Remington's fine art. How was the average cowhand different from the westerner played by movie actors?

wore leather trousers, called **chaps,** over regular overalls. Chaps were fastened to a broad belt buckled at the back. They protected a rider's legs from injury if he fell from his horse or when he had to ride through cactus, sagebrush, or other thorny plants.

The cowhand's **western saddle** had a sturdy horn, or *pommel,* for help in roping powerful steers and horses. These western saddles were heavy but comfortable. A weary cowhand could doze in the saddle while he rode. At night his saddle became a pillow and his saddlecloth a blanket when he stretched out beside the campfire and settled down to sleep.

Cowhands drank potfuls of thick, strong coffee to stay awake on the trail. They ate mostly stews, kidney beans, biscuits, and corn bread.

It was a lonely life. This explains why cowhands were famous for letting off steam when they reached cattle towns such as **Dodge City,** Kansas, the "Cowboy's Capital." Many cowhands were big drinkers and heavy gamblers when they came to town. Sometimes there were brawls and gunfights, but the violence and disorder have been exaggerated. Life in the West was much calmer and more orderly than it is usually pictured in the movies. Nevertheless, many cattle towns did have **boot hills**—cemeteries for those who "died with their boots on," either from overwork or on a spree.

■ What are some inventions of the Mexican–American *vaqueros?*

THE END OF THE OPEN RANGE

The cowhand rode tall on the open range. In the 1880s, however, the days of the open range were ending. By 1884 there were more than 4.5 million head of cattle roaming free on the Great Plains. The range was becoming overstocked. Good grazing land was scarce. In the foothills of the Rockies sheepherders squared off against cattle ranchers. Their sheep cropped the grass right down to the roots so that cattle could no longer find it. Many **range wars** broke out between cattle ranchers and sheep ranchers for control of the grasslands.

Farmers also competed with ranchers for land. Longhorns sometimes trampled their crops. The farmers feared the free-roaming herds would infect their own cattle with a dread disease called "Texas fever."

Then came two terrible winters. In 1885-86 and in 1886-87 blizzards howled across the plains. Theodore Roosevelt, then a "gentleman rancher" in Dakota Territory, wrote: "Furious gales blow down from the north, driving before them the clouds of blinding snow-dust, wrapping the mantle of death around every unsheltered being. . ." When the spring came in 1887, ranchers discovered that the storms had all but wiped out their herds.

CHAPTER 18 REVIEW

Identification
Tell briefly why each of the following persons, terms, or events is important.

1. Red Cloud
2. Sitting Bull
3. Chief Joseph
4. William Cody
5. Helen Hunt Jackson
6. Sarah Winnemucca
7. Joseph G. McCoy
8. Great American Desert
9. Concentration
10. Transcontinental railroads
11. Chivington Massacre
12. Battle of the Little Bighorn
13. Comstock Lode
14. Anaconda
15. Boom town
16. Chisholm Trail
17. Open range
18. *Vaqueros*
19. Range wars
20. Dry farming

Understanding American History

1. Explain why the buffalo and horse were important to the Plains Indians.
2. How was the system called concentration used to remove the Plains Indians?
3. How did the government encourage the building of transcontinental railroads?
4. How did transcontinental railroads affect the settlement of the West?
5. How were Chief Joseph's views on owning land similar to those of Tecumseh (pages 265–67)? How did they differ from the views held by most whites?
6. How did the slaughter of the buffalo lead to the end of Indian independence?
7. Describe life in a typical mining town.
8. Describe the life of a cowhand. How did cowhands depend upon the inventions of the *vaqueros*?
9. What ended the open range?
10. Describe the inventions and farming techniques that helped turn the Great American Desert into the breadbasket of America.

Activities

1. Do research in your library on Custer's Last Stand. Then use historical imagination to pretend you are a newspaper reporter assigned to cover the story for your paper back East. With your classmates prepare a special section for the newspaper describing the Battle of the Little Bighorn. Prepare biographical sketches of the key figures. Create your own illustrations and prepare a relief map of the battle site, using papier-mâché.
2. A *diorama* is an exhibit of lifelike figures in natural settings in the foreground with a painting in the background. As a class activity make a diorama of the Great American Desert, of a mining boom town, or of a farm on the Great Plains in the 1880s.
3. The two great artists of the West were Frederic Remington and Charles Marion Russell. Good examples of Remington's work are on pages 537, 543, and 546. Examples of Russell's work are on pages 253–55, 524, and 539–40. Report on one of these popular artists and show reproductions of his works, or make your own drawings of the cowhands of the Old West.
4. Make a scale model of a sod house that might have stood on the Great Plains. Design a roof that will lift off so you can show how the inside of the house might have been furnished. The staff of a local museum or historical society can help you here.
5. Use historical imagination to place yourself in one of the mining boom towns of the 1860s. Write a letter home to your family in the East telling about your life in the West. Describe your life as a miner and the town where you trade.

CHAPTER 18 TEST

Matching (45 points)
Number your paper 1–15 and match the description in the first column with the name in the second column.

1. Technique that permitted farmers to raise crops when very little rain fell
2. Aimed at turning Indians into farmers and destroying their tribal organizations
3. Policy in which the government would give Indians food, money, and presents if the Indians would live in specific, limited areas
4. Author of a book that showed how the government had broken promises to the Indians
5. Name given to large finds of extremely valuable ore
6. Granted a charter for building a transcontinental railroad
7. Gave lectures on unfair treatment of Indians and demanded that the U.S. return Indian lands
8. Nez Perce chief who felt that Indians had no right to sell the land they lived on
9. Basic social and economic unit of each Plains tribe
10. Sioux chief who led warriors in the Battle of the Little Bighorn
11. Early shelter for farmers on the Great Plains
12. An enormous deposit of gold and silver discovered in Nevada in 1859
13. What the Great American Desert became after farmers used new methods and inventions
14. Sioux chief who fought to keep whites from using the Bozeman Trail
15. Mobs who took law and order into their own hands in the Old West

a. Bands
b. Sitting Bull
c. Bonanza
d. Concentration
e. Red Cloud
f. Sod house
g. Helen Hunt Jackson
h. Chief Joseph
i. Dawes Severalty Act
j. Sarah Winnemucca
k. Dry farming
l. Pacific Railway Act
m. Breadbasket of America
n. Vigilantes
o. Comstock Lode

Completion (25 points)
Number your paper 16–20 and next to each number write the words that best complete each sentence.

16. The two-months' journey of cowhands leading cattle northward was the ____.
17. On the ____ cattle roamed freely and grazed on prairie grass.
18. A rancher could control thousands of acres without actually owning them by buying up the ____ along a stream.
19. Cowhands had to ____ cattle each spring and fall.
20. A ____ marked each calf for its owner.

Essay (30 points)
In a brief essay explain how the horse and buffalo were essential to the lives of the Plains. Plan your paper carefully.

CHAPTER 19
The Rise of Industrial America

Between 1860 and 1900 the United States went through one of the most dramatic periods of change in its entire history. In 1860 about 80 per cent of the nation's 31 million inhabitants lived on farms. About 1.5 million, less than 5 per cent, worked in factories. By the 1890s about 5 million Americans worked in factories. America's manufactured products were worth almost as much as the manufactured goods of Great Britain, France, and Germany combined.

By the end of the century the new industrial growth was visible nearly everywhere. Railroads crossed and recrossed the continent. Small towns had been changed as if by magic into great cities.

In 1900 about 40 per cent of America's 76 million people lived in towns and cities. The steel, oil, and electrical industries, tiny in 1865, had become giants. In 1900 the United States would have seemed a new world to a person who had been out of the country since the Civil War.

A railway switching yard at night is alive with activity in this Currier & Ives engraving. It was published in 1885. At work are yardmen, baggage masters, switchmen, brakemen, and signalmen as well as conductors and engineers. How did railways show America's economic growth?

▨ What changes were there in the U.S. from 1860 to 1900?

Library of Congress

Commodore Cornelius Vanderbilt posed for this photograph c. 1870. That year his railway network ran all the way from New York to Chicago. What was the travel time by railway between those two cities?

THE RAILROAD NETWORK

Americans were fascinated by railroads. Poets celebrated the "pant and roar" of the locomotives, so powerful as to shake the ground, and the elaborate decorations painted on their sides. They even praised the "dense and murky" clouds that belched from the locomotives' smokestacks. To all sorts of people railroads symbolized the boundless energy of the nation.

When the Civil War began, there were only 30,000 miles (48,000 kilometers) of railroad track in the United States. Most railroads were very short, averaging only about 100 miles (160 kilometers). They had been built to serve local needs. Few direct lines connected distant cities. Passengers and freight traveling between New York and Chicago, for example, had to be transferred from one line to another 17 times! The trip took at least 50 hours.

The main task of the postwar generation was to connect these lines into one network. "Commodore" Cornelius Vanderbilt was a pioneer in this work. Vanderbilt could barely read and write, but he was aggressive and hard-nosed. He had made a fortune in shipping, but when river traffic fell during the Civil War, he invested in railroads. By 1869 he had control of the New York Central Railroad, which ran between Buffalo and Albany, and two other lines that connected the Central with New York City.

In 1870 Vanderbilt bought the Lake Shore and Michigan Southern Railroads. His growing New York Central system then extended 965 miles (1,544 kilometers) from New York to Chicago by way of Cleveland and Toledo. Passengers could travel between New York and Chicago in less than 24 hours without leaving their seats. When Vanderbilt died in 1877, he left a railroad system of over 4,500 miles (7,200 kilometers) serving a vast region. He left a personal fortune of $100 million.

In much the same way J. Edgar Thomson, head of the Pennsylvania Railroad, built up direct routes from Philadelphia to St. Louis and Chicago by way of Pittsburgh. In 1871 the Pennsylvania Railroad extended its tracks to New York City. Other lines were extended by wealthy developers such as Jay Gould, Jim Fisk, and James J. Hill.

Besides combining railroads to make through connections, the **railroad barons** built many new lines. By 1900 the United States had about 200,000 miles (320,000 kilometers) of railroad track. This was more than were in all the nations of Europe combined.

In addition to speeding the movement of goods and passengers, the railroads supplied thousands of jobs for laborers, train crews, repair workers, and clerks. By 1891 the Pennsylvania Railroad alone employed over 110,000 workers. The largest United States government employer, the post office, had only 95,000 on its payroll in 1891.

Railroads stimulated the national economy in countless ways. They were great users of wood, copper, and steel. They made it possible to move bulky products like coal and iron ore cheaply over long distances. This made such products available at reasonable prices in regions where they had formerly been very expensive. Railroads enabled farmers in California to sell their fruits and vegetables in New York. Flour milled in Minneapolis could be purchased in Boston. Wherever railroads went, new towns sprang up almost overnight, and older towns grew to be big cities.

- What did railroads symbolize to many Americans?
- What was the main task of postwar railroad builders?
- How did railroads stimulate the national economy?

THE CORPORATION

Railroads were very expensive to build and operate. The sums needed to build even a small one were far larger than the amount John C. Calhoun had to raise to buy his South Carolina plantation, more than John Ellerton Lodge had invested in his fleet of merchant ships, greater than Francis Cabot Lowell and the Boston Associates needed when they built their first textile mill.

One person or family or even a group of partners rarely had enough money to construct and operate a railroad. Railroad developers had to raise money from investors all over the nation and around the world. To do this, they set up their businesses as **corporations.**

When a corporation is formed, the organizers sell shares called **stock certificates.** People who buy shares are called **stockholders.** These stockholders own the corporation, which is usually run by a **board of directors.** Stockholders can sell their shares to anyone for whatever price they can get. If the business is doing poorly, the value of the shares will fall.

For the organizers of big businesses the chief advantage of the corporation is that it brings together the money of many investors. For the investors the chief advantage is **limited liability.** This means that the individual investors risk only the money they have paid for their stocks. In a **partnership,** on the other hand, all the partners are responsible for the debts of the firm. For example, a partner who had invested only $100 could be held responsible for a $5,000 debt of a partnership. The same person investing $100 in the stock of a corporation could lose only that $100, no matter how much money the corporation owed.

- How did the high cost of railroads lead developers to set up corporations?
- What is an advantage of a corporation over a partnership?

READING PRACTICE IN SOCIAL STUDIES

Cause and Effect

What happened to America between 1860 and 1900? Why did it undergo such a dramatic economic change? What kind of nation did it become?

The answers to such questions may be found when you read for *cause and effect*. Each defines the other: A *cause* is an action that brings about an event. An *effect* is the event brought about by an action.

In the simplest kind of diagram, the relationship of cause and effect may be shown:

Cause ⟶ Effect

Whenever you ask why something happened, you are looking for causes. Whenever you ask what will happen when a certain action is taken, you are looking for effects.

History is a tale of causes and effects. Why were 2,898 American soldiers barefoot in the winter of 1777 at Valley Forge? Poor organization, selfish civilians, not enough horses and wagons to haul supplies—all of these are causes. What happened when 9 million buffalo were killed between 1872 and 1874? Its effect was to put an end to Indian independence.

When reading for cause and effect, a number of clues act as signals. Words and phrases such as *because, since, if . . . then, as a result, therefore,* and *for this reason* all signal cause and effect.

To find cause and effect most simply, ask yourself two questions as you read: What happened? The answer will give you the effect. Why did it happen? The answer will give you the cause.

Sometimes you will find more than one cause leading to one effect. Or one cause may bring about several effects. One kind of cause and effect relationship sets up what is called a *chain reaction.* This happens when a cause brings about an effect and the effect becomes a cause for another effect, and so on.

A simple diagram of a chain reaction may be shown in the following fashion:

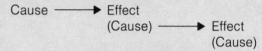

Cause ⟶ Effect
(Cause) ⟶ Effect
(Cause)

Here one cause triggers a series of causes and effects.

When you take notes on a section organized by cause and effect, it may be helpful to make a simple chart like the one below:

Cause(s)	Effect(s)

Briefly state each cause and each effect in the appropriate column. If the cause and effect relationship is a chain reaction, you may prefer to use the pattern in the diagram at the top of this column.

The following questions will give you practice in reading for cause and effect. First read the section "Changing Iron into Steel" on page 555. Then make a simple chart to show cause and effect. Number your paper 1–5. For the first four sentences write the part of each that gives the cause under *Cause* and the part that gives the effect under *Effect.*

1. The Bessemer converter made possible the mass production of steel.
2. Railroad executives wanted to replace iron rails with steel rails because steel was stronger and lasted longer.
3. Before the 1870s steel was too expensive to be widely used. It was made by a slow and expensive process of heating, stirring, and reheating iron.
4. The Mesabi deposits were so near the surface that they could be mined with steam shovels.
5. Which of the following best describes the topic of the section?
   a. making steel
   b. the Bessemer converter
   c. growth of the steel industry

The Metropolitan Museum of Art

CHANGING IRON INTO STEEL

The railroad industry could not have grown as large as it did without steel. The first rails were made of iron. But iron rails were not strong enough to support heavy trains running at high speeds. Railroad executives wanted to replace them with steel rails because steel was 10 or 15 times stronger and lasted 20 times longer. Before the 1870s, however, steel was too expensive to be widely used. It was made by a slow and expensive process of heating, stirring, and reheating iron ore.

Then an English inventor, Henry Bessemer, discovered that directing a blast of air at melted iron in a furnace would burn out the impurities that made the iron brittle. As the air shot through the furnace, the bubbling metal would erupt in showers of sparks. When the fire cooled, the metal had been changed, or *converted,* to steel. The **Bessemer converter** made possible the mass production of steel. Now three to five tons of iron could be changed into steel in a matter of minutes.

"Forging the Shaft: A Welding Heat" was painted in 1877 by John F. Weir. It captures the glow of molten metal that filled American steel factories in the 19th century. How was steel produced before the invention of the Bessemer converter?

The young Andrew Carnegie sat for this photograph shortly after he came to America from Scotland. He worked first as a bobbin boy in a cotton mill, then as a telegrapher, and later as a railroad superintendent. Why did he build his Bessemer steel plant?

Just when the demand for more and more steel developed, prospectors discovered huge new deposits of iron ore in the **Mesabi Range,** a 120-mile-long region (192 kilometers) in Minnesota near Lake Superior. The Mesabi deposits were so near the surface that they could be mined with steam shovels.

Barges and steamers carried the iron ore through Lake Superior to depots on the southern shores of Lake Michigan and Lake Erie. With dizzying speed Gary, Indiana, and Toledo, Youngstown, and Cleveland, Ohio, became major steel-manufacturing centers. Pittsburgh was the greatest steel city of all. The large coal fields near Pittsburgh supplied cheap fuel to **smelt** the ore—that is, to melt it down to remove impurities.

Steel was the basic building material of the industrial age. After steel rails came steel bridges. Next came steel skeletons for tall buildings. Nails, wire, and other everyday objects were also made of steel. Production skyrocketed from 77,000 tons in 1870 to over 11 million tons in 1900.

Andrew Carnegie was by far the most important producer of steel. Early in his career as an ironmaster, Carnegie visited a plant in

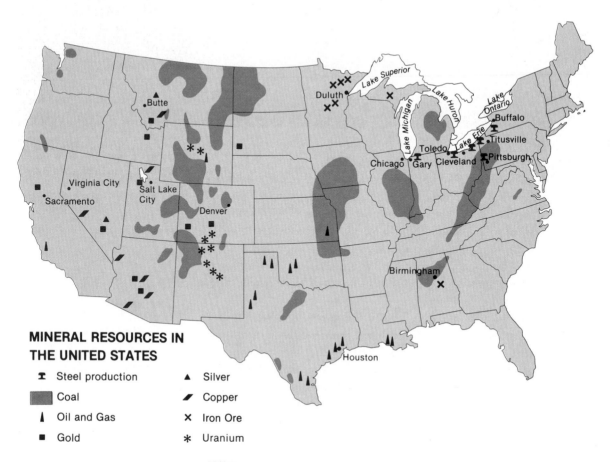

MINERAL RESOURCES IN THE UNITED STATES

- ⊥ Steel production
- ▲ Silver
- ◼ Coal
- ◢ Copper
- ▌ Oil and Gas
- ✕ Iron Ore
- ◼ Gold
- ✳ Uranium

England where the Bessemer process was being used. He had known about this method of making steel for some time. Now he became convinced that the day of cheap steel had arrived. He rushed home and built the largest Bessemer steel plant in America. He did so in the midst of the worst depression in the history of the United States. Labor and materials were cheap. Thus Carnegie got a large, up-to-date steel mill at a bargain price.

- How did the railroad industry depend upon steel to grow?
- What effect on the production of steel did the Bessemer converter have?

An important new industry, oil refining, grew after the Civil War. Crude oil, or petroleum—a dark, thick ooze from the earth—had been known for hundreds of years. But little use had ever been made of it. In the 1850s Samuel M. Kier, a manufacturer in western Pennsylvania, began collecting the oil from local seepages and refining it into kerosene. Refining, like smelting, is a process of removing impurities from a raw material.

Kerosene was used to light lamps. It was a cheap substitute for whale oil, which was becoming harder to get. Soon there was a large demand for kerosene. People began to search for new supplies of petroleum.

The first oil well was drilled by E. L. Drake, a retired railroad conductor. In 1859 he began drilling in Titusville, Pennsylvania. The whole venture seemed so impractical and foolish that onlookers called it "Drake's Folly." But when he had drilled down about 70 feet (21 meters), Drake struck oil. His well began to yield 20 barrels of crude oil a day.

News of Drake's success brought oil prospectors to the scene. By the early 1860s these wildcatters were drilling for "black gold" all over western Pennsylvania. The boom rivaled the California gold rush of 1848 in its excitement and Wild West atmosphere. And it brought far more wealth to the prospectors than any gold rush.

At first oil was shipped to refineries in barrels. The barrel was replaced first by railroad tank cars and then by oil pipelines. Crude oil could be refined into many products. For some years kerosene continued to be the principal one. It was sold in grocery stores and door-to-door. In the 1880s and 1890s refiners learned how to make other petroleum products such as waxes and lubricating oils. Petroleum was not then used to make gasoline or heating oil.

"Black Gold"

Drake Well Museum

Edwin L. Drake wears a top hat in this 1866 photograph of his oil well drilled in 1859 at Titusville, Pennsylvania.

THE COMMUNICATIONS REVOLUTION

Rapid, cheap communication over long distances is an essential part of modern industrial society. The **communications revolution** began in the 1840s when Samuel F. B. Morse invented the **telegraph.** By 1861 telegraph lines connected all parts of the country. One line stretched all the way across the still-unsettled Great Plains to the Pacific Coast.

The telegraph made it possible for people to communicate over great distances in seconds. It took much of the guesswork out of business. Managers could know when supplies would arrive, where demand was greatest for their products, and what prices were being charged across the country.

In front of Western Union's tower, electric lines over telephone wires cross and recross on New York City's Broadway. Perhaps no scene better illustrates the coming of the electrical age than this lithograph c. 1880s. But the wet snows of the Blizzard of 1888 snapped these wires and sent them to the street below. Which invention led the communications revolution?

New York Historical Society

In 1866 the **Western Union Telegraph Company** obtained control of the national telegraph network. The same year Cyrus W. Field succeeded in laying the first successful **telegraph cable** across the Atlantic Ocean to Europe. Not long after that, a telegraph network gave the United States almost instant communication with countries all over the world.

Next came the **telephone.** The telephone was invented by Alexander Graham Bell, a teacher of the deaf in Boston. Work with the deaf had led Bell to the study of *acoustics,* the science of sound. His telephone turned sound waves into an electrical current. The current passed through a long wire and was then changed back into sound in a distant receiver.

Bell first demonstrated the telephone in 1876. When he offered Western Union the right to use his invention, the telegraph company turned him down. President William Orton of Western Union called the telephone an "electrical toy."

Fortunately, other people realized the telephone's usefulness. By 1880 85 towns and cities had telephone systems. Five years later, more than 100 telephone companies were combined to create the **American Telephone and Telegraph Company.** Telephone wires soon wove spidery webs across the skies of America.

▨ How did the communications revolution affect business?

American Telephone and Telegraph Company

Cyrus W. Field, *above,* stands with one hand on the globe made smaller by his Atlantic cable. On August 16, 1858, the first message clicked over the transatlantic telegraph. In three weeks, however, the cable suddenly fell silent. Field persisted, and in 1866 he succeeded in laying another cable. He later lay a cable to Asia and Australia via Hawaii. Matthew Brady took this artful photograph. Below is Alexander Graham Bell in the act of placing the first telephone call over the long lines in October 1892. The call was made from New York to Chicago. What work had Bell done that led to his invention of the telephone?

The Wizard of Menlo Park

In the same year that Bell invented the telephone, Thomas Alva Edison established the nation's first industrial research laboratory at Menlo Park, New Jersey. Edison was the greatest inventor of the age. He was an inspired tinkerer and a hard worker, not a great thinker. "Sticking to it is the genius," he once said. He had only four years of off-and-on schooling.

Edison's first major invention, the **quadruplex telegraph**, was a machine that could send four messages over one wire at the same time. At Menlo Park he made several improvements on Bell's telephone. He invented the **phonograph** in 1877. But the **electric light** was his most important invention.

Using electricity to make light was not a new idea. In 1867 the boulevards of Paris were illuminated with arc lights. Arc lights were noisy and smoky. They could only be used outdoors. Edison was able to design a small light for homes and offices. His basic idea was to pass electricity through a fine wire inside an airless glass globe. The electricity heated the wire white hot, causing it to glow brightly. The wire could not burn up because there was no oxygen in the globe.

Edison spent two years experimenting with different filaments, or wires, that would glow for long periods without breaking. In December 1879 he found one. Soon "the Wizard of Menlo Park" was setting up city lighting companies and power stations and selling light bulbs by the millions. Later, electricity would run machinery. But in 1900 only about 2 per cent of America's manufacturing plants were powered by electricity.

Edison National Historic Site

At five o'clock in the morning, June 16, 1888, Thomas Edison first heard his own voice reciting "Mary Had a Little Lamb" on his talking machine. He perfected it by going without sleep for 72 hours.

COMPETITION AMONG THE RAILROADS

The railroad industry had extremely heavy **fixed costs.** Track and stations had to be maintained. Cars had to be cleaned and painted. It cost almost as much to run an empty train as one crowded with passengers or freight. These fixed costs, or **overhead,** were the same whether business was good or bad.

To attract more business, railroads often used what was called **cutthroat competition**—using any means to shoulder aside rival companies. Railroads often reduced rates. Between February and July 1869 the cost of sending 100 pounds (45 kilograms) of wheat from Chicago to New York fell from $1.80 to 25 cents.

Railroads also gave large shippers illegal kickbacks called **rebates.** In return for their business they would give these shippers lower rates than those charged their smaller competitors. In this way railroad competition was a force leading to **monopoly** in other fields. Monopoly is the domination of a field by a small number of businesses.

Sometimes railroads tried to make up for low, competitive rates by charging high rates for shipping goods from places where no other railroad existed. It often cost more to ship a product from a small "one-railroad town" a short distance from the market than from a large city much farther away. This **long and short haul** pricing also led to monopoly because it favored producers in large cities where railroads competed for traffic.

Railroads tried to reduce competition by making agreements called **pools.** Those who joined the pool agreed to divide up available business and charge a common price for shipments. Pools rarely worked very long. Whenever business fell off, the railroads could not resist the temptation to cut rates. There was no way to enforce pooling agreements when individual companies broke them.

- What fixed costs did railroads have?
- What was cutthroat competition? What were rebates?
- What practice did railroads use to reduce competition?

JOHN D. ROCKEFELLER

Most industries were eager to keep business steady and to avoid costly struggles for customers. A new way of doing this was developed in the oil industry by John D. Rockefeller. The method helped Rockefeller become the richest man in the United States, possibly in the entire world.

Rockefeller was born in Richford, New York, in 1839. After making a modest fortune in the wholesale food business in Cleveland, he decided to go into the oil business. He bought his first refinery in 1865. In 1870 he organized the **Standard Oil Company.** Soon he ex-

John D. Rockefeller was 33 years old in 1872, the date of this photograph. He was already a major figure in the booming oil industry. How much of the U.S. oil industry did he control?

panded from refining into drilling for oil and selling kerosene and other oil-based products to consumers. By the late 1870s Rockefeller controlled 90 per cent of the oil business in the United States.

Rockefeller was a deeply religious person. Even before he became wealthy, he made large contributions to charity. But he was a deadly competitor. He forced railroads to give him rebates on his huge oil shipments. He sold below cost in particular communities to steal business from local refiners. Then he gave the refiners a choice: sell out to Standard Oil or face bankruptcy. He hired spies and paid bribes to informers to tell secrets about other refiners' activities.

Rockefeller was also an excellent businessman. His plants were so efficient that he could undersell competitors and still make sizable profits. He detested waste. He kept close track of every detail of Standard Oil's complicated affairs.

Rockefeller's main objective was to combine all the refineries in the country into one supercompany. Then the industry could develop in a safe, orderly manner. He always gave competitors a chance to join Standard Oil. Only if they refused did he destroy them.

The man who designed Rockefeller's supercompany was Samuel C. T. Dodd. Dodd's creation was called a **trust**—a legal agreement under which stockholders of the separate oil companies turned their stock over to a group of directors called **trustees.** By controlling the stock of all the companies in the supercompany, the trustees could control the industry.

■ How did Rockefeller accomplish his objective of combining the country's refineries?

REGULATION OF BIG BUSINESS

The trust idea soon spread to other businesses. By 1900 almost every branch of manufacturing was dominated by a small number of large producers. The size and power of these trusts alarmed many Americans. They were afraid that the trusts would destroy small companies and cheat consumers by charging high prices once competition had been eliminated. The demand for government regulation of the economy increased steadily. The first target was the railroads.

In 1887 Congress passed the **Interstate Commerce Act.** This law stated that railroad rates must be "reasonable and just." Rates must be made public and could not be changed without public notice. Pools, rebates, and other unfair practices were declared unlawful. To oversee the affairs of railroads and to hear complaints from shippers, the law created the **Interstate Commerce Commission** (ICC), a board of experts. This was the first of the many **regulatory agencies** that control so many aspects of life today.

The ICC had to overcome many difficulties. The Interstate Com-

562

merce Act was vague. How was it possible to decide what a "reasonable and just" freight rate was? The Commission did not have a large enough staff to handle the more than 1,000 complaints it received in its first few months of operation. Nor did the Commission have the power to enforce its decisions. It could only sue violating railroads in court. Of the 16 cases it brought to trial between 1887 and 1905, it won only 1.

The Interstate Commerce Act was supposed to *regulate* competition—that is, to make certain that railroads did not cheat the public. It did not attempt to *control* the size of any railroad company. The way of dealing with the monopoly problem was to break up large businesses into smaller businesses which would compete with one another. This approach was called the **antitrust movement.**

In the late 1880s several states tried to restore competition by passing laws prohibiting trusts. These laws were difficult to enforce because industrial combinations usually did business in more than one state. Under the Constitution only the federal government could regulate such **interstate commerce.**

Then, in 1890, Congress passed the **Sherman Antitrust Act.** This law banned combinations "in the form of trust or otherwise" that restricted interstate trade or commerce. Anyone "who shall monopolize, or attempt to monopolize" such commerce could be fined or sent

When Congress began to debate the Sherman Antitrust Act, Joseph Keppler drew this cartoon for *Puck,* a popular humor magazine. Titled "Bosses of the Senate," the cartoon shows representatives of the various trusts towering over the politicians. The bloated trusts enter through the door at the right, which is marked for "Monopolists." The door at the left is labeled "People's Entrance," but it has been locked shut. What was the antitrust movement?

to jail for up to a year. This law was also difficult to enforce. It did not define "restraint of trade" or monopoly. Every attempt the government made to break up a trust resulted in a lawsuit.

The courts usually sided with the business combinations. The first important Supreme Court case involving the Sherman Act was *U.S. v. E. C. Knight Co.* (1895). It involved an attempt to break up the American Sugar Refining Company. This trust had obtained control of about 90 per cent of the sugar refining of the country by buying up four competing companies. The Court ruled that this combination was not illegal because it did not restrain trade. Since the trust refined its sugar in one state, interstate commerce was not involved. How it could dispose of all its sugar without selling it in many different states, the Court did not say.

The Interstate Commerce Act and the Sherman Antitrust Act had little effect on big business at this time. Most judges still put great stress on the right of individuals to run their affairs more or less as they pleased. Nevertheless, these two laws were extremely important. Both are still in effect and have been greatly strengthened over time. They established the practice of the federal government attempting to control the way American companies do business. After 1890 totally **free enterprise** was diminished in the United States. The Industrial Revolution had made the power of business so great that some public control over business practices came to be increasingly accepted.

- How did the Interstate Commerce Act attempt to regulate the railroads? What difficulties did it have in trying to do so?
- What was banned by the Sherman Antitrust Act? Why was the law not very effective in the 1890s?

WORKERS AND WORK

Post-Civil War industrial changes also greatly affected the men and women who worked in the factories of the United States. Factory jobs became steadily more specialized. More and more workers tended machines. Usually they performed one task over and over, hundreds of times each day. In a steel plant, for example, some laborers shoveled coke and ore. Others loaded furnaces. Still others moved the finished steel. No single worker could make steel alone.

Machines greatly increased the amount a worker could produce. This tended to raise wages and lower prices. Machines brought more goods within the reach of the average family. But they made work less interesting because it took little skill to operate most machines.

Manufacturing corporations grew larger and larger. In 1850 Cyrus McCormick's reaper manufacturing plant in Chicago employed 150 workers. By 1900 it had 4,000.

Culver Pictures

Such large factories had to be run like armies. The boards of directors were the generals. They set policy and appointed the people who carried it out. Next in the chain of command were the plant superintendents. Like the colonels of regiments, they were responsible for actually running the operation. They issued instructions to the foremen of the various departments, who were like army sergeants. The foremen in turn issued orders to the men and women who did the actual work.

These workers were expected to follow orders as obediently as army privates. In a Rochester, New York, carriage factory each worker had a number. To get a drink of water, a worker had to get the foreman's permission. To make sure that the rule was followed, the water faucets were locked up. In a Massachusetts tannery, guards patrolled the shop and reported any worker who talked during the workday.

These were extreme examples. Workers hated all such rules. Many did not meekly submit to them. Instead, they sought ways to get around overly strict regulations.

■ How did the increased use of machines affect workers?
■ How were large factories run?

Pittsburgh in this 1880 engraving is an appropriate symbol of America's great economic change. The smoke from the factories and mills mingles with that from the steamboat on the Ohio River. "Smoky City" it became and then "Steel City." How did jobs change at this time?

UNIONIZATION

In part because large corporations had so much power over their labor force, more workers began to join unions after the Civil War. This was especially true of skilled workers. In 1869 the **Knights of Labor** was founded in Philadelphia by Uriah Stephens, a tailor. At first it was a secret organization, with an elaborate ritual. Soon it expanded and began to work openly to organize workers into a "great brotherhood." By 1879 the Knights claimed to have 9,000 members. In that year Terence V. Powderly, a Pennsylvania machinist and one-time mayor of Scranton, Pennsylvania, became its head.

Under Powderly the Knights admitted women, blacks, immigrants, and unskilled workers. This was a radical step. Most unions would not accept these workers. The Knights advocated the eight-hour workday and strict regulation of trusts. They hoped to avoid strikes. Cooperation between owners, workers, and consumers should be possible, Powderly insisted.

Powderly was a good speechmaker but a very poor administrator. He had little patience with anyone who disagreed with him. He tried to supervise every detail of the union's business.

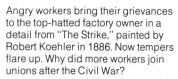

Angry workers bring their grievances to the top-hatted factory owner in a detail from "The Strike," painted by Robert Koehler in 1886. Now tempers flare up. Why did more workers join unions after the Civil War?

Collection of Lee Baxandall, New York (Photo: Gemini-Smith)

In the 1880s local leaders of the Knights organized and won several important strikes against railroads. Membership soared. By 1886 700,000 workers belonged to the organization. This was more than the central leadership could manage. Local units called strikes, which failed. Workers became discouraged and dropped out of the union.

Then the Knights were blamed, quite unfairly, for a terrible bombing incident in **Haymarket Square** in Chicago in 1886. When the police tried to break up a meeting called by radicals during a strike, someone threw a bomb that killed seven policemen. Public opinion turned against unions after the Haymarket bombing. Thousands of workers dropped out of the Knights of Labor as a result.

In 1881, long before the Knights of Labor began to decline, representatives of a number of craft unions founded the Federation of Organized Trade and Labor Unions of the United States and Canada. In 1886 this group changed its name to the **American Federation of Labor** (AFL).

The AFL was led by Samuel Gompers, a cigar maker. Unlike the Knights, the AFL was made up exclusively of skilled workers, organized by particular crafts such as printers, bricklayers, and plumbers. The AFL concentrated on **bread and butter issues**—higher wages, shorter hours, better working conditions. The way to obtain these benefits, Gompers and other leaders of the AFL insisted, was **collective bargaining** with employers. Workers should then be ready to strike to enforce union demands.

- Why was the Knights of Labor organized? How was it changed under the leadership of Terence Powderly?
- Who were the members of the American Federation of Labor?

AFL-CIO

He may look like a sheriff sent to break a strike, but this is the great Samuel Gompers, leader of the AFL. This photograph shows Gompers at the time of an AFL drive to organize West Virginia coal miners. How did the AFL seek to obtain benefits?

THE HOMESTEAD STRIKE

One of the most violent strikes in American history involved an AFL union, the Amalgamated Association of Iron and Steel Workers. In the early 1890s the Amalgamated was the most powerful union in the country. It had 24,000 dues-paying members. Some worked at the Carnegie steel plant in **Homestead,** Pennsylvania. In 1892, when the company reduced wages because of a slump in its business, the union called a strike.

Carnegie was in Scotland when the strike began. The company was being run by one of his partners, Henry Clay Frick. Frick was a tough executive and a bitter opponent of unions. He decided to resist the strike and to try to destroy the Amalgamated. With Carnegie's approval he announced that he would hire strikebreakers and reopen the Homestead mill. To protect the new workers, he hired private police from the Pinkerton Detective Agency, a company known to specialize in strikebreaking.

The Pinkerton Agency sent 300 armed men—**Pinkertons**—to Homestead. They approached the plant on barges on the Monongahela River in the dead of night. The strikers had been warned of their coming. They met them at the docks with gunfire and dynamite. A small-scale war broke out. When it ended, seven Pinkertons and nine strikers were dead. The governor of Pennsylvania then sent 8,000 National Guard troops to Homestead to keep the peace. The strike went on for more than four months. Finally the union gave up the struggle. The workers went back to the plant on Frick's terms.

Frick won the contest, but public opinion turned against him. Then a Russian immigrant, Alexander Berkman, attacked Frick in his Homestead office. To protest the use of Pinkertons, Berkman shot Frick three times in the neck and shoulder. He then stabbed him once in the leg and after that tried to chew a percussion capsule, which guards pried from his mouth. Frick survived, Berkman went to prison, and the public's attitude softened.

■ Why was the Homestead strike called? How did Henry Frick respond? What was the outcome?

THE NEW IMMIGRATION

About three quarters of the workers in the Carnegie steel mills had been born in Europe. Like most immigrants, including Carnegie himself, they had come to America to find work. To millions of poor people in other parts of the world, industrial expansion had made the United States seem like the pot of gold at the end of the rainbow.

It was as though the country were an enormous magnet drawing people into it from every direction. Between 1860 and 1900 about 14 million immigrants arrived. Most settled in large cities. In 1880 87 per cent of the residents of Chicago were either immigrants or the children of immigrants. The situation was similar in New York and San Francisco, in Milwaukee, Cleveland, Boston, and most other cities.

Before the 1880s most immigrants had come from western and northern Europe, especially from England, Ireland, Germany, and the Scandinavian countries. We have already noted that established Americans frequently resented these newcomers. However, people from western Europe had certain advantages that helped them to adjust in their new homeland. British and Irish immigrants spoke English. Many German immigrants were well educated and skilled in one or another useful trade. Scandinavians were experienced farmers and often came with enough money to buy land in the West. Except for the Irish, most of these immigrants were Protestants, as were most Americans.

568

In the 1880s the trend of immigration changed. Thousands of Italians, Poles, Hungarians, Greeks, and Russians flocked in. After 1886 the immigrants' first sight of America was often the **Statue of Liberty.** The words at its base, written by the poet Emma Lazarus, began "Give me your tired, your poor . . ." Most were indeed poor. They had little or no education and no special skills. They knew no English. Their habits and cultures were very different from those of native-born Americans. The majority were Roman or Greek Orthodox Catholics or Jews.

Many of these immigrants came from areas where money was seldom used. People there exchanged food for cloth, a cow for a wagon, and so on. It was difficult for such people to adjust to life in a large industrial city.

Museum of the City of New York

The colossal Statue of Liberty raises the torch of freedom over Upper New York Bay. It was originally known as "Liberty Enlightening the World." In this oil painted by Edward Moran in 1886, its dedication is depicted with flags flying and guns saluting. The sculptor of France's magnificent gift to America was F. A. Bartholdi. It is a tribute to the alliance of France with the American colonies during the American Revolution. The statue is today a national monument and an international symbol of freedom. From which European countries did newcomers of the 1880s arrive?

"The Battery, New York" was painted in oil about 1855 by Samuel B. Waugh. This detail shows immigrants arriving by ship. Castle Garden, at the left, was used to process the immigrants. Why did some Americans resent this new immigration?

The immigrants from each country or district tended to cluster together in the same city neighborhood. In 1890 a New York reporter wrote that a map of the city showing where different nationalities lived would have "more stripes than the skin of a zebra, and more colors than any rainbow." These **ethnic neighborhoods** were like cities within cities. They offered people newly arrived in the strange new world of America a chance to hold on to a few fragments of the world they had left. There the immigrants could find familiar foods, people who spoke their language, churches and clubs based on old-country models.

Many native-born Americans resented this **new immigration.** They insisted that the newcomers were harder to "Americanize" than earlier generations. Workers were disturbed by the new immigrants' willingness to work long hours for low wages. A new nativist organization, the **American Protective Association,** blamed the hard times of the 1890s on immigration. Nativists charged that the new immigrants were physically and mentally inferior. They were dangerous radicals, the nativists said, who wanted to destroy American democratic institutions.

In the 1890s the **Immigration Restriction League** called for a law preventing anyone who could not read and write some language from entering the country. The League knew that such a **literacy test** would keep out many immigrants from southern and eastern Europe.

570

In that part of the world many regions did not have public school systems.

Congress passed a literacy test bill in 1897, but President Grover Cleveland vetoed it. He insisted that America should continue to be a place of refuge for the world's poor and persecuted. Many employers opposed any check on immigration for less humane reasons. They knew that unlimited immigration would assure them a steady force of low-paid but hard-working laborers.

Congress *did* exclude one type of immigrant during this period—the Chinese. By 1880 there were about 75,000 Chinese immigrants in California. They were extremely hard-working people. Because of language and cultural differences, the Chinese tended even more than most immigrants to stick together. They seemed unwilling to try to adapt to American ways, to *assimilate*. Older residents feared and resented them. In 1882 Congress responded to the demands of Californians by passing the **Chinese Exclusion Act.** It prohibited Chinese workers from entering the United States for a period of ten years. Later the ban was extended. It was not lifted until 1965.

By 1900 there were about 80,000 Mexican-Americans in the southwestern part of the nation. Unlike most other immigrants, these newcomers seldom settled in large cities. Many found jobs as laborers building the Southern Pacific and Santa Fe Railroads.

When the lines were completed, they became section hands—men whose job it was to maintain the railroad right of way and repair damaged tracks and ties. This work kept them moving from place to place. Many families had to live in railroad boxcars. Other Mexican

The Granger Collection

Two by two these newcomers enter the U.S. Ark of Refuge, there to be greeted by a kindly Uncle Sam. The Biblical story of Noah is the basis of this lithograph by Joseph Keppler. "Welcome to All" was published in 1880. 'No expensive kings' pledges one sign. Another offers 'free lunch' in a 'free land.' Meanwhile the sky grows stormy and goblins appear in the heavens. But the real flood is that of the immigrants themselves, and soon quotas will be passed to restrict their entry. Who opposed a check on immigration at this time?

immigrants worked as cowhands on cattle ranches. Still others became farm laborers. Like so many immigrants, the Mexican-Americans were poorly paid and oftentimes badly treated.

- How did the immigrants coming to the United States after the 1880s differ from those who had come earlier?
- How did immigrants in cities tend to live?
- How were Chinese immigrants treated? Mexican immigrants?

THE GROWTH OF CITIES

American agriculture was expanding with American industry. But machinery was reducing the need for human labor on farms. Cyrus McCormick's reapers and other new farm machines were displacing thousands of farmhands who had previously plowed, planted, hoed, and harvested the nation's crops. For every city dweller who took up the plow between 1860 and 1900, 20 farmers moved to the city.

The growth of cities after the Civil War was both rapid and widespread. In 1860 places like Birmingham, Denver, Memphis, and Seattle were no more than small towns. By 1900 they were major urban centers. In that same year there were 50 cities of over 100,000 population.

The largest cities were centers of both manufacturing and commerce, and they did not depend on any one activity for their prosperity. Some smaller cities specialized in making a particular product. Dayton, Ohio, manufactured cash registers. Minneapolis, Minnesota, became a flour-milling center.

People moved to cities far more rapidly than housing and other facilities could be built to care for their needs. City land values

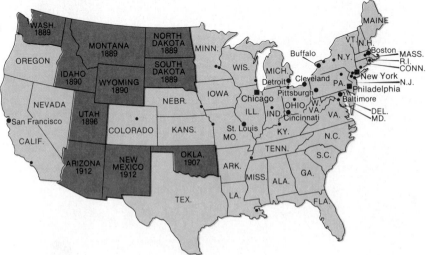

U.S. CITIES IN 1900

- ■ Larger than 1 million people
- ● 300,000 to 1 million people
- · 100,000 to 300,000 people
- New States after 1888

BUILDING SKILLS IN SOCIAL STUDIES

Reading a Table

Several kinds of graphs have been used in this book to show statistics, including a picture (page 95), a bar graph (page 215), and a line graph (page 268). Another useful way to show statistics is by arranging them on a *table*, shown below.

A picture graph gives a quick, general impression. It is used to make broad comparisons when precise figures are not so important. A bar graph is most effective for comparing statistics. And a line graph is particularly helpful in finding trends.

A table is especially valuable for use in organizing several sets of numbers. Exact or round numbers may be used in any number of columns to show growth or change. The table below shows population growth in the United States between the years 1860 and 1900 in twenty-year intervals.

Study the table carefully and then answer the questions in the next column.

1. What is the purpose of this table?
2. What was Boston's population in 1880?
3. Which city had the largest population in each of the years shown on the table? What was its population in each year?
4. Which city had the smallest population in 1860? In 1880? In 1900?
5. Which city had the third largest population in 1880? Where did it rank in 1900?
6. Which city more than tripled in size between 1880 and 1900?
7. Which city doubled in size between 1860 and 1900?
8. To show the trend of a particular city's growth, would you use a line graph or a bar graph? Explain your answer.
9. Which would you use to compare the populations of several cities in 1900: a line graph or a bar graph? Tell why.
10. Draw a bar graph for the populations of cities shown on the table for the year 1900.

POPULATION OF MAJOR U.S. CITIES

City	1860	1880	1900
New York City	1,174,800	1,912,000	3,437,000
Philadelphia	565,500	847,000	1,294,000
Boston	177,800	363,000	561,000
Baltimore	212,400	332,000	509,000
Cincinnati	161,000	255,000	326,000
St. Louis	160,800	350,000	575,000
Chicago	109,300	503,000	1,698,000

soared. A New York City lot selling for $80 in the early 1840s sold for $8,000 in 1880. Because of the high cost of property, builders put up tenement apartments on plots only 25 feet (about 8 meters) wide. They were crowded so closely together that light and moving air were blocked out.

A five- or six-story tenement usually had four apartments on each floor. Front apartments contained four rooms, rear apartments three. Many of the rooms had no windows. In most cases two families had to share a single toilet located in a dark and narrow hallway. Dark, musty, garbage-cluttered "air shafts" separated one tenement building from the next.

Police and fire protection remained inadequate in most cities. Garbage collection was haphazard at best. City water was often impure. Sewers were smelly and often clogged. Disease could spread quickly under these conditions. In one crowded Chicago neighborhood three out of every five babies born in 1900 died before they were three years old.

Of course, many people worked hard trying to solve the cities' problems and improve urban living conditions. Boards of health made studies and established standards for sewage and garbage disposal. Elaborate systems of pipes and reservoirs brought pure water from distant lakes and rivers. Social workers established community centers called **settlement houses** in poor neighborhoods. Settlement houses had something for everyone—day nurseries for little children, gymnasiums and social activities for young and old, English classes for immigrants.

The most famous of the settlement houses was **Hull House** in Chicago, founded in 1889 by Jane Addams. Many of the settlement workers were young women who had graduated from college. They lived in the settlement houses and tried to become part of the community. They believed that they could grow personally by involving themselves in local political and social affairs. At the same time they were helping local people.

As cities grew larger, transportation became a problem. In 1865 most large cities had streetcars drawn by horses. Horses were slow and needed a great deal of care. In 1873 Andrew S. Hallidie installed **cable cars** on the steep hills of San Francisco, which horses could not climb. Hallidie used a long wire cable attached to a stationary steam engine to pull the cars.

Then, in the late 1880s, Frank J. Sprague designed the first electrified street railways in America. In 1887 he opened a 12-mile line (about 19 kilometers) in Richmond, Virginia. By 1890 51 American cities had **electric trolley** systems.

As time passed, hundreds of bridges, paved roads, parks, and grand public buildings improved the appearance of cities and the

Jane Addams as a young woman sat for this photograph in about 1890. She founded Hull House in Chicago with Ellen Gates Starr. In 1931 Addams was awarded the Nobel Peace Prize. What were settlement houses?

Culver Pictures

quality of city life. The most famous symbol of the modern city was the **Brooklyn Bridge** in New York City. The Brooklyn Bridge took 13 years to build. It was designed by John A. Roebling and built by his son Washington. Washington Roebling was disabled during the construction and unable to walk about. He supervised the project from a nearby apartment, keeping track of progress with binoculars and a telescope.

Thus arose industrial America. In 1865 most people lived much the same way as their parents and grandparents had. The lives of the people of 1900 were far different—closer to what we know today.

■ What problems were faced by cities during their rapid growth?

The rise of industrial America has a fitting symbol in the Brooklyn Bridge, which spans New York's East River. It cost $15 million and 20 lives, one that of its designer, John Roebling. His son Washington, *above*, was disabled for life by working in the compressed air of its caissons. He watched over the work from a nearby apartment. On May 24, 1883, the bridge was opened with fireworks and a water parade, shown below. A pedestrian of that era paid a penny to cross or ten cents for horse and carriage. What other advances in transportation were made in this era?

Metropolitan Museum of Art

CHAPTER 19 REVIEW

Identification

Tell briefly why each of the following persons, terms, or events is important.

1. Cornelius Vanderbilt
2. Henry Bessemer
3. Andrew Carnegie
4. Samuel F. B. Morse
5. Alexander Graham Bell
6. Thomas Alva Edison
7. John D. Rockefeller
8. Terence V. Powderly
9. Samuel Gompers
10. Jane Addams
11. Corporations
12. Monopoly
13. Trust
14. Interstate Commerce Act
15. Sherman Antitrust Act
16. American Federation of Labor
17. Collective bargaining
18. Homestead strike
19. Chinese Exclusion Act
20. Settlement houses

Understanding American History

1. What were some of the major changes in the United States in the years between the Civil War and 1900?
2. How did the railroad network help to build up the American economy?
3. Explain how the railroads and the steel industry helped each other grow.
4. What was the communications revolution? How did it affect the American economy?
5. What is a monopoly? How did railroad competition lead to monopoly in other fields?
6. Why were many Americans alarmed by the supercompanies called trusts?
7. How were the Interstate Commerce Act and Sherman Antitrust Act supposed to regulate business? Were they successful? Explain.
8. How did industrialization and the increased use of machines affect the men and women who worked in factories?
9. Why did many Americans oppose the new immigration in the 1880s and 1890s? Why did others favor it?
10. What were some problems faced by growing cities between 1860 and 1900? What were some attempts to improve city life?

Activities

1. Write a story on the following idea: An ordinary citizen who lived in 1800 returns for a look at America in 1900. What are the reactions of this traveler from the time of Jefferson's "nation of farmers" to the sprawling cities and industries of 1900? Which changes impress your time traveler, and which might be upsetting? In another version of the same story imagine a time traveler from 1900 who visits the America of the year 2000.
2. Prepare a multimedia presentation on the railroad network that was built after the Civil War. In pictures, stories, and perhaps songs, show how Americans have been fascinated with railroads.
3. Use your library or other American histories to report on the life of one of the following figures in industrial America:

Cornelius Vanderbilt	Samuel F. B. Morse
Andrew Carnegie	Alexander Graham Bell
John D. Rockefeller	Thomas A. Edison
Cyrus W. Field	Samuel Gompers
Terence V. Powderly	Jane Addams

4. Using historical imagination, place yourself in the year 1890. A few months ago, on your twenty-first birthday, you moved from your parents' farm to find work in the city. Write a letter to the folks at home telling them about city life.
5. Use historical imagination to place yourself in a telegraph office in Homestead, Pennsylvania, in 1892. Send off a report on the clash of strikers and Pinkertons. Include the views of both sides in the Homestead strike.

CHAPTER 19 TEST

Matching (45 points)
Number your paper 1–15 and match the description in the first column with the name in the second column.

1. Inventor of the telegraph
2. Founder of Standard Oil
3. Inventor of the telephone
4. President of the American Federation of Labor
5. Helped improve the lives of city dwellers at Hull House in Chicago
6. Developed a process to quickly and cheaply convert iron into steel
7. Made a fortune in the steel industry
8. President of the Knights of Labor when it admitted women, blacks, immigrants, and unskilled workers
9. Organizer of the New York Central Railroad
10. Inventor of the phonograph and the first practical electric light
11. Laid a telegraph cable across the Atlantic
12. Driller of the first oil well, in Pennsylvania
13. Designer of Rockefeller's supercompany, the trust
14. Builder of the Brooklyn Bridge
15. Poet whose words appear with the Statue of Liberty

a. John D. Rockefeller
b. Samuel Gompers
c. Samuel, C. T. Dodd
d. Jane Addams
e. Washington Roebling
f. Cornelius Vanderbilt
g. Alexander Graham Bell
h. Emma Lazarus
i. Andrew Carnegie
j. Henry Bessemer
k. Thomas A. Edison
l. E. L. Drake
m. Samuel F. B. Morse
n. Terence V. Powderly
o. Cyrus W. Field

Completion (25 points)
Number your paper 16–25 and next to each number write the words from the list below that best complete each sentence.

trust	overhead
cutthroat competition	regulatory agencies
communications revolution	"black gold"
Knights of Labor	corporations
collective bargaining	literacy test

16. Businesses called _____ issue stock in order to raise large amounts of money.
17. Railroads had heavy _____, or fixed operating costs.
18. Members of the Immigration Restriction League proposed a _____ to keep out many eastern and southern Europeans.
19. The telegraph and telephone led to a time known as the _____ in America.
20. The _____ admitted unskilled as well as skilled workers to its membership.
21. The United States government set up _____ to give the public greater control over large industries.
22. A supercompany known as a _____ controls an industry by controlling the stock of several companies.
23. Prospectors for oil, called wildcatters, drilled for what they called _____.
24. Railroads often used _____ to run rival companies out of business.
25. Unions called for _____ in order to get better wages and working conditions.

Essay (30 points)
Explain how the growth of railroads and the growth of the steel industry were related, *or* Explain the effect the growth of business had on immigration and U.S. cities.

CHAPTER 20
National Politics, 1867–1896

A Good Summary

The Civil War and the rapid expansion of the economy that followed it had important effects on American government and politics. So did the great social changes, especially the flood of new immigrants and the shift of population from the farms to the cities. New issues arose as conditions changed. Older political questions had to be reconsidered too.

The Democratic and Republican parties had to deal with difficult and confusing problems. By and large, they failed to find clear solutions to these problems. But their efforts are worth studying closely.

REFIGHTING THE CIVIL WAR

From a political point of view, the Civil War did not end in 1865. Nor did it end in 1877 when the North gave up trying to control the South by force. Indeed, the effects of that war are with us today, more than a century after the Confederacy collapsed.

In the 1850s the controversy over slavery in the territories led most white southerners to become Democrats. When the war ended, most stayed Democrats. After southern whites regained control of their local governments in the 1870s, they voted Democratic in national elections almost to a man. With southern blacks not permitted to vote, the Republican party had no chance at all in any southern states. People spoke of the **Solid South.** Every state that had seceded from the Union cast its electoral votes for the Democratic candidate in every Presidential election from 1880 until 1928.

The Republican party had become the leading party in the North and West by 1860. It remained so throughout the decades after the Civil War. Memories of the war stirred up strong emotions and had a great influence on how people voted. Tens of thousands saw the Republicans as the saviors of the Union, the Democrats as the disloyal dividers of the United States. These views held long after slavery had been done away with and the idea of secession abandoned by even its most extreme southern supporters.

After the war Congress had dozens of important issues to decide. Few of these issues had any connection with the geographical division that separated Democrats from Republicans. Yet Republican politicians constantly made emotional appeals to voters by reminding them that the Democrats were "ex-rebels."

Culver Pictures

food and small sums of money. The machines ran community picnics on holidays. They helped local youngsters who got in trouble with the law.

In return for their help the bosses expected the people to vote for the machine's candidates. By controlling elections, the bosses could reward their friends or line their own pockets. For example, companies that wanted to operate streetcar lines or sell gas or electricity for lighting homes or businesses needed permits called **franchises.** Bosses often demanded large bribes before they would have these franchises issued by the local officials they controlled. They also made deals with contractors who put up public buildings or did other work for the city. The bosses agreed to pay needlessly high prices for the work in return for large **kickbacks** from the contractors.

The machines did both good and harm in their day. Not all of them were associated with the Democratic party. The powerful Philadelphia machine, for example, was a Republican organization. So were many of the machines in middle-sized cities. But most of the big-city machines were run by the Democrats. They were very useful to the national Democratic party in Presidential elections in close states like New York.

  How did the political machines in northern cities attract the votes of recent immigrants?

On the eve of New York City's 1871 election Thomas Nast first drew the Tammany tiger. When this cartoon appeared in *Harper's* magazine, the city bosses threatened to cancel all orders of Harper Brother's textbooks. "The Tammany Tiger Loose" upset Boss Tweed, who had said, "as long as I count the votes, what are you going to do about it?" Nast asked the same question to his readers in the subtitle of this cartoon: "What Are You Going to Do About It?" In what ways did the political bosses make deals?

American Politics

Election campaigns in the 1870s and 1880s were colorful, exciting affairs. Political meetings, called rallies, were held in every community. Bands played. Local party workers wearing badges and campaign ribbons paraded by the thousands through the streets. They carried flags, banners, torches, and posters bearing the names of candidates and party slogans.

Popular speakers were in great demand. For months before elections they traveled on tight schedules from place to place, saying more or less the same thing over and over again. Their speeches sometimes went on for hours. Some received as must as $150 for a single speech, a very large sum in those days.

Ordinary people paid a great deal of attention to politics. A much larger proportion of eligible voters actually voted than has been true in recent times. Did they do so because the campaigns were so intense and colorful? Or were the campaigns intense and colorful because the people were so interested in politics? Unfortunately, these kinds of questions are almost impossible for historians to answer!

Colorado Historical Society

Torchlight and fireworks illuminate this parade for Benjamin Harrison, candidate for President in 1888.

SITTING ON THE FENCE

Extremely important social and economic problems were being discussed and settled at this time. There were problems caused by industrial expansion and technological change. Other problems resulted from the growth of cities. Still other problems related to racial questions and to immigration. Logically, the parties should have fought their campaigns on these issues.

They rarely did so. Each was afraid that a strong stand on any controversial question would cost votes. It seemed politically safer to make vague statements that everyone could accept, even if no one entirely agreed with them. This was called **sitting on the fence.**

Still, the issues remained, and politicians had to deal with them in one way or another. For example, the need to regulate railroads and other big businesses resulted in the Interstate Commerce Act and the Sherman Antitrust Act. The Indian lands of the West were seized and divided up. During these years Congress and the Presidents struggled with high protective tariffs on imported manufactured goods. They tried to solve what was known as "the money question." And they attempted to reform the way government employees were hired and fired.

- What problems arose after the Civil War?
- What was meant by "sitting on the fence"?

THE TARIFF ISSUE

When the United States first began to develop manufacturing about the time of the War of 1812, a strong case could be made for tariffs which heavily taxed foreign manufactured goods. American "infant industries" needed protection in order to compete with larger, more efficient producers in Europe.

After the Civil War the need for protection was much less clear. America was rapidly becoming the largest manufacturing nation in the world. Its factories were efficient. The costs of doing business were lower than in many foreign countries. Manufacturers did not, however, want to give up the extra profits that the **protective tariffs** made possible.

High tariffs raised the prices that farmers and other consumers had to pay for manufactured goods. Many, therefore, were opposed to the policy of protection. A number of tariff laws were passed by Congress between 1865 and 1900. Democrats and Republicans devoted much time to arguing about tariff policy. Neither party took a clear stand on the question. The rates of various imported products were raised and lowered, then lowered and raised, then raised again. No firm decision was ever made about whether protection was good for the nation as a whole.

C. J. Taylor drew this cartoon to show the plight of the farmer, who opposed high tariffs. The caption reads "The Tariff Cow—the Farmer Feeds Her—the Monopolist Gets the Milk." What were protective tariffs?

HBJ Photo

The Democrats tended to be for lowering the tariff, the Republicans for keeping it high. But so many members of Congress from each party voted the other way that it is impossible to say that the tariff was a clear-cut party issue.

- Why did manufacturers favor keeping protective tariffs?
- Why did farmers and other consumers oppose high tariffs?

THE MONEY QUESTION

From the days of Andrew Jackson to the Civil War, the United States had followed a **monetary policy** that was conservative and cautious. All paper money in circulation could be exchanged for gold or silver coins at a bank. Yet during the Civil War, as we have seen, the government could not raise enough money by taxing and borrowing to pay all its expenses. It had to print $492 million in paper money called **greenbacks,** which could not be exchanged for coin. The back sides of these bills were printed in green ink. Paper money printed in yellow ink, popularly called **hard money,** could be exchanged for gold.

The question after the war was what should be done about the greenbacks? Most people believed either that they should be able to exchange greenbacks for gold or silver or that greenbacks should be withdrawn from circulation entirely.

What was done about the greenbacks was sure to affect the lives of most Americans. People who had bought government bonds during the war had paid for them with greenback dollars, which were worth much less than gold or silver coins of the same face value. If these purchasers were paid back in gold when the bonds fell due, they would make very large profits. If the greenbacks were withdrawn by the government, the amount of money in circulation would decline. This would cause **deflation.** Prices of all goods would fall. Every dollar would buy more. Once again, those with money on hand would make large gains. But those people who had borrowed greenbacks would have to repay their loans with more valuable money. They would lose.

Farmers in particular tended to be hurt by deflation after the Civil War. During the war they had borrowed money to buy more land and machinery. They had paid high prices because of the wartime inflation. If the price level fell, the money they paid out to cancel their debts would be more valuable than the money they had borrowed. If wheat sold for $1.50 a bushel when the money was borrowed and for only 50 cents a bushel when it had to be repaid, the farmer would have to produce three times as much wheat to pay off the debt.

Cooper-Hewitt Museum/Smithsonian Institution

Peter Cooper was the candidate of the Greenback party in the election of 1876. He received 80,000 votes. This campaign poster celebrates Cooper's career, which ranged from glue maker and iron worker to head of North American Telegraph. He is remembered as the builder of *Tom Thumb,* one of the first locomotives (page 312), and Cooper Union, seen in the lower right-hand corner of the poster. It provided an education for working folks. Why had greenbacks come into existence?

Beginning in 1866, the government gradually withdrew greenbacks from circulation. This was called **retiring the greenbacks.** The fewer greenbacks in public hands, the less people would fear that the government would print more and cause **inflation.** As Secretary of the Treasury Hugh McCulloch explained, the purpose of retiring the greenbacks was to end uncertainty about the money supply and encourage people to be "industrious, economical [and] honest."

However, reducing the money supply alarmed many business leaders. Early in 1868 Congress decided not to allow any further retirement of greenbacks. The argument continued until 1879 when the remaining greenbacks were made convertible into gold. Thereafter, greenback dollars were the same as any other American bank notes.

- How did greenbacks differ from hard money?
- Who favored retiring the greenbacks? Which group would be hurt by deflation if the greenbacks were retired?

Calvin Curtis painted this portrait of President James A. Garfield. In what way did federal employment change as the U.S. grew larger?

CIVIL SERVICE REFORM

As the United States grew larger, the number of people who worked for the government increased rapidly. There were about 27,000 postmasters in 1869 and over 75,000 in 1900. In the same period the Treasury Department payroll grew from about 4,000 persons to over 24,000. In the 1830s the entire government had employed fewer than 24,000 people.

Much of the work done by the government became increasingly technical. This meant that federal workers needed more skills and experience to perform their jobs efficiently. The new Department of Agriculture, created in the 1860s, employed chemists and biologists in large numbers. Even so-called routine jobs called for people with specialized skills. The introduction of the typewriter in the 1880s, for example, affected the training needed to become a government secretary or clerk.

These developments made the **spoils system** and the Jacksonians' idea of **rotation in office** badly out of date. The dismissal of large numbers of government workers each time a new President took office caused much confusion and waste. The President and other high officials had to spend weeks deciding who of the tens of thousands of employees was to be kept, who fired, and who hired.

At the same time it became difficult to recruit properly trained people for government service. Men and women of ability did not want to give up good jobs to work for a government department. They knew that they might be fired after the next election no matter how well they had done their work.

After the Civil War many thoughtful people began to urge **civil service reform.** Most government jobs below the level of policy makers like Cabinet members and their assistants should be taken out of politics, the reformers said. Applicants should have to take tests, and those with the best scores should be selected without regard for which political party they supported. Once appointed, civil service workers should be discharged only if they failed to perform their duties properly. This was known as the **merit system.**

The problem with civil service reform was that the political parties depended upon the spoils system for rewarding the organizers who ran political campaigns. Presidents and state governors used their powers of appointment, called **patronage,** to persuade legislators to support their programs. They would promise to give government jobs to friends and supporters of the legislators in exchange for the legislators' votes on key issues.

Civil service reform was not an issue that a particular party favored. When the Republicans were in office, the Democrats called for reform. When the Democrats won elections, the Republicans became civil service reformers. The party that controlled the govern-

The New York Historical Society

The good ship *Democracy* tosses in stormy seas while its captain at the stern, President Grover Cleveland, cuts away at mutineers who promote a silver purchase bill. W. A. Rogers is the artist of this *Harper's Weekly* cartoon, published in 1894. Reforms in civil service and tariffs are about to be "deep sixed." On deck is the Tammany tiger gorging itself. What event led to civil service reform?

ment tended to resist reform. Its leaders needed the jobs to reward their supporters. Nevertheless, the need for government efficiency could not be ignored much longer. By 1880 the reformers were increasing in number.

Then came the tragic assassination of President James A. Garfield shortly after he took office in 1881. Garfield was shot in a Washington railroad station by Charles Guiteau, a Republican who had been trying without success to get a job in the State Department. Chester A. Arthur succeeded to the Presidency. A great public cry went up for taking government jobs out of politics. Finally, in 1883, Congress passed the **Pendleton Act** creating a **Civil Service Commission.**

President Chester A. Arthur is the subject of Daniel Huntington's oil. He succeeded to the Presidency after Garfield's assassination in 1881. Arthur was said to look every inch a President. Which reform took place during his Presidency?

Its charge was to make up and administer examinations for applicants seeking certain government jobs. Those with the best scores on the tests were to get the appointments. The Pendleton Act also outlawed the practice of making government employees contribute to political campaign funds.

At first only 15,000 jobs were **classified,** or placed under civil service rules, by the 1883 law. But the number of posts covered was steadily increased over the years. By 1900 about half of all federal employees were under the civil service system.

- Why did the spoils system and rotation of office become badly out of date by the 1870s?
- What proposals did civil service reformers make? How did the Pendleton Act bring reforms in civil service?

POLITICAL "MUSICAL CHAIRS"

Since neither Democrats nor Republicans took firm stands on the real issues, there were few real differences between them. This helps explain why elections were usually close.

In 1880 James A. Garfield got 48.3 per cent of the popular vote for President. He defeated the Democrat, Winfield Scott Hancock, by only 7,000 votes out of nearly 9.2 million cast. Four years later, Grover Cleveland, a Democrat, won with 48.5 per cent of the popular vote. His margin over Republican James G. Blaine was 4.87 million to 4.85 million.

In 1888 Cleveland was defeated by Benjamin Harrison. Although President Cleveland got more popular votes, Harrison had a majority of the electoral vote, 233 to 168. In the next Presidential election Cleveland defeated Harrison and returned to the White

Presidents Cleveland and Harrison, *left to right,* twice opposed each other for the White House. In 1888 Benjamin Harrison was elected and in 1892 Grover Cleveland returned to the White House, where he had been President from 1885 to 1889. Harrison's portrait is by Eastman Johnson, c. 1889. Why were there few differences between Democrats and Republicans at this time?

House. Yet he got only 46 per cent of the popular vote to Harrison's 43 per cent.

In all of these elections no one got a majority of the popular vote because third-party candidates were in the field. These candidates *did* stand for "real issues." There were Greenback party candidates running in 1880 and 1884, for example. They demanded that more rather than fewer greenbacks be put in circulation. Other candidates ran on platforms calling for prohibition of liquor.

The Presidents were elected by such narrow margins that they had relatively little influence while in office. They could not claim to have a **mandate**—the backing of a solid majority of the people—when they presented their programs to Congress.

"His grandfather's hat was too big for his head," sang opponents of Benjamin Harrison when he sought the Presidency. A bust of William Henry Harrison, the Presidential grandfather, gazes down. Joseph Keppler drew this caricature. Why did no candidate get a majority of the popular vote during the era of political "musical chairs"?

In Congress the Democrats had a majority of the House of Representatives from 1874 to 1880 and from 1882 to 1888. But they had a majority of the Senate for only two years during this entire period. Turnover among representatives was extremely rapid. Often more than half the members of the House were first-termers. Without experienced members, Congress was inefficient. With narrow, shifting majorities, it was difficult to pass controversial measures.

■ Why did the Presidents elected after the Civil War have little influence? Why was Congress inefficient?

HARD TIMES FOR THE FARMER

The times were particularly frustrating for farmers. Falling agricultural prices hurt them badly. So did the protective tariffs which

"I Pay for All" says the legend below this sturdy Granger. The lithograph is dated 1873. Rural scenes surround an ideal farmer, including the Biblical Ruth and Boaz, *lower right;* a harvest dance, *lower left;* a farmer's fireside, *upper left;* and the Grange in session, *upper right.* How did the purpose of the Grange change in the 1870s?

raised the prices of the manufactured goods they purchased. But neither party was willing to work for laws that would bring much relief. Farmers turned elsewhere in search of help.

In the 1870s many farmers joined the **National Grange.** The Grange was originally a kind of social club. It soon became a political organization as well. Many branches sprang up, especially in the northeastern quarter of the nation.

Granger leaders believed that railroad freight charges were too high. Because railroads had a monopoly on moving bulky goods to distant markets, Granger leaders demanded government regulation of rates. Their efforts led to the passage of **Granger Laws** in many states. These measures set the rates that railroads and grain warehouses could collect so farmers would not be overcharged.

This raised the question of whether businesses like railroads could be regulated "in the public interest." Yes, ruled the Supreme Court in the case of *Munn v. Illinois* (1877). Granger laws were constitutional. Businesses like railroads that provided broad public services could not be considered completely private.

- What made hard times for farmers after the Civil War?
- How were Granger Laws supposed to help farmers?

THE SILVER ISSUE

Lower freight and storage charges did not help farmers as much as the Grangers had hoped. Costs were not reduced much. So farmers tried instead to raise the prices of their produce. The best way to push up prices seemed to be by causing inflation. Farmers looked for a way to put more money in circulation so their prices would rise. One way was by **coining silver** money.

Throughout the period before the Civil War both gold and silver had been minted into coins and used to back bank notes. But in 1873 Congress had voted to stop coining silver. That seemed a terrible mistake to those who favored inflation.

Many new silver mines had been discovered. If miners could bring their silver to the United States mint for coining, more money would be created. With more money in circulation, prices would rise. Yet silver was a relatively scarce metal. The amount that could be mined would place a limit on the amount of new money that could be put into circulation. This would prevent **runaway inflation,** which might result if there was no limit on how much paper money could be printed.

Farmers and silver miners joined to make a powerful political force. People began to refer to the law that had discontinued the coining of silver as the **Crime of 1873.** They demanded that the government once again coin all the silver brought to the Mint.

The silver issue eventually led to a split in the Democratic party, shown by this 1896 political cartoon by J. S. Pughe. The Silverite runs away with the party's donkey while the "Sound Money" Democrat pursues. Which side of the split does this political cartoonist seem to take?

The result of their pressure was a political compromise. In 1878 Congress passed a bill sponsored by Representative Richard Bland of Missouri and Senator William B. Allison of Iowa. Bland was a Democrat who believed sincerely in coining both gold and silver. Allison, a Republican, was a shrewd political manipulator. (It was said of Allison that he would make no more noise walking across the Senate floor in wooden shoes than a fly made walking on the ceiling.)

The **Bland-Allison Act** ordered the Secretary of the Treasury to purchase and coin between $2 and $4 million in silver each month. In 1890 another coinage law, the **Sherman Silver Purchase Act,** increased the amount of silver coined to 4.5 million ounces a month. This came to about the total being mined at that time.

The price of silver was usually expressed by comparing it to the price of gold. In 1873, when the Mint had stopped coining silver, an ounce of gold was worth about 16 times as much as an ounce of silver. By 1890, when the Sherman Silver Purchase Act was passed, an ounce of gold was worth 20 times as much. This was because the price of silver was falling steeply at the same time as the supply was increasing from new mines in the West.

Farmers and others who favored inflation wanted as much silver coined as possible in order to increase the money supply. If the United States would coin all the world's silver, the price of other products would rise because more money would be in circulation. Those who favored inflation therefore urged **free coinage**—that is, a law requiring the Mint to turn all the silver offered it into silver dollars.

The silver miners were more interested in driving up the price of their silver than in what was done with it. They wanted the United States to exchange an ounce of gold for 16 ounces of silver. Thus, farmers and silver miners combined their interests. They demanded free coinage of silver at a ratio of **16 to 1** with gold.

- Why did farmers favor coining silver money?
- What did people describe as "the Crime of 1873"?
- What is meant by free coinage?
- What did the ratio of 16 to 1 express in coinage?

THE POPULIST PARTY

While the demand for free silver was developing, farmers were looking for other ways out of their hard times. First in Texas, and then elsewhere in the South, a new movement was spreading. It was the **Farmers Alliance.**

Like the earlier National Grange, the Alliance began as a social organization. In many areas local Alliance clubs formed **co-ops** to sell their crops at better prices. These co-ops also purchased goods wholesale to save money for their members. By 1890 the Alliance movement had spread northward into Kansas, Nebraska, and the Dakotas.

Like the Grange, the Alliance became an important political force. Its leaders campaigned against high railroad freight rates and high interest rates charged by banks for mortgages and other loans. Alliance members began to run for local offices, promising if elected to help farmers.

In 1890 several southern states elected governors backed by the Alliance. More than 45 "Alliancemen" were elected to Congress. Alliance officials were encouraged by these results. They decided to establish a new political party and run a candidate for President in 1892. To broaden their appeal, they persuaded representatives of labor unions to join with them. They named their new organization the **People's party,** but it is usually referred to as the **Populist party.**

In July 1892 the first Populist nominating convention met at Omaha, Nebraska. The delegates adopted a platform that called for a long list of specific reforms. One was government ownership of railroads and of the telegraph and telephone network. Another was a federal income tax. Still another was a program of government loans to farmers who would store their crops in government warehouses as security for the loans.

To win the support of industrial workers, the Populist platform called for the eight-hour workday and for restrictions on immigration. It also demanded the "free and unlimited coinage of silver and gold at . . . 16 to 1."

Nebraska Historical Society

James B. Weaver was the nominee chosen by the People's party at its convention held in Omaha in 1892. One spectator saved the ticket at the right as a souvenir. How did the party "balance" its ticket?

PEOPLES PARTY
NATIONAL CONVENTION
OMAHA,   JULY 2ND 1892.
ADMIT ONE
TO SEAT AND SECTION INDICATED ON MARGIN OF THIS TICKET.

ADMISSION AT ➤ EAST ENTRANCE ➤
Thos. Swobe
CHAIRMAN
OF GENERAL CITIZENS COMMITTEE OF ARRANGEMENTS.

SECTION 9
SEAT NO. 7

The Populists chose James Baird Weaver of Iowa as their candidate for President in 1892. He had fought bravely for the Union in the Civil War, rising from lieutenant to brigadier general. Their candidate for Vice President was James G. Field of Virginia, a former general in the Confederate army.

The Populists took clear stands on controversial issues, seeking voters who agreed with their ideas. Democratic and Republican leaders continued to duck controversial questions. In the South the Populists tried to unite black and white farmers. There were many blacks in the Alliance movement in the southern states, although their groups were segregated from the whites.

The 1892 Presidential election was an exciting one. General Weaver got over a million votes, a large number for a third-party candidate. The Populist party won many local contests. On balance, however, the results disappointed the Populists. They lost many votes in the South because large numbers of their white supporters refused to vote for candidates who appealed openly for black support.

- Why did local Farmers Alliance clubs form co-ops?
- How did the Populists differ from Republicans and Democrats in the election of 1892?

596

BUILDING SKILLS IN SOCIAL STUDIES

Reading Election Maps

The maps below are called *election maps*. They show the electoral votes cast by each state in the Presidential elections of 1888 and 1892. The percentages of the electoral and popular vote are given in *circle graphs* with each map.

To be elected President, a candidate must win a simple majority (more than half) of the electoral votes. If no candidate wins a majority, the House of Representatives must choose from the three leading candidates.

1. Which candidate carried the Solid South in 1888? in 1892? Who won each election?
2. Which candidate carried the close states of Indiana and New York in 1888? Which won these states in 1892?
3. Which states divided their electoral votes in 1892?
4. In which states did the third-party Populists win electoral votes in 1892?
5. Name two states that changed from Republican in 1888 to Democratic in 1892.

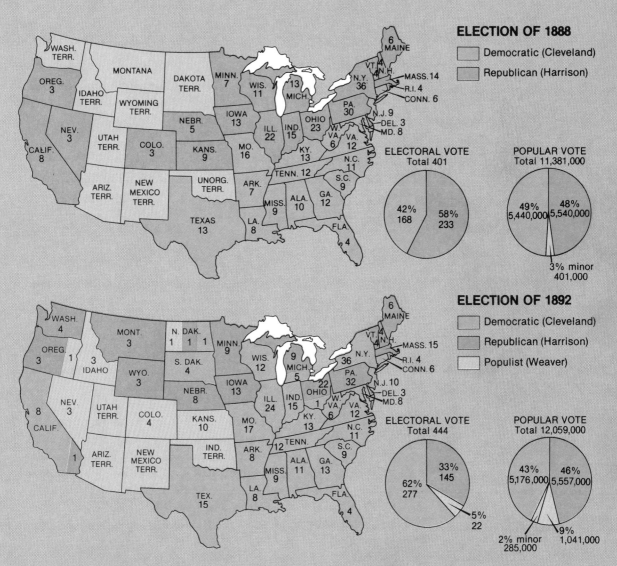

ELECTION OF 1888

- Democratic (Cleveland)
- Republican (Harrison)

ELECTORAL VOTE
Total 401

42% 168
58% 233

POPULAR VOTE
Total 11,381,000

49% 5,440,000
48% 5,540,000
3% minor 401,000

ELECTION OF 1892

- Democratic (Cleveland)
- Republican (Harrison)
- Populist (Weaver)

ELECTORAL VOTE
Total 444

33% 145
62% 277
5% 22

POPULAR VOTE
Total 12,059,000

43% 5,176,000
46% 5,557,000
2% minor 285,000
9% 1,041,000

THE DEPRESSION OF 1893

Shortly after the Presidential election, which Grover Cleveland won, the country entered into the worst period of hard times in its history. Business activity slowed down. Unemployment increased. By the end of 1893 more than a hundred railroads had gone bankrupt. People began to hoard money, withdrawing their savings in gold from the banks.

The long period of deflation that began in the 1870s was an important cause of this depression. But President Cleveland believed the business decline was caused by the uncertainty people had about the safety of their money. The government should stop coining silver, he insisted, and go back to the single **gold standard.** In October 1893 he persuaded Congress to repeal the Sherman Silver Purchase Act.

This action angered those who favored coining silver as well as gold. It split the Democratic party. And it did not end the depression. During 1894-95, economic conditions got worse rather than better.

■ How was the country affected by the Depression of 1893?
■ Why did President Cleveland want to return to the single gold standard?

COXEY'S ARMY

As the depression dragged on, large numbers of unemployed men took to wandering about the countryside. These people were called tramps. Some thought them dangerous troublemakers, perhaps even revolutionaries who wanted to overthrow the government. In truth, they only wanted work.

Small groups of unemployed workers began making protest marches to seek government relief. This increased fear of the "tramp problem." The most important of these marches was headed by Jacob Coxey, who was himself a prosperous business leader.

Coxey's Army marched from Massillon, Ohio, to Washington, attracting an enormous amount of attention. One observer claimed that for every two marchers there was at least one newspaper reporter tagging along to describe the happenings.

Coxey's Army set out in March 1894 and reached Washington in May. There were only a few hundred marchers, most of them obviously harmless people. But when Coxey tried to present a petition to Congress, he was arrested for trespassing on the grounds of the Capitol. The army then broke up Coxey's followers and sent the marchers straggling home. Their march came to nothing.

What makes Coxey's Army important historically is the plan that Coxey worked out for dealing with the depression. The federal government should spend $500 million improving rural roads, he

The Granger Collection

Jacob Coxey of Ohio was arrested in 1894 for walking on the Capitol lawn. This photograph was taken on June 10 as he left the district jail in Washington, D.C. What was the success of Coxey's Army?

said. It should also lend money to state and local governments for other public works projects. The work itself should be done by the unemployed. Anyone without a job should be put to work.

Coxey further proposed that both the $500 million spent by the federal government and the money lent to local governments should simply be printed by the Treasury. Like the Civil War greenbacks, this money would not be backed by gold or silver. This inflation of the money supply would cause prices to rise. That would help farmers and debtors of all sorts. Coxey's program seemed radical and impractical in 1894. Forty years later it appeared a perfectly reasonable way to deal with deflation and unemployment in a depression.

Jacob Coxey, at center, is closely watched by police as he advances with his small army just outside Washington, D.C. A crowd of boys expectantly awaits trouble. What was the size of Coxey's Army?

- Why did Coxey's Army march to Washington?
- How would Coxey's plan have put people to work and caused prices to rise?

THE PULLMAN STRIKE

Since he was President when the depression struck, Cleveland was blamed for the hard times. Emergency soup kitchens were set up to feed the long lines of hungry people who could not find work. Critics unfairly called them "Cleveland Cafes." But Cleveland did little to help the jobless or to stimulate the lagging economy.

More people turned against Cleveland when a great strike broke out in May 1894, shortly after the arrest of Jacob Coxey. The strike had begun in the factory of the Pullman Palace Car Company in Illinois, which manufactured and operated sleeping and dining cars for the railroads. After the strike had gone on for several weeks, engi-

599

neers, conductors, and other workers of the American Railway Union, in sympathy with the strikers, voted not to handle trains to which Pullman cars were attached. This paralyzed the railroads in and around Chicago. It threatened to disrupt the nation's already depressed economy.

A federal judge ordered the railroad workers back to work. When they refused, President Cleveland sent troops into Chicago to make sure that the United States mail was not held up. The union was willing to operate mail trains. However, the railroad officials insisted on attaching Pullman cars to these trains. The **Pullman Strike** continued.

Rioting broke out when blue-coated soldiers entered the Chicago rail yards. The violence turned public opinion against the union. Its president, Eugene Victor Debs, was arrested and thrown in jail. The strike collapsed.

During the Pullman Strike some 600 freight cars were set afire south of 50th Street in Chicago. Strikers are held back by army officers while the fire fighters pour water on these cars of the Panhandle line. What caused this riot to break out?

Conservatives praised Cleveland's defense of "law and order." But thousands of union members were alarmed by his use of the army to break a strike. The governor of Illinois, John Peter Altgeld, had bitterly objected to the use of federal troops in his state. Altgeld claimed that Chicago police and state militia units could preserve order. He accused Cleveland of being a strikebreaker. Altgeld's opposition weakened Cleveland politically since Altgeld, like Cleveland, was a Democrat.

■ Why did many people turn against President Cleveland after the Pullman Strike? Why was the President hurt by Governor Altgeld's criticism?

600

THE DEMOCRATS CHOOSE SILVER

As the election of 1896 drew near, the Democrats had to make a difficult decision. President Cleveland was extremely unpopular. Rightly or wrongly, he was being blamed for the continuing depression. Furthermore, the public knew he was totally opposed to measures that would stimulate the economy by raising prices, especially the coining of silver.

In the southern states where the Democrats were in control, the Populist party was making large gains by calling for the free coinage of silver. Southern farmers were hard hit by the depression. If the Democrats again chose Cleveland, who defended the gold standard, they seemed sure to be defeated in the national election. They might even lose the South to the Populists.

The 1896 election was one which gave the Democrats a chance to hold the Presidency and to take Republican seats in Congress. This was because the Republican party convention in June 1896 had nominated Congressman William McKinley of Ohio as its candidate for President. McKinley would be running on a platform that declared squarely for the gold standard. "We are . . . opposed to the free coinage of silver," the platform stated.

Many normally Republican farmers in the Middle West and nearly all the miners in the Rocky Mountain states were in favor of free silver. The Republican platform made them furious. States like Nebraska and Colorado, traditionally Republican, might go Democratic if that party would come out for free silver.

The Democratic convention met in St. Louis in July. Before picking a candidate, the delegates had to adopt a platform. The key issue to be decided was the money question. A formal debate took place. Three speakers defended the gold standard. Three others spoke in favor of the free coinage of silver.

The final debater was William Jennings Bryan, a young ex-congressman from Nebraska. Bryan was not a particularly thoughtful person, but he had a deep faith in democracy. He believed that legislators should represent the ideas of the people who elected them. As early as 1892 he said, "The people of Nebraska are for free silver, and [therefore] I am for free silver. I will look up the arguments later."

Bryan had served two terms in Congress. But few people outside Nebraska had ever heard of him. He was only 36, barely a year older than the minimum age set by the Constitution for becoming President. Nevertheless, he decided that he had a good chance of getting the 1896 Presidential nomination.

Bryan's speech on the silver question was his great opportunity to attract attention. He succeeded brilliantly. Bryan was one of the greatest political orators in American history. He did not make any new economic arguments for free silver. Instead, like a skillful

William McKinley, the Republican candidate for President in 1896, is the subject of this oil painting by Charles Ayer Whipple. What office did McKinley hold in 1896?

601

William Jennings Bryan was seen as a despoiler of the Bible in this political cartoon by Grant Hamilton. But the same Bryan was actually a very religious person who based courtroom arguments on the Bible. What was Bryan's Cross of Gold speech?

musician, he played upon the emotions of the delegates. His voice rang through the hall like a mighty organ in a great cathedral. As he approached the climax of his appeal, almost every sentence brought forth a burst of applause.

He likened those who favored coining silver to the Crusaders who had freed Jerusalem from the Moslems. He praised western farmers as "hardy pioneers who have braved the dangers of the wilderness" and "made the desert bloom." The country could exist without the cities, Bryan said, but without the nation's farms, "grass will grow in the streets of every city in the country." He concluded by likening the silver forces to Jesus Christ, saying to the defenders of the gold standard, "You shall not press down upon the brow of labor this crown of thorns, you shall not crucify mankind upon a cross of gold."

After cheering this **Cross of Gold** speech, the Democratic convention adopted a platform calling for "the free and unlimited coinage of both silver and gold at the . . . ratio of 16 to 1." The next day the delegates nominated the "Nebraska Cyclone," William Jennings Bryan, for President.

- What difficult decision did Democrats have to make for the Presidential election of 1896?
- What stand did the Republicans take on the money issue in their platform of 1896?
- What actions did Democrats take at their convention after hearing the "Cross of Gold" speech?

THE ELECTION OF 1896

The Presidential campaign of 1896 roused people throughout the nation. When it was over, many Republicans and Democrats had changed sides.

Nearly all business people and manufacturers supported McKinley. Like most other wealthy citizens, these people felt that the issue of silver inflation versus the gold standard and "sound money" was more important than party loyalty. They believed that if Bryan were elected, their businesses would collapse and their wealth would vanish.

Beyond question these people were wrong. There was nothing magical about the gold standard, and Bryan was no threat to their wealth. But they misunderstood the situation. They saw the campaign as a crusade. They thought that McKinley was a great patriotic hero, almost a Washington or a Lincoln, who would save the nation in an hour of terrible danger.

Actually, McKinley was a rather ordinary person. He was hard working, forward looking, and politically shrewd. But he was not

especially intelligent, imaginative, or creative. His greatest advantage in the election was the solid support of his business backers.

The Republican campaign was organized by Marcus Alonzo Hanna, an Ohio industrialist. "Mark" Hanna and his assistants raised enormous amounts of money for the contest. Some of the contributions came from wealthy individuals, many of whom were normally Democrats. But most of the money came from large corporations. As one bank president explained, "We have never before contributed a cent to politics, but the present crisis we believe to be as important as the [Civil] war." It was not then illegal for corporations to give money to political candidates.

Hanna used this money very cleverly. Republican speakers spread across the country. At one point 250 Republican orators were campaigning in 27 states. Pamphlets explaining the Republican program were printed and 250 million distributed. Over 15 million pamphlets on the money question alone were handed out in one two-week period.

Committees were set up to win the support of all kinds of special groups. One committee tried to influence black voters, another those of German descent, and so on. There was even a committee assigned

Free Silverites have unhitched their wagon from the Democratic donkey as they roll over the brink. This is the view of C. J. Taylor, who made this lithograph in 1896. Bryan has his hands stubbornly folded while Governor Altgeld of Illinois waves a firebrand. Why did big business fear Bryan?

603

Marcus Alonzo Hanna planned the Republican strategy in 1896. He is shown in this 1904 etching done by Jacques Reich. What were some of Hanna's campaign schemes?

to campaign among bicycle riders, for bicycling was an especially popular sport in the 1890s.

The Democrats had very little campaign money, in part because so many wealthy Democrats were supporting the Republican candidate. The party organization was also weak. In many of the industrial states Democratic politicians would not support free silver. These **Gold Democrats** formed a **National Democratic party** and nominated Senator John M. Palmer of Illinois for President.

The Democrats did have one very valuable asset—Bryan himself. His magnetic personality and his brilliance as a speaker made him a great campaigner. He traveled constantly, speaking all over the nation. Sometimes he addressed huge crowds in city auditoriums. Sometimes he spoke to only a handful of listeners at rural railroad stations from the back platform of his train. All told, he made over 600 speeches between August and election day in November.

Most important newspapers supported McKinley. Their reporters frequently misquoted Bryan in order to make him appear foolish or radical. *The New York Times* even suggested that he might well be insane. But the papers did report Bryan's speeches in detail. In this election voters could readily learn where both candidates stood on all the issues of the day.

The election caused major shifts in voting patterns. After much debate the Populists nominated Bryan instead of running a candidate of their own. The effect was to end the Populist movement. Yet if the Populist party had run someone else, the free silver vote would have been split. Then McKinley would have been certain to win the election.

Populist strongholds in the South and West went solidly for Bryan in November. So did the mountain states, where silver mining was important. But thousands of formerly Democratic industrial workers voted Republican. City people did not find Bryan as attractive as did farmers and residents of small towns. McKinley was popular with workers, despite his close connections with big business. He convinced workers that free silver would be bad for the economy. And he argued that a high tariff would protect their jobs by keeping out goods made by low-paid foreign laborers.

Boston, New York City, Baltimore, Chicago, and many other cities that had gone Democratic in the Presidential election of 1892 voted Republican in 1896. Chicago, for example, had given Grover Cleveland a majority of over 35,000 in 1892. In 1896 McKinley carried the city by more than 56,000 votes.

- How did the Republicans conduct the campaign of 1896?
- Why was Bryan the Democrats' one valuable asset?
- What was the fate of the Populist movement?

604

McKinley ran what was called a front-porch campaign for the Presidency. He stayed home in Canton, Ohio, partly to be near his wife, Ida, who had epilepsy. Groups from all over the country came to hear his views on various subjects.

These visits were carefully planned. Each delegation was greeted at the railroad station by the "Canton Home Guards" mounted on horses. The visitors then marched to McKinley's modest house. The town took on the appearance of one long Fourth of July celebration. The streets were lined with flags and banners. Pictures of McKinley were everywhere. Stands along the route sold hot dogs, lemonade, and souvenirs.

When a delegation reached McKinley's house, the candidate came out to meet them, usually with his wife and mother at his side. He called their leaders by name and seemed to show keen interest in their problems. A member of the delegation would make a brief speech while McKinley listened to him "like a child looking at Santa Claus."

McKinley's responses showed how well he knew his audiences. To a group of Civil War veterans he might speak about pensions. To manufacturers or factory workers he might stress the importance of the protective tariff. Always he pictured himself as a patriot defending America and the gold standard against the dangerous free-silver position of the Democrats. "Patriotism," he would say, "is above party and National honor is dearer than party name. The currency and credit of the government are good, and must be kept good forever."

Newspaper reporters covered each of these visits. They wrote articles describing the crowds. They quoted the remarks of the candidate in detail. In this way McKinley reached voters all over the country without stepping off the front porch of his house.

The Front-Porch Campaign

White House Historical Association

This watercolor miniature of Ida McKinley was painted by Emily Drayton Taylor in April 1899.

THE ELECTION ENDS AN ERA

The election was a solid Republican triumph. The electoral vote was 271 for McKinley, 176 for Bryan. Looked at one way, McKinley won simply because his party spent more money and was better organized than the Democrats. He carried all the crucial close states of the Northeast by relatively small margins. If Bryan had won in New York, Ohio, Indiana, and Illinois, he would have been President.

In a larger sense, however, McKinley's victory marked the end of the post-Civil War era. Within a year or two, new gold discoveries and improved methods of refining gold ore ended the money short-

Museum of Fine Arts, Boston

The century ends with the glow of lamplight in Boston Common. The time of the scene is at twilight in the early 1900s. This detail comes from a large oil painted by Childe Hassam. How did the political "musical chairs" of the late 19th century end?

age. Free silver was not needed. But the changes in voting patterns caused by the Depression of 1893 and the free-silver fight continued long after those problems were settled.

The farm states voted for Bryan, the industrial states for McKinley. But the election was not a victory for industry nor a defeat for American farmers. Agriculture remained important. As Bryan had said in his Cross of Gold speech, the cities and their industries could not prosper unless farmers were prosperous too.

The election marked the birth of the modern industrial age. To most people of that day, Bryan seemed to be pressing for change, McKinley defending the old, established order. In fact, McKinley was far more forward looking than Bryan. His view of the future was much closer to what the reality of the 20th century would be.

■ What was marked by McKinley's victory in the Presidential election of 1896?

606

CHAPTER 20 REVIEW

Identification
Tell briefly why each of the following persons, terms, or events is important.
1. James A. Garfield
2. Grover Cleveland
3. Benjamin Harrison
4. James B. Weaver
5. Jacob Coxey
6. William McKinley
7. William Jennings Bryan
8. Solid South
9. Political machines
10. Greenbacks
11. Civil service reform
12. National Grange
13. Crime of 1873
14. Bland-Allison Act
15. Free coinage of silver
16. Farmers Alliance
17. Co-ops
18. Populist party
19. Pullman Strike
20. Front-porch campaign

Understanding American History
1. Explain what was meant by "waving the bloody shirt."
2. Why did the Democrats and Republicans nominate so many Presidential candidates from close states after the Civil War?
3. In what ways were political machines corrupt? How did they help supporters?
4. What reforms were made in civil service after Congress acted in 1883?
5. What were the important political issues in the years following the Civil War? Why did the major parties "sit on the fence" rather than take firm stands?
6. What was the money question? How were greenbacks a part of it?
7. What was the position of farmers on tariffs? On regulating railroads? On coining silver?
8. Which groups supported the Populist party? What was its platform in 1892?
9. Explain Jacob Coxey's plan to end the Depression of 1893. How did he act?
10. Which groups supported the Republicans in 1896? Which supported the Democrats?

Activities
1. Presidential campaigns after the Civil War were hard fought and much discussed. Yet time seems to drop a veil over the occupants of the White House during this period, to say nothing of the candidates they defeated. Research and report on one of the following campaigns:

1868	Grant v. Seymour
1872	Grant v. Greeley
1876	Hayes v. Tilden
1880	Garfield v. Hancock
1884	Cleveland v. Blaine, Butler
1888	Harrison v. Cleveland
1892	Cleveland v. Harrison, Weaver

2. In your library and other American history books find examples of the cartoons of Thomas Nast. It was Nast who created the symbols of the tiger to represent Tammany Hall, the Republican elephant, and the Democratic donkey. Explain Nast's use of one of these symbols in a political cartoon from the post-Civil War era.
3. Each state has a Federal Job Information Center that will send you pamphlets, including "Working for the USA" and "First, See Us," to explain today's civil service. Use these to report on present-day government service.
4. Research and report on the founding of co-ops in the Middle West in the 1880s. Consult telephone directories to find co-ops still operating today.
5. Use historical imagination to write a letter to a friend describing what you saw and heard at the Democratic convention in July 1896 when Bryan delivered his "Cross of Gold" speech. Or describe a visit to McKinley during his front-porch campaign.

CHAPTER 20 TEST

Matching (30 points)
Number your paper 1–10 and match the description in the first column with the name in the second column.

1. The power of appointing persons to political jobs in exchange for their support in elections
2. Provided for the purchase and coinage of silver
3. Paper money which could not be exchanged for coin
4. Provided many benefits to poor city dwellers in exchange for their votes
5. Plans that determine how much money will be in circulation
6. Name opponents gave the law that ended the coining of silver
7. Provided for civil service reform
8. Nominated by both parties in an effort to win Presidential elections in close states
9. Farmers' social club that became a powerful political organization
10. Formed by the Farmers Alliance and some labor groups to get reforms passed into law

a. Political machines
b. Bland-Allison Act
c. Crime of 1873
d. Greenbacks
e. National Grange
f. Native sons
g. Patronage
h. Pendleton Act
i. Monetary policy
j. Populist party

Matching (20 points)
Number your paper 11–15 and match the description in the first column with the name in the second column.

11. Populist candidate for President in 1892
12. Republican candidate for President who opposed free coinage of silver
13. Orator who delivered the "Cross of Gold" speech
14. Wanted to end the Depression of 1893 by having the government spend money to get the economy moving
15. His assassination led to the passage of civil service reforms

a. Jacob Coxey
b. James A. Garfield
c. William Jennings Bryan
d. James B. Weaver
e. William McKinley

Classifying (20 points)
Number your paper 16–20. For each of the following statements tell who gave support. Write *F* for farmers, *B* for business leaders.

16. Favored a protective tariff
17. Favored coinage of silver
18. Favored immigration
19. Favored the gold standard
20. Favored inflation

Essay (30 points)
In a brief essay tell why the Populist party was formed and give its main ideas. Proofread your paper carefully.

UNIT SIX TEST

Multiple Choice (20 points)

Number your paper 1–5 and write the letter of the phrase that best completes each sentence.

1. The economy of the Great Plains was based mostly on
   a. agriculture.
   b. industry.
   c. trade.
   d. silver mining.
2. Railroads were important to the growth of the American economy because
   a. they brought people to the West.
   b. people found railway travel exciting.
   c. they created a demand for free silver.
   d. they helped other industries grow.
3. Monopolies were created to
   a. please the farmers.
   b. regulate the government.
   c. eliminate competition.
   d. encourage the growth of unions.
4. Settlement houses attempted to improve
   a. relations with the Indians.
   b. life in frontier towns.
   c. political elections.
   d. the lives of city dwellers.
5. Big city political machines were usually supported by
   a. business leaders.
   b. immigrants.
   c. women.
   d. Civil War veterans.

Chronological Order (25 points)

Number your paper 6–10 and place the following events in order by numbering 1 for the first, 2 for the second, and so on.

6. The Populist party is formed.
7. Custer makes his last stand.
8. The first transcontinental railroad is completed.
9. The Civil War ends.
10. William McKinley is elected President.

Matching (25 points)

Number your paper 11–15 and match the person in the second column with his or her description in the first column.

11. Inventor of the first successful electric light
12. Wrote a book that showed how the government had been unfair to the American Indians
13. Founder of Standard Oil
14. Democratic candidate for President in 1896 who favored free coinage of silver
15. Established Hull House, the most famous of the settlement houses for poor people

a. Jane Addams
b. John D. Rockefeller
c. Helen Hunt Jackson
d. Thomas A. Edison
e. William Jennings Bryan

Essay (30 points)

Write a brief essay on *one* of the following topics. Explain how the growth of railroads helped the American economy to grow, *or* Explain the conditions that led to civil service reform and tell which reforms were achieved after passage of the Pendleton Act in 1883.

1890
McKinley Tariff

1891
Chilean Crisis

1892
Liliuokalani becomes Hawaii's absolute monarch

1893

1894

1895
Venezuela Boundary Dispute
•
Cuba revolts against Spain

1896

1897

Niagara Movement

Hepburn Act
•
Pure Food and Drug Act

Panama Canal begun

William Howard Taft elected President

NAACP founded

Triangle Fire

1905

1906

1907

1908

1909

1910

1911

THE PROGRESSIVE ERA

AN EXPANDING AMERICA

1898
U.S.S. *Maine*
explodes in
Havana
•
Spanish-
American
War
•
Battle of
Manila Bay
•
Hawaii
annexed

1899
First
Open Door
Note

1900
McKinley
reelected
President
•
Boxer
Rebellion

1901
McKinley
assassinated
•
Roosevelt
succeeds to
Presidency
•
U.S. Steel
founded

1902

1903
Republic
of Panama
•
Hay-Bunau-
Varilla
Treaty

1904
Roosevelt
elected
President
•
*The Shame
of the
Cities*

Wilson
elected
resident
•
ogressive
party

Sixteenth,
Seventeenth
Amendments
•
Federal
Reserve
Act

Panama
Canal
completed
•
Federal
Trade
Commission
•
Clayton
Antitrust
Act

U.S. enters
Great War

Nineteenth
Amendment,
Prohibition
begins
•
Armistice

1912

1913

1914

1915

1916

1917

1918

1919

GREAT WORLD WAR

CHAPTER 21
America in World Affairs, 1865-1912

ISOLATIONISM

America's longtime suspicions of Europe had increased during the Civil War. Great Britain and France had sympathized with the Confederate government. British companies had built ships for the southerners. This had enabled the Confederacy to get around the United States blockade of southern ports. The *Alabama,* a British-built warship flying the Confederate flag, destroyed many American merchant ships during the rebellion. For a time Great Britain even considered entering the war on the side of the Confederacy.

While the United States was fighting its desperate struggle, France boldly sent an army into Mexico. The French then named a European prince, Maximilian of Austria, as Emperor of Mexico. This was a direct challenge to the Monroe Doctrine, which had stated that no European colonies were to be established in the Americas.

Once the Civil War ended, the United States sent 50,000 soldiers to the Mexican border and demanded that France withdraw its army. The French pulled out. Then the Mexicans revolted against Maximilian. In June 1867 Mexican patriots led by Benito Juárez entered Mexico City. Maximilian was captured and put to death.

These events demonstrated that European powers were eager to take advantage of any weakness of the United States. Americans wanted nothing from Europe except the right to buy and sell goods. They considered European governments undemocratic. They also believed that European diplomats were tricky and untrustworthy. To get involved with a European diplomat meant the risk of becoming involved in the wars and rivalries of Europe. Better, believed the average American, to have as little as possible to do with Europe.

This was the popular view. American political leaders never took such an extreme position. But the spirit of American relations with the European powers was **isolationist.** The United States should keep pretty much to itself. It should not meddle in European affairs. And it should not permit Europeans to meddle in American affairs.

Americans were taking no serious risks by this **isolationism.** As the nation grew in wealth and numbers, the possibility that any European country might attack it rapidly disappeared.

■ What was the isolationist position most Americans took?

Keystone Press

Benito Juárez was the high-minded leader of the resistance to France's attempt to make Mexico its colony. This engraved portrait shows Juárez as president of Mexico. Why were U.S. troops sent to Mexico?

AMERICAN EXPANSIONISM

Americans never adopted an isolationist attitude toward the rest of the world. Many people believed that the same manifest destiny that had brought the Great West into the Union would eventually bring all of North and South America under the control of the Stars and Stripes—and the islands of the Pacific Ocean as well. This attitude was known as **American expansionism.**

Remember that the Monroe Doctrine had stated that no more *European* colonies should be established in the Americas. It said nothing about the United States extending its control in the Western Hemisphere.

In the years after the Civil War, Americans began to extend their influence in Latin America and in the Pacific Ocean. In August 1867 the United States Navy occupied the **Midway Islands,** located about 1,000 miles (1,600 kilometers) northwest of Hawaii. Most Americans then gave not another thought to these uninhabited flyspecks on the map of the vast Pacific until the great American-Japanese naval battle there in World War II.

■ What was American expansionism?

The British Library/HBJ Photo

A signal event in U.S. expansionism was the opening of Japan to American trade by Commodore Matthew Perry. This detail from a Japanese painted scroll shows one of Perry's four ships in Edo Bay. His arrival by steamship in July 1853 seemed to the Japanese like "four black dragons" in the calm harbor. In March 1854 they agreed to open two ports to U.S. trade. What did many people think would be the ultimate result of manifest destiny?

The Seward House

Present at the signing of the Alaska Purchase Treaty on March 30, 1867, are, left to right, Robert S. Chew, William H. Seward, William Hunter, Waldemar de Bodisco, and Baron Edouard de Stoeckl. What was the price of the Alaska Purchase?

THE PURCHASE OF ALASKA

Americans also knew little to nothing about Alaska, then called Russian America, until Secretary of State William H. Seward purchased it from Russia in March 1867. Russian explorers, fur trappers, and merchants had been in the area since the 1790s. But Alaska had never brought them the riches they sought. The Russian government decided to sell the vast land. The United States seemed the logical customer. Seward jumped at the opportunity to add more territory to the United States. He agreed to a purchase price of $7.2 million.

News of this **Alaska Purchase** surprised everyone in America. Congress knew little about the negotiations until the treaty was presented to it, along with the bill for $7.2 million.

To win support, Seward launched a nationwide campaign. Alaska was worth far more than $7.2 million, he claimed. Its fish, furs, and lumber were very valuable. By controlling it, America would increase its influence in the North Pacific. These arguments convinced the senators. They accepted the treaty by a vote of 37 to 2.

The House of Representatives, however, hesitated to provide the $7.2 million. Seward again ran through his arguments about the virtues of this land in the frozen North. The Russian minister to the United States, Baron Edouard de Stoeckl, wined, dined, and probably bribed a number of House members. Stoeckl later claimed that he had spent almost $200,000 getting the House to appropriate the money.

Many Americans thought buying Alaska was a mistake. They called the territory **"Seward's Folly,"** "Frigidia," and "President Andrew Johnson's Polar Bear Garden." One joke said that in Alaska a cow would give ice cream instead of milk. But most people were pleased. What a bargain Seward made! For about two cents an acre he had obtained nearly 600,000 square miles (1,560,000 square kilometers) of land, a region twice the size of the state of Texas. The land contained immense resources of lumber, gold, copper, and other metals. More recently, rich deposits of oil and natural gas have been discovered there.

- Why did Russia decide to sell Alaska? What arguments did Secretary of State Seward make for purchasing it?
- How did "Seward's Folly" turn out to be an immense bargain?

HAWAII

At this time Americans also became interested in the **Hawaiian Islands.** This archipelago, or island group, is located in the Pacific about 2,000 miles (3,200 kilometers) southwest of San Francisco.

The first Americans to reach these beautiful, sunny islands were New England whalers and traders. Beginning in the late 1700s, they stopped there for rest and fresh supplies on their lonely voyages.

The Hawaiian island of Oahu is seen as it appeared to C. E. Bensell, who visited in 1821. In this watercolor the whaleship *Russel* lies at anchor in the foreground. When did sailors from America first reach Hawaii?

Peabody Museum of Salem (Photo: Mark Sexton)

These sailors were followed by missionaries who came to Hawaii hoping to convert the inhabitants to Christianity. The missionaries settled down, built houses, and raised crops. In the 1840s and 1850s their children and grandchildren were beginning to cultivate sugar.

By the time of the American Civil War, the missionary families dominated the Islands' economy and government. Sugar was the Hawaiians' most important export. They sold most of it in the United States.

The Hawaiians were ruled by a king who made all decisions and owned all the land. But in 1840 King Kamehameha III issued a constitution modeled after the United States Constitution. This was not surprising since many of Kamehameha's advisers were Americans. In 1875 the two countries signed a treaty which allowed Hawaiian sugar to enter the United States without payment of a tariff. In exchange, the Hawaiian government agreed not to give territory or special privileges in the islands to any other nation.

The 1875 treaty greatly encouraged sugar production. The missionary families formed corporations and imported thousands of low-paid Chinese and Japanese immigrants to work on the plantations. Most of these laborers signed long-term contracts similar to the ones that indentured servants had signed with Virginia tobacco planters 250 years earlier.

Between 1875 and 1890 the amount of Hawaiian sugar shipped to the United States jumped from 18 million to 160 million pounds (about 8 million to 72 million kilograms). But the Hawaiian sugar boom came to a sudden end when Congress passed the **McKinley Tariff** of 1890, a law that took away the special advantage of the Hawaiians. Their sugar now had to compete with sugar grown in the

Culver Pictures

The Bishop Museum/Liliuokalani Trust

Hawaii's King Kamehameha III and Queen Liliuokalani are the subjects of these royal portraits. In 1824, at the age of ten, Kamehameha became king. Liliuokalani became queen in 1891. She wrote the popular song "Aloha Oe" or "Farewell to Thee." How did American influence expand under each of these rulers?

616

United States and also with sugar produced in Cuba and other countries. Prices fell, and the economy of the Hawaiian Islands suffered a serious depression.

Along with Hawaii's economic crisis came a political crisis. In 1890 the government changed hands. The new ruler was Queen Liliuokalani. She was intelligent and fiercely patriotic. She resented the influence of American planters and merchants in her country. Her attitude was expressed in the slogan "Hawaii for the Hawaiians."

Queen Liliuokalani was determined to break the power of the white-dominated Hawaiian legislature. In January 1893 she proclaimed a new constitution making her an **absolute monarch** with complete power.

The Americans responded by organizing a revolution. John L. Stevens, the American minister to Hawaii, supported the rebels. He ordered 150 marines ashore from an American warship in Honolulu harbor. They did not have to fire a shot to persuade Liliuokalani and the Hawaiians not to resist. The revolutionaries promptly raised the American flag.

Stevens announced that Hawaii was now under the protection of the United States. A delegation hurried off to Washington to negotiate a **treaty of annexation** to bring Hawaii under American control. In February 1893 President Benjamin Harrison sent this treaty to the Senate for approval. But Harrison's term was about to end. President-elect Cleveland asked the Senate not to vote on the treaty until he had a chance to consider it. The Senate therefore postponed action.

After taking office, Cleveland withdrew the treaty from the Senate. He sent a special commission headed by James H. Blount of Georgia to investigate conditions in the islands. Blount reported that the Hawaiian people did not want to be annexed to the United States.

After reading Blount's report, Cleveland decided to scrap the treaty. He recalled John L. Stevens and sent a new representative to the islands. This new United States minister met with the president of the revolutionary government, Sanford B. Dole, and urged him to resign. Cleveland wanted to return control of the islands to Queen Liliuokalani, who by this time was popularly known in America as "Queen Lil."

Dole (whose pineapples would soon be well-known in the United States) refused to sign. If the United States did not want Hawaii, the revolutionaries would remain independent. On July 4, 1894, they proclaimed Hawaii a republic.

- Who were the first Americans to reach Hawaii? Which groups of immigrants followed?
- Why did Americans living in Hawaii overthrow Queen Liliuokalani and her government?

Sanford B. Dole was born in Hawaii to American missionaries. He held a number of posts in government of the islands, including president and, in 1900, first governor of the Territory of Hawaii. Who ruled before Dole?

This photograph of James G. Blaine was taken by Napoleon Sarony in about 1880. Blaine served in both houses of Congress and was twice named Secretary of State. But the office of President eluded him. He sought the Republican nomination in 1876, 1880, 1884, and 1892. In 1889 what did Blaine accomplish at the Pan-American Conference?

PAN-AMERICANISM

American interest in the nations of Latin America also increased after the Civil War. These countries sold large quantities of coffee, bananas, fertilizer, and many other products to the United States. But they bought most of their manufactured goods in Europe. In the 1890s James G. Blaine, who was Secretary of State under Presidents Garfield and Harrison, set out to develop closer trade ties with Latin America.

Blaine wanted all the nations of the Western Hemisphere to see themselves as belonging to a group with common interests. In his opinion the United States would obviously dominate such a group. This was one reason why many Latin American nations hesitated to cooperate with Blaine. In 1889 Blaine invited the Latin American countries to send representatives to Washington for a meeting. After a whirlwind tour of 41 cities, these representatives assembled for the first **Pan-American Conference.**

The conference did not accomplish much. The delegates rejected Blaine's suggestion that they lower their tariffs on American goods. Still, it was the first time the nations of North and South America had come together. They began to sense their common interests, different from those of other nations.

■ Why did Secretary of State Blaine want to bring the nations of the Western Hemisphere together?

THE CHILEAN CRISIS

Any goodwill that the Pan-American Conference generated suffered a setback in the **Chilean Crisis** of 1891-92. During a civil war in Chile between a faction supporting its president and one backing its congress, the United States supported the presidential side. Unfortunately for the United States, the other side won the war. The Chileans called people from the United States *Yanquis.* Anti-*Yanqui* feeling was now high.

In this heated atmosphere some sailors from the U.S.S. *Baltimore,* on shore leave in the city of Valparaiso, got in a fight outside the True Blue saloon. Apparently a local civilian had spat in the face of one of the sailors. A mob attacked the sailors, and the Valparaiso police did nothing to stop the fighting. Two sailors were killed and 16 injured.

President Harrison then threatened to break diplomatic relations unless the Chilean government apologized. A war scare resulted. Fortunately, the Chilean government did apologize. It also paid $75,000 in damages to the injured sailors and to the families of the dead.

■ What caused high anti-*Yanqui* feeling in Chile in 1891-92?

618

THE VENEZUELA BOUNDARY DISPUTE

In 1895 the United States again flexed its muscles in South America. For decades Great Britain and Venezuela had haggled over the boundary line separating Venezuela and British Guiana, a small British colony on the north coast of South America. Venezuela had tried to settle the dispute in the past, but Great Britain had always refused to permit an outside judge to draw the boundary. Tensions increased in the 1880s when the largest gold nugget ever found—509 ounces (14,252 grams)—was discovered in the territory both countries claimed.

President Grover Cleveland was afraid that if the British took any more American territory, other European powers might follow. Then the economic and political interests of the United States in Latin America would be injured. He was determined to make Great Britain agree to settle the argument by **arbitration**—that is, to allow a neutral judge to decide who owned the territory. He therefore ordered Secretary of State Richard Olney to send a stern message to the British government.

Olney's note of July 20, 1895, was extremely strong and quite insulting in tone. Cleveland described it as a **20-inch gun.** The United States, said Olney, was the supreme power in the hemisphere. The Monroe Doctrine prohibited further European expansion in the Western Hemisphere. The United States would intervene in disputes between European and Latin American nations to make certain that the Monroe Doctrine was not violated.

Despite the harsh tone of Olney's message, the British prime minister, Lord Salisbury, dismissed it as a bluff. He thought Cleveland was playing the political game called **twisting the British lion's tail.** Any statement threatening Great Britain was sure to be popular with Americans of Irish origin. Most Irish-Americans hated the British because they refused to give Ireland its independence. Instead of answering the note promptly, Salisbury delayed nearly four months.

When he did reply, Salisbury rejected Olney's argument that the Monroe Doctrine applied to the boundary dispute. Britain's dispute with Venezuela, he said politely but firmly, was no business of the United States.

This response made Cleveland "mad clean through." The Monroe Doctrine *did* apply to the situation. The nation would "resist by every means in its power" any British seizure of Venezuelan territory. The President asked Congress for money to finance a United States commission that would investigate the dispute. If the British refused to accept its findings, the United States would use force.

Nearly all people seemed to approve of Cleveland's tough stand. Venezuelans were delighted. When the news reached Caracas, the

Richard Olney of Massachusetts is the subject of this photograph. He was President Cleveland's Attorney General and later Secretary of State. It was Olney who urged Cleveland to send federal troops to Chicago to break the Pullman Strike (page 600). What political game did the British accuse Olney of playing?

capital of Venezuela, a cheering crowd of at least 200,000 people gathered at the home of the United States legation.

For a brief time war between the United States and Great Britain seemed possible. But neither government wanted war. Cleveland was mainly interested in reminding the world of the Monroe Doctrine. Great Britain had too many other diplomatic problems to be willing to fight over what they considered a relatively unimportant piece of land in South America.

As soon as he realized that the situation had become dangerous, Lord Salisbury agreed to let an impartial commission decide where to place the boundary. In 1899 this commission gave Britain nearly all the land in question.

On the surface the United States seemed to be defending a small Latin American nation against a great European power in this **Venezuela Boundary Dispute.** In fact, it was putting both Europe and Latin America on notice that the United States was the most important nation in the Western Hemisphere. Throughout the crisis Cleveland ignored Venezuela. Its minister in Washington was never once consulted.

- Why did President Cleveland want to arbitrate the Venezuela Boundary Dispute with Great Britain?
- What was the United States' notice to Europe and Latin America in the Venezuela Boundary Dispute?

CUBA AND SPAIN

Early in 1895, shortly before Secretary Olney fired his "20-inch gun" over the Venezuela boundary, real gunfire broke out in Cuba. The Spanish had called their colony in Cuba the "Ever-Faithful Isle." Cuba was one of Spain's few colonies in America that had not revolted in the early 1800s. It was Spain's last important possession in the Americas.

In 1868 there had been a revolution in Cuba which lasted for ten years. It had failed, but now, in 1895, Cuban patriots again took up arms. Independence was their objective. The rebels engaged in the surprise attacks of **guerrilla warfare.** They burned sugar cane fields, blocked railroads, and ambushed small parties of Spanish soldiers. By the end of 1896 they controlled most of rural Cuba.

In an effort to regain control of the countryside, the Spanish Governor-General, Valeriano Weyler, began herding farm people into what were called **reconcentrados**—concentration camps. He penned up about 500,000 Cubans in these camps. Weyler did this for two reasons. First, Cubans in the camps could not supply the rebels with food. Second, anyone outside the camps could be considered an enemy of Spain and arrested or shot.

The Granger Collection

Conditions inside the concentration camps were unspeakably bad. About 200,000 Cubans died in the camps, victims of disease and malnutrition.

Most people in the United States sympathized with the Cubans' wish to be independent. They were horrified by the stories of Spanish cruelty. Cuban revolutionaries fanned these fires. They established committees called **juntas** in the United States to raise money, spread propaganda, and recruit volunteers.

■ Why had the Spanish called Cuba their "Ever-Faithful Isle"?

■ Why did General Weyler place farm people in concentration camps?

The inspiration for this lithograph cartoon by Louis Dalrymple, made in 1898, is the old saying, "Out of the fat and into the fire." A young woman representing Cuba is caught between "Spanish Misrule" and the flames of "Anarchy" (or political chaos) burning on the isle of Cuba. The caption of the cartoon is "The Duty of the Hour—To Save Her Not Only from Spain, but from a Worse Fate." Which of Cuba's troubles were caused by patriots? Which by Spanish rule?

EXPLOSION IN HAVANA

Both President Cleveland and President McKinley had tried to persuade Spain to give the Cuban people more say about their government. They failed to make much impression. Tension increased. Then, in January 1898, President McKinley sent a battleship, the U.S.S. *Maine,* to Cuba. There had been riots in Havana, the capital city. McKinley sent the *Maine* to protect American citizens there against possible attack.

On February 15, while the *Maine* lay at anchor in Havana Harbor, a tremendous explosion rocked the ship. Of the 350 men aboard, 266 were killed. The *Maine* sank to the bottom.

In strong detail this 1898 lithograph shows the destruction of the *Maine* in Havana Harbor. The panel at the right is titled "Recovering the Dead Bodies." What were the casualties when the *Maine* exploded?

Chicago Historical Society

To this day no one knows for sure what happened. Many Americans jumped to the conclusion that the Spanish had sunk the ship with a mine, a kind of underwater bomb. The navy conducted an investigation. It concluded that the *Maine* had been destroyed by a mine. Another American investigation in 1911 also judged that an explosion from outside had destroyed the ship.

The Spanish government claimed the disaster was caused by an explosion inside the *Maine.* This is certainly possible. A short circuit in the ship's wiring might have caused the *Maine*'s ammunition to explode, for example. It is difficult to imagine that the Spanish would have blown up the ship. The last thing Spain wanted was a war with the United States.

Emotions were inflamed on all sides. The Spanish government, or some individual officer, may indeed have been responsible. Or it is possible that the Cuban rebels did the job, knowing that Spain would be blamed.

In any case, a demand for war against Spain swept the United States. In New York City a man in a Broadway bar raised his glass and proclaimed, "Remember the *Maine!*" This became a battle cry similar to "Remember the Alamo!" during the Texas Revolution of the 1830s.

- Why was the *Maine* sent to Cuba?
- How did the explosion of the *Maine* bring the United States and Spain to the brink of war?

In the 1890s two popular New York newspapers, the *Journal*, owned by William Randolph Hearst, and the *World*, owned by Joseph Pulitzer, were competing bitterly for readers. Both played up crime and scandals to increase sales. This type of writing was called yellow journalism because the *World* printed a comic strip called "The Yellow Kid."

Both the *World* and the *Journal* supported the Cuban revolution. General Weyler's *reconcentrado* policy provided the raw material for many of their stories about Spanish brutality. The actual conditions in Cuba were bad enough. But Hearst and Pulitzer made the camps seem even more shocking. Their exaggerated and untrue stories were topped by screaming headlines and accompanied by spine-chilling drawings and ugly cartoons.

This one-sided picture of the revolution no doubt influenced the United States' decision to go to war with Spain. How much influence the newspapers had is not an easy question to answer. It had some effect on many people. What is more clear is that Hearst and Pulitzer favored war partly for selfish reasons. They knew it would produce exciting news that would help them sell more papers.

Yellow Journalism

The Granger Collection

WAR IS DECLARED

President McKinley wanted to avoid war. He did not let the sinking of the *Maine* cause a break with Spain. But he also wanted to stop the bloodletting in Cuba. He believed the Spanish must do away with the concentration camps and negotiate a truce with the Cubans. Obviously, more self-government should be granted Cuba.

Spain was willing to do this. However, the rebels demanded total independence. The Spanish government did not dare to give in completely. The Spanish people were proud and patriotic. Any government that "gave away" Cuba would surely be overthrown. Perhaps the king himself would be deposed. These unsettling thoughts made Spain stand firmly against Cuban independence.

Still, some peaceful solution might have been found if all sides had been patient. McKinley knew that Spain was earnestly exploring several possible compromises. He had also been promised that in time all his demands would be met. But he finally made up his mind that Spain would never give up Cuba voluntarily.

On April 11, 1898, the President told Congress that he had "exhausted every effort" to end the "intolerable" situation in Cuba. He asked Congress to give him the power to secure in Cuba "a stable government, capable of . . . insuring peace."

WAR.

This elaborate political cartoon by Victor Gillam, 1898, assembles the entire cast who argued the question of whether or not to go to war with Spain over the sinking of the *Maine*. The central figure, in a plumed hat, is President McKinley as Hamlet, the Shakespearean character who is unable to make up his mind. "To be, or not to be," he intones. McKinley cannot decide between the pleas of Uncle Sam, Cuba, *reconcentrados* starved to death, and victims of the sinking *Maine* (at left); the threats of Spain, who taunts, "Uncle Sam will never fight;" and, on the other side, two stockbrokers and a banker, who hope there will be no war. "War or Peace?" McKinley must decide. What had Congress decided?

Congress had been thundering for war for weeks. By huge majorities it passed a joint resolution stating that the people of Cuba "are, and of right ought to be, free and independent." If the Spanish did not withdraw "at once" from the island, the President should use "the entire land and naval forces of the United States" to drive them out. Then Congress protected itself against being accused of going to war for selfish reasons. Its members approved a resolution proposed by Senator Henry M. Teller of Colorado. This **Teller Amendment** stated that the United States had no intention of taking Cuba for itself or trying to control its government.

McKinley gave the Spanish government three days to accept his terms or face war. Unwilling to yield to McKinley's **ultimatum**—do this or face the consequences—the Spanish broke relations with the United States.

- How did President McKinley try to prevent war with Spain?
- What was the attitude of Congress?
- What was the purpose of the Teller Amendment?

THE BATTLE OF MANILA BAY

The first important battle of the **Spanish-American War** did not take place in Cuba but rather in the Far East in the Spanish-held Philippine Islands. The United States had a naval squadron stationed in Hong Kong, China, under the command of Commodore George Dewey. When war was declared, Dewey's ships were ready for instant action. He had been ordered weeks earlier to prepare for battle by the Assistant Secretary of the Navy, Theodore Roosevelt.

624

Dewey steamed swiftly from Hong Kong across the China Sea to Manila, capital of the Philippines. His fleet entered **Manila Bay** on the night of April 30. Early the next morning, he gave the captain of his flagship, the cruiser *Olympia,* the famous command "You may fire when ready, Gridley." The American fleet far outgunned the Spanish warships guarding Manila. By noon the Spanish fleet had been smashed. Not one American sailor was killed. It was a marvelous triumph.

Dewey's victory made him an instant hero in the United States. Many people named babies after him. A chewing gum manufacturer came out with a gum named "Dewey's Chewies." However, until troops arrived from America, Dewey did not have enough men to occupy Manila or conquer any other part of the Philippine archipelago. So he set up a blockade of Manila harbor. When reinforcements reached him in August, he captured the city.

■ Why was Dewey's victory at Manila Bay a triumph?

GETTING TO CUBA

The war in Cuba did not begin so quickly. McKinley called for volunteers and received an enthusiastic response. In two months 200,000 recruits enlisted. Theodore Roosevelt, for example, promptly resigned as Assistant Secretary of the Navy. Although he was nearly 40, he announced that he would organize a regiment and go off to fight in Cuba. He was commissioned a lieutenant colonel in the First Volunteer Cavalry.

Roosevelt led people as easily as the fabled Pied Piper of Hamelin. He came from a wealthy New York family of Dutch origin. He had been a sickly child with poor eyesight, but he had enormous determination. He built up his scrawny body and became a skillful boxer. He loved hunting, hiking, and horseback riding. He also loved politics and scholarship. While still in college, he wrote an excellent history of the naval side of the War of 1812.

Roosevelt had served in the New York state legislature. He had been police commissioner of New York City. And he had run a cattle ranch on the open range of the Dakota Territory until the terrible winter of 1885-86 wiped out his herds.

Roosevelt's call for volunteers brought forth no fewer than 23,000 applicants. The colorful colonel chose a remarkable collection of soldiers from this mass. He enlisted several hundred cowboys, many of whom he had known in his ranching days, and 20 Indians. Several well-known athletes and some police who had worked for him in New York City also joined up. The chaplain of the regiment was a former football player. The outfit became known to the public as the **Rough Riders.**

Commodore George Dewey is atop the observation platform of his ship, painted battle-gray, at the Battle of Manila Bay. With four cruisers and two gunboats Dewey sank all ten of the Spanish ships. Rufus Zogbaum painted this oil in 1898. Who sent Dewey to Manila?

In 1898 Frederic Remington painted this masterful oil, "Charge of the Rough Riders Up San Juan Hill." The scene is as Remington saw it, for he was a war correspondent in Cuba for the Hearst newspapers. Teddy Roosevelt leads the charge on horseback. How were the Rough Riders formed?

With men like Roosevelt recruiting, the army soon had more volunteers than it could efficiently organize in so short a time. Dozens of new units were shipped off to **Tampa,** Florida, where the invasion force was to be trained and supplied. That city became a near madhouse.

All the railroad lines around Tampa were clogged by long lines of unopened freight cars jammed with guns and ammunition, uniforms, and food. The trainees sweated in heavy blue woolen uniforms while the temperature mounted into the humid 90s. Lightweight summer uniforms for the **expeditionary force** did not arrive at Tampa until after the soldiers had sailed off for Cuba. Tropical fevers and other diseases raged through camp. Spoiled foods caused outbreaks of diarrhea and more serious illnesses. The longer the army remained at Tampa, the worse conditions became.

- How were the Rough Riders a remarkable collection of soldiers?
- What problems did the army face in getting its expeditionary force off for Cuba?

THE CAPTURE OF SANTIAGO

The slow-moving transport ships that would carry the army to Cuba could not put to sea until the Spanish fleet in the Atlantic had been located. That fleet could not stand up against American warships, but it could raise havoc with the transports.

626

The Spanish commander, Admiral Pascual Cervera, had tried to avoid the American navy by putting into the harbor of **Santiago,** a city on the southern coast of Cuba. In late May an American squadron discovered his fleet there and blockaded the entrance to the harbor. It was then safe for the army transports to set out.

In mid-June 17,000 men boarded ship in Tampa. There was incredible confusion. Many lost contact with their units. Fearful of being left behind, dozens simply climbed aboard whatever ship they could find. The impatient Roosevelt became furious with the top military command. But at last the expedition managed to set off.

American strategy called for an attack on Santiago. The army, commanded by General William R. Shafter, landed at Daiquiri, a town to the east of Santiago. Once ashore, it began its advance. The Spanish put up a stiff resistance.

Major battles were fought at **El Caney** and at **San Juan Hill.** At El Caney a member of the Second Massachusetts regiment complained, "[the Spaniards] are hidden behind rocks, in weeds and in underbrush, and we just simply can't locate them. They are shooting our men all to pieces."

THE SPANISH-AMERICAN WAR IN CUBA 1898

Library of Congress

The photographer William Dinwiddie posed Colonel Roosevelt and some of his Rough Riders for this picture atop San Juan Hill in 1898. Why did American soldiers have difficulty fighting the Spaniards?

The Rough Riders and black soldiers of the Ninth Cavalry took San Juan Hill by storm on July 1. In this battle Colonel Roosevelt seemed to have no care for his own safety. He galloped back and forth along the line, urging his men forward. Luckily, Roosevelt was not hit. Many of his men were not so fortunate. Most were firing bullets charged with black powder. Each time they fired, a puff of black smoke marked their location for Spanish gunners on top of the hill.

After the capture of San Juan Hill the American artillery could be moved within range of Santiago harbor. Admiral Cervera's fleet had to put to sea. When it did, the powerful American blockade swiftly blasted it. Every one of the Spanish vessels was lost. Only one American sailor was killed in this one-sided fight.

On July 16 the Spanish army commander surrendered Santiago. A few days later another American force completed the occupation of the Spanish island of **Puerto Rico,** about 500 miles (800 kilometers) east of Cuba. The Spanish-American War was over.

▪ Why was the Spanish fleet in the Atlantic blockaded?
▪ What was Roosevelt's behavior at San Juan Hill?

THE TREATY OF PARIS

On July 30 President McKinley sent the Spanish government his peace terms. Spain must leave Cuba. It must give Puerto Rico and an island in the Pacific midway between Hawaii and the Philippines to the United States. American troops would continue to hold the city

This oil painting shows the "Signing of the Peace Protocol Between Spain and the United States" on August 12, 1898. The protocol was an agreement to stop fighting and negotiate peace. President McKinley watches at the left as Secretary of State William R. Day and French Ambassador Jules Cambon, seated together, sign the document. The French were acting as a neutral party. What actions put an end to the fighting in Cuba?

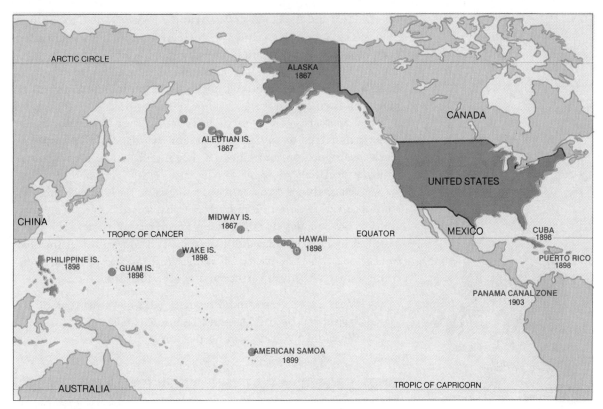

THE UNITED STATES
AND ITS POSSESSIONS IN 1903

■ United States possession in 1903

(In 1902 Cuba became an independent nation)

of Manila until the future of the Philippine Islands could be settled at a peace conference.

These demands were far greater than the original aim of winning independence for Cuba. The excitement of military victory caused McKinley and many other Americans to forget why they had first gone to war.

There was little the Spaniards could do. They accepted McKinley's preliminary terms. Representatives of the two nations then met in Paris in the autumn of 1898. There they framed a formal treaty of peace.

McKinley appointed five American peace commissioners. Three of these were United States senators. The President put the senators on the commission because he expected them to influence their fellow senators. Under the Constitution the treaty would be submitted to the Senate for its approval.

The Spanish commissioners agreed to give up Cuba and to turn

Puerto Rico and the island of **Guam** in the Pacific over to the United States. The Americans, acting on McKinley's order, also demanded possession of the Philippines. The Spaniards objected strongly. The United States had not conquered the islands, they argued. Even Manila had not been captured until after the preliminary terms of peace had been agreed to.

The Spaniards had to give in. To make it easier for them, the Americans agreed to pay $20 million for the islands. This **Treaty of Paris** was signed on December 10, 1898, only ten months after the war was declared.

At relatively little cost in money and lives, the United States had accomplished its objective of freeing Cuba. It had also won itself an empire. No wonder that McKinley's Secretary of State, John Hay, called the conflict "a splendid little war." Of course, it was splendid only if one put aside the fact that the United States had defeated a country that was much smaller and poorer than itself.

- What peace terms did President McKinley demand of the Spanish? Why had he increased his demands?
- What did the U.S. win by the war?

THE FIGHT AGAINST THE TREATY

Many people in the United States opposed the treaty with Spain. They insisted that owning colonies was un-American. Taking Puerto Rico was bad enough, but it was one small island. It might be needed for national defense in case of another war. However, ruling the Philippine Islands without the consent of the Filipinos would make the United States an **imperialist nation,** like Britain, France, Germany, and other European countries that owned colonies.

The Filipinos certainly would not consent to American rule. They wanted their independence. After his victory at Manila Bay, Commodore Dewey had returned the exiled leader of the Filipino patriots, Emilio Aguinaldo, on an American warship. Dewey encouraged Aguinaldo to resume his fight against the Spanish. Aguinaldo did so. He assumed that the United States was there to help liberate his country, just as it had promised to free Cuba.

The **anti-imperialists,** as they were called, included many important Americans. Among the best-known were Andrew Carnegie, the steel manufacturer; Samuel Gompers, the labor leader; Jane Addams, the social worker; and Mark Twain, the author of *Tom Sawyer, Huckleberry Finn,* and many other novels. The anti-imperialists in the Senate were led by George F. Hoar of Massachusetts.

Many anti-imperialists were not opposed to expansion. Senator Hoar, for example, voted for the annexation of Hawaii, which was finally approved during the Spanish-American War. Andrew Carnegie

Emilio Aguinaldo led an insurrection against Spain by Filipinos in 1896. When it was put down, he went into exile in Hong Kong. George Dewey returned Aguinaldo to the Philippines in 1898. Later Aguinaldo fought the occupation of the Philippines by the U.S. What did Aguinaldo assume to be the reason for the U.S. fighting in his country?

630

always favored adding Canada to the United States. But they all believed that it was morally wrong to annex the Filipinos without their consent.

The anti-imperialists needed the votes of only one more than one third of the Senate to defeat the treaty. They seemed likely to succeed. Many Democratic senators would vote against the treaty to embarrass President McKinley and the Republican party.

But the McKinley administration received unexpected help from William Jennings Bryan. Although Bryan was against taking the Philippines, he believed that the Senate should consent to the treaty in order to bring an official end to the war.

Bryan planned to run for President again in 1900. He would make imperialism an issue in the campaign. He was convinced that a majority of the people were opposed to annexing the Philippines. After winning the election, he intended to grant the Filipinos their independence.

Bryan persuaded enough Democratic senators to vote for the treaty to get it through. The vote was 57 to 27, only one vote more than the two thirds necessary. Senator Henry Cabot Lodge of Massachusetts, a leading supporter of the treaty, called the Senate debate "the closest, most bitter, and most exciting struggle I have ever known."

- How would ruling the Philippines make the United States an imperialist nation?
- What position did many anti-imperialists take on annexing the Philippines?
- What role did William Jennings Bryan play in gaining Senate approval of the treaty ending the war?

FIGHTING IN THE PHILIPPINES

William Jennings Bryan's strategy backfired. He was nominated again for President in 1900, and he did make the Philippines a prominent issue in the campaign. But McKinley, running for reelection, defeated him easily. The electoral vote was 292 to 155.

The Republican ticket had been strengthened by the nomination of the popular Rough Rider Theodore Roosevelt for Vice President. After returning from Cuba in triumph, Roosevelt had been elected governor of New York. He had intended to run for reelection as governor in 1900. However, in November 1899 McKinley's first term Vice President, Garret A. Hobart, had died. Roosevelt was persuaded to accept the Republican Vice Presidential nomination.

Then, less than a year after the election, President McKinley was shot and killed by an **anarchist** named Leon Czolgosz. Anarchists believed that all government should be done away with. Theodore

William Jennings Bryan and William McKinley were again candidates for President in 1900. McKinley was the representative of "Sound Money" and his poster has representatives from all walks of life—some in top hats of silk and others in folded caps of paper. Bryan's poster has mementos of his Cross of Gold speech of 1896. How was the Philippines an issue in the election?

By wagon these U.S. soldiers move toward Malabon in the Philippines. This photograph shows ammunition being carried to the front during the Filipino uprising in 1898. What were the death tolls for both sides?

Roosevelt had been a mere assistant secretary two and one-half years earlier. Now he was President of the United States.

There was still another unforeseen result of the Treaty of Paris. Even before the Senate voted for the treaty, the Filipino leader Emilio Aguinaldo had organized a revolution against American rule. Bloody jungle fighting broke out.

Peace was not restored until 1902. By that time more than 4,000 Americans and tens of thousands of Filipinos had been killed.

The United States continued to have great influence in many regions. Often it acted in ways that the local people resented. But opposition to imperialism was growing. Most Americans quickly lost their taste for owning colonies in distant parts of the world.

▨ How was the Republican ticket stengthened in 1900?

BUILDING SKILLS
IN SOCIAL STUDIES

Statistics—numerical facts—may be displayed in various graphic ways, as you know from previous lessons. You have seen examples of picture graphs, bar graphs, line graphs, circle graphs, and tables. The way statistics are organized depends upon the purpose of the graph and also upon the limitations of size.

The table below shows U.S. casualties in wartime. Study it carefully. Then explain why this information is best organized by a table. What would be the difficulty of displaying the casualties on a bar graph? A line graph?

Unlike the table on page 573, this table uses exact figures. Such information would obviously have to be rounded off for display on a graph.

Further, the *range* of the figures on this table—from 385 deaths in the Spanish-American War to 292,131 deaths in World War II—is such that comparison is difficult to show on a graph. For example, a bar graph that allowed one space for each 1,000 deaths would take 292 spaces for World War II.

Answer the following questions based on your reading of the table below.
1. When did the U.S. suffer greatest loss?
2. When did the U.S. suffer least loss?
3. What is the range of U.S. casualties?
4. Which foreign wars were most deadly?
5. Contrast America's first and last wars.

U.S. CASUALTIES IN WAR

	Deaths	Total Casualties
War for American Independence	6,824	33,769
War of 1812	2,260	6,765
Mexican War	1,733	17,435
Civil War		
Union	140,414	646,392
Confederate	74,524	133,821
Total	214,938	780,213
Spanish-American War	385	4,108
World War I	53,513	320,710
World War II	292,131	1,078,162
Korean War	33,629	157,530
Vietnam War	47,192	213,514

THE OPEN DOOR NOTES

The annexation of the Philippines made the United States a power in the Far East. For many years Great Britain, France, Germany, and other European nations had been seizing **spheres of influence** in China. They forced the weak Chinese government to grant them the right to develop particular areas, mostly around Chinese seaports. China's undeveloped resources and its huge population of about 400 million made such spheres seem likely to bring in large profits for the Europeans.

If the practice continued, American businesses might be cut off entirely from the China market. To prevent that from happening, in 1899 Secretary of State John Hay asked all the nations with such spheres of influence to agree not to close their doors to traders from other countries. All businesses should be allowed to trade with China on equal terms. Hay's **Open Door Note** was intended to protect America's trade rather than China's rights.

The European powers sent vague answers to Hay's note. Certainly they did not accept the "Open Door" principle. However, Hay boldly announced that they *had* agreed with him.

T'zu Hsi was the dowager empress of China who encouraged the Boxer Rebellion. Her portrait is by Hubert Vos. To the right is a member of the Righteous, Harmonious Fists, also known as Boxers. Who put down the Boxer Rebellion?

The Fogg Museum

National Archives

None of this exchange involved the Chinese, whose trade and territory were being carved up. Then, members of a secret society of Chinese nationalists known as the "Righteous, Harmonious Fists," or **Boxers,** launched an attack on foreigners in Peking, the capital, and in other parts of China.

Armed with swords and spears, the Boxers destroyed foreign property and killed missionaries and business people. Frightened foreigners fled for protection to the buildings which housed their governments' representatives in Peking. They remained there for weeks, virtual prisoners cut off from all contact with the outside world.

The western nations quickly organized an international army to put down this **Boxer Rebellion** of 1900. A force of 20,000, including 2,500 Americans, was rushed to the area. They rescued the trapped foreign civilians and crushed the Boxers.

Meanwhile, Hay feared that the European powers would use the Boxer Rebellion as an excuse to expand their spheres of influence. He sent off a **Second Open Door Note.** This one stated that the United States opposed any further carving up of China by foreign nations. The Open Door thus included two principles: equal trade rights for all in China and a guarantee of independence for China.

None of the European nations officially accepted these principles. In practice, however, Hay got what he wanted. American business interests were able to trade freely in the spheres and throughout the sprawling Chinese Empire.

- What were spheres of influence in China?
- What was the Boxer Rebellion?
- What two principles were stated by the Open Door Notes?

This is a watercolor caricature of Secretary of State John Hay. It was painted in 1897 by Sir Leslie Ward, who signed his work "Spy." What prompted Hay's Open Door Note?

THE PANAMA CANAL

The United States needed to link the Atlantic and Pacific Oceans. The Spanish-American War and the expansion of the United States into the Pacific made it obvious that a canal across Central America would be extremely valuable.

During the war the new American battleship *Oregon* had to steam 12,000 miles (19,200 kilometers) from the West Coast around South America in order to help destroy Admiral Cervera's fleet at Santiago. It took the *Oregon* 68 days, traveling at top speed. A canal would have reduced the *Oregon*'s voyage to 4,000 miles (6,400 kilometers) or one third the distance.

The United States government was eager to build a canal. The first step was to get rid of the **Clayton-Bulwer Treaty** of 1850 with Great Britain. That agreement stated that any such canal would be controlled by *both* nations.

The treaty had made sense in 1850 when the United States had barely reached the Pacific. It did not make sense in 1900. Therefore, in 1901, Secretary Hay negotiated a new agreement with the British. This **Hay-Pauncefote Treaty** gave the United States the right to build and control a canal by itself. In return the United States promised that ships of all nations would be allowed to use the canal on equal terms.

There were two possible canal routes across Central America. One roughly followed the path the explorer Balboa had taken across the **Isthmus of Panama** when he discovered the Pacific in 1513. It was short, but it passed through mountainous country covered by dense tropical jungles. The other was in the **Republic of Nicaragua.** There the land was more level, and part of the route could make use of Lake Nicaragua, which was 50 miles (80 kilometers) wide. The total distance was much longer, but Nicaragua was closer to the United States.

A private French company had obtained the right to build a canal across Panama, which was then part of the Republic of Colombia. This company had spent a fortune but made little progress. Thousands of its laborers had died of yellow fever and malaria. The company was now bankrupt. There was no chance that it would ever be

Nicaragua was very nearly the site of the canal connecting Atlantic and Pacific. This engraving shows Lake Managua and Momotombo Volcano. What use might have been made of Lake Nicaragua?

Culver Pictures

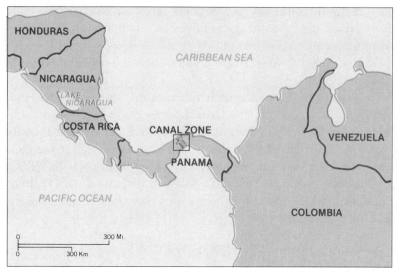

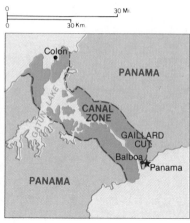

THE PANAMA CANAL ZONE

able to complete a canal. In an effort to regain some of its losses, the company offered to sell its right to build a canal to the United States for $40 million.

A representative of the bankrupt company, Philippe Bunau-Varilla, worked to persuade Congress to take over the canal project. His campaign succeeded. By 1903 President Roosevelt had made up his mind to build the canal in Panama. Congress went along with this decision.

> ▓ What were the arguments for and against building a canal across the Isthmus of Panama? What for and against the Republic of Nicaragua?

THE PANAMA "REVOLUTION"

Next, Secretary of State Hay and the Colombian representative in Washington negotiated a treaty in which Colombia leased a **canal zone** across Panama to the United States. Colombia was to receive $10 million and a rent of $250,000 a year. The United States Senate promptly consented to this treaty.

But the Colombian senate rejected it. The reason was simple. The Colombians wanted more money. The bankrupt French company was being offered four times as much for its rights in Colombia. And Colombia had granted those rights in the first place.

When Colombia rejected the treaty, Bunau-Varilla organized a revolution in Panama. There had been many such uprisings against Colombia there in the past. All had been easily put down. But this time the rebels had the support of the United States. Their "revolution" therefore succeeded.

637

The small rebel army was made up of railroad workers and members of the Panama City fire department. But when Colombian troops, sent by sea, landed at the port of Colón, they were met by the powerful U.S.S. *Nashville.* The Colombians were forced to return to their home port.

Thus was born the **Republic of Panama.** Only three days later, on November 6, 1903, the United States recognized Panama. On November 18, in Washington, Secretary Hay signed a canal treaty with a representative of the new nation. This representative was none other than Philippe Bunau-Varilla. The **Hay-Bunau-Varilla Treaty** granted the United States a ten-mile-wide Canal Zone (16 kilometers). The financial arrangements were the same ones that Colombia had turned down.

■ Why did the Colombian senate reject the treaty for the canal zone across Panama?
■ Why did Bunau-Varilla's "revolution" in Panama succeed?

The One-Centavo Stamp

To persuade Congress to choose Panama over Nicaragua for the new canal, Philippe Bunau-Varilla depended heavily on 90 one-centavo stamps. Bunau-Varilla represented the bankrupt French company that had begun the canal in France.

Bunau-Varilla had mailed out 13,000 copies of a pamphlet, *Panama or Nicaragua?* One of his arguments against a Nicaraguan canal was that there were volcanoes in the republic. No matter that nearly all had long been inactive. He wrote, "What have the Nicaraguans chosen to characterize their country . . . on their postage stamps? Volcanoes!"

The Senate was about to begin debate on the canal site. Far from Washington (and from Nicaragua) rumblings began coming from Mount Pelée, a long-dormant volcano on the island of Martinique. On May 8, 1902, the entire mountain exploded, killing nearly 30,000 people in two minutes. "What an unexpected turn of the wheel of fortune," wrote Bunau-Varilla. He thought again of the Nicaraguan stamp.

Bunau-Varilla went to every stamp dealer in Washington until he had 90 of the one-centavo Nicaraguan stamps. Each showed a puffing locomotive in the foreground and an erupting volcano in the background. Bunau-Varilla pasted the stamps on sheets of paper. Then he mailed one to each of the 90 United States senators with the neatly typed caption: "An official witness of the volcanic activity on the isthmus of Nicaragua."

BUILDING THE CANAL

Before work on the canal could begin, malaria and yellow fever had to be stamped out. Colonel William Gorgas, who had eliminated yellow fever in Cuba, was sent to Panama to rid the area of the mosquitoes which carried the disease. He drained the swamps and ponds where the mosquitoes laid their eggs.

Now the actual construction could begin. Colonel George Goethals of the Army Engineers had charge of the project. The level of the canal had to be raised as high as 85 feet (over 25 meters) above the sea. Water-filled chambers called **locks** would raise and lower ships from one level to another.

For seven years, from 1907 to 1914, a small army of workers drilled and blasted, dug and dredged. They had to cut a 9-mile-long channel (over 14 kilometers) through the mountains of solid rock. The channel was named the **Gaillard Cut** after Colonel David Gaillard, the engineer in charge of this part of the project.

The canal was finally finished in 1914. It was a magnificent achievement. President Roosevelt took full credit for the project and for its swift completion. "I am interested in the Panama Canal because I started it," he said in 1911. "If I had followed traditional conservative methods . . . debate would have been going on yet. *But I took the Canal Zone* and let Congress debate, and while the debate goes on the canal does also."

Roosevelt blamed Colombia for the revolution in Panama. He once told a friend that trying to make a deal with that country was like trying to nail jelly to a wall. Yet many Americans at that time and many more in later times felt that Roosevelt's behavior had been

William Gorgas, *top,* and George Goethals brought American know-how to the Panama Canal project. At left is an oil painted by Jonas Lie in 1913, "Dawn at Culebra." What did Gorgas and Goethals accomplish in Panama?

entirely wrong. In 1921, after Roosevelt was dead, Congress gave Colombia $25 million to make up for the loss of Panama. And in 1978 a new treaty provided that at the end of the century the Canal Zone itself would be turned back to Panama.

■ Why did President Roosevelt take full credit for the swift completion of the Panama Canal?

This powerful portrait of Theodore Roosevelt was painted c. 1908 by John Singer Sargent. It hangs with other Presidential portraits in the White House. Sargent's portraits show the vitality of his subjects. In Roosevelt Sargent had an ideal subject. What caused Roosevelt to issue his famous Corollary?

THE ROOSEVELT COROLLARY

President Roosevelt was eager to prevent any European country from interfering in the affairs of the small nations of the Caribbean. These countries were all poor, and most of them were badly governed. Their governments frequently borrowed money from European banks and investors and did not repay them when the loans fell due. Sometimes, European governments sent in warships and marines to force them to pay their debts.

Before he became President, Roosevelt did not object. "If any South American state misbehaves toward any European country," he wrote, "let the European country spank it." After Roosevelt became President, he had second thoughts. Any European interference in the affairs of Latin American nations violated the Monroe Doctrine, he decided.

Debts, however, must be paid. If a nation in the Western Hemisphere did not pay its debts, the United States must make it do so. That way justice could be done to the lenders, but there would be no European interference in the hemisphere. This policy became known as the **Roosevelt Corollary** to the Monroe Doctrine. *Corollary* means "result" or "what follows from."

Roosevelt always said that he applied the Corollary with the greatest reluctance. When he sent marines into the Dominican Republic in 1905, he insisted that he had no more desire to make that nation a colony of the United States than a snake would have to swallow a porcupine backwards. Many Americans always protested the use of force in such situations.

After William Howard Taft became President in 1909, it seemed shrewder to try to control the nations of the region indirectly. By investing money in countries like Cuba, Nicaragua, and the Dominican Republic, more stable economies would result. Then the governments of these countries would also be more stable. This policy came to be known as **dollar diplomacy** to distinguish it from the **gunboat diplomacy** of the Roosevelt Corollary.

The difficulty with dollar diplomacy was that, without meaning to, it often injured the people of the countries involved. An American company might purchase a number of small tobacco farms in Cuba. Then it might convert the land into a vast sugar plantation. The plan-

The Granger Collection

The American eagle stretches south past Panama and west to cover the Philippines. This 1904 cartoon is by Joseph Keppler, Jr. He gave it this caption: "His 126th Birthday — 'Gee, But This Is an Awful Stretch.'" What is the meaning of this cartoon?

tation would be more efficient. Its crops could be sold for larger amounts of money. But the Cubans who had been independent tobacco farmers now became hired plantation laborers. They were forced to change their entire way of life.

At this time people were just beginning to realize how heavy-handed the United States had become in the Western Hemisphere. Most people still assumed that the Latin American nations shared the values of the United States. Later they would understand that they were seriously mistaken.

- What was the Roosevelt Corollary?
- Why did dollar diplomacy replace gunboat diplomacy?

CHAPTER 21 REVIEW

Identification
Tell briefly why each of the following persons, terms, or events is important.
1. William H. Seward
2. Queen Liliuokalani
3. Sanford B. Dole
4. Valeriano Weyler
5. George Dewey
6. Theodore Roosevelt
7. John Hay
8. Emilio Aguinaldo
9. Philippe Bunau-Varilla
10. Isolationism
11. Expansionism
12. Chilean Crisis
13. Venezuela Boundary Dispute
14. Yellow journalism
15. U.S.S. *Maine*
16. Rough Riders
17. Open Door Notes
18. Boxer Rebellion
19. Roosevelt Corollary
20. Dollar diplomacy

Understanding American History
1. What events during the Civil War caused Americans to be suspicious of Europe?
2. What is isolationism? Why did most Americans favor this policy?
3. What was the purpose of the Pan-American Conference? How was its goodwill set back by the Chilean Crisis?
4. What conditions and events led to the Spanish-American War?
5. What were the U.S. gains from the Spanish-American War?
6. Why did many people in the U.S. oppose the peace treaty of 1898? By what name were opponents of the treaty known? Why was it finally accepted?
7. Explain what John Hay called for in the Open Door Notes.
8. Explain the steps the U.S. took to build and control the Panama Canal.
9. What was the Roosevelt Corollary? Why did the President issue this policy?
10. What was the difference between gunboat diplomacy and dollar diplomacy?

Activities
1. Prepare multimedia presentations on the states of Alaska and Hawaii, past and present. Tell how each was acquired and trace its history from territory to statehood. Describe present-day concerns of each state, including ecology, economy, and social well being.
2. Reread the description of yellow journalism on page 623. What examples of this kind of reporting can you find in early newspapers and magazines? These publications are usually available on microfilm or microfiche in your school library or in the morgue file of your local newspaper.
3. Make a model of the Isthmus of Panama, using clay, plaster of paris, or papier-mâché. Show the route of the Panama Canal and label the locks. Use the model to explain the stages by which a ship passes through the canal.
4. Choose one of the nations of Latin America and present a short report in class on its historical and present-day relationships with the U.S. Include these countries:

Argentina	Guatemala
Bolivia	Haiti
Brazil	Honduras
Chile	Mexico
Colombia	Nicaragua
Costa Rica	Panama
Cuba	Paraguay
Dominican Republic	Peru
Ecuador	Uruguay
El Salvador	Venezuela

5. Use historical imagination to write a letter describing your first view of a new U.S. territory between 1865–1912.

CHAPTER 21 TEST

Matching (45 points)

Number your paper 1–15 and match the description in the first column with the name in the second column.

1. General Weyler placed 500,000 Cuban farmers in these camps to regain control of the countryside
2. Popular name in the late 1860s for Alaska Purchase
3. Volunteer group raised by Theodore Roosevelt to fight against Spain
4. Idea that the U.S. should take land in North and South America and in the Pacific
5. Its explosion in Havana Harbor inflamed U.S.
6. Began when a mob attacked U.S. sailors in Valparaiso
7. Exaggerated stories that play up crime or scandal
8. Name given to U.S. attempts to influence Latin American economies
9. Held that the U.S. would police South America
10. Opposed American annexation of distant lands
11. The idea that Europeans and Americans should not meddle in each other's affairs.
12. First time North and South American nations came together to discuss common interests
13. Attack in Peking on foreigners and their property
14. Written policy intended to keep China trade open to American business
15. Nine-mile (14-kilometer) channel through what had once been mountains of solid rock

a. Chilean Crisis
b. Isolationism
c. Expansionism
d. Pan-American Conference
e. Yellow journalism
f. U.S.S. *Maine*
g. *Reconcentrados*
h. Gaillard Cut
i. Anti-imperialists
j. Open Door Notes
k. Boxer Rebellion
l. "Seward's Folly"
m. Roosevelt Corollary
n. Dollar diplomacy
o. Rough Riders

Matching (25 points)

Number your paper 16–25 and match the description in the first column with the person in the second column.

16. Leader of the Mexican revolt against Maximilian
17. Secretary of State who purchased Alaska
18. Queen who believed in "Hawaii for the Hawaiians"
19. Hero of the Battle of Manila Bay
20. Promoter who lobbied for U.S. to build Panama Canal
21. Author of the Open Door Notes
22. King who owned all Hawaiian land
23. Engineer in charge of building the Panama Canal
24. Eliminated yellow fever in Cuba and Panama
25. Organizer of the Pan-American Conference

a. Kamehameha III
b. James G. Blaine
c. William Gorgas
d. George Goethals
e. William H. Seward
f. Philippe Bunau-Varilla
g. Benito Juárez
h. Liliuokalani
i. John Hay
j. George Dewey

Essay (30 points)

In a two-part essay explain the conditions that led to the Spanish-American War and then describe the U.S. gains from the war. Prepare a simple outline before you begin writing.

CHAPTER 22
Reformers and the Progressive Movement

The Cleveland Museum of Art

Hopeful and expectant at the turn of the century, these strollers in New York's Central Park were painted in about 1905 by William Glackens. He belonged to a school of art known as Impressionism. Rather than trying to paint a photographic likeness, these artists gave their impressions of the light and shadows that played upon their subjects. What was the name of the period after 1900 in America?

THE TURN OF THE CENTURY

Around the turn of the century a new mood spread through the nation. People seemed to be full of hope about the future. This mood lasted for about 15 years in the early 1900s and was known as the **Progressive Era.** It was a time when large numbers of people were working to improve society. These reformers were called **progressives.** They were trying to make progress. They hoped to make a better world.

This belief in progress was part of the American character. Thomas Jefferson and nearly every westward-moving pioneer shared it. During the Progressive Era the feeling was especially strong. People consciously spoke of themselves and the times as "progressive."

Some progressives belonged to the Republican party, some to the Democratic. Theodore Roosevelt, one of the two great Presidents of the era, was a Republican. The other, Woodrow Wilson, was a Democrat. Progressivism was a point of view about society and politics, not a political organization. (Toward the end of the period there was a Progressive party, but we shall come to that later.)

What causes shifts of public feeling such as the Progressive Movement is a mystery. There were several reasons, but no one can say exactly how they were related to one another.

People looked forward because they were beginning the 20th century. They sensed they were at the beginning of new and probably better times. The return of prosperity after the long depression of the 1890s had changed their mood. The easy victory in the Spanish-American War increased their self-confidence. They seemed likely to accomplish whatever they set out to do. They felt stronger and more important because the war had added new territory to the nation in many parts of the world. When Senator Albert J. Beveridge of Indiana made a speech describing "the march of the flag" in the Caribbean and Pacific, he was cheered to the rafters.

■ Who were the progressives?
■ What changes were there in the national mood at the turn of the century?

PROBLEMS OF GROWTH

The same Americans who were so confident and hopeful were aware that conditions in the country were far from perfect. Many serious problems remained unsolved. Speaking broadly, these problems were produced by the Industrial Revolution.

The Cleveland Museum of Art

John Sloan, who painted this oil in about 1911, and William Glackens, whose oil is on page 644, belonged to the Eight, a group of American artists who painted common scenes from everyday life rather than fancy, formal pictures. This painting of a line of wash hung out to dry is one example. Critics called this group the "ashcan" school, but the work is valuable today to give us a good idea of life at the turn of the century. This painting is called "Woman's Work." What caused problems in America at this time?

In the great cities of the United States lived both the richest and poorest people in the country. The mansions of millionaire manufacturers stood only a few blocks from ugly, unhealthy slum districts that housed the poor families who labored in their factories. Few Americans objected to the Carnegies and Rockefellers and Morgans being so wealthy. But sometimes the rich seemed too powerful, the poor too weak. What power the poor did have was in the control of the big-city political machines, which used their votes to steal from the rich and the middle class.

The continued growth of great corporations and trusts was another cause of concern. The revival of the economy increased business profits. This encouraged businesses to expand their operations. Big companies bought out small ones. In the year 1899 alone, over 1,000 firms were swallowed up.

The largest corporations were merging with each other to form giant monopolies. In 1901 the banker J. P. Morgan bought Andrew Carnegie's huge steel company. He then combined it with corporations that made finished steel products like pipe and wire and rails. He called the result the **United States Steel Corporation.**

U.S. Steel became the world's first billion-dollar corporation. Because it was so large and powerful, many people considered such a supercompany dangerous no matter what the policies of its owners and managers.

> How did the world's first billion-dollar corporation come into being?

THE PROGRESSIVE MOOD

None of the reformers' concerns came in with the 20th century. The problems of the Industrial Revolution existed long before 1900. Reformers had been fighting political bosses and machine politics for years. Efforts had been made to improve conditions in the slums. Many state laws had been passed to protect workers. The federal government had tried to check the growth of monopolies by the Sherman Antitrust Act. It had regulated the great railroad corporations through the Interstate Commerce Act. In the 1890s the Populists had vigorously attacked the evils they saw in the industrial age.

What was different about progressives was their new mood. They were happy, cheerful reformers. Most Populists had seen themselves as underdogs being taken advantage of by powerful bankers and railroad tycoons. Progressives attacked bankers and tycoons of all sorts. But they did so more to protect others than to help themselves. Good times made it possible for people to be more generous. Progressives wanted to share their prosperity with people less fortunate than themselves.

The Granger Collection

Like Thomas Jefferson, the progressives believed that if the people knew the truth, they would do what was right. Like Alexander Hamilton, they believed that the government should act forcefully to increase the national wealth and to improve the standard of living for all.

This is how the typical progressive reasoned: First of all, most ordinary people are basically decent and public spirited. When they realize what needs to be done to improve society, they will do it. Informing the people is the first step toward reform.

Next, the political system must be thoroughly democratic. If the wishes of the people are to be carried out, the government must respond to public opinion. Government officials must be both honest and efficient. It must be easy to remove dishonest or lazy officials and replace them with good public servants.

Then, with the will of the people behind it, the government should take action. It should check and control greedy special interests seeking selfish benefits at the expense of the people. It should try to improve the condition of weaker members of society—children, old people, the poor.

On a paper horse William Jennings Bryan rides to awaken his longtime Populist followers. "The Populist Paul Revere" is a color lithograph made by J. S. Pughe in 1904. The horse is made of *The Commoner,* a newspaper read by Populists. What does the age of Bryan's followers suggest was the status of Populism in the early 1900s?

■ How did the progressives differ from reformers of the past?
■ What was the role of the government as progressives saw it?

THE MUCKRAKERS

Progressives depended heavily on newspapers and magazines to get their messages to the people. They placed more stress on describing what was wrong with society than on offering specific plans for reform. They assumed that once the people knew what was wrong, they would do something to correct the problem.

A small army of writers and researchers were soon engaged in what we today call **investigative journalism.** These writers dug into public records. They talked to politicians and business people, to city clerks and police officers, to factory workers and recent immigrants. Then they published their results in hard-hitting articles and books. They were specific. They named names. They demanded that "something be done." Improvements in printing and better ways of reproducing photographs added greatly to the effectiveness of their writing.

Theodore Roosevelt called the authors who exposed the evils of the time **muckrakers.** They were raking up muck, or dirt, in order to make people aware of it. Muckrakers exposed the corrupt activities of political bosses. They described the terrible living conditions of the slums. They showed children laboring in factories and sweatshops. They wrote about the sale of impure foods and drugs. There were even articles describing secret payments of money to college football players and other evils resulting from an "overemphasis" on college sports.

Among the best-known of the muckrakers were Lincoln Steffens and Ida Tarbell. Steffens specialized in exposing corrupt city governments. In *McClure's* magazine, which was the most important muckraking periodical, he reported on conditions in St. Louis, Min-

Ida M. Tarbell and Lincoln Steffens were two of the leading muckrakers of the early 1900s. Tarbell's writings include a life of Abraham Lincoln as well as her articles exposing fraud and corruption. Steffens examined city governments. Why were these writers called *muckrakers?*

neapolis, Cincinnati, and other "boss-ridden" cities. In 1904 Steffens published these articles in a book, *The Shame of the Cities*. He also wrote about corruption in state governments. But Steffens was not a mere scandal seeker. When he discovered well-run cities and honest officials, he praised them highly.

Ida Tarbell was one of the leading journalists of her day. She was also an important historian. Before she turned to muckraking, she wrote biographies of the French Emperor Napoleon and of Abraham Lincoln. But she specialized in economic and business investigations. Her detailed study of the methods used by John D. Rockefeller's Standard Oil Company was published in 19 installments in *McClure's*.

- How did the investigative journalists called muckrakers help progressive causes?
- What did Lincoln Steffens and Ida Tarbell write about?

REFORMING CITY GOVERNMENTS

The struggle to rid cities of corrupt political bosses and their powerful machines was almost endless because more large cities were developing as the nation grew larger and more industrialized. By 1910 there were 50 American cities with populations of more than 100,000.

Among the notable reformer mayors of the Progressive Era was Samuel M. Jones. Jones was a poor farm boy who made a fortune drilling for oil. Then he sold out to Standard Oil and became a manufacturer of oil-drilling equipment in Toledo, Ohio.

During the depression of the 1890s Jones was shocked by the condition of the unemployed men who came to his plant looking for jobs. He set out to apply the **Golden Rule** in his factory: "Do unto others as you would have them do unto you." He raised wages. He reduced the workday to eight hours. He sold lunches to workers at cost. He created a park, gave picnics for his employees, and invited them to his home.

In 1897 "Golden Rule" Jones was elected mayor of Toledo. He held this office until his death in 1904. His election was a victory for honest government. He stressed political independence rather than party loyalty. He established the eight-hour day for many city workers. He built playgrounds and a city golf course. He provided kindergartens for young children.

Another progressive mayor, also from Ohio, was Tom L. Johnson of Cleveland. Johnson was less idealistic than Jones, but he got even more done. He forced the local streetcar company to lower its fares. He reduced taxes by cutting out wasteful city agencies and running others more efficiently. He improved the Cleveland parks. And he reformed the city prisons. After his investigation of Cleveland, Lincoln Steffens called Johnson "the best mayor of the best-governed city in the United States."

Other cities where important reform movements were organized by progressives included Philadelphia, Chicago, and Los Angeles. In San Francisco the corrupt machine of Boss Abraham Ruef was defeated by reformers led by Fremont Older, editor of the San Francisco *Bulletin,* and Rudolph Spreckles, a wealthy sugar manufacturer. In St. Louis a lawyer, Joseph W. Folk, headed the reformers.

■ What made Samuel Jones a remarkable employer? What made him a remarkable mayor?

■ What were some of Tom Johnson's accomplishments as mayor of Cleveland?

REFORMING STATE GOVERNMENTS

Progressives also tried to make state governments more responsive to the wishes of the people. The most "progressive" state by far was Wisconsin. The leading Wisconsin progressive was Robert M. La Follette, who was elected governor of the state in 1900.

La Follette's program was known as the **Wisconsin Idea.** To give voters more control over who ran for public office, he persuaded the legislature to pass a **direct primary** law. Instead of being chosen by politicians, candidates had to campaign for party nominations in **primary elections.** The people, not the politicians, could then select the candidates who would compete in the final election.

While La Follette was governor, the Wisconsin legislature also passed a law limiting the amount of money candidates for office could spend. Another law restricted the activities of **lobbyists** seeking to persuade legislatures to pass laws favorable to special interests.

La Follette had great faith in the good judgment of the people. If they were "thoroughly informed," he said, they would always do what was right. La Follette also realized that state government had to perform many tasks which called for special technical knowledge that ordinary citizens did not have.

La Follette believed that complicated matters such as the regulation of railroads and banks and the setting of tax rates should *not* be decided by popular vote. Appointed commissions of experts ought to handle these tasks. This idea was not original with La Follette. There were state boards of education and railroad commissions in nearly every state long before 1900. But the spread of such organizations in the Progressive Era was rapid.

The Wisconsin Idea was copied in other states. Many passed direct primary laws. Some allowed ordinary citizens to sign petitions which would force the legislature to vote on particular bills. Others

Robert M. La Follette speaks from a wagon to farmers of Cumberland, Wisconsin, in this 1897 photograph. In 1900 he became governor and in 1906 a U.S. senator. His strongest adviser was his wife, Belle Case La Follette, who studied law and worked for women's suffrage. How was Wisconsin progressive?

authorized what was called the **referendum.** Under this system a particular proposal could be placed on the ballot to be decided by the yes or no votes of the people at a regular election.

Many states responded to the demands of women that they be allowed to vote. By 1915 two thirds of the states permitted women to vote in certain elections, such as for members of school boards. About a dozen states had given women full voting rights by that date.

These crusaders for women's rights, called suffragettes, march for votes in New York City in this early 20th-century photograph. Their name is one of the distinctions made at the time between men and women: there were poets and poetesses, postmen and postmistresses, suffragists and suffragettes. How many states gave women voting rights at this time?

Carrie Lane Chapman Catt sat for this oil portrait in 1927. It is the work of Mary Foote. Carrie Lane was superintendent of schools in Mason City, Iowa (the model for the River City of *The Music Man*). She later founded the League of Women Voters. Which group was led by Catt in the early 1900s?

The **National American Women's Suffrage Association** (NAWSA) led this fight. The president of the association from 1900 to 1904 was Carrie Lane Chapman Catt. She was an intelligent person and certainly better informed about public issues than the average man. But she could not vote. She had become active in the fight for women's rights in her home state of Iowa in the 1880s and later in the NAWSA.

One further progressive effort to give the people more control over elected officials was the **Seventeenth Amendment** to the Constitution, which was ratified in 1913. Article I of the Constitution had provided that United States senators should be elected by members of the state legislatures. Sometimes, such as in the contest in Illinois between Abraham Lincoln and Stephen A. Douglas in 1858, the voters were able to make their wishes clear before the legislators acted. Often they were not. The Seventeenth Amendment changed the system. Thereafter, senators were to be "elected by the people" of the state.

- How did the Wisconsin Idea give voters more choice in selecting their candidates for public office?
- What matters did progressives believe should *not* be settled by public vote?
- For what cause did Carrie Lane Chapman Catt fight?
- What did the Seventeenth Amendment provide?

SOCIAL AND ECONOMIC REFORMS

Progressives were making state and local governments more democratic. At the same time they were insisting that these governments do something about the social and economic problems of the times. Many city governments responded by taking over waterworks that had been privately owned. Some extended what was called **municipal socialism** to the public ownership of streetcar lines and to gas and electric companies.

Not many progressives were **socialists.** Socialists favored government ownership of all the means of production. Most progressives believed in the **free enterprise** system—that is, the right of a business to take its own course without government controls. But many progressives made an exception for local public utilities. To have more than one privately owned gas company or to set up competing streetcar lines would have been inefficient. Believers in municipal socialism thought the best way to protect the public against being overcharged was to have the people, through their local governments, own all public utilities.

The progressives continued the efforts to improve the health and housing of poor city dwellers begun by earlier reformers. In New

York City, for example, an improved tenement house law was passed in 1901. Better plumbing and ventilation had to be installed in all new tenements. Older buildings had to be remodeled to meet the new standards. During the Progressive Era more than 40 other cities passed similar tenement house laws.

Conditions in factories also attracted much attention, especially after the terrible tragedy known as the **Triangle Fire.** In 1911 a fire in the Triangle Shirtwaist Company factory on the upper floors of a building in New York City caused the deaths of over 140 women. Some were burned to death. Others were overcome by smoke. Many died jumping from the windows in a desperate effort to escape the flames. After this disaster New York state passed 35 new factory inspection laws. Other states also passed stronger laws to improve the safety of factories. Many began to require manufacturers to insure their workers against accidents.

Urged on by progressives, most states outlawed the employment of young children in factories. Many also limited the hours that women and older children could work. Most people agreed that states had the power to regulate child labor. But many employers and large numbers of workers claimed that laws regulating where or how long adults could work took away the right of individuals to decide such matters for themselves.

Look closely at this room. At these sewing machines once sat women of the Triangle Shirtwaist Company in New York City. From these windows workers leaped to their deaths when flames consumed the upper floors of this building in 1911. Twisted metal is all that remains to testify to the terrible working conditions of this establishment. How did lawmakers respond to this disaster?

The Fourteenth Amendment, these people argued, says a state may not "deprive any person of life, liberty, or property." Laws that say women cannot work more than ten hours a day, or that coal miners cannot work more than eight hours a day, violate this amendment, they claimed. These employers and workers ignored the fact that the Fourteenth Amendment had been added to the Constitution to protect the civil rights of blacks in the southern states after the Civil War.

This poster proclaims the national eight-hour workday. A woman who symbolizes Liberty hands a laurel wreath to a seated worker. Other symbols include a beehive, an arm and hammer, and a Roman numeral eight. What arguments were made against limiting the workday?

Those favoring reforms argued back by stressing the power of the state to protect the public. Despite the Fourteenth Amendment, criminals can be jailed or fined. Such actions must deprive them of liberty and property in order to protect the public against crime. By the same reasoning, laws that prevent people from working long hours or under unhealthy conditions protect their families and society in general, not only the workers themselves. Reformers even insisted that the state had the right to make laws setting a **minimum wage.** They argued that if workers did not earn a certain minimum wage, their families would suffer. Crime and disease and a general loss of energy would result. This would injure the entire society.

- What is meant by municipal socialism? What, by contrast, is free enterprise?
- Why did reformers believe states should make laws to protect workers?

READING PRACTICE IN SOCIAL STUDIES

Making Inferences and Drawing Conclusions

Think how often you have been told to "read between the lines." When you do so, you make *inferences.* Inferences are arrived at by your own reasoning. You *infer* by understanding what is indicated in your reading but not stated outright.

For example, at the beginning of this chapter you read, on page 644:

Some progressives belonged to the Republican party, some to the Democratic. Theodore Roosevelt, one of the two great Presidents of the era, was a Republican. The other, Woodrow Wilson, was a Democrat.

Using good reasoning, you can infer the next sentence:

Progressivism was a point of view about society and politics, not a political organization.

When you draw *conclusions,* you are making a type of inference. A sound conclusion comes from both inference and common sense. To return to the example above, it is reasonable to infer that progressivism was more important in the early 1900s than simply being a Republican or Democrat. And common sense helps you conclude that progressivism appealed to many people if it crossed party lines.

Read the following selection carefully. It was written by a muckraker in 1903, whose subject was child labor in a southern cotton mill. Then do the exercises that follow in order to practice the skills of making inferences and drawing conclusions.

"How old are you?"

"Ten."

She looks six. It is impossible to know if this is true. The children are commanded both by parents and bosses to advance their ages when asked.

"Tired?"

She nods without stopping . . . They have no time to talk. Indeed, conversation is not well looked upon by the bosses . . . and at noon I have no heart to take their leisure. At twelve o'clock Minnie, a little spooler, scarcely higher than her spools, lifts her hands above her head and exclaims: *"Thank God, there's the whistle!"* I watch them disperse; some run like mad, always bareheaded, to fetch the dinner pail for mother or father, who work in the mill and who choose to spend these little legs and spare their own. It takes ten minutes to go, ten to return, and the little laborer has ten to devour its own food, which, half the time, he is too exhausted to eat.

I watch the children crouch on the floor by the frames; some fall asleep between mouthfuls of food, and so lie asleep with food in their mouths until the overseer rouses them to their tasks again. Here and there totters a little child just learning to walk; it runs and crawls the length of the mill. Mothers who have no one with whom to leave their babies bring them to the workshop, and their lives begin, continue, and end in the horrible pandemonium.

Number your paper 1–5. For each statement write *D* if it is stated directly in the selection above or *I* if it must be inferred.
1. Mothers who have no one with whom to leave their babies bring them to the workshop.
2. The bosses believe that talking would cause the children to work more slowly.
3. The noonday meal break lasts a half hour.
4. Some children fall asleep between mouthfuls of food.
5. The author feels pity for these children.

Now state the conclusion that you draw from this reading.

Louis D. Brandeis was author of the famous Brandeis brief. It persuaded the Supreme Court that limiting work hours for women was reasonable. He was called "the people's attorney." In 1916 President Wilson appointed Brandeis to the Supreme Court. Who prepared the research for Brandeis's famous brief?

REFORMERS IN THE COURTS

Both state and federal courts tried to resolve the conflict between the Fourteenth Amendment and the need for state governments to look after the common good. In 1905, in the case of *Lochner v. New York,* the Supreme Court decided that a New York law limiting bakers to ten hours work a day was unconstitutional. Such laws were "meddlesome interference with the rights of the individual," the Court ruled. Bakers could work as long as they liked.

Three years later, however, the Supreme Court took the opposite position. This time the case involved an Oregon law that limited women laundry workers to a ten-hour workday. The Court decided that this law was a proper use of a state's power. Women laundry workers are also mothers, the Court noted. If working too long injured their health, the health of any children they might have would suffer. Therefore, said the Court, "the well-being of the race" would be threatened.

This case, known as *Muller v. Oregon* (1908), is particularly important. For the first time the Supreme Court paid attention to economic and social evidence, not only to legal arguments. A lawyer for Oregon, Louis D. Brandeis, presented a detailed brief, or argument, showing that long hours of work in fact injured the health of women and thus the public health.

The research on which this **Brandeis brief** was based was done by two remarkable women, Florence Kelley and Josephine Goldmark. Kelley and Goldmark were officials of the **National Consumers' League.** They were deeply interested in many progressive reforms. The material they collected for Brandeis had a direct influence on the justices. More important, it changed the way future cases of this type were argued and decided.

Muller v. Oregon did not end the controversy about the power of a state to protect its weaker members. But by the end of the Progressive Era, many state laws had been passed to help workers and poor people.

■ What is the importance of the Supreme Court's decision in the case of *Muller v. Oregon?*

PROGRESSIVES AND BIG BUSINESS

The "trust problem" of the 1880s and 1890s continued to be a matter of great concern in the early 1900s. All progressives looked with some alarm at large corporations—the supercompanies. They argued that supercompanies like U.S. Steel had too much power over important industries. Some sort of government check or control on these large corporations was necessary. But progressives did not agree as to how these giants should be regulated.

unless the owners agreed to a settlement. Then he appointed a special commission to work out the terms to end the dispute.

Because he was a great nature lover, Roosevelt was particularly interested in **conservation** of the nation's natural resources. He used his power as President very effectively in this area. He did not object to allowing lumber companies to cut down trees on government lands. But he believed in **scientific forestry.** Bypassing Congress, he placed large forest areas in federal reserves by executive order. Reserved land could not be claimed or purchased by special interests. But it could be leased to lumber companies. Their cutting, however, was strictly controlled by government experts.

Roosevelt applied the same principle to resources such as coal, waterpower, and grazing lands. He did a great deal to focus public attention on the importance of conserving natural resources. In this respect he was a typical progressive. He assumed that when the people were informed, they would bring pressure on their representatives to do the right thing.

- Why is Roosevelt described as an activist President?
- Why did Roosevelt believe that decision making should be centralized?
- How did Roosevelt work for conservation of the nation's natural resources?

WILLIAM HOWARD TAFT

Roosevelt's views about federal regulation of business and about Presidential power eventually caused a split in the Republican party. They also divided the Progressive Movement.

When he completed his second term as President, Roosevelt did not run again. Instead he used his influence to get the Republican nomination for his close friend William Howard Taft. Taft was easily elected, defeating William Jennings Bryan, who was running for President for the third and last time.

Taft was from Cincinnati, where he had been a federal judge. After the Spanish-American War he had moved from the court of appeals to the post of governor general of the Philippine Islands. In 1904 Roosevelt had appointed him Secretary of War.

By the time he became President, Taft weighed over 300 pounds. He was good natured. He had an excellent sense of humor. When he laughed, his belly shook like the well-known bowlful of jelly. But Taft was not a success as President, and his great weight was partly to blame.

Taft found it hard to get all his work done. Because he was so overweight, he needed much rest and relaxation. Further, he was a poor politician. Theodore Roosevelt had often been able to keep both

The Presidential portrait of William Howard Taft was painted in oil by Anders L. Zorn while Taft was in the White House. Who promoted Taft for President?

sides happy by taking a middle position on controversial questions. When Taft took a middle position, he usually made both sides angry with him.

Taft tried to continue the policies of the Roosevelt administration. He supported a new law to further increase the powers of the Interstate Commerce Commission. He added more forest lands to the national reserves. He also continued Roosevelt's policy of attacking "bad" trusts under the Sherman Act.

Taft allowed conservative Republicans to influence his policies in many ways. He bungled a well-meant attempt to get Congress to lower the tariffs on manufactured goods. There was a nasty fight within his administration over conservation policy between Secretary of the Interior Richard A. Ballinger and Gifford Pinchot, the chief forester of the department. Alaskan coal lands were involved in this **Ballinger-Pinchot controversy.** Taft sided with Ballinger and dismissed Pinchot. He was probably correct in doing so. But Pinchot then persuaded ex-President Roosevelt that Ballinger and the President were not true friends of conservation.

■ Why was President Taft expected to carry on the policies of ex-President Roosevelt?

THE PROGRESSIVE PARTY

Roosevelt did not want to interfere with Taft's handling of the Presidency. Nor did he want to second-guess him. As soon as Taft was inaugurated, Roosevelt went off to hunt big game in Africa. But when he returned to the United States in 1910, he quickly came into conflict with Taft. He soon decided that Taft was not really a progressive. Taft was not using the powers of his office forcefully, the way Roosevelt had. Roosevelt decided that Taft was a weak leader.

In particular Roosevelt objected to the President's antitrust policy. When Taft ordered an antitrust suit against the U.S. Steel Corporation, Roosevelt was furious. In his opinion U.S. Steel was a "good" trust. Its officers had cooperated faithfully with the Bureau of Corporations.

By 1911 all sorts of Republican leaders, conservatives as well as progressives, were telling Roosevelt that Taft was so unpopular that he could not be reelected in 1912. They urged Roosevelt to seek the nomination. Roosevelt finally agreed. He entered and won nearly all the Republican primaries.

However, there were far fewer Presidential primaries in 1912 than there are today. In most states party professionals chose the convention delegates, and Taft got nearly all of them. When the Republican convention met in June, the Taft delegates were in the majority. The President was renominated on the first ballot.

Roosevelt was now ready for a fight. Large numbers of Republican progressives urged him to make the run for President. He agreed to form a new **Progressive party** and seek the Presidency under its banner.

In his enthusiasm for the coming battle for the White House, Roosevelt announced that he felt "as strong as a bull moose." Cartoonists promptly began to use a moose as the symbol for the Progressive party to go along with the Republican elephant and the Democratic donkey. Soon people were referring to the party as the **Bull Moose party.**

Roosevelt's 1912 platform was ahead of its time. Corporations should be brought "under complete federal control," he said. Presidential candidates should be chosen by the people in primary elections, not by machine politicians at conventions. He also came out for a law to insure workers who were injured on the job, minimum-wage protection for women, and doing away with child labor. He supported a Constitutional amendment giving women the right to vote.

Roosevelt called his program the **New Nationalism.** By nationalism he meant a stronger and more active national government. He was thinking of something similar to what we today call the **welfare state.** The government should be prepared to do "whatever . . . the public welfare may require," he said.

"Suffering snakes," the Republican elephant says. "How Theodore has changed." The Democratic donkey agrees. Theodore Roosevelt is now a bull moose in this cartoon from a 1912 *Harper's Weekly*. By what other name was his party known?

- How did President Taft win the nomination to run again for the Presidency?
- Why did ex-President Roosevelt form the Progressive party?
- What did Roosevelt mean by the New Nationalism?

THE ELECTION OF 1912

Roosevelt hoped to attract Democratic as well as Republican voters to the Progressive party. But since he had been a lifelong Republican, the new party was sure to draw most of its support from Republicans. This presented Democrats with a golden opportunity. With Republican voters split between Taft and Roosevelt, the Democrats' chances of winning the election were excellent. All they needed to nail down the victory was an attractive Presidential candidate.

The struggle for the nomination at the Democratic convention was hard fought. The person who won it was Woodrow Wilson, the governor of New Jersey.

Wilson was a newcomer to politics. He had been born in Virginia in 1856. After graduating from Princeton College and studying law, he studied political science and became a professor. Most of his teaching was done at Princeton, where he was very popular. In 1902 he had been elected president of Princeton. As president

This 1919 oil portrait of Woodrow Wilson was painted from life by Harriet Murphy. It shows Wilson in a formal pose during the last year of his Presidency. What did he call his progressive program?

he introduced several important reforms in education. He hired more teachers and encouraged closer contacts between professors and students. He also added a large number of courses to the curriculum.

In 1910, however, Wilson resigned as president of Princeton to run for governor of New Jersey on the Democratic ticket. He was elected. He immediately proposed a number of progressive reforms. More important, he displayed remarkable political skill in getting the state legislature to enact his proposals into law. This success explains how he defeated the other Democratic Presidential hopefuls in 1912.

The Democratic program was in the progressive tradition. Wilson called it the **New Freedom.** The *objectives* of the New Freedom were quite similar to those of the New Nationalism. The *methods* proposed were quite different.

Wilson did not believe in close government regulation of big business. Instead he wished to rely on antitrust laws to break up monopolies. Unlike Roosevelt, who thought that competition was wasteful, Wilson thought competition made business more efficient. The federal government should pass laws defining fair competition, Wilson believed. Any company or individuals who broke those laws should be severely punished.

Wilson also disliked Roosevelt's New Nationalism because he thought it would make government too big and let it interfere too much in the affairs of citizens. He opposed federal laws that told large corporations how to manage their affairs. He also opposed laws that gave special privileges to labor unions or farmers or women or any other group.

In a way, Wilson wanted the federal government to act like the referee in a football game. The government should enforce the rules of the game strictly but evenhandedly. It should keep a sharp eye on the players and penalize any team that broke the rules. But it should not try to call the plays or choose sides.

- Why did the Presidential election of 1912 offer the Democrats a golden opportunity?
- How did Woodrow Wilson's New Freedom differ from Theodore Roosevelt's New Nationalism?

A VICTORY FOR REFORM

Wilson won the election of 1912 easily. He received 435 electoral votes to Roosevelt's 88 and Taft's 8. However, he got less than 42 per cent of the popular vote. Slightly over half the voters cast their ballots for either Roosevelt or Taft. In other words, Wilson was elected because of the breakup of the Republican party.

Nevertheless, the election was an overwhelming victory for progressivism and reform. Together, Wilson and Roosevelt received almost 70 per cent of the popular vote. In addition almost 900,000 voters, about 6 per cent of the total, cast their ballots for the Socialist party. The Socialists were demanding government ownership of railroads, banks, and "all large-scale industries."

The Socialist Presidential candidate was Eugene V. Debs, the leader of the railroad workers who had been jailed for his role in the Pullman strike in 1894. While in prison, Debs had done a good deal of reading about government and politics. He became a socialist. He had run for President on the Socialist ticket in 1904 and in 1908, each time receiving about 400,000 votes. In 1912 his vote more than doubled. Clearly the American people were in a reform-minded mood.

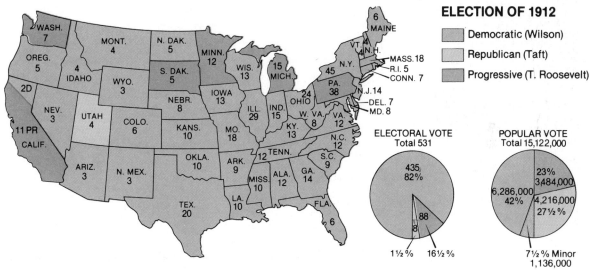

ELECTION OF 1912

Democratic (Wilson)
Republican (Taft)
Progressive (T. Roosevelt)

ELECTORAL VOTE
Total 531

435
82%

88
8
1½%   16½%

POPULAR VOTE
Total 15,122,000

23%
3,484,000
6,286,000
42%   4,216,000
27½%

7½% Minor
1,136,000

Was the election a victory for Wilson's New Freedom philosophy? The answer to this question is unclear. The argument between Wilson and Roosevelt was the same one that Jefferson had with Hamilton in the 1790s about the role of the federal government. On the one hand, the large Socialist vote suggests increased support for the Hamilton (and Roosevelt) "big government" position. On the other hand, both Taft and Wilson believed, as Jefferson had, in competition rather than government regulations. Both promised to enforce the antitrust law strictly. When the Taft and Wilson votes are combined, they come to about 65 per cent of the total.

Probably most citizens did not have a firm opinion about how reform should be accomplished. Most were voting for "a reformer" but not for a particular program.

■ Why did Wilson win the Presidency so easily?
■ Why is it unclear whether Wilson's victory was also a victory for his New Freedom philosophy?

665

A cartoon criminal representing the Money Trust hangs his head as he hears the death sentence spoken by President Wilson in 1913. What banking law was passed in 1913?

WILSON'S NEW FREEDOM

As soon as he took office, President Wilson set out to put his ideas into practice. The Democrats had majorities in both houses of Congress, so he confidently expected to see his proposals enacted into law.

He first urged Congress to lower the high protective tariff. The resulting **Underwood Tariff** of 1913 allowed food products, iron and steel, agricultural machinery—things that could be produced more cheaply in the United States than abroad—to enter the country without any tariff at all. For goods that needed some protection, the duties were lowered but not done away with. In addition, the Underwood Act provided for an **income tax.** This was possible because another progressive reform, the **Sixteenth Amendment** authorizing federal income taxes, had just been added to the Constitution.

Congress also passed the **Federal Reserve Act** in 1913. This law created 12 Federal Reserve Banks. These were banks for banks. When ordinary commercial banks lent money to business borrowers, they received as security for the loans such things as warehouse receipts, bills owed the borrower by customers, and other forms of what is known as **commercial paper.** Under the Federal Reserve system the banks could use this commercial paper as security in order to borrow Federal Reserve Notes issued by the Reserve Banks. They could then lend these notes to other borrowers.

The process of exchanging commercial paper for Federal Reserve Notes is called **rediscounting.** The **rediscount rate** is the interest rate charged by the Federal Reserve Banks on the money they lend commercial banks. A **Federal Reserve Board** in Washington controls the rediscount rate. This Board uses the rate to stimulate or slow down business activity.

Under the law, if the Federal Reserve Board believed that the nation's economy was expanding too rapidly, it raised the rediscount rate. The banks would then have to increase the interest they charged when they lent money. This would discourage business borrowing and cause a slowdown in the economy. During a depression or slump the Federal Reserve Board could lower the rediscount rate. This would make it possible for banks to lower their interest rates. Businesses could borrow more cheaply. They could then increase their output or lower prices, and the national economy would pick up.

In practice the Federal Reserve system did not work quite so smoothly. It was not always easy to know whether to stimulate the economy or slow it down. Still, the Federal Reserve was a great improvement over the old national banking system established during the Civil War. Although somewhat changed by later legislation, it is still in operation.

666

Then, in 1914, Congress passed the **Clayton Antitrust Act.** This law made it illegal for directors of one corporation to be directors of other corporations in the same field. It provided that the officers and managers of a company that violated the antitrust laws could be held personally responsible for the violations. It also stated that labor unions were *not* to be considered "combinations . . . in restraint of trade under the antitrust laws."

In 1914 Congress also created the **Federal Trade Commission.** This Commission conducted investigations of large business corporations. If it found them acting unfairly toward competitors or the public, it issued **cease and desist orders,** making them stop.

The Federal Trade Commission was closer in spirit to Theodore Roosevelt's New Nationalism than to the New Freedom. So was the Federal Reserve system. Wilson was not a rigid believer in old-style competition. Like Roosevelt, he was willing to use more than one technique in order to check the power of big business.

■ What did the Sixteenth Amendment provide?
■ Under the Federal Reserve Act, what is the rediscount rate? Who controls this rate? What is the rate used for?

PROHIBITION

During the Progressive Era there was strong popular support for prohibiting the manufacture, transportation, and sale of alcoholic beverages. By 1914 **prohibition** was in force in more than a quarter of the states, known as the **dry states.** In 1919 the **Eighteenth Amendment** was ratified, making the entire nation dry. This amendment was enforced by the **Volstead Act.**

People who favored prohibition pointed to the sharp decline in arrests for drunkenness and to the lower number of deaths from alcoholism in the 1920s. Fewer workers spent their hard-earned dollars on drink. However, prohibition was impossible to enforce, even with the tough Volstead Act. Private individuals bought liquor smuggled by **bootleggers** or drank gin from teacups in **speakeasys**— secret bars or clubs.

Crime statistics soared in the 1920s. Most of the liquor was sold by gangsters such as "Scarface Al" Capone of Chicago. Hoodlums fought for territories with guns and bombs, killing innocent bystanders as well as their rivals. Still, powerful dry forces kept politicians in both parties from proposing that prohibition be lifted, or **repealed.** It remained in force until December 1933, when it was repealed by the **Twenty-first Amendment.**

■ What arguments were made for prohibition?
■ What made prohibition impossible to enforce?

A federal agent padlocks shut the door to a saloon in the 1920s. Its owners have violated the National Prohibition Act by serving alcohol on the premises. What made the entire nation dry?

LIMITS OF PROGRESSIVISM

By the end of 1914 the Progressive Movement had accomplished many political, social, and economic reforms. But the progressives had prejudices and blind spots that limited their achievements. Most were not very sympathetic to immigrants. It was a time of heavy immigration. During some years at the height of the progressive period, more than 1 million newcomers settled in the United States.

Progressives who were alarmed about corruption in politics blamed the recent immigrants. These people cast a large proportion of the votes that kept corrupt bosses in power. Social workers and many others who were trying to help the poor thought that too many immigrants were crowding into the slums. They argued that the famous American **melting pot** could not absorb so many people so quickly. They were afraid that the character of American life would be undermined unless immigration was somehow limited.

■ Why were progressives not sympathetic to immigrants?

BLACKS IN THE PROGRESSIVE ERA

The most glaring weakness of the progressive reformers was their attitude toward racial problems. The Progressive Era was probably the low point in the history of racial relations after the Civil War.

There was no one progressive point of view on the racial question. A few progressives were strong believers in racial equality. Northern progressives tended to be less prejudiced against blacks than southerners. But most progressives believed that blacks were entitled at best to second-class citizenship. The most common attitude was that of the Alabama progressive who said that blacks were meant "to be protected by Government, rather than to be the directors of Government."

Most progressives claimed not to be prejudiced and to want to help blacks. But being white and comfortably well off in most cases, they had little understanding of the effects of racial discrimination on black people. Theodore Roosevelt once invited Booker T. Washington to have a meal with him at the White House. When newspapers reported that the President had eaten with a black man, Roosevelt was flooded with complaints, many from progressives. Instead of defending his invitation, Roosevelt practically apologized for it. It had been a spur-of-the-moment act, he explained. Washington had just happened to be there on public business at mealtime. Roosevelt never invited another black to dine at the White House.

Still, the early 20th century marked a turning point in the history of racial relations. Booker T. Washington remained an important figure. He raised a great deal of money for black schools. He worked cleverly behind the scenes to get political jobs for blacks and

to fight racial discrimination cases in the courts. However, he was no longer the only significant black public figure. Younger leaders were beginning to reject his whole approach to the racial problem.

William E. B. Du Bois was the most important of the new black leaders. Du Bois was a historian and sociologist. Although he had very light skin, he was proud of being black. He set out to make other blacks realize that they must speak out for their rights. If they did not, they would actually be inferior, he warned. The trouble with Booker T. Washington is that he "apologizes for injustice," Du Bois wrote in 1903. Blacks will never get their "reasonable rights" unless they stop "voluntarily throwing them away," Du Bois said.

In 1905, at a meeting at Niagara Falls, Canada, Du Bois and a few other black leaders began the **Niagara Movement.** They demanded equality of economic and educational opportunities for blacks, an end to racial segregation, and protection of the right to

Leaders of the Niagara Movement posed for this photograph taken in front of a studio backdrop after their meeting in 1905. W. E. B. Du Bois is second from the right in the second row. The pastel portrait of Du Bois was made by Winold Reiss in 1925. What was the Niagara Movement?

669

vote. Then, in 1909, Du Bois joined with seven white liberals to form the **National Association for the Advancement of Colored People** (NAACP). Du Bois became editor of the NAACP journal, *The Crisis.*

The NAACP's chief purpose in its early years was to try to put an end to lynching. Lynching was a terrible American problem. Ku Klux Klan mobs had killed many blacks during the Reconstruction period, and western vigilantes had hanged large numbers of gunslingers, horse thieves, and other outlaws.

During the 1880s and 1890s about 150 to 200 persons a year were lynched. Many were white. Of 638 persons lynched between 1882 and 1886, 411 were whites. Throughout the Progressive Era about 100 persons were lynched each year in the United States. More than 90 per cent of the victims were black.

The NAACP did not succeed in reducing the number of black lynchings, which remained high until well into the 1920s. Yet the organization grew rapidly both in members and in influence. By the end of the Progressive Era more and more blacks were speaking out strongly for their rights.

- What was the attitude of most progressives toward blacks?
- How did Booker T. Washington continue to work for black people? How did William E. B. Du Bois work for blacks?
- What was the chief purpose of the NAACP at the time of its founding?

THE GREAT WAR

After 1914 the pace of progressive reform slowed. President Wilson announced that the major goals of the New Freedom had been reached. Former President Roosevelt turned his attention to other matters.

This does not mean that the national mood that we call progressivism came to an end. Such movements rarely stop suddenly. Indeed, the basic beliefs of the progressives still influence American life. But in 1914 what was soon to be called the **Great War** broke out in Europe. After 1914 that war turned the thoughts of Americans from local problems to international ones.

- What event slowed the pace of progressive reform?

CHAPTER 22 REVIEW

Identification
Tell briefly why each of the following persons, terms, or events is important.
1. Lincoln Steffens
2. Ida Tarbell
3. Robert M. La Follette
4. Theodore Roosevelt
5. William Howard Taft
6. Woodrow Wilson
7. Eugene V. Debs
8. William E. B. Du Bois
9. Muckrakers
10. Direct primary
11. Municipal socialism
12. Free enterprise
13. Trust busting
14. Pure Food and Drug Act
15. Progressive party
16. Sixteenth Amendment
17. Prohibition
18. Federal Reserve Act
19. Clayton Antitrust Act
20. NAACP

Understanding American History
1. Explain what was meant by the Progressive Era at the turn of the century.
2. What national problems did the progressives hope to solve?
3. How did progressives propose to make local and state governments more responsive to society's needs? What arguments did their opponents use against them?
4. Contrast the Supreme Court's rulings in the cases of *Lochner v. New York* (work hours for bakers) and *Muller v. Oregon* (hours for women laundry workers). What was the importance of these rulings?
5. Why did Roosevelt strengthen the powers of the Presidency?
6. What caused the split between Roosevelt and Taft in 1910? How did this lead to the formation of the Progressive party?
7. Compare and contrast Roosevelt's New Nationalism with Wilson's New Freedom.
8. Explain how the result of the election of 1912 was a victory for reform.
9. Explain how the Federal Reserve Board can act either to stimulate or to slow down the economy.
10. What were the views of most progressives toward immigrants and blacks?

Activities
1. Use historical imagination to place yourself in the America of the early 1900s. You are filled with the spirit of the Progressive Movement. Write a letter to an older member of your family telling why you are so hopeful about the events at the turn of the century. Let others in class answer your letter. They should tell whether or not they share your optimism.
2. Bring to class stories from magazines and newspapers or notes on a TV news report that show examples of present-day investigative journalism. Report on any action taken as a result of the investigation.
3. Report in class on your state's primary election laws, as well as those of neighboring states. How are candidates for public office chosen? What qualifications must they meet? What restrictions are placed on their campaigns for office? You can obtain this information from local leaders of the Republican or Democratic parties.
4. Read further in your library and other American history books into the life of Theodore Roosevelt. Report on one of the following topics, or on a topic of your own:
   Roosevelt the Young Naturalist
   Roosevelt the Rancher
   Roosevelt the Rough Rider
   Roosevelt the Trust Buster
   Roosevelt the Conservationist
   Roosevelt the Family Man
5. Choose an issue that calls for reform. Write a letter to your representative in Congress stating your views and ask what stand he or she takes.

CHAPTER 22 TEST

Matching (30 points)
Number your paper 1–10 and match the description in the first column with the term in the second column.

1. Formed by Theodore Roosevelt, its candidate in the election of 1912
2. Placing an issue on the ballot to be decided by yes or no votes in the next regular election
3. Increased the power of the Interstate Commerce Commission to regulate railroads
4. Writers who tried to expose the evils of society
5. Group formed to help blacks achieve equal rights
6. Held that the public, through its government, should own certain utilities
7. The right of a business to take its own course without government controls
8. Approved collection of a federal income tax
9. Allowed people to choose their own candidates for regular elections
10. Enforced the prohibition against the manufacture, sale, or transportation of alcoholic beverages.

a. Muckrakers
b. Direct primary
c. Referendum
d. Free enterprise
e. Municipal socialism
f. Hepburn Act
g. Progressive party
h. Sixteenth Amendment
i. Volstead Act
j. NAACP

Matching (20 points)
Number your paper 11–15 and match the description in the first column with the person in the second column.

11. Winner of the Presidential election in 1912
12. Reformer who promoted the Wisconsin Idea
13. Leader who urged other blacks to gain equal rights
14. Reporter who investigated Standard Oil
15. McKinley's Vice President who succeeded to the Presidency

a. Ida Tarbell
b. Robert M. La Follette
c. Theodore Roosevelt
d. Woodrow Wilson
e. William E. B. Du Bois

Classifying (20 points)
Number your paper 16–20. For each of the following statements, write *FE* if it is an example of free enterprise, *MS* if it is an example of municipal socialism.

16. A local company manufactures and sells synthetic fuel.
17. People's Electric Company supplies water and electricity.
18. Johanson & Garcia, Inc. makes solar collectors.
19. River City Municipal Gas Company extends its pipelines.
20. New England citizens buy and sell crude oil in order to purchase their fuel oil at cost.

Essay (30 points)
In a brief essay compare and contrast the platforms of the Democratic and Progressive parties in the Presidential election of 1912.

UNIT SEVEN TEST

Multiple Choice (20 points)

Number your paper 1–5 and write the letter of the phrase that best completes each sentence.

1. Yellow journalism is an example of
   a. dollar diplomacy.
   b. propaganda.
   c. gunboat diplomacy.
   d. muckraking.
2. The main purpose of the Open Door Notes was to
   a. protect U.S. trade rights in China.
   b. end the Boxer Rebellion.
   c. help blacks get jobs in the North.
   d. end the Spanish-American War.
3. Which of the following was *not* a cause of the Spanish-American War.?
   a. Yellow journalism
   b. Sympathy for Cuba
   c. Sinking of the U.S.S. *Maine*
   d. Desire to build the Panama Canal
4. The Federal Reserve System uses the rediscount rate to
   a. speed up or slow down the economy.
   b. decide who to draft into the army.
   c. buy goods cheaply for government use.
   d. regulate corporations.
5. Theodore Roosevelt tried to
   a. destroy all trusts.
   b. expand the power of the Presidency.
   c. gain control of Cuba for the U.S.
   d. stop the spread of yellow journalism.

Matching (25 points)

Number your paper 6–10 and match the person in the second column with his or her description in the first column.

6. Secretary of State who issued the Open Door Notes
7. Proposed progressive reforms known as the New Freedom
8. An early investigative reporter
9. Hero of the Battle of Manila Bay
10. Progressive governor of Wisconsin

a. Ida Tarbell
b. Woodrow Wilson
c. Robert M. La Follette
d. George Dewey
e. John Hay

Chronological Order (25 points)

Number your paper 11–15 and place the following events in order by numbering 1 for the first, 2 for the second, and so on.

11. Roosevelt runs for President on the Progressive ticket.
12. Roosevelt leads the Rough Riders up San Juan Hill.
13. The Spanish-American War begins.
14. The U.S.S. *Maine* is sunk in Havana Harbor.
15. The Panama Canal is completed.

Essay (30 points)

Write a brief essay on *one* of the following topics. Explain how events from 1865 to 1912, including the Spanish-American War, made the United States a world power, *or* Explain what is meant by progressivism by identifying and explaining at least four progressive reforms of the early 1900s. Plan your paper carefully.

UNIT EIGHT

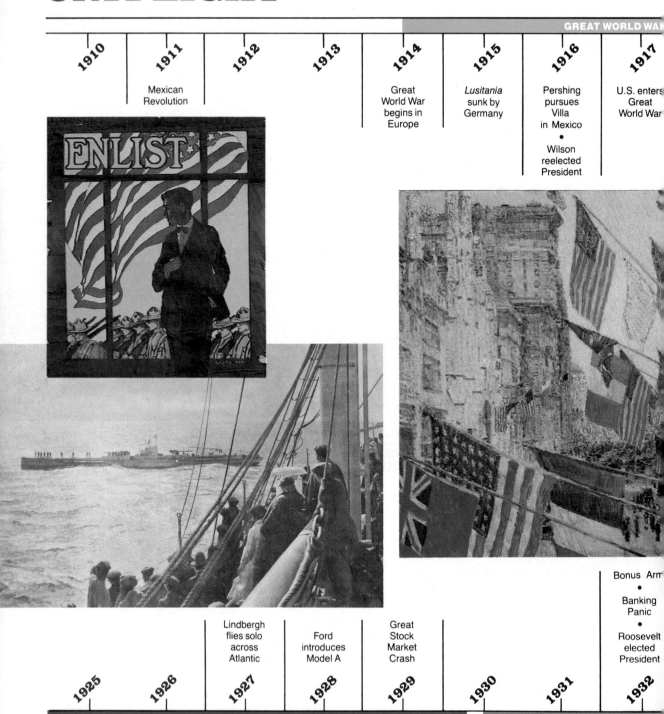

1910

1911
Mexican Revolution

1912

1913

1914
Great World War begins in Europe

1915
Lusitania sunk by Germany

1916
Pershing pursues Villa in Mexico
•
Wilson reelected President

1917
U.S. enters Great World War

Bonus Arm
•
Banking Panic
•
Roosevelt elected President

1925

1926

1927
Lindbergh flies solo across Atlantic

1928
Ford introduces Model A

1929
Great Stock Market Crash

1930

1931

1932

674

A TROUBLED AMERICA

1918

Wilson's Fourteen Points

•

Armistice ends Great World War

1919

Versailles Peace Conference

1920

Senate rejects Versailles Treaty

•

Women receive the vote

•

Harding elected President

1921

Washington Disarmament Conference

•

Five-Power Naval Treaty

1922

1923

Coolidge succeeds to Presidency

•

Teapot Dome Scandal

1924

Coolidge elected President

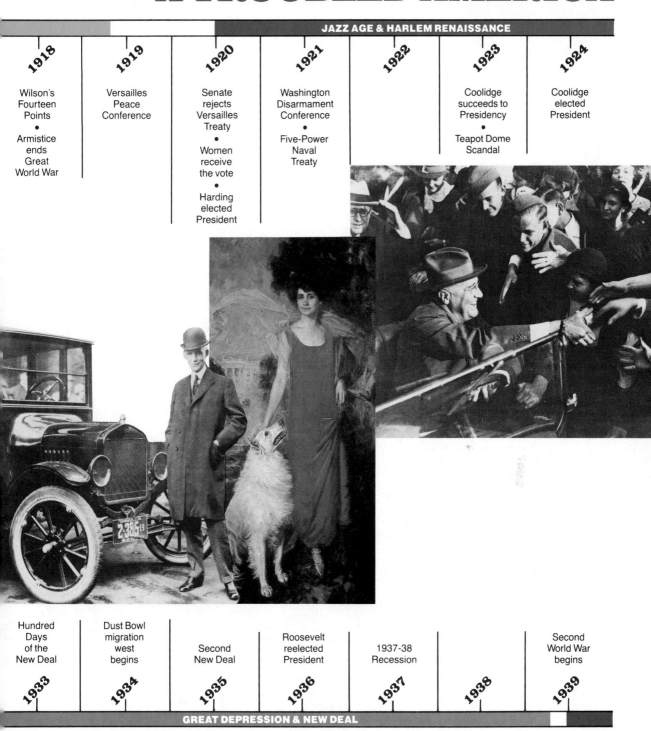

Hundred Days of the New Deal

1933

Dust Bowl migration west begins

1934

Second New Deal

1935

Roosevelt reelected President

1936

1937-38 Recession

1937

1938

Second World War begins

1939

GREAT DEPRESSION & NEW DEAL

CHAPTER 23

The Great World War

WAR IN EUROPE

The **Great War** began in Europe during the summer of 1914. It broke out following the assassination of an Austro-Hungarian prince and his wife in the city of Sarajevo in what is now Yugoslavia. The killer was a member of the **Black Hand,** a terrorist organization in the part of Yugoslavia that was then the nation of Serbia. Serbians wanted the Austro-Hungarians out of their country.

At first there seemed no reason why these murders would lead to a long and terrible war. However, through the years the major nations of Europe had signed a complicated network of treaties. Two powerful groups called **alliances** had been created. When a member of one alliance was threatened, the other members were pledged to support it. Austria and Serbia belonged to rival alliances. Austria held Serbia responsible for the assassinations. Quickly their allies became involved, and their conflict resulted in a war that spread throughout Europe.

In the streets of Sarajevo, sabers flash moments after an assassin's bullets sparked the Great World War. In this rare photograph the assassin of the Austro-Hungarian archduke and duchess is dragged from the street. He was a student still in high school and a member of the terrorist Black Hand. Four years later Gavrilo Princip died of tuberculosis in prison. Why did the violence in Sarajevo set off the Great World War?

Brown Brothers

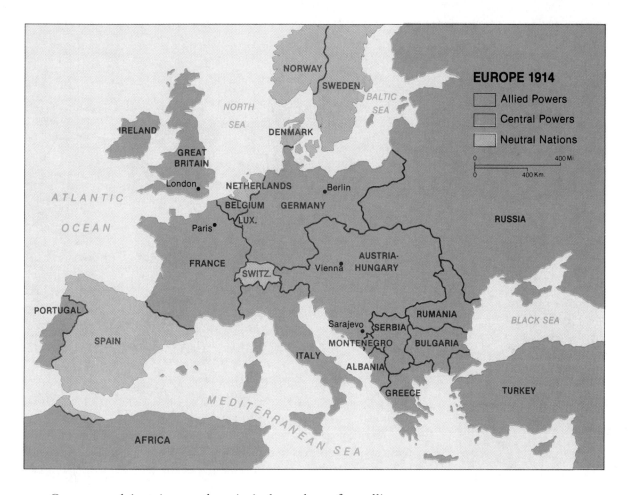

EUROPE 1914

- Allied Powers
- Central Powers
- Neutral Nations

0 _____ 400 Mi.
0 _____ 400 Km.

NORWAY
SWEDEN
BALTIC SEA
NORTH SEA
IRELAND
DENMARK
GREAT BRITAIN
London
NETHERLANDS
Berlin
BELGIUM GERMANY
LUX.
Paris
RUSSIA
ATLANTIC OCEAN
FRANCE
AUSTRIA-HUNGARY
Vienna
SWITZ.
PORTUGAL
SPAIN
RUMANIA
Sarajevo SERBIA
BLACK SEA
MONTENEGRO BULGARIA
ITALY
ALBANIA
GREECE
TURKEY
MEDITERRANEAN SEA
AFRICA

Germany and Austria were the principal members of one alliance. They were known as the **Central Powers** because they dominated the middle of Europe. Later they were joined in the war by Bulgaria and Turkey. Opposing them were a number of nations known as the **Allies.** Great Britain, France, and Russia were the leading members of this alliance. The United States was most concerned by the fighting between Great Britain and Germany.

■ Who were the Central Powers? Who were the Allies?

AMERICAN NEUTRALITY

News of the outbreak of war caught Americans by surprise. There had not been a major war in Europe since the defeat of Napoleon at the battle of Waterloo in 1815. Prosperity and progress had encouraged people to hope that the nations of the world had become too "civilized" to resort to warfare to settle their disagreements.

Under Presidents Taft and Wilson the United States had negotiated **arbitration treaties** with a number of nations. The signers

Culver Pictures

The more this contented cow is fed, the more she gives the German who milks her. Neutral nations carrying foreign merchandise simply played into German hands, in the view of this editorial cartoonist. Americans tried to be neutral, but which hoped the Central Powers would win?

agreed in advance to discuss any differences during a "cooling off" period to last about a year. Only if a solution could not be found would they consider going to war.

This American attitude explains why President McKinley hesitated to ask Congress to declare war on Spain in 1898. Wars were to be fought only for a noble purpose and only after every reasonable effort had been made to negotiate a settlement.

Nearly all Americans believed the United States should not become involved in the war in Europe. Many persons of German or Austrian origin hoped that the Central Powers would win. So did large numbers of Irish-Americans, who were anti-British because Great Britain still refused to grant Ireland its independence. People whose ancestors had come from the Allied nations tended to favor that side in the war. But for the vast majority of Americans the obvious policy for the United States was **neutrality.** Europe was far away. Its rivalries and conflicts had always been viewed by Americans with distrust.

President Wilson expressed the general attitude clearly on August 18, 1914. Every American ought to "act and speak in the true spirit of neutrality," he said. This meant behaving with "impartiality and fairness and friendliness" to all the nations at war.

- What did signers of arbitration treaties agree to do?
- Why did most Americans favor a neutrality policy at the outset of the Great War?

678

WILSON'S FOREIGN POLICY

As President of the United States, Woodrow Wilson had the chief responsibility for deciding the country's foreign policy. He had run for President, however, on the domestic issues of the Progressive Era. Foreign questions had not played much part in the 1912 campaign. Before 1912 Wilson had never been especially concerned with foreign affairs. Nevertheless, he had very strong opinions about what was morally correct in foreign affairs.

This is how Wilson reasoned: The United States did not need any more territory. It had no enemies. It did not want to injure any foreign country. Indeed, being rich and powerful, the United States had a duty to help less fortunate nations, particularly its neighbors in Central and South America. America's destiny was not to control other countries but to encourage the spread of democratic ideas. After all, no other country knew as much about democracy as the United States. The brief period of American imperialism had been a bad mistake, the President insisted.

Wilson thought the United States should help other nations and try to make life better for their people. His trouble was that he was convinced that he knew what was best for the rest of the world. He frequently tried to impose his ideas on people who did not agree with him.

Wilson did not seem to understand that nations with different cultures and traditions often saw things differently than he did. Even nations which sought the same goals as Wilson sometimes resented his efforts to assist them. Perhaps because he had been a teacher for so many years, the President had a tendency to lecture to the officials of other nations. His manner, rather than his actual words, created the impression that Wilson thought he knew better than foreign leaders what was best for their countries.

- What did President Wilson believe should be the role of the United States in foreign affairs?
- Why did leaders of foreign nations sometimes resent President Wilson's efforts to assist them?

REVOLUTION IN MEXICO

Even before the war in Europe began, Wilson had to deal with an important foreign problem. This was the **Mexican Revolution.** This upheaval had begun in 1910. It was of concern to Wilson because United States investments in Mexico were threatened by the troubles. Also, many Mexican refugees from the fighting were crossing the border into Texas, New Mexico, Arizona, and California.

Before Wilson became President, the revolution had been led by Francisco Madero, a progressive-type reformer. Early in 1913 Ma-

Culver Pictures

Victoriano Huerta became military dictator of Mexico in 1913. He was a heavy-handed ruler, opposed at home and by President Wilson. In this photograph Huerta is in uniform with decorations and awards. He died in exile in El Paso, Texas. How did Wilson describe Huerta's government?

dero was murdered by General Victoriano Huerta. Huerta set up a **military dictatorship.** Wilson called this "a government of butchers." He refused to recognize Huerta as the legitimate leader of the Mexican people.

Many Mexicans agreed with Wilson. A new revolt broke out, led by Venustiano Carranza. Wilson was urged on by United States companies whose Mexican properties were in danger. He asked Huerta to order free elections and promise not to be a candidate himself. If he agreed, the United States would try to persuade the Carranza forces to stop fighting.

Wilson meant well. But even supporters of Carranza resented Wilson's interference. Mexico's problems were none of his business, insisted both sides. If we agreed to United States interference, said an official of the Huerta government, "all the future elections for president would be submitted to the veto of any President of the United States."

Then, in April 1914, some American sailors on shore leave in Tampico, Mexico, were arrested. They were soon released, but by this time Wilson was so angry at Huerta that he used the incident to try to overthrow him. He sent a naval force to occupy the city of Veracruz.

Wilson did not intend to start a war. He expected his "show of force" would cause the downfall of Huerta. But 19 United States sailors and 126 Mexicans were killed before Veracruz was captured. Again, Carranza joined with his enemy Huerta in speaking out against the interference of the United States in Mexican affairs.

Fortunately, the ambassadors of the **ABC Powers**—Argentina, Brazil, and Chile—offered to **mediate** the dispute—that is, to act as neutral go-betweens to find a peaceful settlement. Wilson eagerly accepted their offer. The crisis ended. By summer Carranza had forced Huerta from power. The United States then withdrew its naval force from Veracruz.

Yet Wilson's troubles in Mexico were far from over. No sooner had Carranza defeated Huerta than one of his own generals, Francisco "Pancho" Villa, rebelled against him. Wilson supported Villa. He had resented Carranza's independence and refusal to follow United States advice. Villa seemed to be sincerely interested in improving the lives of poor Mexicans. Wilson also thought Villa could be more easily influenced by the United States.

Supporting Pancho Villa was probably the President's worst mistake. Villa was little better than a bandit, while Carranza was genuinely interested in improving the condition of the people of Mexico. From a practical point of view, Carranza had the stronger forces. His troops soon drove the **Villistas** into the mountains of northern Mexico.

680

Culver Pictures

To some Mexicans Pancho Villa and Emiliano Zapata were Robin Hood and Little John. To others they were simply bandits. In this photograph the two leaders and their followers have taken over the presidential palace in Mexico City in December 1914. Villa is seated at the center, and Zapata is to his left, holding a sombrero. Why did President Wilson support the Villistas?

At last, in October 1915, Wilson realized that the best policy for the United States was to keep hands off Mexico and let the people of that nation decide for themselves how they were to be governed. He then officially recognized the Carranza government.

This decision angered Pancho Villa. In January 1916 the Villistas stopped a train in northern Mexico and killed 17 citizens of the United States in cold blood. Then Villa and his men crossed the border in March and attacked the town of Columbus, New Mexico. They killed 17 more United States citizens and set the town on fire.

Wilson ordered troops under General John J. Pershing to capture Villa. This meant invading Mexico. Pershing was an experienced soldier. He had served during the Indian fighting of the 1880s, in Cuba during the Spanish-American War, and in the Philippine Islands. He earned the nickname "Black Jack" while commanding the 10th Cavalry regiment, which was made up entirely of black enlisted men. One of his first decisions when he was ordered to hunt down Villa was to include part of the 10th Cavalry in his expedition.

Pershing's men pursued Villa vigorously, but they could not catch him on his home ground. As had happened when Veracruz was occupied in 1914, United States interference angered Carranza. Wilson was forced to call off the invasion, which accomplished nothing.

Culver Pictures

General John J. Pershing is shown crossing the Santa Maria River with his expeditionary force in pursuit of Pancho Villa in 1916. What were the orders given to this expedition?

- ▓ Why did the United States become involved in the Mexican Revolution?
- ▓ Why was General Pershing unsuccessful in his pursuit of Villa?

681

THE WAR ON THE WESTERN FRONT

As early as 1915 the Great World War had become the bloodiest conflict ever fought. On the **Eastern Front** Russian troops clashed with Austrian and German armies in a series of seesaw battles. There was also fighting in Turkey and Serbia. In Africa and on the islands of the Pacific, Allied troops clashed with German colonial forces. In May 1915 Italy entered the war on the side of the Allies and attacked Austria-Hungary from the south.

The greatest interest of the United States at this time was in the fighting on the so-called **Western Front** in Europe and on the high seas. When the war began, the Germans marched into Belgium on their way to invade France. No matter that they had promised by treaty in 1870 to respect the neutrality of tiny Belgium in the event of war with France.

The Belgians resisted bravely, but they could not stop the invaders. By September 1914 the German armies had swept across Belgium and were within 20 miles (36 kilometers) of Paris. There they were checked by French and British troops.

The two armies then dug trenches to protect themselves from bullets and artillery shells. They put up mazes of barbed wire in front of their positions. Lines of these trenches ran all the way across northern France from the sea to Switzerland. Between the opposing trenches lay a narrow "no man's land."

In the Argonne Forest in France these weary American soldiers collapse into captured German trenches. They were photographed on September 26, 1918. Where was the Western Front?

Culver Pictures

This was **trench warfare.** Soldiers ate and slept in the gravelike damp. First one side, then the other would try to break through at some point along the line. The artillery would begin the attack by firing exploding shells for hours at the enemy trenches. Soldiers would then climb from their trenches and rush "over the top" with fixed bayonets at the enemy line. The defender's artillery would rain shells upon them while sharpshooters and machine gunners from the trenches riddled the attackers with a hail of bullets. These attacks resembled the British attack at Breed's Hill in the first weeks of the American Revolution. But millions, not hundreds, of soldiers were involved. And their weapons were far more deadly.

The armies were **stalemated**—neither side could ever win a decisive victory despite repeated attacks and counterattacks which cost hundreds of thousands of lives. No man's land came to look like the surface of the moon. No tree or house stood there. Scarcely a blade of grass could be found, so heavy was the fire. The surface, like the moon, was pockmarked by tens of thousands of craters where artillery shells had exploded.

The war on the Western Front was unlike any other war in history. The battle between the Union and Confederate armies around the city of Petersburg, Virginia, in the last stages of the Civil War comes closest to it. That battle lasted only a few months. The terrible struggle on the Western Front went on for years.

■ How was trench warfare fought in France?

THE WAR ON THE ATLANTIC

On the Atlantic Ocean a new kind of struggle developed in 1914-15. The British navy was far stronger than Germany's. It attempted to blockade all northern European ports in order to keep Germany from obtaining supplies from the United States and other neutral nations. The Germans, in turn, tried to keep supplies from the British by using submarines, which they called "Undersea ships" or **U-boats.**

All the major navies had submarines by 1914. Both Great Britain and the United States had more in operation at that time than Germany. Submarines were small, relatively slow vessels. Most naval authorities did not consider them important weapons. However, the German navy did not have enough surface ships to operate in the Atlantic against the Allied fleets. U-boats were the only naval weapon the Germans could use.

Like privateers during the American Revolution and the War of 1812, U-boats roamed the seas looking for unarmed merchant vessels to attack. When they sighted powerful enemy warships, they slipped away beneath the surface. These tactics worked so well that the Germans began to build more U-boats as fast as possible.

Culver Pictures

Passengers on this Spanish steamer suspiciously watch the sleek German submarine that prowls the North Sea. Their neutral vessel has been halted for inspection in this 1917 photograph. Why were the Germans building more U-boats at this time?

Both the British blockade and the German submarine campaign hurt American interests. Both of these activities on the high seas also violated the rights of neutral nations according to international law. British warships stopped American ships and forced them to put into Allied ports for inspection. Goods headed for Germany were seized. The British even tried to limit the amount of goods shipped to neutral countries like Norway and Sweden. Otherwise, they claimed, those nations could import more American products than they needed for themselves and ship the surplus to the Central Powers.

The Germans refused to follow the international rules for stopping merchant ships in wartime. These rules provided that ships could be stopped and their cargoes examined. Enemy vessels and neutrals carrying war materials to enemy ports could be taken as prizes or sunk. Before destroying a merchant ship, the attacker was supposed to take the crew prisoner or give it time to get clear of the vessel in lifeboats.

It was extremely dangerous for submarines to obey these rules. If a submarine surfaced and ordered a merchant ship to stop, the merchant ship might turn suddenly and ram the submarine before it could react. Some merchant ships carried concealed cannon. A single cannon shell could send a submarine to the bottom in seconds. If an enemy warship should appear on the horizon while part of a U-boat's

684

crew was examining the cargo of a merchant ship, the U-boat would almost certainly be blown out of the water before it could call back its men and submerge.

Therefore the U-boats attacked their targets from below the surface, firing torpedoes packed with **TNT**—a powerful explosive—without warning. Many sailors and passengers lost their lives when their ships went down.

■ How did the British blockade hurt American interests?
■ How did German U-boats break rules on the high seas?

WILSON ON NEUTRAL RIGHTS

President Wilson protested strongly against both British and German violations of the international rules. If he had threatened to cut off trade with Great Britain the way Jefferson had in 1807, the British would undoubtedly have obeyed the rules. They could not fight the war without supplies from America. But Wilson was unwilling to go that far, in large part because the profitable trade with the Allies was extremely important to the United States.

Wilson took a much stronger stand against Germany. When U-boats began to sink ships without warning, he announced in February 1915 that Germany would be held to **strict accountability** for any American property destroyed or lives lost. In the language of diplomacy the phrase "strict accountability" was a polite way of saying, "If you don't do what we ask, we will probably declare war."

The danger of war over submarine attacks became suddenly critical on May 7, 1915, when the German *U-20* torpedoed the British liner **Lusitania** without warning. Technically this sinking could be defended. The *Lusitania* had deck guns. It was carrying a cargo of guns and ammunition. Its captain was guilty at least of carelessness, for a slow-moving submarine should never have been able to get close enough to a swift ocean liner to hit it with a torpedo.

The *Lusitania* was crowded with civilian passengers. About 1,200 of them, including 128 American citizens, lost their lives in the sinking. The American public was shocked and furious. If Wilson had called for a declaration of war, Congress would probably have acted promptly. Instead, Wilson demanded only that the Germans apologize, pay damages, and promise not to attack passenger ships in the future. Long negotiations followed. In March 1916, after another passenger vessel, the *Sussex,* was torpedoed with the loss of 80 lives, Germany finally gave in. It promised not to sink any more merchant ships without warning. This promise is known as the **Sussex pledge.**

■ What did "strict accountability" mean in diplomacy?
■ Why did the sinking of the *Lusitania* shock Americans?

Brown Brothers

Culver Pictures

Just as the *Lusitania* sailed in May 1915, morning newspapers warned American passengers that they were in peril. At sea a German U-boat torpedoed the ship, shown above as it set sail from New York. Among the dead were 128 Americans. When President Wilson accepted cash for damages, *Life* magazine printed the cover above on April 13, 1916. With a few coins flung to the ground, the German kaiser says, "Here's money for the Americans. I may drown some more." Why did the Germans sink the *Lusitania*?

Torpedo Warfare

This photograph was taken on board a German U-boat only seconds after it fired the torpedo that is slamming into the side of an Allied cargo ship.

Aiming a torpedo accurately from a German U-boat was very difficult. Torpedoes were launched from tubes in the bow of the submarine. The submarine captain's vision was limited because he had to view the target through a periscope. He had to point the entire submarine in the direction he wanted to aim the torpedo.

The captain aimed ahead of his target the way a hunter "leads" a flying duck. He had to estimate the speed of the target and compare it to the speed of the torpedo, which traveled at about 30 miles (48 kilometers) an hour. Nowadays such calculations can be made accurately by computers. In 1915 such equipment was not available. Once fired, the torpedo traveled in a fairly straight line. Its direction could not be changed by the captain, although waves and currents might cause it to veer off course.

The *Lusitania* had a top speed of about 25 miles (40 kilometers) per hour. If it had simply changed direction every few minutes, traveling in a zigzag course, it would have been practically impossible for the slow-moving *U-20* to get close enough to aim a torpedo. If by great luck he did get within range, the captain, Lieutenant Walter Schwieger, would not have known where to aim a torpedo if the *Lusitania* were zigzagging. Between the time the torpedo was fired and the time its course intersected with the *Lusitania*'s, the liner would have changed direction. Obviously, Captain William T. Turner assumed the *Lusitania* was in no danger and took no evasive action.

THE ELECTION OF 1916

By late 1916 some Americans, including ex-President Theodore Roosevelt, were arguing that the United States should enter the war on the side of the Allies. A larger number believed that the United States should at least prepare for war by building up the armed forces. Still, a majority of the people wanted to remain neutral. They appreciated Wilson's patient attempts to avoid involvement and his efforts to persuade the warring nations to make peace.

The depth of their feelings came out during the 1916 Presidential campaign. One Democratic slogan, "He kept us out of war," proved to have enormous appeal. Wilson was not particularly popular in 1916. Many progressives who had voted for him in 1912 felt that he had not done enough for reform. Blacks considered him a racist, for he had actually increased the amount of segregation in government offices in Washington. Women found him reluctant to support their drive to obtain the right to vote. Yet the Progressive party, led by Theodore Roosevelt, had decided not to run a separate candidate in 1916. Instead the Progressives nominated the Republican candidate, Charles Evans Hughes, a justice of the Supreme Court.

Wilson tried to hold his progressive supporters in 1916 by backing a bill making child labor illegal and another making it easier for farmers to obtain low-interest loans. He approved a strong workman's compensation law. He appointed the liberal lawyer, Louis D. Brandeis, famous for the "Brandeis brief" in the *Muller v. Oregon* case, to a vacancy on the Supreme Court. Many liberals applauded the choice of Brandeis, who was Jewish. But large numbers of Americans were prejudiced against Jews and probably voted against Wilson because he appointed Brandeis.

The Presidential election was very close. Wilson got 277 electoral votes to Hughes's 254. Nearly everyone agreed that the President's success in keeping out of the Great War saved him from defeat.

Wilson was too intelligent to take comfort from this fact. He knew that if the Germans ever decided to sink merchant ships again without warning, America could not stay neutral.

- What popular slogan helped Wilson to be reelected President?
- Which groups opposed the reelection of Woodrow Wilson?

Charles Evans Hughes, *above*, was defeated by Woodrow Wilson in the 1916 Presidential election. Below is a Wilson campaign van with one version of his popular slogan, "He kept us out of war." What did the President fear after his reelection?

AMERICA GOES TO WAR

Wilson's fear of being forced into the war led him to make a strong effort to end it by negotiation. On January 22, 1917, he made a moving speech calling for **peace without victory.** If either side tried to profit from the war by taking land or money from the other, Wilson said, the only result would be hatred that would cause more wars. All the nations, including the United States, must try to make a peace based on "justice throughout the world."

Unfortunately, neither the Allies nor the Central Powers would settle for peace without victory. The cost in lives and money had been so great after two and one-half years of war that neither side could face the idea that all that expense had been wasted. At the very least each intended to make the other pay the entire monetary cost of the war. The German government already had secretly decided to resume submarine attacks on shipping without warning.

The Germans realized that unleashing their sharklike U-boats would probably cause the United States to declare war. Nevertheless, they expected that "ruthless submarine warfare" would keep food and munitions from reaching Great Britain. Then the British would have to surrender. The war would be over before the United States could raise and train an army and get its soldiers across the Atlantic to France.

Less than two weeks after Wilson's "peace without victory" speech, an American merchant ship was sunk by a U-boat. Wilson then broke diplomatic relations with Germany. He ordered the German ambassador out of the United States and recalled his own ambassador from Germany.

Late in February the President learned that German Foreign Relations Secretary Arthur Zimmermann was trying to make an alliance with Mexico. In the event of war with the United States, Mexico was to "reconquer" the "lost territory" of Texas, New Mexico, and Arizona. Nothing came of this **Zimmermann Note.** Yet when it was made public, it caused many Americans to call for war against Germany.

Throughout March the number of merchant ships sunk by U-boats increased steadily. The *Housatonic,* the Cunard liner *Laconia,* the *Algonquin* were all torpedoed. Against this grim background the President took the oath of office for his second term. Almost a month later, on April 2, 1917, Wilson asked Congress to declare war. The reason, he said, was to make a just peace possible. "The world," he added in a famous sentence, "must be made **safe for democracy."**

Wilson did not mean by this that the purpose of the war was to make all nations democracies. Rather he meant that the world must be made a place where democracies could exist and flourish. He believed that if the United States did not help to bring the conflict to an early end, the losses and hatreds would be so great that no democratic government could survive.

All eyes are upon the President of the United States as Wilson asks the assembled Congress to declare war on Germany. This photograph was taken on April 2, 1917. What incidents provoked Wilson to call for war?

- What did President Wilson mean by "peace without victory"?
- Why did the Zimmermann Note alarm many Americans?
- What did President Wilson mean by his statement "The world must be made safe for democracy"?

689

William G. McAdoo, *above*, served as manager of the nation's railroads during the Great War. He was also President Wilson's Secretary of the Treasury. In 1914 McAdoo married the President's daughter Eleanor. Below is Bernard Baruch, brilliant head of the War Industries Board. Why were these agencies set up?

THE WAR ON THE HOME FRONT

Building an army and supplying it in a hurry was a huge task. Many changes had to be made in the way goods were manufactured and businesses run. The antitrust laws were suspended. In wartime Wilson agreed with Theodore Roosevelt's argument that large-scale organizations supervised by the government were more efficient than small competing firms. Because so many goods had to be moved, it became necessary to place all the nation's railroads under government management. Wilson appointed Secretary of the Treasury William G. McAdoo to run the entire system.

The President also set up a **War Industries Board** to oversee the production and distribution of manufactured goods. The head of this board was Bernard Baruch, a millionaire stockbroker. Baruch was active in Democratic party politics at a time when most wealthy stockbrokers were Republicans. A friend and adviser of Wilson, he was a natural choice to head the War Industries Board. In this post he performed brilliantly.

Baruch's idea was to organize American industry as though it were one big factory. He decided what was to be made and where the raw materials were to come from. He controlled the distribution of scarce commodities and in some cases even set the price at which they were to be sold. His job was made easier because most producers were eager to cooperate with the War Industries Board. Profit and patriotism were pushing them in the same direction.

Baruch's board had to supply both American needs and much of the war supplies, called **matériel,** and food of the Allied nations. Great Britain, in particular, depended on American wheat, meat, and other products for its survival. Wilson appointed Herbert Hoover as **United States Food Administrator.** It was Hoover's job to make sure that enough foodstuffs were produced and distributed fairly.

Hoover had been head of the Commission for the Relief of Belgium early in the war. As Food Administrator he set out both to increase production and to reduce domestic consumption. At the same time it was important to keep prices from skyrocketing.

Hoover had little trouble increasing production. It was in the farmers' interest to grow more because the demand for their crops was increasing. For example, they raised 619 million bushels (218 million hectoliters) of wheat in 1917 and 904 million bushels (318 million hectoliters) in 1918.

Getting Americans to consume less was more difficult. Hoover organized a vast campaign to convince the public of the need for conservation. Catchy slogans carried his message. "Food will win the war" was the best known. Others included "When in doubt, eat potatoes," which was designed to save wheat, and "If you have a sweet tooth, pull it," to reduce sugar consumption.

United Press International

The third of Wilson's advisers for the war on the home front is shown at right supervising a shipment of supplies to Europe. Herbert Hoover campaigned to persuade Americans to eat less. What catchy slogans did he use?

Culver Pictures

Hoover also organized "Meatless Tuesdays" when no one was supposed to eat meat and "Wheatless Wednesdays" too. He even started a campaign to get every American family to raise a pig. Pigs could live on scraps and garbage and eventually be turned into bacon and pork chops. Hoover's rules could not be enforced. His technique was to depend on (and praise) **voluntary cooperation.** He made it clear that patriotic citizens were *expected* to obey the rules. The results were excellent.

- How did Bernard Baruch organize American industry?
- What were Herbert Hoover's main goals as United States Food Administrator?

LABOR IN WARTIME

Organizing the human resources of the nation was also complicated. During the war the United States Employment Service directed almost 4 million people to new jobs. When war was declared, thousands of young men volunteered for military service. To raise the huge **American Expeditionary Force** (AEF) that was to fight in Europe, however, it was necessary to pass a draft law, the **Selective Service Act** of 1917.

For those men who were not drafted, and for women workers, the war brought many benefits. Wages rose. Unskilled workers got opportunities to move to better jobs. Union membership rose from about 3 million to over 4 million in a year.

This dapper young man must answer the question asked by the wartime recruiting poster: "On which side of the window are you?" Which law might have answered the question for this onlooker?

It was important to prevent strikes from slowing down the production of vital goods. In December 1917 a **National War Labor Conference Board** was set up to try to settle disputes between workers and their employers. This board also tried to make sure that workers were not fired for trying to organize unions.

The American Federation of Labor grew to about 3 million members in 1918. AFL unions cooperated with the Conference Board in most cases. Samuel Gompers, president of the AFL, served as a Presidential adviser. Gompers never promised that union members would not strike during the war. But he went along with the government's request that workers agree to arbitrate conflicts with their employers whenever possible.

The need for laborers especially helped blacks, women, and other groups that had been discriminated against in the job market in the past. Thousands of black workers had already migrated from the South to northern cities before the war began. Half a million more followed between 1914 and 1919. Most of these newcomers earned far more in war plants than they could make raising cotton or tobacco in the South.

The Selective Service System drafted both blacks and whites. Although they were still segregated in the armed forces, blacks were better treated and were given more opportunities than 20 years earlier during the Spanish-American War. About a thousand blacks became officers. Emmett J. Scott of Tuskegee Institute was appointed an assistant to the Secretary of War.

Of course, this did not amount to equal treatment. Yet while some blacks protested, the strong-minded William E. B. Du Bois did not. "Fight for your rights but . . . have sense enough to know when you are getting what you are fighting for," Du Bois urged.

Women were not drafted under the Selective Service Act, although many served as army nurses and as volunteer workers overseas. Thousands of women found jobs in factories and offices they could not have hoped to get before the war. "This is the woman's age!" the head of the National Women's Trade Union League announced in 1917. "Women are coming into the labor [movement] on equal terms with men." This was an exaggeration. Yet women workers did make important gains. Recognizing how necessary women were to the war effort, the Wilson administration established a **Women's Bureau** in the Department of Labor.

Mexican-Americans also benefited from the labor shortage in the United States. Beginning in 1911, thousands had crossed the border to escape the disorder resulting from the Mexican Revolution. Even more came after the Great World War began. Besides working in the cotton fields of Texas and Arizona and on farms in Colorado and California, the Mexican-Americans became railroad laborers,

Among the jobs opened to women by the Great War was carrying the mail. Above the steps trod by this worker are these familiar words: "Neither snow nor rain nor heat nor gloom of night stays these couriers from the swift completion of their appointed rounds." They were written B.C. 500 by the Greek historian Herodotus. Was wartime "the women's age," as one speaker declared?

construction workers, and miners. Some settled in the northern cities, attracted by jobs in war plants. The jobs were mostly low paid and unskilled. Nevertheless, these workers could earn much more than they could by farming. By the end of the war there were communities of Mexican-born families in St. Louis, Chicago, Detroit, and several other northern cities.

- Why was the Selective Service Act of 1917 passed?
- What was the purpose of the National War Labor Conference Board?
- What was the role of blacks during the war? Of women? Of Mexican-Americans?

THE TREATMENT OF PROTESTERS

Despite the urgings of union leaders like Samuel Gompers, some workers were unwilling to go along with the government's labor policies. Radicals in the labor movement had founded a new organization, the **Industrial Workers of the World** (IWW), in 1905. According to the IWW, "the working class and the employing class have nothing in common." Workers should organize, "take possession of the earth and the machinery of production, and abolish the wage system."

One of the founders of the IWW was William D. Haywood. "Big Bill" Haywood had gone to work as a miner in Colorado at the age of 15. In 1896 he joined the Western Federation of Miners. A few years later he became a socialist. In 1904 he led a violent strike of miners in Cripple Creek, Colorado. The next year he was accused of planning the assassination of the governor of Idaho. He was successfully defended by the famous attorney Clarence Darrow. When the

Culver Pictures

William D. Haywood, *above,* was a radical founder of the IWW. He led a violent strike of miners in Cripple Creek, Colorado, seen at left. In this picture miners are herded off to bull pens by vigilantes and deputies. Their strike has failed. Why was the IWW organized?

Colorado Historical Society

Great War broke out, Haywood was secretary-treasurer of the IWW, whose members were known as **Wobblies,** probably because of the way some mispronounced its initials.

If workers would stick together, Haywood said in 1915, they could "stop every wheel in the United States . . . and sweep off your capitalists and state legislatures and politicians into the sea." In 1917 the IWW staged strikes in the lumber and copper-mining industries. The reaction of the government was swift. Federal agents raided IWW headquarters looking for evidence that the Wobblies were trying to slow war production. Over a hundred members, including Haywood, were arrested.

The Wobblies were revolutionaries. Their arrest when they deliberately interfered with the war effort was perfectly proper. But the times made people fearful and uncertain. This led the government to violate the civil rights of many radicals who did nothing but speak or write unpopular words. In 1917 Congress passed the **Espionage Act.** This law made it a crime to aid enemy nations or to interfere with the recruiting of soldiers. It also allowed the Postmaster General to censor mail. The next year a much stronger law, the **Sedition Act,** was passed. This law even cracked down on expressions of opinion. Heavy fines and prison sentences of up to 20 years could be imposed on persons who spoke or wrote anything critical of the government, the army or navy, or even the uniforms worn by soldiers and sailors.

An unreasoning hatred of anything German swept the country. Persons with German names were likely to be insulted by strangers. Schools stopped teaching the German language. Libraries took books by long-dead German authors off the shelves. German-born immigrants who had not become United States citizens were forced to register so that they could be watched closely.

The nation seemed to be in constant fear that radicals and spies would cause the country to lose the war. This was especially true after November 1917, when a **Communist Revolution** occurred in Russia. The Russian communist government quickly made peace with Germany. That enabled the Germans to transfer troops from the Eastern Front to France just when large numbers of American soldiers were going into battle.

A sensible limit on freedom of speech in wartime was finally set by the Supreme Court in *Schenck v. United States* (1919), a case that questioned the constitutionality of the Espionage Act. The decision, written by Justice Oliver Wendell Holmes, one of the greatest of American legal thinkers, upheld the law.

The right of free speech is not an unlimited right, Holmes declared. No one has the right, for example, of "falsely shouting *'Fire!'* in a theater and causing a panic." If there is "a clear and present

Oliver Wendell Holmes served with distinction on the Supreme Court. Holmes was known as the Great Dissenter for his carefully reasoned minority opinions. What was the climate of the country when Holmes wrote his famous decision in the case *Schenck v. United States?*

READING PRACTICE IN SOCIAL STUDIES

Recognizing Propaganda

A German leader once wrote, "The people can be made to see Heaven as Hell, or the most wretched life as paradise, by the skillful and sustained use of propaganda."

Day after day we are exposed to *propaganda* in one form or another. Propaganda is a collection of facts or ideas used to persuade people to support certain ideas, attitudes, or beliefs. It may be true or false, good or evil.

Propaganda may be used for the public good in raising an army or fighting prejudice. But propaganda has come increasingly to mean persuasion by lies or half-truths which give a false, misleading picture. "The larger and more brazen the lie," wrote the German leader, "the more willing the world is to believe it." It is this kind of propaganda to which we need to remain alert.

Among the many techniques of propaganda are the following few:

The bandwagon encourages you to do something because everybody else is doing it.

Card-stacking presents information only favorable to one side.

The *testimonial* uses a famous person to support a product or a point of view.

Transference borrows strong feelings about a subject and applies them to another subject.

Glittering generalities use language for its sound rather than its meaning.

Name-calling attacks reputation or one's good name.

Propaganda played an important role in the U.S. entry into the Great War. Skillful Allied propagandists flooded the U.S. with stories of German cruelty. Once the U.S. entered the war, propagandists at home joined the war of words to persuade Americans to strengthen the war effort.

The following excerpt is from a book published in 1917, the year the U.S. entered the Great War. *The German Terror in Belgium: an Historical Record* was written by the British historian Arnold J. Toynbee. Page after page the book describes German cruelty in the takeover of Belgium.

When Germany declared war on Russia, Belgium, and France in the first days of August 1914, German armies immediately invaded Russian, Belgian, and French territory, and as soon as the frontiers were crossed, these armies began to wage war, not merely against the troops and fortifications of the invaded states, but against the lives and property of the civil population.

Outrages were committed during the whole advance and retreat of the Germans through Belgium and France, and only abated when open maneuvering gave place to trench warfare along all the line from Switzerland to the sea.

In the hamlet of Fécher the whole population—about 1,000 women, children, and men—was penned into the church on August 5th, and next morning the men (412 of them) were herded off as a living screen for the German troops advancing between the forts (the first man to come out of the church being wantonly shot down as an example to the rest). The 411 were driven by byroads to the Chartreuse Monastery, above the Meuse, overlooking the bridge into the city of Liége, and on the 7th they were planted as hostages on the bridge while the Germans marched across. They were held there without food or shelter or relief for a hundred hours.

Reread this account of the German invasion carefully. Then tell which of the propaganda techniques listed in the first column is used by Toynbee. Cite specific passages to support your answer. Discuss in class why Toynbee probably wrote the book.

danger" that something said or written might hurt the war effort, the government may take action. The Supreme Court did not hand down this decision until after the war was over. Before it did so, local, state, and national officials frequently punished persons whose words had no effect on the war effort at all.

- Why did the Wobblies alarm most people during the war?
- What was the Espionage Act? The Sedition Act?
- What did Justice Holmes declare about the right of free speech?

AMERICANS IN THE GREAT WAR

President Wilson put General Pershing in command of the American Expeditionary Force. The AEF went into action in France just in the nick of time. In March 1918 the Germans launched a tremendous attack at the section of the Western Front nearest Paris. With the help of thousands of veterans transferred to France after the Russians left the war, the Germans advanced as far as **Château-Thierry,** a town on the Marne River northeast of Paris. There, in late May, American units were thrown into battle to reinforce French troops. The German advance was stopped.

Norman Rockwell, a popular artist for several decades, painted these four soldiers around the campfire for the songsheet of George M. Cohan's "Over There." The song inspired all kinds of people to sing, "The Yanks are coming, the Yanks are coming." The Yanks in the picture at the right string lines of communication while they advance from Verdun. The bleak landscape testifies to the constant shelling. For these soldiers the war is aboveground at last. They have come up from the trenches, and now they march to victory. What kinds of conditions were discovered by soldiers 'over there'?

After nearly four years of war, many new weapons had been developed. The fighting became more and more mechanized. The British and French were the first to use **tanks**—armored, trucklike vehicles that ran on treads rather than wheels. The first tanks were slow, clumsy, and unreliable. They were used to protect advancing troops rather than to attack enemy forces directly.

Another new weapon was **poison gas.** The Germans used gas first, but the Allies soon copied them. Gas was a horrible weapon, choking and blinding its victims. It was not very effective, however. If the wind shifted, it might blow back on those who released it. In close combat it hampered the attackers as well as the defenders.

Airplanes were used increasingly as time passed. There were some bombing planes but none powerful enough to carry heavy loads of bombs for great distances. Mostly planes were used to locate enemy positions and signal artillery units where their shells were hitting so they could aim more effectively.

Yet control of the air was important. There were many exciting air battles called **dogfights** between Allied and German pilots. In this huge war of faceless fighters, pilots were individual heroes. Those who shot down five or more enemy planes were known as **aces.** René Fonck, a French ace, shot down 75 enemy planes. Edward Mannock, an Englishman, bagged 73. The most famous German ace, Baron Manfred von Richthofen, claimed 80 kills, but this was probably an exaggeration. Captain "Eddie" Rickenbacker was the leading American ace. He shot down 26 German planes.

But the deadliest weapons remained the artillery and **machine guns.** By 1917 each side had tens of thousands of cannon ranged behind the lines. To prepare for one offensive, the French fired 6 million shells into an area only 20 miles long (32 kilometers). The number of machine guns increased even more rapidly. Before the war American regiments were equipped with four machine guns. By the end of the war each regiment had 336.

Yet all these death-dealing weapons did not give either side enough advantage to end the long struggle quickly. Throughout the summer of 1918 the fighting continued with few movements in either direction. Day by day the number of Americans in the trenches increased from about 27,000 in early June to 500,000 by the end of August.

Finally the long stalemate began to break. In mid-September American and French forces pushed the Germans back from a wedge-shaped section of the front known as the **Saint-Mihiel salient.** Next came the long, desperate **Battle of the Argonne Forest.** The Argonne lay northwest of Saint-Mihiel. It was a rocky, hilly region crisscrossed by streams and blasted by constant shelling. Between September 26 and mid-October the Americans struggled through this

Captain Edward V. Rickenbacker was America's most famous ace. What were air battles called during the war?

Smithsonian Institution

"Troops Waiting to Advance" is a pastel sketch made at Hattonchatel on Saint-Mihiel Drive. The artist is W. J. Aylward. He sketched the U.S. soldiers amidst the rubble of war as they awaited orders. What was the importance of the Allies taking the Saint-Mihiel salient?

hellish wilderness. German artillery rained high explosives upon them from the hills on their right flank.

Beyond the Argonne the Allies advanced against the **Hindenburg Line.** The line was actually three rows of trenches several miles apart. It bristled with machine gun nests and was guarded by mile after mile of rusty tangles of barbed wire. By this time over a million Americans were in combat. Another million had landed in France and more were arriving steadily.

On November 7 American units finally broke through the Hindenburg Line. They then advanced more swiftly toward Sedan, a city near the Belgian border. All along the front, French and British armies were also driving the Germans back, rapidly gaining ground. On November 11, 1918, the Germans gave up the hopeless fight. They signed an **armistice,** or truce, that was actually a surrender.

698

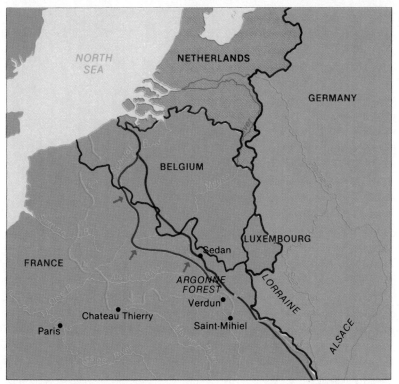

THE WESTERN FRONT

——— Hindenburg line

→ Allied advance Fall 1918

→| German advance Summer 1918

——— Armistice line Nov. 1918

0   100 Mi.

0   100 Km.

Some 53,000 Americans were killed during the Great War. Another 230,000 were wounded. An even larger number died of disease, many of **Spanish influenza.** This world-wide epidemic killed 20 million people. America's war losses were much smaller than those of any of the other major nations. Still, during the last few months Americans bore their full share of the fighting and suffered their full share of the casualties.

■ How did the Allies finally bring the war to an end?

MAKING PEACE

President Wilson had been preparing for making peace even before the United States entered the war. As we have seen, he wanted a peace without victory. Wilson believed the terms must not be so hard on the Central Powers as to cause them to begin planning another war to regain what was taken from them.

In January 1918 Wilson made a speech to Congress describing his plans for peace. "The world must be made safe for every peace-loving nation," he said. Unless all the nations are treated fairly, none can count on being treated fairly. In this respect "all the peoples of the world are in effect partners." The President then listed **Fourteen Points** that he said made up "the only possible program" for peace.

699

The National Gallery

The flags of Great Britain, France, and the United States fly on Fifth Avenue in New York. "Allies Day, May 1917" was painted in oil by Childe Hassam in celebration of the alliance of these three nations. This is an Impressionist painting which pays attention to light and shadow. Another Childe Hassam painting is on page 606. How did Wilson plan for peace?

The first of Wilson's points promised that the peace treaty would not contain secret clauses. "Diplomacy shall proceed . . . in the public view." Another point called for freedom of the seas "in peace and in war." Restrictions like the ones the Germans and the Allies had imposed on neutral shipping must not be permitted. But this point, like urging disarmament and calling for the lowering of protective tariffs "so far as possible," was more hopeful than practical.

A more important point dealt with the future of colonies. In settling "all colonial claims," the interests of those who lived in the colonies must be taken into account, not merely the interests of the ruling powers.

Most of Wilson's other points concerned redrawing the boundaries of European nations. Belgium should get back all the territory occupied by Germany during the war. France should regain the province of Alsace-Lorraine on its eastern border. This region had been lost to Germany in an earlier war.

Elsewhere the boundaries should follow "lines of allegiance and nationality." Areas where the inhabitants thought of themselves as Italians should be part of Italy, Poles part of Poland, and so on. This became known as the **right of self-determination.** All peoples should be able to determine for themselves what nation they belonged to.

The 14th point was to Wilson the most important. It called for the creation of an "association of nations." The purpose of this international organization would be to guarantee the independence and the territory "of great and small nations alike." This **League of Nations,** as it was soon named, was to be a kind of international congress that would settle disputes between nations. When necessary, the League would use force against any nation that defied its rulings.

The "just peace" that Wilson was proposing appealed powerfully to millions of people all over the world. It helped to shorten the Great War by encouraging the Germans to surrender when their armies began to suffer defeats in the autumn of 1918.

After the signing of the armistice on November 11, 1918, Wilson became a world hero. Millions of people believed that his idealism, backed by the wealth and power of the United States, would bring about basic changes in international relations. A new era of peace and prosperity seemed about to begin.

- Why did President Wilson make his Fourteen-Points speech to Congress?
- What did Wilson mean by "the right of self-determination"?
- What was to be the purpose of the League of Nations?

THE VERSAILLES PEACE CONFERENCE

In January 1919 representatives of the victorious Allies gathered at the Palace of Versailles, outside Paris, to write a formal treaty of peace. President Wilson headed the American delegation himself. No earlier President had ever left the nation while in office or personally negotiated a treaty. The chief British representative was Prime Minister David Lloyd George. The French premier, Georges Clemenceau, and the Italian prime minister, Vittorio Orlando, completed the Council of Four, popularly called the **Big Four.** Working under them were many hundreds of lawyers, mapmakers, economists, historians, military leaders, and all sorts of other experts.

Wilson had a difficult time persuading the other leaders to accept his idea of peace without victory. Clemenceau wanted to make Germany pay the entire cost of the war. France especially had been bled white. Most of the fighting had taken place on French soil. The northwestern part of the country was a vast no man's land. And almost

BUILDING SKILLS
IN SOCIAL STUDIES

Comparing National Boundaries

When the Great War was over, the map of Europe was redrawn. Mapmakers were among the participants at the Versailles Peace Conference. Their task was to prepare a new map of Europe's national boundaries that reflected the goal of self-determination. When the conference ended, more people in Europe lived under the flag of their choice than ever before.

The best way to understand the changes in national boundaries is by comparing maps. On page 677 is a map of Europe in 1914, before the fighting began. The map below shows Europe in 1919. The two maps are drawn to the same scale. By looking carefully at both, you can readily see the changes brought about by the war and the peace settlement.

1. Which large Central Power nation shared Germany's border in 1914?
2. Which nations existed in 1914 but not in 1919?
3. Which new, independent nations were created in 1919?
4. From which nations that existed in 1914 was Poland created?
5. Which nations were created from Austria-Hungary after the war?

Brown Brothers

The "Big Four" are shown here in Paris in 1919 for the Versailles Peace Conference. They are, left to right, David Lloyd George from Great Britain, Vittorio Orlando of Italy, Georges Clemenceau from France, and Woodrow Wilson of the United States. What famous first was this conference for the President of the United States?

1.4 million French soldiers had been killed out of the country's total population of only about 40 million, including women, children, and old people.

Lloyd George and Orlando also put the interests of their own nations first. Wilson was forced to agree to a clause in the treaty stating that Germany alone had caused the war. He even accepted a clause making Germany pay "for all damage done to the civilian population of the Allies and their property."

This sum, called **reparations,** was so enormous that the Allies were not able to decide an actual amount. They made the Germans sign "a blank check" agreeing to pay whatever the victors finally demanded. The amount eventually named was $33 billion. This was far more than the Germans could possibly pay, whether or not they were entirely responsible for the war. This was certainly not the peace without victory Wilson had promised.

Even if the Big Four had wanted to do so, putting all the 14 Points into practice would have been impossible. Self-determination was an excellent idea, but in many parts of Europe people of different nationalities were mixed together. There were villages of Germans living in Polish areas, Slavs in the midst of Italians or Hungarians.

Many agreements already in existence conflicted with the idea of self-determination. The victorious nations had made promises in order to win the war that violated this and other of Wilson's points. Britain and France had promised Italy parts of Austria-Hungary. The British had agreed to back an Arab nation in the Middle East and also to support a homeland for the Jews in the same region.

Yet, on balance, the final **Versailles Peace Treaty** did come close to the goal Wilson had aimed at in his 14 Points speech. Poland and Czechoslovakia became new states based on the principle of self-determination. The new map of Europe probably came closer to putting all the people of that continent under the flag of their choice than had ever been done before.

The treaty included what Wilson considered his most important point of all. This was the Covenant, or constitution, of the League of Nations.

The League consisted of a General Assembly of representatives of 42 Allied and neutral nations and a Council controlled by the Big Four and Japan. All League members were required to protect one another's territories against attack. All disputes between members were to be submitted to arbitration. Nations which did not obey League decisions could be punished by **sanctions.** These could take the form of a ban on trade with the offending country or even military force.

Furthermore, the former German colonies in Africa and the Far East and the parts of the Middle East that were taken from Turkey were made **mandates,** or dependencies, of the League as a whole. They were to be managed by individual Allied nations. Great Britain, France, and Japan held most of them. The entire League was made responsible for seeing that the interests of the local inhabitants were properly protected.

The League of Nations was Woodrow Wilson's proudest accomplishment. He believed that its founding marked the beginning of an era of permanent world peace. He knew that the Versailles Treaty was not the true "peace without victory" he had sought. Yet he was absolutely certain that the League would be able to deal with the problems the treaty had created. He believed that the entire arrangement made at Versailles depended on the acceptance and support of the League by all the powers. This was the message he brought when he returned to the United States from France. In July 1919 he submitted the treaty to the Senate.

- Who were the Big Four? On what issue were they divided in their meeting at Versailles?
- What were some outcomes of the Treaty of Versailles? Of what was President Wilson most proud?

CHAPTER 23 REVIEW

Identification

Tell briefly why each of the following persons, terms, or events is important.

1. Woodrow Wilson
2. Victoriano Huerta
3. Venustiano Carranza
4. Francisco "Pancho" Villa
5. John J. Pershing
6. William G. McAdoo
7. Bernard Baruch
8. Herbert Hoover
9. Central Powers
10. Allies
11. Trench warfare
12. Blockade
13. U-boats
14. *Lusitania*
15. American Expeditionary Force
16. Selective Service Act
17. Wobblies
18. Fourteen-Points plan
19. League of Nations
20. Versailles Peace Treaty

Understanding American History

1. Explain the role of the U.S. in world affairs as President Wilson saw it.
2. Why was the Mexican Revolution of concern to the United States?
3. Why was Wilson's interference in Mexican affairs resented by both the leaders he opposed and those he tried to support?
4. Describe trench warfare on the Western Front.
5. Explain how both the British blockade and German submarine warfare hurt American interests in 1914–15.
6. Why did the Central Powers and the Allies not accept Wilson's idea of peace without victory?
7. Give at least three reasons why the U.S. declared war on Germany in 1917.
8. Explain the purpose of the War Industries Board.
9. Describe five new weapons of World War I. Which were the most deadly, and why?
10. What was Wilson's Fourteen-Points plan? Why did he consider the League of Nations his most important point?

Activities

1. Use your historical imagination to take a role as an adviser to President Wilson as he considers U.S. involvement in the Great War. One classmate should take the role of President Wilson. In a White House meeting the following positions should be heard: a) remain neutral, b) remain neutral but provide food to Allies such as Britain, Belgium, and France, c) protest strongly to Britain and Germany for violations of international shipping rules, d) place an embargo on trade with Great Britain, e) hold Germany "strictly accountable" for attacks on American ships, f) declare war on Germany.
2. Make a model of a battlefield on the Western Front, using clay, plaster of paris, or papier-mâché. Include trenches, machine gun nests, barbed-wire mazes, and no man's land.
3. Use an opaque projector to illustrate a report on the war on the home front. Show posters for recruiting, for the war effort in the U.S., or for the Food Administrator (such as "Food will win the war" or the campaign for "Meatless Tuesdays"). Discuss wartime propaganda.
4. Do research and report on one of these European leaders in 1914–19:
   - Kaiser William of Germany
   - Czar Nicholas of Russia
   - Emperor Franz Josef of Austria-Hungary
   - David Lloyd George of England
   - Georges Clemenceau of France
   - Vittorio Orlando of Italy
5. Using the resources of your library, report on the Spanish influenza pandemic of 1918, which took 20 million lives. Describe its toll on the American army.

CHAPTER 23 TEST

Completion (45 points)
Number your paper 1–15 and next to each number write the words from the list below that best complete each sentence.

War Industries Board   neutrality
Fourteen-Points plan   Sedition Act
Western Front   submarine warfare
reparations   Zimmermann Note
Selective Service Act   armistice
Central Powers   Allies
blockade   dogfights
matériel

1. The _____ included Germany, Austria-Hungary, Turkey, and Bulgaria.
2. The U.S. fought on the side of the _____ in the Great War.
3. At the start of the Great War most Americans favored a policy of _____.
4. Fighting on the _____ was characterized by trench warfare.
5. The British _____ was intended to keep Germany from receiving supplies from neutral countries.
6. The Germans used _____ to keep supplies from reaching Britain.
7. The _____ angered Americans because it was evidence that Germany was trying to form an alliance with Mexico.
8. The task of the _____ was to organize the nation's economy for war production.
9. A draft law known as the _____ was passed to raise the U.S. army for the war.
10. Congress passed the _____ in order to prevent criticism of the U.S. war effort.
11. War supplies are called _____.
12. Air battles, called _____, were fought for control of the skies during the war.
13. The Great War ended when Germany signed a truce known as the _____.
14. President Wilson insisted that his _____ was the only possible program for peace.
15. The Versailles Peace Treaty ordered Germany to pay fines or _____ for damages.

Matching (25 points)
Number your paper 16–20 and match the name in the second column with the description in the first column.

16. United States Food Administrator who made sure enough foodstuffs were produced and distributed fairly
17. Commander of the American Expeditionary Force
18. Mexican general who led raids against U.S. border towns in 1917
19. Head of the War Industries Board
20. President who argued that the League of Nations would lead to an era of permanent world peace

a. Woodrow Wilson
b. Francisco "Pancho" Villa
c. John J. Pershing
d. Bernard Baruch
e. Herbert Hoover

Essay (30 points)
Choose one of the following topics for a brief essay. Explain how the need for workers during the Great War helped women, blacks, and Mexican-Americans, *or* Explain how the British blockade and German submarine warfare violated U.S. rights. Tell which did the most damage to U.S. trade. Plan your essay by preparing a brief outline as a checklist to make sure you fully cover the topic you choose.

CHAPTER 24

The 1920s

When President Wilson returned to the United States with the Versailles Treaty, almost everyone believed the Senate would ratify it. Certainly everyone wanted the war to be officially over. And the idea of an organization like the League of Nations seemed a good one. A large majority of Americans probably favored the League, although few understood it entirely or were happy with its every detail. Now came the task of winning over the American people. But a difficult time lay ahead for the President.

POLITICAL PROBLEMS

In the 1918 Congressional elections the Republicans won majorities in both the House and the Senate. Wilson now needed the support of a large number of Republican senators to get the two-thirds majority necessary to ratify the Versailles Treaty.

Wilson had expected the Democrats would continue to control the Senate. He had campaigned for Democrats so that his peace policies would be carried out smoothly. After the election he made matters worse for himself by not including any Republican senators on the peace commission.

Why he did not is a mystery. Perhaps the President assumed the peace treaty would be so popular that senators would not dare vote against it. "The Senate must take its medicine," he said privately.

Wilson did not realize that some parts of any complicated document like the Versailles Treaty were sure to displease many different people. When its details became known, various special interest groups demanded many changes in the treaty. But Wilson refused to agree to *any* changes whatsoever.

The most important criticism involved the League of Nations. The United States would be only one among many members. Suppose the League voted to use force against a nation. Was it not up to Congress to say when American troops were sent into battle? Old suspicions of tricky European diplomats now began to reappear.

- What problem did the 1918 Congressional elections create for President Wilson?
- What position did the President take on changes in the Versailles Treaty?

Henry Cabot Lodge, senator from Massachusetts, is the subject of this portrait in oil by John Singer Sargent. It was painted in 1890. The rich, dark colors are typical of Sargent and of the turn-of-the-century period as well. Another Sargent portrait appears on page 640, this one of Lodge's close friend Theodore Roosevelt. Lodge was a biographer of Washington, Alexander Hamilton, and Daniel Webster. What conflict did he have with President Wilson?

THE SENATE DEBATE

In the Senate debate nearly all the Democrats supported the League without question. Many Republican senators also favored joining the League. Some of these, known as **mild reservationists,** were willing to vote for the treaty if a few minor changes were made. They had reservations about the League, but their reservations would not block American membership.

Other Republicans were willing to vote for the League only if more important changes were made. These **strong reservationists** were led by Senator Henry Cabot Lodge of Massachusetts. He introduced what were called the **Lodge Reservations** to the treaty. The most important of these stated that American armed forces could not be sent into action by the League of Nations until Congress gave its approval.

If Wilson had been willing to accept the Lodge Reservations, the Versailles Treaty would have been ratified easily. Only a small group of senators, known as the **Irreconcilables,** refused to vote for it on any terms. The President could probably have gotten the two-thirds vote by making some small concessions to the mild reservationists alone. Yet he refused to budge. It had to be all or nothing.

- Who were the mild reservationists? The strong reservationists? The irreconcilables?
- What was the most important Lodge Reservation?

THE TRAGEDY OF WOODROW WILSON

For Wilson the basic issue of the treaty ratification was the idea of a truly international government. He argued that the United States must join the League on the same terms as all the other nations. His position was reasonable but not realistic. America had too long seen itself as "different" from the countries of Europe.

Americans were being asked to enter into the kind of "entangling alliance" that Jefferson had warned against in his first inaugural address back in 1801. It was true that the United States had become an international power. But people needed to adjust gradually to modern conditions. "All or nothing" was not the way to educate them.

If the President had been in good health, he would probably not have taken such a rigid stand. But he was in very poor health. While in Paris, he had suffered a mild stroke—the breaking of a blood vessel in his brain. It had not been recognized as a stroke at the time by his doctor. The attack seriously affected Wilson's judgment. Then, in September 1919, while he was trying to rally support for the League, he suffered another stroke. This time there was no mistake about it. His left side was partly paralyzed.

Brown Brothers

Partially paralyzed by the stroke he suffered in 1919, Woodrow Wilson is assisted by a servant as he leaves his home in 1923. He has just made an Armistice Day radio broadcast. Why would Wilson not compromise with moderate Republicans in the Senate debate of 1919?

For weeks Wilson was an invalid in the White House. As he slowly recovered, his advisers pleaded with him to compromise with the moderate Republicans. Otherwise the treaty was sure to be defeated. Wilson refused. It was better "to go down fighting," he told his friends.

On November 19, 1919, the treaty, with the Lodge Reservations attached, came to a vote in the Senate. It was defeated by Democratic votes. Then it was voted on without reservations. This time the Republicans defeated it. The following March, after further debate, the Senate again voted on the treaty with reservations. This time some Democratic senators refused to follow Wilson's urging. They voted for ratification. Not enough of them did so, however, and for a third and final time the treaty was rejected.

- What was the tragedy of Woodrow Wilson?
- What was the outcome of the final vote on the treaty?

THE ELECTION OF 1920

Wilson had hoped that the Presidential election of 1920 would prove that the people of the United States wanted to join the League. The Democratic candidate, Governor James M. Cox of Ohio, campaigned on a platform which called for joining. The Vice Presidential candidate, Franklin D. Roosevelt, a distant cousin of Theodore Roosevelt, also supported the League strongly.

The Republican candidate, Senator Warren G. Harding, refused to take a clear position on the issue. Harding was an expert at avoiding controversial questions. During the Presidential campaign he used a technique called "bloviating." This meant talking about a subject in a way that sounded intelligent but which actually made little or no sense. Citizens who favored the League could think that Harding favored it. Those who opposed it could interpret his statements the other way.

The 1920 Presidential campaign was between Warren G. Harding and James M. Cox, both of Ohio. *Left,* Harding campaigns from his front porch in Marion, Ohio. Cox and his running mate Franklin D. Roosevelt are on the right as they lead a parade through Columbus, Ohio, after receiving official word of their nomination. Roosevelt is the taller man. A year after this picture was taken, he was struck with polio and largely lost the use of his legs. What name was given to Harding's campaign technique in 1920?

On Election Day, Harding won by a huge majority. The new **Nineteenth Amendment,** which gave women the vote, caused a large voter turnout in 1920. The vote for President was nearly twice what it had been in 1916. Harding got 61 per cent of the total, over 16 million votes to Cox's 9.1 million.

Once elected, Harding stopped bloviating about the League. He made it clear that he did not want the United States to join it. Since the League could not be separated from the Versailles Treaty, Congress simply passed a resolution in the summer of 1921 declaring that the war was over.

- What position did Governor Cox take on the League in the 1920 election? What position did Senator Harding take?
- Why was the voter turnout so large in 1920?

United Press International

Women voted for the first time in 1920. This picture was posed for the newspapers in New York City. Three generations of women line up at the ballot box, watched by the male officials. Who was the first President elected with votes cast by both women and men?

FOREIGN POLICY IN THE 1920s

The American people were not ready to assume the kind of international responsibilities that Wilson called for, but they really had little choice. The United States had become the leading industrial and financial power in the world. After the huge foreign loans made by the United States during the war, the rest of the world owed the United States $13 billion. America could not retreat into an isolated cocoon.

In practice the Presidents of the 1920s tried to follow a middle road between the narrow view of **isolationism** and the broader view of **internationalism.** They wanted to enjoy the benefits of America's commanding economic position in the world. Yet they did not want to make binding promises to other countries. This attitude was clearly revealed in the way President Harding approached the question of reducing the size of the navy.

After the huge cost of the Great War the public was eager to avoid building still more warships. In 1921 Harding invited nine European and Asian nations to Washington to discuss **disarmament**— limiting the manufacture of weapons of war. Far Eastern issues were also discussed at this **Washington Disarmament Conference.**

Culver Pictures

"Putting His Foot Down" is the title of this editorial cartoon. Uncle Sam holds a copy of a "Trade Treaty with China" that began America's Open Door policy. He says, "Gentlemen, you may cut up this map as much as you like, but remember that I'm here to stay and that you can't divide me up into spheres of influence." With scissors are, *left to right,* Germany, Italy, England, Austria, Russia, and France. For a full discussion of the Open Door policy see page 634. What did this policy provide?

Several treaties were negotiated by the delegates. The most important was the **Five-Power Naval Treaty.** In this treaty the United States, Great Britain, Japan, France, and Italy agreed to a ten-year "holiday" on the construction of battleships. They also agreed to maintain a fixed ratio, or balance, on all major warships. The United States and Great Britain were to have no more than 525,000 tons of such vessels. Japan's limit was 315,000 tons, France and Italy's 175,000 each. In another agreement all nine nations promised to uphold the principle of the **Open Door** in China. This was the policy which assured all nations equal trade rights with an independent China.

President Harding insisted that the Washington Conference treaties did not commit the United States "to any kind of alliance, entanglement, or involvement." This was true enough. The treaties were backed only by the good will of the nations that signed them. This satisfied most Americans. They wanted peace without the responsibility for maintaining it. They could accept the treaties and still believe that they could remain isolated in the old way from foreign "entanglements."

■ How were American Presidents in the 1920s divided between isolationism and internationalism?

THE POSTWAR REACTION

Isolation was an aspect of a larger **postwar reaction** in the United States. The Great War had been a Great Mistake, most people now thought. Millions of lives had been lost. Billions of dollars had been wasted. And for what purpose? The world had certainly not been made safe for democracy, as Wilson had promised.

In 1919 most Americans seemed more worried about making the United States safe for themselves. Many seriously believed that a communist revolution might break out in the United States at any moment. They were mindful that a tiny group of communists had taken over all of Russia in 1917. Now there were perhaps seventy thousand communists (popularly called **Reds**) in the United States.

Communists wanted workers to raise the red flag of revolution, take up arms, and destroy the capitalist system. At the same time **anarchists,** who wanted all governments abolished, stirred up workers. But most workers were simply trying to keep their jobs. Going from war to peace had been difficult for American industry. Without contracts for war supplies, many plants shut down temporarily or slowed down their operations. Hundreds of thousands of wage earners were thrown out of work. Soldiers returning to civilian life found it almost impossible to get jobs.

Culver Pictures

"Seeking More Freedom" was drawn by a cartoonist named McCutcheon for the *Chicago Tribune* in 1921. In this 1920s political comment nothing is subtle. A "flood of undesirable immigrants" spills from the ship to bypass the "American army of the unemployed." Why were people out of work at this time?

As the flag goes by these watchers at the parade of the 309th Colored Infantry pay their respects. But one little girl cannot keep her eyes on the marchers. Perhaps she admires the soldier's uniform as much as she wonders what terrible wounds come from war. This photograph is from 1919. Why were soldiers who returned to civilian life depressed at this time?

As a result a wave of strikes spread over the land. At one time or another during 1919, 4 million workers were on strike. Seattle was paralyzed. In Boston even the police walked off their jobs. Strikes by police were unheard of at that time. With the streets of Boston unprotected, looters began breaking into stores. The governor of Massachusetts, Calvin Coolidge, finally called in troops to restore order in the city.

At the same time a series of bombings by terrorists took place. To this day no one knows who was responsible for most of the bombings. But the tendency was to blame "the Reds." A **Big Red Scare** swept over America.

President Wilson's Attorney General, A. Mitchell Palmer, became convinced that a massive communist plot to overthrow the federal government was being organized. He ordered raids on the headquarters of suspected radical groups. These **Palmer raids** were often conducted without search warrants. Many suspected communists were held for weeks without formal charges. There was no evidence of a nationwide uprising. Yet in 1921 Palmer announced that such a revolution would take place on May 1, the communist Labor Day. When May 1 passed quietly, Americans realized that the danger of a revolution had been only in their minds. As quickly as it had begun, the Big Red Scare ended.

The nervous mood of the 1920s then took other forms. One was a revival of the Ku Klux Klan. Klan membership grew between 1920 and 1923 from about 5,000 members to several million. Unlike the Klan of Reconstruction days, this one spread into the northern states. It became a powerful but short-lived force in the early 1920s and did much harm to many innocent persons.

Library of Congress

In 1921 Congress reacted to the isolationism of the times by taking steps to control the entry of foreigners into the United States. This made some sense at the time. The frontier had disappeared. In a machine age the nation no longer needed to import large numbers of unskilled laborers. The **Emergency Quota Act** limited the number of immigrants by nationality, reducing the number of newcomers from eastern and southern Europe. A still stiffer quota law, the **National Origins Act,** was passed in 1924. Beginning in 1929, a total of only 150,000 immigrants a year could enter the United States. In practice the number of actual immigrants fell below 100,000 every year from 1931 to 1946.

"I pledge allegiance to the flag of the United States of America, and to the republic for which it stands, one nation under God, indivisible, with liberty and justice for all."

In this 1923 editorial cartoon from *Life* magazine a moth resembling a hooded member of the Ku Klux Klan chews holes in the American flag. The cartoon is captioned, "Like the moth, it works in the dark." Why was the Klan feared?

■ What effect did peacetime have on industry?
■ What was the Big Red Scare?

BUILDING SKILLS IN SOCIAL STUDIES

Finding Trends in Immigration

In 1921 Congress passed the **Emergency Quota Act.** This law limited the number of immigrants by nationality. Each year only 3 per cent of the number of foreign-born people who had been in the United States in 1910 could enter.

In 1924 the **National Origins Act** was passed. It changed the quota year to 1890 and reduced the percentage admitted from 3 per cent to 2 per cent. This change cut immigration from southern and eastern Europe still further. Far fewer people from that part of the world were living in the United States in 1890 than in 1910. Under the 1924 law the quotas of Russia and Italy together were smaller than the quota of Norway, a nation with fewer people than either.

Beginning in 1929, a total of only 150,000 immigrants could enter the U.S. each year. For example, the number of Italians allowed into the U.S. each year after 1929 would be computed this way:

$$\frac{\text{Italian quota}}{150,000} = \frac{\text{Italian-Americans, 1920}}{\text{White population, 1920}}$$

$$\frac{\text{Italian quota}}{150,000} = \frac{3,800,000}{95,500,000}$$

$$\text{Italian quota} = 6,000$$

In practice the number of actual immigrants fell below 100,000 every year from 1931 to 1946. Not many people from northern European countries with large quotas wanted to immigrate, and their quotas went unfilled.

The *trend* of immigration from 1880 to 1940 is best shown on the *bar graph* at right. Form general statements about immigration from northern and western Europe and from southern and eastern Europe in the period from 1890 to 1940. Then describe the trends of immigration from northern and western Europe and from southern and eastern Europe.

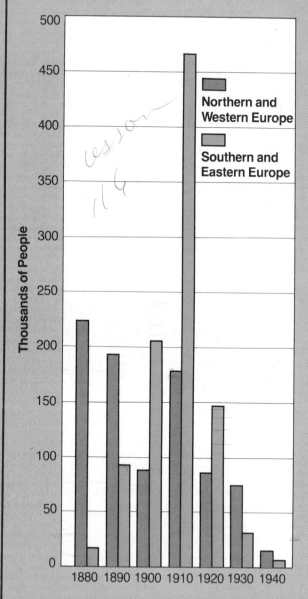

IMMIGRATION FROM EUROPE 1880-1940

Northern and Western Europe

Southern and Eastern Europe

Thousands of People

THE JAZZ AGE

Not all Americans were so troubled in the 1920s. Many were finding new ways to enjoy life. Industry continued to grow, producing new wealth and providing more leisure time for many millions of people. Change was in the air, and the speed of change was increasing. People everywhere were casting off old ways and seeking new ways to express themselves.

Consider the typical music of the period. The music that most Americans listened to and danced to during the 1920s was called **jazz.** Jazz was created by black musicians in New Orleans in the late 1800s. It grew out of the "blues"—music that reflected the hard life of most blacks in America and the tough-minded humor that many displayed in trying to cope with it. W. C. Handy of Alabama was the "father of the blues." His most famous composition was "St. Louis Blues" (1914).

Most of the early black jazz musicians had little or no formal training in music. Yet they were superb performers. Their music was often the only outlet for their emotions. Bessie Smith, a leading singer of the 1920s, sang movingly about her own sorrowful experiences. Louis "Satchmo" Armstrong was the most famous jazz musician of the day. He won international fame both as a trumpeter and as a singer.

W. C. Handy and Bessie Smith are two of the greatest jazz performers. Handy arrived in New York in 1917, already the composer of "Memphis Blues" and "Beale Street Blues." Although Bessie Smith lived only 40 years, she is widely remembered as the "Empress of the Blues." She was perhaps the best jazz artist of all time. Where did jazz begin?

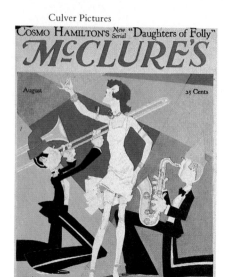

A typical flapper of the 1920s graces this *McClure's* magazine cover. The artist, John Held, Jr., was popular for the sharp angles of his pictures, which captured the special energy of the Jazz Age. Who were flappers?

Jazz musicians *improvised* much of their music. Taking a theme or musical idea, they chased a tune up and down the scales as they played. This gave musicians and listeners alike a sense of freedom.

Jazz spread from New Orleans to Chicago and New York and then throughout most of the world. White musicians as well as black performed it. It became in its own way a powerful force for breaking down racial barriers, both among the players and for those who simply listened.

The decade of the 1920s is sometimes called the **Jazz Age.** In part the popularity of its music is enough to explain this. But jazz also symbolized the way many young people of the time felt about life in general. They sought to break away from rigid, conventional rules and traditions, just as jazz trumpeters and saxophonists departed from written notes in order to express themselves.

Young women in particular seemed determined to free themselves from restricting "out-of date" ideas and rules. They cast off uncomfortable (and unhealthy) corsets and thick petticoats in favor of short skirts and loose-fitting clothing. They cut their hair short. They wore makeup. They drank and smoked in public.

The behavior of these "new women" shocked older people deeply. They called them **flappers** and predicted they would come to a bad end. Actually most of these young women were trying to liberate themselves. Not all of them were conscious feminists. Some were merely trying to keep up with the latest fads and fashions. Still, consciously or not, they were demanding the right to behave the same way men behaved.

■ What was the origin of jazz? How did jazz reflect the 1920s?

■ What were "new women" of the 1920s seeking?

THE GOLDEN AGE OF SPORTS

The 1920s had its full share of gangsters, corrupt politicians, and other villains. It also had its heroes. Athletes were among the most popular. Mass spectator sports were booming. The 1920s was truly the **Golden Age of Sports.**

Some 91,000 boxing fans paid more than $1 million in July 1921 to watch the heavyweight champion, Jack Dempsey, knock out Georges Carpentier of France. Every fall weekend thousands of people jammed football stadiums to cheer for players like Harold "Red" Grange, the "Galloping Ghost" of the University of Illinois. One Saturday afternoon in 1924 Grange took the University of Michigan's opening kickoff 95 yards for a touchdown. He scored three more touchdowns in the first quarter and another before the game ended, Illinois winning 39-14. Grange carried the ball 21 times and gained an incredible 402 yards.

Both, Culver Pictures

The most famous football coach of the 1920s was Knute Rockne of Notre Dame's "Fighting Irish." He began the decade with an unbeaten season. For many the 1920 highlight was Notre Dame's defeat of Army, 27-17, owing largely to the 357 yards gained by the team's captain, George Gipp.

In 1927 one of the most famous **barnstorming,** or traveling, basketball teams in the world was formed by Abe Saperstein. He recruited his players from the slums of Chicago's South Side, but he called his team of all black athletes the Harlem Globetrotters. They became magicians with the basketball and drew fans throughout the world.

Baseball was the national game. Its most famous hero was Babe Ruth, the "Sultan of Swat." Ruth was originally a pitcher—and a very good one. He was also a tremendous hitter. The New York Yankees bought Ruth from the Boston Red Sox and made him an outfielder so he could play every day. Thereafter, year after year, he was baseball's home run leader. In 1927 he hit 60. By the end of his career he had knocked out 714 home runs.

Americans were good at nearly all sports. The tennis players William "Big Bill" Tilden and Helen Wills both won many national championships. Johnny Weismuller held a dozen world swimming records. Gertrude Ederle became the first woman to swim across the English Channel.

His legs were thought to be funny, hers lovely. He is the immortal Babe Ruth, the most popular athlete of the 1920s. She is Helen Wills, believed to be the greatest women's tennis player of her time. In the third game of the 1932 World Series, Ruth chose a spot in the stands of the Chicago Cubs' ball park, pointed to it, and slugged one of his 714 home runs to the astonished fans. Which kinds of sports boomed in the 1920s?

- Why was the 1920s the Golden Age of Sports?
- What was America's national game? Who was its most famous hero?

719

The Lone Eagle

Culver Pictures

The most popular American hero of the 1920s was Charles A. Lindbergh. On May 20, 1927, Lindbergh took off from a muddy, rain-drenched airfield near New York City in a tiny, one-engine plane, the *Spirit of St. Louis*. He was headed for France. Alone, hour after hour, he guided his plane eastward across the Atlantic. He flew with a map in his lap and only some coffee and a few sandwiches to keep up his strength. Staying awake called for a tremendous feat of willpower. If he dozed off, even for a minute, the *Spirit of St. Louis* might have crashed into the sea. Lindbergh did not doze off. About 33½ hours after takeoff he landed safely at Le Bourget airport on the outskirts of Paris. He was the first aviator to fly alone from America to Europe.

Lindbergh's achievement caught the imagination of the entire world. Here is how *The New York Times* described his landing at Le Bourget:

> PARIS, May 21—Lindbergh did it. Twenty minutes after 10 o'clock tonight suddenly and softly there slipped out of the darkness a gray-white airplane as 25,000 pairs of eyes strained toward it. At 10:24 the Spirit of St. Louis landed and lines of soldiers, ranks of policemen and stout steel fences went down before a mad rush as irresistible as the tides of the ocean.

Lindbergh returned home a grinning, modest hero. The idol of millions, he was given a tremendous ticker tape parade through New York City. The newspapers named him "The Lone Eagle." He was also known as "Lucky Lindy," but his success was due far more to courage and skill than luck.

Now that dozens of giant jets fly across the Atlantic every day, Lindbergh's flight may not seem very important. To play down his achievement would be a big mistake. The flight marked the coming of age of the airplane. Lindbergh himself is the perfect symbol of the Air Age. He was two years old when Wilbur and Orville Wright made the first successful airplane flights at Kitty Hawk, North Carolina, in 1903. Those flights lasted only a few seconds and covered only a few hundred yards at most. Yet before Lindbergh died, American astronauts had landed on the moon.

MOTION PICTURES

Lindbergh's achievement combined his own human abilities and the mechanical perfection of his plane. This combination was characteristic of the period. It explains the rapid growth of motion pictures, which, like the airplane, came of age in the 1920s.

Culver Pictures

Movies were popular even before the Great War. The early movie theaters were often installed in vacant stores. These "nickelodeons"—the usual admission charge was five cents—showed jerky, badly lit scenes. In the 1920s motion pictures became an important art form and one of the ten largest industries in the nation. In 1922 40 million people a week went to the movies. By 1930 weekly attendance was averaging 100 million.

Every large city had its movie palaces—large, elaborate theaters seating several thousand people. Hollywood, California, became the motion picture capital of the world. The state's warm, sunny climate was ideal for outdoor movie making.

Americans in the 1920s flocked to every kind of film. There were historical pictures and the most durable of all movies—westerns. The leading actors and actresses were loved by millions. Movie fans followed the careers and personal lives of their favorites as though they were members of their families.

Movies influenced the way people dressed and talked. Women styled their hair like Greta Garbo or Mary Pickford. Men tried to copy Rudolph Valentino, the great lover of *The Sheik,* or Douglas Fairbanks, the sword-fighting hero of *The Three Musketeers.*

The greatest star of the 1920s was Charlie Chaplin. He wrote and directed his own films. In 1915 he created his world-famous character, the sad-looking "little tramp" who wore baggy pants and

For many fans of the 1920s this was Hollywood. Searchlights illuminate Grauman's Chinese Theater as this Hollywood crowd surges forward to glimpse their favorite stars. What were early movies called?

721

Charlie Chaplin and Jackie Cooper starred in "The Kid" in 1920. In an era of silent pictures, movies were truly universal. Chaplin was easily the most famous person in the world. The advertisement below appeared in the 1923 Christmas issue of *Life*. It is an early appearance for Nipper, the Victor dog. How important did movies become as an industry?

Both, Culver Pictures

a battered derby hat and carried a springy bamboo cane. Chaplin was a marvelous slapstick comedian and a gifted mimic. He was also a superb actor, who could literally make audiences laugh and cry at the same time.

For years the movies were silent. Usually a pianist in each theater played mood music to accompany the action on the screen. Then, in 1927, Warner Brothers, an important film company, released the first "talkie," a film that projected the actors' voices as well as their movements. This film was *The Jazz Singer,* starring Al Jolson. He sang three songs and then told the film audience, "You ain't heard nothin' yet, folks." The next year Walt Disney made the first sound cartoon, *Steamboat Willie,* which introduced Mickey Mouse to the world.

- How did movies change from the days of the nickelodeon to the 1920s?
- How did movies influence people?

RADIO

Radio had an even more powerful hold on the public in the 1920s than movies. Like the movies, it could not have been developed without the remarkable scientific and technological advances of the times.

Everyone could enjoy and profit from radio, even sick and bed-ridden people who could not get to the movies. Radio could be listened to without cost and in the privacy of one's home. It was also "live." What people heard was taking place at that very moment: a politician making a speech, the crack of the bat when Babe Ruth hit another home run, the roar of the crowd at a football game, the sound of a jazz band or a symphony orchestra.

The first commercial radio station was KDKA in Pittsburgh. It was operated by the **Westinghouse Electric Company.** KDKA began broadcasting in 1920. Two years later there were more than 500 commercial stations. The **National Broadcasting Company** (NBC) began combining local stations into a nationwide radio network in 1926. A year later the **Columbia Broadcasting System** (CBS) created a competing network. Thereafter, people all over the country could hear the same program at the same time. Audiences grew to the millions.

Radio became still another giant industry. Large companies sprang up to manufacture radio sets and broadcasting equipment. Department stores devoted entire floors to radios. Repairing radios became an important craft. By 1922 3 million families already had radios. In the single year 1929 5 million sets were sold.

Radio brought an enormous variety of information and entertainment into American homes. News, music, plays, political speeches, and sports events filled the airwaves. Radio also influenced what Americans bought in stores. Audiences were bombarded with commercials by manufacturers of all sorts. These advertisers paid large sums to broadcast their "sales pitches."

- What advantage did radio have over movies?
- In what ways did radio become a giant industry?

HENRY FORD'S AUTOMOBILE

Of all the forces reshaping American life in the 1920s, the automobile probably had the most influence. The first gasoline-powered vehicles were built in the 1890s. By the time the United States entered the Great War, over 1 million cars a year were being produced. In the 1920s an average of more than 3 million a year were turned out.

Henry Ford was the key figure in this new industry. Ford had come to Detroit, Michigan, because he hated farm work. He had talent for all kinds of mechanical subjects. While working in Detroit for the Edison Illuminating Company in the 1890s, Ford designed and built an automobile in his home workshop. A little later he built a famous racing car, "999," which he drove to several speed records himself. In 1903 he founded the **Ford Motor Company.**

The first American automobiles were very expensive. They were toys for the rich. Henry Ford dreamed of producing cars cheaply so that ordinary people could own them. (The name of the well-known

Culver Pictures

Henry Ford and his Model T Ford strongly shaped the 1920s. Henry Ford saw 15 million Model T cars produced. This one has a license plate marked "Demonstration" but the date is obscured. What dream led Ford to produce the Model T?

723

Ford Motor Company

At the Ford assembly plant located in Highland Park, Michigan, the body of a Model T Ford was slid down a chute to be placed on the waiting chassis. This is an early photograph of the mass production that made Fords available to so many people. How was this mass production achieved?

German automobile, the *Volkswagen,* or "people's car," expresses his idea exactly.) In 1908 he achieved his goal with his **Model T** Ford. It sold for only $850. And by 1916 Ford had reduced the cost of the new Model T's to $360.

Ford's secret was **mass production** achieved through the use of the **moving assembly line.** His cars were put together, or assembled, while being moved past a line of workers. Each worker or team performed only one fairly simple task.

This method of production was highly efficient. Prices were also held down by Ford's policy of keeping his cars simple and making the same basic model year after year. The Model T was not changed in any important way until 1928, when the **Model A** replaced it. According to a joke of the day, you could have a Model T in any color you wanted as long as you chose black.

Other automobile manufacturers copied Ford's methods. But most made expensive cars. In prosperous times many customers were willing to pay for larger and more comfortable cars than the Model T. By the end of the 1920s Ford was no longer the largest manufacturer. The **General Motors Company** had taken the lead.

■ How did Henry Ford change the automobile industry?

NEW WEALTH FROM THE AUTOMOBILE

The 3 million or more cars produced each year were worth about $3.5 billion even before the car dealers added their expenses and profits. This was only part of the new wealth the automobile created. A huge **rubber tire industry** sprang up. Manufacturers of steel, glass, paint, and dozens of other products greatly increased their output.

The automobile revolutionized the **petroleum-refining industry.** Before the war the most important petroleum product was kerosene. By 1919 ten times as much gasoline as kerosene was being refined. The total amount of petroleum refined in the United States soared from about 50 million barrels to 1 billion barrels a day.

Then there were the effects of the automobile on **road building** and on the **tourist business.** So long as people traveled no faster than a horse could pull a coach or wagon, the bumps and ruts of dirt and gravel roads did not matter much. By the 1920s, however, ordinary cars could speed along at 50 or 60 miles an hour or more. Such speeds were impossible on uneven surfaces. Hundreds of thousands of miles of smooth paved roads had to be built. Great amounts of asphalt and concrete were manufactured to surface them. New road-building machinery was designed and constructed. Thousands of new jobs were created in this road-building industry.

Culver Pictures

Here are two symbols of the 20th century — the Model T hooked to a gasoline pump. This picture was taken in 1920. The man wearing a straw "boater" is an inspector for the Department of Combustibles. It was his job to examine recently installed gasoline pumps. What was the primary use of petroleum before it began to be refined for gasoline?

Better roads for cars meant more traveling, both for business and for pleasure. Gasoline stations appeared alongside each new highway. Roadside restaurants opened side by side with motor hotels—a new way of housing travelers, soon to be known as motels.

■ What were some of the industries that grew because of the automobile?

Motor car advertisements printed in the 1920s stressed the fashionable people who rode in the vehicles. The Pierce-Arrow and Studebaker today are collector's items. To what area did people flock with the advent of the automobile?

AN AUTOMOBILE CIVILIZATION

For thousands of years the power to move about freely and easily was a sign that a person had social status. That is why in ancient times and throughout the Middle Ages ownership of a horse meant that a person belonged to the upper class. Now, because of Henry Ford and the other pioneers of the auto industry, nearly everyone in the United States could afford a car. A *new* Model T could cost as little as $300 in the early 1920s. A secondhand Ford still capable of good service could be bought for $25 to $50.

Automobiles freed ordinary people. Cars let them travel far more widely and rapidly than medieval knights. They could live in **suburbs** surrounded by trees and green fields and drive daily to jobs in the cities. They could visit places hundreds of miles away on weekends or cover thousands of miles on a two-week summer vacation.

Little wonder that automobiles became status symbols for many people. Owners spent Sunday mornings washing and polishing their cars the way a trainer grooms a racehorse or a pedigreed dog before a show. Car owners decorated their autos with shiny hood ornaments and put flowers in small vases on the inside.

The personalities of many car owners seemed to be affected by their vehicles. Once behind the wheel, drivers were in command of half a ton or more of speeding metal. They often became "roadhogs" who turned into cursing bullies when another driver got in their way or tried to pass them on the road.

Automobiles had both good and bad effects on family life. Family picnics and sightseeing trips brought parents and children closer together. However, crowding five or six people into a small space on a hot summer afternoon hardly made for family harmony. Quarrels developed about where to go and how to get there. People complained about "back-seat drivers"—those passengers who made a habit of criticizing the driver.

The automobile also tended to separate family members. Once children were old enough to drive, they generally preferred to be off by themselves or with friends their own age. Soon "two-car" and "three-car" families came into being. In extreme cases the home became little more than a motel or garage. Family members rested there before zooming off again in their Fords and Chevrolets or, if they were wealthy, in their Packards and Pierce-Arrows.

The new automobile civilization had other unfortunate side effects. Between 1915 and 1930 the number of road accidents soared. By 1930 automobile crashes caused more than half the accidental deaths in the nation.

As the number of cars on the roads increased, traffic tie-ups became common. The exhaust fumes of millions of cars caused serious **air pollution** in some areas.

Culver Pictures

Because of the automobile, the oil resources of the nation were being used up at a rapidly increasing rate. Anyone who thought about the question realized that there was only so much petroleum in the ground. It had taken millions of years to be formed and could never be replaced. Still, the supply was so large that most people assumed that it would last practically forever. During the 1920s huge new oil fields were discovered in Texas and Oklahoma. Only a tiny percentage of the petroleum used in America then came from foreign sources. That percentage was actually declining in those years.

The nation was becoming more and more dependent upon gasoline and other petroleum products. Giant industries could not exist without oil in one form or another. Neither could the new life style that was developing in the United States. Yet in the 1920s few people worried about these matters. Gasoline was cheap. There was plenty of it. Let us enjoy life while we can, most people reasoned.

On a Sunday afternoon in the 1920s there are nearly as many motor cars as there are people. A photographer captured this early traffic jam in a suburb of St. Louis, Missouri. The large numbers of Model T's shows how successful Henry Ford was by this time. How did the automobile make the nation more dependent?

- What freedom did the automobile bring to ordinary people?
- How did the automobile have both good and bad effects on family life?
- What were some unfortunate side effects of the automobile?

HARDING AND COOLIDGE

The 1920s was a time when politics seemed to have little connection with how people lived and thought. While society was changing in dramatic and significant ways, most political leaders were conservative, slow moving, and lacking in imagination.

President Warren G. Harding looked like a statesman. He was friendly, good looking, firm jawed, and silver haired. He worked for conservative policies that favored big business. But he was not a strong or creative leader. His programs included high protective tariffs on manufactured goods, lower taxes for the wealthy, and reducing the national debt. Harding was careless about the appointments he made to important public offices. Some people he appointed were incompetent. Others were plainly corrupt.

Harding died of a heart attack in 1923. Soon thereafter a series of scandals were uncovered. Harding himself was not involved. It turned out that various members of his administration had stolen money intended for a veterans' hospital, mishandled government property, and accepted bribes.

The worst scandal involved Albert Fall, Harding's Secretary of the Interior. Fall leased government-owned land containing rich deposits of oil to private companies at very low rents. These included the **Elk Hills** reserve in California and the **Teapot Dome** reserve in Wyoming. In return the heads of the oil companies gave Fall bribes amounting to $400,000. When the facts were discovered by a government investigation, Fall was convicted and put in prison.

It was fortunate for the Republican party that Harding died before the scandals broke. His successor, Vice President Calvin Coolidge, had nothing to do with the corruption. Coolidge's person-

Howard Chandler Christy came to the White House in 1924 to paint the Presidential portrait of Calvin Coolidge. But the President was busy, so Christy instead painted Grace Goodhue Coolidge with her collie Rob Roy. She was a popular and gracious First Lady. Left and right are Presidents Harding and Coolidge. Harding's portrait is by Margaret Lindsay Williams, 1923, and Coolidge's likeness was made by Joseph Burgess in 1956. Calvin Coolidge was a man of few words. A guest at a White House dinner once told President Coolidge that she had bet her friends that she could coax at least three words from him. "You lose," he told her. How was Coolidge different from Harding?

ality was almost the exact opposite of Harding's. He was quiet and very reserved. He hated to spend money. Indeed, he was the only modern President who was able to save part of his salary while in office. He was thoroughly honest. His no-nonsense attitude made it difficult for the Democrats to take political advantage of the scandals.

In 1924 Coolidge easily received the Republican nomination for a second term. The Democratic nomination was decided only after a long and bitter struggle. The eastern wing of the party supported Governor Alfred E. Smith of New York. Most southern and western delegates favored William G. McAdoo, who had been President Wilson's Secretary of the Treasury.

Culver Pictures

Delegates attending the Democratic national convention in 1924 rise to show their support for Al Smith. Who eventually won the 1924 nomination of the Democratic party?

Under the rules of the convention a candidate needed a two-thirds majority to be nominated. Since neither Smith nor McAdoo could get two thirds, a **deadlock** developed. It lasted for days. Finally, on the 103rd ballot, the exhausted delegates nominated John W. Davis, a conservative lawyer from West Virginia.

The deadlock between Smith and McAdoo reflected the basic divisions within the Democratic party and within the nation itself. Smith was a Catholic. Many people were prejudiced against Catholics and would not vote for a Catholic for President. Some even feared that such a person would be a servant of the Pope rather than a servant of the American people.

Many rural people disliked Smith because he had been raised "on the sidewalks of New York." Yet the nation was becoming more and more urban. By the 1920s farmers no longer made up the majority of the population. Many resented this fact. In Smith's candidacy they saw a symbol of the shift from a rural to an urban nation.

In addition to Coolidge and Davis, Senator Robert La Follette of Wisconsin ran for President in 1924. La Follette had been a leading progressive before the Great War. He found both the major parties too conservative for his taste after the war. He therefore formed a new Progressive party. La Follette campaigned on a platform calling for government ownership of railroads, protection of the right of workers to bargain collectively, aid for farmers, and other reforms. "The great issue before the American people," La Follette believed, was "the control of government and industry by private monopoly."

Coolidge won the election easily. He received more than 15 million votes to Davis's 8.4 million and La Follette's 4.8 million. Clearly the national mood was politically conservative at a time when society was going through radical change.

- How did the political mood of the 1920s differ from the way people behaved?
- What scandals were uncovered after President Harding's death?
- What shift in population was evident in the 1920s?

BUSINESS GROWTH IN THE 1920s

The policies of the federal government in the 1920s had large effects on the economy. These policies greatly influenced the lives of nearly everyone. President Coolidge believed that "the business of America is business." He also said, "The man who builds a factory builds a temple." His policies were designed to help business interests and other large investors.

The friendly attitude of the government encouraged businesses to make new investments. Once the switch back to peacetime production had been completed, the American economy certainly prospered. Many industries that had been established before the Great War expanded rapidly.

Between 1915 and 1930 the number of telephone users in the United States doubled. **Dial phones** and improved switchboards speeded communication and cut costs. Electric light companies prospered. As more and more homes were hooked up for electricity, the **electric appliance industry** grew. Most families now had electric irons. Many had electric vacuum cleaners and washing machines and refrigerators as well. Electricity also became an important source of power for industry. By 1930 the United States was using more electricity than all the rest of the world *combined*.

Chain stores grew rapidly in the 1920s. The A&P grocery chain expanded from 400 outlets in 1912 to 15,000 in 1932. Woolworth "five and tens" were opened by the dozens in big cities and small towns. By the end of the decade Americans were buying more than 25

Culver Pictures

These long-distance operators are on duty at the American Telephone and Telegraph office in New York City. Their supervisor watches as they manually complete each call in 1926. How was communication by telephone soon made faster?

per cent of their food and clothing in chain stores. With more and more people living in cities, sales of canned fruits and vegetables rose rapidly.

Even more impressive was the growth of entirely new industries. Chemical plants began turning out many **synthetics**—artificial substances such as rayon for clothing and Bakelite for radio cases. Other new mass-produced products included cigarette lighters, wristwatches, improved cameras, and Pyrex glass for cooking.

- What advances were made in the telephone industry in the 1920s?
- What was the success of chain stores in the 1920s?
- What were some synthetic products made in the 1920s?

"SICK" INDUSTRIES

Despite the general economic expansion of the 1920s, there were several weak areas in the economy. **Sick industries** like coal and textiles did not prosper at all. Coal was meeting stiff competition from oil, natural gas, and electricity. Over 1,000 coal mines were shut down in the 1920s, and nearly 200,000 miners lost their jobs.

Manufacturers of cotton and woolen cloth did not prosper either. Partly because of competition from rayon, the new synthetic textile, these manufacturers were soon producing more cloth than the public was buying. Their profits therefore shrank, and the number of unemployed textile workers rose.

731

Two technologies meet in a farmer's field. Working side by side are this team of horses and a tractor pulling harvesting machinery. When grain is separated from chaff, it is blown into the wagon through the curving stack. How did farmers suffer after the end of the Great War?

American argriculture also suffered. Once the Great War was over, European farmers quickly recaptured their local markets. The price of wheat and other farm products fell sharply. Farmers' incomes declined, but their expenses for mortgage interest, taxes, tractors, harvesters, and supplies did not.

In 1921 a group of congressmen from the South and West organized an informal **Farm Bloc,** or common interest group. Their purpose was to unite congressmen from farm districts behind legislation favorable to agriculture. The Farm Bloc pushed through a bill providing for **subsidies** for farmers through government purchase of farm surpluses. President Coolidge was not sympathetic to proposals to subsidize farm prices. He vetoed the bill.

- Which were the "sick" industries in the 1920s?
- What was the purpose of the Farm Bloc organized in 1921?

THE ELECTION OF 1928

President Coolidge played down the problems of farmers and workers in the "sick" industries. He believed the future was bright. In his 1928 State of the Union message he said, "No Congress has met with a more pleasing prospect than that which appears at the present time."

Most people agreed with Coolidge. Americans were enjoying the greatest period of prosperity in their history. Most were earning more money and working shorter hours than ever before. They had cars, radios, and household gadgets. Life was easy. It seemed likely to become easier still. The Republican party naturally took the credit for the good times.

In the 1928 Presidential campaign, Secretary of Commerce Herbert Hoover received the Republican nomination. The Democratic candidate was Alfred E. Smith. Smith had a record of solid accomplishment as governor of New York. He could not be denied the nomination. But his Catholic religion and his "big city" background hurt him in rural areas.

Hoover won the election with 21 million votes to Smith's 15 million. The electoral vote was 444 to 87. Smith even lost his own state of New York as well as several Democratic states in the once Solid South. The main cause of Smith's defeat was the prosperity issue. A majority of the American people had come to believe that the Republican party was the symbol of economic progress and the guardian of good times.

■ Why did the Republicans win the election of 1928 so easily?

During his campaign for President in 1928, Al Smith was persuaded to pose with two miniature donkeys. The Republican candidate, Herbert Hoover, appears more dignified as he makes his final speech of the campaign on national radio. What was the electoral vote in the 1928 election?

Both, Brown Brothers

THE GREAT CRASH

Prosperity tended to make people ambitious and optimistic. A "get-rich-quick" attitude developed in the United States as the decade advanced. More and more people set out to make fortunes in the stock market. They followed the prices of stocks in the newspapers as closely as they followed Babe Ruth's batting average. By mid-1929 stocks had been climbing steadily in price for several months. The profits of most corporations were on the rise. By 1929 the companies

Variety is a newspaper for people in the entertainment industry. In one of its most famous headlines the Crash of 1929 was announced by the banner at the right Another widely quoted headline told how rural people were rejecting movies about agricultural America. It said, "Sticks Nix Hick Pix." What name was given to October 29, 1929?

listed on the New York Stock Exchange were paying out three times as much money in dividends as they had in 1920.

This boom could not go on forever. Quite suddenly, on October 24, 1929, everyone wanted to sell stocks instead of buying them. Investors jammed telephone lines and crowded into brokers' offices, desperate to turn their stocks into cash. With many sellers and few buyers, the prices of stocks plunged. General Electric Company shares dropped from $315 to $283 in that one day. U.S. Steel skidded from $205 to $193.

Then, on October 29, a day known as **Black Tuesday,** came an even steeper decline. The **Great Stock Market Crash** reached panic proportions. Day after day the drop continued. By the middle of November General Electric stock was down to $168, U.S. Steel to $150.

The prosperity of the 1920s was over. The country was about to enter the **Great Depression.**

- What attitude did the prosperity of the 1920s tend to develop?
- What caused the price of stocks to plunge after October 24, 1929?

CHAPTER 24 REVIEW

Identification

Tell briefly why each of the following persons, terms, or events is important.

1. Henry Cabot Lodge
2. Warren G. Harding
3. Calvin Coolidge
4. W. C. Handy
5. Bessie Smith
6. Harold "Red" Grange
7. Knute Rockne
8. Harlem Globetrotters
9. Babe Ruth
10. Charles A. Lindbergh
11. Charlie Chaplin
12. Henry Ford
13. Nineteenth Amendment
14. Washington Disarmament Conference
15. Big Red Scare
16. Mass production
17. Teapot Dome
18. Jazz Age
19. "Sick" industries
20. Black Tuesday

Understanding American History

1. Explain why the Versailles Treaty was rejected by the U.S. Senate.
2. What were the results of the Washington Disarmament Conference? How did it show both isolationism and internationalism?
3. What were some happenings of the 1920s that were part of the postwar reaction?
4. What was meant by the term "the Jazz Age?" Why was jazz music a symbol for the times?
5. What were some reasons the 1920s was the Golden Age of Sports?
6. How did movies and radio become big businesses of the 1920s?
7. What methods did Henry Ford use to produce automobiles that ordinary people could afford?
8. In what ways did the automobile stimulate the American economy?
9. How did the automobile affect the life of the average American in the 1920s?
10. Which were the "sick" industries of the 1920s? Why were they called "sick"?

Activities

1. Present a classroom discussion on the different views held in the 1920s by isolationists and by internationalists. Follow with another group who will discuss the same topic in the 1980s. Be sure to support each general statement with specific examples so that all may understand your point of view.
2. Use your historical imagination to prepare and present on tape a radio broadcast from the 1920s. In your program include news of the day, music, interviews with famous persons, comedy routines, and commercials. Research the 1920s carefully so that your broadcast seems true to the times.
3. Use your historical imagination to present a series of interviews between prominent people of the 1920s and the press. Include figures from sports, movies, and radio such as the following:

Knute Rockne   Charlie Chaplin
Harold "Red" Grange   Mary Pickford
Jack Dempsey   Douglas Fairbanks
Helen Wills   Rudolph Valentino
Gertrude Ederle   Al Jolson

4. With your classmates present a series of reports on the great hero of the 1920s, Charles A. Lindbergh. Research topics to include a) Lindbergh's barnstorming days, b) the planning and building of the *Spirit of St. Louis,* c) the day before the transatlantic flight, d) the May 1927 flight itself, e) the reception in Paris, and f) Lindbergh's welcome home to the United States. Then explain how Lindbergh's flight was a triumph for both man and machine.
5. Prepare a classroom display to show how the automobile changed American life.

CHAPTER 24 TEST

Completion (20 points)

Number your paper 1–10 and next to each number write the words from the list below that best complete each sentence.

Warren G. Harding   Big Red Scare
James M. Cox   Irreconcilables
National Origins Act   postwar reaction
Versailles Treaty   League of Nations
Nineteenth Amendment   strong reservationists

An important reason why the __1__ was not ratified by the Senate in 1919–20 was fear that U.S. armed forces could be sent into action by the __2__. The treaty was most strongly opposed by a group of senators known as the __3__. Other Republicans who sought important changes in the treaty were called __4__ and led by Henry Cabot Lodge.

In the election of 1920 the __5__ gave women the vote for the first time. Senator __6__ defeated Governor __7__ for President.

In the early 1920s an anxious time of __8__ led to fear of a communist uprising, known as the __9__. Suspicion of immigrants led to the passage of the __10__, which restricted immigration from southern and eastern Europe.

Matching (30 points)

Number your paper 11–25 and match the name in the second column with his or her description in the first column.

11. Progressive candidate for President in 1924
12. Formed the Harlem Globetrotters in Chicago
13. Swam across the English Channel
14. Notre Dame football coach of the 1920s
15. President when the stock market crashed
16. Senate fighter against the League of Nations
17. Baseball hero, the "Sultan of Swat"
18. Movie star who influenced women's fashion
19. First to fly solo over the Atlantic Ocean
20. "Father of the blues" from Alabama
21. Beloved "little tramp" of the movies
22. Senator from Ohio who became President
23. Sang the blues about her sorrowful experiences
24. Pioneer of the Model T and moving assembly line
25. Internationally famous trumpeter and singer

    a. Henry Cabot Lodge
    b. Mary Pickford
    c. Warren G. Harding
    d. Louis Armstrong
    e. Charles A. Lindbergh
    f. Gertrude Ederle
    g. W. C. Handy
    h. Robert M. La Follette
    i. Henry Ford
    j. Bessie Smith
    k. Herbert Hoover
    l. Babe Ruth
    m. Charlie Chaplin
    n. Knute Rockne
    o. Abe Saperstein

Matching (20 points)

Number your paper 26–30 and match the term in the second column with its description in the first column.

26. Congressional supporters of agriculture
27. Weak areas in American economy in the 1920s
28. Artificial substances manufactured in the 1920s
29. Food and clothing outlets across the U.S.
30. Henry Ford's method of mass production

    a. chain stores
    b. "sick" industries
    c. moving assembly line
    d. synthetics
    e. Farm Bloc

Essay (30 points)

Explain how American life in the 1920s was affected by the automobile *or* by spectator sports, movies, and radio.

CHAPTER 25
The Great Depression and the New Deal

The stock market crash in 1929 was the first major event of what we call the **Great Depression.** There had been many earlier depressions in the United States, but the Great Depression lasted longer and was more severe than any before in the nation's history.

THE "NORMAL" BUSINESS CYCLE

People had come to accept depressions as a regular part of the **business cycle.** This is how business cycles worked:

In good times economic activity tended to expand. More goods were produced. Prices rose. More workers were hired. Eventually output increased faster than goods could be sold. Surpluses then piled

Culver Pictures

This picture is a testimonial to the American spirit. In front of a shack of tar paper in a 'Hooverville,' one man poses with his pet cat and dog. Overhead flies the tattered flag of a nation deep in its Great Depression. This picture was taken c. 1932. In what year did the depression begin?

up in company warehouses and in retail stores. Manufacturers had to slow down their production. They let go some of their workers. These unemployed people had less money to buy goods. More manufacturers then had to reduce output and fire more workers. Prices fell. Producers who were losing money began to go out of business. The general economy was **depressed.**

People believed that depressions were self-correcting. When output became very low, the surpluses were gradually used up. Then the efficient producers who had not gone out of business increased output. They rehired workers. These workers, with wages in their pockets, increased their own purchases. Demand increased. Prices rose. The economy entered the **recovery** stage. Recovery eventually led to **prosperity**—a time of high prices, full production, and almost no unemployment.

▨ How were depressions supposed to be self-correcting?

THE GREAT DEPRESSION

A complete business cycle might last anywhere from two or three to five or six years. What made the Great Depression different was that it lasted for more than ten years. The economy declined steeply from late 1929 until the winter of 1932-33. Then it appeared to be stuck. Recovery was slow and irregular. The output of goods remained far below what it had been in 1929. Only in 1940, after the outbreak of the Second World War, did a strong recovery begin.

Throughout this long period at least 10 per cent of the work force was unemployed. At the low point, early in 1933, about 25 per cent of all Americans were without jobs. Americans spent $10.9 billion in food stores in 1929. Although the population increased in every year, Americans did not spend that much on food again until 1941. This was true also of money spent on furniture, clothing, automobiles, jewelry, recreation, medical care, and nearly all other items.

These cold figures tell us little about the human suffering and discouragement that the Great Depression caused. Thousands of shopkeepers who had worked for years to develop their businesses lost everything. Other thousands of people lost their savings in bank failures. Millions of workers who had risen through the ranks to well-paid jobs found themselves unemployed. Those who had developed skills found that their skills were useless. Students graduating from schools and colleges could find no one willing to hire them.

The weakest and poorest suffered most. Many married women lost their jobs because employers thought they did not need to work. Unemployment was far higher among blacks and other minority groups than among whites. In the southwestern states thousands of

United Press International

Christmas Day, 1931, in New York City. A breadline winds down this street for at least three blocks. In line for a charitable meal are these ranks of the unemployed, victims of the Great Depression. Who were hurt hardest by the depression?

Culver Pictures

Mexican-born farm laborers who were unable to find work were rounded up and shipped back to Mexico. Officials excused this cruel policy by arguing that there was not enough relief money to care for them. Many Mexican-born workers who had *not* lost their jobs were also shipped back. In this case the excuse was that they were holding down jobs that United States citizens needed.

The term "depression" describes the mood of the people as well as the state of the economy. Until the middle of the 1930s there was no system of unemployment insurance and no national welfare assistance program to help the unemployed and their families. People in desperate need had no sure place they could turn to.

Great efforts were made to assist the jobless. State and city governments and private charities raised money to feed the poor and provide them with a little cash for their other needs. Special "drives" were conducted to collect clothing for the unemployed and their families. There were **soup kitchens** and **breadlines** where hungry people could get a free meal and **lodging houses** where the homeless could spend the night.

Many victims of the depression received help from relatives and friends. But others stood on street corners trying to sell apples or pencils. Some simply held out their hands, begging for a few pennies. Some became tramps, wandering aimlessly around the country, stealing rides on railroad freight cars. Some became thieves. And some people actually starved to death.

A young worker in his prime can do no better than sell apples from his little cart in 1932. Some Americans had to support themselves by doing odd jobs or selling pencils in the street during the hard times. What efforts were made to help jobless persons?

▨ How did the Great Depression differ from other depressions in the nation's history?

Dorothea Lange's photographs are powerful images which document the Great Depression. "Woman of the High Plains, Texas Panhandle" is a 1938 study. Like many Lange subjects, this woman is dignified even in desolated fields. How were farmers hurt by the depression?

HOOVER FIGHTS THE DEPRESSION

Herbert Hoover's work during the Great World War seemed good training for dealing with the depression. He had helped the Belgians after the Germans invaded their country. He had run the American food program after 1917. As Secretary of Commerce during the 1920s he had won the confidence of most business leaders.

Hoover also understood economics better than most politicians. When he realized that the nation had entered a serious depression, he tried to stimulate recovery quickly. He urged Congress to lower taxes so that people would have more money to spend on goods and services. He called for more government spending on **public works,** such as road construction or building dams. These measures would increase the demand for goods and put jobless people back to work, he said.

Farmers in particular were hard hit by the depression. The price of most farm products fell sharply. Hoover urged farmers to form cooperatives and to raise smaller crops until prices rose. He also favored holding down interest rates so businesses could borrow money more easily.

Above all, the President recognized that the American people had lost confidence in the economic system. This was part of their psychological depression. He tried to encourage them to have faith in the future. "Prosperity," he said, "is just around the corner."

But Hoover's strength as an organizer in wartime proved to be a weakness during the depression. In both situations he insisted that voluntary cooperation would solve the nation's problems. In wartime his appeals to patriotism and self-sacrifice were effective. During the war people knew who the enemy was and what to do to protect themselves. In the depression they could not identify any particular enemy. Therefore they did not have much confidence that they could protect themselves.

Hoover displayed still another weakness. He believed that the federal government should not increase its authority just because times were hard. If the United States took over powers that normally belonged to state and local governments, it would become a "superstate." Even when city after city proved unable to raise enough money to take care of the unemployed, Hoover opposed federal grants for relief purposes. Such aid would destroy the "real liberty" of the people, he said.

He supported federal assistance to banks and big industries. These loans were sound investments, he said. The money would be used to produce goods and earn profits. Then the loans could be repaid. Lending money to a farmer to buy pig feed or more seed or a tractor was also proper, according to Hoover's theory. But he opposed giving federal aid to farmers so that they could feed their children. That

740

would be giving them something for nothing. Under the American system charity was the business of state and local governments and private organizations like the Red Cross and the Salvation Army.

As the Great Depression dragged on, Hoover became more and more unpopular. People began to think that he was hardhearted. He seemed not to care about the sufferings of the poor. His critics even claimed that he was responsible for the depression.

Both charges were untrue. Hoover cared deeply about the suffering the depression was causing. He sincerely believed that his policies were the proper ones. These policies had certainly not caused the depression. After all, every industrial nation in the world then had high unemployment. The Great Depression affected all of Europe and most of the rest of the world.

The economies of nations that depended on agriculture were badly depressed. There was a depression in wheat-growing Australia and in beef-raising Argentina. The price of Brazilian coffee fell so low that farmers there burned the coffee beans in cookstoves. Coffee made a cheaper fuel than coal or kerosene.

"Home Relief Station" was painted to make the point that waiting and humiliation are often part of private charity. These victims of the Great Depression await their turns before the woman investigating claims for assistance. Louis Ribak painted the scene during the depression. Which private charities gave people aid?

741

Still, even if he was not responsible for the long depression, Hoover's rigid policies were not working. He was in charge of the government. Therefore people tended to blame him.

- How did President Hoover try to stimulate the economy?
- What weaknesses did Hoover show in dealing with the Great Depression?
- How widespread was the Great Depression?

THE BONUS ARMY

Public opinion turned further against Hoover after the **Bonus March** of the summer of 1932. Some years earlier Congress had passed a law giving veterans of the Great World War an **adjusted compensation bonus.** Its purpose was to make up for the low pay that soldiers had received during the war while workers at home were earning high wages. The bonus money, however, was not to be paid until 1945.

During the depression veterans began to demand that the bonus be paid at once. In July 1932 about 20,000 former soldiers marched on Washington to demonstrate before the Capitol. When Congress refused to change the law, some of the marchers settled down on vacant land on the edge of Washington. They put up a camp of tents and flimsy tar-paper shacks. They announced that they would not leave until the bonus was paid.

Culver Pictures

A multitude of people gather around members of the Bonus Army in this 1932 photograph. In the background are tar-paper shacks and placards to keep up the spirits of these war veterans. Where was this camp?

Hoover had opposed the bonus to begin with. Such giveaways threatened to destroy the "self-reliance" of the people, he said. He believed, wrongly as it turned out, that the Bonus Marchers were being led by dangerous radicals. When trouble broke out, Hoover ordered army units to assist police in driving out the veterans.

Troops commanded by General Douglas MacArthur then went into action. Infantrymen backed by cavalry units and five tanks swiftly cleared the camp. No shots were fired and no one was killed. However, news film of steel-helmeted, rifle-bearing soldiers firing tear gas grenades at ragged, unarmed war veterans shocked millions of Americans. Hoover's popularity touched rock bottom.

- Why did the Bonus Marchers come to Washington?
- How did Hoover respond to the Bonus Marchers?

FRANKLIN D. ROOSEVELT

It is safe to say that in 1932 any Democratic Presidential candidate could have defeated the Republican Hoover. Somewhere between 13 and 16 million workers were unemployed. The total income of all Americans had fallen from $87 billion in 1929 to $42 billion in 1932. All the shares of the stocks listed on the New York Stock Exchange were worth only a quarter of what they had been worth before the Great Crash.

The particular Democrat who profited from this situation was Franklin D. Roosevelt, the governor of New York. Roosevelt came from a wealthy family. He had graduated from Harvard College, studied law, and gone into politics. As we have seen, he had run for Vice President in 1920 on the ticket with James M. Cox, who was defeated by Warren G. Harding.

The next year Roosevelt spent his usual vacation at his summer home in Campobello, Canada. One day in August 1921 he helped put out a brush fire while on an outing with his children. He returned home tired and chilled to the bone in his wet swimming suit. That night he burned with fever. Within a few days his legs were almost completely paralyzed. He had a severe case of polio. He recovered from the disease, but for the rest of his life he could walk only with the aid of metal braces and two canes. More often he was carried or used a wheelchair.

Roosevelt's usual high spirits sagged, but only briefly. He went on with his political career. In 1928, when Governor Alfred E. Smith of New York ran for President against Hoover, Roosevelt was chosen to run for governor. Hoover defeated Smith in New York, but Roosevelt was elected governor. Two years later he was re-elected by a huge majority. This evidence of popular support won him the 1932 Democratic Presidential nomination.

Roosevelt's Little White House and Museum, Warm Springs

This portrait of Franklin Roosevelt is by Elizabeth Shoumatoff. It was left unfinished when the President died in 1945 while posing for the artist in Warm Springs, Georgia. What illness afflicted Roosevelt? How did he overcome its effects?

Roosevelt was almost the exact opposite of Hoover. Hoover was restrained, stiff, and by 1932 very glum. Roosevelt had a cheerful, relaxed, almost carefree personality. Indeed, in 1932 many observers thought he had more style than substance. He was no more radical than Hoover, but he was a much less rigid person. Hoover worked out careful theories and tried to apply them to the practical problems of government. Roosevelt mistrusted theories. Yet he was willing to apply any theory to any particular problem if there seemed a good chance it would work.

Roosevelt turned out to be a most popular political campaigner. He made excellent speeches. He had tremendous energy. Moreover, he was an optimist. At a time when most people were deeply depressed, his cheer encouraged and uplifted millions. The crowds that gathered when he campaigned seemed to inspire him as well. In November he defeated Hoover easily. His electoral majority was 472 to 59. The popular vote was 22.8 million to 15.8 million. The voters also gave the Democrats large majorities in both houses of Congress.

> Why would any Democratic candidate have been likely to defeat President Hoover in 1932?
> How did Franklin D. Roosevelt contrast with Herbert Hoover?

"NOTHING TO FEAR BUT FEAR ITSELF"

Roosevelt was elected in November, but he could not by law take his oath as President until March 4. Meanwhile, the economy seemed to drift downward aimlessly, like a falling leaf in a winter forest. Suddenly, in February 1933, people all over the country began to rush fearfully to withdraw their savings from the banks. This **banking panic** forced even most of the soundest banks to close their doors.

The banking crisis turned out to be a great advantage for Roosevelt and indirectly for the entire country. It forced people to put politics aside and treat the depression as a great national emergency.

Inauguration Day in Washington was raw and damp. In this dark hour Roosevelt's speech came like a ray of summer sunshine. "This great nation," he said, "will revive and will prosper. So first of all let me assert . . . that the only thing we have to fear is fear itself."

Roosevelt spoke only generally about measures for fighting the depression. But he made his approach crystal clear. He was going to do something. "Action, and action now," was his theme. His first priority would be to put people back to work, he said.

> How did the banking crisis turn out to have an advantage for the entire country?
> What did Roosevelt promise in his inaugural address?

Brown Brothers

THE HUNDRED DAYS

In his inaugural address the President called upon Congress to meet in a special session on March 9 to deal with the emergency. From March 9 to June 16, when this special session ended, was 100 days. No one planned to have the session last exactly 100 days. The fact that it did dramatized how much that Congress accomplished.

In his campaign for President, Roosevelt had called for a **New Deal.** The flood of new laws passed during the **Hundred Days** had the effect of convincing people that old ways were indeed being tossed out, like a worn deck of cards. The country seemed to be making a fresh start.

Even before Congress met, Roosevelt declared a **Bank Holiday,** closing all the banks so that a general plan to protect the savings of the public could be developed. Congress then passed new banking laws, the most important being a measure which created the **Federal Deposit Insurance Corporation** (FDIC). The FDIC insured every-

Anxious depositors fill the lobby of this Cleveland, Ohio, bank in 1933. In the uncertain times they line up to withdraw their savings. As a result banks closed all across the country. What was the Bank Holiday?

Frances E. Perkins, standing, was the first woman Cabinet member. As Secretary of Labor she visited this textile plant in Georgia in 1933. At this time what benefits were given to workers?

one's savings up to $5,000. Runs on banks stopped. Depositors knew that even if their bank failed, they would get their money back. Nothing did more than this measure to restore public confidence.

New banking laws could not create jobs or cause farm prices to rise or stimulate business activity directly. So Congress quickly passed laws to accomplish these objectives. The most important and controversial measure was the **National Industrial Recovery Act** (NIRA).

The NIRA was supposed to stimulate private business by permitting manufacturers to cooperate with one another without fear of violating the antitrust laws. Firms in every industry were to draw up rules, called **codes of fair competition.** The firms were allowed to set limits on how much each could produce in order to avoid flooding markets with goods that could not be sold. They could also fix prices to avoid cutthroat competition.

In addition the codes provided certain benefits for workers. One was the right to freely join unions. Through these unions workers could **bargain collectively** with their employers. **Minimum wage** rates and maximum hours of work were also guaranteed under the codes. Each industrial code had to be approved, supervised, and enforced by the federal government through the **National Recovery Administration** (NRA).

NRA officials made great efforts to persuade workers and employers to accept the new system. "We Do Our Part" was the slogan of the NRA. Its symbol was a picture of a **Blue Eagle.** Soon Blue Eagle stickers were being displayed in the windows of giant factories and small shops all over the country. This symbol was also printed on the labels of products of all kinds.

The NRA was expected to get the sluggish industrial economy moving again. Congress next dealt with the farm problem by passing the **Agricultural Adjustment Act** (AAA). During the depression farm prices had fallen even further than the prices of manufactured goods. The basic idea of the AAA was to push prices up by cutting down on the amount of crops produced.

The Blue Eagle of the NRA appeared everywhere in the 1930s. There are three seals on this cafeteria window in New York. What was the function of the NRA?

Brown Brothers

Under this law the government rented some of the land that was normally planted in so-called basic crops, such as wheat, cotton, tobacco, and corn. No crops were planted on the land the government rented. Farmers benefited in two ways. They got the rent money from the government, and they got higher prices for what they grew on the rest of their land because the total amount grown was smaller.

The AAA raised the money to rent the land taken out of production by **processing taxes.** These were taxes paid by each business that processed, or prepared, the basic crops for general use—the miller who ground wheat into flour, the cotton manufacturer, the cigarette manufacturer, and so on.

The Tennessee Valley Authority had control of this dam located in north Alabama. Wilson Dam opened in 1925 during a time of prosperity. In the Great Depression it controlled floods and helped bring electricity to rural areas. Senator George W. Norris, *below,* was the "father" of the TVA. What other projects were carried out by this agency?

Congress also created the **Tennessee Valley Authority** (TVA) during the Hundred Days. This New Deal agency had no direct relation to the fight against the depression. Its "father" was Senator George W. Norris of Nebraska. During the 1920s Norris had fought efforts to get the government to sell to private interests the dam it had built at Muscle Shoals on the Tennessee River. He wanted the electricity produced at Muscle Shoals to be used as part of a broad plan to develop the resources of the entire Tennessee Valley.

Although Norris was a Republican, Roosevelt accepted his proposal. Under the TVA, Muscle Shoals was an efficient producer of electricity. The Authority had accurate information about how much electricity should cost consumers. The project therefore served as a kind of "yardstick" for measuring the fairness of prices charged by private electric power companies.

The TVA also manufactured fertilizers, built more dams for flood control, and developed a network of parks and lakes for recreation. It planted new forests and developed other conservation projects.

Another achievement of the Hundred Days was the passage of the **Federal Securities Act,** which regulated the way companies could issue and sell stock. Still another was the creation of the **Home Owners' Loan Corporation,** which helped people who were unable to meet mortgage payments hold on to their homes. These measures brought many benefits. But the greatest benefits of the New Deal came from what was done about the unemployed and the poor.

Roosevelt rejected Hoover's ideas about what the federal government could and could not do about unemployment and poverty. Soon after Roosevelt took office, the New Deal **Federal Emergency Relief Administration** was created. This agency was headed by Harry Hopkins, a New York social worker. It distributed $500 million in federal grants among state organizations that cared for the poor. The following fall and winter another New Deal agency, the **Civil Works Authority,** also headed by Hopkins, found jobs for more than 4 million people out of work.

During the Hundred Days, Congress also created the **Civilian Conservation Corps** (CCC). This agency put unemployed young men from poor families to work on various conservation projects. CCC workers lived in camps run by the army. They cleared brush, planted trees, built small dams, and performed dozens of other useful tasks. The CCC provides a good example of how swiftly New Deal measures were put into effect. The law that created the program passed Congress on March 31, 1933. By July there were 300,000 corpsmen at work in 1,300 camps all over the country.

Harry Hopkins, *above,* was a close friend of President Roosevelt's. He was Secretary of Commerce until ill health forced him to resign. Below are Civilian Conservation Corpsmen clearing brush from scrubland in the western United States. What kinds of projects did the CCC carry out?

■ What was the overall effect of the flood of laws passed during the Hundred Days?
■ How did President Roosevelt deal with the bank crisis?
■ How did the New Deal stimulate private business?
■ How did the New Deal push up farm prices?
■ How did the New Deal help the poor and the unemployed?

The Dust Bowl

This photograph of a migrant mother in Nipomo, California, is probably the most famous by Dorothea Lange. It was taken in 1936.

Nature had seemed to smile upon the young nation in the 1830s. In the 1930s nature seemed particularly cruel. As times got harder, weather and even the land seemed to turn against the poor. Perhaps the hardest hit were the farmers of the high plains—the states from Texas and Oklahoma to South and North Dakota. This region rarely gets much rain. In the early 1930s almost none fell.

By 1934 the drought had become so bad that winds picked up powder-dry topsoil and blew it across the plains in dense, black clouds. The region came to be known as the **Dust Bowl**. It was impossible to grow anything.

Broke and discouraged, many Oklahoma farm families loaded into their secondhand Model T Fords and headed west toward California. There they became **migrant workers**, picking fruit, vegetables, cotton, and other crops. They followed the harvest in their overheated cars and spent their nights in roadside camps. Old people died alongside the unfamiliar roads. Babies grew up hungry, their eyes big with suspicion.

One of the migrant workers was a young folksinger named Woodrow Wilson Guthrie, who went to California from Oklahoma in 1937. Californians "needed more and more people to pick their fruits," Woody Guthrie said. "But they looked down for some reason on the people that came in there from other states to do that kind of work." The times were dangerous. "In most towns . . . it is a jailhouse offense to be unemployed," he wrote.

One of Woody Guthrie's songs put the plight of the migrant workers this way:

California is a garden of Eden,
A paradise to live in or see.
But, believe it or not, you won't find it so hot,
If you ain't got the do-re-mi[1]

[1]From "Do Re Mi," words and music by Woody Guthrie. TRO © copyright 1961 and 1963 Ludlow Music Inc., New York, N.Y. Used by permission.

WHY THE NEW DEAL WAS POPULAR

The New Deal was very popular. Democrats increased their majorities in Congress in the 1934 elections. When Franklin D. Roosevelt ran for a second term in 1936, against Alfred Landon of Kansas, he won every state in the Union except Maine and Vermont. He did so despite the fact that New Deal legislation had not ended the depression. Unemployment remained extremely high. Industrial production picked up, but only very slowly.

Dallas Museum

The personality of FDR, as the newspapers came to call him, had a great deal to do with the success of the New Deal. He was an optimist. His hope for better conditions was always cheerful and encouraging, but never silly or foolish. He had a way of reaching people that was truly remarkable. He spoke frequently on the radio. These **fireside chats** were not speeches in the usual sense. The President seemed to come right into the room with his listeners. He explained what problems lay before the nation, how he proposed to deal with them, and what people could do to help him.

Roosevelt made great use of experts. His close advisers, mostly college professors, were known as the **Brain Trust.** Yet ordinary citizens never got the idea that Roosevelt was listening to theories that were not practical and down to earth.

The President never put all the nation's eggs in one basket. This made sense to most people. The economic mess was so complicated

Farms like this one were abandoned to the dust and vultures in the 1930s. A slat-sided cow searches for water in the shadow of the silent windmill. Alexander Hogue painted this scene titled "Drought Stricken Area." How did the drought make the depression worse for farmers?

751

President Roosevelt speaks from the Oval Office. Here he describes his plan to spend billions of dollars to "prime the pump" for economic recovery. He said in part: "We are a rich nation; we can afford to pay for security and prosperity without having to sacrifice our liberties into the bargain." What were these radio addresses called?

that no single plan or project was likely to untangle it. Roosevelt's way was to experiment with many things at once. This created the impression that the best minds in the country were hard at work fighting the depression. Of course, they were not winning an immediate and complete victory. But what seemed important was that *something* was being done.

The New Deal was also popular because it made large groups of people feel that the government was genuinely trying to improve their lives. This had little to do with the depression itself. For example, workers in industries like steel and automobiles were not organized in 1933. It was not the policy of the federal government to promote unions, but the spirit of the New Deal encouraged many workers to join unions. Roosevelt certainly wanted workers to be treated more fairly and with greater respect by their employers than had been common in the past.

President Roosevelt's greatest sympathy was for farmers. New Deal farm legislation was aimed at increasing their shrunken incomes and improving the quality of rural life. The **Rural Electrification Administration,** which brought electricity to remote farm districts, is a good illustration of how the lives of farmers could be made more comfortable.

Most important, the New Deal relieved much of the human suffering caused by the depression. The Civil Works Administration, and later the **Works Progress Administration** (WPA), found useful work for millions of idle men and women. Most of the jobs were of the pick-and-shovel type but not all of them. Harry Hopkins insisted that the full skills of the unemployed be used whenever possible.

In the city of Boston, for example, New Deal work projects included building a subway, expanding the East Boston Airport, and improving a municipal golf course. Other Boston relief workers taught in nursery schools, catalogued books in the Boston Public Library, and read to blind people. College students employed by the **National Youth Administration** graded papers and did office chores in their schools. Singers performed in hospitals. Musicians gave concerts. Troupes of actors put on plays, including a revival of *Uncle Tom's Cabin.* Artists designed posters and painted murals on the walls of schools and libraries.

- How did Roosevelt's personality help to make the New Deal popular?
- How did Roosevelt make use of experts? How did he balance the many theories he listened to?
- How did New Deal work projects go beyond pick-and-shovel jobs?

BUILDING SKILLS IN SOCIAL STUDIES

Art in the Service of Peace

All kinds of work projects were carried out in the 1930s with the federal government as the sponsor. These ranged from pick-and-shovel work such as building sidewalks and clearing brush to painting murals in public buildings. Artists were often given commissions by the Works Progress Administration. Close to 10,000 drawings, paintings, and sculptures were produced as part of the Federal Art Project. Much of the work decorated buildings such as post offices and libraries. Three such murals are reproduced on this page.

U.S. Department of the Interior, Uniphoto

Archives of American Art, Smithsonian Institution, WPA photograph

At the top is "Construction of a Dam" by William Gropper. The heroic figures and the strong curves of the steel reinforcing rods are typical of the period. In the center is Lucienne Bloch's "Childhood." This mural panel is from "Cycle of a Woman's Life," and was painted for a wall in tne New York House of Detention for Women. On the right is "City Building" from a series titled "City Life" by Thomas Hart Benton, a famous artist of the period. Can you identify similar works of art in this chapter?

New School for Social Research

BUILDING SKILLS IN SOCIAL STUDIES

Comparison by Bar Graph

Two sets of statistics may be compared on one graph. Usually the units compared must be similar. Dollars are compared to dollars, people to people. However, it is possible to compare different units on a bar graph by using two *vertical axes*.

The bar graph below compares unemployment and federal spending for the years 1933–39. The vertical axis on the left shows people by millions. The vertical axis on the right shows federal spending by billions. Only a single horizontal axis is needed to show years.

Study the bar graph carefully before answering the questions in the next column.

1. Which axis and color show unemployment? Which show federal spending?
2. Which years show highest unemployment? About how many people were out of work?
3. Which year shows greatest federal spending? About how many billions were spent?
4. What was the trend of unemployment from 1933 to 1939?
5. What was the trend of federal spending from 1933 to 1939?
6. Compare unemployment and federal spending, 1933 with 1934 and 1937 with 1938.
7. Did unemployment go up or down as federal spending was increased?

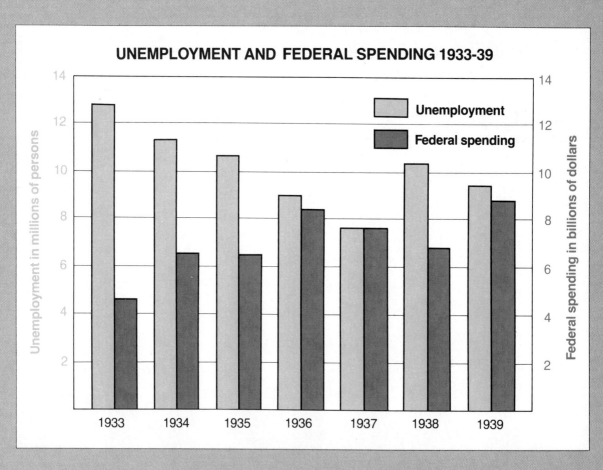

UNEMPLOYMENT AND FEDERAL SPENDING 1933-39

CRITICISM OF THE NEW DEAL

The laws passed during the Hundred Days greatly increased the power of the federal government and particularly of the President. Many day-to-day decisions had to made under these laws. The President and his appointees seemed the logical persons to make them. New Deal laws are full of such phrases as "The President is authorized . . ." and "The Secretary of Agriculture shall have the power to . . ." and "The Board shall have power, in the name of the United States of America, to . . ."

Some people found this trend alarming. Business leaders in particular objected to the new restrictions placed on how they conducted their affairs. The New Deal would destroy the free enterprise system, they charged. They therefore brought suits against the government in the courts, claiming that the new laws were unconstitutional.

Library of Congress

THIS IS ONE RABBIT THAT NEVER FAILED ME!

SPENDING

OLD RELIABLE!

"Old Reliable" is the name given to this cartoon by Clifford Berryman. It appeared in 1938. How is it critical of the New Deal philosophy?

Three outspoken critics of the New Deal are shown above. Huey Long of Louisiana favored what he called "Share-Our-Wealth." He is pictured at a rally of Arkansas Democrats in 1932. In the center is Dr. Francis E. Townshend talking in Newark, New Jersey, in 1936. He advocated Old-Age Revolving Pensions. At right is Father Charles Couglin addressing supporters in Ohio in 1936. He was highly critical of the President. In what ways did the New Deal fail in the eyes of its critics?

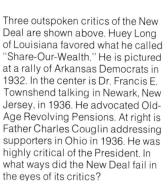

In 1935 and 1936 the Supreme Court ruled that the National Industrial Recovery Act and the Agricultural Adjustment Act were indeed unconstitutional. The Court also declared unconstitutional some important state laws regulating economic affairs, such as a New York minimum-wage law. In the NIRA case, *Schechter v. U.S.* (1935), the Court decided unanimously that Congress had delegated too much of its law-making power to the boards that watched over industrial codes.

Conservatives charged that the New Deal was trying to do too much. Other critics argued that the government was not doing enough. As time passed, the excitement of the Hundred Days disappeared. Perhaps prosperity was "just around the corner," but the corner never seemed to be reached.

Many people who had originally supported Roosevelt now turned against him. One was Senator Huey Long of Louisiana, who ruled like a king in his home state. The "Kingfish," as he was called, had great pity for the little person. He claimed that the President had become a tool of Wall Street investors and other special interests. Long wanted to tax away all incomes of more than $1 million a year. With that money, he said, everyone would be guaranteed a large enough income to own a house, a car, and everything else needed to live decently. Long's **Share-Our-Wealth** organization had over 4.6 million members in 1935.

Francis Townshend, a California doctor, called for granting **Old-Age Revolving Pensions** to every American over 60. He attracted a very large following. A Catholic priest, Father Charles E. Coughlin, spoke to millions in his weekly radio broadcasts. He criticized various New Deal programs. Eventually he made bitter personal attacks on President Roosevelt.

There were even critics within the Roosevelt administration. Some were complaining by 1935 and 1936 that the President was not fighting the depression vigorously enough. They wanted the government to spend more money in order to stimulate the economy and put more people to work.

- What alarmed some people about the laws passed during the Hundred Days?
- What did the Supreme Court rule on some New Deal laws?

THE SECOND NEW DEAL

Roosevelt responded to the criticisms of the mid-1930s by proposing more reforms. We call his new program the **Second New Deal.**

After the Supreme Court struck down the National Industrial Recovery Act, Congress passed the **Wagner Labor Relations Act** of 1935. This law again gave labor unions the right to organize and bargain collectively. It set up a **National Labor Relations Board** (NLRB) to run union elections and settle disputes. When a majority of the workers in the plant voted to join a union in a NLRB election, that union became the representative of all the workers in the plant, not merely of those who had voted to join it.

Library of Congress

"New Deal Remedies" is another of the political cartoons drawn in the 1930s by Clifford Berryman. Uncle Sam has nostrums and prescriptions of all sorts for his recovery. How did Roosevelt respond to critics of his New Deal?

In 1935 Congress also passed the **Social Security Act.** This law set up a system of old-age insurance, paid for partly by workers and partly by their employers. It provided for unemployment insurance too. Many workers, such as farmhands and maids, were not covered by the original Social Security Act. Nevertheless, the law marked a great turning point for American society.

Other laws passed in 1935 included a "soak-the-rich" income tax and an act regulating banks more strictly. Another law was aimed at breaking up combinations among electric light and gas companies.

These measures marked a change of tactics in Roosevelt's battle against the depression. In 1933 he had tried to unite all groups and classes. By 1936 he had given up on holding the support of big business and rich people. During his campaign for reelection he attacked these people, whom he called "an enemy within our gates." He and his campaign managers turned instead to the labor movement, to women voters, and to blacks and other minorities for support. Their efforts were successful. As we have already noted, Roosevelt was reelected by a landslide in 1936.

■ How did Roosevelt change his tactics in his battle against the depression?

BLACKS BEFORE THE NEW DEAL

In 1936 a majority of black American voters cast their ballots for Roosevelt and other Democratic candidates. This marked one of the most significant political shifts of the 20th century. Before the New Deal most blacks had supported "the party of Lincoln." The Republicans had not done much to win or hold the loyalty of blacks since Lincoln's day. The southerners who dominated the Democratic party had usually offered blacks nothing at all.

During the 1920s black Americans lost many of the gains they had won during the Great World War when their labor had been so much in demand. The revived Ku Klux Klan was a constant source of worry. The migration of southern blacks to northern cities continued. Indeed, blacks were the immigrants of the 1920s. They replaced the European immigrants, whose numbers had declined because of the new immigration laws.

So many blacks moved to northern cities that they were crowded into slums or **ghettos.** Harlem, in New York City, was the best known of the black ghettos. By 1930 165,000 blacks were crowded into Harlem's run-down row houses and decaying tenements.

Like the earlier immigrants, most black newcomers were able to get only the dirtiest, most exhausting, and lowest paid kinds of work. Most labor unions shut out black members. This kept blacks from working in industries and crafts where organized labor was strong.

Yet even in segregated sections like Harlem, blacks were able to improve themselves. In such places they were actually the majority. They did not have to stand aside for white people. They could vote and elect black officials. Blacks came to have considerable influence on the larger politics of the city and state. They became more self-confident and more conscious of their rights.

Black writers, musicians, actors, and journalists found audiences in the ghettos. Black doctors and lawyers and other professionals could practice and prosper too. New York City blacks experienced what is called the **Harlem Renaissance** in the 1920s. Artists and poets such as Langston Hughes made the district the black intellectual and cultural capital of the nation. Ambitious young blacks from other states moved there, believing Harlem was the best place to develop their talents.

However, the Great Depression struck black Americans with cruel force. As always in hard times, minority workers were "the last hired and the first fired." By 1932 more than 30 per cent of all black workers were unemployed.

National Portrait Gallery

United Press International

Langston Hughes achieved fame as a poet of the Harlem Renaissance. His photograph above was taken by Edward Weston, himself famous as a photographer. Below is the world heavyweight boxing champion, Joe Louis, with Marva Trotter Louis on the streets of Harlem in 1935. In the era of the Harlem Renaissance how did many blacks suffer?

Still, most blacks voted the Republican ticket in 1932. In Chicago, for example, Hoover got 76 per cent of the black vote. In Cincinnati he got 71 per cent. In 1936 most blacks in Chicago and Cincinnati voted for Roosevelt.

- What significant political shift occurred among black voters between 1932 and 1936?
- In what ways were blacks the immigrants of the 1920s?
- What was the Harlem Renaissance?

BLACKS AND THE NEW DEAL

Today it is hard to understand why black Americans found Roosevelt and the New Deal so attractive. Many of the most important New Deal programs did little or nothing to help blacks. Most of the NRA industrial codes permitted employers to pay lower wages to black workers than to whites. New Deal farm policy badly hurt black tenant farmers and sharecroppers in the South. The AAA payments went to land *owners*. They were paid for taking tobacco land out of production. The tenants and sharecroppers who had farmed these acres lost their jobs and often their homes as well. Unemployed blacks in all parts of the country rarely got a full share of federal relief money or jobs.

The social security program did not discriminate directly against blacks. However, it left out farm laborers and household workers. The millions of blacks who did work of this kind received no share of the new pension and unemployment benefits.

Yet black Americans liked the New Deal. Many blacks became enthusiastic admirers of Franklin Roosevelt. Thousands of black parents in the 1930s named babies after the President. The reasons for such strong feelings are best understood by keeping in mind how white society treated blacks at that time. This is another example of the need to use historical imagination. For example, the Civilian Conservation Corps camps in the South were segregated. If black youths had *not* been sent to separate camps when they joined the CCC, the program could not have functioned in the southern states. More important, the program almost certainly would not have been created by Congress. Blacks realized this. Most blacks therefore accepted the segregation of the camps as a lesser evil than being without work.

Most blacks thought the main point was that they were included in New Deal programs and that some effort to treat them fairly was being made by important officials. Because so many of the unemployed and poor were blacks, WPA and the federal relief programs were particularly important to them. President Roosevelt ordered state relief officials not to "discriminate . . . because of race or religion or politics" in distributing government aid. This order was not always obeyed, but Harry Hopkins and other key WPA officials tried hard to enforce it.

With the approval of Roosevelt, Secretary of the Interior Harold L. Ickes appointed a black, Clark Foreman, to his staff. Ickes instructed Foreman to seek out qualified blacks and try to get them jobs in government bureaus. Foreman also served as a kind of watchdog, checking on cases of racial discrimination in various New Deal programs. Among other distinguished blacks whose government service began in New Deal agencies were Robert Weaver, who became the first head of the Department of Housing and Urban Development in the 1960s, and William Hastie, later a federal judge.

Perhaps the most prominent black woman who served in government during the New Deal was Mary McLeod Bethune. She was the 15th child of former slaves. Some of her brothers and sisters had been sold away from her parents before the Civil War. Mary McLeod was fiercely independent. After completing her education in South Carolina, she taught at several schools for blacks in the South. In 1898 she married Albertus Bethune, also a teacher. She founded a school of her own in Florida during the Progressive Era.

In 1936 Mary McLeod Bethune was put in charge of the Office of Minority Affairs in the National Youth Administration. As with male black officials like Clark Foreman, her role was broader than her title indicated. She always had access to President Roosevelt. During the New Deal period, she later recalled, she conferred with him privately about six or seven times a year.

In a way their relationship points up the strengths and weaknesses of Roosevelt's way of dealing with the race question. His intentions were good, but he was unwilling to take political risks. Once Bethune asked him to act quickly on some important matter. He refused. "Mrs. Bethune, if we must do that now, we'll hurt our progress," he said. "We must do this thing stride by stride."

Mary McLeod Bethune worked strongly for minority rights. She had served as president of the National Association of Colored Women. She was a vice president of the two most important organizations in the United States that worked for racial equality—the National Association for the Advancement of Colored People and the **Urban League.** Yet she was not offended by Roosevelt's attitude. Indeed, she admired him enormously. Her reaction tells us a great deal about racial attitudes and the problems faced by minorities at that time.

- How did many New Deal programs discriminate against blacks directly or indirectly?
- What did most blacks think was the main point in their support of New Deal programs?

This formal portrait of Mary McLeod Bethune was painted by Betsy Graves Reyneau in 1943. In what ways was Mary Bethune a remarkable person?

The First Lady

After Eleanor Roosevelt posed for Douglas Chandor's 1949 oil, she wrote, "A trial made pleasant by the painter."

Eleanor Roosevelt, the First Lady, had worked to improve the treatment of American blacks long before her husband became President. No prominent white person in the United States worked harder than she during the New Deal in the struggle for racial equality. She was also a leader in women's rights organizations, a promoter of consumer protection, a friend of working people, and a believer in the rights of young people.

As a young woman Eleanor Roosevelt attended exclusive private schools and spent holidays with her rich cousins in high society. Her uncle, President Theodore Roosevelt, gave her in marriage to her handsome distant cousin Franklin.

Eleanor Roosevelt had decided early to prepare herself for a life of social service. This was difficult for her. She was a shy person. She had five children to raise. She saw her husband through his crippling polio. But in the 1920s she began timidly to speak in public.

During the New Deal Eleanor Roosevelt traveled everywhere to find out the mood of the country. "You must be my eyes and ears," the President had told her. A famous cartoon of the late 1930s showed two grime-covered coal miners looking up from their work as one said to the other, "For gosh sakes, here comes Mrs. Roosevelt."

THE END OF THE NEW DEAL

Despite his great victory in the election of 1936, President Roosevelt feared that much of the important New Deal legislation would be declared unconstitutional by the Supreme Court. These laws had greatly increased the powers of the federal government. The more conservative justices of the Supreme Court believed, for instance, that Congress had no right under the Constitution to control the negotiations of workers and their employers. Nor could it force workers to contribute to an old-age pension fund without their consent.

Roosevelt was not a constitutional expert. He felt that the election had proved that the people were behind the New Deal. Necessary reforms should not be held up by technical legal questions. He therefore proposed that Congress enable him to increase the number of Supreme Court justices. That way he could be sure that a majority of the Court would uphold key New Deal laws. This **Supreme Court Reform Plan** of 1937 produced a bitter, long, drawn-out fight. Roosevelt had misjudged the attitude of Congress and the public. The plan seemed to most people to threaten the independence of the Court. Roosevelt tried hard, but Congress rejected the plan.

READING PRACTICE
IN SOCIAL STUDIES

Organization by Question and Answer

Among the ways writers organize information are by time sequence (page 441), by comparison and contrast (459), by items in a list (511), and by cause and effect (554). Yet another important type of organization is by *question and answer*.

Question and answer is particularly useful for the historian, whose task it often is to examine broad questions having to do with *trends* or *movements*. Like the quotation marks which enclose a sentence, question and answer may enclose a section—a question in the introduction, an answer in the conclusion.

Organization by question and answer is easy to recognize. The question is usually stated outright and quickly found by skimming a section. Some questions must be formed by changing the order of a few words in a title or a topic sentence.

Once the question is located, the task is to find its answer (or answers). Again skimming is helpful. Often the answer is broken into parts. Words such as *first, second, third, also,* and *too* provide clues to the parts of the answer Other clues lie in phrases such as *for one thing, another reason,* or *yet another effect.*

When you read a section organized by question and answer, you will often find that the parts of the answer each serve as a main idea for a paragraph. In this case the rest of the paragraph is used to support its main idea. Be careful not to confuse details that support the main idea with the main idea itself.

It you take notes on a section organized by question and answer, begin by jotting down the question itself. Then read until you find the parts of the answer. Write down each one. This gives you the main ideas of the section. Write down details that support each part of the answer only if your notes are fairly complete. Otherwise, the question and its answer or answers should be sufficient.

The section of this chapter titled "Significance of the New Deal" on pages 765–68 is a good example of organization by question and answer. Number your paper 1–6 and answer the following questions.

1. What is the question that is being answered in this section?

For each of the following sets of sentences write *A* for the sentence that gives part of the answer to the question. Write *D* for the sentence that is a detail that supports or expands part of the answer.

2. a. One reason is that the New Deal produced a revolution in the relations between workers and their employers.
   b. The New Deal laws encouraged workers to form new industrial unions.
3. a. Unions made contributions to candidates for public office.
   b. Labor became a force in politics too.
4. a. After the New Deal nearly all people agreed that the federal government ought to do whatever was necessary to advance and protect the general welfare.
   b. The New Deal also created what we think of as the welfare state.
5. a. The New Deal years also saw a shift in the balance of power within the federal government.
   b. Under Franklin Roosevelt this trend became an avalanche.
6. a. The normal reaction of people during depressions had always been to cut down on their expenses.
   b. One more change that resulted from the New Deal was not fully clear until a number of years later. Economists and political leaders learned from their experiences during the Great Depression that the economy could be stimulated by unbalancing the federal budget.

This 1937 cartoon by Bruce Russell recalls the Biblical injunction "It is easier for a camel to go through the eye of a needle than for a rich man to enter the Kingdom of God." How did Roosevelt finally succeed in changing the Supreme Court?

However, the justices who had opposed New Deal laws eventually died or resigned. Roosevelt then appointed justices favorable to his program to replace them. The Wagner Labor Relations Act, the Social Security Act, and all other New Deal laws attacked in the courts were eventually declared to be constitutional. Nevertheless, the Court fight was a serious setback for Roosevelt.

Another setback soon followed. Roosevelt had never understood modern economics. When he was running for President in 1932, he had criticized President Hoover for spending federal money recklessly and unbalancing the budget. Yet Roosevelt had never given up the hope of cutting government expenses and eventually reducing the national debt.

During 1936 and early 1937 the economy had been gradually improving. In June 1937 Roosevelt therefore decided to cut back sharply on money spent for federal relief.

The result was to bring the recovery to a sudden stop. Businesss activity fell off sharply. Unemployment increased. This **1937-38 Recession** was deeply discouraging. Just when prosperity appeared to be *really* around the corner, things turned again for the worse. Was the Great Depression going to last forever?

Roosevelt quickly agreed to increase government spending again. Congress provided money for a big new public works program to pick up the economy. At about this time Congress also passed a new **Agricultural Adjustment Act.** This law established the **Commodity Credit Corporation.** It provided that when prices were low, producers of wheat, cotton, and certain other crops could store their crops in government warehouses instead of selling them. The Corporation would lend them money for their crops in storage.

When prices rose, the farmers could take their crops out of storage, sell them, and pay back the loans. This new system was called the **ever-normal granary.** (A granary is a storehouse for grain and other farm crops.) The new system raised prices by keeping surpluses off the market. Then, in bad years, there would be reserves to prevent shortages.

Another important law passed in 1938 officially outlawed child labor. This measure was the **Fair Labor Standards Act.** It also set the length of a normal work week at 40 hours and established a national minimum wage. Many New Dealers were uneasy with this law. It contained many loopholes "protecting" particular industries from having to meet "fair standards." Still, the principles the law established were important. Eventually most of the loopholes were closed.

The Fair Labor Standards Act of 1938 was the last important New Deal law. In 1939 a new World War broke out in Europe. As during the Great World War (which now became known as World War I), European purchases caused the American economy to pick up.

- Why did the Supreme Court Reform Plan produce a bitter fight?
- What caused the 1937-38 Recession?
- What was the system called the ever-normal granary?

SIGNIFICANCE OF THE NEW DEAL

All laws passed by Congress during the New Deal and all the new agencies and boards did not end the Great Depression. Why then is the New Deal considered so important? One reason is that the New Deal produced a revolution in relations between workers and their employers.

Under the National Recovery Administration and then under the National Labor Relations Board, industrial workers formed strong national unions. The old-fashioned AFL unions had been organized along craft lines. Carpenters were in one union, plumbers in another, machinists in a third, and so on. This system made organizing the workers of a large industry, such as steel or rubber or

John L. Lewis was son of a coal miner who emigrated from Wales. Young Lewis was also a miner and rose through the ranks to head the United Mine Workers. In 1935 he founded the CIO. What influence did labor have on politics?

farm machinery, very difficult. The New Deal laws encouraged workers to form new **industrial unions.** These joined together in a new **Congress of Industrial Organizations** (CIO), which soon rivaled the AFL in size and importance.

There were some bitter strikes during the New Deal. In 1937 workers staged "sit-down" strikes in which they took over plants and refused to leave until their demands were met. New Deal legislation protected workers' rights and established orderly methods of settling labor-management disputes. Labor became a force that manufacturers could neither ignore nor hold back.

Labor became a force in politics too. Unions made contributions to candidates for public office. Union leaders campaigned for candidates who supported policies favorable to organized labor. Union lobbyists put pressure on Congress to pass pro-labor legislation.

The New Deal also created what we think of as the **welfare state.** The popularity of New Deal relief programs and programs to create jobs was so great that it was impossible to depend only on state and local agencies after the depression was over. After the New Deal nearly all people agreed that the federal government ought to do whatever was necessary to advance and protect the general welfare. Later Republican administrations accepted this idea as enthusiastically as the Democrats did.

Increasing the power of the federal government meant that state and local governments had less power. It also meant that the government had more control over individuals and private organizations. Looking back, most Americans lost some freedom of choice. This seems to have been a necessary price to pay if such a complex society was to function smoothly. Still, the loss was large.

The New Deal years also saw a shift in the balance of power within the federal government. Congress came to have less power as the Presidency grew stronger. Ever since it created the Interstate Commerce Commission in 1887, Congress had relied on special agencies and boards to carry out and enforce complicated laws. Since the Presidents appointed the members of these organizations, the White House had gained more power and influence.

Under Franklin Roosevelt this trend became an avalanche. The crisis atmosphere of the times encouraged Congress to put more responsibility on the shoulders of Roosevelt and his appointees. Dozens of new agencies, each known by its initials, such as NRA, AAA, TVA, CCC, and NLRB, made up the confusing **alphabet soup** of the New Deal.

Roosevelt's great power and remarkable personal popularity made the Presidency the strongest force in the government. At the time most liberals considered this both necessary and desirable. Conservatives such as Herbert Hoover were greatly alarmed by this

trend. We shall see in a later chapter that both liberals and conservatives eventually changed their attitudes.

One more change that resulted from the New Deal was not fully
clear until a number of years later. Economists and political leaders
learned from their experiences during the Great Depression that the
economy could be stimulated by unbalancing the federal budget.

The normal reaction of people during depressions had always
been to cut down on their expenses. Most ordinary citizens believed
that the government should also economize in hard times.

The long depression of the 1930s demonstrated that government
economizing only made things worse. When the government spent
more than it received in taxes, it put money into the pockets of citizens. When people spent this money, they encouraged producers to
increase output. Indirectly they were causing employers to hire more

In Jonathan Swift's famous satire
Gulliver's Travels, Captain Lemuel
Gulliver is staked to the ground by
tiny people called Lilliputians. The
same fate befalls Uncle Sam in a
1935 magazine cover illustration.
New Deal agencies are used for
rope in this updated version. What
was the 'alphabet soup' of the New
Deal era?

United Press International

In this 1933 photograph well wishers greet Franklin Roosevelt at Warm Springs, Georgia. Roosevelt often traveled there for the relief he found in the hot mineral waters. What great strength of the President's is shown in this photograph?

workers. This was soon fairly obvious. However, most economists and political leaders hesitated early in the New Deal era to carry the technique far enough. Roosevelt's decision to reduce spending in 1937 illustrates this point very well. Larger government spending would probably have ended the depression sooner.

After their experience with unbalanced budgets during the Second World War, most governments got over their fear of what was called **deficit spending.** Everyone learned this lesson of the Great Depression. However, as we shall see in a later chapter, attitudes on this subject would once again change with the passage of time.

■ How did labor unions change during the New Deal?
■ What was the "welfare state" created in the 1930s?
■ How did the balance of power shift within the federal government during the New Deal?
■ What lesson about deficit spending was taught by the Great Depression?

CHAPTER 25 REVIEW

Identification
Tell briefly why each of the following persons, terms, or events is important.
1. Herbert Hoover
2. Franklin D. Roosevelt
3. George W. Norris
4. Harry Hopkins
5. Huey Long
6. Mary McLeod Bethune
7. Eleanor Roosevelt
8. Great Depression
9. Bonus March
10. New Deal
11. Hundred Days
12. Bank Holiday
13. Blue Eagle
14. Rural Electrification Administration
15. Civilian Conservation Corps
16. Fireside chats
17. Brain Trust
18. Social Security Act
19. Harlem Renaissance
20. Alphabet soup

Understanding American History
1. Describe how the business cycle worked.
2. How were each of the following affected by the Great Depression: shopkeepers? people with savings in the bank? workers who had risen through the ranks? students? women? blacks? Mexican-born workers?
3. Compare and contrast the Presidencies of Herbert Hoover and Franklin D. Roosevelt.
4. What did Roosevelt mean when he told the American people "that the only thing we have to fear is fear itself"?
5. Describe some of the actions taken by Congress during the Hundred Days.
6. Explain the term "alphabet soup" as it applies to the New Deal. Then explain the following New Deal agencies:
   Civilian Conservation Corps (CCC)
   Agricultural Adjustment Act (AAA)
   Works Progress Administration (WPA)
7. Why was the New Deal so popular?
8. What criticisms did various groups make of the New Deal?
9. How did the Second New Deal differ from the first?
10. Give examples to show how most blacks responded to the New Deal.

Activities
1. Prepare a diagram for the bulletin board to show the business cycle. Use the diagram to explain the "normal" business cycle and to describe what happened during the Great Depression.
2. Use an almanac to find unemployment statistics for the years 1929–39. Plot these statistics on a graph large enough to be seen by the entire class. Use the graph to illustrate how unemployment declined, rose, and fell during Roosevelt's Presidency.
3. Present-day historians sometimes record *oral history.* These interviews are tape recorded (and sometimes video recorded) and later set down on paper. In oral history we read the actual words of a subject who lived at a particular time and recalls history firsthand. With your classmates prepare an oral history of the Great Depression by interviewing people in your community who lived through the events of 1929–39.
4. Make a chart for the bulletin board to show the "alphabet soup" of the New Deal. List each agency and briefly describe its function. Some classmates might illustrate the chart with appropriate symbols for the various agencies.
5. Use your historical imagination to write a series of diary entries to describe what you see and hear during the Great Depression. Describe how your family copes with hard times. Describe people both more fortunate and less fortunate than you. What thoughts have you about President Franklin D. Roosevelt and his New Deal?

CHAPTER 25 TEST

Matching (45 points)
Number your paper 1–15 and match the description in the first column with the term in the second column.

1. Industrial union that grew to rival the AFL both in size and importance
2. Insured savings accounts to restore confidence in banks
3. Program of Senator Huey Long of Louisiana
4. Radio talks by Franklin Roosevelt that helped build people's confidence
5. Provided flood control and electricity to thousands of people in the Tennessee Valley
6. Experts who served as advisers to FDR
7. Provided old age and unemployment insurance for workers
8. Set up a government agency to run union elections and settle disputes
9. Outlawed child labor and established a 40-hour work week and a minimum wage
10. Time of great intellectual and cultural achievements for blacks in New York City
11. Intended to stimulate business by allowing manufacturers to cooperate without fear of antitrust laws
12. Proposed by FDR because he feared New Deal laws would be found unconstitutional
13. Term used to describe economic ups and downs
14. Plan that employed young men in conservation work
15. Plan for government storage of farm crops which could later be taken out and sold by farmers who paid back loans

a. FDIC
b. Social Security Act
c. NIRA
d. TVA
e. CCC
f. CIO
g. Supreme Court Reform Plan of 1937
h. Fair Labor Standards Act
i. Harlem Renaissance
j. Wagner Labor Relations Act
k. Brain Trust
l. Fireside chats
m. Share-Our-Wealth
n. Ever-normal granary
o. Business cycle

Chronological Order (25 points)
Number your paper 16–20 and place the following events in order by numbering 1 for the first, 2 for the second, and so on.

16. Great Depression begins.
17. Hoover elected President.
18. Second New Deal begins.
19. Bonus Army marches on Washington.
20. Congress meets for the Hundred Days.

Essay (30 points)
In a short essay explain at least four changes that the New Deal made in American life. Then state your opinion about which changes were for the good and which were not.

UNIT EIGHT TEST

Multiple Choice (20 points)

Number your paper 1–5 and write the letter of the phrase that best completes each sentence.

1. Prior to 1917 the U.S. opposed both the British blockade and German submarine warfare because they
   a. violated U.S. neutral rights.
   b. threatened U.S. imports.
   c. hurt U.S. trade with Mexico.
   d. violated the Versailles Peace Treaty.
2. The Versailles Peace Treaty
   a. brought peace without victory.
   b. included a League of Nations.
   c. was lenient toward Germany.
   d. left European boundaries unchanged.
3. During the 1920s the policy most Americans favored in foreign affairs was
   a. expansionism.
   b. internationalism.
   c. warlike.
   d. isolationism.
4. During the 1920s the automobile was important to the economy because it
   a. gave people mobility.
   b. led to the growth of suburbs.
   c. stimulated other industries.
   d. broke traditional family ties.
5. A major result of the New Deal was
   a. increased involvement by the federal government in all aspects of life.
   b. the destruction of labor unions.
   c. the beginning of World War II.
   d. fewer opportunities for minorities.

Matching (25 points)

Number your paper 6–10 and match the person in the second column with his or her description in the first column.

6. Commander of the American Expeditionary Force
7. A vice president of the Urban League and NAACP
8. Aviator who was a great hero of the 1920s
9. Champion of the rights of young people
10. President who believed in piece without victory

a. Woodrow Wilson
b. Charles A. Lindbergh
c. Mary McLeod Bethune
d. John J. Pershing
e. Eleanor Roosevelt

Chronological Order (25 points)

Number your paper 11–15 and place the following events in order by numbering 1 for first, 2 for second, and so on.

11. The stock market crashes.
12. Major laws regulating immigration are passed.
13. The U.S. enters the Great War.
14. The U.S. becomes involved in the Mexican Revolution.
15. The New Deal begins.

Essay (30 points)

Write a brief essay on *one* of the following topics. Explain what was meant by the Hundred Days of the New Deal? Why was it an important time? Describe five New Deal measures passed during the Hundred Days, *or* Describe some of the hardships people endured in the Great Depression. Tell how the depression affected people from all walks of American life.

UNIT NINE

1940

Draft
Lottery
•
Roosevelt
reelected
President

1941

Atlantic Charter
•
Japanese bomb
Pearl Harbor
•
U.S. enters
Second World War

1942

Battle of
the Coral Sea
•
Battles of
Midway and
Guadalcanal

1943

Battle of
Kasserine
Pass
•
Italian
Campaign

1944

D-Day
•
Battle of
Leyte Gulf
•
Roosevelt
reelected Preside
•
Battle of the Bulg

The New York Times.

EXTRA

GERMAN ARMY ATTACKS POLAND;
BOMBED, PORT BLOCKADED;
IS ACCEPTED INTO REICH

ope's Conflict   HOSTILITIES BEGUN   FREE CITY IS SEIZED   Hitler Acts Against Poland   HITLER GIVES WORD

Korean War
begins

Eisenhower
elected
President

Korean War
ends

*Brown v.
Board of Education*
•
Army-McCarthy
Hearings

1950

1951

1952

1953

1954

A GLOBAL AMERICA

1945
Truman
succeeds to
Presidency
•
Atomic bombing
of Japan
•
V-E, V-J Days
•
United Nations
formed

1946
Republicans
win majority
in Congress

1947
Taft-Hartley
Act
•
Truman
Doctrine
•
Marshall Plan
•
Berlin Airlift
begins

1948
U.S. supports
new state
of Israel
•
Truman
elected President

1949
NATO
formed

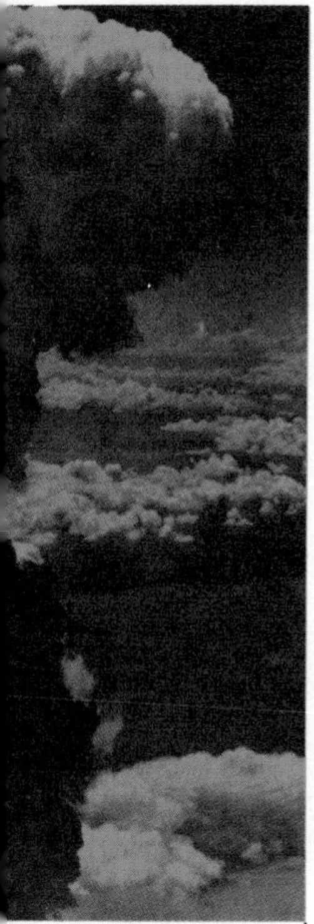

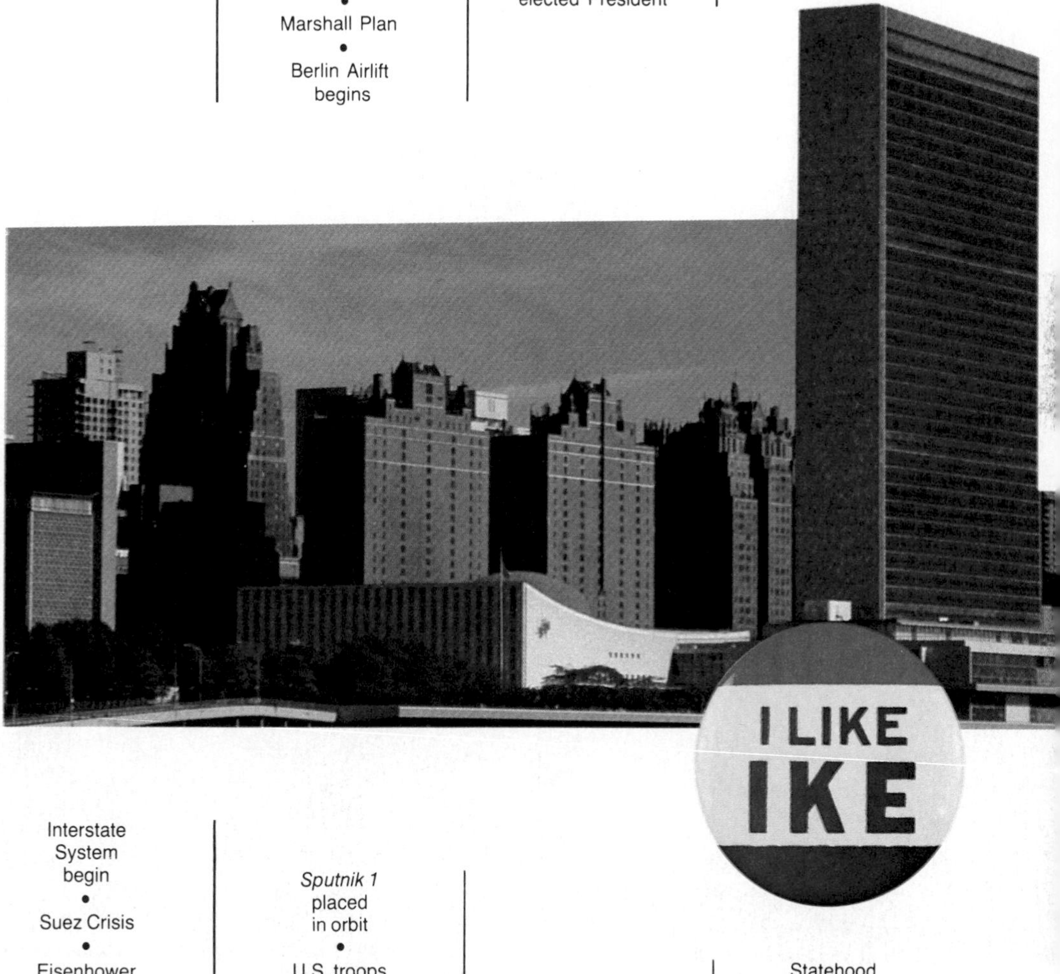

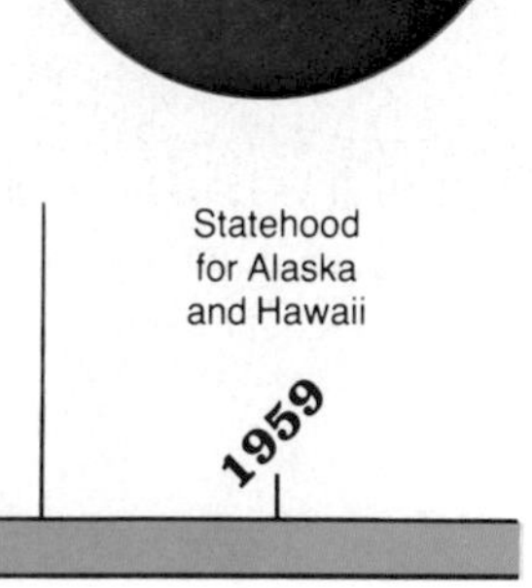

I LIKE
IKE

Montgomery
Bus Strike
•
Geneva
Summit

1955

Interstate
System
begin
•
Suez Crisis
•
Eisenhower
reelected
President

1956

Sputnik 1
placed
in orbit
•
U.S. troops
ordered to
Little Rock

1957

1958

Statehood
for Alaska
and Hawaii

1959

CHAPTER 26

World War II

On September 1, 1939, an enormous German army of 1.7 million men invaded Poland. Two days later Poland's allies—Great Britain and France—responded to this attack by declaring war on Germany. The **Second World War** had begun.

This great world conflict immediately affected the United States. It ended the economic depression. It forced President Roosevelt to direct nearly all of his attention to foreign affairs. And it caused the American people to look once again at their alliances in Europe and the Pacific.

The Second World War began when Germany invaded Poland in 1939. In this photograph German soldiers are in the streets of Warsaw, swastikas of the Third Reich upon their arms. Who were Poland's allies?

Dever, Black Star

THE TOTALITARIAN STATES

The war resulted from the efforts of three nations—Germany, Italy, and Japan—to conquer and control new territories. These nations developed what are called **totalitarian** governments. Their basic principle was that the state was everything, the individual citizen nothing. Totalitarian governments stamped out opposition. The only political party was controlled by the state. All power was in the hands of one leader, or **dictator.** The dictators allowed no criticism of their policies. They claimed absolute authority over the lives of their citizens.

Totalitarianism first developed in Italy in the 1920s. Benito Mussolini became the country's dictator. He called his political system **fascism.** The name came from the ancient Roman symbol of authority, the *fasces,* a bundle of rods tied tightly around an ax. The rods and ax represented the power of the state. Binding them closely together represented national unity.

In Germany the **National Socialists,** or **Nazis,** led by Adolf Hitler, established a totalitarian government in 1933. The Japanese system was somewhat different. The official head of the Japanese government was the emperor, Hirohito. He was considered to be a god, and he took no part in the day-to-day running of the government. In practice, however, the Japanese government was equally committed to the idea that the interests of the state were all-important.

■ What was the basic principle of totalitarian governments?

Il Duce, Benito Mussolini, and the Führer, Adolf Hitler, ruled Italy and Germany with jackboots and fists of steel. Mussolini, here saluting as troops pass in review, wanted Italy to once again have greatness. But his Fascist government turned him out in 1943. He remained Hitler's ally. By 1945 both were dead, one hanged in a public square in Milan, the other a suicide in Berlin. Both left their nations devastated. How did totalitarian governments treat their citizens?

AMERICAN ISOLATIONISM

Totalitarian ideas had little appeal to Americans. Totalitarian states silenced their political opponents and stormed over the borders of weaker nations during the 1930s. This shocked and angered nearly everyone in the United States. When a totalitarian nation attacked another country, the danger of war spreading was on everyone's mind. Americans nearly always sympathized with the victims of the invaders. But they did not want to become involved in another foreign war. Most Americans favored a policy of **isolationism.**

Fighting the Great World War to make the world safe for democracy now seemed a terrible mistake. The totalitarian governments that arose after the war were enemies of democracy. America's allies had failed to pay back the money that the United States had lent them in their hour of desperate need. Looking back, the only Americans who appeared to have profited from the war were the manufacturers of guns and other munitions. It became popular to refer to these manufacturers as **merchants of death.**

■ Why did most Americans favor a policy of isolationism?

JAPANESE AGGRESSION

In 1931 a Japanese army marched into Manchuria, a province in northern China. Although the attack challenged the Open Door policy, President Herbert Hoover refused to take either military or economic measures against Japan. He instead announced that the United States would not recognize Japan's right to any Chinese territory seized by force.

This policy of **nonrecognition** had no effect on Japan. In 1932 the Japanese navy attacked the Chinese port of Shanghai. On March 4, 1933, the same day that Franklin D. Roosevelt took his oath of office as President, the Japanese marched into Jehol, a province in northern China.

■ What was President Hoover's policy of nonrecognition?

THE NEUTRALITY ACTS

Japan's attacks in China worried Roosevelt. Still, he could not ignore the strong isolationist and antiwar sentiment in the United States. On April 6, 1935, the 18th anniversary of America's entrance into the Great World War, 50,000 veterans paraded through Washington in a march for peace. A few days later some 175,000 college students across the country staged a one-hour strike against war. The government should build "schools not battleships," they claimed.

In August 1935 Congress responded by passing the first of a series of **neutrality acts.** This law prohibited the sale of weapons to either side in any war. Later neutrality acts directed the President to warn American citizens that if they traveled on the ships of warring nations, they did so at their own risk.

The idea behind the neutrality laws was to keep the country from repeating what now seemed to be the mistakes of the 1914-17 period. At that time, it will be remembered, President Wilson had insisted on American neutral rights. American ships, citizens, and goods, he stated, had the right to travel without interference on the high seas. That policy had led to submarine attacks and eventually to America entering the war.

■ What events caused Congress to pass the neutrality acts?

ROOSEVELT'S STRATEGY

Soon after the passage of the first neutrality act, Italian troops invaded the African nation of Ethiopia. Roosevelt immediately applied the neutrality law. Nearly all Americans sympathized with the Ethiopians, who had done nothing to provoke Italy. Yet since the Ethiopians had few modern weapons to use against the heavily armed Italians, the neutrality act hurt them far more than their enemy.

America Firsters wanted the U.S. to stay out of the European war brewing in the 1930s. Here they demonstrate against Clarence Streit, the author of *Union Now*, a book that urged the U.S. to join other nations in fighting fascism. What were the neutrality acts passed by Congress?

Therefore, when Japan launched an all-out attack against China in 1937, Roosevelt refused to apply the neutrality law. Using the technicality that Japan had not formally declared war, he allowed the Chinese to buy weapons from American manufacturers.

Roosevelt was looking for a way to check the totalitarian nations without getting involved in a shooting war. In a speech in October 1937 he warned that "mere isolation or neutrality" was no protection. Peaceful nations must work together to isolate, or **quarantine,** aggressor nations. He was talking about what was called **collective security.** Safety required that democratic countries cooperate in the effort to prevent the aggressors from seizing whatever they wanted. However, Congress took no action, and Roosevelt let the matter drop.

■ Why did Roosevelt urge a quarantine of aggressor nations by peaceful nations?

WESTERN EUROPE FALLS TO HITLER

In the summer of 1939 Germany invaded Poland. Great Britain and France then declared war on Germany. The Soviet Union, which had signed a nonaggression treaty with Germany, seized the eastern part of Poland. In a little more than a month, Poland was swallowed up.

In September President Roosevelt called Congress into special session to revise the neutrality laws. After several weeks of debate Congress agreed to allow warring nations to purchase arms and other goods provided that they paid for them in cash and transported their purchases in foreign ships. This **cash-and-carry** policy favored the Allies. As in the First World War, the British and French navies controlled the Atlantic Ocean. German merchant ships could not reach American ports.

■ What was Poland's fate in 1939?
■ What was America's cash-and-carry policy?

Imperial War Museum

Across the English Channel came boats of every size in the spring of 1940. This rescue fleet carried some 340,000 soldiers from France to safety in England. Above them flew the fighters of the Royal Air Force. Charles Cundall painted this oil of Operation Dynamo, the heroic mission. Why were these soldiers trapped?

HITLER'S WAR MACHINE ROLLS ON

Cash and carry was not enough to prevent Hitler's powerful armies from crushing Poland. His war machine rolled on. In April 1940 Hitler invaded Denmark and Norway. On May 10 Nazi tanks swept into the Netherlands and Belgium. A few days later German troops broke through the French defenses at Sedan. Soon they reached the English Channel, trapping thousands of British, French, and Belgian troops at **Dunkirk.** Between May 26 and June 4 British ships managed to rescue about 340,000 soldiers from the beach at Dunkirk and carry them safely to England. But it was a crushing defeat. Swift German armored divisions rolled on through France. Before the end of June the French had surrendered. Hitler was master of most of western Europe. Only Britain and its Atlantic fleet stood between Hitler and victory.

Nearly everyone in the United States was horrified by the thought of such a victory. Hitler was a dictator who used terror and brute force to crush those Germans who opposed him. Democratic principles such as freedom of speech and the press were destroyed in Germany and wherever the Nazis were victorious in the war. Hitler believed that the Germans belonged to a special breed of humans, a "master race" that was supposed to be superior to all others. In particular he considered Jews to be morally and physically inferior. He seized Jewish-owned property, denied Jews the right to higher edu-

As the United States moved closer to war, Congress voted to draft men between the ages of 21 and 35 for military service. In September 1940 Congress authorized a draft to be made by a lottery.

On October 16 more than 16 million men reported to their local draft boards to register for a possible call to military duty. Each was assigned a number from 1 to 8,500. Then all the numbers were placed in small capsules and dropped into a large fishbowl. On October 29 Secretary of War Henry L. Stimson, blindfolded, reached into the bowl and drew out the first capsule. It was number 158. Then others took out the rest, one by one. This determined the order in which men were called up for duty.

cation, and threw tens of thousands of Jews into **concentration camps** simply because they were Jewish.

Hitler intended to round up the millions of Jewish people in the conquered countries of Europe, force them to work in concentration camps until they dropped, and then kill them in cold blood. This was the **Holocaust,** the destruction of a people. By the time the war ended, about 6 million Jews—men, women, and children alike—had been murdered on Hitler's orders.

Hitler was both cruel and power-mad. If he conquered Great Britain, would the United States be safe from his mighty armies? Without massive American aid, Great Britain seemed in danger of being invaded and overwhelmed. German U-boats and bombers had sunk many British destroyers needed to protect Atlantic shipping and prevent a German invasion of England. In July 1940 British Prime Minister Winston Churchill appealed to President Roosevelt for help. He needed 40 or 50 American destroyers. These vessels were not being used because the United States had replaced them with more modern ships.

Roosevelt wanted to help the British. He knew that it would take time to get Congress to act. Therefore he issued an **executive order** turning over 50 destroyers to the British in exchange for 99-year leases on several naval and air bases in the British West Indies. This **destroyers-for-bases** trade was acceptable to those people who would have objected to simply giving the ships to Great Britain.

- How powerful was Hitler by June of 1940?
- What was the Holocaust?
- What was Roosevelt's destroyers-for-bases trade?

Night after night Britain burned in 1940 when Nazi incendiary bombs rained upon the island. Above is a view of London aflame in 1941. At the center is St. Paul's Cathedral. Below is Edward R. Murrow, whose radio broadcasts home to America captured the nightmare of this war. How did the Battle of Britain play a part in the election of 1940?

THE ELECTION OF 1940

Hitler expected to crush British resistance with massive air raids and then invade the shattered island. The Nazi bombings brought the war uncomfortably close to the United States. In the fall of 1940 an American news commentator, Edward R. Murrow, began a series of radio broadcasts from London. Listeners could hear the thud of bombs and the firing of antiaircraft guns. Murrow's broadcasts won much sympathy for the British people.

The **Battle of Britain** formed the background of the Presidential election of 1940. Republicans could not decide between Senator Robert A. Taft, the son of the former President, and Thomas E. Dewey of New York. After six ballots the convention turned to a dark horse, Wendell Willkie of Indiana. Willkie, a former Democrat, was the head of a large public utility corporation. He had led the opposition to the creation of the Tennessee Valley Authority in 1933. Willkie was a strong supporter of aid to Britain. His nomination was a victory for the Republican **internationalists** over the isolationist wing of the party, led by Senator Taft.

When the Democratic convention met in Chicago, not even Roosevelt's closest advisers knew if he would seek renomination. No President had ever run for a third term. However, Roosevelt felt he was needed because of the critical international situation. He won the nomination easily.

Roosevelt ran on his record. Willkie tried to play up the third term issue and the failures of the New Deal to get the economy moving. Late in the campaign he also accused the President of planning to involve the United States in the war. "If you reelect him," Willkie told one audience, "you may expect war in April 1941."

Roosevelt responded quickly. "I have said this before, but I shall say it again and again and again: your boys are not going to be sent into any foreign wars." In the November election Roosevelt received 449 electoral votes, Willkie only 82.

- What was the Battle of Britain?
- How did President Roosevelt face the war issue in his campaign for a third term?

THE LEND-LEASE ACT

Roosevelt interpreted his reelection as an endorsement of his policy of aiding Great Britain. The British were now running desperately short of money to pay for American supplies. Therefore Roosevelt proposed lending them the weapons and goods they needed to continue the struggle against Hitler. In a fireside chat he told the people that the United States "must become the great arsenal of democracy." He asked them to support increased aid to Great Britain even at the risk of becoming involved in the war.

In January 1941 Roosevelt called for support for those who were fighting in defense of what he called the **Four Freedoms**—freedom of speech and religion, freedom from want and fear. A few days later he asked Congress to pass his program for aid to Britain, the **Lend-Lease Act.** This measure gave the President authority to sell or lend war supplies, or matériel, to any nation whose defense was essential to America's security.

The Lend-Lease bill aroused fierce opposition. "Lending war equipment is a good deal like lending chewing gum," said Senator Taft. "You don't want it back." But the public was behind the President. One poll showed that 70 per cent of those questioned supported aid to Britain—even at the risk of war. Congress passed the Lend-Lease Act in March.

- What were Roosevelt's Four Freedoms?

THE BATTLE OF THE ATLANTIC

To stop the flow of supplies to Britain, swarms of German U-boats, called **wolf packs,** ranged the Atlantic. Hitler also shifted part of his air force to attack Atlantic shipping. The **Battle of the Atlantic** was a desperate struggle. During the first half of 1941, U-boats sank ships faster than the British could build them. Roosevelt authorized the United States naval yards to repair damaged British ships, and he transferred ten Coast Guard cutters to the British navy.

In April the United States set up bases in Greenland. American naval vessels began to patrol the Atlantic. These American ships did not try to sink German submarines. Their purpose was to track the submarines and radio their location to British planes and destroyers.

Out of the icy Atlantic waters rises a German submarine ready to attack this helpless Allied cargo ship. In wolf packs these U-boats restlessly ranged the Atlantic waters. This oil was painted by Anton Otto Fischer. Why was the Battle of the Atlantic a desperate struggle?

On June 22, 1941, Hitler broke his 1939 nonaggression agreement with Joseph Stalin and invaded the Soviet Union. Roosevelt quickly announced that lend-lease aid would be extended to Russia. In July he ordered 4,000 Marines to Iceland. This move pushed the area under American protection farther into the Atlantic.

■ What was the Battle of the Atlantic?
■ In what ways did America become more involved in the European war?

THE ATLANTIC CHARTER

In August 1941 President Roosevelt met with Prime Minister Churchill aboard the destroyer *Augusta* at Argentia Bay in Newfoundland. There the two leaders outlined their aims for the postwar world. This **Atlantic Charter,** as it became known, is an inspiring statement of eight democratic principles. In the conclusion the President and the prime minister called for gradual disarmament:

> Eighth, they believe that all of the nations of the world, for realistic as well as spiritual reasons, must come to the abandonment of the use of force. Since no future peace can be maintained if land, sea, or air armaments continue to be employed by nations which threaten, or may threaten, aggression outside of their frontiers, they believe, pending the establishment of a wider and permanent system of general security, that the disarmament of

such nations is essential. They will likewise aid and encourage all other practicable measures which will lighten for peace-loving peoples the crushing burden of armaments.

■ What was the purpose of the Atlantic Charter?

THE UNDECLARED WAR

In September 1941 a German submarine fired a torpedo at the United States destroyer *Greer* off Iceland. The destroyer had been trailing the U-boat and relaying its position to a British plane, which had dropped four depth charges. Although the *Greer* provoked the attack, Roosevelt called the attack "piracy legally and morally." He compared Hitler to a rattlesnake. He ordered naval vessels to escort, or **convoy,** merchant ships carrying lend-lease goods across the Atlantic. And he ordered naval vessels to "shoot on sight" any German submarines they encountered.

After a submarine sank the destroyer *Reuben James* on October 30, killing over 100 sailors, Congress authorized the arming of merchant ships. All restrictions on American commerce were removed. The United States was now engaged in an undeclared war with Germany.

■ What incidents led to the undeclared war with Germany?

NEGOTIATIONS WITH JAPAN

Meanwhile Japan continued to increase its control in east Asia. In September 1940 Japanese troops had conquered part of French Indochina. Later that month Japan, Germany, and Italy signed a mutual defense treaty, the **Tripartite Pact.** This treaty created what was called the **Rome-Berlin-Tokyo Axis.**

Roosevelt hoped to check Japanese aggression with economic weapons. In July 1940 he stopped the export of aviation gasoline and scrap iron to Japan. To prevent a total breakdown of communications with Japan, he did not cut off oil, which Japan needed most. Japan depended upon the United States for 80 per cent of its oil.

In July 1941, after Hitler invaded Russia, Japanese troops moved into French Indochina (now Vietnam), obviously preparing to attack the Dutch East Indies, where there were important oil wells. Roosevelt then cut off all oil shipments to Japan.

The oil embargo stunned the Japanese. They would either have to come to terms with the United States or strike for an independent supply. Since the United States insisted that Japan withdraw from China and Indochina, Japan decided to attack the United States.

■ What economic steps did Roosevelt take to check Japan?

During the meetings that produced the Atlantic Charter, Roosevelt and Churchill were photographed during shipboard church services in 1941. What did they urge in concluding the Charter?

ATTACK ON PEARL HARBOR

The Japanese planned a surprise air attack to destroy the American fleet stationed at **Pearl Harbor** in Hawaii. They believed that by the time the United States could rebuild its Pacific forces, Japan would have further expanded its control of the Far East. Then it would be able to defeat any American counterattack. The attack date was set for Sunday, December 7.

American intelligence experts had broken Japan's diplomatic code. Decoded radio messages indicated that war was near. As early as November 22 one dispatch from Tokyo revealed that "something was going to happen" if the United States did not lift the oil embargo and stop demanding that Japanese troops leave China.

On November 27 all American commanders in the Pacific were warned to expect a "surprise aggressive move" by Japan. The Americans thought the attack was coming in southeast Asia, possibly in the Philippines. Hawaii seemed beyond the range of Japanese forces. The commanders at Pearl Harbor, Admiral Husband E. Kimmel and General Walter C. Short, took precautions only against sabotage by Japanese secret agents in Hawaii.

By the early morning hours of December 7 the Japanese naval task force was in position about 200 miles (320 kilometers) north of the Hawaiian Islands. The ship's crews sent their planes off with shouts of "Banzai! Banzai!"—the Japanese battle cry which means "forever." The first wave of 183 planes left the aircraft carriers and headed for Pearl Harbor.

The lead pilots reached their target about 7:30 on a peaceful and

The U.S. destroyer *Shaw*, attacked at Pearl Harbor on December 7, 1941, is shown at the moment its magazine exploded. Why did Japan attack this U.S. naval base?

United Press International

quiet Sunday morning in Honolulu. On the ships some sailors were still asleep. Others were getting breakfast or lounging on deck. Some were getting ready to go ashore for a swim at Waikiki Beach. Admiral Kimmel and General Short had a date to play a game of golf.

At 7:55 the Japanese struck. Screaming dive bombers swooped down for the kill. Explosions shattered the air. Fortunately, the American aircraft carriers were all at sea. But seven battleships were lined up on **Battleship Row** in the harbor. The bombers came so low over these ships that sailors could see the faces of Japanese pilots as they released their bombs.

The destruction was terrible. The worst blow came when the U.S.S. *Arizona* blew apart and sank, trapping more than a thousand men inside. The Japanese planes rained bombs on every ship in the harbor. They ranged up and down the coast, attacking airfields and barracks. In less than two hours 18 warships were sunk or disabled. Three others were damaged. One hundred and seventy-seven planes were destroyed, most of them on the ground. Then the Japanese returned to their carriers. The task force sped back to Japanese waters. The attack on Pearl Harbor was by far the worst defeat the United States Navy has suffered in all its history.

Americans were shocked and angered by the attack on Pearl Harbor. President Roosevelt went before Congress on December 8 to ask that war be declared on Japan. He called December 7, 1941, "a date which will live in infamy." He had the whole country behind him. Germany and Italy, in turn, carried out the terms of their Tripartite Pact and, on December 11, declared war on the United States.

- What was the extent of the damage done by the Japanese in their attack on Pearl Harbor on December 7, 1941?
- How did Americans react to Pearl Harbor?

THE HOME FRONT

The United States was much better prepared to fight World War II than it had been to fight the Great World War. Long before the attack on Pearl Harbor, Roosevelt had established councils to oversee the production and distribution of war matériel. After war was declared, similar boards were given broad powers to control the distribution of raw materials to manufacturers and to stop the production of many nonessential goods. The government rationed scarce foods, such as meat, butter, and sugar, to make sure that all citizens got their fair share.

The demand for weapons and supplies finally ended the Great Depression. Suddenly steel, aluminum, rubber, and other raw materials needed to make weapons were in extremely short supply. There

"THE GIRL HE LEFT BEHIND" IS STILL BEHIND HIM She's a WOW WOMAN ORDNANCE WORKER

American home life changed with the nation's entry into World War II. At the top of the page are ration stamps which had to be used to buy scarce foods and gasoline. Women went to work in factories. The WOW on this poster stands for Women Ordnance Workers, or makers of weapons. In what ways were women changed by their wartime work?

was no serious shortage of gasoline, but gas was rationed in order to discourage unnecessary travel. Gasoline rationing also saved rubber by keeping drivers from wearing out their tires.

Many manufacturers shifted their plants from the production of consumer goods to weapons. A typical example was the producer of orange juice squeezers who made bullet molds during the war. The automobile companies, of course, turned out tanks and trucks, and airplanes too. The output of airplanes increased from less than 6,000 in 1939 to 96,000 in 1944.

Hundreds of thousands of new workers were needed to produce the tools of war. Unemployment ceased to be a national problem for the first time since 1929. Men and women flocked from farms, towns, and great cities to the East Coast shipyards, to the steel plants and former automobile factories of the Midwest, and to the aircraft plants of the West.

About 6 million women were employed during the war. Songs like "Rosie the Riveter" helped persuade women to take jobs traditionally held only by men. Movies pictured the wives and sweethearts of servicemen working at these jobs while their loved ones fought against the Germans and the Japanese.

The wartime labor shortage cemented the gains that organized labor had made under the New Deal. A **National War Labor Board** was established in 1942 to regulate wages and prevent labor disputes.

Farmers experienced boom times. The demand for food to feed American and Allied troops was enormous. Farm income more than doubled during the war. Farmers who had suffered during the 1920s and 1930s were soon able to pay off their mortgages, improve their property, and put aside savings too.

During the war Congress adopted the **withholding system** of payroll deductions for collecting income taxes. Employers withheld a percentage of their workers' pay and sent the money directly to the treasury. The withholding system made paying taxes a little less painful. It also supplied the government with a steady flow of funds and made evading taxes almost impossible.

High taxes on personal incomes (up to 94 per cent) and on the profits of corporations helped persuade Americans that no one was benefiting too much from the war while soldiers were risking their lives overseas. To boost the morale of those in uniform, Congress passed the Serviceman's Readjustment Act of 1944. This **G.I. Bill of Rights** made low-cost loans available to veterans who wished to buy houses or start new businesses. It also provided money for expenses such as tuition and books for those who wished to resume their education after the war.

■ How did the war finally bring the Great Depression to an end?

National Archives

These are three generations of the Mochida family. They are tagged for evacuation from their home in Hayward, California, to live in an internment camp because they are Japanese-Americans. How many of these West Coast people went to the internment camps?

SUSPICION OF JAPANESE-AMERICANS

World War II was a popular war. Almost no one questioned the decision to fight the Axis powers. Assured of the solid backing of the people, the Roosevelt administration adopted a relaxed attitude toward freedom of speech in wartime. There was no persecution of German-Americans as had occurred during the Great World War.

The one blot on the Roosevelt record of civil liberties was the treatment of Japanese-Americans. About 112,000 lived on the West Coast. They were forced to move to **internment camps** in a barren section of the country. The government was afraid that some were disloyal and would try to interfere with the war effort and help Japan. Others were placed in the camps for their own protection.

The white population of the Far West had always been suspicious of the Chinese and Japanese who settled there. Partly this was the typical dislike of immigrants with different customs. Partly it was a matter of racial prejudice. The suspicion was greatly increased by the sneak Japanese attack on Pearl Harbor. Many people were convinced that unless everyone of Japanese origin was cleared out of the Pacific Coast region, the Japanese would soon be bombing San Francisco.

There was absolutely no evidence that the Japanese-Americans were less loyal than other Americans. Most of them had been born in the United States. Immigration from Japan had been ended by the so-called Gentlemen's Agreement of 1907. Nevertheless, all were forced to sell their homes and property and leave for the camps.

- What reasons did the government give for placing Japanese-Americans in internment camps?
- How was the internment of the Japanese-Americans a blot on Roosevelt's record of civil liberties?

787

BUILDING SKILLS IN SOCIAL STUDIES

Art in the Service of War

Patriotic art abounds in wartime. Recruiting posters, requests for volunteers, reminders to keep wartime secrets ("Loose lips sink ships"), and remembrances of past glory are displayed everywhere. The Marine Corps recruiting poster and "Your Red Cross Needs You!" are by James Montgomery Flagg, a popular illustrator of the period. The Office of War Information prepared "Remember December 7th!" with its quotation from Abraham Lincoln and "Americans Will Always Fight for Liberty." Can you find other examples of art in the service of war in this book?

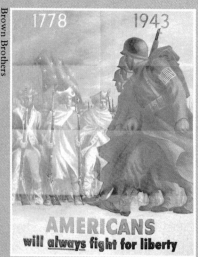

BLACKS IN WARTIME

American blacks also had a difficult time during the war. Black servicemen were expected to risk their lives for the country. Still they were kept in segregated units and frequently treated with disrespect by both officers and enlisted men. Yet by comparison with their treatment during earlier wars, there was some improvement. More black officers were commissioned. A number of blacks became pilots in the air force.

As during the Great World War, the labor shortage benefited black workers. Thousands got a chance to learn new skills and therefore earn higher wages. Yet racial discrimination did not end. For this reason, early in 1941 a black leader, A. Philip Randolph, decided to organize a **March on Washington** to protest the way blacks were being treated.

President Roosevelt feared that such a march would split public opinion at a time when national unity was essential. To persuade Randolph to cancel the march, he issued an executive order prohibiting racial discrimination in defense plants. This rule was enforced by a **Fair Employment Practices Committee.** Randolph then called off the march.

This did not mean that blacks were satisfied with their treatment after 1941. Many whites resented the concessions Roosevelt had made. There was a good deal of racial trouble in the armed services and in industrial plants throughout the war years. More and more blacks were demanding their rights as members of a democratic society. It was clear that when the war ended, demands by blacks for fair treatment were sure to increase.

- What problems were there for blacks in the military during the war? In labor? What advances were there?
- Why did President Roosevelt create the Fair Employment Practices Committee?

Culver Pictures

Asa Philips Randolph was a writer and editor of *The Messenger*, a magazine he helped found. Later he was head of the Brotherhood of Sleeping Car Porters. In what way did he influence Roosevelt?

NEW WEAPONS OF WAR

Amazing changes in the nature of warfare took place between 1918 and 1941. Tanks, which had served mostly as shields for advancing infantry, became swift and powerful offensive weapons. Airplanes, which had been used mainly as scouts and observation posts, now served more as bombers and as mobile machine gun nests. They could drop deadly loads of high explosives on distant factories, railroad yards, and troop concentrations. They also carried supplies to troops in the field and dropped specially trained soldiers called **paratroopers** behind enemy lines. These daring fighters would slip one after another from planes high over Hitler's Europe and scramble to reassemble on the ground below.

THE U.S. ENTERS WORLD WAR II

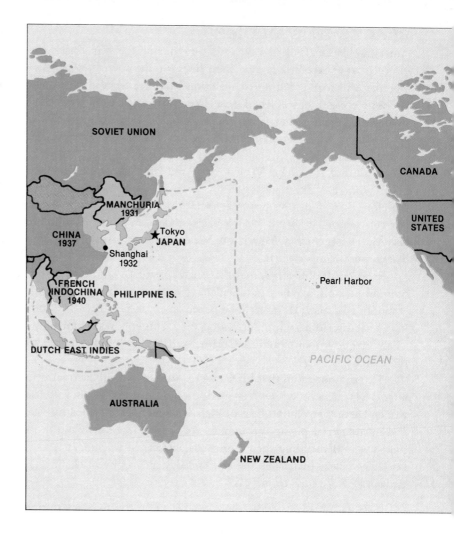

`1940`	Territory controlled by Axis countries and date invaded.
▨	Allied countries
▨	Neutral countries

Air power revolutionized naval warfare. A new kind of warship, the **aircraft carrier,** served as a kind of seagoing airport. Squadrons of carrier-based planes could fly great distances and drop their bombs accurately on enemy ships and shore positions. They could then return to the carrier to refuel and take on another load of bombs. Many crucial naval battles were fought and won in World War II without any warship actually coming within sight of an enemy vessel.

Another new weapon was the **rocket.** Rockets differed from bullets and explosive shells in that they carried the fuel that drove them. In this respect they were like the torpedoes fired by submarines. Large rockets could be fired like artillery at far-distant targets. Smaller ones were fired from planes. There were even small rocket launchers called **bazookas** that two-man infantry teams used against tanks and armored vehicles.

Two British inventions were extremely important in helping to

locate enemy planes, ships, and submarines. One was **radar,** which stands for "radio detection and ranging." Radar bounces radio waves off objects. The reflected waves reveal the shape of the object and its distance from the source. The other tracking device, **sonar,** short for "sound navigation ranging," locates objects that are underwater, where radar is useless. Sonar machines bounce sound waves off objects and record the echoes, thus indicating where the object is. Sonar devices can also pick up the vibrations caused by the propellers of submarines.

- How did the use of tanks change between World War I and World War II?
- How did the use of airplanes change between wars?
- How did air power revolutionize naval warfare?
- How is radar used? How is sonar used?

THE INVASION OF NORTH AFRICA

American military strategists hoped to hold the line against further Japanese advances in the Pacific. Their first major effort would be to defeat Germany. By early 1942 Hitler controlled nearly all of Europe and most of North Africa as well.

The nations that fought the Axis powers in World War II were known as the **Allies.** Chief among the Allies were the United States, Great Britain, France, the Soviet Union, China, Australia, and Canada. In June 1942 President Roosevelt put General Dwight D. Eisenhower in command of American troops in Europe. "Ike" was a first-rate military planner. He also got on well with all kinds of people. Managing and directing the huge and complicated Allied war machine required diplomacy as much as military talent.

Frank Scherschel, LIFE Ⓒ, Time, Inc.

Ullstein Bilderdienst

In North Africa the 'Desert Fox,' Erwin Rommel, pointing at right, led German soldiers against the Allied troops under the command of Dwight Eisenhower and Sir Bernard Montgomery — 'Ike' and 'Monty' to their loyal soldiers. They are pictured left and center in North Africa. What strengths did Eisenhower show?

The first important campaign that Eisenhower directed was an attack on **Morocco** and **Algeria,** in North Africa. An invasion of Europe was not believed possible until more troops and supplies had gathered in England. On November 8, 1942, three separate task forces, one from America, two from England, landed at three points in North Africa. About 110,000 troops, mostly American, were put ashore quickly and efficiently. There was little resistance, and Morocco and Algeria were soon firmly in Allied control.

Then, in February 1943, the first real battle took place at Kasserine Pass in Tunisia. The brilliant German general, Erwin Rommel, deployed his *Afrika Korps* tanks against American tanks in desert warfare. This **Battle of Kasserine Pass** ended in a standoff. But soon the Germans were driven out of the rest of North Africa.

■ Who were the Allies?

THE ITALIAN CAMPAIGN

In July 1943 Eisenhower's forces invaded the Italian island of **Sicily,** the first step in an attack on what Prime Minister Churchill mistakenly called "the soft underbelly of Europe." In a little more than a month Sicily was conquered. The Italians then revolted against the dictator Mussolini and tried to surrender. Unfortunately, the German army in Italy simply took over control of the country. The Americans made a successful landing on the Italian mainland. But the conquest of the country against fierce German resistance was a long and bloody process.

■ What turn of events in Italy prolonged the campaign?

D-DAY

Now the long-awaited invasion of France, **Operation Overlord,** was about to begin. For months the United States and British air forces had been bombing industrial targets and railroad yards in Germany in preparation for the invasion. Now, on **D-Day**—June 6, 1944— 4,000 landing craft and 600 warships carried 176,000 soldiers across the English Channel. They went ashore at several beaches along the coast of **Normandy,** a province in northern France. Naval guns and 11,000 planes bombarded the German defense positions. By nightfall 120,000 men were ashore. The reconquest of Europe had begun.

With the jaws of their landing craft open wide, these American soldiers wade ashore at Normandy on D-Day. This dramatic photograph was taken on June 6, 1944. Why was this such an important landing?

Wide World Photos

The Germans fought skillfully and bravely, but the invaders held the beaches. Reinforcements were brought over. In a single week 326,000 men, 50,000 tanks and trucks, and over 100,000 tons of supplies were ferried across the Channel. By the end of July more than 1 million Allied soldiers were safely landed and established on French soil.

■ What was Operation Overlord? In what ways was it a massive military operation?

THE ALLIES ENTER PARIS

In August the American Third Army under General George S. Patton broke through the German defenses and raced toward Paris. Patton was a colorful and controversial general. He wore ivory-handled pistols more suitable to a cowboy than a lieutenant general. He insisted that all his soldiers, in or out of combat, wear a combat helmet and tie. He once slapped two battle-weary soldiers because he thought they were cowards seeking to avoid combat. But Patton had a first-rate military mind. He was a master of tank warfare. Troops under General Patton's command moved quickly and decisively. They won victories.

Allied troops entered Paris amid great rejoicing in late August. By the end of September almost all of France was liberated. Everyone expected that the invasion of Germany would soon follow.

■ Why was General Patton controversial? What were some of his strengths?

THE ELECTION OF 1944

With victory in sight Roosevelt had to decide whether to run for a fourth term in 1944. He should not have done so because he was in very poor health. He had a bad heart, high blood pressure, and other physical ailments. Still, he was determined to bring the war to a victorious conclusion. The need for a new world organization to replace the League of Nations was also on his mind.

The President was renominated by the Democrats without opposition. Senator Harry Truman of Missouri was chosen as his running mate. The Republican candidate was Governor Thomas E. Dewey of New York. Dewey was not a particularly effective campaigner, but no one could have defeated the popular Roosevelt on the eve of victory. The election was never in doubt. The popular vote was 25.6 million for Roosevelt, 22 million for Dewey. The electoral count was 432 to 99.

■ For what reasons did Roosevelt run for a fourth term?

General George S. Patton surveys the Sicilian landscape. At his side are his ivory-handled pistols. In 1944 what was his destination?

READING PRACTICE IN SOCIAL STUDIES

Facts, Opinions, and Generalizations

Reading history presents us with many *facts*. A fact is something known to be true, to exist, or to have happened. For example, you read on page 774: "On September 1, 1939, an enormous German army of 1.7 million men invaded Poland." This is a statement of fact.

But history also presents us with *opinions*. When the facts are sorted through, it remains for the historian to offer an opinion about larger events. An opinion is something believed to be true yet not absolutely certain. For example: "Most Americans favored a policy of isolationism. Fighting the Great World War to make the world safe for democracy now seemed a terrible mistake." Although election results and writings of the 1930s indicate the last two sentences to be true, they are still the historian's opinion. There is no way to be absolutely certain about the beliefs then held by most Americans.

Opinions are sometimes signaled in writing by words like *believe* or *think*.

Historians also make *generalizations*. A generalization is a general statement that is formed from particular facts or data. These are "usually" or "most of the time" statements, such as: "World War II was a popular war. Almost no one questioned the decision to fight the Axis powers."

Signals for generalizations are words such as *some, many, often, most,* and *usually.*

A good generalization must be supported by fact. When generalizations are supported by opinions, they are weak and often unsound. Furthermore, generalizations are not 100 per cent accurate. They do not cover every situation every time.

Generalizations help make writing efficient. History would be boring indeed if all of the exceptions had to be stated. Better to read: "Americans were shocked and angered by the attack on Pearl Harbor. President Roosevelt went before Congress on December 8 to ask that war be declared on Japan. He called December 7, 1941, 'a date which will live in infamy.' He had the whole country behind him." Here facts and opinions join to form a generalization that is known to be historically accurate.

Number your paper 1–10 and write *F* if the statement is fact, *O* if it is opinion.
1. Benito Mussolini, Italy's dictator, called his system fascism.
2. In Germany the Nazis, led by Adolf Hitler, established a totalitarian government in 1933.
3. Erwin Rommel was one of Germany's most brilliant generals.
4. The United States should not have allowed a Japanese army to march into Manchuria.
5. In August 1944 the American Third Army under General Patton broke through the German defenses and raced toward Paris.
6. General Patton had a first-rate military mind.
7. Roosevelt should not have run for reelection in 1944 because his health was so poor.
8. Dwight Eisenhower was the commander of Operation Overlord.
9. On December 7, 1941, the Japanese bombed Pearl Harbor.
10. If Wendell Willkie had won the election of 1940, the U.S. would not have gotten into World War II.

For the following three statements, tell which is the generalization and which, if any, supports the generalization.
a. Congress passed the first neutrality act in August 1935.
b. Most Americans favored a policy of isolationism during the 1930s.
c. On May 10, 1940, Nazi tanks swept into the Netherlands and Belgium.

THE BATTLE OF THE BULGE

In December 1944 the Allied armies were poised along the German border from Holland to Switzerland. On December 16, before they could march, Hitler threw his last reserves—250,000 men—into a desperate counterattack. The Germans hoped to break through the Allied line and drive on to the Belgium port of Antwerp. That would split the Allied force in two.

The German attack was a total surprise. Within ten days the Germans had driven a wedge, or bulge, 50 miles (80 kilometers) deep into the Allied lines. This was the **Battle of the Bulge.** American troops of the 101st Airborne Division were surrounded at the important road junction of **Bastogne.** The Germans demanded that the American commander, General Anthony C. McAuliffe, surrender his troops. "Nuts!" replied the general. Bastogne was held and the German advance stopped. By January the bulge had been flattened. The Allies were now ready to storm into Germany.

> What was Hitler's strategy in the Battle of the Bulge? What was the outcome of the long battle?

VICTORY IN EUROPE

The Battle of the Bulge shattered Hitler's hope of winning the war. The end came swiftly. In March Allied forces crossed the Rhine River into Germany. By the middle of April British and French troops were within 50 miles (80 kilometers) of **Berlin,** the German capital. Russian armies were approaching the city from the east. On April 25 American and Russian troops met at the Elbe River. Five days later Adolf Hitler killed himself in his bombproof air raid shelter in Berlin. On May 8 Germany surrendered. This became known as **V-E Day** (Victory in Europe).

American joy at the ending of the war was restrained, for President Roosevelt was dead. On April 12, while working on a speech at his winter home in Warm Springs, Georgia, he had died of a massive stroke. The burdens of the Presidency were now upon the shoulders of Harry S. Truman.

> Which allied nations marched on Berlin to end the war?
> Why was American joy restrained on V-E Day?

THE WAR IN THE PACIFIC

The war against Japan was now approaching its climax. The strategy, it will be recalled, was first to prevent further Japanese advances. After Pearl Harbor the Japanese had conquered the **Philippine Islands,** capturing large numbers of American troops. General Douglas

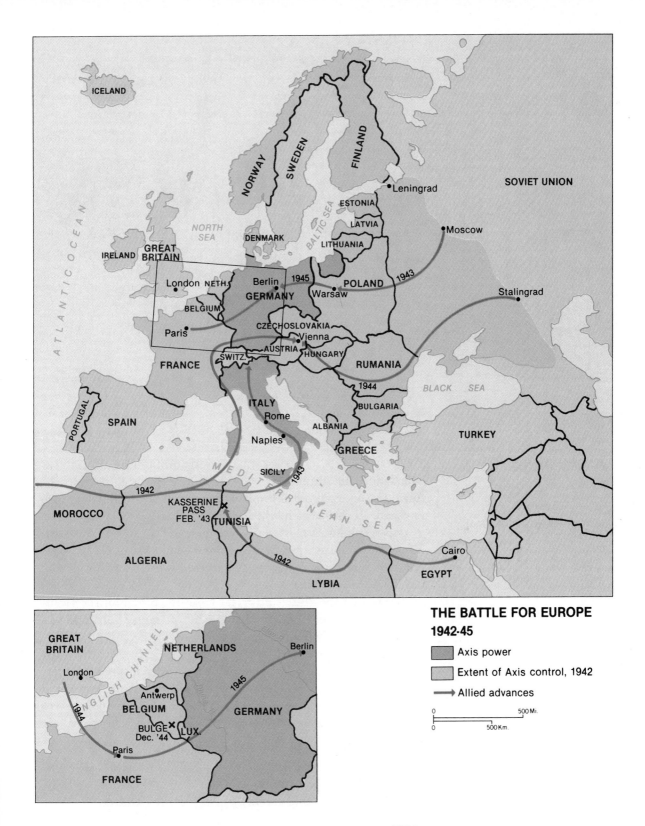

ICELAND

NORWAY SWEDEN FINLAND

SOVIET UNION

ATLANTIC OCEAN

NORTH SEA

BALTIC SEA

Leningrad

ESTONIA

LATVIA

LITHUANIA

Moscow

1943

Stalingrad

IRELAND

GREAT BRITAIN

DENMARK

London NETH. Berlin 1945 POLAND

GERMANY Warsaw

BELGIUM

Paris

CZECHOSLOVAKIA

Vienna

AUSTRIA

SWITZ. HUNGARY

FRANCE

RUMANIA

BLACK SEA

1944

ITALY

Rome

BULGARIA

SPAIN

PORTUGAL

Naples

ALBANIA

GREECE

TURKEY

1943

SICILY

M E D I T E R R A N E A N   S E A

1942

MOROCCO

KASSERINE PASS FEB. '43 × TUNISIA

Cairo

ALGERIA

1942

LYBIA

EGYPT

THE BATTLE FOR EUROPE
1942-45

■ Axis power

□ Extent of Axis control, 1942

→ Allied advances

0 _____ 500 Mi.
0 _____ 500 Km.

GREAT BRITAIN

NETHERLANDS

Berlin

London

ENGLISH CHANNEL

Antwerp

1945

1944

BELGIUM

GERMANY

BULGE Dec. '44 × LUX.

Paris

FRANCE

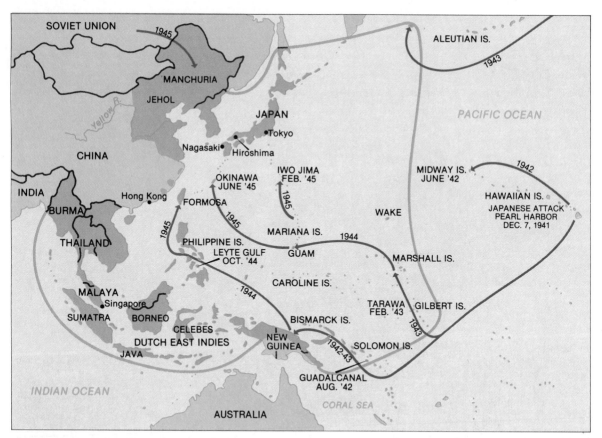

THE WAR IN THE PACIFIC
1942-45

→ Allied advances

⬛ Extent of Japanese control, 1942

MacArthur, the commander in the Philippines, was evacuated by submarine on the order of President Roosevelt before his troops surrendered. "I shall return," he had promised.

Japan, confident of victory, next prepared to invade Australia. But in the great naval **Battle of the Coral Sea** in May 1942 the Japanese fleet was badly damaged. The Japanese were forced to give up their planned invasion.

Then, in June 1942, a powerful Japanese fleet advanced toward the American-owned Midway Island west of Hawaii. The plan was to force a showdown with the American Pacific fleet. But the Japanese ships never reached Midway. American radar picked up their movements. On June 4 dive bombers from American aircraft carriers pounded the Japanese vessels. They sank four Japanese aircraft carriers and destroyed 300 Japanese planes. Again the Japanese fleet had to withdraw. This **Battle of Midway** gave the United States control of the central Pacific.

⬛ What had General MacArthur pledged in 1942?
⬛ What was the significance of the Battle of the Coral Sea?
⬛ What was the significance of the Battle of Midway?

THE PACIFIC CAMPAIGN

To defeat Japan, the strategists believed, the Japanese islands must be invaded. But how to get there? The Japanese controlled thousands of small islands in the Pacific—the Bismarcks, the Carolines, the Gilberts, the Solomons, the Marshalls, and others. Capturing all these islands would be too costly, both in lives and in time.

General MacArthur, the commander of the army forces in the Pacific, was set on returning to the Philippines. He favored a sweep through the Bismarck Islands to the Philippine Sea. The Philippines could then be regained and the captive American soldiers set free.

Admiral Chester W. Nimitz, commander of the Pacific fleet, argued for advancing directly toward Japan itself. The military planners in Washington, the Joint Chiefs of Staff, decided on a two-pronged campaign. MacArthur was to clean out the Bismarcks and then head for the Philippines. Nimitz would attack the Japanese-held islands in the central Pacific and press on toward Japan.

■ What was General MacArthur's strategy in the Pacific? What was Admiral Nimitz's strategy?

Palm trees sway in the tropical sky above Guadalcanal. On the balmy islands of the South Pacific bloody battles were waged. Here American troops wade ashore in their part of the Pacific campaign. Why was it necessary to invade these islands?

Black Star

799

Black Star

Fleet Admiral Chester W. Nimitz is the subject of this photograph. He was made commander of the Pacific Fleet in 1941 after Pearl Harbor was attacked. With whom did he share his command?

FROM GUADALCANAL TO LEYTE

First the Solomon Islands had to be captured. Early in August 1942 American troops landed on three islands of the group. Two of the islands were captured quickly. But in the jungles of **Guadalcanal** Island some of the hardest fighting of the Pacific war took place. For six months the Americans struggled slowly ahead through dense jungles. The Japanese troops resisted stubbornly. They were ready to die to the last man for their country. Japanese sharpshooters tied themselves high in trees. Machine gun teams set up their weapons in caves from which retreat was impossible. Before Guadalcanal was finally cleared in February 1943, 20,000 Japanese were killed.

As Nimitz's forces advanced, every island they attacked was defended with equal determination. The Japanese fought desperately for every inch of ground. When American marines went ashore on the island of Tarawa, they were opposed by 4,500 troops. Only 17 of these Japanese soldiers were taken prisoner. All the rest died in battle.

To the south MacArthur's army was carrying out its part of the plan. In October 1944 it recaptured the Philippines. In the **Battle of Leyte Gulf** the navy destroyed the last major Japanese fleet. Now the United States had complete control of Philippine waters.

■ How did Japanese troops in the Pacific resist the American advance?

IWO JIMA AND OKINAWA

The Allies next secured the bases needed for the invasion of Japan. The marines first fought hard to capture the tiny island of **Iwo Jima,** 750 miles (1,200 kilometers) south of Japan. Two weeks after taking Iwo Jima, American troops went ashore on **Okinawa,** a much larger island only 350 miles (560 kilometers) from Japan. Before the battle for Okinawa ended in June 1945, the Japanese had suffered over 100,000 casualties, the Americans over 11,000.

The United States now had complete control of both air and sea. From airfields in Okinawa, American planes bombed Japan mercilessly. American battleships and cruisers moved in closer to pound industrial targets with their heaviest guns. Soon every important Japanese city was a smoking ruin.

■ What use did the Americans make of Okinawa after its capture?

THE ATOMIC BOMB

Victory was now certain. Still, military experts expected that the cost of invading Japan would be enormous. Japanese soldiers had demonstrated repeatedly that they would fight every battle to the last man. Some authorities believed that the United States would suffer

800

In February 1945 marines landed on Iwo Jima, a tiny island that would become a valuable base in the Pacific for the invasion of Japan. The fight to capture Iwo Jima was bitter. On February 23 the victorious marines reached the top of Mount Suribachi, a volcano on the southern tip of the island. As they crawled toward the rim of the crater, they came under fire from Japanese soldiers dug in on the other side of the mountain. A fierce fight developed. One marine picked up an iron pipe, bound it to a small American flag he was carrying, and raised it. Later another marine arrived with a larger flag. A photographer took a picture of this famous second flag raising over Iwo Jima.

Joe Rosenthal, Wide World Photos

1 million more casualties before Japan was completely conquered.

This was the situation President Truman faced when he learned that American scientists had produced a new and terrible weapon—the **atomic bomb.** On orders from President Roosevelt, scientists had been working on the top-secret **Manhattan Project** since early 1942. Now they had produced a weapon with the explosive force of 20,000 tons of TNT. This tremendous power was released by the splitting of atoms of uranium and plutonium, two highly radioactive elements.

President Truman had to make an extremely difficult decision. Dropping an atomic bomb on a Japanese city would kill thousands of innocent civilians. Yet Truman felt that he had no choice. Without the atomic bomb far more people would be killed before the war was over. He believed that the only way to convince the proud Japanese that further resistance was useless was to use this revolutionary bomb against them.

On August 6, 1945, an American bomber dropped the first atomic bomb upon **Hiroshima,** a city of 344,000. In one blinding flash 75,000 people died. Another 100,000 were injured. When the Japanese still hesitated to surrender, another atomic bomb was dropped on the city of **Nagasaki.** This convinced the Japanese. On August 14, **V-J Day** (Victory in Japan), they surrendered unconditionally. World War II was finally over.

The terrible destruction caused by the atom bombing of Hiroshima and Nagasaki has resulted in a long controversy about President Truman's decision. Even today, people disagree on whether or not the President did the right thing. Aside from the immediate loss of so many lives, the radioactivity released by the explosions caused hundreds of persons to die horrible, lingering deaths. Later many children were born deformed because of radioactive damage suffered

United Press International

With the explosive force of 20,000 tons of TNT, this is the atom bomb that fell on Nagasaki. Never since has its mushroom cloud risen in wartime. Why did the U.S. drop the atomic bomb on Nagasaki?

by their parents. Was there no way that the Japanese could have been shown the power of the bomb without using it on human beings?

On the other hand, the bomb did save lives—Japanese as well as American. Far more people would have died in an all-out invasion. There was also the hope that a demonstration of the horrors of atomic warfare would convince the entire world that such a weapon must never be used again. So far none has.

The final judgment on President Truman's decision lies in the future. It depends upon what all of us and all our descendants do with our knowledge of the dreadful consequences of atomic explosions.

- What was the result of the Manhattan Project?
- What decision did President Truman have to make about the new atomic bomb?
- What arguments are made in support of the atomic bombing of Hiroshima and Nagasaki? What arguments are made against the bombing?

CHAPTER 26 REVIEW

Identification
Tell briefly why each of the following persons, terms, or events is important.
1. Benito Mussolini
2. Adolf Hitler
3. Winston Churchill
4. Franklin D. Roosevelt
5. Edward R. Murrow
6. Wendell Willkie
7. Joseph Stalin
8. Dwight D. Eisenhower
9. George S. Patton
10. Douglas MacArthur
11. Holocaust
12. Four Freedoms
13. Lend-Lease Act
14. Atlantic Charter
15. Rome-Berlin-Tokyo Axis
16. Pearl Harbor
17. Allies
18. G.I. Bill of Rights
19. Operation Overlord
20. Manhattan Project

Understanding American History
1. What was the reaction of most Americans to totalitarian aggression during the early and middle 1930s? How were the neutrality acts part of this reaction?
2. Explain the effect of World War II on the election of 1940.
3. Describe the series of U.S. government actions that showed the step-by-step movement away from the neutrality of the 1930s to open aid for the Allies by 1941.
4. Why did the Japanese attack Pearl Harbor?
5. By 1942 which were the major Axis and Allied countries?
6. How did World War II finally bring an end to the Great Depression?
7. How were minorities affected by World War II, including Japanese-Americans?
8. Explain the importance of Operation Overlord and D-Day.
9. Why were the Battles of the Coral Sea and Midway important in the war against Japan?
10. What arguments did President Truman consider for and against using the atomic bomb at the end of World War II?

Activities
1. Try to obtain recordings of speeches delivered during World War II by Franklin D. Roosevelt and Winston Churchill or news reports from Britain by Edward R. Murrow. Use these speeches as part of a class program on "The World at War." You may also be able to obtain motion pictures of Allied and Axis leaders taken during the war.
2. With your classmates prepare two large maps to show the war in Europe and in the Pacific. Label the sites of the major battles and have classmates give short reports on each.
3. As a class oral history project, locate and interview men and women who fought in World War II or worked on the home front. Ask your subjects to describe their experiences. Remember that the secret of all good interviews is to do your homework beforehand so that your questions lead the interview in a purposeful way.
4. Use historical imagination to write letters home to your family from the front in the European or Pacific war. Tell of your experiences and describe one of the U.S. generals. Other classmates might write letters to you from home telling of their work in the U.S. for the war effort.
5. On April 12, 1945, Franklin D. Roosevelt died suddenly in Warm Springs, Georgia. The new President, Harry S. Truman, told reporters, "I felt like the moon, the stars, and all the planets had fallen on me." Use historical imagination to place yourself with President Truman in his first day in the White House. Discuss some of the major decisions he must make, including use of the atomic bomb.

CHAPTER 26 TEST

Completion (30 points)

Number your paper 1–10 and next to each number write the words from the list below that best complete each sentence.

Four Freedoms   Atlantic Charter
G.I. Bill of Rights   Battle of Midway
Operation Overlord   Axis
Manhattan Project   internment camps
totalitarian governments   Iwo Jima

1. The _____ held that the state was everything, the individual nothing.
2. Loans to be available to veterans after World War II under the _____ boosted their morale in 1944.
3. Roosevelt and Churchill issued the _____ to outline their aims for the postwar world.
4. Germany, Italy, and Japan made up what was called the _____.
5. Japanese-Americans were placed in _____ in the U.S. during World War II.
6. The Allied invasion of France, called _____, began with D-Day on June 6, 1944.
7. The _____ was a turning point in the war when the U.S. gained control of the central Pacific.
8. The secret plan to build the atomic bomb was called the _____.
9. U.S. marines raised the flag over _____ when they reached the top of Mount Suribachi.
10. In January 1941 President Roosevelt spoke of the _____ Americans were defending.

Matching (20 points)

Number your paper 11–20 and match the person in the first column with the description in the second column.

11. Commander of the U.S. Pacific fleet
12. Fascist dictator of Italy
13. Commander of Operation Overlord
14. Prime Minister of Great Britain
15. American general, master of tank warfare
16. Successor of Franklin D. Roosevelt
17. Nazi dictator of Germany
18. Only U.S. President elected to four terms
19. U.S. news commentator who broadcast from London
20. American commander in the Pacific

a. Adolf Hitler
b. Winston Churchill
c. Edward R. Murrow
d. Douglas MacArthur
e. Dwight D. Eisenhower
f. George S. Patton
g. Benito Mussolini
h. Harry S. Truman
i. Franklin D. Roosevelt
j. Chester W. Nimitz

Chronological Order (20 points)

Number your paper 21–25 and place the following events in order by numbering 1 for the first, 2 for the second, and so on.

21. D-Day
22. V-E Day
23. The Battle of the Bulge
24. V-J Day
25. Bombing of Hiroshima and Nagasaki

Essay (30 points)

In a short essay tell what effect World War II had on each of the following groups: factory workers, farmers, women, blacks, and Japanese-Americans. Write at least one paragraph for each group, as well as an introduction and a conclusion.

CHAPTER 27
America in the Cold War

THE SEARCH FOR WORLD PEACE

Any war as widespread and destructive as World War II was bound to cause difficulties and conflicts that would not disappear simply because the shooting had stopped. President Roosevelt had realized this. During the war he prepared to face postwar problems. In particular he hoped to avoid the mistakes that Woodrow Wilson had made after World War I. Wilson's policies had led to the rejection of the Versailles Treaty by the Senate.

Roosevelt succeeded in avoiding Wilson's mistake of not consulting the opposition party about the peace treaty. He made Senator Arthur Vandenberg of Michigan, who was the leading Republican on the Foreign Relations Committee, a delegate to the 1945 **San Francisco Conference.** There the United Nations charter was drafted. As a result the Senate approved the treaty creating the **United Nations** (UN) by a vote of 87 to 2.

Flanked by the flags of 50 nations, Secretary of State Edward Stettinius signs the United Nations Charter on behalf of the United States. To his right stands President Truman. The Charter was approved in June 1945 at the San Francisco Conference. What was the purpose of the UN?

Culver Pictures

The new international organization was created to replace the League of Nations. The United Nations did not have the power to make the United States or any other major power do anything it did not want to do. Under the UN charter the United States, Soviet Union, Great Britain, France, and China all had the right to block any UN action by their **veto power.**

■ How did President Roosevelt's preparation to face postwar problems differ from President Wilson's after World War I?
■ What was the result of the San Francisco Conference?

On the United Nations flag olive branches, traditional symbols of peace, surround the world map. At the San Francisco Conference in 1945 how many nations gathered to sign the UN Charter?

THE UNITED NATIONS

Delegates from 50 nations gathered in San Francisco in April 1945 to draw up the **United Nations Charter.** Three fourths of the people on the planet were represented. Long weeks of discussion and debate were necessary for the delegates to agree on the precise wording of the Charter. It was then ratified by the separate nations. On October 24, 1945, the world organization officially came into being.

The preamble to the Charter is a fine statement of the hopes of the postwar world:

We the peoples of the United Nations, determined to save succeeding generations from the scourge of war, which twice in our lifetime has brought untold sorrow to mankind, and

To reaffirm faith in fundamental human rights, in the dignity and worth of the human person, in the equal rights of men and women and of nations large and small, and

To establish conditions under which justice and respect for the obligations arising from treaties and other sources of international law can be maintained, and

To promote social progress and better standards of life in larger freedom,

And for these ends

To practice tolerance and live together in peace with one another as good neighbors, and

To unite our strength to maintain international peace and security, and

To ensure, by the acceptance of principles and the institution of methods, that armed force shall not be used, save in the common interest, and

To employ international machinery for the promotion of the economic and social advancement of all peoples,

Have resolved to combine our efforts to accomplish these aims.

■ How was the United Nations created?

THE YALTA CONFERENCE

President Roosevelt and Prime Minister Churchill worked closely together on military and diplomatic problems during the war. Both also consulted frequently with the Russian dictator Joseph Stalin. The most important meeting of the **Big Three,** as they were called, took place at the Russian seaside resort of Yalta in February 1945.

At Yalta in the Crimea the Big Three, Churchill, Roosevelt, and Stalin, sit on the grounds of Livadio Palace in February 1945. War has made them old men, Roosevelt in particular. He is clearly in ill health. Behind stand, left to right, Anthony Eden, Edward Stettinius, Alexander Cadogan, V.M. Molotov, and Averill Harriman. For what purpose would the Big Three hold their meetings?

At the time of this **Yalta Conference** the war in Europe was almost over. The war had started back in 1939 when Germany had invaded Poland. The Allies had entered the war with the intention of restoring an independent Polish government. Yet by 1945 Poland had been entirely occupied by the Russian troops who were driving the Germans out of the territory they had conquered. Roosevelt and Churchill hoped to prevent Russia from keeping too much territory in Poland.

Stalin, however, was determined to prevent any government unfriendly to the Soviet Union from controlling Poland. The Germans had invaded his country from Poland in 1941. Many times in the past other enemies had attacked Russia from Polish bases.

The difficulty was that no freely elected Polish government was likely to be friendly to Russia. After all, Russia had joined Germany in dividing up Poland in 1939. Russian troops had treated the Poles brutally. Thousands of Polish officers had been murdered in cold blood by the Russians in the **Kaytn Forest Massacre** of 1943.

After considerable discussion the Big Three worked out a compromise. Russia was to add a large part of eastern Poland to its territory. In the rest of Poland free elections were to be held. The Poles could choose whomever they wished to govern them.

The trouble was that Stalin did not keep his promise to permit free elections in the new Polish republic. Instead he set up a **puppet government,** one that he could control as completely as a puppeteer controls a doll. This government was bitterly resented by the vast majority of the Polish people.

Probably nothing could have prevented Russia from dominating Poland. Russian troops had already occupied the country. The Allies could have driven them out only by going to war. And war with Russia at that time was unthinkable.

Most Americans admired and respected the Russians in 1945, even though the Soviet Union was a communist society ruled by a dictator. The Russians had defended their country bravely and had contributed their full share to the Allied destruction of the Nazi armies. Indeed, 7 million Russians died in the war, many of them civilians who starved during the two-year **Siege of Leningrad** by the Germans.

Even General Eisenhower referred at this time to the long record of "unbroken friendship" between the United States and Russia. He said, "The ordinary Russian seems to me to bear a marked similarity to what we call an 'average American.'"

■ Who were the Big Three? Why did they meet at Yalta in 1945?

Every Russian schoolchild can recite a long rhyme about the Crocodile and his travels. This statue in Volgograd (once Stalingrad) still stands after an incendiary bombing. What toll did the war take on Russia?

TASS/Sovfoto

GETTING BACK TO "NORMAL"

President Roosevelt died a few weeks after returning from Yalta. Less than a month later Germany surrendered. The Russians then declared war on Japan, keeping a promise Stalin had made to Roosevelt at Yalta. However, their contribution to the defeat of Japan was not needed because the United States ended the war by dropping the atomic bomb.

The new President, Harry S. Truman, was more suspicious of Russian motives than Roosevelt had been. He believed that the Russians expected the United States to suffer a serious postwar economic depression. They were "planning to take advantage of our setback," he later wrote.

Truman was eager to frustrate the Russians' plans by preventing a depression. But could he handle the complicated task of converting the economy from wartime to peacetime production?

Truman had grown up on a Missouri farm. He had been an artillery captain in World War I. During the 1920s he got involved in Missouri politics. He served as a local judge, and in 1934 he was elected to the United States Senate. He received the 1944 Democratic Vice Presidential nomination because party leaders needed a likable candidate without any enemies to replace Vice President Henry A. Wallace, whom they considered too radical.

Truman had a reputation for being honest and reasonably liberal, but he seemed a rather ordinary politician. Yet no one had ever accused him of being unwilling to accept responsibility. When he became President, he put a sign on his desk in the White House that said "The Buck Stops Here." However, many people, Truman himself included, wondered whether he would be "big enough" to fill Franklin Roosevelt's shoes.

The depression that Truman feared never occurred. War contracts were canceled and thousands of war workers lost their jobs. However, millions of consumers had saved money during the war when there were few civilian goods to buy. The demand for all sorts of products from houses and automobiles to washing machines and nylon stockings was enormous. No automobiles had been manufactured for civilian use since 1941. Millions of people wanted to replace their worn-out cars. Returning soldiers and laid-off war workers quickly found new jobs.

Unfortunately, the huge demand for goods could not be satisfied quickly. Shortages developed. A period of confusion and bickering followed. After four years of going without and paying high taxes, people wanted to enjoy themselves. They believed that they had sacrificed enough for the common good and the national interest. Now they hoped to concentrate on their own private interests. Workers demanded higher wages but protested angrily against

Harry S. Truman's oil portrait is the work of Martha G. Kempton. Behind him is the U.S. Capitol. What motto did President Truman display on his desk in the White House?

The CIO Political Action Committee sponsored this 1944 poster done by Ben Shahn, an artist known for his strong, brilliant graphics. Why did veterans find work easily after they returned from World War II?

increases in consumer prices. Manufacturers wanted all controls lifted and their taxes reduced.

President Truman tried to resist these selfish demands. He proposed a group of reforms that he called the **Fair Deal.** It called for larger social security benefits, a national health insurance plan, a higher minimum wage, money for public housing, and a continuation of the Fair Employment Practices Commission. At the same time the President resisted efforts to do away with price and wage controls.

Congress refused to pass most of the laws Truman requested. Few workers or employers supported any of Truman's proposals ex-

A *Chicago Tribune* cartoonist took this view of President Truman and his Fair Deal programs in 1951. It has the title "News Item: Truman Requests More Powers." What is Congress offering in this cartoon? What stand did it actually take?

cept those that benefited them directly. The President became more and more frustrated and less and less popular.

Finally, in late 1946, nearly all wartime economic controls were removed. Prices then rose sharply. Workers responded by demanding higher wages. When they got them, their increased spending caused prices to go up again. An upward spiral of wages and prices was set in motion, one that has continued almost without interruption to the present day.

- Why was President Truman anxious to prevent a postwar depression? Why didn't the depression occur?
- What reforms did President Truman propose in his Fair Deal? How did Congress respond?

TURNING OUT THE DEMOCRATS

By the fall of 1946 even large numbers of Democrats had decided that Truman was incompetent. "To err is Truman," became a commonly heard wisecrack. "Had enough?" Republican candidates asked during the 1946 Congressional campaign. "Vote Republican."

A majority of the voters in 1946 did just that. The Republican party won control of both houses of Congress for the first time since the 1920s.

This new Congress set out to reverse the trend toward liberal legislation that had begun with the election of Franklin Roosevelt. First it passed the **Twenty-second Amendment** to the Constitution, limiting future Presidents to two terms. This was a slap at Roosevelt's memory. The Congress also reduced appropriations for many social welfare programs. It tried to lower the income taxes of people with large incomes, but Truman vetoed that bill.

The most controversial measure of the session was the **Taft-Hartley Act,** passed in June 1947. The Wagner Labor Relations Act of 1935 had banned unfair labor practices by employers. The new Taft-Hartley law prohibited unfair practices by unions. It outlawed the **closed shop**—the clause in many labor contracts that required job applicants to join the union before they could be hired. It also gave the President the right to get court injunctions which would force striking unions to call off their strikes for an **80-day "cooling-off" period.** The President could only seek these injunctions when strikes threatened the national interest. Yet judges seldom refused to issue injunctions when the President asked for them. Truman vetoed the Taft-Hartley bill, but Congress repassed it over his veto.

- What was the result of the 1946 Congressional elections?
- What did the Twenty-second Amendment provide?
- What are the two main provisions of the Taft-Hartley Act? How did Truman respond to this bill?

Senator Robert Taft was known as "Mr. Republican" to both friends and foes. He was the son of the 27th President and sponsor of the Taft-Hartley Act. What stand did Congress take on this bill?

811

From the air the destruction of the German city of Cologne is vividly revealed. The famous Cathedral is in the background. What was the war toll for Europeans?

THE TRUMAN DOCTRINE

Truman's domestic difficulties did not prevent him from developing an effective foreign policy. Because he was suspicious of Stalin's motives, he worried a great deal about the danger of Soviet expansion.

In Europe the change from war to peace had not been easy. The American economy had expanded during the war. In Europe the reverse was true. Thirty million Europeans had been killed. The loss of so many potential workers was a terrible blow to the economies of every nation. More millions were homeless and hungry. Such people could not produce very effectively. In every country railroads had been wrecked, bridges blown up, factories smashed. About 25 per cent of all the wealth of Great Britain was destroyed during the war. In Germany there were shortages of everything. A package of American cigarettes cost as much as a German laborer could earn in a month.

These conditions caused a rapid increase in the strength of communist parties in many European countries. Whether or not the Soviet government had anything to do with this trend, it was certainly willing to take advantage of it. Experience had shown that once the communists got control of a government, they did away with free elections and prevented their opponents from getting back in power.

It therefore seemed absolutely necessary to Truman that the spread of communism in Europe be checked. But how could this be done without starting another war? The question became urgent in early 1947. Another country seemed about to fall behind what Churchill described as the **Iron Curtain.** Communist guerrillas in Greece were seeking to overthrow the conservative Greek government. Great Britain had been providing aid to that government. In February 1947 the British informed President Truman that because of their own economic problems they could no longer afford to help Greece.

Truman believed that if Greece became communist, its neighbor, Turkey, might also fall under Russian influence. American economic interests in both countries would surely suffer. The President therefore asked Congress for $400 million to aid these two nations. "It must be the policy of the United States," he said, "to support free peoples who are resisting . . . outside pressures. . . . Our help should be primarily through economic and financial aid."

This idea became known as the **Truman Doctrine.** Congress appropriated the money and the communist threat to Greece and Turkey was checked.

- What was Europe's economic condition after the war?
- What tactics did communist parties use after the war?
- What was the Truman Doctrine?

THE MARSHALL PLAN

The Truman Doctrine was popular in the United States because it appealed to both liberals and conservatives. Liberals liked the idea of helping the people of other countries defend their independence and rebuild their war-torn economies. Conservatives liked the idea of resisting communism and thus preserving the free enterprise system. Nearly everyone took pride in the great influence and prestige that came to the United States in other parts of the world.

Critics of the Truman Doctrine argued that it was a disguised form of imperialism. They saw it as a revived form of dollar diplomacy, similar to the old technique of encouraging American investments in nations like Nicaragua and Haiti before World War I. They also thought that the doctrine aimed too much at attacking communism and not enough at helping people in need.

To counter these objections, George C. Marshall, whom Truman had appointed Secretary of State, proposed his **Marshall Plan** in a speech at Harvard University in June 1947. All the nations of Europe, including Russia, needed American help in rebuilding their war-damaged societies, Marshall said. But they also had to help themselves. The plan could not be imposed on the Europeans from the outside.

Marshall's offer to include Russia was a bluff, or at least a gamble. If the Russians had accepted it, Congress would probably not have provided the money to make the plan work. But Marshall did not think the Russians would accept this plan, and he was right. The communists had no desire to contribute to the revival of the capitalist nations.

While the Soviet Union and the countries of eastern Europe under its control rejected the Marshall Plan, the western Europeans adopted it eagerly. They soon created the **Committee for European Economic Cooperation** (CEEC) to decide what needed to be done and how much it would cost. Over the next few years the United States gave CEEC about $13 billion to carry out its plans.

The Marshall Plan was a brilliant success. By 1951 the economies of the participating nations were booming. Still, the plan had further divided Europe into two competing systems. When Czechoslovakia showed signs of accepting Marshall Plan aid, the local communist party seized power with Russian support. Democracy was destroyed. Czechoslovakia, like Poland, Hungary, and the other states of eastern Europe, fell into Russia's orbit.

■ Why was the Truman Doctrine popular?
■ What was the Marshall Plan? What effect did it have on the economy of Europe? What effect did it have on the politics of Europe?

This oil portrait of General George C. Marshall was painted in 1949 by Anthony Wills. In 1953 the general was awarded the Nobel Peace Prize for his Marshall Plan. How was it a part of the Truman Doctrine?

THE BERLIN AIRLIFT

The United States and its western European friends responded to the communist takeover of Czechoslovakia by strengthening their own alliance. After the war the victors had divided Germany into four zones. One zone was controlled by the United States, one by Great Britain, one by France, and one by Russia. Berlin, the capital city, was located in the Russian zone. Because of Berlin's large size and importance, however, the western nations were unwilling to let Russia control it all. It too was divided into four zones.

In 1948 the United States, Great Britain, and France announced plans to create an independent **Republic of West Germany.** This step led the Russians to close all the roads leading across their zone to Berlin. They could not block the formation of the West German republic. But they might force the Allies to give up their zones in the capital city.

The Russian action caused a serious crisis. If the Americans tried to ship supplies to Berlin by truck or train, they would run into a Russian roadblock. Then they would either have to turn back or start a fight. Truman therefore decided to *fly* supplies to Berlin. Fortunately, Tempelhof Airport lay within the United States zone, in the heart of the city.

An American DC-6 airlifts supplies to West Berlin in 1948. The Berlin Airlift brought some 8,000 tons of goods daily in 277,000 missions, some leaving three minutes apart. Why did Russia blockade Berlin?

Fenno Jacobs, Black Star

U.S. Air Force

Missions to Berlin

"Return for a Reload" (detail) is an oil painted by Herb Mott which was commissioned to commemorate the Berlin Airlift of 1948–49.

The Berlin Airlift was assigned to the United States Air Force. Bulky products usually shipped by river barge or freight car had to be flown in on military planes. At one point General Lucius D. Clay, who had charge of the airlift, telephoned to an American Air Force general in Frankfurt, Germany. "Have you any planes that can carry coal? he asked

"We must have a bad phone connection," the Air Force general replied. "It sounds as if you are asking if we have planes for carrying coal."

"Yes, that's what I said — coal."

"The Air Force can deliver anything," the astonished general then responded. And he proved that it could indeed. Over the next 11 months American and British planes flew some 277,000 missions into Berlin. Their cargoes kept the Berliners fed and working.

Truman's **Berlin Airlift** turned the tables on the Russians. There was no way to block the air lanes. Now the Russians would have to decide whether to allow the supplies to reach West Berlin or start fighting.

The Russians chose to do nothing. They probably believed that it would be impossible to keep the 2 million residents of West Berlin supplied with food and other necessities by air alone.

In May 1949 the Russians gave up trying to squeeze the western powers out of Berlin. They lifted the land blockade. The city, however, remained divided into Soviet and Allied zones.

- How was Germany divided after the war? Why was Berlin also divided?
- How did Truman respond to the Russian blockade of Berlin?

CONTAINMENT: THE COLD WAR

In April 1949 the United States, Great Britain, France, Italy, and eight other nations signed a treaty creating the **North Atlantic Treaty Organization** (NATO). The signers agreed to defend one another in case of attack and to form a unified military force for this purpose. By the time the NATO force was organized, the Soviet

THE COLD WAR IN EUROPE 1950s

- Warsaw Pact Members
- ★ Capital Cities
- NATO Members*
- Nonaligned Countries

*Other members not shown: U.S., Canada, Iceland

0   500 Mi.

0   500 Km.

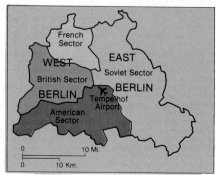

Union had exploded its first atomic bomb. The American monopoly on nuclear weapons had been broken.

Rivalry between the communist and capitalist worlds grew steadily more intense. Neither side dared risk open warfare in the atomic age. Instead they waged what was called the **Cold War.** For American leaders the main objective of the Cold War was to prevent the expansion of Russian influence in every way possible short of all-out war. In 1947 George F. Kennan, a professional diplomat who had served for many years at the American embassy in Moscow, explained how the Cold War could be won. America must build up its armed forces and be prepared to *contain* Soviet expansion wherever it was attempted.

The **containment policy,** according to Kennan, President Truman, and most other Americans, was purely defensive in purpose. The Russians, however, feared that the containment policy, particularly the NATO force, would provoke war. Each side suspected the other of preparing all kinds of evil schemes. In part the tensions of the Cold War were caused by poor communications between the communist and noncommunist diplomats. For this the secretive and overly suspicious Russians were chiefly to blame.

The containment policy worked well for the United States and its allies. It prevented a major war. It enabled the western European nations to rebuild their economies and preserve their democratic political systems. The chief difficulty with containment, from anyone's point of view, was that it tended to prolong the Cold War. A policy of negotiation and compromise might have ended it or at least avoided some of the crises it produced.

- What agreements were made by signers of the NATO treaty?
- What was the containment policy? How did the policy work well for the western allies? What was the chief difficulty with containment?

THE ELECTION OF 1948

While the success of the Berlin Airlift was still in doubt, the 1948 Presidential election campaign took place. The Democratic party was badly divided. Almost none of its leaders wanted to renominate Truman. Some supported Henry A. Wallace, who was running as the candidate of a new **Progressive party.** Wallace had been Truman's Secretary of Commerce. He believed that the Russians' intentions were good and that the Cold War strategy was likely to lead to a real war. When Wallace criticized the Truman Doctrine, the President had forced him to resign. Wallace went on to attack the Marshall Plan and waged war against every aspect of Truman's containment policy.

On the other hand, conservative southern Democrats opposed Truman because of his civil rights policy. In 1947 his **Civil Rights Committee** recommended laws protecting the right of blacks to vote and banning segregation on railroads and buses. It also called for a federal law punishing lynching and the creation of a permanent Fair Employment Practices Committee.

Truman had urged Congress to adopt all these recommendations. He issued executive orders ending segregation in the armed forces and prohibiting job discrimination in all government agencies. The Democratic convention nominated Truman and made his proposals part of the party platform in 1948. Southern Democrats who were known as Dixiecrats then organized a **States' Rights party** and nominated Strom Thurmond, the governor of South Carolina, for President.

With three Democrats running, the Republican candidate, who was again Thomas E. Dewey, seemed sure of victory. Dewey's strategy was to avoid taking stands on controversial issues while the Democrats fought among themselves. But Truman conducted a hard-hitting campaign. He attacked the record of the "do-nothing" Republican-controlled Congress. The Republican party, he claimed, wanted to "turn the clock back" and do away with all the reforms of the New Deal era.

These tactics worked well. Organized labor supported Truman because of his veto of the Taft-Hartley Act. Blacks voted for him because of his civil rights stand. Many farmers were persuaded by his argument that Congress had refused to provide adequate storage space for surplus farm products. Former New Dealers reponded to his charge that the Republicans intended to repeal important New Deal laws.

Still, nearly all the experts continued to predict that Dewey would be elected. How could Truman win with two other candidates competing with him for Democratic votes? The editor of the *Chicago Tribune* was so sure that Dewey would win that he approved the headline "DEWEY DEFEATS TRUMAN" and went to press on election night before all the votes had been counted.

But the experts were wrong. Truman received over 2 million more votes than Dewey and won a solid majority in the electoral college. The States' Rights ticket won only in four southern states. Wallace's Progressive party was swamped everywhere. Truman had proved himself a clever politician. His energy, courage, and determination in fighting so hard when his cause seemed hopeless was part of the reason for his success. Another reason was that a majority of the voters wished to continue the policies of the New Deal.

▪ Who were the four candidates for President in 1948?
▪ What are some reasons Truman was elected in 1948?

In a famous photograph President Truman's glee is evident. He holds the *Chicago Tribune* with its wrong call of the 1948 election. Why did the editor of the *Tribune* print this headline?

THE NEW RED SCARE

Despite his remarkable victory, Truman was unable to get much of his Fair Deal program passed by Congress during his second term. More and more, the Cold War was occupying everyone's attention. A number of events in 1949 and 1950 produced widespread fear of communism similar to the Red Scare of 1919-20. One was the sensational trial of Alger Hiss, the president of the Carnegie Foundation for International Peace. Hiss had been a State Department official before and during World War II. Whittaker Chambers, a former associate, charged that Hiss had been a member of the Communist party and had given him secret State Department documents for the Russians. When Hiss denied this, he was tried and found guilty of lying. He was sentenced to five years in prison.

Next came the arrest and conviction of several Americans who had turned over secret information about the manufacture of atomic bombs to the Russians. People panicked. Some believed that a Russian spy was hiding behind every bush and that the American government was little more than a nest of traitors.

Then came what many called the loss of China to communism. In 1949 Chinese Communists had defeated the armies of General Chiang Kai-shek. Chiang and his supporters were forced to flee to the island of **Formosa** (Taiwan). China, with its hundreds of millions of people, was now part of the communist world.

Culver Pictures

Generalissimo Chiang Kai-shek is astride his Mongolian pony in this photograph from the late 1930s. He led the Chinese government exiled on the island of Formosa. Why had he fled the Chinese mainland?

In the feverish atmosphere caused by the spy trials, many Americans believed that conspiracy lay behind the communists' victory in China. During the Chinese civil war State Department experts had reported that the Chiang government was hopelessly corrupt and inefficient. Now these same experts were accused of being secret communists. The fact that their reports had been accurate did not protect them. If the United States had given more military and economic aid to Chiang, the critics claimed, he could have defeated the Red Chinese forces.

■ What events in 1949 and 1950 made Americans fear a communist conspiracy?

THE RISE OF McCARTHYISM

Early in 1950 a Republican senator, Joseph R. McCarthy of Wisconsin, charged that the State Department was riddled with traitors. He claimed to know the names of 205 communists who held policy-making posts in the department.

This accusation naturally caused a sensation. McCarthy had been almost unknown outside Wisconsin. Suddenly he was making headlines in newspapers all over the country. He quickly took advantage of his new fame. He began to make even more astonishing charges. For example, General Marshall had for a time been a special ambassador to China. Now McCarthy accused him of being part of a conspiracy to turn that country over to the communists.

McCarthy was a total fraud. His charges were false. One of the first Americans to see through McCarthy was Edward R. Murrow, the news commentator who described the Battle of Britain. Still, thousands of Americans assumed that no high public official would make such serious charges without evidence. Politicians often exaggerated. Sometimes they deliberately misled people. But flagrant lying was a different matter. If McCarthy announced that he had a list of 205 or 81 or even 57 communists, people thought surely there must be *some* truth in what he was saying.

In this atmosphere McCarthy did not have to prove his charges. He never showed anyone the 205 names or told anyone where he had obtained this information. The people whom he accused of being "soft on communism" found their careers in government ruined. This was **McCarthyism.** When he attacked other politicians who tried to expose his lies, he was believed, not they. For a time McCarthy became one of the most powerful men in the entire United States.

■ What did Joseph McCarthy charge? Why did many Americans believe Senator McCarthy? What was *McCarthyism?*

Senator Joseph R. McCarthy was photographed in March 1950 as he pulled material from his briefcase for his testimony before the Senate Foreign Relations Subcommittee. How did the public respond to the charges made by the senator?

THE KOREAN WAR

McCarthy's rise came at a time when war broke out in Korea, a nation on the east coast of Asia. Japan had absorbed the Kingdom of Korea in 1910. After World War II Korea was taken from Japan and divided in two. **North Korea** was supported by the Soviet Union, **South Korea** by the United States.

In June 1950 the North Korean army invaded South Korea. President Truman assumed that the Soviet Union was behind the invasion. It is possible that he was incorrect and that the North Koreans acted on their own. Truman had no time to investigate the situation in detail. He decided to apply the containment policy to the situation. In the name of the United Nations he ordered American forces stationed in Japan into Korea. General MacArthur was put in command of the campaign.

The North Koreans had the advantage of surprise. By September they had conquered nearly all of South Korea. Then the UN army, which consisted mainly of Americans and South Koreans, managed to check their advance. Next General MacArthur planned and executed a brilliant counterattack. He landed troops at **Inchon,** far behind the North Korean lines. The tide of battle turned swiftly. The North Koreans, attacked from two sides, retreated. Soon MacArthur's troops had driven the invaders out of South Korea.

"American Caesar" is the name one biographer gave to five-star general Douglas MacArthur. He accepted the surrender of Japan and headed the U.S. occupation in 1945. When President Truman recalled him from Korea, he told an emotional Congress that "old soldiers never die." Why was he ordered to Korea?

In November 1952 this cartoon was published in *The New York Times* to comment on the growing friendship of Russia and China. Stalin leans over the shoulder of Mao Tse-Tung to play against George F. Kennan, the U.S. ambassador to Russia at the time. "Chinese Checkers — We Win or We Don't Play" is the title given by the cartoonist. What role did Russia play in the Korean War?

United Press International

Atop "Old Baldy," one of the barren sites of the Korean War, this U.S. soldier surveys the waste of war. What action caused the Chinese to enter the Korean War?

THE KOREAN WAR 1950-53

▨ Smallest area held by U.N. forces, Sept. 1950

— Farthest advance of U.N. forces, Nov. 1950

— Armistice line, July 1953

→ Communist forces

→ U.N. forces

However, instead of stopping at this point, MacArthur obtained permission from Truman to invade North Korea. By November his troops were approaching the **Yalu River,** the boundary between North Korea and China. This action caused the Chinese to enter the war. Striking suddenly and with tremendous force, they routed MacArthur's army, driving it back into South Korea. Finally, in the spring of 1951, the battle line was stabilized along the original border between the two Koreas.

MacArthur then requested permission to bomb China and to use anticommunist Chinese troops from Taiwan in Korea. President Truman refused to allow this expansion of the war. Still, MacArthur continued to argue for his plan. Truman was forced to remove him from command. The fighting in Korea continued.

The **Korean War** added to the public's worry about communist spying and therefore to the influence of Senator McCarthy. Early in the war Congress passed the **McCarran Internal Security Act.** This law required all communist organizations to register and open their financial records to the government. A special board was set up to investigate organizations that might be subversive—that is, out to overthrow the government. By 1952 Senator McCarthy was describing the Roosevelt and Truman administrations as "20 years of treason."

▪ What provoked the Korean War? How did Truman respond?
▪ What was General MacArthur's strategy at Inchon? What was his fate at the Yalu River?
▪ Why did Truman remove MacArthur from command?
▪ What was the McCarran Act?

THE ELECTION OF 1952

Although the Twenty-second Amendment did not apply to him, President Truman decided not to seek reelection in 1952. Instead he gave his support at the Democratic convention to Governor Adlai Stevenson of Illinois. Stevenson was an excellent speaker, witty and thoughtful at the same time. He had the courage to attack McCarthy head-on during the campaign, something few Democrats dared do.

Dwight D. Eisenhower Presidential Library   Katherine Young

Dwight D. Eisenhower and Adlai E. Stevenson were the candidates for President in the 1952 election. One was a war hero, the other a hero to American intellectuals. What stand did Stevenson take on McCarthy?

Yet Stevenson had little chance of being elected. Many people thought he was too intellectual—an egghead. More important, a majority of the voters believed that it was "time for a change." After all, the nation had not elected a Republican President since Hoover's victory in 1928. The Republican candidate was Dwight D. Eisenhower, the outstanding hero of World War II.

Aside from his fame as a general, Eisenhower had the advantage of never having been involved in party politics. Thousands of normally Democratic citizens could vote for him without feeling that they were voting for a Republican. As a matter of fact, before deciding to back Stevenson, President Truman had tried to persuade Eisenhower to run on the Democratic ticket!

In addition, Eisenhower's warm, easygoing personality appealed to millions. The campaign slogan "I like Ike" perfectly expressed the general reaction. Liberals of both parties who were worried about Senator McCarthy voted for Eisenhower in hopes that he would be able to silence or control the senator. Further, Eisenhower announced during the campaign that if elected he would go to Korea to negotiate a settlement of the war there. Any last doubts about his victory evaporated. Eisenhower won by more than 6 million votes.

Dwight D. Eisenhower
Presidential Library

When asked how he felt after being so badly beaten, Stevenson said that he felt like a small boy who had stubbed his toe—too grown-up to cry but too hurt to laugh. These were the same words used to concede defeat in 1858 by another candidate from Illinois, Abraham Lincoln.

▪ Why did Adlai Stevenson have little chance of defeating Dwight Eisenhower in the 1952 election?

In this portrait John Foster Dulles holds a copy of his pamphlet "The Threat of Red Asia" while pointing to Asia on the globe. He served as Secretary of State for Eisenhower. What name was given to his policy to contain communism?

EISENHOWER'S FOREIGN POLICY

President Eisenhower made no basic changes in the containment policy. But he was under great pressure from conservative Republicans to reduce government spending. He and his Secretary of State, John Foster Dulles, developed a strategy called **massive retaliation.** In simple terms, massive retaliation meant threatening to respond to Soviet aggression anywhere in the world by dropping nuclear bombs on Moscow and other Russian cities. It meant being willing to go "to the brink" of all-out war to contain communism. This policy came to be known as **brinkmanship.**

Atom bombs were replacing "what used to be called conventional weapons," Dulles said. There was no need, he argued, to spend huge amounts on tanks, battleships, and other expensive "military hardware."

Dulles's policy was pure bluff. By 1953 both Russia and the United States had made hydrogen bombs hundreds of times more deadly than the bomb that destroyed Hiroshima. Neither Dulles nor Eisenhower ever seriously considered dropping a nuclear bomb on anyone. It would have been suicidal to do so because a nuclear strike would almost surely have caused a world catastrophe.

The warlike language Dulles used tended to keep Cold War tensions high at a time when the Russians were taking a less aggressive position. Joseph Stalin died in 1953. The new Russian leaders claimed to favor "peaceful coexistence and competition" with the western nations. This gave them an advantage in the worldwide competition to influence public opinion, for Dulles seemed unable to back off from his policy of brinkmanship.

The Eisenhower-Dulles foreign policy also increased Senator McCarthy's influence in the United States because it focused attention on the danger of a clash with the communist powers. The popular President Eisenhower detested McCarthy and his tactics, but he was unwilling to criticize the senator openly.

Eisenhower stiffened the already harsh loyalty program that Truman had set up to clean out possible communist sympathizers in the government. Employees found to be "security risks" were to be fired even if they had not actually done anything wrong. For ex-

Robert Phillips, Black Star

ample, persons who had been convicted of crimes in the past might be classified as security risks. The idea was that communist agents might threaten to expose such people's pasts unless they turned over secret information. Under this program about 3,000 employees were fired. An even larger number resigned. Yet almost none of these people had actually done anything disloyal.

McCarthy finally went too far. Early in 1954 one of his assistants was drafted into the army. McCarthy tried to get him excused from service, but he was without success. He then announced an investigation of "subversive activities" in the army. These **Army-McCarthy Hearings** were televised. They destroyed McCarthy completely. Day after day the emptiness of his charges and his snarling cruelty and insensitivity were seen by millions of viewers. The people he attacked were aware that they were being watched and judged by this enormous audience. They *had* to fight back. When they fought and survived, McCarthy's spell was broken.

The hearings produced no specific results. Later, in August 1954, the Senate voted to investigate McCarthy's behavior. In December the Senate voted to censure him. By a vote of 67 to 22 the Senate resolved "that the conduct of the Senator from Wisconsin, Mr. McCarthy, is contrary to senatorial traditions and is hereby condemned." McCarthy's power to do harm was gone. He remained in the Senate until his death in 1957, ignored if not forgotten.

■ How did the Eisenhower-Dulles foreign policy tend to prolong the cold war?

During the Army-McCarthy Hearings of 1954 Joseph Welch, seated, who represented the army, asked, "Have you no decency left, sir?" McCarthy, standing, made reckless accusations but never proved his charges. How was his spell broken?

READING PRACTICE
IN SOCIAL STUDIES

Organization by Generalizations

Historians sometimes organize their information by making *generalizations*. These are "usually" or "most of the time" statements formed from particular facts or data. For the differences between facts, opinions, and generalizations, turn back to the Reading Practice which appears on page 795.

A generalization is only as strong as the details which support it. For example, earlier in this chapter, on page 812, you read:

In Europe the change from war to peace had not been easy.

Most people would readily agree with this statement. But it becomes a sounder generalization when these details are added:

Thirty million Europeans had been killed. The loss of so many potential workers was a terrible blow to the economies of every nation. More millions were homeless and hungry. Such people could not produce very effectively. In every country railroads had been wrecked, bridges blown up, factories smashed. About 25 per cent of all the wealth of Great Britain was destroyed during the war. In Germany there were shortages of everything. A pack of American cigarettes cost as much as a German laborer could earn in a month.

The original generalization is well supported by facts—casualty figures, examples of the destruction of war, percentages, and the small detail which compares the cost of a pack of American cigarettes to a German worker's monthly wage.

There are three main types of generalizations. First, a generalization may be a definition. For example, on page 816 you read this statement:

Rivalry between the communist and capitalist worlds grew steadily more intense. Neither side dared risk open warfare in the atomic age. Instead they waged what was called the **Cold War.**

From these sentences a generalization may be formed: "The Cold War was a political struggle, not a shooting match."

A second type of generalization is a broad statement. On page 813 you read:

The Truman Doctrine was popular in the United States because it appealed to both liberals and conservatives.

This generalization is supported by specifics:

Liberals liked the idea of helping the peoples of other countries defend their independence and rebuild their war-torn economies. Conservatives liked the idea of resisting communism and thus preserving the free enterprise system. Nearly everyone took pride in the great influence and prestige that came to the United States in other parts of the world.

A third type of generalization is the conclusion. You read on page 812:

The containment policy worked well for the United States.

This generalization seems a valid conclusion because it is backed by facts:

It prevented a major war. It enabled the western European nations to rebuild their economies and preserve their democratic political systems.

Read the section "Eisenhower and the Cold War" on page 827. Then answer the following questions.
1. Which type of generalization is "President Eisenhower avoided military solutions to international problems"?
2. Which details support the opening generalization in the first paragraph?
3. Which sentence in the second paragraph supports the opening generalization?
4. Which details in the next three paragraphs support the opening generalization?
5. Which generalization opens "Eisenhower's Domestic Policies" on page 828?

EISENHOWER AND THE COLD WAR

President Eisenhower avoided military solutions to international problems. Dulles had spoken of "liberating" the people of East Europe who had been forced to accept communist governments after World War II. There were revolts against these governments in **East Germany** in 1953 and in **Hungary** in 1956. But Eisenhower did not intervene.

When the French were being driven out of **Vietnam** in southeast Asia by local communists in 1954, Eisenhower rejected the suggestion that the air force bomb communist positions. Instead the United States supported the division of Vietnam into a northern, procommunist section and a southern, pro-Western government.

Another example of Eisenhower's restraint occurred in 1956 in the Middle East. In 1948 the state of **Israel,** which had formerly been the British mandate, or colony, of Palestine, declared its independence. Many Jews who had somehow escaped Hitler's Holocaust flocked to Israel after the war to start a new life. So did thousands of Jews from all over the world, many of them former residents of the United States.

However, the Arab nations surrounding Israel took up arms to prevent what they considered an invasion of their territory. A series of wars resulted. Although outnumbered, the Israelis overcame the Arabs. Nearly 1 million who had lived in the area when it was Palestine fled to neighboring regions. They then conducted raids and terrorist attacks on Israel, determined to recover their homeland and drive the Jews from the Middle East.

A crisis erupted in 1956 when Egypt stepped up its raids against Israel and seized control of the **Suez Canal,** which was an international waterway. Israel fought back, joined by Great Britain and France, who wanted to regain the canal.

Eisenhower faced a serious dilemma. The United States had supported the independence of Israel from the start. Most Americans felt that the Jews were entitled to a country of their own after their terrible suffering during World War II. In addition, Great Britain and France were also close allies of the United States. But Eisenhower objected to their using force to regain the canal. He demanded that the invaders pull back. So did the Russians, who threatened all-out war. As a result the allies withdrew, and Egypt kept control of the Suez Canal.

By 1954 Nikita Khrushchev had become the head of the Russian government. Khrushchev was a difficult person to understand. At one moment he was full of talk about peace, at the next he was threatening to explode nuclear bombs. One historian has described Khrushchev as a mixture of Santa Claus and a "wild, angry Russian bear."

During the Hungarian uprising of 1956 these freedom fighters tore Russian stars from buildings and blocked tanks in the streets of Budapest. Why did Hungarians revolt in 1956?

827

Eisenhower and the heads of the British and French governments met with Khrushchev in Geneva, Switzerland, in July 1955. They accomplished little at this **Geneva Summit Meeting,** but their discussions were friendly. Experts spoke hopefully of a possible end of the Cold War. Yet, little more than a year later, Khrushchev threatened to bomb London and Paris if Great Britain and France did not pull back from their war with Egypt over the Suez Canal.

■ What was Eisenhower's response to the revolts in East Germany and Hungary? To the fall of the French in Vietnam? To the battle for the Suez Canal?

Oveta Culp Hobby served as head of the WAC's. This is her portrait in uniform in 1943 Brass buttons on her collars show the head of Athena, goddess of peace. To what post was Hobby appointed by Eisenhower?

EISENHOWER'S DOMESTIC POLICIES

President Eisenhower stood halfway between the conservative domestic policies of the Republicans of the 1920s and the liberal policies of the New Deal. He was eager to reduce government spending. He favored measures designed to help private enterprise. He hoped to turn over many federal programs to the individual states.

Yet Eisenhower was unwilling to do away with most of the social welfare legislation of the 1930s. He agreed that it was the government's job to try to regulate economic growth and stimulate the economy during hard times.

While Eisenhower was President, 11 million more workers were brought into the social security and unemployment system. The minimum wage was raised. A start was made in providing public housing for low-income families. Eisenhower also established the new Cabinet-level **Department of Health, Education, and Welfare.** The first head of this important department was Oveta Culp Hobby, the former director of the Women's Army Corps.

Although Eisenhower genuinely wished to hold federal spending to a minimum, he approved two very large new projects. One was the construction of the **St. Lawrence Seaway,** which deepened the channel of the St. Lawrence River so that ocean-going ships could sail directly into the Great Lakes. The other was the **Federal Highway Act** of 1956. This measure authorized the construction of an enormous network of superhighways, the **Interstate System.** Eisenhower considered both these projects necessary for defense in case of a war.

While Eisenhower was President, the last of the 50 states were added to the Union. **Alaska** became a state in January 1959 and **Hawaii** was admitted in August of the same year.

■ How was Eisenhower's domestic policy conservative? How was it liberal?
■ Which two huge federal projects did Eisenhower approve?

BUILDING SKILLS
IN SOCIAL STUDIES

Our Changing Flag

Throughout this book the American flag appears frequently. Indeed, the 48-star flag, which flew longer than any other in our history, is on the cover.

During the American Revolution patriots had many flags. One of the most famous, shown below, grew from Benjamin Franklin's advice to the colonists in 1745 to "Join, or Die." (See page 85.) He illustrated this advice with a rattlesnake cut into eight pieces. An early flag showed the rattlesnake, united and ready to attack, with the motto "Don't Tread on Me."

In 1777 a request came to the Congress assembled in Philadelphia from the Indian Nation for "an American flag." With this request came "three strings of wampum" to cover the cost. Eleven days later Congress passed a Flag Resolution: *Resolved That the Flag of the united states be 13 stripes alternate red and white, that the Union be 13 stars white in a blue field representing a new constellation."* One version of this flag is shown below, another on pages 171 and 200. On page 277 is the 15-star flag that inspired our national anthem. The 34-star flag that flew at the beginning of the Civil War is shown below, and the flag of the Confederacy is on page 455. On page 801 is the famous flag that flew over Iwo Jima. With the admission of Alaska the 49-star flag was created in 1959, and our present 50-star flag first flew on July 4, 1960, after Hawaii became a state. In all, there have been 27 official United States flags since 1777.

The state flags of Texas and California appear on pages 356 and 358. Prepare a report on your state flag. Use reference books or write the office of the secretary of state for the history and meaning of your state flag.

c. 1775   June 14, 1777   July 4, 1861

July 4, 1912   July 4, 1959   July 4, 1960

Earl Warren governed California for ten years before Eisenhower named him Chief Justice. Many landmark decisions were handed down by the Warren Court. Which is today most famous and why?

SCHOOL DESEGREGATION

In 1956 Eisenhower again defeated Adlai Stevenson for President. His margin was even larger than in 1952. Clearly a majority of the voters approved of his middle-of-the-road philosophy.

Yet Eisenhower's most important action during his first term produced radical social changes. Eisenhower himself strongly disapproved of some of these changes. No better modern example exists of how difficult it is to understand the historical significance of events until long after they have occurred.

The action in question was Eisenhower's appointment of Governor Earl Warren of California as Chief Justice of the United States in 1953. Warren had served three terms as governor. He had also run for Vice President in 1948 on the ticket with Thomas E. Dewey.

Although Warren had never been a judge before, he quickly became the most important member of the Supreme Court. Under his leadership the Court became a solid unit, at least where civil rights cases were concerned.

In 1954 this **Warren Court** made one of the most important decisions in the history of the Supreme Court. It decided in the case known as *Brown v. Board of Education of Topeka, Kansas* that it was unconstitutional for states to maintain separate schools for black and white children. This case overturned the "separate but equal" doctrine established in the case of *Plessy v. Ferguson* back in 1896.

The Court ruled that a separate education was by its very nature an unequal education. This would be true even if the conditions in the separate schools were identical. Segregation, in other words, suggests that the people kept out are inferior. As Chief Justice Warren wrote, segregation had harmful effects on all children, white as well as black.

In 1954 all the southern states had separate school systems for whites and blacks. Many northern schools were also segregated in fact if not by law. Putting the **Brown v. Board of Education** decision into effect was bound to be time consuming and difficult. Therefore, a year later the Court announced that the states must go ahead "with all deliberate speed." This actually meant that they could change slowly. Still, they must begin to change promptly and move steadily toward single, racially integrated school systems.

The *Brown* decision was a unanimous one. This was extremely important. If even one of the nine justices had written a dissenting opinion arguing against the ruling, opponents of desegregation could have used his reasoning to justify resisting the law.

Even in the face of a unanimous Court, many southern whites were unwilling to accept school integration, no matter how slowly carried out. There was talk of "massive resistance." This was not mere talk as in the case of John Foster Dulles's "massive retaliation."

Burt Glinn, Magnum

In 1957 the school board of **Little Rock,** Arkansas, following a court order, voted to admit nine black students to a white high school. Governor Orville Faubus then called out the Arkansas National Guard to *prevent* the children from entering the white school.

President Eisenhower was not personally opposed to school integration. He believed, however, that it was "just plain *nuts*" to force white parents to send their children to integrated schools. But Faubus's act was a direct challenge to federal authority. The President promptly sent 10,000 soldiers to Little Rock. With this force behind them, the black children were admitted to the school. Photographs and motion pictures showed the nine, neatly dressed black youngsters being taunted by crowds of angry grownups or walking beside army paratroopers in battle dress. These scenes had a powerful impact on millions of people, southerners as well as northerners.

President Eisenhower ordered U.S. troops to escort these young black students into Central High School in Little Rock, Arkansas, in 1957. What effect did photographs such as this one have on the American public in the late 1950s?

- What did the Warren Court rule in *Brown v. Board of Education?* Why was it important that the decision be unanimous?
- How did Eisenhower respond to the crisis at Little Rock?

831

THE STRUGGLE FOR EQUAL RIGHTS

Black Americans had been fighting for their rights long before *Brown v. Board of Education*. After the Supreme Court declared school segregation unconstitutional, blacks began to speak out even more vigorously against all forms of racial prejudice. In December 1955 Rosa Parks, a black woman in Montgomery, Alabama, was arrested because she refused to give up her seat on a city bus to a white man. Her arrest led the blacks of Montgomery to refuse to ride the buses until the rule requiring blacks to sit in the rear was changed. This boycott was a heavy financial loss for the city's bus system.

Rosa Parks sits at the front of a bus in Montgomery, Alabama, in December 1956. One year earlier she was arrested for refusing to give up her seat to a white man. How was her victory won?

United Press International

The **Montgomery Bus Strike** lasted for nearly a year. It ended with a victory for the blacks. The Supreme Court ruled that the Alabama segregation laws were unconstitutional. It was in leading the strike that a young black clergyman, Martin Luther King, Jr., first became well known. Throughout the long contest he advised the blacks to avoid violence no matter how badly provoked by the whites.

King believed in nonviolent resistance for basically religious reasons. He argued that love was a more effective weapon than hate or force. There were also practical reasons for nonviolence. Blacks were a minority in the United States. To obtain fair treatment, they needed the help of white moderates. They were more likely to get that help by appeals to reason and decency than by force.

By the end of Eisenhower's second term real progress had been made. School desegregation was moving ahead slowly. Other forms of segregation were being ended. In 1960 blacks began an attempt to desegregate lunch counters and similar facilities by staging **sit-ins.** A group would enter a place that served only whites, sit down quietly, and refuse to leave. They were either served or arrested. In either case their actions attracted wide attention and strengthened the drive for fair treatment.

New black organizations had sprung up by 1960 to organize and direct the campaign for equal rights. Martin Luther King, Jr. founded the **Southern Christian Leadership Conference** shortly after the successful Montgomery bus strike. An older organization, the **Congress of Racial Equality** (CORE) and the new **Student Nonviolent Coordinating Council** (SNCC) were two other such groups.

- What prompted the Montgomery Bus Strike? What was the outcome?
- Why did Martin Luther King, Jr., argue for nonviolence?

THE ELECTION OF 1960

In 1960 the Republicans nominated Richard M. Nixon for President. Nixon was Eisenhower's Vice President. Before that he had been a congressman and senator from California.

In Congress Nixon had been a leading communist-hunter. Long before most people took the charges against Alger Hiss seriously, Nixon was convinced of Hiss's guilt. He worked closely with Senator McCarthy in his search for traitors in the government. He was almost as reckless in his charges as McCarthy. While running for Vice President in 1952, for example, Nixon claimed that Adlai Stevenson was "soft on communism."

Nixon was a clever politician, but victory was more important to him than fair play. He was an intelligent and hardworking legislator. He had sympathized with the civil rights movement, and he strongly supported President Truman's foreign policy. While Vice President he had toned down his talk about traitors in the government. He tried to act more like a statesman. This "new Nixon" persuaded Eisenhower and other Republican leaders to back him for President.

Still, many people did not trust Nixon. A joke of the day displayed his photograph over the caption "Would you buy a used car from this man?" Nixon tried hard to explain his controversial reputation. "I believe in the battle," he said. "It's always been there, wherever I go." He wrote that his life had been a series of crises. In each one, he claimed, he had triumphed by being "cool and calm" and working hard.

Martin Luther King, Jr., is seen here marching in Montgomery in 1956. He became the most famous black leader in the United States, winner of the Nobel Peace Prize in 1964. What organization did King found after the Montgomery Bus Strike?

Crowds pressed forward to see John F. Kennedy when he campaigned for President in 1960. Both Kennedy and Richard Nixon traveled extensively between Labor Day, the traditional campaign kickoff day, and Election Day. What were the electoral totals for Kennedy and Nixon?

The Democratic candidate for President in 1960 was Senator John F. Kennedy of Massachusetts. Kennedy was young, handsome, intelligent, and rich. He was a war hero, seriously injured in a rescue mission in the Pacific. He was a Pulitzer prize-winning author and a shrewd politician. And he was an excellent campaigner. Kennedy appealed to liberals because he seemed imaginative and forward looking. Many conservatives supported him too because his policies were moderate.

Kennedy's major handicap was his Catholic religion. Al Smith's crushing defeat by Herbert Hoover in 1928 suggested that the anti-Catholic prejudices of voters in normally Democratic states might be difficult to overcome.

During the campaign Kennedy argued that Eisenhower had been too cautious and conservative. The economy was not growing rapidly enough. The nation needed new ideas. He called his program the **New Frontier.** He would open up new fields for development by being imaginative and vigorous. Nixon, on the other hand, defended Eisenhower's record and promised to go ahead along the same lines. In the election the popular vote was extremly close. Kennedy won by only 100,000 votes out of a total of more than 68 million. But in the electoral vote his margin was 303 to 219.

- What were Nixon's strengths and weaknesses as a candidate for President in 1960? What were Kennedy's strengths and weaknesses?
- What did Kennedy mean by the New Frontier?

834

CHAPTER 27 REVIEW

Identification
Tell briefly why each of the following persons, terms, or events is important.

1. Harry S. Truman
2. Joseph Stalin
3. George C. Marshall
4. Henry A. Wallace
5. Joseph R. McCarthy
6. Dwight D. Eisenhower
7. John Foster Dulles
8. Martin Luther King, Jr.
9. United Nations
10. Yalta Conference
11. Fair Deal
12. Twenty-second Amendment
13. Taft-Hartley Act
14. Iron Curtain
15. Truman Doctrine
16. Marshall Plan
17. Berlin Airlift
18. NATO
19. Cold War
20. *Brown v. Board of Education*

Understanding American History

1. What major decision about Poland did the Big Three make at Yalta? How did Russia come to dominate Poland?
2. Explain why the depression feared by Truman did not occur after World War II.
3. How were the Twenty-second Amendment and the Taft-Hartley Act examples of the Republican reaction against the New Deal?
4. Explain how the Truman Doctrine and the Marshall Plan were intended to stop the spread of communism.
5. Describe the three-way split in the Democratic party in the election of 1948.
6. What is meant by McCarthyism? How did events of 1949–50 help create an atmosphere favorable for McCarthyism?
7. Explain the U.S. foreign policies of containment and massive retaliation. How did they help prolong the Cold War?
8. Why did President Truman order U.S. troops into Korea? Why did he remove General MacArthur from command?
9. What were two major transportation programs carried out during the Eisenhower Presidency?
10. Explain the case of *Brown v. Board of Education.* What did the Supreme Court direct in its unanimous decision?

Activities

1. Prepare a large version of the map on page 816 to show Europe during the Cold War. Use the map to illustrate a series of oral reports on major events and policies of the Cold War. Topics should include the Marshall Plan, containment, Churchill's Iron Curtain speech, the Berlin Airlift, uprisings in East Germany and Hungary, the establishment of NATO and of the Warsaw Pact, the Suez Crisis, the brinkmanship of John Foster Dulles, and the 1955 Geneva Summit Conference.
2. Use historical imagination to write a thank you letter from a Berliner for the airlift of 1948–49.
3. Recordings are available of the Army-McCarthy Hearings of 1954. Listen to them in class and discuss McCarthyism.
4. Prepare a report on the life of Martin Luther King, Jr., and his long struggle for equal rights.
5. In your library use periodicals and reference books to find out how the Security Council of the United Nations is conducted. Have 15 classmates represent the members of the council and discuss a matter of current world interest. Try to bring the matter to some resolution. The permanent council members are the U.S., China, Great Britain, France, and the U.S.S.R. The other ten members in your discussion should represent five African and Asian countries, one from Eastern Europe, two from Latin America, and two from Western Europe.

CHAPTER 27 TEST

Matching (45 points)
Number your paper 1–15 and match the name or term in the second column with its description in the first column.

1. Founder of the Southern Christian Leadership Conference and leader of American blacks
2. Eisenhower's Vice President and a candidate for President in 1960
3. International organization founded to promote world peace and cooperation
4. U.S foreign policy that threatened to bomb Russia if the U.S.S.R. violated peace anywhere in the world
5. Winner of the 1960 Presidential election
6. Dictator of the U.S.S.R. during World War II
7. Treaty signed by eight noncommunist nations to form a unified military force
8. The political and economic struggle after World War II between the U.S. and the U.S.S.R.
9. Senator from Wisconsin who claimed that communists had infiltrated the U.S. government
10. President who approved the St Lawrence Seaway and the Federal Highway Act
11. Truman's plan of reforms, largely rejected by Congress
12. Outlawed closed shops and provided for an 80-day cooling off period when strikes threatened the national interest
13. Meeting of the Big Three near the end of the war
14. Elected President in 1948 in a four-way race
15. American assistance to European nations which were rebuilding their economies after the war

a. Yalta Conference
b. Fair Deal
c. Joseph Stalin
d. Harry S. Truman
e. Marshall Plan
f. NATO
g. Martin Luther King, Jr
h. John F. Kennedy
i. Richard M. Nixon
j. Dwight D. Eisenhower
k. Massive retaliation
l. Joseph R McCarthy
m. United Nations
n. Taft-Hartley Act
o. Cold War

Chronology (25 points)
Number your paper 16- 20 and place the following events in order by numbering 1 for the first. 2 for the second, and so on.
16. The Supreme Court orders school desegregation.
17. John F. Kennedy is elected President.
18. The United Nations is formed.
19. The Marshall Plan is proposed.
20. The Korean War begins.

Essay (30 points)
In a brief essay explain the mood and some of the policies of the Cold War. Plan your essay by preparing a simple outline.

UNIT NINE TEST

Multiple Choice (20 points)
Number your paper 1–5 and write the letter of the phrase that best completes each sentence.

1. Passage of the neutrality acts of the 1930s was an example of
   a. The Big Red Scare.
   b. fear of totalitarianism.
   c. America's isolationist attitude.
   d. the cash-and-carry policy.
2. One effect of World War II on farmers and factory workers was
   a. greater demand for their products.
   b. increased discrimination against blacks.
   c. more competition with Europe.
   d. higher unemployment

3. Passage of the Twenty-second Amendment and the Taft Hartley Act are examples of
   a. attempts to end racial discrimination.
   b. Republican reaction to the New Deal
   c. fear of communism.
   d. McCarthyism
4. The Marshall Plan was an attempt to rebuild European economies in order to
   a. stop a Nazi takeover of Europe.
   b. provide a market for American goods
   c. strengthen the League of Nations.
   d. prevent the spread of communism.
5. A major effect of the Supreme Court's ruling in *Brown v. Board of Education* was
   a. greater demand for racial equality.
   b. the ending of the Cold War.
   c. increased segregation in public schools.
   d. Eisenhower's reelection as President

Matching (25 points)
Number your paper 6–10 and match the person in the second column with the description in the first column.

6. Leader in the fight for racial equality
7. U.S. commander in Europe during World War II
8. English prime minister, one of the Big Three
9. Only U.S. President elected more than twice
10. U.S. President who ended World War II

a. Winston Churchill
b. Harry S. Truman
c. Dwight D. Eisenhower
d. Martin Luther King, Jr.
e. Franklin D. Roosevelt

Chronological Order (25 points)
Number your paper 11–15 and place the following events in order by numbering 1 for the first, 2 for the second, and so on.

11. The atomic bomb is dropped on Hiroshima and Nagasaki.
12. Germany invades Poland.
13. The Supreme Court rules in *Brown v. Board of Education.*
14. The Cold War begins.
15. The Japanese bomb Pearl Harbor.

Essay (30 points)
Write a brief essay on *one* of the following topics. Explain why relations between the U.S. and Russia changed from friendship during World War II to suspicion after the war, *or* Discuss one foreign and one domestic problem that the U.S. faced following World War II. Explain how the U.S. attempted to solve each problem.

UNIT TEN

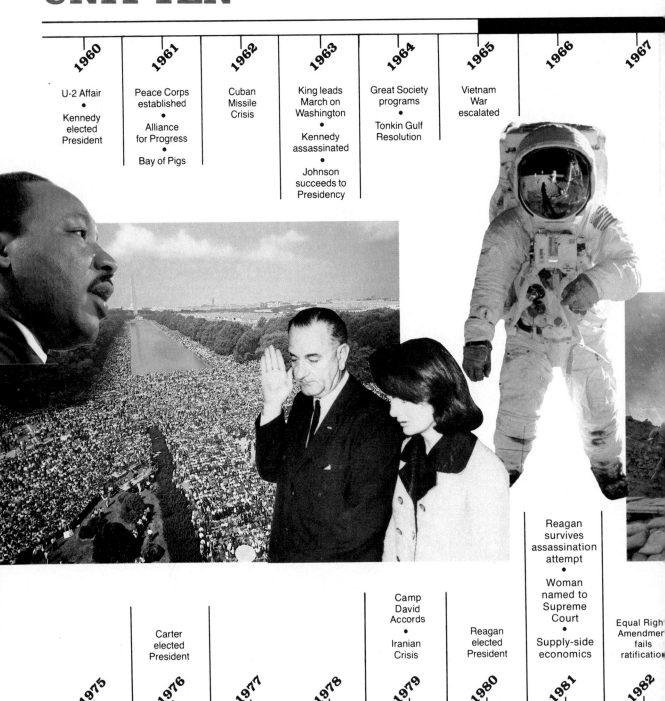

1960
- U-2 Affair
- Kennedy elected President

1961
- Peace Corps established
- Alliance for Progress
- Bay of Pigs

1962
- Cuban Missile Crisis

1963
- King leads March on Washington
- Kennedy assassinated
- Johnson succeeds to Presidency

1964
- Great Society programs
- Tonkin Gulf Resolution

1965
- Vietnam War escalated

1966

1967

1975

1976
- Carter elected President

1977

1978

1979
- Camp David Accords
- Iranian Crisis

1980
- Reagan elected President

1981
- Reagan survives assassination attempt
- Woman named to Supreme Court
- Supply-side economics

1982
- Equal Rights Amendment fails ratification

For three days the world held its breath. Then Khrushchev agreed to remove the missiles. Kennedy won a great personal victory. More important, the possibility of a nuclear war between the United States and the Soviet Union seemed less likely. Both sides had finally come to the brink that John Foster Dulles had foreseen but never actually faced in the 1950s. Both sides had stepped back rather than risk the destruction of the whole world.

Following the Cuban Missile Crisis, a **"hot line"** telephone connection was set up between Washington and Moscow. In any future crisis American and Russian leaders could talk to each other. In the summer of 1963 the two nations took a small first step toward disarmament. They agreed to stop testing nuclear weapons above ground, where the explosions would release dangerous radioactivity into the atmosphere.

- What provoked the Cuban Missile Crisis? What was Kennedy's response? What was Khrushchev's response?
- What small steps toward peace were taken by the United States and the Soviet Union after the Cuban Missile Crisis?

KENNEDY IS ASSASSINATED

After his success in dealing with the missile crisis, Kennedy seemed sure of being reelected in 1964. Nevertheless, he was not able to get Congress to enact much of his domestic program into law. For example, in 1963 he came out for a large tax cut. Reducing taxes would stimulate the economy, he claimed. If people paid lower taxes, they would have more money left to spend on goods. Their purchases would cause producers to increase output. More workers would be hired. Unemployment would go down. Personal and business incomes would rise.

In the long run, the President argued, the lower tax rates would actually produce more income for the government. But conservative members of Congress in both parties objected to lowering taxes while the government's budget remained in the red.

Kennedy also introduced a strong civil rights bill in 1963. His proposal outlawed racial discrimination in all places serving the public, such as hotels, restaurants, and theaters. It too failed to pass Congress.

On November 22, 1963, President Kennedy paid a visit to Dallas, Texas. While riding through the city in an open car, he was shot dead by an assassin. The deed was done so quickly that onlookers scarcely saw the President slump into his wife's lap. The governor of Texas, riding in the front of the car, was wounded by the assassin. Vice President Johnson, two cars behind in the motorcade, was safe. He was sworn in as President two hours later on *Air Force 1*

This haunting picture from the 1960s is at once sorrowful and reassuring. Lyndon B. Johnson takes the oath of office as President from Judge Sarah T. Hughes with his wife, Lady Bird, to his right and Jacqueline Kennedy on his left. Only two hours earlier the young First Lady witnessed her husband's assassination. Now she witnesses this solemn and orderly transfer of power, the iron test of a democracy. What fate befell the President's assassin?

as it carried the slain President's body home for burial in Arlington National Cemetery. Millions saw the orderly transfer of power on television, as well as the stately funeral procession of world heads of state led by the President's widow Jacqueline.

The assassin was Lee Harvey Oswald, a mysterious figure who, it turned out, had at one time lived in Russia. Before Oswald could be properly questioned, *he* was murdered while being transferred from one jail to another. This amazing incident caused many people to believe that Oswald had been killed to keep him from confessing that he had acted for a group of powerful people. There have been many investigations of the assassination and many theories put forth to explain it. But no evidence has ever been found that proves that Oswald did not act entirely on his own. The full truth about this tragedy will never be known.

- What was the fate of President Kennedy's domestic program in 1963?
- How was the orderly transfer of Presidential power demonstrated after the assassination of President Kennedy?

THE JOHNSON PRESIDENCY

Lyndon B. Johnson had grown up in the west Texas ranch country. Before becoming Vice President, he had served for many years in the House and Senate. A lifelong Democrat, he had worshiped Franklin Roosevelt and admired Harry Truman. Yet he had been able to cooperate with President Eisenhower in most legislative matters.

In personality and style Johnson resembled Andrew Jackson more than any other President. He was both warm hearted and hot tempered. He was extremely hardworking and energetic. Johnson seemed to be everywhere—inspecting offices, signing bills, greeting tourists, settling disputes. One Christmas Eve his helicopter even swooped into the garden of the Vatican in Rome. The President had come to present a gift to the Pope. Inside the papal chambers Johnson proudly revealed a plastic bust of himself as President.

Johnson was determined to get Kennedy's program adopted by Congress. This would honor Kennedy's memory and establish Johnson's own reputation. His long service in Congress was an enormous advantage. So was the general feeling that Kennedy's plans should be enacted as a kind of memorial.

President Johnson would bully, wheedle, and bargain. He had a way of brushing aside or smothering other people's objections and doubts. He would call in a hesitating lawmaker, grab him by the lapels of his suitcoat, and say, "Come, let us reason together." More often than not the legislator would do what Johnson wanted, moved by a combination of awe and fear.

Wide World Photos

Lyndon Johnson was perhaps the most physical of Presidents. He poked and prodded to find every person's soft spots. But he was genuinely friendly and a master politician. Here he is seen at a banquet with Congressman John Rooney of Brooklyn. What made Johnson so persuasive?

This young VISTA worker, like her Peace Corps counterpart on page 840, is living with disadvantaged Americans. Here she visits with Navajo children in Arizona. What were some other programs of the Economic Opportunity Act?

As a result Congress passed in 1964 a bill reducing taxes by over $10 billion and a **Civil Rights Act** prohibiting racial discrimination in restaurants, theaters, hotels, hospitals, and public facilities of all sorts. This Civil Rights Act also made it easier and safer for southern blacks to register and vote.

Congress also passed the **Economic Opportunity Act** of 1964, at Johnson's urging. This law sought to help poor people improve their ability to earn money. It attacked the problem at every level. It set up the **Head Start** program to give extra help to disadvantaged children even before they were old enough to go to school. There was a **Job Corps** to train school dropouts as well as an adult education program. The law also founded **VISTA,** a domestic parallel to the overseas Peace Corps.

- For what reasons was Johnson determined to get Kennedy's program adopted by Congress?
- What did the Civil Rights Act of 1964 provide?
- What was the Economic Opportunity Act of 1964?

THE GREAT SOCIETY

Lyndon Johnson easily won the Democratic nomination for President in 1964. His Republican opponent was Senator Barry Goldwater of Arizona. Even people who disliked Goldwater's ideas tended to like him personally. He was sincere and frank, not the kind of politician who adjusts what he says to the mood and prejudices of the voters. Goldwater was extremely conservative. He spoke critically of such basic policies as the social security system. He favored selling all the facilities of the Tennessee Valley Authority to private companies. He wanted to cut back or eliminate many other long-established functions of the federal government.

Most voters found Goldwater's ideas too extreme. Johnson defeated him easily. Kennedy had received only 100,000 votes more than Nixon in 1960. In 1964 Johnson's margin over Goldwater was 16 million.

The Democrats increased their majorities in Congress too. Johnson then proposed what he called the **Great Society** program. With typical energy, he sent Congress 63 messages calling for legislation in a single year.

Congress approved nearly everything Johnson asked for. It created **Medicare,** providing health insurance for people over 65. It supplied huge grants to improve elementary and secondary education. The **Immigration Act** of 1965 abolished the system of favoring immigrants from the nations of northern and western Europe. Future admission to the United States was to be based on the skills and abilities of the newcomers, regardless of nationality.

There was also a **Housing Act** to help pay the rent of poor people and a **Highway Safety Act.** Another civil rights measure, the **Voting Rights Act,** was passed. This law appointed new federal officials called registrars in districts where local white officials were refusing to allow blacks to register to vote. Within a year and a half a million southern blacks were added to the voter lists.

- Why was Lyndon Johnson's margin of victory over Barry Goldwater so large in 1964?
- What were some Great Society measures passed by Congress?

THE AFFLUENT SOCIETY

In the mid-1960s the United States seemed to be entering a new Golden Age. Looking back over the 20 years since the end of World War II, most observers were struck by the tremendous advances that had been made. The **standard of living** of the nation as a whole had never been so high. The percentage of poor people had fallen sharply and would probably be further reduced by President Johnson's Great Society program. The worst tensions of the Cold War with the Soviet Union seemed over. Science and technology had produced many new marvels and promised still further advances. America was the richest country that had ever existed. The question now, wrote the economist John Kenneth Galbraith in 1958, was how to use the abundant wealth created by this **Affluent Society.**

The dominant mood of the 1950s and early 1960s was one of optimism. This does not mean that everyone was satisfied with the state of American society. On the contrary, optimism made many people dissatisfied. They felt that society had serious weaknesses. But because they were optimistic, they believed that these weaknesses could be eliminated.

This hopeful, forward-looking mood had many roots. Victory in World War II was certainly one of the most important. Millions of soldiers and sailors came home confirmed optimists, if only because they had survived amidst the death and destruction of battle. They and other millions who had not actually fought in the war found that victory strengthened their belief that the American way of life was superior to all others. The contrast between America and war-torn Europe further strengthened this belief, as did the dependence on American aid of both the Allies and the defeated Germans and Japanese.

- What was the standard of living in America by the mid-1960s? What is meant by the Affluent Society?
- What were some of the reasons that Americans were so optimistic after World War II?

THE WONDERS OF SCIENCE

Many recent scientific discoveries and the products of the new technology that these discoveries made possible added to the general optimism. The most exciting of these was **nuclear energy.** The same laws of physics that had led to the atom bomb could be used to produce controlled nuclear reactions instead of violent explosions. The enormous energy released by these reactions could be converted into electricity. Some experts predicted that energy would soon be almost as plentiful as water and air. What this would mean in more wealth and leisure for everyone was easy to imagine. By 1955 nuclear power plants could make and distribute electricity.

The race to conquer space began in earnest in the late 1950s. After 1945 progress in rocket research was rapid in many countries. In 1957 the Russians startled the world and shocked millions of Americans by launching the first earth-orbiting vehicle, **Sputnik I.** (*Sputnik* is the Russian word for "traveling companion.") This was a massive blow to Americans' pride. It sparked competition. The first American satellite soared around the earth in 1958. In 1962 John Glenn became the first American astronaut to orbit the globe.

SOVFOTO

The Russian magazine *Krokodil* (for the popular traveling Crocodile of a childhood poem) placed this drawing on its cover. It celebrates the first cosmonaut, Yuri Gagarin, who flew in earth orbit in April 1961. How did the Russians gain an early lead in the space race?

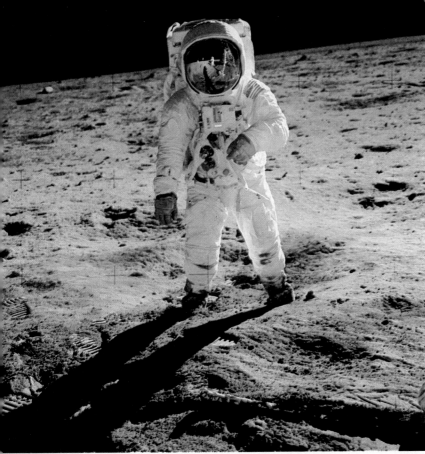

NASA

The historical significance of this picture cannot be fully appreciated. In its way it is as rare as Columbus's journal describing the first sighting of land in the Americas. When two American astronauts walked on the moon in July 1969, Neil Armstrong took this photograph of his partner, Edwin Aldrin. How did Armstrong describe the moon landing?

Once again, a Russian cosmonaut had been first to orbit earth. President Kennedy then boldly announced a program to land astronauts on the moon before the Russians. The public supported the **space program** wholeheartedly, despite its heavy cost. Gradually, the United States began to close the gap with the Russians. It triumphed in July 1969 when Neil Armstrong and Edwin Aldrin walked on the moon. Live television showed the astronaut's first steps and relayed Armstrong's message: "That's one small step for a man, one giant leap for mankind."

Dozens of products and techniques that made life more comfortable and interesting were introduced in the years after the war. All added to the general optimism. Television and jet airliners and home air conditioners changed the way people used their spare time and where they lived and worked. Items like Edwin H. Land's Polaroid camera and long-playing (LP) phonograph records improved upon already existing products. New products included such **synthetic textiles** as orlon and dacron, water-based latex paint, small portable radios and even smaller hearing aids, both using tiny **transistors** instead of bulky vacuum tubes. Electronic **computers** simplified office work and made possible thousands of labor-saving techniques.

United Press International

Paralytic polio was a dreaded killer until 1954. That year Dr. Jonas Salk perfected a vaccine. His work, with that of Albert Sabin, helped eliminate the crippling disease for those who were injected or took the Sabin oral vaccine. What was another advance in medicine after World War II?

Medical advances contributed to the general optimism. Penicillin, first used in military hospitals during the war, became available to everyone. Along with other new **antibiotics,** penicillin practically eliminated most infectious diseases as major causes of death. The discovery by Dr. Jonas Salk of a **polio vaccine** did away with infantile paralysis, a particularly frightening killer.

In still another area, economists seemed to have figured out a way to prevent depressions. When business activity began to slow down, they said, the government should stimulate it. There were two ways to do this. One, called **fiscal policy,** involved the federal budget. The government must increase spending and lower taxes. Its spending would increase the demand for goods and services. Lower taxes would leave consumers with more money to buy goods.

The other method was called **monetary policy.** It involved having the Federal Reserve Board lower interest rates so that businesses and consumers could borrow money more easily in order to expand output and increase consumption.

If the economy began to grow too rapidly, causing prices to rise, fiscal and monetary policies could be reversed. If that happened, economists said, the government should reduce its expenditures, increase taxes, and raise interest rates. The economists claimed that it was possible to "fine tune" the economy by shifting these policies back and forth. A steady rate of economic growth would follow.

- What peacetime use of nuclear energy began in the 1950s?
- What provoked the space race between the U.S. and Russia?
- What were some products developed after World War II?

850

THE POPULATION EXPLOSION

One result of prosperity and public optimism was a rapid increase in the population of the United States. During the Great Depression many people had been too poor to marry and have children. During the war millions of men were overseas. Between 1929 and 1946 the population rose quite slowly, from about 122 million to about 145 million. This was a rate of a little more than 1 million persons a year.

In 1946 the population increased by nearly 3 million. The new trend continued for about 20 years. By the end of 1965 the population of the United States had reached 195 million.

F.P.G.

AFL-CIO

George Meany began his career as a plumber. He was president of the American Federation of Labor in 1955 when it merged with the Congress of Industrial Organizations. The union seal is shown above. How large was the new AFL-CIO?

The labor force grew in size as the population increased. Unemployment remained relatively low. In 1955 the two major branches of the labor movement—the American Federation of Labor and the Congress of Industrial Organizations—resolved their differences. They united to form the **AFL-CIO,** with George Meany, head of the AFL Plumbers Union, as president. The new union had 16 million members.

▨ Why did the population of the United States begin to grow so rapidly in 1946?

BUILDING SKILLS IN SOCIAL STUDIES

Reading the Census

The Constitution requires that a *census*, or counting, be made of the United States population every ten years. The primary purpose of the census has remained unchanged from 1790 through 1980—to see that seats in the House of Representatives reflect the distribution of the national population. Under the principle *one person, one vote*, states must redraw Congressional election districts to reflect national population shifts. By law the number of representatives has been set at 435.

The census is also a *human inventory*. It provides a wealth of information about the main resource of the United States—its people. The 1980 census asked questions about race and ethnic background, energy use, the overall cost of housing, the disabled population, and commuting patterns. All of the information tabulated from the census is closely studied by the various states, partly to determine their fair shares of federal revenue-sharing programs which total some $50 billion annually.

Among the findings of the 1980 census were that the number of housing units has increased as the number of households has gone down. The population has shifted further from the northeast and north central regions to those southern and western states known as the Sun Belt. Most surprising, the Census Bureau's projection of 222 million citizens was quite low. Some 226.5 million citizens were tabulated.

The census information shown on the table below gives land area in square miles, total population, percentage increase since the last census, and population density. Use the information to prepare large graphs for display in the classroom. The kind and number of graphs will be determined by your purpose. Use other Building Skills lessons to plan your graphs.

Census year	Land area (square miles)	Population	% Change over last census	Density per square mile of land
1790	864,746	3,929,214	—	4.5
1800	864,746	5,308,483	35.1	6.1
1810	1,681,828	7,239,881	36.4	4.3
1820	1,749,462	9,638,453	33.1	5.5
1830	1,749,462	12,866,020	33.5	7.4
1840	1,749,462	17,069,453	32.7	9.8
1850	2,940,042	23,191,876	35.9	7.9
1860	2,969,640	31,443,321	35.6	10.6
1870	2,969,640	39,818,449	26.6	13.4
1880	2,969,640	50,155,783	26.0	16.9
1890	2,969,640	62,947,714	25.5	21.2
1900	2,969,834	75,994,575	20.7	25.6
1910	2,969,565	91,972,266	21.0	31.0
1920	2,969,451	105,710,620	14.9	35.6
1930	2,977,128	122,775,046	16.1	41.2
1940	2,977,128	131,669,275	7.2	44.2
1950	3,552,206	151,325,798	14.5	42.6
1960	3,540,911	179,323,175	18.5	50.6
1970	3,540,023	203,211,926	13.3	57.4
1980	3,540,023	226,504,825	11.5	64.0

The Sun Belt

Millions of Americans were moving about the country after the war. The major shift was westward. The territories of Hawaii and Alaska were admitted to statehood in 1959. This was both a sign of their growth and a way to stimulate their further growth. But all the western states grew very rapidly. So also did Florida and other states of the South.

The South and Southwest came to be called the Sun Belt because so many people were being drawn there by the warm climate. Retired people in particular moved to Florida and the Southwest to avoid the harsh northern winters. The new home air conditioners made life comfortable during the hot southern summers.

There were other reasons for the migration to the West and South. Many firms in the aircraft and electronics industries tended to locate in these sections. Thousands of young families followed, attracted by the high wages and pleasant working conditions these industries provided. The new federal highway network made it possible for people to move long distances easily. Travel was swift by jet airplanes.

The federal government encouraged the shift by establishing huge new facilities in the Sun Belt. The best known were the John F. Kennedy rocket-launching base in Florida and the headquarters of the National Aeronautics and Space Administration (NASA) in Texas.

Richard Weiss/Peter Arnold

THE SHIFT TO THE SUBURBS

In every part of the United States people began moving from cities to their surrounding **suburbs.** These suburbanites, as they were called, were looking for the space, fresh air, privacy, and contact with nature that country life provided. Still, they needed to remain near the cities where most of them worked. They also wanted to take advantage of the excitement, conveniences, and cultural opportunities of city life.

Young, recently married couples with small children were particularly attracted to the suburbs. Builders responded to their demand for homes by constructing huge **developments.** Levittown, Pennsylvania, which became a suburb in itself, was the best known of these developments. Its comfortable, relatively cheap **tract houses** stretched row upon row with a sameness that later came to disturb many Americans. But nearly all purchasers were delighted with the houses. Most had three bedrooms and an extra bathroom. Dishwashers, washing machines, and dryers were already installed.

In and around the developments **shopping centers** sprang up, complete with supermarkets, department store branches, movie the-

This Chicago suburb, with its long rows of houses, is made interesting by winding roads, fast-growing fir trees, and, for many homeowners, outdoor swimming pools. How did tract houses attract buyers?

aters, and dozens of small shops. The shopping centers were surrounded by acres of paved parking lots, for suburbanites traveled everywhere by automobile. Almost any product that local residents might want could be purchased in these shopping centers.

Few poor people lived in the new suburbs. The poor could not afford even the smallest tract homes. There were almost no apartment houses or other places to rent. In other words, suburbs were mostly for members of the middle class—office workers, shopkeepers, teachers and other government employees, and well-paid blue collar wage earners such as carpenters, electricians, and automobile assembly-line workers.

The government tried to improve the living conditions of poor people in the cities by putting up large **public housing projects.** These nonprofit apartments were rented at relatively low rates. Usually the rents were based on the income of the tenants.

The problem was that when the percentage of poor people in the cities increased, more and more middle class people moved out to the suburbs. This seriously strained the finances of city governments because when the well-to-do left, income from taxes fell off.

854

Many manufacturers shifted to the suburbs to gain space and because property taxes were lower. This shift caused many of their employees to become suburbanites. Department stores built suburban branches, and chain stores followed their customers. Since many of the poor who remained in the cities were nonwhites, a new kind of segregation developed.

The worst effects of this segregation were not felt until after 1965. Until then well-meaning people had high hopes that President Johnson's Great Society programs would solve this problem along with others.

- For what reasons did many Americans move to the suburbs after World War II?
- What change did the shift to the suburbs bring in housing? In shopping?
- How did the shift to the suburbs cause segregation?

THE EDUCATION BOOM

With so many children being born after the war, thousands of new schools had to be built. Most schools in the suburbs were low, light, and airy brick buildings. In addition to ordinary classrooms, space was provided for teaching arts and crafts and for sports activities. Teachers' salaries rose, for the increased enrollments created a teacher shortage.

Solar panels on the sloping roof of the Madeira School in Virginia heat this fashionable suburban building. How is it typical of those suburban schools built during the education boom after World War II?

Everett Johnson, DeWys

Schools in the cities suffered when the tax revenues that supported them declined. The **Elementary and Secondary Education Act** of 1965 supplied large amounts of federal money to improve these schools.

Changes in higher education were even more dramatic in the affluent society of the 1950s. College enrollments jumped from 1.6 million in 1946 to 3.5 million in 1960. Clearly, many young people, whose parents had not had the opportunity, were going to college. Actually, the number of years of schooling that the average American received had been increasing steadily since the 1820s. Making a college education available to so many more people had important economic and social effects. There was a close relationship between the amount of education people got and the kinds of lives they led when their training was completed.

In business and in many other fields people with intelligence, imagination, and energy often succeeded brilliantly with little formal schooling. Education helped, but it was not essential. College training, however, was required for entry into the professions—medicine, law, teaching, and the like. The easy access to a college education after World War II opened the professions to a much broader section of the population than ever before.

- What caused the education boom? How did suburbs profit? How did cities suffer?
- What happened to college enrollments after the war?

THE IMPACT OF TELEVISION

Even before World War II inventors had developed a way to transmit pictures similar to the way sound is transmitted by radio. As everyone knows, this technique was called **television.** Only in the late 1940s, however, did manufacturers first offer reliable television sets at prices that ordinary people could afford. The demand proved to be tremendous. Throughout the 1950s television sets were sold at a rate of about 7 million a year. By 1960 nearly every family in America had at least one set. Television was one modern advance that even the poorest people seemed able to afford.

Television combined the virtues of radio and motion pictures. Sports events such as baseball and football games were popular from the start. So were musical programs, comedy hours, and serial dramatic shows. Serials were known as **soap operas** because many of them were sponsored by manufacturers of soap and similar household products. News programs kept viewers informed.

Television soon became a force that influenced public events as well as one that reported them. For example, many observers believed that John F. Kennedy won the 1960 Presidential election

United Press International

Baseball and football attracted new audiences with the rise of television in the 1950s. Among the players was Jack Roosevelt Robinson. When he joined the Brooklyn Dodgers in 1947, he was the first black to play in the major leagues. Which sports were popular on television in the 1950s?

because he made a better impression before the TV camera than Richard Nixon. It was even suggested that if Nixon had used better makeup in the first of his televised debates with Kennedy, the election might have gone to him. This was almost certainly an exaggeration. Still, the fact that people could think it was so shows how important television had become.

■ What impact did television have on public events?

The western was a staple for both the movie industry and television. These children gather around the television set in the 1950s. From the outside of homes only a blue glow escaped to the night. What other kinds of programs were first popular on television?

PROGRESS FOR BLACKS

American blacks did not receive their fair share of the new affluence. As late as 1960 about half were still either poor or barely keeping their heads above the so-called **poverty line.** But in 1965 the economic condition of the average black seemed to be improving. More opportunities were opening up. The new AFL-CIO labor federation had promised "to encourage all workers without regard for . . . color" to join their organization. Although some unions shut out black workers, the leaders of the AFL-CIO spoke out strongly against this practice. The United Automobile Workers and a number of other big unions achieved excellent records in promoting harmony between black and white workers.

Blacks were breaking barriers in many fields. In 1947 Jack Roosevelt Robinson proved that Branch Rickey of the Brooklyn Dodgers was a shrewd judge of baseball talent as well as a believer in equal opportunity. In that year Robinson got his chance in the big leagues, the first black to do so. He quickly won a place in the

857

Dodgers' starting lineup as second baseman. He went on to become a great star. In 1949 he was the batting champion of the National League.

Once Robinson had broken in, other good black players were given tryouts. Ball clubs opened to players from Puerto Rico, Mexico, Cuba, and other Latin American countries where baseball had become a popular sport. By 1960 there were black and Hispanic players on every team in the major leagues.

Racial barriers collapsed in all the professional sports. Of course, only a handful of talented athletes could "make it" in sports. But these players were heroes to millions of youngsters. They gave hope to all for the future and made people proud of their heritage.

The greatest leadership for blacks, however, was provided by the Reverend Martin Luther King, Jr. After his success in leading the Montgomery bus boycott, King became a national figure. Everywhere he preached the idea of nonviolence or **passive resistance** as the best way to achieve racial equality. "Nonviolent resistance is not a method for cowards," he said. One must "accept blows from the opponent without striking back." Love, not hate or force, was the way to change people's minds.

In April 1963 King led a campaign in **Birmingham,** Alabama, against segregation. The local police turned fierce dogs on the peaceful demonstrators and drove them from the streets with jets of water from powerful fire hoses. King was thrown in jail. Yet this horrible incident proved the value of King's approach. Millions of Americans were impressed by the demonstrators' courage and outraged by the brutality of the police. They reacted strongly in the blacks behalf.

A few months later 200,000 people gathered in Washington to demonstrate peacefully in favor of President Kennedy's civil rights legislation. During the proceedings King made his famous "I Have a Dream" speech. He dreamed of a time, he told the huge audience who had come to this **March on Washington,** when all white and black Americans could live together in peace and harmony. He concluded with these words:

> From every mountainside, let freedom ring. When we let freedom ring, when we let it ring from every village and every hamlet, from every state and every city, we will be able to speed up that day when all of God's children, black men and white men, Jews and Gentiles, Protestants and Catholics, will be able to join hands and sing in the words of the old Negro spiritual: "Free at last! Free at last! Thank God almighty, we are free at last!"[1]

[1] From Martin Luther King, Jr.'s "I Have a Dream" speech. Copyright © 1963 by Martin Luther King, Jr. Reprinted by permission of Joan Daves.

Fred Ward, Black Star

"Free at last!" With these words Martin Luther King, Jr., concluded his famous speech supporting the civil rights legislation favored by President Kennedy in 1963. Where was this speech delivered?

Francis Kelley, *Life* Magazine, © Time, Inc.

King was an exceptional person. Yet he was typical of the times in his optimism. "The believer in nonviolence has deep faith in the future," he once said.

No one knew better than Martin Luther King that American society was far from perfect. Yet he believed sincerely that the nation was making progress toward the goals that he was seeking. Millions of other Americans, black and white alike, faced the future in the mid-1960s as hopefully as he did.

- What did Martin Luther King hope to accomplish by his policy of passive resistance?
- How did King share in the optimism that was typical of the early 1960s?

The crowd assembled alongside the reflecting pool in Washington, D.C., numbered more than 200,000 people. This march was organized by Martin Luther King, Jr. What policy did he favor for achieving racial equality?

CHAPTER 28 REVIEW

Identification
Tell briefly why each of the following persons, terms, or events is important.
1. John F. Kennedy
2. Fidel Castro
3. Nikita Khrushchev
4. Lyndon B. Johnson
5. John Glenn
6. Neil Armstrong
7. Barry Goldwater
8. Jonas Salk
9. Jack Roosevelt Robinson
10. Martin Luther King, Jr.
11. Peace Corps
12. Bay of Pigs
13. U-2 Affair
14. Berlin Wall
15. Cuban Missile Crisis
16. Great Society
17. Affluent Society
18. Sun Belt
19. Civil Rights Act of 1964
20. March on Washington

Understanding American History
1. Describe three events of the Kennedy years that show how the Cold War continued.
2. Describe the major programs of the Great Society and tell the purpose of each.
3. Explain in what ways Lyndon Johnson was a strong President.
4. Explain why the United States was called the Affluent Society in the mid-1960s.
5. What were some wonders of science that were developed after World War II?
6. Describe the major events in the race for space between the U.S. and Russia.
7. Explain the difference between monetary policy and fiscal policy. Tell how economists planned to use each to prevent future depressions.
8. Why did the population of states in the Sun Belt grow rapidly after World War II?
9. What were the good and bad effects of the growth of suburbs following World War II?
10. Describe the progress made by blacks in the 20 years following World War II.

Activities
1. John Kennedy, like Theodore Roosevelt, was popular with the press. After he was assassinated, the youthful vigor and optimism of his administration reminded his widow of Camelot—the Court of King Arthur and his knights of the round table. Report in class on the legend of Camelot. Then tell in what ways the Kennedy years reminded some press people of that fabled time.
2. Use your historical imagination to write diary entries on two events in the race for space. First describe your reaction in 1957 to word that a space satellite launched by the Soviet Union was circling the globe. Then give your thoughts in 1969 upon seeing two U.S. astronauts walk on the moon.
3. In the early 1980s Congress, under the persistent urging of President Reagan, began to dismantle many programs of Franklin Roosevelt's New Deal and Lyndon Johnson's Great Society. Prepare a series of brief reports on some of these programs, from social security to medicare, and describe their present-day status.
4. Use an almanac or other reference source to find statistics on the populations of city and suburban areas for the years 1960 to 1980. Show these statistics on a line graph. Then write a brief essay describing the trends of suburban and urban population growth.
5. This chapter is titled "An America of Many Riches." Write a letter to a friend living in another country. Tell which of America's riches you most appreciate. Try to make your letter informative rather than boastful. Tell what benefits come to you and your family from a rich America.

CHAPTER 28 TEST

Completion (30 points)
Number your paper 1–10 and next to each number write the words from the list below that best complete each sentence.

Cuban Missile Crisis   Sun Belt
Great Society   suburbs
NASA   Peace Corps
passive resistance   Berlin Wall
Bay of Pigs   VISTA

1 The failure of the American-supported invasion of Cuba at the ____ dealt a blow to the prestige of the United States
2 President Kennedy forced the Soviet Union to back down and withdraw nuclear warheads during the ____.
3. The agency created during the Johnson administration as a domestic parallel to the Peace Corps was known as ____.
4. The agency in charge of the U.S. space program is known as ____.
5. In the regions known as the ____, population grew rapidly after World War II.
6. A sign of communist weakness, the ____ reminded the world that thousands of persons who lived in eastern Europe were captives of communism.
7. A large movement of the middle class to the ____ took place after World War II.
8. Under President Johnson's ____, programs such as Head Start, the Job Corps, and VISTA were created.
9. The tactic of ____ advocated by Martin Luther King, Jr., helped lead many Americans to support equal rights for blacks.
10. President Kennedy created the ____ to send volunteer workers to needy countries.

Matching (20 points)
Number your paper 11–15 and match the description in the first column with the name in the second column.
11. Astronaut who walked on the moon
12. President who created the Peace Corps
13. President who sought the Civil Rights Act of 1964
14. Discoverer of a vaccine for polio
15. Advocate of nonviolence and passive resistance

a. John F. Kennedy
b. Lyndon B. Johnson
c. Martin Luther King, Jr.
d. Jonas Salk
e. Neil Armstrong

Chronological Order (20 points)
Number your paper 16–20 and place the following events in order by numbering 1 for the first, 2 for the second, and so on.
16. President Kennedy is assassinated.
17. Congress passes the Civil Rights Act.
18. President Kennedy stands firm in the Cuban Missile Crisis.
19. Martin Luther King, Jr., leads the March on Washington.
20. U.S. prestige suffers at the Bay of Pigs.

Essay (30 points)
In a brief essay explain how the events of President Kennedy's administration continued the Cold War with Russia that began in the 1950s, *or* Describe advances in science and technology, population growth and shifts, and the higher standard of living that arose after World War II. Tell how these changes affected American life in the 1950s and 1960s.

CHAPTER 29
America Is
Put to the Test

In August 1964 President Johnson announced that North Vietnamese gunboats had attacked the American destroyer *Maddox* in the Gulf of Tonkin, off the coast of Southeast Asia. He called upon Congress to approve and support in advance "the determination of the President, as commander in chief, to take all necessary measures to repel any armed attack against the forces of the United States." Congress voted for this **Tonkin Gulf Resolution** almost unanimously. As we shall soon see, this is another example of how an event that seems unimportant at the time can have far-reaching and unexpected historical significance.

WAR IN VIETNAM

In the summer of 1964 the former French colony of Vietnam was torn by war. Communist North Vietnam was supplying aid to pro-communist South Vietnamese guerrillas, who were known as the **Viet Cong.** The Viet Cong had been seeking to overthrow the pro-American government of South Vietnam ever since Vietnam had been divided into two countries in 1954. They controlled large parts of the country, especially the rural regions.

While Dwight Eisenhower was President, a small number of American military advisers had been sent to South Vietnam to help train the South Vietnamese army. The United States also gave South Vietnam large sums of money for military supplies and economic aid. President Kennedy continued this policy.

The President of South Vietnam, Ngo Dinh Diem, was incompetent and unpopular. Many of the men around him were openly corrupt. A few days before President Kennedy was assassinated, a group of Vietnamese army officers overthrew the Diem government and killed Diem. Unfortunately, they proved no better than he at defeating the Viet Cong.

President Johnson did not change American policy toward Vietnam until the Gulf of Tonkin affair. Even then he was mainly interested in *appearing* to be more aggressive. His Republican opponent in the 1964 Presidential election, Senator Barry Goldwater, demanded that the United States make a bigger effort to "check communism" in Vietnam. Johnson hoped that the Tonkin Gulf Resolution would convince the voters that he was pursuing that objective vigorously.

Robert Ellison, Black Star

Three American soldiers in Vietnam take cover in their muddy dugout as a shell bursts in the distance. This photograph was taken in 1968. Who sent the first American advisers to serve in Vietnam?

But he made a special point of not getting *too* involved in Vietnam. He insisted that he "would never send American boys to do the fighting that Asian boys should do themselves."

After winning the election, however, Johnson decided to step up American military activity in Vietnam. President Eisenhower had warned of a "falling domino" effect if communist expansion were allowed to go unchallenged. "You have a row of dominoes set up, you knock over the first one, and . . . the last one . . . will go over very quickly," Eisenhower said in 1954. According to the **domino theory,** if South Vietnam were controlled by the communists, its neighbors, Laos and Cambodia, would also go communist. Then all Southeast Asia, and perhaps even India with its hundreds of millions of people, would follow.

Recent events such as the war in Korea and the Cuban missile crisis seemed to show that the way to check communist expansion was by firmness and force. President Johnson felt he could not stand down. "We could tuck our tails between our legs and run for cover," he said. "That would just whet the enemy's appetite for greater aggression and more territory, and solve nothing."

The assumption behind this reasoning was that the fighting in South Vietnam was between local Vietnamese patriots and "outside" communists. If the outsiders were allowed to conquer the country, the argument ran, they would be encouraged to press farther. In reality the struggle in South Vietnam was a civil war between supporters of the government and the Viet Cong. "Outside" communists from China and Russia were supplying the Viet Cong with weapons and advice, just as the United States was helping the anticommunist government of South Vietnam. The communist government of North Vietnam was deeply involved too. Its objective was to unite the two Vietnams under a communist regime.

- What was the role of the Viet Cong in the Vietnam War?
- What was Eisenhower's domino theory?
- How did Johnson respond to communist expansion?

AMERICAN ESCALATION IN VIETNAM

In February 1965 Johnson made a fateful decision. He ordered the air force to bomb selected targets in North Vietnam. In March he sent two battalions of marines to Vietnam. Their job was to protect the air base from which the bombers were operating. Soon more troops had to be sent in to reinforce the marines!

These three American soldiers run across a sandbagged fortification in Vietnam as the war moves closer to them. When did the escalation of the war begin in Vietnam?

Robert Ellison, Black Star

A few months later the American forces in Vietnam were given permission to seek out and attack Viet Cong units. More troops were shipped to Vietnam. By the end of 1965 there were 185,000 American fighting men in the country.

This steady **escalation,** or increase, in American military strength in Vietnam went on for three years. Each increase brought more North Vietnamese into the conflict in support of the Viet Cong. By 1968 more than half a million Americans were fighting there. Yet Congress never officially declared war. Johnson instead waged war by the authority of the Tonkin Gulf Resolution, which had seemed to have little historical significance when it was passed by Congress in 1964.

The President and his advisers thought they were acting with great restraint. The enormous difference in size and wealth between the United States and North Vietnam lulled them into believing that the United States could win the war whenever it chose. How, asked the advisers, could a tiny country like North Vietnam successfully resist the United States? They wanted to risk the lives of as few Americans as possible. When each escalation proved to be not enough, they hoped just one more increase would do the job.

Time passed without victory. Large numbers of Americans decided that the war was a terrible mistake. Some claimed that keeping the weak and unpopular government of South Vietnam in power was not worth the cost in American lives and money. Others argued that it was wrong for Americans to be killing people in a small country that was quite literally on the other side of the world.

The fighting in Vietnam was savage. Both sides were capable of extreme cruelty. Prisoners were sometimes killed or tortured. Hundreds of civilians died in air raids. Peaceful villages were burned to the ground to root out possible Viet Cong sympathizers. Local South Vietnamese officials were murdered by Viet Cong terrorists.

Americans who wanted to stop the war were called **doves,** after the traditional bird of peace. Those who insisted that the war must be fought until it was won were known as **hawks.** For a long time the hawks were in the majority. National pride and hatred of communism made many of the hawks believe that it would be cowardly and shameful to pull out of South Vietnam.

Early in 1968 the American commander in Vietnam, General William C. Westmoreland, announced that victory was near. Soon the Viet Cong would be crushed. But on January 31, the Vietnamese New Year's Day, *Tet,* the Viet Cong suddenly attacked cities all over South Vietnam. They even gained control of a large part of **Saigon,** the capital. They held a number of important cities for weeks.

The American and South Vietnamese troops fought back, as one historian has put it, "with the fury of a blinded giant." Eventually

Paul Slade, Globe Photos

Barry Goldwater, the Presidential candidate of the Republican party in 1964, was a hawk in the debate during the Vietnam War. "In your heart you know he's right," was his campaign slogan. Why did hawks oppose leaving Vietnam?

they regained control of the cities. In doing so, however, they destroyed even more of Vietnam. In a remark that soon became famous, an American officer justified the smashing of the town of Ben Tre. "We had to destroy it in order to save it," he said.

The American counterattack crushed the **Tet offensive.** Viet Cong and North Vietnamese losses were enormous. Still, the American public was profoundly shocked at the strength shown by the communists after so many years of war. The tide of opinion turned against the war. When General Westmoreland asked for another 200,000 men, President Johnson turned him down.

- Why did President Johnson and his advisers believe they were acting with restraint in Vietnam?
- Who were the doves? Who were the hawks?
- What was the effect on Americans of the Tet offensive?

1968: A YEAR OF TRAGEDY

In March 1968 President Johnson acknowledged that his Vietnam policy had failed. He had been planning to run for a second full term in 1968. Senator Eugene McCarthy of Minnesota had announced that he would oppose Johnson for the Democratic nomination. McCarthy was a leading dove. Before the Tet offensive no one gave him any chance of defeating Johnson.

After Tet, however, the situation changed: McCarthy almost defeated Johnson in the New Hampshire Presidential primary. Then Robert F. Kennedy, brother of the slain President, declared that he too was a candidate. Faced with a difficult fight that would probably divide the country still further, Johnson announced that he would not seek reelection.

On April 4, less than a week after Johnson's withdrawal, came another shock. Martin Luther King, Jr., was murdered in Memphis, Tennessee, where he had gone to support a strike of garbage collectors. King's murder caused an explosion of anger in black communities all over the country. Riots broke out in 125 cities in 28 states. Whole sections of Washington were aflame in the shadow of the Capitol.

Next, in June, Robert Kennedy was assassinated by an Arab immigrant who objected to the support the United States was giving the state of Israel. Kennedy had just won the California Presidential primary. He had seemed likely to win the nomination at the Democratic national convention in Chicago. His death made the favorite Vice President Hubert H. Humphrey, who had the backing of President Johnson.

Humphrey loyally supported Johnson's policy in Vietnam. (If he had not, Johnson would not have supported him for President.)

Cornell Capa, Magnum

Robert Kennedy was a senator from New York when he decided to seek the 1968 Presidential nomination. He opposed Lyndon Johnson, who had been President Kennedy's Vice President. What were his chances of receiving the nomination before he was assassinated?

Delcan Haun-Black Star

Mourners of Martin Luther King, Jr., make their way through the streets of Atlanta behind a caisson drawn by mules. This symbolic "poor people's funeral" was a tribute to the slain civil rights leader. What cause was King supporting at the time he was assassinated?

When the convention met, large numbers of antiwar protesters, many of whom favored Senator McCarthy for President, flocked to Chicago to demonstrate. Mayor Richard Daley, a Humphrey supporter, then packed the area around the convention hall with city police.

Radicals among the demonstrators insulted and taunted the police. They called them "pigs" and other vulgar names. The police responded by rushing into the crowd, clubs swinging. Millions of television viewers who had tuned in to watch the convention debates saw instead burly, helmeted policemen hitting women with their night sticks and herding dazed and bloody demonstrators into police wagons.

- How did Lyndon Johnson acknowledge that his Vietnam policy had failed?
- How did many Americans react to the assassination of Martin Luther King, Jr.?
- Who rioted at the 1968 Democratic convention?

Claus Meyer, Black Star

Both, Dennis Brack, Black Star

Three candidates sought the White House in 1968. George Wallace, at left, a former governor of Alabama, ran as an independent. Nominee of the Democrats, center, was Hubert Humphrey, the Vice President. The Republican entrant, right, Richard Nixon, had been the Vice President from 1953 to 1960. Which candidate won this election?

THE ELECTION OF 1968

Humphrey won the Democratic nomination easily. But thousands of Democrats blamed him, quite unfairly, for the police riot in Chicago. Most of these same Democrats resented his support of the war in Vietnam.

This split in the Democratic party benefited the Republican candidate, Richard M. Nixon, the former Vice President whom Kennedy had defeated in 1960. Few had expected Nixon to get a second chance to run for President. In 1962 he had run unsuccessfully for governor of California. He seemed a sore loser, blaming reporters for his defeat.

However, Nixon had worked hard for the Republican party during the Kennedy and Johnson administrations. Hundreds of local Republican officials felt that he deserved a second chance for the Presidency. When the 1968 Republican convention met, he had a majority of the delegates in his camp and was easily nominated.

Governor George C. Wallace of Alabama, an outspoken foe of racial integration, also ran for President in 1968 on an independent ticket. For this reason Nixon chose Spiro T. Agnew of Maryland as his running mate. Agnew had taken a tough stand against blacks, urban crime, and protesters of all kinds. He was not well known nationally, but his record made him attractive to many voters who might otherwise have supported Wallace.

In the three-way contest for President, Nixon won. He got only about 43 per cent of the popular vote, less than 1 per cent more than Humphrey. But he received a solid majority of the electoral vote.

- How did Richard Nixon gain the Republican nomination in 1968?
- How did Nixon counter the challenge of George Wallace?

BUILDING SKILLS IN SOCIAL STUDIES

The Electoral College

Every four years the President of the United States is chosen by the *electoral college*. This important decision is made by persons who are faceless and, in two thirds of the states, nameless on the ballot. The members of the electoral college never assemble as a group but meet instead in their respective states after each general election to cast their votes for President. A full explanation of the electoral system is on page 200.

Every state has one electoral vote for each senator and representative. Thus, even the states with the least population have three votes. In addition, the District of Columbia now has three votes. There are a total of 538 electoral votes. In order to be elected, a candidate must receive a simple majority, or 270 votes.

The electoral system has often been criticized for its tradition of *unit rule*. That is, in each state the winner takes all. A candidate who receives one more vote than the closest rival gets all the state's electoral votes. Further, the unit rule gives the largest, most populated states a dominant role in Presidential elections.

The map below shows the states scaled to their electoral votes. Study it carefully. Then plan campaign strategies for candidates of your own invention. In which states will you concentrate your efforts for a candidate with appeal to the Sun Belt? For a candidate from the rural Middle West? For a candidate from the industrial East? For each, give the electoral totals needed to win the election

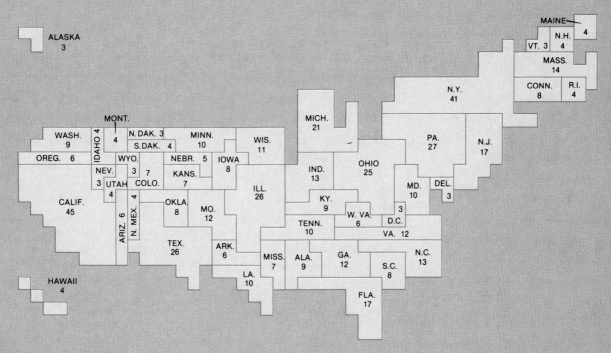

THE STATES SCALED TO THEIR ELECTORAL VOTES 538

NIXON AND THE ECONOMY

The new President favored **moderation.** He sought to please middle-income voters and persons who were neither radicals nor reactionaries. Such people were worried about high taxes and rising prices. Inflation in particular seemed the most alarming trend of the times. President Nixon set out to end it.

President Johnson was partly responsible for the inflation. Each time he ordered an escalation of the war in Vietnam, the government had to spend billions of additional dollars on weapons and other supplies. Johnson had not asked Congress to increase taxes to pay for the war, partly because he feared that his domestic programs would be cut back if he did so. In the saying of the day, he refused to choose between **guns or butter.** Therefore the federal budget was badly unbalanced. With government purchases putting huge sums into the economy without producing more consumer goods, the prices of goods rose sharply.

Nixon used both fiscal and monetary policy to check the inflation. He reduced government spending and persuaded the Federal Reserve Board to raise interest rates to discourage borrowing. The economy slowed down. However, these policies caused unemployment to go up. For some reason prices continued to go up too. Economists were as puzzled by the trend as the President. Throughout 1969 and 1970 the trend continued.

Finally, in August 1971, Nixon took a drastic step. He suddenly ordered a 90-day **wage and price freeze.** During the 90-day period he set up new government boards to supervise wages and prices. Then he announced **guidelines** which placed maximum limits on future increases in wages and prices. This program did not stop inflation, but it did slow it down.

- What was a major cause of the inflation that President Nixon set out to check?
- How did Nixon attempt to check inflation?

NIXON AND THE WAR

Nixon also sought a middle-of-the-road solution to the war in Vietnam. He was unwilling to give up the American goal of keeping the communists from conquering South Vietnam. Yet every report of new American casualties in Vietnam increased the strength of the **antiwar movement.** Nixon's problem was how to reduce the casualties without losing the war.

He decided to shift the burden of fighting the Viet Cong and North Vietnamese to the South Vietnamese army. Gradually, as that army grew stronger, American troops could be withdrawn. This was called the **Vietnamization** of the war.

Robert Ellison, Black Star

This Vietnamese army nurse attends a fallen soldier as American G I s offer assistance. The picture was taken during the Vietnamization of the war. Why was there doubt from the start about this policy?

Whether Vietnamization would work was doubtful from the start. After all, the escalation of the American effort in Vietnam had been necessary because the South Vietnamese had not been able to defeat the communists on their own. At best, Vietnamization would take a long time. The first reduction of American strength amounted to only 25,000 out of an army of more than 540,000.

As time passed, however, Nixon was able to reduce the size of the American force in Vietnam considerably. By the spring of 1970 it was down to 430,000. Nixon proudly announced that he intended to pull out another 150,000 men within a year.

Instead, only a few days later, on April 30, the President announced an expansion of the war. He was sending American troops into **Cambodia,** the nation on the western border of Vietnam. The reason for this invasion, Nixon said, was that the North Vietnamese were using Cambodia as a **sanctuary,** or safe base of operations, from

871

**THE WAR IN VIETNAM
1965-1973**

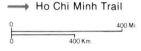 Ho Chi Minh Trail

0   400 Mi.

0   400 Km.

Americans everywhere were deeply upset by this picture taken in 1970 at Kent State University. National Guardsmen opened fire on students during a campus protest. How did other students react to Kent State?

which to launch attacks on South Vietnam. The Americans were going to destroy these bases.

The North Vietnamese had been moving soldiers and supplies into South Vietnam along the **Ho Chi Minh Trail** in Cambodia for years. (Ho Chi Minh had been the president of North Vietnam.) The Americans had responded by bombing the trail. Since Cambodia was a neutral country, this bombing was done secretly.

Nixon's public announcement of the invasion of Cambodia set off a new storm of protest in the United States. In November 1969 250,000 people had staged a protest demonstration in Washington against the war. But the antiwar movement had become less vigorous as Nixon reduced the number of American soldiers in Vietnam. Now it suddenly revived. If Vietnamization was a success, why was it necessary to send Americans into Cambodia?

College students in particular reacted angrily to news of the invasion. There were strikes and demonstrations on campuses all over the country. Much property was destroyed. The worst trouble occurred at **Kent State** University in Ohio. Rioting there led the governor of Ohio to send National Guard troops to the campus to preserve order. After several days of troubles in May, an overly tense guard unit opened fire on protesting students on the campus. Four students were killed and nearly a dozen more were wounded. Many of the victims had merely been walking across the campus on their way to classes when the guardsmen began shooting.

Valley News Dispatch-John Filo

Several days later, two students were shot down by Mississippi state police at **Jackson State.** The killings at Kent State and Jackson State caused still more student protests. Some colleges were forced to close down for the remainder of the school year. Parents were shaken by the spectacle of their children under fire at home in the United States, not on some foreign battlefield of war.

The Cambodian invasion did not lead immediately to much heavy fighting. Nixon depended increasingly on air attacks on North Vietnam to weaken the communists. Soon the American troops in Cambodia were ordered back into South Vietnam. Nixon continued the troop withdrawals. By 1972 fewer than 100,000 Americans were still fighting the war, and the number was declining steadily.

■ What was President Nixon's policy of Vietnamization?
■ Why did Nixon order American troops into Cambodia?
■ What was the response in the United States to the invasion of Cambodia?

NIXON VISITS CHINA AND RUSSIA

As American soldiers withdrew from Vietnam, President Nixon tried to end the war by diplomacy. His chief foreign policy adviser, Henry Kissinger, entered into quiet discussions with North Vietnamese leaders in Paris. In February 1972 Nixon himself made a dramatic trip to China, a nation that supported North Vietnam.

The United States had never officially recognized the communists as the legal rulers of China. At the time of the civil war that brought the communists to power in China, Nixon had been a leader of the group in Congress that opposed recognizing the new government. Like Senator Joseph McCarthy, Nixon had blamed the State Department for the loss of China. Over the years he had opposed having any dealings with the Red Chinese.

Now Nixon reversed himself completely. His visit to China was a great success. The Chinese leaders greeted him warmly. He agreed to support the admission of China to the United Nations. Important trade agreements were worked out. It was clear that the two nations would soon establish regular diplomatic relations.

A few months later Nixon made another important diplomatic move. This time he went to the Soviet Union. Again he was given an extremely friendly welcome. This happened despite the fact that Russia, like China, was supporting the North Vietnamese in the war. Out of this visit came the first **Strategic Arms Limitation Treaty** (SALT). This treaty placed limits on the use of nuclear weapons by the two powers.

■ What diplomatic moves did President Nixon make in 1972?

Henry Kissinger was Secretary of State under President Nixon. With North Vietnam's foreign minister, he received the Nobel Peace Prize in 1973 after negotiating a cease-fire. Where did he meet with the North Vietnamese?

President Nixon is greeted by Mao Tse-Tung, the communist leader of China. This historic visit was one of two missions for peace made by Nixon in 1972. How was he greeted by the Chinese?

A. Bernhaut, FPG

THE ELECTION OF 1972

President Nixon rose in popularity after his successful diplomatic visits and his efforts to wind down the war in Vietnam. The Republicans renominated him for a second term without opposition. The Democrats, however, had no obvious leader in 1972. Hubert Humphrey hoped to face Nixon again. Senator Edmund Muskie of Maine had many supporters. But the nomination went to Senator George McGovern of South Dakota, who had campaigned hard in the primaries on an antiwar platform.

McGovern's campaign was bungled from the start. His running mate, Senator Thomas Eagleton of Missouri, was discovered to have been hospitalized in the past for mental trouble. At first McGovern announced that he would stand behind Eagleton "one thousand per cent." Then he changed his mind. He forced Eagleton to withdraw. Sargent Shriver, a brother-in-law of John F. Kennedy, was chosen instead to run for Vice President. This incident made McGovern seem both indecisive and unfaithful to a loyal supporter.

Shortly before the election, Nixon's negotiator, Henry Kissinger, announced that he had reached an agreement with North Vietnamese leaders. "Peace is at hand," he said. As a result Nixon won an overwhelming victory on election day. He got more than 60 per cent of the popular vote and carried every state but Massachusetts.

■ What were some of the reasons that Richard Nixon won reelection by such an overwhelming majority?

AMERICA LEAVES VIETNAM

After Kissinger's "peace is at hand" announcement, Nixon stopped the bombing of North Vietnam. The agreement Kissinger had negotiated called for a cease fire, a joint North and South Vietnamese administration of the country, and free elections. Then the last of the American troops would go home and the American prisoners of war held by the North Vietnamese would be released.

After the Presidential election this agreement fell through. According to the Americans, the Vietnamese communists backed away from terms they had accepted earlier. The South Vietnamese government also objected to parts of the agreement. President Nixon then resumed the air strikes.

This time the President sent B-52 bombers, the largest in the air force, to strike at **Hanoi,** the capital of North Vietnam. These were far heavier attacks than any launched on Germany during World War II.

While the B-52s pounded Hanoi, peace negotiations were resumed in Paris. Finally, in January 1973, a treaty was signed. So far as the United States was concerned, the war was over. It had cost more than $100 billion and the lives of nearly 50,000 Americans and a much larger number of Vietnamese.

- What were the terms of the first peace agreement negotiated by Henry Kissinger? What reasons were given for its failure?
- What were the costs for the U.S. of the Vietnam War?

THE WATERGATE AFFAIR

The ending of the war and his landslide victory in the 1972 election made Richard Nixon seem one of the most powerful of American Presidents. He cut back sharply on various New Deal and Great Society programs designed to help poor people, blacks, and other disadvantaged groups. He also announced that it was time to crack down hard on crime. He criticized what he called the "permissiveness" of many Americans.

Yet, at the very moment of his greatest success, Nixon's power began to crumble. The cause was the **Watergate Affair,** one of the strangest episodes in the entire history of the United States.

On the night of June 17, 1972, shortly before the Presidential nominating conventions, five burglars were arrested in the headquarters of the Democratic National Committee in Washington, D.C. The headquarters were located in the Watergate, a modern office building and apartment house development on the Potomac River, in the heart of the city.

The burglars had large sums of money in new $100 bills in their wallets when they were arrested. They were carrying two expensive cameras, 40 rolls of film, and a number of tiny listening devices, or "bugs." They had obviously intended to copy Democratic party records and attach the bugs to the office telephones.

Suspicion naturally fell on the Republican party. One of the men arrested was James W. McCord, a former CIA employee who was working for Nixon's campaign organization, the Committee for the Reelection of the President (CREEP). Soon it was discovered that two other campaign officials had been involved in the break-in.

Both Nixon's campaign manager, former Attorney General John Mitchell, and the President himself denied that anyone on the White House staff had anything to do with the incident. Nixon's press secretary described it as a "third-rate burglary." Vice President Spiro Agnew suggested that the *Democrats* might have staged the affair to throw suspicion on the Republican party. Most people accepted the President's denial. The Watergate Affair had no effect on the election.

- What was the Watergate Affair?
- What stand did the White House take on Watergate?

THE COVER-UP

Early in 1973 the Watergate burglars were put on trial in Washington. Most of them pleaded guilty. This meant that they could not be questioned about the case. But one of them, James McCord, told the trial judge, John Sirica, that a number of important Republican officials had been involved in planning the burglary.

McCord's charges were found to be true. The Justice Department renewed its efforts to locate the persons behind the break-in. One by one, important members of the Nixon administration admitted that they had known about the incident. The head of the FBI confessed that he had destroyed documents related to the affair. Clearly there had been a **cover-up** of evidence. The Senate began an investigation.

John Dean, the President's lawyer, provided particularly damaging evidence to investigators. The President fired Dean, whom he considered a traitor. Nixon's two closest aides, H. R. Haldeman and John Ehrlichman, were forced to resign. Still, Nixon insisted that they were loyal public servants who had done nothing wrong.

As the Senate investigation proceeded, witnesses brought out more and more details about Watergate and other illegal activities connected with Nixon's campaign for reelection. It was shown that many large corporations had made secret contributions to the campaign fund. Such gifts were illegal. John Dean testified that the President had helped plan the cover-up from the beginning. When he had gone on television to deny that anyone in the White House was involved, the President had lied, Dean said.

John Dean begins his testimony to the Senate committee investigating Watergate in 1973. What made this testimony particularly important?

Dean's testimony was extremely important because it so directly involved the President. He appeared to be telling the truth. When details of his testimony could be checked against other sources, they proved to be correct. But Nixon denied the charges. It seemed to be his word against Dean's.

Then another witness testified that Nixon had been secretly recording all the conversations that had taken place in his office. These tape recordings would show whether or not Dean had told the truth! At once the Senate investigators demanded that the President allow them to listen to these and other **White House tapes** that might reveal important information.

Nixon refused to allow anyone to listen to the tapes. He claimed what he called **executive privilege**—the right to keep information secret when it related to Presidential business.

Senators Howard Baker and Sam Ervin confer during their Senate investigation into Watergate. It was Senator Baker who asked a key question about the President: "What did he know and when did he know it?" What evidence did this committe demand?

More and more people came to the conclusion that Nixon was lying. Charges that he had cheated on his income taxes while President by claiming large illegal deductions further turned public opinion against him. Yet how could the full truth be discovered while persons Nixon had appointed ran the Justice Department? To end the criticism, Nixon agreed to the appointment of a distinguished law professor, Archibald Cox, as a **special prosecutor** for the Justice Department to take charge of the Watergate case. Cox was promised a free hand and told to pursue the truth wherever the facts led him.

Professor Cox also demanded that the White House tapes be turned over to his investigators for study. Again Nixon refused. A federal judge then ordered him to give Cox the tapes. Instead of doing so, Nixon ordered Attorney General Elliot L. Richardson, head of the Justice Department, to fire Cox!

Richardson resigned rather than carry out this order. So did the assistant attorney general. Nixon persisted and finally the number-three man in the Justice Department discharged Cox. These events occurred on the evening of Saturday, October 20, 1973. The affair was called the **Saturday Night Massacre.**

Nixon's entire administration seemed riddled with scandal. Only ten days before the Saturday Night Massacre, Vice President Spiro Agnew admitted that he had been cheating on his income taxes. He resigned from office. Actually, the official record of his case revealed that he had also accepted $200,000 in bribes while serving as a public official in Maryland. To avoid the national shame of having a Vice President in prison, government lawyers had allowed him to plead guilty only of income tax evasion. Agnew was fined and placed on probation.

The **Twenty-fifth Amendment** of the Constitution, ratified in 1967, includes a provision that when the Vice Presidency falls vacant, the President shall appoint a new Vice President. Nixon chose Congressman Gerald R. Ford of Michigan. The appointment was approved by Congress and Ford became Vice President.

■ What was the cover-up in the Watergate Affair?

NIXON FALLS FROM POWER

The Saturday Night Massacre led many people to demand that Nixon be impeached. (*Impeachment* is the legal means to charge a high official with wrongdoing.) To quiet those demanding his impeachment, Nixon promised to cooperate with Cox's successor as Watergate prosecutor, Leon Jaworski, a Texas lawyer. Nevertheless, the **Judiciary Committee** of the House of Representatives began an investigation to see if there were grounds for impeaching Nixon.

While the Judiciary Committee studied the evidence of Nixon's involvement, prosecutor Jaworski proceeded against others. One after another, men who had been involved in Nixon's campaign for reelection were charged and convicted of crimes. Some had lied under oath, others had obstructed justice, one had raised money for the campaign in an unlawful manner.

Late in April 1974 Nixon released edited transcripts of some of his taped conversations. These, he said, would prove his innocence. However, important parts of conversations were left out in these printed versions. At many places the typescripts contained blanks because, Nixon claimed, the tapes had not recorded what was said clearly enough to be understood. Still he refused to let others check on the editing by listening to the tapes.

Both what the transcripts revealed and what they left out led to increased demands that the President allow investigators to listen to the key tapes themselves. Nixon still refused. He would not turn them over to either the House Judiciary Committee or to special prosecutor Jaworski.

Jaworski therefore asked the Supreme Court to order the President to give him the tapes of 64 specific conversations known to have taken place in the White House. While the Court considered the matter, the Judiciary Committee decided to allow its sessions to be broadcast and televised. In July 1974 the committee passed three **articles of impeachment,** or charges against the President. One accused Nixon of obstructing justice. Another accused him of misusing the powers of the Presidency. The third concerned his refusal to let the committee listen to the tapes.

Under the Constitution the Judiciary Committee's report would be submitted to the full House of Representatives. If the report was accepted, the House would then impeach Nixon by presenting the articles of impeachment to the Senate. The Senate would act as a court hearing the charges. If two thirds of the senators voted in favor of any of the three articles, Nixon would be removed from office.

While the Judiciary Committee was still debating, the Supreme Court ruled that Nixon must turn the tapes over to prosecutor Jaworski. Nixon hesitated. If he defied the Court's order, it was difficult to see how it could be enforced. But Nixon's advisers convinced him that if he refused to obey the court order, the Senate was certain to remove him from office. Therefore he gave up the tapes.

The tapes proved conclusively that Nixon had known about the Watergate cover-up from the start. Only one day after he had said on television that no one in the White House had anything to do with the affair, he had ordered his chief assistant, H. R. Haldeman, to persuade the FBI not to investigate the break-in too vigorously. The FBI could be told that national security was involved, the President suggested.

Dennis Brack, Black Star

After their final hours in the White House Richard and Patricia Nixon, right, are escorted by Gerald and Betty Ford on August 9, 1974. Why did Nixon choose to resign?

Nixon now had the choice of resigning before the House voted to impeach him or going on trial in hopes that the Senate might not remove him. He resigned. On August 9, at noon, he officially surrendered his powers. Gerald R. Ford then took the oath of office and became President of the United States. One of President Ford's first actions was to offer Nixon a pardon for any crimes he may have committed. Nixon promptly accepted the pardon. Thus we close this sad chapter with the full truth about the Watergate Affair still not known.

▪ What three articles of impeachment were passed by the House Judiciary Committee against Nixon?
▪ What did the Supreme Court order in the case against Nixon?
▪ Why were the transcripts of the White House tapes unable to prove the President's claim of innocence?

880

CHAPTER 29 REVIEW

Identification

Tell briefly why each of the following persons, terms, or events is important.

1. Lyndon B. Johnson
2. Eugene McCarthy
3. Robert F. Kennedy
4. Hubert H. Humphrey
5. Richard M. Nixon
6. George McGovern
7. George C. Wallace
8. Henry Kissinger
9. Leon Jaworski
10. Gerald R. Ford
11. Tonkin Gulf Resolution
12. Viet Cong
13. Domino theory
14. Hawks
15. Doves
16. Tet offensive
17. Wage and price freeze
18. SALT
19. CREEP
20. Watergate Affair

Understanding American History

1. How did belief in the domino theory lead the United States to an escalation in the Vietnam War?
2. Distinguish between supporters of South Vietnam, North Vietnam, and the Viet Cong.
3. Identify the events that made 1968 a year of tragedy for the United States.
4. What was President Nixon's plan of Vietnamization? Why did he send American troops into Cambodia? What reaction did this set off in the United States?
5. What were the results of President Nixon's visits to China and Russia?
6. What was the cost, in lives and dollars, of the Vietnam War?
7. What was the Watergate Affair?
8. What was the extent of President Nixon's victory in his reelection in 1972? How was the Democratic campaign bungled?
9. What was the Watergate cover-up? How did it cause President Nixon to resign from the Presidency?
10. How did Gerald R. Ford become Vice President and then President of the United States?

Activities

1. Use a large map of Asia and the Pacific Ocean to trace the possible course of the Vietnam War according to the domino theory. How might the war have spread? Use the map to show where Vietnam was once divided into North and South. Identify the Gulf of Tonkin, Hanoi, Saigon (now Ho Chi Minh City), and the Ho Chi Minh Trail located in Cambodia.
2. Use reference works such as an atlas and almanac to gather statistics on the election of 1968, state by state, Then prepare a large map showing popular and electoral totals. Use the maps on page 597 as models.
3. As an oral history project, ask older members of your family to describe their reactions to major events of the late 1960s and early 1970s. Topics should include the Vietnam War and the antiwar movement; the assassinations of Martin Luther King, Jr., and Robert Kennedy in 1968; the Chicago riot between antiwar demonstrators and police; the opening of China by President Nixon; and the Watergate Affair.
4. As Secretary of State under President Nixon, Henry Kissinger won the Nobel Peace Prize in 1973. Present a report on one of these Secretaries of State: John Quincy Adams (pages 283–85), William H. Seward (614–15), James G. Blaine (618), Richard Olney (619), John Hay (634–35), John Foster Dulles (824), or Henry Kissinger (873–75).
5. Use the resources of your library to prepare a Watergate chronology. Find newspaper and magazine accounts of the events from the break-in to Richard Nixon's resignation.

CHAPTER 29 TEST

Completion (40 points)
Number your paper 1–20 and next to each number write the words from the list below that best complete each sentence.

Watergate cover-up
domino theory
hawks
escalation
Lyndon B. Johnson
Robert F. Kennedy
Watergate Affair
Viet Cong
Cambodia
George C. Wallace

Tonkin Gulf Resolution
Richard M. Nixon
wage and price freeze
Eugene McCarthy
Vietnamization
George McGovern
Tet offensive
inflation
doves
Hubert H. Humphrey

The 1960s saw the __1__ of America's involvement in the Vietnam War. Congress gave President Johnson broad powers to wage this war under the __2__. Most Americans supported the President because they feared the loss of Southeast Asia to communism under the __3__. American and South Vietnamese soldiers fought the __4__ and the North Vietnamese.

Supporters of the Vietnam War were called __5__, and its opponents were called __6__. After America and South Vietnam suffered heavy losses during the __7__, the tide of opinion in the United States turned against the war.

With America in turmoil, __8__ decided not to seek reelection as President. He had been opposed in the New Hampshire primary by __9__. Then __10__ entered the race but was assassinated after winning the California primary. The President supported __11__, who won the Democratic nomination.

The Republicans nominated __12__, who went on to win the election, defeating the Democratic candidate and __13__ of Alabama. The new President planned to end America's involvement in Vietnam with a program called __14__. But he drew protest by ordering U.S. soldiers over the Vietnamese border into __15__.

The new President also fought the economic problem of __16__. In 1971 he used a 90-day __17__ to slow down the rising cost of living.

In 1972 members of the Committee to Reelect the President burgled the Democratic party headquarters in what came to be known as the __18__. A few months later the President easily defeated __19__. But he was forced to resign during his second term because of his part in the __20__.

Chronological Order (30 points)
Number your paper 21–30 and place each set of events in order by numbering 1 for the first, 2 for the second, and so on.
21. President Nixon orders Vietnamization of the war.
22. Congress approves the Tonkin Gulf Resolution.
23. President Nixon orders U.S. troops into Cambodia.
24. American morale falls after the Tet offensive.
25. President Johnson orders escalation of the Vietnam War.

— Vietnam War

26. Robert F. Kennedy is assassinated while campaigning.
27. Richard Nixon is elected President.
28. McCarthy challenges Johnson in New Hampshire.
29. President Johnson decides not to seek reelection.
30. Hubert H. Humphrey wins the Democratic nomination.

— 1968 Election

Essay (30 points)
Write a brief essay describing Richard M. Nixon's successes and failures as President, *or* Describe the events of 1968 that made it a year of tragedy for America.

CHAPTER 30

Modern Times

Before he became President, Gerald Ford was known as an honest, hard-working politician. Nearly everyone in Congress liked him. He got on easily with people. But he had never been noted for vision or originality. During his 25 years in Congress he had seemed more comfortable working for or against the programs of others than developing his own ideas.

Ford was modest about his abilities. When he became President, he announced that he intended to work closely with Congress. "My office door has always been open," he said, "and that is how it is going to be in the White House." Since both Ford and his Vice President, Nelson Rockefeller, had been appointed rather than elected by the people, Ford's style seemed the proper one to adopt.

THE FORD PRESIDENCY

By 1974 business activity had slowed down. Unemployment was increasing. The Democrats blamed this economic recession on Nixon and Ford. They wanted to increase government spending in order to speed recovery. On the other hand, most Republicans feared the economic slump less than they feared inflation. Even when the economy was slowing down, prices continued to rise. More government spending would push prices still higher, Republicans said.

In 1974 the Democrats increased their majorities in both houses of Congress. When the new Congress met, they were able to pass bills designed to help poor people and to create new jobs. Measures providing for construction of public housing, aid to education, and health care were soon sent to President Ford. He vetoed all of them. They involved spending huge sums of money, he explained. Therefore they would lead to still greater inflation. In a little over one year he vetoed 39 bills. In most cases the Democrats were not able to get the two-thirds majorities needed to override the President's veto.

The recession continued. Economists began to describe the country as passing through a period of **stagflation**—a word coined by combining "*stag*nation" and "*inflation*." Finally, in the spring of 1975, Ford reluctantly signed a bill reducing taxes. This helped to end the downturn. By early 1976 the recession was over.

■ What helped end the stagflation of 1975?

Fred Ward, Black Star

When Gerald R. Ford succeeded to the Presidency, he became the only chief executive who was appointed to office rather than elected. Ford's Congressional colleagues cheered his appointment as Vice President in 1973 and later supported him as President. How did Ford show his willingness to work with Congress?

WOMEN SEEK EQUAL RIGHTS

The 1964 Civil Rights Act had banned discrimination on the basis of sex as well as race. Still, women's organizations had pressed for a Constitutional amendment that would guarantee their equality under law. After much debate in 1972 Congress passed an **Equal Rights Amendment** (ERA). This amendment provided that "equality of rights under the law shall not be denied or abridged by the United States or by any state on account of sex." It was submitted to the states for ratification.

The proposed amendment had wide support among women and men from all walks of life. One of the most important women to speak out for the ERA was Elizabeth Bloomer Ford, the First Lady. Like millions of American wives and mothers, she had raised her family in the prosperous years after World War II. She had given up her own career as a dancer when her husband was first elected to Congress in 1948. Thereafter he was rarely home, dividing his time between Congress and trips back to Michigan to campaign for reelection. Betty Ford, at home with the children, quietly questioned her situation.

Tens of thousands of women from relatively poor families had always had to work. Middle-class women, however, had tended to remain in the home after marriage. In the 1950s more and more of these women were taking jobs. They discovered what every working

When the Equal Rights Amendment was not ratified by three fourths of the state legislatures, marchers such as these urged an extension. This demonstration took place in Washington, D.C. in 1978. When did Congress pass the ERA?

Chie Nishio, Nancy Palmer

The Cincinnati Art Museum, The Edwin and Virginia Irwin Memorial, © Estate of Grant Wood, courtesy Associated American Artists, 1981

woman could have told them: in nearly every field the wages and salaries paid to women were lower than those earned by men doing the same work. Moreover, the best jobs were rarely open to women. It was much harder for women to gain admission to law schools and medical colleges. In the business world women were rarely promoted to important positions, especially to those where they might be issuing orders to men.

Most male employers justified their practice by claiming that women usually worked only while waiting to be married. There was no use in promoting women, they said, because most would soon leave in order to marry and raise a family. When it was pointed out that more and more married women were taking jobs, employers shifted their argument. They claimed that it was all right to pay married women less than men because married women did not have to support a family on their own!

Working women naturally resented being discriminated against in the job market. When their numbers increased in the 1950s and 1960s, their resentment burst forth in the **Women's Liberation Movement.** "Women's Lib" first attracted widespread public attention with the publication in 1963 of *The Feminine Mystique* by Betty Friedan.

Friedan had become interested in the problems of well-educated women after she made a study of graduates of Smith College, one of the nation's leading women's colleges. She discovered that a large percentage of these women were unhappy and full of feelings of inadequacy. Why, she wondered, were so many intelligent women so dissatisfied with their lives?

Grant Wood was one of America's finest 20th-century painters. He titled this painting "Daughters of the Revolution." Study the faces of these three women. Might they oppose or support the ERA? Below is Betty Friedan. For what book is she known?

Frederick De Van, Nancy Palmer

The answer, Friedan decided, was that women felt held back by their family responsibilities. They did not see themselves as people. In her own mind the typical woman was "Mrs. Jones" or "Billy Jones's mother." Not even her name could she call her own.

Most women thought that they *ought* to be completely satisfied with their roles as wives and mothers, Friedan wrote. Were not popular magazines like the *Ladies' Home Journal* full of articles describing the satisfactions of raising a large family and running a complicated household efficiently?

Women who read *The Feminine Mystique* experienced what has come to be called **consciousness-raising.** They became aware that their personal doubts and dissatisfactions were shared by others.

Betty Friedan was not a radical. She did not argue that caring for a family was a bad thing. While she was writing her book, she was also bringing up three children of her own. But she insisted that the way to have a satisfying life was the same for women as for men: they must find some sort of "creative work."

In 1966 Friedan helped found the **National Organization for Women** (NOW). Its purpose was to lift legal restrictions on women and see that they got equal employment opportunities in all fields. The government should provide aids like day-care centers for working women with small children, NOW officials argued.

Like Betty Friedan, thousands of prominent women and men vigorously sought equal rights for women. But opposition to the proposed Equal Rights Amendment proved to be strong. Its approval by three fourths of the state legislatures was not forthcoming, even after the deadline for ratification was extended. Some people considered ERA unnecessary because of existing laws against discrimination. Others feared that it would do more harm than good by doing away with laws providing special benefits and protections for women, such as those limiting the hours of women workers. Women would have to be drafted into the armed services in the event of war, opponents of the ERA claimed.

Thus hope dimmed for supporters of the ERA. In 1980 the Republican party refused to endorse the amendment. President Reagan did, however, show his support for equal rights early in his Presidency by appointing Sandra Day O'Connor to the Supreme Court. The President stressed that the Arizona judge was appointed for her ability, not because she was a woman. O'Connor was easily confirmed by the Senate, 99–0, and in October 1981 she became the first woman to sit on the high court.

■ What did the proposed Equal Rights Amendment provide?
■ What did Betty Friedan discover in her survey of women?
■ How did President Reagan show support for equal rights?

Justice Sandra Day O'Connor began her service on the Supreme Court in October 1981. Her appointment won unanimous approval by the Senate. What reason did President Reagan give for her nomination?

The Bicentennial

In 1976 the United States celebrated its **Bicentennial**, the 200th anniversary of the signing of the Declaration of Independence. The celebration was carried out in grand style. Communities all over the country organized and carried out hundreds of special programs—some sensible, some foolish, some pure fun.

In Miami Beach, Florida, 7,000 immigrants were sworn in as citizens of the United States in a mass ceremony at Convention Hall. A man in Oro Grande, California, unfurled a giant American flag measuring 102 by 67 feet (about 30 by 20 meters). There was a balloon race to celebrate the occasion in San Antonio, Texas, and a cherry-pie eating contest in Traverse City, Michigan. In other cities and towns there were parades, fireworks, and reenactments of Revolutionary War battles.

President Ford spoke at Valley Forge, where Washington's army had spent the hard winter of 1777, and at Independence Hall in Philadelphia, where the Declaration had been signed.

The highlight of the Bicentennial Day was **Operation Sail**, a majestic procession of gaily decorated ships in New York harbor. No less than 16 great, high-masted sailing ships from many nations participated. Millions of people lined the New York waterfront and crowded the windows of skyscrapers to watch these "tall ships" and the hundreds of other craft that accompanied them.

Somehow the tall ships became a symbol of pride and hope. They had come to New York from all over the world, sent by nations friendly and not-so-friendly to help celebrate the anniversary. This was a recognition of the importance of the United States and even more of what America had meant over the centuries to the people of other nations.

And the tall ships had endured, just as the United States had endured, in a time of enormous change. They were old but still strong, sound, and very beautiful. Although dwarfed by the great Verrazano Bridge across the harbor entrance and by the skyscrapers of Manhattan, they seemed to tower over their surroundings. They had a quiet dignity in contrast to the noise and bustle of the tugs, ferries, and other craft that swarmed about them. They stood for the value of tradition, for past achievements, for history. Better than any military parade or other display of modern power, they reflected the true strength of the American people.

Fred Ward, Black Star

THE ELECTION OF 1976

Among the people who enjoyed Operation Sail were the delegates to the Democratic convention, which met in New York City. On July 14 the convention nominated James Earl Carter, Jr., for President. Jimmy Carter, as he preferred to be known, had been a little-known Georgia peanut farmer and businessman. His earlier political experience had been limited to service in the Georgia legislature and one term as governor of Georgia.

Carter had begun his campaign for the Presidency in 1974. No one then thought he had much chance. But he worked hard. He studied the issues. He answered reporters' questions carefully and fully. He smiled constantly for the television cameras. In 1976 he won several important primaries, and by the time of the Democratic convention his nomination was a certainty.

At the Republican convention in Kansas City, President Ford won a narrow victory by beating back the challenge of Ronald Reagan, the former governor of California.

At first Carter seemed sure to defeat Ford easily in the election. His strategy was to picture himself as an "outsider" who had no connection with the corruption and scandal that seemed to surround Washington in the age of Watergate. In television advertisements and in his public speeches he stressed his sincerity, his honesty, and above all, his deep religious faith. "I'll never lie to you," he promised the voters. He also stressed his business skills. He would run the federal government efficiently, he said, and he would balance the budget.

Ford emphasized his political experience. He compared his 27 years in national politics to Carter's brief stint at the state level. As the campaign progressed, Ford seemed to gain ground.

Public interest in the campaign was low, however. Barely half the eligible voters actually went to the polls. It was particularly discouraging that relatively few of the 18- to 20-year-olds who had been given the vote by the **Twenty-sixth Amendment** (ratified in 1971) bothered to cast ballots.

The election was very close. Carter won in the electoral college by 297 votes to 240. This was the narrowest margin since Woodrow Wilson defeated Charles Evans Hughes in 1916 by an electoral vote of 277 to 254. Carter carried the northern industrial states and the South. A major reason for his victory was the support he received from Mexican-Americans, particularly in south Texas, and from blacks. Almost 95 out of every 100 black voters cast their ballots for Carter.

- What was Carter's strategy in his campaign against Ford for the Presidency in 1976?
- What was a major reason for Carter's victory?

888

THE CARTER PRESIDENCY

Jimmy Carter tried to make himself more available to ordinary people than most recent Presidents. Instead of riding back to the White House in a limousine after his inauguration, he and his wife and small daughter walked down Pennsylvania Avenue at the head of the inaugural parade, waving and smiling to the crowd.

In office Carter continued to stress this informal style. He appeared on television wearing a sweater instead of a suit coat. He had a "call-in" on television in which he answered questions phoned in by ordinary citizens. He held "town meetings" in different parts of the country in order to sound out public opinion.

As the months passed, critics began to claim that Carter was a poor leader. The economic and social problems of the times were too much for him, these critics charged. He changed his mind too often, they said. Members of his administration frequently did not seem to know what was the President's policy on important issues.

Some members of his own party insisted that Carter was not doing enough to stimulate the economy. He should urge Congress to increase government spending, they said. But others argued that the programs he did support were too expensive.

Many blacks complained bitterly that Carter had forgotten how important black voters had been to him in the election. He had not

At his home in Plains, Georgia, the President-elect, Jimmy Carter, talks with reporters. His Vice President, Walter Mondale, is to his left. The Carters stressed informality in the White House. Why did they believe this approach was important?

Ron Sherman, Nancy Palmer

appointed enough blacks to posts in his administration, they said. He had not done enough about unemployment and other issues important to the poor. Still other people attacked Carter for not doing something about the shortage of petroleum products and the soaring price of gasoline and heating oil.

Carter did win public praise for his efforts to bring peace to the troubled Middle East. He brought Israel's premier, Menachem Begin, and Egypt's president, Anwar Sadat, to Camp David, the Presidential retreat. There the three leaders hammered out an agreement to work for peace, known as the **Camp David Accords.**

■ In what ways did Carter stress his informal style?

IMMIGRATION IN THE 1970s

Newcomers to America are more likely to have come from different parts of the world than the immigrants of the past. Southern and eastern Europeans now come in much larger numbers than people from northern and western Europe. But the greatest change has been in the number of Asians arriving.

In 1965, under the old regulations, the entire continent of Asia supplied only 20,000 immigrants to America. In 1973 over 124,000 Asians entered the United States. The majority came from Korea, the Philippine Islands, and more recently from Vietnam and Cambodia.

The Korean War and the stern policies of the South Korean government led thousands of **Koreans** to apply for entry into the United States. Most settled in California and Hawaii, but considerable numbers came to New York City and other eastern cities. There were no more than 2,000 Koreans in the United States before the Korean War. By 1970 there were about 70,000. In 1975 alone more than 28,000 Korean immigrants arrived.

Still larger numbers of **Filipinos** were becoming Americans. When the Philippine Islands was a colony of the United States, there was no limit on Filipino entry. By 1930 over 100,000 had come. More than half settled in the Hawaiian Islands, where they worked mostly on sugar and pineapple plantations. Many Filipinos enlisted in the navy during this time. However, because of prejudice against Orientals, nearly all were assigned to duty as mess boys (kitchen workers) or as servants to officers.

When the Philippines became independent after World War II, Filipino immigration declined to a trickle. But after the Immigration Act of 1965 it soared. As in the case of the South Koreans, many of the new arrivals came for political reasons. Unlike the earlier Filipino immigrants, many were skilled workers and professional people.

The **Vietnamese** who came to America were nearly all victims of the Vietnam War. In 1975 about 140,000 of these refugees were

Sipa Press, Black Star

admitted without regard for the limits imposed by the immigration law. In that year South Vietnamese resistance to Viet Cong and North Vietnamese military pressure collapsed. The communists gained control of all Vietnam. Many Vietnamese who had been friendly to America were driven from their country after the fall of Saigon, when the capital of South Vietnam was seized by the victorious communists. The United States government helped these Vietnamese to settle in America.

Later, thousands of other South Vietnamese and **Cambodians** fled their homelands to escape communist rule. Nearly all left on small ships, many of which were not seaworthy. Many of these **boat people** were drowned. Others died in refugee camps in nearby lands. In 1979 the United States admitted large numbers of the boat people.

■ For what reasons did immigrants come from Korea, the Philippines, Vietnam, and Cambodia?

MEXICAN-AMERICANS MOVE NORTH

By far the largest number of immigrants admitted under the 1965 law came from Mexico. Before World War II the ebb and flow of Mexican immigration had depended almost entirely on economic conditions. During the Great Depression, when jobs were scarce, far more Mexicans left the United States than came in.

When the United States entered World War II, however, the demand for labor in the Southwest soared. The United States and

Fighting between the Khmer Rouge and the Vietnamese army in Phom Malai drove these refugees from their Cambodian homeland. Many suffered from malaria and hunger. In what way did the U.S. assist the Cambodian boat people?

891

Mexico signed an agreement allowing Mexicans to work temporarily in the United States. These workers were known as *braceros,* a name that comes from the Spanish word for "arm." The *braceros* were brought north to harvest crops and sent back when the season ended. Their employers supplied them with food and housing, usually of very poor quality. Their wages were extremely low. Nevertheless, between 1942 and 1964 almost 5 million Mexicans came to the United States under the *bracero* program.

As with immigrants all through history, many of the Mexicans who had settled permanently in the United States found that the country was indeed the land of opportunity. Many obtained farms of their own. Others landed good jobs. Some became successful professionals. Their example caused thousands of other Mexicans to want to come to the United States. After the 1965 immigration law put a limit on the number of newcomers from the Western Hemisphere, many Mexicans entered the United States illegally by swimming across the Rio Grande. They came north because there was no work for them in Mexico. In the United States they found work, but at very low wages.

Most employers treated the illegal immigrants even more badly than they treated the *braceros* because these workers could not complain without risk of being arrested and sent back to Mexico. Still they continued to flock northward. As one explained, "The life is better than any I can hope to have back home."

Throughout the postwar years Mexican-born workers harvested most of the crops grown in California and the rest of the Southwest. Gradually a leader emerged for these **migrant workers,** who followed the harvest. César Chávez, who had grown up in the migrant camps of California, founded a labor union, the **National Farm Workers Association.** Three years later this union joined with an organization of Filipino farm laborers to form the **United Farm Workers Organizing Committee.** Then Chávez called for a great *huelga,* or strike, against the California grape growers.

The strikers won a great deal of public sympathy. When Chávez called for a national boycott of grapes, supporters across the country began picketing supermarkets and grocery stores. They urged shoppers not to buy California grapes until the growers came to terms with the strikers. Protesters in Boston staged a "Boston Grape Party." They dumped grapes into the harbor just as the colonists had dumped East India Company tea in 1773.

Chávez's own dedication was almost as important as the low wages earned by the pickers in winning public support. He led a long march on the state capital to put pressure on the California legislature. He staged a 25-day hunger strike. It took five years before the grape growers recognized the union and settled the strike.

César Chávez was photographed in 1966 standing in front of a National Farm Workers standard. *Huelga* is Spanish for "strike." Which people did Chavez lead?

Chávez inspired migrant workers with a sense of their own worth. "We . . . stood tall outside the vineyards where we had stooped for years," the grape pickers stated proudly. Some who called themselves **Chicanos** spoke of *La Causa* (the cause) which was to make all members of *La Raza* (the race) conscious of their common history and culture.

- Why did many Mexicans immigrate to the United States?
- How did the California migrant farm workers organize?

SPANISH-SPEAKING NEWCOMERS

After the Cuban Revolution of 1959 many thousands of Cubans who were opposed to the new government of Fidel Castro emigrated to the United States. After Castro announced that he was a communist and made an alliance with the Soviet Union, these Cubans were admitted to the United States under laws that allowed refugees from communist countries to come in without regard for any limits set by the immigration laws. All told, about 750,000 entered. About half settled in southern Florida, in and around Miami.

For the next 20 years Castro made it next to impossible for Cubans to leave their country. In 1980, however, he changed his mind. In a few weeks' time more than 100,000 Cubans entered the United States. As with the Vietnamese in 1975, restrictions on immigration were temporarily set aside.

The other major group of Spanish-speaking newcomers came from Puerto Rico. Since Puerto Rico was part of the United States, these people were American citizens. The immigration laws did not apply to them.

Living conditions were hard in Puerto Rico, and unemployment was extremely high. The airlines ran many low-cost jet flights from the island to the mainland. Hundreds of thousands of Puerto Ricans came north in search of work. Most settled in New York City, which soon had a larger Puerto Rican population than San Juan, the capital of Puerto Rico.

In many ways the Puerto Ricans were like the European immigrants of the years before the Great World War. Most were very poor. Most came from rural backgrounds and were not accustomed to city life. Few could speak English. Few had the skills needed to get well-paid jobs. All these things made life hard for the Puerto Ricans. Many were crowded into neglected pockets of the city called **barrios.**

Yet many Puerto Ricans were able to improve their lives. Herman Badillo came to New York from Puerto Rico in 1941, when he was 12. He worked as a dishwasher and as a pin boy in a bowling alley. He went to college and earned a law degree. In 1965 he was elected borough president of the Bronx, the part of New York City with the largest Puerto Rican population. In 1970 he was elected to Congress. He later ran for mayor of New York but was defeated.

By the 1970s there were large clusters of other Caribbean island people in the large eastern cities, especially in New York. Many came from Haiti, the Dominican Republic, and Colombia.

- Why were restrictions on immigration set aside for Cubans?
- How were the Puerto Rican immigrants like the European immigrants who arrived after the Great World War?

BLACKS EXAMINE THEIR HERITAGE

While many of the postwar immigrants had dark skins, their backgrounds were far different from that of the native-born American blacks. Indeed, black Americans had been part of the country's history for some 350 years. Only the American Indians had been in the country longer.

The same interests that made immigrants cling to their traditions encouraged blacks to look into their past and take pride in their long struggle for freedom and fair treatment.

Increased knowledge of past injustices made American blacks even more determined to gain respect and equal treatment. Martin Luther King, Jr.'s policy of persuasion and passive resistance had not satisfied some **black activists.** Their leaders talked of **Black Power.** Their goal was not integration. They believed in separating themselves entirely from white society. Even well-meaning whites were unwelcome, explained Stokley Carmichael, a leader of the Black Power movement. White people "cannot understand the black experience," Carmichael insisted.

As we have seen, one of the many injustices of slavery was the way it cut off its victims from contact with family and relatives and from nearly all knowledge of their lost homeland. Blacks became eager to recover some of their hidden history. The study of African history and culture increased in the schools and colleges in the 1960s and 1970s.

One reflection of this interest in origins and influences was the enormous popularity of Alex Haley's book *Roots*. Haley set out to try to reconstruct his personal family history. After much work he believed he had traced it back to an African named Kunta Kinte, who had been captured and carried off to slavery in America in the 1700s. Haley's reconstruction of his distant past was, of course, part truth and part fiction. The book and a television serial based upon it were enormously popular, read and seen by millions of people.

- What belief did black activists hold?
- What did the enormous interest in *Roots* reflect?

THE AMERICAN INDIAN MOVEMENT

The same emphasis on reviving lost cultures and values affected American Indians. During the New Deal period the federal government had given up the effort begun with the Dawes Act of 1887 to force Indians to copy white ways and adopt white values. Instead, the **Indian Reorganization Act** of 1934 encouraged the revival of tribal life. Indians should choose their own leaders and run their own affairs, supporters of the new policy believed. Many did so.

Indian schools began to teach Indian languages and history. Ancient arts and crafts were relearned and developed. A **National Indian Youth Council,** founded in 1961, began to press for the return of Indian lands in many parts of the nation. Some Indians coined the term **Red Power** to rally supporters.

In 1968 Congress passed what was known as the **Indian Rights Act.** This law was intended to protect Indians against discrimination and mistreatment. But it had the unintended effect of weakening the new tribal governments. These were often dominated by powerful chiefs who did not respect the needs and opinions of all tribe members. Many Indians objected and sought relief under the law.

In 1972 a new organization, the **American Indian Movement** (AIM) began to use more drastic techniques in an effort to achieve its goals. Its members staged sit-ins at various sites. They occupied the

Paul Fusco, Magnum

These Kiowa Sioux seek justice for American Indians They carry the AIM rainbow banner What was an unintended effect of the Indian Rights Act of 1968?

offices of the Bureau of Indian Affairs in Washington for several days to call attention to their demands for fairer treatment.

The most dramatic of the Indian occupations occurred in 1973 at the town of **Wounded Knee** in South Dakota. The AIM leaders chose Wounded Knee because it had been the site of a terrible massacre of Indian women and children by white soldiers in 1891. The Indian activists held the town for weeks before laying down arms.

■ Which recent laws assisted American Indians?

CRISIS IN AMERICA'S CITIES

By the 1970s about three quarters of the American people were living in cities and their surrounding suburbs. These **metropolitan areas** were growing steadily larger. As they expanded, metropolitan areas began to meet one another. They formed supercities.

One **urban complex** or megalopolis (from the Greek for "great city") stretched from Portland, Maine, through Boston, New York City, Philadelphia, Baltimore, and Washington to Richmond, Virginia. It was known as BosWash. Another, ChiPitt, reached from

J. R. Eyerman, Black Star

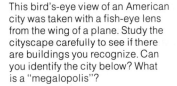

This bird's-eye view of an American city was taken with a fish-eye lens from the wing of a plane. Study the cityscape carefully to see if there are buildings you recognize. Can you identify the city below? What is a "megalopolis"?

Chicago to Pittsburgh. A third, SanSan, extended from San Francisco to San Diego in California.

Within these metropolitan areas the central or **inner cities** wasted away. Large numbers of their well-to-do and middle-class residents moved to the suburbs. Poor city dwellers, many of them blacks, Puerto Ricans, or Mexican-Americans, remained behind.

A vicious circle of decay resulted from this population shift. When the better-off citizens with money to spend began to leave, department stores and other businesses followed these good customers to the suburbs. This meant that there were fewer jobs for inner-city residents. It meant also that city tax collections fell off.

Public services began to decline as a result. Often the city governments raised tax rates to make up for the loss. This caused still more middle-income citizens to move away. Higher property taxes also made it difficult for landlords to make a profit. They therefore skimped on maintaining their buildings. Heating systems broke down in winter. Roofs leaked. Corridors were dark and dirty. Basically sound buildings soon deteriorated beyond repair, and decent neighborhoods became slums.

This general decline made life harder and more discouraging for the people who had to remain in the inner cities. Their children had little hope of getting decent jobs when they completed their schooling. Since the cities had less money, the schools began to suffer too. Classes were overcrowded. Supplies were inadequate. Equipment broke down.

Faced with such conditions, many students lost interest in school. They became **dropouts.** Unable to find jobs, many of these dropouts idled about causing trouble. Hopeless and resentful, some turned to crime.

Poor schools and increasing crime statistics led still more middle-class people to move away. As the population of the inner cities fell, whole sections were abandoned. Empty buildings attracted vandals and criminals. Windows were soon smashed, pipes, fixtures, and wiring ripped out. Fires broke out in the ruins.

One of the worst examples of this **urban decay** was the section of New York City called the South Bronx. In 1977 President Carter visited this district. He was deeply shocked. The area looked as though it had been bombed in an air raid. It contained about 1,500 buildings. Most were fire-blackened, empty shells. Yet just a few minutes' drive from the South Bronx, fashionable shoppers bought their gold cuff links at Tiffany's and perfume at Saks Fifth Avenue.

- Which were the three primary urban complexes?
- What vicious circle developed with the decay of the inner cities?

THE UNITED STATES

POPULATION DISTRIBUTION

Travelers who cross the United States by night sometimes see the lights of America's cities in much the same way as this map shows. Can you locate BosWash, ChiPitt, and SanSan?

RBAN AND RURAL, IN THE UNITED STATES

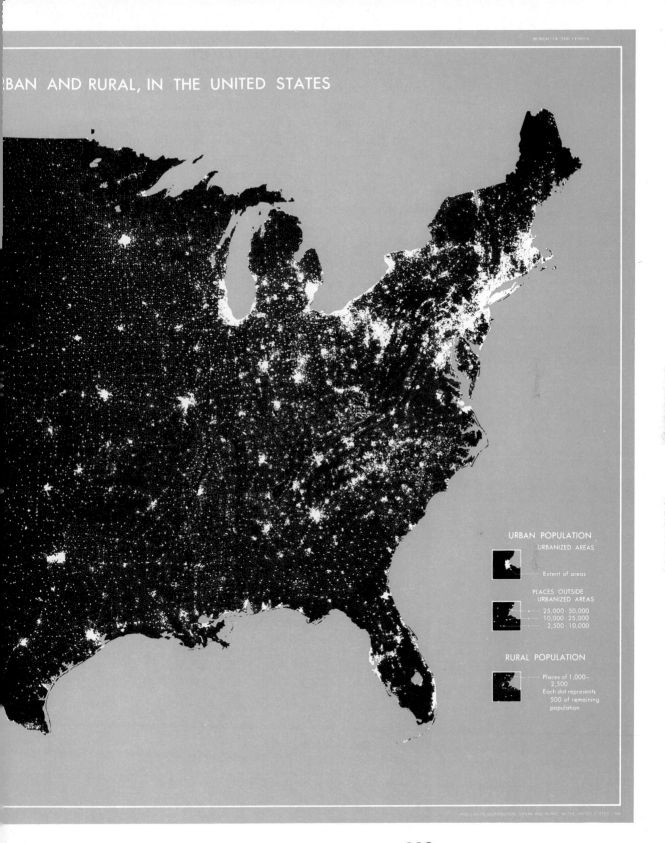

URBAN POPULATION

URBANIZED AREAS

← Extent of areas

PLACES OUTSIDE
URBANIZED AREAS

• 25,000 - 50,000
• 10,000 - 25,000
· 2,500 - 10,000

RURAL POPULATION

· Places of 1,000 -
2,500
Each dot represents
500 of remaining
population

COPING WITH POLLUTION

The concentration of so many people and so much manufacturing in metropolitan areas caused serious **pollution.** Millions of automobiles, buses, and trucks poured harmful exhaust fumes into the air in increasing amounts. The furnaces of factories and utility companies released black clouds of smoke and cinders. The mile-high city of Denver was veiled in haze. At certain times health officials warned the residents of Los Angeles not to exercise outdoors. Polluting substances called **smog** (the word comes from *smoke* plus *fog*) were so thick that deep breathing could be dangerous. At such times some

The sun is nearly obscured by the cloud of smoke in this photograph. The poisonous fumes have taken a heavy toll on the trees at the left. Where might this smoke originate?

Charles Steinhacker, Black Star

people with heart trouble, allergies, and lung diseases took to wearing gas masks outdoors to protect themselves!

Pollution was one of the prices that Americans paid for the rapid industrial expansion that followed World War II. Air pollution was not the only form this problem took. Many factories were dumping poisonous chemical waste products into rivers and lakes. Accidents to off-shore oil wells and to huge oil tankers released tons of thick, black crude oil into the oceans. The oil killed birds and fish and covered miles of beaches with tar and grease.

Chemicals used to kill insects and to fertilize the soil proved dangerous too. According to one expert, in 1969 18 million fish were killed by the pollution of American waters. Many scientists also believed that the gases used in spray cans caused damage to the upper atmosphere. Apparently these gases weaken the layer of ozone that protects the earth from heavy radiation from the sun.

Public support for the fight against pollution was vigorous. In 1970 more than 20 million people celebrated **Earth Day.** All across the country people gathered to call attention to the pollution problem and discuss ways to improve the environment. In that year Congress established an **Environmental Protection Agency** to try to prevent all forms of pollution.

▓ What was a cause of air pollution? Of water pollution?

COPING WITH ENERGY SHORTAGES

Americans in the 1970s faced a severe shortage of energy. Because of the enormous increase in the consumption of petroleum products, the United States had become an importer rather than an exporter of crude oil. This was possible because huge deposits of oil had been found in the Middle East, in Venezuela, and in other parts of the world. Much of this oil had been discovered and refined by American and European countries. They paid very little for it. The countries where the oil fields were located were very poor. Their rulers were grateful for whatever revenues the oil developers brought them.

Gradually, however, these oil-producing nations became more demanding. In 1960 Venezuela and the leading Middle Eastern producers—Saudi Arabia, Iran, Kuwait, and Iraq—joined in forming the **Organization of Petroleum Exporting Countries** (OPEC).

For some years OPEC was little more than a paper organization. But as world demand soared, OPEC added new members. Little by little it obtained price increases from the oil companies. By 1973 the OPEC nations were receiving about $3 a barrel for crude oil.

Then war broke out in the Middle East between Israel and its Arab neighbors. The United States was supplying its ally, Israel, with planes and supplies. The Arab states reacted by cutting off all oil.

The Arab-Israeli war ended quickly, but the oil embargo went on for months. When it was finally lifted, OPEC raised the price of crude oil to $11.65 a barrel. There seemed to be nothing that the United States and the other oil-importing countries could do to break the OPEC monopoly. The opening up of new American oil fields in northern Alaska in the 1970s could not reverse the trend. OPEC continued to push the price of oil higher, over $20 a barrel.

By 1980 the American people knew that they would have to cut down on their use of petroleum products. They began to buy smaller, lighter automobiles to replace the heavy "gas guzzlers" they had previously favored.

Meanwhile, a desperate search began for other sources of energy. One source, **nuclear energy,** was already producing large amounts of electricity.

Nuclear power plants make electricity by controlled splitting of atoms of uranium, the same element that was used in atom bombs. The uranium atoms are slowly broken up to release enormous amounts of heat without causing an explosion. The heat is used to turn water into steam, just as coal or oil are used in conventional power plants.

Nuclear plants are very expensive to build. And there is also the concern that an accident might cause an explosion and release death-dealing radioactive particles into the air. In 1979, for example, at **Three Mile Island** nuclear plant near Harrisburg, Pennsylvania, a breakdown caused rods of uranium to overheat and melt. People nearby feared for their lives. Eventually the danger subsided. The plant, which had been closed for more than five years, reopened in October 1985. The reopening, however, reminded people about the accident, which had led many people to ask whether nuclear power

NUCLEAR POWER PLANTS IN THE U.S. 1980

▲ Operating

△ Under construction

• Planned

Tony O'Brien, Nancy Palmer

In the shadows of these cooling towers for a nuclear power plant in the West, cows contentedly graze. What questions do many people ask about nuclear power?

was too dangerous to be used. Most experts think not. Still, the future of this form of energy seems, at best, quite limited.

Many scientists argued that the sun itself was the best source of yet-unused energy. By using **solar collectors** to gather the heat of the sun, it is possible to heat water and produce electricity. Solar energy is totally safe. It does no damage to the environment. The collectors cost nothing to operate once they are installed.

Another possible solution to the energy problem is the manufacture of **synthetic petroleum.** Coal could be converted into liquid or gas forms. Shale rock contains oil, as do certain tar sands. All these minerals exist in huge amounts in the United States.

▨ How does OPEC control the price of oil?
▨ What are some alternative sources of energy?

903

THE ELECTION OF 1980

The energy crisis aggravated one of the most frustrating problems of modern times—inflation. The skyrocketing price of oil caused the prices of gasoline, heating oil, and all other petroleum products to go up rapidly. By 1979 the **inflation rate** was 13 per cent. Inflation was the most frightening problem of the age. It became the main issue in the 1980 Presidential election.

President Carter won the Democratic nomination after a hard campaign against Senator Edward M. Kennedy of Massachusetts, a brother of President John F. Kennedy. Carter was helped during the primaries by an international crisis that broke out in November 1979. A mob in Teheran, the capital of **Iran,** invaded the American embassy and held all the people in the building hostage. The leaders demanded that the United States turn over to them the former shah, or king, of Iran, who had fled to America a year earlier during a revolution. They also demanded all the shah's large fortune, which they insisted he had stolen from the Iranian people.

A stalemate resulted. For months the Iranians held 53 Americans prisoner in the embassy in Teheran. Despite the pressure of world public opinion, they would not yield. In desperation President Carter finally ordered a team of marine commandos flown into Iran at night. Their mission was to rescue the hostages by force. The commandos landed in the Iranian desert without being detected. The mission had to be canceled, however, when several of the American helicopters broke down. Eight of the marines were killed by an accident and much equipment had to be abandoned. The hostages remained in captivity. Still the public tended to back the President, who was obviously doing his best.

The Republican party nominated Ronald Reagan for President. As the election approached, most experts said the contest between Reagan and Carter was "too close to call." But they misread the American people. On election day Ronald Reagan won a sweeping victory. His majority of the electoral vote was 489 to 49. The Republican party also gained heavily in the Congressional elections. For the first time since Eisenhower's Presidency, a majority of the Senate was Republican.

After his defeat Carter devoted all his energies to trying to free the hostages in Iran. Fear that the new President might take strong action in the matter probably convinced the Iranian leaders to give way. On January 20, 1981, Ronald Reagan took the oath of office as the 40th President of the United States. Shortly afterwards, he announced that the hostages had left Iran.

- How was Carter helped in the primaries by the crisis in Iran?
- What was the extent of Reagan's victory?

Wide World Photos

On the west steps of the Capitol, facing their native California, are Ronald Reagan and Nancy Reagan just after his inauguration as the 40th President. What change was there in the U.S. Senate after the election of 1980?

REAGAN AS PRESIDENT

President Reagan's policy was to increase the amount of money spent on defense but to cut back on other government spending. He also intended to reduce taxes by 10 per cent a year for three years. He claimed that the budget could be balanced despite the lower taxes. Americans would invest the money they saved on taxes in new business enterprises. This would cause the economy to boom. More jobs would be created, and profits would rise. People would have more money. Tax *revenues* would go up even though tax *rates* were lower. This theory was known as **supply-side economics.**

If the theory did not work, Reagan's program was likely to result in a large increase in the national debt and therefore in very high inflation. The Democratic leaders spoke strongly against the program, especially the tax cut.

By the time Reagan had been in the White House half a year everyone realized that he was both a determined leader and an extremely skillful politician. Since the Republicans had a majority in the Senate, he could get his bills passed easily in that branch of Congress. But the House of Representatives was still Democratic. Its leaders hoped to defeat the President's proposed tax cuts and to increase the amounts spent on education, welfare, and other social measures. Nevertheless, by midsummer both the Reagan budget and bills reducing the federal income tax by 25 percent over three years had been enacted into law.

In the midst of the budget fight a would-be assassin shot the President in the chest. One of his assistants, a police officer, and a secret service agent were also wounded. The President showed great courage in the face of near death and a sense of humor as well. When he was wheeled into the operating room, he said to the doctors, "I hope you fellows are all Republicans." When his wife arrived at his side, he told her, "Honey, I guess I forgot to duck." Naturally, the injured President attracted an outpouring of public sympathy and support.

Until well into Reagan's term, however, the nation's economic problems persisted. A serious recession developed. Business activity lagged. Unemployment rose above ten percent and interest rates remained high. With tax revenues down and the government spending billions on defense, the deficit rose to nearly $200 billion in 1983.

The recession finally did have one desirable result—the inflation rate tumbled from over 12 percent to below four percent by early 1984. When inflation fell, so did interest rates. Business began to pick up. Many idle workers were able to find jobs.

But the huge budget deficit remained. Some advisers urged Reagan to reduce it by cutting down on military spending. He refused to do so because he believed that the Soviet Union was an

BUILDING SKILLS IN SOCIAL STUDIES

Reading Editorial Cartoons

Throughout our history editorial cartoonists have been sharp observers of national politics. Pat Oliphant drew the airlift of the last liberals from Washington, D.C. after President Reagan's legislative victories. It recalls the airlift of the last Americans from Vietnam. Jack Ohman drew the auto graveyard. The figure on blocks is Thomas "Tip" O'Neill, the Democratic Speaker of the House. Frank Evers drew the economic cartoon in early 1981. What is its message? Find other editorial cartoons on a similar theme to discuss in class.

Pat Oliphant, © 1981, Washington Star.
Reprinted with permission of Universal Press
Syndicate. All rights reserved.

Jack Ohman, Chicago Tribune–New York News Syndicate

New York News

United Press International

In a hospital robe President Ronald Reagan flashes his familiar smile. Nancy Reagan is at his side. This was the first picture released after a would-be assassin shot Reagan in Washington, D.C. How did the President react to the shooting?

"evil empire" out to dominate the world. The only thing the Russians respected, he said, was strength. If they knew that the United States was as strong as they were and ready to meet any attack with overwhelming force they would restrain themselves.

This policy caused Reagan to take a particularly militant stand against possible Soviet "penetration" of Central America. Some years earlier, rebels in Nicaragua known as **Sandinistas** had overthrown a reactionary dictator. These Sandinistas had set up a government friendly to the Soviet Union. They were also supporting rebel forces in the neighboring nation of El Salvador.

Reagan provided advisers and military and economic aid to the El Salvador government and backed anti-government Nicaraguans who were seeking to overthrow the Sandinistas. The sums spent were not large enough to have much effect on the deficit. Nevertheless, many Americans feared that involvement of any kind might lead to "another Vietnam"—the sending, step by step, of more and more weapons and soldiers into the conflict.

▨ What is supply-side economics?
▨ What program did Reagan persuade Congress to pass?
▨ Why did Americans fear involvement in Nicaragua?

THE ELECTION OF 1984

Reagan's Central American policy was controversial but he remained personally popular. In 1984 the Republican convention unanimously nominated him for a second term as president. The fight for the Democratic nomination was long-drawn-out and bitter. At the start of the primary season the leading candidates seemed to be Walter Mondale, who had been Carter's vice president, and the former astronaut John Glenn (see p. 848), who had entered politics and been elected to the Senate from Ohio. Mondale was well known and had the support of many Democratic leaders and of most labor union officials. Glenn was hailed by his backers as a popular hero, another Eisenhower.

But most of the early primaries were won by Senator Gary Hart of Colorado, who promised the voters "new ideas." Glenn proved to be a dull campaigner and soon dropped out. Mondale, however, rallied his forces and won some key primaries. Hart continued to do well, but he lost momentum when it became clear that he had few really new ideas about how to deal with the nation's problems. Another candidate, the Reverend Jesse Jackson, the first black to wage a serious campaign for the presidency, attracted wide support by denouncing Reagan's economic policies as harmful to the poor. Jackson also charged that the Republicans were out to weaken civil rights legislation.

Jockeying for votes at the convention was intense, but Mondale had a majority on the first ballot. He then electrified the country by selecting a woman, Representative Geraldine Ferraro of New York, as his vice-presidential running mate. He also announced that if elected he would ask Congress to raise taxes in order to reduce the budget deficit. This was a direct challenge to President Reagan, who had sworn not to increase taxes under any circumstances.

Democratic hopes were high. They believed that Mondale's courage in facing the deficit problem directly, Jackson's ability to persuade blacks to register and vote, and Ferraro's appeal to women would counterbalance Reagan's popularity.

They were wrong. Mondale emphasized the difficulties the nation faced.. He claimed to be as determined as the President to resist Soviet aggression, but insisted that Reagan was taking *too* tough a stand toward the Russians. He charged that the Republicans had been unfair to poor people and minorities.

Mondale made a good argument for these propositions. But his tone was quarrelsome, his mood dark. Reagan, on the other hand, was the eternal optimist. His tone was friendly, his mood sunny. Mondale stressed the danger of inflation and a new depression. Reagan talked about continuing prosperity and the fact that the inflation problem had been "licked."

The result was a Reagan landslide. The president won nearly 60 percent of the popular vote. The Electoral College vote was even more lopsided: 525 to 13. Mondale carried only his home state of Minnesota and the District of Columbia.

Studying these results, many political analysts decided that the country had turned sharply in a conservative direction. They said that an era had ended. The New Deal coalition of industrial workers, farmers, poor people, blacks, and other minorities had collapsed. Of these groups, only the blacks had voted overwhelmingly Democratic.

Whether the analysts were correct remained to be seen. Although Reagan was certainly the popular choice, his party had not done particularly well in the election. The Democrats still controlled the House of Representatives. And the nation's economic and social problems remained. As always, how the President and Congress and the American people dealt with these problems would determine the future.

- Why did the Democrats think they would win the 1984 election?
- By how large a margin did Reagan win?

CHAPTER 30 REVIEW

Identification
Tell briefly why each of the following persons, terms, or events is important.
1. Gerald R. Ford
2. Elizabeth Bloomer Ford
3. Betty Friedan
4. Sandra Day O'Connor
5. Jimmy Carter
6. César Chávez
7. Herman Badillo
8. Edward M. Kennedy
9. Ronald Reagan
10. Stagflation
11. Equal Rights Amendment
12. Women's Liberation
13. Operation Sail
14. Twenty-sixth Amendment
15. United Farm Workers
16. Black Power
17. American Indian Movement
18. Environmental Protection Agency
19. OPEC
20. Supply-side economics

Understanding American History
1. Why did President Ford veto spending projects approved by Congress in the mid-1970s? What action did he later take to end stagflation?
2. What question led Betty Friedan to write *The Feminine Mystique*? What was the purpose of the National Organization for Women?
3. What arguments were made for and against the proposed Equal Rights Amendment?
4. What position did the Republican party take on ERA in 1980? How did President Reagan show support for equal rights?
5. For what reasons did President Carter's popularity decline?
6. From what countries did most immigrants come after 1965?
7. How did the United Farm Workers attempt to win sympathy in their strike against California grape growers?
8. What was meant by Black Power? How did American blacks react to increased knowledge of past injustices?
9. What are three major problems Americans coped with in the 1970s?
10. What economic actions did Ronald Reagan take after his 1980 election? By 1984 what were the results of his actions?

Activities
1. Throughout *American History* you have been encouraged to use your historical imagination. You have also been asked to think about historical significance. Two good examples of historical significance are the Monroe Doctrine and the Tonkin Gulf Resolution. Neither seemed particularly important when first announced. Yet 35 Presidents have based Latin American policy on the Monroe Doctrine. And Lyndon Johnson waged war in Vietnam under the Tonkin Gulf Resolution. As a class discussion project, ask what actions of the President and Congress in the 1980s might have particular historical significance.
2. Prepare a collage for the bulletin board on the theme that America is a country of many peoples and special interest groups.
3. Use an atlas or gazetteer to prepare a map of a major metropolitan area. Show the most important city or cities, suburbs, and transportation links.
4. Prepare classroom displays to show various forms of energy in use today or proposed for tomorrow. In a series of brief talks give the strengths and weaknesses of each.
5. Ronald Reagan is the oldest President to take office. Yet not even a would-be assassin's bullet could slow his pace during his first months in office. Use the *Readers' Guide to Periodical Literature* to find an article describing a typical day in the President's life or write the White House for a copy of the President's calendar.

CHAPTER 30 TEST

Matching (25 points)
Number your paper 1–10 and match the description in the first column with the name or term in the second column.
1. Oil-producing nations formed this organization to set oil prices
2. President elected by a broad majority
3. President elected by a thin majority
4. Period of mild economic recession
5. First woman appointed to the Supreme Court
6. Walter Mondale's vice–presidential running mate for the 1984 election
7. Power produced by splitting atoms of uranium
8. Another term for a megalopolis or "super city"
9. Movement that began when working women resented discrimination on the job market
10. Legislation passed in 1965 to fight pollution

a. Ronald Reagan
b. Stagflation
c. Sandra Day O'Connor
d. Jimmy Carter
e. Geraldine Ferraro
f. Urban complex
g. Nuclear energy
h. Clear Air Act
i. OPEC
j. Women's Liberation

Classifying (25 points)
Number your paper 11–20. For each of the following statements, write *F* if it describes President Ford, *C* for President Carter, and *R* for President Reagan.
11. He appointed the first woman to the Supreme Court.
12. He vetoed 39 spending measures approved by Congress.
13. His election marked a turning point in American politics.
14. He stressed an informal style and easy availability.
15. His program of economic reforms was passed by Congress.
16. He struggled with a period of stagflation.
17. He struggled to free American hostages in Iran.
18. He was appointed Vice President by Congress.
19. He was accused of not doing enough to stimulate the economy.
20. He survived a would-be assassin's bullet.

Chronological Order (20 points)
Number your paper 21–25 and place the following events in order by writing 1 for the first, 2 for the second, and so on.
21. Reagan defeats Carter for President.
22. Ford defeats Reagan for the Republican nomination.
23. Carter defeats Kennedy for the Democratic nomination.
24. Carter defeats Ford for President.
25. Ford succeeds to the Presidency.

Essay (30 points)
Write a brief essay stating possible solutions to one of these problems: urban decay, pollution, or energy shortages.

UNIT TEN TEST

Multiple Choice (20 points)
Number your paper 1–5 and write the letter of the phrase that best completes each sentence.

1. By the mid-1960s progress since World War II in the standard of living caused America to be described as the
   a. Great Society.
   b. Affluent Society.
   c. Alliance for Progress.
   d. Sun Belt.
2. By 1970 an increasing number of immigrants were coming to the United States from
   a. northwest Europe.
   b. Asia.
   c. Africa.
   d. Greece and Italy.
3. Because of the Watergate Affair and its cover-up, President Nixon
   a. was impeached.
   b. resigned.
   c. visited China and Russia.
   d. withdrew U.S. troops from Vietnam.
4. Before World War II the United States
   a. used little oil.
   b. imported large quantities of oil.
   c. produced oil for itself and others.
   d. purchased its oil from OPEC.
5. The United States withdrew from Vietnam
   a. when it won the war.
   b. when Vietnamization succeeded.
   c. when a peace treaty was agreed upon.
   d. when South Vietnam won the war.

Matching (30 points)
Number your paper 6–15 and match the person in the second column with his or her description in the first column.

6. President who ordered commandos into Iran
7. Leader who favored passive resistance
8. President who ordered nuclear warheads out of Cuba
9. President whose election marked a turning point
10. First U.S. President to visit China while in office
11. President not elected by the American public
12. Organized migrant farm workers
13. First woman appointed to the Supreme Court
14. President who escalated the Vietnam War
15. First black to wage a serious campaign for the presidency

a. John F. Kennedy
b. Martin Luther King, Jr.
c. Lyndon B. Johnson
d. Richard M. Nixon
e. Gerald R. Ford
f. Jimmy Carter
g. Ronald Reagan
h. Reverend Jesse Jackson
i. César Chávez
j. Sandra Day O'Connor

Chronological Order (20 points)
Number your paper 16–20 and place the following events in order by numbering 1 for the first, 2 for the second, and so on.

16. America celebrates its Bicentennial.
17. President Nixon visits Russia.
18. President Reagan makes broad economic changes.
19. President Johnson creates the Great Society.
20. President Kennedy is assassinated.

Essay (30 points)
In a carefully planned essay tell what you think is the most important challenge facing the United States today. How can our sense of American history help us to meet that challenge?

GLOSSARY

Page numbers in boldface type tell where each word appears in boldface type in the book. By turning back to the page, you can review each word in context. For some words phonetic pronunciations are given and primary and secondary stresses are marked. Use the simple pronunciation key below.

---

add, āce, câre, pälm, end, ēven, it, īce, odd, ōpen, ôrder, tŏŏk, pōōl, up, bûrn, oil, pout, check, go, ring, thin, **th**is, zh in vision. The schwa ə is the sound of *a* in above, *e* in sicken, *i* in flexible, *o* in melon, and *u* in focus. The **yoo** is the *u* in fuse.

A

ABC Powers. The countries of Argentina, Brazil, and Chile. **680**

Abolitionists (ab'ə-lish'ə-nists). People who wanted to end slavery in the U.S. **387**

Advice and consent. The Senate approval required by the Constitution for major appointments made by the President. **202**

Affluent (af'loo-ənt) **Society.** An economist's term to describe the wealthy America of post-World War II. **847**

AFL-CIO. An organization of labor unions formed when the American Federation of Labor and the Congress of Industrial Organizations were merged in 1955. **851**

Age of Reform. The period in America between 1830 and 1850 of social concern and improvement. **396**

Alamo (al'ə-mō). The San Antonio fort where 187 Texans died fighting for independence. **347**

Alien and Sedition Acts. Four 1798 laws aimed at foreigners and others in the U.S. who were supposedly undermining the government by helping France. **232**

Alliance for Progress. President Kennedy's program to provide economic assistance for Latin American countries. **841**

Alliances. Unions made between nations, states, or individuals. **676**

Allies (al'īz). Nations which fought together in World War II, including the U.S., Great Britain, France, and the U.S.S.R. **677**

Alphabet soup. The many agencies formed during the New Deal that were known by their initials. **766**

American expansionism. The belief that North and South America and the islands of the Pacific Ocean should be under the control of the U.S. **613**

American Expeditionary Force. The military forces that fought in Europe during World War I. **691**

American Indian Movement of 1972 (AIM). An organization that supported fairer treatment of American Indians. **895**

Amnesty (am'nəs-tē). An official pardon for offenses committed against the government. **492**

Anarchist (an'ər-kist). One who opposes all forms of government. **631, 713**

Anthropologists. Scientists who study the physical, social, and cultural development of people. **10**

Antibiotic (an'ti-bī-ot'ik). A substance such as penicillin which is produced to fight disease. **850**

Antitrust movement. An attempt to regulate business practices that placed restraints on trade. **563**

Appellate (ə-pel'it) **courts.** The two lower federal appeals courts. **202**

Arbitration (är'bə-trā'shən). The hearing and settlement of a dispute between two parties by a third neutral party. **619**

Archeologists. Scientists who study history and culture by examining the remains of early human cultures. **10**

Armistice. A truce or an agreement to stop fighting. **698**

Army of Northern Virginia. The Confederate army commanded by Robert E. Lee. **463**

Army of the Potomac. The Union army during the Civil War. **462**

Articles of Confederation. The agreement under which the thirteen original colonies established a government of states in 1781. **162**

Artifact (är'tə-fakt). Anything made by human work such as jewelry, tools, or weapons. **10**

Assassination. Killing a high official by surprise attack. **492**

Astrolabe (as'trə-lāb). An instrument used to measure a ship's latitude or distance from the equator. **17**

Atlantic Charter. An agreement between Great Britain and the U.S. to work for a world free of war, signed by Roosevelt and Churchill on August 14, 1941. **782**

B

Bacon's Rebellion. A revolt of Virginia colonists led by Nathaniel Bacon in 1676 which resulted in an expedition to kill Indians, the burning of Jamestown, and the removal of its governor. **89**

Bank Holiday. An order by Franklin Roosevelt closing all banks for several days in 1933 while a program was developed to protect the savings of the public. **745**

Bank notes. Paper money issued to represent a certain sum of gold or silver coins. **217, 335**

Bank of the United States. Created by Congress in 1816 to set up a central banking system and to protect American industries. **217, 294**

Banking Panic. An event in February 1933 when people throughout the country rapidly withdrew their savings from banks. **744**

Bay of Pigs. Scene of a failed invasion of Cuba in April 1961 by exiles trained by the U.S. **841**

Beecher's Bibles. The name given to the weapons bought in Kansas in the 1850s with money raised by Rev. Henry Ward Beecher of New York. **428**

Berlin Airlift. Period during the Cold War when the U.S. flew supplies to West Berlin after Russia blocked entry roads. **815**

Bessemer (bes'ə-mər) **converter.** The invention of Henry Bessemer for mass production of steel. **555**

Big Knives. Name used by Tecumseh (ti-kum'sə), a Shawnee chief, to refer to white people. **266**

Bill of Rights. Name given to the first ten amendments to the Constitution. **160, 212**

Black Codes. Regulations passed by southern governments during Reconstruction to prohibit blacks from voting. **494**

"Black gold." Another name for oil. **557**

Black Hand. A terrorist organization in Serbia before World War I. **676**

"Black Republican." A name given to the post-Civil War governments in the South. **502**

Black Tuesday. The day the stock market crashed, October 29, 1929. **734**

"Bleeding Kansas." Name given in eastern newspaper accounts to fighting in Kansas in the 1850s between proslavery and antislavery forces. **430**

Blockade runners. Small, fast ships used during the Civil War. **467**

Bonanza (bə-nan'zə). A rich deposit of ore. **537**

Bonanza farms. Gigantic farms that spread over thousands of acres. **548**

Bonus Marchers. Veterans who marched on Washington in July 1932 to protest slowness in compensation for their low pay as soldiers in World War I. **742**

Border states. During the Civil War, Maryland, West Virginia, Kentucky, and Missouri. **445**

Bosses. Leaders of political machines. **581**

Boxer Rebellion. A 1900 uprising in China during which foreign property was destroyed and foreign missionaries and business people were held captive. **635**

Boycott (boi'kot). A refusal to buy certain goods as a protest. **112**

Brain Trust. Close advisers of Franklin Roosevelt who were mostly college professors. **751**

Brand. A mark burned on a calve's hide with a hot iron to show ownership. **543**

Brandeis (bran'dīs) **brief.** The argument presented by Louis D. Brandeis before the Supreme Court that stated that long work hours

injured the health of women and children; research for the brief was done by Florence Kelley and Josephine Goldmark. **656**

Bread and butter issues. Labor's concerns of higher wages, shorter hours, and better working conditions. **567**

Breadlines. Lines of persons waiting to be given food during the Great Depression. **739**

Brinkmanship. The policy under President Eisenhower to risk all-out war to contain communism. **824**

Brown v. Board of Education. The landmark decision of the Supreme Court in 1954 that schools must be integrated. **830**

Bull Moose party. The nickname given to the Progressive party when Theodore Roosevelt ran for President in 1912. **663**

C

Cabinet. Appointed officials who head government agencies and advise the President. **210**

Canal Zone. The strip of territory leased to the U.S. by Panama that extends five miles on each side of the Panama Canal. **637**

Carbon-14 dating. A process used to determine the age of an ancient object by measuring its radioactive content. **10**

Carpetbaggers. Northerners who went South after the Civil War to profit financially from confused and unsettled conditions. **503**

Cash crops. Crops raised to bring growers money for manufactured goods such as farm tools, clothing, and ammunition. **73**

Cattle kingdom. Grasslands of the High Plains that stretched from Texas to Canada and from the Rockies to eastern Kansas. **540**

Central Powers. Germany, Austria, Hungary, Turkey, and Bulgaria during World War I. **677**

Charter. An official document given by a government granting special rights and privileges to a person or company. **36**

Circular Letter. A letter issued by the Massachusetts legislature to other colonial assemblies which stated that the colonists should act together to resist taxation without representation. **114**

Circumnavigate (sûr'kəm-nav'ə-gāt). To sail completely around the globe. **25**

Civil Service Commission. Agency established in 1883 to design and

administer examinations for certain government positions. **590**

Claim jumpers. People who took ore deposits that had been staked out by others. **539**

Clipper ship. Sailing ship of the 19th century built for speed. **366**

Closed shop. Business that hires only members of a labor union. **811**

Cold War. The diplomatic and economic rivalry of the U.S. and Russia after World War II. **817**

Collective bargaining. Negotiations between employers and workers on wages, benefits, or working conditions. **567**

Commercial Revolution. The economic expansion in Europe that occured from 1450 to the 1700s. **14**

Commonwealth. A state in which there is self-government. **53**

Comstock (kum'stok) **Lode.** An extremely rich silver deposit in Nevada. **537**

Conestoga (kon'is-tō'gə) **wagon.** A sturdy covered wagon used by pioneers who moved westward. **322**

Confederate States of America. A federation of 11 independent southern states formed after their secession from the Union in 1860–61. **452**

Conquistadors (kon-kēs'tə-dôrs). Spanish soldiers who conquered Mexico and Peru. **28**

Conscience Whigs. Northern members of the Whig party who were against slavery (see **Cotton Whigs**). **430**

Conscript. To draft men to serve as soldiers by law. **469**

Conservation. Protecting or preserving from waste or loss, such as natural resources. **661**

Containment policy. A strategy used by the U.S. to limit the spread of communism in the 1950s. **817**

Continental dollars. Paper money printed by Congress after the Revolutionary War to pay its debts. **172**

Contrabands (kon'trə-bands). Black slaves who crossed Union lines during the Civil War. **470**

Co-ops (kō'ops). Groups formed through the Farmers' Alliance in order to sell crops at better prices and to purchase goods wholesale for members. **595**

Copperheads. Northerners who opposed the Civil War. **465**

Cotton boll (bōl). The seed pod of a cotton plant. **377**

Cotton diplomacy. The belief that England and France would support the Confederacy to insure their supply of cotton. **469**

Cotton gin. A machine invented by Eli Whitney in 1793 which separated cotton fibers from cotton seeds. **378**

"Cotton Is King." Southern slogan which meant that cotton was essential to the country as well as to Europe. **385**

Cotton Whigs. Southern members of the Whig party who were for slavery (see **Conscience Whigs**). **430**

Crop-lien (krop′lēn) **system.** An agreement in which supplies were lent to farmers by merchants or landowners in exchange for portions of the crops. **506**

Culture. The special characteristics of the people who make up a society, such as their language, government, how they make a living, family relationships, and how they educate their children. **4**

Cutthroat competition. Ruthless business practices between companies striving for the same market. **561**

D

D-Day. The Allied invasion of France on June 6, 1944, to drive out Hitler's occupying armies. **793**

Dark horse. A political candidate who unexpectedly wins a party's nomination. **347**

Deficit (def′ə-sit) **spending.** The spending of public funds raised by borrowing rather than by taxation. **768**

Deflation (di-flā′shən). A decline in prices caused by a decrease in money supply or spending. **587**

Democracy. A form of government in which power is vested in the people and exercised by them through a system of representation that involves free elections. **68, 139.**

Depression. A severe decline in business activity especially marked by high levels of unemployment. **170, 338**

Dictator (dik′tā-tər). A person who rules a country with absolute power. **775**

Direct primary. A preliminary election to choose candidates to run for public office. **650**

Disarmament (dis-är′mə-mənt). A reduction or limitation in the manufacture of weapons of war. **711**

Doctrine of nullification (nul′ə-fi-cā′shən). The theory put forth in 1798 that any state had the right to refuse acceptance of national law because of the limited powers of the Constitution. **239**

Dollar diplomacy. A policy in the early 1900s of investing U.S. money in Latin American countries in hopes that more stable governments would result. **640**

Domino theory. The idea in the 1950s–1970s that if a country fell to communism, the countries on its borders would also fall. **863**

"Drake's Folly." Nickname for the first oil well, drilled by E. L. Drake of Titusville, Pennsylvania. **557**

Dred Scott. The Supreme Court decision in 1854 that Scott, a former slave who sued for his freedom, would remain a slave. **433**

Dry farming. A technique used to raise crops in areas with less than 15 to 20 inches of rain a year. **547**

Dumping. The practice of selling goods at extremely low prices in order to attract customers. **171**

Dust Bowl. A region in the south and central U.S. where eroded topsoil was blown away during the droughts of 1934–37. **750**

Duty. A tariff or tax placed on foreign goods. **294**

E

East India Company. The tea company that was given assistance by the British Parliament in 1773. **122**

Elastic clause. The "necessary and proper" clause of the Constitution often used to expand the powers of Congress. **218**

Electors. Persons selected in each state to vote for President. **200**

Enclosure movement. Period when British landowners fenced in their fields and began raising sheep. **37**

Equal Rights Amendment (ERA). A Constitutional amendment proposed in 1972 which would provide that "equality of rights under the law shall not be denied or abridged by the U.S. or by any state on account of sex." **884**

Era of Good Feelings. The period from 1817 to 1821 when the country was prosperous and at peace under President Monroe. **318**

Ever-normal granary. A system of storing grain in government granaries that regulated prices and kept surpluses off the market. **765**

F

Fair Deal. President Truman's proposals for larger social security benefits, national health insurance, a higher minimum wage, and programs to extend the New Deal. **810**

Farmers' Alliance. A social organization that became a political force by finding ways to sell crops at better prices. **595**

Federal Deposit Insurance Corporation (FDIC). A federal agency created to give government protection to savings deposits. **745**

Federal Reserve Act. A 1913 law that created a national banking system of 12 Federal Reserve Banks. **666**

Federal Reserve Board. A government agency that controls interest rates charged by the Federal Reserve Bank on money lent to commercial banks. **666**

Federal Trade Commission. A commission created in 1914 to help eliminate unfair business practices and to enforce antitrust laws. **667**

Federalist Papers. A series of newspaper articles written in 1787–88 that explained and defended the Constitution. **205**

Fifty-Niners. Name given to prospectors who went west in 1859. **528**

Fireside Chats. Informal Presidential speeches given by Franklin Roosevelt in the 1930s. **751**

Fiscal (fis′kəl) **policy.** A means of stimulating business activity by having the federal government increase spending and lower taxes. **850**

Five-Power Naval Treaty. A 1921 agreement between the U.S., Great Britain, Japan, France, and Italy to a ten-year "holiday" on the construction of battleships. **712**

Forty-Niners. The nickname given to prospectors who went to California in search of gold in 1849. **366**

Four Freedoms. Freedom of speech and religion, freedom from want and fear, according to Franklin Roosevelt. **781**

Fourteen Points. A peace program outlined by President Wilson in 1918. **699**

Franchises (fran′chīz-əs). Contracts for public works or services granted by the government. **583**

Free enterprise. An economic system in which there is limited public control over business practices. **652**

Free-Soil party. A political party founded in 1848 by northern Democrats who were opposed to popular sovereignty. **370**

Freedmen. Former slaves. **494**

Freedmen's Bureau. Organization run by the army to care for refugees and to protect southern blacks. **496**

Frigates. American naval warships built in the early 1800s. **232, 269**

Frontier. The edge of a settled region that borders on unsettled territory. **68**

G

Gettysburg Address. A speech delivered by President Lincoln at a wartime burial site in Gettysburg, Pennsylvania, which has become a classic expression of American democratic ideals. **478**

Ghettos. Sections of a city where members of minority groups live because of economic needs or social pressures. **758**

G.I. Bill of Rights. A program under the Servicemen's Readjustment Act of 1944 which enabled veterans to obtain low-cost loans to buy homes or start businesses. **786**

Gold Rush. The surge of 80,000 miners who came to California to look for gold in 1848. **366**

Gold standard. The monetary system that used gold to mint coins and to back bank notes. **598**

Grandfather clause. A law which eliminated literacy tests and poll taxes for persons who had voted before 1867 and their descendents. **512**

Great Awakening. In the 1740s a time of widespread religious fervor in the colonies and a force for toleration. **82**

Great Compromise. The agreement made at the Constitutional Convention in 1787 to create a House of Representatives elected by the people on the basis of population and a Senate elected by the state legislatures, two members from each state. **198**

Great Depression. The national economic crisis from 1929–1940. **734, 737**

Great Plains. The region which extends from western Texas north to the Dakotas and into Canada. **8**

Great Society. The social and economic program of Lyndon Johnson. **846**

Great Stock Market Crash. The disastrous fall in the stock market in 1929 which ended the prosperity of the 1920s. **734**

Great War. The first world war, which broke out in Europe in 1914. **670, 676**

Greenbacks. U.S. paper money which was not exchangeable for gold or silver coins. **586**

Gunboat diplomacy. Popular name for the policy of the Roosevelt Corollary, which meant the U.S. would make a show of force to prevent European interference in the Western Hemisphere. **640**

Guns or butter. A reference to Lyndon Johnson's unbalanced federal budget because of his unwillingness to sacrifice domestic programs while fighting the Vietnam War. **870**

H

Hard money. Gold or silver coins. **172, 335, 586**

Harlem Renaissance (ren′ə-säns′). Period during the 1920s when New York City's Harlem became an intellectual and cultural capital for blacks. **759**

Headright. An agreement by colonists in 1618 to pay their way or that of others to settle in Virginia in exchange for 50 acres of land for each "head" transported from England. **44**

Hiroshima (hir′ə·shē′mə). Japanese city, site of the first atomic bombing by the U.S. in August 1945, killing 75,000 people but ending World War II. **801**

Historical imagination. The ability to look at past events objectively by appreciating what people knew and did not know at a particular time. **3**

Historical significance. A reference to an event whose importance is not clear and whose outcome seldom can be predicted at the time it occurs. **288, 862**

Holocaust. Hitler's programs to exterminate the Jewish people in the 1930s–40s. **779**

Homestead Act. A law that granted free public land to farmers who agreed to cultivate the land for a given period of time. **444**

Houses of refuge. Places built to protect delinquent and homeless children and separate them from adult criminals. **409**

Hull House. A Chicago settlement house founded in 1889 by social worker Jane Addams which became a model for others in the country. **574**

Hundred Days. The time it took Congress to pass Roosevelt's New Deal programs to revive the country during the Great Depression. **745**

I

Ice Age. An epoch when icecaps and glaciers covered large parts of the earth's surface. **2**

Ideal communities. Settlements established between 1820 and 1850 by reformers who favored a communal way of life. **405**

Impeachment. A formal charge of wrongdoing brought against a high official of the federal government. **203, 498**

Impressment. A practice used by the British in the early 1800s to force sailors to serve in the British navy. **258**

Indentured servant. Name for a colonist who worked for a period of time without wages for the owner of a work contract. **44**

Indigo (in′də-gō). A plant that produces a dark blue dye used in manufacturing cloth. **75**

Indirect taxes. Taxes on imports that were collected from shippers and paid by consumers in the form of higher prices. **113**

Industrial Revolution. The change in the early 1800s from handicraft to production by machine and factory. **298**

Industrial technology. The tools and machines used to produce goods. **296**

Inflation. A rise in price levels resulting from an increase in the amount of money or credit and a decrease in the amount of goods available for sale. **172, 588**

Inflationary (in-flā′shən-er′ē) **spiral.** A continuous rise in prices that occurs when the higher cost of one product or service causes the prices of other goods and services to rise. **337**

Inner city. Usually the older and more densely populated central section of a city. **897**

Interchangeable parts. Mechanical parts that can be substituted one for the other, an essential for mass production. **297**

Internal improvements. The roads and canals needed in the 1820s to get western goods to market cheaply. **326**

Internment (in-tûrn′mənt) **camp.** A military station where prisoners of war are held, but in this case home for some 112,000 Japanese-Americans who were removed to barren sections of the U.S. during World War II. **787**

Interstate commerce. Trading between different states. **563**

Interstate System. A network of superhighways begun in 1956 under President Eisenhower. **828**

Intolerable Acts. Name colonists

gave to the Coercive Acts passed by the British government in 1774 to punish the colonists for the Boston Tea Party. **125**

Iron Curtain. Winston Churchill's name to describe the barrier of censorship and secrecy between communist countries and the rest of the western world. **812**

Isolationism. A policy that advocates national self-sufficiency and freedom from foreign alliances. **612, 711**

J

Jazz. Music created by black musicians in New Orleans in the late 1800s that became popular during the 1920s. **717**

Jazz Age. One name for the 1920s in America. **718**

Job Corps. A Great Society program to train poor, unskilled workers. **846**

Joint-stock companies. A group of investors formed to outfit colonial expeditions in the early 1600s. **39**

Juntas (hōon′täz). In this case, committees established in the U.S. by Cuban revolutionaries to gather support in the late 1890s. **621**

K

Kentucky and Virginia Resolutions. Statements written in 1798 by Jefferson and Madison to question the power of the federal government over states' rights. **239**

Knights of Labor. Labor union of skilled and unskilled workers founded in 1869. **566**

Know-Nothings. The name given to members of the Native American party during the 1850s. **430**

Korean War. War in 1950–52 between North and South Korea in which South Korea was supported by U.N. troops, mainly from the U.S. **822**

Ku Klux Klan. A secret organization which attempted to keep blacks down by terror. **508, 715**

L

L'Anse aux Meadows (läns′ō me-dō′). Site of the only Viking camp found in North America. **11**

League of Nations. An international organization established in 1920 to seek world peace; dissolved in 1946 when many of the League's functions were taken over by the United Nations. **701**

Lexington and Concord. Massachusetts towns where the first battles of the American Revolution were fought. **127**

Literacy test. A test of a person's ability to read and write as a requirement for voting. **512, 570**

Lobbyists. People representing special interest groups who try to influence legislators. **650**

Long drive. A two-month journey that brought cattle to the railroads. **541**

Lost Colony. English colony settled at Roanoke, Virginia, in 1587; by 1591 all of its members had disappeared. **37**

Lowell system. A method first used in 1813 to recruit laborers for factories in Lowell, Massachusetts, in which young women were employed to operate power looms. **301**

Loyalists. Also called **Tories;** Americans during the Revolution who remained loyal to the king of England. **138**

Lusitania. The British liner carrying American passengers sunk by a German torpedo in 1915. **685**

M

Manhattan Project. The code name of the top-secret plan to develop the atom bomb. **801**

Manifest destiny. The belief in the 1840s that the obvious future role of the U.S. was to extend its boundaries to the Pacific Ocean. **351**

Mason-Dixon line. The boundary between Maryland and Pennsylvania, traditional line separating North and South. **87**

Mass production. The manufacture, usually by machinery, of goods in large quantities. **296**

Massive retaliation (ri-tal′ē-ā′shən). The stated U.S. policy under Eisenhower to respond to Soviet agression anywhere in the world with nuclear weapons. **824**

Matériel (mə-tir′ē-el′). The equipment and supplies used by a military force. **690**

Mayflower Compact. A document drawn up by the Pilgrims in 1620 that provided a legal basis for self-government. **46**

Mechanical reaper. Machine invented by Cyrus McCormick to harvest wheat. **465**

Mediate (mē′dē-āt). To settle differences between parties by acting as a peacemaker. **680**

Medicare. A Great Society program that provided health insurance for people over 65. **846**

Melting pot. The idea that immigrants of various racial and cultural backgrounds eventually become adapted to American ways. **668**

Mercenaries (mûr′sə-ner′ez). Soldiers hired to fight for money. **147**

Merchant adventurers. English merchants in the early 1600s who backed exploration and colonization. **39**

Merit system. The policy adopted by the U.S. Civil Service to make government appointments and promotions on the basis of ability rather than politics. **589**

Middlemen. Traders who buy products from one person and sell them at higher prices to a merchant or directly to the consumer. **18**

Middle Passage. A dreaded part of the voyage by slaves across the Atlantic. **72**

Migrant workers. Farm workers who follow the harvests. **750**

Military dictatorship. Absolute military rule over a country. **680**

Minimum wage. The least amount of wages a worker can receive by law. **654**

Minute Men. Civilian-soldiers who were trained to fight in the Revolutionary War on short notice. **126**

Missouri Compromise. An 1820 plan which allowed Missouri to become a slave state and Maine a free state. **369**

Monetary (mon′ə-ter′ē) **policy.** A means of stimulating business activity by having the Federal Reserve Board lower interest rates. **850**

Monopoly (mə-nop′ə-lē). The exclusive control of a product or service that results in fixed prices and elimination of competition. **561**

Mormon Trail. A route to Salt Lake City used by Mormon pioneers. **364**

Moving assembly line. A method of mass production used by Henry Ford in which each worker or team performed only one simple task. **724**

Muckrakers. Reporters who exposed corruption in the early 1900s. **648**

Municipal socialism. A plan which transferred private ownership of streetcar lines and gas and electric companies to city governments. **652**

N

National Association for the Advancement of Colored People (NAACP). A civil rights organization formed in 1909. **670**

National Grange. A farmers' organization that became politically active during the 1870s. **593**

Nationalism. Patriotic feelings for one's country. **176**

Native sons. Political candidates who are nominated because of their ability to carry their home states in a national election. **580**

Naval stores. Products that were produced from the pine forests of the South. **75**

Navigation. The science of charting the position or course of a ship, aircraft, or similar vehicle. **18**

Neutrality. The policy of avoiding permanent ties with other nations. **226, 678**

New Deal. Franklin Roosevelt's program to revive the country from the Great Depression. **745**

New Freedom. Woodrow Wilson's Democratic program proposed in 1912. **664**

New Frontier. John F. Kennedy's social and economic programs of the early 1960s. **834**

New Nationalism. Theodore Roosevelt's Progressive program in 1912. **663**

North Atlantic Treaty Organization (NATO). An agreement to stand firm against Soviet military threats, made between the U.S., Great Britain, France, and eight other nations in 1949. **816**

Nullify (nul′ə-fī). To cancel or take away the legal force of a law. **239**

O

"Old Ironsides." Nickname for the American warship *Constitution* used in the War of 1812. **271**

One person, one vote. The principle of electing legislators on the basis of population. **87**

Open Door. An 1889 U.S. policy that assured all nations equal trade rights with China. **634, 712**

Open range. Government-owned grazing land used by ranchers to feed their herds. **542**

Operation Sail. A procession of decorated ships in New York Harbor in honor of the American Bicentennial. **887**

Ordinance. A public act or law made by the authority of the government. **332**

Ordinance of nullification. A proposal made by John C. Calhoun to permit a state to cancel a law it believed unconstitutional. **331**

Oregon Trail. The route followed by pioneers to the Northwest. **355**

Organization of Petroleum Exporting Countries (OPEC). An oil cartel founded in 1960 that included Venezuela, Saudi Arabia, Iran, Kuwait, and Iraq. **901**

Overhead. Fixed costs or expenses in business that do not yield a profit. **561**

Override. The privilege of Congress to overrule a Presidential veto by a two-thirds vote. **203, 497**

Overseer. A person who supervises other workers. **321**

P

Parliament. The law-making body of England. **93**

Passive resistance. A method of demonstrating nonviolent opposition to a policy or program considered unjust. **858**

Patriots. During the American Revolution, groups who favored independence for the American colonies. **126**

Patronage. The awarding of government positions by office holders. **589**

Peace Corps. A program established by President Kennedy that sent trained American volunteers to needy countries. **841**

"Peculiar institution." A name some gave to slaveholding. **71**

Picaroons (pik′ə-rōōnz′). French merchant ships that seized cargo from American merchant ships in the 1790s. **229**

Pilgrims. A community of people who settled in Massachusetts in the 1620s to practice their religion freely. **45**

Pinkertons. Armed men who worked as agents for the Pinkerton Detective Agency. **568**

Plains Indians. Indian tribes that lived on the grasslands between the Rocky Mountains and the Mississippi River. **8**

Poison gas. A chemical weapon first used by the Germans during World War I. **697**

Polio vaccine (vak′sēn). An innoculation developed by Dr. Jonas Salk which protected polio victims from paralysis. **850**

Political machines. Big city organizations run by bosses who won elections by controlling poor and immigrant voters. **581**

Poll tax. A fee charged for voting. **512**

Pollution. The amount of harmful substances that affect the quality of the environment. **900**

Popular sovereignty (sov′rən-tē). A system that allowed settlers in each territory to decide whether or not they would have slavery. **369, 425**

Precedent. A guide for later action. **209, 435**

Primary elections. Elections to select candidates to run for public office. **650**

Privateers (prī-və-tirz′). American merchant ships or their crews who flew the French flag and attacked unarmed British ships in the early 1800s. **220**

Processing taxes. Taxes paid by businesses that used agricultural crops as their raw materials. **747**

Prohibition. The act of forbidding the manufacture, transportation, and sale of alcoholic beverages. **410, 557**

Prospect. To search for gold. **365**

Prosperity. A time of high production and low unemployment. **738**

Protective tariffs. High taxes on imported goods to give an advantage to American manufacturers. **293, 585**

Public servants. Government officials or people who work for the government. **160**

Puritans. English Protestants who wished to "purify" the Church of England and came to America in the early 1600s for religious freedom. **53**

Putting-out system. A method by which workers wove cloth on looms in their own homes from thread "put out" by the manufacturer. **300**

Q

Quadruplex (kwod′rōō-pleks) **telegraph.** Edison's first major invention, a machine that could send four messages over one wire at the same time. **560**

Quarantine (kwôr′ən-tēn). A policy of isolating aggressor nations in the 1930s. **777**

R

Radar. Electronic pulses used to locate traveling objects and determine their size and rate of speed. **791**

Rancheros (ran-char′os). Mexican landholders who owned *ranchos*. **361**

Rancho. A vast estate with cattle-grazing lands owned by a Mexican citizen. **361**

Range rights. Water rights to control the land surrounding a water supply. **542**

Range wars. Battles in the 1880s

between sheep and cattle ranchers for control of grasslands. **544**

Ratifying conventions. Meetings first held in 1787 for the purpose of approving the Constitution. **209**

Rebates (rē′bāts). Illegal kickbacks, or money returned, to preferred shippers by the railroads in the 1870s. **561**

Reconcentrados. (ri·kon′sen·trä′dōz) Concentration camps in Cuba where farm people were kept in the late 1890s. **620**

Reconstruction Act. A four-part measure passed in 1867 that ordered a military occupation of the South and forced Southerners to give blacks equal rights. **498**

Red Stick Confederacy. An alliance formed by Tecumseh of all Indian tribes east of the Mississippi to resist white expansion. **266**

Referendum (ref′ə-ren′dəm). A legal procedure by which the people can revoke a law passed by the legislature. **651**

Regulatory (reg′yə-lə-tôr′ē) **agencies.** Government watchdog groups that supervise business operations. **562**

Reparations (rep′ə-rā′shənz). Money given by defeated nations as payment for wrongs, damages, or injuries suffered by other nations during a war. **703**

Repeal. To reject or revoke a law. **333, 667**

Republic. A government characterized by power that lies in representatives elected by the people. **169**

Republican party. A political party formed in 1854 by Northern Whigs and Democrats who opposed slavery. **431**

Restraint of trade. Interference with the free flow of goods or with fair competition. **657**

Rhode Island System. A labor force of children who operated spinning machines in Rhode Island mills. **300**

Right of self-determination. The principle that all peoples should be able to determine for themselves which nation they belong to; what Southerners argued they were fighting for during the Civil War. **701**

Right of way. The strip of land granted by the government to railroad companies laying down tracks. **526**

Rotation in office. Replacing of government jobholders with other members of the political party in power. **331, 588**

Rough Riders. Theodore Roosevelt's regiment sent to Cuba during the Spanish-American War. **625**

Round-up. Bringing together cattle scattered over the open range. **543**

Runaway inflation. An uncontrollable rise in prices due to a high circulation of paper money. **593**

S

San Francisco Conference. The meeting held in 1945 to draft the United Nations Charter. **805**

Sanctions. Penalties for violating a treaty. **704**

Sandinistas. Rebels in Nicaragua who set up government friendly to the Soviets. **907**

Scalawags (skal′ə-wagz). Southern whites in the Republican party during Reconstruction. **503**

Scientific forestry. A form of conservation which set aside large forest areas in protected federal reserves and placed strict controls over lumber companies. **661**

Sea dogs. An affectionate nickname the English gave to sea captains in the 16th century. **35**

Sea Island cotton. Cotton that grew well only on the Sea Islands along the coasts of Georgia and South Carolina. **377**

Secession (si-sesh′ən). The withdrawal from an association with a political or religious group. **249**

Second World War. The war that broke out in 1939 when England and France declared war on Germany and later involved the Allies (England, France, Russia, and the U.S.) against the Axis (Germany, Italy, and Japan). **774**

Sectionalism (sek′shən-əl-iz′əm). Period following the Era of Good Feelings when regional conflicts arose. **319**

Segregation. The separation of people in public places on the basis of racial, religious, or social differences. **421, 512**

Seneca (sen′ə-kə) **Falls Declaration.** A statement issued by delegates to the 1840 women's rights convention who proposed that women be given the same rights and privileges as men. **401**

Separate-but-equal. The argument which supported the legality of segregation when races were separated in supposedly equal public schools. **513**

Serf. A person who lived under the feudal system and was bound to work a master's land. **12**

Settlement houses. Community centers in poor neighborhoods. **574**

"Seward's Folly." What Americans called the purchase of Alaska in 1867 by Secretary of State William Seward. **615**

Shakers. A religious group founded in England in 1747. **405**

Sharecropping. A system in which landowners provided laborers with the supplies needed for farming in exchange for a portion of their crops. **505**

Ships of the line. The British fleet armed with 70 or more cannons used in the War of 1812. **269**

Sick industries. Coal and textile industries which did not prosper during the 1920s. **731**

Sitting on the fence. Not taking a strong stand on any political issue. **585**

Smelt. To melt away impurities in ore to obtain metal. **556**

Smog. "Smoke" plus "fog" produced by smoke and chemical fumes. **900**

Society. A group of families who live and work together and share similar values and patterns of behavior. **4**

Sod houses. Houses made of grassy surface soil and wooden roofs built by the pioneers of the Great Plains. **546**

Solar collectors. Devices that gather and convert heat from the sun into electricity. **903**

Soldier of fortune. A professional fighter who was willing to sell his sword for money. **41**

Solid South. The southern states who traditionally supported the Democratic party. **578**

Sonar. An electronic device that locates underwater objects by sending out high-frequency sound waves. **791**

Soup kitchens. Places where food was served to the needy during the Great Depression. **739**

Southern hospitality. A reference to the friendly welcome given strangers by southerners. **65**

Specialization (spesh′əl-ə-zā′shən). A concentration on the manufacture of a particular product. **319**

Speculators. People who invest money where there is a considerable risk but also the possibility of large profits. **216**

Spheres of influence. Particular areas in China in the 19th century whose development was controlled by various European nations. **634**

Spinning jenny. A mechanical spinning wheel invented by James Hargreaves in 1765. **298**

Spoils of office. The dividing up of political rewards by the party in power. **330, 588**

Sputnik I. Russian for "traveling companion," in 1957 the first earth-orbiting satellite. **848**

Squatters. People who cleared and settled a tract of land. **68**

Stagflation. A word coined by combining parts of "*stag*nation" and "*inflation*." **883**

Stalemate (stāl'mīt). A deadlock in which neither opposing side can act effectively. **683**

Stamp Act. The 1765 British law that placed a tax on all printed matter in the colonies. **110**

Standard of living. The average quantity and quality of goods, services, and comforts that a person requires in daily life. **847**

Starving time. The period of starvation in Jamestown that lasted from 1609 to 1611. **42**

States' rights. The doctrine that holds that the states have the final power in the Union. **240, 447**

States' Rights party. A political party formed by Southern Democrats (Dixiecrats) in 1948. **818**

Steam engine. An engine driven by steam patented by James Watt in 1769. **310**

Steel plow. A farming tool manufactured by James Oliver in 1868. **548**

Stockholders. People who buy shares in a corporation. **553**

Stone Age. The earliest known period of human culture when stone was used to make tools and weapons. **4**

Strait of Magellan. A water passage between the Atlantic and Pacific Oceans. **26**

Strategic Arms Limitation Treaty (SALT). An agreement between the U.S. and the Soviet Union to limit nuclear weapons. **873**

Student Nonviolent Coordinating Council (SNCC). An organization set up to direct and organize a campaign for equal rights for blacks. **833**

Subsidies (sub'sə-dēz). Financial aid from the government for a purpose that benefits the public. **732**

Suburbs. Residential areas located outside a city. **726**

Suez Canal. Waterway in the Middle East invaded by British, French, and Israeli troops in 1956. **827**

Sugar Act. A law passed in 1764 which taxed the colonists' imports of sugar, wine, and coffee. **109**

Sun Belt. The states in the South and Southwest where population is increasing. **853**

"Sunshine patriots." An expression used by Thomas Paine to describe Americans who supported independence only when things were going well. **147**

Supply—side Economics. Lowering tax rates in order to increase tax revenues. **905**

Supreme Court. The highest U.S. court of appeals, composed of nine justices. **198**

Sutter's Fort. Fortified town built by John Sutter on California's American River in 1839. **354**

Synthetics. Artificial substances and materials. **731**

T

Taft-Hartley Act. A law passed in 1947 to regulate the growing influence of labor unions. **811**

Tammany (tam'ə-nē) **Hall.** A political machine run by New York City Democrats. **581**

Tariffs. Taxes placed on imported and exported goods. **171**

Taxation without representation. The argument by colonists that they were taxed by the British without being represented in Parliment. **110**

Tea Act. A 1773 law that gave the East India Company exclusive rights to sell tea directly to American retailers. **122**

Teapot Dome. A high-yielding government oil reserve in Wyoming that was the subject of a scandal involving leases on federal lands during President Harding's administration. **728**

Temperance (tem'pər-əns). The effort to restrict alcoholic drinking. **410**

Tenements (ten'ə-mənts). Buildings in which several families live crowded together, often in unsafe and unsanitary conditions. **304**

Tennessee Valley Authority (TVA). A federal agency established in 1933 to prevent flooding in the upper valley of the Tennessee River. **748**

Texas longhorns. Cattle with low, wide horns that once grazed freely in Texas. **540**

Three-Fifths Compromise. An agreement made by the framers of the Constitution to include three fifths of black slaves in counting a state's population. **199**

Three R's. The fundamental subjects of reading, writing, and 'rithmetic. **404**

Three sisters. The main crops of corn, beans, and squash raised by southwestern Indians. **6**

Tidewater. Name given southern coastal areas where rivers were affected by the ocean tides. **74**

TNT. An explosive containing nitrogen, used in blasting and warfare. **685**

Tom Thumb. The first steam-driven locomotive, built by Peter Cooper in 1830. **311**

Tonkin Gulf Resolution. An authority granted by Congress to Lyndon Johnson in 1964 to approve and support in advance "the determination of the President, as Commander in Chief, to take all necessary measures to repel any armed attack against the forces of the U.S." **862**

Tories. Colonists who remained loyal to England during the Revolutionary War. **138**

"Trail of Tears." Name given to the forced removal of Cherokee Indians from Georgia in 1838. **341**

Transcontinental Treaty. An 1818 treaty between the U.S. and Spain that extended America's western boundaries to the Pacific Coast. **284**

Transistors. Miniature electronic devices used to control and increase an electronic current. **849**

Transportation Revolution. An increase in transportation systems during the mid-1800s which joined people in the West with those in the East. **312**

Trench warfare. The fighting during World War I that took place in trenches that ran across northern France from the sea to Switzerland. **682**

Triangular trade. The profitable trade between the northern colonies, the West Indies, and England, with variations. **78**

Truman Doctrine. A U.S. policy to give financial and military aid to nations so they could resist communist rule. **812**

Trust. A group of corporations formed by a legal agreement made especially for the purpose of reducing competition. **562**

Trust buster. A person who wants to dissolve an established trust. **657**

Turnpikes. Roads on which tolls are collected. **306**

Tuskegee (tus-kē′gē) **Institute.** A school for blacks located in Alabama, founded by Booker T. Washington. **515**

Twine binder. A machine invented by John Appleby in the 1870s that gathered and bound wheat with string. **548**

Twisting the British lion's tail. Name given to political attacks on Great Britain made to appeal to anti-British sentiment in the U.S. **619**

Two-party system. A political system characterized by two major parties of similar strength, Democratic and Republican in the U.S. **226**

U

U-boats. German submarines or "undersea ships." **683**

Ultimatum. (ul′tə-mā′təm). A final offer or demand. **624**

Upland cotton. A variety of cotton that withstood cold temperatures. **377**

Urban complex. Connected cities, or a megalopolis, from the Greek for "great city." **896**

Urban frontier. Western cities that developed on the edge of settled areas and were used as outposts and depots from which settlers spread out. **303**

Urban League. An organization founded in 1910 to work for equal rights for blacks. **761**

U-2 Affair. A 1960 incident when an American spy plane was shot down over Russia. **841**

V

V-E Day. World War II victory in Europe when Germany surrendered to the Allies on May 8, 1945. **796**

V-J Day. World War II victory in Japan when Japan surrendered to the U.S. on August 14, 1945. **801**

Vaqueros (vä-kā′rōs). The first cowhands who invented almost all the tools of the cowhand's trade. **543**

Veto. The power of the President to reject bills passed by Congress. **203, 496**

Viet Cong. Procommunist South Vietnamese guerrilla soldiers. **862**

Vietnamization. Policy of building up the South Vietnamese army so that American troops could be withdrawn. **870**

Villistas. (və·lēs′təz) The armed troops of Pancho Villa who fought during the Mexican Revolution in the 1910s. **680**

Volunteers in Service to America (VISTA). An organization similar to the overseas Peace Corps but operating on a domestic level. **846**

Voting Rights Act. A Great Society law that appointed federal officials called "registrars" in districts where local officials were refusing to allow blacks to register to vote. **847**

W

Wage and price freeze. A 90-day period imposed by President Nixon in 1971 to regulate the economy. **870**

Wagner Labor Relations Act. A 1935 law that gave labor unions the right to organize and bargain collectively. **757**

War for American Independence. The war of revolution against the British from 1775 to 1781. **129**

War Hawks. Westerners and southerners who favored the War of 1812 against England. **264**

War of 1812. The war of the U.S. against Great Britain from 1812 to 1814. **269**

Water-frame. A spinning machine invented in 1768 by Richard Arkwright. **298**

Watergate Affair. A government scandal touched off when five burglars were arrested in 1972 in the headquarters of the Democratic National Committee in Washington. **875**

Waving the bloody shirt. A reference to the tactic made by Republican politicians in the late 1800s to remind voters that Democrats were "ex-rebels." **579**

Welfare state. A policy in which the government assumes a large measure of responsibility for the social well-being of its members. **663**

Western saddle. A deep-seated saddle with a high pommel used by the early cowhands. **544**

Whigs. Political party in opposition to the Democrats. **341**

Wildcatters. Name given to oil prospectors in the 1860s. **557**

Wisconsin Idea. The progressive program of reforms by Robert M. La Follette of Wisconsin in the early 1900s. **650**

Women's Liberation Movement. A program of political action and demonstrations begun in the late 1960s to attain equal rights for women. **885**

Women's Rights Convention. A meeting in Seneca Falls, New York, in 1840 to seek equal rights for women. **401**

Works Progress Administration (WPA). A New Deal agency that found useful work for millions of unemployed persons. **752**

X

XYZ correspondence. Name given letters which revealed that the American delegates sent to France in 1797 had been asked for a bribe by the French. **231**

Y

Yankee ingenuity. A knack for solving difficult problems in clever ways. **77**

Yellow journalism. The writing style of newspapers that played up crime and scandal during the 1890s. **623**

Z

Zimmermann Note. A document which showed that Germany was trying to make an alliance with Mexico in 1917. **688**

PRESIDENTS OF THE UNITED STATES

No.	Name	Born-Died	Years in office	Political party	Home state	Vice President
1	George Washington	1732–1799	1789–97	None	Va.	John Adams
2	John Adams	1735–1826	1797–1801	Federalist	Mass.	Thomas Jefferson
3	Thomas Jefferson	1743–1826	1801–09	Republican*	Va.	Aaron Burr
						George Clinton
4	James Madison	1751–1836	1809–17	Republican	Va.	George Clinton
						Elbridge Gerry
5	James Monroe	1758–1831	1817–25	Republican	Va.	Daniel D. Tompkins
6	John Quincy Adams	1767–1848	1825–29	Republican	Mass.	John C. Calhoun
7	Andrew Jackson	1767–1845	1829–37	Democratic	Tenn.	John C. Calhoun
						Martin Van Buren
8	Martin Van Buren	1782–1862	1837–41	Democratic	N.Y.	Richard M. Johnson
9	William Henry Harrison	1773–1841	1841	Whig	Ohio	John Tyler
10	John Tyler	1790–1862	1841–45	Whig	Va.	
11	James K. Polk	1795–1849	1845–49	Democratic	Tenn.	George M. Dallas
12	Zachary Taylor	1784–1850	1849–50	Whig	La.	Millard Fillmore
13	Millard Fillmore	1800–1874	1850–53	Whig	N.Y.	
14	Franklin Pierce	1804–1869	1853–57	Democratic	N.H.	William R. King
15	James Buchanan	1791–1868	1857–61	Democratic	Pa.	John C. Breckinridge
16	Abraham Lincoln	1809–1865	1861–65	Republican	Ill.	Hannibal Hamlin
						Andrew Johnson
17	Andrew Johnson	1808–1875	1865–69	Republican	Tenn.	
18	Ulysses S. Grant	1822–1885	1869–77	Republican	Ill.	Schuyler Colfax
						Henry Wilson
19	Rutherford B. Hayes	1822–1893	1877–81	Republican	Ohio	William A. Wheeler
20	James A. Garfield	1831–1881	1881	Republican	Ohio	Chester A. Arthur
21	Chester A. Arthur	1830–1886	1881–85	Republican	N.Y.	
22	Grover Cleveland	1837–1908	1885–89	Democratic	N.Y.	Thomas A. Hendricks
23	Benjamin Harrison	1833–1901	1889–93	Republican	Ind.	Levi P. Morton
24	Grover Cleveland		1893–97	Democratic	N.Y.	Adlai E. Stevenson
25	William McKinley	1843–1901	1897–1901	Republican	Ohio	Garret A. Hobart
						Theodore Roosevelt
26	Theodore Roosevelt	1858–1919	1901–09	Republican	N.Y.	
						Charles W. Fairbanks
27	William Howard Taft	1857–1930	1909–13	Republican	Ohio	James S. Sherman
28	Woodrow Wilson	1856–1924	1913–21	Democratic	N.J.	Thomas R. Marshall
29	Warren G. Harding	1865–1923	1921–23	Republican	Ohio	Calvin Coolidge
30	Calvin Coolidge	1872–1933	1923–29	Republican	Mass.	
						Charles G. Dawes
31	Herbert Hoover	1874–1964	1929–33	Republican	Calif.	Charles Curtis
32	Franklin D. Roosevelt	1882–1945	1933–45	Democratic	N.Y.	John Nance Garner
						Henry Wallace
						Harry S. Truman
33	Harry S. Truman	1884–1972	1945–53	Democratic	Mo.	
						Alben W. Barkley
34	Dwight D. Eisenhower	1890–1969	1953–61	Republican	Kans.	Richard M. Nixon
35	John F. Kennedy	1917–1963	1961–63	Democratic	Mass.	Lyndon B. Johnson
36	Lyndon B. Johnson	1908–1973	1963–69	Democratic	Texas	
						Hubert H. Humphrey
37	Richard M. Nixon	1913–	1969–74	Republican	Calif.	Spiro T. Agnew
						Gerald R. Ford
38	Gerald R. Ford	1913–	1974–77	Republican	Mich.	Nelson A. Rockefeller
39	Jimmy Carter	1924–	1977–81	Democratic	Ga.	Walter F. Mondale
40	Ronald Reagan	1911–	1981–	Republican	Calif.	George H. Bush

*The Republican party of the third through sixth Presidents is not the party of Abraham Lincoln, which was founded in 1854.

FACTS ABOUT THE STATES

State	Year of Statehood	1980 Population	Reps. in Congress	Area (Sq. mi.)	Capital	Largest City
Alabama	1819	3,890,061	7	51,609	Montgomery	Birmingham
Alaska	1959	400,481	1	586,412	Juneau	Anchorage
Arizona	1912	2,717,866	5	113,909	Phoenix	Phoenix
Arkansas	1836	2,285,513	4	53,104	Little Rock	Little Rock
California	1850	23,668,562	45	158,693	Sacramento	Los Angeles
Colorado	1876	2,888,834	6	104,247	Denver	Denver
Connecticut	1788	3,107,576	6	5,009	Hartford	Hartford
Delaware	1787	595,225	1	2,057	Dover	Wilmington
District of Columbia	1791	637,651	—	69		Washington
Florida	1845	9,739,992	19	58,560	Tallahassee	Jacksonville
Georgia	1788	5,464,265	10	58,876	Atlanta	Atlanta
Hawaii	1959	965,000	2	6,450	Honolulu	Honolulu
Idaho	1890	943,935	2	83,557	Boise	Boise
Illinois	1818	11,418,461	22	56,400	Springfield	Chicago
Indiana	1816	5,490,179	10	36,291	Indianapolis	Indianapolis
Iowa	1846	2,913,387	6	56,290	Des Moines	Des Moines
Kansas	1861	2,363,208	5	82,264	Topeka	Wichita
Kentucky	1792	3,661,433	7	40,395	Frankfort	Louisville
Louisiana	1812	4,203,972	8	48,523	Baton Rouge	New Orleans
Maine	1820	1,124,660	2	33,215	Augusta	Portland
Maryland	1788	4,216,446	8	10,577	Annapolis	Baltimore
Massachusetts	1788	5,737,037	11	8,257	Boston	Boston
Michigan	1837	9,258,344	18	58,216	Lansing	Detroit
Minnesota	1858	4,077,148	8	84,068	St. Paul	Minneapolis
Mississippi	1817	2,520,638	5	47,716	Jackson	Jackson
Missouri	1821	4,917,444	9	69,686	Jefferson City	St. Louis
Montana	1889	786,690	2	147,138	Helena	Billings
Nebraska	1867	1,570,006	3	77,227	Lincoln	Omaha
Nevada	1864	799,184	2	110,540	Carson City	Las Vegas
New Hampshire	1788	920,610	2	9,304	Concord	Manchester
New Jersey	1787	7,364,158	14	7,836	Trenton	Newark
New Mexico	1912	1,299,968	3	121,666	Santa Fe	Albuquerque
New York	1788	17,557,288	34	49,576	Albany	New York City
North Carolina	1789	5,874,429	11	52,586	Raleigh	Charlotte
North Dakota	1889	652,695	1	70,665	Bismarck	Fargo
Ohio	1803	10,797,419	21	41,222	Columbus	Cleveland
Oklahoma	1907	3,025,266	6	69,919	Oklahoma City	Oklahoma City
Oregon	1859	2,632,663	5	96,981	Salem	Portland
Pennsylvania	1787	11,866,728	23	45,333	Harrisburg	Philadelphia
Rhode Island	1790	947,154	2	1,214	Providence	Providence
South Carolina	1788	3,119,208	6	31,055	Columbia	Columbia
South Dakota	1889	690,178	1	77,047	Pierre	Sioux Falls
Tennessee	1796	4,590,750	9	42,244	Nashville	Memphis
Texas	1845	14,228,383	27	267,339	Austin	Houston
Utah	1896	1,461,037	3	84,916	Salt Lake City	Salt Lake City
Vermont	1791	511,456	1	9,609	Montpelier	Burlington
Virginia	1788	5,346,279	10	40,817	Richmond	Norfolk
Washington	1889	4,130,163	8	68,192	Olympia	Seattle
West Virginia	1863	1,949,644	4	24,181	Charleston	Huntington
Wisconsin	1848	4,705,335	9	56,154	Madison	Milwaukee
Wyoming	1890	470,816	1	97,914	Cheyenne	Cheyenne

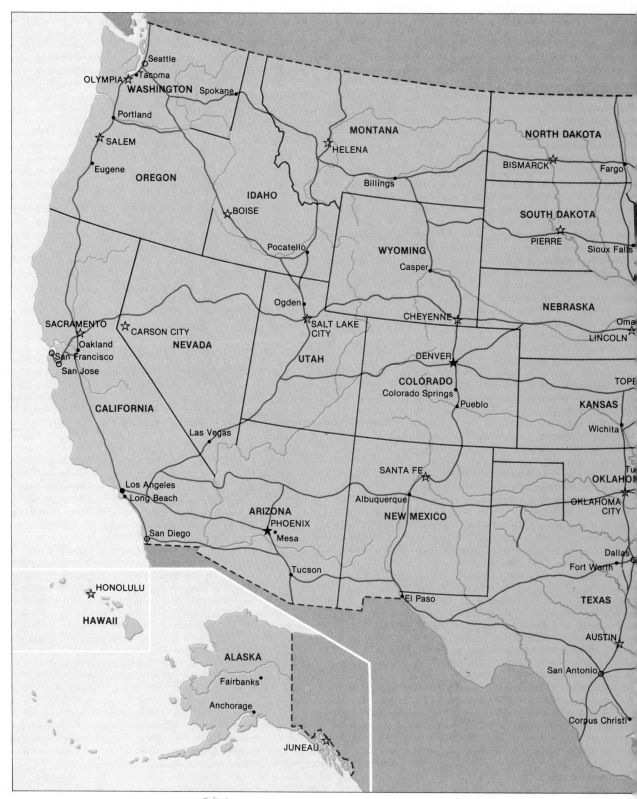

Seattle
Tacoma
OLYMPIA☆
WASHINGTON Spokane
Portland
☆ SALEM
Eugene
OREGON

MONTANA
☆ HELENA

NORTH DAKOTA
BISMARCK☆
Fargo

IDAHO
☆ BOISE
Pocatello

Billings

SOUTH DAKOTA
☆
PIERRE
Sioux Falls

WYOMING
Casper

NEBRASKA
Oma
LINCOLN

SACRAMENTO
☆ CARSON CITY
Oakland
San Francisco
San Jose

NEVADA

Ogden
SALT LAKE
CITY

CHEYENNE
☆

DENVER
★
COLORADO
Colorado Springs
Pueblo

TOPE

KANSAS
Wichita

UTAH

CALIFORNIA

Las Vegas

Los Angeles
Long Beach

San Diego

ARIZONA
PHOENIX
★
Mesa

Tucson

SANTA FE
☆
Albuquerque
NEW MEXICO

El Paso

Tu
OKLAHO
OKLAHOMA
CITY
☆

Dallas
Fort Worth

TEXAS

AUSTIN
☆

HONOLULU
☆
HAWAII

ALASKA
Fairbanks
Anchorage

San Antonio

Corpus Christi

JUNEAU ☆

924

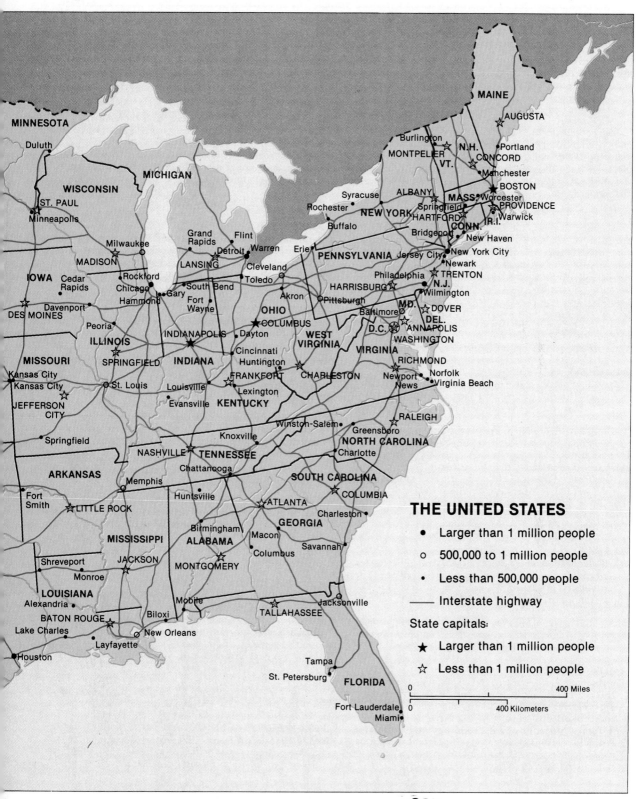

THE UNITED STATES

- • Larger than 1 million people
- ○ 500,000 to 1 million people
- • Less than 500,000 people
- — Interstate highway

State capitals:

- ★ Larger than 1 million people
- ☆ Less than 1 million people

0   400 Miles

0   400 Kilometers

MINNESOTA
Duluth
WISCONSIN
ST. PAUL
Minneapolis
MICHIGAN
MADISON
Milwaukee
Grand Rapids
Flint
Detroit
Warren
Erie
Lansing
IOWA
Cedar Rapids
Rockford
Chicago
South Bend
Cleveland
Toledo
Akron
Davenport
DES MOINES
Hammond
Gary
Fort Wayne
Pittsburgh
Peoria
OHIO
COLUMBUS
ILLINOIS
INDIANAPOLIS
Dayton
MISSOURI
SPRINGFIELD
INDIANA
Cincinnati
Huntington
WEST VIRGINIA
Kansas City
Kansas City
St. Louis
Louisville
FRANKFORT
CHARLESTON
JEFFERSON CITY
Evansville
Lexington
KENTUCKY
Springfield
Winston-Salem
ARKANSAS
Knoxville
NASHVILLE
TENNESSEE
Chattanooga
Fort Smith
LITTLE ROCK
Memphis
Huntsville
Birmingham
ATLANTA
MISSISSIPPI
GEORGIA
ALABAMA
Macon
Shreveport
JACKSON
MONTGOMERY
Columbus
Savannah
Monroe
LOUISIANA
Alexandria
Mobile
BATON ROUGE
Biloxi
Lake Charles
New Orleans
Layfayette
Houston
TALLAHASSEE
Jacksonville
Tampa
St. Petersburg
FLORIDA
Fort Lauderdale
Miami

MAINE
AUGUSTA
Burlington
N.H.
Portland
MONTPELIER
CONCORD
VT.
Manchester
BOSTON
ALBANY
Syracuse
MASS.
Worcester
Rochester
Springfield
PROVIDENCE
NEW YORK
HARTFORD
Warwick
Buffalo
CONN.
R.I.
Bridgeport
New Haven
PENNSYLVANIA
Jersey City
New York City
Newark
Philadelphia
TRENTON
HARRISBURG
N.J.
Wilmington
MD.
DOVER
Baltimore
DEL.
D.C.
ANNAPOLIS
WASHINGTON
VIRGINIA
RICHMOND
Norfolk
Newport News
Virginia Beach
RALEIGH
Greensboro
NORTH CAROLINA
Charlotte
SOUTH CAROLINA
COLUMBIA
Charleston

925

OUR LIVING HERITAGE

One of the best ways to use your historical imagination is by visiting the sites of important events or the homes of famous persons. The places listed here are but a few of the many historic sites in the United States. For more information about sites in your community or state, write your county or state historical society.

Many of the sites listed below are under the care of the federal government. These national historic locales are abbreviated **NMP** for military parks, **NHP** for historic parks, **NHL** for landmarks, **NHB** for battlefields, **NHS** for sites, and **NM** for national monuments. Page references are included to help you review the importance of most sites in this book. For further information write the appropriate regional office of the National Park Service:

Western Region, 450 Golden Gate Avenue, San Francisco CA 94102; **Midwest Region,** 1709 Jackson, Omaha NB 68102; **North Atlantic Region,** 15 State Street, Boston MA 02109; **National Capital Region,** 1100 Ohio Drive, SW, Washington DC 20242; **Southeast Region,** 75 Spring Street, SW, Atlanta GA 30303; **Rocky Mountain Region,** 655 Parfet Street, PO Box 25287, Denver CO 80225; **Southwest Region,** PO Box 728, Santa Fe NM 87501; **Pacific Northwest Region,** Westin Building, Room 1920, Seattle WA 98121; **Alaska Area,** 540 West 5th Avenue, Room 202, Anchorage AK 99501.

ALABAMA
Horseshoe Bend NMP north of Dadeville is the site of Andrew Jackson's victory over the Creek nation in 1814. The visitor center has exhibits of Creek culture and frontier life. **275**

Tuskegee Institute NHS in Tuskegee is the site of the pioneer school founded for blacks in 1881 by Booker T. Washington. **515**

Alabama Space and Rocket Center in Huntsville features space exhibits including simulated travel to the moon and tours of the Marshall Space Flight Center. **848**

The First White House of the Confederacy and the **Alabama State Capital** in Montgomery commemorate the role of Jefferson Davis as President. **451**

ALASKA
Alaskaland-Pioneer Park in Fairbanks is a 40-acre park recreating a gold rush town and an Indian village. **The University of Alaska Museum** in Fairbanks has displays on Eskimo culture as well as on Russian and gold rush history of the state.

Sitka NHP north of Sitka is a memorial to the Tlingit Indians. The visitor center also has exhibits on life during the time Russia owned Alaska. **9, 614**

ARIZONA
Tombstone NHS preserves this silver rush town of the 1880s. Visitors can see exhibits of the town's history at Schieffelin Hall and the Wells Fargo Museum and tour the underground silver mines.

The Heard Museum of Anthropology and Primitive Art in Phoenix displays arts and crafts of southwestern Indians and Mexicans. It has exhibits on South American cultures and Spanish colonial days.

Casa Grande Ruins in Casa Grande, **Montezuma Castle** east of Prescott, and the **Navajo National Monument** east of Kaibab all have ruins of prehistoric Indian cultures.

ARKANSAS
Arkansas Territorial Restoration in downtown Little Rock is one of the nation's finest, consisting of 13 buildings dating from the 1820s and 1830s.

Ozark Folk Center at Mountain View is an 80-acre living museum that features arts, crafts, music, and Ozarks lore.

Fort Smith NHS features Indian and pioneer artifacts in the commissary building, all that remains of a fort that was famous as a gateway to the West.

CALIFORNIA
Hearst San Simeon State Historic Park south of Monterey contains the castle built by publishing tycoon William Randolph Hearst and designed by Julia Morgan. **623**

Marshall Gold Discovery State Historic Site at Coloma, near Sacramento, is where the Gold Rush began in 1848. Attractions include Sutter's Mill, Marshall's cabin, a museum, and the Wah Hop store, which explains the role of the Chinese in the Gold Rush. **365**

Sutter's Fort NHL in Sacramento is a reconstruction of that early settlement. The **State Indian Museum** is also located in Sacramento. **354**

Santa Barbara Mission NHL at Santa Barbara is one of the 21 missions founded by Father Junípero Serra. It has a fine collection of original mission treasures. **360**

Bodie NHL near Bridgeport is a ghost town of 170 buildings, reminders of its days during the Gold Rush. **365**

Fort Ross NHL near Jenner is a restoration of a Russian fort used by seal and otter hunters on the Pacific. **325**

COLORADO
Central City is the site of Colorado's first important gold discovery in 1859. **Cripple Creek, Telluride,** and **Georgetown** are other restored mining towns. **528**

Mesa Verde National Park near Cortez contains hundreds of dwellings inhabited by Indians between 400 and 1300 A.D. **7**

Bent's Old Fort NHS near La Junta preserves a fort and trading post on the Santa Fe Trail. **364**

CONNECTICUT
Old New-Gate Prison in East Granby was originally a copper mine opened in 1707. It was used during the Revolutionary War to house prisoners of war. Attractions include the prison yard with its scaffold, a museum, and tours of the restored mine and dungeons.

Mystic Seaport and Museum is one of the oldest shipbuilding and whaling ports in the U.S. The seaport preserves the atmosphere of a mid-19th century New England maritime village. At berth is the *Charles W. Morgan,* the last of the 19th-century wooden whaleships.

DELAWARE
Henry Francis du Pont Winterthur Museum in Winterthur contains almost 200 period rooms and displays devoted to American furniture and decorative arts.

The **Delaware State Museum** in Dover has exhibits on state history, the plantation home of Revolutionary War leader John Dickinson, and the Octagonal School House, a restored school house built in 1836.

Fort Christina NHL in Wilmington marks the landing place of Swedish colonists in 1638. **51**

DISTRICT OF COLUMBIA

The White House, home of every President but Washington, has tours of its splendid public rooms. **243**

The Smithsonian Institution includes the National Air and Space Museum, showing the history of aviation and space travel, the National Collection of Fine Arts; the National Portrait Gallery, from which many portraits in this book were obtained; and the National Museum of History and Technology.

The Library of Congress began with the purchase of Thomas Jefferson's library. On display are Jefferson's rough draft of the Declaration of Independence and Lincoln's drafts of the Gettysburg Address.

The National Archives displays the original Declaration of Independence, the Constitution, and the Bill of Rights.

The U.S. Capitol, seat of Congress, features murals of historic events and statues of Presidents and other famous Americans. **243.**

FLORIDA

Cape Canaveral Air Force Station and **John F. Kennedy Space Center,** both near Titusville, are the launching sites of the U.S. manned space flights and the space shuttle. There are tours of the Moon Launch Pad, Vehicle Assembly Building, Mission Control Center, and the Air Force Museum. **853**

St. Augustine NHL reflects the Spanish heritage of the oldest city in the U.S. The city has many restored buildings and ships. **102**

GEORGIA

New Echota in Calhoun is a restoration of the Cherokee capital. It explains the Cherokees' efforts to establish a republican form of government. **341**

Fort Benning in Columbus has exhibits of U.S. history from the Revolutionary War to the present.

Andersonville NHS preserves this infamous Civil War prison camp.

HAWAII

Pu'uhonua o Honaunau (City of Refuge) NHP features exhibits on life in Hawaii before outsiders arrived in the 1700s.

U.S.S. Arizona NM at Pearl Harbor on Oahu is the site of the Japanese bombardment on December 7, 1941. **784**

IDAHO

Massacre Rocks State Park west of American Falls marks an 1862 ambush on a wagon train on the Oregon Trail.

Nez Perce NHP near Spaulding contains 23 historic sites showing the tribe's history and culture. **533**

Fort Hall NHL north of Pocatello is a reconstruction of a fort that was important in the westward migration.

ILLINOIS

Nauvoo Restoration was a Fox Indian village until the Mormons arrived in 1839. **363**

Among Chicago's great museums are the **Chicago Historical Society,** which recreates the Great Chicago Fire, and the **Art Institute,** with its splendid American art.

The Ulysses S. Grant Home is in Galena, once the wealthiest city in Illinois. **484**

Springfield has memorials to Abraham Lincoln including the **Lincoln Home** and the **Old State Capitol** NHL where Lincoln served in the state legislature. Nearby is **New Salem State Park,** a reconstruction of the town as Lincoln knew it in the 1830s. **437**

INDIANA

Lincoln Boyhood National Memorial south of Lincoln City and **Lincoln Pioneer Village** in Rockport preserve the childhood residences of Abraham Lincoln. **324**

The Benjamin Harrison Home NHL in Indianapolis features many of the original furnishings in the home of the 23rd President. **590**

Vincennes, the oldest town in Indiana, has many historic sites, including George Rogers Clark NHP and Grouseland, the home of William Henry Harrison. **153, 343**

The Tippecanoe County Historical Museum in Lafayette has relics of the Battle of Tippecanoe. **267**

IOWA

Herbert Hoover NHS in West Branch features the two-room cottage where the 31st President was born and his Presidential library. **733**

The Living History Farm near Des Moines is a working pioneer farm with an 1870 mansion.

Amana Village NHL west of Iowa City gives a view of life in this ideal community founded in the 19th century. **406**

KANSAS

Dodge City, founded in 1872, features Boot Hill; Old Fort Dodge Jail, which houses a museum; and a replica of Old Front Street. **541**

Pawnee Indian Village in Belleville features Pawnee earth lodges from the early 1800s and a museum. **523**

Dwight D. Eisenhower Home in Abilene is the boyhood home of the 34th President and site of his library. **823**

The John Brown Memorial Park and **John Brown Cabin** in Osawatomie commemorate the abolitionist in Kansas. **429**

KENTUCKY

Cumberland Gap NHP south of Middlesboro marks this pathway to the West first blazed by Daniel Boone. The park includes parts of Boone's Wilderness Road and Hensley Settlement, a reconstructed mountain community. **308**

The Appalachian Museum in Berea features a smokehouse, blacksmith shop, and a country store.

Ashland NHL, a reconstruction of Henry Clay's mansion, is in Lexington. His law office may also be visited. **326**

LOUISIANA

New Orleans Jazz Museum traces the history of jazz and honors jazz greats like Louis Armstrong. **717**

The Vieux Carre Historic District in New Orleans preserves the flavor of the city when it was Spanish and French. Among landmarks are the Cabildo and Jackson Square, where the U.S. flag was first raised over Lousiana Territory. **247**

Chalmette NHP near New Orleans marks the site of the Battle of New Orleans. **277**

MAINE

Shaker Village near Poland is maintained as a living museum of life in this religious community. **405**

Boothbay Railway Museum, the **Grand Banks Schooner Museum,** and the **Boothbay Regional Museum** are all in Boothbay.

The Old Conway House Complex in Camden is an 18th-century farmhouse and restored community.

The Bath Maritime Museum honors the state's ties to the sea. Several grand mansions also stand in Bath.

Roosevelt Campobello International Park on Campobello Island features the summer home of Franklin and Eleanor Roosevelt. **743**

MARYLAND

The U.S. Frigate <u>Constellation</u> NHL, the nation's oldest warship, is in Baltimore. **Mount Clare Station** is the nation's first railroad station and the **Baltimore & Ohio Transportation Museum** has a collection of antique railroad engines and cars. **The Peale Museum** NHL features paintings by the Peales, several of which appear in this book. **269, 311**

Fort McHenry NM in Baltimore is the site where Francis Scott Key composed "The Star-Spangled Banner" during the War of 1812. **276**

Antietam National Battlefield near Sharpsburg marks the site of a decisive but costly battle of the Civil War. **471**

MASSACHUSETTS

Lexington Green NHL commemorates the Battle of Lexington and Concord. Nearby are the Buckman Tavern, where the Minute Men gathered before battle, Hancock-Clarke House, where Sam Adams and John Hancock stayed, and Monroe Tavern, headquarters of the British troops. **126**

Freedom Trail in Boston takes visitors past many historic sites, including Faneuil Hall, Paul Revere's House, Old North Church, and the Old State House. At the Boston Naval Shipyard is the U.S.S. *Constitution.* **260**

Among the numerous restored, recreated, or preserved historic towns are **Old Deerfield** (102), **Hancock, Shaker Village** near Pittsfield (405), **Plymouth Plantation** at Plymouth (46), **Quincy** with the Adams NHS (228, 327), **Salem,** and **Old Sturbridge Village.**

Lowell NHP features seven mills, a canal, and the 19th-century buildings of a factory town. **301**

MICHIGAN

Greenfield Village in Dearborn is a recreated American community of the early 19th century. The Henry Ford Museum includes exhibits on American arts and crafts.

The International Afro-American Museum in Detroit tells the history of blacks in America. Also in Detroit are the **Historical Museum** and **Fort Wayne Military Museum.**

Mackinaw Island NHL features many historic buildings, including one of the oldest existing forts in the U.S.

The Gerald R. Ford Museum in Grand Rapids has Presidential papers. **883**

MINNESOTA

Winona is an old steamboat town which features an 1898 Mississippi riverboat at the **Steamboat Museum,** the **Bunnell House,** a pioneer home, and a country museum.

Old Mendota, the oldest permanent settlement in the state, has historic buildings that recall that days when Mendota was a trading post village.

Fort Snelling State Park NHL has been restored near Minneapolis and St. Paul. **The Gibbs Farm Museum** in St. Paul features the farm's original equipment.

MISSISSIPPI

Natchez features many historical sites reflecting its steamboat days and ante-bellum mansions. Attractions include Connelly's Tavern, Stanton Hall, and Longwood.

Beauvoir near Biloxi was the home of Jefferson Davis after the Civil War. **452**

Vicksburg National Military Park features extensive remains of forts, breastworks, and gun emplacements. **483**

Old Natchez Trace Museum is near Tupelo. The trace was a road used by people who floated their goods down the Mississippi.

MISSOURI

The Trail of Tears State Park near Cape Giradeau contains part of the trail taken by the Cherokees in 1838. **340**

Among the many sites in St. Louis is the sweeping arch of the **Jefferson National Expansion Memorial.** Within the park, site of the original French village, is the **Old Courthouse,** where the Dred Scott case was heard. **433**

Harry S. Truman Memorial Library, with its Presidential memorabilia, is in Independence. **809**

Sainte Genevieve, the oldest permanent settlement in Missouri, has many buildings in the French style.

MONTANA

Custer Battlefield NM on the Crow reservation marks the site where Sioux and Cheyenne defeated Custer. **531**

Fort Benton Museum features dioramas recalling the days when the site was a stopping point for the Lewis and Clark Expedition and later a trading post. **253**

Virginia City, home of Montana's 1863 gold strike, has restored buildings and museums.

The Grant-Kohrs Ranch NHS near Deer Lodge recaptures life on a large 19th-century cattle ranch. **542**

The C. M. Russell Gallery in Helena holds a good collection of Russell's work, which appears frequently in this book; dioramas; and a recreated 1880 street scene.

NEBRASKA

Buffalo Bill Ranch State Historic Park near North Platte was the ranch of Buffalo Bill Cody. **534**

Brownville, a steamboat town founded in 1854, features a museum with exhibits on pioneer life.

The Stuhr Museum of the Prairie Pioneer in Grand Island recreates a prairie town of the 19th century.

The Bryan House NHL in Lincoln was the home of William Jennings Bryan. **601**

NEVADA

The Nevada State Museum in Carson City features Indian and pioneer history and an underground mine tour.

Virginia City NHL near Carson City is the mining boom town that made fortunes. **539**

NEW HAMPSHIRE

Old Fort No. 4 in Claremont, a replica of a 1744 fort, has exhibits and demonstrations of early means of defense.

The **Historic Information Center** in Portsmouth, housed in a grand 1784 mansion, can provide information on many buildings of historic interest including the **Strawberry Banks** restoration.

NEW JERSEY
Waterloo Village near Morristown has been restored as a pre-Revolutionary War village. **Morristown** NHP was winter headquarters for Washington. The park includes the Ford Mansion, where the Washingtons stayed, Fort Nonsense, and Jockey Hollow. **145**

Edison NHS in West Orange is a complex of buildings in which Thomas A. Edison worked. **560**

Monmouth Battlefield NHL near Freehold is the site of Washington's victory in 1778, which boosted American morale. **153**

NEW YORK
Among the many museums in New York City is **Castle Clinton** NM, a restored fort built to protect New York City during the War of 1812. **The Statue of Liberty** NM, off the tip of Manhattan, features the American Museum of Immigration. **569**

Richmondtown Restoration on Staten Island is a group of 40 buildings that show the evolution of the American village.

The Black History Museum in Hempstead traces the history of American blacks from colonial times. Also on Long Island are **Old Bethpage Village** restoration and **Sagamore Hill** NHS, home of the Theodore Roosevelt family. **658**

The Vanderbilt Mansion NHS and the **Franklin D. Roosevelt Home** and Presidential library are in Hyde Park. **743**

Washington's Headquarters NHL at Newburgh is the site where the Washingtons lived in 1782–83. Also at Newburgh are the **Knox Headquarters** and the **Windsor Cantonment,** a military village planned by General von Steuben. **150**

Saratoga NHP near Stillwater marks the site where General Burgoyne surrendered his British army. **148**

West Point NHL is the site chosen by Washington for the U.S. Military Academy. **153**

NEW MEXICO
The Indian Pueblo Cultural Center in Albuquerque explains the Pueblo culture through demonstrations and tours. **6**

Los Alamos Scientific Laboratory has exhibits at Bradbury Science Hall on the uses and applications of nuclear energy. **902**

The Taos Pueblo NHL, two large five-story pueblos that are still inhabited, and the **Mission of St. Francis of Assisi,** built in the early 1700s, are both near Taos.

Impressive Indian village remains are at **Aztec Ruins** NM near Farmington, **Gila Cliff Dwellings** NM, **Chaco Canyon** NM, and **Bandelier** NM.

NORTH CAROLINA
Oconaluftee Indian Village near Cherokee is a replica of an 18th-century Cherokee village with a museum. **341**

Wright Brothers NM south of Kitty Hawk is the site of the first successful flight in 1903. **720**

Fort Raleigh NHS on Roanoke Island is a reconstruction of the Lost Colony of Roanoke. **36**

Guilford Court House NMP near Greensboro is the site of the Revolutionary War battle that sent Cornwallis in retreat to the coast. **153**

NORTH DAKOTA
Fort Abercrombie State Historic Site near Wahpeton contains reconstructed blockhouses, a stockade, and a museum.

Bonanzaville U.S.A. near Fargo is a recreated village in the Red River Valley, where gigantic farms flourished. **548**

Frontier Museum and Pioneer Village near Williston has two museums and a reconstructed village.

Fort Mandan State Historic Site near Washburn is a reconstruction of the fort where the Lewis and Clark Expedition spent the winter of 1804–05. **252**

OKLAHOMA
Cherokee National Capitol NHL in Tahlequah was the site of the capital city of the Cherokee Nation. **340**

Indian City U.S.A. near Anadarko is a reconstruction of villages of the Plains Indians. **523**

The National Cowboy Hall of Fame and Western Heritage Center outside Oklahoma City has exhibits on the Old West, including a sod house and an Indian village. **543**

OHIO
Mound City Group NM near Chillicothe is an excavation of a cultural center of the prehistoric Hopewell Indians. **9**

Harriet Beecher Stowe House in Cincinnati is a museum dedicated to the author of *Uncle Tom's Cabin.* **422**

Au Glaize Village near Defiance, **Geauga County Historical Society Century Village** at Burton, **Hale Farm** and **Western Reserve Village** at Bath and **Zoar Village** at Zoar are all 19th-century villages.

Fort Recovery is a state memorial near Fort Recovery and includes a partially restored fort and museum with exhibits on the Indian wars of the 1790s. **264**

OREGON
Fort Clatsop National Memorial near Astoria is a replica of the fort erected by Lewis and Clark in 1805. **252**

Collier Memorial State Park near Klamath Falls has a logging museum and pioneer village.

Jacksonville Historic District is a restored 1880s gold rush town.

PENNSYLVANIA
In Philadelphia a visitor center provides maps and information about **Independence** NHP, which includes the Liberty Bell, Independence Hall, Congress Hall, and buildings dating from 1732 to 1834. **175**

Gettysburg NMP is the site of a major battle of the Civil War fought in 1863. Here Lincoln later delivered his famous address. **477**

Valley Forge NHP is the place where the American army spent the hard winter of 1777–78. **150**

Fort Duquesne and **Fort Pitt** are landmark sites on the Ohio. **103**

PUERTO RICO
San Juan NHS contains the Spanish fortresses Castillo El Morro and Castillo San Cristobal, the San Juan Gate, and La Fortaleza, the governor's palace built in 1530.

RHODE ISLAND

Old Slater Mill in Pawtucket consists of restored buildings of the 1793 mill built for early mass production. **299**

Bowen's Wharf of Newport has been restored to show houses and public buildings dating from 1675 to 1820.

Mount Zion Black Museum in Newport exhibits black history and culture in a pre-Civil War church.

SOUTH CAROLINA

In or near Charleston are the sites of **Old Charles Towne,** a restoration of the state's first permanent settlement (57), **Fort Sumter** NM (454), and the **Old Slave Mart Museum.** This beautiful city preserves many gracious homes.

Historic Camden is a restoration of the town the British burnt during the Revolutionary War. **153**

King's Mountain NMP near Spartanburg is the 4,000-acre site of the decisive American victory in 1780. **153**

The Calhoun House (also known as Fort Hill) on the campus of Clemson University in Clemson is the plantation home of John and Floride Calhoun. **321**

Lexington County Homestead Museum, near Columbia, honors Swiss-German settlers.

SOUTH DAKOTA

Wounded Knee Battlefield NHL near Hot Springs is a museum and mass grave commemorating the last important battle between Plains Indians and U.S. army soldiers. **896**

Prairie Village at Madison is a reconstructed late 19th-century town.

Deadwood near Rapid City preserves buildings of a mining town of the Old West. **542**

TENNESSEE

The American Museum of Atomic Energy in Oak Ridge has tours explaining atomic energy and its uses. **902**

Cades Cove near Gatlinburg is a living museum of pioneer homesteads along an 11-mile stretch of road.

The Hermitage NHL near Nashville is the beautiful home of Andrew and Rachel Jackson, kept as it was when Jackson died in 1845. **328**

Shiloh NMP, the Civil War site, is near Savannah. **482**

TEXAS

The rich historical heritage of San Antonio includes the **Alamo** NHL; **La Villita,** a restoration of San Antonio's earliest community, and the **Spanish Governor's Palace. The San Antonio Mission** NHP includes four of the finest missions in the United States. **347**

Square House Carson County Historical Museum near Amarillo is an 1893 ranch with displays on life in the West. **540**

The NASA Lyndon B. Johnson Space Center in Houston has a visitor center and self-guiding tours. **853.**

The Sam Houston Memorial Museum in Huntsville has exhibits on Texas pioneers and the Texas Revolution. **349**

The Lyndon B. Johnson Presidential Library in Austin has a replica of the Oval Office and excellent displays. **845**

UTAH

Pioneer Museum near Provo has a fine collection of regional pioneer artifacts and a pioneer village.

The Golden Spike NHS at Promontory marks the spot where the last spike was driven to lay tracks for the first transcontinental railroad. **526**

Salt Lake City Temple Square NHL commemorates achievements of the Mormons. **The Utah Pioneer Village** recreates their pioneer life. **362**

VERMONT

The President Coolidge Homestead near White River Junction is the home where Coolidge was sworn in as President. A museum exhibits 19th-century tools. **728**

The Outdoor Shelburne Museum at Shelburne includes 18th-and 19th-century houses and a 1903 side-wheel steamboat.

VIRGINIA

Williamsburg NHL, with its over 100 restored buildings in the colonial capital, is a living demonstration of colonial life. **63**

Colonial NHP includes Jamestown Island, site of the Jamestown Colony, and Yorktown, the site where Cornwallis surrendered to Washinton in 1781. **40, 154**

Mount Vernon is the lovely home of George and Martha Washington. **243**

Monticello near Charlottesville is the elegant and functional home designed by Thomas Jefferson. **241**

The Appomattox Court House NHP at Appomattox was the scene of Lee's surrender to Grant in 1865. **488**

Manassas National Battlefield Park commemorates the Civil War battles of Bull Run and Richmond. **456, 470**

WASHINGTON

The U.S.S. Missouri in the Naval Shipyard at Bremerton was the scene of the Japanese surrender in 1945. **801**

The Whitman Mission NHS near Walla Walla depicts missionary activity in the West. **355**

The Willis Carey Historical Museum near Wenatchee features a typical 19th-century community and many Indian artifacts.

Point Defiance Park at Tacoma holds a replica of the first fort built by the Hudson Bay Company on the Pacific Coast, an old logging camp, and a pioneer home.

WEST VIRGINIA

Lewisburg near White Sulphur Springs features a restoration of the colonial town.

Harpers Ferry NHP preserves the town as it was at the time of John Brown's raid in 1859. **442**

Fort New Salem at Salem is a reconstruction of a settlement founded in 1792.

WISCONSIN

Historic Galloway House and Village in Fond du Lac is a replica of an 1890 village, including a 30-room Victorian mansion.

Stonefield at Cassfield includes a 19th-century frontier village, the home of a gentleman farmer, and a museum.

La Follette Home NHL in Maple Bluff was the home of Robert and Belle Case La Follette. **650**

WYOMING

Fort Laramie NHS near Torrington was an important stop for travelers on the Oregon Trail. **525**

South Pass City near Lander offers a museum and restoration of this gold rush town.

The Oregon Trail Ruts NHL near Guernsey shows the ruts made by wagons on the Oregon Trail, some six feet deep. **355**

INDEX

A

Abilene, Kansas, 541
Abolitionists, 387–93, 422, 428, 442–44
Adams, Abigail, 211, *il* 211, 212
Adams, John, 115, 132, 139, 165, 206, 228–31, 240–42, *il* 132, 166, 211, 228
Adams, John Quincy, 283–86, 288, 326–29, *il* 283
Adams, Samuel, 115, 124, 127, 132, 176, 205, *il* 116, 132
Addams, Jane, 574, 630, *il* 574
"Advice and consent," 202
Affluent Society, 847
AFL-CIO, 851, 857
Africa, 18–19, 70, 78, 894
Agnew, Spiro T., 868, 876, 878
Agricultural Adjustment Act, 747, 756, 765
Agriculture. *See* Farming
Aguinaldo, Emilio, 630, 632, *il* 630
Airplanes, 697, 720, 780, 789–90, 814–15, 853
Alabama, 319, 832
Alamo, 347–48
Alaska, 614–15, 828, 853
Albany Plan of Union, 85–86
Aldrin, Edwin, 849, *il* 849
Algeria, 792
Alien Act, 232, 239, 245
Alliance for Progress, 841
Allies: World War I, 677–78, 682, 688, 698, 701–04; World War II, 778–79, 792–96, 814–15
Altgeld, John Peter, 600
Amalgamated Association of Iron and Steel Workers, 567–68
Amana community, 406
Amendments: Bill of Rights, 212, 214; 12th, 243; 13th, 494; 14th, 497–98, 654, 656; 15th, 500; 16th, 666; 17th, 652; 18th, 667; 19th, 710; 21st, 667; 22nd, 811; 25th, 878; 26th, 888
American Anti-Slavery Society, 388
American Colonization Society, 376
American Expeditionary Force, 691, 696
American Federation of Labor, 567–68, 692, 765–66. *See also* AFL-CIO

American Indian Movement (AIM), 895–96
American Railway Union, 599–600
American System, 326
American Temperance Union, 410
Anarchists, 631, 713
Anderson, Robert, 451, 454
André, John, 154
Andros, Sir Edmund, 97, *il* 97
Anthony, Susan B., 401
Anthropologists, 10
Antietam, 471–72; *il* 471
Antifederalists, 204–05
Anti-imperialists, 630–32
Antiwar movement (Vietnam), 867, 870–72
Appalachian Mountains, 86
Appomattox Court House, Va., 488
Arapaho Indians, 528–29, *il* 528
Archeology and archeologists, 10
Argentina, 680
Argonne Forest, 697–98, *il* 682
U.S.S. Arizona, 785, *il* 784
Arkansas, 456
Arkwright, Richard, 298–99
Armstrong, Louis, 717
Armstrong, Neil, 849
Army: and strikes, 600, *il* 600; used against veterans, 743. *See also* names of individual wars
Army-McCarthy Hearings, 825, *il* 825
Arnold, Benedict, 149, 153–54
Arthur, Chester A., 589, *il* 590
Articles of Confederation, 162–63, 174–75
Asia, 14, 634–35. *See also* names of individual countries
Asians in America, 890–91. *See also* Chinese in America; Japanese in America
Assemblies, colonial, 87–88, 94, 159
Atlanta, Ga., 486
Atlanta Compromise, 515–16
Atlantic Charter, 782–83
Atlantic Ocean, 66, 72, 683–85, 688, 778–79, 781–82, *il* 782
Atomic bombs, 801–02, 819, 824, 843, 848, *il* 802
Attorney General, 209
Austin, Stephen F., 347
Australia, 792, 798

Austria, 676–77, 682
Automobile industry, 723–27, *il* 723, 724, 725, 726, 727
Axis (Rome-Berlin-Tokyo), 783
Aztecs, 27, *il* 27

B

Bacon's Rebellion, 88–89, *il* 88
Badillo, Herman, 893–94
Baker, Howard, *il* 877
Balboa, Vasco Núñez de, 24
Ballinger-Pinchot controversy, 662
Baltimore, Md., 145, 276–77, *il* 65
Bank Holiday, 745–46
Bank of the United States: First, 217–19, *il* 217, 218; Second, 294, 333–37, *il* 335
Banks and banking, 217–19, 333–35, 506–07, 666, 744–46, *il* 666, 745
Barton, Clara, 479, *il* 479
Bartram, John, 83
Baruch, Bernard, 690, *il* 690
Baseball, 719, 857
Basketball, 718
Bastogne, 796
Battles. *See* names and locations of individual battles
Bay of Pigs, 840–41
Beauregard, Pierre, 458, *il* 484
Beecher, Henry Ward, 428, *il* 428
Begin, Menachem, 890
Bell, Alexander Graham, 559, *il* 559
Bell, John, 445–46, *il* 446
Bering Strait, 2
Berkeley, Sir William, 89
Berlin, Germany, 796, 814–15, 841
Bessemer converter, 555, 557, *il* 555
Bethune, Mary McLeod, 761, *il* 761
Bicentennial, 887
Biddle, Nicholas, 335–37, *il* 335, 336
"Big Four," 701, 703, *il* 703
"Big Three," 807–08, *il* 807
Bill of Rights, 212, 214, 238–39
Bills of Rights (states), 160
Bingham, George Caleb, *il* 386
Birmingham, Ala., 858
Bismarck Islands, 799–800
Black Codes, 494
Black Hills, 529, 531–32

Civil rights: Committee, 818; movement, 832–33, 858–59, 894; of radicals, 694; and Reconstruction, 496–98, 510–14, *il* 497

Civil Rights Acts: of 1866, 496–97; of 1875, 513; of 1964, 843, 846

Civil service, 588–90

Civil War, 454–88, 578–80, *il* 460, 462, 468, 471, 473, 474, 476, 478, 479, 483, 487, 488

Civil War Amendments, 494, 497–98, 500–01

Civil Works Authority, 749, 752

Clark, George Rogers, 153, *il* 153

Clark, William, 251–56, *il* 253, 255, *il* 256

Clay, Henry, 326–28, 337, 346, 372–73, *il* 326, 372

Clay, Lucius, 815

Clayton Antitrust Act, 667

"Clear and present danger," 694, 696

Clemenceau, Georges, 701, 703, *il* 703

Cleveland, Grover, 571, 590–91, 598–601, 617, 619–20, *il* 589, 590

Cleveland, Ohio, 649–50

Clinton, De Witt, 308

Clinton, Henry, 147, 151, 153–154

Clipper ships, 366–67, *il* 367

Closed shop, 757, 811

Cloth industry, 37, 298–301, 379, 731

Coal industry, 660–61, 731

Cody, William, 534, *il* 534

Coercive Acts, 124–25

Cold Harbor, 485–86

Cold War, 816–17, 819–22, 824, 827–28, 840–43

Cole, Thomas, *il* 292

Collective bargaining, 567, 746, 757

Cologne, Germany, *il* 812

Colombia, 636–40

Colonies: of France, 48–49; of Great Britain, 34–60, 63–89, 92–100, 109, 112–13, 116, 132; of Holland, 49–51; of Sweden, 50–51; of the United States, 630

Colonizationists, 376, 391

Columbia River, 255, *il* 255

Columbus, Christopher, 19–23, *il* 19, 21

Columbus, N.M., 681

Commercial Revolution, 14–15

Committee for European Economic Cooperation (CEEC), 813

Committee for the Reelection of the President (CREEP), 876

Committees of Correspondence, 126

Commodity Credit Corporation, 765

Common Sense, 138, *il* 138

Commonwealth v. Hunt, 414

Communists, 694, 713–15, 812–13, 817, 819–20, 822, 824–25, 827, 840, 862–64

Compromise of 1850, 370–73

Compromise of 1877, 510

Comstock Lode, 536–38

Concentration camps, 620–21, 623, 632, 779. *See also* Internment camps

Concord, Mass., 127–28, *il* 128

Conestoga wagons, 322, *il* 322

Confederate States of America, 451–52, 454, 456–61, 463, 467, 469–70, 488

Congress: creation of, 198, 206; in 1880s, 592; election to, 200, 202; Farm Bloc in, 732; and Hundred Days, 745–49; and Northwest territories, 168–69; powers of, 218, 766; and Presidents, 510, 766, 810–11, 883, *il* 689; and Reconstruction, 495–99; routine of, 242. *See also* House of Representatives; Senate

Congress of Industrial Organizations, 766. *See also* AFL-CIO

Congress of Racial Equality (CORE), 833

Connecticut, 53, 204

Conquistadors, 27–30, *il* 27, 28

Conservation, 661–62, 749

Conservative parties, 509

Conservatives, 728, 756, 766–67, 813, 824, 846

Constitution, 176–205, 239, 762. *See also* Amendments

U.S.S. **Constitution,** 257, 270–71, *il* 257, 270

Constitutional Convention, 175–77, 198–202

Constitutional conventions (state), 161

Constitutional Unionist party, 445

Constitutions (state), 159–60, 169

Containment policy, 817, 824

Continental Army, 134, 150–51

Continental Congress: First, 126; Second, 132–33, 138–39, 162, *il* 132, 163

Continental Divide, 254

Convention of 1800, 240

Conventions. *See* Nominating conventions

Coolidge, Calvin, 714, 728–30, 732, *il* 728

Coolidge, Grace Goodhue, *il* 728

Cooper, Sir Anthony Ashley, 57

Cooper, Peter, 311, *il* 587

Co-ops, 595

Copley, John Singleton, *il* 283

Copper mining, 538

Copperheads, 465–66, *il* 466

Coral Sea, 798

Cornwallis, Lord George, 153–54, *il* 155

Corporations, 553, 646, 656–58, 663, 667

Corruption in politics, 509–10, 581, 583, 648–49, 668, 728, 875–80

Cortés, Hernán, 27, *il* 27

Cotton, 298, 377–81, *il* 379, 380, 385, 505

"Cotton diplomacy," 469

Cotton gin, 378–81

Coughlin, Charles E., 756, *il* 756

Council Bluffs, Iowa, 253

Councils, colonial, 40–42, 93–94

Courts: federal, 202, 656, 811; state, 656. *See also* Supreme Court

Cowhands, 543–44, *il* 543

Cowpens, Battle of, 153

Cox, Archibald, 878

Cox, James M., 709–10, *il* 710

Coxey's Army, 598–99, *il* 598, 599

Crawford, William H., 326–27

Creek Indians, 9, 274–75

Cripple Creek, Colo., 693, *il* 693

Crisis, The, 670

Crockett, Davy, 348, *il* 348

Crook, George, *il* 481

Crop-lien system, 506–07, *il* 507

Cross of Gold speech, 602

Crusades, 13–14

Cuba, 21, 620–30, 640–41, 840–43, 893, *il* 621, 624, 626, 627

Cuffe, Paul, 391

Currier and Ives, *il* 351, 379, 424

Custer, George Armstrong, 531–32, *il* 481, 531, 532

Czolgosz, Leon, 631

D

da Gama, Vasco, 19

Dale, Thomas, 42–43

Daley, Richard, 867

Dallas, Tex., 843

Dare, Virginia, 37

Darrow, Clarence, 693

Davis, Jefferson, 452–54, 486, *il* 452

Davis, Jefferson Columbus, *il* 481

Davis, John W., 729
Dawes Severalty Act, 536
Dawes, William, 127
D-Day, 793–94, il 793
Dean, John, 876–77, il 877
Debs, Eugene V., 600, 665
Decatur, Stephen, 271
Declaration of Independence, 139–43
Declaratory Act, 112
Deficit spending, 768
Deflation, 587–88, 598. See also Depressions; Economy; Inflation; Recessions
Delany, Martin R., il 473
Delaware, 59, 204
Delaware Indians, 59, 86, il 59
del Cano, Juan, 25
De Leon, Ponce, 29
Democracy, 68–69, 139, 245, 329–31, 403
Democratic party, 328, 346, 349, 370, 430–31, 436, 444, 510, 578–83, 598, 601–02, 604–06, 663–64, 707–09, 729, 750, 780, 817–18, 874, 883, 888, il 579, 581, 583, 663, 729
Democratic-Republican party, 227, 232, 238, 241–43
Dempsey, Jack, 718
Department of Agriculture, 588
Department of Health, Education, and Welfare, 828
Department of Justice, 878
Department of the Navy, 231
Department of State, 209–10, 819–20
Department of the Treasury, 209–10, 216, 341
Department of War, 209–10
Depressions: of 1784, 170; of 1837, 338, 341; of 1893, 598, 601; Great Depression of 1930s, 737–52, 756–60, 764–68
Detroit, Mich., 272, 274
Devin, Thomas C., il 481
Dewey, George, 624–25, 630, il 625
Dewey, Thomas E., 780, 794, 818
Diem, Ngo Dinh, 862
Dinwiddie, Robert, 103
Direct election of senators, 652
Disarmament, 711–12, 843
Discoveries of America, 2–4, 11–12, 17–20
District of Columbia, 228, 242, 472. See also Washington, D.C.
Dix, Dorothea, 407–08, il 407
Dole, Sanford B., 617, il 617

Dollar diplomacy, 640–41, 813
Dominican Republic, 640
Domino theory, 863
Donelson, Fort, 482
Douglas, Stephen A., 424–25, 436–40, 444–47, il 436, 446
Douglass, Frederick, 393, 420, il 393
Doves (Vietnam War), 865–67
Draft laws, 469, 474, 691
Draft riots, 474, il 474
Drake, Edwin L., 557, il 557
Drake, Sir Francis, 35, 43, il 35
Du Bois, W.E.B., 669–70, 692, il 669
Dulles, John Foster, 824, 827, il 824
Dunkirk, 778, il 778
Duquesne, Fort, 103, 105
Dust Bowl, 750, il 751
Duties. See Tariffs

E
Eastern Europe, 813, 827
East Germany, 827, 841
East India Company, 122
Economic Opportunity Act, 846
Economy: Civil War, 464–65; Confederate, 467; government regulation of, 562–64, 666, 764–65, 767–68, 843, 850, 883, 903, 905; growth of, 292–93, 551, 553, 646, 730–31, 809–11. See also Deflation; Depressions; Inflation; Recessions; various sectors of the economy
Eden, Anthony, il 807
Edison, Thomas Alva, 560, il 560
Education: of blacks, 501–02, 513–14, 669, 830–31, il 502, 514; boom (1960s), 855–56; in cities, 856; early public, 403–04, il 403; of women, 397–98, il 398
Egypt, 827–28
Ehrlichman, John, 876
Eight-hour workday, 566, 654
Eisenhower, Dwight, 792, 808, 823–31, 840–41, il 792, 823
Elastic clause, 218
El Caney, 627
Elections: direct primary, 650; of senators, 652; of 1789, 206; of 1796, 228–29; of 1800, 241–43; of 1824, 326–27; of 1828, 328–29; of 1832, 337; of 1836, 341; of 1840, 343; of 1848, 369–70; of 1856, 432–33; of 1860, 444–46, il 446; of 1864, 486; of 1868, 500; of 1876, 509–10; in 1880s, 590–91; of 1892, 596; of 1896, 602–06; of 1900,

631; of 1912, 663–65, il 663; of 1916, 686–87; of 1920, 709–10; of 1924, 730; of 1928, 732–33; of 1932, 744; of 1936, 750; of 1940, 780–81; of 1944, 794; of 1948, 817–18; of 1952, 823; of 1960, 834; of 1964, 846; of 1968, 868; of 1972, 874; of 1976, 888; of 1980, 904; of 1984, 908
Electors and electoral college, 200, 206, 228, 242–43, 330, 446, 509–10, 590
Electronics industry, 849, 853
Elementary and Secondary Education Act, 856
Elizabeth I (queen of Great Britain), 35–36, il 35
Elliott, Robert B., il 503
Emancipation Proclamation, 472–73, il 472
Embargo Act, 259–61, il 260
Emory, William H., il 481
Enclosure movement, 37, il 39
England. See Great Britain
English Channel, 778, 793–94, il 778
Enlightenment, the, 83–84
Enumerated articles, 99–100
Environmental Protection Agency, 901
Equal Rights Amendment (ERA), 884, 886
Era of Good Feelings, 318–19
Eric the Red, 11
Ericson, Leif, 11–12
Erie Canal, 308–09, 322
Ervin, Sam, il 877
Eskimos, 8
Espionage Act, 694
Essex, 272
Ethiopia, 776
Europe: in middle ages, 12–17; United States and, 612, 812–13; wars in, 676–78, 682, 765, 778, 792. See also names of individual countries
Evans, George Henry, 413
Ewell, Richard S., il 484
Executive branch of government, 198–200. See also President
Executive branch (states) 159–60
Expansionism, 613. See also Imperialism
Exports, 73–79, 170, 259–60. See also Trade

F
Factories, 299–301, 414, 564–65, 653, il 299, 653

937

Lincoln, Mary Todd, 491, *il* 454
Lincoln, "Tad," 491, *il* 491
Lindbergh, Charles A., 720, *il* 720
Line of Demarcation, 22
Literacy tests, 512, 570–71
Little Bighorn, 531–32, *il* 532
Little Rock, Ark., 831, *il* 831
Little Turtle (Michikinikua), 221–22, *il* 221
Livingston, Robert, 139, 246–49, *il* 249
Lloyd George, David, 701, 703, *il* 703
Lochner v. New York, 656
Lodge, Henry Cabot, 631, 708–09, *il* 708
Lodge, John Ellerton, 320, *il* 320
Logan, John Alexander, *il* 481
Log Cabin Campaign, 343
London, England, 780, *il* 780
London Company, 40, 42, 44, 92
Long, Huey, 756, *il* 756
Long Island, 145
Longstreet, James, *il* 484
Lords of Trade, 92, 98
Los Angeles, Calif., 650
Louis, Joe, *il* 759
Louisiana Purchase, 246–49, *il* 249
Louisiana Territory, 249, 283, 369
L'Ouverture, Toussaint, 246
Lowell system, 301
Loyalists, 138, 145, 153, 167
Lucas, Eliza, 75
Lundy, Benjamin, 387–88
Luther, Seth, 414
Lusitania, 685–86, *il* 685
Lynchings, 515, 670

M

McAdoo, William G., 690, 729, *il* 690
MacArthur, Douglas, 743, 798–800, 821–22, *il* 821
McAuliffe, Anthony C., 796
McCarran Internal Security Act, 822
McCarthy, Eugene, 866–67
McCarthy, Joseph, 820, 822–25, 833, *il* 820, 825
McCarthyism, 820, 822
McClellan, George B., 462–64, 470–71, 475, 486, *il* 462
McClure's magazine, 648–49, *il* 718
McCord, James, 876
McCormick, Cyrus, 465
McCoy, Joseph G., 541
McCulloch v. Maryland, 333, 335
McDowell, Irvin, 458, 461

McGovern, George, 874
McHenry, Fort, 276–77
McKinley, Ida, *il* 605
McKinley, William, 601–06, 621–24, 628–31, *il* 601, 624, 631
McKinley Tariff, 616–17
McPherson, James Birdseye, *il* 481
Madero, Francisco, 679–80
Madison, Dolley, 276, *il* 276
Madison, James, 175, 205, 227, 239, 261, 276, *il* 239
Magellan, Ferdinand, 24–25, *il* 24
Maine, 52, 319, 369
U.S.S. Maine, 621–24, *il* 622, 624
Malaria, 75, 639
Manassas, Va., 458, 461–62
Manchuria, 776
Manhattan Project, 801
Manifest destiny, 351
Manila Bay, 624–25, *il* 624
Mann, Horace, 403–05, *il* 403
Manufacturing, 100, 293–301, 690, 785–86, 855. *See also* Factories; Industry
Mao Tse-Tung, *il* 874
Marbury v. Madison, 435
March on Washington (1963), 858–59, *il* 859
Marion, Francis, 153, *il* 153
Marquette, Jacques, 48
Marshall, George C., 813, 820, *il* 813
Marshall, James W., 365
Marshall, John, 229–31, 339, 435, *il* 231, 435
Marshall Plan, 813
Marye's Heights, 475–76, *il* 476
Maryland, 55, 57, 163–64
Mason-Dixon line, 86–87
Massachusetts, 53, 125, 126–31, 173–74, 204–05, 403–04
Massachusetts Anti-Slavery Society, 393
Massachusetts Bay Colony, 53
Massachusetts Emigrant Aid Society, 427
Mass production, 296–97, 724, *il* 724
Maximilian (emperor of Mexico), 612
Mayflower Compact, 46
Meade, George G., 477–78, *il* 478, 481
Meany, George, 851
Medicare, 846
Medicine, 479, 850
Memphis, Tenn., 866

Mental illness, 407–08
Merchants, 15, 17, 37, 39–40, 122–23
Merritt, Wesley, *il* 481
Mesabi Range, 556
Mexican-Americans, 543, 571–72, 692–93, 738–39, 888, 891–93
Mexican War, 357–60
Mexico, 347–48, 357–60, 612, 679–81, 688, 891–92
Mexico City, 359, *il* 358
Michigan, 169, 272
Middle East, 827–28, 901–02
Midway Islands, 613, 798
Midwest, 522–27. *See also* Northwest Territories
Migrant workers, 571–72, 750, 892–93
Mining and miners, 365–68, 536–40, 593, 595, 693–94, 731, *il* 367, 368, 536, 539, 693
Minimum-wage laws, 654, 746, 756, 765, 828
Mint, 593–95
Minuit, Peter, 50
Minute Men, 126–31, *il* 126, 127, 129
Missions and missionaries, 360–61, 616
Mississippi, 319
Mississippi River, 48–49, 223–24, 246, 481, 483, *il* 483
Missouri, 319, 369, 427–29, *il* 429
Missouri Compromise, 369, 434–35
Missouri River, 253
Mitchell, John, 876
Molotov, V. M., *il* 807
Mondale, Walter, *il* 889, 908–09
Money, 172–73, 177, 217–18, 335, 337, 586–88, 593–95, 601–02, 666, 850, *il* 172, 218
Monmouth Court House, 153
Monopolies, 561, 563–64, 646, 664, 730. *See also* Trusts
Monroe, Elizabeth, *il* 288
Monroe, James, 247, 249, 282, 286–88, 318, *il* 249, 288
Monroe Doctrine, 287–88, 612, 619–20, 640
Montana, 529–30, 538
Montcalm, Louis Joseph de, 105
Montezuma, 27, *il* 27
Montgomery, Sir Bernard, *il* 792
Montgomery, Ala., 451, 832, *il* 832, 833
Moon landing, 849, *il* 849
Morgan, J. P., 646, 657, *il* 657
Mormons, 363–65, 405, *il* 364

Penn, William, 58–59, il 86
Pennsylvania, 59, 204
Pensions, 756
People's party. See Populist party
Perry, Matthew, il 613
Perry, Oliver Hazard, 272, 274, il 274
Pershing, John J., 681, 696, il 681
Petersburg, Va., 486, 488
Petroleum industry, 557, 561–62, 725, 727–28, 901–02
Philadelphia, Pa., 59, 125, 132, 145, 175, 650, il 158, 175
Philip II (king of Spain), 35
Philippine Islands, 25, 624–25, 629–32, 796–800, 890
Pickering, Timothy, 249
Pickett, George E., 477
Pierce, Franklin, 425, il 425
Pikes Peak, 528–29
Pilgrims, 45–48, il 45, 47
Pinckney, Charles C., 229–31, 241, il 231
Pinckney, Thomas, 225, 228–29
Pinckney's Treaty, 224–25
Pinkertons, 567–68
Pirates, 35
Pitcairn, John, 127–28, il 127, 128
Pitt, William, 104, il 93
Pittsburgh, Pa., 105, 556, il 310, 565
Pizarro, Francisco, 29–30
Plains Indians, 8, 523–25, 528–36, il 528, 531, 532
Plantations, 320–21, 380–82, 616, 640–41, il 321, 379, 382
Plessy v. Ferguson, 513, 830
Plymouth, Mass., 46, 48
Plymouth Company, 52
Poison gas, 697
Poland, 704, 774, 777, 807–08, il 774
Political bosses, 581, 583, 648–49, 668, il 581
Political campaigns, 330, 343, 584, 603–05, il 584. See also Elections
Political machines, 580–81, 583, 646, il 581, 583
Political parties, 226–27, 243, 330, 430–31, 585, 589. See also names of parties
Polk, James K., 346–47, 349, 356–58, 360, il 347
Poll tax laws, 512
Pollution, 304, 726, 900–01, il 900
Pontiac's Rebellion, 108
Poor Richard's Almanack, 84–85, il 84
Pope, John, 470–71

Popular sovereignty, 369, 372, 425, 427, 436, 440
Population, 63–65, 291, 304, 461, 551, 572, 729, 851, 896–97
Populist party, 595–96, 601, 604, 646, il 647
Porter, David, 272
Port Hudson, La., 483, il 483
Pottawatomie Massacre, 429–30
Poverty, 304, 408–09, 411, 413, 574, 646, 738–39, 749, 854, 857, 897, il 409, 580
Powderly, Terence V., 566–67
Power: of Congress, 162, 203, 218, 766; of federal government, 162–63, 174, 177, 198, 203, 664–65, 740, 766; of Parliament, 112; of President, 199–200, 660, 755, 766; of states, 177, 214, 656
Prejudice and discrimination against: Asians, 787, 890; blacks, 69, 385, 421, 434, 438–39, 494, 496, 500, 502, 508–09, 512–16, 668, 760, 789, il 508, 514; Catholics, 729, 834; immigrants, 570–71, 890; Indians, 69; Jews, 687; women, 397, 400, 885
Prescott, Samuel, 127
Prescott, William, 130–31
President, Office of the, 199–200, 660, 755, 766, 811
Primary election, 650, 662, 866
Princip, Gavrilo, 676, il 676
Privateers, 220, 229, 232, 271
Privy Council (of Great Britain), 92
Proclamation of 1763, 108
Progressive Era, 644–70
Progressive parties, 663, 687, 730, 817–18
Progressives, 644–70, 686–87, 730
Prohibition, 410, 667, il 667
Providence, R.I., 54
Public housing projects, 854
Public utilities, 652, 748
Public works, 740, 749, 752, 765
Pueblos, 6, il 6
Puerto Ricans, 893
Puerto Rico, 628, 630
Pulitzer, Joseph, 623
Pullman Strike, 599–600, il 600
Pure Food and Drug Act, 658
Puritans, 53–55, il 52
Put-in-Bay, 274

Q
Quakers, 58–59
Quebec, 48, 105, il 107
Queen Anne's War, 102
Quota system, 715, 846

R
Radar and sonar, 790–91, 798
Radical Republicans, 492, 498–99
Radicals, 115, 124–26, 387–88, 393, 414, 693–94, 867
Radio, 722–23, 780
Railroads, 311–12, 424, 526–28, 552–55, 561–63, 593, 598, 599–600, 657–58, 690, il 424, 526, 527, 551
Raleigh, Sir Walter, 36, 43, il 36
Ramona, 535
Rancheros, 360–61, il 361
Randolph, A. Philip, 789, il 789
Randolph, Edmund, 198, 209
Rawlins, John Aaron, il 481
Reactionaries, 227
Reagan, Nancy, il 904, 906
Reagan, Ronald, 886, 888, 904–09, il 904, 907
Recessions, 713, 764–65, 883. See also Depressions
Reconstruction, 496–504, 508–09
Reconstruction Acts, 497–98, 500
Red Cloud, Chief, 530, il 530
Redcoats. See Great Britain
Red Cross, 479
Red Eagle, 275
Red scares, 713–15, 819–20, 822, 824–25
Red Shirts, 509
Red Stick Confederacy, 266–67
Referendum, 650–51
Reformers: in Age of Reform, 396, 400–14; in Progressive Era, 644–57, 661, 664–70
Religious persecution, 45, 53, 54–55, 58, 302, 363
Removal Act, 239
Representation, 87–88, 112, 198–99
Republican party, 431, 436, 492, 495–500, 509–10, 578–81, 583, 601, 603–04, 662, 707–09, 780, 811, 818, 868, 888, 904
Reservations, 529, 536
Revere, Paul, 114–15, 127, il 114, 115
Revolution, American, 127–206
Revolutions: in Cuba, 620–23, 840; fear of, 694, 713–15; French, 219; Mexican, 679–81; in Philippines, 632; Russian, 694
Rhine River, 796
Rhode Island, 54–55, 172–73
Rice, 74–75
Richardson, Elliot, 878
Richmond, Va., 456, 465–66, 487–88, il 456, 487

64–65, 853; and secession, 446–47, 450–51; and Reconstruction, 492, 494–98, 502–04, 508–10, 512–16, *il* 503, 508; and slavery, 377–85, 390. *See also* Confederate States of America

South America, 619–20. *See also* Latin America; names of individual countries

South Carolina, 57–58, 331–33, 447

Southern Christian Leadership Conference, 833

Southwest, 6, 360, 368–70, 372, 571–72, 738–39, 853, 891–92, *il* 6

Soviet Union, 694, 777, 782, 792, 807–09, 812–17, 819, 821–22, 824, 827–28, 841, 848–49, 873, *il* 821

Space program, 848–49, 853, *il* 849

Spain, 20–31, 34–36, 107, 150, 165–67, 223–24, 246–47, 264, 282–85, 360–61, 620–30

Spanish-American War, 624–30, *il* 625, 626, 627, 628

Spanish Armada, 35–36

Spinning jenny, 298, *il* 298

Spirit of St. Louis, 720

Spoils system, 330–31, 588

Sports, 718–19

Spotsylvania Court House, 485

Sputnik I, 848

Squanto, 47

Stagflation, 883

Stalin, Joseph, 807–08, 824, *il* 807

Stamp Act, 110–12, *il* 111

Standard Oil Company, 561–62, 649, 657

Stanton, Edwin M., 499

Stanton, Elizabeth Cady, 397, 400–01, *il* 400

"Star-Spangled Banner, The," 277, *il* 277

States, creation of, 159–60, 168–69

States' rights, 162–65, 214, 239–40, 447

States Rights party (Dixiecrats), 818

Statue of Liberty, 569, *il* 569

Steamboats, 310–11, *il* 310

Steel. *See* Iron and steel industry

Steffens, Lincoln, 648–50, *il* 648

Steichen, Edward, *il* 657

Stephens, Alexander, 452, 494

Stettinius, Edward, *il* 805, 807

Stevens, John L., 617

Stevens, Thaddeus, 492

Stevenson, Adlai, 823–24, 830, 833, *il* 823

Stocks and stock market, 553, 733–34, 748

Stoeckl, Baron Edouard de, 614, *il* 614

Stone Age, 4, *il* 2, 4

Stowe, Harriet Beecher, 422–23, *il* 422

Strait of Magellan, 25

Strategic Arms Limitation Treaty, 873

Streit, Clarence, *il* 776

Strikes, 567–68, 599–600, 660–61, 692–94, 714, 766, 811, 892–93, *il* 566, 693

Stuart, E. B. "Jeb," *il* 484

Stuart, Gilbert, *il* 239

Student Nonviolent Coordinating Council (SNCC), 833

Stuyvesant, Peter, 51, *il* 51

Subsidies, agricultural, 732

Suburbs, 726, 853–55, 897, *il* 854

Suez Canal, 827–28

Sugar, 73, 77, 109, 616, 640–41, *il* 73, 109

Sugar Act, 109

Sullivan, Anne, 407, *il* 407

Sumter, Fort, 451, 454, *il* 451, 454

Sunbelt, 853. *See also* Southwest

Supply-side economics, 903

Supreme Court, 198, 202, 434–36, 513–14, 564, 593, 656–57, 694, 696, 762, 764, 830, 832, 879, 886, *il* 764

Sutter, John A., 354, 365

Sutter's Fort, 354, 365, *il* 354

Synthetic petroleum, 903

T

Taft, Robert A., 780–81, *il* 811

Taft, William Howard, 640, 661–62, 664–65, *il* 661

Taft-Hartley Act, 811

Taiwan (Formosa), 819–20

Talleyrand, Charles Maurice de, 229–31, 240, 246–49, *il* 230, 249

Tammany Hall, 581, *il* 581, 583, 589

Taney, Roger, 434, *il* 435

Tarbell, Ida, 648–49, *il* 648

Tariffs, 171, 177, 214, 293–96, 326, 331–33, 585–86, 662, 666, *il* 586

Taxes and taxation, 109–13, 122–23, 163, 171, 666, 747, 758, 786, 843, 846, 850, 905

Taylor, Zachary, 357–59, 370, 379, *il* 357, 370

Tea Act, 122–23

Teapot Dome, 728

Tecumseh, 265–67, 272, 274, *il* 267

Telephone and telegraph, 558–59, 730, *il* 731

Television, 825, 856–57, *il* 857

Teller Amendment, 624

Temperance societies, 410, *il* 411

Ten-hour workday, 656

Tenements, 304, 574, 653, *il* 580

Tennessee, 456

Tennessee Valley Authority (TVA), 748, *il* 748

Tenochtitlán, 27

Tenskwatawa (the Prophet), 267–68, *il* 267

Tenure of Office Act, 499

Terrorists, 508–09, 515, 676, 827

Terry, Alfred Howe, *il* 481

Tet offensive, 865–66

Texas, 347–49, 356–57, 360, 372–73, 540–41

Thames, Battle of the, 274

Thomas, George Henry, *il* 481

Three-Fifths Compromise, 199

Three Mile Island, 902–03

Thurmond, Strom, 818

Ticonderoga, Fort, 129, 137, 149, *il* 137

Tilden, Samuel J., 509–10, *il* 509

Tippecanoe, 267

Tobacco, 43–44, 51, 73–74

Toleration Act of 1649, 57

Tompkins, Sally L., 479

Tom Thumb, 311, *il* 312

Tonkin Gulf Resolution, 862, 865

Tools and machinery, 296–99, 547–48, 564, *il* 547

Topeka, Kansas, 428, *il* 428

Tories. *See* Loyalists

Totalitarian governments, 775

Tourist industry, 725

Towns and villages, 64–65, 80, 94, 168, *il* 96

Townsend, Francis, 756, *il* 756

Townshend Acts, 113–16

Trade, 14–15, 77–79, 98–100, 116, 170–71, 259–61, 562–64, 634–35, 657

Transcontinental Treaty, 282–84

Transportation, 306–12, 574. *See also* various modes of transportation

Treaty of Dancing Rabbit Creek, 339–40

Treaty of Greenville, 223, *il* 223

Treaty of Paris, 628–30, *il* 628

Treaty of Utrecht, 102

Trenton, 147

Trevett v. Weeden, 173

Trial by jury, 212, 214

Triangle Fire, 653, *il* 653

Triangular trade, 77–79